Greens Solicitors Professional Handbook
2014/2015

Greens Solicitors Professional Handbook 2014/2015

REPRINTED FROM DIVISION F (SOLICITORS) OF
THE PARLIAMENT HOUSE BOOK

W. GREEN

THOMSON REUTERS

Published in 2014 by
W. Green, 21 Alva Street, Edinburgh EH2 4PS
Part of Thomson Reuters (Professional) UK Limited
(Registered in England & Wales, Company No 1679046.
Registered Office and address for service:
Aldgate House, 33 Aldgate High Street, London EC3N 1DL)
Printed and bound by CPI Group (UK) Ltd, Croydon, CR0 4YY
No natural forests were destroyed to make this product;
only farmed timber was used and replanted
A CIP catalogue record for this book is available from the British Library

ISBN 9780414031432

Thomson Reuters and the Thomson Reuters Logo are trademarks of Thomson
Reuters.
Rules, Codes and Practice Guidelines reproduced with kind permission of The
Law Society of Scotland

Reprinted from the *Parliament House Book*, published in looseleaf form and updated five times a year by W. Green, the Scottish Law Publisher

The following paperback titles are also available in the series:	
Annotated Rules of the Court of Session 2014/2015	
Sheriff Court Rules 2014/2015	
Parliament House Book consists of the following Divisions:	
A Fees and Stamps	
B Courts, Upper	
C Court of Session Practice	
D Courts, Lower	
E Licensing	
F Solicitors	
G Legal Aid	
H Bankruptcy and other Mercantile Statutes	
I Companies	
J Conveyancing, Land Tenure and Registration	
K Family Law	
L Landlord and Tenant	
M Succession, Trusts, Liferents and Judicial Factors	

MAIN TABLE OF CONTENTS

Volume 1

SOLICITORS: PRACTICE GUIDELINES
Professional Practice—Where Can I Find It?   F 3001

SOLICITORS (SCOTLAND) ACT 1980

(1980 c. 46)

An Act to consolidate certain enactments relating to solicitors and notaries public in Scotland.

[1st August 1980]

PART I – ORGANISATION

The Law Society of Scotland

Establishment and objects of Law Society of Scotland

1.—[1](1)   The Law Society of Scotland (referred to in this Act as "the Society") shall continue to exist and shall exercise the functions conferred upon it by this Act and sections 16 to 23 (which relate to the provision of conveyancing and executry services) of the 1990 Act.

(2)   The object of the Society shall include the promotion of—

    (a)   the interests of the solicitors' profession in Scotland; and

    (b)   the interests of the public in relation to that profession.

(3)   The Society may do anything that is incidental or conducive to the exercise of these functions or the attainment of those objects.

(4)   Schedule 1 shall have effect in relation to the Society.

Power to act as statutory regulator

1A.[2]   The Society may—

    (a)   act as an approved regulator within the meaning of Part 2 of the 2010 Act,

    (b)   do anything that is necessary or expedient for the purposes of doing so.

Membership of Society

2.—[3](1)   Every solicitor having in force a practising certificate shall be a member of the Society.

(2)   Notwithstanding any other provisions of this Act, the Council may admit as a member of the Society any solicitor not having in force a practising certificate on such terms and conditions (including the payment by him of a reduced annual subscription) as they may determine.

(3)   Subject to subsection (2), a solicitor shall—

    (a)   be treated as if he were not a member of the Society while suspended from practice as a solicitor under any enactment;

    (b)   cease to be a member of the Society when his practising certificate ceases to have effect.

---

[1] As amended by the Public Appointments and Public Bodies etc. (Scotland) Act 2003 (asp 4), s.12 (effective August 15, 2003).

[2] As inserted by the Legal Services (Scotland) Act 2010 (asp 16) Pt 4 c.3 s.131 (effective April 1, 2011).

[3] Read in conjunction with the European Communities (Lawyer's Practice) (Scotland) Regulations 2000 (SSI 2000/121), reg.37(2) and Sch.2 (effective May 22, 2000).

The Council of the Law Society

Establishment and functions of Council of Law Society

3.—[1](1) The business of the Society shall continue to be conducted by the Council of the Society (referred to in this Act as "the Council") the members of which shall be elected, co-opted or appointed in accordance with the provisions of the scheme made under paragraph 2 of Schedule 1.

(2)[2] The Council shall have the functions conferred upon them by this Act and sections 16 to 23 of the 1990 Act.

Discharge of functions of Council of the Law Society

3A.—[3](1) The Council may arrange for any of their functions (other than excepted functions) to be discharged on their behalf by—

    (a) a committee of the Council;

    (b) a sub-committee of such a committee; or

    (c) an individual (whether or not a member of the Society's staff).

(2) Where, under subsection (1)(a), the Council have arranged for any of their functions to be discharged by a committee, the committee may, with the approval of the Council, arrange for that function to be discharged on behalf of the Council by—

    (a) a sub-committee of the committee; or

    (b) an individual (whether or not a member of the Society's staff).

(3) Where, under subsection (1) or (2), the Council or a committee have arranged for any of the Council's functions to be discharged by a subcommittee, the sub-committee may, with the approval of the Council, arrange for that function to be discharged on behalf of the Council by a member of the Society's staff.

(4) A power given by subsection (1), (2) or (3) may be exercised so as to impose restrictions or conditions on the body or person by whom the function concerned is to be discharged.

(5) Any arrangement made under this section shall not arrange for any of the following functions of the Council to be discharged by an individual—

    (aa)[4] that under section 47(2) of the 2007 Act of determining what action to propose, or take, as respects a conduct complaint remitted to them under section 6(a) or 15(5)(a) of that Act;

    (ab)[5] that under—

        (i) section 42ZA(1) or (2) of this Act or section 20ZB(1) or (2) of the 1990 Act of determining whether or not to uphold a conduct complaint so remitted which suggests unsatisfactory professional conduct;

---

[1] As amended by the Legal Services (Scotland) Act 2010 (asp 16) Pt 4 c.3 s.132(1) (effective June 30, 2011).

[2] As amended by the Public Appointments and Public Bodies etc. (Scotland) Act 2003 (asp 4), s.12 (effective August 15, 2003).

[3] Inserted by the Council of the Law Society of Scotland Act 2003 (asp 14), s.1 (effective May 31, 2003).

[4] As inserted by the Legal Profession and Legal Aid (Scotland) Act 2007 (asp 5) Sch.5 para. 1 (2)(a) (effective October 1, 2008; subject to savings and transitional provisions specified in SSI 2008/332 art.4).

[5] As inserted by the Legal Profession and Legal Aid (Scotland) Act 2007 (asp 5) Sch.5 para. 1 (2)(a) (effective October 1, 2008; subject to savings and transitional provisions specified in SSI 2008/332 art.4).

    (ii) section 42ZA(3)(b) of this Act or section 20ZB(3)(b) of the 1990 Act of determining what steps to take when upholding such a conduct complaint;

  (ac)[1] that under section 51(1) of this Act of determining whether or not to make a complaint to the Tribunal as respects a conduct complaint so remitted which suggests professional misconduct;

  (a) *[Repealed by the Legal Services Act 2007 (c.29) Sch.23 para.1 (effective October 1, 2008 as SI 2008/1436; repeal has effect subject to savings and transitional provisions specified in SSI 2008/332 art.4).]*

  (b)[2] that under section 20(1) or (2) of the 1990 Act of determining—

    (i) whether paragraph (a) or (d) of the said section 20(1) applies to the practitioner; and

    (ii) what action to take in the matter.

 (6) An arrangement made under this section may identify an individual by name or by reference to an office or post which the individual holds.

 (7) An arrangement under this section for the discharge of any of the functions of the Council may extend to any of the functions of the Society which is exercisable by the Council.

 (8) Where any arrangement is made under this section for the discharge of any of the functions of the Council by a body or person, the function shall be exercised by that body or person in the name of the Council, except that, where the function in question is a function of the Society which is exercisable by the Council, it shall be exercised in the name of the Society.

 (9) Any arrangement under this section for the discharge of any of the functions of the Council—

  (a) does not affect the responsibility of the Council for the exercise of the function or any liability arising therefrom;

  (b) does not prevent the Council from exercising the function; and

  (c) may be revoked at any time by the Council and also, in the case of any arrangement made under subsection (2) or (3), by the committee or sub-committee which made that arrangement.

 (10) In this section, "excepted functions" means—

  (a) any function of the Council to make rules or regulations under this Act or any other enactment; and

  (b) any function of the Council under paragraph 2 of Schedule 1 to prepare a scheme (scheme for the constitution of the Council etc.).

 (11)[3] This section is—

  (a) subject to sections 3B to 3G, and

  (b) without prejudice to any other power which the Council may have to arrange for the discharge of their functions.

 (12) During any period before—

  (a) paragraph 14(6)(a) of Schedule 4 to the Public Appointments and Public

---

[1] As inserted by the Legal Profession and Legal Aid (Scotland) Act 2007 (asp 5) Sch.5 para. 1 (2)(a) (effective October 1, 2008; subject to savings and transitional provisions specified in SSI 2008/332 art.4).

[2] As amended by the Legal Profession and Legal Aid (Scotland) Act 2007 (asp 5) Sch.5 para.1(2)(b) (effective October 1, 2008; subject to savings and transitional provisions specified in SSI 2008/332 art.4) and the Legal Profession and Legal Aid (Scotland) Act 2007 (Modification and Consequential Provisions) Order 2011 (SSI 2011/235) art.3(2) (effective March 23, 2011).

[3] As substituted by the Legal Services (Scotland) Act 2010 (asp 16) Pt 4 c.3 s.133(1) (effective April 1, 2011 for the purpose of enabling regulations to be made; June 1, 2011 otherwise).

Bodies etc. (Scotland) Act 2003 (asp 4) comes into force, subsection (5) applies as if paragraph (b) and the word "and" that precedes it were omitted;

(b) section 12(c) of that Act comes into force, subsection (5)(a) applies as if for the words "the 1990 Act" there were substituted "the Law Reform (Miscellaneous Provisions) (Scotland) Act 1990 (c.40) ("the 1990 Act")".

Regulatory committee

3B.—[1](1) The Council must, for the purpose mentioned in subsection (2)—

(a) arrange under section 3A(1)(a) for their regulatory functions to be exercised on their behalf by a regulatory committee, and

(b) ensure that the committee continues so to exercise those functions (in particular, for the discharge of the Council's responsibility as mentioned in section 3A(9)(a)).

(2) The purpose is of ensuring that the Council's regulatory functions are exercised—

(a) independently of any other person or interest,

(b) properly in other respects (in particular, with a view to achieving public confidence).

(3) Accordingly, the Council must not—

(a) exercise their regulatory functions through any other means, or

(b) interfere unduly in the regulatory committee's business.

(4) Subsection (3)(a) is subject to—

(a) any determination made by the regulatory committee in a particular case that it is necessary, for ensuring that something falling within the Council's regulatory functions is achieved appropriately, that specific action be taken otherwise than through the regulatory committee, and

(b) such directions as the regulatory committee gives the Council (acting in any other capacity) in connection with the determination.

Particular rules applying

3C.—[2](1) The following particular rules apply as respects the regulatory committee—

(a) the committee's membership may include persons who are not members of the Council,

(b) at least 50% of the committee's membership is to comprise lay persons,

(c) lay persons, where they are not members of the Council, are appointable to the committee if they would be appointable to the Council as nonsolicitor members (see paragraph 3A(3) of Schedule 1),

(d) the committee is to appoint one of its lay members as its convener,

(e) if the convener is not present at a meeting of the committee, another of its lay members is to chair the meeting.

---

[1] As inserted by the Legal Services (Scotland) Act 2010 (asp 16) Pt 4 c.3 s.133(2) (effective April 1, 2011 for the purpose of enabling regulations to be made; June 1, 2011 otherwise).
[2] As inserted by the Legal Services (Scotland) Act 2010 (asp 16) Pt 4 c.3 s.133(2) (effective April 1, 2011 for the purpose of enabling regulations to be made; June 1, 2011 otherwise).

(2) Any sub-committee of the regulatory committee (formed under section 3A(2)(a)) is subject to the particular rules applying as respects the regulatory committee, except that—

(a) a meeting of the sub-committee need not be chaired by one of its lay members,

(b) it may co-opt members from outside the membership of the regulatory committee.

(3) Nothing done by the regulatory committee (or a sub-committee of it) is invalid solely because of a temporary shortfall in the number of its lay members.

(4) In subsection (1)(b), "lay persons" are persons who are not—

(a) solicitors,

(b) advocates,

(c) conveyancing or executry practitioners as defined in section 23 of the 1990 Act,

(d) those having a right to conduct litigation, or a right of audience, by virtue of section 27 of the 1990 Act, or

(e) confirmation agents or will writers within the meaning of Part 3 of the 2010 Act.

Resolving regulatory disputes

3D.—[1](1) This section applies in relation to any dispute arising between the regulatory committee and the Council (acting in any other capacity) with respect to the application of section 3B.

(2) If the dispute cannot be settled by the parties, it is to be submitted to (and resolved by) arbitration.

(3) The arbitrator is to be appointed—

(a) jointly by the parties, or

(b) in the absence of agreement for joint appointment, by the Lord President on a request made by either (or both) of them.

(4) The arbitrator's resolution of the dispute is final and binding on the parties.

Further provision for section 3B etc.

3E.—[2](1) The Scottish Ministers may by regulations—

(a) prescribe a maximum—

(i) number of members that the regulatory committee, or any subcommittee of it, may have,

(ii) proportion of the membership (of either) that may comprise coopted members,

(b) make further provision about the Council's regulatory functions if they believe that such provision is necessary for ensuring that those functions are exercised in accordance with the purpose stated in section 3B(2),

(c) modify (by elaboration or exception) the definition in sections 3F and 3G if they believe that such modification is appropriate.

---

[1] As inserted by the Legal Services (Scotland) Act 2010 (asp 16) Pt 4 c.3 s.133(2) (effective April 1, 2011 for the purpose of enabling regulations to be made; June 1, 2011 otherwise).
[2] As inserted by the Legal Services (Scotland) Act 2010 (asp 16) Pt 4 c.3 s.133(2) (effective April 1, 2011 for the purpose of enabling regulations to be made; June 1, 2011 otherwise).

(2)   Before making regulations under subsection (1), the Scottish Ministers must consult the Council (and take account of sections 4 and 5 of the 2010 Act).

(3)   The power to make regulations under subsection (1) is exercisable by statutory instrument; but—

(a)   a statutory instrument containing regulations under subsection (1)(a) is subject to annulment in pursuance of a resolution of the Scottish Parliament,

(b)   a statutory instrument containing regulations under subsection (1)(b) or (c) is not to be made unless a draft of the instrument has been laid before, and approved by a resolution of, the Parliament.

Meaning of "regulatory functions"

3F.—[1](1)   For the purposes of sections 3B to 3E, the Council's "regulatory functions" are their functions of regulating in respect of any matter the professional practice, conduct and discipline of—

(a)   solicitors (including firms of solicitors) and incorporated practices,

(b)   other legal practitioners, for example—

(i)   registered European or foreign lawyers,

(ii)   conveyancing or executry practitioners.

(2)   Those functions include (in particular) their functions as to—

(a)   setting standards of qualification, education and training,

(b)   admission of persons to the profession,

(c)   keeping the roll and other registers,

(d)   administering the Guarantee Fund,

(e)   making regulatory rules under any relevant enactment.

(3)   In subsection (1)(b)(ii), the reference to conveyancing or executry practitioners is to be construed in accordance with section 23 of the 1990 Act.

Extended meaning under section 3F

3G.[2]   If the Society acts as an approved regulator as mentioned in section 1A, the Council's "regulatory functions" for the purposes of sections 3B to 3E also comprise such regulatory functions as—[3]

(a)   fall within the meaning of that expression as given for the purposes of Part 2 of the 2010 Act (by section 30(1) of that Act), and

(b)   are exercisable under that Part of that Act by the Society in its capacity as an approved regulator as so mentioned.

PART II – RIGHT TO PRACTISE AS A SOLICITOR

Qualifications and Training

Qualifications for practising as solicitor

4.   No person shall be qualified to practise as a solicitor unless—

---

[1] As inserted by the Legal Services (Scotland) Act 2010 (asp 16) Pt 4 c.3 s.133(2) (effective April 1, 2011 for the purpose of enabling regulations to be made; June 1, 2011 otherwise).

[2] As inserted by the Legal Services (Scotland) Act 2010 (asp 16) Pt 4 c.3 s.133(2) (effective April 1, 2011 for the purpose of enabling regulations to be made; June 1, 2011 otherwise).

[3] As inserted by the Legal Services (Scotland) Act 2010 (asp 16) Pt 4 c.3 s.133(2) (effective April 1, 2011 for the purpose of enabling regulations to be made; June 1, 2011 otherwise).

(a) he has been admitted as a solicitor; and
(b) his name is on the roll; and
(c) subject to section 24, he has in force a certificate issued by the Council in accordance with the provisions of this Part authorising him to practise as a solicitor (referred to in this Act as a "practising certificate").

Training regulations

5.—¹(1) The Council may, with the concurrence of the Lord President, make regulations for—
(a) practical training;
(b) attendance at a course of legal education;
(c) the passing of examinations.
(2) Regulations under this section—
(a) may make such incidental, consequential and supplemental provisions as the Council consider necessary or proper in relation to the matters specified in subsection (1);
(b) may include provision for the charging by the Council of fees and the application thereof; and
(c) may make different provisions for different circumstances.

Admission

Admission as solicitor

6.—(1) Subject to the provisions of this section, no person shall be admitted as a solicitor in Scotland unless—
(a) *[Repealed by the Employment Equality (Age) Regulations 2006 (SI 2006/1031) (effective October 1, 2006).]*
(b)² he has satisfied the Council—
(i) that he has complied with the provisions of any regulations made under section 5 that apply to him, and
(ii) that he is a fit and proper person to be a solicitor, and has obtained from the Council a certificate to that effect; and
(c) he has paid such sum in respect of his admission as has been fixed by the Council with the approval of the Lord President.
(2)³ Where—
(a) a person has complied with the requirements of subsection (1); but
(b) the Council have not lodged a petition for his admission as a solicitor within one month of his having so complied,
he may apply by petition to the court for admission as a solicitor; and if he produces the certificate mentioned in paragraph (b) of subsection (1) the court shall make an order admitting him as a solicitor.
(3) If any person has not obtained from the Council a certificate to the effect mentioned in paragraph (b) of subsection (1) but has otherwise satisfied the require-

---

¹ Read in conjunction with the European Communities (Lawyer's Practice) (Scotland) Regulations 2000 (SSI 2000/121), reg.37(2) and Sch.2 (effective May 22, 2000).
² As amended by the Law Reform (Miscellaneous Provisions) (Scotland) Act 1985 (c.73), Sch.1, Pt II, para.2(a) and Sch.4.
³ As substituted by the Law Reform (Miscellaneous Provisions) (Scotland) Act 1990 (c.40), s.37(1) (effective July 10, 1992: SI 1992/1599).

ments of that subsection the court, on such an application being made by him and on being satisfied after such inquiry as it thinks fit, that—

    (a) he is a fit and proper person to be admitted as a solicitor, and

    (b) he is competent to be a solicitor,

may make an order admitting him as a solicitor.

(3A)[1] The Council may petition the court for the admission as a solicitor of an applicant who has complied with the requirements of subsection (1) above; and, where it does so it shall lodge the petition not later than one month after the applicant has first so complied.

(3B)[2] The Court shall, on a petition being made to it under subsection (3A) above, make an order admitting the applicant as a solicitor.

(4) Any order admitting a person as a solicitor under this section shall include a direction to the Council to enter the name of that person in the roll.

(5) Nothing in this section affects the operation of the Colonial Solicitors Act 1900 or any Order in Council made under that Act (admission as solicitors in Scotland of solicitors of certain overseas territories).

(6) Every person who has been enrolled as a law agent shall be deemed to be admitted as a solicitor.

The Roll

Keeping the roll

7.—(1) The Council shall continue to be the registrar of solicitors and shall keep at the office of their secretary a roll of solicitors (in this Act referred to as "the roll").

(2) The roll shall consist of the names in alphabetical order of all solicitors entered on it in accordance with section 8.

(2A)[3] The roll is also to record against the name of each enrolled solicitor the address of the place of business of that solicitor (as given under subsection (2) of that section).

(3) Any person may inspect the roll during office hours without payment.

(4)[4] Schedule 2 (powers of Council in relation to roll of solicitors) shall have effect.

Entry in the roll

8.—(1) On production to the Council of an order under section 6 admitting a person as a solicitor and directing that his name be entered on the roll the Council shall enter the name of that person on the roll.

(2) Any solicitor whose name is entered on the roll (in this Act referred to as "an enrolled solicitor") shall, on such enrolment, inform the Council in writing of the address of his place of business, and shall on any change of that address, inform them in writing of his new address.

---

[1] Inserted by the Law Reform (Miscellaneous Provisions) (Scotland) Act 1985 (c.73), Sch.1, Pt II, para.2(b).

[2] Inserted by the Law Reform (Miscellaneous Provisions) (Scotland) Act 1985 (c.73), Sch.1, Pt II, para.2(b).

[3] As inserted by the Legal Services (Scotland) Act 2010 (asp 16) Pt 4 c.3 s.134(1) (effective May 1, 2011).

[4] As inserted by the Solicitors (Scotland) Act 1988 (c.42) Sch.1 para.2.

(3)   The Council shall issue a certificate of enrolment to any enrolled solicitor who applies for it.

Removal of name from roll on request

9.—(1)[1]   An enrolled solicitor who wishes his name to be removed from the roll of solicitors may make an application to the Council in that behalf, and the Council shall remove the name of that solicitor or, as the case may be, the annotation against his name, or any annotation made against his name under section 25A(3) from the roll.

(2)[2]   But the Council are required to remove the name or annotation only if they are satisfied that—

      (a)   the solicitor has made adequate arrangements with respect to the business which the solicitor then has in hand, and

      (b)   it is otherwise appropriate to do so.

Restoration of name to roll on request

10.—[3](1)   A solicitor whose name has been struck off the roll other than by order of the court, shall only be entitled to have his name restored to the roll, if on an application in that behalf made by him to the Tribunal and after such inquiry as the Tribunal thinks proper, the Tribunal so orders.

(1ZA)[4]   Where the restoration of a solicitor's name to the roll has been prohibited under section 53(2)(aa), the solicitor is entitled to have the solicitor's name restored to the roll if (but only if) the Tribunal so orders—

      (a)   on an application made to it by the solicitor, and

      (b)   after such enquiry as it thinks proper.

(1A)[5]   On an application to the Council from a solicitor whose name, or any annotation against whose name, has been removed from the roll under section 9 (except where subsection (1ZA) applies) the Council may, after such inquiry as they think proper, restore the name of that solicitor or, as the case may be, the annotation, to the roll.

(2)   Rules made by the Tribunal under section 52 may—

      (a)[6]   regulate the making, hearing and determining of applications under subsection (1) or (1ZA);

      (b)   *[Repealed by the Solicitors (Scotland) Act 1988 (c.42), s.6(2) Sch.2.]*

---

[1] As amended by the Solicitors (Scotland) Act 1988 (c.42) Sch.1 para.3, the Law Reform (Miscellaneous Provisions) (Scotland) Act 1990 (c.40) Sch.8 para.29(2) and by the Legal Services (Scotland) Act 2010 (asp 16) Pt 4 c.3 s.135(1)(b) (effective May 1, 2011).
[2] As inserted by the Legal Services (Scotland) Act 2010 (asp 16) Pt 4 c.3 s.135(1)(c) (effective May 1, 2011).
[3] As amended by the Solicitors (Scotland) Act 1988 (c.42), Sch.1, para.4, and the Law Reform (Miscellaneous Provisions) (Scotland) Act 1990 (c.40), Sch.8, para.29(3).
[4] As inserted by the Legal Services (Scotland) Act 2010 (asp 16) Pt 4 c.3 s.136(1)(a) (effective May 1, 2011).
[5] As amended by the Legal Services (Scotland) Act 2010 (asp 16) Pt 4 c.3 s.136(1) (effective May 1, 2011).
[6] As amended by the Legal Services (Scotland) Act 2010 (asp 16) Pt 4 c.3 s.136(1) (effective May 1, 2011).

Directions by Lord President

11.—(1)   The Lord President may give directions to the Council in relation to the carrying out of their duties in connection with the keeping of the roll and they shall give effect to any such directions.

(2)   *[Repealed by the Solicitors (Scotland) Act 1988 (c.42), Sch.2.]*

Power of court to prescribe fees

12.   *[Repealed by the Solicitors (Scotland) Act 1988 (c.42), Sch.2.]*

Register of European lawyers

Keeping the register

12A.—[1](1)   The Council shall establish and maintain the register referred to in regulation 15 of the European Communities (Lawyer's Practice) (Scotland) Regulations 2000, and shall keep the register at the office of their secretary.

(2)   The register shall consist of the names in alphabetical order of all European lawyers entered on it in accordance with regulation 17 of those regulations.

(2A)[2]   The register is also to record against the name of each lawyer entered on it the address of the place of business of that lawyer and related information (as given under section 12B(1)).

(3)   Any person may inspect the register during office hours without payment.

(4)   Schedule 2 (powers of Council in relation to roll of solicitors) shall apply to the register as it does to the roll and in its application to the register the words "section 7(3)" in paragraph 4 shall be read as if the words "section 12A" were substituted therefor.

Information to be provided by registered European lawyers

12B.—[3](1)   Any registered European lawyer—

    (a)   shall, on registration, inform the Council in writing of the address of his place of business, his home professional title, and the name and address of the competent authority with which he is registered in his home state; and

    (b)   shall thereafter inform the Council of any change to the information required under paragraph (a) above.

(2)   The Council shall issue a registration to any registered European lawyer who applies for it.

Removal of name from register on request

12C.—[4](1)   A registered European lawyer who wishes his name, or any annotation made against his name under section 25A(3), to be removed from the register

---

[1] As inserted by the European Communities (Lawyer's Practice) (Scotland) Regulations 2000 (SSI 2000/121) reg.37(1) and Sch.1 para.1(2) (effective May 22, 2000).

[2] As inserted by the Legal Services (Scotland) Act 2010 (asp 16) Pt 4 c.3 s.134(2) (effective May 1, 2011).

[3] Inserted by the European Communities (Lawyer's Practice) (Scotland) Regulations 2000 (SSI 2000/121), reg.37(1) and Sch.1, para.1(2) (effective May 22, 2000).

[4] As inserted by the European Communities (Lawyer's Practice) (Scotland) Regulations 2000 (SSI 2000/121) reg.37(1) and Sch.1 para. 1(2) (effective May 22, 2000) and amended by the Legal Services (Scotland) Act 2010 (asp 16) Pt 4 c.3 s.135(2) (effective May 1, 2011).

may make an application to the Council in that behalf, and the Council shall remove the name of that solicitor, or, as the case may be, the annotation against his name, from the register.

(2)[1] But the Council are required to remove the name or annotation only if they are satisfied that—

    (a)   the solicitor has made adequate arrangements with respect to the business which the solicitor then has in hand, and

    (b)   it is otherwise appropriate to do so.

Restoration of name to register on request

12D.—[2](1)   Subject to subsection (2), a registered European lawyer whose name has been removed from the register shall be entitled to have his name restored to the register only if, on an application in that behalf made by him to the Tribunaland after such enquiry as the Tribunal thinks proper, the Tribunal so orders.

(2)   On an application to the Council by a registered European lawyer whose name, or any annotation against whose name, has been removed from the register under section 12C, the Council may, after such inquiry as they think proper, restore the name of the registered European lawyer or, as the case may be, the annotation, to the register.

(3)   Rules made by the Tribunal under section 52 may—

    (a)   regulate the making, hearing and determining of applications under subsection (1);

    (b)   provide for payment by the applicant to the council of such fee in respect of restoration to the register as the rules may specify.

Practising Certificates

Applications for practising certificates

13.—(1)   Subject to this section and sections 14 to 24, the Council may make rules with respect to—

    (a)   applications for practising certificates;

    (b)   the issue of practising certificates;

    (c)   the keeping of a register of applications for and the issue of practising certificates.

(2)   Any person may inspect the register during office hours without payment.

(3)   The making of a false statement by a solicitor in an application for a practising certificate may be treated as professional misconduct by him for the purposes of Part IV, unless he proves the statement was made without intention to deceive.

Issue of practising certificate

14.—(1)   The Council shall issue to an enrolled solicitor on application being duly made by him, a practising certificate in accordance with rules made by them under section 13.

(2)   The Council shall not issue a practising certificate to a solicitor while he is suspended from practice.

---

[1] As inserted by the Legal Services (Scotland) Act 2010 (asp 16) Pt 4 c.3 s.135(2)(c) (effective May 1, 2011).

[2] Inserted by the European Communities (Lawyer's Practice) (Scotland) Regulations 2000 (SSI 2000/121), reg.37(1) and Sch.1, para.1(2) (effective May 22, 2000).

Discretion of Council in special cases

15.—(1) In any case where this section has effect, the applicant shall, unless the Council otherwise order, give to the Council, not less than 6 weeks before he applies for a practising certificate, notice of his intention to do so; and the Council may in their discretion—

    (a) grant or refuse the application, or

    (b) decide to issue a certificate to the applicant subject to such conditions as the Council may think fit.

(2)[1] Subject to subsections (3) and (4), this section shall have effect in any case where a solicitor applies for a practising certificate—

    (a) *[Repealed by the Law Reform (Miscellaneous Provisions) (Scotland) Act 1985 (c.73), Sch.1, Pt II, para.3 and Sch.4.]*

    (b) not having held a practising certificate in force within the period of 12 months following the date of his admission; or

    (c) when a period of 12 months or more has elapsed since he held a practising certificate in force; or

    (d) without having paid in full any fine imposed on him under section 42ZA(4)(b) or Part IV; or

    (e)[2] without having paid in full any expenses for which he has been found liable under section 62A or Part IV; or

    (f) when, having been suspended from practice, the period of suspension has expired; or

    (g) when, having had his name struck off the roll, his name has been restored to the roll; or

    (h) after his estate has been sequestrated or he has granted a trust deed for behoof of creditors, whether he has obtained his discharge or not; or

        (i) when—

            (i) the Council are investigating a conduct complaint remitted to them under section 6(a) or 15(5)(a) of the 2007 Act, his attention has been drawn by the Council to the matter, and he has not replied or has not furnished a reply which would enable the Council to dispose of the matter; or

            (ii) after a complaint has been made of delay in the disposal of the business of a client he has not completed that business within such period as the Council may fix as being a reasonable period within which to do so,

        and in either case has been notified in writing by the Council accordingly,

    (j) *[Repealed by the Legal Services Act 2007 (c.29) Sch.23 para.1 (effective October 1, 2008 as SI 2008/1436; repeal has effect subject to savings and transitional provisions specified in SSI 2008/332 art.4).]*

(3) Where a practising certificate free of conditions is issued by the Council under subsection (1) to a solicitor in relation to whom this section has effect by reason of any such circumstances as are mentioned in paragraphs (b), (c), (f), (g) or (h) of subsection (2), this section shall not thereafter have effect in relation to that solicitor by reason of those circumstances.

---

[1] As amended by the Legal Profession and Legal Aid (Scotland) Act 2007 (asp 5) Sch.5 para. 1(3) (effective October 1, 2008).

[2] As substituted by the Legal Services Act 2007 (c.29) Sch.20 para.1(3)(a) (effective October 1, 2008).

(4)   Where the Council decide to issue a practising certificate subject to conditions, they may, if they think fit, postpone the issue of the certificate pending the hearing and determination of an appeal under section 16.

Appeals from decisions of Council

16.—¹(1)   Where

    (a)   an application for a practising certificate is duly made to the Council otherwise than in a case where section 15 has effect and the Council refuse or neglect to issue a practising certificate, the applicant;

    (b)   the Council refuse to recognise a body corporate as being suitable in terms of section 34(1A)(b), the body corporate

may apply to the court, who may make such order in the matter as it thinks fit.

(2)   Where the Council in exercise of the power conferred on them by section 15, refuse to issue a practising certificate, or issue a practising certificate subject to conditions, the applicant may appeal to the court against that decision within 14 days of being notified of it.

(3)   On an appeal to the court under subsection (2) the court may—

    (a)   affirm the decision of the Council; or

    (b)   direct the Council to issue a practising certificate to the applicant subject to such conditions if any as the court may think fit; or

    (c)   make such other order as it thinks fit.

Date and expiry of practising certificates

17.—(1)   Every practising certificate issued in November of any year shall bear the date of 1st November in that year, and every other practising certificate shall bear the date of the day on which it was issued.

(2)   Every practising certificate shall have effect from the date it bears under subsection (1).

(3)   Subject to subsection (4), every practising certificate shall expire on 31st October next after it is issued.

(4)   On the name of any solicitor being struck off the roll or on a solicitor being suspended from practice as a solicitor, any practising certificate for the time being in force of that solicitor shall cease to have effect, but in the case of suspension, if he ceases to be so suspended during the period for which the practising certificate would otherwise have continued in force, the certificate shall thereupon again have effect.

Suspension of practising certificates

18.—²(1)[3,4]   If—

    (a)   in pursuance of the Mental Health (Care and Treatment) (Scotland) Act 2003 a solicitor is, by reason of mental disorder, detained in hospital;

    (b)   a guardian is appointed to a solicitor under the Adults with Incapacity (Scotland) Act 2000 (asp 4);

---

[1] As amended by the Law Reform (Miscellaneous Provisions) (Scotland) Act 1985 (c.73), Sch.1, Pt.I, para.1.

[2] As amended by the Mental Health (Scotland) Act 1984 (c.36) Sch.3 para.46.

[3] As amended by the Mental Health (Care and Treatment) (Scotland) Act 2003 (Modification of Enactments) Order (SSI 2005/465) art.2 and Sch.1 (effective September 27, 2005).

[4] As amended by the Adults with Incapacity (Scotland) Act 2000 (asp 4) s.88 and Sch.5, para.15 (effective April 1, 2002).

    (c)   the estate of the solicitor is sequestrated;

    (d)   a solicitor grants a trust deed for behoof of creditors;

    (e)   a judicial factor is appointed on the estate of the solicitor under section 41;

any practising certificate for the time being in force of that solicitor shall cease to have effect, and he shall be suspended from practice as a solicitor.

    (1ZA)[1]   The Council may suspend from practice a solicitor who—

    (a)   has been convicted of an offence involving dishonesty, or

    (b)   in respect of an offence, has been—

        (i)   fined an amount equivalent to level 4 on the standard scale or more (whether on summary or solemn conviction), or

        (ii)   sentenced to imprisonment for a term of 12 months or more.

    (1A)[2]   If—

    (a)   an administration or winding up order, or an appointment of a provisional liquidator, liquidator, receiver or judicial factor has been made in relation to the incorporated practice; or

    (b)   a resolution has been passed for the voluntary winding-up of an incorporated practice (other than a resolution passed solely for the purposes of reconstruction or amalgamation of the incorporated practice with another incorporated practice),

the recognition under section 34(1A) of the incorporated practice shall be thereby revoked.

    (2)[3, 4]   On the occurrence of any of the circumstances mentioned in subsection (1) or (1ZA), the solicitor in question shall intimate those circumstances to the Council in writing immediately.

    (3)   On the occurrence of the circumstances mentioned in paragraphs (d) or (e) of subsection (1) the trustee or as the case may be the judicial factor shall intimate his appointment to the Council in writing immediately.

    (3A)[5]   On the occurrence of the circumstances mentioned in—

    (a)   paragraph (a) of subsection (1A), the administrator, provisional liquidator, liquidator, receiver or, as the case may be, judicial factor appointed in relation to the incorporated practice;

    (b)   paragraph (b) of subsection (1A), the incorporated practice shall immediately intimate that fact to the Council.

Further provisions relating to suspension of practising certificates

    19.—(1)   The provisions of this section have effect in relation to a practising certificate which has ceased to have effect by virtue of section 18 during the period when that certificate would, but for that section, have continued in force.

    (2), (3)   *[Repealed by the Solicitors (Scotland) Act 1988 (c.42) Sch.2.]*

---

[1] As inserted by the Legal Services (Scotland) Act 2010 (asp 16) Pt 4 c.3 s.137(1)(a) (effective May 1, 2011).
[2] Inserted by the Law Reform (Miscellaneous Provisions) (Scotland) Act 1985 (c.73) Sch.1, Pt.I para.2.
[3] As amended by the Solicitors (Scotland) Act 1988 (c.42) Sch.2.
[4] As amended by the Legal Services (Scotland) Act 2010 (asp 16) Pt 4 c.3 s.137(1)(b) (effective May 1, 2011).
[5] Inserted by the Law Reform (Miscellaneous Provisions) (Scotland) Act 1985 (c.73) Sch.1, Pt.I para.2.

(4)   A practising certificate which has ceased to have effect by virtue of paragraphs (c) or (d) of section 18(1) shall again have effect on the solicitor being granted his discharge.

(5)   A practising certificate which has ceased to have effect by virtue of paragraph (e) of section 18(1) shall again have effect on the judicial factor being granted his discharge.

(5A)[1, 2]   Where a solicitor is suspended from practice as a solicitor by virtue of paragraph (a) or (b) of section 18(1), the period of suspension shall, for the purposes of section 15(2)(f), expire on the solicitor ceasing to be detained in hospital or subject to guardianship or, as the case may be, on the curator bonis being discharged.

(5B)[3]   A suspension from practice arising by virtue of section 18(1ZA) expires if the grounds for it no longer apply.

(5C)   On the occurrence of any of the circumstances mentioned in subsections (4) to (5B), the solicitor concerned must notify the Council in writing (and without delay).

(6)[4]   Where a solicitor is suspended from practice as a solicitor by virtue of paragraphs (c), (d) or (e) of section 18(1) or by virtue of section 18(1ZA), he may at any time apply to the Council to terminate the suspension.

(7)   On an application under subsection (6), the Council may either—
    (a)   grant the application with or without conditions; or
    (b)   refuse the application.

(8)   If on an application by a solicitor under subsection (6), the Council refuse the application or grant it subject to conditions, the solicitor may appeal against the decision to the court, who may—
    (a)   affirm the decision; or
    (b)   vary any conditions imposed by the Council; or
    (c)   terminate the suspension either with or without conditions.

Council's duty to supply lists of solicitors holding practising certificates

20.—[5, 6](1)   The Council shall send a list of all solicitors holding practising certificates for the practice year then current—
    (a)   to the Keeper of the Registers of Scotland;
    (ab)   to the Principal Clerk of Session;
    (b)   to each sheriff clerk;
as soon as practicable after 1st December in each year.

(2)   The Council shall send a list of all solicitors who have rights of audience in—
    (a)   the Court of Session, to—
        (i)   the Principal Clerk of Session;

---

[1] Inserted by the Solicitors (Scotland) Act 1988 (c.42), Sch.1, para.6.

[2] As substituted by the Mental Health (Care and Treatment) (Scotland) Act 2003 (Modification of Enactments) Order (SSI 2005/465), art.2 and Sch.1 (effective September 27, 2005).

[3] As inserted by the Legal Services (Scotland) Act 2010 (asp 16) Pt 4 c.3 s.137(2)(a) (effective May 1, 2011).

[4] As inserted by the Legal Services (Scotland) Act 2010 (asp 16) Pt 4 c.3 s.137(2)(b) (effective May 1, 2011).

[5] As amended by the Law Reform (Miscellaneous Provisions) (Scotland) Act 1990 (c.40), Sch.8, para.29(4) and Sch.9.

[6] Read in conjunction with the European Communities (Lawyer's Practice) (Scotland) Regulations 2000 (SSI 2000/121), reg.37(2) and Sch.2 (effective May 22, 2000).

(ii)[1] the Supreme Court; and

(iii) the Registrar to the Judicial Committee of the Privy Council; and

(b)[2] the High Court of Justiciary, to the Principal Clerk of Justiciary, as soon as practicable after 1st December in each year; and where, by virtue of an order under section 53(2)(ba) or 55(1)(ba) or (bb), a solicitor's right of audience in any of those courts is suspended or revoked, the Council shall forthwith inform the persons mentioned in this subsection of that fact.

(3) The Council shall notify those persons to whom they have sent lists under this section of any changes in those lists.

Consultants to hold practising certificates

21.—[3](1) A consultant shall be treated for the purposes of this Act as a practising solicitor and the provisions relating to practising certificates and, subject to subsection (2), the Guarantee Fund shall apply to him.

(2) The Council may if they think fit exempt a consultant from any of the provisions of section 43 or Schedule 3 (the Guarantee Fund).

(3)[4] In this section "consultant" means any solicitor who

(a) not being in partnership with a solicitor or other solicitors causes or permits his name to be associated with the name of that solicitor or those solicitors or their firm's name,

(b) not being a director of an incorporated practice, causes or permits his name to be associated with that incorporated practice,

whether he is described as a consultant or adviser or in any other way.

Evidence as to holding of practising certificates

22.—(1) Any list purporting to be issued by the Council and to contain the names of solicitors in Scotland who have before 1st December in any year obtained practising certificates for the period of 12 months from 1st November in that year shall, until the contrary is proved, be evidence that the persons named in that list are solicitors holding such certificates.

(2) The absence from any such list of the name of any person shall, until the contrary is proved, be evidence that the person is not qualified to practise as a solicitor under a certificate for the current year, but in the case of any such person an extract from the roll certified as correct by the Council shall be evidence of the facts appearing in the extract.

Offence to practise without practising certificate

23.—(1) Any person who practises as a solicitor or in any way holds himself out as entitled by law to practise as a solicitor without having in force a practising

---

[1] As substituted by the Constitutional Reform Act 2005 (c.4) Sch.9(1) para.32(2) (effective October 1, 2009).

[2] As amended by the Legal Services Act 2007 (c.29) Sch.23 para.1 (effective October 1, 2008 as SI 2008/1436; amendment has effect subject to savings and transitional provisions specified in SSI 2008/332 art.4).

[3] Read in conjunction with the European Communities (Lawyer's Practice) (Scotland) Regulations 2000 (SSI 2000/121) reg.37(2) and Sch.2 (effective May 22, 2000).

[4] As amended by the Law Reform (Miscellaneous Provisions) (Scotland) Act 1985 (c.73) Sch.1, Pt I, para.3.

certificate shall be guilty of an offence under this Act unless he proves that he acted without receiving or without expectation of any fee, gain or reward, directly or indirectly.

(2)   Without prejudice to any proceedings under subsection (1), failure on the part of a solicitor in practice to have in force a practising certificate may be treated as professional misconduct for the purposes of Part IV.

Professional misconduct for registered European lawyer to practise without a registration certificate

23A.[1]   Failure on the part of a registered European lawyer in practice to have in force a current registration certificate may be treated as professional misconduct for the purposes of Part IV.

23B.[2]   Failure on the part of a registered foreign lawyer in practice to have in force a current registration certificate may be treated as professional misconduct for the purposes of Part IV.

Saving of public officials

24.   Nothing in this Act shall require a practising certificate to be taken out by a person who is by law authorised to act as a solicitor to a public department without admission, or by any assistant or officer appointed to act under the direction of any such solicitor.

Registration certficates for registered European Lawyers

Applications for registration certificates

24A.—[3](1)   Subject to sections 24B to 24G below, the Council may make rules with respect to—

    (a)   applications for;

    (b)   the issue of;

    (c)   the keeping of a register for and the issue of, registration certificates for registered European lawyers as it would make rules under section 13 with respect to practising certificates for enrolled solicitors.

(2)   Any person may inspect the register referred to in subsection (1)(c) during office hours without payment.

(3)   The making of a false statement by a registered European lawyer in an application for a registration certificate may be treated as professional misconduct by him for the purposes of Part IV, unless he proves the statement was made without intention to deceive.

---

[1] As inserted by the European Communities (Lawyer's Practice) (Scotland) Regulations 2000 (SSI 2000/121) reg.37(1) and Sch.1 para. 1(4) (effective May 22, 2000).
[2] As inserted by the Solicitors (Scotland) Act 1980 (Foreign Lawyers and Multi-national Practices) Regulations 2004 (SSI 2004/383) reg.3.
[3] As inserted by the European Communities (Lawyer's Practice) (Scotland) Regulations 2000 (SSI 2000/121) reg.37(1) and Sch.1 para.1(3) (effective May 22, 2000).

Issue of registration certificates

24B.—[1](1)   The Council shall issue to a registered European lawyer on application being made by him, a registration certificate in accordance with rules made by them under section 24A.

(2)   The Council shall not issue a registration certificate to a registered European lawyer while his registration is suspended or withdrawn.

Discretion of Council in special cases

24C.—[2](1)   In any case where this section has effect, the applicant shall, unless the Council otherwise order, give to the Council, not less than 6 weeks before he applies for a renewal of a registration certificate, notice of his intention to do so; and the Council may in their discretion—

    (a)   grant or refuse the application; or

    (b)   decide to issue a registration certificate to the applicant subject to such conditions as the Council may think fit.

(2)   Subject to subsections (3) and (4) below, this section shall have effect in any case where a registered European lawyer applies for a renewal of a registration certificate—

    (a)   not having held a registration certificate in force within the period of 12 months following the date of his registration; or

    (b)   when a period of 12 months or more has elapsed since he held a registration certificate in force; or

    (c)   without having paid in full any fine imposed on him under Part IV; or

    (d)[3]   without having paid in full any expenses for which he has been found liable under section 62A or Part IV; or

    (e)   when, having been suspended from practice, the period of suspension has expired; or

    (f)   when, having had his registration withdrawn, he has been registered again; or

    (g)   after his estate has been sequestrated or he has granted a trust deed for behoof of creditors, whether he has obtained his discharge or not; or

    (h)[4]   when, after a complaint has been made—

        (i)   relating to his conduct of the business of a client his attention has been drawn by the Council to the matter, and he has not replied or has not furnished a reply which would enable the Council to dispose of the matter; or

        (ii)   of delay in disposal of the business of a client he has not completed that business within such period as the Council may fix as being a reasonable period within which to do so,

and in either case has been notified in writing by the Council accordingly.

---

[1] As inserted by the European Communities (Lawyer's Practice) (Scotland) Regulations 2000 (SSI 2000/121) reg.37(1) and Sch.1 para.1(3) (effective May 22, 2000).

[2] Inserted by the European Communities (Lawyer's Practice) (Scotland) Regulations 2000 (SSI 2000/121), reg.37(1) and Sch.1, para. 1(3) (effective May 22, 2000).

[3] As substituted by the Legal Services Act 2007 (c.29) Sch.20 para.1(5)(a) (effective October 1, 2008).

[4] As amended by the Legal Services Act 2007 (c.29) Sch.23 para.1 (effective October 1, 2008 as SI 2008/1436; repeal has effect subject to savings and transitional provisions specified in SSI 2008/332 art.4).

(3) Where a registration certificate free of conditions is issued by the Council under subsection (1) to a registered European lawyer to whom that subsection has effect by reason of any such circumstances as are mentioned in paragraphs (a), (b), (e), (f) or (g) of subsection (2), this section shall not thereafter have effect in relation to that registered European lawyer by reason of those circumstances.

(4) Where the Council decide to issue a registration certificate subject to conditions, they may, if they think fit, postpone the issue of the registration certificate pending the hearing and determination of an appeal under section 24D.

Appeals from decisions of Council

24D—[1](1) Where—
- (a) an application for a registration certificate is duly made to the Council otherwise than in a case where section 24C has effect and the Council refuse or neglect to issue a registration certificate, the applicant;
- (b) the Council refuse to recognise a body corporate as being suitable in terms of section 34(1A) (b), the body corporate,

may apply to the court, who may make such order in the matter as it thinks fit.

(2) Where the Council in exercise of the power conferred on them by section 24C, refuse to issue a registration certificate, or issue a registration certificate subject to conditions, the applicant may appeal to the court against that decision within 14 days of being notified of it.

(3) On an appeal to the court under subsection (2) the court may—
- (a) affirm the decision of the Council; or
- (b) direct the Council to issue a registration certificate to the applicant subject to such conditions if any as the court thinks fit; or
- (c) make such order as it thinks fit.

Date and expiry of registration certificate

24E.—[2](1) Every registration certificate issued in November of any year shall bear the date of 1st November in that year, and every other registration certificate shall bear the date on which it was issued.

(2) Every registration certificate shall have effect from the date it bears under subsection (1).

(3) Subject to subsection (4), every registration certificate shall expire on 31st October next after it is issued.

(4) On the name of a registered European lawyer being withdrawn from the register or on a registered European lawyer being suspended from practice as a registered European lawyer, any registration certificate for the time being in force of that registered European lawyer shall cease to have effect, but in the case of suspension, if he ceases to be so suspended during the period for which the registration would otherwise have continued in force, the registration certificate shall thereupon again have effect.

---

[1] Inserted by the European Communities (Lawyer's Practice) (Scotland) Regulations 2000 (SSI 2000/121), reg.37(1) and Sch.1, para. 1(3) (effective May 22, 2000).
[2] Inserted by the European Communities (Lawyer's Practice) (Scotland) Regulations 2000 (SSI 2000/121), reg.37(1) and Sch.1, para. 1(3) (effective May 22, 2000).

Suspension of registration certificate

24F.—[1](1) [2] If—

    (a) in pursuance of the Mental Health (Care and Treatment) (Scotland) Act 2003 a registered European lawyer is, by reason of mental disorder, detained in hospital;

    (b) *[Repealed by the Adult Support and Protection (Scotland) Act 2007 (asp 10) Sch.2, para.1 (effective October 5, 2007).]*

    (c) the estate of a registered European lawyer is sequestrated;

    (d) a registered European lawyer grants a trust deed for behoof of creditors;

    (e) a judicial factor is appointed on the estate of a registered European lawyer;

any registration certificate for the time being in force of that registered European lawyer shall cease to have effect, and he shall be suspended from practice as a registered European lawyer.

    (1A)[3] The Council may suspend from practice a registered European lawyer who—

    (a) has been convicted of an offence involving dishonesty, or

    (b) in respect of an offence, has been—

        (i) fined an amount equivalent to level 4 on the standard scale or more (whether on summary or solemn conviction), or

        (ii) sentenced to imprisonment for a term of 12 months or more.

    (2)[4] On the occurrence of any of the circumstances mentioned in subsection (1) or (1A), the registered European lawyer in question shall intimate those circumstances to the Council in writing immediately.

    (3) On the occurrence of the circumstances mentioned in paragraph (d) or (e) of subsection (1) the trustee or as the case may be the judicial factor shall intimate his appointment to the Council in writing immediately.

Further provisions relating to suspension of registration certificate

24G.—[5](1) The provisions of this section shall have effect in relation to a registration certificate which has ceased to have effect by virtue of section 24F during the period when that registration certificate would, but for that section, have continued in force.

    (2) A registration certificate which has ceased to have effect by virtue of paragraph (c) or (d) of section 24F(1) shall again have effect on the registered European lawyer being granted his discharge.

    (3) A registration certificate which has ceased to have effect by virtue of paragraph (e) of section 24F(1) shall again have effect on the judicial factor being granted his discharge.

---

[1] Inserted by the European Communities (Lawyer's Practice) (Scotland) Regulations 2000 (SSI 2000/121), reg.37(1) and Sch.1, para. 1(3) (effective May 22, 2000).

[2] As amended by the Mental Health (Care and Treatment) (Scotland) Act 2003 (Modification of Enactments) Order 2005, art.2 and Sch.1 (effective September 27, 2005).

[3] As inserted by the Legal Services (Scotland) Act 2010 (asp 16) Pt 4 c.3 s.137(3)(a) (effective May 1, 2011).

[4] As amended by the Legal Services (Scotland) Act 2010 (asp 16) Pt 4 c.3 s.137(3)(b) (effective May 1, 2011).

[5] Inserted by the European Communities (Lawyer's Practice) (Scotland) Regulations 2000 (SSI 2000/121), reg.37(1) and Sch.1, para. 1(3) (effective May 22, 2000).

(4)[1, 2]   Where a registered European lawyer is suspended from practice as a registered European lawyer by virtue of paragraph (a) of section 24F(1), the period of suspension shall, for the purposes of section 24C(2)(e), expire on the registered European lawyer ceasing to be detained.

(4A)[3]   A suspension from practice arising by virtue of section 24F(1A) expires if the grounds for it no longer apply.

(4B)[4]   On the occurrence of any of the circumstances mentioned in subsections (2) to (4A), the lawyer concerned must notify the Council in writing (and without delay).

(5)[5]   Where a registered European lawyer is suspended from practice as a registered European lawyer by virtue of paragraph (c), (d) or (e) of section 24F(1) or by virtue of section 24F(1A), he may at any time apply to the Council to terminate the suspension.

(6)   On an application under subsection (5), the Council may either—
    (a)   grant the application with or without conditions; or
    (b)   refuse the application.

(7)   If on an application by a registered European lawyer under subsection (5) the Council refuse the application or grant it subject to conditions, the registered European lawyer may appeal against the decision to the court, who may—
    (a)   affirm the decision; or
    (b)   vary any conditions imposed by the Council; or
    (c)   terminate the suspension either with or without conditions.

Rights of Solicitors

Rights of practising   F1.46

25.   Every person qualified to practise as a solicitor in accordance with section 4 may practise as a solicitor in any court in Scotland.

Rights of audience in the Court of Session, the Supreme Court, the Judicial   F1.47
Committee of the Privy Council and the High Court of Justiciary[6]

25A.—[7](1)[8, 9]   Subject to regulations 6 and 11 of the European Communities (Lawyer's Practice) (Scotland) Regulations 2000 and without prejudice to section 103(8) of the Criminal Procedure (Scotland) Act 1995 (right of solicitor to appear before single judge) and section 48(2)(b) (extension of rights of audience by act of sederunt) of the Court of Session Act 1988, a solicitor who—

---

[1] As amended by the Mental Health (Care and Treatment) (Scotland) Act 2003 (Modification of Enactments) Order 2005, art.2 and Sch.1 (effective September 27, 2005).

[2] As amended by the Adult Support and Protection (Scotland) Act 2007 (asp 10) Sch.2, para.1 (effective October 5, 2007).

[3] As inserted by the Legal Services (Scotland) Act 2010 (asp 16) Pt 4 c.3 s.137(4)(a) (effective May 1, 2011).

[4] As inserted by the Legal Services (Scotland) Act 2010 (asp 16) Pt 4 c.3 s.137(4)(a) (effective May 1, 2011).

[5] As amended by the Legal Services (Scotland) Act 2010 (asp 16) Pt 4 c.3 s.137(4)(b) (effective May 1, 2011).

[6] As amended by the Constitutional Reform Act 2005 (c.4) Sch.9 para.32 (effective October 1, 2009).

[7] As inserted by the Law Reform (Miscellaneous Provisions) (Scotland) Act 1990 (c.40) s. 24.

[8] As amended by the Criminal Procedure (Consequential Provisions) (Scotland) Act 1995 (c.40) Sch.4 para.31 (effective April 1, 1996: s.7(2)).

[9] As amended by the European Communities (Lawyer's Practice) (Scotland) Regulations 2000 (SSI 2000/121) reg.37(1) and Sch.1 para.1(5) (effective May 22, 2000).

(a)[1, 2]   seeks a right of audience in, on the one hand, the Court of Session, the Supreme Court and the Judicial Committee of the Privy Council or, on the other hand, the High Court of Justiciary and the Judicial Committee of the Privy Council; and

(b)   has satisfied the Council as to the requirements provided for in this section,

shall have a right of audience in those courts or, as the case may be, that court.

(2)   The requirements mentioned in subsection (1), in relation to the courts or, as the case may be, the court in which a solicitor seeks a right of audience, are that—

(a)   he has completed, to the satisfaction of the Council, a course of training in evidence and pleading in relation to proceedings in those courts or that court;

(b)   he has such knowledge as appears to the Council to be appropriate of—

    (i)   the practice and procedure of; and

    (ii)   professional conduct in regard to, those courts or that court; and

(c)   he has satisfied the Council that he is, having regard among other things to his experience in appropriate proceedings in the sheriff court, otherwise a fit and proper person to have a right of audience in those courts or that court.

(3)   Where a solicitor has satisfied the Council as to the requirements of subsection (2) in relation to the courts or, as the case may be, the court in which he seeks a right of audience the Council shall make an appropriate annotation on the roll against his name.

(4)[3]   The Council shall make rules under this section as to—

(a)   the matters to be included in, the methods of instruction to be employed in, and the qualifications of the person who will conduct, any course of training such as is mentioned in subsection (2)(a); and

(b)[4]   the manner in which a solicitor's knowledge of the practice and procedure and professional conduct mentioned in subsection (2)(b) is to be demonstrated, and separate rules shall be so made in relation to, on the one hand, the Court of Session, the Supreme Court and, on the other hand, the High Court of Justiciary.

(5)   The Council shall make rules of conduct in relation to the exercising of any right of audience held by virtue of this section.

(6)   Where a solicitor having a right of audience in any of the courts mentioned in subsection (1) is instructed to appear in that court, those instructions shall take precedence before any of his other professional obligations, and the Council shall make rules—

(a)   stating the order of precedence of those courts for the purposes of this subsection;

(b)   stating general criteria to which solicitors should have regard in determining whether to accept instructions in particular circumstances; and

---

[1] As amended by SI 1999/1042, Art. 4, Sch.2, para.7 (effective on commencement of s.44(1)(c) of the Scotland Act (c.44): May 20, 1999).

[2] As amended by the Constitutional Reform Act 2005 (c.4) Sch.9(1) para.32(3) (effective October 1, 2009).

[3] As amended by the Constitutional Reform Act 2005 (c.4) Sch.9(1) para.32(3) (effective October 1, 2009).

[4] As amended by SI 1999/1042, Art. 4, Sch.2, para.7 (effective on commencement of s.44(1)(c) of the Scotland Act (c.44): May 20, 1999).

   (c)   securing, through such of their officers as they think appropriate, that, where reasonably practicable, any person wishing to be represented before any of those courts by a solicitor holding an appropriate right of audience is so represented,

and for the purposes of rules made under this subsection the Inner and Outer Houses of the Court of Session, and the High Court of Justiciary exercising its appellate jurisdiction, may be treated as separate courts.

(7)   Subsection (6) does not apply to an employed solicitor whose contract of employment prevents him from acting for persons other than his employer.

(8)   Subject to subsections (9) and (10), the provisions of section 34(2) and (3) apply to rules made under this section as they apply to rules made under that section and, in considering any rules made by the Council under subsection (5), the Lord President shall have regard to the desirability of there being common principles applying in relation to the exercising of rights of audience by all practitioners appearing before the Court of Session and the High Court of Justiciary.

(9)[1]   The Council shall, after any rules made under subsection (4) have been approved by the Lord President, submit such rules to the Secretary of State, and no such rules shall have effect unless the Secretary of State, after consulting the CMA in accordance with section 64A, has approved them.

(10)   The Council shall, after any rules made under subsection (5) have been approved by the Lord President, submit such rules to the Secretary of State.

(11)[2]   Where the Secretary of State considers that any rule submitted to him under section (10) would directly or indirectly inhibit the freedom of a solicitor to appear in court or undertake all the work preparatory thereto he shall consult the CMA in accordance with section 64A.

(12)   The Council may bring into force the rules submitted by them to the Secretary of State under subsection (10) with the exception of any such rule which he has, in accordance with section 64B, refused to approve.

(13)   Nothing in this section affects the powers of any court in relation to any proceedings—

   (a)   to hear a person who would not otherwise have a right of audience before the court in relation to those proceedings; or

   (b)   to refuse to hear a person (for reasons which apply to him as an individual) who would otherwise have a right of audience before the court in relation to those proceedings, and where a court so refuses it shall give its reasons for that decision.

(14)   Where a complaint has been made that a solicitor has been guilty of professional misconduct in the exercise of any right of audience held by him by virtue of this section, the Council may, or if so requested by the Lord President shall, suspend him from exercising that right pending determination of that complaint under Part IV.

(14A)[3]   Where the Commission makes a determination under section 9(1) of the 2007 Act upholding a services complaint against a solicitor, the Council may, if

---

[1] As amended by the Enterprise and Regulatory Reform Act 2013 (c.24) Sch.6 para.10 (effective April 1, 2014).
[2] As amended by the Enterprise and Regulatory Reform Act 2013 (c.24) Sch.6 para.10 (effective April 1, 2014).
[3] As inserted by the Legal Profession and Legal Aid (Scotland) Act 2007 (asp 5) Sch.5 para.1(5) (effective October 1, 2008).

they consider that the complaint has a bearing on his fitness to exercise any right of audience held by him by virtue of this section and that it is appropriate to do so, suspend or revoke the right.

(15) Where a function is conferred on any person or body by this section he or, as the case may be, they shall exercise that function as soon as is reasonably practicable.

Restriction on rights of practising

F1.48

Offence for solicitors to act as agents for unqualified persons

26.—[1](1)   Any solicitor to whom this subsection applies who or incorporated practice which upon the account or for the profit of any unqualified person—

(a)   acts as agent in any action or proceedings in any court, or

(b)   permits or suffers his or, as the case may be, its name to be made use of in any way in any such action or proceedings; or

(c)   subject to subsection (4) draws or prepares any writ to which section 32 applies; or

(d)   subject to subsection (4) permits or suffers his or, as the case may be, its name to be made use of in the drawing or preparing of any such writ; or

(e)   does any other act to enable that person to appear, act or practise in any respect as a solicitor or notary public,

knowing that person not to be a qualified solicitor or notary public, as the case may be, shall be guilty of an offence.

(2)[2, 3]   Subsection (1) applies to any solicitor, registered foreign lawyer or registered European lawyer pursuing professional activities within the meaning of the European Communities (Lawyer's Practice) (Scotland) Regulations 2000, not being a solicitor, registered foreign lawyer or registered European lawyer pursuing professional activities within the meaning of the European Communities (Lawyer's Practice) (Scotland) Regulations 2000 who is employed full-time on a fixed salary by a body corporate or employed by a law centre or a citizens advice body.

(3)[4, 5, 6]   In this section "person" includes a body corporate but "unqualified person" does not include a licensed legal services provider, an incorporated practice, registered foreign lawyer, multi national practice or a registered European lawyer pursuing professional activities within the meaning of the European Communities (Lawyer's Practice) (Scotland) Regulations 2000.

---

[1] As amended by the Law Reform (Miscellaneous Provisions) (Scotland) Act 1985 (c.73), Sch.1, Pt I, para.4, and the Law Reform (Miscellaneous Provisions) (Scotland) Act 1990 (c.40), Sch.8, para.29(5).
[2] As amended by the European Communities (Lawyer's Practice) (Scotland) Regulations 2000 (SSI 2000/121), reg.37(1) and Sch.1, para.1(6) and by the Solicitors (Scotland) Act 1980 (Foreign Lawyers and Multi-national Practices) Regulations 2004 (SSI 2004/383), reg.4.
[3] As amended by the Legal Services (Scotland) Act 2010 (asp 16) Pt 4 c.3 s.125(1) (effective April 1, 2011).
[4] As amended by the Law Reform (Miscellaneous Provisions) (Scotland) Act 1985 (c.73), Sch.1, Pt I, para.4, and the Law Reform (Miscellaneous Provisions) (Scotland) Act 1990 (c.40), Sch.8, para.29(5).
[5] As amended by the European Communities (Lawyer's Practice) (Scotland) Regulations 2000 (SSI 2000/121), reg.37(1) and Sch.1, para.1(6) and by the Solicitors (Scotland) Act 1980 (Foreign Lawyers and Multi-national Practices) Regulations 2004 (SSI 2004/383), reg.4.
[6] As amended by the Legal Services (Scotland) Act 2010 (asp 16) Pt 4 c.3 s.123(1) (effective July 2, 2012).

(4)[1] Subsection (1)(c) and (d) shall not apply in relation to—

    (a) writs relating to heritable or moveable property drawn or prepared upon the account of or for the profit of independent qualified conveyancers

---

[1] As inserted by the Law Reform (Miscellaneous Provisions) (Scotland) Act 1990 (c.40) Sch.8(II) para.29(5)(d) (effective March 1, 1997 for purposes specified in SI 1996/2894 art.3 and Sch.1; not yet in force otherwise).

providing conveyancing services within the meaning of section 23 (interpretation of sections 16 to 22) of the Law Reform (Miscellaneous Provisions) (Scotland) Act 1990; or

(b) papers to found or oppose an application for a grant of confirmation in favour of executors drawn or prepared upon the account of or for the profit of an executry practitioner or recognised financial institution providing executry services within the meaning of the said section 23.

Offence for solicitors to share fees with unqualified persons

27. *[Repealed by the Law Reform (Miscellaneous Provisions) (Scotland) Act 1990 (c.40) Sch.9 (effective March 17, 1993: SI 1993/641).]*

Offence for solicitors who are disqualified to seek employment without informing employer

28.[1] Any person who—

(a) has been struck off the roll; or
(b) suspended from practice as a solicitor; or
(c)[2] has had his registration as a registered European lawyer withdrawn; or
(d)[3] has been suspended from practice as a registered European lawyer, and while so disqualified from practice seeks or accepts employment by a solicitor in connection with that solicitor's practice or by an incorporated practice or multi-national practice without previously informing him or, as the case may be, it that he is so disqualified shall be guilty of an offence; or
(e) has had his registration as a registered foreign lawyer withdrawn; or
(f) has been suspended from practice as a registered foreign lawyer.

29. *[Repealed by the Law Reform (Miscellaneous Provisions) (Scotland) Act 1990 (c.40) s.39 and Sch.9.]*

Liability for fees of other solicitor

30.[4, 5, 6] Where a solicitor or an incorporated practice authorised by and acting for a client employs another solicitor or incorporated practice or a licensed legal services provider he or, as the case may be, it shall (whether or not he or, as the case may be, it discloses the client) be liable to the employed party for that party's fees and outlays, unless at the time of the employment he or, as the case may be, it expressly disclaims any such liability.

---

[1] As amended by the Law Reform (Miscellaneous Provisions) (Scotland) Act 1985 (c.73), Sch.1, Pt I, para.6.
[2] As amended by the European Communities (Lawyer's Practice) (Scotland) Regulations 2000 (SSI 2000/121), reg.37(1) and Sch.1, para.1(7) and by the Solicitors (Scotland) Act 1980 (Foreign Lawyers and Multi-national Practices) Regulations 2004 (SSI 2004/383), reg.5.
[3] As amended by the European Communities (Lawyer's Practice) (Scotland) Regulations 2000 (SSI 2000/121), reg.37(1) and Sch.1, para.1(7) and by the Solicitors (Scotland) Act 1980 (Foreign Lawyers and Multi-national Practices) Regulations 2004 (SSI 2004/383), reg.5.
[4] As amended by the Law Reform (Miscellaneous Provisions) (Scotland) Act 1985 (c.73), Sch.1, Pt I, para.7.
[5] Read in conjunction with the European Communities (Lawyer's Practice) (Scotland) Regulations 2000 (SSI 2000/121), reg.37(2) and Sch.2 and the Solicitors (Scotland) Act 1980 (Foreign Lawyers and Multi-national Practices) Regulations 2004 (SSI 2004/383), reg.13.
[6] As substituted by the Legal Services (Scotland) Act 2010 (asp 16) Pt 4 c.3 s.123(2) (effective July 2, 2012).

Unqualified persons acting as solicitors

Offence for persons to pretend to be solicitor or notary public[1]

31.—[2](1)[3, 4] Any person (including a body corporate) who, not having the relevant qualification, either by himself or together with others, wilfully and falsely—

    (a)   pretends to be a solicitor or notary public; or

    (aa)[5] pretends to be a registered European lawyer; or

    (ab)[6] pretends to be a registered foreign lawyer; or

    (b)[7]   takes or uses any name, title, addition or description implying that he is duly qualified to act as a solicitor or a notary public, registered European lawyer or registered foreign lawyer, as the case may be, or recognised by law as so qualified;

shall be guilty of an offence.

(2) Any person (including a body corporate) who either by himself or together with others, wilfully and falsely—

    (a)   pretends to be an incorporated practice;

    (b)   takes or uses any name, title, addition or description implying that he is an incorporated practice,

shall be guilty of an offence.

(2A)[8] This section does not apply to an incorporated practice.

(2B)[9] This section does not apply in relation to the taking or using by a licensed legal services provider of a name, title, addition or description if the licensed provider has the Society's written authority for using it.

(2C)[10] For the purpose of subsection (2B), the Council are to make rules which—

    (a)   set the procedure for getting the Society's authority (and specify the conditions that the Society may impose if it gives that authority),

---

[1] As amended by the European Communities (Lawyer's Practice) (Scotland) Regulations 2000 (SSI 2000/121), reg.37(1) and Sch.1, para.1(8) and by the Solicitors (Scotland) Act 1980 (Foreign Lawyers and Multi-national Practices) Regulations 2004 (SSI 2004/383), reg.56.

[2] As amended by the Law Reform (Miscellaneous Provisions) (Scotland) Act 1985 (c.73), Sch.1, Pt I, para.8. Modified by the Copyright, Designs and Patents Act 1988 (c.48), s.278 (patent attorneys).

[3] As amended by the European Communities (Lawyer's Practice) (Scotland) Regulations 2000 (SSI 2000/121), reg.37(1) and Sch.1, para.1(8) and by the Solicitors (Scotland) Act 1980 (Foreign Lawyers and Multi-national Practices) Regulations 2004 (SSI 2004/383), reg.56.

[4] As amended by the Legal Services (Scotland) Act 2010 (asp 16) Pt 4 c.3 s.123(3) (effective July 2, 2012).

[5] Inserted by the European Communities (Lawyer's Practice) (Scotland) Regulations 2000 (SSI 2000/121), reg.37(1) and Sch.1, para.1(7)(c) (effective May 22, 2000).

[6] Inserted by the Solicitors (Scotland) Act 1980 (Foreign Lawyers and Multi-national Practices) Regulations 2004 (SSI 2004/383), reg.6.

[7] As amended by the European Communities (Lawyer's Practice) (Scotland) Regulations 2000 (SSI 2000/121), reg.37(1) and Sch.1, para.1(8) and by the Solicitors (Scotland) Act 1980 (Foreign Lawyers and Multi-national Practices) Regulations 2004 (SSI 2004/383), reg.56.

[8] As inserted by the Legal Services (Scotland) Act 2010 (asp 16) Pt 4 c.3 s.123(3) (effective July 2, 2012).

[9] As inserted by the Legal Services (Scotland) Act 2010 (asp 16) Pt 4 c.3 s.123(3) (effective July 2, 2012).

[10] As inserted by the Legal Services (Scotland) Act 2010 (asp 16) Pt 4 c.3 s.123(3) (effective July 2, 2012).

    (b)   specify the grounds on which the Society may refuse to give that authority (and require the Society to give rea sons in writing if it refuses to give that authority).

(3)   *[Repealed by the Law Reform (Miscellaneous Provisions) (Scotland) Act 1990 (c.40), Sch.9.]*

Offence for unqualified persons to prepare certain documents

32.—[1, 2](1)[3]   Subject to the provisions of this section and regulations 6, 11, 12 and 13 of the European Communities (Lawyer's Practice) (Scotland) Regulations 2000, any unqualified person (including a body corporate) who draws or prepares—

    (a)   any writ relating to heritable or moveable estate; or

    (b)[4]   any writ relating to any action or proceedings in any court; or

    (c)   any papers on which to found or oppose an application for a grant of confirmation in favour of executors,

shall be guilty of an offence.

(2)   Subsection (1) shall not apply—

    (a)   to an unqualified person if he proves that he drew or prepared the writ or papers in question without receiving, or without expecting to receive, either directly or indirectly, any fee, gain or reward (other than by remuneration paid under a contract of employment); or

    (b)   to an advocate; or

    (c)   to any public officer drawing or preparing writs in the course of his duty; or

    (d)   to any person employed merely to engross any writ; or

    (e)[5]   an incorporated practice; or

    (ea)[6]   a licensed legal services provider;

    (f)[7]   to a member of a body which has made a successful application under section 25 of the 1990 Act but only to the extent to which the member is exercising rights acquired by virtue of section 27 of that Act.

(2A)[8]   Subsection (1)(a) shall not apply to a conveyancing practitioner providing conveyancing services within the meaning of section 23 of the Law Reform (Miscellaneous Provisions) (Scotland) Act 1990.

(2B)[9]   Subsection (1)(b) shall not apply to—

    (a)   a person who is, by virtue of an act of sederunt made under section 32

---

[1] As amended by the Law Reform (Miscellaneous Provisions) (Scotland) Act 1990 (c.40), Sch.8, para.29(6).

[2] As inserted by the Legal Profession and Legal Aid (Scotland) Act 2007 (asp 5) s.61 (effective March 19, 2007).

[3] As amended by the European Communities (Lawyer's Practice) (Scotland) Regulations 2000 (SSI 2000/121), reg.37(1) and Sch.1, para.1(9) (effective May 22, 2000).

[4] As amended by the Solicitors (Scotland) Act 1988 (c.42), Sch.1, para.7.

[5] Added by the Law Reform (Miscellaneous Provisions) (Scotland) Act 1985 (c.73), Sch.1, Pt I, para.9.

[6] As inserted by the Legal Services (Scotland) Act 2010 (asp 16) Pt 4 c.3 s.123(4) (effective July 2, 2012).

[7] As inserted by the Legal Profession and Legal Aid (Scotland) Act 2007 (asp 5) s.61 (effective March 19, 2007).

[8] As amended by the Public Appointments and Public Bodies etc. (Scotland) Act 2003 (asp 4), Sch.4, para.7 (effective August 15, 2003).

[9] As amended by the Consumer Credit Act 2006 (c.14) s.16(5) (effective October 1, 2008) and existing text renumbered as s.32(2B)(a) and s.32(2B)(b) inserted by the Home Owner and Debtor Protection (Scotland) Act 2010 (asp 6) Pt 1 s.7(3) (effective October 3, 2010 subject to transitional provisions and savings specified in SSI 2010/316 arts 5 and 6).

(power of Court of Session to regulate procedure) of the Sheriff Courts (Scotland) Act 1971, permitted to represent—

    (a)   a party to a summary cause;

    (b)   a debtor or hirer in proceedings for—

        (i)   a time order under section 129 of the Consumer Credit Act 1974 (time orders); or

        (ii)   variation or revocation, under section 130(6) of that Act (variation and revocation of time orders), of a time order made under section 129.

    (b)   an approved lay representative within the meaning of section 5F of the Heritable Securities (Scotland) Act 1894 or section 24E of the Conveyancing and Feudal Reform (Scotland) Act 1970 (lay representation in proceedings by creditors for repossession of residential property) while acting in pursuance of the section in question.

(2C)   Subsection (1)(c) shall not apply to an executry practitioner or a recognised financial institution providing executry services within the meaning of section 23 of the Law Reform (Miscellaneous Provisions) (Scotland) Act 1990.

(3)   In this section "writ" does not include—

    (a)   a will or other testamentary writing;

    (b)   a document in *re mercatoria*, missive or mandate;

    (c)   a letter or power of attorney;

    (d)   a transfer of stock containing no trust or limitation thereof.

(4)[1]   For the purposes of this section, "unqualified person" includes a registered foreign lawyer.

Unqualified persons not entitled to fees, etc.

33.—[2, 3](1)   Subject to the provisions of regulations 12 and 13 of the European Communities (Lawyer's Practice) (Scotland) Regulations 2000, no fee, reward, outlay or expenses on account of or in relation to any act or proceeding done or taken by any person who—

    (a)   acts as a solicitor or as a notary public without being duly qualified so to act; or

    (b)   not being so qualified, frames or draws any writs to which section 32 applies,

shall be recoverable by any person in any action or matter.

(2)   This section does not apply to an incorporated practice or a licensed legal services provider or in relation to writs framed or drawn by a person who is, by virtue of an act of sederunt made under section 32 of the Sheriff Courts (Scotland) Act 1971, permitted to represent a party to a summary cause.

---

[1] Added by the Solicitors (Scotland) Act 1980 (Foreign Lawyers and Multi-national Practices) Regulations 2004 (SSI 2004/383), reg.7 (effective October 1, 2004).

[2] As amended by the Law Reform (Miscellaneous Provisions) (Scotland) Act 1985 (c.73), Sch.1, Pt 1, para.10, the Solicitors (Scotland) Act 1988 (c.42), Sch.1, para.8 and Sch.2, and the Law Reform (Miscellaneous Provisions) (Scotland) Act 1990 (c.40), Sch.8, para.29(7); further amended by the European Communities (Lawyer's Practice) (Scotland) Regulations 2000 (SSI 2000/121), reg.37(1) and Sch.1, para.1(10) (effective May 22, 2000).

[3] As amended by the Legal Services (Scotland) Act 2010 (asp 16) Pt 4 c.3 s.123(5) (effective July 2, 2012).

Privilege of incorporated practices from disclosure etc.

33A.—[1, 2](1)   Any communication made to or by an incorporated practice in the course of its acting as such for a client shall in any legal proceedings be privileged from disclosure in like manner as if the body had at all material times been a solicitor acting for the client.

(2)   Any enactment or instrument making special provision in relation to a solicitor or other legal representative as to the disclosure of information, or as to the production, seizure or removal of documents, with respect to which a claim to professional privilege could be maintained, shall, with any necessary modifications, have effect in relation to an incorporated practice as it has effect in relation to a solicitor.

33B.(1)   Any communication made to or by a registered foreign lawyer in the course of his actings as such for a client shall in any legal proceedings be privileged from disclosure in like manner as if the registered foreign lawyer had at all material times been a solicitor acting for a client.

(2)   Any enactment or instrument making special provision in relation to a solicitor or other legal representative as to the disclosure of information, or as to the production, seizure or removal of documents, with respect to which a claim to professional privilege could be maintained, shall, with any necessary modifications, have effect in relation to a registered foreign lawyer as it has effect in relation to a solicitor.

NOTE

[1] As inserted by the Solicitors (Scotland) Act 1980 (Foreign Lawyers and Multi-national Practices) Regulations 2004 (SSI 2004/383), reg.8.

Licensed legal services providers

F1.2

33C.—[3](1)   Subsection (2) applies to any rule made under section 34 which prohibits or unduly restricts the—

    (a)   involvement of solicitors in or with, or employment of solicitors by, licensed legal services providers,

    (b)   provision of services by licensed providers, or

    (c)   operation of licensed providers in other respects.

(2)   The rule is of no effect in so far as it does so (and for this purpose it is immaterial when the rule was made).

(3)   The reference in subsection (1)(a) to solicitors does not include a solicitor who is disqualified from practice by reason of having been—

    (a)   struck off (or removed from) the roll, or

    (b)   suspended from practice.

---

[1] As inserted by the Law Reform (Miscellaneous Provisions) (Scotland) Act 1985 (c.73), Sch.1, Pt I, para.11.
[2] Read in conjunction with the European Communities (Lawyer's Practice) (Scotland) Regulations 2000 (SSI 2000/121), reg.37(2) and Sch.2 (effective May 22, 2000).
[3] As inserted by the Legal Services (Scotland) Act 2010 (asp 16) Pt 4 c.3 s.124(1) (effective July 2, 2012).

PART III – PROFESSIONAL PRACTICE, CONDUCT AND DISCIPLINE OF SOLICITORS

Practice rules

Rules as to professional practice, conduct and discipline

34.—[1, 2, 3](1)   Subject to subsections (2) and (3), the Council may, if they think fit, make rules for regulating in respect of any matter the professional practice, conduct and discipline of solicitors and incorporated practices.

(1A)[4]   Rules made under this section may—

    (a)   provide as to the management and control by—

        (i)   solicitors holding practising certificates or their executors;

        (ii)   other incorporated practices

        of bodies corporate carrying on businesses consisting of the provision of professional services such as are provided by individuals and firms practising as solicitors being bodies the membership of which is restricted to such solicitors, executors and other incorporated practices;

    (b)   prescribe the circumstances in which such bodies may be recognised by the Council as being suitable to undertake the provision of any such services;

    (c)   prescribe the conditions which (subject to any exceptions provided by the rules) must at all times be satisfied by bodies corporate so recognised if they are to remain so recognised (which bodies, when and for so long as so recognised, are in this Act referred to as "incorporated practices");

    (d)   regulate the conduct of the affairs of incorporated practices; and

    (e)   provide—

        (i)   for the manner and form in which applications for recognition under this section are to be made, and for the payment of fees in connection with such applications;

        (ii)   for regulating the names that may be used by incorporated practices;

        (iii)   as to the period for which any recognition granted under this section shall (subject to the provisions of this Act) remain in force;

        (iv)   for the revocation of any such recognition on the grounds that it was granted as a result of any error or fraud;

        (v)   for the keeping by the Society of a list containing the names and places of business of all incorporated practices and for the information contained in any such list to be available for inspection;

        (vi)   for the rules made under any provision of this Act to have effect

---

[1] As amended by the Law Reform (Miscellaneous Provisions) (Scotland) Act 1985 (c.73), Sch.1, Pt. I, para.12.

[2] As amended by the Law Reform (Miscellaneous Provisions) (Scotland) Act 1990 (c.40), s.31(3) (effective March 17, 1993 by SI 1993/641).

[3] Read in conjunction with the European Communities (Lawyer's Practice) (Scotland) Regulations 2000 (SSI 2000/121), reg.37(2) and Sch.2 and the Solicitors (Scotland) Act 1980 (Foreign Lawyers and Multi-national Practices) Regulations 2004 (SSI 2004/383), reg.14.

[4] Inserted by the Law Reform (Miscellaneous Provisions) (Scotland) Act 1985 (c.73), Sch.1, Pt. I, para.12(b) and (c).

in relation to incorporated practices with such additions, omissions or other modifications as appear to the Council to be necessary or expedient;

    (vii) for empowering the Council to take such steps as they consider necessary or expedient to ascertain whether or not any rules applicable to incorporated practices by virtue of this section are being complied with; and

  (f)[1] make such additional or different provision as the Council think fit in relation to solicitors who have an interest in or are employed by (or otherwise within) licensed legal services providers.

(1B)[2] Rules made under this section may—

  (a) prevent a solicitor from entering a multi-national practice without the approval of the Council; and

  (b) make different provision for the regulation of solicitors and registered foreign lawyers in a multi-national practice in the following different cases—

    (i) where the principal place of business of the practice is outside Scotland and it has a place of business in Scotland;

    (ii) where the principal place of business of the practice is in Scotland and it has a place of business outside Scotland;

    (iii) where the principal place of business of the practice is in Scotland and it has no place of business outside Scotland.

(1C)[3] For the purposes of subsection (1B)(b), the principal place of business of a multi-national practice shall be determined by the Council who shall take into account factors set out in rules which may be made under this section.

(2) The Council shall, before making any rules under this section or section 35—

  (a) send to each member of the Society a draft of the rules; and

  (b) thereafter submit the draft rules to a meeting of the Society; and

  (c) take into consideration any resolution passed at that meeting relating to amendments to the draft rules.

(3) Rules made under this section or section 35 shall not have effect unless the Lord President after considering any objections he thinks relevant has approved the rules so made.

(3A) *[Repealed by the Legal Services (Scotland) Act 2010 (asp 16) Pt 4 c.3 s.124(2)(a) (effective July 2, 2012).]*

(4) *[Repealed by the Legal Services Act 2007 (c.29) Sch.23 para.1 (effective October 1, 2008 as SI 2008/1436; repeal has effect subject to savings and transitional provisions specified in SSI 2008/332 art.4).]*

(4ZA)[4] If any solicitor fails to comply with any rule made under this section, that failure may be treated as professional misconduct or unsatisfactory professional conduct.

---

[1] As substituted by the Legal Services (Scotland) Act 2010 (asp 16) Pt 4 c.3 s.124(2)(a)(i) (effective July 2, 2012).

[2] Inserted by the Solicitors (Scotland) Act 1980 (Foreign Lawyers and Multi-national Practices) Regulations 2004 (SSI 2004/383), reg.9.

[3] Inserted by the Solicitors (Scotland) Act 1980 (Foreign Lawyers and Multi-national Practices) Regulations 2004 (SSI 2004/383), reg.9.

[4] As inserted by the Legal Profession and Legal Aid (Scotland) Act 2007 (asp 5) Sch.5 para.1(6)(a) (effective October 1, 2008).

(4A)[1]   A certificate purporting to be signed by an officer of the Society and stating that any body corporate is or is not an incorporated practice shall, unless the contrary is proved, be sufficient evidence of that fact.

(4B)[2]   Subject to the provisions of this Act, the Secretary of State may, by order made by statutory instrument subject to annulment in pursuance of a resolution of either House of Parliament, provide for any enactment or instrument passed or made before the commencement of [sub]section (1A) above and having effect in relation to solicitors to have effect in relation to incorporated practices with such additions, omissions, or other modifications as appear to him to be necessary or expedient.

Accounts rules

Accounts rules

35.—[3, 4](1)[5]   The Council shall, subject to section 34(2) and (3), make rules (in this Act referred to as "accounts rules")—

    (a)   as to the opening and keeping by solicitors and incorporated practices of accounts and deposits at the banks specified in subsection (2) or with a building society for moneys not belonging to them received by them in the course of their practice;

    (b)   as to the opening and keeping by solicitors and incorporated practices of—

        (i)   a deposit or share account with a building society, or

        (ii)   an account showing sums on loan to a local authority, being in either case for a client whose name is specified in the title of the account;

    (c)   as to the keeping by solicitors and incorporated practices of books and accounts containing particulars and information as to money not belonging to them received, held or paid by them in the course of their practice;

    (d)   as to the action which the Council may take to enable them to ascertain whether or not the rules are being complied with; and

    (e)   as to the recovery from solicitors of fees and other costs incurred by the Council in ascertaining whether or not a solicitor who has failed to comply with the accounts rules has remedied that failure and is complying with the rules.

(2)[6]   The banks mentioned in paragraph (a) of subsection (1) are—

    (a)   the Bank of England;

    (b)   *[Repealed by the Trustee Savings Banks Act 1985 (c.58), Sch.4.]*

    (c)   the National Savings Bank;

    (d)   *[Repealed by the Postal Services Act 2000 (Consequential Modifica-*

---

[1] Inserted by the Law Reform (Miscellaneous Provisions) (Scotland) Act 1985 (c.73), Sch.1, Pt. I, para.12(b) and (c).

[2] Inserted by the Law Reform (Miscellaneous Provisions) (Scotland) Act 1985 (c.73), Sch.1, Pt. I, para.12(b) and (c).

[3] Extended by the Trustee Savings Banks Act 1985 (c.58), Sch.1, para.11(2)(b).

[4] Read in conjunction with the European Communities (Lawyer's Practice) (Scotland) Regulations 2000 (SSI 2000/121), reg.37(2) and Sch.2 and the Solicitors (Scotland) Act 1980 (Foreign Lawyers and Multi-national Practices) Regulations 2004 (SSI 2004/383), reg.14.

[5] As amended by the Law Reform (Miscellaneous Provisions) (Scotland) Act 1985 (c.73), Sch.1, Pt. I, para.13, Pt. II, para.4 and Sch.4, and the Solicitors (Scotland) Act 1988 (c.42), Sch.1, para.9 and Sch.2.

[6] As amended by the Banking Act 1987 (c.22), Sch.6, para.9.

tions No.1) Order 2001, (SI 2001/1149), Art.3, Sch.2 (effective March 26, 2001).]

(e)[1]   a person (other than a building society) who has permission under Part 4 of the Financial Services and Markets Act 2000 to accept deposits;

(ea)[2]   an EEA firm of the kind mentioned in paragraph 5(b) of Schedule 3 to the Financial Services and Markets Act 2000 which has permission under paragraph 15 of that Schedule (as a result of qualifying for authorisation under paragraph 12 of that Schedule) to accept deposits;

(2A)[3]   Paragraphs (e) and (ea) of subsection (2) must be read with—

(a)   section 22 of the Financial Services and Markets Act 2000;

(b)   any relevant order under that section; and

(c)   Schedule 2 to that Act.

(3)[4]   If any solicitor fails to comply with any rule made under this section that failure may be treated as professional misconduct or as unsatisfactory professional conduct.

(4)   Rules made under this section shall not apply to a solicitor—

(a)   who is in employment as solicitor to a Minister of the Crown or a Government Department or as an assistant or officer appointed to act under the direction of such solicitor; or

(b)[5]   who is in employment to which Part V of the Legal Aid (Scotland) Act 1986 applies; or

(c)   who is in employment in an office connected with the administration of a local authority or a statutory undertaking or a designated body to which he has been appointed by the authority or the statutory undertakers or the persons responsible for the management of that body by reason of his being a solicitor,

so far as regards monies received, held or paid by him in the course of that employment.

In this subsection—

"local authority" means a local authority within the meaning of the Local Government (Scotland) Act 1973;

"statutory undertakers" means any persons (including a local authority) authorised by any enactment or statutory order or any scheme made under or confirmed by an enactment to construct, work or carry on any railway, light railway, tramway, road transport, water transport, canal, inland navigation, dock, harbour, pier or lighthouse undertaking or any undertaking for the supply of gas, electricity, hydraulic power or water;

"designated body" means any body whether corporate or unincorporate for the time being designated by the Council for the purposes of this section.

---

[1] Inserted by the Financial Services and Markets Act 2000 (Consequential Amendments and Repeals) Order 2001, (SI 2001/3649), art.222.
[2] Inserted by the Financial Services and Markets Act 2000 (Consequential Amendments and Repeals) Order 2001, (SI 2001/3649), art.222.
[3] Inserted by the Financial Services and Markets Act 2000 (Consequential Amendments and Repeals) Order 2001, (SI 2001/3649), art.222.
[4] As substituted by the Legal Profession and Legal Aid (Scotland) Act 2007 (asp 5) Sch.5 para.1(7) (effective October 1, 2008).
[5] As amended by the Legal Aid (Scotland) Act 1986 (c.47), Sch.3, para.7.

Interest on client's money

36.—[1, 2](1) [3]   Accounts rules shall make provision for requiring a solicitor or an incorporated practice, in such cases as may be prescribed by the rules—

    (a)   to keep in a separate deposit or savings account at a bank or with a building society, or on a separate deposit receipt at a bank, for the benefit of the client money received for or on account of a client; or

    (aa) to keep in—

        (i)   a deposit or share account with a building society; or

        (ii) an account showing sums on loan to a local authority,

being in either case an account kept by the solicitor in his or, as the case may be, by the incorporated practice in its own name for a specified client, money so received; or

    (b)   to make good to the client out of the solicitor's or, as the case may be, the incorporated practice's own money a sum equivalent to the interest which would have accrued if the money so received had been kept as mentioned in paragraph (a) or (*aa*).

(2)   The cases in which a solicitor or incorporated practice may be required to act as mentioned in subsection (1) may be defined among other things by reference to the amount of any sum received or balance held or the period for which it is or is likely to be retained or held or both; and the rules may include provision for enabling a client (without prejudice to any other remedy) to require that any question arising under the rules in relation to the client's money be referred to and determined by the Society.

(3)   Except as provided by the rules, a solicitor or incorporated practice shall not be liable by virtue of the relation between solicitor and client to account to any client for interest received by the solicitor or, as the case may be, the incorporated practice on monies lodged in an account at a bank or with a building society, or on deposit receipt, at a bank, being monies received or held for or on account of his or, as the case may be, its clients generally.

(4)   Nothing in this section or in the rules shall affect any arrangement in writing whenever made between a solicitor and his client or an incorporated practice and its client as to the application of the client's money or interest on it.

Accountant's certificates

37.—[4, 5](1)   This section shall have effect for the purpose of securing satisfactory evidence of compliance with the accounts rules.

(2)   Subject to the following provisions of this section, every solicitor and incorporated practice to whom the accounts rules apply shall, in accordance with the rules made under subsection (3), deliver to the Council a certificate by an accountant (in this section referred to as an "accountant's certificate").

[1] As amended by the Law Reform (Miscellaneous Provisions) (Scotland) Act 1985 (c.73), Sched. 1, Pt. I, para.14, and the Solicitors (Scotland) Act 1988 (c.42), Sched. 1, para.10 and Sched. 2.

[2] Read in conjunction with the European Communities (Lawyer's Practice) (Scotland) Regulations 2000 (SSI 2000/121), reg.37(2) and Sch.2 and the Solicitors (Scotland) Act 1980 (Foreign Lawyers and Multi-national Practices) Regulations 2004 (SSI 2004/383), reg.14.

[3] As amended by the Law Reform (Miscellaneous Provisions) (Scotland) Act 1980 (c.55), s.25.

[4] As amended by the Law Reform (Miscellaneous Provisions) (Scotland) Act 1985 (c.73), Sched. 1, Pt. I, para.15 (reading the word "substituted" in para.15(c)(i) as "inserted").

[5] Read in conjunction with the European Communities (Lawyer's Practice) (Scotland) Regulations 2000 (SSI 2000/121), reg.37(2) and Sch.2 and the Solicitors (Scotland) Act 1980 (Foreign Lawyers and Multi-national Practices) Regulations 2004 (SSI 2004/383), reg.13 and 14.

(3)   The council shall make rules (in this Act referred to as "accountant's certificate rules") prescribing—

    (a)   the qualifications to be held by an accountant by whom an accountant's certificate may be given;

    (b)   the nature and extent of the examination to be made by an accountant of the books and accounts of a solicitor or his firm or of an incorporated practice and of any other relative documents with a view to the signing of an accountant's certificate;

    (c)   the intervals at which an accountant's certificate shall be delivered to the Council, not being more frequent than once in each practice year;

    (d)   the accounting period for which an accountant's certificate shall be delivered or the different accounting periods for which in different circumstances an accountant's certificate shall be delivered;

    (e)   the period within which an accountant's certificate shall be delivered; and

    (f)   the form and content of an accountant's certificate.

(4)   The accountant's certificate rules may include such other provisions as the Council consider necessary or proper for the purpose of giving effect to the foregoing provisions of this section and for regulating any incidental, consequential or supplementary matters.

(5)   The delivery of an accountant's certificate in pursuance of subsection (2) shall not be required in the case of—

    (a)   a solicitor who or incorporated practice which, in agreement with the Council, furnishes to the Council and keeps in force a fidelity bond by an insurance office or other institution accepted by the court as cautioners for a judicial factor appointed by the court for such amount as the Council may determine, guaranteeing the intromissions of the solicitor or his firm or, as the case may be, of the incorporated practice with money held by him or them or, as the case may be, it for or on behalf of clients; or

    (b)   a solicitor or incorporated practice who satisfies the Council that during the accounting period to which the accountant's certificate would ordinarily relate he has not in the course of his practice or, as the case may be, it has not held or received any money on behalf of clients.

(6)   If the Council are of opinion that satisfactory evidence of compliance with the accounts rules for the time being in force will be secured by some method other than by delivery of an accountant's certificate under subsection (2), they may make rules—

    (a)   prescribing—

        (i)   that other method;

        (ii)   the terms and conditions to be observed in connection therewith; and

        (iii)   the procedure to be followed by solicitors or incorporated practices desiring to adopt that other method, and

    (b)   containing such incidental, consequential and supplementary provisions relative thereto as the Council may consider necessary or proper;

and a solicitor who satisfies the Council that he or, as the case may be, an incorporated practice which satisfies the Council that it is complying with rules made under this subsection shall not be required to deliver an accountant's certificate in pursuance of subsection (2).

(7)   A certificate under the hand of the secretary of the Society certifying that a specified solicitor or incorporated practice has or has not, as the case may be, delivered to the Council an accountant's certificate, or supplied any evidence required from him or, as the case may be, it under this section or under the accountant's certificate rules or, as the case may be, under any rules made under subsection (6), shall, unless the contrary is proved, be evidence of the fact so certified.

(8)[1]   Failure by a solicitor to comply with any provision of this section or of the accountant's certificate rules or of any rules made under subsection (6), so far as applicable to him, may be treated as professional misconduct or as unsatisfactory professional misconduct.

Accounts fee

37A.—[2](1)   An annual fee set in accordance with this section (the "accounts fee") is to be paid by each—

    (a)   solicitor who is required by paragraph 1 of Schedule 3 (as read with section 43(7)) to pay an annual contribution on behalf of the Guarantee Fund,

    (b)   incorporated practice that is required by that paragraph of that Schedule to pay an annual corporate contribution on that behalf.

(2)   The accounts fee is also to be paid by each—

    (a)   registered European lawyer or registered foreign lawyer who is required by virtue of paragraph 1A or 1B of that Schedule to pay an annual contribution on that behalf,

    (b)   multi-national practice to which the accounts rules apply by virtue of an enactment.

(3)   The accounts fee is to be set by the Council for the purpose of funding the exercise of their function of securing compliance (by the categories specified in subsections (1) and (2)) with the accounts rules.

(4)   The accounts fee is to be—

    (a)   set—

        (i)   no later than 30 September each year in respect of the 12 month period beginning with 1 November that year, or

        (ii)   by reference to such other dates as the Council may fix,

    (b)   paid to the Council by such date as they may fix.

(5)   The accounts fee may be set—

    (a)   so as to involve different amounts (including nil) for different—

        (i)   categories (as specified in subsections (1) and (2)),

        (ii)   circumstances (by reference to all relevant factors),

    (b)   in the case of incorporated practices, by particular reference to the number of solicitors that they have as directors, members or employees.

(6)   The Council may take such steps as they consider necessary for recovering the accounts fee due in accordance with this section.

---

[1] As substituted by the Legal Profession and Legal Aid (Scotland) Act 2007 (asp 5) Sch.5 para. 1(8) (effective October 1, 2008).

[2] As inserted by the Legal Services (Scotland) Act 2010 (asp 16) Pt 4 c.3 s.138(1) (effective May 1, 2011).

Powers of Council to intervene

Powers where dishonesty alleged

38. *[Repealed by the Legal Services Act 2007 (c.29) Sch.23 para.1 (effective October 1, 2008 as SI 2008/1436; repeal has effect subject to savings and transitional provisions specified in SSI 2008/332 art.4).]*

Powers where delay alleged

39. *[Repealed by the Legal Services Act 2007 (c.29) Sch.23 para.1 (effective October 1, 2008 as SI 2008/1436; repeal has effect subject to savings and transitional provisions specified in SSI 2008/332 art.4).]*

Powers where excessive fees etc. charged

39A.—[1, 2](1) This section applies where the Council are satisfied, in the case of any solicitor or incorporated practice, after inquiry and after giving the solicitor or incorporated practice an opportunity of being heard, that the solicitor or incorporated practice has issued an account for professional fees and outlays of an amount which is grossly excessive (whether or not the account has been paid by or on behalf of the client or debited by the solicitor or incorporated practice to the account of any sums held on behalf of the client).

(2) Where this section applies the Council may—

    (a) in the case of a solicitor, withdraw his practising certificate; or

    (b) in the case of an incorporated practice, withdraw the practising certificates of all or any of the solicitors who are directors of the incorporated practice;

and a certificate so withdrawn shall cease to have effect and the solicitor shall be suspended from practice as a solicitor.

(3) On being satisfied by the solicitor or, as the case may be, incorporated practice that he or it has complied with the requirements of subsection (4) the Council, unless they are of the opinion that the solicitor or incorporated practice is liable to disciplinary proceedings under Part IV, shall terminate the suspension from practice of the solicitor or solicitors concerned and shall restore to him or them any practising certificates held by him or them for the practice year then current.

(4) The requirements referred to in subsection (3) are—

    (a) to submit the account to the Auditor of the Court of Session for taxation together with all documents in the possession or control of the solicitor or incorporated practice which relate to the matters in respect of which the account was issued; and

    (b) to refund to the client a sum not less than the relevant amount.

(5) The Council shall be entitled to be represented at a diet for taxation by virtue of subsection (4)(a) and to make representations to the Auditor of Court.

(6) Where, on taxation of an account by virtue of subsection (4)(a), the amount due in respect of the account as taxed is the amount specified in the account as is-

---

[1] Inserted by the Solicitors (Scotland) Act 1988 (c.42), s.4.

[2] Read in conjunction with the European Communities (Lawyer's Practice) (Scotland) Regulations 2000 (SSI 2000/121), reg.37(2) and Sch.2 and the Solicitors (Scotland) Act 1980 (Foreign Lawyers and Multi-national Practices) Regulations 2004 (SSI 2004/383), reg.13.

sued, the fee of the Auditor of Court shall be paid by the Council; but in any other case the fee shall be paid by the solicitor or, as the case may be, the incorporated practice.

(7) In subsection (4)(b) "the relevant amount" is the amount (if any) by which the sum received by the solicitor or incorporated practice in respect of the accouint exceeds the amount due in respect of the account as taxed.

(8) A solicitor may, within 21 days of receiving written notice of a decision of the Council under subsection (2) to withdraw his practising certificate, appeal to the Court against that decision; and on any such appeal the Court may give such directions in the matter, including directions as to the expenses of the proceedings before the Court, as it may think fit; and the order of the Court shall be final.

(9) The withdrawal of a solicitor's practising certificate under subsection

(2) shall be without prejudice to the operation of section 35(3) or section 37(8).

(10)[1] The Council shall notify the Commission of any case—

    (a) where any of the following things occur—

        (i) they withdraw a practising certificate under subsection (2);

        (ii) they terminate a suspension from practice and restore a practising certificate under subsection (3);

        (iii) the Court makes an order under subsection (8); and

    (b) which does not involve a complaint remitted to the Council under section 6(a) or 15(5)(a) of the 2007 Act.

Powers where failure to comply with accounts rules, etc.

40.—[2], [3](1) [4] Where the Council are satisfied, in the case of any solicitor or incorporated practice, after enquiry and after giving the solicitor or, as the case may be, incorporated practice an opportunity of being heard, that the solicitor or, as the case may be, incorporated practice has failed or is failing to comply with any provisions of—

    (a) section 35 or the accounts rules made under that section, or

    (b) section 37 or the accountant's certificate rules or other rules made under that section,

so far as applicable in his or, as the case may be, its case (in this section referred to as "the applicable provisions"), the Council may, subject to the provisions of this section,

    (a) withdraw the practising certificate held by the solicitor; or as the case may be—

    (b) withdraw the practising certificate or certificates or any or all of the solicitors who are directors of the incorporated practice,

and a certificate so withdrawn shall thereupon cease to have effect and the solicitor shall be suspended from practice as a solicitor.

(2) On being satisfied by the solicitor that he or, as the case may be, by the incorporated practice that it is able and willing to comply with the applicable provi-

---

[1] As inserted by the Legal Profession and Legal Aid (Scotland) Act 2007 (asp 5) Sch.5 para. 1(11) (effective October 1, 2008).

[2] As amended by the Law Reform (Miscellaneous Provisions) (Scotland) Act 1985 (c.73), Sched. 1, Pt. I, para. 18.

[3] Read in conjunction with the European Communities (Lawyer's Practice) (Scotland) Regulations 2000 (SSI 2000/121), reg.37(2) and Sch.2 and the Solicitors (Scotland) Act 1980 (Foreign Lawyers and Multi-national Practices) Regulations 2004 (SSI 2004/383), reg.13.

[4] As amended by the Solicitors (Scotland) Act 1988 (c.42), Sch.1, para. 12.

sions, the Council, unless they are of opinion that the solicitor or, as the case may be, the incorporated practice is liable to disciplinary proceedings under Part IV, shall terminate the suspension from practice of the solicitor or solicitors concerned and shall restore to him or them any practising certificate or certificates held by him or them for the practice year then current.

(3)   Within 21 days after receiving written notice of a decision of the Council under this section to withdraw his practising certificate, or to refuse to terminate his suspension from practice, a solicitor may appeal to the court against the decision; and on any such appeal the court may give such directions in the matter, including directions as to the expenses of the proceedings before the court, as it may think fit; and the order of the court shall be final.

(4)   Any withdrawal of a solicitor's practising certificate by the Council in exercise of the power conferred by subsection (1) shall be without prejudice to the operation of section 35(3) or section 37(8).

(5)[1]   The Council shall notify the Commission of any case—
   (a)   where any of the following things occur—
      (i)   they withdraw a practising certificate under subsection (1);
      (ii)   they terminate a suspension from practice and restore a practising certificate under subsection (2);
      (iii)   the Court makes an order under subsection (3); and
   (b)   which does not involve a complaint remitted to the Council under section 6(a) or 15(5)(a) of the 2007 Act.

Appointment of judicial factor

41.[2, 3]   Where the Council, in exercise of any power conferred on them by the accounts rules, have caused an investigation to be made of the books, accounts and other documents of a solicitor or an incorporated practice, and, on consideration of the report of the investigation, the Council are satisfied—
   (a)   that the solicitor or, as the case may be the incorporated practice has failed to comply with the provisions of those rules, and
   (b)   that, in the case of a solicitor, in connection with his practice as such either—
      (i)   his liabilities exceed his assets in the business, or
      (ii)   his books, accounts and other documents are in such a condition that it is not reasonably practicable to ascertain definitely whether his liabilities exceed his assets, or
      (iii)   there is reasonable ground for apprehending that a claim on the Guarantee Fund may arise; or
   (c)   that, in the case of an incorporated practice, either—
      (i)   its liabilities exceed its assets, or
      (ii)   its books, accounts and other documents are in such a condition that it is not reasonably practicable to ascertain definitely whether its liabilities exceed its assets, or

---

[1] As inserted by the Legal Profession and Legal Aid (Scotland) Act 2007 (asp 5) Sch.5 para. 1(12) (effective October 1, 2008).
[2] As amended by the Law Reform (Miscellaneous Provisions) (Scotland) Act 1985 (c.73), Sched. 1, Pt. I, para. 19, and the Solicitors (Scotland) Act 1988 (c.42), Sched. 1, para. 13 and Sched. 2.
[3] Read in conjunction with the European Communities (Lawyer's Practice) (Scotland) Regulations 2000 (SSI 2000/121), reg.37(2) and Sch.2 and the Solicitors (Scotland) Act 1980 (Foreign Lawyers and Multi-national Practices) Regulations 2004 (SSI 2004/383), reg.13.

(iii) there is reasonable ground for apprehending that a claim on the guarantee fund may arise,

the Council may apply to the court for the appointment of a judicial factor on the estate of the solicitor or as the case may be, of the incorporated practice; and the court, on consideration of the said report and after giving the solicitor or as the case may be, the incorporated practice an opportunity of being heard, may appoint a judicial factor on such estate, or do otherwise as seems proper to it.

Distribution of sums in client bank account

42.—[1, 2](1) Subject to the provisions of this section, where, in any of the events mentioned in subsection (2) or (2A), the sum at the credit of any client account kept by a solicitor or an incorporated practice (or where several such accounts are kept by him or, as the case may be, by it the total of the sums at the credit of those accounts) is less than the total of the sums received by him in the course of his practice on behalf of his clients or, as the case may be, by it on behalf of its clients and remaining due by him or, as the case may be, by it to them, then, notwithstanding any rule of law to the contrary, the sum at the credit of the client account (or where several such accounts are kept, the total of the sums at the credit of those accounts) shall be divisible proportionately among the clients of the solicitor or, as the case may be, the incorporated practice according to the respective sums received by him in the course of his practice on their behalf or, as the case may be, by it on their behalf and remaining due by him or as the case may be, by it to them.

(2) The events to which subsection (1) applies are in relation to any solicitor—

    (a) the sequestration of his estate;

    (b) the granting by him of a trust deed for behoof of creditors;

    (c) the appointment of a judicial factor on his estate.

(2A) The events to which subsection (1) applies are in relation to any incorporated practice—

    (a) the making of an administration or winding up order or the appointment of a provisional liquidator, liquidator, receiver or judicial factor; or

    (b) the passing of a resolution for voluntary winding up (other than one passed solely for the purposes of reconstruction or amalgamation with another incorporated practice).

(3)[3] Where a solicitor or an incorporated practice keeps an account at a bank in his or, as the case may be, its own name for a specified client no regard shall be had for the purposes of this section to the sum at the credit of that account or to any sums received by the solicitor in the course of his practice on behalf of that client or, as the case may be, by the incorporated practice on that behalf and remaining due by him or, as the case may be, by it to that client, so far as these are represented by the sum at the credit of that bank account; nor shall any regard be had for such purposes to any—

    (a) deposit or share account with a society; or

    (b) account showing sums on loan to a local authority,

---

[1] As amended by the Law Reform (Miscellaneous Provisions) (Scotland) Act 1985 (c.73), Sched. 1, Pt. I, para.20.

[2] As amended by the Law Reform (Miscellaneous Provisions) (Scotland) Act 1980 (c.55), s.25, and the Solicitors (Scotland) Act 1988 (c.42), Sch.2.

[3] As amended by the Law Reform (Miscellaneous Provisions) (Scotland) Act 1980 (c.55), s.25, and the Solicitors (Scotland) Act 1988 (c.42), Sch.2.

being in either case an account kept by the solicitor in his own name or, as the case may be, by the incorporated practice in its own name for a specified client.

(4)   For the purposes of this section any reference to an account at a bank includes a reference to a deposit receipt at a bank.

Notes

[3] Read in conjunction with the European Communities (Lawyer's Practice) (Scotland) Regulations 2000 (SSI 2000/121), reg.37(2) and Sch.2 and the Solicitors (Scotland) Act 1980 (Foreign Lawyers and Multi-national Practices) Regulations 2004 (SSI 2004/383), reg.13.

Unsatisfactory professional conduct: Council's powers   F1.3

42ZA.—[1](1)   Where a conduct complaint suggesting unsatisfactory professional conduct by a practitioner who is a solicitor is remitted to the Council under section 6(a) or 15(5)(a) of the 2007 Act, the Council must having—

(a)   investigated the complaint under section 47(1) of that Act and made a written report under section 47(2) of that Act;

(b)   given the solicitor an opportunity to make representations, determine the complaint.

(2)   Where a complaint is remitted to the Council under section 53ZA, the Council—

(a)   must—

(i)   notify the solicitor specified in it and the complainer of that fact and that the Council are required to investigate the complaint as a complaint of unsatisfactory professional conduct;

(ii)   so investigate the complaint;

(iii)   having so investigated the complaint and given the solicitor an opportunity to make representations, determine the complaint;

(b)   may rely, in their investigation, on any findings in fact which the Tribunal makes available to them under section 53ZA(2) as respects the complaint.

(3)   Where the Council make a determination under subsection (1) or (2) upholding the complaint, they—

(a)   shall censure the solicitor;

(b)   may take any of the steps mentioned in subsection (4) which they consider appropriate.

(4)   The steps are—

(a)   where the Council consider that the solicitor does not have sufficient competence in relation to any aspect of the law or legal practice, to direct the solicitor to undertake such education or training as regards the law or legal practice as the Council consider appropriate in that respect;

(b)   subject to subsection (6), to direct the solicitor to pay a fine not exceeding £2,000;

(c)   where the Council consider that the complainer has been directly affected by the conduct, to direct the solicitor to pay compensation of such amount, not exceeding £5,000, as they may specify to the complainer for loss, inconvenience or distress resulting from the conduct.

[1] As inserted by the Legal Profession and Legal Aid (Scotland) Act 2007 (asp 5) Pt 2 s.53(2) (effective October 1, 2008).

(5)   The Council may, in considering the complaint, take account of any previous determination by them, the Tribunal or the Court upholding a complaint against the solicitor of unsatisfactory professional conduct or professional misconduct (but not a complaint in respect of which an appeal is pending or which has been quashed ultimately on appeal).

(6)   The Council shall not direct the solicitor to pay a fine under subsection (4)(b) where, in relation to the subject matter of the complaint, the solicitor has been convicted by any court of an act involving dishonesty and sentenced to a term of imprisonment of not less than 2 years.

(7)   Any fine directed to be paid under subsection (4)(b) above shall be treated for the purposes of section 211(5) of the Criminal Procedure (Scotland) Act 1995 (fines payable to HM Exchequer) as if it were a fine imposed in the High Court.

(8)   The Council shall intimate—

  (a)   a determination under subsection (1) or (2);
  (b)   any censure under subsection (3)(a);
  (c)   any direction under subsection (4),

to the complainer and the solicitor specified in it by sending to each of them a copy of the determination, censure or, as the case may be, the direction and by specifying the reasons for the determination.

(9)   A solicitor in respect of whom a determination upholding a conduct complaint has been made under subsection (1) or (2), or a direction has been made under subsection (4) may, before the expiry of the period of 21 days beginning with the day on which the determination or, as the case may be, the direction is intimated to him, appeal to the Tribunal against the—

  (a)   determination;
  (b)   direction (whether or not he is appealing against the determination).

(10)   A complainer may, before the expiry of the period of 21 days beginning with the day on which a determination under subsection (1) or (2) not upholding the conduct complaint is intimated to him, appeal to the Tribunal against the determination.

(11)   Where the Council have upheld the conduct complaint but have not directed the solicitor under subsection (4)(c) to pay compensation, the complainer may, before the expiry of the period of 21 days beginning with the day on which the determination upholding the complaint is intimated to him, appeal to the Tribunal against the Council's decision not to make a direction under that subsection.

(12)   A complainer to whom the Council have directed a solicitor under subsection (4)(c) to pay compensation may, before the expiry of the period of 21 days beginning with the day on which the direction under that subsection is intimated to him, appeal to the Tribunal against the amount of the compensation directed to be paid.

(13)   The Scottish Ministers may by order made by statutory instrument—

  (a)   amend subsection (4)(b) by substituting for the amount for the time being specified in that subsection such other amount as appears to them to be justified by a change in the value of money;
  (b)   after consulting the Council and such groups of persons representing consumer interests as they consider appropriate, amend subsection (4)(c) by substituting for the amount for the time being specified in that subsection such other amount as they consider appropriate.

(14)   A statutory instrument containing an order under—

  (a)   subsection (13)(a) is subject to annulment in pursuance of a resolution of the Scottish Parliament;

(b)   subsection (13)(b) is not to be made unless a draft of the instrument has been laid before, and approved by resolution of, the Scottish Parliament.

(15)   In this section, "complainer" means the person who made the complaint and, where the complaint was made by the person on behalf of another person, includes that other person.

Unsatisfactory professional conduct: Council's powers to monitor compliance with direction under section 42ZA(4)

42ZB.—[1](1)   The Council shall, by notice in writing, require every solicitor who is specified in—

(a)   a direction made under section 42ZA(4); or

(b)   such a direction as confirmed or varied on appeal by—

(i)   the Tribunal; or

(ii)   the Court,

to give, before the expiry of such period being not less than 21 days as the notice specifies, an explanation of the steps which he has taken to comply with the direction.

(2)   Where an appeal is made under section 42ZA(9) or (12) or 54A(1) or (2) against a direction made under section 42ZA(4), any notice under subsection (1)(a) above relating to the direction shall cease to have effect pending the outcome of the appeal.

Report by Commission to Council under section 10(2)(e) of the 2007 Act: Council's powers

42ZC.—[2](1)   Where the Council receive a report from the Commission under section 10(2)(e) of the 2007 Act as respects a practitioner who is a solicitor, they may direct him to undertake such education or training as regards the law or legal practice as the Council consider appropriate in the circumstances.

(2)   The Council shall by notice in writing—

(a)   intimate a direction under subsection (1) to the solicitor;

(b)   require the solicitor to give, before the expiry of such period being not less than 21 days as the notice specifies, an explanation of the steps which he has taken to comply with the direction.

(3)   Where an appeal is made under section 42ZD(1) or (3) against a direction under subsection (1), any notice under subsection (2)(b) relating to the direction shall cease to have effect pending the outcome of the appeal.

Direction under section 42ZC(2): appeal by practitioner

42ZD.—[3](1)   A solicitor in respect of whom a direction has been made under section 42ZC(1) may, before the expiry of the period of 21 days beginning with the day on which it is intimated to him, appeal to the Tribunal against the direction.

(2)   On an appeal to the Tribunal under subsection (1), the Tribunal may quash, confirm or vary the direction being appealed against.

---

[1] As inserted by the Legal Profession and Legal Aid (Scotland) Act 2007 (asp 5) Pt 2 s.53(2) (effective October 1, 2008).
[2] As inserted by the Legal Profession and Legal Aid (Scotland) Act 2007 (asp 5) Pt 2 s.55(1) (effective October 1, 2008).
[3] As inserted by the Legal Profession and Legal Aid (Scotland) Act 2007 (asp 5) Pt 2 s.55(1) (effective October 1, 2008).

(3)   The solicitor may, before the expiry of the period of 21 days beginning with the day on which the Tribunal's decision under subsection (2) is intimated to him, appeal to the Court against the decision.

(4)   On an appeal to the Court under subsection (3), the Court may give such directions in the matter as it thinks fit, including directions as to the expenses of the proceedings before the Court and as to any order by the Tribunal relating to expenses.

(5)   A decision of the Court on an appeal under subsection (3) shall be final.

Powers where inadequate professional services alleged

42A.   *[Repealed by the Legal Services Act 2007 (c.29) Sch.23 para.1 (effective October 1, 2008 as SI 2008/1436; repeal has effect subject to savings and transitional provisions specified in SSI 2008/332 art.4).]*

Inadequate professional services: Council's powers to monitor compliance with directions

42B.   *[Repealed by the Legal Services Act 2007 (c.29) Sch.23 para.1 (effective October 1, 2008 as SI 2008/1436; repeal has effect subject to savings and transitional provisions specified in SSI 2008/332 art.4).]*

Powers to examine documents and demand explanations in connection with complaints

42C.—[1, 2, 3](1)   Where the Council are satisfied that it is necessary for them to do so for the purpose of investigating a complaint made to them or remitted to them by the Tribunal alleging—

(a)   *[Repealed by the Legal Services Act 2007 (c.29) Sch.23 para.1 (effective October 1, 2008 as SI 2008/1436; repeal has effect subject to savings and transitional provisions specified in SSI 2008/332 art.4).]*

(b)   the failure of an incorporated practice to comply with any provision of this Act or of rules made under this Act applicable to that practice,

(c)   *[Repealed by the Legal Services Act 2007 (c.29) Sch.23 para.1 (effective October 1, 2008).]*

the Council may give notice in writing in accordance with subsection (2) to the incorporated practice.

(2)   A notice under subsection (1) may require—

(a)   the production or delivery to any person appointed by the Council, at a time and place specified in the notice, of all documents to which this section applies which are in the possession or control of the incorporated practice and relate to the matters to which the complaint relates (whether or not they relate also to other matters); and

(b)   an explanation, within such period, not being less than 21 days, as the notice may specify, from the incorporated practice regarding the matters to which the complaint relates.

---

[1] Inserted by the Solicitors (Scotland) Act 1988 (c.42), s.2.
[2] Read in conjunction with the European Communities (Lawyer's Practice) (Scotland) Regulations 2000 (SSI 2000/121), reg.37(2) and Sch.2 and the Solicitors (Scotland) Act 1980 (Foreign Lawyers and Multi-national Practices) Regulations 2004 (SSI 2004/383), reg.13.
[3] As amended by the Legal Services Act 2007 (c.29) Sch.23 para.1 (effective October 1, 2008 as SI 2008/1436 subject to savings and transitional provisions specified in SSI 2008/332 art.4).

(3)[1]   This section applies to the following documents—
- (a)   all books, accounts, deeds, securities, papers and other documents in the possession or control of the incorporated practice;
- (b)   all books, accounts, deeds, securities, papers and other documents relating to any trust of which the incorporated practice or one of its employees is a sole trustee or of which the practice is a co-trustee only with one or more of its employees.

(4)   Part II of Schedule 3 shall have effect in relation to the powers conferred by subsection (1) to require the production or delivery of documents as it has effect in relation to the powers conferred by section 38, but with the following modifications—
- (a)   for the references in that Part to section 38 there shall be substituted references to this section; and
- (b)   for the reference in paragraph 5(1) in that Part to a person failing to produce or deliver documents immediately on being required by the Council to do so there shall be substituted a reference to a person failing to produce or deliver the documents within the time specified in the notice under subsection (1) of this section.

Protection of clients

Guarantee Fund

43.—[2, 3](1)   There shall be a fund to be called "The Scottish Solicitors Guarantee Fund" (in this Act referred to as "the Guarantee Fund"), which shall be vested in the Society and shall be under the control and management of the Council.

(2)   Subject to the provisions of this section and of Schedule 3 the Guarantee Fund shall be held by the Society for the purpose of making grants in order to compensate persons who in the opinion of the Council suffer pecuniary loss by reason of dishonesty on the part of—
- (a)[4]   any solicitor, registered foreign lawyer or registered European lawyer in practice in the United Kingdom, or any employee of such solicitor, registered foreign lawyer or registered European lawyer in connection with the practice of the solicitor, registered foreign lawyer or registered European lawyer, whether or not he had a practising certificate in force when the act of dishonesty was committed, and notwithstanding that subsequent to the commission of that act he may have died or had his name removed from or struck off the roll or may have ceased to practise or been suspended from practice;
- (aa)[5]   any conveyancing or executry practitioner or an employee of the

---

[1] As substituted by the Legal Profession and Legal Aid (Scotland) Act 2007 (asp 5) Sch.5 para.1(13)(a) (effective October 1, 2008).
[2] Read in conjunction with the Solicitors (Scotland) Act 1980 (Foreign Lawyers and Multinational Practices) Regulations 2004 (SSI 2004/383), reg.13.
[3] As amended by the Legal Services (Scotland) Act 2010 (asp 16) Pt 4 c.3 s.128 (effective July 2, 2012).
[4] As amended by the European Communities (Lawyer's Practice) (Scotland) Regulations 2000 (SSI 2000/121), reg.37(1) and Sch.1, para.1(11)(a) and by the Solicitors (Scotland) Act 1980 (Foreign Lawyers and Multi-national Practices) Regulations 2004 (SSI 2004/383), reg.10.
[5] As inserted by the Legal Services (Scotland) Act 2010 (asp 16) Pt 4 c.3 s.128(2) (effective April 1, 2011).

practitioner in connection with the practitioner's practice as such, even if subsequent to the act concerned the practitioner has ceased to provide conveyancing or executry services;

(b)[1, 2] any incorporated practice or any director, member, manager, secretary or other employee of an incorporated practice, notwithstanding that subsequent to the commission of that act it may have ceased to be recognised under section 34(1A) or have been wound up; or

(c)[3] any licensed legal services provider or person within it in connection with its provision of legal services (with the same meaning as for Part 2 of the 2010 Act), even if—

(i) the Society is not its approved regulator, or

(ii) subsequent to the act concerned it has ceased to operate.

(3) No grant may be made under this section—

(a) in respect of a loss made good otherwise;

(b) in respect of a loss which in the opinion of the Council has arisen while the solicitor was suspended from practice;

(c) to a solicitor or his representatives in respect of a loss suffered by him or them in connection with his practice as a solicitor by reason of dishonesty on the part of a partner or employee of his;

(ca)[4] to a conveyancing or executry practitioner in respect of a loss suffered by reason of dishonesty on the part of a partner or employee of the practitioner in connection with the practitioner's practice as such;

(cc)[5, 6] to an incorporated practice or any director or member thereof in respect of a loss suffered by it or him by reason of dishonesty on the part of any director, member, manager, secretary or other employee of the incorporated practice in connection with the practice;

(cd)[7] to a licensed provider or any investor or person who owns, manages or controls or is within the licensed provider in respect of a loss suffered by it or any such person in connection with the licensed provider's provision of legal services by reason of dishonesty on the part of any such persons;

(d) unless an application for a grant is made to the Society in such manner, and within such period after the date on which the loss first came to the knowledge of the applicant, as may be prescribed by rules made under Schedule 3;

(e)[8] in respect of any default of a registered European lawyer, or any of his employees or partners, where such act or default takes place outside Scotland, unless the Council is satisfied that the act or default is closely

---

[1] As amended by the European Communities (Lawyer's Practice) (Scotland) Regulations 2000 (SSI 2000/121), reg.37(1) and Sch.1, para.1(11)(a) and by the Solicitors (Scotland) Act 1980 (Foreign Lawyers and Multi-national Practices) Regulations 2004 (SSI 2004/383), reg.10.

[2] As amended by the Legal Services (Scotland) Act 2010 (asp 16) Pt 4 c.3 s.128(1) (effective April 1, 2011).

[3] As inserted by the Legal Services (Scotland) Act 2010 (asp 16) Pt 4 c.3 s.128 (effective July 2, 2012).

[4] As inserted by the Legal Services (Scotland) Act 2010 (asp 16) Pt 4 c.3 s.128(2) (effective April 1, 2011).

[5] Inserted by the Law Reform (Miscellaneous Provisions) (Scotland) Act 1985 (c.73), s. 56 and Sched. 1, Pt. I, para.21.

[6] As amended by the Legal Services (Scotland) Act 2010 (asp 16) Pt 4 c.3 s.128(1) (effective April 1, 2011).

[7] As inserted by the Legal Services (Scotland) Act 2010 (asp 16) Pt 4 c.3 s.128 (effective July 2, 2012).

[8] Inserted by the European Communities (Lawyer's Practice) (Scotland) Regulations 2000 (SSI 2000/121), reg.37(1) and Sch.1, para.1(11)(b) (effective May 22, 2000).

connected with the registered European lawyer's practice in Scotland;

(f)[1] in respect of any act or default of a registered foreign lawyer, or any of his employees or partners, where such act or default takes place outside Scotland, unless the Council is satisfied that the act or default is closely connected with the registered foreign lawyer's practice, or any of his partners' practice, in Scotland; or

(g)[2] in respect of any act or default of any member, director, manager, secretary or other employee of an incorporated practice which is a multi-national practice, where such act or default takes place outside Scotland, unless the Council is satisfied that the act or default is closely connected with the incorporated practice's practice in Scotland.

(4)   The decision of the Council with respect to any application for a grant shall be final.

(5)   The Council may refuse to make a grant, or may make a grant only to a limited extent, if they are of opinion that there has been negligence on the part of the applicant or of any person for whom he is responsible which has contributed to the loss in question.

(6)   The Council or any committee appointed by them may administer oaths for the purpose of inquiry into any matters which affect the making or refusal of a grant from the Guarantee Fund.

(7)   Part I of Schedule 3 shall have effect with respect to the Guarantee Fund, including the making of contributions thereto by solicitors and the administration and management of the Fund by the Council; but nothing in that Schedule shall apply to or in the case of a solicitor—

(a)   who is not in practice as a solicitor; or

(b)   who is suspended from practice as a solicitor during suspension; or

(c)   who is in any such employment as is specified in section 35(4) or in the employment of an incorporated practice or a licensed provider;

but where any solicitor in any such employment as is mentioned in paragraph (c) engages in private practice as a solicitor, the said Schedule and the other provisions of this Act relating to the Guarantee Fund shall apply to him and in his case so far as regards such private practice.

(8)[3]   In the case of licensed providers, this section and Part I of Schedule 3 apply in relation to (and only to) such licensed providers as are regulated by an approved regulator that in furtherance of section 24(4) of the 2010 Act does not maintain its own compensation fund as referred to in that section.

(9)[4]   In this section and paragraph 1 of Schedule 3—"approved regulator", "investor", are to be construed in accordance with Part 2 of the 2010 Act.

NOTES

[2] As amended by the Law Reform (Miscellaneous Provisions) (Scotland) Act 1985 (c.73), s.56 and Sched.1, Pt 1, para.21(c).

---

[1] Inserted by the Solicitors (Scotland) Act 1980 (Foreign Lawyers and Multi-national Practices) Regulations 2004 (SSI 2004/383), reg.10.

[2] Inserted by the Solicitors (Scotland) Act 1980 (Foreign Lawyers and Multi-national Practices) Regulations 2004 (SSI 2004/383), reg.10.

[3] As inserted by the Legal Services (Scotland) Act 2010 (asp 16) Pt 4 c.3 s.128 (effective July 2, 2012).

[4] As inserted by the Legal Services (Scotland) Act 2010 (asp 16) Pt 4 c.3 s.128 (effective July 2, 2012).

F1.4

Professional indemnity

44.—[1, 2](1)   The Council may make rules with the concurrence of the Lord President concerning indemnity for solicitors and incorporated practices and former solicitors against any class of professional liability, and the rules may for the purpose of providing such indemnity do all or any of the following things, namely—

(a) authorise or require the Society to establish and maintain a fund or funds;

(b) authorise or require the Society to take out and maintain insurance with an authorised insurer;

(c) require solicitors or any specified class of solicitors and incorporated practices or any specified class thereof to take out and maintain insurance with an authorised insurer.

(2)   The Society shall have power, without prejudice to any of its other powers, to carry into effect any arrangements which it considers necessary or expedient for the purpose of the rules.

(3)   Without prejudice to the generality of subsections (1) and (2) rules made under this section—

(a) may specify the terms and conditions on which indemnity is to be available, and any circumstances in which the right to it is to be excluded or modified;

(b) may provide for the management, administration and protection of any fund maintained by virtue of subsection (1)(a) and require solicitors or any class of solicitors and incorporated practices or any class of incorporated practices to make payments to any such fund;

(c) may require solicitors or any class of solicitors and incorporated practices or any class of incorporated practices to make payments by way of premium on any insurance policy maintained by the Society by virtue of subsection (1)(b);

(d) may prescribe the conditions which an insurance policy must satisfy for the purpose of subsection (1)(c);

(e) may authorise the Society to determine the amount of any payments required by the rules subject to such limits, or in accordance with such provisions, as may be prescribed by the rules;

(f) may specify circumstances in which, where a solicitor or incorporated practice for whom indemnity is provided has failed to comply with the rules, proceedings in respect of sums paid by way of indemnity in connection with a matter in relation to which he or, as the case may be, it has failed to comply may be taken against him or, as the case may be, it by the Society or by insurers;

(g) may specify circumstances in which solicitors and incorporated practices are exempt from the rules;

(h) may empower the Council to take such steps as they consider necessary or expedient to ascertain whether or not the rules are being complied with; and

(i) may contain incidental, procedural or supplementary provisions.

---

[1] As amended by the Law Reform (Miscellaneous Provisions) (Scotland) Act 1985 (c.73), Sch.1 Pt I para.22 (effective December 30, 1985).

[2] Read in conjunction with the European Communities (Lawyer's Practice) (Scotland) Regulations 2000 (SSI 2000/121), reg.37(2) and Sch.2 and the Solicitors (Scotland) Act 1980 (Foreign Lawyers and Multi-national Practices) Regulations 2004 (SSI 2004/383), reg.14.

(4)[1]   Failure to comply with rules made under this section may be treated as professional misconduct or unsatisfactory professional conduct.

(5)[2]   In this section an "authorised insurer" is—

(a)   a person who has permission under Part 4 of the Financial Services and Markets Act 2000 to effect or carry out contracts of general liability insurance;

(b)   a person who has permission under Part 4 of that Act to effect or carry out contracts of insurance relating to accident, sickness, credit, suretyship, miscellaneous financial loss and legal expenses;

(c)   an EEA firm of the kind mentioned in paragraph 5(d) of Schedule 3 to that Act, which has permission under paragraph 15 of that Schedule (as a result of qualifying for authorisation under paragraph 12 of that Schedule) to effect or carry out contracts of general liability insurance; or

(d)   an EEA firm of the kind mentioned in paragraph 5(d) of Schedule 3 to that Act, which has permission under paragraph 15 of that Schedule (as a result of qualifying for authorisation under paragraph 12 of that Schedule) to effect or carry out contracts relating to accident, sickness, credit, suretyship, miscellaneous financial loss and legal expenses;

"professional liability" means any civil liability incurred by a solicitor or former solicitor in connection with his practice or in connection with any trust of which he is or formerly was a trustee and, as respects incorporated practices, means any liability incurred by it which if it had been incurred by a solicitor would constitute such civil liability.

(6)[3]   The definition of "authorised insurer" in subsection (5) must be read with—

(a)   section 22 of the Financial Services and Markets Act 2000;

(b)   any relevant order under that section; and

(c)   Schedule 2 to that Act.

Safeguarding interests of clients of solicitor struck off or suspended

45.—[4, 5](1)   The following provisions of this section shall have effect in relation to the practice of a solicitor whose name is struck off the roll or who is suspended from practice as a solicitor under any provision of this Act and, in relation to any incorporated practice, the recognition under section 34(1A) of which is revoked.

(2)   In the case of a solicitor, the solicitor shall within 21 days of the material date satisfy the Council that he has made suitable arrangements for making available to his clients or to some other solicitor or solicitors or incorporated practice instructed by his clients or by himself—

(a)   all deeds, wills, securities, papers, books of accounts, records, vouchers

---

[1] As substituted by the Legal Profession and Legal Aid (Scotland) Act 2007 (asp 5) Sch.5 para.1(14) (effective October 1, 2008).

[2] Inserted by the Financial Services and Markets Act 2000 (Consequential Amendments and Repeals) Order 2001 (SI 2001/3649) art.223.

[3] Inserted by the Financial Services and Markets Act 2000 (Consequential Amendments and Repeals) Order 2001 (SI 2001/3649) art.223.

[4] As amended by the Law Reform (Miscellaneous Provisions) (Scotland) Act 1985 (c.73), Sched. 1, Pt. I, para.23, with effect from 30th December 1985.

[5] Read in conjunction with the European Communities (Lawyer's Practice) (Scotland) Regulations 2000 (SSI 2000/121), reg.37(2) and Sch.2 and the Solicitors (Scotland) Act 1980 (Foreign Lawyers and Multi-national Practices) Regulations 2004 (SSI 2004/383), reg.13 (except with regard to s.45(4).

and other documents in his or his firm's possession or control which are held on behalf of his clients or which relate to any trust of which he is sole trustee or co-trustee only with one or more of his partners or employees, and

(b) all sums of money due from him or his firm or held by him or his firm on behalf of his clients or subject to any such trust as aforesaid.

(2A) In the case of an incorporated practice, it shall within 21 days of the material date satisfy the Council that it has made suitable arrangements for making available to its clients or to some other solicitor or solicitors or incorporated practice instructed by its clients or itself—

(a) all deeds, wills, securities, papers, books of accounts, records, vouchers and other documents in its possession or control which are held on behalf of its clients or which relate to any trust of which it is sole trustee or co-trustee only with one or more of its employees; and

(b) all sums of money due from it or held by it on behalf of its clients or subject to any trust as aforesaid.

(3A)[1] If the solicitor or, as the case may be, the incorporated practice fails so to satisfy the Council, the Council may—

(a) require the production or delivery to any person appointed by them at a time and place fixed by them of the documents mentioned in subsection (3B);

(b) take possession of all such documents; and

(c) apply to the Court for an order that no payment be made by any banker, building society or other body named in the order out of any banking account or any sum deposited in the name of the solicitor or his firm or, as the case may be, the incorporated practice without the leave of the Court and the Court may make such order.

(3B)[2] The documents are—

(a) all books, accounts, deeds, securities, papers and other documents in the possession or control of the solicitor or his firm or, as the case may be, the incorporated practice;

(b) all books, accounts, deeds, securities, papers and other documents relating to any trust of which the solicitor is a sole trustee or is a cotrustee only with one or more of his partners or employees or, as the case may be, of which the incorporated practice or one of its employees is a sole trustee or of which the practice is a co-trustee only with one or more of its employees.

(4) If the solicitor, immediately before the striking off or, as the case may be, the suspension, was a sole solicitor, the right to operate on, or otherwise deal with, any client account in the name of the solicitor or his firm shall on the occurrence of that event vest in the Society (notwithstanding any enactment or rule of law to the contrary) to the exclusion of any other person.

(4A)[3] Where—

(a) a solicitor is restricted from acting as a principal; and

---

[1] As substituted for s.45(3) by the Legal Profession and Legal Aid (Scotland) Act 2007 (asp 5) Sch.5 para.1(15)(b) (effective November 23, 2007).

[2] As substituted for s.45(3) by the Legal Profession and Legal Aid (Scotland) Act 2007 (asp 5) Sch.5 para.1(15)(b) (effective November 23, 2007).

[3] As inserted by the Legal Profession and Legal Aid (Scotland) Act 2007 (asp 5) Pt 3 s.60(2)(a) (effective November 23, 2007).

(b)   immediately before the restriction the solicitor was a sole solicitor, the right to operate on, or otherwise deal with, any client account in the name of the solicitor or the solicitor's firm shall on the occurrence of those circumstances vest in the Society (notwithstanding any enactment or rule of law to the contrary) to the exclusion of any other person until such time as the Council have approved acceptable other arrangements in respect of the client account.

(4B)[1]   Part II of Schedule 3 has effect in relation to the powers of the Council under subsection (3A).

(5)   In this section—

"material date" means whichever is the latest of—
> (a)   the date when the order of the Tribunal or court by or in pursuance of which the solicitor is struck off the roll or suspended from practice or, as the case may be, the recognition under section 34(1A) is revoked is to take effect;
> (b)   the last date on which
>> (i)   an appeal against that order may be lodged or an application may be made to the court under section 54(2), or
>> (ii)   an appeal against a decision of the Council under section 40 may be lodged;
> (c)   the date on which any such appeal is dismissed or abandoned;

"principal" means a solicitor who is a sole practitioner or is a partner in a firm of two or more solicitors or is a director of an incorporated practice which is a company or a solicitor who is a member of a multi-national practice having its principal place of business in Scotland;[2]

"sole solicitor" means a solicitor practising under his own name or as a single solicitor under a firm name.

Safeguarding interests of clients in certain other cases

46.—[3](1)   Where the Council are satisfied that a sole solicitor is incapacitated by illness or accident to such an extent as to be unable to operate on, or otherwise deal with, any client account in the name of the solicitor or his firm, and that no other arrangements acceptable to the Council have been made, the right to operate on, or otherwise deal with, that account shall vest in the Society (notwithstanding any enactment or rule of law to the contrary) to the exclusion of any other person so long, but only so long, as the Council are satisfied that such incapacity and absence of other acceptable arrangements continues.

(2)[4]   Where a sole solicitor ceases to practise for any reason other than that his name has been struck off the roll or that he has been suspended from practice, and the Council are not satisfied that suitable arrangements have been made for making available to his clients or to some other solicitor or solicitors instructed by his clients or on their behalf—

---

[1] As inserted by the Legal Profession and Legal Aid (Scotland) Act 2007 (asp 5) Sch.5 para.1(15)(c) (effective November 23, 2007).

[2] As inserted by the Legal Profession and Legal Aid (Scotland) Act 2007 (asp 5) s.60(2)(b) (effective November 23, 2007).

[3] Read in conjunction with the European Communities (Lawyer's Practice) (Scotland) Regulations 2000 (SSI 2000/121), reg.37(2) and Sch.2 (effective May 22, 2000).

[4] As substituted by Legal Profession and Legal Aid (Scotland) Act 2007 (asp 5) Sch.5 para.1(16) (effective November 23, 2007).

    (a)   all deeds, wills, securities, papers, books of accounts, records, vouchers and other documents in his or his firm's possession or control which are held on behalf of his clients or which relate to any trust of which he is the sole trustee, or a co-trustee only with one or more of his employees, and

    (b)   all sums of money due from him or his firm or held by him or his firm on behalf of his clients or subject to any such trust as aforesaid, the Council may do any of the things mentioned in subsection (3A).

  (3)   Where a sole solicitor dies—

    (a)   the right to operate on or otherwise deal with any client account in the name of the solicitor or his firm shall vest in the Society (notwithstanding any enactment or rule of law to the contrary) to the exclusion of any personal representatives of the solicitor, and shall be exercisable as from the death of the solicitor; and

    (b)   if the Council are not satisfied that suitable arrangements have been made for making available to the solicitor's clients or to some other solicitor or solicitors instructed by his clients or on their behalf—

        (i)   all deeds, wills, securities, papers, books of accounts, records, vouchers and other documents which were in his or his firm's possession or control which were held on behalf of his clients or which relate to any trust of which he was the sole trustee, or a co-trustee only with one or more of his employees, and

       (ii)   all sums of money which were due from him or his firm or were held by him or his firm on behalf of his clients or subject to any such trust as aforesaid,

the provisions of section 38 shall apply in relation to that solicitor notwithstanding that the Council may not have reasonable cause to believe that he had been guilty of any such dishonesty as is mentioned in section 43(2).

  (3A)[1] The things are to—

    (a)   require the production or delivery to any person appointed by the Council at a time and a place fixed by them of the documents mentioned in subsection (3B);

    (b)   take possession of all such documents; and

    (c)   apply to the Court for an order that no payment be made by any banker, building society or other body named in the order out of any banking account or any sum deposited in the name of the solicitor or his firm without the leave of the Court and the Court may make such order.

  (3B)[2] The documents are—

    (a)   all books, accounts, deeds, securities, papers and other documents in the possession or control of the solicitor or his firm;

    (b)   all books, accounts, deeds, securities, papers and other documents relating to any trust of which he is a sole trustee or is a co-trustee only with one or more of his employees.

---

[1] As inserted by the Legal Profession and Legal Aid (Scotland) Act 2007 (asp 5) Sch.5, para. 1(16) (effective November 23, 2007).

[2] As inserted by the Legal Profession and Legal Aid (Scotland) Act 2007 (asp 5) Sch.5, para. 1(16) (effective November 23, 2007).

(4)   In a case where the Society have operated on or otherwise dealt with a client account by virtue of subsection (3) the Society shall be entitled to recover from the estate of the solicitor who has died such reasonable expenses as the Society have thereby incurred.

(4A)¹   Part II of Schedule 3 has effect in relation to the powers of the Council under subsection (2) or (3).

(5)   In this section "sole solicitor" has the same meaning as in section 45.

Restriction on employing solicitor struck off or suspended

47.—²,³(1)   Unless he has the written permission of the Council to do so, a solicitor shall not, in connection with his practice as a solicitor and, unless it has such permission, an incorporated practice shall not, employ or remunerate any person who to his or, as the case may be, its knowledge is disqualified from practising as a solicitor by reason of the fact that his name has been struck off the roll or that he is suspended from practice as a solicitor.

(2)   Any permission given by the Council for the purposes of subsection (1) may be given for such period and subject to such conditions as the Council think fit.

(3)   A solicitor or, as the case may be, incorporated practice aggrieved by the refusal of the Council to grant any such permission as aforesaid, or by any conditions attached by the Council to the grant thereof, may appeal to the court; and on any such appeal the court may give such directions in the matter as it thinks fit.

(4)   If any solicitor acts in contravention of this section or of any condition subject to which any permission has been given thereunder, his name shall be struck off the roll or he shall be suspended from practice as a solicitor for such period as the Tribunal, or, in the case of an appeal, the court, may think fit and if any incorporated practice so acts its recognition under section 34(1A) shall be revoked.

48.   *[Repealed by the Law Reform (Miscellaneous Provisions) (Scotland) Act 1985, Sch.1, Pt II, para.5.]*

PART IV – COMPLAINTS AND DISCIPLINARY PROCEEDINGS

Lay Observer

49.   *[Repealed by the Law Reform (Miscellaneous Provisions) (Scotland) Act 1990, Sch.9.]*

The Scottish Solicitors' Discipline Tribunal

The Tribunal

50.—⁴(1)   For the purposes of this Part of this Act and sections 16 to 23 (which relate to the provision of conveyancing and executry services) of the 1990 Act there

---

¹ As inserted by the Legal Profession and Legal Aid (Scotland) Act 2007 (asp 5) Sch.5, para. 1(16) (effective November 23, 2007).
² As amended by the Law Reform (Miscellaneous Provisions) (Scotland) Act 1985 (c.73), Sch.1, Pt I, para.24.
³ Read in conjunction with the European Communities (Lawyer's Practice) (Scotland) Regulations 2000 (SSI 2000/121), reg.37(2) and Sch.2 and the Solicitors (Scotland) Act 1980 (Foreign Lawyers and Multi-national Practices) Regulations 2004 (SSI 2004/383), reg.13.
⁴ As amended by the Public Appointments and Public Bodies etc. (Scotland) Act 2003 (asp 4), s.13 (effective August 15, 2003).

shall be a tribunal, which shall be known as the Scottish Solicitors' Discipline Tribunal and is in this Act referred to as "the Tribunal".

(2)   Part I of Schedule 4 shall have effect in relation to the constitution of the Tribunal.

Complaints to Tribunal

51.—[1, 2](1)   A complaint may be made to the Tribunal by the Council; and, for the purpose of investigating and prosecuting complaints, the Council may appoint a solicitor to act as fiscal.

(1A)[3]   In subsection (1) above, without prejudice to the generality of that subsection, the reference to a complaint includes a complaint in respect of conveyancing and executry practitioners and the provision by them of conveyancing and executry services (those expressions having the meanings given in section 23 of the 1990 Act).

(2)[4]   The persons mentioned in subsection (3) may report to the Tribunal any case where it appears that an incorporated practice may have failed to comply with any provision of this Act or of rules made under this Act applicable to it and any such report shall be treated by the Tribunal as a complaint under subsection (1).

(3)[5]   The persons referred to in subsection (2) are—

    (a)   the Lord Advocate;

          (aa)[6]   the Advocate General for Scotland;

    (b)   any judge;

          (ba)   the Dean of the Faculty of Advocates;

    (c)   the Auditor of the Court of Session;

    (d)   the Auditor of any sheriff court;

    (e)   the Scottish Legal Aid Board;

    (f)   *[Repealed by the Legal Profession and Legal Aid (Scotland) Act 2007 (Transitional, Savings and Consequential Provisions) Order (SSI 2008/ 332) art.4(3) (effective October 1, 2008).]*

(4)   Where a report is made to the Tribunal under subsection (2) the Tribunal may, if it thinks fit, appoint a solicitor to prosecute the complaint and the expenses of the solicitor, so far as not recoverable from the solicitor complained against, shall be paid out of the funds of the Tribunal.

---

[1] As amended by the Law Reform (Miscellaneous Provisions) (Scotland) Act 1985, Sch.1, Pt I, para.26, the Legal Aid (Scotland) Act 1986, Sched. 3, para.8, and the Solicitors (Scotland) Act 1988, Sched. 1, para. 14.

[2] Read in conjunction with the European Communities (Lawyer's Practice) (Scotland) Regulations 2000 (SSI 2000/121), reg.37(2) and Sch.2 and the Solicitors (Scotland) Act 1980 (Foreign Lawyers and Multi-national Practices) Regulations 2004 (SSI 2004/383), reg.13 (except the references to a solicitor appointed under subsections (1) and (4)).

[3] Inserted by the Public Appointments and Public Bodies etc. (Scotland) Act 2003 (asp 4), s.13 (effective August 15, 2003).

[4] As amended by the Legal Services Act 2007 (c. 29) Sch.23 para.1 (effective October 1, 2008 as SI 2008/1436; amendment has effect subject to savings and transitional provisions specified in SSI 2008/ 332 art.4).

[5] As amended by the Law Reform (Miscellaneous Provisions) (Scotland) Act 1990, Sched. 8, para.29(9).

[6] As amended by SI 1999/1042, Art. 4, Sch.2, para.7 (effective on commencement of s.44(1)(c) of the Scotland Act (c.44): May 20, 1999).

Procedure on complaints and appeals to Tribunal

52.—[1, 2, 3](1)[4]   Part II of Schedule 4 shall have effect in relation to the procedure and powers of the Tribunal in relation to any complaint or appeal concerning a solicitor or an incorporated practice.

(2)[5]   Subject to the other provisions of this Part, the provisions of sections 16 to 23 of the 1990 Act, and of any rules of court made under this Act, the Tribunal, with the concurrence of the Lord President, may make rules—

(a)   for regulating the making, hearing and determining of complaints made to it under this Act; and

(aa)   for regulating the making, hearing and determining of appeals made to it under section 42ZA(9), (10), (11) or (12), 42ZD(1) or 53D(1);

(ab)   for regulating the making, hearing and determining of—

(i)   inquiries under subsection (2A) of section 20 of the 1990 Act;

(ii)   appeals under subsection (8A)(b), (11)(b) or (11ZC) of that section; and

(iii)   appeals under section 20ZB(9), (10), (11) or (12) or 20ZE(1) of that Act.

(b)   generally as to the procedure of the Tribunal (including provision for hearings taking place in public or wholly or partly in private).

(3)   Rules made by the Tribunal under subsection (2) for regulating the making, hearing or determining of appeals referred to in paragraph (aa) or (ab)(ii) of that subsection may include provision as to persons being entitled, or required by the Tribunal, to appear or be represented at the appeal.

Powers of Tribunal

53.—[6, 7](1)   Subject to the other provisions of this Part, the powers exercisable by the Tribunal under subsection (2) shall be exercisable if—

(a)   after holding an inquiry into a complaint against a solicitor the Tribunal is satisfied that he has been guilty of professional misconduct, or

(b)[8]   a solicitor has (whether before or after enrolment as a solicitor), been convicted by any court of an act involving dishonesty or has been fined

---

[1] As amended by the Law Reform (Miscellaneous Provisions) (Scotland) Act 1985, Sched. 1, Pt I, para.27, the Solicitors (Scotland) Act 1988, Sched. 1, para.15 and the Public Appointments and Public Bodies etc. (Scotland) Act 2003 (asp 4), s.13 (effective August 15, 2003).

[2] Read in conjunction with the European Communities (Lawyer's Practice) (Scotland) Regulations 2000 (SSI 2000/121), reg.37(2) and Sch.2 (effective May 22, 2000).

[3] As amended by the Legal Profession and Legal Aid (Scotland) Act 2007 (asp 5) Sch.5 para. 1(18) (effective October 1, 2008: insertion has effect subject to savings and transitional provisions specified in SSI 2008/332 art.4).

[4] Read in conjunction with the Solicitors (Scotland) Act 1980 (Foreign Lawyers and Multinational Practices) Regulations 2004 (SSI 2004/383), reg.13.

[5] Read in conjunction with the Solicitors (Scotland) Act 1980 (Foreign Lawyers and Multinational Practices) Regulations 2004 (SSI 2004/383), reg.14.

[6] As amended by the Law Reform (Miscellaneous Provisions) (Scotland) Act 1985, Sch.1, Pt. I, para.28, the Solicitors (Scotland) Act 1988 Sch.1, para.16, and the Law Reform (Miscellaneous Provisions) (Scotland) Act 1990 Sch.8, para.29(10).

[7] Read in conjunction with the European Communities (Lawyer's Practice) (Scotland) Regulations 2000 (SSI 2000/121) reg.37(2) and Sch.2 and the Solicitors (Scotland) Act 1980 (Foreign Lawyers and Multi-national Practices) Regulations 2004 (SSI 2004/383) reg.13 (except with regard to subsections (2)(g), (6B) and (8)(b)).

[8] As substituted by the Legal Services (Scotland) Act 2010 (asp 16) Pt 4 c.3 s.139(1) (effective May 1, 2011).

an amount equivalent to level 4 on the standard scale or more (whether on summary or solemn conviction) or sentenced to imprisonment for a term of 12 months or more; or

(c) an incorporated practice has been convicted by any court of an offence, which conviction the Tribunal is satisfied renders it unsuitable to continue to be recognised under section 34(1A); or

(d) after holding an inquiry into a complaint, the Tribunal is satisfied that an incorporated practice has failed to comply with any provision of this Act or of rules made under this Act applicable to it.

(2)[1] Subject to subsection (1), the Tribunal may—

(a) order that the name of the solicitor be struck off the roll;

(aa)[2] if the solicitor's name has been removed from the roll under section 9, by order prohibit the restoration of the solicitor's name to the roll;

(b) order that the solicitor be suspended from practice as a solicitor for such time as it may determine;

(ba) order that any right of audience held by the solicitor by virtue of section 25A be suspended or revoked;

(bb)[3] where the solicitor has been guilty of professional misconduct, and where the Tribunal consider that the complainer has been directly affected by the misconduct, direct the solicitor to pay compensation of such amount, not exceeding £5,000, as the Tribunal may specify to the complainer for loss, inconvenience or distress resulting from the misconduct;

(bc)[4] where—

(i) an incorporated practice has been convicted, or has been found to have failed, as referred to in subsection (1)(c) or (d), and

(ii) the Tribunal consider that the complainer has been directly affected by any misconduct by the practice to which the conviction or failure is (to any extent) attributable, direct the practice to pay to the complainer compensation (for loss, inconvenience or distress resulting from the misconduct) of such amount not exceeding £5,000 as the Tribunal may specify;

(c)[5] subject to subsection (3ZA), impose on the solicitor or, as the case may be, the incorporated practice, a fine not exceeding £10,000; or

(d) censure the solicitor or, as the case may be, the incorporated practice; or

(e) impose such fine and censure him or, as the case may be, it;

(f) order that the recognition under section 34(1A) of the incorporated practice be revoked; or

(g) order that an investment business certificate issued to a solicitor, a firm of solicitors or an incorporated practice be—

(i) suspended for such time as they may determine; or

---

[1] As amended by the Law Reform (Miscellaneous Provisions) (Scotland) Act 1980 s.24, and SI 1987/333.

[2] As inserted by the Legal Services (Scotland) Act 2010 (asp 16) Pt 4 c.3 s.136(2) (effective May 1, 2011).

[3] Repealed by the Legal Profession and Legal Aid (Scotland) Act 2007 (Transitional, Savings and Consequential Provisions) Order (SSI 2008/332) art.4(3) (effective October 1, 2008).

[4] As inserted by the Legal Services (Scotland) Act 2010 (asp 16) Pt 4 c.3 s.139(1) (effective May 1, 2011).

[5] As amended by the Legal Profession and Legal Aid (Scotland) Act 2007 (Modification and Consequential Provisions) Order 2011 (SSI 2011/235) art.3(3) (effective March 23, 2011).

(ii) subject to such terms and conditions as it may direct; or

(iii) revoked.

(3) *[Repealed by the Legal Services Act 2007 (c.29) Sch.23 para.1 (effective October 1, 2008 as SI 2008/1436; repeal has effect subject to savings and transitional provisions specified in SSI 2008/332 art.4).]*

(3ZA)[1] The Tribunal shall not impose a fine under subsection (2)(c)—

(a) where the Tribunal is proceeding on the ground referred to in subsection (1)(a) and the solicitor, in relation to the subject matter of the Tribunal's inquiry, has been convicted by any court of an act involving dishonesty and sentenced to a term of imprisonment of not less than 2 years;

(b) where the Tribunal is proceeding on the ground referred to in subsection (1)(b).

(3A)[2] The powers conferred by subsection (2)(bb) to (e) may be exercised by the Tribunal—

(a) in relation to a former solicitor, notwithstanding that his name has been struck off the roll or that he has, since the date of the misconduct, conviction or sentence referred to in subsection (1)(a) or (b), ceased to practise as a solicitor or been suspended from practice;

(b) in relation to a body corporate which was formerly an incorporated practice, notwithstanding that the body has, since the date of the conviction or failure referred to in subsection (1)(c) or (d), ceased to be recognised as an incorporated practice by virtue of section 34(1A).

(3B) The power conferred by subsection (2)(ba) may be exercised by the Tribunal either independently of, or in conjunction with, any other power conferred by that subsection.

(4) Any fine imposed by the Tribunal under subsection (2) shall be forfeit to Her Majesty.

(5) Where the Tribunal have exercised the power conferred by subsection (2) to censure, or impose a fine on, a solicitor, or both to censure and impose a fine, the Tribunal may order that the solicitor's practising certificate shall be subject to such terms and conditions as the Tribunal may direct; and the Council shall give effect to any such order of the Tribunal.

(6)[3] Where the Tribunal order that the name of a solicitor be struck off the roll, or that the solicitor be suspended from practice as a solicitor, or that any right of audience held by the solicitor by virtue of section 25A be suspended or revoked, the Tribunal may direct that the order shall take effect on the date on which it is intimated to the solicitor; and if any such direction is given the order shall take effect accordingly.

(6A) Where the Tribunal order that the recognition under section 34(1A) of an incorporated practice be revoked, the Tribunal shall direct that the order shall take

---

[1] As inserted by the Legal Profession and Legal Aid (Scotland) Act 2007 (asp 5) Sch.5 para.1(19)(a) (effective October 1, 2008: insertion has effect subject to savings and transitional provisions specified in SSI 2008/332 art.4).

[2] As amended by the Legal Services (Scotland) Act 2010 (asp 16) Pt 4 c.3 s.139(1) (effective May 1, 2011).

[3] As amended by the Law Reform (Miscellaneous Provisions) (Scotland) Act 1985 Sch.1, Pt. I, para.28, the Solicitors (Scotland) Act 1988 Sch.1, para.16, and the Law Reform (Miscellaneous Provisions) (Scotland) Act 1990 Sch.8, para.29(10).

effect on such date as the Tribunal specifies, being a date not earlier than 60 days after its order is intimated to the incorporated practice, and such an order shall take effect accordingly.

(6B)   Where the Tribunal make an order under subsection (2)(g), they may direct that the order shall take effect on the date on which it is intimated to the solicitor, firm or incorporated practice; and if any such direction is given the order shall take effect accordingly.

(7)   Where in relation to any such order as is mentioned in subsection (6), (6A) or (6B) the Tribunal give a direction under subsection (6) or, as the case may be, subsection (6A) or (6B) and an appeal against the order is taken to the court under section 54, the order shall continue to have effect pending the determination or abandonment of the appeal unless, on an application under subsection (2) of section 54, the court otherwise directs.

(7A)[1]   In subsection (2)(g), section 53D(1) and paragraph 16(h) of Schedule 4, "investment business certificate" means a certificate issued by the Council under Rule 2.2 of the Solicitors (Scotland) (Conduct of Investment Business) Practice Rules 1988.

(7B)[2]   A direction of the Tribunal under this section is enforceable in like manner as an extract registered decree arbitral in its favour bearing a warrant for execution issued by the sheriff court of any sheriffdom in Scotland.

(7C)[3, 4]   The Scottish Ministers may by order made by statutory instrument, after consulting the Council and such groups of persons representing consumer interests as they consider appropriate, amend paragraph (bb) or (bc) of subsection (2) by substituting for the amount for the time being specified in that paragraph such other amount as they consider appropriate.

(7D)[5]   A statutory instrument containing an order under subsection (7C) is not to be made unless a draft of the instrument has been laid before, and approved by resolution of, the Scottish Parliament.

(8)[6]   The Secretary of State may, by order made by statutory instrument subject to annulment in pursuance of a resolution of either House of Parliament, amend—

(a)   paragraph (c) of subsection (2) by substituting for the amount for the time being specified in that paragraph such other amount as appears to him to be justified by a change in the value of money;

(b)   the definition of "investment business certificate" in subsection (7A) by substituting for the reference to Rule 2.2 of the Solicitors (Scotland) (Conduct of Investment Business) Practice Rules 1988, or such refer-

---

[1] As inserted by the Solicitors (Scotland) Act 1988 (c.42), s.6(1), Sch.1 para. 16(e).

[2] As inserted by the Legal Profession and Legal Aid (Scotland) Act 2007 (asp 5) Sch.5 para.1(19)(b) (effective October 1, 2008: insertion has effect subject to savings and transitional provisions specified in SSI 2008/332 art.4).

[3] As inserted by the Legal Profession and Legal Aid (Scotland) Act 2007 (asp 5) Pt 2 s.56 (effective October 1, 2008: insertion has effect subject to savings and transitional provisions specified in SSI 2008/332 art.4).

[4] As amended by the Legal Services (Scotland) Act 2010 (asp 16) Pt 4 c.3 s.139(1) (effective May 1, 2011).

[5] As inserted by the Legal Profession and Legal Aid (Scotland) Act 2007 (asp 5) Pt 2 s.56 (effective October 1, 2008: insertion has effect subject to savings and transitional provisions specified in SSI 2008/332 art.4).

[6] Inserted by the Law Reform (Miscellaneous Provisions) (Scotland) Act 1980, s.24 and as amended by the 1988 Act as noted above.

ence replacing that reference as may for the time being be specified in that subsection, a reference to such Practice Rule as may from time to time replace Rule 2.2.

(9) *[Repealed by the Legal Profession and Legal Aid (Scotland) Act 2007 (Transitional, Savings and Consequential Provisions) Order (SSI 2008/332) art.4(3) (effective October 1, 2008).]*[1] In subsection (2)(bb) and (bc), "complainer" has the same meaning as in section 42ZA.

Remission of complaint by Tribunal to Council

53ZA.—[2](1) Where, after holding an inquiry under section 53(1) into a complaint of professional misconduct against a solicitor, the Tribunal—

   (a) is not satisfied that he has been guilty of professional misconduct;

   (b) considers that he may be guilty of unsatisfactory professional conduct,

it must remit the complaint to the Council.

   (2) Where the Tribunal remits a complaint to the Council under subsection (1), it may make available to the Council any of its findings in fact in its inquiry into the complaint under section 53(1).

Powers of Tribunal on appeal: unsatisfactory professional conduct

53ZB.—[3](1) On an appeal to the Tribunal under section 42ZA(9) the Tribunal—

   (a) may quash or confirm the determination being appealed against;

   (b) if it quashes the determination, shall quash the censure accompanying the determination;

   (c) may quash, confirm or vary the direction being appealed against;

   (d) may, where it considers that the solicitor does not have sufficient competence in relation to any aspect of the law or legal practice, direct the solicitor to undertake such education or training as regards the law or legal practice as the Tribunal considers appropriate in that respect;

   (e) may, subject to subsection (5), fine the solicitor an amount not exceeding £2000;

   (f) may, where it considers that the complainer has been directly affected by the conduct, direct the solicitor to pay compensation of such amount, not exceeding £5,000, as it may specify to the complainer for loss, inconvenience or distress resulting from the conduct.

   (2) On an appeal to the Tribunal under section 42ZA(10) the Tribunal—

   (a) may quash the determination being appealed against and make a determination upholding the complaint;

   (b) if it does so, may, where it considers that the complainer has been directly affected by the conduct, direct the solicitor to pay compensation of such amount, not exceeding £5,000, as it may specify to the complainer for loss, inconvenience or distress resulting from the conduct;

---

[1] As amended by the Legal Services (Scotland) Act 2010 (asp 16) Pt 4 c.3 s.139(1) (effective May 1, 2011).

[2] As inserted by the Legal Profession and Legal Aid (Scotland) Act 2007 (asp 5) Pt 2 s.53(3) (effective October 1, 2008: insertion has effect subject to savings and transitional provisions specified in SSI 2008/332).

[3] As inserted by the Legal Profession and Legal Aid (Scotland) Act 2007 (asp 5) Pt 2, s.53(3) (effective October 1, 2008: insertion has effect subject to savings and transitional provisions specified in SSI 2008/332).

(c)   may confirm the determination.

(3)   On an appeal to the Tribunal under section 42ZA(11) the Tribunal may, where it considers that the complainer has been directly affected by the conduct, direct the solicitor to pay compensation of such amount, not exceeding £5,000, as it may specify to the complainer for loss, inconvenience or distress resulting from the conduct.

(4)   On an appeal under section 42ZA(12) the Tribunal may quash, confirm or vary the direction being appealed against.

(5)   The Tribunal shall not direct the solicitor to pay a fine under subsection (1)(e) where, in relation to the subject matter of the complaint, the solicitor has been convicted by any court of an act involving dishonesty and sentenced to a term of imprisonment of not less than 2 years.

(6)   Any fine directed to be paid under subsection (1)(e) above shall be treated for the purposes of section 211(5) of the Criminal Procedure (Scotland) act 1995 (fines payable to HM Exchequer) as if it were a fine imposed in the High Court.

(7)   A direction of the Tribunal under this section is enforceable in like manner as an extract registered decree arbitral in favour of the Council bearing a warrant for execution issued by the sheriff court of any sheriffdom in Scotland.

(8)   The Scottish Ministers may by order made by statutory instrument—

(a)   amend subsection (1)(e) by substituting for the amount for the time being specified in that subsection such other amount as appears to them to be justified by a change in the value of money;

(b)   after consulting the Council and such groups of persons representing consumer interests as they consider appropriate, amend subsection (1)(f) by substituting for the amount for the time being specified in that subsection such other amount as they consider appropriate.

(9)   A statutory instrument containing an order under—

(a)   subsection (8)(a) is subject to annulment in pursuance of a resolution of the Scottish Parliament;

(b)   subsection (8)(b) is not to be made unless a draft of the instrument has been laid before, and approved by resolution of, the Scottish Parliament.

(10)   In this section, "complainer" has the same meaning as in section 42ZA.

Enforcement of Council direction: unsatisfactory professional conduct

53ZC.[1]   Where a solicitor fails to comply with a direction given by the Council under section 42ZA(4) (including such a direction as confirmed or varied on appeal by the Tribunal or, as the case may be, the Court) before the expiry of the period specified in the notice relating to that direction given to him under section 42ZB(1), or such longer period as the Council may allow, the direction shall be enforceable in like manner as an extract registered decree arbitral in favour of the Council bearing a warrant for execution issued by the sheriff court of any sheriffdom in Scotland.

---

[1] As inserted by the Legal Profession and Legal Aid (Scotland) Act 2007 (asp 5) Pt 2 s.53(3) (effective October 1, 2008: insertion has effect subject to savings and transitional provisions specified in SSI 2008/332).

PART IV – COMPLAINTS AND DISCIPLINARY PROCEEDINGS

The Scottish Solicitors' Discipline Tribunal

53A.-53C. *[Repealed by the Legal Services Act 2007 (c.29) Sch.23 para.1 (effective October 1, 2008 as SI 2008/1436; repeal has effect subject to savings and transitional provisions specified in SSI 2008/332 art.4).]*

Suspension etc. of investment business certificates: appeal to Tribunal

53D.—[1, 2](1)   Where, in accordance with rules made under this Act, the Council suspend or withdraw an investment business certificate or impose conditions or restrictions on it the solicitor, firm of solicitors or incorporated practice to whom it was issued may, within 21 days of the date of intimation of the decision of the Council, appeal to the Tribunal against that decision.

(2)   On an appeal to the Tribunal under subsection (1) the Tribunal may quash, confirm or vary the decision being appealed against.

(2A)[3]   The solicitor, firm of solicitors or, as the case may be, the incorporated practice may, before the expiry of the period of 21 days beginning with the day on which the decision of the Tribunal under subsection (2) is intimated to him or, as the case may be, it, appeal to the Court against the decision.

(2B)[4]   The Council may, before the expiry of the period of 21 days beginning with the day on which the decision of the Tribunal under subsection (2) is intimated to them, appeal to the Court against the decision.

(2C)[5]   On an appeal under subsection (2A), the Court may give such directions in the matter as it thinks fit, including directions as to the expenses of the proceedings before the Court and as to any order by the Tribunal relating to expenses.

(2D)[6]   A decision of the Court under subsection (2C) shall be final.

Appeals from decisions of Tribunal

54.—[7, 8](1)   *[Repealed by Legal Services Act 2007 (c.29) Sch.23 para.1 (effective October 1, 2008 as SI 2008/1436; repeal has effect subject to savings and transitional provisions specified in SSI 2008/332 art.4).]*

---

[1] Inserted by the Solicitors (Scotland) Act 1988 (c.42), Sched. 1, para.17.

[2] Read in conjunction with the European Communities (Lawyer's Practice) (Scotland) Regulations 2000 (SSI 2000/121), reg.37(2) and Sch.2 (effective May 22, 2000).

[3] (2A)-(2D) as substituted for s.53(3) by the Legal Profession and Legal Aid (Scotland) Act 2007 (asp 5) Sch.5 para.1(20) (effective October 1, 2008: substitution has effect subject to savings and transitional provisions specified in SSI 2008/332 art.4).

[4] (2A)-(2D) as substituted for s.53(3) by the Legal Profession and Legal Aid (Scotland) Act 2007 (asp 5) Sch.5 para.1(20) (effective October 1, 2008: substitution has effect subject to savings and transitional provisions specified in SSI 2008/332 art.4).

[5] (2A)-(2D) as substituted for s.53(3) by the Legal Profession and Legal Aid (Scotland) Act 2007 (asp 5) Sch.5 para.1(20) (effective October 1, 2008: substitution has effect subject to savings and transitional provisions specified in SSI 2008/332 art.4).

[6] (2A)-(2D) as substituted for s.53(3) by the Legal Profession and Legal Aid (Scotland) Act 2007 (asp 5) Sch.5 para.1(20) (effective October 1, 2008: substitution has effect subject to savings and transitional provisions specified in SSI 2008/332 art.4).

[7] As amended by the Law Reform (Miscellaneous Provisions) (Scotland) Act 1985 (c.73), Sched. 1, Pt. I, para.29.

[8] Read in conjunction with the European Communities (Lawyer's Practice) (Scotland) Regulations 2000 (SSI 2000/121), reg.37(2) and Sch.2 and the Solicitors (Scotland) Act 1980 (Foreign Lawyers and Multi-national Practices) Regulations 2004 (SSI 2004/383), reg.13.

(1A)[1] A solicitor or an incorporated practice may, before the expiry of the period of 21 days beginning with the day on which any decision by the Tribunal mentioned in subsection (1B) is intimated to him or, as the case may be, it appeal to the Court against the decision.

(1B)[2] The decision is—

    (a) where the Tribunal was satisfied as mentioned in section 53(1)(a), the finding that the solicitor has been guilty of professional misconduct;

    (b) where the Tribunal was satisfied as mentioned in section 53(1)(d), the finding that the incorporated practice has failed to comply with any provision of this Act or of any rule made under this Act applicable to the practice;

    (c) in any case falling within paragraph (a) or (b), or where the decision was made because of the circumstances mentioned in section 53(1)(b) or (c), any decision under section 53(2) or (5).

(1C)[3, 4] The Council may, before the expiry of the period of 21 days beginning with the day on which a decision by the Tribunal under section 53(2) or (5) is intimated to them, appeal to the Court against the decision; but the Council may not appeal to the Court against a decision of the Tribunal under section 53(2)(bb) or (bc).

(1D)[5, 6] Where the Tribunal has found that a solicitor has been guilty of professional misconduct but has not directed him under section 53(2)(bb) or (bc) to pay compensation, the complainer may, before the expiry of the period of 21 days beginning with the day on which the Tribunal's finding is intimated to him, appeal to the Court against the decision of the Tribunal not to make a direction under that subsection.

(1E)[7, 8] A complainer to whom the Tribunal has directed a solicitor under section 53(2)(bb) or (bc) to pay compensation may, before the expiry of the period of 21 days beginning with the day on which the direction under that subsection is intimated to him, appeal to the Court against the amount of the compensation directed to be paid.

---

[1] As inserted by the Legal Profession and Legal Aid (Scotland) Act 2007 (asp 5) Pt 2 s.57(1) (effective October 1, 2008: insertion has effect subject to savings and transitional provisions specified in SSI 2008/332 art.4).

[2] As inserted by the Legal Profession and Legal Aid (Scotland) Act 2007 (asp 5) Pt 2 s.57(1) (effective October 1, 2008: insertion has effect subject to savings and transitional provisions specified in SSI 2008/332 art.4).

[3] As inserted by the Legal Profession and Legal Aid (Scotland) Act 2007 (asp 5) Pt 2 s.57(1) (effective October 1, 2008: insertion has effect subject to savings and transitional provisions specified in SSI 2008/332 art.4).

[4] As amended by the Legal Services (Scotland) Act 2010 (asp 16) Pt 4 c.3 s.139(2) (effective May 1, 2011).

[5] As inserted by the Legal Profession and Legal Aid (Scotland) Act 2007 (asp 5) Pt 2 s.57(1) (effective October 1, 2008: insertion has effect subject to savings and transitional provisions specified in SSI 2008/332 art.4).

[6] As amended by the Legal Services (Scotland) Act 2010 (asp 16) Pt 4 c.3 s.139(2) (effective May 1, 2011).

[7] As inserted by the Legal Profession and Legal Aid (Scotland) Act 2007 (asp 5) Pt 2 s.57(1) (effective October 1, 2008: insertion has effect subject to savings and transitional provisions specified in SSI 2008/332 art.4).

[8] As amended by the Legal Services (Scotland) Act 2010 (asp 16) Pt 4 c.3 s.139(2) (effective May 1, 2011).

(1F)[1]   On an appeal under any of subsections (1A) to (1E), the Court may give such directions in the matter as it thinks fit, including directions as to the expenses of the proceedings before the Court and as to any order by the Tribunal relating to expenses.

(1G)[2]   A decision of the Court under subsection (1A), (1B), (1C), (1D), (1E) or (1F) shall be final.

(2)   Where

(a)   the Tribunal has exercised the power conferred by section 53(6) to direct that its decision shall take effect on the date on which it is intimated to the solicitor concerned, the solicitor may, within 21 days of that date, apply to the court for an order varying or quashing the direction in so far as it relates to the date of taking effect;

(b)   the Tribunal has ordered the revocation of the recognition under section 34(1A) of an incorporated practice, the incorporated practice may within 21 days of the date when the order is intimated to it apply to the court for an order varying (subject to the limit of 60 days referred to in subsection (6A) of section 53) the direction under that subsection;

(c)[3]   the Tribunal has exercised the power conferred by section 53(6B) to direct that its order shall take effect on the day on which it is intimated to the solicitor, firm of solicitors or incorporated practice concerned, the solicitor, firm of solicitors or incorporated practice may, before the expiry of the period of 21 days beginning with that day, apply to the court for an order varying or quashing the direction in so far as it relates to the day on which the order takes effect; and on any such application the Court may make the order applied for or such other order with respect to the matter as it thinks fit.

(2A)[4]   In subsections (1D) and (1E), "complainer" has the same meaning as in section 42ZA.

Appeals from decisions of Tribunal: unsatisfactory professional conduct

54A.—[5](1)   A solicitor in respect of whom a decision has been made by the Tribunal under section 53ZB(1), (2), (3) or (4) may, before the expiry of the period of 21 days beginning with the day on which the decision is intimated to him, appeal to the Court against the decision.

(2)   A complainer may, before the expiry of the period of 21 days beginning with the day on which a decision by the Tribunal under section 53ZB to which this subsection applies is intimated to him, appeal to the Court against the decision.

---

[1] As inserted by the Legal Profession and Legal Aid (Scotland) Act 2007 (asp 5) Pt 2 s.57(1) (effective October 1, 2008: insertion has effect subject to savings and transitional provisions specified in SSI 2008/332 art.4).

[2] As inserted by the Legal Profession and Legal Aid (Scotland) Act 2007 (asp 5) Pt 2 s.57(1) (effective October 1, 2008: insertion has effect subject to savings and transitional provisions specified in SSI 2008/332 art.4).

[3] As inserted by the Legal Profession and Legal Aid (Scotland) Act 2007 (asp 5) Pt 2 s.57(1) (effective October 1, 2008: insertion has effect subject to savings and transitional provisions specified in SSI 2008/332 art.4).

[4] As inserted by the Legal Profession and Legal Aid (Scotland) Act 2007 (asp 5) Pt 2 s.57(1) (effective October 1, 2008: insertion has effect subject to savings and transitional provisions specified in SSI 2008/332 art.4).

[5] As inserted by the Legal Profession and Legal Aid (Scotland) Act 2007 (asp 5) Pt 2 s.53(4) (effective October 1, 2008: insertion has effect subject to savings and transitional provisions specified in SSI 2008/332).

(3)   Subsection (2) applies to the following decisions of the Tribunal under section 53ZB—

    (a)   a decision under subsection (1)(a) quashing the Council's determination upholding the complaint;

    (b)   a decision under subsection (1)(c) quashing or varying a direction by the Council that the solicitor pay compensation;

    (c)   a decision under subsection (1)(f) directing the solicitor to pay compensation;

    (d)   a decision under subsection (2)(b) not to direct the solicitor to pay compensation;

    (e)   a decision under subsection (2)(c) confirming the Council's decision not to uphold the complaint;

    (f)   a decision under subsection (3) confirming the Council's decision not to direct the solicitor to pay compensation;

    (g)   a decision under subsection (4) quashing the Council's direction that the solicitor pay compensation or varying the amount of compensation directed to be paid.

(4)   On an appeal under subsection (1) or (2), the Court may give such directions in the matter as it thinks fit, including directions as to the expenses of the proceedings before the Court and as to any order by the Tribunal relating to expenses.

(5)   A decision of the Court under subsection (4) shall be final.

(6)   In this section, "complainer" has the same meaning as in section 42ZA.

The Court

Powers of court

55.—[1](1)[2]   In the case of professional misconduct by any solicitor the court may—

    (a)   cause the name of that solicitor to be struck off the roll; or

    (b)   suspend the solicitor from practice as a solicitor for such period as the court may determine; or

    (ba) suspend the solicitor from exercising any right of audience held by him by virtue of section 25A for such period as the court may determine; or

    (bb) revoke any right of audience so acquired by him; or

    (bc)[3] where the Court considers that the complainer has been directly affected by the misconduct, direct the solicitor to pay compensation of such amount, not exceeding £5,000, as it may specify to the complainer for loss, inconvenience or distress resulting from the misconduct; or

    (c)[4]   fine the solicitor an amount not exceeding £10,000; or

    (d)   censure him; and in any of those events,

---

[1] Read in conjunction with the European Communities (Lawyer's Practice) (Scotland) Regulations 2000 (SSI 2000/121), reg.37(2) and Sch.2 and the Solicitors (Scotland) Act 1980 (Foreign Lawyers and Multi-national Practices) Regulations 2004 (SSI 2004/383), reg.13 (except with regard to subsections (1)(ba) and (bb) and (3A)).

[2] As amended by the Law Reform (Miscellaneous Provisions) (Scotland) Act 1990 (c.40), Sched. 8, para.29(12).

[3] As inserted by the Legal Profession and Legal Aid (Scotland) Act 2007 (asp 5) Pt 2 s.56(2) (effective October 1, 2008: insertion has effect subject to savings and transitional provisions specified in SSI 2008/332).

[4] As amended by the Legal Profession and Legal Aid (Scotland) Act 2007 (asp 5) Pt 2 s.56(2) (effective October 1, 2008: amendment has effect subject to savings and transitional provisions specified in SSI 2008/332).

    (e)   find him liable in any expenses which may be involved in the proceedings before the court.

(2)   Subject to subsection (3), a decision of the court under this section shall be final.

(3)   A solicitor whose name has been struck off the roll in pursuance of an order made by the court under subsection (1), may apply to the court for an order directing his name to be restored to the roll and the court may make such order.

(3A)[1]   A solicitor whose rights of audience under section 25A have been revoked in pursuance of an order made by the court under subsection (1) may apply to the court for an order restoring those rights, and the court may make such order.

(4)   An application under subsection (3) shall be by way of petition and intimation of any such petition shall be made to the Tribunal who shall be entitled to appear and to be heard in respect of the application.

(5)[2]   The Scottish Ministers may by order made by statutory instrument—

    (a)   after consulting the Council and such groups of persons representing consumer interests as they consider appropriate, amend paragraph (bc) of subsection (1) by substituting for the amount for the time being specified in that paragraph such other amount as they consider appropriate;

    (b)   amend paragraph (c) of subsection (1) by substituting for the amount for the time being specified in that subsection such other amount as appears to them to be justified by a change in the value of money.

(6)[3]   A statutory instrument containing an order under—

    (a)   subsection (5)(a) is not to be made unless a draft of the instrument has been laid before, and approved by resolution of, the Scottish Parliament;

    (b)   subsection (5)(b) is subject to annulment in pursuance of a resolution of the Scottish Parliament.

(7)[4]   In this section, "complainer" has the same meaning as in section 42ZA.

Powers of Court: unsatisfactory professional conduct

55A.—(1)[5]   In the case of unsatisfactory professional conduct by a solicitor the Court may—

    (a)   fine the solicitor an amount not exceeding £2000;

    (b)   where it considers that the complainer has been directly affected by the conduct, direct the solicitor to pay compensation of such amount, not exceeding £5,000, as it may specify to the complainer for loss, inconvenience or distress resulting from the conduct;

---

[1] Inserted by the Law Reform (Miscellaneous Provisions) (Scotland) Act 1990 (c.40), Sch.8, para.29(12).

[2] As inserted by the Legal Profession and Legal Aid (Scotland) Act 2007 (asp 5) Pt 2 s.56(2) (effective October 1, 2008: insertion has effect subject to savings and transitional provisions specified in SSI 2008/332).

[3] As inserted by the Legal Profession and Legal Aid (Scotland) Act 2007 (asp 5) Pt 2 s.56(2) (effective October 1, 2008: insertion has effect subject to savings and transitional provisions specified in SSI 2008/332).

[4] As inserted by the Legal Profession and Legal Aid (Scotland) Act 2007 (asp 5) Pt 2 s.56(2) (effective October 1, 2008: insertion has effect subject to savings and transitional provisions specified in SSI 2008/332).

[5] As inserted by the Legal Profession and Legal Aid (Scotland) Act 2007 (asp 5) Pt 2 s.53(5) (effective October 1, 2008: insertion has effect subject to savings and transitional provisions specified in SSI 2008/332).

    (c) find the solicitor liable in any expenses which may be involved in the proceedings before it.

(2) A decision of the Court under subsection (1) shall be final.

(3) The Scottish Ministers may by order made by statutory instrument—

    (a) amend subsection (1)(a) by substituting for the amount for the time being specified in that subsection such other amount as appears to them to be justified by a change in the value of money;

    (b) after consulting the Council and such groups of persons representing consumer interests as they consider appropriate, amend subsection (1)(b) by substituting for the amount for the time being specified in that subsection such other amount as they consider appropriate.

(4) A statutory instrument containing an order under—

    (a) subsection (3)(a) is subject to annulment in pursuance of a resolution of the Scottish Parliament;

    (b) subsection (3)(b) is not to be made unless a draft of the instrument has been laid before, and approved by resolution of, the Scottish Parliament.

(5) In this section, "complainer" has the same meaning as in section 42ZA.

Saving for jurisdiction of courts

56.[1] Except as otherwise expressly provided, nothing in this Part shall affect the jurisdiction exercisable by the court, or by any inferior court, over solicitors.

Further provision as to compensation awards

56A. *[Repealed by the Legal Services Act 2007 (c.29) Sch.23 para.1 (effective October 1, 2008 as SI 2008/1436; repeal has effect subject to savings and transitional provisions specified in SSI 2008/332 art.4).]*

PART V – NOTARIES PUBLIC

Admission and enrolment of solicitors as notaries public

57.—[2](1) The offices and functions of—

    (a) the clerk to the admission of notaries public; and

    (b) the keeper of the register of notaries public,

are hereby transferred to the Council.

(2)[3] Any solicitor qualified to practise in accordance with section 4 may apply to the court to be admitted as a notary public; and on any such application the court may so admit the applicant and may direct the Council to register him in the register of notaries public.

(2A) A petition by the Council under section 6(3A) for the admission of a person as a solicitor may, if the person so requests, include an application for the person's admission as a notary public; and an order on any such petition admitting that person as a solicitor may admit him as a notary public and direct the Council to register him in the register of notaries public.

---

[1] Read in conjunction with the European Communities (Lawyer's Practice) (Scotland) Regulations 2000 (SSI 2000/121), reg.37(2) and Sch.2 and the Solicitors (Scotland) Act 1980 (Foreign Lawyers and Multi-national Practices) Regulations 2004 (SSI 2004/383), reg.13.

[2] As amended by the Law Reform (Miscellaneous Provisions) (Scotland) Act 1990 (c.40), s.37(2) (effective 20th July 1992: SI 1992/1599).

[3] As amended by the Legal Profession and Legal Aid (Scotland) Act 2007 (asp 5) s.62(2) (effective November 23, 2007).

(2B)   A petition by a person under section 6(2) for his admission as a solicitor may include an application for his admission as a notary public; and an order on any such petition admitting that person as a solicitor may admit him as a notary public and direct the Council to register him in the register of notaries public.

(3)   It shall not be necessary for any person to find caution on his admission as a notary public.

(4)[1]   The procedure to be followed on any application by a person to be admitted a notary public may be prescribed by rules of court.

(5)   The Council may charge such reasonable fees as they consider appropriate in respect of the admission of any person as a notary public.

Removal from and restoration to register of names of notaries public

58.—[2](1)   In the case of any person who is both a solicitor and a notary public, if his name is struck off the roll of solicitors or is removed from that roll in pursuance of an order under any provision of this Act, the Council shall forthwith strike off or, as the case may be, remove his name from the register of notaries public.

(2)   If the name of any such person, having been struck off or removed from the roll as aforesaid, is subsequently restored thereto in pursuance of an order under any provision of this Act, the Council shall forthwith restore the name to the register of notaries public.

(3)   Where a person who is both a solicitor and a notary public is suspended from practising as a solicitor under this Act the Council shall forthwith remove the person's name from the register of notaries public.

(4)   If the suspension of such a person as is mentioned in subsection (3) is terminated or otherwise comes to an end the Council shall restore the person's name to the register.

(5)[3]   Where a person who is a solicitor and a notary public no longer has in force a practising certificate, the Council shall forthwith remove the person's name from the register of notaries public.

(6)[4]   If the person mentioned in subsection (5) becomes qualified to practise as a solicitor in accordance with section 4, the Council shall restore the person's name to the register of notaries public.

Authority of notaries public to administer oaths, etc.

59.—(1)   Subject to subsection (2), in any case where the administration of an oath, or the receipt of an affidavit or solemn affirmation, is authorised by or under any enactment, it shall be lawful for the oath to be administered, or, as the case may be, for the affidavit or affirmation to be received, by a notary public.

(2)[5]   Nothing in this section applies to an oath or affirmation relating to any matter or thing relating to the preservation of the peace or to the prosecution, trial or punishment of an offence, or to any proceedings before either House of Parliament or any committee thereof or before the Scottish Parliament or any committee thereof.

---

[1] As amended by the Solicitors (Scotland) Act 1988 (c.42), Sch.1, para.18 and Sch.2.
[2] As amended by the Law Reform (Miscellaneous Provisions) (Scotland) Act 1990 (c.40), s.37(3) (effective 20th July 1992: SI 1992/1599).
[3] As inserted by the Legal Profession and Legal Aid (Scotland) Act 2007 (asp 5) s.62(3) (effective November 23, 2007).
[4] As inserted by the Legal Profession and Legal Aid (Scotland) Act 2007 (asp 5) s.62(3) (effective November 23, 2007).
[5] As amended by SI 1999/1042, art.3, Sch.1, Pt I, para.8 (effective May 6, 1999).

(3)   This section is without prejudice to any other statutory provision relating to the administration of oaths by notaries public.

Rules regarding notaries public

59A.—[1](1)   Subject to subsections (2) and (3), the Council may, if they think fit, make rules for regulating in respect of any matter the admission, enrolment and professional practice of notaries public.

(2)   The Council shall, before making any rules under this section—

    (a)   send to each notary public a draft of the rules; and

    (b)   take into consideration any representations made by any notary public on the draft.

(3)   Rules made under this section shall not have effect unless the Lord President, after considering any representations the Lord President thinks relevant, has approved the rules so made.

(4)   If a notary public fails to comply with any rule made under this section that failure may be treated as professional misconduct or unsatisfactory professional conduct on the part of the solicitor who is the notary public.

Offence for notaries public to act for unqualified persons

60.   *[Repealed by the Solicitors (Scotland) Act 1988 (c.42), Sch.2.]*

Registered foreign lawyers[2]

60A.—[3, 4, 5](1)   Subject to the provisions of this section, solicitors and incorporated practices may enter into multi-national practices with registered foreign lawyers.

(2)   The Council shall maintain a register of foreign lawyers, and may make rules with regard to registration; and, without prejudice to the generality of the foregoing, such rules may include provision as to—

    (a)   the manner in which applications for registration are to be made;

  (aa)[6]   the information which shall accompany such applications;

    (b)   the fees payable in respect of such applications;

    (c)   conditions which may be imposed in respect of registration; and

    (d)   the period for which any such registration is to run.

(3)   Section 34(2) and (3) apply to rules made under subsection (2) as they apply to rules made under that section.

(4)[7]   A foreign lawyer may apply to the Council to be registered as such for the purposes of—

---

[1] As inserted by the Legal Profession and Legal Aid (Scotland) Act 2007 (asp 5) s.63 (effective November 23, 2007).

[2] As substituted by the Legal Services (Scotland) Act 2010 (Ancillary Provision) Regulations 2012 (SSI 2012/212) reg.2 (effective July 2, 2012).

[3] Inserted by the Law Reform (Miscellaneous Provisions) (Scotland) Act 1990 (c.40), s.32 (in force March 17, 1993, only in respect of the provisions relating to the making of rules and orders in s.60A(2), (3) and (5)–(8): SI 1993/641).

[4] Read in conjunction with the European Communities (Lawyer's Practice) (Scotland) Regulations 2000 (SSI 2000/121), reg.37(2) and Sch.2 (effective May 22, 2000).

[5] Brought into force by SSI 2004/382 (effective October 1, 2004), in so far as not already in force.

[6] Inserted by the Solicitors (Scotland) Act 1980 (Foreign Lawyers and Multi-national Practices) Regulations 2004 (SSI 2004/383), reg.11.

[7] As substituted by the Legal Services (Scotland) Act 2010 (Ancillary Provision) Regulations 2012 (SSI 2012/212) reg.2 (effective July 2, 2012).

(a)   subsection (1); or

(b)   having an interest in a licensed legal services provider as a solicitor investor within the meaning given by section 67(6) of the 2010 Act.

(4ZA)[1]   Where an application is made under subsection (4), the Council are to enter the lawyer's name on the register of foreign lawyers if they are satisfied that the legal profession of which the applicant is a member is so regulated as to make it appropriate for the applicant to be registered for those purposes.

(4A)[2]   Any person may inspect the register of foreign lawyers during office hours without payment.

(4B)[3]   A registered foreign lawyer who wishes his name to be removed from the register of foreign lawyers may make an application to the Council in that behalf, and the Council shall, if the registered foreign lawyer satisfies the Council that he has made adequate arrangements with respect to the business that he has then in hand, remove the name of that foreign lawyer from the register of foreign lawyers.

(4C)[4]   On an application to the Council by a foreign lawyer whose name has been removed from the register of foreign lawyers under subsection (4B), the Council may, after such inquiry as they think proper, restore the name of the foreign lawyer to the register of foreign lawyers.

(4D)[5]   A foreign lawyer whose name has been removed (other than pursuant to an application made under subsection (4B)) from the register of foreign lawyers shall have his name restored to that register only if, on an application in that behalf made by him to the Tribunal and after such inquiry as the Tribunal thinks proper, the Tribunal so orders.

(4E)[6]   Rules made by the Tribunal under section 52 (procedure on complaints to the Tribunal) may—

(a)   regulate the making, hearing and determining of applications under subsection (4D); and

(b)   provide for payment by the applicant to the Council of such fee in respect of restoration to the register of foreign lawyers as the rules may specify.

(4F)[7]   Where, following an application under subsection (4), the Council decide not to enter the name of a foreign lawyer in the register of foreign lawyers the applicant may, within three months of the notification to him of the Council's decision (or later with the permission of the court), appeal to the court against the decision and, on such an appeal, the court may—

(a)   order the Council to register the foreign lawyer;

(b)   refuse the appeal; or

(c)   remit the matter to the Council with such directions as it sees fit.

---

[1] As substituted by the Legal Services (Scotland) Act 2010 (Ancillary Provision) Regulations 2012 (SSI 2012/212) reg.2 (effective July 2, 2012).

[2] Inserted by the Solicitors (Scotland) Act 1980 (Foreign Lawyers and Multi-national Practices) Regulations 2004 (SSI 2004/383), reg.11.

[3] Inserted by the Solicitors (Scotland) Act 1980 (Foreign Lawyers and Multi-national Practices) Regulations 2004 (SSI 2004/383), reg.11.

[4] Inserted by the Solicitors (Scotland) Act 1980 (Foreign Lawyers and Multi-national Practices) Regulations 2004 (SSI 2004/383), reg.11.

[5] Inserted by the Solicitors (Scotland) Act 1980 (Foreign Lawyers and Multi-national Practices) Regulations 2004 (SSI 2004/383), reg.11.

[6] Inserted by the Solicitors (Scotland) Act 1980 (Foreign Lawyers and Multi-national Practices) Regulations 2004 (SSI 2004/383), reg.11.

[7] Inserted by the Solicitors (Scotland) Act 1980 (Foreign Lawyers and Multi-national Practices) Regulations 2004 (SSI 2004/383), reg.11.

(4G)[1] Sections 24A to 24G (registration certificates for registered European lawyers) shall apply to registered foreign lawyers as they apply to registered European lawyers and any reference in those sections (as so applied) to a registration certificate shall be construed as a reference to a registration certificate for a registered foreign lawyer.

(5) Subject to subsection (6), the Secretary of State may by order made by statutory instrument provide that any enactment or instrument—

    (a) *[Repealed by the Solicitors (Scotland) Act 1980 (Foreign Lawyers and Multi-national Practices) Regulations 2004 (SSI 2004/383), reg.11.]*

    (b) having effect in relation to solicitors; and

    (c) specified in the order,

shall have effect with respect to registered foreign lawyers as it has effect with respect to solicitors.

(6) Before making any order under subsection (5), the Secretary of State shall consult the Council.

(7) An order under subsection (5) may provide for an enactment or instrument to have effect with respect to registered foreign lawyers subject to such additions, omissions or other modifications as the Secretary of State specifies in the order.

(8) No order shall be made under subsection (5) unless a draft of the order has been approved by both Houses of Parliament.

PART VI – MISCELLANEOUS AND GENERAL

Miscellaneous

Protection of banks

61.—[2, 3](1) Subject to the provisions of this section, no bank or building society shall, in connection with any transaction on any account of a solicitor or an incorporated practice kept with it or with any other bank or building society—

    (a) incur any liability, or

    (b) be under any obligation to make any inquiry, or

    (c) be deemed to have any knowledge of any right of any person to any money paid or credited to the account,

which it would not incur, or be under, or be deemed to have (as the case may be) in the case of an account kept by a person entitled absolutely to all money paid or credited to it; but nothing in this subsection shall relieve the bank or building society from any liability or obligation under which it would be apart from this Act.

(2) In subsection (1) "account" does not include an account kept by a solicitor or an incorporated practice as trustee for a specified beneficiary.

(3) Notwithstanding anything in the preceding provisions of this section a bank or building society at which a solicitor or an incorporated practice keeps a special account for clients' money shall not, in respect of any liability of the solicitor or, as the case may be, the incorporated practice to the bank or building society (not being

---

[1] Inserted by the Solicitors (Scotland) Act 1980 (Foreign Lawyers and Multi-national Practices) Regulations 2004 (SSI 2004/383), reg.11.

[2] As amended by the Law Reform (Miscellaneous Provisions) (Scotland) Act 1985 (c.73), Sched. 1, Pt. I, para.31, and the Solicitors (Scotland) Act 1988 (c.42), Sch.1, para.19.

[3] Read in conjunction with the European Communities (Lawyer's Practice) (Scotland) Regulations 2000 (SSI 2000/121), reg.37(2) and Sch.2 and the Solicitors (Scotland) Act 1980 (Foreign Lawyers and Multi-national Practices) Regulations 2004 (SSI 2004/383), reg.13.

a liability in connection with that account) have or obtain any recourse or right, whether by way of set-off, counter-claim, charge or otherwise, against money standing to the credit of that account.

Solicitors' fees

61A.—[1, 2](1)   Subject to the provisions of this section, and without prejudice to—

(a)   section 32(1)(i) of the Sheriff Courts (Scotland) Act 1971; or

(b)   section 5(h) of the Court of Session Act 1988,

where a solicitor and his client have reached an agreement in writing as to the solicitor's fees in respect of any work done or to be done by him for his client it shall not be competent, in any litigation arising out of any dispute as to the amount due to be paid under any such agreement, for the court to remit the solicitor's account for taxation.

(2)   Subsection (1) is without prejudice to the court's power to remit a solicitor's account for taxation in a case where there has been no written agreement as to the fees to be charged.

(3)   A solicitor and his client may agree, in relation to a litigation undertaken on a speculative basis, that, in the event of the litigation being successful, the solicitor's fee shall be increased by such a percentage as may, subject to subsection (4), be agreed.

(4)[3]   The percentage increase which may be agreed under subsection (3) shall not exceed such limit as the court may, after consultation with the Council, prescribe by act of sederunt.

Charge for expenses out of property recovered

62.—[4](1)   Where a solicitor has been employed by a client to pursue or defend any action or proceeding, the court before which the action or proceeding has been heard or is depending may declare the solicitor entitled, in respect of the taxed expenses of or in reference to the action or proceeding, to a charge upon, and a right to payment out of, any property (of whatsoever nature, tenure or kind it may be) which has been recovered or preserved on behalf of the client by the solicitor in the action or proceeding; and the court may make such order for the taxation of, and for the raising and payment of, those expenses out of the said property as the court thinks just.

(2)   Where a declaration has been made under subsection (1) any act done or deed granted by the client after the date of the declaration except an act or deed in favour of a bona fide purchaser or lender, shall be absolutely void as against the charge or right.

---

[1] Inserted by the Law Reform (Miscellaneous Provisions) (Scotland) Act 1990 (c.40), s. 36(3) (effective 4th July 1992: SI 1992/1599).
[2] Read in conjunction with the European Communities (Lawyer's Practice) (Scotland) Regulations 2000 (SSI 2000/121), reg.37(2) and Sch.2 and the Solicitors (Scotland) Act 1980 (Foreign Lawyers and Multi-national Practices) Regulations 2004 (SSI 2004/383), reg.13.
[3] The court's power to enact an act of sederunt under subss. (3) and (4) was brought into force on July 4, 1992 by SI 1992/1599.
[4] Read in conjunction with the European Communities (Lawyer's Practice) (Scotland) Regulations 2000 (SSI 2000/121), reg.37(2) and Sch.2 (effective May 22, 2000).

Council's power to recover expenses incurred under section 45 or 46

62A.—[1, 2, 3](1)   Without prejudice to the Society's entitlement under section 46(4) to recover expenses, the Council shall be entitled to recover from a solicitor or incorporated practice in respect of whom it has taken action under section 45, or 46, any expenditure reasonably incurred by it in so doing.

(2)   Expenditure incurred in taking action under section 38 is recoverable under subsection (1) above only where notice has been served under paragraph 5(2) of Schedule 3 in connection with that action and—

(a)   no application has been made in consequence under paragraph 5(4) of that Schedule; or

(b)   the Court, on such an application, has made a direction under paragraph 5(5) of that Schedule.

General

Penalties and time limit for prosecution of offences

63.—[4, 5](1)   Any person guilty of an offence under this Act shall be liable on summary conviction to a fine not exceeding level 4 on the standard scale.

(2)   Notwithstanding any provision of the Criminal Procedure (Scotland) Act 1975, the prosecution of any offence under this Act shall be commenced within 6 months of its first discovery by the prosecutor or in any event within 2 years after the commission of that offence.

(3)   Where an offence under this Act is committed by a body corporate and is proved to have been committed with the consent or connivance of or to be attributable to any neglect on the part of—

(a)   any director, secretary or other similar officer of the body corporate; or

(b)   any person who was purporting to act in any such capacity,

he (as well as the body corporate) shall be guilty of the offence and shall be liable to be proceeded against and punished accordingly.

(4)   Where an offence under this Act is committed by a partnership or by an unincorporated association (other than a partnership) and is proved to have been committed with the consent or connivance of a partner in the partnership or, as the case may be, a person concerned in the management or control of the association, he (as well as the partnership or association) shall be guilty of the offence and shall be liable to be proceeded against and punished accordingly.

---

[1] Inserted by the Law Reform (Miscellaneous Provisions) (Scotland) Act 1985 (c.73) Sch.1, Pt. II, para.6.

[2] Read in conjunction with the European Communities (Lawyer's Practice) (Scotland) Regulations 2000 (SSI 2000/121) reg.37(2) and Sch.2 and the Solicitors (Scotland) Act 1980 (Foreign Lawyers and Multi-national Practices) Regulations 2004 (SSI 2004/383) reg.13 (except with regard to references to s.46).

[3] As amended by the Legal Services Act 2007 (c.29) Sch.23 para.1 (effective October 1, 2008 as SI 2008/1436; amendment has effect subject to savings and transitional provisions specified in SSI 2008/332 art.4).

[4] As amended by virtue of the Criminal Procedure (Scotland) Act 1975 (c.21), ss. 289F and 289G, and by the Law Reform (Miscellaneous Provisions) (Scotland) Act 1990 (c.40), Sch.8, para.29(14) and Sch.9.

[5] Read in conjunction with the European Communities (Lawyer's Practice) (Scotland) Regulations 2000 (SSI 2000/121) reg.37(2) and Sch.2 and the Solicitors (Scotland) Act 1980 (Foreign Lawyers and Multi-national Practices) Regulations 2004 (SSI 2004/383) reg.13.

Service of notices, etc. F1.110

64.[1, 2] Any notice or other document which is required or authorised under this Act to be given to, or served on, any person shall be taken to be duly given or served if it is delivered to him or left at, or sent by post to, his last-known place of business or residence or, in the case of an incorporated practice, if it is left at, or delivered or sent by post to, its registered office.

Advisory and supervisory functions of the Competition and Markets Authority F1.111

64A.—[3, 4](1) Before considering any rule—
- (a) made under section 25A(4) or (5);
- (b) *[As repealed by the Legal Services (Scotland) Act 2010 (asp 16) Pt 4 c.3 s.124(2)(b) (effective July 2, 2012).]*

the Secretary of State shall send a copy of the proposed rule in question to the CMA.

(2) The CMA shall consider whether the rule in question would have, or would be likely to have, the effect of restricting, distorting or preventing competition to any significant extent.

(3) When the CMA has completed its consideration the CMA shall give such advice to the Secretary of State as it thinks fit.

(4) The CMA may publish any advice given under subsection (3).

(5) The CMA shall, so far as practicable, exclude from anything published under subsection (4) any matter—
- (a) which relates to the affairs of a particular person; and
- (b) the publication of which would, or might in the CMA's opinion, seriously and prejudicially affect the interests of that person.

(6) For the purposes of the law of defamation, the publication of any advice or report by the CMA under this section shall be absolutely privileged.

Duty of Secretary of State F1.112

64B.[5, 6] When he has received advice under section 64A(3) in relation to a rule made under section 25A(4) or (5), the Secretary of State may, having considered—
- (a) that advice;
- (b) whether the interests of justice require that there should be such a rule; and
- (c) in relation to a rule made under section 25A(5), any relevant practice obtaining in the sheriff court,

approve or refuse to approve the rule.

---

[1] As amended by the Law Reform (Miscellaneous Provisions) (Scotland) Act 1985 (c.73) Sch.1, Pt. I, para.32.

[2] Read in conjunction with the European Communities (Lawyer's Practice) (Scotland) Regulations 2000 (SSI 2000/121) reg.37(2) and Sch.2 and the Solicitors (Scotland) Act 1980 (Foreign Lawyers and Multi-national Practices) Regulations 2004 (SSI 2004/383) reg.13.

[3] Inserted by the Law Reform (Miscellaneous Provisions) (Scotland) Act 1990 (c.40) s.43 (effective June 3, 1991).

[4] As amended by the Enterprise and Regulatory Reform Act 2013 (c.24) Sch.6 para.11 (effective April 1, 2014).

[5] Inserted by the Law Reform (Miscellaneous Provisions) (Scotland) Act 1990 (c.40) s.43 (effective June 3, 1991).

[6] As amended by the Legal Services (Scotland) Act 2010 (asp 16) Pt 4 c.3 s.124(2) (effective July 2, 2012).

F1.113   **Investigatory powers of the Competition and Markets Authority**[1]

64C.—[2](1)   For the purpose of investigating any matter under section 64A, the CMA may by notice in writing—

    (a)   require any person to produce to the CMA or to any person appointed by the CMA for the purpose, at a time and place specified in the notice, any documents which are specified or described in the notice and which—

        (i)   are in that person's custody or under that person's control; and

        (ii)   relate to any matter relevant to the investigation; or

    (b)   require any person carrying on any business to furnish to him (within such time and in such manner and form as the notice may specify) such information as may be specified or described in the notice.

(2)   A person shall not be required under this section to produce any document or disclose any information which he would be entitled to refuse to produce or disclose on the grounds of confidentiality between a client and his professional legal adviser in any civil proceedings.

(2A)[3]   A notice under this section may be issued on the CMA's behalf by any member of the CMA Board.

(3)   *[As repealed by the Enterprise Act 2002 (Consequential and Supplemental Provisions) Order 2003 (SI 2003/1398) Sch.1 para.2(2) (effective June 20, 2003).]*

F1.114   **Enforcement of notices under section 64C**

64CA.—[4](1)[5]   The court may, on an application by the CMA, enquire into whether any person ("the defaulter") has refused or otherwise failed, without reasonable excuse, to comply with a notice under section 64C(1).

(2)[6]   An application under subsection (1) shall include details of the possible failure which the CMA considers has occurred.

(3)   In enquiring into a case under subsection (1), the court shall hear any witness who may be produced against or on behalf of the defaulter and any statement which may be offered in defence.

(4)   Subsections (5) and (6) apply where the court is satisfied, after hearing any witnesses and statements as mentioned in subsection (3), that the defaulter has refused or otherwise failed, without reasonable excuse, to comply with a notice under section 64C(1).

(5)   The court may punish the defaulter as it would have been able to punish him had he been guilty of contempt of court.

(6)   Where the defaulter is a body corporate or is a partnership constituted under the law of Scotland, the court may punish any director, officer or (as the case may be) partner of the defaulter as it would have been able to punish that director, officer

---

[1] As amended by the Enterprise and Regulatory Reform Act 2013 (c.24) Sch.6 para.11 (effective April 1, 2014).

[2] Inserted by the Law Reform (Miscellaneous Provisions) (Scotland) Act 1990 (c.40) s.43 (effective June 3, 1991).

[3] As inserted by the Enterprise and Regulatory Reform Act 2013 (c.24) Sch.6 para.11 (effective April 1, 2014).

[4] As inserted by the Enterprise Act 2002 (Consequential and Supplemental Provisions) Order 2003 (SI 2003/1398) art.2 Sch.1 para.2(3) (effective June 20, 2003).

[5] As amended by the Enterprise and Regulatory Reform Act 2013 (c.24) Sch.6 para.13 (effective April 1, 2014).

[6] As amended by the Enterprise and Regulatory Reform Act 2013 (c.24) Sch.6 para.13 (effective April 1, 2014).

or partner had he been guilty of contempt of court.

Altering, etc. documents required to be produced under section 64C

F1.115

64CB.—[1](1) A person commits an offence if he intentionally alters, suppresses or destroys a document which he has been required to produce by a notice under section 64C(1).

(2) A person who commits an offence under subsection (1) shall be liable—

    (a) on summary conviction, to a fine not exceeding the statutory maximum;

    (b) on conviction on indictment, to imprisonment for a term not exceeding two years or to a fine or to both.

Review of rules approved by the Secretary of State

F1.116

64D.—[2](1) Without prejudice to the power of the Council to review any rule made by them, where the Secretary of State has approved a rule under section 64B he may, and if so requested by the Lord President shall, require the Council to review its terms.

(2) When they have reviewed a rule following a requirement made under subsection (1), the Council may revise the rule in the light of that review, and shall then submit the rule as revised or, if they have not revised it, as previously approved to the Lord President and the Secretary of State.

(3) Where the Lord President and the Secretary of State are agreed that the terms of [any] rule as submitted to them are satisfactory, the Secretary of State shall approve the rule, and may direct the Council to bring it into force as soon as is practicable.

(4) Where either the Secretary of State or the Lord President is of the view that any rule, as submitted to them, is not satisfactory, but they do not agree as to what the terms of the rule should be, the rule shall continue to have effect as previously approved.

(5) Where the Secretary of State and the Lord President agree both that any rule submitted to them under subsection (2) is not satisfactory, and as to what the terms of the rule should be, the Secretary of State may direct the Council—

    (a) to amend the rule in such manner as he and the Lord President consider appropriate; and

    (b) to bring the rule, as so amended, into force as soon as is practicable.

(6)[3] The provisions of sections 64A and 64B apply to rules submitted to the Secretary of State under this section as they apply to rules submitted to him under sections 25A(9) or (10).

Interpretation

F1.117

65.—[4], [5](1)[6], [7] In this Act, except in so far as the context otherwise requires—

---

[1] Inserted by the Enterprise Act 2002 (Consequential and Supplemental Provisions) Order 2003 (SI 2003/1398) art.2, Sch.1 para.2(3) (effective June 20, 2003).

[2] As inserted by the Law Reform (Miscellaneous Provisions) (Scotland) Act 1990 (c.40) s.43.

[3] As amended by the Legal Services (Scotland) Act 2010 (asp 16) Pt 4 c.3 s.124(2) (effective July 2, 2012).

[4] As amended by the Legal Services (Scotland) Act 2010 (asp 16) Pt 4 c.3 s.124(2) (effective July 2, 2012).

[5] As amended by the Enterprise and Regulatory Reform Act 2013 (c.24) Sch.6 para.13 (effective April 1, 2014).

"the 1990 Act" means the Law Reform (Miscellaneous Provisions) (Scotland) Act 1990 (c.40);[1]

"the 2007 Act" means the Legal Profession and Legal Aid (Scotland) Act 2007 (asp 5);[2]

"the 2010 Act" means the Legal Services (Scotland) Act 2010;[3]

"accounts fee" has the meaning given by section 37A(1);[4]

"accounts rules" has the meaning given by section 35;

"accountant's certificate rules" has the meaning given by section 37(3);

"advocate" means a member of the Faculty of Advocates;

"building society" means a building society within the meaning of the Building Societies Act 1986;

"citizens advice body" means an association which is formed (and operates)—

    (a) otherwise than for the purpose of making a profit, and

    (b) with the sole or primary objective of providing legal and other advice (including information) to the public for no fee, gain or reward;[5]

"client account" means a current or deposit or savings account at a bank or with a building society, or a deposit receipt, at a bank, being an account or, as the case may be, a deposit receipt in the title of which the word "client", "trustee", "trust" or other fiducial term appears, including—

    (a) an account or deposit receipt for a client whose name is specified in the title of the account on deposit receipt, and

    (b) an account such as is mentioned in paragraphs (a) and (b) of section 35(1);

"the Commission" means the Scottish Legal Complaints Commission;[6]

"the Council" has the meaning given by section 3;

[7]"the CMA" means the Competition and Markets Authority;

"the CMA Board" has the same meaning as in Schedule 4 to the Enterprise and Regulatory Reform Act 2013;

"the court" means the Court of Session;

---

[6] As amended by the Law Reform (Miscellaneous Provisions) (Scotland) Act 1985 (c.73), Sched., Pt. I, para.33, the Solicitors (Scotland) Act 1988 (c.42), s.5(1), Sch.1, para.20 and Sch.2, and the Law Reform (Miscellaneous Provisions) (Scotland) Act 1990 (c.40), Sch.8, para.29(15) and Sch.9 (all in force by 17th March 1993: SI 1993/641).

[7] As amended by the Legal Services Act 2007 (c.29) Sch.23 para.1 (effective October 1, 2008 as SI 2008/1436; amendment has effect subject to savings and transitional provisions specified in SSI 2008/332 art.4).

[1] As inserted by the Public Appointments and Public Bodies etc. (Scotland) Act 2003 (asp 4) s.12 (effective August 15, 2003).

[2] As inserted by the Legal Profession and Legal Aid (Scotland) Act 2007 (asp 5) Sch.5 para.1(23) (effective October 1, 2008: insertion has effect subject to savings and transitional provisions specified in SSI 2008/332).

[3] As inserted by the Legal Services (Scotland) Act 2010 (asp 16) Pt 4 c.3 s.123(6) (effective July 2, 2012).

[4] As inserted by the Legal Services (Scotland) Act 2010 (asp 16) Pt 4 c.3 s.138(2) (effective May 1, 2011).

[5] As inserted by the Legal Services (Scotland) Act 2010 (asp 16) Pt 4 c.3 s.125(2) (effective April 1, 2011).

[6] As inserted by the Legal Profession and Legal Aid (Scotland) Act 2007 (asp 5) Sch.5 para.1(23) (effective October 1, 2008: insertion has effect subject to savings and transitional provisions specified in SSI 2008/332).

[7] As amended by the Enterprise and Regulatory Reform Act 2013 (c.24) Sch.6 para.14 (effective April 1, 2014).

[As repealed by the Enterprise and Regulatory Reform Act 2013 (c.24) Sch.6 para.14 (effective April 1, 2014).]

"foreign lawyer" means a person who is not a solicitor or an advocate but who is a member, and entitled to practise as such, of a legal profession regulated within a jurisdiction outwith Scotland;

"functions" includes powers and duties;

"incorporated practice" has the meaning given by section 34(1A)(c);

"judge" includes sheriff;

"law centre" means a body—

    (a) established for the purpose of providing legal services to the public generally as well as to individual members of the public; and

    (b) which does not distribute any profits made either to its members or otherwise, but reinvests any such profits for the purposes of the law centre;

"licensed legal services provider" (or "licensed provider") is to be construed in accordance with Part 2 of the 2010 Act;[1]

"Lord President" means the Lord President of the Court of Session;

"multi-national practice" means—

    (a) a partnership whose members are solicitors or incorporated practices and registered foreign lawyers; or

    (b) a body corporate whose members include registered foreign lawyers, and membership of which is restricted to solicitors, incorporated practices, registered foreign lawyers and other multi-national practices;

""notary public" means a notary public duly admitted in Scotland;

"practice year" means the year ending on 31st October;

"practising certificate" has the meaning given by section 4;

"property" includes property, whether heritable or moveable, and rights and interests in, to or over such property;

"registered European lawyer" means a person registered with the Society in accordance with regulation 17 of the European Communities (Lawyer's Practice) (Scotland) Regulations 2000;[2]

"registered foreign lawyer" means a foreign lawyer who is registered under section 60A;

"regulatory committee" means the regulatory committee formed in accordance with section 3B(1);[3]

"the roll" has the meaning given by section 7;

"the Society" has the meaning given by section 1;

"Scottish legal services ombudsman" means the ombudsman appointed under section 34 of the Law Reform (Miscellaneous Provisions) (Scotland) Act 1990;

"solicitor" means any person enrolled or deemed to have been enrolled as a solicitor in pursuance of this Act;

"the Tribunal" has the meaning given by section 50;

---

[1] As inserted by the Legal Services (Scotland) Act 2010 (asp 16) Pt 4 c.3 s.123(6) (effective July 2, 2012).

[2] Inserted by the European Communities (Lawyer's Practice) (Scotland) Regulations 2000 (SSI 2000/121), reg.37(2) and Sch.1, para.1(12)(a) (effective May 22, 2000).

[3] As inserted by the Legal Services (Scotland) Act 2010 (asp 16) Pt 4 c.3 s.133(3) (effective April 1, 2011 for the purpose of enabling regulations to be made; June 1, 2011 otherwise).

"unqualified person" means a person who is not qualified under section 4 to act as a solicitor;

"unsatisfactory professional conduct" as respects a solicitor has the meaning given (as respects a practitioner who is a solicitor) by section 46 of the 2007 Act.[1]

(2) Unless the context otherwise requires a reference—

    (a)[2] in any enactment to law agents includes solicitors and registered European lawyers;

    (b) in any enactment to the register of law agents kept in pursuance of the Law Agents (Scotland) Act 1873 includes the roll;

    (c) in any enactment or instrument to the Solicitors Discipline (Scotland) Committee shall be construed as a reference to the Tribunal.

    (d) in any enactment or instrument or other document to the General Council of Solicitors in Scotland shall be construed as a reference to the Council.

    (e) in any enactment to a solicitor's or registered European lawyer's being entitled to practise in the court, or in any other court, or to act in any matter, by reason of his being enrolled in, or of his having subscribed, the list of solicitors practising in that court, shall be construed as a reference to his being entitled so to practise or act by reason of his name being included in the appropriate list provided under section 20.

(3) In this Act references to any enactment shall, except in so far as the context otherwise requires, be construed as references to that enactment as amended, extended or applied by or under any other enactment, including any enactment contained in this Act.

(4) In this Act, except in so far as the context otherwise requires—

    (a) any reference to a numbered Part, section or Schedule is a reference to the Part or section of, or the Schedule to, this Act so numbered;

    (b) a reference in a section to a numbered subsection is a reference to the subsection of that section so numbered;

    (c) a reference in a section, subsection or Schedule to a numbered or lettered paragraph is a reference to the paragraph of that section, subsection or Schedule so numbered or lettered; and

    (d) a reference to any provision of an Act (including this Act) includes a reference to any Schedule incorporated in the Act by that provision.

Transitional and savings provisions, and repeals

66.—(1) Schedule 6 (transitional and savings provisions) shall have effect, but the provisions of that Schedule shall not be taken as prejudicing the operation of section 16 of the Interpretation Act 1978 (general savings in respect of repeals).

(2) The enactments specified in Schedule 7 are hereby repealed to the extent shown in column 3 of that Schedule.

---

[1] As inserted by the Legal Profession and Legal Aid (Scotland) Act 2007 (asp 5) Pt 2 s.53(6) (effective October 1, 2008: insertion has effect subject to savings and transitional provisions specified in SSI 2008/332).

Citation, extent and commencement

67.—(1)   This Act may be cited as the Solicitors (Scotland) Act 1980.

(2)   This Act extends to Scotland only.

(3)   This Act shall come into operation on the expiration of one month from the date on which it is passed.

SCHEDULES

SCHEDULE 1[1]

Section 1

THE LAW SOCIETY OF SCOTLAND   **F1.5**

Constitution and Proceedings

1.   The Society shall be a body corporate with a common seal and may sue and be sued in its own name.

2.   The Council shall prepare a scheme providing for—

---

[1] As amended by the European Communities (Lawyer's Practice) (Scotland) Regulations 2000 (SSI 2000/121) reg.37(1) (effective May 22, 2000).

(a)[1] the constitution and proceedings of the Council;
(aa)[2] election, co-option and appointment to the Council;
(b) the meetings of the Society;
(c) the appointment of a chairman, vice-chairman, secretary and other officers and employees of the Society;
(d)[3] the appointment and constitution of committees and sub-committees.

3. The scheme prepared under paragraph 2—
(a) may make provision enabling the Council to admit as honorary members of the Society persons who have ceased to be practising solicitors, no such honorary member being entitled to vote at meetings of the Society or liable to pay an annual subscription;
(b) shall make provision for the admission on application made in that behalf and on payment of the annual subscription as a member of the Society of any solicitor who by virtue of the provisions of section 24 is exempted from taking out a practising certificate;
(bza)[4] shall make provision for—
(i) the election or co-option of solicitor members to the Council,
(ii) the appointment of non-solicitor members to the Council;
(ba)[5] may make provision for persons other than solicitors to be members of a committee or sub-committee of the Council (including provision for such persons to constitute a majority of the members of the committee or sub-committee);
(c) may contain such other provisions with respect to the administration, management and proceedings of the Society as are considered necessary or proper and are consistent with the provisions of this Act.

3A.—[6](1) This paragraph applies for the purpose of paragraph 3(bza).
(2) Persons are electable, or eligible to be co-opted, as solicitor members if they are members of the Society.
(3) Persons are appointable as non-solicitor members if they appear to the Council—
(a) to be qualified to represent the interests of the public in relation to the provision of legal services in Scotland, or
(b) having regard to the Society's functions, to be suitable in other respects.

4. A scheme prepared under paragraph 2 shall have effect on being approved by a resolution passed by a majority of the members present in person or by proxy at a general meeting of the Society, or at an adjournment of such meeting.

5. The Society may by a resolution passed by a majority consisting of not less than two-thirds of the members of the Society present in person or by proxy at a meeting of the Society of which due notice specifying the intention to propose the resolution has been given, or at any adjournment of such meeting, rescind, add to or amend any of the provisions of the scheme so approved.

Revenue

6.[7] Subject to paragraph 7, every member of the Society shall, for each year, pay to the Society such subscription as may be fixed from time to time by the Society in general meeting.

6A.[8] The subscription payable under paragraph 6 by a practising member (or the proportion of it so payable, calculated by reference to the number of months remaining in the practice year) shall be paid at the time of submission of his application for a practising certificate.

---

[1] As amended by the Legal Services (Scotland) Act 2010 (asp 16) Pt 4 c.3 s.132(2)(a) (effective June 30, 2011).
[2] As inserted by the Legal Services (Scotland) Act 2010 (asp 16) Pt 4 c.3 s.132(2)(a) (effective June 30, 2011).
[3] As amended by the Council of the Law Society of Scotland Act 2003 (asp 14) s.2(2) (effective June 1, 2003).
[4] As inserted by the Legal Services (Scotland) Act 2010 (asp 16) Pt 4 c.3 s.132(2)(b) (effective June 30, 2011).
[5] As inserted by the Council of the Law Society of Scotland Act 2003 (asp 14) s.2(3) (effective June 1, 2003).
[6] As inserted by the Legal Services (Scotland) Act 2010 (asp 16) Pt 4 c.3 s.132(2) (effective June 30, 2011).
[7] As substituted by the Law Reform (Miscellaneous Provisions) (Scotland) Act 1985 Sch.1, Pt II, para.7.
[8] As inserted by the Law Reform (Miscellaneous Provisions) (Scotland) Act 1985 Sch.1, Pt II, para.7.

7.[1]   The subscription payable by a solicitor in respect of the year or part thereof in which he is first included in the roll of solicitors and in respect of each of the two years immediately following shall be one half of the amount of the subscription fixed under paragraph 6 (reduced, in the case of a solicitor first included in the roll for only part of a year, in that year proportionately).

7A.[2]   The Society shall have power, subject to paragraphs 7B to 7D, to impose in respect of any year a special subscription on all members of the Society of such amount and payable at such time and for such specified purpose as it may determine.

7B.[3]   The Society may determine that an imposition under paragraph 7A shall not be payable by any category of member or shall be abated as respects any category of member.

7C.[4]   An imposition under paragraph 7A or a determination under that paragraph or paragraph 7B may be made only in general meeting.

7D.[5]   No imposition may be made under paragraph 7A above unless a majority of those members voting at the general meeting at which it is proposed has, whether by proxy or otherwise, voted in favour of its being made.

8.   Except as otherwise provided in this Act, the expenses of the Society shall be defrayed out of the subscriptions and other income received by the Society or the Council and out of other property belonging to the Society.

In this paragraph "expenses of the Society" includes the expenses of the Tribunal so far as not otherwise defrayed and any expenses incurred by the Council in exercise of their functions under this Act, and the reasonable travelling and maintenance expenses of members of the Council or committees of the Council incurred in attending meetings of the Council or committees, or otherwise incurred in the business of the Society.

9.   Paragraph 8 does not affect any trust constituted for a special purpose.

Powers

10.   The Society may—
    (a)   purchase or otherwise acquire land for any of the purposes of this Act;
    (b)   sell, lease or otherwise dispose of land so acquired;
    (c)   borrow for any of the purposes of this Act in such manner and on such security as they may determine;
    (d)   invest any monies not immediately required to meet expenses and other outlays of the Society in any investment in which trustees in Scotland are by law authorised to invest (but nothing in this sub-paragraph prevents the investment of any monies forming any part of any property held in trust for a special purpose in any class of investment authorised by the deed constituting the trust);
    (e)   accept any gift of property for the purposes of the Society;
    (f)   accept, hold and administer any gift of property or hold as trustees any property for any purpose which the Society consider to be for the benefit of solicitors in Scotland or their dependants or employees or any substantial body of such solicitors or dependants or employees; and
    (g)   subject to the provisions of this Act exercise the functions formerly exercised by the General Council of Solicitors in Scotland.

11.   The Council may—
    (a)   act for and in the name of the Society in any matter other than a matter which in accordance with the provisions of this Schedule is to be determined by the Society in general meeting;
    (b)   without prejudice to any other powers they may have, take into consideration and make recommendations or representations with regard to any matters which are in their opinion of importance to solicitors in Scotland.

---

[1] As amended by the Law Reform (Miscellaneous Provisions) (Scotland) Act 1985 Sch.1, Pt II, para.7 and Sch.4.
[2] Paras. 7A to 7D inserted by the Law Reform (Miscellaneous Provisions) (Scotland) Act 1985, Sch.1, Pt II, para.7. Para.7D amended by the Solicitors (Scotland) Act 1988, Sch.1, para.21.
[3] Paras. 7A to 7D inserted by the Law Reform (Miscellaneous Provisions) (Scotland) Act 1985, Sch.1, Pt II, para.7. Para.7D amended by the Solicitors (Scotland) Act 1988, Sch.1, para.21.
[4] Paras. 7A to 7D inserted by the Law Reform (Miscellaneous Provisions) (Scotland) Act 1985, Sch.1, Pt II, para.7. Para.7D amended by the Solicitors (Scotland) Act 1988, Sch.1, para.21.
[5] Paras. 7A to 7D inserted by the Law Reform (Miscellaneous Provisions) (Scotland) Act 1985, Sch.1, Pt II, para.7. Para.7D amended by the Solicitors (Scotland) Act 1988, Sch.1, para.21.

Exemption from liability for damages

11A.[1]   Neither the Society nor any of its officers or servants shall be liable in damages for anything done or omitted in the discharge or purported discharge of its functions unless the act or omission is shown to have been in bad faith.

Attestation

12.   *[Repealed by the Requirements of Writing (Scotland) Act 1995 (c.7), Sch.5 (effective August 1, 1995: s.15(2)).]*

SCHEDULE 2[2]

Section 11

THE ROLL: POWERS OF THE COUNCIL AND ANCILLARY PROVISIONS

1.   The Council (as registrar of solicitors) for the purpose of maintaining the roll as correctly as is reasonably practicable shall have power—

(a)   to remove from the roll the name of any solicitor who has died;

(b)   to send to any solicitor at his address as shown in the roll a letter enquiring whether he wishes to continue to have his name included in the roll and intimating that if no reply is made within the period of 6 months beginning with the date of the posting of the letter his name may be removed from the roll;

(c)   to send any solicitor on the roll who has for at least 3 years been so enrolled in pursuance of regulations made by the Council under section 5 on an undertaking by him to serve a post qualifying year for practical training which the Council are not satisfied that he has implemented, a letter enquiring whether he intends to fulfil that undertaking and intimating that unless a reply which the Council regard as satisfactory is received within the period of 6 months beginning with the date of the posting of the letter his name may be removed from the roll; and

(d)   if a reply indicating that he does not wish that his name shall continue to be included in the roll is returned by any solicitor to whom a letter has been so sent, or if no reply or in a case of a letter sent under subparagraph (c) a reply which the Council do not regard as satisfactory is returned within the period mentioned in subparagraph (b) or (c), as the case may be, by any such solicitor, to remove the name of that solicitor from the roll.

2.   The Council may, on the application of a solicitor whose name has been removed from the roll in pursuance of paragraph 1(d), and on payment by him to the Council of such reasonable fee in respect of restoration as the Council may fix, order that his name shall be restored to the roll.

3.   Any person aggrieved by a decision of the Council under paragraph 2 may appeal against the decision to the Court, and the provisions of section 40(3) shall, subject to any necessary modifications, apply to any such appeal.

---

[1] Inserted by the Law Reform (Miscellaneous Provisions) (Scotland) Act 1990, Sch.8, para.29(16).
[2] As amended by the Solicitors (Scotland) Act 1988 (c.42), Sch.1, para.22 and Sch.2 and by the Solicitors (Scotland) Act 1980 (c.46) Pt II, s.12A(4) (effective May 22, 2000).

4. Subject to section 7(3), the Council may charge such reasonable fees (including an annual fee payable by enrolled solicitors) as they may fix in connection with the keeping of the roll.

SCHEDULE 3

Section 43

PART I

THE SCOTTISH SOLICITORS GUARANTEE FUND

Contributions by Solicitors

1.—[1, 2, 3](1)   Subject to the provisions of this Act, there shall be paid to the Society on behalf of the Guarantee Fund by every solicitor in respect of each year during which, or part of which, he is in practice as a solicitor, along with his application for a practising certificate, a contribution (hereafter referred to as an "annual contribution").

(2)   The sum payable by a solicitor in respect of the year in which he first commences to practise after admission and in respect of each of the two years immediately following shall be one half of the annual contribution.

(2A)   Sub-paragraphs (1) and (2) do not apply to solicitors who are—
    (a)   directors or members of incorporated practices, or
    (b)   investors in licensed legal services providers.

(2B)   Subject to the provisions of this Act, there shall be paid to the Society on behalf of the Guarantee Fund—
    (a)   by every incorporated practice in respect of each year during which, or part of which, it is recognised under section 34(1A) a contribution (hereafter referred to as an "annual corporate contribution") in accordance with the relevant scale of annual corporate contributions referred to in sub-paragraph (3), and
    (b)   by every licensed provider, in respect of each year during which or part of which it operates as such under the licence issued by its approved regulator, a contribution (also an "annual corporate contribution") in accordance with the relevant scale of annual corporate contributions referred to in sub-paragraph (3).

(3)   The Council shall not later than 30th September in each year fix the amount, if any, of the annual contribution to be paid in respect of the following year and the scales of the annual corporate contributions to be so paid.

(3A)   The scales of annual corporate contributions—
    (a)   are to be fixed under sub-paragraph (3) by reference to all relevant factors, including—
        (i)   in the case of incorporated practices, the number of solicitors that they have as directors, members or employees,
        (ii)   in the case of licensed providers, the number of solicitors that they have as investors or employees,
    (b)   may otherwise make different provision as between incorporated practices and licensed providers.

(4)   No annual contribution shall be payable by a solicitor and no annual corporate contribution by an incorporated practice or a licensed provider so long as the amount of the Guarantee Fund including the value of all investments forming part of the Fund and after providing for all outstanding liabilities, is in the opinion of the Council not less than £250,000 or such other sum as the Council may from time to time determine.

(5)   If at any time the Council are of opinion that the liabilities of the Guarantee Fund render it expedient in order to secure the financial stability of the Fund, the Council may, by resolution of which not less than 10 days' previous notice in writing has been given to each member of the Council, impose upon every solicitor a contribution (hereafter referred to as a "special contribution") of the amount specified in the resolution, and upon every incorporated practice and licensed provider a contribution (hereafter referred to as a "special corporate contribution") in accordance with a scale of such contributions fixed by

---

[1] As amended by the Law Reform (Miscellaneous Provisions) (Scotland) Act 1985 (c.73) s.56 and, Sch.1, Pt I, para.34, Pt II, para.8, and Sch.4.
[2] As amended by the Legal Services (Scotland) Act 2010 (asp 16) Pt 4 c.3 s.129(1)(a) (effective April 1, 2011).
[3] As amended by the Legal Services (Scotland) Act 2010 (asp 16) Pt 4 c.3 s.129(1) (effective July 2, 2012).

the Council as under sub-paragraph (3), and a special or special corporate contribution shall be payable to the Society in one sum or, if the Council so determine, by instalments on or before such date or dates as may be specified in the resolution.

(6) No special contribution shall be payable by a solicitor in the year in which he first commences to practice after admission nor in either of the 2 years immediately following.

(7) *[Repealed by the Law Reform (Miscellaneous Provisions) (Scotland) Act 1985, Sch.1, Pt. II, para.8(c), with effect from December 30, 1985.]*

(8) No annual contribution and no special contribution shall be payable by any solicitor who is in the employment of another solicitor or of a firm of solicitors or of an incorporated practice or a licensed provider and who does not engage in practice as a solicitor on his own account.

(9) Without prejudice to any other method of recovering contributions payable to the Society under this Schedule whether annual or special a practising certificate shall not be issued to a solicitor except on production of evidence of payment of the contributions (if any) due by him to the Fund on or before the issue of the certificate.

(10) In this Schedule the expression "year" means the period of 12 months commencing on 1st November or such other day as may be fixed by the Council.

Contributions by registered European lawyers

1A.—[1](1) Subject to the provisions of this paragraph, paragraph (1) above shall apply to registered European lawyers as it applies to solicitors and references to a practising certificate shall include references to a registered European lawyer's registration certificate.

(2) Where a registered European lawyer can prove that—

    (a) he is covered by a guarantee provided in accordance with the professional rules of his home State; and

    (b the guarantee is equivalent in terms of the conditions and the extent of its cover to the Guarantee Fund, then to the extent that there is such equivalence that lawyer shall be exempt from the requirements of paragraph (1).

(3) Where the equivalence under sub paragraph (2) is only partial, the Society may specify the guarantee obligations a registered European lawyer is required to meet to comply with paragraph (1).

(4) Subparagraphs (2), (6) and (8) of paragraph (1) shall not apply.

(5) For the purposes of this paragraph the words "home State" have the same meaning as provided for in regulation 2 of the European Communities (Lawyer's Practice) (Scotland) Regulations 2000.

Contributions by registered foreign lawyers

1B.—[2](1) Subject to the provisions of this paragraph, paragraph 1 above shall apply to registered foreign lawyers as it applies to solicitors and in that paragraph as so applied references to a practising certificate shall be construed as references to a registered foreign lawyer's registration certificate.

(2) Where a registered foreign lawyer can prove that—

    (a) he is covered by a guarantee provided in accordance with the rules of the legal profession of which he is a member; and

    (b) the guarantee is equivalent in terms of the conditions and the extent of its cover to the Guarantee Fund,

then to the extent that there is such equivalence that lawyer shall be exempt from the requirements of paragraph 1.

(3) Where the equivalence referred to in sub paragraph (2) is only partial, the Society may specify the guarantee obligations a registered foreign lawyer is required to meet to comply with paragraph 1.

(4) The Council may, where it is satisfied that any acts or defaults on the part of a registered foreign lawyer would not result in a grant being made from the Guarantee Fund held under section 43, exempt that lawyer from the requirements of paragraph 1.

(5) Sub paragraphs (2), (6) and (8) of paragraph 1 shall not apply to registered foreign lawyers.

Contributions by Solicitors

1C.—[3](1) Paragraph 1 applies to a conveyancing or executry practitioner as it applies to a solicitor.

(2) But it does so with the following of its provisions to be disregarded—

---

[1] As inserted by the European Communities (Lawyer's Practice) (Scotland) Regulations 2000 (SSI 2000/121) reg.37(1) and Sch.1 para.1(13) (effective May 22, 2000).

[2] As inserted by the Solicitors (Scotland) Act 1980 (Foreign Lawyers and Multi-national Practices) Regulations 2004 (SSI 2004/383) reg.12.

[3] As inserted by the Legal Services (Scotland) Act 2010 (asp 16) Pt 4 c.3 s.129(2) (effective April 1, 2011).

(a)   the reference in sub-paragraph (1) to an application for a practising certificate,

(b)   sub-paragraphs (2), (2A), (6) and (9).

(3)   If a conveyancing or executry practitioner fails to pay an annual contribution due by virtue of this paragraph, the Council may suspend (pending payment) the relevant entry in the register maintained by them under section 17(1) or 18(1) of the 1990 Act.

(4)   For the purposes of section 43 and this paragraph, the references to a conveyancing or executry practitioner (or conveyancing or executry services) are to be construed in accordance with section 23 of the 1990 Act.

Investment etc.

2.—(1)   Monies not immediately required to meet sums payable out of the Guarantee Fund may be invested by the Society in any investments in which trustees in Scotland are by law authorised to invest.

(2)   The Society may borrow money for the purposes of the Guarantee Fund in such manner and on such security as they may determine but the total sum due at any time in respect of any such loans shall not exceed[1] £1,250,000.

(3)   The accounts of the Guarantee Fund shall be made up annually for the year ending 31st October or on such other day as may be fixed by the Council and shall be audited by an auditor appointed by the Society.

(4)   As soon as the audit is completed the audited accounts and the auditor's report on the accounts shall be submitted to the Council and a copy of the audited accounts and the auditor's report shall be sent to the Lord Advocate and to every solicitor who is contributing to the Fund.

(5)   All investments and other monies forming part of the Guarantee Fund and the books and accounts relating to that Fund shall be kept separate from the other investments and monies, books and accounts of the Society, and the investments and other monies forming part of the Guarantee Fund shall not be liable for any obligations, debts or liabilities incurred by the Society or the Council in relation to any business of the Society other than the business of the Guarantee Fund, nor shall the investments and other monies of the Society held for the purposes other than those relating to the Guarantee Fund be liable for any obligations, debts or liabilities incurred by the Society or the Council in relation to the Guarantee Fund.

Insurance

3.—(1)   The Society may enter into a contract of insurance with any person, body of persons or corporation authorised by law to carry on insurance business for guaranteeing the sufficiency of the Guarantee Fund or for any other purpose in relation to the Fund.

(2)[2]   Any such contract of insurance may be entered into in relation to solicitors, incorporated practices and licensed providers generally or in relation to any solicitor or solicitors, incorporated practice or practices or licensed provider or providers named therein.

(3)   No person other than the Society shall have any right of action against a person, body or corporation with whom any such contract of insurance was entered into or have any right to any monies payable under that contract.

Grants

4.—[3](1)   Every application for a grant from the Guarantee Fund shall be in such form as may be prescribed by rules made under this Schedule and shall be accompanied, if so required by the Council, by a statutory declaration and the applicant shall produce to the Council such documents and other evidence as they demand.

(2)[4]   The Council may, as a condition of making a grant out of the Guarantee Fund, require the person to whom the grant is made to assign to the Society at the expense of the Society any rights and remedies competent to him against the solicitor in question, his partner or employee or the incorporated practice in question or its employee or any other person in respect of the loss.

---

[1] Figure substituted by the Legal Profession and Legal Aid (Scotland) Act 2007 (asp 5) s.59 (effective November 23, 2007).

[2] As substituted by the Legal Services (Scotland) Act 2010 (asp 16) Pt 4 c.3 s.129(3) (effective July 2, 2012).

[3] Read in conjunction with the European Communities (Lawyer's Practice) (Scotland) Regulations 2000 (SSI 2000/121) reg.37(2) and Sch.2 of the Solicitors (Scotland) Act 1980 (Foreign Lawyers and Multi-national Practices) Regulations 2004 (SSI 2004/383) reg.14.

[4] As amended by the Law Reform (Miscellaneous Provisions) (Scotland) Act 1985, Sched. 1, Pt. I, para. 34.

(3)   A grant from the Guarantee Fund may at the discretion of the Council be paid in one sum or in such instalments as the Council may determine.

(3A)[1]   The amount of an individual grant from the Guarantee Fund may not exceed £1.25 million.

(4)[2]   The Council may make rules with regard to the procedure to be followed in giving effect to the provisions of this Act relating to the Guarantee Fund, including matters to be prescribed thereunder, and also with respect to any matters incidental, ancillary or supplemental to those provisions or concerning the administration, management or protection of the Guarantee Fund.

5.—[3](1)   The Scottish Ministers may by regulations amend the sum specified in paragraph 4(3A).

(2)   Before making regulations under sub-paragraph (1), the Scottish Ministers must consult the Council (and take account of sections 4 and 5 of the 2010 Act).

(3)   The power to make regulations under sub-paragraph (1) is exercisable by statutory instrument; but a statutory instrument containing any such regulations is not to be made unless a draft of the instrument has been laid before, and approved by resolution of, the Scottish Parliament.

PART II

Section 38

Power of Council to investigate

5.—[4, 5](1)   If under section 45 or 46 any person (whether a solicitor or not) having possession or control of any documents mentioned in that section refuses or fails to produce or deliver them immediately on being required by the Council to do so or cause them to be so produced or delivered, the Council may apply to the court for an order requiring that person to produce or deliver the documents or to cause them to be produced or delivered to the person appointed at the place fixed by the Council within such time as the court may order.

(2)[6]   Upon taking possession of any such documents which have been produced or delivered to the Council, the Council shall serve upon the solicitor or incorporated practice mentioned in section 45 or 46, and every such person, a notice giving particulars and the date on which they took possession.

(3)   Every requirement made or notice given under section 45 or 46 or under this Part of this Schedule shall be in writing under the hand of such person as may be appointed by the Council for the purpose and may be served either personally or by registered letter or by a letter sent by recorded delivery service addressed to the last known place of business or residence of the person to whom the requirement is made or notice given.

(4)   Within 14 days after service of a notice under sub-paragraph (2) the person upon whom such notice has been served may apply to the court for an order directing the Council to return such documents to the person from whom they were received by the Council or to such other person as the applicant may request and on the hearing of any such application the court may make the order applied for or such other order as they think fit.

(5)   If no application is made to the court under sub-paragraph (4) or if the court on any such application directs that the documents in question remain in the custody or control of the Council, the Council may make enquiries to ascertain the person to whom they belong and may deal with the documents in accordance with the directions of that person.

[1] As inserted by the Legal Services (Scotland) Act 2010 (asp 16) Pt 4 c.3 s.130(a) (effective April 1, 2011).

[2] Read in conjunction with the European Communities (Lawyer's Practice) (Scotland) Regulations 2000 (SSI 2000/121) reg.37(2) and Sch.2 of the Solicitors (Scotland) Act 1980 (Foreign Lawyers and Multi-national Practices) Regulations 2004 (SSI 2004/383) reg.14.

[3] As inserted by the Legal Services (Scotland) Act 2010 (asp 16) Pt 4 c.3 s.130(b) (effective April 1, 2011). Possible drafting error—should be numbered 4A.

[4] Read in conjunction with the European Communities (Lawyer's Practice) (Scotland) Regulations 2000 (SSI 2000/121), reg.37(2) and Sch.2 and the Solicitors (Scotland) Act 1980 (Foreign Lawyers and Multi-national Practices) Regulations 2004 (SSI 2004/383), reg.13.

[5] As amended by the Legal Services Act 2007 (c.29) Sch.23 para.1 (effective October 1, 2008 as SI 2008/1436; amendment has effect subject to savings and transitional provisions specified in SSI 2008/332 art.4).

[6] As amended by the Law Reform (Miscellaneous Provisions) (Scotland) Act 1985, Sched. 1, Pt. I, para. 34.

SCHEDULE 4[1]

Sections 50, 52

CONSTITUTION, PROCEDURE AND POWERS OF TRIBUNAL

PART I

Constitution

1.[2]   The Tribunal shall consist of not more than 28 members.

1A.[3]   The Tribunal shall consist of equal numbers of—

(a)   members (in this Part referred to as "solicitor members") appointed by the Lord President, who are solicitors recommended by the Council as representatives of the solicitors' profession throughout Scotland; and

(b)   members (in this Part referred to as "non-lawyer members") appointed by the Lord President after consultation with the Scottish Ministers, who are not—

(i)   solicitors;

(ii)   advocates;

(iii)   conveyancing practitioners or executry practitioners, within the meaning of section 23 of the Law Reform (Miscellaneous Provisions) (Scotland) Act 1990 (c.40) ("the 1990 Act");

(iv)   persons exercising a right to conduct litigation or a right of audience acquired by virtue of section 27 of the 1990 Act.

1B.[4]   The validity of any proceedings of the Tribunal is not affected by a vacancy in membership of the Tribunal nor by any defect in the appointment of a member.

1C.[5]   The Scottish Ministers may by order made by statutory instrument amend paragraph 1 so as to vary the maximum number of members of the Tribunal.

1D.[6]   A statutory instrument containing an order made under paragraph 1C is subject to annulment in pursuance of a resolution of the Scottish Parliament.

2.[7]   Each member of the Tribunal shall retire from office on the expiry of 5 years from the date of his appointment, but in the case

(a)[8]   of a non-lawyer, may be re-appointed by the Lord President after consultation with the Secretary of State; and

(b)   of a solicitor member, may be re-appointed by the Lord President on the recommendation of the Council.

---

[1] Read in conjunction with the European Communities (Lawyer's Practice) (Scotland) Regulations 2000 (SSI 2000/121), reg.37(2) and Sch.2 and the Solicitors (Scotland) Act 1980 (Foreign Lawyers and Multi-national Practices) Regulations 2004 (SSI 2004/383), reg.13.

[2] As substituted by the Legal Profession and Legal Aid (Scotland) Act 2007 (asp 5) s.58(2) (effective November 23, 2007).

[3] As inserted by the Legal Profession and Legal Aid (Scotland) Act 2007 (asp 5) s.58(2) (effective November 23, 2007).

[4] As inserted by the Legal Profession and Legal Aid (Scotland) Act 2007 (asp 5) s.58(2) (effective November 23, 2007).

[5] As inserted by the Legal Profession and Legal Aid (Scotland) Act 2007 (asp 5) s.58(2) (effective November 23, 2007).

[6] As inserted by the Legal Profession and Legal Aid (Scotland) Act 2007 (asp 5) s.58(2) (effective November 23, 2007).

[7] As amended by the Law Reform (Miscellaneous Provisions) (Scotland) Act 1980, s. 24, and the Law Reform (Miscellaneous Provisions) (Scotland) Act 1990 (c. 40), Sch.8, para.29(17) (effective 20th July 1992: SI 1992/1599).

[8] As substituted by the Legal Profession and Legal Aid (Scotland) Act 2007 (asp 5) s.58(3) (effective November 23, 2007).

3.[1, 2]   The Lord President may from time to time terminate the appointment of any member of the Tribunal, and may fill any vacancy therein by the appointment of a solicitor recommended by the Council or, as the case may be, after consultation with the Secretary of State, by the appointment of a non-lawyer member.

4.   The Tribunal may appoint one of their number to be chairman, and may also appoint a clerk, who shall not be a member of the Tribunal, and, subject to the provisions of this Act, may regulate their procedure in such way as they may think fit.

5.[3]   The Tribunal shall be deemed to be properly constituted if—

(a)   at least 4 members are present, and

(b)   at least 2 solicitor members are present, and

(c)   at least 2 non-lawyer members are present.

(d)   *[Repealed by the Legal Profession and Legal Aid (Scotland) Act 2007 (asp 5) s.58(5)(c) (effective November 23, 2007).]*

6.[4, 5]   There shall be paid to the non-lawyer members of the Tribunal out of money provided by Parliament such fees and allowances as the Secretary of State may determine.

PART II[6]

PROCEDURE AND POWERS OF TRIBUNAL

Complaints

7.   The making of a complaint to the Tribunal or the giving of any information in connection with a complaint shall confer qualified privilege.

8.   A complaint made to the Tribunal shall not be withdrawn except with the Tribunal's leave and subject to such conditions with respect to expenses or otherwise as the Tribunal thinks fit.

8A.   *[Repealed by the Legal Profession and Legal Aid (Scotland) Act 2007 (asp 5) Sch.5 para. 1 (26) (a) (effective October 1, 2008: repeal has effect subject to savings and transitional provisions specified in SSI 2008/332 art.4).]*

9.[7, 8]   Subject to Part IV, the Tribunal may dismiss a complaint against a solicitor or an incorporated practice—

(a)   without requiring the solicitor or the incorporated practice to answer the allegations made against him or, as the case may be, it or without holding any inquiry if—

(i)   they are of the opinion that the complaint discloses no prima facie case of professional misconduct on the part of the solicitor or, of failure on the part of the incorporated practice to comply with any provision of this Act; or

(ii)   the complainer fails to comply with any rule made under section 52; or

(b)   without hearing parties if they are of the opinion upon consideration of the complaint and other documents that they disclose no case of professional misconduct on the part of the solicitor or, of failure on the part of the incorporated practice to comply with any provision of this Act or of rules made under this Act.

10.[9]   The Tribunal shall give notice of the complaint to the solicitor or incorporated practice against whom the complaint is made ("the respondent") and shall inquire into the complaint, giving him or, as the case may be, it reasonable opportunity of making his or, as the case may be, its defence.

---

[1] As amended by the Law Reform (Miscellaneous Provisions) (Scotland) Act 1990 (c. 40), Sch.8, para.29(17) (effective July 20, 1992: SI 1992/1599).

[2] As substituted by the Legal Profession and Legal Aid (Scotland) Act 2007 (asp 5) s.58(4) (effective November 23, 2007).

[3] As substituted by the Legal Profession and Legal Aid (Scotland) Act 2007 (asp 5) Pt 3 s.58(5) (effective November 23, 2007).

[4] As amended by SI 1999/1820, Art. 4, Sch.2, para.65 (effective July 1, 1999).

[5] As substituted by the Legal Profession and Legal Aid (Scotland) Act 2007 (asp 5) s.58(6) (effective November 23, 2007).

[6] Applied by the Legal Aid (Scotland) Act 1986, s.31(10).

[7] As amended by the Law Reform (Miscellaneous Provisions) (Scotland) Act 1985, Sch.1, Pt I, para.35, and the Solicitors (Scotland) Act 1988, Sch.1, para.23.

[8] As amended by the Legal Services Act 2007 (c.29) Sch.23 para.1 (effective October 1, 2008 as SI 2008/1436; amendment has effect subject to savings and transitional provisions specified in SSI 2008/332 art.4).

[9] As amended by the Law Reform (Miscellaneous Provisions) (Scotland) Act 1985, Sch.1, Pt I, para.35.

11. For the purpose of inquiring into the complaint the Tribunal may administer oaths and receive affirmations; and the complainer and respondent shall each be entitled—

(a) to require the evidence of parties, witnesses and others interested, and

(b) to call for and recover such evidence and documents, and examine such witnesses, as they think proper, but no person shall be compelled to produce any document which he could not be compelled to produce in an action.

12. On a petition by the complainer or the respondent to the court, or to the sheriff having jurisdiction in any place in which the respondent carries on business, the court or, as the case may be, the sheriff, on production of copies (certified by the clerk of the Tribunal) of the complaint and answers, if lodged, together with a statement signed by the clerk specifying the place and date of the hearing of the complaint and certifying that notice to that effect has been given to the complainer and to the respondent, and on being satisfied that it would be proper to compel the giving of evidence by any witness or the production of documents by any haver, may—

(a) grant warrant for the citation of witnesses and havers to give evidence or to produce documents before the Tribunal, and for the issue of letters of second diligence against any witness or haver failing to appear after due citation;

(b) grant warrant for the recovery of documents; and

(c) appoint commissioners to take the evidence of witnesses, to examine havers, and to receive exhibits and productions.

Decisions

13. The Tribunal shall set out in their decision—

(a) in the case of a complaint, the facts proved, and

(b) in the case of a conviction, particulars of the conviction and sentence,

and shall in the case of a complaint add to their decision a note stating the grounds on which the decision has been arrived at.

14.[1] Every decision of the Tribunal shall be signed by the chairman or other person presiding and shall, subject to paragraph 14A, be published in full.

14A.[2] In carrying out their duty under paragraph 14, the Tribunal may refrain from publishing any names, places or other facts the publication of which would, in their opinion, damage, or be likely to damage, the interests of persons other than—

(a) the solicitor against whom the complaint was made; or

(b) his partners; or

(c) his or their families,

but where they so refrain they shall publish their reasons for so doing.

15.[3] A copy of every decision by the Tribunal certified by the clerk shall be sent forthwith by the clerk to the respondent, the complainer and, as the case may be, the person who made the complaint as respects which the appeal was made to the Tribunal intimating the right of appeal available from that decision under this Act.

16.[4] In the case of a decision by the Tribunal—

(a) ordering a solicitor to be struck off the roll; or

(b) ordering a solicitor to be suspended from practice; or

(c) censuring a solicitor or an incorporated practice; or

(d) fining a solicitor or an incorporated practice; or,

(e) ordering that the recognition under section 34(1A) of an incorporated practice be revoked; or,

(f)-(g) *[Repealed by the Legal Services Act 2007 (c.29) Sch.23 para.1 (effective October 1, 2008 as SI 2008/1436; repeal has effect subject to savings and transitional provisions specified in SSI 2008/332 art.4).]*

---

[1] As substituted by the Law Reform (Miscellaneous Provisions) (Scotland) Act 1990 (c.40), Sch.8, para.29(17) (effective July 20, 1992: SI 1992/1599).

[2] As inserted by the Law Reform (Miscellaneous Provisions) (Scotland) Act 1990 (c.40), Sch.8, para.29(17) (effective July 20, 1992: SI 1992/1599).

[3] As substituted by the Legal Profession and Legal Aid (Scotland) Act 2007 (asp 5) Sch.5 para. 1(26) (effective October 1, 2008).

[4] As amended by the Law Reform (Miscellaneous Provisions) (Scotland) Act 1985, Sch.1, Pt I, para.35, the Solicitors (Scotland) Act 1988, Sch.1, para.23, and the Law Reform (Miscellaneous Provisions) (Scotland) Act 1990, Sch.8.

    (h)   ordering that an investment business certificate issued to a solicitor, a firm of solicitors or an incorporated practice be—

        (i)   suspended; or

        (ii)   subject to such terms and conditions as they may direct; or

        (iii)   revoked,

on the expiration of the days of appeal if any without an appeal being lodged or, where an appeal has been lodged, if and as soon as the appeal is withdrawn or a decision by the court is given in terms of subparagraphs (a) to (h) or in the case of a decision of the Tribunal under section 53(6) or (6B) which has not been varied or quashed by the court or under section 53(6A) which has not been varied by the court, the clerk of the Tribunal shall immediately send to the Council a copy of the decision of the Tribunal certified by him and a copy of the decision by the court in any appeal, and the Council shall forthwith give effect to any order as to striking the solicitor off the roll or as to revoking the recognition under section 34(1A) of an incorporated practice and to any terms and conditions directed by the Tribunal under section 53(5); and in any other case shall cause a note of the effect of the decision to be entered against the name of the solicitor in the roll.

    17.[1]   The Council shall forthwith intimate any order striking a solicitor off the roll or suspending a solicitor from practice to each sheriff clerk and to the Principal Clerk of Session, and shall, without prejudice to paragraph 14, cause a notice of the operative part of the order to be published in the *Edinburgh Gazette*.

    18.   The file of orders under this Act striking solicitors off the roll, suspending solicitors from practice, or restoring persons to the roll shall be open for inspection at the office of the Society at any reasonable hour by any person without payment of any fee.

    18A.[2]   Without prejudice to paragraph 18, the Council shall ensure that a copy of every decision published under paragraph 14 is open for inspection at the office of the Society during office hours by any person without payment of any fee.

Expenses

    19.   Subject to the provisions of Part IV, the Tribunal may make in relation to any complaint against a solicitor such order as it thinks fit as to the payment by the complainer or by the respondent of the expenses incurred by the other party and by the Tribunal or a reasonable contribution towards those expenses.

    20.   On the application of the person in whose favour an order for expenses under paragraph 19 is made and on production of a certificate by the clerk of the Tribunal that the days of appeal against the order have expired without an appeal being lodged or, where such an appeal has been lodged, that the appeal has been dismissed or withdrawn, the court may grant warrant authorising that person to recover those expenses from the person against whom the order was made.

    21.   Such warrant shall have effect for execution and for all other purposes as if it were an extracted decree of court awarded against the person against whom the order of the Tribunal was made.

    22.   The expenses of the Tribunal so far as not otherwise defrayed shall be paid by the Society as part of the expenses of the Society.

Appeals[3]

    23.[4]   The foregoing provisions of Part II of this Schedule shall apply in relation to an appeal to the Tribunal under section 42ZA(9), (10), (11) or (12), 42ZD(1) or section 53D(1) as they apply in relation to a complaint, but with the following modifications—

    (a)   for references to a complaint (except in paragraph 14A) there shall be substituted references to an appeal;

    (b)   *[Repealed by the Legal Profession and Legal Aid (Scotland) Act 2007 (asp 5) Sch.5 para.1(26)(c) (effective October 1, 2008).]*

    (c)   paragraphs 9 and 10 shall not apply; and

---

[1] As amended by the Law Reform (Miscellaneous Provisions) (Scotland) Act 1990 (c.40), Sch.8, para.29(17), and 9.

[2] Inserted by the Law Reform (Miscellaneous Provisions) (Scotland) Act 1990 (c.40), Sch.8, para.29(17) (effective July 20, 1992: SI 1992/1599).

[3] Paras. 23-25 added by the Solicitors (Scotland) Act 1988, Sched. 1, para.23.

[4] As substituted by the Legal Profession and Legal Aid (Scotland) Act 2007 (asp 5) Sch.5 para.1(26) (effective October 1, 2008).

    (ca)   in paragraph 11, for the words "complainer and respondent" there shall be substituted "parties to the appeal";

    (cb)   in paragraph 12—

        (i)   for the words "the complainer or the respondent" there shall be substituted "any party to the appeal";

        (ii)   for the word "respondent" where it second appears there shall be substituted "solicitor, the firm of solicitors or, as the case may be, the incorporated practice";

        (iii)   for the words "complainer and to the respondent" there shall be substituted "parties to the appeal";

    (cc)   in paragraph 14A(a), after the word "complaint" there shall be inserted "(as respects which the appeal was made)";

    (cd)   in paragraph 15, for the words "respondent, the complainer and, as the case may be, the person who made the complaint as respects which the appeal was made to the Tribunal" there shall be substituted "parties to the appeal and, if the person who made the complaint as respects which the appeal was made was not a party to the appeal, to that person";

    (ce)   in paragraph 16, after paragraph (e) there shall be inserted—

        "(ea)   under section 42ZD(2); or

        (eb)   under section 53ZB(1), (2), (3) or (4); or";

    (d)   in paragraph 19, for the words from the beginning to "respondent" there shall be substituted "The Tribunal may make such order as it thinks fit as to the payment by any party to the appeal";

24.   Subject to Part IV, the Tribunal may dismiss an appeal without holding an inquiry if—

    (a)   they are of the opinion that the appeal is manifestly ill-founded; or

    (b)   the appellant fails to comply with any rule made under section 52.

25.[1]   The Tribunal shall give notice of the appeal to the solicitor, the firm of solicitors or, as the case may be, the incorporated practice, to the person who made the complaint in respect of which the appeal was made and, as the case may be, to the Council and shall enquire into the matter, giving the appellant and the complainer reasonable opportunity to make representations to the Tribunal.

SCHEDULE 5

1.-9.   *[Repealed by the Law Reform (Miscellaneous Provisions) (Scotland) Act 1990 Sch.9.]*

10.   *[Not reproduced.]*

SCHEDULE 6

Section 66

TRANSITIONAL AND SAVINGS PROVISIONS

General

1.—(1)   In so far as—

    (a)   any agreement, appointment, operation, authorisation, determination, scheme, instrument, order or regulation made by virtue of an enactment repealed by this Act, or

    (b)   any approval, consent, direction or notice given by virtue of such an enactment, or

    (c)   any complaint made or investigation begun by virtue of such enactment, or

    (d)   any other proceedings begun by virtue of such an enactment, or

    (e)   anything done or having effect as if done,

could, if a corresponding enactment in this Act were in force at the relevant time, have been made, given, begun or done by virtue of the corresponding enactment, it shall, if effective immediately before the corresponding enactment comes into force, continue to have effect thereafter as if made, given, begun or done by virtue of that corresponding enactment.

    (2)   Where—

    (a)   there is any reference in this Act (whether expressed or implied) to a thing done or required or authorised to be done, or a thing omitted, or to an event which has occurred, under or for the purposes of or by reference to or in contravention of this Act, then

    (b)   that reference shall be construed (subject to its context) as including a reference to the corresponding thing, done or required or authorised to be done, or omitted, or to the cor-

---

[1] As substituted by the Legal Profession and Legal Aid (Scotland) Act 2007 (asp 5) Sch.5 para.1(26) (effective October 1, 2008).

responding events which occurred, as the case may be, under or for the purposes of or by reference to or in contravention of any of the corresponding provisions of the repealed enactments.

2.   Where any enactment passed before this Act or any instrument or document refers either expressly or by implication to an enactment repealed by this Act, the reference shall (subject to its context) be construed as or as including a reference to the corresponding provision of this Act.

3.   Where any period of time specified in an enactment repealed by this Act is current at the commencement of this Act, this Act has effect as if its corresponding provision has been in force when that period began to run.

Admission of enrolled law agent

4.   Notwithstanding the repeal by this Act of section 15 of the Solicitors (Scotland) Act 1933, the court may grant an application to be admitted as a solicitor to any applicant who was on 28th June 1933 entitled to be admitted as an enrolled law agent according to the regulations for admission then in force under the Law Agents (Scotland) Act 1873.

Restriction of grant under Guarantee Fund

5.   Notwithstanding the repeal by this Act of section 22(2)(b) of the Legal Aid and Solicitors (Scotland) Act 1949, no grant shall be made by the Council under section 43 in respect of a loss which in the opinion of the Council arose before 1st November 1951.

Rights of banks

6.   Nothing in section 61(3) shall deprive a bank of any right existing on 1st November 1949.

Admission to societies

7.   Notwithstanding the repeal by this Act of sections 44 and 45 of the Solicitors (Scotland) Act 1933 any society may—
    (a)   admit a solicitor as a member on such conditions as it thinks fit;
    (b)   accept as a qualification for admission an apprenticeship served under the provisions of this Act with a solicitor who is not a member.

8.   The repeal of Section 35 of the Solicitors (Scotland) Act 1933 is without prejudice to powers of control exercisable by any society over its members, being powers the society were entitled to exercise immediately before 1st March 1934.

In this paragraph and in paragraph 7, "society" means a faculty or society of solicitors in Scotland, incorporated by Royal Charter or otherwise formed in accordance with law, other than the Law Society of Scotland.

Saving for non-qualified person to conduct certain proceedings

9.[1]   Nothing in this Act shall affect any enactment empowering any person, not being a person qualified to act as a solicitor, to conduct, defend or otherwise act in relation to any action or proceedings in any court.

Register of law agents

10.   Notwithstanding the repeal by this Act of section 18(1) of the Solicitors (Scotland) Act 1933, the Council shall continue to keep in their custody the Register of Law Agents kept under the Law Agents (Scotland) Act 1873 and any relative documents transferred to their custody by virtue of section 18(4) of the Solicitors (Scotland) Act 1949.

Certificate of admission

11.   Notwithstanding the repeal by this Act of section 14 of the Solicitors (Scotland) Act 1933, the certificate of admission of a solicitor shall be in writing and signed by a judge of the court.

SCHEDULE 7

ARRANGEMENT OF PROVISIONS

[Not reproduced.]

---

[1] As substituted by the Solicitors (Scotland) Act 1988 Sch.1 para.24.

LAW REFORM (MISCELLANEOUS PROVISIONS) (SCOTLAND) ACT 1990

F1.6

(1990 c. 40)

An Act, as respects Scotland, . . . to provide as to rights of audience in courts of law, legal services and judicial appointments, and for the establishment and functions of an ombudsman in relation to legal services; . . . and to make certain other miscellaneous reforms of the law.

[November 1, 1990]

PART I – CHARITIES

1.–15. *[Not reproduced.]*

PART II – LEGAL SERVICES

Conveyancing and Executry Services

16.–19. *[Not reproduced.]*

Professional misconduct, etc.

20.—[1,2](1) Where, after such inquiry as they consider appropriate into a conduct complaint remitted to them under section 6(a) or 15(5)(a) of the 2007 Act suggesting professional misconduct by a practitioner or that the circumstances referred to in paragraph (a)(ii) of section 2(1) of the 2007 Act apply as respects a practitioner and after giving the practitioner concerned an opportunity to make representations, the Council are satisfied that a practitioner—

    (a)   is guilty of professional misconduct;

  (b)-(c) *[Repealed by the Legal Profession and Legal Aid (Scotland) Act 2007 (asp 5) Sch.5 para.3(4) (effective October 1, 2008).]*

    (d)   has been convicted of a criminal offence rendering him no longer a fit and proper person to provide conveyancing services as a conveyancing practitioner or, as the case may be, executry services as an executry practitioner,

they may take such of the steps out in subsection (2) below as they think fit and shall, without prejudice to subsection (6) below, intimate their decision to the practitioner by notice in writing.

    (2)   The steps referred to in subsection (1) above are—

  (a)–(b) *[Repealed by the Legal Profession and Legal Aid (Scotland) Act 2007 (asp 5) Sch.5 para.3(4) (effective October 1, 2008).]*

    (c)   to attach conditions (or, as the case may be, further conditions) to the registration of the practitioner or to vary any condition so attached;

    (ca) where the Council consider that the complainer has been directly affected by the professional misconduct or, as the case may be, the matter referred to in paragraph (d) of subsection (1), to direct the practitioner to pay compensation of such amount, not exceeding £5,000, as the

---

[1] Brought into force on March 1, 1997 by SI 1996/2894; as amended by SI 1996/2966 and the Public Appointments and Public Bodies etc. (Scotland) Act 2003 (asp 4), Sch.4, para. 12(6) (effective August 15, 2003).

[2] As substituted in part by the Legal Profession and Legal Aid (Scotland) Act 2007 (asp 5) Sch.5 para.3 and Pt 2 ss.56 and 57 (effective October 1, 2008).

Council may specify to the complainer for loss, inconvenience or distress resulting from the misconduct or, as the case may be, the matter;

(cb) subject to subsection (2ZA) below, to impose on the practitioner a fine not exceeding £2,000;

(d)–(e) *[Repealed by Public Appointments and Public Bodies etc. (Scotland) Act 2003 (asp 4) Sch.4 para.12(6) (effective August 15, 2003).]*

(f) *[Repealed by the Legal Profession and Legal Aid (Scotland) Act 2007 (asp 5) Sch.5 para.3(4) (effective October 1, 2008).]*

(g) *[Repealed by Public Appointments and Public Bodies etc. (Scotland) Act 2003 (asp 4) Sch.4 para.12(6) (effective August 15, 2003).]*

(h) to make a report of the Council's findings to any other person exercising functions with respect to—

    (i) the practitioner; or

    (ii) any person employed by or acting on behalf of the practitioner in connection with the provision of the services.

(2ZA) The Council shall not impose a fine under subsection (2)(cb) above where, in relation to the subject matter of the complaint, the practitioner has been convicted by any court of an offence involving dishonesty and sentenced to a term of imprisonment of not less than 2 years.

(2ZB) Any fine imposed under subsection (2)(cb) above shall be treated for the purposes of section 211(5) of the Criminal Procedure (Scotland) Act 1995 (fines payable to HM Exchequer) as if it were a fine imposed in the High Court.

(2A) Where—

(a) after holding an inquiry into a conduct complaint against a practitioner, the Tribunal are satisfied that—

    (i) he has been guilty of professional misconduct; or

    (ii) *[Repealed by the Legal Profession and Legal Aid (Scotland) Act 2007 (asp 5) Sch.5 para.3(4) (effective October 1, 2008).]*

(b) a practitioner has been convicted by any court of an act involving dishonesty or has been sentenced to a term of imprisonment of not less than 2 years,

the Tribunal may take such of the steps set out in subsection (2B) below as they think fit.

(2B) The steps referred to in subsection (2A) above are—

(a) to suspend or revoke the registration of the practitioner;

(aa) where the practitioner has been guilty of professional misconduct, and where the Tribunal consider that the complainer has been directly affected by the misconduct, to direct the practitioner to pay compensation of such amount, not exceeding £5,000, as the Tribunal may specify to the complainer for loss, inconvenience or distress resulting from the misconduct;

(b) subject to subsection (3) below, to impose on the practitioner a fine not exceeding £10,000;

(c) to censure the practitioner; and

(d)[1] a step which the Council may take in respect of a practitioner under subsection (2)(c) above.

(3) The Tribunal shall not impose a fine under subsection (2B)(b) above where, in relation to the subject matter of the Tribunal's inquiry, the practitioner has been

---

[1] As amended by the Legal Profession and Legal Aid (Scotland) Act 2007 (Modification and Consequential Provisions) Order 2011 (SSI 2011/235) para.6(2) (effective March 23, 2011).

convicted by any court of an offence involving dishonesty and sentenced to a term of imprisonment of not less than two years.

(4)   Any fine imposed under subsection (2B)(b) above shall be treated for the purposes of section 211(5) of the Criminal Procedure (Scotland) Act 1995 (fines payable to HM Exchequer) as if it were a fine imposed in the High Court.

(5)   *[Repealed by the Legal Profession and Legal Aid (Scotland) Act 2007 (Modification and Consequential Provisions) Order 2011 (SSI 2011/235) para.6(2)(b) (effective March 23, 2011).]*

(6)[1]   Where the Council make a direction under subsection (2)(ca) or the Tribunal make a direction under subsection (2B)(aa), the Council or (as the case may be) the Tribunal shall, by notice in writing, require the practitioner to which the direction relates to give to the Council, within such period being not less than 21 days as the notice may specify, an explanation of the steps which he has taken to comply with the direction.

(7)   Where a practitioner—
  (a)   fails to comply with a notice under subsection (6) above; or
  (b)   complies with such a notice but the Council are not satisfied as to the steps taken by the practitioner to comply with the direction to which the notice relates,
the Council may apply to the court for an order requiring the practitioner to comply with the direction to which the notice relates within such time as the court may order.

(8)   Where the Council take a step set out in subsection (2)(c) above or the Tribunal, by virtue of subsection (2B)(d) above, take a similar step or the Tribunal take a step set out in subsection (2B)(a) above and—
  (a)   any period specified in this section for applying for review or for the making of an appeal in respect of the matter has expired without such a review having been applied for or such an appeal having been made;
  (b)   where such an application or appeal is made, the matter is finally determined in favour of the Council's or, as the case may be, Tribunal's decision or the application or appeal is withdrawn,
the Council shall amend the register of executry practitioners or, as the case may be, the register of conveyancing practitioners accordingly.

(8A)   Where the Council are satisfied that a practitioner is guilty of professional misconduct or that the circumstances referred to in subsection (1)(d) apply as respects a practitioner, the practitioner may—
  (a)   before the expiry of the period of 21 days beginning with the day on which the finding by the Council to that effect is intimated to him, apply to the Council for a review by them of the finding;
  (b)   before the expiry of the period of 21 days beginning with the day on which the outcome of the review is intimated to him, appeal to the Tribunal against the decision of the Council in the review; and the Tribunal may quash or confirm the decision.

(9)–(10)   *[Repealed by the Public Appointments and Public Bodies etc. (Scotland) Act 2003 (asp 4), Sch.4, para.12(6)(j) (effective August 15, 2003).]*

---

[1] As amended by the Legal Profession and Legal Aid (Scotland) Act 2007 (Modification and Consequential Provisions) Order 2011 (SSI 2011/235) para.6(2) (effective March 23, 2011).

(11)[1] Where the Council take a step set out in subsection (2)(c) to (cb) above, the practitioner concerned may—

(a) within 21 days of the date on which the Council's decision is intimated to him, apply to the Council to review their decision; and

(b) within 21 days of the date on which the outcome of such review is intimated to him, appeal to the Tribunal against the decision made in any such review; and the Tribunal may quash, confirm or vary that decision.

(11ZA) Where the Council find that a practitioner is guilty of professional misconduct or that the circumstances referred to in subsection (1)(d) apply as respects a practitioner but do not direct him under subsection (2)(ca) to pay compensation, the complainer may, before the expiry of the period of 21 days beginning with the day on which the Council's finding is intimated to him, apply to the Council for a review by them of their decision not to direct the practitioner under subsection (2)(ca) to pay compensation.

(11ZB) A complainer to whom the Council have directed a practitioner under subsection (2)(ca) to pay compensation may, before the expiry of the period of 21 days beginning with the day on which the direction under that subsection is intimated to him, apply to the Council for a review by them of the direction.

(11ZC) The complainer may, before the expiry of the period of 21 days beginning with the day on which the outcome of the review under subsection (11ZA) or (11ZB) is intimated to him, appeal to the Tribunal against the decision of the Council in the review; and the Tribunal may quash, confirm or vary the decision.

(11A) Within 21 days of the date on which—

(a) the outcome of any appeal under subsection (8A)(b) or (11)(b) above; or

(aa) a finding by the Tribunal that a practitioner is guilty of professional misconduct or that the circumstances mentioned in subsection (1)(d) apply as respects the practitioner; or

(b) the taking of any step referred to in subsection (2B) above,

is intimated to the practitioner concerned, he may appeal to the court against the decision made by the Tribunal in the appeal the finding referred to in paragraph (aa) or, as the case may be, the decision to take such a step; and the court may make such order in the matter as it thinks fit.

(11B) The complainer may, before the expiry of the period of 21 days beginning with the day on which the outcome of any appeal under subsection (11ZC) is intimated to him, appeal to the court against the Tribunal's decision in the appeal.

(11C) Where after holding an inquiry into a complaint against a practitioner, the Tribunal find that he has been guilty of professional misconduct or that the circumstances referred to in subsection (2A)(b) apply as respects him, but do not direct the practitioner under subsection (2B)(aa) to pay compensation, the complainer may, before the expiry of the period of 21 days beginning with the day on which the Tribunal's finding is intimated to him, appeal to the court against the decision of the Tribunal not to make a direction under that subsection.

(11D) A complainer to whom the Tribunal have directed a practitioner under subsection (2B)(aa) to pay compensation may, before the expiry of the period of 21

---

[1] As amended by the Legal Profession and Legal Aid (Scotland) Act 2007 (Modification and Consequential Provisions) Order 2011 (SSI 2011/235) para.6(2) (effective March 23, 2011).

days beginning with the day on which the direction under that subsection is intimated to him, appeal to the court against the amount of the compensation directed to be paid.

(11E) In an appeal under subsection (11C) or (11D), the court may make such order in the matter as it thinks fit.

(11F) A direction of the Tribunal under this section is enforceable in like manner as an extract registered decree arbitral in its favour bearing a warrant for execution issued by the sheriff court of any sheriffdom in Scotland.

(11G) The Scottish Ministers may by order made by statutory instrument, after consulting the Council and such groups of persons representing consumer interests as they consider appropriate, amend subsection (2)(ca) or (2B)(aa) by substituting for the amount for the time being specified in that provision such other amount as they consider appropriate.

(11H) A statutory instrument containing an order under subsection (11G) is not to be made unless a draft of the instrument has been laid before, and approved by resolution of, the Scottish Parliament.

(12) *[Repealed by Public Appointments and Public Bodies etc. (Scotland) Act 2003 (asp 4) Sch.4 para.12(6) (effective August 15, 2003).]*

(13)-(15) *>[Repealed by the Legal Profession and Legal Aid (Scotland) Act 2007 (asp 5) Sch.5 para.3(4) (effective October 1, 2008).]*

(16) The Secretary of State may, by order made by statutory instrument subject to annulment in pursuance of a resolution of either House of Parliament, amend subsection (2)(cb) or (2B)(b) above by substituting for the amount for the time being specified in that provision such other amount as appears to him to be justified by a change in the value of money.

(17) In this section "executry practitioner" and "conveyancing practitioner" respectively include any executry practitioner or conveyancing practitioner whether or not he was registered as such at the time when the subject matter of the Council's or, as the case may be, Tribunal's inquiry occurred and notwithstanding that subsequent to that time he has ceased to be so registered.

Remission of complaint by Tribunal to Council

20ZA.—[1](1) Where, after holding an inquiry under section 20(2A) into a complaint of professional misconduct against a practitioner, the Tribunal—

    (a) are not satisfied that he has been guilty of professional misconduct;

    (b) consider that he may be guilty of unsatisfactory professional conduct,

they must remit the complaint to the Council.

(2) Where the Tribunal remit a complaint to the Council under subsection (1), they may make available to the Council any of their findings in fact in their inquiry into the complaint under section 20(2A).

Unsatisfactory professional conduct

20ZB.—[2](1) Where a conduct complaint suggesting unsatisfactory professional conduct by a practitioner is remitted to the Council under section 6(a) or 15(5)(a) of the 2007 Act, the Council must having—

---

[1] As inserted by the Legal Profession and Legal Aid (Scotland) Act 2007 (asp 5) Pt 2 s.54(2) (effective October 1, 2008).

[2] As inserted by the Legal Profession and Legal Aid (Scotland) Act 2007 (asp 5) Pt 2 s.54(2) (effective October 1, 2008).

   (a) investigated the complaint under section 47(1) of that Act and made a written report under section 47(2) of that Act;

   (b) given the practitioner an opportunity to make representations, determine the complaint.

  (2) Where a complaint is remitted to the Council under section 20ZA, the Council—

   (a) must—

     (i) notify the practitioner specified in it and the complainer of that fact and that the Council are required to investigate the complaint as a complaint of unsatisfactory professional conduct;

     (ii) so investigate the complaint;

     (iii) having so investigated the complaint and given the practitioner an opportunity to make representations, determine the complaint;

   (b) may rely, in their investigation, on any findings in fact which the Tribunal make available to them under section 20ZA(2) as respects the complaint.

  (3) Where the Council make a determination under subsection (1) or (2) upholding the complaint, they—

   (a) shall censure the practitioner;

   (b) may take any of the steps mentioned in subsection (4) which they consider appropriate.

  (4) The steps are—

   (a) where the Council consider that the practitioner does not have sufficient competence in relation to any aspect of conveyancing law or legal practice or, as the case may be, executry law or legal practice, to direct him to undertake such education or training as regards the law or legal practice concerned as the Council consider appropriate in that respect;

   (b) subject to subsection (6) below, to direct the practitioner to pay a fine not exceeding £2,000;

   (c) where the Council consider that the complainer has been directly affected by the conduct, to direct the practitioner to pay compensation of such amount, not exceeding £5,000, as they may specify to the complainer for loss, inconvenience or distress resulting from the conduct.

  (5) The Council may, in considering the complaint, take account of any previous determination by them, the Tribunal or the court upholding a complaint against the practitioner of unsatisfactory professional conduct or professional misconduct (but not a complaint in respect of which an appeal is pending or which has been quashed ultimately on appeal).

  (6) The Council shall not direct the practitioner to pay a fine under subsection (4)(b) above where, in relation to the subject matter of the complaint, he has been convicted by any court of an offence involving dishonesty and sentenced to a term of imprisonment of not less than 2 years.

  (7) Any fine directed to be paid under subsection (4)(b) above shall be treated for the purposes of section 211(5) of the Criminal Procedure (Scotland) Act 1995 (fines payable to HM Exchequer) as if it were a fine imposed in the High Court.

  (8) The Council shall intimate—

   (a) a determination under subsection (1) or (2);

   (b) any censure under subsection (3)(a);

   (c) any direction under subsection (4),

to the complainer and the practitioner by sending to each of them a copy of the determination, the censure or, as the case may be, the direction and by specifying the reasons for the determination.

(9)   A practitioner in respect of whom a determination upholding a conduct complaint has been made under subsection (1) or (2), or a direction has been made under subsection (4) may, before the expiry of the period of 21 days beginning with the day on which the determination or, as the case may be, the direction is intimated to him, appeal to the Tribunal against the—

(a)   determination;

(b)   direction (whether or not he is appealing against the determination).

(10)   A complainer may, before the expiry of the period of 21 days beginning with the day on which a determination under subsection (1) or (2) not upholding the conduct complaint is intimated to him, appeal to the Tribunal against the determination.

(11)   Where the Council have upheld the conduct complaint but have not directed the practitioner under subsection (4)(c) to pay compensation, the complainer may, before the expiry of the period of 21 days beginning with the day on which the determination upholding the complaint is intimated to him, appeal to the Tribunal against the Council's decision not to make a direction under that subsection.

(12)   A complainer to whom the Council have directed a practitioner under subsection (4)(c) to pay compensation may, before the expiry of the period of 21 days beginning with the day on which the direction under that subsection is intimated to him, appeal to the Tribunal against the amount of the compensation directed to be paid.

(13)   The Scottish Ministers may by order made by statutory instrument—

(a)   amend subsection (4)(b) by substituting for the amount for the time being specified in that subsection such other amount as appears to them to be justified by a change in the value of money;

(b)   after consulting the Council and such groups of persons representing consumer interests as they consider appropriate, amend subsection (4)(c) by substituting for the amount for the time being specified in that subsection such other amount as they consider appropriate.

(14)   A statutory instrument containing an order under—

(a)   subsection (13)(a) is subject to annulment in pursuance of a resolution of the Scottish Parliament;

(b)   subsection (13)(b) is not to be made unless a draft of the instrument has been laid before, and approved by resolution of, the Scottish Parliament.

Unsatisfactory professional conduct: Council's powers to monitor compliance with direction under section 20ZB(4)

20ZC.—[1](1)   The Council shall, by notice in writing, require every practitioner who is specified in—

(a)   a direction made under section 20ZB(4); or

(b)   such a direction as confirmed or varied on appeal by—

(i)   the Tribunal; or

(ii)   the court,

---

[1] As inserted by the Legal Profession and Legal Aid (Scotland) Act 2007 (asp 5) Pt 2 s.54(2) (effective October 1, 2008).

to give, before the expiry of such period being not less than 21 days as the notice specifies, an explanation of the steps which he has taken to comply with the direction.

(2)   Where an appeal is made under section 20ZB(9) or (12) or 20D(1) or (2) against a direction made under section 20ZB(4), any notice under subsection (1) above relating to the direction shall cease to have effect pending the outcome of the appeal.

Report by Commission to Council under section 10(2)(e) of the 2007 Act: Council's powers

20ZD.—[1](1)   Where the Council receive a report from the Commission under section 10(2)(e) of the 2007 Act as respects a practitioner, they may direct him to undertake such education or training as regards conveyancing law or legal practice or, as the case may be, executry law or legal practice as they consider appropriate in the circumstances.

(2)   The Council shall by notice in writing—
   (a)   intimate a direction under subsection (1) to the practitioner;
   (b)   require the practitioner to give, before the expiry of such period being not less than 21 days as the notice specifies, an explanation of the steps which he has taken to comply with the direction.

(3)   Where an appeal is made under section 20ZE(1) or (3) against a direction under subsection (1), any notice under subsection (2)(b) relating to the direction shall cease to have effect pending the outcome of the appeal.

Direction under section 20ZD(1): appeal by practitioner

20ZE.—[2](1)   A practitioner in respect of whom a direction has been made under section 20ZD(1) may, before the expiry of the period of 21 days beginning with the day on which it is intimated to him, appeal to the Tribunal against the direction.

(2)   On an appeal to the Tribunal under subsection (1), the Tribunal may quash, confirm or vary the direction being appealed against.

(3)   The practitioner may, before the expiry of the period of 21 days beginning with the day on which the Tribunal's decision under subsection (2) is intimated to him, appeal to the court against the decision.

(4)   On an appeal to the court under subsection (3), the court may give such directions in the matter as it thinks fit, including directions as to the expenses of the proceedings before the court and as to any order by the Tribunal relating to expenses.

(5)   A decision of the court on an appeal under subsection (3) shall be final.

Review of decisions

20A.—[3](1)   The Council shall establish a procedure under which they shall, on the application of any aggrieved person, review any relevant decision made by them.

(2)   In subsection (1) above—

---

[1] As inserted by the Legal Profession and Legal Aid (Scotland) Act 2007 (asp 5) Pt 2 s.54(2) (effective October 1, 2008).
[2] As inserted by the Legal Profession and Legal Aid (Scotland) Act 2007 (asp 5) Pt 2 s.54(2) (effective October 1, 2008).
[3] As inserted by the Public Appointments and Public Bodies etc. (Scotland) Act 2003 (asp 4), Sch.4, para. 12(7) (effective August 15, 2003).

(a) "relevant decision" means—
  (i) a refusal to grant an application for registration as a practitioner;
  (ii) a decision to grant an application for registration as a practitioner subject to conditions; or
  (iii)[1] a decision to take any step set out in subsection (2)(c) to (cb) of section 20 of this Act; and
(b) "aggrieved person" means the applicant or, as the case may be, the practitioner concerned.

Unsatisfactory professional conduct: powers of Tribunal on appeal

20B.—[2](1) On an appeal to the Tribunal under section 20ZB(9) the Tribunal—
  (a) may quash or confirm the determination being appealed against;
  (b) if they quash the determination, shall quash the censure accompanying the determination;
  (c) may quash, confirm or vary the direction being appealed against;
  (d) may, where they consider that the practitioner does not have sufficient competence in relation to any aspect of conveyancing law or legal practice or, as the case may be, executry law or legal practice, direct him to undertake such education or training as regards the law or legal practice concerned as the Tribunal consider appropriate in that respect;
  (e) may, subject to subsection (5), fine the practitioner an amount not exceeding £2000;
  (f) may, where they consider that the complainer has been directly affected by the conduct, direct the practitioner to pay compensation of such amount, not exceeding £5,000, as they may specify to the complainer for loss, inconvenience or distress resulting from the conduct.
  (2) On an appeal to the Tribunal under section 20ZB(10) the Tribunal—
  (a) may quash the determination being appealed against and make a determination upholding the complaint;
  (b) if they do so, may, where they consider that the complainer has been directly affected by the conduct, direct the practitioner to pay compensation of such amount, not exceeding £5,000, as they may specify to the complainer for loss, inconvenience or distress resulting from the conduct;
  (c) may confirm the determination.
  (3) On an appeal to the Tribunal under section 20ZB(11) the Tribunal may, where they consider that the complainer has been directly affected by the conduct, direct the practitioner to pay compensation of such amount, not exceeding £5,000, as they may specify to the complainer for loss, inconvenience or distress resulting from the conduct.
  (4) On an appeal under section 20ZB(12) the Tribunal may quash, confirm or vary the direction being appealed against.
  (5) The Tribunal shall not direct the practitioner to pay a fine under subsection (1)(e) where, in relation to the subject matter of the complaint, he has been convicted by any court of an offence involving dishonesty and sentenced to a term of imprisonment of not less than 2 years.

---

[1] As amended by the Legal Profession and Legal Aid (Scotland) Act 2007 (Modification and Consequential Provisions) Order 2011 (SSI 2011/235) para.6(3) (effective March 23, 2011).
[2] As inserted by the Legal Profession and Legal Aid (Scotland) Act 2007 (asp 5) Pt 2 s.54(3) (effective October 1, 2008).

(6)   Any fine directed to be paid under subsection (1)(e) shall be treated for the purposes of section 211(5) of the Criminal Procedure (Scotland) Act 1995 (fines payable to HM Exchequer) as if it were a fine imposed in the High Court.

(7)   A direction of the Tribunal under this section is enforceable in like manner as an extract registered decree arbitral in favour of the Council bearing a warrant for execution issued by the sheriff court of any sheriffdom in Scotland.

(8)   The Scottish Ministers may by order made by statutory instrument—

(a)   amend subsection (1)(e) by substituting for the amount for the time being specified in that subsection such other amount as appears to them to be justified by a change in the value of money;

(b)   after consulting the Council and such groups of persons representing consumer interests as they consider appropriate, amend subsection (1)(f) by substituting for the amount for the time being specified in that subsection such other amount as they consider appropriate.

(9)   A statutory instrument containing an order under—

(a)   subsection (8)(a) is subject to annulment in pursuance of a resolution of the Scottish Parliament;

(b)   subsection (8)(b) is not to be made unless a draft of the instrument has been laid before, and approved by resolution of, the Scottish Parliament.

Unsatisfactory professional conduct: enforcement of Council direction

20C.[1]   Where a practitioner fails to comply with a direction given by the Council under section 20ZB(4) (including such a direction as confirmed or varied on appeal by the Tribunal or, as the case may be, the court) before the expiry of the period specified in the notice relating to that direction given to the practitioner under section 20ZC(1), or such longer period as the Council may allow, the direction shall be enforceable in like manner as an extract registered decree arbitral in favour of the Council bearing a warrant for execution issued by the sheriff court of any sheriffdom in Scotland.

Unsatisfactory professional conduct: appeal from decisions of Tribunal

20D.—[2](1)   A practitioner in respect of whom a decision has been made by the Tribunal under section 20B(1), (2), (3) or (4) may, before the expiry of the period of 21 days beginning with the day on which the decision is intimated to him, appeal to the court against the decision.

(2)   A complainer may, before the expiry of the period of 21 days beginning with the day on which a decision by the Tribunal under section 20B to which this subsection applies is intimated to him, appeal to the court against the decision.

(3)   Subsection (2) applies to the following decisions of the Tribunal under section 20B—

(a)   a decision under subsection (1)(a) quashing the Council's determination upholding the complaint;

(b)   a decision under subsection (1)(c) quashing or varying a direction by the Council that the practitioner pay compensation;

---

[1] As inserted by the Legal Profession and Legal Aid (Scotland) Act 2007 (asp 5) Pt 2 s.54(3) (effective October 1, 2008).
[2] As inserted by the Legal Profession and Legal Aid (Scotland) Act 2007 (asp 5) Pt 2 s.54(3) (effective October 1, 2008).

   (c)   a decision under subsection (1)(f) directing the practitioner to pay compensation;

   (d)   a decision under subsection (2)(b) not to direct the practitioner to pay compensation;

   (e)   a decision under subsection (2)(c) confirming the Council's decision not to uphold the complaint;

   (f)   a decision under subsection (3) confirming the Council's decision not to direct the practitioner to pay compensation;

   (g)   a decision under subsection (4) quashing the Council's direction that the practitioner pay compensation or varying the amount of compensation directed to be paid.

(4)   On an appeal under subsection (1) or (2), the court may give such directions in the matter as it thinks fit, including directions as to the expenses of the proceedings before the court and as to any order by the Tribunal relating to expenses.

(5)   A decision of the court under subsection (4) shall be final.

Unsatisfactory professional conduct: powers of court on appeal

20E.—[1](1)   On an appeal under section 20D, the court may—

   (a)   fine the practitioner an amount not exceeding £2000;

   (b)   where it considers that the complainer has been directly affected by the conduct, direct the practitioner to pay compensation of such amount, not exceeding £5,000, as it may specify to the complainer for loss, inconvenience or distress resulting from the conduct;

   (c)   find the practitioner liable in any expenses which may be involved in the proceedings before it.

(2)   A decision of the court under subsection (1) shall be final.

(3)   The Scottish Ministers may by order made by statutory instrument—

   (a)   amend subsection (1)(a) by substituting for the amount for the time being specified in that subsection such other amount as appears to them to be justified by a change in the value of money;

   (b)   after consulting the Council and such groups of persons representing consumer interests as they consider appropriate, amend subsection (1)(b) by substituting for the amount for the time being specified in that subsection such other amount as they consider appropriate.

(4)   A statutory instrument containing an order under—

   (a)   subsection (3)(a) is subject to annulment in pursuance of a resolution of the Scottish Parliament;

   (b)   subsection (3)(b) is not to be made unless a draft of the instrument has been laid before, and approved by resolution of, the Scottish Parliament.

Council's intervention powers

21.—[2, 3](1)   The powers conferred on the Council by this section may be exercised if, after such inquiry (if any) as the Council consider appropriate, it ap-

---

[1] As inserted by the Legal Profession and Legal Aid (Scotland) Act 2007 (asp 5) Pt 2 s.54(3) (effective October 1, 2008).

[2] Brought into force on March 1, 1997 by SI 1996/2894, as amended by SI 1996/2966 and the Public Appointments and Public Bodies etc. (Scotland) Act 2003 (asp 4), Sch.4, para. 12(8) (effective August 15, 2003).

[3] As amended by the Legal Profession and Legal Aid (Scotland) Act 2007 (asp 5) Sch.5 para.3(5) (effective October 1, 2008).

pears to them to be desirable to do so for the purpose of protecting the interests of the clients, or prospective clients, of an independent conveyancing practitioner or an executry practitioner (each of which is in this section referred to as a "relevant practitioner").

(2) The Council may, in particular, exercise any such power where it appears to them that a relevant practitioner—

(a) is no longer a fit and proper person to provide conveyancing services or, as the case may be, executry services; or

(b) has ceased, for whatever reason, to provide such services.

(c) *[Repealed by the Legal Profession and Legal Aid (Scotland) Act 2007 (asp 5) Sch.5 para.3(6) (effective October 1, 2008).]*

(3) The Council may direct the relevant practitioner not to dispose of, or otherwise deal with, except in accordance with the terms of the direction—

(a) any assets belonging to any client of the practitioner and held by or under the control of the practitioner in connection with his business as an independent conveyancing practitioner or, as the case may be, an executry practitioner; or

(b) any assets of the practitioner which are specified, or of a kind specified, in the direction.

(4) The Council may direct the relevant practitioner to transfer to the Council, or to such persons (in this section referred to as "the trustees") as may be specified in the direction—

(a) all assets belonging to any client of the practitioner and held by or under the control of the practitioner in connection with his business as an independent conveyancing practitioner or, as the case may be, an executry practitioner; or

(b) any assets of the practitioner which are specified, or of a kind specified, in the direction.

(5) A relevant practitioner to whom a direction is given may, within 21 days of the date on which the direction is received by him, apply to the court, which may make such order in the matter as it thinks fit.

(6) A relevant practitioner to whom a direction is given shall comply with it as soon as it takes effect (and whether or not he proposes to apply to the court under subsection (5) above).

(7) If, on an application to the court by the Council, the court is satisfied—

(a) that a relevant practitioner has failed, within a reasonable time, to comply with any direction given to him; or

(b) that there is a reasonable likelihood that a relevant practitioner will so fail,

the court may make an order requiring the practitioner, and any other person whom the court considers it appropriate to subject to its order, to take such steps as the court may direct with a view to securing compliance with the direction.

(8) Any assets which have been transferred as a result of a direction given under subsection (4) above shall be held by the Council, or by the trustees, on trust for the client or, as the case may be, the practitioner concerned.

(9) The trustees may deal with any assets which have been transferred to them only in accordance with directions given to them by the Council.

(10) If the Council have reasonable cause to believe that a relevant practitioner or an employee of a relevant practitioner has been guilty of dishonesty resulting in pecuniary loss to a client of the relevant practitioner, they may apply to the Court of Session for an order that no payment be made by any bank, building society or other

body named in the order out of any bank, building society or other account or any sum deposited in the name of the relevant practitioner without the leave of the court and the court may make such an order.

(11)   Any direction under this section—

    (a)   shall be given in writing;

    (b)   shall state the reason why it is being given;

    (c)   shall take effect on such date as may be specified in the direction (which may be the date on which it is served on the relevant practitioner); and

    (d)   may be varied or revoked by a further direction given by the Council.

(11A)   Where the Council make a direction under subsection (3) or (4) or apply to the court for an order under subsection (10), the Council shall notify the Commission to that effect and provide it with details of their findings in any inquiry held by virtue of subsection (1) as respects the practitioner concerned.

(12)   In this section—

"assets" includes any sum of money (in whatever form and whether or not in any bank, building society or other account) and any book, account, deed or other document held by the relevant practitioner on his own behalf in connection with his business as a relevant practitioner or on behalf of the client concerned; and

"independent conveyancing practitioner" and "executry practitioner" respectively include any independent conveyancing practitioner or executry practitioner whether or not he was registered as such at the time when the matter in relation to which the Council exercise or propose to exercise their powers under this section arose and notwithstanding that subsequent to that time he has ceased to be so registered.

Powers of investigation

21A.—[1, 2](1)   The Council may exercise the power conferred by subsection (3) below for the purpose of—

    (a)–(b)   *[Repealed by the Legal Profession and Legal Aid (Scotland) Act 2007 (asp 5) Sch.5 para.3(7) (effective October 1, 2008).]*

    (c)   consideration by the Council whether to exercise the powers conferred on them by section 21 of this Act.

(2)   The Tribunal may exercise the power conferred by subsection (3) below for any of the following purposes—

    (a)   an inquiry under subsection (2A) of section 20 of this Act; and

    (b)   an appeal under subsection (8A)(b), (11)(b) or (11ZC) of that section.

(3)   The Council or, as the case may be, the Tribunal may give notice in writing to a practitioner specifying the subject matter of their investigation and requiring either or both of the following—

    (a)   the production or delivery to any person appointed by the Council or, as the case may be, the Tribunal, at a time and place specified in the notice, of such documents so specified as are in the possession or control of the practitioner and relate to the subject matter of the investigation;

---

[1] As inserted by the Public Appointments and Public Bodies etc. (Scotland) Act 2003 (asp 4) Sch.4, para.12(9) (effective August 15, 2003).

[2] As amended by the Legal Profession and Legal Aid (Scotland) Act 2007 (asp 5) Sch.5 para.3(7) (effective October 1, 2008).

    (b)   an explanation, within such period being not less than 21 days as the notice may specify, from the practitioner regarding the subject matter of the investigation.

(4)   If a practitioner fails to comply with a notice under subsection (3)(a) above, the Council or, as the case may be, the Tribunal may apply to the Court of Session for an order requiring him to produce or deliver the documents to the person appointed at the place specified in the notice within such time as the court may order.

Procedures of the Tribunal etc.

21B.—[1, 2](1)   Paragraphs 7 to 9, 11, 13 to 15 and 18A to 22 of Schedule 4 to the Solicitors (Scotland) Act 1980 (c.46) (which make provision as to certain powers and procedures of the Tribunal) apply in relation to complaints made against conveyancing and executry practitioners as they apply in relation to complaints against solicitors, but as if—

    (a)   in paragraph 9(a)(i) and (b), the words "or, as the case may be, of provision of inadequate professional services" were omitted;

    (b)   in paragraphs 9 and 19, the references to Part IV of that Act were references to sections 20 and 21A of this Act.

(2)   Paragraphs 7, 8, 11, 13 to 15 and 18A to 22 of that Schedule to that Act apply in relation to any appeal under subsection (8A)(b), (11)(b) or (11ZC) of section 20, 20ZB(9), (10), (11) or (12) or 20ZE(1) of this Act as they apply, by virtue of subsection (1) above, in relation to any complaint against conveyancing and executry practitioners, and—

    (a)   the modifications made to those paragraphs by paragraph 23(a), (ca), (cc), (cd) and (d) of that Schedule apply for the purposes of that application of those paragraphs; and

    (b)   paragraphs 24 and 25 of that Schedule apply in relation to any such appeal as they apply in relation to an appeal to which those paragraphs apply, but as if the reference in paragraph 24 to Part IV of that Act were a reference to sections 20 and 21A of this Act and as regards paragraph 25 also as if for the words "the solicitor, the firm of solicitors or, as the case may be, the incorporated practice" there were substituted "the practitioner".

(3)   In the case of a decision by the Tribunal—

    (a)   to take any of the steps set out in subsection (2B) of section 20 of this Act; or

    (b)   in an appeal under subsection (8A)(b), (11)(b) or (11ZC) of that section, subsection (4) below applies.

(4)   Where this subsection applies and—

    (a)   no appeal has been made to the court under subsection (11A), (11B), (11C) or (11D) of section 20 of this Act against the decision; or

    (b)   such an appeal has been made but has—

        (i)   been withdrawn; or

        (ii)   resulted in the Tribunal's decision being upheld,

the clerk of the Tribunal shall send to the Council a copy of the decision of the Tribunal certified by him and the decision of the court in any such appeal.

---

[1] Inserted by the Public Appointments and Public Bodies etc. (Scotland) Act 2003 (asp 4), Sch.4, para.12(9) (effective August 15, 2003).

[2] As substituted by the Legal Profession and Legal Aid (Scotland) Act 2007 (asp 5) Sch.5 para.3(8) (effective October 1, 2008).

(5) If the decision of the Tribunal so certified is to suspend or revoke the registration of the practitioner under paragraph (a) of subsection (2B) of section 20 of this Act, the Council shall—

    (a)   give effect to the decision; and

    (b)   cause a note of the effect of the decision to be entered against the name of the practitioner in the register of conveyancing practitioners or, as the case may be, of executry practitioners.

Compensation fund

21C. *[Repealed by the Legal Services (Scotland) Act 2010 (asp 16) Pt 4 c.3 s.128(3) (effective April 1, 2011: repeal has effect subject to savings specified in 2010 (asp 16) s.128(3)(a) and (b)).]*

Disclosure of documents etc.

22.—[1](1)   Any communication made to or by—

    (a)   an independent conveyancing practitioner or an executry practitioner in the course of his acting as such for a client;

shall in any action or proceedings in any court be protected from disclosure on the ground of confidentiality between client and professional legal adviser in like manner as if the practitioner had at all material times been a solicitor acting for the client.

(2)   Any enactment or instrument making special provision in relation to a solicitor or other legal representative as to the disclosure of information, or as to the production, seizure or removal of documents, with respect to which a claim to confidentiality between client and professional legal adviser could be maintained, shall, with any necessary modifications, have effect in relation to—

    (a)   an independent conveyancing practitioner; and

    (b)   an executry practitioner;

as it has effect in relation to a solicitor.

Interpretation of sections 16 to 22

23.[2, 3]   In sections 16 to 22 of this Act and this section, except where the context otherwise requires—

    "complainer" means the person who made the complaint and, where the complaint was made by the person on behalf of another person, includes that other person;

    "conveyancing practitioner" means a person registered under section 17 in the register of conveyancing practitioners;

    "conveyancing services" means the preparation of writs, contracts and other documents in connection with the transfer of heritable property and loans

---

[1] Brought into force on March 1, 1997 by SI 1996/2894, as amended by SI 1996/2966 and the Public Appointments and Public Bodies etc. (Scotland) Act 2003 (asp 4), Sch.4, para.12(10) (effective August 15, 2003).

[2] Brought into force on April 1, 1991 by SI 1991/822. As amended by the Public Appointments and Public Bodies etc. (Scotland) Act 2003 (asp 4), Sch.4, para.12(11) (effective August 15, 2003).

[3] As amended by the Legal Profession and Legal Aid (Scotland) Act 2007 (asp 5) Sch.5 para.3(9) (effective October 1, 2008).

secured over such property, and services ancillary thereto, including (in the case of independent conveyancing practitioners) relevant notarial services, but does not include any services—
    (a) relating to the arranging of loans; or
    (b) falling within section 1(1)(a) of the Estate Agents Act 1979;
"the Council" means the Council of the Law Society of Scotland;
"the court" means the Court of Session;
"executry practitioner" means a person registered under section 18 in the register of executry practitioners;
"executry services" means the drawing and preparation of papers on which to found or oppose an application for a grant of confirmation of executors and services in connection with the administration, ingathering, distribution and winding up of the estate of a deceased person by executors, but does not include anything which constitutes carrying on a regulated activity within the meaning of the Financial Services and Markets Act 2000
"independent conveyancing practitioner" means a conveyancing practitioner whose entry in the register of conveyancing practitioners has been annotated to that effect under section 17(1B);
"practitioner" means an executry practitioner or a conveyancing practitioner; and
"relevant notarial services" means the functions exercisable by independent conveyancing practitioners by virtue of section 14(1) and (2) of the Public Appointments and Public Bodies etc. (Scotland) Act 2003 (asp 4).
"the Tribunal" means the Scottish Solicitors' Discipline Tribunal; and
"unsatisfactory professional conduct" has the meaning given (as respects a conveyancing practitioner or, as the case may be, an executry practitioner) by section 46 of the 2007 Act.

Rights of audience

Rights of audience in the Court of Session, the House of Lords, the Judicial Committee of the Privy Council and the High Court of Justiciary   F1.153

24.   *[Inserts S.25A in the Solicitors (Scotland) Act 1980 (c.46), supra.]*

Rights to conduct litigation and rights of audience   F1.154

25.—(1)   Any professional or other body may, for the purpose of enabling any of their members who is a natural person to acquire—
    (a) rights to conduct litigation on behalf of members of the public; and
    (b) rights of audience,
make an application in that regard to the Lord President and the Secretary of State.
    (2)   An application under subsection (1) above shall include a draft scheme—
    (a) specifying—
        (i)   the courts;
        (ii)   the categories of proceedings;
        (iii) the nature of the business; and
        (iv)   the rights to conduct litigation and the rights of audience,
        in relation to which the application is made;
    (b) describing—
        (i)   the training requirements which the body would impose upon any of their members who sought to acquire any right such as is mentioned in subsection (1) above; and

      (ii)   the code of practice which they would impose upon their members in relation to the exercise by those members of any rights acquired by them by virtue of this section,

in the event of the application being granted; and

  (c) proposing arrangements for—

      (i)   the indemnification of members of the public against loss suffered by them through the actings of the body's members in the exercise by those members of any rights acquired by them by virtue of this section; and

      (ii) the treatment by the body of complaints made to them by members of the public in relation to the actings of members of the body exercising rights acquired by virtue of this section,

and shall state that the body have complied with the provisions of Schedule 2 to this Act.

(3)[1] A code of practice such as is mentioned in subsection (2)(b)(ii) above shall include provision with regard to revoking, suspending or attaching conditions to the exercise of any right acquired by a member of the body by virtue of section 27 of this Act in consequence of a breach by that member of that code of practice; and shall in particular include provision enabling the body to comply with the provisions of section 27(4) of this Act.

(4) A draft scheme submitted under this section shall also include the proposals of the body in relation to such other matters as may be prescribed by the Secretary of State in regulations made under this section.

(5) Regulations under this section shall be made by statutory instrument subject to annulment in pursuance of a resolution of either House of Parliament.

(6) Schedule 2 shall have effect in relation to the publication of applications made under subsection (1) above.

F1.155 **Consideration of applications made under section 25**

26.—(1) The Lord President shall consider the provision made in any draft scheme submitted to him under section 25(1) of this Act in relation to the matters mentioned in section 25(2); and the Secretary of State shall, subject to subsection (5) below and to section 40 of this Act, consider the provision so made in section 25(2)(b) and (c).

(2) In considering the code of practice included in the draft scheme by virtue of section 25(2)(b)(ii), the Lord President shall have regard to the desirability of there being common principles applying in relation to the exercising of rights to conduct litigation and rights of audience by all practitioners in relation to the court or, as the case may be, the courts, mentioned in the application.

(3)[2] The Lord President and the Secretary of State shall—

  (a) consult each other in considering a draft scheme submitted to them under section 25(1); and

  (b) consider any written representations timeously made to them under Schedule 2 to this Act,

and may, either jointly or severally, make preliminary observations to the body concerned in relation to that draft; and the body may make such adjustments to the

---

[1] As substituted by the Legal Profession and Legal Aid (Scotland) Act 2007 (asp 5) Sch.5 para.3(10)(d) (effective March 19, 2007).

[2] As amended by the Enterprise and Regulatory Reform Act 2013 (c.24) Sch.6 para.46 (effective April 1, 2014).

draft as appear to them to be appropriate, and the Lord President and the Secretaryof State (who shall, in accordance with section 40, consult the CMA in respect of any adjustments made in relation to the matters mentioned in section 25(2)(6) or (c)) shall thereafter consider the draft scheme as so adjusted.

(4)   In considering a draft scheme under subsection (1) or (3) above, the Lord President and the Secretary of State shall have regard to whether the provisions of the draft scheme are such as—

(a)   to achieve; and

(b)   to ensure the maintenance of,

appropriate standards of conduct and practice by persons who may acquire rights to conduct litigation or rights of audience in the event of the draft scheme being approved.

(5)   In relation to any code of practice such as is mentioned in section 25(2)(b)(ii), the duty of the Secretary of State under subsection (1) above is limited to a consideration of any provision of such a code as would, in his view, directly or indirectly inhibit the freedom of a member of the body concerned to undertake all the work necessary for the preparation of a case or for the presentation of a case before the court, other than such a provision which has that effect only by reason of the provision made in the draft scheme with respect to the matters mentioned in section 25(2)(a).

(6)   After they have considered a draft scheme under subsections (1) and (3) above, if the Lord President and the Secretary of State—

(a)   are satisfied with the draft scheme, the Lord President shall grant the application, and shall so inform the body;

(b)   are not satisfied with the scheme, the Lord President shall refuse the application, and shall so inform the body, giving written reasons for the refusal,

and the Lord President shall send a copy of the letter granting or refusing the application to any person who has made representations in relation to the draft scheme under Schedule 2 to this Act.

(7)   Where the Lord President has granted an application under subsection (6)(a) above, in relation to—

(a)   civil proceedings, the Court of Session may by act of sederunt; and

(b)   criminal proceedings, the High Court of Justiciary may by act of adjournal,

make such provision for giving effect to the scheme as appears to it to be appropriate.

Exercise of rights to conduct litigation and rights of audience

F1.156

27.—(1)   Where an application made under section 25 of this Act has been granted under section 26 of this Act, any member of the body concerned who has complied with the terms of the scheme in relation to the matters mentioned in section 25(2)(b)(i), and who appears to the body to be a fit and proper person, shall have the right to conduct litigation or rights of audience to which that compliance entitles him.

(2)   Where a function is, whether expressly or by implication, conferred on any person or body by section 26 or this section he or, as the case may be, they shall exercise that function as soon as is reasonably practicable.

(3)   Nothing in subsection (1) above affects the power of any court in relation to any proceedings—

(a)   to hear a person who would not otherwise have a right of audience before that court in relation to those proceedings; or

(b) to refuse to hear a person (for reasons which apply to him as an individual) who would otherwise have a right of audience before that court in relation to those proceedings, and where a court so refuses it shall give its reasons for that decision.

(4)   Where a complaint has been made that a person has been guilty of professional misconduct in the exercise of any right to conduct litigation or right of audience held by him by virtue of this section, the body of which he is a member may, or if so requested by the Lord President shall, suspend that person from exercising that right pending determination of that complaint by the body.

(5)   Where a person holding a right of audience in any court by virtue of this section is instructed to appear in that court, those instructions shall take precedence before any of his other professional or business obligations, and the code of practice mentioned in section 25(2)(6)(ii) shall include rules—

(a) stating the order of precedence of courts for the purposes of this subsection;

(b) stating general criteria to which members of the body should have regard in determining whether to accept instructions in particular circumstances; and

(c) securing, through such of their officers as they think appropriate, that, where reasonably practicable, any person wishing to be represented before any court by one of their members holding an appropriate right of audience is so represented,

and, for the purposes of such rules, the Inner and Outer Houses of the Court of Session, and the High Court of Justiciary exercising its appellate jurisdiction, may be treated as separate courts.

(6)   A person exercising any right of audience held by virtue of this section shall have the same immunity from liability for negligence in respect of his acts or omissions as if he were an advocate, and no act or omission on the part of any such person shall give rise to an action for breach of contract in relation to the exercise by him of such a right of audience.

(7)   Any person who wilfully and falsely—

(a) pretends to have any right to conduct litigation or right of audience by virtue of this section; or

(b) where he has any such right, pretends to have any further such right which he does not have; or

(c) takes or uses any name, title, addition or description implying that he has any such right or, as the case may be, any further such right,

shall be guilty of an offence and liable on summary conviction to a fine not exceeding level 4 on the standard scale.

(8)   For the purposes of section 25, section 26 and this section—

"right of audience" includes, in relation to any court, any such right exercisable by an advocate; and

"right to conduct litigation" means the right to exercise on behalf of a client all or any of the functions, other than any right of audience, which may be exercised by a solicitor in relation to litigation.

F1.157   Surrender of rights to conduct litigation and rights of audience

28.—(1)   Subject to the provisions of this section, where an application made under section 25 of this Act has been granted under section 26(6) of this Act, the body concerned may apply to the Lord President and the Secretary of State for permission to surrender any entitlement of their members to acquire rights to conduct litigation or rights of audience.

(2)   The Lord President and the Secretary of State shall jointly issue directions as to the requirements with which any body wishing to surrender their members' entitlement will have to comply, and, without prejudice to the generality of the foregoing, any such directions may include provision—

(a)   where members of a body have acquired rights to conduct litigation or rights of audience, as to the arrangements to be made for the completion of any work outstanding at the time the application is made; and

(b)   relating to the particular circumstances of a particular body.

(3)   An application under subsection (1) above shall describe the manner in which the body have complied, or will comply, with the directions issued under subsection (2) above.

(4)   Where the Lord President and the Secretary of State are satisfied that the body concerned have complied, or will comply, with the directions issued under subsection (2) above, the Lord President shall grant the application, and shall so inform the body.

(5)   With effect from the date on which an application under subsection (1) above is granted, any member of the body concerned who has acquired rights to conduct litigation or rights of audience by virtue of the scheme shall cease to hold those rights.

Revocation of rights granted under section 26   F1.158

29.—(1)   Where it appears to the Secretary of State that a body has failed to comply with a direction under section 42(6) of this Act, he may by order made by statutory instrument revoke the grant of the application made by that body under section 25 of this Act.

(2)   No instrument shall be made under subsection (1) above unless a draft of the instrument has been laid before and approved by each House of Parliament.

(3)   With effect from the date on which an order under subsection (1) above takes effect, any member of the body concerned who has acquired rights to conduct litigation or rights of audience by virtue of the scheme shall cease to hold those rights.

Regulation of right of English, Welsh and Northern Irish practitioners to practise in Scotland   F1.159

30.—[1](1)   The Secretary of State, after consulting the Lord President, may by regulations prescribe circumstances in which, and conditions subject to which, practitioners who are qualified to practise in England and Wales or Northern Ireland may, in such capacity as may be prescribed, exercise in Scotland—

(a)   prescribed rights of audience; or

(b)   prescribed rights to conduct litigation,

without being entitled to do so apart from the regulations.

(2)   The Secretary of State, after consulting the Lord President, may by regulations make provision for the purpose of enabling practitioners who are entitled to practise in England and Wales or Northern Ireland to become qualified to practise in

---

[1] In force June 3, 1991: SI 1991/1252.

Scotland on terms, and subject to conditions, corresponding or similar to those on which practitioners who are entitled to practise in member States may become qualified to practise in Scotland.

(3)   Regulations made under subsection (1) above may, in particular—

(a)   prescribe any right of audience which may not be exercised by a person in Scotland unless he is instructed to act together with a person who has that right of audience there;

(b)   prescribe legal services which may not be provided by any person practising by virtue of the regulations;

(c)   prescribe the title or description which must be used by any person practising by virtue of the regulations;

(d)   provide for the body by whom and the means by which the qualification of any person claiming to be entitled to practise by virtue of the regulations is to be verified; and

(e)   provide for such professional or other body as may be prescribed to have power to investigate and deal with any complaint made against a person practising by virtue of the regulations.

(4)   Regulations made under subsection (1) or (2) above may modify any rule of law or practice which the Secretary of State considers should be modified in order to give effect to the regulations.

(5)   Regulations under this section shall be made by statutory instrument subject to annulment in pursuance of a resolution of either House of Parliament.

(6)   In this section "practitioner" means, in relation to England and Wales and Northern Ireland—

(a)   a barrister or solicitor; and

(b)   any person falling within such category as may be prescribed in regulations made by the Secretary of State after consultation with the Lord President.

Rules of Conduct

F1.160   Rules of conduct etc.

31.—[1](1)   *[As repealed by the Legal Services (Scotland) Act 2010 (asp 16) Pt 4 c.2 s.122(4) (effective June 1, 2011).]*

(2)[2]   Where it appears to the Faculty of Advocates that any rule of conduct in relation to the exercise of an advocate's right of audience in the Court of Session is more restrictive than the equivalent rule in relation to the exercise of the equivalent right in the sheriff court, they may submit that rule to the Secretary of State for his approval, and the Secretary of State shall consult the CMA in accordance with section 40 of this Act, and thereafter, having—

(a)   considered any advice tendered to him by the CMA;

(b)   compared the rule applicable in the Court of Session with the equivalent rule applicable in the sheriff court; and

(c)   considered whether the interests of justice require that there should be such a rule in the Court of Session,

he may approve or refuse to approve the rule.

---

[1] In force March 17, 1993: SI 1993/641.
[2] As amended by the Enterprise and Regulatory Reform Act 2013 (c.24) Sch.6 para.47 (effective April 1, 2014).

(3)   In section 34 of the 1980 Act (rules as to professional practice, conduct and discipline)—

(a)   at the end of subsection (1A) there shall be inserted—
"and

(f)   make such additional or different provision as the Council think fit in relation to solicitors who, or incorporated practices which, are partners in or directors of multi-disciplinary practices."; and

(b)   after subsection (3) there shall be inserted—

"(3A)   Without prejudice to subsection (3), any rule made, whether before or after the coming into force of this subsection, by the Council under this section or section 35 which has the effect of prohibiting the formation of multi-disciplinary practices shall not have effect unless the Secretary of State, after consulting the Director in accordance with section 64A, has approved it.".

Multi-national practices

Multi-national practices   F1.161

32.   *[Inserts S.60A in Solicitors (Scotland) Act 1980 (c.46) above.]*

Complaints in relation to legal services

Complaints in relation to legal services   F1.162

33.   *[As repealed by the Legal Services Act 2007 (c.29) Sch.23 para.1 (effective October 1, 2008 as SI 2008/1436; repeal has effect subject to savings and transitional provisions specified in SSI 2008/332 arts 2 and 4).]*

Scottish legal services ombudsman

Scottish legal services ombudsman   F1.163

34.   *[As repealed by the Legal Profession and Legal Aid (Scotland) Act 2007 (Transitional, Savings and Consequential Provisions) Order (SSI 2008/332) art.3(1)(a) (effective October 1, 2008: repeal has effect subject to savings and transitional provisions specified in SSI 2008/332 arts 3 and 4).]*

Ombudsman's final report and recommendations   F1.164

34A.   *[As repealed by the Legal Profession and Legal Aid (Scotland) Act 2007 (Transitional, Savings and Consequential Provisions) Order (SSI 2008/332) art.3(1)(b) (effective October 1, 2008: repeal has effect subject to savings and transitional provisions specified in SSI 2008/332 arts 3 and 4).]*

Advisory functions of ombudsman   F1.165

34B.   *[As repealed by the Legal Profession and Legal Aid (Scotland) Act 2007 (Transitional, Savings and Consequential Provisions) Order (SSI 2008/332) art.3(1)(c) (effective October 1, 2008: repeal has effect subject to savings and transitional provisions specified in SSI 2008/332 arts 3 and 4).]*

Judicial appointments

35.   *[See Division B.]*

Solicitors' and counsel's fees

F1.166   **Solicitors' and counsel's fees**

36.   *[Inserts new section 61A into the Solicitors (Scotland) Act 1980 (c.46), above.]*

Miscellaneous and supplementary

F1.167   **Admission of solicitors and notaries public**

37.—(1)   *[Amends s.6(2) of the Solicitors (Scotland) Act 1980 (c.46), above].*

(2)   *[Amends s.57 of the Solicitors (Scotland) Act 1980 (c.46), above].*

(3)   *[Amends s.58 of the Solicitors (Scotland) Act 1980 (c.46), above].*

F1.168   **Availability of legal aid in relation to services provided under this Act**

38.   *[Inserts new section 43A in the Legal Aid (Scotland) Act 1986 (c.47): Div. G below]*

F1.169   **Removal of certain restrictions on the borrowing of the court process**

39.   *[Repeals s.29 of the Solicitors (Scotland) Act 1980 (c.46), above].*

F1.170   **Advisory and supervisory functions of the CMA**

40.—[1, 2](1)   Before—

    (a)[3]   approving any rules made under section 17(11) or 18(10) of this Act; or

    (b)[4]   approving any rules—

        (i)   ...

        (ii)   such as are mentioned in section 31(1) or (2), of this Act; or

    (c)   considering any provisions of a draft scheme under section 26(1) or (3) of this Act,

the Secretary of State shall first send a copy of the proposed regulations, rules or provisions to the CMA.

(2)[5]   The CMA shall consider whether any such rules or provisions as are mentioned in subsection (1) above would have, or would be likely to have, the effect of restricting, distorting or preventing competition to any significant extent.

(3)   When CMA has completed its consideration it shall give such advice to the Secretary of State as it thinks fit.

(4)   The CMA may publish any advice given under subsection (3) above.

(5)   The CMA shall, so far as practicable, exclude from anything published under subsection (4) above any matter—

    (a)   which relates to the affairs of a particular person; and

---

[1] In force September 30, 1991: SI 1991/2152.

[2] As amended by the Enterprise and Regulatory Reform Act 2013 (c.24) Sch.6 para.48 (effective April 1, 2014).

[3] As amended by the Public Appointments and Public Bodies etc. (Scotland) Act 2003 (asp 4) Sch.4 para.12(14) (effective August 15, 2003).

[4] As amended by the Public Appointments and Public Bodies etc. (Scotland) Act 2003 (asp 4) Sch.4 para.12(14) (effective August 15, 2003).

[5] As amended by the Public Appointments and Public Bodies etc. (Scotland) Act 2003 (asp 4) Sch.4 para.12(14) (effective August 15, 2003).

(b) the publication of which would, or might in the CMA's opinion, seriously and prejudicially affect the interests of that person.

(6) For the purposes of the law of defamation, the publication of any advice by the CMA under this section shall be absolutely privileged.

Investigatory powers of the CMA

F1.171

41.—[1](1)[2] For the purpose of investigating any matter under section 40 of this Act, the CMA may by notice in writing—

(a) require any person to produce to the CMA or to any person appointed by the CMA for the purpose, at a time and place specified in the notice, any documents which are specified or described in the notice and which—
  (i) are in that person's custody or under that person's control; and
  (ii) relate to any matter relevant to the investigation; or
(b) require any person carrying on any business to furnish to the CMA (within such time and in such manner and form as the notice may specify) such information as may be specified or described in the notice.

(2) A person shall not be required under this section to produce any document or disclose any information which he would be entitled to refuse to produce or disclose on the grounds of confidentiality between a client and his professional legal adviser in any civil proceedings.

(3) *[As repealed by the Enterprise Act 2002 (Consequential and Supplemental Provisions) Order 2003 (SI 2003/1398) Sch.1 para.12(2) (effective June 20, 2003).]*

Enforcement of notices under section 41

F1.172

41A.—[3](1)[4] The court may, on an application by the CMA, enquire into whether any person ("the defaulter") has refused or otherwise failed, without reasonable excuse, to comply with a notice under section 41(1).

(2)[5] An application under subsection (1) shall include details of the possible failure which the CMA considers has occurred.

(3) In enquiring into a case under subsection (1), the court shall hear any witness who may be produced against or on behalf of the defaulter and any statement which may be offered in defence.

(4) Subsections (5) and (6) apply where the court is satisfied, after hearing any witnesses and statements as mentioned in subsection (3), that the defaulter has refused or otherwise failed, without reasonable excuse, to comply with a notice under section 41(1).

(5) The court may punish the defaulter as it would have been able to punish him had he been guilty of contempt of court.

(6) Where the defaulter is a body corporate or is a partnership constituted under the law of Scotland, the court may punish any director, officer or (as the case may

---

[1] In force September 30, 1991: SI 1991/2152.
[2] As amended by the Enterprise and Regulatory Reform Act 2013 (c.24) Sch.6 para.49 (effective April 1, 2014).
[3] As inserted by the Enterprise Act 2002 (Consequential and Supplemental Provisions) Order 2003 (SI 2003/1398) Sch.1 para.12(3) (effective June 20, 2003).
[4] As amended by the Enterprise and Regulatory Reform Act 2013 (c.24) Sch.6 para.50 (effective April 1, 2014).
[5] As amended by the Enterprise and Regulatory Reform Act 2013 (c.24) Sch.6 para.50 (effective April 1, 2014).

be) partner of the defaulter as it would have been able to punish that director, officer or partner had he been guilty of contempt of court.

(7)   In this section "the court" means the Court of Session.

F1.173   **Altering, etc. documents required to be produced under section 41**

41B.—[1](1)   A person commits an offence if he intentionally alters, suppresses or destroys a document which he has been required to produce by a notice under section 41(1).

(2)   A person who commits an offence under subsection (1) shall be liable—

    (a)   on summary conviction, to a fine not exceeding the statutory maximum;

    (b)   on conviction on indictment, to imprisonment for a term not exceeding two years or to a fine or to both.

F1.174   **Review of rules approved by the Secretary of State**

42.—[2](1)   Where the Secretary of State has approved—

    (a)[3]   a rule under section 31(2) of this Act; or

    (b)   a draft scheme under section 26(6) of this Act,

he may and, where the Lord President, in the case of a draft scheme such as is mentioned in paragraph (b), so requests shall, require the body which made the rule or, as the case may be, the scheme to review its terms.

(2)   When they have reviewed a rule or, as the case may be, a scheme, following a requirement made under subsection (1) above, the body concerned may revise the rule or scheme in the light of that review, and shall then submit the rule or scheme as revised or, if they have not revised it, as previously approved—

    (a)   in the case of a rule such as is mentioned in subsection (1)(a) above, to the Secretary of State; or

    (b)   in the case of a draft scheme such as is mentioned in subsection (1)(b) above, to the Secretary of State and the Lord President.

(3)   Where a rule, whether revised or as previously approved, is submitted to the Secretary of State under subsection (2)(a) above, he may—

    (a)   approve the rule as submitted to him; or

    (b)   amend the rule in such manner as he considers appropriate,

and (except where the rule remains in the form previously approved) he may direct the body concerned to bring it into operation as soon as is practicable.

(4)   Where the Lord President and the Secretary of State are agreed that the terms of a draft scheme submitted to them under subsection (2)(b) above are satisfactory, the Secretary of State may—

    (a)   approve the scheme; and

    (b)   (except where the scheme remains in the form previously approved) direct the body concerned to bring the scheme, as so amended, into force as soon as is practicable.

---

[1] Inserted by the Enterprise Act 2002 (Consequential and Supplemental Provisions) Order 2003 (SI 2003/1398) Sch.1 para.12(3) (effective June 20, 2003).

[2] In force September 30, 1991: SI 1991/2152.

[3] As amended by the Public Appointments and Public Bodies etc. (Scotland) Act 2003 (asp 4) Sch.4 para.12(15) (effective August 15, 2003).

(5)   Where either the Secretary of State or the Lord President is of the view that the terms of any such scheme so submitted to them are not satisfactory, but they do not agree as to what the terms of the scheme should be, the scheme shall continue to have effect as previously approved.

(6)   Where the Secretary of State and the Lord President agree both that the terms of a scheme so submitted to them are not satisfactory, and as to what the terms of the scheme should be, the Secretary of State may amend the scheme in such manner as he and the Lord President consider appropriate; and may direct the body concerned to bring the scheme, as so amended, into force as soon as is practicable.

(7)   The provisions of section 40(1)(b) and (c) of this Act shall apply to rules and schemes submitted under subsection (2) of this section as they apply to rules submitted under sections 17(15) and 31(2) and schemes submitted under section 25(1) of this Act.

Functions of Director in relation to certain rules made under the 1980 Act   F1.175

43.   *[New ss.64A-64D of the Solicitors (Scotland) Act 1980 (c.46) appear in the print of that Act, above.]*

Interpretation of Part II   F1.176

44.[1]   In this Part of this Act, unless the context otherwise requires—

"advocate" means a member of the Faculty of Advocates practising as such;
[2]"the CMA" means the Competition and Markets Authority;
[As repealed by the Enterprise and Regulatory Reform Act 2013 (c.24) Sch.6 para.51 (effective April 1, 2014).]
"Lord President" means the Lord President of the Court of Session;
"solicitor" has the same meaning as in section 65(1) of the 1980 Act;
"the 1980 Act" means the Solicitors (Scotland) Act 1980; and
"the 2007 Act" means the Legal Profession and Legal Aid (Scotland) Act 2007 (asp 5).[3]

PART III – THE LICENSING (SCOTLAND) ACT 1976

45.-55.   *[See Division E.]*   F1.177

PART IV

56.-72.   *[See Divisions B, I and M.]*

PART V – GENERAL

Finance

73.   *[Not printed.]*

Amendments and repeals   F1.178

74.—(1)   The enactments mentioned in Schedule 8 to this Act shall have effect subject to the amendments specified in that Schedule.

---

[1] In force April 1, 1991: SI 1991/822.
[2] As amended by the Enterprise and Regulatory Reform Act 2013 (c.24) Sch.6 para.51 (effective April 1, 2014).
[3] As inserted by the Legal Profession and Legal Aid (Scotland) Act 2007 (asp 5) Sch.5 para.3(12) (effective October 1, 2008).

(2)   The enactments mentioned in Schedule 9 to this Act are hereby repealed to the extent specified in the third column of that Schedule.

F1.179   **Citation, commencement and extent**

75.—(1)   This Act may be cited as the Law Reform (Miscellaneous Provisions) (Scotland) Act 1990.

(2)   Subject to subsections (3) and (4) below, this Act shall come into force on such day as the Secretary of State may appoint by order made by statutory instrument and different days may be appointed for different provisions and for different purposes.

(3)   The provisions of—

    (a)   Part III and section 66 of this Act and so much of section 74 as relates to those provisions; and

    (b)   sections 67, 70 and 71 of this Act and paragraphs 21 and 34 of Schedule 8 to this Act,

shall come into force at the end of the period of two months beginning with the day on which this Act is passed.

(4)   Paragraph 27(3) of Schedule 8 to this Act shall come into force on the day on which this Act is passed.

(5)   Subject to subsections (6) and (7) below, this Act extends to Scotland only.

(6)   *[Repealed by the Requirements of Writing Scotland Act 1995, Sch.5]*

(7)   Paragraph 17 of Schedule 1 to this Act, paragraph 11 of Schedule 3 to this Act and Schedule 9 to this Act so far as relating to the House of Commons Disqualification Act 1975 extend also to England and Wales and Northern Ireland.

SCHEDULES

F1.180   SCHEDULE 1

[Repealed by the Public Appointments and Public Bodies etc. (Scotland) Act 2003 (asp 4) Sch.4 para.12(16) (effective August 15, 2003).]

F1.181   SCHEDULE 2

PUBLICATION OF APPLICATIONS MADE UNDER SECTION 25

1.   Any professional or other body making an application under section 25 of this Act shall, for a period of six weeks beginning with the date on which the application is submitted to the Lord President and the Secretary of State—

    (a)   make a copy of the draft scheme referred to in section 25(2) of this Act available for public inspection at a specified place; and

    (b)   on a request from any person—

        (i)   send him a copy of the draft scheme; or

        (ii)   make a copy of the draft scheme available for public inspection at a suitable place in his locality.

2.   Any person may make written representations concerning any draft scheme submitted under section 25 of this Act, and such representations shall—

    (a)   be made to both the Lord President and the Secretary of State; and

    (b)   be delivered to both the Lord President and the Secretary of State before the expiry of the period of six weeks beginning with the date on which the application is made.

3.   At the same time as an application under section 25 is submitted to the Lord President and the Secretary of State, the body making the application shall place an advertisement mentioning the matters referred to in paragraph 4 below in the Edinburgh Gazette and in a daily newspaper circulating throughout Scotland.

4. An advertisement such as referred to in paragraph 3 above shall state that—

(a) a copy of the draft scheme referred to in section 25(2) of this Act will be available for public inspection at a specified place for a period of six weeks beginning with the date on which the advertisement appears;

(b) a copy of the draft scheme will be—

(i) sent, free of charge, to any person on request; or

(ii) made available for public inspection at a suitable place in that person's locality;

(c) any person may make written representations concerning the draft scheme to the Lord President and the Secretary of State; and

(d) any such representations are to be delivered within the period of six weeks beginning with the date on which the application is made.

SCHEDULE 3

SCOTTISH LEGAL SERVICES OMBUDSMAN

[Repealed by the Legal Profession and Legal Aid (Scotland) Act 2007 (Transitional, Savings and Consequential Provisions) Order (SSI 2008/332) art.3(1)(d) (effective October 1, 2008: repeal has effect subject to savings and transitional provisions specified in SSI 2008/332 arts 3 and 4).]

SCHEDULES 4-7

[Not reproduced.]

PROPERTY MISDESCRIPTIONS ACT 1991

(1991 c. 29)   F1.7

[Repealed by the Property Misdescriptions Act 1991 (Repeal) Order 2013 (SI 2013/1575) art.2 (effective October 1, 2013).]

PROCEEDS OF CRIME ACT 2002

(2002 c. 29)   F1.8

Sections 1.–239. *[Not reproduced.]*

PART 5 – CIVIL RECOVERY OF THE PROCEEDS ETC. OF UNLAWFUL CONDUCT

Chapter 1 – Introductory

General purpose of this Part

240.—(1) This Part has effect for the purposes of—

(a) enabling the enforcement authority to recover, in civil proceedings before the High Court or Court of Session, property which is, or represents, property obtained through unlawful conduct,

(b) enabling cash which is, or represents, property obtained through unlawful conduct, or which is intended to be used in unlawful conduct, to be forfeited in civil proceedings before a magistrates' court or (in Scotland) the sheriff.

(2) The powers conferred by this Part are exercisable in relation to any property (including cash) whether or not any proceedings have been brought for an offence in connection with the property.

"Unlawful conduct"

241.—(1) Conduct occurring in any part of the United Kingdom is unlawful conduct if it is unlawful under the criminal law of that part.

(2) Conduct which—

    (a)[1] occurs in a country or territory outside the United Kingdom and is unlawful under the criminal law applying in that country or territory, and

    (b) if it occurred in a part of the United Kingdom, would be unlawful under the criminal law of that part,

is also unlawful conduct.

(3) The court or sheriff must decide on a balance of probabilities whether it is proved—

    (a) that any matters alleged to constitute unlawful conduct have occurred, or

    (b) that any person intended to use any cash in unlawful conduct.

"Property obtained through unlawful conduct"

242.(1) A person obtains property through unlawful conduct (whether his own conduct or another's) if he obtains property by or in return for the conduct.

(2) In deciding whether any property was obtained through unlawful conduct—

---

[1] As substituted by the Serious Organised Crime and Police Act 2005 (c.15), Sch.6, para.8 (effective January 1, 2006).

    (a)   it is immaterial whether or not any money, goods or services were provided in order to put the person in question in a position to carry out the conduct,

    (b)   it is not necessary to show that the conduct was of a particular kind if it is shown that the property was obtained through conduct of one of a number of kinds, each of which would have been unlawful conduct.

Chapter 2 – Civil Recovery in the High Court or Court of Session

Proceedings for recovery orders

Proceedings for recovery orders in England and Wales or Northern Ireland

243.—(1)   Proceedings for a recovery order may be taken by the enforcement authority in the High Court against any person who the authority thinks holds recoverable property.

(2)   The enforcement authority must serve the claim form—

    (a)   on the respondent, and

    (b)   unless the court dispenses with service, on any other person who the authority thinks holds any associated property which the authority wishes to be subject to a recovery order,

wherever domiciled, resident or present.

(3)   If any property which the enforcement authority wishes to be subject to a recovery order is not specified in the claim form it must be described in the form in general terms; and the form must state whether it is alleged to be recoverable property or associated property.

(4)   The references above to the claim form include the particulars of claim, where they are served subsequently.

Proceedings for recovery orders in Scotland

244.—(1)   Proceedings for a recovery order may be taken by the enforcement authority in the Court of Session against any person who the authority thinks holds recoverable property.

(2)   The enforcement authority must serve the application—

    (a)   on the respondent, and

    (b)   unless the court dispenses with service, on any other person who the authority thinks holds any associated property which the authority wishes to be subject to a recovery order,

wherever domiciled, resident or present.

(3)   If any property which the enforcement authority wishes to be subject to a recovery order is not specified in the application it must be described in the application in general terms; and the application must state whether it is alleged to be recoverable property or associated property.

"Associated property"

245.—(1)

"Associated property" means property of any of the following descriptions (including property held by the respondent) which is not itself the recoverable property—

    (a)   any interest in the recoverable property,

(b) any other interest in the property in which the recoverable property subsists,

(c) if the recoverable property is a tenancy in common, the tenancy of the other tenant,

(d) if (in Scotland) the recoverable property is owned in common, the interest of the other owner,

(e) if the recoverable property is part of a larger property, but not a separate part, the remainder of that property.

(2) References to property being associated with recoverable property are to be read accordingly.

(3) No property is to be treated as associated with recoverable property consisting of rights under a pension scheme (within the meaning of sections 273 to 275).

Property freezing orders (England and Wales and Northern Ireland)

245A–245G. [England, Wales and Northern Ireland.]

Interim receiving orders (England and Wales and Northern Ireland)

246.–249. *[Not reproduced.]*

Interim receiving orders: further provisions[1]

250.–255. *[Not reproduced.]*

Application for prohibitory property order

255A.—(1) Where the enforcement authority may take proceedings for a recovery order in the Court of Session, the authority may apply to the court for a prohibitory property order (whether before or after starting the proceedings).

(2) A prohibitory property order is an order that—

(a) specifies or describes the property to which it applies, and

(b) subject to any exclusions (see section 255C(1)(b) and (2)), prohibits any person to whose property the order applies from in any way dealing with the property.

(3) An application for a prohibitory property order may be made without notice if the circumstances are such that notice of the application would prejudice any right of the enforcement authority to obtain a recovery order in respect of any property.

(4) The court may make a prohibitory property order on an application if it is satisfied that the condition in subsection (5) is met and, where applicable, that the condition in subsection (6) is met.

(5) The first condition is that there is a good arguable case—

(a) that the property to which the application for the order relates is or includes recoverable property, and

(b) that, if any of it is not recoverable property, it is associated property.

(6) The second condition is that, if—

(a) the property to which the application for the order relates includes property alleged to be associated property, and

(b) the enforcement authority has not established the identity of the person who holds it,

---

[1] Sections 250–255F moved into a new section group by the Serious Organised Crime and Police Act 2005 (c.15) Sch.6 para. 13 (effective January 1, 2006).

the authority has taken all reasonable steps to do so.

Variation and recall of prohibitory property order

255B.—(1)   The court may at any time vary or recall a prohibitory property order.

(2)   If the court makes an interim administration order that applies to all of the property to which a prohibitory property order applies, it must recall the prohibitory property order.

(3)   If the court makes an interim administration order that applies to some but not all of the property to which a prohibitory property order applies, it must vary the prohibitory property order so as to exclude any property to which the interim administration order applies.

(4)   If the court decides that any property to which a prohibitory property order applies is neither recoverable property nor associated property, it must vary the order so as to exclude the property.

(5)   Before exercising power under this Chapter to vary or recall a prohibitory property order, the court must (as well as giving the parties to the proceedings an opportunity to be heard) give such an opportunity to any person who may be affected by its decision.

(6)   Subsection (5) does not apply where the court is acting as required by subsection (2) or (3).

Exclusions

255C.—(1)   The power to vary a prohibitory property order includes (in particular) power to make exclusions as follows—

(a)   power to exclude property from the order, and

(b)   power, otherwise than by excluding property from the order, to make exclusions from the prohibition on dealing with the property to which the order applies.

(2)   Exclusions from the prohibition on dealing with the property to which the order applies (other than exclusions of property from the order) may also be made when the order is made.

(3)   An exclusion may, in particular, make provision for the purpose of enabling any person—

(a)   to meet his reasonable living expenses, or

(b)   to carry on any trade, business, profession or occupation.

(4)   An exclusion may be made subject to conditions.

(5)   An exclusion may not be made for the purpose of enabling any person to meet any legal expenses in respect of proceedings under this Part.

(6)   If excluded property is not specified in the order it must be described in the order in general terms.

(7)   The power to make exclusions must be exercised with a view to ensuring, so far as practicable, that the satisfaction of any right of the enforcement authority to recover the property obtained through unlawful conduct is not unduly prejudiced.

(8)   Subsection (7) does not apply where the court is acting as required by section 255B(3) or (4).

Restriction on proceedings and remedies

255D.—(1) While a prohibitory property order has effect the court may sist any action, execution or other legal process in respect of the property to which the order applies.

(2) If a court (whether the Court of Session or any other court) in which proceedings are pending in respect of any property is satisfied that a prohibitory property order has been applied for or made in respect of the property, it may either sist the proceedings or allow them to continue on any terms it thinks fit.

(3) Before exercising any power conferred by this section, the court must (as well as giving the parties to any of the proceedings concerned an opportunity to be heard) give such an opportunity to any person who may be affected by the court's decision.

Arrestment of property affected by prohibitory property order

255E.—(1) On the application of the enforcement authority the Court of Session may, in relation to moveable recoverable property to which a prohibitory property order applies (whether generally or to such of it as is specified in the application), grant warrant for arrestment.

(2) An application under subsection (1) may be made at the same time as the application for the prohibitory property order or at any time thereafter.

(3) Such a warrant for arrestment may be granted only if the property would be arrestable if the person entitled to it were a debtor.

(4) A warrant under subsection (1) has effect as if granted on the dependence of an action for debt at the instance of the enforcement authority against the person and may be executed, recalled, loosed or restricted accordingly.

(5) An arrestment executed under this section ceases to have effect when, or in so far as, the prohibitory property order ceases to apply in respect of the property in relation to which the warrant for arrestment was granted.

(6) If an arrestment ceases to have effect to any extent by virtue of subsection (5) the enforcement authority must apply to the Court of Session for an order recalling or, as the case may be, restricting the arrestment.

Inhibition of property affected by prohibitory property order

255F.—(1) On the application of the enforcement authority, the Court of Session may, in relation to the property mentioned in subsection (2), grant warrant for inhibition against any person specified in a prohibitory property order.

(2) That property is heritable property situated in Scotland to which the prohibitory property order applies (whether generally or to such of it as is specified in the application).

(3) The warrant for inhibition—

    (a) has effect as if granted on the dependence of an action for debt by the enforcement authority against the person and may be executed, recalled, loosed or restricted accordingly, and

    (b) has the effect of letters of inhibition and must forthwith be registered by the enforcement authority in the register of inhibitions and adjudications.

(4) Section 155 of the Titles to Land Consolidation (Scotland) Act 1868 (c. 101) (effective date of inhibition) applies in relation to an inhibition for which warrant is granted under subsection (1) as it applies to an inhibition by separate letters or contained in a summons.

(5)   An inhibition executed under this section ceases to have effect when, or in so far as, the prohibitory property order ceases to apply in respect of the property in relation to which the warrant for inhibition was granted.

(6)   If an inhibition ceases to have effect to any extent by virtue of subsection (5) the enforcement authority must—

(a)   apply for the recall or, as the case may be, the restriction of the inhibition, and

(b)   ensure that the recall or restriction is reflected in the register of inhibitions and adjudications.

Interim administration orders (Scotland)

Application for interim administration order

256.—(1)   Where the enforcement authority may take proceedings for a recovery order in the Court of Session, the authority may apply to the court for an interim administration order (whether before or after starting the proceedings).

(2)   An interim administration order is an order for—

(a)   the detention, custody or preservation of property, and

(b)   the appointment of an interim administrator.

(3)   An application for an interim administration order may be made without notice if the circumstances are such that notice of the application would prejudice any right of the enforcement authority to obtain a recovery order in respect of any property.

(4)   The court may make an interim administration order on the application if it is satisfied that the conditions in subsections (5) and, where applicable, (6) are met.

(5)   The first condition is that there is a probabilis causa litigandi—

(a)   that the property to which the application for the order relates is or includes recoverable property, and

(b)   that, if any of it is not recoverable property, it is associated property.

(6)   The second condition is that, if—

(a)   the property to which the application for the order relates includes property alleged to be associated property, and

(b)   the enforcement authority has not established the identity of the person who holds it,

the authority has taken all reasonable steps to do so.

(7)   In its application for an interim administration order, the enforcement authority must nominate a suitably qualified person for appointment as interim administrator, but the nominee may not be a member of the staff of the Scottish Administration.

(8)   The extent of the power to make an interim administration order is not limited by sections 257 to 264.

Functions of interim administrator

257.—(1)   An interim administration order may authorise or require the interim administrator—

(a)   to exercise any of the powers mentioned in Schedule 6,

(b)   to take any other steps the court thinks appropriate,

for the purpose of securing the detention, custody or preservation of the property to which the order applies or of taking any steps under subsection (2).

(2)   An interim administration order must require the interim administrator to take any steps which the court thinks necessary to establish—

(a)   whether or not the property to which the order applies is recoverable property or associated property,

(b)   whether or not any other property is recoverable property (in relation to the same unlawful conduct) and, if it is, who holds it.

(3)   If—

(a)   the interim administrator deals with any property which is not property to which the order applies, and

(b)   at the time he deals with the property he believes on reasonable grounds that he is entitled to do so in pursuance of the order,

the interim administrator is not liable to any person in respect of any loss or damage resulting from his dealing with the property except so far as the loss or damage is caused by his negligence.

Inhibition of property affected by order

258.—(1)   On the application of the enforcement authority, the Court of Session may, in relation to the property mentioned in subsection (2), grant warrant for inhibition against any person specified in an interim administration order.

(2)   That property is heritable property situated in Scotland to which the interim administration order applies (whether generally or such of it as is specified in the application).

(3)   The warrant for inhibition—

(a)   has effect as if granted on the dependence of an action for debt by the enforcement authority against the person and may be executed, recalled, loosed or restricted accordingly, and

(b)   has the effect of letters of inhibition and must forthwith be registered by the enforcement authority in the register of inhibitions and adjudications.

(4)   Section 155 of the Titles to Land Consolidation (Scotland) Act 1868 (c. 101) (effective date of inhibition) applies in relation to an inhibition for which warrant is granted under subsection (1) as it applies to an inhibition by separate letters or contained in a summons.

(5)   The execution of an inhibition under this section in respect of property does not prejudice the exercise of an interim administrator's powers under or for the purposes of this Part in respect of that property.

(6)   An inhibition executed under this section ceases to have effect when, or in so far as, the interim administration order ceases to apply in respect of the property in relation to which the warrant for inhibition was granted.

(7)   If an inhibition ceases to have effect to any extent by virtue of subsection (6) the enforcement authority must—

(a)   apply for the recall or, as the case may be, the restriction of the inhibition, and

(b)   ensure that the recall or restriction is reflected in the register of inhibitions and adjudications.

Duties of respondent etc.

259.—(1)   An interim administration order may require any person to whose property the order applies—

(a) to bring the property to a place (in Scotland) specified by the interim administrator or place it in the custody of the interim administrator (if, in either case, he is able to do so),

(b) to do anything he is reasonably required to do by the interim administrator for the preservation of the property.

(2) An interim administration order may require any person to whose property the order applies to bring any documents relating to the property which are in his possession or control to a place (in Scotland) specified by the interim administrator or to place them in the custody of the interim administrator.

"Document" means anything in which information of any description is recorded.

Supervision of interim administrator and variation of order

260.—(1) The interim administrator, any party to the proceedings and any person affected by any action taken by the interim administrator, or who may be affected by any action proposed to be taken by him, may at any time apply to the court for directions as to the exercise of the interim administrator's functions.

(2) Before giving any directions under subsection (1), the court must (as well as giving the parties to the proceedings an opportunity to be heard) give such an opportunity to the interim administrator and to any person who may be interested in the application.

(3) The court may at any time vary or recall an interim administration order.

(4) Before exercising any power under this Chapter to vary or set aside an interim administration order, the court must (as well as giving the parties to the proceedings an opportunity to be heard) give such an opportunity to the interim administrator and to any person who may be affected by the court's decision.

Restrictions on dealing etc. with property

261.—(1) An interim administration order must, subject to any exclusions made in accordance with this section, prohibit any person to whose property the order applies from dealing with the property.

(2) Exclusions may be made when the interim administration order is made or on an application to vary the order.

(3) An exclusion may, in particular, make provision for the purpose of enabling any person—

(a) to meet his reasonable living expenses, or

(b) to carry on any trade, business, profession or occupation,

and may be made subject to conditions.

(4) But an exclusion may not be made for the purpose of enabling any person to meet any legal expenses in respect of proceedings under this Part.

(5) If the excluded property is not specified in the order it must be described in the order in general terms.

(6) The power to make exclusions must be exercised with a view to ensuring, so far as practicable, that the satisfaction of any right of the enforcement authority to recover the property obtained through unlawful conduct is not unduly prejudiced.

Restriction on proceedings and remedies

262.—(1)   While an interim administration order has effect, the court may sist any action, execution or other legal process in respect of the property to which the order applies.

(2)   If a court (whether the Court of Session or any other court) in which proceedings are pending in respect of any property is satisfied that an interim administration order has been applied for or made in respect of the property, the court may either sist the proceedings or allow them to continue on any terms it thinks fit.

(3)   Before exercising any power conferred by this section, the court must (as well as giving the parties to any of the proceedings in question an opportunity to be heard) give such an opportunity to the interim administrator (if appointed) and any person who may be affected by the court's decision.

Exclusion of property which is not recoverable etc.

263.—(1)   If the court decides that any property to which an interim administration order applies is neither recoverable property nor associated property, it must vary the order so as to exclude it.

(2)   The court may vary an interim administration order so as to exclude from the property to which the order applies any property which is alleged to be associated property if the court thinks that the satisfaction of any right of the enforcement authority to recover the property obtained through unlawful conduct will not be prejudiced.

(3)   The court may exclude any property within subsection (2) on any terms or conditions, applying while the interim administration order has effect, which the court thinks necessary or expedient.

Reporting

264.—(1)   An interim administration order must require the interim administrator to inform the enforcement authority and the court as soon as reasonably practicable if he thinks that—

    (a)   any property to which the order applies by virtue of a claim that it is recoverable property is not recoverable property,

    (b)   any property to which the order applies by virtue of a claim that it is associated property is not associated property,

    (c)   any property to which the order does not apply is recoverable property (in relation to the same unlawful conduct) or associated property, or

    (d)   any property to which the order applies is held by a person who is different from the person it is claimed holds it,

or if he thinks that there has been any other material change of circumstances.

(2)   An interim administration order must require the interim administrator—

    (a)   to report his findings to the court,

    (b)   to serve copies of his report on the enforcement authority and on any person who holds any property to which the order applies or who may otherwise be affected by the report.

Arrestment of property affected by interim administration order

265.—(1)   On the application of the enforcement authority or the interim administrator the Court of Session may, in relation to moveable recoverable property to which an interim administration order applies (whether generally or such of it as is specified in the application), grant warrant for arrestment.

(2) An application by the enforcement authority under subsection (1) may be made at the same time as the application for the interim administration order or at any time thereafter.

(3) Such a warrant for arrestment may be granted only if the property would be arrestable if the person entitled to it were a debtor.

(4) A warrant under subsection (1) has effect as if granted on the dependence of an action for debt at the instance of the enforcement authority or, as the case may be, the interim administrator against the person and may be executed, recalled, loosed or restricted accordingly.

(5) The execution of an arrestment under this section in respect of property does not prejudice the exercise of an interim administrator's powers under or for the purposes of this Part in respect of that property.

(6) An arrestment executed under this section ceases to have effect when, or in so far as, the interim administration order ceases to apply in respect of the property in relation to which the warrant for arrestment was granted.

(7) If an arrestment ceases to have effect to any extent by virtue of subsection (6) the enforcement authority or, as the case may be, the interim administrator must apply to the Court of Session for an order recalling or, as the case may be, restricting the arrestment.

Vesting and realisation of recoverable property

Recovery orders

266.—(1) If in proceedings under this Chapter the court is satisfied that any property is recoverable, the court must make a recovery order.

(2) The recovery order must vest the recoverable property in the trustee for civil recovery.

(3) But the court may not make in a recovery order—

    (a) any provision in respect of any recoverable property if each of the conditions in subsection (4) or (as the case may be) (5) is met and it would not be just and equitable to do so, or

    (b) any provision which is incompatible with any of the Convention rights (within the meaning of the Human Rights Act 1998 (c. 42)).

(4) In relation to a court in England and Wales or Northern Ireland, the conditions referred to in subsection (3)(a) are that—

    (a) the respondent obtained the recoverable property in good faith,

    (b) he took steps after obtaining the property which he would not have taken if he had not obtained it or he took steps before obtaining theproperty which he would not have taken if he had not believed he was going to obtain it,

    (c) when he took the steps, he had no notice that the property was recoverable,

    (d) if a recovery order were made in respect of the property, it would, by reason of the steps, be detrimental to him.

(5) In relation to a court in Scotland, the conditions referred to in subsection (3)(a) are that—

    (a) the respondent obtained the recoverable property in good faith,

    (b) he took steps after obtaining the property which he would not have taken if he had not obtained it or he took steps before obtaining the property which he would not have taken if he had not believed he was going to obtain it,

(c)   when he took the steps, he had no reasonable grounds for believing that the property was recoverable,

(d)   if a recovery order were made in respect of the property, it would, by reason of the steps, be detrimental to him.

(6)   In deciding whether it would be just and equitable to make the provision in the recovery order where the conditions in subsection (4) or (as the case may be) (5) are met, the court must have regard to—

(a)   the degree of detriment that would be suffered by the respondent if the provision were made,

(b)   the enforcement authority's interest in receiving the realised proceeds of the recoverable property.

(7)   A recovery order may sever any property.

(8)   A recovery order may impose conditions as to the manner in which the trustee for civil recovery may deal with any property vested by the order for the purpose of realising it.

(8A)[1]   A recovery order made by a court in England and Wales or Northern Ireland may provide for payment under section 280 of reasonable legal expenses that a person has reasonably incurred, or may reasonably incur, in respect of—

(a)   the proceedings under this Part in which the order is made, or

(b)   any related proceedings under this Part.

(8B)[2]   If regulations under section 286B apply to an item of expenditure, a sum in respect of the item is not payable under section 280 in pursuance of provision under subsection (8A) unless—

(a)   the enforcement authority agrees to its payment, or

(b)   the court has assessed the amount allowed by the regulations in respect of that item and the sum is paid in respect of the assessed amount.

(9)   This section is subject to sections 270 to 278.

Functions of the trustee for civil recovery

267.—(1)   The trustee for civil recovery is a person appointed by the court to give effect to a recovery order.

(2)   The enforcement authority must nominate a suitably qualified person for appointment as the trustee.

(3)   The functions of the trustee are—

(a)   to secure the detention, custody or preservation of any property vested in him by the recovery order,

(b)   in the case of property other than money, to realise the value of the property for the benefit of the enforcement authority, and

(c)   to perform any other functions conferred on him by virtue of this Chapter.

(4)   In performing his functions, the trustee acts on behalf of the enforcement authority and must comply with any directions given by the authority.

---

[1] As inserted by the Serious Organised Crime and Police Act 2005 (c.15), Sch.6, para. 15 (effective January 1, 2006).

[2] As inserted by the Serious Organised Crime and Police Act 2005 (c.15), Sch.6, para. 15 (effective January 1, 2006).

(5)   The trustee is to realise the value of property vested in him by the recovery order, so far as practicable, in the manner best calculated to maximise the amount payable to the enforcement authority.

(6)   The trustee has the powers mentioned in Schedule 7.

(7)   References in this section to a recovery order include an order under section 276 and references to property vested in the trustee by a recovery order include property vested in him in pursuance of an order under section 276.

Recording of recovery order (Scotland)

268.—(1)   The clerk of the court must immediately after the making of a recovery order which relates to heritable property situated in Scotland send a certified copy of it to the keeper of the register of inhibitions and adjudications for recording in that register.

(2)   Recording under subsection (1) is to have the effect, as from the date of the recovery order, of an inhibition at the instance of the trustee for civil recovery against the person in whom the heritable property was vest prior to that date.

Rights of pre-emption, etc.

269.—(1)   A recovery order is to have effect in relation to any property despite any provision (of whatever nature) which would otherwise prevent, penalise or restrict the vesting of the property.

(2)   A right of pre-emption, right of irritancy, right of return or other similar right does not operate or become exercisable as a result of the vesting of any property under a recovery order.

A right of return means any right under a provision for the return or reversion of property in specified circumstances.

(3)   Where property is vested under a recovery order, any such right is to have effect as if the person in whom the property is vested were the same person in law as the person who held the property and as if no transfer of the property had taken place.

(4)   References to rights in subsections (2) and (3) do not include any rights in respect of which the recovery order was made.

(5)   This section applies in relation to the creation of interests, or the doing of anything else, by a recovery order as it applies in relation to the vesting of property.

Associated and joint property

270.—(1)   Sections 271 and 272 apply if the court makes a recovery order in respect of any recoverable property in a case within subsection (2) or (3).

(2)   A case is within this subsection if—
  (a)   the property to which the proceedings relate includes property which is associated with the recoverable property and is specified or described in the claim form or (in Scotland) application, and
  (b)   if the associated property is not the respondent's property, the claim form or application has been served on the person whose property it is or the court has dispensed with service.

(3)   A case is within this subsection if—
  (a)   the recoverable property belongs to joint tenants, and
  (b)   one of the tenants is an excepted joint owner.

(4)   An excepted joint owner is a person who obtained the property in circumstances in which it would not be recoverable as against him; and references to the

excepted joint owner's share of the recoverable property are to so much of the recoverable property as would have been his if the joint tenancy had been severed.

(5)   Subsections (3) and (4) do not extend to Scotland.

Agreements about associated and joint property

271.—(1)   Where—

    (a)   this section applies, and

    (b)   the enforcement authority (on the one hand) and the person who holds the associated property or who is the excepted joint owner (on the other) agree,

the recovery order may, instead of vesting the recoverable property in the trustee for civil recovery, require the person who holds the associated property or who is the excepted joint owner to make a payment to the trustee.

(2)   A recovery order which makes any requirement under subsection (1) may, so far as required for giving effect to the agreement, include provision for vesting, creating or extinguishing any interest in property.

(3)   The amount of the payment is to be the amount which the enforcement authority and that person agree represents—

    (a)   in a case within section 270(2), the value of the recoverable property,

    (b)   in a case within section 270(3), the value of the recoverable property less the value of the excepted joint owner's share.

(4)[1]   But if—

    (a)   a property freezing order, an interim receiving order, a prohibitory property order or an interim administration order applied at any time to the associated property or joint tenancy, and

    (b)   the enforcement authority agrees that the person has suffered loss as a result of the order mentioned in paragraph (a),

the amount of the payment may be reduced by any amount the enforcement authority and that person agree is reasonable, having regard to that loss and to any other relevant circumstances.

(5)   If there is more than one such item of associated property or excepted joint owner, the total amount to be paid to the trustee, and the part of that amount which is to be provided by each person who holds any such associated property or who is an excepted joint owner, is to be agreed between both (or all) of them and the enforcement authority.

(6)   A recovery order which makes any requirement under subsection (1) must make provision for any recoverable property to cease to be recoverable.

Associated and joint property: default of agreement

272.—(1)   Where this section applies, the court may make the following provision if—

    (a)   there is no agreement under section 271, and

    (b)   the court thinks it just and equitable to do so.

(2)   The recovery order may provide—

---

[1] As substituted by the Serious Organised Crime and Police Act 2005 (c.15), Sch.6, para. 16 (effective January 1, 2006).

(a) for the associated property to vest in the trustee for civil recovery or (as the case may be) for the excepted joint owner's interest to be extinguished, or

(b) in the case of an excepted joint owner, for the severance of his interest.

(3) A recovery order making any provision by virtue of subsection (2)(a) may provide—

(a) for the trustee to pay an amount to the person who holds the associated property or who is an excepted joint owner, or

(b) for the creation of interests in favour of that person, or the imposition of liabilities or conditions, in relation to the property vested in the trustee,

or for both.

(4) In making any provision in a recovery order by virtue of subsection (2) or (3), the court must have regard to—

(a) the rights of any person who holds the associated property or who is an excepted joint owner and the value to him of that property or, as the case may be, of his share (including any value which cannot be assessed in terms of money),

(b) the enforcement authority's interest in receiving the realised proceeds of the recoverable property.

(5)[1] If—

(a) a property freezing order, an interim receiving order, a prohibitory property order or an interim administration order applied at any time to the associated property or joint tenancy, and

(b) the court is satisfied that the person who holds the associated property or who is an excepted joint owner has suffered loss as a result of the order mentioned in paragraph (a),

a recovery order making any provision by virtue of subsection (2) or (3) may require the enforcement authority to pay compensation to that person.

(6) The amount of compensation to be paid under subsection (5) is the amount the court thinks reasonable, having regard to the person's loss and to any other relevant circumstances.

(7)[2] In subsection (5) the reference to the enforcement authority is, in the case of an enforcement authority in relation to England and Wales or Northern Ireland, a reference to the enforcement authority which obtained the property freezing order or interim receiving order concerned.

Payments in respect of rights under pension schemes

273.—(1) This section applies to recoverable property consisting of rights under a pension scheme.

(2) A recovery order in respect of the property must, instead of vesting the property in the trustee for civil recovery, require the trustees or managers of the pension scheme—

(a) to pay to the trustee for civil recovery within a prescribed period the amount determined by the trustees or managers to be equal to the value of the rights, and

---

[1] As substituted by the Serious Organised Crime and Police Act 2005 (c.15) Sch.6 para.17 (effective January 1, 2006).
[2] As inserted by the Serious Crime Act 2007 (c.27) Sch.8(2) para.87 (effective April 1, 2008).

(b) to give effect to any other provision made by virtue of this section and the two following sections in respect of the scheme.

This subsection is subject to sections 276 to 278.

(3) A recovery order made by virtue of subsection (2) overrides the provisions of the pension scheme to the extent that they conflict with the provisions of the order.

(4) A recovery order made by virtue of subsection (2) may provide for the recovery by the trustees or managers of the scheme (whether by deduction from any amount which they are required to pay to the trustee for civil recovery or otherwise) of costs incurred by them in—

(a) complying with the recovery order, or

(b)[1] providing information, before the order was made, to the enforcement authority, receiver appointed under section 245E, interim receiver or interim administrator.

(5) None of the following provisions applies to a court making a recovery order by virtue of subsection (2)—

(a) any provision of section 159 of the Pension Schemes Act 1993 (c. 48), section 155 of the Pension Schemes (Northern Ireland) Act 1993 (c.49), section 91 of the Pensions Act 1995 (c. 26) or Article 89 of the Pensions (Northern Ireland) Order 1995 (S.I. 1995/3213 (N.I. 22)) (which prevent assignment and the making of orders that restrain a person from receiving anything which he is prevented from assigning),

(b) any provision of any enactment (whenever passed or made) corresponding to any of the provisions mentioned in paragraph (a),

(c) any provision of the pension scheme in question corresponding to any of those provisions.

Consequential adjustment of liabilities under pension schemes

274.—(1) A recovery order made by virtue of section 273(2) must require the trustees or managers of the pension scheme to make such reduction in the liabilities of the scheme as they think necessary in consequence of the payment made in pursuance of that subsection.

(2) Accordingly, the order must require the trustees or managers to provide for the liabilities of the pension scheme in respect of the respondent's recoverable property to which section 273 applies to cease.

(3) So far as the trustees or managers are required by the recovery order to provide for the liabilities of the pension scheme in respect of the respondent's recoverable property to which section 273 applies to cease, their powers include (in particular) power to reduce the amount of—

(a) any benefit or future benefit to which the respondent is or may be entitled under the scheme,

(b) any future benefit to which any other person may be entitled under the scheme in respect of that property.

---

[1] As inserted by the Serious Crime Act 2007 (c.27) Pt 3 s.83(2) (effective April 6, 2008 subject to transitional and transitory provisions and savings as specified in SI 2008/755 art.17(2) and (3)).

Pension schemes: supplementary

275.—(1) Regulations may make provision as to the exercise by trustees or managers of their powers under sections 273 and 274, including provision about the calculation and verification of the value at any time of rights or liabilities.

(2) The power conferred by subsection (1) includes power to provide for any values to be calculated or verified—

(a) in a manner which, in the particular case, is approved by a prescribed person, or

(b) in accordance with guidance from time to time prepared by a prescribed person.

(3)[1] Regulations means regulations made by the Secretary of State after consultation with the Scottish Ministers or, in relation to Northern Ireland, regulations made by the Department of Justice; and prescribed means prescribed by regulations.

(4) A pension scheme means an occupational pension scheme or a personal pension scheme; and those expressions have the same meaning as in the Pension Schemes Act 1993 (c. 48) or, in relation to Northern Ireland, the Pension Schemes (Northern Ireland) Act 1993 (c. 49).

(5) In relation to an occupational pension scheme or a personal pension scheme, the trustees or managers means—

(a) in the case of a scheme established under a trust, the trustees,

(b) in any other case, the managers.

(6) References to a pension scheme include—

(a) a retirement annuity contract (within the meaning of Part 3 of the Welfare Reform and Pensions Act 1999 (c. 30) or, in relation to Northern Ireland, Part 4 of the Welfare Reform and Pensions (Northern Ireland) Order 1999),

(b) an annuity or insurance policy purchased, or transferred, for the purpose of giving effect to rights under an occupational pension scheme or a personal pension scheme,

(c) an annuity purchased, or entered into, for the purpose of discharging any liability in respect of a pension credit under section 29(1)(b) of the Welfare Reform and Pensions Act 1999 (c. 30) or, in relation to Northern Ireland, Article 26(1)(b) of the Welfare Reform and Pensions (Northern Ireland) Order 1999.

(7) References to the trustees or managers—

(a) in relation to a retirement annuity contract or other annuity, are to the provider of the annuity,

(b) in relation to an insurance policy, are to the insurer.

(8) Subsections (3) to (7) have effect for the purposes of this group of sections (that is, sections 273 and 274 and this section).

Consent orders

276.—(1) The court may make an order staying (in Scotland, sisting) any proceedings for a recovery order on terms agreed by the parties for the disposal of

---

[1] As amended by the Northern Ireland Act 1998 (Devolution of Policing and Justice Functions) Order 2010 (SI 2010/976) Sch.14 para.54 (effective April 12, 2010: amendment has effect subject to transitional provision specified in SI 2010/976 art.28).

the proceedings if each person to whose property the proceedings, or the agreement, relates is a party both to the proceedings and the agreement.

(2) An order under subsection (1) may, as well as staying (or sisting) the proceedings on terms—

(a) make provision for any property which may be recoverable property to cease to be recoverable,

(b) make any further provision which the court thinks appropriate.

(3) Section 280 applies to property vested in the trustee for civil recovery, or money paid to him, in pursuance of the agreement as it applies to property vested in him by a recovery order or money paid under section 271.

Consent orders: pensions

277.—(1) This section applies where recoverable property to which proceedings under this Chapter relate includes rights under a pension scheme.

(2) An order made under section 276—

(a) may not stay (in Scotland, sist) the proceedings on terms that the rights are vested in any other person, but

(b) may include provision imposing the following requirement, if the trustees or managers of the scheme are parties to the agreement by virtue of which the order is made.

(3) The requirement is that the trustees or managers of the pension scheme—

(a) make a payment in accordance with the agreement, and

(b) give effect to any other provision made by virtue of this section in respect of the scheme.

(4) The trustees or managers of the pension scheme have power to enter into an agreement in respect of the proceedings on any terms on which an order made under section 276 may stay (in Scotland, sist) the proceedings.

(5) The following provisions apply in respect of an order under section 276, so far as it includes the requirement mentioned in subsection (3).

(6) The order overrides the provisions of the pension scheme to the extent that they conflict with the requirement.

(7) The order may provide for the recovery by the trustees or managers of the scheme (whether by deduction from any amount which they are required to pay in pursuance of the agreement or otherwise) of costs incurred by them in—

(a) complying with the order, or

(b)[1] providing information, before the order was made, to the enforcement authority, receiver appointed under section 245E, interim receiver or interim administrator.

(8) Sections 273(5) and 274 (read with section 275) apply as if the requirement were included in an order made by virtue of section 273(2).

(9) Section 275(4) to (7) has effect for the purposes of this section.

Limit on recovery

278.—(1) This section applies if the enforcement authority seeks a recovery order—

---

[1] As amended by the Serious Crime Act 2007 (c.27) Pt 3 s.83(2) (effective April 6, 2008 subject to transitional and transitory provisions and savings as specified in SI 2008/755 art. 17(2) and (3)).

    (a)   in respect of both property which is or represents property obtained through unlawful conduct and related property, or

    (b)   in respect of property which is or represents property obtained through unlawful conduct where such an order, or an order under section 276, has previously been made in respect of related property.

(2)   For the purposes of this section—

    (a)   the original property means the property obtained through unlawful conduct,

    (b)   the original property, and any items of property which represent the original property, are to be treated as related to each other.

(3)   The court is not to make a recovery order if it thinks that the enforcement authority's right to recover the original property has been satisfied by a previous recovery order or order under section 276.

(4)   Subject to subsection (3), the court may act under subsection (5) if it thinks that—

    (a)   a recovery order may be made in respect of two or more related items of recoverable property, but

    (b)   the making of a recovery order in respect of both or all of them is not required in order to satisfy the enforcement authority's right to recover the original property.

(5)   The court may in order to satisfy that right to the extent required make a recovery order in respect of—

    (a)   only some of the related items of property, or

    (b)   only a part of any of the related items of property, or both.

(6)   Where the court may make a recovery order in respect of any property, this section does not prevent the recovery of any profits which have accrued in respect of the property.

(6A)[1]   If—

    (a)   recoverable property is forfeited in pursuance of a forfeiture notice under section 297A, and

    (b)   the enforcement authority subsequently seeks a recovery order in respect of related property,

       the forfeiture notice is to be treated for the purposes of this section as if it were a recovery order obtained by the enforcement authority in respect of the forfeited property.

(7)   If—

    (a)   an order is made under section 298 for the forfeiture of recoverable property, and

    (b)   the enforcement authority subsequently seeks a recovery order in respect of related property,

the order under section 298 is to be treated for the purposes of this section as if it were a recovery order obtained by the enforcement authority in respect of the forfeited property.

(8)   If—

    (a)   in pursuance of a judgment in civil proceedings (whether in the United Kingdom or elsewhere), the claimant has obtained property from the defendant ("the judgment property"),

---

[1] Prospectively inserted by the Policing and Crime Act 2009 (c.26) Sch.7(7) para.106 (not yet in force).

    (b)   the claim was based on the defendant's having obtained the judgment property or related property through unlawful conduct, and

    (c)   the enforcement authority subsequently seeks a recovery order in respect of property which is related to the judgment property,

the judgment is to be treated for the purposes of this section as if it were a recovery order obtained by the enforcement authority in respect of the judgment property.

In relation to Scotland, "claimant" and "defendant" are to be read as "pursuer" and "defender".

    (9) If—

    (a)   property has been taken into account in deciding the amount of a person's benefit from criminal conduct for the purpose of making a confiscation order, and

    (b)   the enforcement authority subsequently seeks a recovery order in respect of related property,

the confiscation order is to be treated for the purposes of this section as if it were a recovery order obtained by the enforcement authority in respect of the property referred to in paragraph (a).

    (10) In subsection (9), a confiscation order means—

    (a)   an order under section 6, 92 or 156, or

    (b)   an order under a corresponding provision of an enactment mentioned in section 8(7)(a) to (g),

and, in relation to an order mentioned in paragraph (b), the reference to the amount of a person's benefit from criminal conduct is to be read as a reference to the corresponding amount under the enactment in question.

Section 278: supplementary

279.—(1) Subsections (2) and (3) give examples of the satisfaction of the enforcement authority's right to recover the original property.

    (2) If—

    (a)   there is a disposal, other than a part disposal, of the original property, and

    (b)   other property (the representative property) is obtained in its place, the enforcement authority's right to recover the original property is satisfied by the making of a recovery order in respect of either the original property or the representative property.

    (3) If—

    (a)   there is a part disposal of the original property, and

    (b)   other property (the representative property) is obtained in place of the property disposed of,

the enforcement authority's right to recover the original property is satisfied by the making of a recovery order in respect of the remainder of the original property together with either the representative property or the property disposed of.

    (4) In this section—

    (a)   a part disposal means a disposal to which section 314(1) applies,

    (b)   the original property has the same meaning as in section 278.

Applying realised proceeds

280.—(1) This section applies to—

    (a)   sums which represent the realised proceeds of property which was vested in the trustee for civil recovery by a recovery order or which he obtained in pursuance of a recovery order,

    (b)   sums vested in the trustee by a recovery order or obtained by him in pursuance of a recovery order.

  (2) The trustee is to make out of the sums—

    (a)   first, any payment required to be made by him by virtue of section 272,

    (aa)[1] next, any payment of legal expenses which, after giving effect to section 266(8B), are payable under this subsection in pursuance of provision under section 266(8A) contained in the recovery order,

    (b)[2] then, any payment of expenses incurred by a person acting as an insolvency practitioner which are payable under this subsection by virtue of section 432(10),

and any sum which remains is to be paid to the enforcement authority.

  (3)[3] The enforcement authority (unless it is the Scottish Ministers) may apply a sum received by it under subsection (2) in making payment of the remuneration and expenses of—

    (a)   the trustee; or

    (b)   any interim receiver appointed in, or in anticipation of, the proceedings for the recovery order.

  (4)[4] Subsection (3)(a) does not apply in relation to remuneration of the trustee if the trustee is a member of the staff of the enforcement authority concerned.

Exemptions etc.

Victims of theft, etc.

281.—(1) In proceedings for a recovery order, a person who claims that any property alleged to be recoverable property, or any part of the property, belongs to him may apply for a declaration under this section.

  (2) If the applicant appears to the court to meet the following condition, the court may make a declaration to that effect.

  (3) The condition is that—

    (a)   the person was deprived of the property he claims, or of property which it represents, by unlawful conduct,

    (b)   the property he was deprived of was not recoverable property immediately before he was deprived of it, and

    (c)   the property he claims belongs to him.

  (4) Property to which a declaration under this section applies is not recoverable property.

---

[1] As inserted by the Serious Organised Crime and Police Act 2005 (c.15), Sch.6, para.18 (effective January 1, 2006).

[2] As substituted by the Serious Organised Crime and Police Act 2005 (c.15), Sch.6, para.18 (effective January 1, 2006).

[3] As inserted by the Serious Organised Crime and Police Act 2005 (c.15) para.99 (effective July 1, 2005) and substituted by the Serious Crime Act 2007, Sch.8(2), para.88 (effective April 1, 2008).

[4] As inserted by the Serious Organised Crime and Police Act 2005 (c.15) para.99 (effective July 1, 2005) and substituted by the Serious Crime Act 2007, Sch.8(2), para.88 (effective April 1, 2008).

Other exemptions

282.—[1](1)   Proceedings for a recovery order may not be taken against any person in circumstances of a prescribed description; and the circumstances may relate to the person himself or to the property or to any other matter.

In this subsection, prescribed means prescribed by an order made by the Secretary of State after consultation with the Scottish Ministers or, in relation to Northern Ireland, prescribed by an order made by the Department of Justice.

(2)   Proceedings for a recovery order may not be taken in respect of cash found at any place in the United Kingdom unless the proceedings are also taken in respect of property other than cash which is property of the same person.

(3)[2]   Proceedings for a recovery order may not be taken against the Financial Conduct Authority or the Prudential Regulation Authority in respect of any recoverable property held by it.

(4)   Proceedings for a recovery order may not be taken in respect of any property which is subject to any of the following charges—

    (a)   a collateral security charge, within the meaning of the Financial Markets and Insolvency (Settlement Finality) Regulations 1999 (S.I. 1999/2979),

    (b)   a market charge, within the meaning of Part 7 of the Companies Act 1989 (c. 40),

    (c)   a money market charge, within the meaning of the Financial Markets and Insolvency (Money Market) Regulations 1995 (S.I. 1995/2049),

    (d)   a system charge, within the meaning of the Financial Markets and Insolvency Regulations 1996 (S.I. 1996/1469) or the Financial Markets and Insolvency Regulations (Northern Ireland) 1996 (S.R. 1996/252).

(5)   Proceedings for a recovery order may not be taken against any person in respect of any recoverable property which he holds by reason of his acting, or having acted, as an insolvency practitioner.

Acting as an insolvency practitioner has the same meaning as in section 433.

Miscellaneous

Compensation

283.—[3](1)   If, in the case of any property to which a property freezing order, an interim receiving order, a prohibitory property order or an interim administration order has at any time applied, the court does not in the course of the proceedings decide that the property is recoverable property or associated property, the person whose property it is may make an application to the court for compensation.

(2)   Subsection (1) does not apply if the court—

    (a)   has made a declaration in respect of the property by virtue of section 281, or

    (b)   makes an order under section 276.

(3)   If the court has made a decision by reason of which no recovery order could be made in respect of the property, the application for compensation must be made

---

[1] As amended by the Northern Ireland Act 1998 (Devolution of Policing and Justice Functions) Order 2010 (SI 2010/976) Sch.14 para.55 (effective April 12, 2010: amendment has effect subject to transitional provision specified in SI 2010/976 art.28).
[2] As amended by the Financial Services Act 2012 (c.21) Sch.18(2) para.94(2) (effective April 1, 2013).
[3] As substituted by the Serious Organised Crime and Police Act 2005 (c.15) Sch.6 para. 19 (effective January 1, 2006).

within the period of three months beginning—

(a) in relation to a decision of the High Court in England and Wales, with the date of the decision or, if any application is made for leave to appeal, with the date on which the application is withdrawn or refused or (if the application is granted) on which any proceedings on appeal are finally concluded,

(b) in relation to a decision of the Court of Session or of the High Court in Northern Ireland, with the date of the decision or, if there is an appeal against the decision, with the date on which any proceedings on appeal are finally concluded.

(4) If, in England and Wales or Northern Ireland, the proceedings in respect of the property have been discontinued, the application for compensation must be made within the period of three months beginning with the discontinuance.

(5)[1] If the court is satisfied that the applicant has suffered loss as a result of the order mentioned in subsection (1), it may require the enforcement authority to pay compensation to him.

(6) If, but for section 269(2), any right mentioned there would have operated in favour of, or become exercisable by, any person, he may make an application to the court for compensation.

(7) The application for compensation under subsection (6) must be made within the period of three months beginning with the vesting referred to in section 269(2).

(8) If the court is satisfied that, in consequence of the operation of section 269, the right in question cannot subsequently operate in favour of the applicant or (as the case may be) become exercisable by him, it may require the enforcement authority to pay compensation to him.

(9) The amount of compensation to be paid under this section is the amount the court thinks reasonable, having regard to the loss suffered and any other relevant circumstances.

(10)[2] In the case of an enforcement authority in relation to England and Wales or Northern Ireland—

(a) the reference in subsection (5) to the enforcement authority is a reference to the enforcement authority which obtained the property freezing order or interim receiving order concerned, and

(b) the reference in subsection (8) to the enforcement authority is a reference to the enforcement authority which obtained the recovery order concerned.

Payment of interim administrator or trustee (Scotland)

284.—[3](1) Any fees or expenses incurred by an interim administrator, or a trustee for civil recovery appointed by the Court of Session, in the exercise of his functions are to be reimbursed by the Scottish Ministers as soon as is practicable after they have been incurred.

(2) The Scottish Ministers may apply a sum received by them under section 280(2) in making payment of such fees or expenses.

---

[1] As substituted by the Serious Organised Crime and Police Act 2005 (c.15) Sch.6 para. 19 (effective January 1, 2006).

[2] As inserted by the Serious Crime Act 2007 (c.27) Sch.8(2) para.89 (effective April 1, 2008).

[3] Existing s.284 renumbered as s.284(1) and s.284(2)–(3) inserted by the Serious Organised Crime and Police Act 2005 (c.15) s.99(3) (effective July 1, 2005).

(3)   Subsection (2) does not apply in relation to the fees of a trustee for civil recovery if the trustee is a member of their staff.

Effect on diligence of recovery order (Scotland)

285.—[1](1)   An arrestment or attachment of any recoverable property executed on or after the appointment of the trustee for civil recovery is ineffectual in a question with the trustee.

(2)[2]   Any recoverable property so arrested or attached, or (if the property has been sold) the proceeds of sale, must be handed over to the trustee for civil recovery.

(3)   A poinding of the ground in respect of recoverable property on or after such an appointment is ineffectual in a question with the trustee for civil recovery except for the interest mentioned in subsection (4).

(4)   That interest is—

    (a)   interest on the debt of a secured creditor for the current half yearly term, and

    (b)   arrears of interest on that debt for one year immediately before the commencement of that term.

(5)   On and after such appointment no other person may raise or insist in an adjudication against recoverable property or be confirmed as an executor-creditor on that property.

(6)   An inhibition on recoverable property shall cease to have effect in relation to any heritable property comprised in the recoverable property on such appointment.

(7)   *[Repealed by the Bankruptcy and Diligence etc. (Scotland) Act 2007 (asp.3) Sch.6(1), para.1 (effective April 1, 2008 for the purpose specified in SSI 2008/115 art.3(2)–(3) and Sch.2; not yet in force otherwise).]*

Scope of powers (Scotland)

286.—(1)   Orders under this Chapter may be made by the Court of Session in respect of a person wherever domiciled, resident or present.

(2)   Such an order may be made by the Court of Session in respect of moveable property wherever situated.

(3)   But such an order in respect of a person's moveable property may not be made by the Court of Session where—

    (a)   the person is not domiciled, resident or present in Scotland, and

    (b)   the property is not situated in Scotland,

unless the unlawful conduct took place in Scotland.

Legal expenses excluded from freezing: required conditions

286A.—[3](1)   The Lord Chancellor may by regulations specify the required conditions for the purposes of section 245C(5) or 252(4).

(2)   A required condition may (in particular)—

---

[1] As substituted by the Debt Arrangement and Attachment (Scotland) Act 2002 (asp 17) Sch.3(1) para.29(1)(a) (effective February 24, 2003: substitution came into force on December 30, 2002 but could not take effect until the commencement of 2002 c.29 s.285 on February 24, 2003).

[2] As substituted by the Debt Arrangement and Attachment (Scotland) Act 2002 (asp 17) Sch.3(1) para.29(1)(a) (effective February 24, 2003: substitution came into force on December 30, 2002 but could not take effect until the commencement of 2002 c.29 s.285 on February 24, 2003).

[3] As inserted by the Serious Organised Crime and Police Act 2005 (c.15) Sch.6, para.20 (effective August 1, 2005).

    (a)   restrict who may receive sums released in pursuance of the exclusion (by, for example, requiring released sums to be paid to professional legal advisers), or

    (b)   be made for the purpose of controlling the amount of any sum released in pursuance of the exclusion in respect of an item of expenditure.

    (3)   A required condition made for the purpose mentioned in subsection (2)(b) may (for example)—

    (a)   provide for sums to be released only with the agreement of the enforcement authority;

    (b)   provide for a sum to be released in respect of an item of expenditure only if the court has assessed the amount allowed by regulations under section 286B in respect of that item and the sum is released for payment of the assessed amount;

    (c)   provide for a sum to be released in respect of an item of expenditure only if—

        (i)   the enforcement authority agrees to its release, or

        (ii)   the court has assessed the amount allowed by regulations under section 286B in respect of that item and the sum is released for payment of the assessed amount.

    (4)   Before making regulations under this section, the Lord Chancellor must consult such persons as he considers appropriate.

Legal expenses: regulations for purposes of section 266(8B) or 286A(3)

    286B.—[1](1)   The Lord Chancellor may by regulations—

    (a)   make provision for the purposes of section 266(8B);

    (b)   make provision for the purposes of required conditions that make provision of the kind mentioned in section 286A(3)(b) or (c).

    (2)   Regulations under this section may (in particular)—

    (a)   limit the amount of remuneration allowable to representatives for a unit of time worked;

    (b)   limit the total amount of remuneration allowable to representatives for work done in connection with proceedings or a step in proceedings;

    (c)   limit the amount allowable in respect of an item of expense incurred by a representative or incurred, otherwise than in respect of the remuneration of a representative, by a party to proceedings.

    (3)   Before making regulations under this section, the Lord Chancellor must consult such persons as he considers appropriate.

Financial threshold

    287.—(1)   At any time when an order specifying an amount for the purposes of this section has effect, the enforcement authority may not start proceedings for a recovery order unless the authority reasonably believes that the aggregate value of the recoverable property which the authority wishes to be subject to a recovery order is not less than the specified amount.

---

[1] As inserted by the Serious Organised Crime and Police Act 2005 (c.15) Sch.6, para.20 (effective August 1, 2005).

(2)[1]   The power to make an order under subsection (1) is exercisable by the Secretary of State after consultation with the Scottish Ministers or, in relation to Northern Ireland, exercisable by the Department of Justice.

(3)[2]   If the authority applies for a property freezing order, an interim receiving order, a prohibitory property order or an interim administration order before starting the proceedings, subsection (1) applies to the application instead of to the start of the proceedings.

(4)[3]   This section does not affect the continuation of proceedings for a recovery order which have been properly started or the making or continuing effect of a property freezing order, an interim receiving order, a prohibitory property order or an interim administration order which has been properly applied for.

Limitation

288.   *[Not reproduced]*

Chapter 3 – Recovery of Cash in Summary Proceedings

Searches

Searches

289.—[4, 5](1)   If an officer of Revenue and Customs, a constable or an accredited financial investigator is lawfully on any premises and has reasonable grounds for suspecting that there is on the premises cash—

    (a)   which is recoverable property or is intended by any person for use in unlawful conduct, and

    (b)   the amount of which is not less than the minimum amount,

he may search for the cash there.

(2)   If an officer of Revenue and Customs, a constable or an accredited financial investigator has reasonable grounds for suspecting that a person (the suspect) is carrying cash—

    (a)   which is recoverable property or is intended by any person for use in unlawful conduct, and

    (b)   the amount of which is not less than the minimum amount,

he may exercise the following powers.

(3)   The officer, constable or accredited financial investigator may, so far as he thinks it necessary or expedient, require the suspect—

    (a)   to permit a search of any article he has with him,

    (b)   to permit a search of his person.

---

[1] As amended by the Northern Ireland Act 1998 (Devolution of Policing and Justice Functions) Order 2010 (SI 2010/976) Sch.14 para.56 (effective April 12, 2010: amendment has effect subject to transitional provision specified in SI 2010/976 art.28).

[2] As substituted by the Serious Organised Crime and Police Act 2005 (c.15) Sch.6, para.21 (effective January 1, 2006).

[3] As substituted by the Serious Organised Crime and Police Act 2005 (c.15) Sch.6, para.21 (effective January 1, 2006).

[4] As amended by the Finance Act 2013 (c.29) Sch.48 para.2(2) (effective July 17, 2013).

[5] As amended by the Serious Crime Act 2007 (c.27) Sch.11 para.2 (effective April 6, 2008 subject to transitional and transitory provisions and savings as specified in SI 2008/755 art. 17(2) and (3)).

(4)   An officer, constable or accredited financial investigator exercising powers by virtue of subsection (3)(b) may detain the suspect for so long as is necessary for their exercise.

(5)   The powers conferred by this section—

    (a)   are exercisable only so far as reasonably required for the purpose of finding cash,

    (b)   are exercisable by a customs officer only if he has reasonable grounds for suspecting that the unlawful conduct in question relates to an assigned matter (within the meaning of the Customs and Excise Management Act 1979 (c. 2)),

    [1](ba)   are exercisable by an officer of Revenue and Customs only so far as the officer is exercising a function relating to a matter other than an excluded matter,

    (c)   are exercisable by an accredited financial investigator only in relation to premises or (as the case may be) suspects in England, Wales or Northern Ireland.

[2](5A)   The reference in subsection (5)(ba) to an excluded matter is to a matter specified in section 54(4)(b) of, or in any of paragraphs 3, 5, 7, 10, 12 and 14 to 30 of Schedule 1 to, the Commissioners for Revenue and Customs Act 2005.

(6)   Cash means—

    (a)   notes and coins in any currency,

    (b)   postal orders,

    (c)   cheques of any kind, including travellers' cheques,

    (d)   bankers' drafts,

    (e)   bearer bonds and bearer shares,

found at any place in the United Kingdom.

(7)[3]   Cash also includes any kind of monetary instrument which is found at any place in the United Kingdom, if the instrument is specified by the Secretary of State by an order made after consultation with the Scottish Ministers or, in relation to Northern Ireland, is specified by the Department of Justice by an order.

(8)   This section does not require a person to submit to an intimate search or strip search (within the meaning of section 164 of the Customs and Excise Management Act 1979 (c. 2)).

Prior approval

290.—[4, 5, 6](1)   The powers conferred by section 289 may be exercised only with the appropriate approval unless, in the circumstances, it is not practicable to obtain that approval before exercising the power.

(2)   The appropriate approval means the approval of a judicial officer or (if that is not practicable in any case) the approval of a senior officer.

(3)   A judicial officer means—

---

[1] As inserted by the Finance Act 2013 (c.29) Sch.48 para.2(2) (effective July 17, 2013).

[2] As inserted by the Finance Act 2013 (c.29) Sch.48 para.2(2) (effective July 17, 2013).

[3] As amended by the Northern Ireland Act 1998 (Devolution of Policing and Justice Functions) Order 2010 (SI 2010/976) Sch.14 para.57 (effective April 12, 2010: amendment has effect subject to transitional provision specified in SI 2010/976 art.28).

[4] As amended by the Serious Crime Act 2007 (c.27) Sch.11 para.3 (effective April 6, 2008 subject to transitional and transitory provisions and savings as specified in SI 2008/755 art. 17(2) and (3)).

[5] As amended by the Finance Act 2013 (c.29) Sch.48 para.2(2) (effective July 17, 2013).

[6] As amended by the Serious Crime Act 2007 (c.27) Sch.11 para.3 (effective April 6, 2008 subject to transitional and transitory provisions and savings as specified in SI 2008/755 art. 17(2) and (3)).

(a) in relation to England and Wales and Northern Ireland, a justice of the peace,

(b) in relation to Scotland, the sheriff.

(4) A senior officer means—

[1](a) in relation to the exercise of the power by an officer of Revenue and Customs, such an officer of a rank designated by the Commissioners of Customs and Excise as equivalent to that of a senior police officer,

(b) in relation to the exercise of the power by a constable, a senior police officer.

(c) in relation to the exercise of the power by an accredited financial investigator, an accredited financial investigator who falls within a description specified in an order made for this purpose by the Secretary of State under section 453.

(5) A senior police officer means a police officer of at least the rank of inspector.

(6) If the powers are exercised without the approval of a judicial officer in a case where—

(a) no cash is seized by virtue of section 294, or

(b)[2, 3] any cash so seized is not detained for more than 48 hours (calculated in accordance with section 295(1B))

officer of Revenue and Customs, constable or accredited financial investigator who exercised the powers must give a written report to the appointed person.

(7) The report must give particulars of the circumstances which led him to believe that—

(a) the powers were exercisable, and

(b) it was not practicable to obtain the approval of a judicial officer.

(8) In this section and section 291, the appointed person means—

(a)[4] in relation to England and Wales, a person appointed by the Secretary of State,

(b) in relation to Scotland, a person appointed by the Scottish Ministers,

(c)[5] in relation to Northern Ireland, a person appointed by the Department of Justice.

(9) The appointed person must not be a person employed under or for the purposes of a government department or of the Scottish Administration; and the terms and conditions of his appointment, including any remuneration or expenses to be paid to him, are to be determined by the person appointing him.

Report on exercise of powers

291.—(1) As soon as possible after the end of each financial year, the appointed person must prepare a report for that year.

"Financial year" means—

---

[1] As amended by the Finance Act 2013 (c.29) Sch.48 para.3 (effective July 17, 2013).
[2] As amended by the Serious Organised Crime and Police Act 2005 (c.15) s.100(3) (effective July 1, 2005).
[3] As amended by the Finance Act 2013 (c.29) Sch.48 para.3 (effective July 17, 2013).
[4] As amended by the Northern Ireland Act 1998 (Devolution of Policing and Justice Functions) Order 2010 (SI 2010/976) Sch.14 para.58(a) (effective April 12, 2010: amendment has effect subject to transitional provision specified in SI 2010/976 art.28).
[5] As inserted by the Northern Ireland Act 1998 (Devolution of Policing and Justice Functions) Order 2010 (SI 2010/976) Sch.14 para.58(b) (effective April 12, 2010: insertion has effect subject to transitional provision specified in SI 2010/976 art.28).

(a)   the period beginning with the day on which this section comes into force and ending with the next 31 March (which is the first financial year), and

(b)   each subsequent period of twelve months beginning with 1 April.

[1](2)[2]   The report must give his opinion as to the circumstances and manner in which the powers conferred by section 289 are being exercised in cases where the officer of Revenue and Customs, constable or accredited financial investigator who exercised them is required to give a report under section 290(6).

(3)   In the report, he may make any recommendations he considers appropriate.

(4)[3]   He must send a copy of his report to the Secretary of State or, as the case may be, the Scottish Ministers or the Department of Justice, who must arrange for it to be published.

(5)[4]   The Secretary of State must lay a copy of any report he receives under this section before Parliament; and the Scottish Ministers must lay a copy of any report they receive under this section before the Scottish Parliament; and the Department of Justice must lay a copy of any report it receives under this section before the Northern Ireland Assembly.

(6)[5]   Section 41(3) of the Interpretation Act (Northern Ireland) 1954 applies for the purposes of subsection (5) in relation to the laying of a copy of a report as it applies in relation to the laying of a statutory document under an enactment.

Code of practice

292.—[6, 7](1)[8]   The Secretary of State must make a code of practice in connection with the exercise by officers of Revenue and Customs and (in relation to England and Wales) constables and accredited financial investigators of the powers conferred by virtue of section 289.

(2)   Where he proposes to issue a code of practice he must—

(a)   publish a draft,

(b)[9]   consider any representations made to him about the draft by the Scottish Ministers, the Department of Justice or any other person,

(c)   if he thinks it appropriate, modify the draft in the light of any such representations.

---

[1] As amended by the Finance Act 2013 (c.29) Sch.48 para.4 (effective July 17, 2013).

[2] As amended by the Serious Crime Act 2007 (c.27) Sch.11 para.4 (effective April 6, 2008 subject to transitional and transitory provisions and savings as specified in SI 2008/755 art. 17(2) and (3)).

[3] As amended by the Northern Ireland Act 1998 (Devolution of Policing and Justice Functions) Order 2010 (SI 2010/976) Sch.14 para.59 (effective April 12, 2010: amendment has effect subject to transitional provision specified in SI 2010/976 art.28).

[4] As amended by the Northern Ireland Act 1998 (Devolution of Policing and Justice Functions) Order 2010 (SI 2010/976) Sch.14 para.59 (effective April 12, 2010: amendment has effect subject to transitional provision specified in SI 2010/976 art.28).

[5] As inserted by the Northern Ireland Act 1998 (Devolution of Policing and Justice Functions) Order 2010 (SI 2010/976) Sch.14 para.59 (effective April 12, 2010: insertion has effect subject to transitional provision specified in SI 2010/976 art.28).

[6] As amended by the Finance Act 2013 (c.29) Sch.48 para.5 (effective July 17, 2013).

[7] As amended by the Serious Crime Act 2007 (c.27) Sch.11 para.5 (effective April 6, 2008 subject to transitional and transitory provisions and savings as specified in SI 2008/755 art. 17(2) and (3)).

[8] As amended by the Northern Ireland Act 1998 (Devolution of Policing and Justice Functions) Order 2010 (SI 2010/976) Sch.14 para.60 (effective April 12, 2010: amendment has effect subject to transitional provision specified in SI 2010/976 art.28).

[9] As amended by the Northern Ireland Act 1998 (Devolution of Policing and Justice Functions) Order 2010 (SI 2010/976) Sch.14 para.60 (effective April 12, 2010: amendment has effect subject to transitional provision specified in SI 2010/976 art.28).

(3)   He must lay a draft of the code before Parliament.

(4)   When he has laid a draft of the code before Parliament he may bring it into operation by order.

(5)   He may revise the whole or any part of the code issued by him and issue the code as revised; and subsections (2) to (4) apply to such a revised code as they apply to the original code.

[1](6)   A failure by an officer of Revenue and Customs, a constable or an accredited financial investigator to comply with a provision of the code does not of itself make him liable to criminal or civil proceedings.

(7)   The code is admissible in evidence in criminal or civil proceedings and is to be taken into account by a court or tribunal in any case in which it appears to the court or tribunal to be relevant.

Code of practice (Scotland)

293.—(1)   The Scottish Ministers must make a code of practice in connection with the exercise by constables in relation to Scotland of the powers conferred by virtue of section 289.

(2)   Where they propose to issue a code of practice they must—
   (a)   publish a draft,
   (b)   consider any representations made to them about the draft,
   (c)   if they think it appropriate, modify the draft in the light of any such representations.

(3)   They must lay a draft of the code before the Scottish Parliament.

(4)   When they have laid a draft of the code before the Scottish Parliament they may bring it into operation by order.

(5)   They may revise the whole or any part of the code issued by them and issue the code as revised; and subsections (2) to (4) apply to such a revised code as they apply to the original code.

(6)   A failure by a constable to comply with a provision of the code does not of itself make him liable to criminal or civil proceedings.

(7)   The code is admissible in evidence in criminal or civil proceedings and is to be taken into account by a court or tribunal in any case in which it appears to the court or tribunal to be relevant.

Code of practice (Northern Ireland)

293A.—[2](1)   The Department of Justice must make a code of practice in connection with the exercise by constables and accredited financial investigators, in relation to Northern Ireland, of the powers conferred by virtue of section 289.

(2)   Where the Department of Justice proposes to issue a code of practice it must—
   (a)   publish a draft,
   (b)   consider any representations made to the Department of Justice about the draft,
   (c)   if the Department of Justice thinks it appropriate, modify the draft in the light of any such representations.

---

[1] As amended by the Finance Act 2013 (c.29) Sch.48 para.5 (effective July 17, 2013).
[2] As inserted by the Northern Ireland Act 1998 (Devolution of Policing and Justice Functions) Order 2010 (SI 2010/976) Sch.14 para.61 (effective April 12, 2010: insertion has effect subject to transitional provision specified in SI 2010/976 art.28).

(3)   The Department of Justice must lay a draft of the code before the Northern Ireland Assembly.

(4)   When the Department of Justice has laid a draft of the code before the Northern Ireland Assembly, the Department of Justice may bring it into operation by order.

(5)   Section 41(3) of the Interpretation Act (Northern Ireland) 1954 applies for the purposes of subsections (3) and (4) in relation to the laying of a draft as it applies in relation to the laying of a statutory document under an enactment.

(6)   The Department of Justice may revise the whole or any part of the code issued by it and issue the code as revised; and subsections (2) to (5) apply to such a revised code as they apply to the original code.

(7)   A failure by a constable or accredited financial investigator to comply with a provision of the code does not of itself make him liable to criminal or civil proceedings.

(8)   The code is admissible in evidence in criminal or civil proceedings and is to be taken into account by a court or tribunal in any case in which it appears to the court or tribunal to be relevant.

Seizure and detention

Seizure of cash   F1.239

294.—[1, 2](1)   An officer of Revenue and Customs, a constable or an accredited financial investigator may seize any cash if he has reasonable grounds for suspecting that it is—

(a)   recoverable property, or

(b)   intended by any person for use in unlawful conduct.

(2)   An officer of Revenue and Customs, a constable or an accredited financial investigator may also seize cash part of which he has reasonable grounds for suspecting to be—

(a)   recoverable property, or

(b)   intended by any person for use in unlawful conduct,

if it is not reasonably practicable to seize only that part.

[3](2A)   The powers conferred by this section are exercisable by an officer of Revenue and Customs only so far as the officer is exercising a function relating to a matter other than an excluded matter.

[4](2B)   But the powers may be exercised by the officer in reliance on a suspicion that relates to an excluded matter.

[5](2C)   The reference in subsection (2A) to an excluded matter is to a matter specified in section 54(4)(b) of, or in any of paragraphs 3, 5, 7, 10, 12 and 14 to 30 of Schedule 1 to, the Commissioners for Revenue and Customs Act 2005.

(3)   This section does not authorise the seizure of an amount of cash if it or, as the case may be, the part to which his suspicion relates, is less than the minimum amount.

---

[1] As amended by the Serious Crime Act 2007 (c.27) Sch.11 para.6 (effective April 6, 2008 subject to transitional and transitory provisions and savings as specified in SI 2008/755 art. 17(2) and (3)).

[2] As amended by the Finance Act 2013 (c.29) Sch.48 para.6 (effective July 17, 2013).

[3] As inserted by the Finance Act 2013 (c.29) Sch.48 para.6 (effective July 17, 2013).

[4] As inserted by the Finance Act 2013 (c.29) Sch.48 para.6 (effective July 17, 2013).

[5] As inserted by the Finance Act 2013 (c.29) Sch.48 para.6 (effective July 17, 2013).

(4)   This section does not authorise the seizure by an accredited financial investigator of cash found in Scotland.

F1.240   **Detention of seized cash**

295.—[12](1)   While the officer of Revenue and Customs, constable or accredited financial investigator continues to have reasonable grounds for his suspicion, cash seized under section 294 may be detained initially for a period of 48 hours.

(1A)[3]   The period of 48 hours mentioned in subsection (1) is to be calculated in accordance with subsection (1B).

(1B)[4]   In calculating a period of 48 hours in accordance with this subsection, no account shall be taken of—

(a)   any Saturday or Sunday,

(b)   Christmas Day,

(c)   Good Friday,

(d)   any day that is a bank holiday under the Banking and Financial Dealings Act 1971 in the part of the United Kingdom within which the cash is seized, or

(e)   any day prescribed under section 8(2) of the Criminal Procedure (Scotland) Act 1995 as a court holiday in a sheriff court in the sheriff court district within which the cash is seized.

(2)   The period for which the cash or any part of it may be detained may be extended by an order made by a magistrates' court or (in Scotland) the sheriff; but the order may not authorise the detention of any of the cash—

(a)[5]   beyond the end of the period of six months beginning with the date of the order,

(b)   in the case of any further order under this section, beyond the end of the period of two years beginning with the date of the first order.

(3)   A justice of the peace may also exercise the power of a magistrates' court to make the first order under subsection (2) extending the period.

(4)   An application for an order under subsection (2)—

(a)   in relation to England and Wales and Northern Ireland, may be made by the Commissioners of Customs and Excise, a constable or an accredited financial investigator,

(b)   in relation to Scotland, may be made by the Scottish Ministers in connection with their functions under section 298 or by a procurator fiscal,

and the court, sheriff or justice may make the order if satisfied, in relation to any cash to be further detained, that either of the following conditions is met.

(5)   The first condition is that there are reasonable grounds for suspecting that the cash is recoverable property and that either—

(a)   its continued detention is justified while its derivation is further investigated or consideration is given to bringing (in the United

---

[1] As amended by the Serious Crime Act 2007 (c.27) Sch.11 para.7 (effective April 6, 2008 subject to transitional and transitory provisions and savings as specified in SI 2008/755 art. 17(2) and (3)).

[2] As amended by the Finance Act 2013 (c.29) Sch.48 para.7 (effective July 17, 2013).

[3] As inserted by the Serious Organised Crime and Police Act 2005 (c.15) s.100(2) (effective July 1, 2005).

[4] As inserted by the Serious Organised Crime and Police Act 2005 (c.15) s.100(2) (effective July 1, 2005).

[5] As substituted by the Policing and Crime Act 2009 (c.26) Pt 5 s.64(1) (effective January 25, 2010).

Kingdom or elsewhere) proceedings against any person for an offence with which the cash is connected, or

(b) proceedings against any person for an offence with which the cash is connected have been started and have not been concluded.

(6) The second condition is that there are reasonable grounds for suspecting that the cash is intended to be used in unlawful conduct and that either—

(a) its continued detention is justified while its intended use is further investigated or consideration is given to bringing (in the United Kingdom or elsewhere) proceedings against any person for an offence with which the cash is connected, or

(b) proceedings against any person for an offence with which the cash is connected have been started and have not been concluded.

(7) An application for an order under subsection (2) may also be made in respect of any cash seized under section 294(2), and the court, sheriff or justice may make the order if satisfied that—

(a) the condition in subsection (5) or (6) is met in respect of part of the cash, and

(b) it is not reasonably practicable to detain only that part.

(8) An order under subsection (2) must provide for notice to be given to persons affected by it.

Interest

296.—[1](1) If cash is detained under section 295 for more than 48 hours (calculated in accordance with section 295(1B)) it is at the first opportunity to be paid into an interest-bearing account and held there; and the interest accruing on it is to be added to it on its forfeiture or release.

[2, 3](2) In the case of cash detained under section 295 which was seized under section 294(2), the officer of Revenue and Customs, a constable or an accredited financial investigator must, on paying it into the account, release the part of the cash to which the suspicion does not relate.

(3) Subsection (1) does not apply if the cash or, as the case may be, the part to which the suspicion relates is required as evidence of an offence or evidence in proceedings under this Chapter.

Release of detained cash

297.—[4](1) This section applies while any cash is detained under section 295.

(2) A magistrates' court or (in Scotland) the sheriff may direct the release of the whole or any part of the cash if the following condition is met.

(3) The condition is that the court or sheriff is satisfied, on an application by the person from whom the cash was seized, that the conditions in section 295 for the detention of the cash are no longer met in relation to the cash to be released.

---

[1] As amended by the Serious Organised Crime and Police Act 2005 (c.15) s.100(3) (effective July 1, 2005).

[2] As substituted by the Serious Crime Act 2007 (c.27) Sch.11 para.8 (effective April 6, 2008 subject to transitional and transitory provisions and savings as specified in SI 2008/755 art. 17(2) and (3)).

[3] As amended by the Finance Act 2013 (c.29) Sch.48 para.9 (effective July 17, 2013).

[4] As amended by the Serious Crime Act 2007 (c.27) Sch.11 para.9 (effective April 6, 2008 subject to transitional and transitory provisions and savings as specified in SI 2008/755 art. 17(2) and (3)).

[1](4)   An officer of Revenue and Customs, constable or accredited financial investigator or (in Scotland) procurator fiscal may, after notifying the magistrates' court, sheriff or justice under whose order cash is being detained, release the whole or any part of it if satisfied that the detention of the cash to be released is no longer justified.

Forfeiture without court order

Forfeiture notice

297A.—[2](1)   Subsection (2) applies while any cash is detained in pursuance of an order under section 295(2) made by a magistrates' court in England and Wales or Northern Ireland.

(2)   A senior officer may give a notice for the purpose of forfeiting the cash or any part of it if satisfied that the cash or part—

(a)   is recoverable property, or

(b)   is intended by any person for use in unlawful conduct.

(3)   The Secretary of State must make regulations about how a notice is to be given.

(4)   The regulations may provide—

(a)   for a notice to be given to such person or persons, and in such manner, as may be prescribed;

(b)   for a notice to be given by publication in such manner as may be prescribed;

(c)   for circumstances in which, and the time at which, a notice is to be treated as having been given.

(5)   The regulations must ensure that where a notice is given it is, if possible, given to every person to whom notice of an order under section 295(2) in respect of the cash has been given.

(6)   A senior officer means—

(a)   an officer of Revenue and Customs of a rank designated by the Commissioners for Her Majesty's Revenue and Customs as equivalent to that of a senior police officer,

(b)   a senior police officer, or

(c)   an accredited financial investigator.

(7)   A senior police officer means a police officer of at least the rank of inspector.

(8)   A notice under this section is referred to in this Chapter as a forfeiture notice.

Content

297B.—[3](1)   A forfeiture notice must—

(a)   state the amount of cash in respect of which it is given,

(b)   state when and where the cash was seized,

(c)   confirm that the senior officer is satisfied as mentioned in section 297A(2),

---

[1] As amended by the Finance Act 2013 (c.29) Sch.48 para.9 (effective July 17, 2013).

[2] Prospectively inserted by the Policing and Crime Act 2009 (c.26) Pt 5 s.65(1) (date to be appointed and not yet in force).

[3] Prospectively inserted by the Policing and Crime Act 2009 (c.26) Pt 5 s.65(1) (date to be appointed and not yet in force).

(d) specify a period for objecting to the proposed forfeiture and an address to which any objections must be sent, and

(e) explain that the cash will be forfeited unless an objection is received at that address within the period for objecting.

(2) The period for objecting must be at least 30 days starting with the day after the notice is given.

Effect

297C.—[1](1) This section applies if a forfeiture notice is given in respect of any cash.

(2) The cash is to be detained until—

(a) the cash is forfeited under this section,

(b) the notice lapses under this section, or

(c) the cash is released under a power conferred by this Chapter.

(3) If no objection is made within the period for objecting, and the notice has not lapsed, the cash is forfeited (subject to section 297E).

(4) If an objection is made within the period for objecting, the notice lapses.

(5) If an application is made for the forfeiture of the whole or any part of the cash under section 298, the notice lapses.

(6) If the cash or any part of it is released under a power conferred by this Chapter, the notice lapses or (as the case may be) lapses in relation to that part.

(7) An objection may be made by anyone, whether a recipient of the notice or not.

(8) An objection means a written objection sent to the address specified in the notice; and an objection is made when it is received at the address.

(9) An objection does not prevent forfeiture of the cash under section 298.

(10) Nothing in this section affects the validity of an order under section 295(2).

Detention following lapse of notice

297D.—[2](1) This section applies if—

(a) a forfeiture notice is given in respect of any cash,

(b) the notice lapses under section 297C(4), and

(c) the period for which detention of the cash was authorised under section 295(2) has expired.

(2) The cash may be detained for a further period of up to 48 hours (calculated in accordance with section 295(1B)).

(3) But if within that period the Commissioners for Her Majesty's Revenue and Customs, a constable or an accredited financial investigator decides that neither of the applications mentioned in subsection (4) ought to be made, the cash must be released.

(4) The applications are—

(a) an application for a further order under section 295(2);

(b) an application for forfeiture of the cash under section 298.

---

[1] Prospectively inserted by the Policing and Crime Act 2009 (c.26) Pt 5 s.65(1) (date to be appointed and not yet in force).
[2] Prospectively inserted by the Policing and Crime Act 2009 (c.26) Pt 5 s.65(1) (date to be appointed and not yet in force).

(5)   If within that period an application is made for a further order under section 295(2) the cash may be detained until the application is determined or otherwise disposed of.

Application to set aside forfeiture

297E.—[1](1)   This section applies if any cash is forfeited in pursuance of a forfeiture notice.

(2)   A person aggrieved by the forfeiture may apply to a magistrates' court in England and Wales or Northern Ireland for an order setting aside the forfeiture of the cash or any part of it.

(3)   The application must be made before the end of the period of 30 days starting with the day on which the period for objecting ended.

(4)   But the court may give permission for an application to be made after the 30-day period has ended if it thinks that there are exceptional circumstances to explain why the applicant—

    (a)   failed to object to the forfeiture within the period for objecting, and

    (b)   failed to make an application within the 30-day period.

(5)   On an application under this section the court must consider whether the cash to which the application relates could be forfeited under section 298 (ignoring the forfeiture mentioned in subsection (1) above).

(6)   If the court is satisfied that the cash to which the application relates or any part of it could not be forfeited under that section it must set aside the forfeiture of that cash or part.

(7)   Where the court sets aside the forfeiture of any cash—

    (a)   it must order the release of that cash, and

    (b)   that cash is to be treated as never having been forfeited.

Release of cash subject to forfeiture notice

297F.—[2](1)   This section applies while any cash is detained under section 297C or 297D.

(2)   A magistrates' court may direct the release of the whole or any part of the cash if the following condition is met.

(3)   The condition is that the court is not satisfied, on an application by the person from whom the cash was seized, that the cash to be released—

    (a)   is recoverable property, or

    (b)   is intended by any person for use in unlawful conduct.

(4)   An officer of Revenue and Customs, constable or accredited financial investigator may release the cash or any part of it if satisfied that the detention of the cash to be released is no longer justified.

Application of forfeited cash

297G.—[3](1)   Cash forfeited in pursuance of a forfeiture notice, and any accrued interest on it, is to be paid into the Consolidated Fund.

---

[1] Prospectively inserted by the Policing and Crime Act 2009 (c.26) Pt 5 s.65(1) (date to be appointed and not yet in force).

[2] Prospectively inserted by the Policing and Crime Act 2009 (c.26) Pt 5 s.65(1) (date to be appointed and not yet in force).

[3] Prospectively inserted by the Policing and Crime Act 2009 (c.26) Pt 5 s.65(1) (date to be appointed and not yet in force).

(2) But it is not to be paid in—

    (a) before the end of the period within which an application under section 297E may be made (ignoring the possibility of an application by virtue of section 297E(4)), or

    (b) if an application is made within that period, before the application is determined or otherwise disposed of.

Forfeiture

Forfeiture

298.—[1](1) While cash is detained under section 295, an application for the forfeiture of the whole or any part of it may be made—

    (a) to a magistrates' court by the Commissioners of Customs and Excise, an accredited financial investigator or a constable,

    (b) (in Scotland) to the sheriff by the Scottish Ministers.

(2) The court or sheriff may order the forfeiture of the cash or any part of it if satisfied that the cash or part—

    (a) is recoverable property, or

    (b) is intended by any person for use in unlawful conduct.

(3) But in the case of recoverable property which belongs to joint tenants, one of whom is an excepted joint owner, the order may not apply to so much of it as the court thinks is attributable to the excepted joint owner's share.

(4) Where an application for the forfeiture of any cash is made under this section, the cash is to be detained (and may not be released under any power conferred by this Chapter) until any proceedings in pursuance of the application (including any proceedings on appeal) are concluded.

Appeal against decision under section 298

299.—[2](1) Any party to proceedings for an order for the forfeiture of cash under section 298 who is aggrieved by an order under that section or by the decision of the court not to make such an order may appeal—

    (a) in relation to England and Wales, to the Crown Court;

    (b) in relation to Scotland, to the Sheriff Principal;

    (c) in relation to Northern Ireland, to a county court.

(2) An appeal under subsection (1) must be made before the end of the period of 30 days starting with the day on which the court makes the order or decision.

(3) The court hearing the appeal may make any order it thinks appropriate.

(4) If the court upholds an appeal against an order forfeiting the cash, it may order the release of the cash.

Application of forfeited cash

300.—(1) Cash forfeited under this Chapter, and any accrued interest on it—

    (a) if forfeited by a magistrates' court in England and Wales or Northern Ireland, is to be paid into the Consolidated Fund,

---

[1] As amended by the Serious Crime Act 2007 (c.27) Sch.11 para.10 (effective April 6, 2008 subject to transitional and transitory provisions and savings as specified in SI 2008/755 art. 17(2) and (3)).

[2] As substituted by the Serious Organised Crime and Police Act 2005 (c.15) s.101(1) (effective July 1, 2005).

    (b)   if forfeited by the sheriff, is to be paid into the Scottish Consolidated Fund.

(2)   But it is not to be paid in—

    (a)   before the end of the period within which an appeal under section 299 may be made, or

    (b)   if a person appeals under that section, before the appeal is determined or otherwise disposed of.

Supplementary

Victims and other owners

301.—(1)   A person who claims that any cash detained under this Chapter, or any part of it, belongs to him may apply to a magistrates' court or (in Scotland) the sheriff for the cash or part to be released to him.

(2)   The application may be made in the course of proceedings under section 295 or 298 or at any other time.

(3)   If it appears to the court or sheriff concerned that—

    (a)   the applicant was deprived of the cash to which the application relates, or of property which it represents, by unlawful conduct,

    (b)   the property he was deprived of was not, immediately before he was deprived of it, recoverable property, and

    (c)   that cash belongs to him,

the court or sheriff may order the cash to which the application relates to be released to the applicant.

(4)   If—

    (a)   the applicant is not the person from whom the cash to which the application relates was seized,

    (b)   it appears to the court or sheriff that that cash belongs to the applicant,

    (c)   the court or sheriff is satisfied that the conditions in section 295 for the detention of that cash are no longer met or, if an application has been made under section 298, the court or sheriff decides not to make an order under that section in relation to that cash, and

    (d)   no objection to the making of an order under this subsection has been made by the person from whom that cash was seized,

the court or sheriff may order the cash to which the application relates to be released to the applicant or to the person from whom it was seized.

(5)[1]   The release condition is met—

    (a)   in relation to cash detained under section 295, if the conditions in that section for the detention of the cash are no longer met,

    (b)   in relation to cash detained under section 297C or 297D, if the cash is not recoverable property and is not intended by a person for use in unlawful conduct, and

    (c)   in relation to cash detained under 298, if the court or sheriff decides not to make an order under that section in relation to the cash.

---

[1] Prospectively inserted by the Policing and Crime Act 2009 (c.26) Sch.7(7) para.108 (not yet in force).

Compensation   F1.254

302.—(1) If no forfeiture order is made in respect of any cash detained under this Chapter, the person to whom the cash belongs or from whom it was seized may make an application to the magistrates' court or (in Scotland) the sheriff for compensation.

(2)[1] If, for any period beginning with the first opportunity to place the cash in an interest-bearing account after the initial detention of the cash for 48 hours (calculated in accordance with section 295(1B), the cash was not held in an interest-bearing account while detained, the court or sheriff may order an amount of compensation to be paid to the applicant.

(3) The amount of compensation to be paid under subsection (2) is the amount the court or sheriff thinks would have been earned in interest in the period in question if the cash had been held in an interest-bearing account.

(4) If the court or sheriff is satisfied that, taking account of any interest to be paid under section 296 or any amount to be paid under subsection (2), the applicant has suffered loss as a result of the detention of the cash and that the circumstances are exceptional, the court or sheriff may order compensation (or additional compensation) to be paid to him.

(5) The amount of compensation to be paid under subsection (4) is the amount the court or sheriff thinks reasonable, having regard to the loss suffered and any other relevant circumstances.

[2](6) If the cash was seized by an officer of Revenue and Customs, the compensation is to be paid by the Commissioners of Customs and Excise.

[3](7) If the cash was seized by a constable, the compensation is to be paid as follows—

   (a) in the case of a constable of a police force in England and Wales, it is to be paid out of the police fund from which the expenses of the police force are met,

   (b) in the case of a constable of a police force in Scotland, it is to be paid by the Scottish Police Authority,

   (ba) in the case of a constable of the Police Service of Scotland, it is to be paid by the Scottish Police Authority,

   (c) in the case of a police officer within the meaning of the Police (Northern Ireland) Act 2000 (c. 32), it is to be paid out of money provided by the Chief Constable.

(7A)[4] If the cash was seized by an accredited financial investigator who was not an officer of Revenue and Customs or a constable, the compensation is to be paid as follows—

   (a) in the case of an investigator—

---

[1] As amended by the Serious Organised Crime and Police Act 2005 (c.15) s.100(3) (effective July 1, 2005).
[2] As amended by the Finance Act 2013 (c.29) Sch.48 para.10 (effective July 17, 2013).
[3] As amended by the Police and Fire Reform (Scotland) Act 2012 (Consequential Modifications and Savings) Order 2013 (SSI 2013/119) Sch.1(1) para.19(3) (effective April 1, 2013).
[4] As inserted by the Serious Crime Act 2007 (c.27) Sch.11 para.11 (effective April 6, 2008 subject to transitional and transitory provisions and savings as specified in SI 2008/755 art. 17(2) and (3)).

       (i)[1] who was a member of the civilian staff of a police force, including the metropolitan police force, (within the meaning of that Part of that Act), or

      (ii) who was a member of staff of the City of London police force, it is to be paid out of the police fund from which the expenses of the police force are met,

  (b) in the case of an investigator who was a member of staff of the Police Service of Northern Ireland, it is to be paid out of money provided by the Chief Constable,

  (c) in the case of an investigator who was a member of staff of a department of the Government of the United Kingdom, it is to be paid by the Minister of the Crown in charge of the department or by the department,

  (d) in the case of an investigator who was a member of staff of a Northern Ireland department, it is to be paid by the department,

  (e) in any other case, it is to be paid by the employer of the investigator.

(7B)[2] The Secretary of State may by order amend subsection (7A).

(7C)[3] If any cash is detained under this Chapter and part only of the cash is forfeited in pursuance of a forfeiture notice, this section has effect in relation to the other part.

(8) If a forfeiture order is made in respect only of a part of any cash detained under this Chapter, this section has effect in relation to the other part.

(9)[4] The power in subsection (7B) is exercisable by the Department of Justice (and not by the Secretary of State) so far as it may be used to make provision which could be made by an Act of the Northern Ireland Assembly without the consent of the Secretary of State (see sections 6 to 8 of the Northern Ireland Act 1998).

F1.255   **Powers for prosecutors to appear in proceedings**

302A.—[5](1) The Director of Public Prosecutions or the Director of Public Prosecutions for Northern Ireland may appear for a constable or an accredited financial investigator in proceedings under this Chapter if the Director—

  (a) is asked by, or on behalf of, a constable or (as the case may be) an accredited financial investigator to do so, and

  (b) considers it appropriate to do so.

(2)[6] The Director of Public Prosecutions may appear for the Commissioners for Her Majesty's Revenue and Customs or an officer of Revenue and Customs in proceedings under this Chapter if the Director—

  (a) is asked by, or on behalf of, the Commissioners for Her Majesty's

---

[1] As substituted by the Police Reform and Social Responsibility Act 2011 (c.13) Sch.16(3) para.306 (effective January 16, 2012).

[2] As inserted by the Serious Crime Act 2007 (c.27) Sch.11 para.11 (effective April 6, 2008 subject to transitional and transitory provisions and savings as specified in SI 2008/755 art. 17(2) and (3)).

[3] Prospectively inserted by the Policing and Crime Act 2009 (c.26) Sch.7(7) para.109 (not yet in force).

[4] As inserted by the Northern Ireland Act 1998 (Devolution of Policing and Justice Functions) Order 2010 (SI 2010/976) Sch.14 para.62(2) (effective April 12, 2010: insertion has effect subject to transitional provision specified in SI 2010/976 art.28).

[5] As inserted by the Serious Crime Act 2007 (c.27) Pt 3 s.84(1) and Sch.11 para.12 (effective April 6, 2008 subject to transitional and transitory provisions and savings as specified in SI 2008/755 art. 17(2) and (3)).

[6] As amended by the Public Bodies (Merger of the Director of Public Prosecutions and the Director of Revenue and Customs Prosecutions) Order 2014 (SI 2014/834) Sch.2 para.24 (effective March 27, 2014).

Revenue and Customs or (as the case may be) an officer of Revenue and Customs to do so, and

(b)   considers it appropriate to do so.

(3)   The Directors may charge fees for the provision of services under this section.

(4)   The references in subsection (1) to an accredited financial investigator do not include an accredited financial investigator who is an officer of Revenue and Customs but the references in subsection (2) to an officer of Revenue and Customs do include an accredited financial investigator who is an officer of Revenue and Customs.

"The minimum amount"

303.—[1](1)   In this Chapter, the minimum amount is the amount in sterling specified in an order made by the Secretary of State after consultation with the Scottish Ministers and the Department of Justice.

(2)   For that purpose the amount of any cash held in a currency other than sterling must be taken to be its sterling equivalent, calculated in accordance with the prevailing rate of exchange.

Financial investigators

303A.—[2](1)   In this Chapter (apart from this section) any reference in a provision to an accredited financial investigator is a reference to an accredited financial investigator who falls within a description specified in an order made for the purposes of that provision by the Secretary of State under section 453.

(2)   Subsection (1) does not apply to the second reference to an accredited financial investigator in section 290(4)(c).

(3)   Where an accredited financial investigator of a particular description—

(a)   applies for an order under section 295,

(b)   applies for forfeiture under section 298, or

(c)   brings an appeal under, or relating to, this Chapter,

any subsequent step in the application or appeal, or any further application or appeal relating to the same matter, may be taken, made or brought by a different accredited financial investigator of the same description.

Chapter 4 – – General

Recoverable property

Property obtained through unlawful conduct

304.—(1)   Property obtained through unlawful conduct is recoverable property.

(2)   But if property obtained through unlawful conduct has been disposed of (since it was so obtained), it is recoverable property only if it is held by a person into whose hands it may be followed.

---

[1] As amended by the Northern Ireland Act 1998 (Devolution of Policing and Justice Functions) Order 2010 (SI 2010/976) Sch.14 para.63 (effective April 12, 2010: amendment has effect subject to transitional provision specified in SI 2010/976 art.28).
[2] As inserted by the Serious Crime Act 2007 (c.27) Sch.11 para. 13 (effective April 6, 2008 subject to transitional and transitory provisions and savings as specified in SI 2008/755 art. 17(2) and (3)).

(3)   Recoverable property obtained through unlawful conduct may be followed into the hands of a person obtaining it on a disposal by—

  (a)   the person who through the conduct obtained the property, or
  (b)   a person into whose hands it may (by virtue of this subsection) be followed.

Tracing property, etc.

305.—(1)   Where property obtained through unlawful conduct ("the original property") is or has been recoverable, property which represents the original property is also recoverable property.

(2)   If a person enters into a transaction by which—

  (a)   he disposes of recoverable property, whether the original property or property which (by virtue of this Chapter) represents the original property, and
  (b)   he obtains other property in place of it,

the other property represents the original property.

(3)   If a person disposes of recoverable property which represents the original property, the property may be followed into the hands of the person who obtains it (and it continues to represent the original property).

Mixing property

306.—(1)   Subsection (2) applies if a person's recoverable property is mixed with other property (whether his property or another's).

(2)   The portion of the mixed property which is attributable to the recoverable property represents the property obtained through unlawful conduct.

(3)   Recoverable property is mixed with other property if (for example) it is used—

  (a)   to increase funds held in a bank account,
  (b)   in part payment for the acquisition of an asset,
  (c)   for the restoration or improvement of land,
  (d)   by a person holding a leasehold interest in the property to acquire the freehold.

Recoverable property: accruing profits

307.—(1)   This section applies where a person who has recoverable property obtains further property consisting of profits accruing in respect of the recoverable property.

(2)   The further property is to be treated as representing the property obtained through unlawful conduct.

General exceptions

308.—(1)   If—

  (a)   a person disposes of recoverable property, and
  (b)   the person who obtains it on the disposal does so in good faith, for value and without notice that it was recoverable property,

the property may not be followed into that person's hands and, accordingly, it ceases to be recoverable.

(2)   If recoverable property is vested, forfeited or otherwise disposed of in pursuance of powers conferred by virtue of this Part, it ceases to be recoverable.

(3) If—

    (a) in pursuance of a judgment in civil proceedings (whether in the United Kingdom or elsewhere), the defendant makes a payment to the claimant or the claimant otherwise obtains property from the defendant,

    (b) the claimant's claim is based on the defendant's unlawful conduct, and

    (c) apart from this subsection, the sum received, or the property obtained, by the claimant would be recoverable property,

the property ceases to be recoverable.

In relation to Scotland, "claimant" and "defendant" are to be read as "pursuer" and "defender".

(4) If—

    (a)[1] a payment is made to a person in pursuance of a compensation order under Article 14 of the Criminal Justice (Northern Ireland) Order 1994 (S.I. 1994/2795 (N.I. 15)), section 249 of the Criminal Procedure (Scotland) Act 1995 (c. 46) or section 130 of the Powers of Criminal Courts (Sentencing) Act 2000 (c. 6) or in pursuance of a service compensation order under the Armed Forces Act 2006, and

    (b) apart from this subsection, the sum received would be recoverable property,

the property ceases to be recoverable.

(5) If—

    (a) a payment is made to a person in pursuance of a restitution order under section 27 of the Theft Act (Northern Ireland) 1969 (c. 16 (N.I.)) or section 148(2) of the Powers of Criminal Courts (Sentencing) Act 2000 or a person otherwise obtains any property in pursuance of such an order, and

    (b) apart from this subsection, the sum received, or the property obtained, would be recoverable property,

the property ceases to be recoverable.

(6) If—

    (a) in pursuance of an order made by the court under section 382(3) or 383(5) of the Financial Services and Markets Act 2000 (c. 8) (restitution orders), an amount is paid to or distributed among any persons in accordance with the court's directions, and

    (b) apart from this subsection, the sum received by them would be recoverable property,

the property ceases to be recoverable.

(7) If—

    (a)[2] in pursuance of a requirement of the Financial Conduct Authority, the Prudential Regulation Authority or the Bank of England under or by virtue of section 384(5) of the Financial Services and Markets Act 2000 (power to require restitution), an amount is paid to or distributed among any persons, and

    (b) apart from this subsection, the sum received by them would be recoverable property,

the property ceases to be recoverable.

---

[1] As amended by the Armed Forces Act 2006 (c.52) Sch.16 para.197 (effective October 31, 2009).
[2] As amended by the Financial Services Act 2012 (c.21) Sch.18(2) para.94(3) (effective April 1, 2013).

(7A)[1]   If—

(a)   a payment is made to a person in pursuance of an unlawful profit order under section 4 of the Prevention of Social Housing Fraud Act 2013, and

(b)   apart from this subsection, the sum received would be recoverable property, the property ceases to be recoverable.

(8)   Property is not recoverable while a restraint order applies to it, that is—

(a)   an order under section 41, 120 or 190, or

(b)   an order under any corresponding provision of an enactment mentioned in section 8(7)(a) to (g).

(8A)[2]   Property is not recoverable while it is detained under or by virtue of section 44A, 47J, 47K, 47M, 47P, 122A, 127J, 127K, 127M, 127P, 193A, 195J, 195K, 195M or 195P.

(9)   Property is not recoverable if it has been taken into account in deciding the amount of a person's benefit from criminal conduct for the purpose of making a confiscation order, that is—

(a)   an order under section 6, 92 or 156, or

(b)   an order under a corresponding provision of an enactment mentioned in section 8(7)(a) to (g),

and, in relation to an order mentioned in paragraph (b), the reference to the amount of a person's benefit from criminal conduct is to be read as a reference to the corresponding amount under the enactment in question.

(10)   Where—

(a)   a person enters into a transaction to which section 305(2) applies, and

(b)   the disposal is one to which subsection (1) or (2) applies,

this section does not affect the recoverability (by virtue of section 305(2)) of any property obtained on the transaction in place of the property disposed of.

Other exemptions

309.—(1)   An order may provide that property is not recoverable or (as the case may be) associated property if—

(a)   it is prescribed property, or

(b)   it is disposed of in pursuance of a prescribed enactment or an enactment of a prescribed description.

(2)   An order may provide that if property is disposed of in pursuance of a prescribed enactment or an enactment of a prescribed description, it is to be treated for the purposes of section 278 as if it had been disposed of in pursuance of a recovery order.

(3)   An order under this section may be made so as to apply to property, or a disposal of property, only in prescribed circumstances; and the circumstances may relate to the property or disposal itself or to a person who holds or has held the property or to any other matter.

---

[1] Prospectively inserted by the Prevention of Social Housing Fraud Act 2013 (c.3) Sch.1 para.23 (not yet in force).

[2] Prospectively inserted by the Policing and Crime Act 2009 (c.26) Sch.7(7) para.106 (not yet in force).

(4)[1] In this section, an order means an order made by the Secretary of State after consultation with the Scottish Ministers and the Department of Justice, and prescribed means prescribed by the order.

Granting interests

F1.264

310.—(1) If a person grants an interest in his recoverable property, the question whether the interest is also recoverable is to be determined in the same manner as it is on any other disposal of recoverable property.

(2) Accordingly, on his granting an interest in the property ("the property in question")—

   (a) where the property in question is property obtained through unlawful conduct, the interest is also to be treated as obtained through that conduct,

   (b) where the property in question represents in his hands property obtained through unlawful conduct, the interest is also to be treated as representing in his hands the property so obtained.

Insolvency

Insolvency

F1.265

311.—(1) Proceedings for a recovery order may not be taken or continued in respect of property to which subsection (3) applies unless the appropriate court gives leave and the proceedings are taken or (as the case may be) continued in accordance with any terms imposed by that court.

(2) An application for an order for the further detention of any cash to which subsection (3) applies may not be made under section 295 unless the appropriate court gives leave.

(3) This subsection applies to recoverable property, or property associated with it, if—

   (a) it is an asset of a company being wound up in pursuance of a resolution for voluntary winding up,

   (b) it is an asset of a company and a voluntary arrangement under Part 1 of the 1986 Act, or Part 2 of the 1989 Order, has effect in relation to the company,

   (c) an order under section 2 of the 1985 Act, section 286 of the 1986 Act or Article 259 of the 1989 Order (appointment of interim trustee or interim receiver) has effect in relation to the property,

   (d) it is an asset comprised in the estate of an individual who has been adjudged bankrupt or, in relation to Scotland, of a person whose estate has been sequestrated,

   (e) it is an asset of an individual and a voluntary arrangement under Part 8 of the 1986 Act, or Part 8 of the 1989 Order, has effect in relation to him, or

   (f) in relation to Scotland, it is property comprised in the estate of a person who has granted a trust deed within the meaning of the 1985 Act.

---

[1] As amended by the Northern Ireland Act 1998 (Devolution of Policing and Justice Functions) Order 2010 (SI 2010/976) Sch.14 para.64 (effective April 12, 2010: amendment has effect subject to transitional provision specified in SI 2010/976 art.28).

(4)   An application under this section, or under any provision of the 1986 Act or the 1989 Order, for leave to take proceedings for a recovery order may be made without notice to any person.

(5)   Subsection (4) does not affect any requirement for notice of an application to be given to any person acting as an insolvency practitioner or to the official receiver (whether or not acting as an insolvency practitioner).

(6)   References to the provisions of the 1986 Act in sections 420 and 421 of that Act, or to the provisions of the 1989 Order in Articles 364 or 365 of that Order, (insolvent partnerships and estates of deceased persons) include subsections (1) to (3) above.

(7)   In this section—

    (a)   the 1985 Act means the Bankruptcy (Scotland) Act 1985 (c. 66),

    (b)   the 1986 Act means the Insolvency Act 1986 (c. 45),

    (c)   the 1989 Order means the Insolvency (Northern Ireland) Order 1989 (S.I. 1989/2405 (N.I. 19)),

and in subsection (8) "the applicable enactment" means whichever enactment mentioned in paragraphs (a) to (c) is relevant to the resolution, arrangement, order or trust deed mentioned in subsection (3).

(8)   In this section—

    (a)   an asset means any property within the meaning of the applicable enactment or, where the 1985 Act is the applicable enactment, any property comprised in an estate to which the 1985 Act applies,

    (b)   the appropriate court means the court which, in relation to the resolution, arrangement, order or trust deed mentioned in subsection (3), is the court for the purposes of the applicable enactment or, in relation to Northern Ireland, the High Court,

    (c)   acting as an insolvency practitioner has the same meaning as in section 433,

    (d)   other expressions used in this section and in the applicable enactment have the same meaning as in that enactment.

Delegation of enforcement functions

F1.266   **Performance of functions of Scottish Ministers by constables in Scotland**

312.—(1)   In Scotland, a constable engaged in temporary service with the Scottish Ministers in connection with their functions under this Part may perform functions, other than those specified in subsection (2), on behalf of the Scottish Ministers.

(2)   The specified functions are the functions conferred on the Scottish Ministers by—

    (a)   sections 244(1) and (2) and 256(1) and (7) (proceedings in the Court of Session),

    (b)   section 267(2) (trustee for civil recovery),

    (c)   sections 271(3) and (4) and 272(5) (agreements about associated and joint property),

    (d)   section 275(3) (pension schemes),

    (e)   section 282(1) (exemptions),

    (f)   section 283(5) and (8) (compensation),

    (g)   section 287(2) (financial threshold),

    (h)   section 293(1) (code of practice),

    (i)   section 298(1) (forfeiture),

    (j)   section 303(1) (minimum amount).

Restriction on performance of Director's functions by police F1.267

313. *[As repealed subject to transitional and transitory provisions and savings as specified in SI 2008/755 arts 3–14 by the Serious Crime Act 2007 (c.27) Sch.14 para.1 (effective April 1, 2008).]*

Interpretation

Obtaining and disposing of property F1.268

314.—(1) References to a person disposing of his property include a reference—

(a) to his disposing of a part of it, or

(b) to his granting an interest in it,

(or to both); and references to the property disposed of are to any property obtained on the disposal.

(2) A person who makes a payment to another is to be treated as making a disposal of his property to the other, whatever form the payment takes.

(3) Where a person's property passes to another under a will or intestacy or by operation of law, it is to be treated as disposed of by him to the other.

(4) A person is only to be treated as having obtained his property for value in a case where he gave unexecuted consideration if the consideration has become executed consideration.

Northern Ireland courts F1.269

315. In relation to the practice and procedure of courts in Northern Ireland, expressions used in this Part are to be read in accordance with rules of court.

General interpretation F1.270

316.—[1, 2, 3](1) In this Part—

"associated property" has the meaning given by section 245,

"cash" has the meaning given by section 289(6) or (7),

"constable", in relation to Northern Ireland, means a police officer within the meaning of the Police (Northern Ireland) Act 2000 (c. 32),

"country" includes territory,

"the court" (except in sections 253(2) and (3) and 262(2) and (3) and Chapter 3) means the High Court or (in relation to proceedings in Scotland) the Court of Session,

"dealing" with property includes disposing of it, taking possession of it or removing it from the United Kingdom,

[4]"the Department of Justice" means the Department of Justice in Northern Ireland;

"enforcement authority"—

---

[1] As amended by the Serious Crime Act 2007 (c.27) Sch.8(2) para.91 (effective April 1, 2008).

[2] As amended by the Serious Organised Crime and Police Act 2005 (c.15) Sch.6 para.22 (effective January 1, 2006).

[3] As amended by the Crime and Courts Act 2013 (c.22) Sch.8(2) para.121 (effective October 7, 2013).

[4] As inserted by the Northern Ireland Act 1998 (Devolution of Policing and Justice Functions) Order 2010 (SI 2010/976) Sch.14 para.65 (effective April 12, 2010: insertion has effect subject to transitional provision specified in SI 2010/976 art.28).

(a)[1]   in relation to England and Wales, means the National Crime Agency, the Director of Revenue and Customs Prosecutions or the Director of the Serious Fraud Office,

(b)   in relation to Scotland, means the Scottish Ministers,

(c)   in relation to Northern Ireland, means the National Crime Agency, the Director of the Serious Fraud Office or the Director of Public Prosecutions for Northern Ireland,

"excepted joint owner" has the meaning given by section 270(4),

"interest", in relation to land—

(a)   in the case of land in England and Wales or Northern Ireland, means any legal estate and any equitable interest or power,

(b)   in the case of land in Scotland, means any estate, interest, servitude or other heritable right in or over land, including a heritable security,

"interest", in relation to property other than land, includes any right (including a right to possession of the property),

"interim administration order" has the meaning given by section 256(2),

"interim receiving order" has the meaning given by section 246(2),

"the minimum amount" (in Chapter 3) has the meaning given by section 303,

"part", in relation to property, includes a portion,

"premises" has the same meaning as in the Police and Criminal Evidence Act 1984 (c. 60),

"prohibitory property order" has the meaning given by section 255A(2);

"property freezing order" has the meaning given by section 245A(2);

"property obtained through unlawful conduct" has the meaning given by section 242,

"recoverable property" is to be read in accordance with sections 304 to 310,

"recovery order" means an order made under section 266,

"respondent" means—

(a)   where proceedings are brought by the enforcement authority by virtue of Chapter 2, the person against whom the proceedings are brought,

(b)   where no such proceedings have been brought but the enforcement authority has applied for a property freezing order, an interim receiving order, a prohibitory property order or an interim administration order, the person against whom he intends to bring such proceedings,

"share", in relation to an excepted joint owner, has the meaning given by section 270(4),

"unlawful conduct" has the meaning given by section 241,

"value" means market value.

(2)   The following provisions apply for the purposes of this Part.

(3)   For the purpose of deciding whether or not property was recoverable at any time (including times before commencement), it is to be assumed that this Part was in force at that and any other relevant time.

(4)   Property is all property wherever situated and includes—

(a)   money,

---

[1] As amended by the Public Bodies (Merger of the Director of Public Prosecutions and the Director of Revenue and Customs Prosecutions) Order 2014 (SI 2014/834) Sch.2 para.25 (effective March 27, 2014).

(b) all forms of property, real or personal, heritable or moveable,

(c) things in action and other intangible or incorporeal property.

(5) Any reference to a person's property (whether expressed as a reference to the property he holds or otherwise) is to be read as follows.

(6) In relation to land, it is a reference to any interest which he holds in the land.

(7) In relation to property other than land, it is a reference—

(a) to the property (if it belongs to him), or

(b) to any other interest which he holds in the property.

(8) References to the satisfaction of the enforcement authority's right to recover property obtained through unlawful conduct are to be read in accordance with section 279.

(8A) In relation to an order in England and Wales or Northern Ireland which is a recovery order, a property freezing order, an interim receiving order or an order under section 276, references to the enforcement authority are, unless the context otherwise requires, references to the enforcement authority which is seeking, or (as the case may be) has obtained, the order.

(9) Proceedings against any person for an offence are concluded when—

(a) the person is convicted or acquitted,

(b) the prosecution is discontinued or, in Scotland, the trial diet is deserted simpliciter, or

(c)[1] the jury is discharged without a finding otherwise than in circumstances where the proceedings are continued without a jury.

PART 7 – MONEY LAUNDERING   F1.9

Offences

Concealing etc

327.—[2](1) A person commits an offence if he—

(a) conceals criminal property;

(b) disguises criminal property;

(c) converts criminal property;

(d) transfers criminal property;

(e) removes criminal property from England and Wales or from Scotland or from Northern Ireland.

(2) But a person does not commit such an offence if—

(a) he makes an authorised disclosure under section 338 and (if the disclosure is made before he does the act mentioned in subsection (1)) he has the appropriate consent;

(b) he intended to make such a disclosure but had a reasonable excuse for not doing so;

(c) the act he does is done in carrying out a function he has relating to the enforcement of any provision of this Act or of any other enactment relating to criminal conduct or benefit from criminal conduct.

---

[1] As amended by the Criminal Justice Act 2003 (c.44) Sch.36(4) para.78 (effective July 24, 2006 as SI 2006/1835).

[2] As inserted by the Serious Organised Crime and Police Act 2005 s.103 brought into force by SI 2005/1521 (effective July 1, 2005).

(2A)[1] Nor does a person commit an offence under subsection (1) if—

    (a) he knows, or believes on reasonable grounds, that the relevant criminal conduct occurred in a particular country or territory outside the United Kingdom, and

    (b) the relevant criminal conduct—

        (i) was not, at the time it occurred, unlawful under the criminal law then applying in that country or territory, and

        (ii) is not of a description prescribed by an order made by the Secretary of State.

(2B)[2] In subsection (2A) "the relevant criminal conduct" is the criminal conduct by reference to which the property concerned is criminal property.

(2C)[3] A deposit-taking body that does an act mentioned in paragraph (c) or (d) of subsection (1) does not commit an offence under that subsection if—

    (a) it does the act in operating an account maintained with it, and

    (b) the value of the criminal property concerned is less than the threshold amount determined under section 339A for the act.

(3) Concealing or disguising criminal property includes concealing or disguising its nature, source, location, disposition, movement or ownership or any rights with respect to it.

Arrangements

328.—(1) A person commits an offence if he enters into or becomes concerned in an arrangement which he knows or suspects facilitates (by whatever means) the acquisition, retention, use or control of criminal property by or on behalf of another person.

(2) But a person does not commit such an offence if—

    (a) he makes an authorised disclosure under section 338 and (if the disclosure is made before he does the act mentioned in subsection (1)) he has the appropriate consent;

    (b) he intended to make such a disclosure but had a reasonable excuse for not doing so;

    (c) the act he does is done in carrying out a function he has relating to the enforcement of any provision of this Act or of any other enactment relating to criminal conduct or benefit from criminal conduct.

(3)[4] Nor does a person commit an offence under subsection (1) if—

    (a) he knows, or believes on reasonable grounds, that the relevant criminal conduct occurred in a particular country or territory outside the United Kingdom, and

    (b) the relevant criminal conduct—

        (i) was not, at the time it occurred, unlawful under the criminal law then applying in that country or territory, and

---

[1] As inserted by the Serious Organised Crime and Police Act 2005 s.102 brought into force by SI 2006/1085 (effective May 15, 2006).

[2] As inserted by the Serious Organised Crime and Police Act 2005 s.102 brought into force by SI 2006/1085 (effective May 15, 2006).

[3] As inserted by the Serious Organised Crime and Police Act 2005 s.103 brought into force by SI 2005/1521 (effective July 1, 2005).

[4] As inserted by the Serious Organised Crime and Police Act 2005 s.102 brought into force by SI 2006/1085 (effective May 15, 2006).

(ii)   is not of a description prescribed by an order made by the Secretary of State.

(4)[1]   In subsection (3) "the relevant criminal conduct" is the criminal conduct by reference to which the property concerned is criminal property.

(5)[2]   A deposit-taking body that does an act mentioned in subsection (1) does not commit an offence under that subsection if—

(a)   it does the act in operating an account maintained with it, and

(b)   the arrangement facilitates the acquisition, retention, use or control of criminal property of a value that is less than the threshold amount determined under section 339A for the act.

Acquisition, use and possession

329.—(1)   A person commits an offence if he—

(a)   acquires criminal property;

(b)   uses criminal property;

(c)   has possession of criminal property.

(2)   But a person does not commit such an offence if—

(a)   he makes an authorised disclosure under section 338 and (if the disclosure is made before he does the act mentioned in subsection (1)) he has the appropriate consent;

(b)   he intended to make such a disclosure but had a reasonable excuse for not doing so;

(c)   he acquired or used or had possession of the property for adequate consideration;

(d)   the act he does is done in carrying out a function he has relating to the enforcement of any provision of this Act or of any other enactment relating to criminal conduct or benefit from criminal conduct.

(2A)[3]   Nor does a person commit an offence under subsection (1) if—

(a)   he knows, or believes on reasonable grounds, that the relevant criminal conduct occurred in a particular country or territory outside the United Kingdom, and

(b)   the relevant criminal conduct—

(i)   was not, at the time it occurred, unlawful under the criminal law then applying in that country or territory, and

(ii)   is not of a description prescribed by an order made by the Secretary of State.

(2B)[4]   In subsection (2A) "the relevant criminal conduct" is the criminal conduct by reference to which the property concerned is criminal property.

(2C)[5]   A deposit-taking body that does an act mentioned in subsection (1) does not commit an offence under that subsection if—

---

[1] As inserted by the Serious Organised Crime and Police Act 2005 s.102 brought into force by SI 2006/1085 (effective May 15, 2006).

[2] As inserted by the Serious Organised Crime and Police Act 2005 s.103 brought into force by SI 2005/1521 (effective July 1, 2005).

[3] Inserted by the Serious Organised Crime and Police Act 2005, s.102, brought into force by SI 2006/1085 (effective May 15, 2006).

[4] Inserted by the Serious Organised Crime and Police Act 2005, s.102, brought into force by SI 2006/1085 (effective May 15, 2006).

[5] Inserted by the Serious Organised Crime and Police Act 2005, s.103, brought into force by SI 2005/1521 (effective July 1, 2005).

Parliament House Book R.126: May 2014

    (a)   it does the act in operating an account maintained with it, and

    (b)   the value of the criminal property concerned is less than the threshold amount determined under section 339A for the act.

(3)   For the purposes of this section—

    (a)   a person acquires property for inadequate consideration if the value of the consideration is significantly less than the value of the property;

    (b)   a person uses or has possession of property for inadequate consideration if the value of the consideration is significantly less than the value of the use or possession;

    (c)   the provision by a person of goods or services which he knows or suspects may help another to carry out criminal conduct is not consideration.

Failure to disclose: regulated sector

330.—[1](1)   A person commits an offence if each of the conditions in subsections (2) to (4) are satisfied.

(2)   The first condition is that he—

    (a)   knows or suspects, or

    (b)   has reasonable grounds for knowing or suspecting,

that another person is engaged in money laundering.

(3)   The second condition is that the information or other matter—

    (a)   on which his knowledge or suspicion is based, or

    (b)   which gives reasonable grounds for such knowledge or suspicion,

came to him in the course of a business in the regulated sector.

(3A)[2]   The third condition is—

    (a)   that he can identify the other person mentioned in subsection (2) or the whereabouts of any of the laundered property, or

    (b)   that he believes, or it is reasonable to expect him to believe, that the information or other matter mentioned in subsection (3) will or may assist in identifying that other person or the whereabouts of any of the laundered property.

(4)[3]   The fourth condition is that he does not make the required disclosure to—

    (a)   a nominated officer, or

    (b)[4,5]   a person authorised for the purposes of this Part by the Director General of the National Crime Agency, as soon as is practicable after the information or other matter mentioned in subsection (3) comes to him.

(5)[6]   The required disclosure is a disclosure of—

---

[1] s.330 of the Act shall not have effect in relation to a person who engages in any of the activities mentioned in paragraph 1(1)(f) to (n) of Sch.9 where the information or other matter on which knowledge or suspicion that another person is engaged in money laundering is based, or which gives reasonable grounds for such knowledge or suspicion, came to that person before March 1, 2004, the Proceeds of Crime Act 2002 (Business in the Regulated Sector and Supervisory Authorities) Order 2003, (SI 2003/3074), para.4.

[2] Substituted by the Serious Organised Crime and Police Act 2005, s.104, brought into force by SI 2005/1521 (effective July 1, 2005).

[3] Substituted by the Serious Organised Crime and Police Act 2005, s.104, brought into force by SI 2005/1521 (effective July 1, 2005).

[4] As amended by the Serious Crime Act 2007 (c.27) Sch.8(6), para.126 (effective April 1, 2008).

[5] As amended by the Crime and Courts Act 2013 (c.22) Sch.8(2) para.129 (effective October 7, 2013).

[6] Substituted by the Serious Organised Crime and Police Act 2005, s.104, brought into force by SI 2005/1521 (effective July 1, 2005).

    (a)   the identity of the other person mentioned in subsection (2), if he knows it,

    (b)   the whereabouts of the laundered property, so far as he knows it, and

    (c)   the information or other matter mentioned in subsection (3).

(5A)[1]   The laundered property is the property forming the subject-matter of the money laundering that he knows or suspects, or has reasonable grounds for knowing or suspecting, that other person to be engaged in.

(6)[2]   But he does not commit an offence under this section if—

    (a)   he has a reasonable excuse for not making the required disclosure,

    (b)[3]   he is a professional legal adviser or other relevant professional adviser and—

        (i)   if he knows either of the things mentioned in subsection (5)(a) and (b), he knows the thing because of information or other matter that came to him in privileged circumstances, or

        (ii)   the information or other matter mentioned in subsection (3) came to him in privileged circumstances, or

    (c)[4]   subsection (7) or (7B) applies to him.

(7)   This subsection applies to a person if—

    (a)   he does not know or suspect that another person is engaged in money laundering, and

    (b)   he has not been provided by his employer with such training as is specified by the Secretary of State by order for the purposes of this section.

(7A)[5]   Nor does a person commit an offence under this section if—

    (a)   he knows, or believes on reasonable grounds, that the money laundering is occurring in a particular country or territory outside the United Kingdom, and

    (b)   the money laundering—

        (i)   is not unlawful under the criminal law applying in that country or territory, and

        (ii)   is not of a description prescribed in an order made by the Secretary of State.

(7B)[6]   This subsection applies to a person if—

    (a)   he is employed by, or is in partnership with, a professional legal adviser or a relevant professional adviser to provide the adviser with assistance or support,

    (b)   the information or other matter mentioned in subsection (3) comes to the person in connection with the provision of such assistance or support, and

---

[1] Substituted by the Serious Organised Crime and Police Act 2005, s.104, brought into force by SI 2005/1521 (effective July 1, 2005).

[2] As amended by the Serious Organised Crime and Police Act 2005, s.105 and Sch.17, Pt.2, brought into force by SI 2005/1521 (effective July 1, 2005).

[3] As amended by the Proceeds of Crime Act 2002 and Money Laundering Regulations 2003 (Amendment) Order 2006/308 art. 2 (effective February 21, 2006).

[4] As amended by the Proceeds of Crime Act 2002 and Money Laundering Regulations 2003 (Amendment) Order 2006/308 art. 2 (effective February 21, 2006).

[5] Inserted by the Serious Organised Crime and Police Act 2005, s.102, brought into force by SI 2006/1085 (effective May 15, 2006).

[6] Inserted by the Proceeds of Crime Act 2002 and Money Laundering Regulations 2003 (Amendment) Order 2006/308 art. 2 (effective February 21, 2006).

    (c)   the information or other matter came to the adviser in privileged circumstances.

(8)   In deciding whether a person committed an offence under this section the court must consider whether he followed any relevant guidance which was at the time concerned—

    (a)   issued by a supervisory authority or any other appropriate body,

    (b)   approved by the Treasury, and

    (c)   published in a manner it approved as appropriate in its opinion to bring the guidance to the attention of persons likely to be affected by it.

(9)   A disclosure to a nominated officer is a disclosure which—

    (a)   is made to a person nominated by the alleged offender's employer to receive disclosures under this section, and

    (b)[1]   is made in the course of the alleged offender's employment.

(9A)[2]   But a disclosure which satisfies paragraphs (a) and (b) of subsection (9) is not to be taken as a disclosure to a nominated officer if the person making the disclosure—

    (a)[3]   is a professional legal adviser or other relevant professional

    (b)   makes it for the purpose of obtaining advice about making a disclosure under this section, and

    (c)   does not intend it to be a disclosure under this section.

(10)[4]   Information or other matter comes to a professional legal adviser or other relevant professional adviser in privileged circumstances if it is communicated or given to him—

    (a)   by (or by a representative of) a client of his in connection with the giving by the adviser of legal advice to the client,

    (b)   by (or by a representative of) a person seeking legal advice from the adviser, or

    (c)   by a person in connection with legal proceedings or contemplated legal proceedings.

(11)   But subsection (10) does not apply to information or other matter which is communicated or given with the intention of furthering a criminal purpose.

(12)   Schedule 9 has effect for the purpose of determining what is—

    (a)   a business in the regulated sector;

    (b)   a supervisory authority.

(13)   An appropriate body is any body which regulates or is representative of any trade, profession, business or employment carried on by the alleged offender.

(14)[5]   A relevant professional adviser is an accountant, auditor or tax adviser who is a member of a professional body which is established for accountants, auditors or tax advisers (as the case may be) and which makes provision for—

    (a)   testing the competence of those seeking admission to membership of such a body as a condition for such admission; and

---

[1] As amended by the Serious Organised Crime and Police Act 2005, s.105 and Sch.17, Pt.2, brought into force by SI 2005/1521 (effective July 1, 2005).

[2] Inserted by the Serious Organised Crime and Police Act 2005, s.104, brought into force by SI 2005/1521 (effective July 1, 2005).

[3] As amended by the Proceeds of Crime Act 2002 and Money Laundering Regulations 2003 (Amendment) Order 2006/308 art. 2 (effective February 21, 2006).

[4] As amended by the Proceeds of Crime Act 2002 and Money Laundering Regulations 2003 (Amendment) Order 2006/308 art. 2 (effective February 21, 2006).

[5] Inserted by the Proceeds of Crime Act 2002 and Money Laundering Regulations 2003 (Amendment) Order 2006/308 art. 2 (effective February 21, 2006).

(b) imposing and maintaining professional and ethical standards for its members, as well as imposing sanctions for non-compliance with those standards.

Failure to disclose: nominated officers in the regulated sector

331.—[1](1)   A person nominated to receive disclosures under section 330 commits an offence if the conditions in subsections (2) to (4) are satisfied.

(2)   The first condition is that he—

(a)   knows or suspects, or

(b)   has reasonable grounds for knowing or suspecting,

that another person is engaged in money laundering.

(3)   The second condition is that the information or other matter—

(a)   on which his knowledge or suspicion is based, or

(b)   which gives reasonable grounds for such knowledge or suspicion,

came to him in consequence of a disclosure made under section 330.

(3A)[2]   The third condition is—

(a)   that he knows the identity of the other person mentioned in subsection (2), or the whereabouts of any of the laundered property, in consequence of a disclosure made under section 330,

(b)   that that other person, or the whereabouts of any of the laundered property, can be identified from the information or other matter mentioned in subsection (3), or

(c)   that he believes, or it is reasonable to expect him to believe, that the information or other matter will or may assist in identifying that other person or the whereabouts of any of the laundered property.

[3, 4, 5](4)   The fourth condition is that he does not make the required disclosure to a person authorised for the purposes of this Part by the Director General of the National Crime Agency as soon as is practicable after the information or other matter mentioned in subsection (3) comes to him.

(5)[6]   The required disclosure is a disclosure of—

(a)   the identity of the other person mentioned in subsection (2), if disclosed to him under section 330,

(b)   the whereabouts of the laundered property, so far as disclosed to him under section 330, and

(c)   the information or other matter mentioned in subsection (3).

---

[1] s.330 of the Act shall not have effect in relation to a person who engages in any of the activities mentioned in paragraph 1(1)(f) to (n) of Sch.9 where the information or other matter on which knowledge or suspicion that another person is engaged in money laundering is based, or which gives reasonable grounds for such knowledge or suspicion, came to that person before March 1, 2004, the Proceeds of Crime Act 2002 (Business in the Regulated Sector and Supervisory Authorities) Order 2003, (SI 2003/3074), para.4.

[2] Substituted by the Serious Organised Crime and Police Act 2005, s.104, brought into force by SI 2005/1521 (effective July 1, 2005).

[3] Substituted by the Serious Organised Crime and Police Act 2005, s.104, brought into force by SI 2005/1521 (effective July 1, 2005).

[4] As amended by the Serious Crime Act 2007 (c.27) Sch.8(6), para.127 (effective April 1, 2008).

[5] As amended by the Crime and Courts Act 2013 (c.22) Sch.8(2) para.130 (effective October 7, 2013).

[6] Substituted by the Serious Organised Crime and Police Act 2005, s.104, brought into force by SI 2005/1521 (effective July 1, 2005).

(5A)[1] The laundered property is the property forming the subject-matter of the money laundering that he knows or suspects, or has reasonable grounds for knowing or suspecting, that other person to be engaged in.

(6)[2] But he does not commit an offence under this section if he has a reasonable excuse for not making the required disclosure.

(6A)[3] Nor does a person commit an offence under this section if—

    (a) he knows, or believes on reasonable grounds, that the money launder-ing is occurring in a particular country or territory outside the United Kingdom, and

    (b) the money laundering—

        (i) is not unlawful under the criminal law applying in that country or territory, and

        (ii) is not of a description prescribed in an order made by the Secretary of State.

(7) In deciding whether a person committed an offence under this section the court must consider whether he followed any relevant guidance which was at the time concerned—

    (a) issued by a supervisory authority or any other appropriate body,

    (b) approved by the Treasury, and

    (c) published in a manner it approved as appropriate in its opinion to bring the guidance to the attention of persons likely to be affected by it.

(8) Schedule 9 has effect for the purpose of determining what is a supervisory authority.

(9) An appropriate body is a body which regulates or is representative of a trade, profession, business or employment.

Failure to disclose: other nominated officers

332.—(1) A person nominated to receive disclosures under section 337 or 338 commits an offence if the conditions in subsections (2) to (4) are satisfied.

(2) The first condition is that he knows or suspects that another person is engaged in money laundering.

(3)[4] The second condition is that the information or other matter on which his knowledge or suspicion is based came to him in consequence of a disclosure made under the applicable section.

(3A)[5] The third condition is—

    (a) that he knows the identity of the other person mentioned in subsection (2), or the whereabouts of any of the laundered property, in consequence of a disclosure made under the applicable section,

---

[1] Substituted by the Serious Organised Crime and Police Act 2005, s.104, brought into force by SI 2005/1521 (effective July 1, 2005).

[2] Substituted by the Serious Organised Crime and Police Act 2005, s.104, brought into force by SI 2005/1521 (effective July 1, 2005).

[3] Inserted by the Serious Organised Crime and Police Act 2005, s.102, brought into force by SI 2006/1085 (effective May 15, 2006).

[4] As amended by the Serious Organised Crime and Police Act 2005, s.104, brought into force by SI 2005/1521 (effective July 1, 2005).

[5] Substitutedby the Serious Organised Crime and Police Act 2005, s.104, brought into force by SI 2005/1521 (effective July 1, 2005).

(b) that that other person, or the whereabouts of any of the laundered property, can be identified from the information or other matter mentioned in subsection (3), or

(c) that he believes, or it is reasonable to expect him to believe, that the information or other matter will or may assist in identifying that other person or the whereabouts of any of the laundered property.

1, 2, 3(4) The fourth condition is that he does not make the required disclosure to a person authorised for the purposes of this Part by the Director General of SOCA as soon as is practicable after the information or other matter mentioned in subsection (3) comes to him.

(5)[4] The required disclosure is a disclosure of—

(a) the identity of the other person mentioned in subsection (2), if disclosed to him under the applicable section,

(b) the whereabouts of the laundered property, so far as disclosed to him under the applicable section, and

(c) the information or other matter mentioned in subsection (3).

(5A)[5] The laundered property is the property forming the subject-matter of the money laundering that he knows or suspects that other person to be engaged in.

(5B)[6] The applicable section is section 337 or, as the case may be, section 338.

(6)[7] But he does not commit an offence under this section if he has a reasonable excuse for not making the required disclosure.

(7)[8] Nor does a person commit an offence under this section if—

(a) he knows, or believes on reasonable grounds, that the money laundering is occurring in a particular country or territory outside the United Kingdom, and

(b) the money laundering—

(i) is not unlawful under the criminal law applying in that country or territory, and

(ii) is not of a description prescribed in an order made by the Secretary of State.

Tipping off

333. *[Repealed by the Terrorism Act 2000 and Proceeds of Crime Act 2002 (Amendment) Regulations (SI 2007/3398) Sch.2, para.3 (effective December 26, 2007).]*

---

[1] Substitutedby the Serious Organised Crime and Police Act 2005, s.104, brought into force by SI 2005/1521 (effective July 1, 2005).
[2] As amended by the Serious Crime Act 2007 (c.27) Sch.8(6) para.128 (effective April 1, 2008).
[3] As amended by the Crime and Courts Act 2013 (c.22) Sch.8(2) para.131 (effective October 7, 2013).
[4] Substitutedby the Serious Organised Crime and Police Act 2005, s.104, brought into force by SI 2005/1521 (effective July 1, 2005).
[5] Substitutedby the Serious Organised Crime and Police Act 2005, s.104, brought into force by SI 2005/1521 (effective July 1, 2005).
[6] Substitutedby the Serious Organised Crime and Police Act 2005, s.104, brought into force by SI 2005/1521 (effective July 1, 2005).
[7] Substitutedby the Serious Organised Crime and Police Act 2005, s.104, brought into force by SI 2005/1521 (effective July 1, 2005).
[8] Inserted by the Serious Organised Crime and Police Act 2005, s.102, brought into force by SI 2006/1085 (effective May 15, 2006).

Tipping off: regulated sector

333A.—[1](1)   A person commits an offence if—

(a)   the person discloses any matter within subsection (2);

(b)   the disclosure is likely to prejudice any investigation that might be conducted following the disclosure referred to in that subsection; and

(c)   the information on which the disclosure is based came to the person in the course of a business in the regulated sector.

(2)   The matters are that the person or another person has made a disclosure under this Part—

(a)   to a constable,

(b)   to an officer of Revenue and Customs,

(c)   to a nominated officer, or

[2](d)   to a National Crime Agency officer authorised for the purposes of this Part by the Director General of that Agency,

of information that came to that person in the course of a business in the regulated sector.

(3)   A person commits an offence if—

(a)   the person discloses that an investigation into allegations that an offence under this Part has been committed is being contemplated or is being carried out;

(b)   the disclosure is likely to prejudice that investigation; and

(c)   the information on which the disclosure is based came to the person in the course of a business in the regulated sector.

(4)   A person guilty of an offence under this section is liable—

(a)   on summary conviction to imprisonment for a term not exceeding three months, or to a fine not exceeding level 5 on the standard scale, or to both;

(b)   on conviction on indictment to imprisonment for a term not exceeding two years, or to a fine, or to both.

(5)   This section is subject to—

(a)   section 333B (disclosures within an undertaking or group etc),

(b)   section 333C (other permitted disclosures between institutions etc), and

(c)   section 333D (other permitted disclosures etc).

Disclosures within an undertaking or group etc

333B.—[3](1)   An employee, officer or partner of an undertaking does not commit an offence under section 333A if the disclosure is to an employee, officer or partner of the same undertaking.

(2)   A person does not commit an offence under section 333A in respect of a disclosure by a credit institution or a financial institution if—

(a)   the disclosure is to a credit institution or a financial institution,

(b)   the institution to whom the disclosure is made is situated in an EEA State or in a country or territory imposing equivalent money laundering requirements, and

---

[1] As inserted by the Terrorism Act 2000 and Proceeds of Crime Act 2002 (Amendment) Regulations 2007 (SI 2007/3398) Sch.2 para.4 (effective December 26, 2007).

[2] As amended by the Crime and Courts Act 2013 (c.22) Sch.8(2) para.132 (effective October 7, 2013).

[3] As inserted by the Terrorism Act 2000 and Proceeds of Crime Act 2002 (Amendment) Regulations 2007 (SI 2007/3398) Sch.2 para.4 (effective December 26, 2007).

(c) both the institution making the disclosure and the institution to whom it is made belong to the same group.

(3) In subsection (2) "group" has the same meaning as in Directive 2002/87/EC of the European Parliament and of the Council of 16th December 2002 on the supplementary supervision of credit institutions, insurance undertakings and investment firms in a financial conglomerate.

(4) A professional legal adviser or a relevant professional adviser does not commit an offence under section 333A if—

(a) the disclosure is to professional legal adviser or a relevant professional adviser,

(b) both the person making the disclosure and the person to whom it is made carry on business in an EEA State or in a country or territory imposing equivalent money laundering requirements, and

(c) those persons perform their professional activities within different undertakings that share common ownership, management or control.

Other permitted disclosures between institutions etc

333C.—[1](1) This section applies to a disclosure—

(a) by a credit institution to another credit institution,

(b) by a financial institution to another financial institution,

(c) by a professional legal adviser to another professional legal adviser, or

(d) by a relevant professional adviser of a particular kind to another relevant professional adviser of the same kind.

(2) A person does not commit an offence under section 333A in respect of a disclosure to which this section applies if—

(a) the disclosure relates to—

(i) a client or former client of the institution or adviser making the disclosure and the institution or adviser to whom it is made,

(ii) a transaction involving them both, or

(iii) the provision of a service involving them both;

(b) the disclosure is for the purpose only of preventing an offence under this Part of this Act;

(c) the institution or adviser to whom the disclosure is made is situated in an EEA State or in a country or territory imposing equivalent money laundering requirements; and

(d) the institution or adviser making the disclosure and the institution or adviser to whom it is made are subject to equivalent duties of professional confidentiality and the protection of personal data (within the meaning of section 1 of the Data Protection Act 1998).

Other permitted disclosures etc

333D.—[2](1) A person does not commit an offence under section 333A if the disclosure is—

(a) to the authority that is the supervisory authority for that person by virtue of the Money Laundering Regulations 2007 (S.I. 2007/2157); or

---

[1] As inserted by the Terrorism Act 2000 and Proceeds of Crime Act 2002 (Amendment) Regulations 2007 (SI 2007/3398) Sch.2 para.4 (effective December 26, 2007).

[2] As inserted by the Terrorism Act 2000 and Proceeds of Crime Act 2002 (Amendment) Regulations 2007 (SI 2007/3398) Sch.2 para.4 (effective December 26, 2007).

(b) for the purpose of—

    (i) the detection, investigation or prosecution of a criminal offence (whether in the United Kingdom or elsewhere),

    (ii) an investigation under this Act, or

    (iii) the enforcement of any order of a court under this Act.

(2) A professional legal adviser or a relevant professional adviser does not commit an offence under section 333A if the disclosure—

    (a) is to the adviser's client, and

    (b) is made for the purpose of dissuading the client from engaging in conduct amounting to an offence.

(3) A person does not commit an offence under section 333A(1) if the person does not know or suspect that the disclosure is likely to have the effect mentioned in section 333A(1)(b).

(4) A person does not commit an offence under section 333A(3) if the person does not know or suspect that the disclosure is likely to have the effect mentioned in section 333A(3)(b).

Interpretation of sections 333A to 333D

333E.—[1](1) For the purposes of sections 333A to 333D, Schedule 9 has effect for determining—

    (a) what is a business in the regulated sector, and

    (b) what is a supervisory authority.

(2) In those sections—

"credit institution" has the same meaning as in Schedule 9;

"financial institution" means an undertaking that carries on a business in the regulated sector by virtue of any of paragraphs (b) to (i) of paragraph 1(1) of that Schedule.

(3) References in those sections to a disclosure by or to a credit institution or a financial institution include disclosure by or to an employee, officer or partner of the institution acting on its behalf.

(4) For the purposes of those sections a country or territory imposes "equivalent money laundering requirements" if it imposes requirements equivalent to those laid down in Directive 2005/60/EC of the European Parliament and of the Council of 26th October 2005 on the prevention of the use of the financial system for the purpose of money laundering and terrorist financing.

(5) In those sections "relevant professional adviser" means an accountant, auditor or tax adviser who is a member of a professional body which is established for accountants, auditors or tax advisers (as the case may be) and which makes provision for—

    (a) testing the competence of those seeking admission to membership of such a body as a condition for such admission; and

    (b) imposing and maintaining professional and ethical standards for its members, as well as imposing sanctions for non-compliance with those standards.

---

[1] As inserted by the Terrorism Act 2000 and Proceeds of Crime Act 2002 (Amendment) Regulations 2007 (SI 2007/3398) Sch.2 para.4 (effective December 26, 2007).

Penalties

334.—(1)   A person guilty of an offence under section 327, 328 or 329 is liable—

    (a)   on summary conviction, to imprisonment for a term not exceeding six months or to a fine not exceeding the statutory maximum or to both, or

    (b)   on conviction on indictment, to imprisonment for a term not exceeding 14 years or to a fine or to both.

  (2)[1]   A person guilty of an offence under section 330, 331 or 332 is liable—

    (a)   on summary conviction, to imprisonment for a term not exceeding six months or to a fine not exceeding the statutory maximum or to both, or

    (b)   on conviction on indictment, to imprisonment for a term not exceeding five years or to a fine or to both.

  (3)[2]   A person guilty of an offence under section 339(1A) is liable on summary conviction to a fine not exceeding level 5 on the standard scale.

Consent

F1.10

Appropriate consent

335.—(1)   The appropriate consent is—

    (a)   the consent of a nominated officer to do a prohibited act if an authorised disclosure is made to the nominated officer;

    (b)   the consent of a constable to do a prohibited act if an authorised disclosure is made to a constable;

    (c)   the consent of a customs officer to do a prohibited act if an authorised disclosure is made to a customs officer.

  (2)   A person must be treated as having the appropriate consent if—

    (a)   he makes an authorised disclosure to a constable or a customs officer, and

    (b)   the condition in subsection (3) or the condition in subsection (4) is satisfied.

  (3)   The condition is that before the end of the notice period he does not receive notice from a constable or customs officer that consent to the doing of the act is refused.

  (4)   The condition is that—

    (a)   before the end of the notice period he receives notice from a constable or customs officer that consent to the doing of the act is refused, and

    (b)   the moratorium period has expired.

  (5)   The notice period is the period of seven working days starting with the first working day after the person makes the disclosure.

  (6)   The moratorium period is the period of 31 days starting with the day on which the person receives notice that consent to the doing of the act is refused.

  (7)   A working day is a day other than a Saturday, a Sunday, Christmas Day, Good Friday or a day which is a bank holiday under the Banking and Financial Dealings Act 1971 (c.80) in the part of the United Kingdom in which the person is when he makes the disclosure.

---

[1] As substituted by the Terrorism Act 2000 and Proceeds of Crime Act 2002 (Amendment) Regulations 2007 (SI 2007/3398) Sch.2 para.5 (effective December 26, 2007).

[2] Inserted by the Serious Organised Crime and Police Act 2005 s.105 brought into force by SI 2005/1521 (effective July 1, 2005).

(8)   References to a prohibited act are to an act mentioned in section 327(1), 328(1) or 329(1) (as the case may be).

(9)   A nominated officer is a person nominated to receive disclosures under section 338.

(10)   Subsections (1) to (4) apply for the purposes of this Part.

F1.11   **Nominated officer: consent**

336.—(1)   A nominated officer must not give the appropriate consent to the doing of a prohibited act unless the condition in subsection (2), the condition in subsection (3) or the condition in subsection (4) is satisfied.

(2)   The condition is that—

[1,2,3](a)   he makes a disclosure that property is criminal property to a person authorised for the purposes of this Part by the Director General of the National Crime Agency, and

(b)   such a person gives consent to the doing of the act.

(3)   The condition is that—

[4,5](a)   he makes a disclosure that property is criminal property to a person authorised for the purposes of this Part by the Director General of the National Crime Agency, and

(b)   before the end of the notice period he does not receive notice from such a person that consent to the doing of the act is refused.

(4)   The condition is that—

[6,7,8](a)   he makes a disclosure that property is criminal property to a person authorised for the purposes of this Part by the Director General of the National Crime Agency,

(b)   before the end of the notice period he receives notice from such a person that consent to the doing of the act is refused, and

(c)   the moratorium period has expired.

(5)   A person who is a nominated officer commits an offence if—

(a)   he gives consent to a prohibited act in circumstances where none of the conditions in subsections (2), (3) and (4) is satisfied, and

(b)   he knows or suspects that the act is a prohibited act.

(6)   A person guilty of such an offence is liable—

(a)   on summary conviction, to imprisonment for a term not exceeding six months or to a fine not exceeding the statutory maximum or to both, or

(b)   on conviction on indictment, to imprisonment for a term not exceeding five years or to a fine or to both.

---

[1] As amended by the Serious Organised Crime and Police Act 2005, Sch.4, para. 173, brought into force by SI 2006/378 (effective April 1, 2006).

[2] As substituted by the Serious Crime Act 2007 (c.27) Sch.8(6) para.129 (effective April 1, 2008 subject to transitional and transitory provisions and savings as specified in SI 2008/755 arts 3–14).

[3] As amended by the Crime and Courts Act 2013 (c.22) Sch.8(2) para.133 (effective October 7, 2013).

[4] As amended by the Serious Organised Crime and Police Act 2005, Sch.4, para. 173, brought into force by SI 2006/378 (effective April 1, 2006).

[5] As amended by the Crime and Courts Act 2013 (c.22) Sch.8(2) para.133 (effective October 7, 2013).

[6] As amended by the Serious Organised Crime and Police Act 2005, Sch.4, para. 173, brought into force by SI 2006/378 (effective April 1, 2006).

[7] As substituted by the Serious Crime Act 2007 (c.27) Sch.8(6) para.129 (effective April 1, 2008 subject to transitional and transitory provisions and savings as specified in SI 2008/755 arts 3–14).

[8] As amended by the Crime and Courts Act 2013 (c.22) Sch.8(2) para.133 (effective October 7, 2013).

(7)   The notice period is the period of seven working days starting with the first working day after the nominated officer makes the disclosure.

(8)   The moratorium period is the period of 31 days starting with the day on which the nominated officer is given notice that consent to the doing of the act is refused.

(9)   A working day is a day other than a Saturday, a Sunday, Christmas Day, Good Friday or a day which is a bank holiday under the Banking and Financial Dealings Act 1971 (c.80) in the part of the United Kingdom in which the nominated officer is when he gives the appropriate consent.

(10)   References to a prohibited act are to an act mentioned in section 327(1), 328(1) or 329(1) (as the case may be).

(11)   A nominated officer is a person nominated to receive disclosures under section 338.

Disclosures

Protected disclosures

337.—(1)   A disclosure which satisfies the following three conditions is not to be taken to breach any restriction on the disclosure of information (however imposed).

(2)   The first condition is that the information or other matter disclosed came to the person making the disclosure (the discloser) in the course of his trade, profession, business or employment.

(3)   The second condition is that the information or other matter—

(a)   causes the discloser to know or suspect, or

(b)   gives him reasonable grounds for knowing or suspecting,

that another person is engaged in money laundering.

(4)   The third condition is that the disclosure is made to a constable, a customs officer or a nominated officer as soon as is practicable after the information or other matter comes to the discloser.

(4A)[1]   Where a disclosure consists of a disclosure protected under subsection (1) and a disclosure of either or both of—

(a)   the identity of the other person mentioned in subsection (3), and

(b)   the whereabouts of property forming the subject-matter of the money laundering that the discloser knows or suspects, or has reasonable grounds for knowing or suspecting, that other person to be engaged in,

the disclosure of the thing mentioned in paragraph (a) or (b) (as well as the disclosure protected under subsection (1)) is not to be taken to breach any restriction on the disclosure of information (however imposed).

(5)   A disclosure to a nominated officer is a disclosure which—

(a)[2]   is made to a person nominated by the discloser's employer to receive disclosures under section 330 or this section, and

(b)[3]   is made in the course of the discloser's employment.

---

[1] Inserted by the Serious Organised Crime and Police Act 2005, s.104, brought into force by SI 2005/1521 (effective July 1, 2005).

[2] As amended by the Serious Organised Crime and Police Act 2005, s.106, brought into force by SI 2005/1521 (effective July 1, 2005).

[3] As amended by the Serious Organised Crime and Police Act 2005, s.105 and Sch.17, Pt.2, brought into force by SI 2005/1521 (effective July 1, 2005).

Authorised disclosures

338.—(1) For the purposes of this Part a disclosure is authorised if—

    (a) it is a disclosure to a constable, a customs officer or a nominated officer by the alleged offender that property is criminal property, and

    (b) *[Repealed by the Serious Organised Crime and Police Act 2005 (c.15) Sch.17(2) para.1 (effective July 1, 2005 as SI 2005/1521).]*

    (c)[1] the first, second or third condition set out below is satisfied.

(2) The first condition is that the disclosure is made before the alleged offender does the prohibited act.

(2A)[2] The second condition is that—

    (a) the disclosure is made while the alleged offender is doing the prohibited act,

    (b) he began to do the act at a time when, because he did not then know or suspect that the property constituted or represented a person's benefit from criminal conduct, the act was not a prohibited act, and

    (c) the disclosure is made on his own initiative and as soon as is practicable after he first knows or suspects that the property constitutes or represents a person's benefit from criminal conduct.

(3)[3] The third condition is that—

    (a) the disclosure is made after the alleged offender does the prohibited act,

    (b)[4] he has a reasonable excuse for his failure to make the disclosure before he did the act, and

    (c) the disclosure is made on his own initiative and as soon as it is practicable for him to make it.

(4) An authorised disclosure is not to be taken to breach any restriction on the disclosure of information (however imposed).

(5) A disclosure to a nominated officer is a disclosure which—

    (a) is made to a person nominated by the alleged offender's employer to receive authorised disclosures, and

    (b)[5] is made in the course of the alleged offender's employment.

(6) References to the prohibited act are to an act mentioned in section 327(1), 328(1) or 329(1) (as the case may be).

Form and manner of disclosures

339.—(1) The Secretary of State may by order prescribe the form and manner in which a disclosure under section 330, 331, 332 or 338 must be made.

---

[1] As amended by the Serious Organised Crime and Police Act 2005, s.105 and Sch.17, Pt.2, brought into force by SI 2005/1521 (effective July 1, 2005).

[2] Inserted by the Serious Organised Crime and Police Act 2005, s.106, brought into force by SI 2005/1521 (effective July 1, 2005).

[3] As amended by the Serious Organised Crime and Police Act 2005, s.106, brought into force by SI 2005/1521 (effective July 1, 2005).

[4] As substituted by the Terrorism Act 2000 and Proceeds of Crime Act 2002 (Amendment) Regulations (SI 2007/3398) Sch.2, para.6 (effective December 26, 2007).

[5] As amended by the Serious Organised Crime and Police Act 2005, s.105 and Sch.17, Pt.2, brought into force by SI 2005/1521 (effective July 1, 2005).

(1A)[1]   A person commits an offence if he makes a disclosure under section 330, 331, 332 or 338 otherwise than in the form prescribed under subsection (1) or otherwise than in the manner so prescribed.

(1B)[2]   But a person does not commit an offence under subsection (1A) if he has a reasonable excuse for making the disclosure otherwise than in the form prescribed under subsection (1) or (as the case may be) otherwise than in the manner so prescribed.

(2)[3]   The power under subsection (1) to prescribe the form in which a disclosure must be made includes power to provide for the form to include a request to a person making a disclosure that the person provide information specified or described in the form if he has not provided it in making the disclosure.

(3)[4]   Where under subsection (2) a request is included in a form prescribed under subsection (1), the form must—

(a)   state that there is no obligation to comply with the request, and

(b)   explain the protection conferred by subsection (4) on a person who complies with the request.

(4)   A disclosure made in pursuance of a request under subsection (2) is not to be taken to breach any restriction on the disclosure of information (however imposed).

(5)   *[Repealed by the Serious Organised Crime and Police Act 2005, Sch.17, Pt.2, brought into force by SI 2005/1521 (effective July 1, 2005)]*

(6)   *[Repealed by the Serious Organised Crime and Police Act 2005, Sch.17, Pt.2, brought into force by SI 2005/1521 (effective July 1, 2005)]*

(7)   Subsection (2) does not apply to a disclosure made to a nominated officer.

Disclosures to the NCA[5, 6]

339ZA.   Where a disclosure is made under this Part to a constable or an officer of Revenue and Customs, the constable or officer of Revenue and Customs must disclose it in full to a person authorised for the purposes of this Part by the Director General of the National Crime Agency as soon as practicable after it has been made.

Threshold amounts

Threshold amounts

339A—[7](1)   This section applies for the purposes of sections 327(2C), 328(5) and 329(2C).

---

[1] As substituted by the Serious Organised Crime and Police Act 2005, s.105, brought into force by SI 2005/1521 (effective July 1, 2005).
[2] As substituted by the Serious Organised Crime and Police Act 2005, s.105, brought into force by SI 2005/1521 (effective July 1, 2005).
[3] As substituted by the Serious Organised Crime and Police Act 2005, s.105, brought into force by SI 2005/1521 (effective July 1, 2005).
[4] As substituted by the Serious Organised Crime and Police Act 2005, s.105, brought into force by SI 2005/1521 (effective July 1, 2005).
[5] As inserted by the Terrorism Act 2000 and Proceeds of Crime Act 2002 (Amendment) Regulations 2007 (SI 2007/3398) Sch.2 para.7 (effective December 26, 2007).
[6] As amended by the Crime and Courts Act 2013 (c.22) Sch.8(2) para.134 (effective October 7, 2013).
[7] As inserted by the Serious Organised Crime and Police Act 2005, s.103, brought into force by SI 2005/1521 (effective July 1, 2005).

(2) The threshold amount for acts done by a deposit-taking body in operating an account is £250 unless a higher amount is specified under the following provisions of this section (in which event it is that higher amount).

(3) An officer of Revenue and Customs, or a constable, may specify the threshold amount for acts done by a deposit-taking body in operating an account—

    (a) when he gives consent, or gives notice refusing consent, to the deposit-taking body's doing of an act mentioned in section 327(1), 328(1) or 329(1) in opening, or operating, the account or a related account, or

    (b) on a request from the deposit-taking body.

(4) Where the threshold amount for acts done in operating an account is specified under subsection (3) or this subsection, an officer of Revenue and Customs, or a constable, may vary the amount (whether on a request from the deposit-taking body or otherwise) by specifying a different amount.

(5) Different threshold amounts may be specified under subsections (3) and (4) for different acts done in operating the same account.

(6) The amount specified under subsection (3) or (4) as the threshold amount for acts done in operating an account must, when specified, not be less than the amount specified in subsection (2).

(7) The Secretary of State may by order vary the amount for the time being specified in subsection (2).

(8) For the purposes of this section, an account is related to another if each is maintained with the same deposit-taking body and there is a person who, in relation to each account, is the person or one of the persons entitled to instruct the body as respects the operation of the account.

Interpretation

340.—(1) This section applies for the purposes of this Part.

(2) Criminal conduct is conduct which—

    (a) constitutes an offence in any part of the United Kingdom, or

    (b) would constitute an offence in any part of the United Kingdom if it occurred there.

(3) Property is criminal property if—

    (a) it constitutes a person's benefit from criminal conduct or it represents such a benefit (in whole or part and whether directly or indirectly), and

    (b) the alleged offender knows or suspects that it constitutes or represents such a benefit.

(4) It is immaterial—

    (a) who carried out the conduct;

    (b) who benefited from it;

    (c) whether the conduct occurred before or after the passing of this Act.

(5) A person benefits from conduct if he obtains property as a result of or in connection with the conduct.

(6) If a person obtains a pecuniary advantage as a result of or in connection with conduct, he is to be taken to obtain as a result of or in connection with the conduct a sum of money equal to the value of the pecuniary advantage.

(7) References to property or a pecuniary advantage obtained in connection with conduct include references to property or a pecuniary advantage obtained in both that connection and some other.

(8) If a person benefits from conduct his benefit is the property obtained as a result of or in connection with the conduct.

(9) Property is all property wherever situated and includes—
  (a) money;
  (b) all forms of property, real or personal, heritable or moveable;
  (c) things in action and other intangible or incorporeal property.
(10) The following rules apply in relation to property—
  (a) property is obtained by a person if he obtains an interest in it;
  (b) references to an interest, in relation to land in England and Wales or Northern Ireland, are to any legal estate or equitable interest or power;
  (c) references to an interest, in relation to land in Scotland, are to any estate, interest, servitude or other heritable right in or over land, including a heritable security;
  (d) references to an interest, in relation to property other than land, include references to a right (including a right to possession).
(11) Money laundering is an act which—
  (a) constitutes an offence under section 327, 328 or 329,
  (b) constitutes an attempt, conspiracy or incitement to commit an offence specified in paragraph (a),
  (c) constitutes aiding, abetting, counselling or procuring the commission of an offence specified in paragraph (a), or
  (d) would constitute an offence specified in paragraph (a), (b) or (c) if done in the United Kingdom.
(12) For the purposes of a disclosure to a nominated officer—
  (a) references to a person's employer include any body, association or organisation (including a voluntary organisation) in connection with whose activities the person exercises a function (whether or not for gain or reward), and
  (b) references to employment must be construed accordingly.
(13)[1, 2] References to a constable include references to a person authorised for the purposes of this Part by the Director General of the National Crime Agency.
(14)[3] "Deposit-taking body" means—
  (a) a business which engages in the activity of accepting deposits, or
  (b) the National Savings Bank.

PART 8 – INVESTIGATIONS

Chapter 1 – – Introduction

Investigations

341.—(1) For the purposes of this Part a confiscation investigation is an investigation into—
  (a) whether a person has benefited from his criminal conduct, or
  (b) the extent or whereabouts of his benefit from his criminal conduct.
(2) For the purposes of this Part a civil recovery investigation is an investigation into—

---

[1] As amended by the Serious Organised Crime and Police Act 2005, Sch.4, para.173, brought into force by SI 2006/378 (effective April 1, 2006) and the Serious Crime Act 2007 (c.27) Sch.8(6), para. 130 (effective April 1, 2008).
[2] As amended by the Crime and Courts Act 2013 (c.22) Sch.8(2) para.135 (effective October 1, 2013).
[3] Inserted by the Serious Organised Crime and Police Act 2005, s.103, brought into force by SI 2005/ 1521 (effective July 1, 2005).

(a) whether property is recoverable property or associated property,

(b) who holds the property, or

(c) its extent or whereabouts.

(3) But an investigation is not a civil recovery investigation if—

(a) proceedings for a recovery order have been started in respect of the property in question,

(b) an interim receiving order applies to the property in question,

(c) an interim administration order applies to the property in question, or

(d) the property in question is detained under section 295.

(3A)[1] For the purposes of this Part a detained cash investigation is—

(a) an investigation for the purposes of Chapter 3 of Part 5 into the derivation of cash detained under section 295 or a part of such cash, or

(b) an investigation for the purposes of Chapter 3 of Part 5 into whether cash detained under section 295, or a part of such cash, is intended by any person to be used in unlawful conduct.

(4) For the purposes of this Part a money laundering investigation is an investigation into whether a person has committed a money laundering offence.

(5)[2] For the purposes of this Part an exploitation proceeds investigation is an investigation for the purposes of Part 7 of the Coroners and Justice Act 2009 (criminal memoirs etc) into—

(a) whether a person is a qualifying offender,

(b) whether a person has obtained exploitation proceeds from a relevant offence,

(c) the value of any benefits derived by a person from a relevant offence, or

(d) the available amount in respect of a person.

Paragraphs (a) to (d) are to be construed in accordance with that Part of that Act.

Offences of prejudicing investigation

342.—[3, 4](1) This section applies if a person knows or suspects that an appropriate officer or (in Scotland) a proper person is acting (or proposing to act) in connection with a confiscation investigation, a civil recovery investigation, a detained cash investigation, an exploitation proceeds investigation or a money laundering investigation which is being or is about to be conducted.

(2) The person commits an offence if—

(a) he makes a disclosure which is likely to prejudice the investigation, or

(b) he falsifies, conceals, destroys or otherwise disposes of, or causes or permits the falsification, concealment, destruction or disposal of, documents which are relevant to the investigation.

(3) A person does not commit an offence under subsection (2)(a) if—

(a) he does not know or suspect that the disclosure is likely to prejudice the investigation,

(b) the disclosure is made in the exercise of a function under this Act or

---

[1] As inserted by the Serious Crime Act 2007 (c.27) Pt 3 c.2 s.75(1) (effective April 6, 2008 subject to transitional and transitory provisions and savings as specified in SI 2008/755 art. 17(2) and (3)).

[2] As inserted by the Coroners and Justice Act 2009 (c.25) Sch.19 para.2 (effective April 6, 2010).

[3] As amended by the Serious Crime Act 2007 (c.27) Sch.10 para.2 (effective April 6, 2008 subject to transitional and transitory provisions and savings as specified in SI 2008/755 art. 17(2) and (3)).

[4] As amended by the Coroners and Justice Act 2009 (c.25) Sch.19 para.3 (effective April 6, 2010).

any other enactment relating to criminal conduct or benefit from criminal conduct or in compliance with a requirement imposed under or by virtue of this Act, or

(ba)[1] the disclosure is of a matter within section 333A(2) or (3)(a) (money laundering: tipping off) and the information on which the disclosure is based came to the person in the course of a business in the regulated sector,

(bb)[2] the disclosure is made in the exercise of a function under Part 7 of the Coroners and Justice Act 2009 (criminal memoirs etc) or in compliance with a requirement imposed under or by virtue of that Act,

(c) he is a professional legal adviser and the disclosure falls within subsection (4).

(4) A disclosure falls within this subsection if it is a disclosure—

(a) to (or to a representative of) a client of the professional legal adviser in connection with the giving by the adviser of legal advice to the client, or

(b) to any person in connection with legal proceedings or contemplated legal proceedings.

(5) But a disclosure does not fall within subsection (4) if it is made with the intention of furthering a criminal purpose.

(6) A person does not commit an offence under subsection (2)(b) if—

(a) he does not know or suspect that the documents are relevant to the investigation, or

(b) he does not intend to conceal any facts disclosed by the documents from any appropriate officer or (in Scotland) proper person carrying out the investigation.

(7) A person guilty of an offence under subsection (2) is liable—

(a) on summary conviction, to imprisonment for a term not exceeding six months or to a fine not exceeding the statutory maximum or to both, or

(b) on conviction on indictment, to imprisonment for a term not exceeding five years or to a fine or to both.

(8) For the purposes of this section—

(a) "appropriate officer" must be construed in accordance with section 378;

(b) "proper person" must be construed in accordance with section 412;

---

[1] As inserted by the Terrorism Act 2000 and >Proceeds of Crime Act 2002 (Amendment) Regulations 2007 (SI 2007/3398) Sch.2 para.8 (effective December 26, 2007).

[2] As inserted by the Coroners and Justice Act 2009 (c.25) Sch.19 para.3 (effective April 6, 2010).

(c)[1] Schedule 9 has effect for determining what is a business in the regulated sector.

F1.12

Chapter 2 – – England and Wales and Northern Ireland
[Not reproduced.]

Chapter 3 – – Scotland

Production orders

Production orders

380.—(1) The sheriff may, on an application made to him by the appropriate person, make a production order if he is satisfied that each of the requirements for the making of the order is fulfilled.

(2)[2] In making a production order in relation to property subject to a civil recovery investigation or a detained cash investigation, the sheriff shall act in the exercise of his civil jurisdiction.

(3) The application for a production order must state that—

    (a) a person specified in the application is subject to a confiscation investigation or a money laundering investigation, or

    (b)[3] property specified in the application is subject to a civil recovery investigation or a detained cash investigation.

(4) The application must also state that—

    (a) the order is sought for the purposes of the investigation;

    (b) the order is sought in relation to material, or material of a description, specified in the application;

    (c) a person specified in the application appears to be in possession or control of the material.

(5) A production order is an order either—

    (a) requiring the person the application for the order specifies as appearing to be in possession or control of material to produce it to a proper person for him to take away, or

    (b) requiring that person to give a proper person access to the material,

within the period stated in the order.

(6) The period stated in a production order must be a period of seven days beginning with the day on which the order is made, unless it appears to the sheriff that a longer or shorter period would be appropriate in the particular circumstances.

Requirements for making of production order

381.—(1) These are the requirements for the making of a production order.

(2) There must be reasonable grounds for suspecting that—

    (a) in the case of a confiscation investigation, the person the application for the order specifies as being subject to the investigation has benefited from his criminal conduct;

    (b) in the case of a civil recovery investigation, the property the application

---

[1] As inserted by the Terrorism Act 2000 and >Proceeds of Crime Act 2002 (Amendment) Regulations 2007 (SI 2007/3398) Sch.2 para.8 (effective December 26, 2007).
[2] As amended by the Serious Crime Act 2007 (c.27) Sch.10 para.14 (effective June 18, 2009).
[3] As amended by the Coroners and Justice Act 2009 (c.25) Sch.19 para.3 (effective April 6, 2010).

for the order specifies as being subject to the investigation is recoverable property or associated property;

(ba)[1] in the case of a detained cash investigation into the derivation of cash, the property the application for the order specifies as being subject to the investigation, or a part of it, is recoverable property;

(bb)[2] in the case of a detained cash investigation into the intended use of cash, the property the application for the order specifies as being subject to the investigation, or a part of it, is intended by any person to be used in unlawful conduct;

(c) in the case of a money laundering investigation, the person the application for the order specifies as being subject to the investigation has committed a money laundering offence.

(3) There must be reasonable grounds for believing that the person the application specifies as appearing to be in possession or control of the material so specified is in possession or control of it.

(4) There must be reasonable grounds for believing that the material is likely to be of substantial value (whether or not by itself) to the investigation for the purposes of which the order is sought.

(5) There must be reasonable grounds for believing that it is in the public interest for the material to be produced or for access to it to be given, having regard to—

(a) the benefit likely to accrue to the investigation if the material is obtained,

(b) the circumstances under which the person the application specifies as appearing to be in possession or control of the material holds it.

Order to grant entry

382.—(1) This section applies if a sheriff makes a production order requiring a person to give a proper person access to material on any premises.

(2) The sheriff may, on an application made to him by the appropriate person and specifying the premises, make an order to grant entry in relation to the premises.

(3) An order to grant entry is an order requiring any person who appears to the appropriate person to be entitled to grant entry to the premises to allow a proper person to enter the premises to obtain access to the material.

Further provisions

383.—(1) A production order does not require a person to produce, or give access to, any items subject to legal privilege.

(2) A production order has effect in spite of any restriction on the disclosure of information (however imposed).

(3) A proper person may take copies of any material which is produced, or to which access is given, in compliance with a production order.

(4) Material produced in compliance with a production order may be retained for so long as it is necessary to retain it (as opposed to copies of it) in connection with the investigation for the purposes of which the order was made.

(5) But if a proper person has reasonable grounds for believing that—

(a) the material may need to be produced for the purposes of any legal proceedings, and

---

[1] As inserted by the Serious Crime Act 2007 (c.27) Pt 3 c.2 s.75(5) (effective June 18, 2009).
[2] As inserted by the Serious Crime Act 2007 (c.27) Pt 3 c.2 s.75(5) (effective June 18, 2009).

(b)   it might otherwise be unavailable for those purposes,
it may be retained until the proceedings are concluded.

Computer information

384.—(1)   This section applies if any of the material specified in an application for a production order consists of information contained in a computer.

(2)   If the order is an order requiring a person to produce the material to a proper person for him to take away, it has effect as an order to produce the material in a form in which it can be taken away by him and in which it is visible and legible.

(3)   If the order is an order requiring a person to give a proper person access to the material, it has effect as an order to give him access to the material in a form in which it is visible and legible.

Government departments

385.—(1)   A production order may be made in relation to material in the possession or control of an authorised government department.

(2)   An order so made may require any officer of the department (whether named in the order or not) who may for the time being be in possession or control of the material to comply with it.

(3)   If an order contains such a requirement—

(a)   the person on whom it is served must take all reasonable steps to bring it to the attention of the officer concerned;

(b)   any other officer of the department who is in receipt of the order must also take all reasonable steps to bring it to the attention of the officer concerned.

(4)   If the order is not brought to the attention of the officer concerned within the period stated in the order (in pursuance of section 380(5)) the person on whom it is served must report the reasons for the failure to—

(a)   the sheriff in the case of an order made for the purposes of a confiscation investigation or a money laundering investigation;

(b)[1]   the sheriff exercising a civil jurisdiction in the case of an order made for the purposes of a civil recovery investigation or a detained cash investigation.

(5)   In this section, "authorised government department" includes a government department which is an authorised department for the purposes of the Crown Proceedings Act 1947 (c. 44) and the Scottish Administration.

Supplementary

386.—(1)   An application for a production order or an order to grant entry may be made ex parte to a sheriff in chambers.

(2)   Provision may be made by rules of court as to the discharge and variation of production orders and orders to grant entry.

(3)   Rules of court under subsection (2) relating to production orders and orders to grant entry—

(a)   made in a confiscation investigation or a money laundering investigation shall, without prejudice to section 305 of the Criminal Procedure (Scotland) Act 1995 (c. 46) be made by act of adjournal;

---

[1] As amended by the Serious Crime Act 2007 (c.27) Sch.10 para.15 (effective June 18, 2009).

(b)[1] made in a civil recovery investigation or a detained cash investigation shall, without prejudice to section 32 of the Sheriff Courts (Scotland) Act 1971 (c. 58) be made by act of sederunt.

(4) An application to discharge or vary a production order or an order to grant entry may be made to the sheriff by—

(a) the person who applied for the order;

(b) any person affected by the order.

(5) The sheriff may—

(a) discharge the order;

(b) vary the order.

Search warrants

Search warrants

387.—(1) The sheriff may, on an application made to him by the appropriate person, issue a search warrant if he is satisfied that either of the requirements for the issuing of the warrant is fulfilled.

(2)[2] In issuing a search warrant in relation to property subject to a civil recovery investigation or a detained cash investigation, the sheriff shall act in the exercise of his civil jurisdiction.

(3) The application for a search warrant must state that—

(a) a person specified in the application is subject to a confiscation investigation or a money laundering investigation, or

(b)[3] property specified in the application is subject to a civil recovery investigation or a detained cash investigation.

(4) A search warrant is a warrant authorising a proper person—

(a) to enter and search the premises specified in the application for the warrant, and

(b) to seize and retain any material specified in the warrant which is found there and which is likely to be of substantial value (whether or not by itself) to the investigation for the purposes of which the application is made.

(4A)[4] A proper person may, if necessary, use reasonable force in executing a search warrant.

(5) The requirements for the issue of a search warrant are—

(a) that a production order made in relation to material has not been complied with and there are reasonable grounds for believing that the material is on the premises specified in the application for the warrant, or

(b) that section 388 is satisfied in relation to the warrant.

(6) An application for a search warrant may be made ex parte to a sheriff in chambers.

Requirements where production order not available

388.—(1) This section is satisfied in relation to a search warrant if—

---

[1] As amended by the Serious Crime Act 2007 (c.27) Sch.10 para.16 (effective June 18, 2009).
[2] As amended by the Serious Crime Act 2007 (c.27) Sch.10 para.17 (effective June 18, 2009).
[3] As amended by the Serious Crime Act 2007 (c.27) Pt 3 c.2 s.76(4) (effective June 18, 2009).
[4] As inserted by the Serious Crime Act 2007 (c.27) Pt 3 s.86 (effective April 28, 2008).

    (a)   subsection (2) applies, and

    (b)   either the first or the second set of conditions is complied with.

  (2)   This subsection applies if there are reasonable grounds for suspecting that—

    (a)   in the case of a confiscation investigation, the person specified in the application for the warrant has benefited from his criminal conduct;

    (b)   in the case of a civil recovery investigation, the property specified in the application for the warrant is recoverable property or associated property;

  (ba)[1]   in the case of a detained cash investigation into the derivation of cash, the property specified in the application for the warrant, or a part of it, is recoverable property;

  (bb)[2]   in the case of a detained cash investigation into the intended use of cash, the property specified in the application for the warrant, or a part of it, is intended by any person to be used in unlawful conduct;

    (c)   in the case of a money laundering investigation, the person specified in the application for the warrant has committed a money laundering offence.

  (3)   The first set of conditions is that there are reasonable grounds for believing that—

    (a)   any material on the premises specified in the application for the warrant is likely to be of substantial value (whether or not by itself) to the investigation for the purposes of which the warrant is sought,

    (b)   it is in the public interest for the material to be obtained, having regard to the benefit likely to accrue to the investigation if the material is obtained, and

    (c)   it would not be appropriate to make a production order for any one or more of the reasons in subsection (4).

  (4)   The reasons are—

    (a)   that it is not practicable to communicate with any person against whom the production order could be made;

    (b)   that it is not practicable to communicate with any person who would be required to comply with an order to grant access to the material or to grant entry to the premises on which the material is situated;

    (c)   that the investigation might be seriously prejudiced unless a proper person is able to secure immediate access to the material.

  (5)   The second set of conditions is that—

  (a)[3]   there are reasonable grounds for believing that there is material on the premises specified in the application for the warrant and that the material falls within subsection (6), (7), (7A), (7B) or (8),

    (b)   there are reasonable grounds for believing that it is in the public interest for the material to be obtained, having regard to the benefit likely to accrue to the investigation if the material is obtained, and

    (c)   any one or more of the requirements in subsection (9) is met.

  (6)   In the case of a confiscation investigation, material falls within this subsection if it cannot be identified at the time of the application but it—

    (a)   relates to the person specified in the application, the question whether

---

[1] As inserted by the Serious Crime Act 2007 (c.27) Pt 3 c.2 s.76 (effective June 18, 2009).
[2] As inserted by the Serious Crime Act 2007 (c.27) Pt 3 c.2 s.76 (effective June 18, 2009).
[3] As amended by the Serious Crime Act 2007 (c.27) Sch.10 para.18 (effective June 18, 2009).

he has benefited from his criminal conduct or any question as to the extent or whereabouts of his benefit from his criminal conduct, and

(b) is likely to be of substantial value (whether or not by itself) to the investigation for the purposes of which the warrant is sought.

(7) In the case of a civil recovery investigation, material falls within this subsection if it cannot be identified at the time of the application but it—

(a) relates to the property specified in the application, the question whether it is recoverable property or associated property, the question as to who holds any such property, any question as to whether the person who appears to hold any such property holds other property which is recoverable property, or any question as to the extent or whereabouts of any property mentioned in this paragraph, and

(b) is likely to be of substantial value (whether or not by itself) to the investigation for the purposes of which the warrant is sought.

(7A)[1] In the case of a detained cash investigation into the derivation of cash, material falls within this subsection if it cannot be identified at the time of the application but it—

(a) relates to the property specified in the application, the question whether the property, or a part of it, is recoverable property or any other question as to its derivation, and

(b) is likely to be of substantial value (whether or not by itself) to the investigation for the purposes of which the warrant is sought.

(7B)[2] In the case of a detained cash investigation into the intended use of cash, material falls within this subsection if it cannot be identified at the time of the application but it—

(a) relates to the property specified in the application or the question whether the property, or a part of it, is intended by any person to be used in unlawful conduct, and

(b) is likely to be of substantial value (whether or not by itself) to the investigation for the purposes of which the warrant is sought.

(8) In the case of a money laundering investigation, material falls within this subsection if it cannot be identified at the time of the application but it—

(a) relates to the person specified in the application or the question whether he has committed a money laundering offence, and

(b) is likely to be of substantial value (whether or not by itself) to the investigation for the purposes of which the warrant is sought.

(9) The requirements are—

(a) that it is not practicable to communicate with any person entitled to grant entry to the premises;

(b) that entry to the premises will not be granted unless a warrant is produced;

(c) that the investigation might be seriously prejudiced unless a proper person arriving at the premises is able to secure immediate entry to them.

---

[1] As inserted by the Serious Crime Act 2007 (c.27) Pt 3 c.2 s.76 (effective June 18, 2009).
[2] As inserted by the Serious Crime Act 2007 (c.27) Pt 3 c.2 s.76 (effective June 18, 2009).

Further provisions: general

389. A search warrant does not confer the right to seize any items subject to legal privilege.

Further provisions: confiscation, civil recovery, detained cash and money laundering

390.—[1](1) This section applies to search warrants sought for the purposes of confiscation investigations, civil recovery investigations, detained cash investigations or money laundering investigations.

(2) A warrant continues in force until the end of the period of one month starting with the day on which it is issued.

(3) A warrant authorises the person executing it to require any information which is held in a computer and is accessible from the premises specified in the application for the warrant, and which the proper person believes relates to any matter relevant to the investigation, to be produced in a form—

(a) in which it can be taken away, and

(b) in which it is visible and legible.

(4) Copies may be taken of any material seized under a warrant.

(5) A warrant issued in relation to a civil recovery investigation or a detained cash investigation may be issued subject to conditions.

(6) A warrant issued in relation to a civil recovery investigation or a detained cash investigation may include provision authorising the person executing it to do other things which—

(a) are specified in the warrant, and

(b) need to be done in order to give effect to it.

(7) Material seized under a warrant issued in relation to a civil recovery investigation or a detained cash investigation may be retained for so long as it is necessary to retain it (as opposed to copies of it) in connection with the investigation for the purposes of which the warrant was issued.

(8) But if the Scottish Ministers have reasonable grounds for believing that—

(a) the material may need to be produced for the purposes of any legal proceedings, and

(b) it might otherwise be unavailable for those purposes,

it may be retained until the proceedings are concluded.

Disclosure orders

Disclosure orders

391.—(1) The High Court of Justiciary, on an application made to it by the Lord Advocate in relation to confiscation investigations, or the Court of Session, on an application made to it by the Scottish Ministers in relation to civil recovery investigations, may make a disclosure order if it is satisfied that each of the requirements for the making of the order is fulfilled.

(2)[2] No application for a disclosure order may be made in relation to a detained cash investigation or a money laundering investigation.

(3) The application for a disclosure order must state that—

---

[1] As amended by the Serious Crime Act 2007 (c.27) Sch.10 para. 19 (effective June 18, 2009).
[2] As amended by the Serious Crime Act 2007 (c.27) Sch.10 para.20 (effective June 18, 2009).

(a) a person specified in the application is subject to a confiscation investigation and the order is sought for the purposes of the investigation, or

(b) property specified in the application is subject to a civil recovery investigation and the order is sought for the purposes of the investigation.

(4) A disclosure order is an order authorising the Lord Advocate or the Scottish Ministers to give to any person the Lord Advocate considers or the Scottish Ministers consider has relevant information, notice in writing requiring him to do, with respect to any matter relevant to the investigation for the purposes of which the order is sought, any or all of the following—

(a) answer questions, either at a time specified in the notice or at once, at a place so specified;

(b) provide information specified in the notice, by a time and in a manner so specified;

(c) produce documents, or documents of a description, specified in the notice, either at or by a time so specified or at once, and in a manner so specified.

(5) Relevant information is information (whether or not contained in a document) which the Lord Advocate considers or the Scottish Ministers consider to be relevant to the investigation.

(6) A person is not bound to comply with a requirement imposed by a notice given under a disclosure order unless evidence of authority to give the notice is produced to him.

Requirements for making of disclosure order

392.—(1) These are the requirements for the making of a disclosure order.

(2) There must be reasonable grounds for suspecting that—

(a) in the case of a confiscation investigation, the person specified in the application for the order has benefited from his criminal conduct;

(b) in the case of a civil recovery investigation, the property specified in the application for the order is recoverable property or associated property.

(3) There must be reasonable grounds for believing that information which may be provided in compliance with a requirement imposed under the order is likely to be of substantial value (whether or not by itself) to the investigation for the purposes of which the order is sought.

(4) There must be reasonable grounds for believing that it is in the public interest for the information to be provided, having regard to the benefit likely to accrue to the investigation if the information is obtained.

Offences

393.—(1) A person commits an offence if without reasonable excuse he fails to comply with a requirement imposed on him under a disclosure order.

(2) A person guilty of an offence under subsection (1) is liable on summary conviction to—

(a) imprisonment for a term not exceeding six months,

(b) a fine not exceeding level 5 on the standard scale, or

(c) both.

(3) A person commits an offence if, in purported compliance with a requirement imposed on him under a disclosure order, he—

(a)   makes a statement which he knows to be false or misleading in a material particular, or

(b)   recklessly makes a statement which is false or misleading in a material particular.

(4)   A person guilty of an offence under subsection (3) is liable—

(a)   on summary conviction, to imprisonment for a term not exceeding six months or to a fine not exceeding the statutory maximum or to both, or

(b)   on conviction on indictment, to imprisonment for a term not exceeding two years or to a fine or to both.

Statements

394.—(1)   A statement made by a person in response to a requirement imposed on him under a disclosure order may not be used in evidence against him in criminal proceedings.

(2)   But subsection (1) does not apply—

(a)   in the case of proceedings under Part 3,

(b)   on a prosecution for an offence under section 393(1) or (3),

(c)   on a prosecution for perjury, or

(d)   on a prosecution for some other offence where, in giving evidence, the person makes a statement inconsistent with the statement mentioned in subsection (1).

(3)   A statement may not be used by virtue of subsection (2)(d) against a person unless—

(a)   evidence relating to it is adduced, or

(b)   a question relating to it is asked,

by him or on his behalf in the proceedings arising out of the prosecution.

Further provisions

395.—(1)   A disclosure order does not confer the right to require a person to answer any question, provide any information or produce any document which he would be entitled to refuse to answer, provide or produce on grounds of legal privilege.

(2)   A disclosure order has effect in spite of any restriction on the disclosure of information (however imposed).

(3)   The Lord Advocate and the Scottish Ministers may take copies of any documents produced in compliance with a requirement to produce them which is imposed under a disclosure order.

(4)   Documents so produced may be retained for so long as it is necessary to retain them (as opposed to a copy of them) in connection with the investigation for the purposes of which the order was made.

(5)   But if the Lord Advocate has, or the Scottish Ministers have, reasonable grounds for believing that—

(a)   the documents may need to be produced for the purposes of any legal proceedings, and

(b)   they might otherwise be unavailable for those purposes, they may be retained until the proceedings are concluded.

Supplementary

396.—(1)   An application for a disclosure order may be made ex parte to—

    (a)   in the case of an order made in a confiscation investigation, a judge of the High Court of Justiciary;

    (b)   in the case of an order made in a civil recovery investigation, a judge of the Court of Session,

in chambers.

(2)   Provision may be made by rules of court as to the discharge and variation of disclosure orders.

(3)   Rules of court under subsection (2) relating to disclosure orders—

    (a)   made in a confiscation investigation shall, without prejudice to section 305 of the Criminal Procedure (Scotland) Act 1995 (c. 46) be made by act of adjournal;

    (b)   made in a civil recovery investigation shall, without prejudice to section 5 of the Court of Session Act 1988 (c. 36), be made by act of sederunt.

(4)   An application to discharge or vary a disclosure order may be made to a judge of the court which made the order by—

    (a)   the Lord Advocate or the Scottish Ministers;

    (b)   any person affected by the order.

(5)   The court may—

    (a)   discharge the order;

    (b)   vary the order.

Customer information orders

Customer information orders

397.—(1)   The sheriff may, on an application made to him by the appropriate person, make a customer information order if he is satisfied that each of the requirements for the making of the order is fulfilled.

(1A)[1]   No application for a customer information order may be made in relation to a detained cash investigation.

(2)   In making a customer information order in relation to property subject to a civil recovery investigation the sheriff shall act in the exercise of his civil jurisdiction.

(3)   The application for a customer information order must state that—

    (a)   a person specified in the application is subject to a confiscation investigation or a money laundering investigation, or

    (b)   property specified in the application is subject to a civil recovery investigation and a person specified in the application appears to hold the property.

(4)   The application must also state that—

    (a)   the order is sought for the purposes of the investigation;

    (b)   the order is sought against the financial institution or financial institutions specified in the application.

(5)   An application for a customer information order may specify—

    (a)   all financial institutions,

    (b)   a particular description, or particular descriptions, of financial institutions, or

    (c)   a particular financial institution or particular financial institutions.

---

[1] As amended by the Serious Crime Act 2007 (c.27) Sch.10 para.21 (effective June 18, 2009).

(6)　A customer information order is an order that a financial institution covered by the application for the order must, on being required to do so by notice in writing given by the appropriate person, provide any such customer information as it has relating to the person specified in the application.

(7)　A financial institution which is required to provide information under a customer information order must provide the information to a proper person in such manner, and at or by such time, as that person requires.

(8)　If a financial institution on which a requirement is imposed by a notice given under a customer information order requires the production of evidence of authority to give the notice, it is not bound to comply with the requirement unless evidence of the authority has been produced to it.

Meaning of customer information

398.—(1)　"Customer information", in relation to a person and a financial institution, is information whether the person holds, or has held, an account or accounts at the financial institution (whether solely or jointly with another) and (if so) information as to—

(a)　the matters specified in subsection (2) if the person is an individual;

(b)　the matters specified in subsection (3) if the person is a company or limited liability partnership or a similar body incorporated or otherwise established outside the United Kingdom.

(2)　The matters referred to in subsection (1)(a) are—

(a)　the account number or numbers;

(b)　the person's full name;

(c)　his date of birth;

(d)　his most recent address and any previous addresses;

(e)　the date or dates on which he began to hold the account or accounts and, if he has ceased to hold the account or any of the accounts, the date or dates on which he did so;

(f)　such evidence of his identity as was obtained by the financial institution under or for the purposes of any legislation relating to money laundering;

(g)　the full name, date of birth and most recent address, and any previous addresses, of any person who holds, or has held, an account at the financial institution jointly with him;

(h)　the account number or numbers of any other account or accounts held at the financial institution to which he is a signatory and details of the person holding the other account or accounts.

(3)　The matters referred to in subsection (1)(b) are—

(a)　the account number or numbers;

(b)　the person's full name;

(c)　a description of any business which the person carries on;

(d)[1]　the country or territory in which it is incorporated or otherwise established and any number allocated to it under the Companies Act 2006 or corresponding legislation of any country or territory outside the United Kingdom;

---

[1] As substituted by the Companies Act 2006 (Consequential Amendments, Transitional Provisions and Savings) Order 2009 (SI 2009/1941) Sch.1 para.196(3)(a) (effective October 1, 2009).

(e) any number assigned to it for the purposes of value added tax in the United Kingdom;

(f)[1] its registered office, and any previous registered offices, under the Companies Act 2006 (or corresponding earlier legislation) or anything similar under corresponding legislation of any country or territory outside the United Kingdom;

(g) its registered office, and any previous registered offices, under the Limited Liability Partnerships Act 2000 (c. 12) or anything similar under corresponding legislation of any country or territory outside Great Britain;

(h) the date or dates on which it began to hold the account or accounts and, if it has ceased to hold the account or any of the accounts, the date or dates on which it did so;

(i) such evidence of its identity as was obtained by the financial institution under or for the purposes of any legislation relating to money laundering;

(j) the full name, date of birth and most recent address and any previous addresses of any person who is a signatory to the account or any of the accounts.

(4) The Scottish Ministers may by order provide for information of a description specified in the order—

(a) to be customer information, or

(b) no longer to be customer information.

(5)[2] Money laundering is an act which—

(a) constitutes an offence under section 327, 328 or 329 of this Act or section 18 of the Terrorism Act 2000 (c. 11), or

(aa) constitutes an offence specified in section 415(1A) of this Act,

(b) would constitute an offence specified in paragraph (a) or (aa) if done in the United Kingdom.

Requirements for making of customer information order

399.—(1) These are the requirements for the making of a customer information order.

(2) In the case of a confiscation investigation, there must be reasonable grounds for suspecting that the person specified in the application for the order has benefited from his criminal conduct.

(3) In the case of a civil recovery investigation, there must be reasonable grounds for suspecting that—

(a) the property specified in the application for the order is recoverable property or associated property;

(b) the person specified in the application holds all or some of the property.

(4) In the case of a money laundering investigation, there must be reasonable grounds for suspecting that the person specified in the application for the order has committed a money laundering offence.

---

[1] As substituted by the Companies Act 2006 (Consequential Amendments, Transitional Provisions and Savings) Order 2009 (SI 2009/1941) Sch.1 para.196(3)(a) (effective October 1, 2009).
[2] As amended by the Serious Organised Crime and Police Act 2005 (c.15) s.107(3)(b) (effective July 1, 2005).

(5) In the case of any investigation, there must be reasonable grounds for believing that customer information which may be provided in compliance with the order is likely to be of substantial value (whether or not by itself) to the investigation for the purposes of which the order is sought.

(6) In the case of any investigation there must be reasonable grounds for believing that it is in the public interest for the customer information to be provided, having regard to the benefit likely to accrue to the investigation if the information is obtained.

Offences

400.—(1) A financial institution commits an offence if without reasonable excuse it fails to comply with a requirement imposed on it under a customer information order.

(2) A financial institution guilty of an offence under subsection (1) is liable on summary conviction to a fine not exceeding level 5 on the standard scale.

(3) A financial institution commits an offence if, in purported compliance with a customer information order, it—

    (a) makes a statement which it knows to be false or misleading in a material particular, or

    (b) recklessly makes a statement which is false or misleading in a material particular.

(4) A financial institution guilty of an offence under subsection (3) is liable—

    (a) on summary conviction, to a fine not exceeding the statutory maximum, or

    (b) on conviction on indictment, to a fine.

Statements

401.—(1) A statement made by a financial institution in response to a customer information order may not be used in evidence against it in criminal proceedings.

(2) But subsection (1) does not apply—

    (a) in the case of proceedings under Part 3,

    (b) on a prosecution for an offence under section 400(1) or (3), or

    (c) on a prosecution for some other offence where, in giving evidence, the financial institution makes a statement inconsistent with the statement mentioned in subsection (1).

(3) A statement may not be used by virtue of subsection (2)(c) against a financial institution unless—

    (a) evidence relating to it is adduced, or

    (b) a question relating to it is asked,

by or on behalf of the financial institution in the proceedings arising out of the prosecution.

Further provisions

402. A customer information order has effect in spite of any restriction on the disclosure of information (however imposed).

Supplementary

403.—(1) An application for a customer information order may be made ex parte to a sheriff in chambers.

(2)   Provision may be made by rules of court as to the discharge and variation of customer information orders.

(3)   Rules of court under subsection (2) relating to customer information orders—

    (a)   made in a confiscation investigation or a money laundering investigation shall, without prejudice to section 305 of the Criminal Procedure (Scotland) Act 1995 (c. 46), be made by act of adjournal;

    (b)   made in a civil recovery investigation shall, without prejudice to section 32 of the Sheriff Courts (Scotland) Act 1971 (c. 58), be made by act of sederunt.

(4)   An application to discharge or vary a customer information order may be made to the sheriff by—

    (a)   the person who applied for the order;

    (b)   any person affected by the order.

(5)   The sheriff may—

    (a)   discharge the order;

    (b)   vary the order.

Account monitoring orders

Account monitoring orders

404.—(1)   The sheriff may, on an application made to him by the appropriate person, make an account monitoring order if he is satisfied that each of the requirements for the making of the order is fulfilled.

(1A)[1]   No application for an account monitoring order may be made in relation to a detained cash investigation.

(2)   In making an account monitoring order in relation to property subject to a civil recovery investigation, the sheriff shall act in the exercise of his civil jurisdiction.

(3)   The application for an account monitoring order must state that—

    (a)   a person specified in the application is subject to a confiscation investigation or a money laundering investigation, or

    (b)   property specified in the application is subject to a civil recovery investigation and a person specified in the application appears to hold the property.

(4)   The application must also state that—

    (a)   the order is sought for the purposes of the investigation;

    (b)   the order is sought against the financial institution specified in the application in relation to account information of the description so specified.

(5)   Account information is information relating to an account or accounts held at the financial institution specified in the application by the person so specified (whether solely or jointly with another).

(6)   The application for an account monitoring order may specify information relating to—

    (a)   all accounts held by the person specified in the application for the order at the financial institution so specified,

---

[1] As inserted by the Serious Crime Act 2007 (c.27) Sch.10 para.22 (effective June 18, 2009).

    (b)   a particular description, or particular descriptions, of accounts so held, or

    (c)   a particular account, or particular accounts, so held.

(7)   An account monitoring order is an order that the financial institution specified in the application for the order must, for the period stated in the order, provide account information of the description specified in the order to the proper person in the manner, and at or by the time or times, stated in the order.

(8)   The period stated in an account monitoring order must not exceed the period of 90 days beginning with the day on which the order is made.

Requirements for making of account monitoring order

405.—(1)   These are the requirements for the making of an account monitoring order.

(2)   In the case of a confiscation investigation, there must be reasonable grounds for suspecting that the person specified in the application for the order has benefited from his criminal conduct.

(3)   In the case of a civil recovery investigation, there must be reasonable grounds for suspecting that—

    (a)   the property specified in the application for the order is recoverable property or associated property;

    (b)   the person specified in the application holds all or some of the property.

(4)   In the case of a money laundering investigation, there must be reasonable grounds for suspecting that the person specified in the application for the order has committed a money laundering offence.

(5)   In the case of any investigation, there must be reasonable grounds for believing that account information which may be provided in compliance with the order is likely to be of substantial value (whether or not by itself) to the investigation for the purposes of which the order is sought.

(6)   In the case of any investigation, there must be reasonable grounds for believing that it is in the public interest for the account information to be provided, having regard to the benefit likely to accrue to the investigation if the information is obtained.

Statements

406.—(1)   A statement made by a financial institution in response to an account monitoring order may not be used in evidence against it in criminal proceedings.

(2)   But subsection (1) does not apply—

    (a)   in the case of proceedings under Part 3;

    (b)   in the case of proceedings for contempt of court, or

    (c)   on a prosecution for an offence where, in giving evidence, the financial institution makes a statement inconsistent with the statement mentioned in subsection (1).

(3)   A statement may not be used by virtue of subsection (2)(c) against a financial institution unless—

    (a)   evidence relating to it is adduced, or

    (b)   a question relating to it is asked,

by or on behalf of the financial institution in the proceedings arising out of the prosecution.

Further provisions

407. An account monitoring order has effect in spite of any restriction on the disclosure of information (however imposed).

Supplementary

408.—(1) An application for an account monitoring order may be made ex parte to a sheriff in chambers.

(2) Provision may be made by rules of court as to the discharge and variation of account monitoring orders.

(3) Rules of court under subsection (2) relating to account monitoring orders—

    (a) made in a confiscation investigation or a money laundering investigation shall, without prejudice to section 305 of the Criminal Procedure (Scotland) Act 1995 (c. 46), be made by act of adjournal;

    (b) made in a civil recovery investigation shall, without prejudice to section 32 of the Sheriff Courts (Scotland) Act 1971 (c. 58), be made by act of sederunt.

(4) An application to discharge or vary an account monitoring order may be made to the sheriff by—

    (a) the person who applied for the order;

    (b) any person affected by the order.

(5) The sheriff may—

    (a) discharge the order;

    (b) vary the order.

Officers of Revenue and Customs[1]

Restriction on exercise of certain powers conferred on officers of Revenue and Customs

408C.—(1) This section applies to the powers conferred on an officer of Revenue and Customs which are exercisable in connection with—

    (a) a production order made or to be made in relation to a confiscation investigation or a money laundering investigation,

    (b) a search warrant issued or to be issued in relation to a confiscation investigation or a money laundering investigation,

    (c) a customer information order, and

    (d) an account monitoring order.

(2) The powers are exercisable by the officer only so far as the officer is exercising a function relating to a matter other than an excluded matter.

(3) The reference in subsection (2) to an excluded matter is to a matter specified in section 54(4)(b) of, or in any of paragraphs 3, 5, 7, 10, 12 and 14 to 30 of Schedule 1 to, the Commissioners for Revenue and Customs Act 2005.

---

[1] As inserted by the Finance Act 2013 (c.29) Sch.48 para.19 (effective July 17, 2013).

General

Jurisdiction of sheriff

409.—(1)   A sheriff may grant a production order, search warrant, customer information order or account monitoring order under this Act in relation to property situated in any area of Scotland notwithstanding that it is outside the area of that sheriff.

(2)   Any such order or warrant may, without being backed or endorsed by another sheriff, be executed throughout Scotland in the same way as it may be executed within the sheriffdom of the sheriff who granted it.

(3)   This section is without prejudice to any existing rule of law or to any other provision of this Act.

Code of practice

410.—(1)   The Scottish Ministers must prepare a code of practice as to the exercise by proper persons of functions they have under this Chapter.

(2)   After preparing a draft of the code the Scottish Ministers—

    (a)   must publish the draft;

    (b)   must consider any representations made to them about the draft;

    (c)   may amend the draft accordingly.

(3)   After the Scottish Ministers have proceeded under subsection (2) they must lay the code before the Scottish Parliament.

(4)   When they have done so, the Scottish Ministers may bring the code into operation on such day as they may appoint by order.

(5)   A proper person must compy with a code of practice which is in operation under this section in the exercise of any function he has under this Chapter.

(6)   If a proper person fails to comply with any provision of a code of practice issued under this section he is not by reason only of that failure liable in any criminal or civil proceedings.

(7)   But the code of practice is admissible in evidence in such proceedings and a court may take account of any failure to comply with its provisions in determining any questions in the proceedings.

(8)   The Scottish Ministers may from time to time revise a code previously brought into operation under this section; and the preceding provisions of this section apply to a revised code as they apply to the code as first prepared.

Performance of functions of Scottish Ministers by constables in Scotland

411.—(1)   In Scotland, a constable engaged in temporary service with the Scottish Ministers in connection with their functions under this Part may perform functions, other than those specified in subsection (2), on behalf of the Scottish Ministers.

(2)   The specified functions are the functions conferred on the Scottish Ministers by—

    (a)   section 380(1) (production orders),

    (b)   section 382(2) (entry orders),

    (c)   section 386(4) (supplementary to production and entry orders),

    (d)   section 387(1) (search warrants),

    (e)   section 391(1) (disclosure orders),

    (f)   section 396(4) (supplementary to disclosure orders),

    (g)   section 397(1) (customer information orders),

    (h)   section 403(4) (supplementary to customer information orders),

F1.14

(i) section 404(1) (account monitoring orders),
(j) section 408(4) (supplementary to account monitoring orders).

Interpretation

412.[1]   In this Chapter, unless the context otherwise requires—

"appropriate person" means—
    (a) the procurator fiscal, in relation to a confiscation investigation or a money laundering investigation,
    (b) the Scottish Ministers, in relation to a civil recovery investigation or a detained cash investigation;
references to a "constable" include references to an officer of Revenue and Customs;[2]
"legal privilege" means protection in legal proceedings from disclosure, by virtue of any rule of law relating to the confidentiality of communications; and "items subject to legal privilege" are—
    (a) communications between a professional legal adviser and his client, or
    (b) communications made in connection with or in contemplation of legal proceedings and for the purposes of those proceedings,
which would be so protected.
"premises" include any place and, in particular, include—
    (a) any vehicle, vessel, aircraft or hovercraft;
    (b) any offshore installation within the meaning of section 1 of the Mineral Workings (Offshore Installations) Act 1971 (c. 61) and any tent or movable structure;
"proper person" means—
    (a) a constable, in relation to a confiscation investigation or a money laundering investigation;
    (b) the Scottish Ministers or a person named by them, in relation to a civil recovery investigation or a detained cash investigation.

Chapter 4 – Interpretation

Criminal conduct

413.—(1)   Criminal conduct is conduct which—
    (a) constitutes an offence in any part of the United Kingdom, or
    (b) would constitute an offence in any part of the United Kingdom if it occurred there.

(2)   A person benefits from conduct if he obtains property or a pecuniary advantage as a result of or in connection with the conduct.

(3)   References to property or a pecuniary advantage obtained in connection with conduct include references to property or a pecuniary advantage obtained in both that connection and some other.

(4)   If a person benefits from conduct his benefit is the property or pecuniary advantage obtained as a result of or in connection with the conduct.

(5)   It is immaterial—
    (a) whether conduct occurred before or after the passing of this Act, and

---

[1] As inserted by the Serious Crime Act 2007 (c.27) Sch.10 para.23 (effective June 18, 2009).
[2] As inserted by the Finance Act 2013 (c.29) Sch.48 para.20 (effective July 17, 2013).

(b)   whether property or a pecuniary advantage constituting a benefit from conduct was obtained before or after the passing of this Act.

Property

414.—(1)   Property is all property wherever situated and includes—

(a)   money;

(b)   all forms of property, real or personal, heritable or moveable;

(c)   things in action and other intangible or incorporeal property.

(2)   "Recoverable property" and "associated property" have the same meanings as in Part 5.

(3)   The following rules apply in relation to property—

(a)   property is obtained by a person if he obtains an interest in it;

(b)   references to an interest, in relation to land in England and Wales or Northern Ireland, are to any legal estate or equitable interest or power;

(c)   references to an interest, in relation to land in Scotland, are to any estate, interest, servitude or other heritable right in or over land, including a heritable security;

(d)   references to an interest, in relation to property other than land, include references to a right (including a right to possession).

Money laundering offences

415.—(1)   An offence under section 327, 328 or 329 is a money laundering offence.

(1A)[1]   Each of the following is a money laundering offence—

(a)   an offence under section 93A, 93B or 93C of the Criminal Justice Act 1988;

(b)   an offence under section 49, 50 or 51 of the Drug Trafficking Act 1994;

(c)   an offence under section 37 or 38 of the Criminal Law (Consolidation) (Scotland) Act 1995;

(d)   an offence under article 45, 46 or 47 of the Proceeds of Crime (Northern Ireland) Order 1996.

(2)   Each of the following is a money laundering offence—

(a)   an attempt, conspiracy or incitement to commit an offence specified in subsection (1);

(b)   aiding, abetting, counselling or procuring the commission of an offence specified in subsection (1).

Other interpretative provisions

416.—(1)   These expressions are to be construed in accordance with these provisions of this Part—

civil recovery investigation: section 341(2) and (3)
confiscation investigation: section 341(1)
detained cash investigation: section 341(3A)[2]
money laundering investigation: section 341(4)

---

[1] As inserted by the Serious Organised Crime and Police Act 2005 (c.15) s.107(4) (effective July 1, 2005).

[2] As inserted by the Serious Crime Act 2007 (c.27) Sch.10 para.24 (effective April 6, 2008 subject to transitional and transitory provisions and savings as specified in SI 2008/755 art.17(2) and (3)).

[1](2) In the application of this Part to England and Wales and Northern Ireland, these expressions are to be construed in accordance with these provisions of this Part—

> account information: section 370(4)
> account monitoring order: section 370(6)
> appropriate officer: section 378
> customer information: section 364
> customer information order: section 363(5)
> disclosure order: section 357(4)
> document: section 379
> order to grant entry: section 347(3)
> production order: section 345(4)
> [2]relevant authority: section 357(7) to (9)
> [3]relevant Director: section 352(5A)
> search and seizure warrant: section 352(4)
> senior appropriate officer: section 378
> [4]senior National Crime Agency officer: section 378(8).

(3) In the application of this Part to Scotland, these expressions are to be construed in accordance with these provisions of this Part—

> account information: section 404(5)
> account monitoring order: section 404(7)
> customer information: section 398
> customer information order: section 397(6)
> disclosure order: section 391(4)
> production order: section 380(5)
> proper person: section 412
> search warrant: section 387(4).

(4) "Financial institution" means a person carrying on a business in the regulated sector.

(5) But a person who ceases to carry on a business in the regulated sector (whether by virtue of paragraph 5 of Schedule 9 or otherwise) is to continue to be treated as a financial institution for the purposes of any requirement under—

(a) a customer information order, or

(b) an account monitoring order,

to provide information which relates to a time when the person was a financial institution.

(6) References to a business in the regulated sector must be construed in accordance with Schedule 9.

(7) "Recovery order", "interim receiving order" and "interim administration order" have the same meanings as in Part 5.

(7A)[5] "Unlawful conduct" has the meaning given by section 241.

(8) References to notice in writing include references to notice given by electronic means.

(9) This section and sections 413 to 415 apply for the purposes of this Part.

Sections 416.–462, Schs 1–8   *[Not reproduced.]*

---

[1] As inserted by the Crime and Courts Act 2013 (c.22) Sch.8(2) para.145 (effective October 1, 2013).
[2] As inserted by the Serious Crime Act 2007 (c.27) Sch.8(4) para. 117 (effective April 1, 2008).
[3] As inserted by the Serious Crime Act 2007 (c.27) Sch.8(4) para. 117 (effective April 1, 2008).
[4] As inserted by the Serious Crime Act 2007 (c.27) Sch.8(4) para. 117 (effective April 1, 2008).
[5] As inserted by the Serious Crime Act 2007 (c.27) Sch.10 para.24 (effective April 6, 2008 subject to transitional and transitory provisions and savings as specified in SI 2008/755 art.17(2) and (3)).

F1.332

SCHEDULE 9

REGULATED SECTOR AND SUPERVISORY AUTHORITIES

Section 330

PART 1[1]

REGULATED SECTOR

Business in the regulated sector

1.—(1) A business is in the regulated sector to the extent that it consists of—

(a) the acceptance by a credit institution of deposits or other repayable funds from the public, or the granting by a credit institution of credits for its own account;

(b)[2, 3] the carrying on of one or more of the activities listed in points 2 to 12, 14 and 15 of Annex 1 to the Capital Requirements Regulation by an undertaking other than—

   (i) a credit institution; or

   (ii) an undertaking whose only listed activity is trading for own account in one or more of the products listed in point 7 of Annex 1 to the Capital Requirements Regulation and which does not act on behalf of a customer (that is, a third party which is not a member of the same group as the undertaking);

(c) the carrying on of activities covered by the Life Assurance Consolidation Directive by an insurance company authorised in accordance with that Directive;

(d) the provision of investment services or the performance of investment activities by a person (other than a person falling within Article 2 of the Markets in Financial Instruments Directive) whose regular occupation or business is the provision to other persons of an investment service or the performance of an investment activity on a professional basis;

(e) the marketing or other offering of units or shares by a collective investment undertaking;

(f) the activities of an insurance intermediary as defined in Article 2(5) of the Insurance Mediation Directive, other than a tied insurance intermediary as mentioned in Article 2(7) of that Directive, in respect of contracts of long-term insurance within the meaning given by article 3(1) of, and Part II of Schedule 1 to, the Financial Services and Markets Act 2000 (Regulated Activities) Order 2001;

(g) the carrying on of any of the activities mentioned in paragraphs (b) to (f) by a branch located in an EEA State of a person referred to in those paragraphs (or of an equivalent person in any other State), wherever its head office is located;

(h) the activities of the National Savings Bank;

---

[1] As substituted by the Proceeds of Crime Act 2002 (Business in the Regulated Sector and Supervisory Authorities) Order 2007 (SI 2007/3287) art.2 (effective December 15, 2007: substitution has effect subject to transitional provision specified in SI 2007/3287 art.3).

[2] As substituted by the Electronic Money Regulations 2011 (SI 2011/99) Sch.4(1) para.4 (effective April 30, 2011).

[3] As amended by the Capital Requirements Regulations 2013 (SI 2013/3115) Sch.2 para.41 (effective January 1, 2014).

(i)   any activity carried on for the purpose of raising money authorised to be raised under the National Loans Act 1968 under the auspices of the Director of Savings;

(j)   the carrying on of statutory audit work within the meaning of section 1210 of the Companies Act 2006 (meaning of "statutory auditor" etc) by any firm or individual who is a statutory auditor within the meaning of Part 42 of that Act (statutory auditors);

(k)   the activities of a person appointed to act as an insolvency practitioner within the meaning of section 388 of the Insolvency Act 1986 (meaning of "act as insolvency practitioner") or article 3 of the Insolvency (Northern Ireland) Order 1989;

(l)   the provision to other persons of accountancy services by a firm or sole practitioner who by way of business provides such services to other persons;

(m)   the provision of advice about the tax affairs of other persons by a firm or sole practitioner who by way of business provides advice about the tax affairs of other persons;

(n)   the participation in financial or real property transactions concerning—

    (i)   the buying and selling of real property (or, in Scotland, heritable property) or business entities;

    (ii)   the managing of client money, securities or other assets;

    (iii)   the opening or management of bank, savings or securities accounts;

    (iv)   the organisation of contributions necessary for the creation, operation or management of companies; or

    (v)   the creation, operation or management of trusts, companies or similar structures, by a firm or sole practitioner who by way of business provides legal or notarial services to other persons;

(o)   the provision to other persons by way of business by a firm or sole practitioner of any of the services mentioned in sub-paragraph (4);

(p)[1]   the carrying on of estate agency work by a firm or a sole practitioner who carries on, or whose employees carry on, such work;

(q)   the trading in goods (including dealing as an auctioneer) whenever a transaction involves the receipt of a payment or payments in cash of at least 15,000 euros in total, whether the transaction is executed in a single operation or in several operations which appear to be linked, by a firm or sole trader who by way of business trades in goods;

(r)   operating a casino under a casino operating licence (within the meaning given by section 65(2) of the Gambling Act 2005 (nature of licence)).

(s)[2]   the auctioning by an auction platform of two-day spot or five-day futures, within the meanings given by Article 3 of the Emission Allowance Auctioning Regulation;

(t)[3]   bidding directly, on behalf of clients, in auctions of emissions allowances in accordance with the Emission Allowance Auctioning Regulation.

---

[1] As amended by the Terrorism Act 2000 and Proceeds of Crime Act 2002 (Business in the Regulated Sector) (No.2) Order 2012 (SI 2012/2299) art.3(a) (effective October 1, 2012).

[2] As inserted by the Terrorism Act 2000 and Proceeds of Crime Act 2002 (Business in the Regulated Sector) Order 2011 (SI 2011/2701) art.3(2) (effective December 12, 2011).

[3] As inserted by the Terrorism Act 2000 and Proceeds of Crime Act 2002 (Business in the Regulated Sector) Order 2012 (SI 2012/1534) art.3 (effective July 7, 2012).

(2)[1] For the purposes of sub-paragraph (1)(a) and (b) "credit institution" means—

(a)[2] a credit institution as defined in Article 4(1)(1) of the Capital Requirements Regulation; or

(b) a branch (within the meaning of Article 4(1)(17) of that Regulation) located in an EEA state of an institution falling within paragraph (a) (or of an equivalent institution in any other State) wherever its head office is located.

(3) For the purposes of sub-paragraph (1)(n) a person participates in a transaction by assisting in the planning or execution of the transaction or otherwise acting for or on behalf of a client in the transaction.

(4) The services referred to in sub-paragraph (1)(o) are—

(a) forming companies or other legal persons;

(b) acting, or arranging for another person to act—

(i) as a director or secretary of a company;

(ii) as a partner of a partnership; or

(iii) in a similar position in relation to other legal persons;

(c) providing a registered office, business address, correspondence or administrative address or other related services for a company, partnership or any other legal person or arrangement;

(d) acting, or arranging for another person to act, as—

(i) a trustee of an express trust or similar legal arrangement; or

(ii) a nominee shareholder for a person other than a company whose securities are listed on a regulated market.

(5) For the purposes of sub-paragraph (4)(d) "regulated market"—

(a) in relation to any EEA State, has the meaning given by point 14 of Article 4(1) of the Markets in Financial Instruments Directive; and

(b) in relation to any other State, means a regulated financial market which subjects companies whose securities are admitted to trading to disclosure obligations which are contained in international standards and are equivalent to the specified disclosure obligations.

(6) For the purposes of sub-paragraph (5) "the specified disclosure obligations" means disclosure requirements consistent with—

(a) Article 6(1) to (4) of Directive 2003/6/EC of the European Parliament and of the Council of 28th January 2003 on insider dealing and market manipulation;

(b) Articles 3, 5, 7, 8, 10, 14 and 16 of Directive 2003/71/EC of the European Parliament and of the Council of 4th November 2003 on the prospectuses to be published when securities are offered to the public or admitted to trading;

(c) Articles 4 to 6, 14, 16 to 19 and 30 of Directive 2004/109/EC of the European Parliament and of the Council of 15th December 2004 relating to the harmonisation of transparency requirements in relation to information about issuers whose securities are admitted to trading on a regulated market; or

(d) Community legislation made under the provisions mentioned in paragraphs (a) to (c).

(6A)[3] For the purposes of sub-paragraph (1)(p) "estate agency work" is to be read in accordance with section 1 of the Estate Agents Act 1979 (estate agency work), but for those purposes references in that section to disposing of or acquiring an interest in land are (despite anything in section 2 of that Act) to be taken to

---

[1] As amended by the Capital Requirements Regulations 2013 (SI 2013/3115) Sch.2 para.41 (effective January 1, 2014).

[2] As substituted by the Electronic Money Regulations 2011 (SI 2011/99) Sch.4(1) para.4 (effective April 30, 2011).

[3] As amended by the Terrorism Act 2000 and Proceeds of Crime Act 2002 (Business in the Regulated Sector) (No.2) Order 2012 (SI 2012/2299) art.3(b) (effective October 1, 2012).

include references to disposing of or acquiring an estate or interest in land outside the United Kingdom where that estate or interest is capable of being owned or held as a separate interest.

(7) For the purposes of sub-paragraph (1)(j) and (l) to (q) "firm" means any entity, whether or not a legal person, that is not an individual and includes a body corporate and a partnership or other unincorporated association.

(8) For the purposes of sub-paragraph (1)(q) "cash" means notes, coins or travellers' cheques in any currency.

(9)[1] For the purposes of sub-paragraph (1)(s)"auction platform" means a platform on which auctions of emissions allowances are held in accordance with the Emission Allowance Auctioning Regulation.

Excluded activities   **F1.333**

2.—(1) A business is not in the regulated sector to the extent that it consists of—

(a) the issuing of withdrawable share capital within the limit set by section 6 of the Industrial and Provident Societies Act 1965 (maximum shareholding in society), or the acceptance of deposits from the public within the limit set by section 7(3) of that Act (carrying on of banking by societies), by a society registered under that Act;

(b) the issuing of withdrawable share capital within the limit set by section 6 of the Industrial and Provident Societies Act (Northern Ireland) 1969 (maximum shareholding in society), or the acceptance of deposits from the public within the limit set by section 7(3) of that Act (carrying on of banking by societies), by a society registered under that Act;

(c) the carrying on of any activity in respect of which a person who is (or falls within a class of persons) specified in any of paragraphs 2 to 23, 25 to 38 or 40 to 49 of the Schedule to the Financial Services and Markets Act 2000 (Exemption) Order 2001 is exempt;

(d) the exercise of the functions specified in section 45 of the Financial Services Act 1986 (miscellaneous exemptions) by a person who was an exempted person for the purposes of that section immediately before its repeal; or

(e) the engaging in financial activity which fulfils all of the conditions set out in paragraphs (a) to (g) of sub-paragraph (3) of this paragraph by a person whose main activity is that of a high value dealer.

(f) *[Repealed by the Localism Act 2011 (c.20) Sch.25(29) para.1 (effective January 15, 2012).]*

(2) For the purposes of sub-paragraph (1)(e) a "high value dealer" means a person mentioned in paragraph 1(1)(q) when carrying on the activities mentioned in that paragraph.

(3) A business is not in the regulated sector to the extent that it consists of financial activity if—

(a) the person's total annual turnover in respect of the financial activity does not exceed £64,000;

(b) the financial activity is limited in relation to any customer to no more

[1] As inserted by the Terrorism Act 2000 and Proceeds of Crime Act 2002 (Business in the Regulated Sector) Order 2011 (SI 2011/2701) art.3(2) (effective December 12, 2011).

than one transaction exceeding 1,000 euros, whether the transaction is
carried out in a single operation, or a series of operations which appear
to be linked;

    (c)   the financial activity does not exceed 5% of the person's total annual
turnover;

    (d)   the financial activity is ancillary to the person's main activity and
directly related to that activity;

    (e)   the financial activity is not the transmission or remittance of money (or
any representation of monetary value) by any means;

    (f)   the main activity of the person carrying on the financial activity is not
an activity mentioned in paragraph 1(1)(a) to (p) or (r); and

    (g)   the financial activity is provided only to customers of the person's main
activity and is not offered to the public.

(4)   A business is not in the regulated sector if it is carried on by—

    (a)   the Auditor General for Scotland;

    (b)   the Auditor General for Wales;

    (c)   the Bank of England;

    (d)   the Comptroller and Auditor General;

    (e)   the Comptroller and Auditor General for Northern Ireland;

    (f)   the Official Solicitor to the Supreme Court, when acting as trustee in his
official capacity; or

    (g)   the Treasury Solicitor.

F1.334

Interpretation

3.—[1](1)[2] In this Part—

> *[As repealed by the Capital Requirements Regulations 2013 (SI 2013/3115)
> Sch.2 para.41 (effective January 1, 2008).]*
> "the Capital Requirements Regulation" means Regulation (EU) No. 575/2013
> of the European Parliament and of the Council;
> [3]"the Emission Allowance Auctioning Regulation" means Commission
> Regulation (EU) No. 1031/2010 of 12 November 2010 on the timing,
> administration and other aspects of auctioning of greenhouse gas emission
> allowances pursuant to Directive 2003/87/EC of the European Parliament
> and of the Council establishing a scheme for greenhouse gas emission allow-
> ances trading within the Community;
> "the Insurance Mediation Directive" means directive 2002/92/EC of the
> European Parliament and of the Council of 9th December 2002 on insurance
> mediation;
> "the Life Assurance Consolidation Directive" means directive 2002/83/EC of
> the European Parliament and of the Council of 5th November 2002 concern-
> ing life assurance; and
> "the Markets in Financial Instruments Directive" means directive 2004/39/EC
> of the European Parliament and of the Council of 12th April 2004 on markets
> in financial instruments.

---

[1] As amended by the Electronic Money Regulations 2011 (SI 2011/99) Sch.4 para.4 (effective April
30, 2011).

[2] As amended by the Capital Requirements Regulations 2013 (SI 2013/3115) Sch.2 para.41 (effective
January 1, 2014).

[3] As inserted by the Terrorism Act 2000 and Proceeds of Crime Act 2002 (Business in the Regulated
Sector) Order 2011 (SI 2011/2701) art.3(3) (December 12, 2011).

(2)   In this Part references to amounts in euros include references to equivalent amounts in another currency.

(3)   Terms used in this Part and in the Banking Consolidation Directive or the Markets in Financial Instruments Directive have the same meaning in this Part as in those Directives.

PART 2[1]

SUPERVISORY AUTHORITIES

F1.335

4.—(1)   The following bodies are supervisory authorities—

(a)   the Commissioners for Her Majesty's Revenue and Customs;

(b)   the Department of Enterprise, Trade and Investment in Northern Ireland;

(c)[2]   Financial Conduct Authority;

(d)   the Gambling Commission;

(e)   *[As repealed by the Enterprise and Regulatory Reform Act 2013 (Competition) (Consequential, Transitional and Saving Provisions) Order 2014 (SI 2014/892) Sch.1 para.159 (effective April 1, 2014).]*

(ea)[3]   Prudential Regulation Authority;

(f)[4]   the Secretary of State; and

(g)[5, 6]   the professional bodies listed in sub-paragraph (2).

(2)   The professional bodies referred to in sub-paragraph (1)(g) are—

(a)   the Association of Accounting Technicians;

(b)   the Association of Chartered Certified Accountants;

(c)   the Association of International Accountants;

(d)   the Association of Taxation Technicians;

(e)   the Chartered Institute of Management Accountants;

(f)   the Chartered Institute of Public Finance and Accountancy;

(g)   the Chartered Institute of Taxation;

(h)   the Council for Licensed Conveyancers;

(i)   the Faculty of Advocates;

(j)   the Faculty Office of the Archbishop of Canterbury;

(k)   the General Council of the Bar;

(l)   the General Council of the Bar of Northern Ireland;

(m)   the Insolvency Practitioners Association;

(n)   the Institute of Certified Bookkeepers;

(o)   the Institute of Chartered Accountants in England and Wales;

(p)   the Institute of Chartered Accountants in Ireland;

---

[1] As substituted by the Proceeds of Crime Act 2002 (Business in the Regulated Sector and Supervisory Authorities) Order 2007 (SI 2007/3287) art.2 (effective December 15, 2007: substitution has effect subject to transitional provision specified in SI 2007/3287 art.3).

[2] As substituted by the Financial Services Act 2012 (c.21) Sch.18(2) para.94(4)(a) (effective April 1, 2013).

[3] As inserted by the Financial Services Act 2012 (c.21) Sch.18(2) para.94(4)(b) (effective April 1, 2013).

[4] As inserted by the Proceeds of Crime Act 2002 (Business in the Regulated Sector and Supervisory Authorities) Order 2003 (SI 2003/3074) para.3 and substituted by the Pensions Act 2004 (c.35) Sch.12 para.80 (effective April 6, 2005, SI 2005/695).

[5] As inserted by the Proceeds of Crime Act 2002 (Business in the Regulated Sector and Supervisory Authorities) Order 2003 (SI 2003/3074) para.3 and substituted by the Pensions Act 2004 (c.35) Sch.12 para.80 (effective April 6, 2005, SI 2005/695).

[6] As substituted by the Gambling Act 2005 Sch.16 para.19, brought into force by SI 2005/2455 (effective October 1, 2005).

(q)   the Institute of Chartered Accountants of Scotland;
(r)   the Institute of Financial Accountants;
(s)   the International Association of Book-keepers;
(t)   the Law Society;
(u)   the Law Society for Northern Ireland; and
(v)   the Law Society of Scotland.

Part 3

F1.336

Power to Amend

5. The Treasury may by order amend Part 1 or 2 of this Schedule.

Legal Profession and Legal Aid (Scotland) Act 2007

2007 asp 5

CONTENTS

PART 1

THE SCOTTISH LEGAL COMPLAINTS COMMISSION

Establishment

PART 2

PART 2A

PART 2B

PART 3

PART 4

Legal aid

PART 5

General

77. Advice, services or activities to which Act does not apply
78. Ancillary provision
79. Regulations or orders
80. Interpretation
81. Minor and consequential modifications
82. Short title and commencement

Schedule 1   The Scottish Legal Complaints Commission
Schedule 2   Further powers of Commission under section 17 or 37
Schedule 3   Rules as to Commission's practice and procedure
Schedule 4   Further powers of relevant professional organisations under section 48
Schedule 5   Minor and consequential modifications

The Bill for this Act of the Scottish Parliament was passed by the Parliament on 14th December 2006 and received Royal Assent on 19th January 2007.

An Act of the Scottish Parliament to establish the Scottish Legal Complaints Commission; to make provision as regards complaints against members of the legal profession in Scotland and other matters concerning the regulation of that profession; to make provision in connection with the administration of the Scottish Legal Aid Fund, including a register of advice organisations in connection with advice and assistance; and for connected purposes.

PART 1

THE SCOTTISH LEGAL COMPLAINTS COMMISSION

Establishment

The Scottish Legal Complaints Commission

1.—(1) There is established a body to be known as the Scottish Legal Complaints Commission (referred to in this Act as "the Commission").

(2) Schedule 1 makes further provision about the status, constitution, proceedings etc. of the Commission.

Conduct or services complaints against practitioners

Receipt of complaints: preliminary steps

2.—(1) Where the Commission receives a complaint by or on behalf of any of the persons mentioned in subsection (2)—

(a) suggesting—
  (i) professional misconduct or unsatisfactory professional conduct by a practitioner other than a firm of solicitors or an incorporated practice;
  (ii) that a conveyancing practitioner or an executry practitioner has been convicted of a criminal offence rendering the practitioner no longer a fit and proper person to provide conveyancing services as a conveyancing practitioner or, as the case may be, executry services as an executry practitioner,
  (a complaint suggesting any such matter being referred to in this Part as a "conduct complaint");
(b) suggesting that professional services provided by a practitioner in connection with any matter in which the practitioner has been instructed by a client were inadequate (referred to in this Part as a "services complaint"),

it must, subject to subsection (3) and sections 3 and 4 and any provision in rules made under section 32(1) as to eligibility for making complaints, take the preliminary steps mentioned in subsection (4).

(2) The persons are—
(a) as respects a conduct complaint, any person;
(b) as respects a services complaint—

    (i) any person who appears to the Commission to have been directly affected by the suggested inadequate professional services;
    (ii) the Lord Advocate;
    (iii) the Advocate General for Scotland;
    (iv) any judge (including a sheriff);
    (v) the Auditor of the Court of Session;
    (vi) the Auditor of any sheriff court;
    (vii) the Scottish Legal Aid Board;
    (viii) any relevant professional organisation.

(3) The Commission is not to take the preliminary steps mentioned in subsection (4), and is not to take any further action under any other provision of this Part, in relation to any element of a conduct complaint which is about a practitioner acting in a judicial capacity in a court or tribunal specified by order by the Scottish Ministers.

(4) The preliminary steps are—
    (a) to determine whether or not the complaint is frivolous, vexatious or totally without merit;
    (b) where the Commission determines that the complaint is any or all of these things, to—
      (i) reject the complaint;
      (ii) give notice in writing to the complainer and the practitioner that it has rejected the complaint as frivolous, vexatious or totally without merit (or two or all of these things).

Existence of specified regulatory scheme

3.—(1) Where any element of a complaint referred to in section 2(1) is capable of being dealt with under a specified regulatory scheme, the Commission is prevented from dealing with the element but only to the extent that the element is capable of being dealt with under the specified regulatory scheme.

(2) Where the circumstances referred to in subsection (1) apply, the Commission must give notice in writing to that effect to—
    (a) the complainer and the practitioner;
    (b) such other persons as may be specified by the Scottish Ministers by order.

(3) Notice under subsection (2) must specify under which specified regulatory scheme the Commission considers the element is capable of being dealt with.

(4) Where the circumstances referred to in subsection (1) apply, notice under subsection (2) must in addition specify that the fact that the Commission is prevented by subsection (1) from dealing with the complaint to the extent that the complaint is capable of being dealt with under the specified regulatory scheme does not prevent the Commission taking the preliminary steps referred to in section 2(4) and dealing with the complaint under any provision of this Part to the extent that it is able.

(5) In this section "specified regulatory scheme" means a scheme specified as such by the Scottish Ministers by order.

Complaint not made timeously or made prematurely

4.—(1) Where a complaint referred to in section 2(1) is not made timeously, the Commission is not to take the preliminary steps referred to in section 2(4) in relation to it, and is not to take any further action under any other provision of this Part (except this section), in relation to it.

(2) Where a complaint referred to in section 2(1) is made prematurely, the Commission need not take the preliminary steps referred to in section 2(4) in relation to it, and need not take any further action under any other provision of this Part (except this section), in relation to it.

(3) For the purposes of subsection (1), a complaint is not made timeously where—

(a) rules made under section 32(1) fix time limits for the making of complaints;
(b) the complaint is made after the expiry of the time limit applicable to it;
(c) the Commission does not extend the time limit in accordance with the rules.

(4) For the purposes of subsection (2), a complaint is made prematurely where—
(a) the complainer has not previously communicated the substance of it to the practitioner, the practitioner's firm or, as the case may be, where the practitioner is an employee of another practitioner that other practitioner (referred to in this Part as the "employing practitioner") and given the practitioner, the firm or the employing practitioner what the Commission considers is a reasonable opportunity to deal with it;
(b) rules made under section 32(1) either—
 (i) do not provide for circumstances in which the Commission will take the steps and further action referred to in that subsection; or
 (ii) do provide for such circumstances but none is applicable in relation to the complaint.

(5) Where the circumstances referred to in subsection (1) or (2) apply, the Commission must give notice in writing to the complainer and practitioner to that effect.

(6) Where the circumstances referred to in subsection (2) apply, notice under subsection (5) must specify whether or not the Commission is proceeding to take the preliminary steps referred to in section 2(4).

Determining nature of complaint
5.—(1) Where the Commission proceeds to determine under section 2(4) whether a complaint is frivolous, vexatious or totally without merit and determines that it is none of these things, it must determine whether the complaint constitutes—
(a) a conduct complaint;
(b) a services complaint,
including whether (and if so to what extent) the complaint constitutes separate complaints falling within more than one of these categories and if so which of the categories.

(2) Where it appears to the Commission that the complaint may constitute both—
(a) a conduct complaint; and
(b) a separate services complaint,
it must consult, co-operate and liaise with the relevant professional organisation and have regard to any views expressed by the organisation on the matter before making a determination under subsection (1) as respects the complaint.

(3) A relevant professional organisation must co-operate and liaise with the Commission in relation to subsection (2).

Complaint determined to be conduct complaint
6. Where, or to the extent that, the Commission determines under section 5(1) that a complaint is a conduct complaint, it must—
(a) remit the complaint to the relevant professional organisation to deal with (and give to the organisation any material which accompanies the conduct complaint);
(b) give notice in writing to the complainer and the practitioner by sending to each of them a copy of the determination and specifying—
 (i) the reasons for the determination;
 (ii) that the conduct complaint is being remitted under this section for investigation and determination by the relevant professional organisation;

(iii) the relevant professional organisation to which it is being remitted;

(iv) that the relevant professional organisation is under a duty under this Act to deal with the conduct complaint.

Services complaint: notice

7. Where, or to the extent that, the Commission determines under section 5(1) that a complaint is a services complaint, it must give notice in writing to the complainer and the practitioner by sending to each of them a copy of the determination and specifying the reasons for the determination.

Services complaint: local resolution or mediation

8.—(1) This section applies where the Commission determines under section 5(1) that a complaint by or on behalf of a person referred to in section 2(2)(b)(i) is a services complaint.

(2) Where the Commission considers that either—

(a) the complaint has been made prematurely (within the meaning of section 4(4)); or

(b) the practitioner, the practitioner's firm or the employing practitioner has made no attempt, or an insufficient attempt, to achieve a negotiated settlement with the complainer,

the Commission may, by notice in writing to the complainer and the practitioner refer the complaint back to the practitioner, the practitioner's firm or, as the case may be, the employing practitioner requesting that the practitioner, the firm or the employing practitioner attempt to achieve such a settlement.

(3) Where the Commission refers a complaint back to the practitioner, the practitioner's firm or the employing practitioner under subsection (2), it may, by notice in writing, require the practitioner, the firm or the employing practitioner to give, before the end of such period being not less than 21 days as the notice specifies, an account and explanation of the steps which the practitioner, firm or employing practitioner has taken to attempt to achieve a negotiated settlement.

(4) Where the Commission considers it appropriate to do so, it may, by notice in writing to the complainer and the practitioner, offer to mediate in relation to the complaint.

(5) The Commission may enter into mediation in relation to a complaint only if both the complainer and the practitioner accept the offer made under subsection (4).

(6) The Commission must discontinue mediation in relation to a complaint if either the complainer or the practitioner withdraws consent to the mediation and may do so in any other circumstances; and, if mediation is discontinued, the Commission must give notice in writing to the complainer and the practitioner of its decision.

Services complaint: Commission's duty to investigate and determine

9.—(1) Where—

(a) the Commission does not refer a services complaint back to the practitioner, the practitioner's firm or the employing practitioner under section 8(2) (because it considers that the practitioner, firm or employing practitioner has made a sufficient attempt to achieve a negotiated settlement);

(b) the Commission refers a services complaint back to the practitioner, the practitioner's firm or the employing practitioner under that section but—

(i) no attempt to achieve a negotiated settlement takes place;

(ii) such an attempt takes place but is discontinued or a negotiated settlement is not accepted by both the practitioner and the complainer;

(c) mediation by virtue of section 8(5) in relation to the complaint—
  (i) does not take place;
  (ii) takes place but is discontinued or the outcome of the mediation is not accepted by both the complainer and the practitioner;
(d) the Commission determines under section 5(1) that a complaint by or on behalf of any person referred to in sub-paragraphs (ii) to (viii) of section 2(2)(b) is a services complaint,

the Commission must, subject to section 15(2) and (5), investigate the complaint and after giving the complainer and the practitioner an opportunity to make representations, subject to subsections (2) to (4), determine it by reference to what the Commission considers is fair and reasonable in the circumstances.

(2) Where the complainer is a person referred to in section 2(2)(b)(i) the Commission must, subject to subsection (3), propose to the practitioner and the complainer a settlement as respects the complaint which it considers is fair and reasonable in the circumstances.

(3) Where the practitioner was, at the time the services were provided, an employee of an employing practitioner, a proposal under subsection (2) to the practitioner and the complainer must also be made to the employing practitioner.

(4) Where the practitioner and the complainer, and where subsection (3) applies the employing practitioner, accept a settlement proposed by the Commission under subsection (2) as respects the complaint, the Commission is not to determine the complaint under subsection (1).

Commission upholds services complaint

10.—(1) Where the Commission makes a determination under section 9(1) upholding a services complaint, it may take such of the steps mentioned in subsection (2) as it considers fair and reasonable in the circumstances.

(2) The steps are, subject to subsection (3)—
  (a) to determine that the amount of the fees and outlays to which the practitioner is entitled for the services provided to the client and to which the complaint relates, is to be—
    (i) nil; or
    (ii) such amount as the Commission may specify in the determination,
    and to direct the practitioner to comply or secure compliance with such of the requirements set out in subsection (5) as appear to the Commission to be necessary to give effect to the determination;
  (b) to direct the practitioner to secure the rectification at the practitioner's own expense of any such error, omission or other deficiency arising in connection with the services as the Commission may specify;
  (c) to direct the practitioner to take, at the practitioner's own expense, such other action in the interests of the complainer as the Commission may specify;
  (d) where the Commission considers that the complainer has been directly affected by the inadequate professional services, to direct the practitioner to pay compensation of such amount, not exceeding £20,000, as the Commission may specify to the complainer for loss, inconvenience or distress resulting from the inadequate professional services;
  (e) where the Commission considers that the practitioner may not have sufficient competence in relation to any aspect of the law or legal practice, to report the matter to the relevant professional organisation.

(3) Where the practitioner was, at the time when the services were provided, an employee (referred to in this section as an "employee practitioner") of an employing practitioner—

(a) a direction under subsection (2)(a), (b) or (c) must be to the employing practitioner instead of the employee practitioner;

(b) a direction under subsection (2)(d)—

    (i) may be to and direct either the employing practitioner or, if the Commission considers it appropriate, the employee practitioner to pay all of the compensation directed to be paid under that subsection in relation to the complaint concerned;

    (ii) may be to and direct the employee practitioner to pay such part of the total amount of compensation directed to be paid under that subsection in relation to the complaint concerned as the Commission considers appropriate and if it does so, must be to and direct the employing practitioner to pay the remainder of the total amount;

(c) a copy of any report under subsection (2)(e) must be sent to the employing practitioner.

(4) The Commission must, in considering what steps to take under subsection (2), take into account any—

(a) prior direction by it under subsection (2)(d) that the employee practitioner concerned or, where subsection (3) applies, the employing practitioner, pay to the complainer an amount by way of compensation;

(b) award of damages by the court to the complainer;

(c) other compensation ordered (whether by determination, direction or otherwise) by a tribunal or other professional body to be paid to the complainer,

in relation to the subject matter of the complaint.

(5) The requirements referred to in subsection (2)(a) are to—

(a) refund, whether wholly or to any specified extent any amount already paid by or on behalf of the client in respect of fees and outlays of the practitioner in connection with the services;

(b) waive, whether wholly or to any specified extent, the right to recover the fees and outlays.

(6) Before making a determination in accordance with subsection (2)(a), the Commission may submit the practitioner's accounts for the fees and outlays to the Auditor of the Court of Session for taxation.

(7) The Scottish Ministers may by order, after consulting—

(a) the relevant professional organisations;

(b) such groups of persons representing consumer interests as they consider appropriate,

amend subsection (2)(d) by substituting for the amount for the time being specified in that subsection such other amount as they consider appropriate.

Fair and reasonable: matters to be taken into account by Commission

11. In considering what is fair and reasonable in the circumstances, the Commission is to take into account the relevant law (including levels of damages awarded by courts in similar circumstances) and relevant codes of practice, professional rules, standards and guidance.

Services complaint: notice where not upheld or upheld

12.—(1) The Commission must give notice in writing of a—

(a) determination by it under section 9(1) not to uphold a services complaint;

(b) determination by it under that section upholding any such complaint;

(c) determination, direction or report by it under section 10(2),

to the complainer and every practitioner specified in it and, where section 10(3) applies, to the employing practitioner by sending to each of them a copy of the determination, the direction or, as the case may be, the report.

(2) Where the determination is made by a determination committee by virtue of paragraph 13(2)(d)(i) or, as the case may be, (ii) of schedule

1, notice under subsection (1) must specify the reasons for the determination.

Services complaint: reports

13.—(1) The Commission may, if it considers it appropriate to do so in any particular case, publish a report of—

(a) any mediation which has taken place by virtue of section 8(5) in relation to a services complaint, the outcome of which is accepted by both the complainer and the practitioner;

(b) an investigation of a services complaint under section 9 and—

    (i) any settlement proposed under subsection (2) of that section as respects the complaint, which is accepted as mentioned in subsection (4) of that section;

    (ii) any determination of the complaint under subsection (1) of that section;

(c) a determination, direction or report under section 10(2).

(2) A report under subsection (1) must not (unless the complainer consents)—

(a) mention the name of the complainer;

(b) include any particulars which, in the opinion of the Commission, are likely to identify the complainer.

(3) A report under subsection (1) may only—

(a) mention the name of the practitioner complained of; or

(b) include any particulars which, in the opinion of the Commission, are likely to identify the practitioner,

if the practitioner consents or the condition in subsection (4) is met.

(4) The condition is that—

(a) the case is exceptional;

(b) in the opinion of the Commission, it is in the public interest for the identity of the practitioner concerned to be included in the report; and

(c) the Commission has given not less than 4 weeks notice in writing to the practitioner that it intends to identify the practitioner in the report, specifying the reasons for its decision.

Determination under section 9(1) or taking of steps under section 10(2): effect in relation to proceedings

14.—(1) Neither the making of a determination under section 9(1) upholding a complaint, nor the taking of any steps under section 10(2) may be founded upon in any proceedings.

(2) A direction under section 10(2)(d) to a practitioner to pay compensation to a complainer does not prejudice any right of the complainer to take proceedings against the practitioner for damages in respect of any loss which the complainer claims to have suffered; and any amount directed to be paid to the complainer under that section may be taken into account in the computation of any award of damages made to the complainer in any such proceedings.

Complaint appears during mediation or investigation to fall within different category

15.—(1) Where a relevant professional organisation at any time during any mediation by it, or its investigation, of a conduct complaint remitted to it under section 6(a) considers that it is reasonably likely that the complaint (or any element of it) may instead constitute a services complaint, it must—

(a) suspend the mediation or, as the case may be, the investigation;

(b) consult, co-operate and liaise with the Commission as respects the matter;

(c) send the complaint and any material which relates to it and which is in the organisation's possession to the Commission;

(d) give notice in writing to the complainer and the practitioner that it so considers and is so doing.

(2) Where the Commission at any time during its mediation by virtue of section 8(5) in relation to, or investigation by virtue of section 9(1) of, a services complaint considers that it is reasonably likely that the complaint (or any element of it) may instead constitute a conduct complaint, it must—

    (a) suspend the mediation or investigation;

    (b) send a copy of the complaint and any material which relates to it and which is in the Commission's possession to the relevant professional organisation;

    (c) consult, co-operate and liaise with the relevant professional organisation as respects the matter;

    (d) give notice in writing to the complainer, the practitioner and the relevant professional organisation that it so considers and is so doing.

(3) Where, in the circumstances referred to in subsection (1) or (2) the Commission, having regard to the views expressed by the relevant professional organisation as respects the matter, considers that—

    (a) its determination under section 5(1) as respects the complaint should be confirmed (to any extent), it must so determine; and the determination under this paragraph must specify the extent to which the determination under that section is confirmed;

    (b) a complaint (or any element of a complaint) which was determined by it under section 5(1) to constitute—

      (i) a conduct complaint constitutes instead a services complaint;

      (ii) a services complaint constitutes instead a conduct complaint,

it must determine accordingly.

(4) Where, or to the extent that, the Commission determines under subsection (3)(a) to confirm to any extent its determination under section 5(1)—

    (a) it must give notice in writing to the complainer, the practitioner and the relevant professional organisation by sending to each of them a copy of the determination and specifying the reasons for the determination;

    (b) any suspension under subsection (1)(a) or (2)(a) ceases.

(5) Where the Commission determines under subsection (3)(b) that a complaint (or any element of a complaint) which was determined by it under section 5(1) to constitute a services complaint constitutes instead a conduct complaint, it must—

    (a) remit the conduct complaint to the relevant professional organisation to deal with (and give to the organisation any material referred to in section 6(a));

    (b) give notice in writing to the complainer, the practitioner and the relevant professional organisation by sending to each of them a copy of the determination and specifying—

      (i) the reasons for the determination;

      (ii) that the conduct complaint is being remitted under paragraph (a);

      (iii) the relevant professional organisation to which it is being remitted;

      (iv) that the relevant professional organisation is under a duty under this Act to deal with the conduct complaint.

(6) Where the Commission determines under subsection (3)(b) that a complaint (or any element of a complaint) which was determined by it under section 5(1) to constitute a conduct complaint constitutes instead a services complaint—

    (a) it must give notice in writing to the complainer, the practitioner and the relevant professional organisation by sending to each of them a copy of the determination and specifying the reasons for the determination;

    (b) sections 8 to 12 apply to the services complaint as they apply where a determination is made under section 5(1) that a complaint constitutes a services complaint.

Power to monitor compliance with directions under section 10(2)

16.—(1) The Commission must, by notice in writing, require every practitioner specified in any direction under section 10(2) to give, before the end of such period being not less than 21 days as the notice specifies, an account and explanation of the steps which the practitioner has taken to comply with the direction.

(2) Where an appeal against any such direction is made under section 21(1), any notice under subsection (1) relating to the direction ceases to have effect pending the outcome of the appeal.

Power to examine documents and demand explanations in connection with conduct or services complaints

17.—(1) Where the Commission is satisfied that it is necessary for it to do so for the purposes of section 2, 4, 5, 8, 9, 10, 15 or 16, it may give notice in writing in accordance with subsection (2) to the practitioner, the practitioner's firm or, as the case may be, the employing practitioner.

(2) Notice under subsection (1) may require—

(a) the production or delivery to any person appointed by the Commission, at a time and place specified in the notice, of all documents mentioned in subsection (3) which are in the possession or control of the practitioner, the firm or, as the case may be, the employing practitioner and which relate to the matters to which the complaint relates (whether or not they relate also to other matters);

(b) an explanation, within such period being not less than 21 days as the notice specifies, from the practitioner, the firm or, as the case may be, the employing practitioner regarding the matters to which the complaint relates.

(3) The documents are—

(a) all books, accounts, deeds, securities, papers and other documents in the possession or control of the practitioner, the firm or, as the case may be, the employing practitioner;

(b) all books, accounts, deeds, securities, papers and other documents relating to any trust of which the practitioner is the sole trustee or a co-trustee only with one or more of the practitioner's partners or employees or, as the case may be, where the practitioner is an incorporated practice of which the practice or one of its employees is a sole trustee or it is a co-trustee only with one or more of its employees.

(4) Where the Commission is satisfied that it is necessary for it to do so for the purposes of section 2, 4, 5, 8, 9, 10 or 15, it may give notice in writing in accordance with subsection (5) to the complainer.

(5) Notice under subsection (4) may require—

(a) the production or delivery to any person appointed by the Commission at a time and place specified in the notice, of all documents mentioned in subsection (6) which are in the possession or control of the complainer and which relate to the matters to which the complaint relates (whether or not they relate to other matters);

(b) an explanation, within such period being not less than 21 days as the notice specifies, from the complainer regarding the matters to which the complaint relates.

(6) The documents are all books, accounts, deeds, securities, papers and other documents in the possession or control of the complainer.

(7) Schedule 2 makes further provision about the powers of the Commission under this section.

Power of Commission to recover certain expenses

18.—(1) The Commission is, subject to subsection (2), entitled to recover from a practitioner, the practitioner's firm or, as the case may be, the employing practitioner, in respect of whom it has taken any action by virtue of section 17, any expenditure reasonably incurred by it in so doing.

(2) Expenditure incurred in taking action by virtue of section 17 is recoverable under subsection (1) only where notice has been served under paragraph 2(a) of schedule 2 in connection with that action and either—

(a) no application has been made in consequence under paragraph 3 of that schedule; or

(b) the court, on such an application, has made a direction under paragraph 4 of that schedule.

Documents and information from third parties

19.—(1) Where the Commission has requested that documents or information in the possession or control of a person be produced for the purposes of an investigation by it under this Act and the person refuses or fails to produce the documents or information, the Commission may apply to the court for an order under subsection (2).

(2) An order by the court under this subsection may require a person to produce or deliver the documents or information or to cause them or it to be produced or delivered to the person appointed at the place fixed by the Commission within such time as the court may order.

(3) The court may make an order under subsection (2) only if—

(a) it appears—
   (i) the documents sought are; or
   (ii) the information sought is,
   relevant to the investigation; and

(b) it is in the public interest for the documents or information to be produced.

(4) Where the Commission receives possession of any such documents or information which have been produced or delivered to it, it must without delay serve on the person from whom the documents or information were received, a notice giving particulars and the date on which it took possession.

(5) Before the expiry of the period of 14 days after service of a notice under subsection (4) the person on whom the notice has been served may apply to the court for an order directing return of the documents or information to the person from whom they were received by the Commission or to such other person as the applicant may request; and on the hearing of any such application the court may make the order applied for or such other order as it thinks fit.

(6) If no application is made to the court under subsection (5), or if the court on any such application directs that the documents or information in question remain in the custody or control of the Commission, the Commission may make enquiries to ascertain the person to whom they belong and may deal with the documents or information in accordance with the directions of that person.

(7) This section does not apply to documents or information in the possession or control of—

(a) the person who made the complaint from which the investigation arises;

(b) the practitioner concerned;

(c) a relevant professional organisation.

Enforcement of Commission direction under section 10(2)

20. A direction by the Commission under section 10(2) is enforceable in like manner as an extract registered decree arbitral in its favour bearing a warrant for execution issued by the sheriff court of any sheriffdom in Scotland.

Appeals

Appeal against Commission decisions

21.—(1) Any person mentioned in subsection (2) may, with the leave of the court, appeal against any decision of the Commission under the preceding sections of this Part as respects a complaint on any ground set out in subsection (4).

(2) Those persons are—

(a) the complainer;

(b) the practitioner to whom the complaint relates;

(c) the practitioner's firm;

(d) the employing practitioner;

(e) the relevant professional organisation.

(3) An appeal under subsection (1) must be made before the expiry of the period of 28 days beginning with the day on which notice of the decision was given to the complainer and the practitioner; but the court may, on cause shown, consider an appeal made after the expiry of that period.

(4) The grounds referred to in subsection (1) are—

(a) that the Commission's decision was based on an error of law;

(b) that there has been a procedural impropriety in the conduct of any hearing by the Commission on the complaint;

(c) that the Commission has acted irrationally in the exercise of its discretion;

(d) that the Commission's decision was not supported by the facts found to be established by the Commission.

(5) The Commission is to be a party in any proceedings on an appeal under subsection (1).

(6) In this section and in section 22, "decision" includes any determination, direction or other decision and also includes the making of any report under section 10(2)(e).

Appeal: supplementary provision

22.—(1) On any appeal under section 21(1), the court may make such order as it thinks fit (including an order substituting its own decision for the decision appealed against).

(2) Where such an order upholds a services complaint or confirms a decision of the Commission to uphold a services complaint, the court may direct that such of the steps mentioned in 10(2) as it considers fair and reasonable in the circumstances be taken.

(3) On any appeal under section 21(1) the court may make such ancillary order (including an order as to the expenses of the appeal) as it thinks fit.

(4) A decision of the court under this section is final.

Handling by relevant professional organisations of conduct complaints

Handling by relevant professional organisations of conduct complaints: investigation by Commission

23.—(1) The Commission may, subject to subsection (4), carry out such investigation as appears to it to be appropriate of any complaint made to it by or on behalf of any person which relates to the manner in which a conduct complaint made by or on behalf of that person and remitted to a relevant professional organisation under section 6(a) or 15(5)(a) has been dealt with by the organisation (such a complaint being referred to in this Act as a "handling complaint").

(2) The Commission may decide—

(a) not to investigate a handling complaint;

(b) to discontinue the investigation of a handling complaint.

(3) If the Commission decides not to investigate, or to discontinue the investigation of, a handling complaint it must give notice in writing to—

(a) the person who made the handling complaint;
(b) the relevant professional organisation;
(c) the practitioner concerned in the conduct complaint to which the handling complaint relates,

by sending to each of them a copy of the decision and specifying the reasons for the decision.

(4) The Commission must not investigate a handling complaint where either—

(a) the relevant professional organisation has not completed its investigation of the conduct complaint to which the handling complaint relates; or
(b) the handling complaint is made after the expiry of the period of 6 months after such date as the Scottish Ministers may specify by order,

but paragraph (a) does not apply in any of the circumstances mentioned in subsection (5).

(5) The circumstances are that—

(a) the handling complaint is that the relevant professional organisation—
   (i) has acted unreasonably in failing to start an investigation into the complaint; or
   (ii) having started such an investigation, has failed to complete it within a reasonable time; or
(b) the Commission considers that, even though the complaint is being investigated by the organisation, an investigation by the Commission is justified.

(6) Where the Commission decides that subsection (4)(a) does not prevent it investigating a handling complaint because any of the circumstances referred to in subsection (5) apply, it must give notice in writing to—

(a) the person who made the handling complaint;
(b) the relevant professional organisation;
(c) the practitioner concerned in the conduct complaint to which the handling complaint relates,

by sending to each of them a copy of the decision and specifying the reasons for the decision.

(7) An order under subsection (4)(b) may specify different dates for different purposes.

(8) Where the Commission is conducting an investigation under this section, it may at any time make a written interim report in relation to the investigation and must send a copy of any such report to—

(a) the person who made the handling complaint;
(b) the relevant professional organisation;
(c) the practitioner concerned in the conduct complaint to which the handling complaint relates.

(9) The Scottish Ministers may by order amend the period of time referred to in subsection (4)(b).

Investigation under section 23: final report and recommendations

24.—(1) Where the Commission has completed an investigation under section 23 it must—

(a) make a written report of its conclusions;
(b) send a copy of the report to—
   (i) the person who made the handling complaint;
   (ii) the relevant professional organisation;
   (iii) the practitioner concerned in the conduct complaint to which the handling complaint relates.

(2) A report under this section may include one or more of the following recommendations—

(a) that the relevant professional organisation provide to the person making the handling complaint such information about the conduct complaint to which the handling complaint relates, and how it was dealt with, as the Commission considers appropriate;

(b) that the conduct complaint be investigated further by the relevant professional organisation;

(c) that the conduct complaint be reconsidered by the relevant professional organisation;

(d) that the relevant professional organisation consider exercising its powers in relation to the practitioner concerned;

(e) that the relevant professional organisation pay compensation of such amount, not exceeding £5000, as the Commission may specify to the person making the handling complaint for loss, inconvenience or distress resulting from the way in which the conduct complaint was handled by the organisation;

(f) that the relevant professional organisation pay to the person making the handling complaint an amount specified by the Commission by way of reimbursement of the cost, or part of the cost, of making the handling complaint.

(3) Where a report under this section includes any recommendation, the report must state the reasons for making the recommendation.

(4) A relevant professional organisation to whom a report is sent by the Commission under this section must have regard to the conclusions and recommendations set out in the report so far as relating to the organisation.

(5) Where a report sent to a relevant professional organisation under this section includes a recommendation relating to it, the organisation must, before the end of the period of 3 months beginning with the date on which the report was sent, notify the Commission, the person who made the handling complaint and the practitioner concerned, in writing, of—

(a) the action which it has taken to comply with the recommendations or in consequence of further consideration of the matter by it;

(b) its decision not to comply wholly with a recommendation and any reason for that decision.

(6) Where the Commission is either—

(a) notified under subsection (5)(b) that the relevant professional organisation has decided not to comply wholly with a recommendation; or

(b) of the opinion that the relevant professional organisation has not complied wholly with a recommendation before the end of the period of 3 months beginning with the date on which the report was sent to the organisation under this section,

the Commission may direct the professional organisation to comply with that recommendation if the Commission thinks fit; and the organisation must comply with the direction.

(7) For the purposes of subsection (6), a "recommendation" means any recommendation referred to in paragraphs (a) to (c), (e) or (f) of subsection (2).

(8) The Scottish Ministers may by order, after consulting—

(a) the relevant professional organisations;

(b) such groups of persons representing consumer interests as they consider appropriate,

amend subsection (2)(e) by substituting for the amount for the time being specified in that subsection such other amount as they consider appropriate.

Failure to comply with recommendation

25.—(1) If the Commission considers that a relevant professional organisation has failed to comply with a direction under section 24(6), the Commission may apply by petition to the court for the organisation to be dealt with in accordance with subsection (2).

(2) Where such a petition is presented, the court may inquire into the matter and after hearing—

(a) any witnesses who may be produced against or on behalf of the professional organisation; and

(b) any statement that may be offered in defence,

may order the organisation to comply with the recommendation with which the direction under section 24(6) is concerned.

Abolition of Scottish legal services ombudsman

26.—(1) The office of the Scottish legal services ombudsman ("the ombudsman") is abolished on such date as the Scottish Ministers may by order specify.

(2) The Scottish Ministers may not make an order under subsection (1) unless the ombudsman has no exercisable functions.

(3) The functions of the ombudsman cease to be exercisable except in relation to the advice, services and activities mentioned in section 77(2).

Finance

Annual general levy

27.—(1) Each—

(a) advocate practising as such;

(b) conveyancing practitioner or executry practitioner;

(c) person exercising a right to conduct litigation or a right of audience acquired by virtue of section 27 of the 1990 Act;

(d) solicitor who has in force a practising certificate,

must, subject to subsection (2) and section 29(2), pay to the Commission in respect of each financial year a contribution (referred to in this Part as "the annual general levy").

(2) Each relevant professional organisation—

(a) must secure the collection by it, from all of the persons falling within the categories referred to in paragraphs (a) to (d) of subsection (1) as respects whom it is the relevant professional organisation, of the annual general levy due by them;

(b) must pay to the Commission a sum representing the total amount which falls to be collected by it under paragraph (a) in respect of each financial year.

(3) Any—

(a) sum due to the Commission under subsection (2)(b);

(b) interest due on any such sum at such rate as may be specified by the Scottish Ministers by order from the date the sum is due under rules made under section 32(1) until it is paid,

may be recovered by it (as a debt) from the relevant professional organisation which is liable under that subsection to pay the sum.

(4) A relevant professional organisation may recover (as a debt), from any person falling within the categories referred to in paragraphs (a) to (d) of subsection (1) as respects whom it is the relevant professional organisation—

(a) any sum due by the person to the Commission under that subsection;

(b) any interest due on any such sum at such rate as may be specified by the Scottish Ministers by order from the date the sum is due under rules made under section 32(1) until it is paid.

(5) If any person who is liable under subsection (1) to pay the annual general levy fails to pay any amount of the levy, or pays any such amount late, the failure or late payment may be treated as professional misconduct or unsatisfactory professional conduct.

Complaints levy

28.—(1) A practitioner against whom a services complaint is made must pay to the Commission, in the circumstances mentioned in subsection (2), a contribution in relation to the complaint (referred to in this Part as "the complaints levy").

(2) The circumstances are where—
(a) any of the following applies—
(i) mediation by virtue of section 8(5) takes place in relation to the complaint and the outcome of the mediation is accepted by both the complainer and the practitioner;
(ii) a settlement proposed as respects the complaint by the Commission under section 9(2) is accepted as mentioned in section 9(4);
(iii) the Commission makes a determination under section 9(1) upholding the complaint; and
(b) the amount of the levy has not been determined as nil and the Commission does not in accordance with rules made under section 32(1) waive the requirement to pay the levy.
(3) Any—
(a) sum due by a practitioner to the Commission under subsection (1);
(b) interest due on any such sum at such rate as may be specified by the Scottish Ministers by order from the date the sum is due under rules made under section 32(1) until it is paid,
may be recovered by it (as a debt) from the practitioner.
(4) If any person who is liable under subsection (1) to pay the complaints levy fails to pay any amount of the levy, or pays any such amount late, the failure or late payment may be treated as professional misconduct or unsatisfactory professional conduct.

Amount of levies and consultation
29.—(1) The amount of the—
(a) annual general levy;
(b) complaints levy,
in respect of each financial year is such amount as may be determined by the Commission, having had regard to any views expressed in its consultation under subsection (4) in respect of the financial year in question.
(2) The amount of the annual general levy must be the same amount for each of the individuals who are liable under section 27(1) to pay it; but rules made under section 32(1) may provide for circumstances in which the Commission may waive a portion of the amount which would otherwise require to be paid.
(3) The Commission may determine different amounts (including an amount of nil) for the complaints levy in different circumstances.
[1] (4) The Commission must, in January each year, consult each relevant professional organisation and its members, and the Scottish Ministers on the Commission's proposed budget for the next financial year.
(5) The proposed budget must—
(a) include—
(i) an estimate as respects resource requirements;
(ii) the proposed amount of the annual general levy and the complaints levy;
(b) be accompanied by information as to the Commission's projected work plan for the next financial year.
(6) Each relevant professional organisation must, for the purpose of informing the Commission in relation to—
(a) the inclusion in the Commission's proposed budget for each financial year of the proposed amount of the annual general levy;
(b) the Commission's determination under subsection (1) of the amount of the annual general levy in respect of each financial year,
provide the Commission with an estimate of the number of persons as respects whom it is the relevant professional organisation and who it anticipates should be liable under section 27(1) to pay the annual general levy for the financial year concerned.
(7) The Commission must secure so far as is reasonably practicable that,

taking one financial year with another, the amount of the annual general levy and the complaints levy is reasonably sufficient to meet its expenditure.

(8) The Commission must, no later than 31 March in each year, publish the responses it has received in the consultation carried out by it under subsection (4) in the immediately preceding January.

¹ (9) Subsection (8) does not apply to responses which are subject to an express request in writing for confidentiality.

(10) The Commission must lay a copy of the finalised budget before the Parliament no later than 30 April in each year.

NOTE
¹ As amended by the Legal Services (Scotland) Act 2010 (asp 16) Pt 4 c.4 s.144(a) (effective April 1, 2011).

Grants or loans by the Scottish Ministers
30.—(1) The Scottish Ministers may make grants to the Commission of such amounts as they consider appropriate.

(2) Any grant under this section may be made on such terms and subject to such conditions (including conditions as to repayment) as the Scottish Ministers consider appropriate; and the Scottish Ministers may from time to time after the grant is made vary such terms and conditions.

(3) For the purpose of the exercise of any of its duties or powers under this Part—
  (a) the Commission may, subject to such conditions as the Scottish Ministers think fit, borrow from them;
  (b) the Scottish Ministers may lend to the Commission,
sums of such amounts as the Ministers may determine.

(4) Any loan made in pursuance of subsection (3) is to be repaid to the Scottish Ministers at such times and by such methods, and interest on the loan is to be paid to them at such times and at such rates, as they may from time to time direct.

Guarantees
31.—(1) The Scottish Ministers may guarantee, in such manner and on such conditions as they think fit, the discharge of any financial obligation in connection with any sums borrowed by the Commission.

(2) Immediately after any guarantee is given under this section, the Scottish Ministers must lay a statement of the guarantee before the Parliament.

(3) Where any sum is paid out in fulfilment of a guarantee under this section, the Commission must make to the Scottish Ministers, at such times and in such manner as they may from time to time direct—
  (a) payments of such amount as they may so direct in or towards repayment of the sums so paid out;
  (b) payments of interest, at such rate as they may so direct, on the amount outstanding for the time being in respect of sums so paid out.

Rules as to Commission's practice and procedure

Duty of Commission to make rules as to practice and procedure
32.—(1) The Commission must make rules as to its practice and procedure and, as soon as practicable after making or varying those rules, publish them and make them available to the public in a form which is readily accessible.

(2) Schedule 3 makes further provision as respects provision which—
  (a) must be included;
  (b) may in particular be included,
in the rules.

(3) The rules may make different provision for different categories of complaint.

(4) The Commission must keep the rules under review and must vary the provisions of the rules whenever it considers it appropriate to do so.

(5) The Commission must, before making rules or varying the rules, consult with—

(a) the Lord President of the Court of Session;

(b) the Scottish Ministers;

(c) the relevant professional organisations;

(d) such groups of persons representing consumer interests as it considers appropriate,

as to the proposed content of the rules to be made or varied.

Forwarding complaints, advice, monitoring etc.

Duty of relevant professional organisations to forward complaints to Commission

33. Where a relevant professional organisation receives a complaint from a person other than the Commission about—

(a) the conduct of, or any services provided by, a practitioner;

(b) its handling of a conduct complaint remitted to it under section 6(a) or 15(5)(a),

it must without delay send the complaint and any material which accompanies it to the Commission.

Commission's duty to provide advice

34.—(1) The Commission must, so far as is reasonably practicable, provide advice to any person who requests it as respects the process of making a services complaint or a handling complaint to it.

(2) Where the Commission receives a complaint suggesting what purports to be professional misconduct or unsatisfactory professional conduct by a practitioner who is a firm of solicitors or an incorporated practice—

(a) it must inform the person that a complaint to it suggesting such misconduct or such conduct may be made only against a named practitioner who is an individual;

(b) where the complaint received is not about a named practitioner who is an individual, it must so far as is reasonably practicable offer advice to the person with a view to assisting the person to reformulate the complaint so that it is about such a named practitioner.

(3) Where a person in requesting or being offered such advice expresses a preference for receiving it by a particular means (as, for example, in writing, by telephone, by means of a recording or an explanation in person), the Commission must, so far as is reasonably practicable, give effect to the preference.

Services complaints: monitoring, reports, protocols and information sharing

35.—(1) The Commission must monitor practice and identify any trends in practice as respects the way in which practitioners have dealt with matters that result in services complaints being dealt with by the Commission under sections 8 to 12.

(2) The Commission must prepare and publish reports on any trends in practice which it identifies under subsection (1) at such intervals as it considers appropriate.

(3) The Commission must—

(a) enter into protocols with the relevant professional organisations as respects the sharing of information by it with them in relation to—

(i) numbers of services complaints dealt with by it;

(ii) such trends as it may identify in relation to such complaints;

(iii) settlements proposed by it under section 9(2), which are accepted as mentioned in subsection (4) of that section;

(iv) the substance of any services complaints which might be relevant to section 31(3) of the 1986 Act;

(v) determinations by it under section 9(1) upholding services complaints;

(vi) failure by practitioners to comply with directions by it under section 10(2), notice by it under section 16 or 17(1) or requirements by it under section 37(3);

(b) share information with the relevant professional organisations in accordance with the protocols.

(4) The relevant professional organisations must enter into protocols with the Commission for the purposes of subsection (3)(a).

Conduct complaints: monitoring, reports, guidance and recommendations

36.—(1) The Commission must monitor practice and identify any trends in practice as respects the way in which—

(a) practitioners have dealt with matters that result in conduct complaints being remitted to the relevant professional organisations under section 6(a) or 15(5)(a);

(b) the relevant professional organisations have dealt with conduct complaints so remitted.

(2) The Commission must prepare and publish reports on any trends in practice which it identifies under subsection (1) at such intervals as it considers appropriate.

(3) The Commission may—

(a) give guidance to the relevant professional organisations as to the timescales within which they should aim to complete their investigation of or, as the case may be, determine conduct complaints remitted to them under section 6(a) or 15(5)(a);

(b) make recommendations to any relevant professional organisation about the organisation's procedures for, and methods of dealing with, conduct complaints so remitted to it.

(4) Each relevant professional organisation to which the Commission makes a recommendation under subsection (3)(b) must—

(a) consider the recommendation;

(b) notify the Commission in writing of—

(i) the results of the consideration;

(ii) any action the organisation has taken or proposes to take in consequence of the recommendation.

(5) The Commission may carry out, for any of the purposes of this section, audits of the records held by the relevant professional organisations relating to conduct complaints remitted to them under section 6(a) or 15(5)(a).

Obtaining of information from relevant professional organisations

37.—(1) The Commission may require any relevant professional organisation to—

(a) provide it with such information, being information which is within the knowledge of the organisation, as the Commission considers relevant for any of the purposes of section 23, 24 or 36;

(b) to produce to it such documents, being documents which are within the possession or control of the organisation, as the Commission considers relevant for any of those purposes.

(2) The information required to be provided or the documents required to be produced under subsection (1) may include information or, as the case may be, documents obtained by the relevant professional organisation from a practitioner while investigating a conduct complaint against the

practitioner remitted to it under section 6(a) or 15(5)(a); and the organisation must comply with such a requirement.

(3) Where any information required by the Commission under subsection (1) is not within the knowledge of the relevant professional organisation, or any documents required to be produced under that subsection are not within the possession or control of the organisation, the Commission may require the practitioner concerned—

    (a) to provide it with that information in so far as it is within the knowledge of the practitioner;

    (b) to produce to it those documents if they are within the practitioner's possession or control.

(4) Schedule 2 makes further provision about the powers of the Commission under this section.

Efficient and effective working

38.—(1) In relation to any investigation or report undertaken by it under this Act, the Commission must liaise with the relevant professional organisation with a view to minimising any unnecessary duplication in relation to any investigation or report undertaken, or to be undertaken, by the relevant professional organisation.

(2) In relation to any investigation or report undertaken by it under this Act, each relevant professional organisation must liaise with the Commission with a view to minimising any unnecessary duplication in relation to any investigation or report undertaken, or to be undertaken, by the Commission.

Monitoring effectiveness of guarantee funds etc.

39.—(1) The Commission may monitor the effectiveness of—

    (a) the Scottish Solicitors Guarantee Fund vested in the Society and controlled and managed by the Council under section 43(1) of the 1980 Act ("the Guarantee Fund");

    (b) arrangements carried into effect by the Society under section 44(2) of that Act ("the professional indemnity arrangements");

    (c) any funds or arrangements maintained by any relevant professional organisation which are for purposes analogous to those of the Guarantee Fund or the professional indemnity arrangements as respects its members.

(2) The Commission may make recommendations to the relevant professional organisation concerned about the effectiveness (including improvement) of the Guarantee Fund, the professional indemnity arrangements or any such funds or arrangements as are referred to in subsection (1)(c).

(3) The Commission may request from the relevant professional organisation such information as the Commission considers relevant to its functions under subsections (1) and (2).

(4) Where a relevant professional organisation fails to provide information requested under subsection (3), it must give reasons to the Commission in respect of that failure.

How practitioners deal with complaints: best practice notes

40.—The Commission may issue guidance to the relevant professional organisations or to practitioners as respects how practitioners deal with complaints made to them about—

    (a) their professional conduct or the professional services provided by them;

    (b) the professional conduct of, or professional services provided by, any of their employees who are practitioners,

and any such guidance may recommend or include recommendations as respects standards for systems by practitioners for dealing with such complaints.

Miscellaneous

Power by regulations to amend duties and powers of Commission

41.—(1) The Scottish Ministers may, after consulting—

(a) the Commission;

(b) the relevant professional organisations;

(c) such other persons or groups of persons as they consider appropriate,

by regulations modify the provisions of this Part for the purposes of adjusting the duties imposed, or the powers conferred, by it on the Commission (including imposing new duties or conferring new powers).

(2) Regulations under subsection (1) may contain such incidental, supplemental, consequential, transitional, transitory or saving provision as the Scottish Ministers consider necessary or expedient for the purposes of that subsection (including modification of any enactment, instrument or document).

Reports: privilege

42. For the purposes of the law of defamation, the publication of any report under section 13(1), 23(8), 24, 35(2), 36(2) or paragraph 16 of schedule 1 is privileged unless the publication is proved to be made with malice.

Restriction upon disclosure of information: Commission

43.—(1) Except as permitted by subsection (3), no information mentioned in subsection (2) may be disclosed.

(2) The information is information—

(a) contained in a conduct complaint, services complaint or handling complaint;

(b) which is given to or obtained by the Commission or any person acting on its behalf in the course of, or for the purposes of—

(i) any consideration of such a complaint;

(ii) an investigation (including any report of such an investigation) into a services complaint or a handling complaint.

(3) Such information may be disclosed—

(a) for the purpose of enabling or assisting the Commission to exercise any of its functions;

(b) where the disclosure is required by or by virtue of any provision made by or under this Act or by any other enactment or other rule of law.

(4) Any person who, in contravention of subsection (1), knowingly discloses any information obtained when employed by, or acting on behalf of, the Commission is guilty of an offence and liable, on summary conviction, to a fine not exceeding level 4 on the standard scale.

Exemption from liability in damages

44.—(1) Neither the Commission nor any person who is, or is acting as, a member of the Commission or an employee of the Commission is to be liable in damages for anything done or omitted in the discharge, or purported discharge, of the Commission's functions.

(2) Subsection (1) does not apply—

(a) if the act or omission is shown to have been in bad faith;

(b) so as to prevent an award of damages made in respect of an act or omission on the ground that the act or omission was unlawful as a result of section 6(1) of the Human Rights Act 1998 (c.42).

Giving of notices etc. under Part 1

45.—(1) Any notice which is required under this Part to be given in writing is to be treated as being in writing if it is received in a form which is legible and capable of being used for subsequent reference.

(2) Any notice which is required under this Part to be given to any person—
  (a) is duly given—
    (i) where the person is not an incorporated practice, if it is left at, or delivered or sent by post to, the person's last known place of business or residence;
    (ii) where the person is an incorporated practice, if it is left at or delivered or sent by post to the practice's registered office;
    (iii) where the person is a practitioner who is a firm of solicitors or an incorporated practice, if it is sent to the person by electronic means but only if the practitioner agrees to that means of sending;
    (iv) where the person is an individual, if it is sent to the person by electronic means but only if the individual agrees to that means of sending;
    (v) to any person, if it is given in such other manner as may be prescribed by regulations by the Scottish Ministers;
  (b) if permitted by paragraph (a) to be sent, and sent, by electronic means is, unless the contrary is proved, deemed to be delivered on the next working day which follows the day on which the notice is sent.
(3) Regulations under subsection (2)(a)(v) may—
  (a) in particular provide that notice required to be given to a person who is not an individual may be given by addressing or sending it to such person appointed by the person for that purpose or to such person falling within such other categories prescribed in the regulations as appear to the Scottish Ministers to be appropriate;
  (b) make different provision for different purposes.
(4) In subsection (2)(b), "working day" means any day other than a Saturday, a Sunday or a day which, under the Banking and Financial Dealings Act 1971 (c. 80), is a bank holiday in Scotland.

Interpretation of Part 1

46.—(1) In this Part, unless the context otherwise requires—
"advocate" means a member of the Faculty of Advocates;
"annual general levy" has the meaning given by section 27(1);
"client"—
  (a) (in relation to any matter in which the practitioner has been instructed) includes any person on whose behalf the person who gave the instructions was acting;
  (b) where the practitioner is an employee of a person who is not a practitioner, includes (in relation to any matter in which the practitioner has been instructed by the employer) the employer;
"complainer" means the person who makes the complaint and, where the complaint is made by the person on behalf of another person, includes that other person;
"complaint" includes any expression of dissatisfaction;
"complaints levy" has the meaning given by section 28(1);
"the Commission" means the Scottish Legal Complaints Commission;
"conduct complaint" has the meaning given by section 2(1)(a);
"conveyancing practitioner" means a person registered under section 17 of the 1990 Act in the register of conveyancing practitioners;
"the Council" means the Council of the Law Society of Scotland;
"the court" means the Court of Session;
"employing practitioner" has the meaning given by section 4(4)(a);
"executry practitioner" means a person registered under section 18 of the 1990 Act in the register of executry practitioners;
"handling complaint" has the meaning given by section 23(1);
"inadequate professional services"—
  (a) means, as respects a practitioner who is—

(i) an advocate, professional services which are in any respect not of the quality which could reasonably be expected of a competent advocate;

(ii) a conveyancing practitioner or an executry practitioner, professional services which are in any respect not of the quality which could reasonably be expected of a competent conveyancing practitioner or, as the case may be, a competent executry practitioner;

(iii) a firm of solicitors or an incorporated practice, professional services which are in any respect not of the quality which could reasonably be expected of a competent firm of solicitors or, as the case may be, a competent incorporated practice;

(iv) a person exercising a right to conduct litigation or a right of audience acquired by virtue of section 27 of the 1990 Act, professional services which are in any respect not of the quality which could reasonably be expected of a competent person exercising such a right;

(v) a solicitor, professional services which are in any respect not of the quality which could reasonably be expected of a competent solicitor;

[1] (vi) a registered European or foreign lawyer, professional services that are in any respect not of the quality which could reasonably be expected of a competent lawyer of that type;

(b) includes any element of negligence in respect of or in connection with the services,

and cognate expressions are to be construed accordingly;

"incorporated practice" has the meaning given by section 34(1A)(c) of the 1980 Act;

"practising certificate" has the meaning given by section 4 of the 1980 Act;

"practitioner" means—

(a) an advocate and includes any advocate whether or not a member of the Faculty of Advocates at the time when it is suggested the conduct complained of occurred or the services complained of were provided and notwithstanding that subsequent to that time the advocate has ceased to be such a member;

(b) a conveyancing practitioner and includes any such practitioner, whether or not registered at that time and notwithstanding that subsequent to that time the practitioner has ceased to be so registered;

(c) an executry practitioner and includes any such practitioner, whether or not registered at that time and notwithstanding that subsequent to that time the practitioner has ceased to be so registered;

(d) a firm of solicitors, whether or not since that time there has been any change in the firm by the addition of a new partner or the death or resignation of an existing partner or the firm has ceased to practise;

(e) an incorporated practice, whether or not since that time there has been any change in the persons exercising the management and control of the practice or the practice has ceased to be recognised by virtue of section 34(1A) of the 1980 Act or has been wound up;

(f) a person exercising a right to conduct litigation or a right of audience acquired by virtue of section 27 of the 1990 Act and includes any such person, whether or not the person had

acquired the right at that time and notwithstanding that subsequent to that time the person no longer has the right;
   (g) a solicitor, whether or not the solicitor had a practising certificate in force at that time and notwithstanding that subsequent to that time the name of the solicitor has been removed from or struck off the roll or the solicitor has ceased to practise or has been suspended from practice;
  [1] (h) a registered European or foreign lawyer, whether or not registered at that time and notwithstanding that subsequent to that time the lawyer's registration has ceased to have effect or the lawyer has stopped practising;
[1] "registered European or foreign lawyer" is to be construed in accordance with section 65(1) of the 1980 Act;
"relevant professional organisation" means, in relation to a complaint as respects a practitioner who is—
  (a) an advocate, the Faculty of Advocates;
  (b) a conveyancing practitioner, an executry practitioner, a firm of solicitors or an incorporated practice, the Council;
  (c) a person exercising a right to conduct litigation or a right of audience acquired by virtue of section 27 of the 1990 Act, the body which made a successful application under section 25 of that Act and of which the person is a member;
  (d) a solicitor, the Council;
  [1] (e) a registered European or foreign lawyer, the Council;
"the roll" means the roll of solicitors kept by the Council by virtue of section 7(1) of the 1980 Act;
"services complaint" has the meaning given by section 2(1)(b);
"the Society" means the Law Society of Scotland;
"solicitor" means any person enrolled or deemed to have been enrolled as a solicitor in pursuance of the 1980 Act;
"unsatisfactory professional conduct" means, as respects a practitioner who is—
  (a) an advocate, professional conduct which is not of the standard which could reasonably be expected of a competent and reputable advocate;
  (b) a conveyancing practitioner or an executry practitioner, professional conduct which is not of the standard which could reasonably be expected of a competent and reputable conveyancing practitioner or, as the case may be, a competent and reputable executry practitioner;
  [2] (c) a person exercising a right to conduct litigation or a right of audience acquired by virtue of section 27 of the 1990 Act, professional conduct which is not of the standard which could reasonably be expected of a competent and reputable person exercising such a right;
  (d) a solicitor, professional conduct which is not of the standard which could reasonably be expected of a competent and reputable solicitor;
  [1] (e) a registered European or foreign lawyer, conduct that is not of the standard which could reasonably be expected of a competent and reputable lawyer of that type,
but which does not amount to professional misconduct and which does not comprise merely inadequate professional services; and cognate expressions are to be construed accordingly.
(2) For the avoidance of doubt, anything done by any Crown Counsel or procurator fiscal in relation to the prosecution of crime or investigation of deaths is not done in relation to any matter in which the Crown Counsel or procurator fiscal has been instructed by a client.
(3) For the avoidance of doubt, the exercise of discretion by any Crown

Counsel or procurator fiscal in relation to the prosecution of crime or investigation of deaths is not in itself capable of constituting professional misconduct or unsatisfactory professional conduct.

(4) In subsections (2) and (3), "procurator fiscal" has the same meaning as in section 307 of the Criminal Procedure (Scotland) Act 1995 (c.46).

NOTES
[1] As inserted by the Legal Services (Scotland) Act 2010 (asp 16) Pt 4 c.4 s.143 (effective April 1, 2011).
[2] As amended by the Legal Services (Scotland) Act 2010 (asp 16) Pt 4 c.4 s.144(b) (effective April 1, 2011).

PART 2

CONDUCT AND SERVICES COMPLAINTS ETC.: OTHER MATTERS

Conduct complaints: duty of relevant professional organisations to investigate etc.

47.—(1) Where a conduct complaint is remitted to a relevant professional organisation under section 6(a) or 15(5)(a), the organisation must, subject to section 15(1) and (6), investigate it.

(2) After investigating a conduct complaint, the relevant professional organisation must make a written report to the complainer and the practitioner of—
  (a) the facts of the matter as found by the organisation;
  (b) what action the organisation proposes to take, or has taken, in the matter.

(3) Each relevant professional organisation must ensure that its procedures for dealing with conduct complaints do not conflict with the duty imposed on it by section 24(4) or (5) in relation to any report sent to it under that section or any direction by the Commission under section 24(6).

(4) In this section and sections 48 to 52, words and expressions have the same meanings as in section 46.

Conduct complaints and reviews: power of relevant professional organisations to examine documents and demand explanations

48.—(1) Where a relevant professional organisation is satisfied that it is necessary for it to do so for the purposes of an investigation by it into a conduct complaint under section 47 or a review by it of a decision in relation to a conduct complaint, it may—
  (a) give notice in writing in accordance with subsection (2) to the practitioner, the practitioner's firm or, as the case may be, the employing practitioner;
  (b) give notice in writing in accordance with subsection (4) to the complainer.

(2) Notice under subsection (1)(a) may require—
  (a) the production or delivery to any person appointed by the relevant professional organisation, at a time and place specified in the notice, of all documents mentioned in subsection (3) which are in the possession or control of the practitioner, the firm or, as the case may be, the employing practitioner and which relate to the matters to which the complaint relates (whether or not they relate also to other matters);
  (b) an explanation, within such period being not less than 21 days as the notice specifies, from the practitioner, the firm or, as the case may be, the employing practitioner regarding the matters to which the complaint relates.

(3) The documents are—
  (a) all books, accounts, deeds, securities, papers and other documents in the possession or control of the practitioner, the firm or, as the case may be, the employing practitioner;

(b) all books, accounts, deeds, securities, papers and other documents relating to any trust of which the practitioner is the sole trustee or a co-trustee only with one or more of the practitioner's partners or employees or, as the case may be, where the practitioner is an incorporated practice of which the practice or one of its employees is a sole trustee or it is a co-trustee only with one or more of its employees.

(4) Notice under subsection (1)(b) may require—

(a) the production or delivery to any person appointed by the relevant professional organisation at a time and place specified in the notice, of all documents mentioned in subsection (5) which relate to the matters to which the complaint relates (whether or not they relate to other matters);

(b) an explanation, within such period being not less than 21 days as the notice specifies, from the complainer regarding the matters to which the complaint relates.

(5) The documents are all books, accounts, deeds, securities, papers and other documents in the possession or control of the complainer.

(6) Schedule 4 makes further provision about the powers of a relevant professional organisation under this section.

Conduct complaints: financial impropriety

49.—(1) If, in the course of an investigation into a conduct complaint under section 47, a relevant professional organisation has reasonable cause to believe that the practitioner, the practitioner's firm (or any employee thereof) or, as the case may be, the employing practitioner, has been guilty of any financial impropriety it may apply to the court for an order under subsection (2).

(2) An order under this subsection is that no payment be made by any banker, building society or other body named in the order out of—

(a) any banking account in the name of such practitioner or firm; or

(b) any sum deposited in the name of such practitioner or firm,

without the leave of the court.

Power of relevant professional organisations to recover certain expenses

50.—(1) A relevant professional organisation is, subject to subsection (2), entitled to recover from a practitioner, the practitioner's firm or, as the case may be, the employing practitioner, in respect of whom it has taken any action by virtue of section 48(1)(a) or 49, any expenditure reasonably incurred by it in so doing.

(2) Expenditure incurred in taking action by virtue of section 48(1)(a) is recoverable under subsection (1) only where notice has been served under paragraph 2(a) of schedule 4 in connection with that action and—

(a) no application has been made in consequence under paragraph 3 of that schedule; or

(b) the court, on such an application, has made a direction under paragraph 4 of that schedule.

Powers in relation to documents and information from third parties

51.—(1) Where a relevant professional organisation has requested that documents or information in the possession or control of a person be produced for the purposes of an investigation by it into a conduct complaint under section 47 or a review by it of a decision in relation to a conduct complaint, and the person refuses or fails to produce the documents or information, the organisation may apply to the court for an order under subsection (2).

(2) An order by the court under this subsection may require a person to produce or deliver the documents or information or to cause them or it to be produced or delivered to the person appointed at the place fixed by the relevant professional organisation within such time as the court may order.

(3) Subsections (3) to (7) of section 19 apply for the purposes of this section as they apply for the purposes of that section but subject to the modification that for the references in subsections (4) to (6) to "the Commission" substitute "the relevant professional organisation".

Restriction upon disclosure of information: relevant professional organisations

52.—(1) Except as permitted by subsection (3), no information mentioned in subsection (2) may be disclosed.

(2) The information is information—

(a) contained in a conduct complaint;

(b) which is given to or obtained by a relevant professional organisation or any person acting on its behalf in the course of, or for the purposes of—

(i) any consideration of such a complaint;

(ii) an investigation (including any report of such an investigation) into such a complaint.

(3) Such information may be disclosed—

(a) for the purpose of enabling or assisting the relevant professional organisation to exercise any of its functions in relation to such a complaint;

(b) where the disclosure is required by or by virtue of any provision made by or under this Act or by any other enactment or other rule of law.

(4) Any person who, in contravention of subsection (1), knowingly discloses any information obtained when employed by, or acting on behalf of, a relevant professional organisation is guilty of an offence and liable, on summary conviction, to a fine not exceeding level 4 on the standard scale.

Unsatisfactory professional conduct: solicitors

53.—(1) The 1980 Act is amended as follows.

(2) After section 42, insert—

"Unsatisfactory professional conduct: Council's powers

42ZA.—(1) Where a conduct complaint suggesting unsatisfactory professional conduct by a practitioner who is a solicitor is remitted to the Council under section 6(a) or 15(5)(a) of the 2007 Act, the Council must having—

(a) investigated the complaint under section 47(1) of that Act and made a written report under section 47(2) of that Act;

(b) given the solicitor an opportunity to make representations, determine the complaint.

(2) Where a complaint is remitted to the Council under section 53ZA, the Council—

(a) must—

(i) notify the solicitor specified in it and the complainer of that fact and that the Council are required to investigate the complaint as a complaint of unsatisfactory professional conduct;

(ii) so investigate the complaint;

(iii) having so investigated the complaint and given the solicitor an opportunity to make representations, determine the complaint;

(b) may rely, in their investigation, on any findings in fact which the Tribunal makes available to them under section 53ZA(2) as respects the complaint.

(3) Where the Council make a determination under subsection (1) or (2) upholding the complaint, they—

(a) shall censure the solicitor;

(b) may take any of the steps mentioned in subsection (4) which they consider appropriate.

(4) The steps are—

(a) where the Council consider that the solicitor does not have sufficient competence in relation to any aspect of the law or legal practice, to direct the solicitor to undertake such education or training as regards the law or legal practice as the Council consider appropriate in that respect;

(b) subject to subsection (6), to direct the solicitor to pay a fine not exceeding £2,000;

(c) where the Council consider that the complainer has been directly affected by the conduct, to direct the solicitor to pay compensation of such amount, not exceeding £5,000, as they may specify to the complainer for loss, inconvenience or distress resulting from the conduct.

(5) The Council may, in considering the complaint, take account of any previous determination by them, the Tribunal or the Court upholding a complaint against the solicitor of unsatisfactory professional conduct or professional misconduct (but not a complaint in respect of which an appeal is pending or which has been quashed ultimately on appeal).

(6) The Council shall not direct the solicitor to pay a fine under subsection (4)(b) where, in relation to the subject matter of the complaint, the solicitor has been convicted by any court of an act involving dishonesty and sentenced to a term of imprisonment of not less than 2 years.

(7) Any fine directed to be paid under subsection (4)(b) above shall be treated for the purposes of section 211(5) of the Criminal Procedure (Scotland) Act 1995 (fines payable to HM Exchequer) as if it were a fine imposed in the High Court.

(8) The Council shall intimate—
   (a) a determination under subsection (1) or (2);
   (b) any censure under subsection (3)(a);
   (c) any direction under subsection (4),
to the complainer and the solicitor specified in it by sending to each of them a copy of the determination, censure or, as the case may be, the direction and by specifying the reasons for the determination.

(9) A solicitor in respect of whom a determination upholding a conduct complaint has been made under subsection (1) or (2), or a direction has been made under subsection (4) may, before the expiry of the period of 21 days beginning with the day on which the determination or, as the case may be, the direction is intimated to him, appeal to the Tribunal against the—
   (a) determination;
   (b) direction (whether or not he is appealing against the determination).

(10) A complainer may, before the expiry of the period of 21 days beginning with the day on which a determination under subsection (1) or (2) not upholding the conduct complaint is intimated to him, appeal to the Tribunal against the determination.

(11) Where the Council have upheld the conduct complaint but have not directed the solicitor under subsection (4)(c) to pay compensation, the complainer may, before the expiry of the period of 21 days beginning with the day on which the determination upholding the complaint is intimated to him, appeal to the Tribunal against the Council's decision not to make a direction under that subsection.

(12) A complainer to whom the Council have directed a solicitor under subsection (4)(c) to pay compensation may, before the expiry of the period of 21 days beginning with the day on which the direction under that subsection is intimated to him, appeal to the Tribunal against the amount of the compensation directed to be paid.

(13) The Scottish Ministers may by order made by statutory instrument—
   (a) amend subsection (4)(b) by substituting for the amount for the time being specified in that subsection such other amount as appears to them to be justified by a change in the value of money;
   (b) after consulting the Council and such groups of persons representing consumer interests as they consider appropriate, amend subsection (4)(c) by substituting for the amount for the time being specified in that subsection such other amount as they consider appropriate.

(14) A statutory instrument containing an order under—
   (a) subsection (13)(a) is subject to annulment in pursuance of a resolution of the Scottish Parliament;
   (b) subsection (13)(b) is not to be made unless a draft of the instrument has been laid before, and approved by resolution of, the Scottish Parliament.

(15) In this section, "complainer" means the person who made the complaint and, where the complaint was made by the person on behalf of another person, includes that other person.

Unsatisfactory professional conduct: Council's powers to monitor compliance with direction under section 42ZA(4)

42ZB.—(1) The Council shall, by notice in writing, require every solicitor who is specified in—

(a) a direction made under section 42ZA(4); or

(b) such a direction as confirmed or varied on appeal by—

　(i) the Tribunal; or

　(ii) the Court,

to give, before the expiry of such period being not less than 21 days as the notice specifies, an explanation of the steps which he has taken to comply with the direction.

(2) Where an appeal is made under section 42ZA(9) or (12) or 54A(1) or (2) against a direction made under section 42ZA(4), any notice under subsection (1)(a) above relating to the direction shall cease to have effect pending the outcome of the appeal.".

(3) After section 53 (powers of Tribunal), insert—

"Remission of complaint by Tribunal to Council

53ZA.—(1) Where, after holding an inquiry under section 53(1) into a complaint of professional misconduct against a solicitor, the Tribunal—

(a) is not satisfied that he has been guilty of professional misconduct;

(b) considers that he may be guilty of unsatisfactory professional conduct,

it must remit the complaint to the Council.

(2) Where the Tribunal remits a complaint to the Council under subsection (1), it may make available to the Council any of its findings in fact in its inquiry into the complaint under section 53(1).

Powers of Tribunal on appeal: unsatisfactory professional conduct

53ZB.—(1) On an appeal to the Tribunal under section 42ZA(9) the Tribunal—

(a) may quash or confirm the determination being appealed against;

(b) if it quashes the determination, shall quash the censure accompanying the determination;

(c) may quash, confirm or vary the direction being appealed against;

(d) may, where it considers that the solicitor does not have sufficient competence in relation to any aspect of the law or legal practice, direct the solicitor to undertake such education or training as regards the law or legal practice as the Tribunal considers appropriate in that respect;

(e) may, subject to subsection (5), fine the solicitor an amount not exceeding £2000;

(f) may, where it considers that the complainer has been directly affected by the conduct, direct the solicitor to pay compensation of such amount, not exceeding £5,000, as it may specify to the complainer for loss, inconvenience or distress resulting from the conduct.

(2) On an appeal to the Tribunal under section 42ZA(10) the Tribunal—

(a) may quash the determination being appealed against and make a determination upholding the complaint;

(b) if it does so, may, where it considers that the complainer has been directly affected by the conduct, direct the solicitor to pay compensation of such amount, not exceeding £5,000, as it may specify to the complainer for loss, inconvenience or distress resulting from the conduct;

(c) may confirm the determination.

(3) On an appeal to the Tribunal under section 42ZA(11) the Tribunal may, where it considers that the complainer has been directly affected by

the conduct, direct the solicitor to pay compensation of such amount, not exceeding £5,000, as it may specify to the complainer for loss, inconvenience or distress resulting from the conduct.

(4) On an appeal under section 42ZA(12) the Tribunal may quash, confirm or vary the direction being appealed against.

(5) The Tribunal shall not direct the solicitor to pay a fine under subsection (1)(e) where, in relation to the subject matter of the complaint, the solicitor has been convicted by any court of an act involving dishonesty and sentenced to a term of imprisonment of not less than 2 years.

(6) Any fine directed to be paid under subsection (1)(e) above shall be treated for the purposes of section 211(5) of the Criminal Procedure (Scotland) Act 1995 (fines payable to HM Exchequer) as if it were a fine imposed in the High Court.

(7) A direction of the Tribunal under this section is enforceable in like manner as an extract registered decree arbitral in favour of the Council bearing a warrant for execution issued by the sheriff court of any sheriffdom in Scotland.

(8) The Scottish Ministers may by order made by statutory instrument—

    (a) amend subsection (1)(e) by substituting for the amount for the time being specified in that subsection such other amount as appears to them to be justified by a change in the value of money;

    (b) after consulting the Council and such groups of persons representing consumer interests as they consider appropriate, amend subsection (1)(f) by substituting for the amount for the time being specified in that subsection such other amount as they consider appropriate.

(9) A statutory instrument containing an order under—

    (a) subsection (8)(a) is subject to annulment in pursuance of a resolution of the Scottish Parliament;

    (b) subsection (8)(b) is not to be made unless a draft of the instrument has been laid before, and approved by resolution of, the Scottish Parliament.

(10) In this section, "complainer" has the same meaning as in section 42ZA.

Enforcement of Council direction: unsatisfactory professional conduct

53ZC. Where a solicitor fails to comply with a direction given by the Council under section 42ZA(4) (including such a direction as confirmed or varied on appeal by the Tribunal or, as the case may be, the Court) before the expiry of the period specified in the notice relating to that direction given to him under section 42ZB(1), or such longer period as the Council may allow, the direction shall be enforceable in like manner as an extract registered decree arbitral in favour of the Council bearing a warrant for execution issued by the sheriff court of any sheriffdom in Scotland.".

(4) After section 54 (appeals from decisions of Tribunal), insert—

"Appeals from decisions of Tribunal: unsatisfactory professional conduct

54A.—(1) A solicitor in respect of whom a decision has been made by the Tribunal under section 53ZB(1), (2), (3) or (4) may, before the expiry of the period of 21 days beginning with the day on which the decision is intimated to him, appeal to the Court against the decision.

(2) A complainer may, before the expiry of the period of 21 days beginning with the day on which a decision by the Tribunal under section 53ZB to which this subsection applies is intimated to him, appeal to the Court against the decision.

(3) Subsection (2) applies to the following decisions of the Tribunal under section 53ZB—

(a) a decision under subsection (1)(a) quashing the Council's determination upholding the complaint;

(b) a decision under subsection (1)(c) quashing or varying a direction by the Council that the solicitor pay compensation;

(c) a decision under subsection (1)(f) directing the solicitor to pay compensation;

(d) a decision under subsection (2)(b) not to direct the solicitor to pay compensation;

(e) a decision under subsection (2)(c) confirming the Council's decision not to uphold the complaint;

(f) a decision under subsection (3) confirming the Council's decision not to direct the solicitor to pay compensation;

(g) a decision under subsection (4) quashing the Council's direction that the solicitor pay compensation or varying the amount of compensation directed to be paid.

(4) On an appeal under subsection (1) or (2), the Court may give such directions in the matter as it thinks fit, including directions as to the expenses of the proceedings before the Court and as to any order by the Tribunal relating to expenses.

(5) A decision of the Court under subsection (4) shall be final.

(6) In this section, "complainer" has the same meaning as in section 42ZA.".

(5) After section 55 (powers of Court), insert—

"Powers of Court: unsatisfactory professional conduct

55A.—(1) In the case of unsatisfactory professional conduct by a solicitor the Court may—

(a) fine the solicitor an amount not exceeding £2000;

(b) where it considers that the complainer has been directly affected by the conduct, direct the solicitor to pay compensation of such amount, not exceeding £5,000, as it may specify to the complainer for loss, inconvenience or distress resulting from the conduct;

(c) find the solicitor liable in any expenses which may be involved in the proceedings before it.

(2) A decision of the Court under subsection (1) shall be final.

(3) The Scottish Ministers may by order made by statutory instrument—

(a) amend subsection (1)(a) by substituting for the amount for the time being specified in that subsection such other amount as appears to them to be justified by a change in the value of money;

(b) after consulting the Council and such groups of persons representing consumer interests as they consider appropriate, amend subsection (1)(b) by substituting for the amount for the time being specified in that subsection such other amount as they consider appropriate.

(4) A statutory instrument containing an order under—

(a) subsection (3)(a) is subject to annulment in pursuance of a resolution of the Scottish Parliament;

(b) subsection (3)(b) is not to be made unless a draft of the instrument has been laid before, and approved by resolution of, the Scottish Parliament.

(5) In this section, "complainer" has the same meaning as in section 42ZA.".

(6) In section 65(1) (interpretation), after the definition of "unqualified person" insert ";

"unsatisfactory professional conduct" as respects a solicitor has the meaning given (as respects a practitioner who is a solicitor) by section 46 of the 2007 Act".

Unsatisfactory professional conduct: conveyancing or executry practitioners

54.—(1) The 1990 Act is amended as follows.

(2) After section 20 (professional misconduct etc. by conveyancing or executry practitioners), insert—

"Remission of complaint by Tribunal to Council

20ZA.—(1) Where, after holding an inquiry under section 20(2A) into a complaint of professional misconduct against a practitioner, the Tribunal—

(a) are not satisfied that he has been guilty of professional misconduct;

(b) consider that he may be guilty of unsatisfactory professional conduct,

they must remit the complaint to the Council.

(2) Where the Tribunal remit a complaint to the Council under subsection (1), they may make available to the Council any of their findings in fact in their inquiry into the complaint under section 20(2A).

Unsatisfactory professional conduct

20ZB.—(1) Where a conduct complaint suggesting unsatisfactory professional conduct by a practitioner is remitted to the Council under section 6(a) or 15(5)(a) of the 2007 Act, the Council must having—

(a) investigated the complaint under section 47(1) of that Act and made a written report under section 47(2) of that Act;

(b) given the practitioner an opportunity to make representations, determine the complaint.

(2) Where a complaint is remitted to the Council under section 20ZA, the Council—

(a) must—

   (i) notify the practitioner specified in it and the complainer of that fact and that the Council are required to investigate the complaint as a complaint of unsatisfactory professional conduct;

   (ii) so investigate the complaint;

   (iii) having so investigated the complaint and given the practitioner an opportunity to make representations, determine the complaint;

(b) may rely, in their investigation, on any findings in fact which the Tribunal make available to them under section 20ZA(2) as respects the complaint.

(3) Where the Council make a determination under subsection (1) or (2) upholding the complaint, they—

(a) shall censure the practitioner;

(b) may take any of the steps mentioned in subsection (4) which they consider appropriate.

(4) The steps are—

(a) where the Council consider that the practitioner does not have sufficient competence in relation to any aspect of conveyancing law or legal practice or, as the case may be, executry law or legal practice, to direct him to undertake such education or training as regards the law or legal practice concerned as the Council consider appropriate in that respect;

(b) subject to subsection (6) below, to direct the practitioner to pay a fine not exceeding £2,000;

(c) where the Council consider that the complainer has been directly affected by the conduct, to direct the practitioner to pay compensation of such amount, not exceeding £5,000, as they may specify to the complainer for loss, inconvenience or distress resulting from the conduct.

(5) The Council may, in considering the complaint, take account of any previous determination by them, the Tribunal or the court upholding a complaint against the practitioner of unsatisfactory professional conduct or professional misconduct (but not a complaint in respect of which an appeal is pending or which has been quashed ultimately on appeal).

(6) The Council shall not direct the practitioner to pay a fine under subsection (4)(b) above where, in relation to the subject matter of the complaint, he has been convicted by any court of an offence involving dishonesty and sentenced to a term of imprisonment of not less than 2 years.

(7) Any fine directed to be paid under subsection (4)(b) above shall be treated for the purposes of section 211(5) of the Criminal Procedure (Scotland) Act 1995 (fines payable to HM Exchequer) as if it were a fine imposed in the High Court.

(8) The Council shall intimate—
(a) a determination under subsection (1) or (2);
(b) any censure under subsection (3)(a);
(c) any direction under subsection (4),
to the complainer and the practitioner by sending to each of them a copy of the determination, the censure or, as the case may be, the direction and by specifying the reasons for the determination.

(9) A practitioner in respect of whom a determination upholding a conduct complaint has been made under subsection (1) or (2), or a direction has been made under subsection (4) may, before the expiry of the period of 21 days beginning with the day on which the determination or, as the case may be, the direction is intimated to him, appeal to the Tribunal against the—
(a) determination;
(b) direction (whether or not he is appealing against the determination).

(10) A complainer may, before the expiry of the period of 21 days beginning with the day on which a determination under subsection (1) or (2) not upholding the conduct complaint is intimated to him, appeal to the Tribunal against the determination.

(11) Where the Council have upheld the conduct complaint but have not directed the practitioner under subsection (4)(c) to pay compensation, the complainer may, before the expiry of the period of 21 days beginning with the day on which the determination upholding the complaint is intimated to him, appeal to the Tribunal against the Council's decision not to make a direction under that subsection.

(12) A complainer to whom the Council have directed a practitioner under subsection (4)(c) to pay compensation may, before the expiry of the period of 21 days beginning with the day on which the direction under that subsection is intimated to him, appeal to the Tribunal against the amount of the compensation directed to be paid.

(13) The Scottish Ministers may by order made by statutory instrument—
(a) amend subsection (4)(b) by substituting for the amount for the time being specified in that subsection such other amount as appears to them to be justified by a change in the value of money;
(b) after consulting the Council and such groups of persons representing consumer interests as they consider appropriate, amend subsection (4)(c) by substituting for the amount for the time being specified in that subsection such other amount as they consider appropriate.

(14) A statutory instrument containing an order under—
(a) subsection (13)(a) is subject to annulment in pursuance of a resolution of the Scottish Parliament;
(b) subsection (13)(b) is not to be made unless a draft of the instrument has been laid before, and approved by resolution of, the Scottish Parliament.

Unsatisfactory professional conduct: Council's powers to monitor compliance with direction under section 20ZB(4)

20ZC.—(1) The Council shall, by notice in writing, require every practitioner who is specified in—

(a) a direction made under section 20ZB(4); or

(b) such a direction as confirmed or varied on appeal by—

(i) the Tribunal; or

(ii) the court,

to give, before the expiry of such period being not less than 21 days as the notice specifies, an explanation of the steps which he has taken to comply with the direction.

(2) Where an appeal is made under section 20ZB(9) or (12) or 20D(1) or (2) against a direction made under section 20ZB(4), any notice under subsection (1) above relating to the direction shall cease to have effect pending the outcome of the appeal.".

(3) After section 20A (review by Council of certain of their decisions), insert—

"Unsatisfactory professional conduct: powers of Tribunal on appeal

20B.—(1) On an appeal to the Tribunal under section 20ZB(9) the Tribunal—

(a) may quash or confirm the determination being appealed against;

(b) if they quash the determination, shall quash the censure accompanying the determination;

(c) may quash, confirm or vary the direction being appealed against;

(d) may, where they consider that the practitioner does not have sufficient competence in relation to any aspect of conveyancing law or legal practice or, as the case may be, executry law or legal practice, direct him to undertake such education or training as regards the law or legal practice concerned as the Tribunal consider appropriate in that respect;

(e) may, subject to subsection (5), fine the practitioner an amount not exceeding £2000;

(f) may, where they consider that the complainer has been directly affected by the conduct, direct the practitioner to pay compensation of such amount, not exceeding £5,000, as they may specify to the complainer for loss, inconvenience or distress resulting from the conduct.

(2) On an appeal to the Tribunal under section 20ZB(10) the Tribunal—

(a) may quash the determination being appealed against and make a determination upholding the complaint;

(b) if they do so, may, where they consider that the complainer has been directly affected by the conduct, direct the practitioner to pay compensation of such amount, not exceeding £5,000, as they may specify to the complainer for loss, inconvenience or distress resulting from the conduct;

(c) may confirm the determination.

(3) On an appeal to the Tribunal under section 20ZB(11) the Tribunal may, where they consider that the complainer has been directly affected by the conduct, direct the practitioner to pay compensation of such amount, not exceeding £5,000, as they may specify to the complainer for loss, inconvenience or distress resulting from the conduct.

(4) On an appeal under section 20ZB(12) the Tribunal may quash, confirm or vary the direction being appealed against.

(5) The Tribunal shall not direct the practitioner to pay a fine under subsection (1)(e) where, in relation to the subject matter of the complaint, he has been convicted by any court of an offence involving dishonesty and sentenced to a term of imprisonment of not less than 2 years.

(6) Any fine directed to be paid under subsection (1)(e) shall be treated for the purposes of section 211(5) of the Criminal Procedure (Scotland) Act 1995 (fines payable to HM Exchequer) as if it were a fine imposed in the High Court.

(7) A direction of the Tribunal under this section is enforceable in like manner as an extract registered decree arbitral in favour of the Council bearing a warrant for execution issued by the sheriff court of any sheriffdom in Scotland.

(8) The Scottish Ministers may by order made by statutory instrument—

    (a) amend subsection (1)(e) by substituting for the amount for the time being specified in that subsection such other amount as appears to them to be justified by a change in the value of money;

    (b) after consulting the Council and such groups of persons representing consumer interests as they consider appropriate, amend subsection (1)(f) by substituting for the amount for the time being specified in that subsection such other amount as they consider appropriate.

(9) A statutory instrument containing an order under—

    (a) subsection (8)(a) is subject to annulment in pursuance of a resolution of the Scottish Parliament;

    (b) subsection (8)(b) is not to be made unless a draft of the instrument has been laid before, and approved by resolution of, the Scottish Parliament.

Unsatisfactory professional conduct: enforcement of Council direction

20C. Where a practitioner fails to comply with a direction given by the Council under section 20ZB(4) (including such a direction as confirmed or varied on appeal by the Tribunal or, as the case may be, the court) before the expiry of the period specified in the notice relating to that direction given to the practitioner under section 20ZC(1), or such longer period as the Council may allow, the direction shall be enforceable in like manner as an extract registered decree arbitral in favour of the Council bearing a warrant for execution issued by the sheriff court of any sheriffdom in Scotland.

Unsatisfactory professional conduct: appeal from decisions of Tribunal

20D.—(1) A practitioner in respect of whom a decision has been made by the Tribunal under section 20B(1), (2), (3) or (4) may, before the expiry of the period of 21 days beginning with the day on which the decision is intimated to him, appeal to the court against the decision.

(2) A complainer may, before the expiry of the period of 21 days beginning with the day on which a decision by the Tribunal under section 20B to which this subsection applies is intimated to him, appeal to the court against the decision.

(3) Subsection (2) applies to the following decisions of the Tribunal under section 20B—

    (a) a decision under subsection (1)(a) quashing the Council's determination upholding the complaint;

    (b) a decision under subsection (1)(c) quashing or varying a direction by the Council that the practitioner pay compensation;

    (c) a decision under subsection (1)(f) directing the practitioner to pay compensation;

    (d) a decision under subsection (2)(b) not to direct the practitioner to pay compensation;

    (e) a decision under subsection (2)(c) confirming the Council's decision not to uphold the complaint;

    (f) a decision under subsection (3) confirming the Council's decision not to direct the practitioner to pay compensation;

(g) a decision under subsection (4) quashing the Council's direction that the practitioner pay compensation or varying the amount of compensation directed to be paid.

(4) On an appeal under subsection (1) or (2), the court may give such directions in the matter as it thinks fit, including directions as to the expenses of the proceedings before the court and as to any order by the Tribunal relating to expenses.

(5) A decision of the court under subsection (4) shall be final.

Unsatisfactory professional conduct: powers of court on appeal

20E.—(1) On an appeal under section 20D, the court may—

(a) fine the practitioner an amount not exceeding £2000;

(b) where it considers that the complainer has been directly affected by the conduct, direct the practitioner to pay compensation of such amount, not exceeding £5,000, as it may specify to the complainer for loss, inconvenience or distress resulting from the conduct;

(c) find the practitioner liable in any expenses which may be involved in the proceedings before it.

(2) A decision of the court under subsection (1) shall be final.

(3) The Scottish Ministers may by order made by statutory instrument—

(a) amend subsection (1)(a) by substituting for the amount for the time being specified in that subsection such other amount as appears to them to be justified by a change in the value of money;

(b) after consulting the Council and such groups of persons representing consumer interests as they consider appropriate, amend subsection (1)(b) by substituting for the amount for the time being specified in that subsection such other amount as they consider appropriate.

(4) A statutory instrument containing an order under—

(a) subsection (3)(a) is subject to annulment in pursuance of a resolution of the Scottish Parliament;

(b) subsection (3)(b) is not to be made unless a draft of the instrument has been laid before, and approved by resolution of, the Scottish Parliament.".

Report by Commission to Council under section 10(2)(e)

55.—(1) After section 42ZB of the 1980 Act (as inserted by section 53(2) of this Act), insert—

"Report by Commission to Council under section 10(2)(e) of the 2007 Act: Council's powers

42ZC.—(1) Where the Council receive a report from the Commission under section 10(2)(e) of the 2007 Act as respects a practitioner who is a solicitor, they may direct him to undertake such education or training as regards the law or legal practice as the Council consider appropriate in the circumstances.

(2) The Council shall by notice in writing—

(a) intimate a direction under subsection (1) to the solicitor;

(b) require the solicitor to give, before the expiry of such period being not less than 21 days as the notice specifies, an explanation of the steps which he has taken to comply with the direction.

(3) Where an appeal is made under section 42ZD(1) or (3) against a direction under subsection (1), any notice under subsection (2)(b) relating to the direction shall cease to have effect pending the outcome of the appeal.

Direction under section 42ZC(2): appeal by practitioner

42ZD.—(1) A solicitor in respect of whom a direction has been made under section 42ZC(1) may, before the expiry of the period of 21 days beginning with the day on which it is intimated to him, appeal to the Tribunal against the direction.

(2) On an appeal to the Tribunal under subsection (1), the Tribunal may quash, confirm or vary the direction being appealed against.

(3) The solicitor may, before the expiry of the period of 21 days beginning with the day on which the Tribunal's decision under subsection (2) is intimated to him, appeal to the Court against the decision.

(4) On an appeal to the Court under subsection (3), the Court may give such directions in the matter as it thinks fit, including directions as to the expenses of the proceedings before the Court and as to any order by the Tribunal relating to expenses.

(5) A decision of the Court on an appeal under subsection (3) shall be final.".

(2) After section 20ZC of the 1990 Act (as inserted by section 54(2) of this Act), insert—

"Report by Commission to Council under section 10(2)(e) of the 2007 Act: Council's powers

20ZD.—(1) Where the Council receive a report from the Commission under section 10(2)(e) of the 2007 Act as respects a practitioner, they may direct him to undertake such education or training as regards conveyancing law or legal practice or, as the case may be, executry law or legal practice as they consider appropriate in the circumstances.

(2) The Council shall by notice in writing—
   (a) intimate a direction under subsection (1) to the practitioner;
   (b) require the practitioner to give, before the expiry of such period being not less than 21 days as the notice specifies, an explanation of the steps which he has taken to comply with the direction.

(3) Where an appeal is made under section 20ZE(1) or (3) against a direction under subsection (1), any notice under subsection (2)(b) relating to the direction shall cease to have effect pending the outcome of the appeal.

Direction under section 20ZD(1): appeal by practitioner

20ZE.—(1) A practitioner in respect of whom a direction has been made under section 20ZD(1) may, before the expiry of the period of 21 days beginning with the day on which it is intimated to him, appeal to the Tribunal against the direction.

(2) On an appeal to the Tribunal under subsection (1), the Tribunal may quash, confirm or vary the direction being appealed against.

(3) The practitioner may, before the expiry of the period of 21 days beginning with the day on which the Tribunal's decision under subsection (2) is intimated to him, appeal to the court against the decision.

(4) On an appeal to the court under subsection (3), the court may give such directions in the matter as it thinks fit, including directions as to the expenses of the proceedings before the court and as to any order by the Tribunal relating to expenses.

(5) A decision of the court on an appeal under subsection (3) shall be final.".

Powers to fine and award compensation for professional misconduct etc.

56.—(1) In section 53 of the 1980 Act (powers of Tribunal)—
   (a) in subsection (2), after paragraph (ba) insert—
      "(bb) where the solicitor has been guilty of professional misconduct, and where the Tribunal consider that the complainer has been directly affected by the misconduct, direct the solicitor to pay compensation of such amount, not exceeding £5,000, as the Tribunal may specify to the complainer for loss, inconvenience or distress resulting from the misconduct;";
   (b) after subsection (7B) (as inserted by paragraph 1(19)(b) of schedule 5 to this Act), insert—

"(7C) The Scottish Ministers may by order made by statutory instrument, after consulting the Council and such groups of persons representing consumer interests as they consider appropriate, amend paragraph (bb) of subsection (2) by substituting for the amount for the time being specified in that paragraph such other amount as they consider appropriate.

(7D) A statutory instrument containing an order under subsection (7C) is not to be made unless a draft of the instrument has been laid before, and approved by resolution of, the Scottish Parliament.";

(c) after subsection (8), insert—

"(9) In subsection (2)(bb), "complainer" has the same meaning as in section 42ZA.".

(2) In section 55 of the 1980 Act (powers of Court)—

(a) in subsection (1)—

(i) after paragraph (bb), insert—

"(bc) where the Court considers that the complainer has been directly affected by the misconduct, direct the solicitor to pay compensation of such amount, not exceeding £5,000, as it may specify to the complainer for loss, inconvenience or distress resulting from the misconduct; or";

(ii) in paragraph (c), after "solicitor" insert "an amount not exceeding £10,000";

(b) after subsection (4) insert—

"(5) The Scottish Ministers may by order made by statutory instrument—

(a) after consulting the Council and such groups of persons representing consumer interests as they consider appropriate, amend paragraph (bc) of subsection (1) by substituting for the amount for the time being specified in that paragraph such other amount as they consider appropriate;

(b) amend paragraph (c) of subsection (1) by substituting for the amount for the time being specified in that subsection such other amount as appears to them to be justified by a change in the value of money.

(6) A statutory instrument containing an order under—

(a) subsection (5)(a) is not to be made unless a draft of the instrument has been laid before, and approved by resolution of, the Scottish Parliament;

(b) subsection (5)(b) is subject to annulment in pursuance of a resolution of the Scottish Parliament.

(7) In this section, "complainer" has the same meaning as in section 42ZA.".

(3) In section 20 of the 1990 Act (professional misconduct, etc.)—

(a) in subsection (2), after paragraph (c) insert—

"(ca) where the Council consider that the complainer has been directly affected by the professional misconduct or, as the case may be, the matter referred to in paragraph (d) of subsection (1), to direct the practitioner to pay compensation of such amount, not exceeding £5,000, as the Council may specify to the complainer for loss, inconvenience or distress resulting from the misconduct or, as the case may be, the matter;

(cb) subject to subsection (2ZA) below, to impose on the practitioner a fine not exceeding £2,000;";

(b) after that subsection, insert—

"(2ZA) The Council shall not impose a fine under subsection (2)(cb) above where, in relation to the subject matter of the complaint, the practitioner has been convicted by any court of an offence involving dishonesty and sentenced to a term of imprisonment of not less than 2 years.

(2ZB) Any fine imposed under subsection (2)(cb) above shall be treated for the purposes of section 211(5) of the Criminal Procedure (Scotland) Act 1995 (fines payable to HM Exchequer) as if it were a fine imposed in the High Court.";

(c) in subsection (2B), after paragraph (a) insert—

"(aa) where the practitioner has been guilty of professional misconduct, and where the Tribunal consider that the complainer has been directly affected by the misconduct, to direct the practitioner to pay compensation of such amount, not exceeding £5,000, as the Tribunal may specify to the complainer for loss, inconvenience or distress resulting from the misconduct;";

(d) after subsection (11F) (as inserted by paragraph 3(4)(k) of schedule 5 to this Act), insert—

"(11G) The Scottish Ministers may by order made by statutory instrument, after consulting the Council and such groups of persons representing consumer interests as they consider appropriate, amend subsection (2)(ca) or (2B)(aa) by substituting for the amount for the time being specified in that provision such other amount as they consider appropriate.

(11H) A statutory instrument containing an order under subsection (11G) is not to be made unless a draft of the instrument has been laid before, and approved by resolution of, the Scottish Parliament.".

Review of and appeal against decisions on remitted conduct complaints: cases other than unsatisfactory professional conduct

57.—(1) In section 54 of the 1980 Act (appeals from decisions of Tribunal in cases other than unsatisfactory professional conduct)—

(a) after subsection (1), insert—

"(1A) A solicitor or an incorporated practice may, before the expiry of the period of 21 days beginning with the day on which any decision by the Tribunal mentioned in subsection (1B) is intimated to him or, as the case may be, it appeal to the Court against the decision.

(1B) The decision is—

(a) where the Tribunal was satisfied as mentioned in section 53(1)(a), the finding that the solicitor has been guilty of professional misconduct;

(b) where the Tribunal was satisfied as mentioned in section 53(1)(d), the finding that the incorporated practice has failed to comply with any provision of this Act or of any rule made under this Act applicable to the practice;

(c) in any case falling within paragraph (a) or (b), or where the decision was made because of the circumstances mentioned in section 53(1)(b) or (c), any decision under section 53(2) or (5).

(1C) The Council may, before the expiry of the period of 21 days beginning with the day on which a decision by the Tribunal under section 53(2) or (5) is intimated to them, appeal to the Court against the decision; but the Council may not appeal to the Court against a decision of the Tribunal under section 53(2)(bb).

(1D) Where the Tribunal has found that a solicitor has been guilty of professional misconduct but has not directed him under section 53(2)(bb) to pay compensation, the complainer may, before the expiry of the period of 21 days beginning with the day on which the Tribunal's finding is intimated to him, appeal to the Court against the decision of the Tribunal not to make a direction under that subsection.

(1E) A complainer to whom the Tribunal has directed a solicitor under section 53(2)(bb) to pay compensation may, before the expiry of the period of 21 days beginning with the day on which the direction under that subsection is intimated to him, appeal to the Court against the amount of the compensation directed to be paid.

(1F)   On an appeal under any of subsections (1A) to (1E), the Court may give such directions in the matter as it thinks fit, including directions as to the expenses of the proceedings before the Court and as to any order by the Tribunal relating to expenses.

(1G)   A decision of the Court under subsection (1A), (1B), (1C), (1D), (1E) or (1F) shall be final.";

(b)   in subsection (2), after paragraph (b) insert ";

(c)   the Tribunal has exercised the power conferred by section 53(6B) to direct that its order shall take effect on the day on which it is intimated to the solicitor, firm of solicitors or incorporated practice concerned, the solicitor, firm of solicitors or incorporated practice may, before the expiry of the period of 21 days beginning with that day, apply to the court for an order varying or quashing the direction in so far as it relates to the day on which the order takes effect";

(c)   after that subsection, insert—

"(2A)   In subsections (1D) and (1E), "complainer" has the same meaning as in section 42ZA.

(2B)   Subsection (1) does not apply to any element of a decision of the Tribunal to which subsections (1A) to (1G) and paragraph (c) of subsection (2) apply.

(2C)   Subsections (1A) to (1G), and paragraph (c) of subsection (2), apply to any element of a decision of the Tribunal which does not relate to the provision of advice, services or activities referred to in section 77(2) of the 2007 Act.".

(2)   In section 20 of the 1990 Act (professional misconduct etc. by conveyancing or executry practitioners)—

(a)   after subsection (8), insert—

"(8A)   Where the Council are satisfied that a practitioner is guilty of professional misconduct or that the circumstances referred to in subsection (1)(d) apply as respects a practitioner, the practitioner may—

(a)   before the expiry of the period of 21 days beginning with the day on which the finding by the Council to that effect is intimated to him, apply to the Council for a review by them of the finding;

(b)   before the expiry of the period of 21 days beginning with the day on which the outcome of the review is intimated to him, appeal to the Tribunal against the decision of the Council in the review; and the Tribunal may quash or confirm the decision.";

(b)   after subsection (11), insert—

"(11ZA)   Where the Council find that a practitioner is guilty of professional misconduct or that the circumstances referred to in subsection (1)(d) apply as respects a practitioner but do not direct him under subsection (2)(ca) to pay compensation, the complainer may, before the expiry of the period of 21 days beginning with the day on which the Council's finding is intimated to him, apply to the Council for a review by them of their decision not to direct the practitioner under subsection (2)(ca) to pay compensation.

(11ZB)   A complainer to whom the Council have directed a practitioner under subsection (2)(ca) to pay compensation may, before the expiry of the period of 21 days beginning with the day on which the direction under that subsection is intimated to him, apply to the Council for a review by them of the direction.

(11ZC)   The complainer may, before the expiry of the period of 21 days beginning with the day on which the outcome of the review under subsection (11ZA) or (11ZB) is intimated to him, appeal to the Tribunal against the decision of the Council in the review; and the Tribunal may quash, confirm or vary the decision.";

(c)   in subsection (11A)—

(i)   in paragraph (a), after "subsection" insert "(8A)(b) or";

(ii)   after that paragraph, insert—

"(aa)   a finding by the Tribunal that a practitioner is guilty of professional misconduct or that the circumstances mentioned in subsection (1)(d) apply as respects the practitioner; or";

(iii)   for the words "or, as the case may be," substitute "the finding

referred to in paragraph (aa) or, as the case may be, the decision";
(d)   after that subsection, insert—

"(11B)   The complainer may, before the expiry of the period of 21 days beginning with the day on which the outcome of any appeal under subsection (11ZC) is
intimated to him, appeal to the court against the Tribunal's decision in the appeal.

(11C)   Where after holding an inquiry into a complaint against a practitioner,
the Tribunal find that he has been guilty of professional misconduct or that the
circumstances referred to in subsection (2A)(b) apply as respects him, but do not
direct the practitioner under subsection (2B)(aa) to pay compensation, the
complainer may, before the expiry of the period of 21 days beginning with the day
on which the Tribunal's finding is intimated to him, appeal to the court against the
decision of the Tribunal not to make a direction under that subsection.

(11D)   A complainer to whom the Tribunal have directed a practitioner under
subsection (2B)(aa) to pay compensation may, before the expiry of the period of 21
days beginning with the day on which the direction under that subsection is
intimated to him, appeal to the court against the amount of the compensation
directed to be paid.

(11E)   In an appeal under subsection (11C) or (11D), the court may make such
order in the matter as it thinks fit.".

Part 2A[1] – Special provision for licensed providers

Complaints about licensed providers

57A.—(1)   Parts 1 and 2 apply in relation to complaints made about licensed
legal services providers as they apply in relation to complaints made about
practitioners.

(2)   Subsection (1) is subject to—
(a)   subsections (3) and (4), and
(b)   such further modification to the operation of Parts 1 and 2 as the Scottish Ministers may by regulations make for the purposes of—
(i)   subsection (1),
(ii)   section 57B(4) and (5).

(3)   In relation to a services complaint about a licensed provider, its approved
regulator is to be regarded as the relevant professional organisation.

(4)   A conduct complaint may not be made about a licensed provider, but—
(a)   such a complaint may be made about a practitioner within such a
provider,
(b)   the provisions relating to such a complaint remain (subject to such

---

[1] As inserted by the Legal Services (Scotland) Act 2010 (asp 16) Pt 2 c.3 s.81 (effective April 1, 2011
for the purpose of enabling Regulations to be made; July 2, 2012 subject to transitional provision as
specified in SSI 2012/152 art.3 otherwise).

modification as to those provisions as is made under subsection (2)(b)) applicable for the purposes of section 57B(4) and (5).

(5) Where an approved regulator receives (from a person other than the Commission) a complaint about the conduct of, or any services provided by, a practitioner within one of its licensed providers, the approved regulator must without delay send to the Commission the complaint and any material that accompanies it.

Regulatory complaints

57B.—(1) There is an additional type of complaint which applies only in relation to licensed providers (a "regulatory complaint").

(2) A regulatory complaint is where any person suggests that a licensed provider is failing (or has failed) to—

(a) have regard to the regulatory objectives,
(b) adhere to the professional principles,
(c) comply with—
  (i) its approved regulator's regulatory scheme,
  (ii) the terms and conditions of its licence.

(3) In relation to a regulatory complaint about a licensed provider, its approved regulator is to be regarded as the relevant professional organisation.

(4) The procedure in respect of a regulatory complaint is (by virtue of section 57A(4)(b)) the same as it would be for a conduct complaint about a licensed provider, subject to such modification as to that procedure as is made under section 57A(2)(b).

(5) The Commission and the approved regulator have (by virtue of section 57A(4)(b)) the same functions in relation to a regulatory complaint as they would have in relation to a conduct complaint about a licensed provider, subject to such modification as to those functions as is made under section 57A(2)(b).

Levy, advice and guidance

57C.—(1) A licensed provider must pay to the Commission—

(a) the annual general levy, and
(b) the complaints levy (if arising),

in accordance with Part 1 (and in addition to any levy payable under that Part by a solicitor or other person within the licensed provider).

(2) Section 29 applies for the purposes of subsection (1) as it applies for the purposes of sections 27(1) and 28(1).

(3) For the application of sections 27(1), 28(1) and 29 by virtue of subsections (1) and (2)—

(a) an approved regulator is to be regarded as a relevant professional organisation whose members are its licensed providers,
(b) a licensed provider is to be regarded—
  (i) in connection with the annual general levy, as an individual person falling within the relevant category,
  (ii) in connection with the complaints levy, as an individual practitioner of the relevant type.

(4) But the amount of the annual general levy for a licensed provider may be—

(a) different from the amount to be paid by individuals,
(b) of different amounts (including nil) in different circumstances.

(5) The Commission—

(a) must (so far as practicable) provide advice to any person who requests it as respects the process of making a regulatory complaint to the Commission,
(b) may issue guidance under section 40 to approved regulators and licensed providers as respects how licensed providers are to deal with regulatory complaints.

Recovery of levy

57D.—(1) An approved regulator must—

(a) secure the collection by it, from its licensed providers, of the annual general levy due by them, and

(b) pay to the Commission a sum representing the total amount which falls to be collected by it under paragraph (a) in respect of each financial year.

(2) Subsection (3) of section 27 applies in relation to any sum due under subsection (1)(b) (including interest) as it applies in relation to any sum due under subsection (2)(b) of section 27.

(3) Subsection (4) of section 27 applies in relation to any sum due under section 57C(1)(a) (including interest) as it applies in relation to any sum due under subsection (1) of section 27.

(4) Subsection (3) of section 28 applies in relation to any sum due under section 57C(1)(b) (including interest) as it applies in relation to any sum due under subsection (1) of section 28.

(5) For the application of sections 27(3) and (4) and 28(3) by virtue of subsections (2) to (4)—

(a) the approved regulator is to be regarded as the relevant professional organisation,

(b) each of its licensed providers is to be regarded—

(i) in relation to section 27(4), as an individual person falling within the relevant category,

(ii) in relation to section 28(3), as an individual practitioner of the relevant type.

(6) Section 57C(1) is subject to subsection (1).

Handling complaints

57E.—(1) Parts 1 and 2 apply in relation to any complaint made about how an approved regulator has dealt with a regulatory complaint as they apply in relation to a handling complaint (relating to a conduct complaint) made about a relevant professional organisation.

(2) Subsection (1) is subject to such modification to the operation of those Parts as the Scottish Ministers may by regulations make for the purposes of that subsection.

Effectiveness of compensation fund

57F.—(1) Section 39 also applies in relation to a compensation fund of its own that is maintained by an approved regulator in furtherance of section 24(2) of the Legal Services (Scotland) Act 2010.

(2) For the application of section 39 by virtue of subsection (1)—

(a) any such compensation fund is to be regarded as falling within subsection (1)(c) of that section,

(b) the approved regulator is to be regarded as the relevant professional organisation.

Interpretation of Part 2A

57G. For the purposes of this Part—"approved regulator","licensed legal services provider" (or "licensed provider"),"professional principles","regulatory objectives","regulatory scheme", are to be construed in accordance with Part 2 of the Legal Services (Scotland) Act 2010.

[1] PART 2B

SPECIAL PROVISION FOR CONFIRMATION AGENTS AND WILL WRITERS

NOTE
[1] As inserted by the Legal Services (Scotland) Act 2010 (asp 16) Pt 2 c.3 s.114 (effective April 1, 2011 for the purpose of enabling Regulations to be made; not yet in force otherwise).

Complaints about agents and writers

57H.—(1) Parts 1 and 2 apply in relation to complaints made about confirmation agents and will writers as they apply in relation to complaints made about practitioners.

(2) Subsection (1) is subject to—

(a) subsection (3), and

(b) such further modification to the operation of Parts 1 and 2 as the Scottish Ministers may by regulations make for the purposes of subsection (1).

(3) In relation to a services or conduct complaint about a confirmation agent or will writer, the relevant approving body is to be regarded as the relevant professional organisation.

Handling complaints

57I.—(1) Parts 1 and 2 apply in relation to any complaint made about how an approving body has dealt with a conduct complaint as they apply in relation to a handling complaint (relating to a conduct complaint) made about a relevant professional organisation.

(2) Subsection (1) is subject to such modification to the operation of those Parts as the Scottish Ministers may by regulations make for the purposes of that subsection.

Levy payable

57J.—(1) A confirmation agent must pay to the Commission—

(a) the annual general levy, and

(b) the complaints levy (if arising),

in accordance with Part 1.

(2) A will writer must pay to the Commission—

(a) the annual general levy, and

(b) the complaints levy (if arising),

in accordance with Part 1.

(3) Section 29 applies for the purposes of subsections (1) and (2) as it applies for the purposes of sections 27(1) and 28(1).

(4) For the application of sections 27(1), 28(1) and 29 by virtue of subsections (1) to (3)—

(a) an approving body is to be regarded as a relevant professional organisation whose members are its confirmation agents or (as the case may be) will writers,

(b) a confirmation agent or (as the case may be) will writer is to be regarded—

(i) in connection with the annual general levy, as an individual person falling within the relevant category,

(ii) in connection with the complaints levy, as an individual practitioner of the relevant type.

Recovery of levy

57K.—(1) An approving body must—

(a) secure the collection by it, from its confirmation agents or (as the case may be) will writers, of the annual general levy due by them, and

(b) pay to the Commission a sum representing the total amount which falls to be collected by it under paragraph (a) in respect of each financial year.

(2) Subsection (3) of section 27 applies in relation to any sum due under subsection (1)(b) (including interest) as its applies in relation to any sum due under subsection (2)(b) of section 27.

(3) Subsection (4) of section 27 applies in relation to any sum due under section 57J(1)(a) and (2)(a) (including interest) as its applies in relation to any sum due under subsection (1) of section 27.

(4) Subsection (3) of section 28 applies in relation to any sum due under

section 57J(1)(b) and (2)(b) (including interest) as its applies in relation to any sum due under subsection (1) of section 28.

(5) For the application of sections 27(3) and (4) and 28(3) by virtue of subsections (2) to (4)—

    (a) the approving body is to be regarded as the relevant professional organisation,

    (b) each of its confirmation agents or (as the case may be) will writers is to be regarded—

        (i) in relation to section 27(4), as an individual person falling within the relevant category,

        (ii) in relation to section 28(3), as an individual practitioner of the relevant type.

(6) Section 57J(1) and (2) is subject to subsection (1).

Interpretation of Part 2B

57L. For the purposes of this Part—"approving body", "confirmation agent", "will writer", are to be construed in accordance with Part 3 of the Legal Services (Scotland) Act 2010.

PART 3

LEGAL PROFESSION: OTHER MATTERS

Constitution of Scottish Solicitors' Discipline Tribunal

58.—(1) Schedule 4 to the 1980 Act is amended as follows.

(2) For paragraph 1 substitute—

"**1.** The Tribunal shall consist of not more than 28 members.

1A. The Tribunal shall consist of equal numbers of—

    (a) members (in this Part referred to as "solicitor members") appointed by the Lord President, who are solicitors recommended by the Council as representatives of the solicitors' profession throughout Scotland; and

    (b) members (in this Part referred to as "non-lawyer members") appointed by the Lord President after consultation with the Scottish Ministers, who are not—

        (i) solicitors;

        (ii) advocates;

        (iii) conveyancing practitioners or executry practitioners, within the meaning of section 23 of the Law Reform (Miscellaneous Provisions) (Scotland) Act 1990 (c.40) ("the 1990 Act");

        (iv) persons exercising a right to conduct litigation or a right of audience acquired by virtue of section 27 of the 1990 Act.

1B. The validity of any proceedings of the Tribunal is not affected by a vacancy in membership of the Tribunal nor by any defect in the appointment of a member.

1C. The Scottish Ministers may by order made by statutory instrument amend paragraph 1 so as to vary the maximum number of members of the Tribunal.

1D. A statutory instrument containing an order made under paragraph 1C is subject to annulment in pursuance of a resolution of the Scottish Parliament.".

(3) In paragraph 2(a), for "lay" substitute "non-lawyer".

(4) In paragraph 3, for "lay" substitute "non-lawyer".

(5) In paragraph 5—

    (a) in sub-paragraph (b), for "1 lay member is" substitute "2 solicitor members are";

    (b) for sub-paragraph (c) substitute—

"(c) at least 2 non-lawyer members are present.";

    (c) sub-paragraph (d) is repealed.

(6) In paragraph 6, for "lay" substitute "non-lawyer".

Scottish Solicitors Guarantee Fund: borrowing limit
59. In paragraph 2(2) of Schedule 3 (Scottish Solicitors Guarantee Fund) to the 1980 Act, for "£20,000" substitute "£1,250,000".

Safeguarding interests of clients
60.—(1) The 1980 Act is amended as follows.
(2) In section 45 (safeguarding interests of clients of solicitors struck off or suspended)—
    (a) after subsection (4), insert—
    "(4A) Where—
        (a) a solicitor is restricted from acting as a principal; and
        (b) immediately before the restriction the solicitor was a sole solicitor,
    the right to operate on, or otherwise deal with, any client account in the name of the solicitor or the solicitor's firm shall on the occurrence of those circumstances vest in the Society (notwithstanding any enactment or rule of law to the contrary) to the exclusion of any other person until such time as the Council have approved acceptable other arrangements in respect of the client account.";
    (b) in subsection (5), after the definition of "material date", insert—
    " "principal" means a solicitor who is a sole practitioner or is a partner in a firm of two or more solicitors or is a director of an incorporated practice which is a company or a solicitor who is a member of a multi-national practice having its principal place of business in Scotland;".

Offence for unqualified persons to prepare certain documents
61. In section 32(2) of the 1980 Act (offence for unqualified persons to prepare certain documents), after paragraph (e) add "; or
    (f) to a member of a body which has made a successful application under section 25 of the 1990 Act but only to the extent to which the member is exercising rights acquired by virtue of section 27 of that Act".

Notaries public to be practising solicitors
62.—(1) The 1980 Act is amended as follows.
(2) In section 57(2), after "solicitor" insert "qualified to practise in accordance with section 4".
(3) In section 58, after subsection (4) insert—
    "(5) Where a person who is a solicitor and a notary public no longer has in force a practising certificate, the Council shall forthwith remove the person's name from the register of notaries public.
    (6) If the person mentioned in subsection (5) becomes qualified to practise as a solicitor in accordance with section 4, the Council shall restore the person's name to the register of notaries public.".

Regulation of notaries public
63. After section 59 of the 1980 Act, insert—
    "59A Rules regarding notaries public
    (1) Subject to subsections (2) and (3), the Council may, if they think fit, make rules for regulating in respect of any matter the admission, enrolment and professional practice of notaries public.
    (2) The Council shall, before making any rules under this section—
        (a) send to each notary public a draft of the rules; and
        (b) take into consideration any representations made by any notary public on the draft.
    (3) Rules made under this section shall not have effect unless the Lord President, after considering any representations the Lord President thinks relevant, has approved the rules so made.
    (4) If a notary public fails to comply with any rule made under this

section that failure may be treated as professional misconduct or unsatisfactory professional conduct on the part of the solicitor who is the notary public.".

PART 4

LEGAL AID

Criminal legal aid in solemn proceedings

64.—(1) The 1986 Act is amended as follows.

(2) In section 22(1)(b)(i) (automatic availability of criminal legal aid), for "23(1)(a)" substitute "23A(1)".

(3) In section 23 (power of the court to grant legal aid)—

(a) paragraph (a) of subsection (1); and

(b) paragraph (a) of subsection (2),

are repealed.

(4) After that section, insert—

"Legal aid in solemn proceedings

23A.—(1) Criminal legal aid shall be available on an application made to the Board, where a person is being prosecuted under solemn procedure, if the Board is satisfied after consideration of the person's financial circumstances that the expenses of the case cannot be met without undue hardship to the person or the person's dependants.

(2) Legal aid made available to a person under subsection (1) may be subject to such conditions as the Board considers expedient; and such conditions may be imposed at any time.

(3) The Board may require a person receiving legal aid under subsection (1) to comply with such conditions as it considers expedient to enable it to satisfy itself from time to time that it is reasonable for him to continue to receive criminal legal aid.

(4) The Board shall establish a procedure under which any person whose application for legal aid under subsection (1) has been refused may apply to the Board for a review of the application.

(5) The Board shall establish a procedure under which any person receiving criminal legal aid under subsection (1) which is subject to conditions by virtue of subsection (2) may apply to the Board for a review of any such condition.".

(5) In section 25(4) (legal aid in appeals), after "23" insert ", 23A".

(6) In section 25AB(4) (legal aid in references, appeals or applications for special leave to appeal to the Judicial Committee or the Privy Council), after "23" insert ", 23A".

(7) In section 30(3)(a) (legal aid in contempt proceedings), after "23" insert ", 23A".

Criminal legal aid: conditions and reviews

65.—(1) Section 24 (legal aid in summary proceedings) of the 1986 Act is amended in accordance with subsections (2) to (6) of this section.

(2) In subsection (1), for "subsection" substitute "subsections (1A), (2) and".

(3) After subsection (1) insert—

"(1A) Legal aid made available to a person under subsection (1) may be subject to such conditions as the Board considers expedient; and such conditions may be imposed at any time.".

(4) In subsection (2), after "that" insert

"——

(a) after consideration of the financial circumstances of the person, the expenses of the case cannot be met without undue hardship to him or his dependants;

(b) ".

(5) After subsection (5) insert—

"(5A) The Board shall establish a procedure under which any person receiving criminal legal aid under this section which is subject to conditions by virtue of subsection (1A) may apply to the Board for a review of any such condition.".

(6) In subsection (6)—

(a) the word "has either" is repealed;

(b) at the beginning of paragraph (a) insert "has";

(c) at the end of paragraph (a) "or" is repealed;

(d) at the beginning of paragraph (b) insert "has";

(e) at the end of paragraph (b) insert "; or

    (c) is no longer receiving criminal legal aid in connection with proceedings because the Board is no longer satisfied as to the matters mentioned in paragraphs (a) and (b) of subsection (1)".

(7) Section 25 (legal aid in appeals) of the 1986 Act is amended in accordance with subsections (8) and (9) of this section.

(8) After subsection (2A) insert—

"(2B) Where a person is no longer receiving criminal legal aid because the Board is no longer satisfied as mentioned in subsection (2)(c) above the High Court may, at any time prior to the disposal of the appeal, whether or not on application made to it, notwithstanding the Board no longer being so satisfied, determine that it is in the interests of justice that the person should receive criminal legal aid in connection with the appeal, and the Board shall forthwith make such legal aid available to him.

(2C) Legal aid made available to a person under subsection (2) may be subject to such conditions as the Board considers expedient; and such conditions may be imposed at any time.".

(9) After subsection (3) insert—

"(3A) The Board shall establish a procedure under which any person whose application for criminal legal aid under subsection (2) has been refused may apply to the Board for a review of his application.

(3B) The Board shall establish a procedure under which any person receiving criminal legal aid under subsection (2) which is subject to conditions by virtue of subsection (2C) may apply to the Board for a review of any such condition.".

(10) Section 25AB (legal aid in references, appeals or applications for special leave to appeal to the Judicial Committee of the Privy Council) is amended in accordance with subsections (11) and (12) of this section.

(11) After subsection (2) insert—

"(2A) Legal aid made available to a person under subsection (2) may be subject to such conditions as the Board considers expedient; and such conditions may be imposed at any time.".

(12) After subsection (3) insert—

"(3A) The Board shall establish a procedure under which any person whose application for criminal legal aid under subsection (2) has been refused may apply to the Board for a review of his application.

(3B) The Board shall establish a procedure under which any person receiving criminal legal aid under this section which is subject to conditions by virtue of subsection (2A) may apply to the Board for a review of any such condition.".

Criminal Legal Assistance Register: removal of name following failure to comply with code

66.—(1) Section 25D (removal of name from Register following failure to comply with code) of the 1986 Act is amended as follows.

(2) In subsection (1), after "be" insert ", or may not have been,".

(3) After subsection (4), insert—

"(4A) Where, after carrying out the procedures mentioned in subsection (1) above and, where a time limit has been set under subsection (3) above, after the expiry of that time limit, the Board is

satisfied that, regardless of whether or not there is current compliance with the code—
  (a) the firm have not complied with the code in a material regard, it may remove the names of the firm and, subject to subsection (5) below, of any registered solicitors connected with the firm from the Register;
  (b) the solicitor has not complied with the code in a material regard, it may remove his name from the Register.".
(4) In subsection (5), after "(4)(a)" insert "or (4A)(a)".
(5) In subsection (8), after "(4)" insert "or (4A)".

Register of advice organisations: advice and assistance
  67.—(1) The 1986 Act is amended as follows.
  (2) In section 4(2)(a) (Scottish Legal Aid Fund), after "counsel" insert "or registered organisation".
  (3) In section 6 (definitions)—
  (a) in subsection (1)—
    (i) in the definition of "advice and assistance" after paragraph (a) insert—
    "(aa) oral or written advice provided by an adviser—
      (i) on the application of Scots law to any specified categories of circumstances which have arisen in relation to the person seeking advice;
      (ii) as to any steps which that person might appropriately take having regard to the application of Scots law to those circumstances;";
    (ii) in that definition, after paragraph (b) insert—
    "(c) assistance provided to a person by an adviser in taking any steps mentioned in paragraph (aa)(ii) above, by taking such steps on his behalf or by assisting him in so taking them;";
    (iii) in the definition of "assistance by way of representation", after the word "means" insert ", subject to section 12B(3) of this Act,";
  (b) in subsection (2), before the definition of "client" insert—
  " "adviser" means a person who is approved by a registered organisation for the purposes of providing advice and assistance on behalf of the organisation and who is the person by whom advice and assistance is provided;".
  (4) In section 10 (financial limit)—
  (a) in subsection (1)—
    (i) after the word "solicitor" where it first occurs insert "or, as the case may be, adviser";
    (ii) in paragraph (a), after the word "solicitor" insert "or adviser";
  (b) in subsection (3)—
    (i) after paragraph (a) insert—
    "(aa) any outlays which may be incurred by the registered organisation (which approved the adviser) in, or in connection with, the providing of the advice and assistance;";
    (ii) after paragraph (b) insert—
    "(ba) any fees (not being charges for outlays) which, apart from section 11 of this Act, would be properly chargeable by the registered organisation (which approved the adviser) in respect of the advice and assistance;".
  (5) In section 12 (payments of fees or outlays otherwise than through clients' contributions)—
  (a) in subsection (3), after the word "solicitor" where it first occurs insert "or, as the case may be, the registered organisation,";
  (b) in paragraph (d) of that subsection, after "solicitor" insert "or the registered organisation".

(6) After section 12, insert—

"Register of advice organisations

Register of advice organisations
12A.—(1) The Board shall establish and maintain a register of advice organisations ("the register of advice organisations") of organisations approved by the Board as registered organisations in relation to the provision of advice and assistance by persons approved by such organisations as advisers.
(2) A person who—
(a) is a solicitor;
(b) is an advocate;
(c) is a conveyancing practitioner or an executry practitioner, within the meaning of section 23 of the Law Reform (Miscellaneous Provisions) (Scotland) Act 1990 (c.40);
(d) has acquired any right to conduct litigation or right of audience by virtue of section 27 of that Act,
may not be an adviser.
(3) Schedule 1A makes further provision about advisers and registered organisations, the register of advice organisations, code of practice for advisers etc.

Advice and assistance
12B.—(1) The Scottish Ministers may by regulations specify categories of circumstances for the purposes of paragraph (aa) of the definition of "advice and assistance" in section 6(1) of this Act.
(2) The power under subsection (1) may specify different categories for different purposes.
(3) In this Act—
(a) "advice and assistance" as defined in section 6(1)(c) is limited to the extent to which it is competent for the adviser to perform any steps on behalf of the person or by assisting him in so taking them;
(b) "assistance by way of representation" as defined in section 6(1) includes advice and assistance provided by an adviser but only to the extent to which it is competent for the adviser to perform such steps referred to in that definition.".
(7) In section 33 (fees and outlays of solicitors and counsel)—
(a) after subsection (1) insert—
"(1A) A registered organisation shall be paid out of the Fund in accordance with section 4(2)(a) of this Act in respect of any fees or outlays properly incurred by it in respect of the advisers it approves providing advice and assistance under this Act.";
(b) in subsection (2), after "counsel" insert "and, in respect of advice and assistance as mentioned in paragraph (b) of this subsection, advisers".
(8) In section 41 (interpretation)—
(a) after the definition of "advice and assistance" insert—
""adviser" has the meaning given to it in section 6(2) of this Act;
"adviser code" means the code of practice in relation to the register of advice organisations for the time being in force under Schedule 1A to this Act;";
(b) after the definition of "the Register" insert—
" "the register of advice organisations" means the register established and maintained under section 12A of this Act;";
(c) after the definition of "registered firm" insert—
" "registered organisation" means an organisation whose name appears on the register of advice organisations;".
(9) After Schedule 1 (Scottish Legal Aid Board) to the 1986 Act, insert—

"SCHEDULE 1A

Further provision in relation to the Register of Advice Organisations

(introduced by section 12A(3))

Register of advice organisations

1.—(1) An organisation which satisfies the Board that it complies with the relevant provisions of the adviser code shall be approved by the Board as an organisation that may approve a person to provide advice and assistance on behalf of the organisation; and the Board shall make an appropriate entry on the register of advice organisations.

(2) An individual may apply for entry on the register of advice organisations as an organisation; and if the Board is satisfied that the individual complies with the relevant provisions of the adviser code in relation to an organisation, the Board shall approve the individual and treat the individual as an organisation for the purposes of this Schedule.

(3) The Board must make the register of advice organisations available for public inspection, without charge, at all reasonable times.

(4) In this Schedule an "organisation" includes—
  (a) a firm of solicitors;
  (b) an incorporated practice within the meaning of section 34(1A)(c) of the Solicitors (Scotland) Act 1980 (c. 46).

Applications

2.—(1) An application for entry on the register of advice organisations shall be made in such form as the Board may determine, and shall be accompanied by such documents as the Board may specify.

(2) On receipt of an application the Board shall make such enquiries as it thinks appropriate for the purposes of determining whether the applicant complies with the relevant provisions of the adviser code.

(3) The Board may determine an application to be entered on the register of advice organisations by—
  (a) granting the application; or
  (b) refusing the application.

(4) Where the Board decides to refuse an application it shall as soon as practicable thereafter send the applicant, by recorded delivery, a written note of its reasons.

Further provision on applications

3.—(1) In determining any application for entry on the register of advice organisations, the Board may limit the grant of the application to any of the particular categories of circumstances as specified by virtue of section 12B(1).

(2) Where the Board limits the grant of an application as mentioned in sub-paragraph (1), the entry made on the register under paragraph 1(1) must state the categories in relation to which the organisation is registered; and any adviser approved by the organisation may provide advice and assistance under this Act only in relation to those categories.

Adviser code

4.—(1) The Board shall prepare a code of practice (an "adviser code") in relation to advisers and registered organisations.

(2) The adviser code prepared under sub-paragraph (1) must include—
  (a) the conditions to be complied with in order to qualify for registration;
  (b) the types of organisations eligible for registration;
  (c) the conditions to be complied with in order for a person to be approved by a registered organisation as an adviser;
  (d) the laying down of standards, conduct, practice and training expected in relation to—
    (i) the provision of advice and assistance by advisers;
    (ii) the supervision of such activity by registered organisations;
  (e) arrangements for dealing with complaints about the activities of advisers and registered organisations;
  (f) arrangements for monitoring the activities of advisers and registered organisations.

(3) The adviser code prepared under sub-paragraph (1) has effect on such date as the Board may confirm.

(4) But the adviser code may not have effect unless and until it has been—
  (a) approved by the Scottish Ministers; and
  (b) the Board has laid a copy of the prepared code before the Scottish Parliament.

(5) The Board is to publish the adviser code in such way as, in its opinion, is likely to bring it to the attention of those interested in it.

(6) The Board is to—
(a) keep the adviser code under review; and
(b) revise it where appropriate.

(7) The provisions of this paragraph apply in relation to any revision of the adviser code as they apply in relation to the version originally prepared.

(8) Registered organisations shall comply with the relevant requirements of the adviser code.

Monitoring
5. The Board is to monitor—
(a) the provision of advice and assistance and related activities by advisers;
(b) compliance with the adviser code by registered organisations.

Removal of name from the register of advice organisations
6.—(1) Where it appears to the Board (whether or not following a complaint made to it) that a registered organisation may not be, or may not have been, complying with the adviser code, it shall investigate the matter in such manner as it thinks fit.

(2) Where the Board conducts an investigation under sub-paragraph (1) it must allow the registered organisation concerned the opportunity to make representations.

(3) Following an investigation under sub-paragraph (1), the Board may give the registered organisation concerned an opportunity, within such time as it may specify, to remedy any defect in the compliance with the adviser code.

(4) Where, after carrying out the procedures mentioned in sub-paragraph (1) and, where a time limit has been set under sub-paragraph (3), after the expiry of that time limit, the Board is satisfied that the registered organisation is not complying with the adviser code, it shall remove from the register of advice organisations the name of the organisation.

(5) Where, after carrying out the procedures mentioned in sub-paragraph (1) and, where a time limit has been set under sub-paragraph (3), after the expiry of that time limit, the Board is satisfied that, regardless of whether or not there is current compliance with the code, the registered organisation has not complied with the code in a material regard, it may remove the name of the organisation from the register of advice organisations.

(6) Where the Board decides to remove the name of an organisation from the register of advice organisations in accordance with sub-paragraph (4) it shall as soon as practicable thereafter send the organisation, by recorded delivery, a written note of its reasons.

Appeals
7.—(1) A decision by the Board to refuse an application under paragraph 2(3)(b) may be appealed by the applicant to the Court of Session within 21 days of the receipt of the notification of the Board's reasons under paragraph 2(4).

(2) A decision by the Board under paragraph 6(4) or (5) to remove from the register of advice organisations the name of a registered organisation may be appealed to the Court of Session within 21 days of the receipt of the notification of the Board's reasons under paragraph 6(6); but the making of an appeal shall not have the effect of restoring the name to the register of advice organisations.

(3) An appeal under sub-paragraph (1) or (2) may be on questions of both fact and law and the court, after hearing such evidence and representations as it considers appropriate, may make such order as it thinks fit.".

Scottish Legal Aid Board: grants for certain purposes
68.—(1) The 1986 Act is amended as follows.
(2) In section 4 (Scottish Legal Aid Fund)—
(a) at the beginning of subsection (2)(a) insert "subject to section 4A(13),";
(b) after subsection (2)(ab) insert—
"(ac) such sums as are, by virtue of section 4A, due out of the Fund to any person;";
(c) after subsection (3)(ac) insert—
"(ad) any sums recovered from a person in connection with a grant made by the Board in accordance with section 4A;".
(3) After that section insert—

"Power of Board to make grants for certain purposes
4A.—(1) The Board may, on an application made to it by any person,

make grants of such amount and subject to such conditions (including conditions as to repayment) as it may determine to the person in respect of—

    (a) any of the matters mentioned in subsection (2);

    (b) any of the purposes mentioned in subsection (3).

(2) The matters are—

    (a) any civil legal aid or advice and assistance in relation to civil matters provided, or to be provided, by any solicitor or counsel;

    (b) any advice and assistance in relation to civil matters provided, or to be provided, by any adviser;

    (c) any advice, assistance or representation (not falling within paragraphs (a) or (b)) provided, or to be provided, by any person, which is connected to civil matters.

(3) The purposes are facilitating, supporting and developing the provision of any of the matters referred to in subsection (2).

(4) The Scottish Ministers must specify a limit to the total amount that may be paid out of the Fund by virtue of subsection (1).

(5) In specifying any limit under subsection (4) the Scottish Ministers must specify the period in relation to which that limit applies.

(6) Any grant made under subsection (1) must be made in accordance with an approved plan.

(7) The Board must prepare and publish a plan as to the criteria which the Board will apply in considering whether or not to make such a grant; and the Board must submit the plan to the Scottish Ministers for approval.

(8) The Scottish Ministers may approve a plan submitted to them under subsection (7) with or without modification.

(9) The Scottish Ministers may at any time—

    (a) approve a modification of an approved plan proposed by the Board or withdraw approval of such a plan or modification;

    (b) require the Board to prepare and publish a plan under subsection (7).

(10) An application under subsection (1) must include such information as the Board may reasonably require.

(11) In preparing and publishing the plan under subsection (7) the Board must do so in accordance with such directions as the Scottish Ministers may give.

(12) Any money due to a person by virtue of this section shall be paid to the person by the Board out of the Fund.

(13) Any money paid to a person under subsection (1) as provided in subsection (12), in respect of—

    (a) any civil legal aid or advice and assistance provided by any solicitor or counsel;

    (b) any advice and assistance provided by an adviser,

shall be taken to be a payment in accordance with this Act; and no other payment may be made out of the Fund in respect of that civil legal aid or, as the case may be, advice and assistance.

(14) In this section, "approved plan" means a plan approved, for the time being, by the Scottish Ministers under subsection (8); and includes any part or modification of the plan so approved.

(15) For the purposes of this section, "person" includes a body corporate or unincorporate.".

Financial limit: advice and assistance

69.—(1) Section 10 (financial limit) of the 1986 Act is amended as follows.

(2) In subsection (1)(b)—

    (a) after "except" insert ", subject to subsection (4),";

    (b) at the end insert "or in the circumstances set out in subsection (1A)".

(3) After subsection (1) insert—

"(1A)   The circumstances are that—

    (a)   the advice and assistance requires to be given urgently; and

    (b)   it is not possible to seek the approval of the Board before the advice and assistance requires to be given,

and following which an application may be made under subsection (1B) for the Board's approval.

(1B)   If the Board is satisfied that the circumstances set out in subsection (1A) were present it may, on application by the solicitor or adviser concerned, give its approval to the limit having been exceeded.".

(4)   After subsection (3) insert—

"(4)   In the circumstances set out in subsection (5), no application may be made for the Board's approval for the cost of giving the advice and assistance—

    (a)   to exceed the limit applicable under this section; or

    (b)   to that limit having been exceeded.

(5)   The circumstances are that the matter with which the advice and assistance is concerned is not—

    (a)   specified as a distinct matter for the purposes of advice and assistance by virtue of regulations made under this Act; or

    (b)   being treated as if it were a distinct matter by virtue of such regulations.".

Further provision in relation to the Fund: advice and assistance

70.—[1](1)   In section 4 of the 1986 Act (Scottish Legal Aid Fund) in subsection (2), after paragraph (b) insert—

"(ba)   any sums as are, by virtue of section 12C of this Act, due out of the Fund;".

(2)   After section 12B of that Act (inserted by section 67 of this Act) insert—

"Advice and assistance: further provision in relation to the Fund

Further provision in relation to the Fund: advice and assistance

12C.—(1)   This section applies where, in respect of any matter in connection with which advice and assistance has been provided, the sums mentioned in section 4(3)(aa), (ca) and (cb) which are payable into the Fund have been so paid.

(2)   There shall be paid out of the Fund any sum which, in the opinion of the Board the party concerned would have been likely to receive, after the operation of section 12(3), if the advice and assistance provided had not been provided—

    (a)   by virtue of a grant made under section 4A; or

    (b)   by a solicitor in the course of employment to which Part V of this Act applies.".

Availability of civil legal aid for defamation or verbal injury

71.—(1)   The 1986 Act is amended as follows.

(2)   In section 14 (availability of civil legal aid), after subsection (1B) insert—

"(1C)   In the case of proceedings described in paragraph 1 of Part II of Schedule 2 to this Act, civil legal aid shall be available to a person only if, in addition to the requirements which have to be met under subsection (1) and section 15 of this Act and subject to paragraph 2 of Part II of Schedule 2, such criteria as may be set out by the Scottish Ministers in directions given to the Board are met.

(1D)   A direction given under subsection (1C) may—

    (a)   include criteria in respect of which the Board may require to satisfy itself;

    (b)   make different provision for different purposes;

    (c)   be varied or revoked at any time.

(1E)   Where the Scottish Ministers give a direction under subsection (1C)—

    (a)   the Board must comply with it;

    (b)   the Scottish Ministers must arrange for the direction to be published in such manner as they consider appropriate.".

(3)   In Part II of Schedule 2 (excepted proceedings)—

---

[1] This section is not yet in force.

(a) in paragraph 1, after "to" insert "section 14(1C) and";

(b) in paragraph 2, the words ", and legal" to the end are repealed.

Civil legal aid: conditions and reviews

72.—(1) Section 14 (availability of civil legal aid) of the 1986 Act is amended in accordance with subsections (2) and (3) of this section.

(2) In subsection (1), for "subsection" substitute "subsections (1F) and".

(3) After subsection (1E) (inserted by section 71(2) of this Act), insert—

"(1F) Legal aid made available to a person under subsection (1) may be subject to such conditions as the Board considers expedient; and such conditions may be imposed at any time.

(1G) The Board shall establish a procedure under which any person receiving civil legal aid under this section which is subject to conditions by virtue of subsection (1F) may apply to the Board for a review of any such condition.".

(4)–(6) *[As repealed by the Children's Hearings (Scotland) Act 2011 (asp 1) Sch.6 para.1 (effective June 24, 2013.]*

Availability of legal aid: Judicial Committee of the Privy Council

73.—(1) In section 25AB (legal aid in references, appeals or applications for special leave to appeal to the Judicial Committee of the Privy Council) of the 1986 Act—

(a) in subsection (1), for "or 13(a)" substitute ", 13(a) or 33";

(b) in subsection (4), after "11" insert "or 33".

(2) In paragraph 1 of Part 1 of Schedule 2 to that Act, for "and 13(b)" substitute ", 13(b), 32 and 33".

Solicitors employed by the Scottish Legal Aid Board

74.—(1) In section 4 (Scottish Legal Aid Fund) of the 1986 Act, after subsection (2)(a) insert—

"(aza) any expenses incurred by the Board in connection with the provision by solicitors employed by it by virtue of section 27(1) of this Act of—

(i) advice and assistance in relation to civil matters;

(ii) civil legal aid;

(iii) any services as are mentioned in section 26(2) of this Act;".

(2) In section 26 (employment to which Part V applies)—

    (a)   in subsection (2)—

        (i)   the word "local" is repealed;

        (ii) in paragraph (a), for "its function" substitute "any function it has";

    (b)   in subsection (3)(a)—

        (i)   the word "local" is repealed;

        (ii) after "concerned" insert "(whether wholly or partly)".

(3)   In section 27 (arrangements for employment to which Part V applies) of that Act—

    (a)   after subsection (1), insert—

> "(1A) The provisions of paragraph 8 of Schedule 1 to this Act shall apply to solicitors employed by the Board by virtue of subsection (1) as they apply to employees appointed by the Board under that paragraph.";

    (b)   subsections (2) and (3) are repealed.

Contributions, and payments out of property recovered

75.—[1](1)   The 1986 Act is amended as follows.

(2)   In section 4 (Scottish Legal Aid Fund) in subsection (2), after paragraph (ab) insert—

> "(aba)   any sums repayable to a person in accordance with section 17(2C) of this Act;
>
> (abb)   any sums payable to a person in accordance with section 17(2D) of this Act;".

(3)   In that section, after subsection (3)(c) insert—

> "(ca)   any sum recovered as to expenses under an award of a court or an agreement or otherwise in favour of any person in respect of any matter in connection with which advice and assistance has been provided to the person—
>
>   (i)   by virtue of a grant made under section 4A; or
>
>   (ii) by a solicitor in the course of employment to which Part V of this Act applies;
>
> (cb)   any sum which is to be paid out of property (of whatever nature and wherever situated) recovered or preserved for any person in respect of any matter in connection with which advice and assistance has been provided to the person (including his rights under any settlement arrived at in connection with that matter in order to avoid or bring to an end any proceedings)—
>
>   (i)   by virtue of a grant made under section 4A; or
>
>   (ii) by a solicitor in the course of employment to which Part V of this Act applies;".

(4)   In section 17 (contributions, and payments out of property recovered), after subsection (2B) insert—

> "(2C) If the total contribution to the Fund made by a person in respect of any proceedings exceeds the net liability of the Fund on the person's account, the excess shall be repaid to the person.
>
> (2D) Any sums paid to the Board under subsection (2B) which are no longer required to meet the net liability of the Fund on a person's account, having taken into account any relevant sums paid to the Board under subsection (2A), shall be paid to the person.
>
> (2E) Nothing in subsection (2B) shall prejudice the power of the court to allow any damages or expenses to be set off.
>
> (2F) In this section, the reference to a "net liability of the Fund" on a legally assisted person's account is a reference to the aggregate amount of—
>
>   (a)   the sums paid or payable to a solicitor or counsel out of the Fund on the person's account, in respect of the proceedings in question; and
>
>   (b)   any sums paid or payable to a solicitor, counsel or registered organisation (in respect of the advisers it approves) out of the Fund on the person's account, for advice and assistance in connection with the proceedings in question or any matter to which those proceedings relate,

---

[1] Not yet in force.

being sums not recouped by the Fund out of expenses in respect of those proceedings, or as a result of any right which the person may have to be indemnified against such expenses.

(2G)   Where the solicitor for a legally assisted person is employed by the Board for the purposes of Part V of this Act, references in subsection (2F) to sums payable out of the Fund include references to sums which would have been so payable had the legal aid and, as the case may be, advice and assistance been provided in circumstances other than those specified in subsection (2I).

(2H)   Where—

(a)   civil legal aid is or has been provided in respect of the proceedings in question by virtue of a grant made under section 4A; and

(b)   advice and assistance is or has been provided in connection with the proceedings by virtue of a grant made under section 4A,

references in subsection (2F) to sums payable out of the Fund include references to sums which would have been so payable had the legal aid and, as the case may be, advice and assistance been provided in circumstances other than those specified in subsection (2I).

(2I)   The circumstances are that the legal aid and, as the case may be, advice and assistance has been provided—

(a)   by virtue of a grant made under section 4A; or

(b)   by a solicitor in the course of employment to which Part V of this Act applies.".

Regulations under section 36 of the 1986 Act

76.—(1)   Section 36 (regulations) of the 1986 Act is amended as follows.

(2)   After paragraph (c) of subsection (2) insert—

"(ca)   make provision allowing the Board to determine—

(i)   the matters which, subject to subsection (2A), are or are not to be treated as distinct matters for the purposes of advice and assistance;

(ii)   on a case by case basis, matters which may be treated as if they were distinct matters for the purposes of advice and assistance;".

(3)   After subsection (2) insert—

"(2A)   Regulations made under this section which include provision as mentioned in subsection (2)(ca)(i) must include provision to the effect that—

(a)   any determination by the Board as to the matters which are or are not to be so treated as distinct matters may only be made after consultation with the Law Society;

(b)   where a matter has been determined by the Board to be so treated as a distinct matter, the Board may not determine that the matter is no longer to be so treated unless the Scottish Ministers consent.".

PART 5 – GENERAL

Advice, services or activities to which Act does not apply

77.   *[Repealed by the Legal Services Act 2007 (c.29) Sch.23 para.1 (effective October 1, 2008 as SI 2008/1436).]*

Ancillary provision

78.—(1)   The Scottish Ministers may by order make such incidental, supplemental, consequential, transitional, transitory or saving provision as they consider necessary or expedient for the purposes, or in consequence, of, or for giving full effect to, this Act or any provision of it.

[1,2] (1A) The Scottish Ministers may by order make such further provision as, having regard to the effect of the Legal Services Act 2007 so far as concerning the subject matter of Parts 1 and 2 of this Act (and applying in Scotland), they consider necessary or expedient in connection with this Act or any related provisions of the 1980 Act.

(2) An order under this section may—

(a) make different provision for different purposes;

(b) modify any enactment, instrument or document.

NOTES

[1] As inserted by the Legal Services (Scotland) Act 2010 (asp 16) Pt 4 c.4 s.145(1) (effective April 1, 2011).

[2] As amended by the Legal Services (Scotland) Act 2010 (Ancillary Provision) Regulations 2012 (SSI 2012/212) reg.4 (effective July 2, 2012).

Regulations or orders

79.—(1) Any power conferred by this Act on the Scottish Ministers to make orders or regulations—

(a) must be exercised by statutory instrument;

(b) may be exercised so as to make different provision for different purposes.

(2) A statutory instrument containing an order or regulations made under this Act (except an order made under section 26(1) or 82(2)) is, subject to subsection (3), subject to annulment in pursuance of a resolution of the Parliament.

(3) A statutory instrument containing—

(a) an order under section 10(7) or 24(8);

(b) regulations under section 41(1);

(c) an order under—

[1] (i) section 78(1) or (1A) containing provisions which add to, replace or omit any part of the text of an Act;

(ii) paragraph 2(7) of schedule 1,

is not to be made unless a draft of the instrument has been laid before, and approved by resolution of, the Parliament.

NOTE

[1] As substituted by the Legal Services (Scotland) Act 2010 (asp 16) Pt 4 c.4 s.145(2) (effective April 1, 2011).

Interpretation

80. In this Act—

"the 1980 Act" means the Solicitors (Scotland) Act 1980 (c. 46);

"the 1986 Act" means the Legal Aid (Scotland) Act 1986 (c. 47);

"the 1990 Act" means the Law Reform (Miscellaneous Provisions) (Scotland) Act 1990 (c.40).

Minor and consequential modifications

81. Schedule 5 makes—

(a) minor modifications;

(b) modifications consequential on the provisions of this Act.

Short title and commencement

82.—(1) This Act may be cited as the Legal Profession and Legal Aid (Scotland) Act 2007.

(2) The provisions of this Act, except this section and sections 46, 79 and 80 come into force on such day as the Scottish Ministers may by order appoint.

(3) Different days may be appointed under subsection (2) for different purposes.

SCHEDULE 1

The Scottish Legal Complaints Commission

(introduced by section 1(2))

1. *Status*
 (1) The Commission is a body corporate.
 (2) The Commission is not to be regarded as a servant or agent of the Crown, or having any status, immunity or privilege of the Crown, nor are its members or its employees to be regarded as civil servants, nor its property as property of, or held on behalf of, the Crown.

2. *Membership of the Commission*
 (1) The Commission is to consist of the following members—
  (a) a person to chair the Commission ("the chairing member"); and
 [1] (b) 11 other members.
 (2) Members are appointed by the Scottish Ministers, having consulted the Lord President of the Court of Session ("the Lord President").
 [1] (3) The chairing member and 6 other members of the Commission must be members (in this schedule referred to as "non-lawyer members") who are not within any of the categories mentioned in sub-paragraph (6).
 [1] (4) There must be 5 members of the Commission (in this schedule referred to as "lawyer members") who are within any of the categories mentioned in sub-paragraph (6).
 (5) Of the lawyer members 3 must have practised within any, or any combination, of the categories mentioned in sub-paragraph (6) for at least 10 years.
 (6) The categories are—
  (a) solicitors;
  (b) advocates;
  (c) conveyancing practitioners or executry practitioners;
  (d) persons exercising a right to conduct litigation or a right of audience acquired by virtue of section 27 of the 1990 Act.
 (7) The Scottish Ministers may, subject to sub-paragraphs (8) and (9), by order amend—
  (a) sub-paragraph (1)(b) to alter the number of other members referred to there;
  (b) sub-paragraph (3) to alter the number of other members referred to there;
  (c) sub-paragraph (4) to alter the number of members referred to there;
  (d) sub-paragraph (5) to alter the number of lawyer members referred to there.
 (8) The number of non-lawyer members must be greater than the number of lawyer members.
 (9) The number of—
  (a) non-lawyer members must be no fewer than 4 and no greater than 8;
  (b) lawyer members must be no fewer than 3 and no greater than 7.

NOTE
 [1] As substituted by the Legal Profession and Legal Aid (Scotland) Act 2007 (Membership of the Scottish Legal Complaints Commission) Amendment Order 2010 (SSI 2010/415) art.2 (effective November 24, 2010).

3. *Terms of appointment etc.*
 (1) Subject to sub-paragraph (2), each member is to be appointed for a period of 5 years.
 (2) Appointments that constitute the Commission for the first time are to be in accordance with sub-paragraph (3).
 (3) Each member is to be appointed for a period of not less than 4 years and not exceeding 6 years.
 (4) A member—
  (a) may by giving notice in writing to the Scottish Ministers resign office as a member of the Commission;
  (b) otherwise, holds and vacates office in accordance with the terms and conditions of appointment.
 (5) A person is, on ceasing to be a member, eligible for reappointment for a single further period; but not before a period of 3 years has elapsed.

4. *In appointing members, the Scottish Ministers are to have regard to the desirability of including—*
  (a) persons who have experience of, and have shown capacity in—
   (i) consumer affairs or complaints handling;
   (ii) the provision of advice to members of the public on or in relation to such matters;

(b) persons who have experience of, and shown capacity in, the practice and provision of legal education and training;
(c) persons who have experience of, and shown capacity in—
    (i) civil or criminal proceedings;
    (ii) court procedures and practice generally;
    (iii) the practice and provision of other legal services;
    (iv) the monitoring of legal services;
(d) persons who have such other skills, knowledge or experience as the Scottish Ministers consider to be relevant in relation to the exercise of the Commission's functions.

5. *Removal of members*

(1) Subject to sub-paragraph (2), the chairing member may, by written notice, remove a member from office if the chairing member is satisfied as regards any of the following matters—
(a) that the member becomes insolvent;
(b) that the member—
    (i) has been absent from meetings of the Commission for a period longer than 6 consecutive months without the permission of the Commission;
    (ii) has been convicted of a criminal offence;
    (iii) is otherwise unable or unfit to discharge the functions of a member or is unsuitable to continue as a member.
(2) The chairing member may not remove a member from office without the agreement of the Lord President of the Court of Session.
(3) The Lord President may, by written notice, remove the chairing member from office if the Lord President is satisfied as regards any of the matters mentioned in sub-paragraph (1)(a) or (b).
(4) For the purpose of sub-paragraph (1)(a) a member becomes insolvent on—
(a) the approval of a voluntary arrangement proposed by the member;
(b) being adjudged bankrupt;
(c) the member's estate being sequestrated;
(d) entering into a debt arrangement programme under Part 1 of the Debt Arrangement and Attachment (Scotland) Act 2002 (asp 17) as the debtor;
(e) granting a trust deed for creditors.

6. *Disqualification from membership*

(1) A person is disqualified from appointment, and from holding office, as a member of the Commission if that person is—
(a) a member of the House of Commons;
(b) a member of the Scottish Parliament;
(c) a member of the European Parliament.
(2) A person who has held any of the offices set out in sub-paragraph (1)(a) to (c) is also disqualified from appointment as a member of the Commission for a period of one year starting from the day on which the person last held any of those offices.

7. *Remuneration, allowances and pensions for members*

(1) The Commission is to pay to its members such remuneration as the Scottish Ministers may in each case determine.
(2) The Commission is to pay to its members such allowances as the Scottish Ministers may in each case determine.
(3) The Commission may, with the approval of the Scottish Ministers—
(a) pay or make arrangements for the payment;
(b) make payments towards the provision;
(c) provide and maintain schemes (whether contributory or not) for the payment,
of such pensions, allowances or gratuities to or in respect of any person who is or has ceased to be a member of the Commission, as the Commission may determine.
(4) The reference in sub-paragraph (3) to pensions, allowances and gratuities includes a reference to pensions, allowances and gratuities by way of compensation for loss of office.

8. *Chief executive and other employees*

(1) The Commission is to employ a chief executive.
(2) The chief executive is, with the approval of the Scottish Ministers, to be appointed by the Commission on such terms and conditions as the Commission may, with such approval, determine.
(3) The Commission may (subject to any directions given under sub-paragraph (4)) appoint such other employees on such terms and conditions as the Commission may determine.
(4) The Scottish Ministers may give directions to the Commission as regards the appointment of employees under sub-paragraph (3) (including the number of appointments) and as regards terms and conditions of their employment.

(5) The Commission must comply with directions given to it under sub-paragraph (4).

(6) The Commission may, with the approval of the Scottish Ministers—

(a) pay or make arrangements for the payment;

(b) make payments towards the provision;

(c) provide and maintain schemes (whether contributory or not) for the payment,

of such pensions, allowances or gratuities to or in respect of any person who is or has ceased to be an employee of it, as the Commission may determine.

(7) The reference in sub-paragraph (6) to pensions, allowances and gratuities includes a reference to pensions, allowances and gratuities by way of compensation for loss of employment.

9. *Accountable officer*

(1) The chief executive is the accountable officer for the purposes of this paragraph.

(2) The functions of the accountable officer are—

(a) signing the accounts of the expenditure and receipts of the Commission;

(b) ensuring the propriety and regularity of the finances of the Commission;

(c) ensuring that the resources of the Commission are used economically, efficiently and effectively;

(d) the duty mentioned in sub-paragraph (3).

(3) The duty is, where the accountable officer is required by the Commission to act in some way but considers that to do so would be inconsistent with the proper performance of the functions specified in sub-paragraph (2)(a) to (c), to—

(a) obtain written authority from the Commission before taking the action;

(b) send a copy of the authority as soon as possible to the Auditor General for Scotland.

10. *Procedure*

(1) Subject to sub-paragraph (2)—

(a) any quorum of the Commission as contained in rules made under section 32(1) must consist of a greater number of non-lawyer members than lawyer members;

(b) the chairing member must, if present, chair meetings of the Commission or any committee of the Commission;

(c) if the chairing member is not available to be present at a meeting of the Commission or any committee of the Commission, the chairing member is to appoint another non-lawyer member to chair the meeting or committee;

(d) the chairing member has a casting vote; and any person appointed by that member under sub-sub-paragraph (c) has a casting vote for the purposes of that appointment;

(e) the validity of any proceedings of the Commission, or any of its committees, is not affected by a vacancy in membership nor by any defect in the appointment of a member.

(2) Sub-paragraph (1) does not apply to a determination committee established under paragraph 11(1)(a).

11. *Committees*

(1) The Commission—

(a) must establish one or more determination committees in accordance with rules made under section 32(1) for the purpose of exercising any functions mentioned in paragraph 13(2) which a determination committee is authorised by the Commission to exercise;

(b) may establish other committees for any other purposes relating to its functions.

(2) Subject to sub-paragraph (3)—

(a) the Commission is to determine the composition of its committees;

(b) any quorum of a committee as contained in rules made by virtue of section 32 must consist of a greater number of non-lawyer members than lawyer members;

(c) a committee of the Commission is to comply with any directions given to it by the Commission.

(3) Sub-paragraph (2) does not apply to a determination committee established under sub-paragraph (1)(a).

12. *General powers*

(1) The Commission may do anything which appears to it to be necessary or expedient for the purpose of, or in connection with, or appears to it to be conducive to, the exercise of the Commission's functions.

(2) In particular the Commission may—

(a) enter into contracts;

(b) with the consent of the Scottish Ministers, borrow money;

(c) with the consent of the Scottish Ministers, acquire and dispose of land;

(d) obtain advice or assistance from any person who, in the Commission's opinion, is qualified to give it.

(3) The Commission may pay to any person from whom advice or assistance is obtained such fees, remuneration and allowances as the Commission may, with the approval of the Scottish Ministers, determine.

13. *Delegation of functions*

(1) The Commission may, subject to sub-paragraphs (2), (3) and (4), authorise—
   (a) the chief executive;
   (b) any of its committees;
   (c) any of its members;
   (d) any of its other members of staff,
to exercise such of its functions (to such extent) as it may determine.

(2) The Commission may authorise—
   [1](a) a decision under section 2(4)(a) that a complaint is frivolous, vexatious or totally without merit to be taken only by any of its committees or by one of the Commission's members;
   (b) the function of deciding under section 3(1) whether—
      (i) any element of a complaint is capable of being dealt with under a specified regulatory scheme;
      (ii) the extent (if any) to which the Commission is able to take the preliminary steps referred to in section 2(4) in relation to the complaint and to deal with it under Part 1,
   to be exercised only by one of the Commission's members;
   (c) the function of deciding whether any element of a complaint is about the exercise of discretion by any Crown Counsel or procurator fiscal in relation to the prosecution of crime or investigation of deaths to be exercised only by one of the Commission's members;
   (d) the following functions to be exercised only by a determination committee—
      (i) the making of a determination under section 9(1);
      (ii) the making of a determination or direction under section 10(2);
      (iii) the making of any decision or the publication of a report under section 13;
      (iv) the making of a decision under section 23(2);
      (v) the making of a direction under section 24(6).

(3) The Commission may not authorise the exercise of any of the following functions under sub-paragraph (1)—
   (a) the approval of annual reports and accounts;
   (b) making of rules under section 32(1);
   (c) determining the amount of the annual general levy and the complaints levy under section 29(1);
   (d) the approval of any budget or other financial plan.

(4) Sub-paragraph (1) does not affect the responsibility of the Commission for the exercise of its functions.

NOTE
[1] As substituted by the Legal Services (Scotland) Act 2010 (asp 16) Pt 4 c.4 s.144 (effective April 1, 2011).

14. *Location of office*

(1) Subject to sub-paragraph (2), the Commission's determination of the location of the Commission's office premises is subject to the approval of the Scottish Ministers.

(2) The Scottish Ministers may direct the Commission as to the location of the Commission's office premises; and the Commission must comply with any such direction.

15. *Accounts*

(1) The Commission must—
   (a) keep proper accounts and accounting records;
   (b) prepare in respect of each financial year a statement of accounts; and
   (c) send the statement of accounts to the Scottish Ministers,
in accordance with such directions as the Scottish Ministers may give.

(2) The Scottish Ministers must as soon as practicable—
   (a) send the statement of accounts to the Auditor General for Scotland for auditing;
   (b) lay the audited statement before the Parliament.

(3) If requested by any person, the Commission is to make available at any reasonable time, without charge, in printed or electronic form, their audited accounts, so that they may be inspected by that person.

16. *Reports*

(1) As soon as practicable after the end of each financial year, the Commission must prepare a report on—

(a) the discharge of the Commission's functions during that year; and

(b) such action the Commission proposes to take in the following year in pursuance of its functions.

(2) The Commission must—

(a) send a copy of the report to the Scottish Ministers; and

(b) publish the report.

(3) In preparing and publishing the report the Commission must do so in accordance with such directions as the Scottish Ministers may give.

(4) The Scottish Ministers must as soon as practicable lay a copy of the report before the Parliament.

(5) The Commission may publish such other reports on matters relevant to the functions of the Commission as it considers appropriate.

SCHEDULE 2

FURTHER POWERS OF COMMISSION UNDER SECTION 17 OR 37

(introduced by sections 17(7) and 37(4))

1. Where the Commission—

(a) gives notice under subsection (1) of section 17 to any person having possession or control of any documents mentioned in subsection (3) of that section;

(b) gives notice under section 17(4) to any person having possession or control of any documents mentioned in subsection (6) of that section;

(c) requires any person under section 37(1) or (3) to provide it with information or documents referred to in that section,

and the person refuses or fails to produce or deliver any of the documents or the information within the time specified in the notice or requirement or to cause them to be so produced or delivered, the Commission may apply to the court for an order requiring the person to produce or deliver the documents or information or to cause them or it to be produced or delivered to the person appointed at the place fixed by the Commission within such time as the court may order.

2. Where the Commission takes possession of any such documents or information which have or has been produced or delivered to it, it must—

(a) in the case mentioned in paragraph 1(a) or (c), without delay serve on the practitioner against whom the complaint is made, and any other person to whom the notice was given or requirement made;

(b) in the case mentioned in paragraph 1(b), without delay serve on the complainer,

a notice giving particulars and the date on which it took possession.

3. Before the expiry of the period of 14 days after service of a notice under paragraph 2 the person on whom the notice has been served may apply to the court for an order directing the Commission to return such documents or information to the person from whom they were received by the Commission or to such other person as the applicant may request; and on the hearing of any such application the court may make the order applied for or such other order as it thinks fit.

4. If no application is made to the court under paragraph 3, or if the court on any such application directs that the documents or information in question remain in the custody or control of the Commission, the Commission may make enquiries to ascertain the person to whom they belong and may deal with the documents or information in accordance with the directions of the person.

SCHEDULE 3

RULES AS TO COMMISSION'S PRACTICE AND PROCEDURE

(introduced by section 32(2))

Provision which must be included

1. The rules as to the Commission's practice and procedure made under section 32(1) must include provision—

(a) regulating the making to the Commission of complaints under Part 1, including—

      (i) when a complaint is to be regarded as made for the purposes of the Part;

      (ii) the eligibility of persons to make such complaints on behalf of other persons (whether living or not);

(b) requiring the Commission not to—

      (i) investigate a services complaint by virtue of section 9;

      (ii) remit a conduct complaint to a relevant professional body under section 6(a) or 15(5)(a);

      (iii) investigate a handling complaint by virtue of section 23,

unless the complainer has, for the purposes of Parts 1 and 2 of this Act, waived any right of confidentiality in relation to the matters to which the complaint relates;

(c) regulating the handling by it of complaints under Part 1;

(d) regulating the proposal by the Commission under section 9(2) of a settlement of a complaint and how an accepted settlement is to be constituted;

(e) requiring the Commission—

      (i) where it considers it appropriate, to hold a hearing in relation to a complaint being dealt with by it under Part 1;

      (ii) to decide whether such a hearing should be in public or private;

(f) as to—

      (i) the evidence which may be required or admitted;

      (ii) the extent to which it may be oral or written;

      (iii) the consequences of a person's failure to produce any information or document which the person has been required to produce;

(g) as to when reasons are to be given (in circumstances where they are not required by this Act to be given)—

      (i) for the Commission's determinations, directions, decisions or recommendations under Part 1;

      (ii) in respect of what matters relating to the determinations, directions, decisions or recommendations;

(h) as to the membership of a determination committee, including in particular provision requiring—

      (i) that any such committee has at least 3 members, of which the majority are non-lawyer members of the Commission;

      (ii) that any such committee is chaired by a lawyer member of the Commission;

  [1] (iii) where the Commission has under section 9(2) proposed a settlement as respects a complaint and the settlement has not been accepted as mentioned in section 9(4), that the members of the committee determining the complaint under section 9(1) or making a determination or direction under section 10(2), by virtue of paragraph 13(2) of schedule 1, must not have been involved in any aspect of the investigation of the complaint (including deciding under section 2(4)(a) that the complaint was frivolous, vexatious or totally without merit) or the formulation or making by the Commission of the proposed settlement;

(i) requiring, where the Commission itself (and not one of its determination committees) determines a complaint under section 9(1) or makes a determination or direction under section 10(2) in relation to a complaint, that any member of the Commission involved in doing so must not have been involved in any aspect of the investigation of the complaint (including any matter referred to in paragraph 13(2)(a) to (c) of schedule 1) or the formulation or making by the Commission under section 9(2) of a proposed settlement as respects the complaint;

(j) as to the charging of interest at such rate as may be specified by the Scottish Ministers by order under section 27(3)(b) on any amount of the annual general levy due to be paid to the Commission by a relevant professional organisation under section 27(2)(b) from the date the amount is due under the rules until it is paid;

(k) as to the charging of interest at such rate as may be specified by the Scottish Ministers by order under section 28(3)(b) on any amount of the complaints levy due to the Commission from the date the amount is due under the rules until it is paid;

(l) subject to schedule 1, regulating its own meetings (including any quorum) and that of its committees.

NOTE

[1] As substituted by the Legal Services (Scotland) Act 2010 (asp 16) Pt 4 c.4 s.144 (effective April 1, 2011).

Provision which may in particular be included

2. The rules as to the Commission's practice and procedure made under section 32(1) may in particular include provision—

(a) fixing time limits for the making of complaints against practitioners or relevant professional organisations or the stages of its investigation under Part 1;

(b) as to—

    (i) extension of any time limit fixed by it under the rules;

    (ii) the circumstances in which such extension may be made;

(c) as to the circumstances in which the Commission is not prevented by section 4(2) from taking the steps and further action referred to in that section in relation to a complaint which is made prematurely (within the meaning of section 4(4));

(d) as to the circumstances in which the Commission may rely on—

    (i) with the agreement of the body concerned, findings in fact of a relevant professional organisation, the Scottish Solicitors' Discipline Tribunal or such other body as the Scottish Ministers may by order specify which has disciplinary functions;

    (ii) previous findings in fact of the Commission;

(e) securing that a procedural defect in relation to—

    (i) the making of;

    (ii) the Commission dealing with,

a complaint under Part 1 is not to have an effect under the Part where the Commission considers that appropriate in the interests of fairness;

(f) as to the collection of the amount of the annual general levy to be paid to it by the relevant professional organisations and of any complaints levy due to it by practitioners;

(g) as to the recovery by it from the relevant professional organisations of the annual general levy due to be paid to it by them and from practitioners of any complaints levy due by them;

(h) as to the circumstances in which the Commission may—

    (i) waive a portion of the annual general levy which would otherwise be payable under section 27(1);

    (ii) refund any portion of an amount paid under that section;

(i) as to the circumstances in which the Commission may waive the requirement under section 28(1) to pay the complaints levy in any case;

(j) as to the calculation of the total amount of the annual general levy each relevant professional organisation is due to collect under section 27(2)(a) in respect of each financial year and notification of each such organisation of the amount so calculated by the Commission.

3. In this schedule—

"lawyer member" has the meaning given by paragraph 2(4) of schedule 1;

"non-lawyer member" has the meaning given by paragraph 2(3) of that schedule.

SCHEDULE 4

FURTHER POWERS OF RELEVANT PROFESSIONAL ORGANISATIONS UNDER SECTION 48

(introduced by section 48)

1. Where a relevant professional organisation gives notice—

(a) under section 48(1)(a) to any person having possession or control of any documents mentioned in subsection (3) of that section;

(b) under section 48(1)(b) to any person having possession or control of any documents mentioned in subsection (5) of that section,

and the person refuses or fails to produce or deliver any of the documents within the time specified in the notice or to cause them to be so produced or delivered, the relevant professional organisation may apply to the court for an order requiring the person to produce or deliver the documents or to cause them to be produced or delivered to the person appointed at the place fixed by the relevant professional organisation within such time as the court may order.

2. Where a relevant professional organisation takes possession of any such documents which have been produced or delivered to it, it must—

(a) in the case mentioned in paragraph 1(a), without delay serve on the practitioner against whom the complaint is made, and any other person to whom the notice was given;

(b) in the case mentioned in paragraph 1(b), without delay serve on the complainer,

a notice giving particulars and the date on which it took possession.

3. Before the expiry of the period of 14 days after service of a notice under paragraph 2 the person on whom the notice has been served may apply to the court for an order directing the relevant professional organisation to return such documents to the person from whom they

were received by the relevant professional organisation or to such other person as the applicant may request; and on the hearing of any such application the court may make the order applied for or such other order as it thinks fit.

4. If no application is made to the court under paragraph 3, or if the court on any such application directs that the documents in question remain in the custody or control of the relevant professional organisation, the relevant professional organisation may make enquiries to ascertain the person to whom they belong and may deal with the documents in accordance with the directions of that person.

SCHEDULE 5

MINOR AND CONSEQUENTIAL MODIFICATIONS

(introduced by section 81 *)*

[Not reproduced.]

LEGAL SERVICES ACT 2007

(2007 c.29)   **F1.18**

Sections 1.–194. *[Not reproduced.]*

Scotland

Application of the Legal Profession and Legal Aid (Scotland) Act 2007

195.—(1)   The Legal Profession and Legal Aid (Scotland) Act 2007 (asp 5) ("the 2007 Act") applies to—

(a)   any element of a complaint relating to,

(b)   the provision by a practitioner of,

the advice, services and activities mentioned in subsection (2) as it applies to any other advice, services and activities provided by a practitioner.

(2)   The advice, services and activities are—

(a)   *[As repealed by the Financial Services and Markets Act 2000 (Regulated Activities) (Amendment) (No.2) Order 2013 (SI 2013/1881) Sch.1(1) para.13 (effective July 26, 2013).]*

(b)   activities of an insolvency practitioner within the meaning of Part 13 of the Insolvency Act 1986 (c. 45);

(c)   activities mentioned in paragraph (a) of paragraph 5(1) of Schedule 3 to the Financial Services Act 1986 (c. 60);

(d)   immigration advice or immigration services;

(e)[1]   regulated activity within the meaning of section 22 of the Financial Services and Markets Act 2000 (c. 8), other than activity falling within paragraph (f) below, in respect of which the Financial Conduct Authority has by virtue of Part 20 of that Act arranged for its regulatory role to be carried out by the Law Society of Scotland;

(f)   exempt regulated activities within the meaning of section 325(2) of the Financial Services and Markets Act 2000.

(3)   In subsection (1), "complaint" and "practitioner" have the same meaning as in Part 1 of the 2007 Act.

---

[1] As amended by the Financial Services Act 2012 (c.21) Sch.18(2) para.125(4) (effective April 1, 2013).

(4)   Omit section 77 of the 2007 Act (advice services and activities to which Act does not apply).

(5)   Schedule 20 contains minor and consequential amendments in connection with the application of the 2007 Act by virtue of this section.

Scottish legal services ombudsman: functions

F1.19

196.—(1)   The functions of the Scottish legal services ombudsman cease to be exercisable in relation to the advice, services and activities mentioned in section 195(2).

(2)   In the Immigration and Asylum Act 1999 (c. 33)—

    (a)   in section 86(4)(c) (designated professional bodies), for "Scottish Legal Services Ombudsman" substitute "Scottish Legal Complaints Commission", and

    (b)   in paragraph 4(2)(c) of Schedule 5 (the Immigration Services Commissioner), for "Scottish Legal Services Ombudsman" substitute "Scottish Legal Complaints Commission".

LEGAL SERVICES (SCOTLAND) ACT 2010

F1.20

(2010 ASP 16)

An Act of the Scottish Parliament to allow and to make provision for regulating the supply of certain legal services by licensed entities; to extend rights to obtain confirmation to the estates of deceased persons; to regulate will and other testamentary writing by non-lawyers; to make provision concerning the Law Society of Scotland and the Faculty of Advocates and for the professional arrangements to which solicitors and advocates are subject; to allow court rules to permit the making of oral submissions by lay representatives in civil cases; and for connected purposes.

PART 1 – THE REGULATORY OBJECTIVES ETC.

Introduction

Regulatory objectives

1.   For the purposes of this Act, the regulatory objectives are the objectives of—

    (a)   supporting—

        (i)   the constitutional principle of the rule of law,

        (ii)   the interests of justice,

    (b)   protecting and promoting—

        (i)   the interests of consumers,

        (ii)   the public interest generally,

    (c)   promoting—

        (i)   access to justice,

        (ii)   competition in the provision of legal services,

    (d)   promoting an independent, strong, varied and effective legal profession,

    (e)   encouraging equal opportunities (as defined in Section L2 of Part II of Schedule 5 to the Scotland Act 1998) within the legal profession,

    (f)   promoting and maintaining adherence to the professional principles.

Professional principles

2. For the purposes of this Act, the professional principles are the principles that persons providing legal services should—

    (a)   support the proper administration of justice,

    (b)   act with independence (in the interests of justice),

    (c)   act with integrity,

    (d)   act in the best interests of their clients (and keep clients' affairs confidential),

    (e)   maintain good standards of work,

    (f)   where—

        (i)   exercising before any court a right of audience, or

        (ii)   conducting litigation in relation to proceedings in any court,

    comply with such duties as are normally owed to the court by such persons,

    (g)   meet their obligations under any relevant professional rules,

    (h)   act in conformity with professional ethics.

Legal services

3.—(1) For the purposes of this Act, legal services are services which consist of (at least one of)—

    (a)   the provision of legal advice or assistance in connection with—

        (i)   any contract, deed, writ, will or other legal document,

        (ii)   the application of the law, or

        (iii)   any form of resolution of legal disputes,

    (b)   the provision of legal representation in connection with—

        (i)   the application of the law, or

        (ii)   any form of resolution of legal disputes.

  (2) But, for those purposes, legal services do not include—

    (a)   judicial activities,

    (b)   any other activity of a judicial nature,

    (c)   any activity of a quasi-judicial nature (for example, acting as a mediator).

  (3) In subsection (1)(a)(iii) and (b)(ii), "legal disputes" includes disputes as to any matter of fact the resolution of which is relevant to determining the nature of any person's legal rights or obligations.

Role of Ministers

Ministerial oversight

4.—(1) Subsections (2) and (3) apply in relation to the exercise by the Scottish Ministers of their functions—

    (a)   under Parts 2 and 3, or

    (b)   under section 125(3) or otherwise arising by virtue of Part 4 (except sections 141(c) and 145(1)).

  (2) The Scottish Ministers must, so far as practicable, act in a way which—

    (a)   is compatible with the regulatory objectives, and

    (b)   they consider most appropriate with a view to meeting those objectives.

  (3) The Scottish Ministers must adopt best regulatory practice under which (in particular) regulatory activities should be—

    (a)   carried out—

(i)   effectively (but without giving rise to unnecessary burdens),

(ii)   in a way that is transparent, accountable, proportionate and consistent,

(b)   targeted only at such cases as require action.

Consultation by Ministers

5.—(1)   Subsection (2) applies in relation to the exercise by the Scottish Ministers of their functions—

(a)   under Parts 2 and 3, or

(b)   under section 125(3) or otherwise arising by virtue of Part 4 (except sections 141(c) and 145(1)).

(2)   Where (and to the extent that) the Scottish Ministers consider it appropriate to do so in the case of an individual function, they must consult such persons or bodies as appear to them to have a significant interest in the particular subject-matter to which the exercise of the function relates.

(3)   The general requirement to consult under subsection (2) has effect in conjunction with, or in the absence of, any particular consultation requirement to which the Scottish Ministers are subject in a specific (and relevant) context.

PART 2 – REGULATION OF LICENSED LEGAL SERVICES

Chapter 1 – – Approved Regulators

Approved regulators

Approved regulators

6.—(1)   For the purposes of this Part, an approved regulator is a professional or other body which is approved as such by the Scottish Ministers under section 7.

(2)   That is, following an application to them by the body under subsection (3).

(3)   An application to become an approved regulator must include—

(a)   a copy of the applicant's proposed regulatory scheme (see section 7(1)(c)),

(b)   a copy of its proposed statement of policy under section 78(1),

(c)   a description of—

(i)   the applicant's constitution and composition (including internal structure),

(ii)   its internal governance arrangements,

(iii)   its representative functions (if any),

(iv)   its other activities (if any).

(4)   The applicant—

(a)   must provide the Scottish Ministers with such other information as they may reasonably require for their (or the Lord President's) consideration of its application,

(b)   may withdraw its application at any time by giving them written notice to that effect.

(5)   No more than 3 approved regulators may exist at any time.

(6)   The Scottish Ministers may—

(a)   with the agreement of the Lord President, and

(b)   after consulting such other person or body as they consider appropriate, by regulations amend the number specified in subsection (5).

(7) The Scottish Ministers may by regulations prescribe fees that they may charge—

    (a) an applicant to become an approved regulator,

    (b) approved regulators.

Approval of regulators

7.—(1) The Scottish Ministers may approve the applicant as an approved regulator if they are satisfied that—

    (a) for regulating licensed legal services providers in accordance with this Part, the applicant has—

        (i) the necessary expertise as regards the provision of legal services (including as deriving from that of the persons within it),

        (ii) a thorough understanding of the application of the regulatory objectives and the professional principles,

        (iii) sufficient resources (financial and otherwise),

        (iv) the capability in other respects,

    (b) the applicant will always exercise its regulatory functions—

        (i) independently of any other person or interest,

        (ii) properly in other respects (in particular, with a view to achieving public confidence),

    (c) the applicant's proposed regulatory scheme is adequate (as determined with particular reference to section 12),

    (d) the applicant's internal governance arrangements are, or will be, suitable (as determined with particular reference to section 27).

(2) The Scottish Ministers may give their approval subject to conditions.

(3) Their approval may be given—

    (a) with restrictions imposed by reference to particular categories of—

        (i) licensed providers,

        (ii) legal services,

    (b) either—

        (i) without limit of time, or

        (ii) for a fixed period of at least 3 years.

(4) The Scottish Ministers may, after consulting the approved regulator, vary (including by addition or deletion) any conditions or restrictions imposed under subsection (2) or (3).

(5) The Scottish Ministers may by regulations make further provision about approval under this section, including (in particular)—

    (a) the process for seeking their approval,

    (b) in relation to capability to act as an approved regulator, the criteria for their approval

(including things that applicants must be able to demonstrate).

(6) Before making regulations under subsection (5), the Scottish Ministers must consult the Lord President.

Pre-approval consideration

8.—(1) Before deciding whether or not to approve the applicant as an approved regulator under section 7, the Scottish Ministers must consult—

    (a) the Lord President,

    (b) the OFT, and such other organisation (appearing to them to represent the interests of consumers in Scotland) as they consider appropriate,

(c)   such other person or body as they consider appropriate.

(2)   In consulting under subsection (1), the Scottish Ministers—

    (a)   must send a copy of the application to the consultees,

    (b)   may send a copy of any revised application to any (or all) of them.

(3)   The Scottish Ministers must, with reasons, notify the applicant if they intend to—

    (a)   refuse to approve it as an approved regulator, or

    (b)   impose conditions or restrictions under section 7(2) or (3).

(4)   If notification is given to the applicant under subsection (3), it has 28 days beginning with the date of the notification (or such longer period as the Scottish Ministers may allow) to—

    (a)   make representations to the Scottish Ministers,

    (b)   take such steps as it may consider expedient.

Lord President's agreement

9.—(1)   Despite section 7(1), the Scottish Ministers must not approve the applicant as an approved regulator unless the Lord President agrees to its being approved as such.

(2)   The Scottish Ministers are to impose under section 7(2) such particular conditions relating to the expertise mentioned in section 7(1)(a)(i) as are reasonably sought by the Lord President when (and if) notifying them of the Lord President's agreement for the purpose of subsection (1).

(3)   The Lord President's agreement is required for—

    (a)   the imposition of any—

        (i)   conditions under section 7(2) (apart from conditions to which subsection (2) relates),

        (ii)   restrictions under section 7(3),

    (b)   the variation of any such conditions or restrictions under section 7(4).

Authorisation to act

10.—(1)   An approved regulator may not exercise any of its regulatory functions unless it is authorised to do so by the Scottish Ministers under this section.

(2)   The Scottish Ministers may give their authorisation if they are satisfied (or continue to be satisfied)—

    (a)   as mentioned in subsection (1) of section 7,

    (b)   as regards any criteria provided for under subsection (5)(b) of that section.

(3)   Their authorisation may be given with restrictions imposed by reference to particular categories of—

    (a)   licensed provider,

    (b)   legal services.

(4)   Their authorisation may be given—

    (a)   either—

        (i)   without limit of time, or

        (ii)   for a fixed period of at least 3 years,

    (b)   subject to conditions.

(5)   The Scottish Ministers may, after consulting the approved regulator, vary (including by addition or deletion) any restrictions or conditions imposed under subsection (3) or (4)(b).

(6) The Scottish Ministers may by regulations make further provision about authorisation under this section including (in particular) the process for requests for their authorisation.

Request for authorisation

11.—(1) A request for authorisation under section 10 may be—
- (a) made at any reasonable time (including at the same time as applying for approval under section 7),
- (b) withdrawn by the approved regulator (or applicant) at any time by giving the Scottish Ministers written notice to that effect.

(2) The Scottish Ministers must, with reasons, notify the approved regulator (or applicant) if they intend to—
- (a) withhold their authorisation, or
- (b) impose conditions under section 10(4)(b).

(3) If notification is given to the approved regulator (or applicant) under subsection (2), it has 28 days beginning with the date of the notification (or such longer period as the Scottish Ministers may allow) to—
- (a) make representations to the Scottish Ministers,
- (b) take such steps as it may consider expedient.

(4) The approved regulator (or applicant) must provide the Scottish Ministers with such information as they may reasonably require for their consideration of its request for their authorisation.

(5) In section 10 and this section, a reference to authorisation means initial or renewed authorisation.

Regulatory schemes

Regulatory schemes

12.—(1) An approved regulator must—
- (a) make a regulatory scheme for licensing and regulating the provision of legal services by its licensed legal services providers, and
- (b) apply the scheme in relation to them.

(2) The regulatory scheme is to—
- (a) contain—
  - (i) the licensing rules (see section 14),
  - (ii) the practice rules (see section 18),
  - (iii) the compensation rules (see sections 25 and 26(1)),
- (b) include provision for reconciling different sets of regulatory rules (see section 13),
- (c) cover such other regulatory matters as the Scottish Ministers may by regulations specify

(and in such manner as the regulations may specify).

(3) The regulatory scheme may—
- (a) relate to—
  - (i) one or more categories of licensed provider,
  - (ii) some or all legal services,
- (b) make different provision for different cases or types of case.

(4) An approved regulator may amend its regulatory scheme (or any aspect of it), but—

(a) any material amendment is invalid unless it has the prior approval of the Scottish Ministers,

(b) the Scottish Ministers may not give their approval without—

(i) the Lord President's agreement, and

(ii) consulting such other person or body as they consider appropriate.

(5) The Scottish Ministers may by regulations—

(a) confer authority for the regulatory schemes of approved regulators to deal with the provision by their licensed providers of such other services (in addition to legal services) as the regulations may prescribe, and

(b) specify the extent to which (and the manner in which) the regulatory schemes may do so.

F1.452 **Reconciling different rules**

13.—(1) The provision required by section 12(2)(b) to be in the regulatory scheme is such provision as is reasonably practicable (and appropriate in the circumstances) for—

(a) preventing or resolving regulatory conflicts, and

(b) avoiding unnecessary duplication of regulatory rules.

(2) For the purposes of this section, a regulatory conflict is a conflict between—

(a) the regulatory scheme of an approved regulator, and

(b) any professional or regulatory rules made by any other body which regulates the provision of legal or other services.

(3) The Scottish Ministers may by regulations make further provision about regulatory conflicts (such as may involve an approved regulator).

(4) Before making regulations under subsection (3), the Scottish Ministers must have the Lord President's agreement.

Licensing rules

F1.453 **Licensing rules: general**

14.—(1) For the purposes of this Part, the licensing rules are rules about—

(a) the procedure for becoming a licensed provider, including (in particular)—

(i) the making of applications,

(ii) the criteria to be met by applicants,

(iii) the determination of applications,

(iv) the issuing of licences,

(b) the terms of licences and attaching to licences of conditions or restrictions,

(c) the—

(i) renewal of licences,

(ii) circumstances in which licences may be revoked or suspended,

(d) licensing provision affecting non-solicitor investors in licensed providers,

(e) licensing fees that are chargeable by the approved regulator.

(2) Rules made in pursuance of subsection (1)(a) to (c) must allow for review by the approved regulator of any decision made by it under the rules that materially affects an applicant for a licence or (as the case may be) a licensed provider.

(3) Licensing rules may include such further licensing arrangements as to licensed providers for which provision is (in the approved regulator's opinion) necessary or expedient.

(4) See also sections 55(6)(b), 57(4), 62(2), 63(3) and 67(2)(b) and paragraph 4(2) of schedule 8 (as well as sections 15 and 16).

Initial considerations

F1.454

15.—[1](1) Licensing rules must provide for—
- (a) consultation with the CMA, where appropriate in accordance with subsection (2), in relation to a licence application,
- (b) how the approved regulator is to deal with a licence application where it believes that granting it would cause (directly or indirectly) a material and adverse effect on the provision of legal services.

(2) For the purpose of subsection (1)(a), it is appropriate to consult the CMA where the approved regulator believes that the granting of the licence application may have the effect of—
- (a) preventing competition within the legal services market, or
- (b) significantly restricting or distorting such competition.

Other licensing rules

F1.455

16.—(1) Licensing rules may allow for—
- (a) an applicant to be issued with a provisional licence—
    - (i) in anticipation of its becoming (or becoming eligible to be) a licensed provider, and
    - (ii) whose full effect as a licence is conditional on its becoming a licensed provider (and such other relevant matters as the rules may specify), or
- (b) a licensed provider to be issued with a provisional licence—
    - (i) in anticipation of its transferring to the regulation of the approved regulator, and
    - (ii) whose full effect as a licence is conditional on the transfer occurring (and such other relevant matters as the rules may specify).

(2) Licensing rules must—
- (a) state that a licence application may be refused on the ground that the applicant appears to be incapable (for any reason) of complying with the regulatory scheme,
- (b) provide for grounds for non-renewal, revocation or suspension of a licence where the licensed provider is breaching (or has breached) the regulatory scheme.

Licensing appeals

F1.456

17.—(1) An applicant for a licence or (as the case may be) a licensed provider may appeal against a relevant licensing decision taken by virtue of this Part—
- (a) to the sheriff,
- (b) within the period of 3 months beginning with the date on which that decision is intimated to it.

---

[1] As amended by the Enterprise and Regulatory Reform Act 2013 (c.24) Sch.6 para.194 (effective April 1, 2014).

(2)   A relevant licensing decision is a decision to—
    (a)   refuse the licensed provider's application for—
        (i)   a licence, or
        (ii)   renewal of its licence,
    (b)   attach conditions or restrictions to its licence, or
    (c)   revoke or suspend its licence.

Practice rules

Practice rules: general

18.—(1)   For the purposes of this Part, the practice rules are rules about—
    (a)   the—
        (i)   operation and administration of licensed providers,
        (ii)   standards to be met by licensed providers,
    (b)   the operational positions within licensed providers,
    (c)   accounting and auditing (see section 22),
    (d)   professional indemnity (see section 23),
    (e)   the making and handling of any complaint about—
        (i)   a licensed provider,
        (ii)   a designated or other person within a licensed provider,
    (f)   the measures that may be taken by the approved regulator, in relation to a licensed provider, if—
        (i)   there is a breach of the regulatory scheme, or
        (ii)   a complaint referred to in paragraph (e) is upheld.

(2)   Rules made in pursuance of subsection (1)(f) must allow a licensed provider to make representations to the approved regulator before it takes any of the measures available to it under the rules.

(3)   Practice rules may include such further arrangements as to the professional practice, conduct or discipline of licensed providers for which provision is (in the approved regulator's opinion) necessary or expedient.

(4)   See also sections 55(6)(a), 57(5) and 65(4) (as well as sections 19 to 23).

Financial sanctions

19.—(1)   Practice rules made in pursuance of section 18(1)(f) may provide for the imposition of a financial penalty.

(2)   A financial penalty provided for by virtue of subsection (1) must not exceed the maximum amount permitted by the Scottish Ministers when giving their approval under section 7.

(3)   A financial penalty imposed by virtue of this section is payable to the Scottish Ministers (but the approved regulator may collect it on their behalf).

(4)   A licensed provider may appeal against a financial penalty (or the amount of a financial penalty) imposed on it by virtue of this section—
    (a)   to the sheriff,
    (b)   within the period of 3 months beginning with the date on which the penalty is intimated to it.

(5)   Where an appeal is made under subsection (4), no part of the penalty requires to be paid before the appeal is determined or withdrawn.

Enforcement of duties

20.—(1)   Practice rules must include provision that it is a breach of the regulatory scheme for a licensed provider to—
  (a)   fail to comply with section 50, or
  (b)   fail to comply with its—
      (i)   other duties under this Part, or
      (ii)   duties under any other enactment specified in the scheme.
  (2)   Practice rules must require a licensed provider to—
  (a)   review and report on its performance (see section 21), and
  (b)   have its performance and that report assessed by the approved regulator.

Performance report

21.—(1)   Practice rules made by reference to section 20(2)(a) are (in particular) to give the Head of Practice of a licensed provider the functions of—
  (a)   carrying out an annual review, and
  (b)   sending a report (in a specified form) on the review to the approved regulator.
  (2)   The review must include an examination of—
  (a)   the licensed provider's compliance with section 50(1), and
  (b)   the involvement of any non-solicitor investors in the licensed provider.
  (3)   Practice rules made by reference to section 20(2)(b) may describe the approved regulator's functions under section 31.

Accounting and auditing

22.   Practice rules must—
  (a)   require licensed providers to keep in place proper accounting and auditing procedures,
  (b)   include provision corresponding to that applying under sections 35 to 37 (accounts rules) of the 1980 Act in relation to an incorporated practice.

Professional indemnity

23.   Practice rules must—
  (a)   require licensed providers to keep in place sufficient arrangements for professional indemnity,
  (b)   include provision corresponding to that applying under section 44 (professional indemnity) of the 1980 Act in relation to an incorporated practice.

Compensation arrangements

Choice of arrangements

24.—(1)   An approved regulator must proceed with either option A or option B as regards a compensation fund from which to make good such relevant losses as may be suffered by reason of dishonesty on the part of its licensed legal services providers.
  (2)   Option A is for the approved regulator to maintain its own compensation fund (separate from the Guarantee Fund) in relation to its licensed providers.
  (3)   If option A is proceeded with, the compensation fund is to be—

(a) held by the approved regulator for such purpose as corresponds to the purpose for which the Guarantee Fund is held under section 43(2)(c) of the 1980 Act in relation to licensed providers,

(b) administered by it in such way as corresponds to the administration of the Guarantee Fund in accordance with section 43(3) to (7) of, and Part I of Schedule 3 to, the 1980 Act (so far as applicable in relation to licensed providers).

(4) Option B is for the approved regulator, by not maintaining its own compensation fund as mentioned in option A, to cause the Guarantee Fund to be administered as respects its licensed providers.

(5) For the purpose of option B, see section 43(2)(c) to (8) of, and Part I of Schedule 3 to, the 1980 Act.

(6) As soon as it has decided which of options A and B to proceed with, the approved regulator (where not the Law Society) must inform the Law Society of its decision.

F1.464   Compensation rules: general

25.—(1) For the purposes of this Part, the compensation rules are rules in pursuance of (as the case may be)—

(a) option A in section 24, or

(b) option B in that section.

(2) In pursuance of option A, the rules must—

(a) state—
    (i) the purpose of the approved regulator's compensation fund,
    (ii) as a minimum, the monetary amount to be contained in that fund,

(b) describe the way in which that fund is to be administered by the approved regulator,

(c) specify the criteria for qualifying for payment out of that fund,

(d) provide for the procedure for—
    (i) making claims for such payment,
    (ii) determining such claims,

(e) require the making of contributions to that fund by a licensed provider in accordance with the relevant scale of annual contributions fixed by virtue of section 24(3)(b),

(f) make provision for the destination (or distribution) of that fund in the event that the approved regulator ceases to operate.

(3) In pursuance of option B, the rules must require the making of contributions to the Guarantee Fund by a licensed provider in accordance with the relevant scale of annual contributions fixed under paragraph 1(3) of Schedule 3 to the 1980 Act.

F1.465   More about compensation arrangements

26.—(1) Compensation rules may include such further compensation arrangements as to licensed providers for which provision is (in the approved regulator's opinion) necessary or expedient.

(2) The Scottish Ministers may by regulations make further provision about compensation arrangements as to licensed providers, including (in particular)—

(a) for the content of compensation rules,

(b) in connection with a compensation fund, for functions of approved regulators and licensed providers.

(3)   In sections 24 and 25 and this section, the references to the Guarantee Fund are to the Scottish Solicitors Guarantee Fund (which is vested in the Law Society under section 43(1) of the 1980 Act).

Internal governance

Internal governance arrangements   F1.466

27.—(1)   The internal governance arrangements of an approved regulator must incorporate such provision as is necessary with a view to ensuring that the approved regulator will—

    (a)   always exercise its regulatory functions—
        (i)   independently of any other person or interest,
        (ii) properly in other respects (in particular, with a view to achieving public confidence),
    (b)   continue to allocate sufficient resources (financial and otherwise) to the exercise of its regulatory functions,
    (c)   review regularly how effectively it is exercising its regulatory functions (in particular, by reviewing the effectiveness of its regulatory scheme).

(2)   In relation to an approved regulator which has representative functions, relevant factors in connection with subsection (1)(a) include (in particular) the need for—

    (a)   the approved regulator's code of conduct (if any) for its members to be compatible with the regulatory objectives and the professional principles,
    (b)   the approved regulator to—
        (i)   exercise its regulatory functions separately from its other functions (in particular, any representative functions), and
        (ii) avoid conflicts of interest in relation to its regulatory functions,
    (c)   the approved regulator to secure that a reasonable proportion of the individuals who are responsible for the exercise of its regulatory functions are not qualified legal practitioners.

(3)   The approved regulator's regard to the factor mentioned in subsection (2)(b) is demonstrable by (for example) its securing that within its structure its regulatory functions are clearly demarcated.

Communicating outside   F1.467

28.—(1)   The internal governance arrangements of an approved regulator must not, in relation to the persons who are involved in the exercise of its regulatory functions, prevent the persons from engaging in consultation or other communication with—

    (a)   other approved regulators,
    (b)   the Scottish Ministers,
    (c)   the Scottish Legal Aid Board,
    (d)   the Scottish Legal Complaints Commission, or
    (e)[1] the CMA, or any other public body which has functions concerning the application of competition law.

---

[1] As amended by the Enterprise and Regulatory Reform Act 2013 (c.24) Sch.6 para.195 (effective April 1, 2014).

(2)   Where an approved regulator has representative functions, its internal governance arrangements must not, in relation to any person who—

    (a)   is involved in the exercise of its regulatory functions, and

    (b)   considers that the independence or effectiveness of the approved regulator's exercise of its regulatory functions is being (or has been) for any reason adversely affected by the furtherance of its representative functions, prevent the person from notifying the Scottish Ministers accordingly.

(3)   Subsections (1) and (2) are subject to any overriding prohibition or restriction arising by virtue of any relevant—

    (a)   enactment or rule of law, or

    (b)   rule of professional conduct or ethics.

F1.468   **More about governance**

29.—(1)   The Scottish Ministers may by regulations make further provision about the internal governance arrangements of approved regulators.

(2)   However, regulations under subsection (1) must relate to the regulatory functions of approved regulators.

(3)   Before making regulations under subsection (1), the Scottish Ministers must—

    (a)   have the Lord President's agreement, and

    (b)   consult any approved regulator that would be affected by the regulations.

(4)   For the purposes of this Part, the internal governance arrangements of an approved regulator are its own organisational and operational arrangements for the carrying out of its activities.

Regulatory functions etc.

F1.469   **Regulatory and representative functions**

30.—(1)   For the purposes of this Part, the regulatory functions of an approved regulator are the approved regulator's functions of regulating its licensed legal services providers including (in particular) its functions—

(a) in relation to its regulatory scheme,

(b) under section 31.

(2) For the purposes of this Part, the representative functions of an approved regulator are any functions that the approved regulator has, in that or any other capacity, of representing or promoting the interests of the individual persons (taken collectively or otherwise) who form its membership.

(3) Nothing in this Part permits the Scottish Ministers to interfere with an approved regulator's representative functions (but this does not prevent the Scottish Ministers from taking such action under this Part as they consider appropriate for the purpose of ensuring that an approved regulator's regulatory functions are not prejudiced by its representative functions).

Assessment of licensed providers

31.—(1) An approved regulator must assess the performance of each of its licensed providers at least once in every successive period of 3 years from (in each case) the date on which the approved regulator issued the licensed provider with its licence.

(2) The Scottish Ministers may require an approved regulator to carry out a special assessment of a licensed provider if the Scottish Legal Complaints Commission requests that they do so in a case where the Commission has significant concerns about how a complaint about a licensed provider has been dealt with.

(3) An assessment under this section must (in particular) concern—

(a) the licensed provider's compliance with section 50(1), and

(b) such other matters as the approved regulator considers appropriate.

(4) When conducting the assessment, the approved regulator may—

(a) require from the licensed provider the production of any—

    (i) relevant documents,

    (ii) other relevant information,

(b) interview any person within the licensed provider.

(5) The approved regulator must—

(a) prepare a report on the assessment, and

(b) send a copy of the report to the licensed provider (and, if the assessment was required under subsection (2), also send one to the Scottish Ministers and the Commission).

(6) Before finalising the report, the approved regulator must—

(a) send a draft of the report to the licensed provider, and

(b) give it a reasonable opportunity to make representations about—

    (i) the findings of the assessment, and

    (ii) any recommendations contained in the report.

(7) If the assessment discloses (or appears to disclose) any professional misconduct by a member of a professional association, the approved regulator must notify that association accordingly.

(8) An approved regulator may delegate any of its functions under this section to any suitable person or body.

(9) The Scottish Ministers may by regulations make further provision about the assessment of licensed providers.

Relationship with other bodies

Giving information to SLAB

32.—(1) An approved regulator must provide the Scottish Legal Aid Board with such information as the Board may reasonably require for the purpose mentioned in subsection (2).

(2) The purpose is the Board's exercise of its function under section 1(2A) of the 1986 Act.

Solicitors: Statutes

Reporting to Law Society

33.—(1) This section applies in relation to any licensed legal services provider (whose approved regulator is not the Law Society) that is required, by compensation rules made by reference to section 25(3), to make contributions to the Guarantee Fund.

(2) The approved regulator must report to the Law Society any—
  (a) breach of the regulatory scheme by the licensed provider that the approved regulator discovers as regards the procedures arising under practice rules made by reference to section 22,
  (b) suspicion held by the approved regulator that there is engagement in such financial impropriety as may (in the approved regulator's opinion) give rise to the risk of a claim being made on the Guarantee Fund.

(3) The approved regulator must make available to the Law Society any report prepared by the approved regulator about an inspection carried out by it as regards compliance with—
  (a) the procedures arising under practice rules made by reference to section 22,
  (b) any other financial procedure as regards which the approved regulator has functions under this Part.

(4) The approved regulator must inform the Law Society of any further action that it intends to take (or has taken) in relation to any of the matters mentioned in subsections (2) and (3).

(5) In this section and section 34, the references to the Guarantee Fund are to it as defined in section 26(3).

Steps open to Society

34.—(1) Where—
  (a) section 33 applies, and
  (b) the Law Society suspects that the approved regulator is failing to enforce under this Part any financial procedure to which that section relates,
the Society may refer the circumstances to the Scottish Ministers.

(2) But the Society may make a referral under subsection (1) only if—
  (a) it has made representations to the approved regulator in respect of its suspicion, and
  (b) in light of any response to them (or where none is received timeously), its suspicion is not relieved.

(3) In a referral under subsection (1), the Society may—
  (a) request that the Scottish Ministers take such action under this Part as they consider appropriate,
  (b) seek their consent to the Society's taking of the step mentioned in subsection (5).

(4) That consent may be—
  (a) sought only if the Society suspects that the suspected failure may be facilitating to any extent engagement in such financial impropriety as may (in the Society's opinion) give rise to the risk of a claim being made on the Guarantee Fund,
  (b) given only if the Scottish Ministers are satisfied (on information provided by the Society) that—
    (i) the Society's suspicions are reasonable, and
    (ii) it is necessary (by way of investigation) that the step be taken.

(5) The step is that the Society inspect, at the licensed provider's premises, any document, record or other information (in any form) found there which—
  (a) relates to—
    (i) the licensed provider's client account, or
    (ii) any other financial account held by it, and
  (b) is relevant in relation to any financial procedure to which section 33 relates.

Financial inspection by Society

35.—(1) If the relevant consent is given under subsection (4)(b) of section 34, the Law Society may take the step mentioned in subsection (5) of that section.

(2) The licensed provider must co-operate with the Society in connection with the taking of the step.

(3) But the Society does not have authority to take the step (or enter the premises) unless the Society has—

(a) consulted the approved regulator about the taking of it, and

(b) given the licensed provider at least 48 hours notice of the taking of it.

(4) Following the taking of the step, the Society—

(a) must report its findings to—

(i) the approved regulator, and

(ii) the Scottish Ministers,

(b) in the report to the Scottish Ministers, may request that they take such action (or further action) under this Part as they consider appropriate.

(5) In this section, the references to taking the step mentioned in section 34(5) are to its being taken by the Society's representatives as appointed for the purpose of this section.

Review of own performance

36.—(1) An approved regulator must review annually its performance.

(2) In particular, a review is to cover the following matters—

(a) the approved regulator's compliance with section 77,

(b) the exercise of its regulatory functions,

(c) the operation of its internal governance arrangements,

(d) its compliance with any measures applying to it by virtue of section 38(4)(a) or (b).

(3) The approved regulator must send a report on the review to the Scottish Ministers.

(4) The report must contain a copy of the approved regulator's annual accounts (but only so far as they are relevant in connection with its functions under this Part).

(5) The Scottish Ministers must lay a copy of the report before the Scottish Parliament.

(6) The Scottish Ministers may by regulations make further provision about—

(a) the review of approved regulators' performance,

(b) reports on reviews of their performance.

Monitoring by Ministers

37.—(1) The Scottish Ministers may monitor the performance of approved regulators in such manner as they consider appropriate.

(2) Monitoring the performance of an approved regulator includes (in particular) doing so by

reference to—

(a) its compliance with section 77,

(b) the exercise of its regulatory functions,

(c) the operation of its internal governance arrangements,

(d) its compliance with any measures applying to it by virtue of section 38(4)(a) or (b).

(3) An approved regulator must—

(a) provide such information about its performance in relation to its regulatory scheme as the Scottish Ministers may reasonably request,

(b) do so within 21 days beginning with the date of the request (or such longer period as the Scottish Ministers may allow).

Measures open to Ministers

38.—(1) The Scottish Ministers may, in relation to an approved regulator, take one or more of the measures mentioned in subsection (4) if they consider that to be appropriate in the circumstances of the case.

(2) When considering the appropriateness of taking any of those measures, or a combination of them, the Scottish Ministers must (except in the case of a measure mentioned in paragraph (f) of that subsection) have particular regard to the effect that it may have on the approved regulator's observance of the regulatory objectives.

(3) Schedules 1 to 6 (to which subsection (1) is subject) respectively make provision concerning the measures mentioned in subsection (4).

(4) The measures are—

(a) setting performance targets,
(b) directing that action be taken,
(c) publishing a statement of censure,
(d) imposing a financial penalty,
(e) amending an authorisation given under section 10,
(f) rescinding an authorisation given under that section.

(5) The rescission of an authorisation by virtue of subsection (4)(f) has the effect of terminating the associated approval (of the approved regulator) given under section 7, except where it is stated under paragraph 5(3)(b) of schedule 6 that the approval is preserved.

(6) The Lord President's agreement is required for the taking of any of the measures mentioned in subsection (4) except paragraph (d).

(7) The Scottish Ministers may by regulations—

(a) specify other measures that may be taken by them,
(b) make further provision about the measures that they may take (including for the procedures to be followed),

in relation to approved regulators.

(8) Before making regulations under subsection (7), the Scottish Ministers must—

(a) have the Lord President's agreement, and
(b) consult every approved regulator.

Ceasing to regulate

Surrender of authorisation

39.—(1) An approved regulator may, with the prior agreement of the Scottish Ministers, surrender the authorisation given to it under section 10.

(2) Schedule 7 (to which subsection (1) is subject) makes provision concerning the surrender of such an authorisation.

(3) An approved regulator must take all reasonable steps to ensure that the effective regulation of its licensed providers is not interrupted by the surrender of such an authorisation.

(4) The surrender of an authorisation by virtue of subsection (1) has the effect of terminating the associated approval (of the approved regulator) given under section 7.

Cessation directions

40.—(1) This section applies where—

(a) an approved regulator amends its regulatory scheme so as to exclude the regulation of particular categories of licensed providers or legal services, or
(b) the authorisation of an approved regulator is to be (or has been)—
   (i) amended by virtue of section 38(4)(e) so as to exclude the regulation of certain categories of licensed providers or legal services,
   (ii) rescinded by virtue of section 38(4)(f), or
   (iii) surrendered by virtue of section 39(1).

(2) The Scottish Ministers may direct the approved regulator to take specified action (or refrain from doing something) if they consider that to be necessary or expedient for the continued effective regulation of a licensed provider.

(3) The approved regulator must (so far as practicable) comply with a direction given to it under subsection (2).

(4) For the purposes of this section, a reference to an approved regulator includes (as the context requires) a former approved regulator.

Transfer arrangements

41.—(1) This section applies where—
  (a) an approved regulator has amended its regulatory scheme so as to exclude the regulation of particular categories of licensed provider or legal services,
  (b) the authorisation of an approved regulator is to be (or has been)—
    (i) amended by virtue of section 38(4)(e) so as to exclude the regulation of particular categories of licensed provider or legal services,
    (ii) rescinded by virtue of section 38(4)(f), or
    (iii) surrendered by virtue of section 39(1), or
  (c) the approved regulator is otherwise unable to continue to regulate some or all of its licensed providers.

(2) The approved regulator must (as soon as reasonably practicable)—
  (a) notify each of its licensed providers of the relevant situation within subsection (1),
  (b) do so by reference to any effective date.

(3) A notification under subsection (2) must inform each licensed provider as to whether it requires, in consequence of the relevant situation, to transfer to the regulation of a different approved regulator (a "new regulator") from the one which issued its current licence (the "current regulator").

(4) Each licensed provider that is so required to transfer to a new regulator must—
  (a) within 28 days beginning with the date of the notification, or failing which as soon as practicable, take all reasonable steps so as to transfer to the regulation of a new regulator, and
  (b) where it does so transfer, take (as soon as practicable) such steps as are necessary to ensure that it complies with the new regulator's regulatory scheme before the end of the changeover period.

(5) For the purpose of subsection (4)(b), the changeover period is the period of 6 months beginning with the date on which the new regulator takes over the regulation of the licensed provider.

(6) On the coming into effect of a licence issued to the licensed provider by a new regulator, the licence issued to it by the current regulator ceases to have effect.

Extra arrangements

42.—(1) The Scottish Ministers may by regulations make provision in connection with section 41 as to the arrangements for the transfer of licensed providers to the regulation of a different approved regulator (a "new regulator").

(2) Regulations under subsection (1) may (in particular)—
  (a) provide for a licensed provider which has not transferred to the regulation of a new regulator to be regulated by such new regulator as may be appointed by the Scottish Ministers with the new regulator's consent,
  (b) provide for the Scottish Ministers to recover on behalf of the new regulator, or a licensed provider, any fee (or a part of it) paid by the licensed provider to the former approved regulator in connection with the licensed provider's current licence.

Change of approved regulator

43.—(1) A licensed legal services provider may transfer voluntarily to the regulation of a different approved regulator (a "new regulator") from the one which issued its current licence (the "current regulator").

(2) But the transfer requires the new regulator's written consent (and its agreement to issue the licensed provider with a licence having effect from the date on which the transfer is to occur).

(3) Where a licensed provider wishes to do so, it must—
(a) give a notice which complies with subsection (4) to—
  (i) the current regulator, and
  (ii) the Scottish Ministers, and
(b) provide such further information as may reasonably be required by either of them.

(4) A notice complies with this subsection if it—
(a) explains why the licensed provider wishes to transfer to the regulation of a new regulator,
(b) specifies—
  (i) the new regulator,
  (ii) the date on which the transfer is to occur (which must be within 28 days of the date of the notice), and
(c) is accompanied by a copy of the new regulator's written consent to the transfer.

(5) On the coming into effect of a licence issued to the licensed provider by a new regulator, the licence issued to it by the current regulator ceases to have effect.

(6) The Scottish Ministers may by regulations make further provision about the transfer by a licensed provider to the regulation of a new regulator.

Step-in by Ministers

44.—(1) The Scottish Ministers may by regulations make provision which establishes a body with a view to its becoming an approved regulator.

(2) The Scottish Ministers may by regulations make provision which allows them to act as an
approved regulator in such circumstances as the regulations may prescribe.

(3) Regulations under subsection (2) may provide for this Part to apply with or subject to such modifications as the regulations may specify.

(4) No regulations are to be made under subsection (1) or (2)—
(a) without the Lord President's agreement, and
(b) unless the Scottish Ministers believe that their intervention under this section is necessary, as a last resort, in order to ensure that the provision of legal services by licensed providers is regulated effectively.

Additional functions etc.

Additional powers and duties

45.—(1) The Scottish Ministers may by regulations make provision conferring on approved regulators such additional functions as they consider appropriate for the purposes of this Part.

(2) Before making regulations under subsection (1), the Scottish Ministers must—
(a) have the Lord President's agreement, and
(b) consult—
  (i) every approved regulator,
  (ii) such other person or body as they consider appropriate.

Guidance on functions

46.—(1) In exercising its functions under this Part, an approved regulator must have regard to any guidance issued (to approved regulators generally) by the Scottish Ministers for the purposes of or in connection with this Part.

(2) Before issuing such guidance, the Scottish Ministers must consult—

(a) every approved regulator,

(b) such other person or body as they consider appropriate.

(3) The Scottish Ministers must publish any such guidance as issued (or re-issued).

Chapter 2 – Licensed Legal Services Providers

Licensed providers

Licensed providers

47.—(1) For the purposes of this Part, a licensed legal services provider is a business entity which, through the designated and other persons within it—

(a) provides (or offers to provide) legal services—

(i) to the general public or otherwise, and

(ii) for a fee, gain or reward, and

(b) does so under a licence issued by an approved regulator in accordance with the approved regulator's licensing rules.

(2) An entity is eligible to be a licensed provider only if it has within it, for the provision of legal services, at least one solicitor who holds a valid practising certificate that is free of conditions (such as may be imposed under section 15(1)(b) or 53(5) of the 1980 Act).

(3) A licensed provider may not be regulated by more than one approved regulator at the same time.

(4) In this Part, a reference to a licensed provider is to a licensed legal services provider.

Eligibility criteria

48.—(1) This section—

(a) applies for the purposes of licensing an entity as a licensed legal services provider under this Part,

(b) does so in conjunction with section 49.

(2) The following are examples of arrangements which would make an entity eligible to be a licensed provider—

(a) the entity has within it—

(i) at least one solicitor as mentioned in section 47(2), and

(ii) at least one individual practitioner of another type,

for the carrying out of the sort of legal work for which each is qualified,

(b) the entity has within it at least one solicitor as mentioned in section 47(2) but, through also having within it at least one person who is not a solicitor or other type of individual practitioner, additionally provides (or offers to provide)—

(i) other professional services, or

(ii) services of another kind,

(c) the entity has within it at least one solicitor as mentioned in section 47(2) but not every person who has ownership or control of the entity, or another material interest in it, is a solicitor (or a firm of solicitors) or an incorporated practice.

(3) But an entity, to be eligible to be a licensed provider—

    (a) need not be a body corporate or a partnership,

    (b) requires, if it falls—

        (i) under the ownership or control of another entity, or

        (ii) within the structure of another entity,

    to be a separate part of the other entity or otherwise distinct from it.

(4) For the avoidance of doubt, an entity is not eligible to be a licensed provider if it—

    (a) consists of—

        (i) a single solicitor practising under the solicitor's own name, or

        (ii) a solicitor otherwise practising as a sole practitioner,

    (b) is a firm of solicitors or an incorporated practice, or

    (c) is a law centre as defined in section 65(1) of the 1980 Act.

(5) In subsection (2)(a)(ii) and (b), a type of "individual practitioner" (apart from a solicitor) is—

    (a) an advocate,

    (b) a conveyancing or executry practitioner,

    (c) a litigation practitioner, or

    (d) a confirmation agent or will writer within the meaning of Part 3.

(6) The Scottish Ministers may by regulations—

    (a) make—

        (i) provision specifying other categories of entity that are, or are not, eligible to be a licensed provider,

        (ii) further provision about criteria for eligibility to be a licensed provider,

    (b) modify—

        (i) section 47(2) so as to specify an additional type of legally qualified person (as an alternative to a solicitor as mentioned there),

        (ii) subsection (5) so as to add a type of legal practitioner to the list there.

(7) Before making regulations under subsection (6)(b), the Scottish Ministers must consult every approved regulator.

Majority ownership

49.—(1) An entity is eligible to be a licensed provider only if the qualifying investors in it (taken together) have at least a 51% stake in the total ownership or control of the entity.

(2) For the purpose of subsection (1), a "qualifying investor" is—

    (a) a solicitor investor, or

    (b) an investor who is a member of another regulated profession.

(3) In subsection (2)(b), a "regulated profession" is a profession the professional activities of whose members (and qualifications for membership of which) are, under statutory or administrative arrangements, regulated by a professional association.

(4) Despite the generality of subsections (2)(b) and (3), the Scottish Ministers—

    (a) are by regulations to specify in connection with those subsections what is, or is not, to be regarded as a regulated profession,

    (b) may by regulations specify in connection with those subsections what is, or is not, to be regarded as a professional association, professional activities (or qualifications) or membership of a profession.

(5) Before making regulations under subsection (4), the Scottish Ministers must—

    (a) have the Lord President's agreement, and

    (b) consult—

        (i) the Law Society,

        (ii) every approved regulator,

        [1](iii) the CMA, and such other organisation (appearing to them to represent the interests of consumers in Scotland) as they consider appropriate,

        (iv) such other person or body as they consider appropriate.

---

[1] Enterprise and Regulatory Reform Act 2013 (c.24) Sch.6(2) para.196 (effective April 25, 2013).

Key duties and positions

Key duties
50.—(1) A licensed legal services provider must—
(a) have regard to the regulatory objectives,
(b) adhere to the professional principles,
(c) comply with—
(i) its approved regulator's regulatory scheme,
(ii) the terms and conditions of its licence.
(2) A licensed provider must seek to ensure that every designated or other person who is—
(a) within the licensed provider, and
(b) subject to a professional code of conduct,
complies with the code of conduct.
(3) A licensed provider must have within it—
(a) a Head of Legal Services (see section 51), and
(b) either—
(i) a Head of Practice (see section 52), or
(ii) a Practice Committee (see section 53).
(4) A licensed provider must ensure that the following positions are not left unoccupied—
(a) that of its Head of Legal Services, and
(b) that (as the case may be)—
(i) of its Head of Practice, or
(ii) within its Practice Committee by virtue of section 53(3).
(5) However, the same person may (at the same time) be a licensed provider's Head of Legal Services and also its Head of Practice.

Head of Legal Services
51.—(1) It is for a licensed provider to make such administrative arrangements as it considers appropriate in respect of its Head of Legal Services.
(2) A person is eligible for appointment (and to act) as its Head of Legal Services only if the person is a solicitor who holds a valid practising certificate that is free of conditions (such as may be imposed under section 15(1)(b) or 53(5) of the 1980 Act).
(3) But a person becomes disqualified from that position if the person is disqualified from practice as a solicitor by reason of having been—
(a) struck off (or removed from) the roll of solicitors, or
(b) suspended from practice.
(4) A Head of Legal Services has the function of securing the licensed provider's—
(a) compliance with section 50(1)(a) and (b),
(b) fulfilment of its other duties under this Part so far as relevant in connection with its provision of legal services.
(5) A Head of Legal Services is to manage the designated persons within the licensed provider with a view to ensuring that they—
(a) have regard to the Head's function under subsection (4),
(b) adhere to the professional principles,
(c) meet their professional obligations.
(6) A Head of Legal Services is to take such reasonable steps as may be required for the purposes of subsection (4).
(7) If it appears to a Head of Legal Services that the licensed provider is failing (or has failed) to fulfil any of its duties under this Part or another enactment, the Head is to report that fact to the Head of Practice.
(8) Where (and to the extent that) under this section and section 52 a function falls to both—
(a) a Head of Legal Services, and
(b) a Head of Practice,

they are jointly and severally responsible for exercising the function.

(9) The Scottish Ministers may by regulations—

(a) make further provision about—

(i) Heads of Legal Services,

(ii) the functions of such Heads (in their capacity as such),

(b) modify subsection (2) so as to specify an additional type of legally qualified person (as an alternative to a solicitor as mentioned there).

(10) Before making regulations under subsection (9), the Scottish Ministers must consult the Lord President.

Head of Practice

52.—(1) It is for a licensed provider to make such administrative arrangements as it considers appropriate in respect of its Head of Practice.

(2) A person is eligible for appointment (and to act) as its Head of Practice only if the person—

(a) has such qualifications, expertise and experience as are reasonably required, and

(b) in other respects, is fit and proper for the position.

(3) A Head of Practice has the function of securing the licensed provider's—

(a) compliance with section 50(1)(c),

(b) fulfilment of its other duties under this Part.

(4) A Head of Practice is to manage the designated and other persons within the licensed provider with a view to ensuring that they—

(a) have regard to the Head's functions under this Part,

(b) meet any professional obligations to which they are subject.

(5) A Head of Practice is to take such reasonable steps as may be required for the purposes of subsection (3).

(6) If it appears to a Head of Practice that—

(a) the licensed provider is failing (or has failed) to fulfil any of its duties under this Part or another enactment,

(b) an investor in the licensed provider is—

(i) failing (or has failed) to fulfil any of the investor's duties under this Part or another enactment, or

(ii) contravening (or has contravened) section 66(1) or (2),

the Head is to report that fact to the licensed provider's approved regulator.

(7) The Scottish Ministers may by regulations make further provision about—

(a) Heads of Practice,

(b) the functions of such Heads (in their capacity as such).

(8) Before making regulations under subsection (7), the Scottish Ministers must consult the Lord President.

Practice Committee

53.—(1) It is for a licensed provider—

(a) to decide whether to have a Practice Committee (instead of having a Head of Practice),

(b) if it has one, to make such administrative arrangements as it considers appropriate in respect of it.

(2) A Practice Committee has the functions under this Part that would otherwise be exercisable by a Head of Practice (and the specification of any of those functions is to be read accordingly).

(3) A Practice Committee is to have among its members a person who would be eligible for

appointment as its Head of Practice (if there were one).

(4) The members of a Practice Committee are jointly and severally responsible as regards the

Committee's functions.

(5) The Scottish Ministers may by regulations make further provision about—
(a) Practice Committees,
(b) the functions of such Committees.
(6) Before making regulations under subsection (5), the Scottish Ministers must consult the Lord President.

Appointment to position etc.

Notice of appointment
54.—(1) Subsection (2) applies whenever a licensed legal services provider appoints a person as its—
(a) Head of Legal Services, or
(b) Head of Practice.
(2) The licensed provider must—
(a) within 14 days from the date of the appointment—
(i) notify its approved regulator of that fact,
(ii) give the approved regulator the name and other details of the person appointed,
(b) from that date give the approved regulator such further relevant information, and by such time, as it may reasonably require.
(3) Subsections (4) and (5) apply where a licensed provider sets up a Practice Committee.
(4) The licensed provider must—
(a) within 14 days from the date on which the Committee is set up—
(i) notify its approved regulator of that fact,
(ii) give the approved regulator the names and other relevant details of the Committee's members (including with specific reference to section 53(3)),
(b) from that date give the approved regulator such other relevant information, and by such time, as it may reasonably require.
(5) The licensed provider must also—
(a) whenever there is a change in the membership of the Committee, give the approved regulator—
(i) notice of the change,
(ii) the name and other relevant details of any new Committee member,
within 14 days from the date on which the change occurs,
(b) if it ever dissolves the Committee (in favour of having a Head of Practice), notify its approved regulator of that fact within 14 days from the date on which the dissolution occurs,
(c) from the date mentioned in paragraph (a) or (b) (as the case may be) give the approved regulator such further relevant information, and by such time, as it may reasonably require.

Challenge to appointment
55.—(1) An approved regulator may by written notice challenge the appointment by any of its licensed providers of a person ("P")—
(a) as its—
(i) Head of Legal Services, or
(ii) Head of Practice, or
(b) as a member of its Practice Committee.
(2) A notice of a challenge under subsection (1)—
(a) requires to be given by the approved regulator within 14 days of the relevant notification to it under section 54(2), (4) or (5)(a),
(b) is to specify the grounds for the challenge.
(3) A challenge under subsection (1) may be made only if the approved regulator—
(a) believes that P is (or may be)—

(i) ineligible, or

(ii) unsuitable,

for the appointment, or

(b) has other reasonable grounds for the challenge.

(4) If the approved regulator determines (after making a challenge under subsection (1)) that the grounds for the challenge are made out, it may direct the licensed provider to rescind P's appointment.

(5) Before giving a direction under subsection (4), the approved regulator must give the licensed provider and P 28 days (or such longer period as it may allow) to—

(a) make representations to it,

(b) take such steps as the licensed provider or P may consider expedient.

(6) Practice and licensing rules respectively must—

(a) explain the basis on which P's suitability for the appointment is determinable,

(b) provide that the licensed provider's licence is to be revoked or suspended if the licensed provider does not comply with a direction under subsection (4).

(7) A licensed provider which or another person who is aggrieved by a direction under subsection (4) (or both jointly) may appeal against the direction—

(a) to the sheriff,

(b) within the period of 3 months beginning with the date on which the direction is given.

(8) For the purpose of subsections (1) to (6), an example of things relevant as respects P's suitability for the appointment is whether P has a record of misconduct in any professional context.

Disqualification from position

56.—(1) An approved regulator has the functions exercisable—

(a) under this section and section 57, and

(b) by reference to one or more of the conditions specified in section 58, in relation to a person ("P") who holds within any of its licensed providers any of the posts to which those sections relate.

(2) If the first condition is met in relation to P, the approved regulator must disqualify P from—

(a) appointment (or acting) as the Head of Practice,

(b) membership of a Practice Committee.

(3) If the second condition is met in relation to P, the approved regulator—

(a) must disqualify P from—

(i) appointment (or acting) as the Head of Legal Services or Head of Practice,

(ii) membership of a Practice Committee,

(b) may disqualify P from being a designated person.

(4) If the third condition is met in relation to P, the approved regulator must disqualify P from—

(a) appointment (or acting) as the Head of Legal Services or Head of Practice,

(b) membership of a Practice Committee.

(5) If the fourth condition is met in relation to P, the approved regulator—

(a) must disqualify P from—

(i) appointment (or acting) as the Head of Legal Services or Head of Practice,

(ii) membership of a Practice Committee,

(b) may disqualify P from being a designated person.

(6) If the fifth condition is met in relation to P, the approved regulator may disqualify P from—

(a) appointment (or acting) as the Head of Legal Services or Head of Practice,
(b) membership of a Practice Committee,
(c) being a designated person.

Effect of disqualification
57.—(1) A disqualification under section 56—
(a) may be—
    (i) without limit of time, or
    (ii) for a fixed period,
(b) extends so as to apply in relation to every licensed provider (including a licensed provider that is subject to the regulation of a different approved regulator).
(2) Where a disqualification under section 56 is from being a designated person, the disqualification may be framed so as to be limited by reference to—
(a) particular activities, or
(b) activities carried out without appropriate supervision (for example, that of a senior solicitor).
(3) Before disqualifying P under section 56, the approved regulator must give the licensed provider and P 28 days (or such longer period as it may allow) to—
(a) make representations to it,
(b) take such steps as the licensed provider or P may consider expedient.
(4) Licensing rules must provide that the licensed provider's licence may be revoked or suspended if the licensed provider wilfully disregards a disqualification imposed under section 56.
(5) Practice rules must—
(a) set procedure (which the approved regulator is to follow) for imposing a disqualification under section 56,
(b) allow for review (and lifting) by the approved regulator of a disqualification imposed by it under that section.
(6) A person who is disqualified under section 56 may appeal against the disqualification—
(a) to the sheriff,
(b) within the period of 3 months beginning with the date on which the disqualification is imposed.

Conditions for disqualification
58.—(1) This section applies for the purposes of section 56.
(2) The first condition is that—
(a) P—
    (i) is subject to a trust deed granted by P for the benefit of P's creditors,
    (ii) is subject to an individual voluntary arrangement under the Insolvency Act 1986, to repay P's creditors,
    (iii) has been adjudged bankrupt and has not been discharged from bankruptcy, or
    (iv) has been sequestrated (that is, sequestration of P's estate has been awarded) and the sequestration has not been discharged, and
(b) the approved regulator is satisfied accordingly that P is unsuitable for the position.
(3) The second condition is that—
(a) P is subject to a bankruptcy restrictions order or undertaking under the Bankruptcy (Scotland) Act 1985, the Insolvency Act 1986 or corresponding Northern Ireland legislation, and
(b) the approved regulator is satisfied accordingly that P is unsuitable for the position.

(4) The third condition is that—
(a) P—
   (i) is subject to a disqualification order or undertaking under the Company Directors Disqualification Act 1986 or corresponding Northern Ireland legislation,
   (ii) is disqualified by a court from holding, or otherwise has been removed by a court from, a position of business responsibility (for example, from being a director of a charity), and
(b) the approved regulator is satisfied accordingly that P is unsuitable for the position.

(5) The fourth condition is that—
(a) P—
   (i) has been convicted of an offence involving dishonesty, or
   (ii) in respect of an offence, has been fined an amount equivalent to level 4 on the standard scale or more (whether on summary or solemn conviction) or sentenced to imprisonment for a term of 12 months or more, and
(b) the approved regulator is satisfied accordingly that P is unsuitable for the position.

(6) The fifth condition is that—
(a) P (acting in the relevant capacity) has—
   (i) failed in a material regard to fulfil any of P's duties under (or arising by virtue of) this Part, or
   (ii) caused, or substantially contributed to, a material breach of the terms or conditions of the licensed provider's licence, and
(b) the approved regulator is satisfied accordingly that P is unsuitable for the position.

(7) In subsections (3)(a) and (4)(a)(i), "Northern Ireland legislation" has the meaning given in section 24(5) of the Interpretation Act 1978.

Designated persons

Designated persons
59.—(1) In this Part, a "designated person" within a licensed legal services provider is a person who is designated as such under subsection (2).

(2) Designation under this subsection is written designation by the licensed provider to carry out legal work in connection with the licensed provider's provision of legal services.

(3) For the purposes of subsection (2)—
(a) designation by the licensed provider means designation on its behalf by its Head of Legal Services or Head of Practice (who has the function accordingly),
(b) a person is eligible for designation only if the person is an employee of the licensed provider (or otherwise works within it under any arrangement),
(c) it is immaterial whether the person is—
   (i) a member of a professional association, or
   (ii) paid for the work.

Working context
60.—(1) A Head of Legal Services is, in furtherance of section 51(5)(b) and (c), responsible for ensuring that there is (by or under the direction of the Head) adequate supervision of the legal work carried out by the designated persons within the licensed provider.

(2) Only a designated person within a licensed provider may carry out legal work in connection with its provision of legal services.

(3) Nothing in this Part affects the operation of—

(a) section 32 of the 1980 Act or any other enactment which requires that a particular sort of legal work be carried out by an individual of a particular description (or in a particular way), or

(b) any rule of professional practice, conduct or discipline (whether for solicitors or otherwise) which properly so requires.

Listing and information

61.—(1) The Head of Practice of a licensed provider must—

(a) keep a list of the designated persons within the licensed provider, and

(b) give its approved regulator a copy of the list whenever the approved regulator requests it.

(2) The Head of Practice must give its approved regulator such information about the designated persons within the licensed provider as the approved regulator may reasonably request.

Non-solicitor investors

Fitness for involvement

62.—(1) An approved regulator must—

(a) before issuing a licence to a licensed legal services provider, or renewing it, satisfy itself as to the fitness of every non-solicitor investor in the licensed provider for having an interest in the licensed provider,

(b) thereafter, monitor as it considers appropriate the investor's fitness in that regard.

(2) Licensing rules must—

(a) explain the basis on which a non-solicitor investor's fitness for having an interest in a licensed provider is determinable,

(b) provide that, where the approved regulator determines that the investor is unfit in that regard—

(i) a licence is not to be issued to the licensed provider (or renewed),

(ii) if issued, the licence is to be revoked or suspended.

(3) But the approved regulator need not act as required by licensing rules made under subsection (2)(b) if, by such time as it may reasonably appoint, the licensed provider demonstrates to it that (following disqualification as required by section 65(1) or otherwise) the investor no longer has the relevant interest.

(4) The approved regulator must, before making its final determination as to fitness, give the non-solicitor investor 28 days (or such longer period as it may allow) to—

(a) make representations to it,

(b) take such steps as the investor may consider expedient.

(5) A person who is determined as unfit under this section may appeal against the determination—

(a) to the sheriff,

(b) within the period of 3 months beginning with the date on which the determination is made.

Exemption from fitness test

63.—(1) Section 62(1) is subject to this section.

(2) The approved regulator need not act as required by that section in relation to any exemptible investor in the licensed provider.

(3) Licensing rules must explain—

(a) any circumstances in which the approved regulator proposes to rely on subsection (2),

(b) any threshold below the percentage specified in subsection (4) by reference to which it proposes to rely on subsection (2),

(c) where it proposes to rely on subsection (2), its reasons.

(4) In subsection (2), an "exemptible investor" is an investor who has less than a 10% stake in the total ownership or control of the licensed provider.

Factors as to fitness

64.—(1) This section applies for the purposes of section 62.

(2) The following are examples of things relevant as respects a non-solicitor investor's fitness for having an interest in a licensed provider—
- (a) the investor's—
    - (i) financial position and business record,
    - (ii) probity and character,
    - (iii) family, business or other associations (so far as bearing on character),
- (b) whether—
    - (i) the investor has ever caused, or substantially contributed to, a material breach of the terms or conditions of any licensed provider's licence,
    - (ii) the investor's involvement in the licensed provider may (in the approved regulator's opinion) be detrimental to the observance of the regulatory objectives or adherence to the professional principles, or to the compliance with this Part or any other enactment, by any person or body,
    - (iii) the investor has ever contravened section 66(1) or (2) or there is (in the approved regulator's opinion) a significant risk that the investor will ever contravene that section.

(3) A non-solicitor investor is to be presumed to be unfit for having an interest in a licensed provider if one or more of the following conditions is met—
- (a) the first condition is that the investor—
    - (i) is subject to a trust deed granted by the investor for the benefit of the investor's creditors,
    - (ii) is subject to an individual voluntary arrangement under the Insolvency Act 1986, to repay the investor's creditors,
    - (iii) has been adjudged bankrupt and has not been discharged from bankruptcy, or
    - (iv) has been sequestrated (that is, sequestration of the investor's estate has been awarded) and the sequestration has not been discharged,
- (b) the second condition is that the investor is subject to a bankruptcy restrictions order or undertaking under the Bankruptcy (Scotland) Act 1985, the Insolvency Act 1986 or corresponding Northern Ireland legislation,
- (c) the third condition is that the investor—
    - (i) is subject to a disqualification order or undertaking under the Company Directors Disqualification Act 1986 or corresponding Northern Ireland legislation,
    - (ii) is disqualified by a court from holding, or otherwise has been removed by a court from, a position of business responsibility (for example, from being a director of a charity),
- (d) the fourth condition is that the investor—
    - (i) has been convicted of an offence involving dishonesty, or
    - (ii) in respect of an offence, has been fined an amount equivalent to level 4 on the standard scale or more (whether on summary or solemn conviction) or sentenced to imprisonment for a term of 12 months or more.

(4) Where a non-solicitor investor is a body, it is relevant as respects the investor's fitness for having an interest in a licensed provider whether or not the persons having (to any extent)—
- (a) ownership or control of the body, or
- (b) any other material interest in it,

would (if they were investors in the licensed provider in their own right) be held to be fit in that regard.

(5) In subsection (3)(b) and (c)(i), "Northern Ireland legislation" has the meaning given in section 24(5) of the Interpretation Act 1978.

Ban for improper behaviour

65.—(1) Where an approved regulator determines that a non-solicitor investor in a licensed provider has contravened section 66(1) or (2), the approved regulator must disqualify the investor from having an interest in the licensed provider.

(2) A disqualification under subsection (1)—

(a) may be—

  (i) without limit of time, or

  (ii) for a fixed period,

(b) extends so as to apply in relation to every licensed provider (including a licensed provider that is subject to the regulation of a different approved regulator).

(3) Before disqualifying an investor under subsection (1), the approved regulator must give the investor 28 days (or such longer period as it may allow) to—

(a) make representations to it,

(b) take such steps as the investor may consider expedient.

(4) Practice rules must—

(a) set procedure (which the approved regulator is to follow) for imposing a disqualification under subsection (1),

(b) allow for review (and lifting) by the approved regulator of a disqualification imposed by it under that subsection.

(5) A person who is disqualified under subsection (1) may appeal against the disqualification—

(a) to the sheriff,

(b) within the period of 3 months beginning with the date on which the disqualification is imposed.

Behaving properly

66.—(1) A non-solicitor investor in a licensed provider must not (in that capacity) act in a way that is incompatible with—

(a) the regulatory objectives or the professional principles,

(b) the licensed provider's duties under section 50(1), or

(c) its—

  (i) other duties under this Part,

  (ii) duties under any other enactment.

(2) A non-solicitor investor in a licensed provider must not (in that capacity)—

(a) interfere improperly in the provision of legal or other professional services by the licensed provider,

(b) in relation to any designated or other person within the licensed provider—

  (i) exert undue influence,

  (ii) solicit unlawful or unethical conduct, or

  (iii) otherwise behave improperly.

More about investors

67.—(1) Schedule 8 provides for other—

(a) requirements to which licensed legal services providers are subject,

(b) functions of approved regulators,

in relation to interests in licensed providers.

(2) The Scottish Ministers may by regulations make further provision—

(a) relating to interests in licensed providers,

(b) for licensing rules in connection with persons who have an interest in a licensed provider.

(3) The Scottish Ministers may by regulations—

(a) amend the percentage specified in section 63(4) and paragraph 4(3) of schedule 8,

(b) amend (by addition, elaboration or exception) a definition in subsection (6).

(4) Regulations under subsection (2)(a) may (in particular)—

(a) impose requirements to which a licensed provider, or an investor in a licensed provider, is subject,

(b) specify criteria or circumstances by reference to which a non-solicitor investor is to be presumed, or held, to be fit (or unfit),

(c) set out—

  (i) what amounts (to any extent) to ownership, control or another material interest,

  (ii) what interest (or type) is relevant as regards a particular percentage stake in ownership or control,

  (iii) by reference to a family, business or other association, what other interest (or type) also counts towards such a stake,

(d) for circumstances where an interest is held by a body, set out—

  (i) what interest (or type) in the body counts towards the interest held by it,

  (ii) the extent to which the interest in it so counts.

(5) Before making regulations under subsection (3), the Scottish Ministers must have the Lord President's agreement.

(6) In this Part—

(a) an "investor" in a licensed provider is any person who has (to any extent)—

  (i) ownership or control of the licensed provider, or

  (ii) any other material interest in it,

(b) a "non-solicitor investor" in a licensed provider is an investor who is not entitled to practise—

  (i) as a solicitor, a firm of solicitors or an incorporated practice,

  (ii) in England and Wales or Northern Ireland, as a solicitor (outwith the meaning for this Act), or

  (iii) as a registered European or foreign lawyer,

(c) the reference to a "solicitor investor" in a licensed provider is to be construed accordingly.

(7) In sections 62 to 66, this section and schedule 8, a reference to a licensed provider includes an applicant to become one.

Discontinuance of services

Duty to warn

68.—(1) Subsection (2) applies where a licensed legal services provider—

(a) is in serious financial difficulty, or

(b) for any reason (except revocation or suspension of its licence under this Part)—

  (i) intends to stop providing legal services, or

  (ii) is likely to become unable to continue providing legal services.

(2) The licensed provider must—

(a) notify (without delay) its approved regulator accordingly,

(b) provide the approved regulator with such relevant information as the approved regulator may require,

(c) take all reasonable steps to mitigate such disruption to its clients as is likely to result from the difficulty or (as the case may be) its ceasing to provide legal services.

Inability to operate

69.—(1) Subsections (2) to (7) apply where—

(a) through the application of section 48 or 49 or otherwise, a licensed provider is no longer eligible to remain as such,

(b) because of a vacancy within a licensed provider, the licensed provider has within it no person who is eligible to be (or act as) its—

(i) Head of Legal Services, or

(ii) Head of Practice,

(c) in respect of a licensed provider—

(i) a provisional liquidator, liquidator, receiver or judicial factor is appointed,

(ii) an administration or winding up order is made,

(iii) a resolution is passed by it for its voluntary winding up (except where that resolution is solely to facilitate reconstruction or amalgamation with another licensed provider), or

(d) for some other reason (except revocation or suspension of its licence under this Part), a licensed provider stops providing legal services.

(2) The licensed provider must—

(a) notify (without delay and no later than 7 days after the event referred to in subsection (1)) its approved regulator accordingly,

(b) provide the approved regulator with such information about the situation as the approved regulator may require.

(3) The approved regulator must revoke the licensed provider's licence except where the approved regulator is satisfied that—

(a) the situation is temporary, and

(b) there are sufficient arrangements in place to safeguard the interests of the licensed provider's clients until such time as the situation is rectified.

(4) Even if the exception mentioned in subsection (3) is made out, the approved regulator may suspend the licence pending rectification of the situation.

(5) For the purpose of subsections (3) and (4), the approved regulator must review the situation every 14 days (or, if it so chooses, more frequently).

(6) For so long as the licensed provider's licence is not revoked or suspended under subsection (3) or (4) in connection with the situation, the situation alone does not prevent the licensed provider from continuing (or recommencing) to provide legal services.

(7) Where a licensed provider has ceased to exist—

(a) its functions under subsection (2)(a) and (b) fall to its former Head of Practice or (if unavailable) its former Head of Legal Services,

(b) if neither Head is available, its function under subsection (2)(b) falls to a person nominated by its approved regulator.

(8) In this section, a reference to a licensed provider includes (as the context requires) a former licensed provider.

Safeguarding clients

70.—(1) Subsections (2) and (3) apply where—

(a) a licensed provider—

(i) has given (or is required to give) notice to its approved regulator under section 68(2)(a) or 69(2)(a), or

(ii) has had (or is to have) its licence revoked or suspended under this Part, and

(b) the approved regulator has not informed it (or has not had an opportunity to do so) that the approved regulator is satisfied that it has made sufficient arrangements for the safeguarding of its clients' interests.

(2) The licensed provider must—

(a) prepare—

    (i) in the case of revocation, final accounts,
    (ii) in the case of suspension, interim accounts,
    which (in particular) detail all sums held on behalf of clients,
  (b) comply with any directions given under subsection (3).

(3) The approved regulator may direct the licensed provider to take specified action (or refrain from doing something) if the approved regulator considers that to be necessary or expedient for safeguarding the interests of the licensed provider's legal services clients.

(4) Directions given under subsection (3) may (in particular) require the licensed provider to make available to a relevant person or body any—
  (a) document or information (of whatever kind) held in the licensed provider's possession or control which—
    (i) relates to, or is held on behalf of, a client of the licensed provider, or
    (ii) relates to any trust of which the licensed provider (or one of the designated persons within it) is sole trustee or co-trustee only with other designated persons in the licensed provider,
  (b) sum of money held by the licensed provider—
    (i) on behalf of a client,
    (ii) subject to any trust of the kind mentioned in paragraph (a)(ii).

(5) For the purposes of subsection (4), a relevant person or body is—
  (a) the particular client,
  (b) the approved regulator,
  (c) a provider of legal services that is properly instructed by the licensed provider, or the approved regulator, to act in place of the licensed provider.

(6) The Court of Session may, on an application by the approved regulator, make an order—
  (a) confirming that the licensed provider is required to comply with a direction given under subsection (3),
  (b) varying the direction or imposing such conditions as the Court considers appropriate in the circumstances,
  (c) that, without the leave of the Court, no payment be made by any bank, building society or other body named in the order out of any account (or any sum otherwise deposited) in the name of the licensed provider.

(7) Before making such an order, the Court must—
  (a) give the licensed provider and any other person with an interest an opportunity to be heard,
  (b) be satisfied that the direction or (as the case may be) freezing of an account represents an appropriate course of action in all the circumstances of the case.

(8) The approved regulator may recover from the licensed provider any expenditure reasonably incurred by the approved regulator in consequence of its taking action under this section.

(9) Where a licensed provider has ceased to exist, its functions under (or arising by virtue of) this section fall—
  (a) to its former Head of Practice or (if unavailable) its former Head of Legal Services,
  (b) if neither Head is available, to a person nominated by its approved regulator.

(10) The Scottish Ministers may by regulations make further provision about the steps that are, in the circumstances within subsection (1), to be taken to safeguard the interests of clients of licensed providers.

(11) In this section, a reference to a licensed provider includes (as the context requires) a former licensed provider.

Distribution of client account

71.—(1) Any sums of the kind to which section 42 of the 1980 Act applies that are held in a client account (as referred to in that section) kept by a licensed provider are, in any of the events mentioned in subsection (2A) of that section, to be distributed in the same way as they would if they were subject to that section.

(2) For the purpose of subsection (1), any reference in that section to an incorporated practice is to be read as if it were a reference to the licensed provider.

Professional practice etc.

Employing disqualified lawyer

72.—(1) Subsection (2) applies in relation to—

(a) a person who has been struck off the roll of solicitors or suspended from practice as a solicitor,

(b) a person—

  (i) who has been suspended from practice as a registered European lawyer or whose registration as a registered European lawyer has been withdrawn, or

  (ii) who has been suspended from practice as a registered foreign lawyer or whose registration as a registered foreign lawyer has been withdrawn,

(c) a person who has been prohibited (including by reason of a disqualification or another removal of a right to provide services) from—

  (i) practising as an advocate,

  (ii) acting as a conveyancing or executry practitioner,

  (iii) acting as a litigation practitioner, or

  (iv) acting as a confirmation agent or will writer within the meaning of Part 3,

(d) a body whose certificate of recognition as an incorporated practice has been revoked.

(2) A licensed legal services provider must not employ or remunerate as a designated person—

(a) the person while the person is so debarred (however described in subsection (1)), or

(b) the body while the revocation subsists.

(3) But subsection (2) is inoperative in relation to the person or (as the case may be) body if the licensed provider has its approved regulator's written authority that it is so inoperative in the circumstances of the particular case.

(4) Any authority under subsection (3) may be given—

(a) for a specified period,

(b) with conditions attached.

(5) A licensed provider may appeal to the Court of Session if it is aggrieved by—

(a) the withholding of any such authority, or

(b) any conditions attached under subsection (4)(b).

(6) On an appeal under subsection (5)—

(a) the Court may direct the approved regulator on the matter as the Court considers appropriate,

(b) the Court's determination is final.

(7) If a licensed provider wilfully contravenes—

(a) subsection (2), or

(b) any conditions attached under subsection (4)(b),

its approved regulator may revoke or suspend its licence.

Concealing disqualification

73.—(1) Subsection (2) applies to—

(a) a person who has been struck off the roll of solicitors or suspended from practice as a solicitor,

(b) a person—

(i) who has been suspended from practice as a registered European lawyer or whose registration as a registered European lawyer has been withdrawn, or

(ii) who has been suspended from practice as a registered foreign lawyer or whose registration as a registered foreign lawyer has been withdrawn,

(c) a person who has been prohibited (including by reason of a disqualification or another removal of a right to provide services) from—

(i) practising as an advocate,

(ii) acting as a conveyancing or executry practitioner,

(iii) acting as a litigation practitioner, or

(iv) acting as a confirmation agent or will writer within the meaning of Part 3.

(2) The person is guilty of an offence if, while the person is so debarred (however described in subsection (1)), the person seeks or accepts employment by a licensed provider without previously informing it of the debarment.

(3) A person who commits an offence under subsection (2) is liable on summary conviction to a fine not exceeding level 5 on the standard scale.

(4) Subsection (5) applies to a body whose certificate of recognition as an incorporated practice has been revoked.

(5) The body is guilty of an offence if, while the revocation subsists, the body seeks or accepts employment by a licensed provider without previously informing it of the revocation.

(6) A body which commits an offence under subsection (5) is liable on summary conviction to a fine not exceeding level 5 on the standard scale.

Pretending to be licensed

74.—(1) A person commits an offence if the person—

(a) pretends to be a licensed provider, or

(b) takes or uses any name, title, addition or description implying falsely that the person is a licensed provider.

(2) A person who commits an offence under this section is liable on summary conviction to a fine not exceeding level 5 on the standard scale.

Professional privilege

75.—(1) Subsection (2) applies to any communication made to or by—

(a) a licensed provider in the course of its acting as such in its provision of legal services for any of its clients,

(b) a designated person (apart from a solicitor or advocate) within the licensed provider who is acting—

(i) in connection with its provision of such legal services, and

(ii) at the direction, and under the supervision, of a solicitor.

(2) The communication is, in any legal proceedings, privileged from disclosure as if the licensed provider or (as the case may be) the person had at all material times been a solicitor acting for the client.

(3) Subsection (4) applies to any special provision which—

(a) is contained in an enactment or otherwise,

(b) relates to a solicitor, and

(c) concerns—

(i) the disclosure of information with respect to which a claim of professional privilege could be maintained, or

  (ii) the production, seizure or removal of documents with respect to which such a claim could be maintained.

(4) The provision has effect in relation to a licensed provider, and any designated person (apart from a solicitor) within a licensed provider, as it does in relation to a solicitor but with any necessary modifications.

(5) This section is without prejudice to any other enactment or rule of law concerning professional or other privilege from disclosure (in particular, as applicable in relation to a solicitor).

Chapter 3 – Further Provision

Achieving regulatory aims

Input by the CMA   F1.515

76.—[1](1) The Scottish Ministers or (as the case may be) an approved regulator must, whenever consulting the CMA under this Part, request the CMA—

  (a) to give such advice as it considers appropriate in relation to the matter concerned,

  (b) in considering what advice to give, to have particular regard to whether the matter concerned would have (or be likely to have) the effect of preventing, or significantly restricting or distorting, competition within the legal services market.

(2) The Scottish Ministers are or (as the case may be) the approved regulator is to take account of any advice given by the CMA within—

  (a) the relevant consultation period, or

  (b) otherwise—

    (i) in the case of the Scottish Ministers, the period of 90 days beginning with the day on which they request the advice,

    (ii) in the case of the approved regulator, the period of 30 days beginning on the day on which it requests the advice or such longer period not exceeding 90 days as it may agree with the CMA.

(3) The Scottish Ministers may publish any advice duly given to them by the CMA.

Role of approved regulators   F1.516

77.—(1) Subsections (2) to (4) apply in relation to the exercise by an approved regulator of its functions under this Part.

(2) The approved regulator must, so far as practicable, act in a way which—

  (a) is compatible with the regulatory objectives, and

  (b) it considers most appropriate with a view to meeting those objectives.

(3) The approved regulator must adopt best regulatory practice under which (in particular) regulatory activities should be—

  (a) carried out—

    (i) effectively (but without giving rise to unnecessary burdens),

    (ii) in a way that is transparent, accountable, proportionate and consistent,

  (b) targeted only at such cases as require action.

---

[1] As amended by the Enterprise and Regulatory Reform Act 2013 (c.24) Sch.6 para.197 (effective April 1, 2014).

(4)   The approved regulator must seek to ensure that its licensed legal services providers have regard to the regulatory objectives.

F1.517   **Policy statement**

78.—(1)   An approved regulator must prepare and issue a statement of policy as to how, in exercising its functions under this Part, it will comply with its duties under section 77.

(2)   The approved regulator—
  (a)   may revise the policy statement,
  (b)   if it does so, must re-issue the policy statement.

(3)   The approved regulator may issue (or re-issue) the policy statement only with the approval of the Scottish Ministers.

(4)   The approved regulator must publish the policy statement as issued (or re-issued).

(5)   In exercising its functions under this Part, the approved regulator must have regard to the policy statement as issued (or re-issued).

Complaints

F1.518   **Complaints about regulators**

79.—(1)   Any complaint about an approved regulator is to be made to the Scottish Legal Complaints Commission.

(2)   The Commission is to determine whether or not the complaint is—
  (a)   one for which section 57E(1) of the 2007 Act makes provision,
  (b)   frivolous, vexatious or totally without merit.

(3)   And—
  (a)   if the Commission determines that the complaint falls within subsection (2)(a), the Commission is to proceed by reference to section 57E(1) of the 2007 Act,
  (b)   if the Commission determines that the complaint falls within subsection (2)(b), the Commission—
    (i)   must notify the complainer and the approved regulator accordingly (with reasons),
    (ii)   is not required to take any further action,
  (c)   if the Commission determines that the complaint does not fall within subsection (2)(a) or (b), the Commission must refer the complaint to the Scottish Ministers.

(4)   The Scottish Ministers must investigate any complaint about an approved regulator that is referred to them under subsection (3)(c).

(5)   Where the Scottish Ministers do not uphold the complaint, they must notify the complainer and the approved regulator accordingly (with reasons).

(6)   Where the Scottish Ministers uphold the complaint, they must—
  (a)   notify the complainer and the approved regulator accordingly (with reasons), and
  (b)   decide whether to proceed under section 38.

(7)   The Scottish Ministers may delegate to the Commission any of their functions under subsections (4), (5) and (6)(a) (and, if they so delegate their function under subsection (4), they may also waive the referral requirement under subsection (3)(c)).

(8)   The Scottish Ministers may by regulations make further provision about complaints made about approved regulators (and how they are to be dealt with).

Levy payable by regulators   F1.519

80.—(1)   An approved regulator must pay to the Scottish Legal Complaints Commission—

(a)   in respect of each financial year, an annual levy,

(b)   if arising, a complaints levy.

(2)   The amount of the annual levy or complaints levy payable by an approved regulator—

(a)   is to be determined by the Commission,

(b)   may be—

(i)   different from any amount payable as an annual general levy or (as the case may be) a complaints levy under Part 1 of the 2007 Act,

(ii) in either case, of different amounts (including nil) in different circumstances.

(3) The complaints levy arises as respects an approved regulator where—

(a) the Scottish Ministers delegate to the Commission their function under section 79(4) in relation to a complaint made about the approved regulator, and

(b) the Commission upholds the complaint.

(4) Before determining for a financial year the amount of the annual levy or complaints levy, the Commission must consult—

(a) each approved regulator (with particular reference to the proposed amount to be payable by it),

(b) the Scottish Ministers.

Complaints about providers
81. [Not reprinted.]

Registers and lists

Register of approved regulators
82.—(1) The Scottish Ministers—

(a) must keep and publish a register of approved regulators,

(b) may do so in such manner as they consider appropriate.

(2) The register is to include the following information in relation to each approved regulator—

(a) its contact details (including its address, website and telephone number),

(b) the date on which it was given the relevant approval under section 7,

(c) the date on which it was given the relevant authorisation under section 10 (and the duration of that authorisation (unlimited or the fixed period)),

(d) the categories of legal services to which that authorisation relates,

(e) details of any measure taken by the Scottish Ministers under section 38.

Registers of licensed providers
83.—(1) An approved regulator must keep and publish a register of its licensed legal services providers.

(2) The register is to include the following information in relation to each licensed provider—

(a) its name and any place of business,

(b) the relevant details about its licence,

(c) the name of every non-solicitor investor in the licensed provider,

(d) the name of every person intimated to the approved regulator under paragraph 3 of schedule 8,

(e) the names and the dates of appointment of—

(i) its Head of Legal Services, and

(ii) its Head of Practice or, if applicable, each member of its Practice Committee (including with specific reference to section 53(3)),

(f) whether the licensed provider has been the subject of any disciplinary action and (if so) a description of that action.

(3) In subsection (2)(b), the relevant details about a licensed provider's licence are—

(a) the date on which the licence was originally granted,

(b) the date on which it was most recently renewed,

(c) whether it is subject to any conditions,

(d) the date on which it will expire.

(4) But, in the case of a former licensed provider, the relevant details are instead—

(a) the date on which the licence was originally granted,

(b) the period for which the licensed provider held a licence,

(c) the reason for the licensed provider ceasing to hold a licence.

(5) The Scottish Ministers may by regulations-

(a) make further provision about the information to be contained in the registers of licensed providers, and

(b) prescribe the manner in which those registers are to be kept and published.

(6) In this section, a reference to a licensed provider includes a former licensed provider.

Lists of disqualified persons

84.—(1) An approved regulator must keep a list of the persons whom it has disqualified under section 56 (that is, from holding a certain position in a licensed legal services provider).

(2) The list kept under subsection (1) must include the following information in relation to each person concerned—

(a) the person's name,

(b) the—

(i) name of any relevant licensed provider,

(ii) any relevant position held by the person as at the date of the disqualification,

(c) each position from which the person is disqualified,

(d) the date of disqualification and its duration (unlimited or the fixed period),

(e) the reasons for the disqualification.

(3) An approved regulator must keep a list of the persons whom it has—

(a) determined as unfit under section 62 (that is, for being a non-solicitor investor in a licensed provider), or

(b) disqualified under section 65(1) (that is, from having an interest in a licensed provider).

(4) The list kept under subsection (3) must include the following information in relation to each person concerned—

(a) the person's name,

(b) the name of any relevant licensed provider,

(c) the date of the determination or (as the case may be) disqualification,

(d) the grounds for the determination or (as the case may be) disqualification.

(5) A list kept under this section must not include information relating to a person in respect of whom the determination or (as the case may be) disqualification—

(a) has been reversed on appeal, or

(b) otherwise, no longer applies.

(6) The approved regulator must—

(a) publish the lists kept by it under this section, and

(b) notify the Scottish Ministers of any material alterations made to either of them.

(7) The Scottish Ministers may by regulations—

(a) make further provision about the information to be contained in the lists kept under this section,

(b) prescribe the manner in which those lists are to be kept and published.

Miscellaneous

Privileged material

85.—(1) Subsection (2) applies to the publication under this Part of any—

(a) advice, report or notice, or

(b) other material.

(2) For the purposes of the law on defamation, the publication is privileged.

(3) But subsection (2) is ineffective if it is proved that the publication was made with malice.

Immunity from damages

86.—(1) Neither an approved regulator nor any of its officers, members or employees is liable in damages for any act or omission occurring in the exercise (or purported exercise) of its functions under this Part.

(2) But subsection (1) is ineffective if it is shown that the act or omission was in bad faith.

Appeal procedure

87.—(1) This section applies in relation to an appeal to the sheriff under this Part.

(2) The appeal is to be made by way of summary application.

(3) In the appeal, the sheriff may—

(a) uphold, vary or quash the decision that is the subject of the appeal,

(b) make such further order (including for the expenses of the parties) as is necessary in the interests of justice.

(4) The sheriff's determination in the appeal is final.

Corporate offences

88.—(1) Subsection (2) applies where—

(a) an offence under this Part is committed by a relevant organisation, and

(b) the commission of the offence—
    (i) involves the connivance or consent of, or
    (ii) is attributable to the neglect of,
    a responsible official of the organisation.

(2) The official (as well as the organisation) commits the offence.

(3) For the purpose of this section—

(a) a "relevant organisation" is—
    (i) a company,
    (ii) a limited liability partnership,
    (iii) an ordinary partnership, or
    (iv) any other body or association,

(b) a "responsible official" is—
    (i) in the case of a company, a director, secretary, manager or other similar officer,
    (ii) in the case of a limited liability partnership, a member,
    (iii) in the case of an ordinary partnership, a partner,
    (iv) in the case of another body or association, a person who is concerned in the management or control of its affairs,

but in each case also extends to a person purporting to act in such a capacity.

Effect of professional or other rules

89.—(1) Sections 121(5) and 124(3) respectively make provision (in connection with this Part) as to the effect of professional rules to which advocates and solicitors are subject.

(2) Nothing in this Part affects the operation of any rule which regulates in respect of any matter the professional practice, conduct or discipline of other persons who provide professional services (in particular, as it may relate to their involvement in or with licensed legal services providers).

(3) This Part is without prejudice to any function of a person or body—

(a) arising by virtue of the application of another enactment (or a regulatory rule made under another enactment), and

(b) to regulate in any respect the provision of any professional or other services by licensed legal services providers.

PART 3

CONFIRMATION AND WILL WRITING SERVICES

CHAPTER 1

CONFIRMATION SERVICES

Regulation of confirmation agents

Confirmation agents and services
[1] **90.**—(1) For the purposes of this Part, confirmation services are services that are—
  (a) described in subsection (2), and
  (b) provided (or offered)—
    (i) to members of the public, and
    (ii) for a fee, gain or reward.
(2) The services are those of drawing or preparing papers on which to found or oppose an application for the confirmation of a person as the executor nominate or dative in relation to the estate of a deceased person.
(3) It is immaterial for the description in subsection (2) whether or not the services also involve applying to the sheriff on behalf of the person so as to secure the person's confirmation as such (or taking other related action).
(4) For the purposes of this Part, a confirmation agent is a person on whom, in accordance with an approving body's regulatory scheme, the right to provide confirmation services is conferred.

NOTE
[1] Not yet in force.

Approving bodies
[1] **91.**—(1) For the purposes of this Chapter, an approving body is a professional or other body which is certified as such by the Scottish Ministers under section 92.
(2) That is, following an application to them by the body under subsection (3).
(3) An application to become an approving body must include—
  (a) a copy of the applicant's proposed regulatory scheme (see section 92(1)(b)),
  (b) a description of—
    (i) the applicant's constitution and composition (including internal structure),
    (ii) its activities.
(4) The applicant—
  (a) must provide the Scottish Ministers with such other information as they may reasonably require for their consideration of its application,
  (b) may withdraw its application at any time by giving them written notice to that effect.
(5) There is no restriction on the number of approving bodies that may exist at any time.
(6) The Scottish Ministers may by regulations prescribe fees that they may charge an applicant to become an approving body.

NOTE
[1] Partially in force.

Certification of bodies

92.—[1](1)   The Scottish Ministers may certify the applicant as an approving body if they are satisfied that—

(a)   the applicant is suitable to be an approving body,

(b)   the applicant's proposed regulatory scheme is adequate (as determined with particular reference to section 93).

(2)   The Scottish Ministers may certify the applicant as an approving body—

(a)   either—

(i)   without limit of time, or

(ii)   for a fixed period,

(b)   with reference to a specified date from which the approving body may exercise its functions in relation to its regulatory scheme,

(c)   subject to conditions.

(3)   The Scottish Ministers may, after consulting the approving body, vary (including by addition or deletion) any conditions imposed under subsection (2)(c).

(4)   Before deciding whether or not to certify the applicant as an approving body, the Scottish Ministers must consult—

[2](a)   the CMA, and such other organisation (appearing to them to represent the interests of consumers in Scotland) as they consider appropriate,

(b)   such other person or body as they consider appropriate.

(5)   In consulting under subsection (4), the Scottish Ministers—

[3](a)   must send a copy of the application to the CMA,

(b)   may send—

(i)   to any other consultee, a copy of the application,

(ii)   to the OFT or any other consultee, a copy of any revised application.

(6)   The Scottish Ministers must, with reasons, notify the applicant if they intend to—

(a)   refuse to certify it as an approving body, or

(b)   certify it as such subject to conditions.

(7)   If notification is given to the applicant under subsection (6), it has 28 days beginning with the date of the notification (or such longer period as the Scottish Ministers may allow) to—

(a)   make representations to the Scottish Ministers,

(b)   take such steps as it may consider expedient.

(8)   The Scottish Ministers may by regulations make further provision about certification under this section, including (in particular)—

(a)   the process for seeking their certification,

(b)   in relation to capability to act as an approving body, the criteria for their certification (including things that applicants must be able to demonstrate).

Regulatory schemes

93.—[4](1)   An approving body must—

---

[1] Partially in force.
[2] Enterprise and Regulatory Reform Act 2013 (c.24) Sch.6(2) para.199 (effective April 25, 2013).
[3] Enterprise and Regulatory Reform Act 2013 (c.24) Sch.6(2) para.199 (effective April 25, 2013).
[4] Partially in force.

  (a) make a regulatory scheme for—
    (i) conferring on any of the individual persons within its membership the right to provide confirmation services, and
    (ii) regulating the provision of confirmation services by the persons on whom (in accordance with the scheme) that right is conferred, and
  (b) apply the scheme in relation to them.
 (2) The regulatory scheme is to—
  (a) describe the training requirements to be met by a prospective confirmation agent,
  (b) incorporate a code of practice to which a confirmation agent is subject,
  (c) require that a confirmation agent keep in place sufficient arrangements for professional indemnity,
  (d) include rules about—
    (i) the making and handling of any complaint about a confirmation agent,
    (ii) the measures that may be taken by the approving body, in relation to a confirmation agent, if a conduct complaint (as construed by reference to section 2(1)(a) of the 2007 Act (and as if the confirmation agent were a practitioner to whom that section relates)) about the confirmation agent is upheld,
  (e) allow a confirmation agent to make representations to the approving body before it takes any of the measures available to it by virtue of paragraph (d)(ii),
  (f) cover such other regulatory matters as the Scottish Ministers may by regulations specify (and in such manner as they may so specify).
 (3) The code of practice mentioned in subsection (2)(b) must—
  (a) set out the standards to be met by confirmation agents,
  (b) make such further arrangements as to the professional practice, conduct or discipline of confirmation agents for which provision is (in the approving body's opinion) necessary or expedient,
  (c) allow for—
    (i) the rescission or suspension of, or attaching of conditions to the exercise of, the right of a confirmation agent to provide confirmation services if the agent contravenes the code of practice,
    (ii) the suspension of that right of a confirmation agent if a complaint, suggesting that the agent is guilty of professional misconduct in relation to the provision of confirmation services, is made about the agent.
 (4) A confirmation agent may appeal against a decision taken under the regulatory scheme to rescind or suspend, or attach conditions to the exercise of, the agent's right to provide confirmation services—
  (a) to the sheriff,
  (b) within the period of 3 months beginning with the date on which that decision is intimated to the agent.
 (5) An approving body must, so far as practicable when exercising its functions under this Chapter, observe the regulatory objectives.

Financial sanctions

94.—[1](1)   Rules included in a regulatory scheme in pursuance of section 93(2)(d)(ii) may provide for the imposition of a financial penalty.

(2)   A financial penalty provided for by virtue of subsection (1) must not exceed the maximum amount permitted by the Scottish Ministers when giving their certification under section 92.

(3)   A financial penalty imposed by virtue of this section is payable to the Scottish Ministers (but the approving body may collect it on their behalf).

(4)   A confirmation agent may appeal against a financial penalty (or the amount of a financial penalty) imposed on the agent by virtue of this section—

    (a)   to the sheriff,

    (b)   within the period of 3 months beginning with the date on which the penalty is intimated to the agent.

---

[1] Not yet in force.

F 100/112/1

(5) Where an appeal is made under subsection (4), no part of the penalty requires to be paid before the appeal is determined or withdrawn.

NOTE
[1] Not yet in force.

Review of own performance
[1] **95.**—(1) An approving body must review annually its performance.
(2) In particular, a review is to cover the following matters—
(a) the approving body's compliance with section 93(5),
(b) the exercise of its functions in relation to its regulatory scheme,
(c) its compliance with any measures applying to it by virtue of section 100(3).
(3) The approving body must send a report on the review to the Scottish Ministers.
(4) The report must contain a copy of the approving body's annual accounts (but only so far as they are relevant in connection with its functions under this Chapter).
(5) The Scottish Ministers must lay a copy of the report before the Scottish Parliament.
(6) The Scottish Ministers may by regulations make further provision about—
(a) the review of approved bodies' performance,
(b) reports on reviews of their performance.

NOTE
[1] Partially in force.

Pretending to be authorised
[1] **96.**—(1) A person commits an offence if the person—
(a) pretends to be a confirmation agent (or otherwise pretends to have the right to provide confirmation services under this Part), or
(b) takes or uses any name, title, addition or description implying falsely that the person is a confirmation agent (or otherwise so implying that the person has the right to provide confirmation services under this Part).
(2) A person who commits an offence under this section is liable on summary conviction to a fine not exceeding level 5 on the standard scale.

NOTE
[1] Not yet in force.

Other regulatory matters

Revocation of certification
[1] **97.**—(1) Subsection (2) applies where the Scottish Ministers are satisfied that an approving body has failed to comply with a direction under section 100(3).
(2) The Scottish Ministers may—
(a) revoke the certification given to the approving body under section 92,
(b) require the approving body to take specified action (or refrain from doing something) if they consider that to be necessary or expedient in connection with the revocation.
(3) The revocation under subsection (2) of the certification of an approving body has the effect, from the date on which the revocation becomes effective, of rescinding the right of each of its confirmation agents to provide confirmation services (so far as that right is conferred by the approving body in question).

NOTE
[1] Not yet in force.

Surrender of certification

[1] **98.**—(1) An approving body may, with the prior agreement of the Scottish Ministers, surrender the certification given to it under section 92.

(2) The approving body must—
(a) take all reasonable steps to mitigate such disruption to the clients of its confirmation agents as is likely to result from the surrender,
(b) in particular, take steps for ensuring that any relevant work is—
(i) completed, or
(ii) taken over by a suitably qualified person,
before the date from which subsection (5) is operative.

(3) The Scottish Ministers may direct the approving body to take specified action (or refrain from doing something) if they consider that to be necessary or expedient—
(a) for the purpose of subsection (2), or
(b) otherwise in connection with the surrender.

(4) Before the Scottish Ministers may agree to the surrender, they must be satisfied that the approving body has complied (or will comply) with—
(a) subsection (2), and
(b) any directions given to it under subsection (3).

(5) The surrender of an approving body's certification under subsection (1) has, from the date on which the surrender becomes effective, the effect of extinguishing the right of each of its confirmation agents to provide confirmation services (so far as that right is conferred by the approving body in question).

NOTE
[1] Not yet in force.

Register and list

[1] **99.**—(1) The Scottish Ministers—
(a) must keep and publish a register of approving bodies,
(b) may do so in a such manner as they consider appropriate.

(2) The register is to include the following information in relation to each approving body—
(a) its contact details (including its address, website and telephone number),
(b) the date on which it was given the relevant certification under section 92.

(3) An approving body must—
(a) keep a list of its confirmation agents,
(b) give the Scottish Ministers a copy of the list whenever they request it.

(4) An approving body must give the Scottish Ministers such information about its confirmation agents as the Scottish Ministers may reasonably request.

NOTE
[1] Not yet in force.

Ministerial functions

Ministerial intervention

[1] **100.**—(1) An approving body must—
(a) provide such information about its performance in relation to its regulatory scheme as the Scottish Ministers may reasonably request,
(b) do so within 21 days beginning with the date of the request (or such longer period as the Scottish Ministers may allow).

(2) An approving body—

(a) if directed to do so by the Scottish Ministers, must—
  (i) review its regulatory scheme (or any relevant part of it), and
  (ii) report to them its findings and (if appropriate) inform them of any proposed amendment to the scheme,

(b) may amend its regulatory scheme so as to give effect to the proposed amendment, but—
  (i) any material amendment is invalid unless it has the prior approval of the Scottish Ministers,
  (ii) the Scottish Ministers may not give their approval before they have consulted such person or body as they consider appropriate.

(3) The Scottish Ministers may—
  (a) if, after consulting such person or body as they consider appropriate, they consider that an approving body's regulatory scheme is not (or is no longer) adequate, direct the approving body to amend the regulatory scheme in such manner as they may specify,
  (b) if they are satisfied that an approving body has not complied with a requirement imposed on it by or under this Chapter, direct the approving body to take specified remedial action (or refrain from doing something).

(4) An approving body must—
  (a) review annually the performance of its confirmation agents,
  (b) prepare a report on the review,
  (c) send a copy of the report to the Scottish Ministers.

(5) The Scottish Ministers may by regulations make further provision—
  (a) about the review of confirmation agents,
  (b) so far as it appears to them to be necessary for safeguarding the interests of clients of confirmation agents—
    (i) concerning the functions of approving bodies,
    (ii) relating to confirmation agents.

Chapter 2 – Will Writing Services

Regulation of will writers

Will writers and services

101.—[1](1) For the purposes of this Part, will writing services are services that are—
  (a) described in subsection (2), and
  (b) provided (or offered)—
    (i) to members of the public, and
    (ii) for a fee, gain or reward.

(2) The services are those of drawing or preparing wills or other testamentary writings.

(3) For the purposes of this Part, a will writer is a person on whom, in accordance with an approving body's regulatory scheme, the right to provide will writing services is conferred.

---

[1] Not yet in force.

Approving bodies

102.—[1](1) For the purposes of this Chapter, an approving body is a professional or other body which is certified as such by the Scottish Ministers under section 103.

(2) That is, following an application to them by the body under subsection (3).

(3) An application to become an approving body must include—

    (a) a copy of the applicant's proposed regulatory scheme (see section 103(1)(b)),

    (b) a description of—

        (i) the applicant's constitution and composition (including internal structure),

        (ii) its activities.

(4) The applicant—

    (a) must provide the Scottish Ministers with such other information as they may reasonably require for their consideration of its application,

    (b) may withdraw its application at any time by giving them written notice to that effect.

(5) There is no restriction on the number of approving bodies that may exist at any time.

(6) The Scottish Ministers may by regulations prescribe fees that they may charge an applicant to become an approving body.

Certification of bodies

103.—[2](1) The Scottish Ministers may certify the applicant as an approving body if they are satisfied that—

    (a) the applicant is suitable to be an approving body,

    (b) the applicant's proposed regulatory scheme is adequate (as determined with particular reference to section 104).

(2) The Scottish Ministers may certify the applicant as an approving body—

    (a) either—

        (i) without limit of time, or

        (ii) for a fixed period,

    (b) with reference to a specified date from which the approving body may exercise its functions in relation to its regulatory scheme,

    (c) subject to conditions.

(3) The Scottish Ministers may, after consulting the approving body, vary (including by addition or deletion) any conditions imposed under subsection (2)(c).

[3](4) Before deciding whether or not to certify the applicant as an approving body, the Scottish Ministers must consult—

    (a) the CMA, and such other organisation (appearing to them to represent the interests of consumers in Scotland) as they consider appropriate,

    (b) such other person or body as they consider appropriate.

[4](5) In consulting under subsection (4), the Scottish Ministers—

---

[1] Partially in force.

[2] Partially in force.

[3] As amended by the Enterprise and Regulatory Reform Act 2013 (c.24) Sch.6(2) para.199 (effective April 25, 2013).

[4] As amended by the Enterprise and Regulatory Reform Act 2013 (c.24) Sch.6(2) para.199 (effective April 25, 2013).

  (a) must send a copy of the application to the CMA,
  (b) may send—
      (i) to any other consultee, a copy of the application,
      (ii) to the CMA or any other consultee, a copy of any revised application.

(6) The Scottish Ministers must, with reasons, notify the applicant if they intend to—
  (a) refuse to certify it as an approving body, or
  (b) certify it as such subject to conditions.

(7) If notification is given to the applicant under subsection (6), it has 28 days beginning with the date of the notification (or such longer period as the Scottish Ministers may allow) to—
  (a) make representations to the Scottish Ministers,

(b) take such steps as it may consider expedient.

(8) The Scottish Ministers may by regulations make further provision about certification under this section, including (in particular)—

(a) the process for seeking their certification,

(b) in relation to capability to act as an approving body, the criteria for their certification (including things that applicants must be able to demonstrate).

NOTE

[1] Partially in force.

Regulatory schemes

[1] **104.**—(1) An approving body must—

(a) make a regulatory scheme for—

    (i) conferring on any of the individual persons within its membership the right to provide will writing services, and

    (ii) regulating the provision of will writing services by the persons on whom (in accordance with the scheme) that right is conferred, and

(b) apply the scheme in relation to them.

(2) The regulatory scheme is to—

(a) describe the training requirements to be met by a prospective will writer,

(b) incorporate a code of practice to which a will writer (and anyone acting on behalf of the will writer in relation to will writing services) is subject,

(c) require that a will writer keep in place sufficient arrangements for professional indemnity,

(d) include rules about—

    (i) the making and handling of any complaint about a will writer,

    (ii) the measures that may be taken by the approving body, in relation to a will writer, if a conduct complaint (as construed by reference to section 2(1)(a) of the 2007 Act (and as if the will writer were a practitioner to whom that section relates)) about the will writer is upheld,

(e) allow a will writer to make representations to the approving body before it takes any of the measures available to it by virtue of paragraph (d)(ii),

(f) cover such other regulatory matters as the Scottish Ministers may by regulations specify (and in such manner as they may so specify).

(3) The code of practice mentioned in subsection (2)(b) must—

(a) set out the standards to be met by will writers (and persons acting on their behalf in relation to will writing services),

(b) except in such circumstances as the approving body considers appropriate, prohibit the drawing or preparation of a will or other testamentary writing by a will writer which provides for the writer to be a beneficiary,

(c) require a will writer who provides the service of storing wills or other testamentary writings to keep in place sufficient arrangements for the storage of such documents (including arrangements in the event of the writer ceasing to provide will writing services),

(d) make such further arrangements as to the professional practice, conduct or discipline of will writers for which provision is (in the approving body's opinion) necessary or expedient,

(e) provide that it is a breach of the code of practice for a will writer to fail to comply with the writer's duties under any enactment specified in the code,

(f) provide that a breach of the code of practice by a person acting on behalf of a will writer in relation to will writing services constitutes a breach of the code of practice by the writer,

(g) allow for—
  (i) the rescission or suspension of, or attaching of conditions to the exercise of, the right of a will writer to provide will writing services if the writer contravenes the code of practice,
  (ii) the suspension of that right of a will writer if a complaint, suggesting that the writer is guilty of professional misconduct in relation to the provision of will writing services, is made about the writer.

(4) A will writer may appeal against a decision taken under the regulatory scheme to rescind or suspend, or attach conditions to the exercise of, the writer's right to provide will writing services—
  (a) to the sheriff,
  (b) within the period of 3 months beginning with the date on which that decision is intimated to the writer.

(5) An approving body must, so far as practicable when exercising its functions under this Chapter, observe the regulatory objectives.

NOTE
[1] Partially in force.

Financial sanctions
[1] **105.**—(1) Rules included in a regulatory scheme in pursuance of section 104(2)(d)(ii) may provide for the imposition of a financial penalty.

(2) A financial penalty provided for by virtue of subsection (1) must not exceed the maximum amount permitted by the Scottish Ministers when giving their certification under section 103.

(3) A financial penalty imposed by virtue of this section is payable to the Scottish Ministers (but the approving body may collect it on their behalf).

(4) A will writer may appeal against a financial penalty (or the amount of a financial penalty) imposed on the writer by virtue of this section—
  (a) to the sheriff,
  (b) within the period of 3 months beginning with the date on which the penalty is intimated to the writer.

(5) Where an appeal is made under subsection (4), no part of the penalty requires to be paid before the appeal is determined or withdrawn.

NOTE
[1] Not yet in force.

Review of own performance
[1] **106.**—(1) An approving body must review annually its performance.

(2) In particular, a review is to cover the following matters—
  (a) the approving body's compliance with section 104(5),
  (b) the exercise of its functions in relation to its regulatory scheme,
  (c) its compliance with any measures applying to it by virtue of section 111(3).

(3) The approving body must send a report on the review to the Scottish Ministers.

(4) The report must contain a copy of the approving body's annual accounts (but only so far as they are relevant in connection with its functions under this Chapter).

(5) The Scottish Ministers must lay a copy of the report before the Scottish Parliament.

(6) The Scottish Ministers may by regulations make further provision about—
  (a) the review of approved bodies' performance,
  (b) reports on reviews of their performance.

NOTE
  [1] Partially in force.

Pretending to be authorised
  [1] **107.**—(1) A person commits an offence if the person—
  (a) pretends to be a will writer (or otherwise pretends to have the right to provide will writing services under this Part), or
  (b) takes or uses any name, title, addition or description implying falsely that the person is a will writer (or otherwise so implying that the person has the right to provide will writing services under this Part).
  (2) A person who commits an offence under this section is liable on summary conviction to a fine not exceeding level 5 on the standard scale.

NOTE
  [1] Not yet in force.

Other regulatory matters

Revocation of certification
  [1] **108.**—(1) Subsection (2) applies where the Scottish Ministers are satisfied that an approving body has failed to comply with a direction under section 111(3).
  (2) The Scottish Ministers may—
  (a) revoke the certification given to the approving body under section 103,
  (b) require the approving body to take specified action (or refrain from doing something) if they consider that to be necessary or expedient in connection with the revocation.
  (3) The revocation under subsection (2) of the certification of an approving body has the effect, from the date on which the revocation becomes effective, of rescinding the right of each of its will writers to provide will writing services (so far as that right is conferred by the approving body in question).

NOTE
  [1] Not yet in force.

Surrender of certification
  [1] **109.**—(1) An approving body may, with the prior agreement of the Scottish Ministers, surrender the certification given to it under section 103.
  (2) The approving body must—
  (a) take all reasonable steps to mitigate such disruption to the clients of its will writers as is likely to result from the surrender,
  (b) in particular, take steps for ensuring that any relevant work is—
      (i) completed, or
      (ii) taken over by a suitably qualified person,
  before the date from which subsection (5) is operative.
  (3) The Scottish Ministers may direct the approving body to take specified action (or refrain from doing something) if they consider that to be necessary or expedient—
  (a) for the purpose of subsection (2), or
  (b) otherwise in connection with the surrender.
  (4) Before the Scottish Ministers may agree to the surrender, they must be satisfied that the approving body has complied (or will comply) with—
  (a) subsection (2), and
  (b) any direction given to it under subsection (3).
  (5) The surrender of an approving body's certification under subsection (1) has, from the date on which the surrender becomes effective, the effect of extinguishing the right of each of its will writers to provide will writing services (so far as that right is conferred by the approving body in question).

NOTE
[1] Not yet in force.

Register and list
[1] **110.**—(1) The Scottish Ministers—
(a) must keep and publish a register of approving bodies,
(b) may do so in such manner as they consider appropriate.
(2) The register is to include the following information in relation to each approving body—
(a) its contact details (including its address, website and telephone number),
(b) the date on which it was given the relevant certification under section 103.
(3) An approving body must—
(a) keep a list of its will writers,
(b) give the Scottish Ministers a copy of the list whenever they request it.
(4) An approving body must give the Scottish Ministers such information about its will writers as the Scottish Ministers may reasonably request.

NOTE
[1] Not yet in force.

Ministerial functions

Ministerial intervention
[1] **111.**—(1) An approving body must—
(a) provide such information about its performance in relation to its regulatory scheme as the Scottish Ministers may reasonably request,
(b) do so within 21 days beginning with the date of the request (or such longer period as the Scottish Ministers may allow).
(2) An approving body—
(a) if directed to do so by the Scottish Ministers, must—
(i) review its regulatory scheme (or any relevant part of it), and
(ii) report to them its findings and (if appropriate) inform them of any proposed amendments to the scheme,
(b) may amend its regulatory scheme so as to give effect to the proposed amendment, but—
(i) any material amendment is invalid unless it has the prior approval of the Scottish Ministers,
(ii) the Scottish Ministers may not give their approval before they have consulted such person or body as they consider appropriate.
(3) The Scottish Ministers may—
(a) if, after consulting such person or body as they consider appropriate, they consider that an approving body's regulatory scheme is not (or is no longer) adequate, direct the approving body to amend the regulatory scheme in such manner as they may specify,
(b) if they are satisfied that an approving body has not complied with a requirement imposed on it by or under this Chapter, direct the approving body to take specified remedial action (or refrain from doing something).
(4) An approving body must—
(a) review annually the performance of its will writers,
(b) prepare a report on the review,
(c) send a copy of the report to the Scottish Ministers.
(5) The Scottish Ministers may by regulations make further provision—
(a) about the review of will writers,
(b) so far as it appears to them to be necessary for safeguarding the interests of clients of will writers—

(i) concerning the functions of approving bodies,
(ii) relating to will writers.

NOTE
[1] Partially in force.

Step-in by Ministers
[1] **112.**—(1) The Scottish Ministers may by regulations make provision which establishes a body with a view to its becoming an approving body.

(2) The Scottish Ministers may by regulations make provision which allows them to act as an
approving body in such circumstances as the regulations may prescribe.

(3) Regulations under subsection (2) may provide for this Chapter to apply with or subject to such modifications as the regulations may specify.

(4) No regulations are to be made under subsection (1) or (2) unless the Scottish Ministers believe that their intervention under this section is necessary, as a last resort, in order to ensure that the provision of will writing services by will writers is regulated effectively.

NOTE
[1] Partially in force.

CHAPTER 3

FURTHER PROVISION

Regard to OFT input
[1] **113.**—(1) The Scottish Ministers, whenever consulting the OFT under section 92(4)(a) or 103(4)(a), must request the OFT—
  (a) to give such advice as it considers appropriate in relation to the matter concerned,
  (b) in considering what (if any) advice to give, to have particular regard to whether the matter concerned would have (or be likely to have) the effect of preventing, or significantly restricting or distorting, competition within the legal services market.

(2) The Scottish Ministers are to take account of any advice given by the OFT within—
  (a) the relevant consultation period, or
  (b) otherwise, the period of 90 days beginning with the day on which they request the advice.

(3) The Scottish Ministers may publish any advice duly given to them by the OFT.

NOTE
[1] Not yet in force.

Complaints about services
114. [Not reprinted.]

Privilege and immunity
[1] **115.**—(1) For the purposes of the law on defamation, the publication under this Part of any material is privileged unless it is proved that the publication was made with malice.

(2) Neither an approving body nor any of its officers, members or employees is liable in damages for any act or omission occurring in the exercise (or purported exercise) of its functions under this Part unless it is shown that the act or omission was in bad faith.

NOTE
[1] Not yet in force.

Appeal procedure

[1] **116.**—(1) This section applies in relation to an appeal to the sheriff under this Part.

(2) The appeal is to be made by way of summary application.

(3) In the appeal, the sheriff may—

(a) uphold, vary or quash the decision that is the subject of the appeal,

(b) make such further order (including for the expenses of the parties) as is necessary in the interests of justice.

(4) The sheriff's determination in the appeal is final.

NOTE

[1] Not yet in force.

Corporate offences

[1] **117.**—(1) Subsection (2) applies where—

(a) an offence under this Part is committed by a relevant organisation, and

(b) the commission of the offence—

(i) involves the connivance or consent of, or

(ii) is attributable to the neglect of,

a responsible official of the organisation.

(2) The official (as well as the organisation) commits the offence.

(3) For the purpose of this section—

(a) a "relevant organisation" is—

(i) a company,

(ii) a limited liability partnership,

(iii) an ordinary partnership, or

(iv) any other body or association,

(b) a "responsible official" is—

(i) in the case of a company, a director, secretary, manager or other similar officer,

(ii) in the case of a limited liability partnership, a member,

(iii) in the case of an ordinary partnership, a partner,

(iv) in the case of another body or association, a person who is concerned in the management or control of its affairs,

but in each case also extends to a person purporting to act in such a capacity.

NOTE

[1] Not yet in force.

Consequential modification

118. [Not reprinted.]

PART 4

THE LEGAL PROFESSION

CHAPTER 1

APPLYING THE REGULATORY OBJECTIVES

Application by the profession

119.—(1) Each of the regulatory authorities mentioned in subsection (2) must, so far as practicable when exercising the authority's regulatory functions (as defined in subsection (3)), act in a way which—

(a) is compatible with the regulatory objectives, and

(b) it considers most appropriate with a view to meeting those objectives.

(2) For the purpose of this section, the regulatory authorities are—
   (a) the Court of Session,
   (b) the Lord President,
   (c) the Faculty of Advocates,
   (d) the Council of the Law Society,
   (e) any other person who or body that has regulatory functions in relation to the provision of legal services by legal practitioners (of any type).

(3) For the purpose of this section, the regulatory functions of a regulatory authority—
   (a) are its functions of regulating in respect of any matter the professional practice, conduct and discipline of legal practitioners (of any type),
   (b) include its functions of making professional or regulatory rules to which legal practitioners (of any type) are subject.

(4) In subsections (2) and (3), "legal practitioners" means—
   (a) solicitors (including firms of solicitors) or incorporated practices,
   (b) advocates,
   (c) conveyancing or executry practitioners, or
   (d) litigation practitioners.

Chapter 2 – Faculty of Advocates

Regulation of the Faculty   F1.558

120.—(1) The Court of Session is responsible—
   (a) for—
      (i) admitting persons to (and removing persons from) the office of advocate,
      (ii) prescribing the criteria and procedure for admission to (and removal from) the office of advocate,
   (b) for regulating the professional practice, conduct and discipline of advocates.

(2) The Court's responsibilities within subsection (1)(a)(ii) and (b) are exercisable on its behalf, in accordance with such provision as it may make for the purpose, by—
   (a) the Lord President, or
   (b) the Faculty of Advocates.

Professional rules   F1.559

121.—(1) Subsections (2) and (3) apply to any rule which—
   (a) prescribes the criteria or procedure for admission to (or removal from) the office of advocate, or
   (b) regulates in respect of any matter the professional practice, conduct or discipline of advocates.

(2) If the rule is made by the Faculty, the rule—
   (a) is of no effect unless it has been approved by the Lord President (and may not be revoked unless its revocation has been approved by the Lord President),
   (b) must be published by the Faculty.

(3) In any other case, the rule—
   (a) is of no effect unless the Faculty has been consulted on it (and may not be revoked unless the Faculty has been consulted on its revocation),

(b) requires—
   (i) where made by the Lord President, to be published,
   (ii) where made by the Court of Session, to be contained in an Act of Sederunt.
(4) Neither this section nor section 122 affects the validity of any rule—
   (a) that was in force immediately prior to the commencement of this section, and
   (b) which regulates in respect of any matter the professional practice, conduct or discipline of advocates.
(5) Nothing in Part 2 affects the operation of any rule which regulates in respect of any matter the professional practice, conduct or discipline of advocates (in particular, as it may relate to their involvement in or with licensed legal services providers).

F1.560 **Particular rules**

122.—(1) Subsection (2) applies to any rule—
   (a) which regulates in respect of any matter the professional practice, conduct or discipline of advocates, and
   (b) under which an advocate is prohibited from forming a legal relationship with another advocate, or any other person, for the purpose of their jointly offering professional services to the public.
(2)[1] The rule is of no effect unless it has been approved by the Scottish Ministers after they have consulted the CMA.
(3) Subsection (2) is without prejudice to section 121(2) and (3).
(4) In section 31 (rules of conduct etc.) of the 1990 Act, subsection (1) is repealed.

Chapter 3 – Solicitors and Other Representatives
[Not reprinted.]

Chapter 4 – Other Bodies
[Not reprinted.]

F1.561 ### PART 5 – GENERAL

Regulations

146.—(1) Any power of the Scottish Ministers to make regulations under the preceding Parts of this Act is exercisable by statutory instrument.
(2) The regulations may—
   (a) make different provision for different purposes,
   (b) include such incidental, consequential, transitional, transitory or saving provision as the Scottish Ministers consider necessary or expedient for the purposes of or in connection with the regulations.
(3) But—
   (a) a statutory instrument containing regulations under—
      (i) section 6(6),
      (ii) section 12(2)(c) or (5),

---

[1] As amended by the Enterprise and Regulatory Reform Act 2013 (c.24) Sch.6 para.201 (effective April 1, 2014).

(iii)   section 38(7),
(iv)   section 44(1),
(v)   section 45(1),
(vi)   section 48(6)(a)(i),
(vii)   section 49(4),
(viii)   section 67(3),
(ix)   section 70(10),
(x)   section 93(2)(f),
(xi)   section 100(5)(b),
(xii)   section 104(2)(f),
(xiii)   section 111(5)(b), or
(xiv)   section 112(1),

is not to be made unless a draft of the instrument has been laid before, and approved by resolution of, the Scottish Parliament,

(b)   a statutory instrument containing any other regulations under the preceding Parts of this Act is subject to annulment in pursuance of a resolution of the Parliament.

Further modification   F1.562

147.—(1)   The Scottish Ministers may by regulations made by statutory instrument—

(a)   amend the percentage specified in subsection (1) of section 49, or
(b)   repeal section 49 (and consequentially the references in this Act to that section).

(2)   But regulations may be made under subsection (1) only if the Scottish Ministers believe that the effect of the amendment or (as the case may be) repeal would be—

(a)   compatible with the regulatory objectives, and
(b)   appropriate in any other relevant respect.

(3)   Before making regulations under subsection (1), the Scottish Ministers must consult—

(a)   the Lord President,
(b)   the Law Society,
(c)   every approved regulator,
(d)[1]   the CMA, and such other organisation (appearing to them to represent the interests of consumers in Scotland) as they consider appropriate,
(e)   such other person or body as they consider appropriate.

(4)   A statutory instrument containing regulations under subsection (1) is not to be made unless a draft of the instrument has been laid before, and approved by resolution of, the Scottish Parliament.

Ancillary provision   F1.563

148.—[2](1)   The Scottish Ministers may by regulations made by statutory instrument make such—

(a)   supplemental provision, or
(b)   incidental, consequential, transitional, transitory or saving provision,

---

[1] As amended by the Enterprise and Regulatory Reform Act 2013 (c.24) Sch.6 para.203 (effective April 1, 2014).
[2] Partially in force.

as they consider necessary or expedient for the purposes of or in connection with this Act.

(2) But—

    (a) a statutory instrument containing regulations under subsection (1) which adds to, replaces or omits any part of the text of an Act (including this Act) is not to be made unless a draft of the instrument has been laid before, and approved by resolution of, the Scottish Parliament,

    (b) a statutory instrument containing any other regulations under that subsection is subject to annulment in pursuance of a resolution of the Parliament.

F1.564 **Definitions**

149.—[1](1)[2] In this Act (unless the context otherwise requires)—

"the 1980 Act" means the Solicitors (Scotland) Act 1980,

"the 1986 Act" means the Legal Aid (Scotland) Act 1986,

"the 1990 Act" means the Law Reform (Miscellaneous Provisions) (Scotland) Act 1990,

"the 2007 Act" means the Legal Profession and Legal Aid (Scotland) Act 2007,

"CMA" means Competition and Markets Authority,

"Faculty" means Faculty of Advocates,

"Law Society" means Law Society of Scotland,

"Lord President" means Lord President of the Court of Session,

[As repealed by the Enterprise and Regulatory Reform Act 2013 (c.24) Sch.6 para.204 (effective April 1, 2014).]

(2) In this Act (unless the context otherwise requires)—

    (a) the following expressions are to be construed in accordance with section 65(1) (interpretation) of the 1980 Act—"advocate", "incorporated practice", "practising certificate", "registered European lawyer", "registered foreign lawyer", "solicitor",

    (b) the following expressions are to be construed in accordance with section 23 (interpretation) of the 1990 Act—"conveyancing practitioner", "executry practitioner",

    (c) a reference to a litigation practitioner is to a person having a right to conduct litigation, or a right of audience, by virtue of section 27 of the 1990 Act.

(3) In this Act (unless the context otherwise requires), a reference to a professional association or body includes—

    (a) the Law Society,

    (b) any other organisation which serves a profession (for example, the Institute of Chartered Accountants of Scotland).

(4) Schedule 9 is an index of expressions introduced for—

    (a) the whole Act,

    (b) Parts 2 and 3.

---

[1] Partially in force.

[2] As amended by the Enterprise and Regulatory Reform Act 2013 (c.24) Sch.6 para.204 (effective April 1, 2014).

Commencement and short title   F1.565

150.—(1) This section and sections 146 to 149 come into force on the day after Royal Assent.

(2) The other provisions of this Act come into force on the day that the Scottish Ministers by order made by statutory instrument appoint.

(3) An order under subsection (2) may appoint different days for different provisions.

(4) An order under subsection (2) may—

    (a) make different provision for different purposes,

    (b) include such transitional, transitory or saving provision as the Scottish Ministers consider necessary or expedient in connection with the commencement of this Act.

(5) The short title of this Act is the Legal Services (Scotland) Act 2010.

SCHEDULE 1   F1.566

Performance Targets

(introduced by section 38(3))

Application

1. This schedule applies where the Scottish Ministers—

    (a) are satisfied that an act or omission of an approved regulator (or a series of acts or omissions) has had, or is likely to have, an adverse impact on the observance of any of the regulatory objectives, or

    (b) consider that, for any other reason, it is necessary or expedient for one or more performance targets to be set as respects an approved regulator.

Power to set targets

2.—(1) The Scottish Ministers may—

    (a) set one or more performance targets for the approved regulator in relation to its regulatory functions,

    (b) require the approved regulator to set one or more performance targets in relation to its regulatory functions.

(2) The approved regulator must (so far as practicable) comply with a performance target set for it under sub-paragraph (1)(a) or (b).

Notice of intention

3.—(1) Before setting a performance target, or requiring the approved regulator to do so, the Scottish Ministers must give it a notice (a "notice of intention") of their intention to do so.

(2) The notice of intention must—

    (a) state that the Scottish Ministers intend to—

        (i)   set a performance target, or

        (ii) require that the approved regulator set such a target,

    (b) describe the proposed target (including the period within which it would have to be met),

    (c) specify—

        (i)   the act or omission (or series of acts or omissions) to which the proposed target relates,

> (ii) any other facts which, in their opinion, justify the intended target-setting.

Consultation

4.—(1) The approved regulator has 28 days beginning with the date of receipt of the notice of intention (or such longer period as the approved regulator and the Scottish Ministers may agree) to make representations to the Scottish Ministers about the proposed target.

(2) The Scottish Ministers must—

> (a) give a copy of the notice of intention to such persons or bodies as they consider appropriate,
>
> (b) consult them accordingly.

Decision

5.—(1) The Scottish Ministers must have regard to any representations made to them by the approved regulator, or any consultee under paragraph 4(2), when deciding whether to proceed with the target-setting.

(2) The Scottish Ministers must—

> (a) send to the approved regulator a notice (a "decision notice") of their decision,
>
> (b) notify the consultees under paragraph 4(2) of their decision,
>
> (c) publish any target set, or requirement made by them, under paragraph 2(1)(a) or (b) in such manner as they consider most appropriate to bring it to the attention of any relevant person or body.

(3) If the Scottish Ministers' decision is in favour of target-setting, the decision notice must contain the target.

(4) An approved regulator must publish any target set by it following a requirement under paragraph 2(1)(b) in such manner as it considers most appropriate for bringing it to the attention of any relevant person or body.

(5) For the purposes of this schedule, relevant persons or bodies include—

> (a) other approved regulators,
>
> (b) providers of legal services,
>
> (c) organisations representing the interests of consumers,
>
> (d) members of the public.

F1.567

SCHEDULE 2

DIRECTIONS

(introduced by section 38(3))

Application

1. This schedule applies where the Scottish Ministers are satisfied that—

> (a) an act or omission of an approved regulator (or a series of acts or omissions) has had, or is likely to have, an adverse impact on the observance of any of the regulatory objectives,
>
> (b) an approved regulator has failed to comply with a requirement imposed on it by or under this Act (including a direction imposed in accordance with this schedule),
>
> (c) an approved regulator has failed to adhere to its internal governance arrangements (including, in particular, those relating to the independent and effective exercise of its regulatory functions), or

(d)   an approved regulator has made a material amendment to its regulatory scheme under section 12(4).

Power to direct

2.—(1)   The Scottish Ministers may direct the approved regulator to take—

(a)   in a case falling within paragraph 1(a), such action as they consider will counter the adverse impact, mitigate its effect or prevent its recurrence,

(b)   in a case falling within paragraph 1(b) or (c), such action as they consider will remedy the failure, mitigate its effect or prevent its recurrence,

(c)   in a case falling within paragraph 1(d), such action as they consider necessary or expedient in relation to such transitional matters as may arise from the amendment.

(2)   A direction under sub-paragraph (1) may require the approved regulator to modify any part of its regulatory scheme.

(3)   A direction under sub-paragraph (1) must not be framed by reference to—

(a)   a specific disciplinary case, or

(b)   other specific regulatory proceedings.

(4)   A direction under sub-paragraph (1) may require the approved regulator to refrain from doing something.

(5)   The approved regulator must (so far as practicable) comply with a direction given to it in accordance with this schedule.

Notice of intention

3.—(1)   Before giving a direction to an approved regulator under this schedule, the Scottish Ministers must give it a notice (a "notice of intention") of their intention to do so.

(2)   The notice of intention must—

(a)   state that the Scottish Ministers intend to give a direction,

(b)   indicate the terms of the proposed direction (including the date by which it would have to be complied with),

(c)   explain why the Scottish Ministers are satisfied as mentioned in paragraph 1.

Consultation

4.—(1)   The approved regulator has 28 days beginning with the date of receipt of the notice of intention (or such longer period as the approved regulator and the Scottish Ministers may agree) to make representations to the Scottish Ministers about the proposed direction.

(2)   The Scottish Ministers must—

(a)   publish the notice of intention in such manner as they consider most appropriate for bringing it to the attention of any relevant person or body,

(b)   give a copy of the notice of intention to such person or body as they consider appropriate,

(c)   after the expiry of the period for representations—

(i)   give the recipients under paragraph (b) a copy of any representations received from the approved regulator,

(ii)   consult them accordingly in relation to the appropriateness of giving the direction.

(3)[1] Where the Scottish Ministers consider that the proposed direction may have the effect of preventing competition within the legal services market, or significantly restricting or distorting such competition, they must (additionally)—

    (a)   send to the CMA—

        (i)   a copy of the notice of intention,

        (ii)   a copy of any representations received from the approved regulator,

    (b)   consult the CMA accordingly.

Decision

5.—(1) The Scottish Ministers must have regard to any representations made to them by the approved regulator, or any consultee under paragraph 4(2)(c) or (3), when deciding whether to proceed with giving a direction.

    (2)   The Scottish Ministers must—

    (a)   send to the approved regulator a notice (a "decision notice") of their decision,

    (b)   notify the consultees under paragraph 4(2)(c) and (3) of their decision,

---

[1] As amended by the Enterprise and Regulatory Reform Act 2013 (c.24) Sch.6 para.205 (effective April 1, 2014).

(c) publish the decision notice in such manner as they consider most appropriate for bringing it to the attention of any relevant person or body.

(3) If the Scottish Ministers decide to give the direction, the decision notice must contain the direction.

(4) For the purposes of this schedule, relevant persons or bodies include—

(a) other approved regulators,

(b) providers of legal services,

(c) organisations representing the interests of consumers,

(d) members of the public.

Extension of time to comply

6.—(1) The Scottish Ministers may, on an application by an approved regulator made at any time after the giving of a direction, allow an approved regulator additional time to comply with the direction.

(2) Where such additional time is allowed, the Scottish Ministers must publicise that fact in such manner as they consider most likely to bring it to the attention of any relevant person or body.

Enforcement

7.—(1) If at any time it appears to the Scottish Ministers that an approved regulator has failed to comply with a direction given under this schedule, they may make an application to the Court of Session for an order as described in sub-paragraph (2).

(2) On an application under sub-paragraph (1), the Court may (if it decides that the approved regulator has failed to comply with the direction) order the approved regulator to take such steps as the Court thinks fit for securing that the direction is complied with.

SCHEDULE 3

CENSURE

(introduced by section 38(3))

Application

1. This schedule applies where the Scottish Ministers are satisfied that—

(a) an act or omission of an approved regulator (or a series of acts or omissions) has had, or is likely to have, an adverse impact on the observance of any of the regulatory objectives, or

(b) an approved regulator has failed to comply with a requirement imposed on it by or under this Act.

Power to censure

2. The Scottish Ministers may make and publish a statement censuring the approved regulator for—

(a) the act or omission (or series of acts or omissions), or

(b) the failure.

Preliminary advice

3. Before making the statement, the Scottish Ministers must consult such person or body as they consider appropriate about the proposed statement.

Notice of intention

4.—(1) If, after consulting under paragraph 3, the Scottish Ministers intend to proceed with making the statement, they must give the approved regulator a notice (a "notice of intention") of that intention.

(2) The notice of intention must—

(a) state that the Scottish Ministers intend to publish the statement,

(b) specify the date on which they intend to publish the statement (which must be after the expiry of the period mentioned in paragraph 5(1)),

(c) set out the terms of the proposed statement,

(d) specify—

(i) the act or omission (or series of acts or omissions), or

(ii) the failure,

to which the proposed statement relates.

Consultation

5.—(1) The approved regulator has 28 days beginning with the date of receipt of the notice of intention (or such longer period as the approved regulator and the Scottish Ministers may agree) to make representations to the Scottish Ministers about the proposed statement.

(2) The Scottish Ministers must—

    (a) provide the consultees under paragraph 3 with a copy of any representations received from the approved regulator,

    (b) seek their further views in light of the representations.

Decision

6.—(1) The Scottish Ministers must have regard to any representations made to them by the approved regulator, or any consultee under paragraph 3, when deciding whether to proceed with publishing the statement.

(2) The Scottish Ministers must—

    (a) send to the approved regulator a notice (a "decision notice") of their decision,

    (b) notify the consultees under paragraph 3 of their decision,

    (c) publish the decision notice in such manner as they consider most appropriate for bringing it to the attention of any relevant person or body.

(3) If the Scottish Ministers decide to publish the statement, the decision notice must contain the statement (and the statement need not be published separately).

(4) For the purpose of this schedule, relevant persons or bodies include—

    (a) other approved regulators,

    (b) providers of legal services,

    (c) organisations representing the interests of consumers,

    (d) members of the public.

SCHEDULE 4

FINANCIAL PENALTIES

(introduced by section 38(3))

Application

1. This schedule applies where the Scottish Ministers are satisfied that an approved regulator has failed to—

    (a) adhere to its internal governance arrangements (including, in particular, those relating to the independent and effective exercise of its regulatory functions), or

    (b) comply with a direction given in accordance with schedule 2.

Power to impose penalty

2.—(1) The Scottish Ministers may impose on the approved regulator a penalty, in respect of a failure mentioned in paragraph 1, of an amount not exceeding the prescribed maximum.

(2) Here, the prescribed maximum is the maximum amount that is prescribed in regulations made by the Scottish Ministers for the purpose of this paragraph.

(3) A financial penalty imposed under this paragraph is payable to the Scottish Ministers.

Amount of penalty

3.—(1) When considering the appropriate amount of a penalty to be imposed under paragraph 2, the Scottish Ministers must have regard to—

    (a) the seriousness of the failure,

    (b) the nature of the failure in other respects.

(2) It is material for the purpose of sub-paragraph (1)—

    (a) whether the failure was deliberate,

    (b) if the failure is attributable to recklessness or negligence, the degree involved.

(3) The Scottish Ministers may consult such person or body as they consider appropriate when considering—

    (a) whether to impose a penalty,

    (b) the appropriate amount of the penalty.

Notice of intention

4.—(1) Before imposing a financial penalty, the Scottish Ministers must give the approved regulator a notice (a "notice of intention") of their intention to do so.

(2) The notice of intention must—

    (a) state—

    (i)   that the Scottish Ministers intend to impose a financial penalty,

    (ii)   the amount of the proposed penalty,

  (b)   by reference to the failure concerned and any other relevant facts, explain why the Scottish Ministers consider that—

    (i)   it is appropriate to impose a penalty,

    (ii)   the amount of the proposed penalty is appropriate.

Consultation

5.—(1) The approved regulator has 28 days beginning with the date of receipt of the notice of intention (or such longer period as the approved regulator and the Scottish Ministers may agree) to make representations to the Scottish Ministers about the proposed penalty.

(2) The Scottish Ministers must—

  (a)   publish the notice of intention in such manner as they consider most appropriate for bringing it to the attention of any relevant person or body,

  (b)   give a copy of that notice, and a copy of any representations received from the approved regulator, to any person whom or body that they consult under subparagraph (3).

(3) After the expiry of the period for representations, the Scottish Ministers may consult such person or body as they consider appropriate about the appropriateness of—

  (a)   imposing the penalty,

  (b)   its amount.

Decision

6.—(1) The Scottish Ministers must have regard to any representations made to them by the approved regulator, and any consultee under paragraph 5(3), when deciding whether to proceed with imposing the penalty.

(2) The Scottish Ministers must—

  (a)   give a notice to the approved regulator (a "decision notice") of their decision,

  (b)   notify the consultees under paragraph 5(3) of their decision,

  (c)   publish the decision notice in such manner as they consider most appropriate for bringing it to the attention of any relevant person or body.

(3) The decision notice must—

  (a)   state whether or not a financial penalty is being imposed,

  (b)   give the reason for the imposition (or otherwise) of a penalty,

  (c)   if a penalty is being imposed—

    (i)   state the amount of the penalty (and mention any allowance made for payment by instalments),

    (ii)   explain why the Scottish Ministers consider that amount to be appropriate,

    (iii)   specify the date by which the penalty requires to be paid in full.

(4) That date must not be within the 3 months beginning with the day on which the decision notice is given to the approved regulator (but this does not preclude earlier payment at the initiative of the approved regulator).

(5) For the purpose of this schedule, relevant persons or bodies include—

  (a)   other approved regulators,

  (b)   providers of legal services,

  (c)   organisations representing the interests of consumers,

  (d)   members of the public.

Variation of penalty

7.—(1) The Scottish Ministers may, on an application from an approved regulator received within 21 days beginning with the day on which the decision notice is given to the approved regulator—

  (a)   vary the date by which the penalty requires to be paid,

  (b)   allow for the penalty to be paid by—

    (i)   instalments (if not already allowed), or

    (ii)   different instalments (if allowed).

(2) Where an application is made under sub-paragraph (1), no part of the penalty is required to be paid before the Scottish Ministers notify the approved regulator of their determination of the application.

Appeal

8.—(1) An approved regulator on which a financial penalty is imposed under paragraph 2 may appeal to the Court of Session against the penalty on one or more of the appeal grounds.

(2) On an appeal under this paragraph—

  (a)   the Court may—

(i)   uphold, vary or quash the decision that is the subject of the appeal,

(ii)   make such further order as is necessary in the interests of justice,

(b)   the Court's determination is final.

Appeal grounds

9. The grounds for an appeal under paragraph 8 are—

   (a)   that, in the circumstances of the case—

      (i)   it was not appropriate to impose the penalty, or

      (ii)   the amount of the penalty is excessive,

   (b)   that the date specified under paragraph 6(3)(c)(iii) is unreasonable,

   (c)   that the other arrangements for payment are unreasonable, including—

      (i)   the absence of any provision for payment by instalments, or

      (ii)   any provision for payment by instalments that has been allowed,

   (d)   that—

      (i)   the penalty was imposed otherwise than in accordance with this schedule, and

      (ii)   the approved regulator's interests have been substantially prejudiced as a result.

Time for appeal

10.—(1)   An appeal under paragraph 8 is to be made—

   (a)   within the 3 months beginning with the day on which the decision notice is given to the approved regulator, or

   (b)   where the ground of appeal is referable to something done under paragraph 7(1), within the 3 months beginning with the day on which the approved regulator is notified of the thing done.

(2)   Where an appeal is made under paragraph 8, no part of the penalty requires to be paid before the appeal is determined or withdrawn.

Interest

11.—(1)   If the whole or part of a penalty is not paid as required in accordance with this schedule the unpaid amount carries interest at the prescribed rate.

(2)   Here, the prescribed rate is the rate that is prescribed in regulations made by the Scottish Ministers for the purpose of this paragraph.

Default

12.—(1)   Sub-paragraph (2) applies where the whole or part of a penalty is not paid as required in accordance with this schedule.

(2)   The Scottish Ministers may recover from the approved regulator, as a debt due to them—

   (a)   the penalty or (as the case may be) the part of it, and

   (b)   the interest that it carries.

SCHEDULE 5

AMENDMENT OF AUTHORISATION

(introduced by section 38(3))

Application

1. This schedule applies where the Scottish Ministers are satisfied that—

   (a)   an act or omission of an approved regulator (or a series of acts or omissions) has had, or is likely to have, an adverse impact on the observance of any of the regulatory objectives, and

   (b)   the matter cannot be addressed adequately by the Scottish Ministers taking any of the measures mentioned in section 38(4)(a) to (d).

Power to amend

2.—(1)   The Scottish Ministers may amend the authorisation of the approved regulator (given under section 10).

(2)   In particular, the Scottish Ministers may—

   (a)   impose restrictions as respects the authorisation by reference to particular categories of—

      (i)   licensed provider,

      (ii)   legal services,

   (b)   alter the duration of the authorisation (including by imposing a limit of time),

    (c)   impose new conditions, or vary any existing conditions, to which the authorisation is subject.

Notice of intention

3.—(1) Before amending the approved regulator's authorisation, the Scottish Ministers must give it a notice (a "notice of intention") of their intention to do so.

    (2) The notice of intention must—

        (a)   state that the Scottish Ministers intend to amend the approved regulator's authorisation,

        (b)   specify the proposed amendments to the authorisation, and

        (c)   explain why they are satisfied as mentioned in paragraph 1.

Consultation

4.—(1) The approved regulator has 28 days beginning with the date of receipt of the notice of intention (or such longer period as the approved regulator and the Scottish Ministers may agree) to make representations to the Scottish Ministers about the proposed amendments.

    (2) The Scottish Ministers must—

        (a)   publish the notice of intention in such manner as they consider most appropriate for bringing it to the attention of any relevant person or body,

        (b)   give a copy of the notice of intention to—

            (i)[1] the CMA,

            (ii) such other person or body as they consider appropriate,

        (c)   after the expiry of the period for representations—

            (i) give the recipients under paragraph (b) a copy of any representations received from the approved regulator,

            (ii) consult them accordingly in relation to the proposed amendments.

    (3) When consulted under sub-paragraph (2)(c), the Lord President is to—

        (a)   give the Scottish Ministers such advice in respect of the proposed amendments as the Lord President thinks fit,

        (b)   in deciding what advice to give, have regard (in particular) to the likely impact of the proposed amendments on the operation of the Scottish courts.

    (4) For the purpose of sub-paragraph (3)—

        (a)   the approved regulator, or

        (b)   any other person who holds information relevant in relation to proposed amendments, must provide the Lord President with such information about the proposed amendments (or their likely consequences) as the Lord President may reasonably require.

Decision

5.—(1) The Scottish Ministers must have regard to any representations made to them by the approved regulator, or any consultee under paragraph 4(2)(c), when deciding whether to proceed with amending the authorisation.

    (2) The Scottish Ministers must—

        (a)   give a notice of their decision (a "decision notice") to the approved regulator,

        (b)   give reasons in the decision notice for their decision,

---

[1] As amended by the Enterprise and Regulatory Reform Act 2013 (c.24) Sch.6 para.206 (effective April 1, 2014).

(c)   notify the consultees under paragraph 4(2)(c) of their decision,
(d)   publish the decision notice in such manner as they consider most appropriate for bringing it to the attention of any relevant person or body.

(3)   If the Scottish Ministers decide to amend the authorisation, the decision notice must specify the date from which the amendments are to be effective (which may be the date on which that notice is given).

(4)   For the purposes of this schedule, relevant persons or bodies include—
(a)   other approved regulators,
(b)   providers of legal services,
(c)   organisations representing the interests of consumers,
(d)   members of the public.

F1.571

SCHEDULE 6

RESCISSION OF AUTHORISATION

(introduced by section 38(3))

Application

1.   This schedule applies where the Scottish Ministers are satisfied that—
(a)   an act or an omission of an approved regulator (or a series of acts or omissions) has had, or is likely to have, an adverse impact on the observance of any of the regulatory objectives, and
(b)   the matter cannot be adequately addressed by the Scottish Ministers taking any of the measures mentioned in section 38(4)(a) to (e).

Power to rescind

2.   The Scottish Ministers may rescind the authorisation of the approved regulator (given under section 10).

Notice of intention

3.—(1)   Before rescinding the approved regulator's authorisation, the Scottish Ministers must give it a notice (a "notice of intention") of their intention to do so.

(2)   The notice of intention must—
(a)   state that the Scottish Ministers intend to rescind the approved regulator's authorisation,
(b)   explain why they are satisfied as mentioned in paragraph 1.

Consultation

4.—(1)   The approved regulator has 28 days beginning with the date of receipt of the notice of intention (or such longer period as the approved regulator and the Scottish Ministers may agree) to make representations to the Scottish Ministers about the proposed rescission.

(2)   The Scottish Ministers must—
(a)   publish the notice of intention in such manner as they consider most appropriate for bringing it to the attention of any relevant person or body,
(b)   give a copy of the notice of intention to—
(i)[1]   the CMA,

---

[1] As amended by the Enterprise and Regulatory Reform Act 2013 (c.24) Sch.6 para.207 (effective April 1, 2014).

(ii)   such other person or body as they consider appropriate,

(c)   after the expiry of the period for representations, the Scottish Ministers must—

(i)   give the recipients under paragraph (b) a copy of any representations received from the approved regulator,

(ii)   consult them accordingly in relation to the proposed rescission.

Decision

5.—(1)   The Scottish Ministers must have regard to any representations made to them by the approved regulator, or any consultee under paragraph 4(2)(c), when deciding whether to proceed with rescinding the authorisation.

(2)   The Scottish Ministers must—

(a)   give a notice of their decision (a "decision notice") to the approved regulator,

(b)   give reasons in the decision notice for their decision,

(c)   notify the consultees under paragraph 4(2)(c) of their decision,

(d)   publish the decision notice in such manner as they consider most appropriate for bringing it to the attention of any relevant person or body.

(3)   If the Scottish Ministers decide to rescind the authorisation, the decision notice must—

(a)   specify the date from which the rescission is to be effective (which may be the date on which that notice is given),

(b)   state, for the purpose of section 38(5), whether or not the approval of the approved regulator (given under section 7) is preserved.

(4)   For the purposes of this schedule, relevant persons or bodies include—

(a)   other approved regulators,

(b)   providers of legal services,

(c)   organisations representing the interests of consumers,

(d)   members of the public.

SCHEDULE 7

SURRENDER OF AUTHORISATION

(introduced by section 39(2))

F1.572

Application

1.   This schedule applies where an approved regulator proposes to surrender its authorisation under section 39.

Surrender notice

2.—(1)   The approved regulator must give the Scottish Ministers a notice (a "surrender notice") of its proposal to do so.

(2)   The notice must—

(a)   specify the approved regulator's reasons for proposing to surrender its authorisation,

(b)   be published (by the approved regulator) in such manner as the approved regulator considers most appropriate for bringing it to the attention of any relevant person or body.

Consultation

3.—(1) The Scottish Ministers must, as soon as reasonably practicable after receipt of a surrender notice—

    (a) send a copy of the notice to—

        (i) the Lord President,

        (ii)[1] the CMA,

        (iii) each of the approved regulator's licensed providers,

        (iv) such other person or body as they consider appropriate,

    (b) consult them accordingly.

(2) The consultees under sub-paragraph (1) have 6 weeks beginning with the day on which they are sent the copy of the notice to make representations to the Scottish Ministers about the proposed surrender.

(3) When consulted under sub-paragraph (1), the Lord President is to—

    (a) give the Scottish Ministers such advice in respect of the proposed surrender as the Lord President thinks fit,

    (b) in deciding what advice to give, have regard to the likely impact of the proposed surrender on the operation of the Scottish courts.

(4) For the purpose of sub-paragraph (3)—

    (a) the approved regulator, or

    (b) any other person who holds information relevant to the proposed surrender,

must provide the Lord President with such information about the proposed surrender (or its likely consequences) as the Lord President may reasonably require.

Decision

4.—(1) The Scottish Ministers must, within 28 days beginning with the day after the period mentioned in paragraph 3(2) ends, decide whether to agree to the proposed surrender.

(2) In making their decision, the Scottish Ministers must have regard to—

    (a) any advice given to them by the Lord President,

    (b) any representations made to them by the other consultees under paragraph 3(1),

    (c) any further representation made to them by the approved regulator.

(3) The Scottish Ministers must—

    (a) send to the approved regulator a notice (a "decision notice") of their decision,

    (b) notify the consultees under paragraph 3(1) of their decision,

    (c) publish the decision notice in such manner as they consider appropriate for bringing it to the attention of any relevant person or body.

(4) For the purpose of this schedule, relevant persons or bodies include—

    (a) other approved regulators,

    (b) providers of legal services,

    (c) organisations representing the interests of consumers,

    (d) members of the public.

---

[1] As amended by the Enterprise and Regulatory Reform Act 2013 (c.24) Sch.6 para.208 (effective April 1, 2014).

Date of surrender

5.—(1) If the Scottish Ministers agree to the surrender of the authorisation, the decision notice must specify the date from which the surrender is to be effective (which must be within the period of 6 months beginning with the date of the decision notice).

(2) That date—

    (a) is to be fixed having taken account of the wishes of the approved regulator,

    (b) must allow a reasonable amount of time for the carrying out of such transitional arrangements as are necessary in connection with the surrender.

SCHEDULE 8   **F1.573**

INVESTORS IN LICENSED PROVIDERS

(introduced by section 67(1) *)*

Initial notification requirements

1.—(1) An applicant for a licence (issuable in accordance with an approved regulator's licensing rules) must give the approved regulator the standard information about non-solicitor investors when applying for the licence.

(2) The applicant must also—

    (a) give (as soon as practicable) the approved regulator any standard information subsequently coming to light,

    (b) notify (as soon as practicable) the approved regulator of any other change in the standard information.

(3) The standard information is—

    (a) the name and other details of—

        (i) every non-solicitor investor in the applicant,

        (ii) any other person whom the applicant expects to be a non-solicitor investor in the applicant at such time as the licence may be issued,

    (b) in each case, a description of the nature of the person's interest.

2.—(1) It is an offence for a person to fail to comply with a requirement imposed on the person by paragraph 1.

(2) A person who commits an offence under sub-paragraph (1) is liable on summary conviction to a fine not exceeding level 5 on the standard scale.

(3) It is a defence for a person prosecuted for an offence under sub-paragraph (1) to show that at the relevant time the person had no knowledge, and could not reasonably be expected to have knowledge, of the information in question.

Continuing notification requirements

3.—(1) This paragraph applies where—

    (a) a person takes, or proposes to take, a step to acquire such an interest as would result in the person becoming a non-solicitor investor in a licensed provider,

    (b) a non-solicitor investor takes, or proposes to take, a step which would—

        (i) significantly change the investor's interest in the licensed provider, or

        (ii) acquire an additional kind of interest in the licensed provider, or

    (c) a person becomes a non-solicitor investor in a licensed provider—

        (i) as a new investor, or

(ii)   because the person, having ceased to be entitled to practise as mentioned in section 67(6)(b) (while remaining as an investor), comes within the definition there.

(2) In a case falling within sub-paragraph (1)(a) or (b), the licensed provider must (as soon as practicable) notify the approved regulator of the proposal including by giving it—

(a)   the name and other details of the person concerned,

(b)   the details of the interest concerned.

(3) In a case falling within sub-paragraph (1)(c)(i), the licensed provider must (as soon as practicable) notify the approved regulator of the acquisition including by giving it the name and other details of the investor.

(4) In a case falling within sub-paragraph (1)(c)(ii), the licensed provider must (as soon as practicable) notify the approved regulator of the fact.

(5) Sub-paragraph (3) does not apply where sub-paragraph (2) has been complied with in relation to the acquisition.

(6) It is an offence for a person to fail to comply with a requirement imposed on the person by sub-paragraph (2), (3) or (4).

(7) A person who commits an offence under sub-paragraph (6) is liable on summary conviction to a fine not exceeding level 5 on the standard scale.

(8) It is a defence for a person prosecuted for an offence under sub-paragraph (6) to show that at the relevant time the person had no knowledge, and could not reasonably be expected to have knowledge, of the information in question.

Exemption from notification requirements

4.—(1) An approved regulator may in relation to any exemptible investor in a licensed provider waive the requirements to give it information (or notification) under paragraphs 1 and 3.

(2) Licensing rules must explain—

(a)   any circumstances in which the approved regulator proposes to rely on subparagraph (1),

(b)   any threshold below the percentage specified in sub-paragraph (3) by reference to which it proposes to rely on sub-paragraph (1),

(c)   where it proposes to rely on sub-paragraph (1), its reasons.

(3) In sub-paragraph (1), an "exemptible investor" is (as the case may be)—

(a)   an investor who has less than a 10% stake in the total ownership or control of the licensed provider, or

(b)   a person whose intended acquisition of an interest in the licensed provider is of less than a 10% stake in the total ownership or control of the licensed provider.

Requirement to notify investors

5.—(1) Where an applicant gives information under paragraph 1, the applicant must notify any person whom the information concerns—

(a) of—

(i)   the making of the application, and

(ii)   the fact that the identity of the person has been disclosed to the approved regulator,

(b)   of the effect of paragraph 6.

(2) Where a licensed provider gives notification under paragraph 3(2) or (3), the licensed provider must notify any person whom the notification concerns—

(a) of—

(i) the giving of that notification, and

(ii) the fact that the identity of the person has been disclosed to the approved regulator,

(b) of the effect of paragraph 6.

(3) It is an offence for a person to fail without reasonable excuse to comply with a requirement imposed on the person by sub-paragraph (1) or (2).

(4) A person who commits an offence under sub-paragraph (3) is liable on summary conviction to a fine not exceeding level 5 on the standard scale.

Approved regulator may obtain information

6.—(1) An approved regulator may require a person whose identity has been disclosed to it under paragraph 1 or 3 to provide it with such documents and other information as it may reasonably require.

(2) It is an offence for a person who is required to provide information by virtue of subparagraph (1)—

(a) to fail without reasonable excuse to comply with the requirement, or

(b) knowingly to provide false or misleading information.

(3) A person who commits an offence under sub-paragraph (2) is liable—

(a) on summary conviction to a fine not exceeding the statutory maximum,

(b) on conviction on indictment to a term of imprisonment not exceeding 2 years or a fine (or both).

SCHEDULE 9[1]

INDEX OF EXPRESSIONS USED

(introduced by section 149(4) *)*

Whole Act expressions	Relevant provisions
particular expressions	
regulatory objectives	all in Part 1
professional principles	
legal services	
other expressions	
the 1980 Act, the 1986 Act, the 1990 Act & the 2007 Act	all in section 149(1) to (3)
advocate	
conveyancing practitioner	
executry practitioner	
Faculty	
incorporated practice	
Law Society	
litigation practitioner	
Lord President	
OFT	
professional association or body	
registered European lawyer	

---

[1] Not yet in force.

Whole Act expressions	Relevant provisions
registered foreign lawyer	
solicitor	

Part 2 expressions	Relevant provisions
approved regulator (of licensed provider)	section 6
approval and authorisation (of approved regulator)	sections 7 and 10
designated person (within licensed provider)	section 59
Head of Legal Services, Head of Practice and Practice Committee (of licensed provider)	sections 51 to 53
internal governance arrangements (of approved regulator)	section 27
investor, non-solicitor investor and solicitor investor (in licensed provider)	section 67
licensed legal services provider (and licensed provider)	section 47
licensing and practice rules (in regulatory scheme)	sections 14 and 18
regulatory and representative functions (of approved regulator)	section 30

Part 3 expressions	Relevant provisions
regulatory scheme (of approved regulator)	section 12
approving body (of confirmation agent)	section 91
approving body (of will writer)	section 102
confirmation agent and confirmation services	section 90
regulatory scheme (of approving body)	sections 93 and 104
will writer and will writing services	section 101

STATUTORY INSTRUMENTS

PROPERTY MISDESCRIPTIONS (SPECIFIED MATTERS) ORDER 1992

(SI 1992/2834)

11 December 1992.

The Secretary of State, in exercise of the powers conferred upon him by section 1 of the Property Misdescriptions Act 1991, hereby makes the following Order:

1. This Order may be cited as the Property Misdescriptions (Specified Matters) Order 1992 and shall come into force on 4th April 1993.

2. The matters contained in the Schedule to this Order are hereby specified to the extent described in that Schedule for the purposes of section 1(1) of the Property Misdescriptions Act 1991.

SCHEDULE

SPECIFIED MATTERS

Article 2

1. Location or address.

2. Aspect, view, outlook or environment.

3. Availability and nature of services, facilities or amenities.

4. Proximity to any services, places, facilities or amenities.

5. Accommodation, measurements or sizes.

6. Fixtures and fittings.

7. Physical or structural characteristics, form of construction or condition.

8. Fitness for any purpose or strength of any buildings or other structures on land or of land itself.

9. Treatments, processes, repairs or improvements or the effects thereof.

10. Conformity or compliance with any scheme, standard, test or regulations or the existence of any guarantee.

11. Survey, inspection, investigation, valuation or appraisal by any person or the results thereof.

12. The grant or giving of any award or prize for design or construction.

13. History, including the age, ownership or use of land or any building or fixture and the date of any alterations thereto.

14. Person by whom any building, (or part of any building), fixture or component was designed, constructed, built, produced, treated, processed, repaired, reconditioned or tested.

15. The length of time during which land has been available for sale either generally or by or through a particular person.

16. Price (other than the price at which accommodation or facilities are available and are to be provided by means of the creation or disposal of an interest in land in the circumstances specified in section 23(1)(a) and (b) of the Consumer Protection Act 1987 or Article 16(1)(a) and (b) of the Consumer Protection (NI) Order 1987 (which relate to the creation or disposal of certain interests in new dwellings)) and previous price.

17. Tenure or estate.

18. Length of any lease or of the unexpired term of any lease and the terms and conditions of a lease (and, in relation to land in Northern Ireland, any fee farm grant creating the relation of landlord and tenant shall be treated as a lease).

19. Amount of any ground-rent, rent or premium and frequency of any review.

20. Amount of any rent-charge.

21. Where all or any part of any land is let to a tenant or is subject to a licence, particulars of the tenancy or licence, including any rent, premium or other payment due and frequency of any review.

22. Amount of any service or maintenance charge or liability for common repairs.

23. Council tax payable in respect of a dwelling within the meaning of section 3, or in Scotland section 72, of the Local Government Finance Act 1992 or the basis or any part of the basis on which that tax is calculated.

24. Rates payable in respect of a non-domestic hereditament within the meaning of section 64 of the Local Government Finance Act 1988 or, in Scotland, in respect of lands and heritages shown on a valuation roll or the basis or any part of the basis on which those rates are calculated.

25. Rates payable in respect of a hereditament within the meaning of the Rates (Northern Ireland) Order 1977 or the basis or any part of the basis on which those rates are calculated.

26. Existence or nature of any planning permission or proposals for development, construction or change of use.

27. In relation to land in England and Wales, the passing or rejection of any plans of proposed building work in accordance with section 16 of the Building Act 1984 and the giving of any completion certificate in accordance with regulation 15 of the Building Regulations 1991.

28. In relation to land in Scotland, the granting of a warrant under section 6 of the Building (Scotland) Act 1959 or the granting of a certificate of completion under section 9 of that Act.

29. In relation to land in Northern Ireland, the passing or rejection of any plans of proposed building work in accordance with Article 13 of the Building Regulations (Northern Ireland) Order 1979 and the giving of any completion certificate in accordance with building regulations made under that Order.

30. Application of any statutory provision which restricts the use of land or which requires it to be preserved or maintained in a specified manner.

31. Existence or nature of any restrictive covenants, or of any restrictions on resale, restrictions on use, or pre-emption rights and, in relation to land in Scotland, (in addition to the matters mentioned previously in this paragraph) the existence or nature of any reservations or real conditions.

32. Easements, servitudes or wayleaves.

33. Existence and extent of any public or private right of way.

THE MONEY LAUNDERING REGULATIONS 2003

F2.2

(SI 2003/3075)

[Repealed by the Money Laundering Regulations 2007 (SI 2007/2157) reg.1(3) (effective December 15, 2007).]

THE MONEY LAUNDERING REGULATIONS 2007

F2.3

(SI 2007/2157)

15 December 2007.

CONTENTS

PART 1 GENERAL

The Treasury are a government department designated for the purposes of section 2(2) of the European Communities Act 1972 in relation to measures relating to preventing the use of the financial system for the purpose of money laundering;

The Treasury, in exercise of the powers conferred on them by section 2(2) of the European Communities Act 1972 and by sections 168(4)(b), 402(1)(b), 417(1) and 428(3) of the Financial Services and Markets Act 2000, make the following Regulations:

PART 1

GENERAL

Citation, commencement etc.

1.—(1)   These Regulations may be cited as the Money Laundering Regulations 2007 and come into force on 15th December 2007.

(2)   These Regulations are prescribed for the purposes of sections 168(4)(b) (appointment of persons to carry out investigations in particular cases) and 402(1)(b) (power of the Authority to institute proceedings for certain other offences) of the 2000 Act.

(3)   The Money Laundering Regulations 2003 are revoked.

Interpretation

2.—[1, 2](1)   In these Regulations—

"the 2000 Act" means the Financial Services and Markets Act 2000;

"Annex I financial institution" has the meaning given by regulation 22(1);

[3]"auction platform" has the meaning given by regulation 3(13A);

"auditor", except in regulation 17(2)(c) and (d), has the meaning given by regulation 3(4) and (5);

"authorised person" means a person who is authorised for the purposes of the 2000 Act;

[4]"the Authority" means the Financial Conduct Authority;

[As repealed by the Capital Requirements Regulations 2013 (SI 2013/3115) Sch.2 para.68 (effective January 1, 2014).]

"beneficial owner" has the meaning given by regulation 6;

[5]"bill payment service provider" means an undertaking which provides a payment service enabling the payment of utility and other household bills;

"business relationship" means a business, professional or commercial relationship between a relevant person and a customer, which is expected by the relevant person, at the time when contact is established, to have an element of duration;

"the capital requirements directive" means Directive 2013/36/EU of the European Parliament and of the Council of 26 June 2013 relating to the activity of credit institutions and the prudential supervision of credit institutions and investment firms, amending Directive 2002/87/EC and repealing Directives 2006/48/EC and 2006/49/EC;

"the capital requirements regulation" means Regulation (EU) 575/2013 of the European Parliament and of the Council of 26 June 2013 on prudential requirements for credit institutions and investment firms and amending Regulation (EU) No 648/2012;

"cash" means notes, coins or travellers' cheques in any currency;

"casino" has the meaning given by regulation 3(13);

"the Commissioners" means the Commissioners for Her Majesty's Revenue and Customs;

"consumer credit financial institution" has the meaning given by regulation 22(1);

"credit institution" has the meaning given by regulation 3(2);

[...] has the meaning given by regulation 5;

"DETI" means the Department of Enterprise, Trade and Investment in Northern Ireland;

---

[1] As amended by the Financial Services and Markets Act 2000 (Regulated Activities) (Amendment) (No.2) Order 2013 (SI 2013/1881) Sch.1(2) para.31 (effective July 26, 2013).
[2] As amended by the Capital Requirements Regulations 2013 (SI 2013/3115) Sch.2 para.68 (effective January 1, 2014).
[3] As inserted by the Recognised Auction Platforms Regulations 2011 (SI 2011/2699) Pt 4 reg.11(2) (effective December 12, 2011).
[4] As inserted by the Financial Services Act 2012 (Consequential Amendments and Transitional Provisions) Order 2013 (SI 2013/472) Sch.2 para.129(a) (effective April 1, 2013).
[5] As inserted by the Payment Services Regulations 2009 (SI 2009/209) Sch.6(2) para.6(a) (effective November 1, 2009).

"the electronic money directive" means Directive 2009/110/EC of the European Parliament and of the Council of 16th September 2009 on the taking up, pursuit and prudential supervision of the business of electronic money institutions;[1]

"electronic money institution" has the meaning given by regulation 2(1) of the Electronic Money Regulations 2011;[2]

"the emission allowance auctioning regulation" means Commission Regulation (EU) No. 1031/2010 of 12 November 2010 on the timing, administration and other aspects of auctioning of greenhouse gas emission allowances pursuant to Directive 2003/87/EC of the European Parliament and of the Council establishing a scheme for greenhouse gas emission allowances trading within the Community;

"estate agent" has the meaning given by regulation 3(11);

"external accountant" has the meaning given by regulation 3(7);

"financial institution" has the meaning given by regulation 3(3);

"firm" means any entity, whether or not a legal person, that is not an individual and includes a body corporate and a partnership or other unincorporated association;

"high value dealer" has the meaning given by regulation 3(12);

"the implementing measures directive" means Commission Directive 2006/70/EC of 1st August 2006 laying down implementing measures for the money laundering directive;

"independent legal professional" has the meaning given by regulation 3(9);

"insolvency practitioner", except in regulation 17(2)(c) and (d), has the meaning given by regulation 3(6);

"the life assurance consolidation directive" means Directive 2002/83/EC of the European Parliament and of the Council of 5th November 2002 concerning life assurance;

"local weights and measures authority" has the meaning given by section 69 of the Weights and Measures Act 1985(local weights and measures authorities);

"the markets in financial instruments directive" means Directive 2004/39/EC of the European Parliament and of the Council of 12th April 2004 on markets in financial instruments;

"money laundering" means an act which falls within section 340(11) of the Proceeds of Crime Act 2002;

"the money laundering directive" means Directive 2005/60/EC of the European Parliament and of the Council of 26th October 2005 on the prevention of the use of the financial system for the purpose of money laundering and terrorist financing;

"money service business" means an undertaking which by way of business operates a currency exchange office, transmits money (or any representations of monetary value) by any means or cashes cheques which are made payable to customers;

"nominated officer" means a person who is nominated to receive disclosures under Part 7 of the Proceeds of Crime Act 2002 (money laundering) or Part 3 of the Terrorism Act 2000 (terrorist property);

---

[1] As substituted by the Electronic Money Regulations 2011 (SI 2011/99) Sch.4(2) para.19(a) (effective April 30, 2011).

[2] As substituted by the Electronic Money Regulations 2011 (SI 2011/99) Sch.4(2) para.19(a) (effective April 30, 2011).

"non-EEA state" means a state that is not an EEA state;

"notice" means a notice in writing;

"occasional transaction" means a transaction (carried out other than as part of a business relationship) amounting to 15,000 euro or more, whether the transaction is carried out in a single operation or several operations which appear to be linked;

[...] means the Office of Fair Trading;

"ongoing monitoring" has the meaning given by regulation 8(2);

"payment services" has the meaning given by regulation 2(1) of the Payment Services Regulations 2009;[1]

[2]"person who has a qualifying relationship with a PRA-authorised person" is to be read with section 415B(4) of the 2000 Act;

[3]"the PRA" means the Prudential Regulation Authority;

[4]"PRA-authorised person" has the meaning given in section 2B(5) of the 2000 Act;

"regulated market"—

   (a)   within the EEA, has the meaning given by point 14 of Article 4(1) of the markets in financial instruments directive; and

   (b)   outside the EEA, means a regulated financial market which subjects companies whose securities are admitted to trading to disclosure obligations which are contained in international standards and are equivalent to the specified disclosure obligations;

"relevant person" means a person to whom, in accordance with regulations 3 and 4, these Regulations apply;

"the specified disclosure obligations" means disclosure requirements consistent with—

   (a)   Article 6(1) to (4) of Directive 2003/6/EC of the European Parliament and of the Council of 28th January 2003 on insider dealing and market manipulation;

   (b)   Articles 3, 5, 7, 8, 10, 14 and 16 of Directive 2003/71/EC of the European Parliament and of the Council of 4th November 2003 on the prospectuses to be published when securities are offered to the public or admitted to trading;

   (c)   Articles 4 to 6, 14, 16 to 19 and 30 of Directive 2004/109/EC of the European Parliament and of the Council of 15th December 2004 relating to the harmonisation of transparency requirements in relation to information about issuers whose securities are admitted to trading on a regulated market; or

   (d)   Community legislation made under the provisions mentioned in sub-paragraphs (a) to (c);

"supervisory authority" in relation to any relevant person means the supervisory authority specified for such a person by regulation 23;

"tax adviser" (except in regulation 11(3)) has the meaning given by regulation 3(8);

---

[1] As inserted by the Payment Services Regulations 2009 (SI 2009/209) Sch.6(2) para.6(a) (effective November 1, 2009).
[2] As inserted by the Financial Services Act 2012 (c.21) Sch.2 para.129(a)(ii) (effective April 1, 2013).
[3] As inserted by the Financial Services Act 2012 (c.21) Sch.2 para.129(a)(ii) (effective April 1, 2013).
[4] As inserted by the Financial Services Act 2012 (c.21) Sch.2 para.129(a)(ii) (effective April 1, 2013).

"telecommunication, digital and IT payment service provider" means an undertaking which provides payment services falling within paragraph 1(g) of Schedule 1 to the Payment Services Regulations 2009;[1]
"terrorist financing" means an offence under—

(a) section 15 (fund-raising), 16 (use and possession), 17 (funding arrangements), 18 (money laundering) or 63 (terrorist finance: jurisdiction) of the Terrorism Act 2000;

(b) paragraph 7(2) or (3) of Schedule 3 to the Anti-Terrorism, Crime and Security Act 2001 (freezing orders);

(c) *[Revoked by the Terrorist Asset-Freezing etc. Act 2010 (c.38) Sch.2(1) para.1 (effective December 17, 2010).]*

(d)[2] regulation 10 of the Al-Qaida (Asset-Freezing) Regulations 2011;

(e)[3] section 11, 12, 13, 14, 15 or 18 of the Terrorist Asset-Freezing etc. Act 2010 (offences relating to the freezing of funds etc. of designated persons);

"trust or company service provider" has the meaning given by regulation 3(10).

(2) In these Regulations, references to amounts in euro include references to equivalent amounts in another currency.

(3) Unless otherwise defined, expressions used in these Regulations and the money laundering directive have the same meaning as in the money laundering directive and expressions used in these Regulations and in the implementing measures directive have the same meaning as in the implementing measures directive.[4]

Application of the Regulations

3.—(1) Subject to regulation 4, these Regulations apply to the following persons acting in the course of business carried on by them in the United Kingdom ("relevant persons")—

(a) credit institutions;
(b) financial institutions;
(c) auditors, insolvency practitioners, external accountants and tax advisers;
(d) independent legal professionals;
(e) trust or company service providers;
(f) estate agents;
(g) high value dealers;
(h) casinos.

(1A)[5] Regulations 2, 20, 21, 23, 24, 35 to 42, and 44 to 48 apply to an auction platform acting in the course of business carried on by it in the United Kingdom, and such an auction platform is a relevant person for the purposes of those provisions.

---

[1] As inserted by the Payment Services Regulations 2009 (SI 2009/209) Sch.6(2) para.6(a) (effective November 1, 2009).
[2] As inserted by the Recognised Auction Platforms Regulations 2011 (SI 2011/2699) Pt 4 reg.11(2) (effective December 12, 2011).
[3] As substituted by the Terrorist Asset-Freezing etc. Act 2010 (c.38) Sch.1(1) para.6(b) (effective December 17, 2010).
[4] As substituted by the Al-Qaida (Asset-Freezing) Regulations 2011 (SI 2011/2742) Sch.2 para.2 (effective November 16, 2011)
[5] As inserted by the Recognised Auction Platforms Regulations 2011 (SI 2011/2699) Pt 4 reg.11(3) (effective December 12, 2011).

(2)[1, 2] "Credit institution" means—

(a)[3] a credit institution as defined in Article 4(1)(1) of the capital requirements regulation; or

(b) a branch (within the meaning of Article 4(1)(17) of that regulation)
located in an EEA state of an institution falling within sub-paragraph
(a) (or an equivalent institution whose head office is located in a non-
EEA state) wherever its head office is located,

when it accepts deposits or other repayable funds from the public or grants credits
for its own account (within the meaning of the banking consolidation directive), or
when it bids directly in auctions in accordance with the emission allowance auctioning regulation on behalf of its clients.

(3)[4, 5] "Financial institution" means—

(a)[6] an undertaking, including a money service business, when it carries out
one or more of the activities listed in points 2 to 12, 14 and 15 of Annex
1 to the capital requirements directive (the relevant text of which is set
out in Schedule 1 to these Regulations), other than—

---

[1] As amended by the Financial Services and Markets Act 2000 (Regulated Activities) (Amendment)
Order 2012 (SI 2012/1906) Pt 3 art.7 (effective July 20, 2012).
[2] As amended by the Capital Requirements Regulations 2013 (SI 2013/3115) Sch.2 para.68 (effective
January 1, 2014).
[3] As substituted by the Electronic Money Regulations 2011 (SI 2011/99) Sch.4(2) para.19(b) (effective
April 30, 2011).
[4] As amended by the Financial Services and Markets Act 2000 (Regulated Activities) (Amendment)
Order 2012 (SI 2012/1906) Pt 3 art.7 (effective July 20, 2012).
[5] As amended by the Capital Requirements Regulations 2013 (SI 2013/3115) Sch.2 para.68 (effective
January 1, 2014).
[6] As substituted by the Electronic Money Regulations 2011 (SI 2011/99) Sch.4(2) para.19(b) (effective
April 30, 2011).

(i) a credit institution;
(ii)[1] an undertaking whose only listed activity is as a creditor under an agreement which—
  (aa) falls within section 12(a) of the Consumer Credit Act 1974 (debtor-creditor-supplier agreements),
  (bb) provides fixed sum credit (within the meaning given in section 10 of the Consumer Credit Act 1974 (running-account credit and fixed-sum credit)) in relation to the provision of services, and
  (cc) provides financial accommodation by way of deferred payment or payment by instalments over a period not exceeding 12 months;
(iii) an undertaking whose only listed activity is trading for own account in one or more of the products listed in point 7 of Annex 1 to the banking consolidation directive where the undertaking does not have a customer,
and, for this purpose, "customer" means a third party which is not a member of the same group as the undertaking;
(b) an insurance company duly authorised in accordance with the life assurance consolidation directive, when it carries out activities covered by that directive;
(c)[2] a person, other than a person falling within Article 2 of the markets in financial instruments directive, whose regular occupation or business is the provision to other persons of an investment activity on a professional basis, when providing or performing investment services or activities (within the meaning of that directive) or when bidding directly in auctions in accordance with the emission allowance auctioning regulation on behalf of clients;
(ca)[3] a person falling within Article 2(1)(i) of the markets in financial instruments directive, when bidding directly in auctions in accordance with the emission allowance auctioning regulation on behalf of clients of the person's main business.
(d) a collective investment undertaking, when marketing or otherwise offering its units or shares;
(e) an insurance intermediary as defined in Article 2(5) of Directive 2002/92/EC of the European Parliament and of the Council of 9th December 2002 on insurance mediation, with the exception of a tied insurance intermediary as mentioned in Article 2(7) of that Directive, when it acts in respect of contracts of long-term insurance within the meaning given by article 3(1) of, and Part II of Schedule 1 to, the Financial Services and Markets Act 2000 (Regulated Activities) Order 2001;
(f) a branch located in an EEA state of a person referred to in sub-paragraphs (a) to (e) (or an equivalent person whose head office is located in a non-EEA state), wherever its head office is located, when carrying out any activity mentioned in sub-paragraphs (a) to (e);

---

[1] As substituted by the Financial Services Act 2012 (c.21) Sch.2 para.129(a)(i) (effective April 1, 2013).
[2] As substituted by the Financial Services and Markets Act 2000 (Regulated Activities) (Amendment) Order 2012 (SI 2012/1906) Pt 3 art.7 (effective July 20, 2012).
[3] As inserted by the Financial Services and Markets Act 2000 (Regulated Activities) (Amendment) Order 2012 (SI 2012/1906) Pt 3 art.7 (effective July 20, 2012).

(g)   the National Savings Bank;

(h)   the Director of Savings, when money is raised under the auspices of the Director under the National Loans Act 1968.

(4)   "Auditor" means any firm or individual who is a statutory auditor within the meaning of Part 42 of the Companies Act 2006 (statutory auditors), when carrying out statutory audit work within the meaning of section 1210 of that Act.

(5)   Before the entry into force of Part 42 of the Companies Act 2006 the reference in paragraph (4) to—

(a)   a person who is a statutory auditor shall be treated as a reference to a person who is eligible for appointment as a company auditor under section 25 of the Companies Act 1989 (eligibility for appointment) or article 28 of the Companies (Northern Ireland) Order 1990; and

(b)   the carrying out of statutory audit work shall be treated as a reference to the provision of audit services.

(6)   "Insolvency practitioner" means any person who acts as an insolvency practitioner within the meaning of section 388 of the Insolvency Act 1986 (meaning of "act as insolvency practitioner") or article 3 of the Insolvency (Northern Ireland) Order 1989.

(7)   "External accountant" means a firm or sole practitioner who by way of business provides accountancy services to other persons, when providing such services.

(8)   "Tax adviser" means a firm or sole practitioner who by way of business provides advice about the tax affairs of other persons, when providing such services.

(9)   "Independent legal professional" means a firm or sole practitioner who by way of business provides legal or notarial services to other persons, when participating in financial or real property transactions concerning—

(a)   the buying and selling of real property or business entities;

(b)   the managing of client money, securities or other assets;

(c)   the opening or management of bank, savings or securities accounts;

(d)   the organisation of contributions necessary for the creation, operation or management of companies; or

(e)   the creation, operation or management of trusts, companies or similar structures,

and, for this purpose, a person participates in a transaction by assisting in the planning or execution of the transaction or otherwise acting for or on behalf of a client in the transaction.

(10)   "Trust or company service provider" means a firm or sole practitioner who by way of business provides any of the following services to other persons—

(a)   forming companies or other legal persons;

(b)   acting, or arranging for another person to act—

(i)   as a director or secretary of a company;

(ii)   as a partner of a partnership; or

(iii)   in a similar position in relation to other legal persons;

(c)   providing a registered office, business address, correspondence or administrative address or other related services for a company, partnership or any other legal person or arrangement;

(d)   acting, or arranging for another person to act, as—

(i)   a trustee of an express trust or similar legal arrangement; or

(ii)   a nominee shareholder for a person other than a company whose securities are listed on a regulated market,

when providing such services.

(11)[1]   "Estate agent" means—
   (a)   a firm; or
   (b)   sole practitioner,
who, or whose employees, carry out estate agency work , when in the course of carrying out such work.

(11A)[2]   For the purposes of paragraph (11) "estate agency work" is to be read in accordance with section 1 of the Estate Agents Act 1979 (estate agency work), but for those purposes references in that section to disposing of or acquiring an interest in land are (despite anything in section 2 of that Act) to be taken to include references to disposing of or acquiring an estate or interest in land outside the United Kingdom where that estate or interest is capable of being owned or held as a separate interest.

(12)   "High value dealer" means a firm or sole trader who by way of business trades in goods (including an auctioneer dealing in goods), when he receives, in respect of any transaction, a payment or payments in cash of at least 15,000 euros in total, whether the transaction is executed in a single operation or in several operations which appear to be linked.

(13)   "Casino" means the holder of a casino operating licence and, for this purpose, a "casino operating licence" has the meaning given by section 65(2) of the Gambling Act 2005 nature of licence).

(13A)[3]   "Auction platform" means a platform which auctions two-day spot or five-day futures, within the meanings given by Article 3(4) and (5) of the emission allowance auctioning regulation, when it carries out activities covered by that regulation.

(14)   In the application of this regulation to Scotland, for "real property" in paragraph (9) substitute "heritable property".

Exclusions

4.—(1)   These Regulations do not apply to the following persons when carrying out any of the following activities—
   (a)   a society registered under the Industrial and Provident Societies Act 1965 when it—
      (i)   issues withdrawable share capital within the limit set by section 6 of that Act (maximum shareholding in society); or
      (ii)   accepts deposits from the public within the limit set by section 7(3) of that Act (carrying on of banking by societies);
   (b)   a society registered under the Industrial and Provident Societies Act (Northern Ireland) 1969, when it—
      (i)   issues withdrawable share capital within the limit set by section 6 of that Act (maximum shareholding in society); or
      (ii)   accepts deposits from the public within the limit set by section 7(3) of that Act (carrying on of banking by societies);
   (c)   a person who is (or falls within a class of persons) specified in any of paragraphs 2 to 23, 25 to 38 or 40 to 49 of the Schedule to the Financial

---

[1] As amended by the Money Laundering (Amendment) Regulations 2012 (SI 2012/2298) reg.3 (effective October 1, 2012).
[2] As inserted by the Money Laundering (Amendment) Regulations 2012 (SI 2012/2298) reg.3 (effective October 1, 2012).
[3] As inserted by the Recognised Auction Platforms Regulations 2011 (SI 2011/2699) Pt 4 reg.11(3) (effective December 12, 2011).

Services and Markets Act 2000 (Exemption) Order 2001, when carrying out any activity in respect of which he is exempt;

(ca)[1] a local authority within the meaning given in article 3 of the Financial Services and Markets Act 2000 (Regulated Activities) Order 2001, when carrying on an activity which would be a regulated activity for the purposes of the Financial Services and Markets Act 2000 but for article 72G of that Order;

(d) a person who was an exempted person for the purposes of section 45 of the Financial Services Act 1986 (miscellaneous exemptions) immediately before its repeal, when exercising the functions specified in that section;

(e) a person whose main activity is that of a high value dealer, when he engages in financial activity on an occasional or very limited basis as set out in paragraph 1 of Schedule 2 to these Regulations; or

(f)[2] a person, when he prepares a home report.

(2) These Regulations do not apply to a person who falls within regulation 3 solely as a result of his engaging in financial activity on an occasional or very limited basis as set out in paragraph 1 of Schedule 2 to these Regulations.

(3) Parts 2 to 5 of these Regulations do not apply to—

(a) the Auditor General for Scotland;

(b) the Auditor General for Wales;

(c) the Bank of England;

(d) the Comptroller and Auditor General;

(e) the Comptroller and Auditor General for Northern Ireland;

(f) the Official Solicitor to the Supreme Court, when acting as trustee in his official capacity;

(g) the Treasury Solicitor.

(4)[3] In paragraph (1)(f), "home report" means the documents prescribed for the purposes of section 98, 99(1) or 101(2) of the Housing (Scotland) Act 2006.

PART 2

CUSTOMER DUE DILIGENCE

Meaning of customer due diligence measures

5. "Customer due diligence measures" means—

(a) identifying the customer and verifying the customer's identity on the basis of documents, data or information obtained from a reliable and independent source;

(b) identifying, where there is a beneficial owner who is not the customer, the beneficial owner and taking adequate measures, on a risk-sensitive basis, to verify his identity so that the relevant person is satisfied that he knows who the beneficial owner is, including, in the case of a legal person, trust or similar legal arrangement, measures to understand the ownership and control structure of the person, trust or arrangement; and

---

[1] As inserted by the Financial Services and Markets Act 2000 (Consumer Credit) (Miscellaneous Provisions) (No.2) Order 2014 (SI 2014/506) art.4 (effective April 1, 2014).

[2] As amended by the Money Laundering (Amendment) Regulations 2012 (SI 2012/2298) reg.4 (effective October 1, 2012).

[3] As amended by the Money Laundering (Amendment) Regulations 2012 (SI 2012/2298) reg.4 (effective October 1, 2012).

    (c)   obtaining information on the purpose and intended nature of the business relationship.

Meaning of beneficial owner

6.—(1)   In the case of a body corporate, "beneficial owner" means any individual who—

    (a) as respects any body other than a company whose securities are listed on a regulated market, ultimately owns or controls (whether through direct or indirect ownership or control, including through bearer share holdings) more than 25% of the shares or voting rights in the body; or

    (b) as respects any body corporate, otherwise exercises control over the management of the body.

(2) In the case of a partnership (other than a limited liability partnership), "beneficial owner" means any individual who—

    (a) ultimately is entitled to or controls (whether the entitlement or control is direct or indirect) more than a 25% share of the capital or profits of the partnership or more than 25% of the voting rights in the partnership; or

    (b) otherwise exercises control over the management of the partnership.

(3) In the case of a trust, "beneficial owner" means—

    (a) any individual who is entitled to a specified interest in at least 25% of the capital of the trust property;

    (b) as respects any trust other than one which is set up or operates entirely for the benefit of individuals falling within sub-paragraph (a), the class of persons in whose main interest the trust is set up or operates;

    (c) any individual who has control over the trust.

(4) In paragraph (3)—

"specified interest" means a vested interest which is—

    (a) in possession or in remainder or reversion (or, in Scotland, in fee); and

    (b) defeasible or indefeasible;

"control" means a power (whether exercisable alone, jointly with another person or with the consent of another person) under the trust instrument or by law to—

    (a) dispose of, advance, lend, invest, pay or apply trust property;

    (b) vary the trust;

    (c) add or remove a person as a beneficiary or to or from a class of beneficiaries;

    (d) appoint or remove trustees;

    (e) direct, withhold consent to or veto the exercise of a power such as is mentioned in sub-paragraph (a), (b), (c) or (d).

(5) For the purposes of paragraph (3)—

    (a) where an individual is the beneficial owner of a body corporate which is entitled to a specified interest in the capital of the trust property or which has control over the trust, the individual is to be regarded as entitled to the interest or having control over the trust; and

    (b) an individual does not have control solely as a result of—

        (i) his consent being required in accordance with section 32(1)(c) of the Trustee Act 1925 (power of advancement);

        (ii) any discretion delegated to him under section 34 of the Pensions Act 1995 (power of investment and delegation);

        (iii) the power to give a direction conferred on him by section 19(2) of the Trusts of Land and Appointment of Trustees Act 1996 (appointment and retirement of trustee at instance of beneficiaries); or

        (iv) the power exercisable collectively at common law to vary or extinguish a trust where the beneficiaries under the trust are of full age and capacity and (taken together) absolutely entitled to the property subject to the trust (or, in Scotland, have a full and unqualified right to the fee).

(6)   In the case of a legal entity or legal arrangement which does not fall within paragraph (1), (2) or (3), "beneficial owner" means—

(a)   where the individuals who benefit from the entity or arrangement have been determined, any individual who benefits from at least 25% of the property of the entity or arrangement;

(b)   where the individuals who benefit from the entity or arrangement haveyet to be determined, the class of persons in whose main interest the entity or arrangement is set up or operates;

(c)   any individual who exercises control over at least 25% of the property of the entity or arrangement.

(7)   For the purposes of paragraph (6), where an individual is the beneficial owner of a body corporate which benefits from or exercises control over the property of the entity or arrangement, the individual is to be regarded as benefiting from or exercising control over the property of the entity or arrangement.

(8)   In the case of an estate of a deceased person in the course of administration, "beneficial owner" means—

(a)   in England and Wales and Northern Ireland, the executor, original or by representation, or administrator for the time being of a deceased person;

(b)   in Scotland, the executor for the purposes of the Executors (Scotland) Act 1900.

(9)   In any other case, "beneficial owner" means the individual who ultimately owns or controls the customer or on whose behalf a transaction is being conducted.

(10)   In this regulation—

"arrangement", "entity" and "trust" means an arrangement, entity or trust which administers and distributes funds;

"limited liability partnership" has the meaning given by the Limited Liability Partnerships Act 2000.

Application of customer due diligence measures

7.—(1)   Subject to regulations 9, 10, 12, 13, 14, 16(4) and 17, a relevant person must apply customer due diligence measures when he—

(a)   establishes a business relationship;

(b)   carries out an occasional transaction;

(c)   suspects money laundering or terrorist financing;

(d)   doubts the veracity or adequacy of documents, data or information previously obtained for the purposes of identification or verification.

(2)   Subject to regulation 16(4), a relevant person must also apply customer due diligence measures at other appropriate times to existing customers on a risk-sensitive basis.

(3)   A relevant person must—

(a)   determine the extent of customer due diligence measures on a risk-sensitive basis depending on the type of customer, business relationship, product or transaction; and

(b)   be able to demonstrate to his supervisory authority that the extent of the measures is appropriate in view of the risks of money laundering and terrorist financing.

(4)   Where—

(a) a relevant person is required to apply customer due diligence measures in the case of a trust, legal entity (other than a body corporate) or a legal arrangement (other than a trust); and

(b) the class of persons in whose main interest the trust, entity or arrangement is set up or operates is identified as a beneficial owner,

the relevant person is not required to identify all the members of the class.

(5) Paragraph (3)(b) does not apply to the National Savings Bank or the Director of Savings.

Ongoing monitoring

8.—(1) A relevant person must conduct ongoing monitoring of a business relationship.

(2) "Ongoing monitoring" of a business relationship means—

(a) scrutiny of transactions undertaken throughout the course of the relationship (including, where necessary, the source of funds) to ensure that the transactions are consistent with the relevant person's knowledge of the customer, his business and risk profile; and

(b) keeping the documents, data or information obtained for the purpose of applying customer due diligence measures up-to-date.

(3) Regulation 7(3) applies to the duty to conduct ongoing monitoring under paragraph (1) as it applies to customer due diligence measures.

Timing of verification

9.—(1) This regulation applies in respect of the duty under regulation 7(1)(a) and (b) to apply the customer due diligence measures referred to in regulation 5(a) and (b).

(2) Subject to paragraphs (3) to (5) and regulation 10, a relevant person must verify the identity of the customer (and any beneficial owner) before the establishment of a business relationship or the carrying out of an occasional transaction.

(3) Such verification may be completed during the establishment of a business relationship if—

(a) this is necessary not to interrupt the normal conduct of business; and

(a) there is little risk of money laundering or terrorist financing occurring, provided that the verification is completed as soon as practicable after contact is first established.

(4) The verification of the identity of the beneficiary under a life insurance policy may take place after the business relationship has been established provided that it takes place at or before the time of payout or at or before the time the beneficiary exercises a right vested under the policy.

(5) The verification of the identity of a bank account holder may take place after the bank account has been opened provided that there are adequate safeguards in place to ensure that—

(a) the account is not closed; and

(b) transactions are not carried out by or on behalf of the account holder (including any payment from the account to the account holder),

before verification has been completed.

Casinos

10.—(1) A casino must establish and verify the identity of—

    (a)   all customers to whom the casino makes facilities for gaming available—

        (i)   before entry to any premises where such facilities are provided; or

        (ii)   where the facilities are for remote gaming, before access is given to such facilities; or

    (b)   if the specified conditions are met, all customers who, in the course of any period of 24 hours—

        (i)   purchase from, or exchange with, the casino chips with a total value of 2,000 euro or more;

        (ii)[1]   pay the casino 2,000 euro or more for the use of gaming machines; or

        (iii)   pay to, or stake with, the casino 2,000 euro or more in connection with facilities for remote gaming.

  (2)   The specified conditions are—

    (a)   the casino verifies the identity of each customer before or immediately after such purchase, exchange, payment or stake takes place, and

    (b)   the Gambling Commission is satisfied that the casino has appropriate procedures in place to monitor and record—

        (i)   the total value of chips purchased from or exchanged with the casino;

        (ii)   the total money paid for the use of gaming machines; or

        (iii)   the total money paid or staked in connection with facilities for remote gaming,

by each customer.

  (3)   In this regulation—

"gaming", "gaming machine", "remote operating licence" and "stake" have the meanings given by, respectively, sections 6(1) (gaming & game of chance), 235 (gaming machine), 67 (remote gambling) and 353(1) (interpretation) of the Gambling Act 2005;

"premises" means premises subject to—

    (a)   a casino premises licence within the meaning of section 150(1)(a) of the Gambling Act 2005 (nature of licence); or

    (b)   a converted casino premises licence within the meaning of paragraph 65 of Part 7 of Schedule 4 to the Gambling Act 2005 (Commencement No. 6 and Transitional Provisions) Order 2006;

"remote gaming" means gaming provided pursuant to a remote operating licence.

Requirement to cease transactions etc.

  11.—(1) Where, in relation to any customer, a relevant person is unable to apply customer due diligence measures in accordance with the provisions of this Part, he—

    (a)   must not carry out a transaction with or for the customer through a bank account;

    (b)   must not establish a business relationship or carry out an occasional transaction with the customer;

    (c)   must terminate any existing business relationship with the customer;

---

[1] As amended by the Money Laundering (Amendment) Regulations 2007 (SI 2007/3299) reg.2(a) (effective December 15, 2007).

(d) must consider whether he is required to make a disclosure by Part 7 of the Proceeds of Crime Act 2002 or Part 3 of the Terrorism Act 2000.

(2) Paragraph (1) does not apply where a lawyer or other professional adviser is in the course of ascertaining the legal position for his client or performing his task of defending or representing that client in, or concerning, legal proceedings, including advice on the institution or avoidance of proceedings.

(3) In paragraph (2), "other professional adviser" means an auditor, accountant or tax adviser who is a member of a professional body which is established for any such persons and which makes provision for—

(a) testing the competence of those seeking admission to membership of such a body as a condition for such admission; and

(b) imposing and maintaining professional and ethical standards for its members, as well as imposing sanctions for non-compliance with those standards.

Exception for trustees of debt issues

12.—(1) A relevant person—

(a) who is appointed by the issuer of instruments or securities specified in paragraph (2) as trustee of an issue of such instruments or securities; or

(b) whose customer is a trustee of an issue of such instruments or securities,

is not required to apply the customer due diligence measure referred to in regulation 5(b) in respect of the holders of such instruments or securities.

(2) The specified instruments and securities are—

(a)[1] instruments which fall within article 77 or 77A of the Financial Services and Markets Act 2000 (Regulated Activities) Order 2001; and

(b) securities which fall within article 78 of that Order.

Simplified due diligence

13.—(1) A relevant person is not required to apply customer due diligence measures in the circumstances mentioned in regulation 7(1)(a), (b) or (d) where he has reasonable grounds for believing that the customer, transaction or product related to such transaction, falls within any of the following paragraphs.

(2) The customer is—

(a) a credit or financial institution which is subject to the requirements of the money laundering directive; or

(b) a credit or financial institution (or equivalent institution) which—

(i) is situated in a non-EEA state which imposes requirements equivalent to those laid down in the money laundering directive; and

(ii) is supervised for compliance with those requirements.

(3) The customer is a company whose securities are listed on a regulated market subject to specified disclosure obligations.

(4) The customer is an independent legal professional and the product is an account into which monies are pooled, provided that—

(a) where the pooled account is held in a non-EEA state—

---

[1] As amended by the Financial Services and Markets Act 2000 (Regulated Activities) (Amendment) Order 2010 (SI 2010/86) Sch.1 para.10(2) (effective February 24, 2010).

      (i)   that state imposes requirements to combat money laundering and terrorist financing which are consistent with international standards; and

      (ii)   the independent legal professional is supervised in that state for compliance with those requirements; and

  (b)   information on the identity of the persons on whose behalf monies are held in the pooled account is available, on request, to the institution which acts as a depository institution for the account.

(5)   The customer is a public authority in the United Kingdom.

(6)   The customer is a public authority which fulfils all the conditions set out in paragraph 2 of Schedule 2 to these Regulations.

(7)   The product is—

  (a)   a life insurance contract where the annual premium is no more than 1,000 euro or where a single premium of no more than 2,500 euro is paid;

  (b)   an insurance contract for the purposes of a pension scheme where the contract contains no surrender clause and cannot be used as collateral;

  (c)   a pension, superannuation or similar scheme which provides retirement benefits to employees, where contributions are made by an employer or by way of deduction from an employee's wages and the scheme rules do not permit the assignment of a member's interest under the scheme (other than an assignment permitted by section 44 of the Welfare Reform and Pensions Act 1999 (disapplication of restrictions on alienation) or section 91(5)(a) of the Pensions Act 1995 (inalienability of occupational pension)); or

  (d)[1]   electronic money, within the meaning of Article 2(2) of the electronic money directive, where—

      (i)   if the device cannot be recharged, the maximum amount stored in the device is no more than 250 euro or, in the case of electronic money used to carry out payment transactions within the United Kingdom, 500 euro; or

      (ii)   if the device can be recharged, a limit of 2,500 euro is imposed on the total amount transacted in a calendar year, except when an amount of 1,000 euro or more is redeemed in the same calendar year by the electronic money holder (within the meaning of Article 11 of the electronic money directive).

(8)   The product and any transaction related to such product fulfils all the conditions set out in paragraph 3 of Schedule 2 to these Regulations.

(9)   The product is a child trust fund within the meaning given by section 1(2) of the Child Trust Funds Act 2004.

(10)[2]   The product is a junior ISA within the meaning given by regulation 2B of the Individual Savings Account Regulations 1998.

Enhanced customer due diligence and ongoing monitoring

14.—(1)   A relevant person must apply on a risk-sensitive basis enhanced customer due diligence measures and enhanced ongoing monitoring—

---

[1] As substituted by the Electronic Money Regulations 2011 (SI 2011/99) Sch.4(2) para.19(c) (effective April 30, 2011).

[2] As inserted by the Money Laundering (Amendment) Regulations 2011 (SI 2011/1781) reg.2 (effective November 1, 2011).

(a) in accordance with paragraphs (2) to (4);

(b) in any other situation which by its nature can present a higher risk of money laundering or terrorist financing.

(2) Where the customer has not been physically present for identification purposes, a relevant person must take specific and adequate measures to compensate for the higher risk, for example, by applying one or more of the following measures—

(a) ensuring that the customer's identity is established by additional documents, data or information;

(b) supplementary measures to verify or certify the documents supplied, or requiring confirmatory certification by a credit or financial institution which is subject to the money laundering directive;

(c) ensuring that the first payment is carried out through an account opened in the customer's name with a credit institution.

(3) A credit institution ("the correspondent") which has or proposes to have a correspondent banking relationship with a respondent institution ("the respondent") from a non-EEA state must—

(a) gather sufficient information about the respondent to understand fully the nature of its business;

(b) determine from publicly-available information the reputation of the respondent and the quality of its supervision;

(c) assess the respondent's anti-money laundering and anti-terrorist financing controls;

(d) obtain approval from senior management before establishing a new correspondent banking relationship;

(e) document the respective responsibilities of the respondent and correspondent; and

(f) be satisfied that, in respect of those of the respondent's customers who have direct access to accounts of the correspondent, the respondent—

(i) has verified the identity of, and conducts ongoing monitoring in respect of, such customers; and

(ii) is able to provide to the correspondent, upon request, the documents, data or information obtained when applying customer due diligence measures and ongoing monitoring.

(4) A relevant person who proposes to have a business relationship or carry out an occasional transaction with a politically exposed person must—

(a) have approval from senior management for establishing the business relationship with that person;

(b) take adequate measures to establish the source of wealth and source of funds which are involved in the proposed business relationship or occasional transaction; and

(c) where the business relationship is entered into, conduct enhanced ongoing monitoring of the relationship.

(5) In paragraph (4), "a politically exposed person" means a person who is—

(a) an individual who is or has, at any time in the preceding year, been entrusted with a prominent public function by—

(i) a state other than the United Kingdom;

        (ii)[1] an EU institution; or

        (iii)   an international body,

        including a person who falls in any of the categories listed in paragraph 4(1)(a) of Schedule 2;

    (b)   an immediate family member of a person referred to in sub-paragraph (a), including a person who falls in any of the categories listed in paragraph 4(1)(c) of Schedule 2; or

    (c)   a known close associate of a person referred to in sub-paragraph (a), including a person who falls in either of the categories listed in paragraph 4(1)(d) of Schedule 2.

(6)   For the purpose of deciding whether a person is a known close associate of a person referred to in paragraph (5)(a), a relevant person need only have regard to information which is in his possession or is publicly known.

Branches and subsidiaries

15.—(1)   A credit or financial institution must require its branches and subsidiary undertakings which are located in a non-EEA state to apply, to the extent permitted by the law of that state, measures at least equivalent to those set out in these Regulations with regard to customer due diligence measures, ongoing monitoring and record-keeping.

(2)   Where the law of a non-EEA state does not permit the application of such equivalent measures by the branch or subsidiary undertaking located in that state, the credit or financial institution must—

    (a)   inform its supervisory authority accordingly; and

    (b)   take additional measures to handle effectively the risk of money laundering and terrorist financing.

(3)   In this regulation "subsidiary undertaking"—

    (a)   except in relation to an incorporated friendly society, has the meaning given by section 1162 of the Companies Act 2006 (parent and subsidiary undertakings) and, in relation to a body corporate in or formed under the law of an EEA state other than the United Kingdom, includes an undertaking which is a subsidiary undertaking within the meaning of any rule of law in force in that state for purposes connected with implementation of the European Council Seventh Company Law Directive 83/349/EEC of 13th June 1983 on consolidated accounts;

    (b)   in relation to an incorporated friendly society, means a body corporate of which the society has control within the meaning of section 13(9)(a) or (aa) of the Friendly Societies Act 1992 (control of subsidiaries and other bodies corporate).

(4)   Before the entry into force of section 1162 of the Companies Act 2006 the reference to that section in paragraph (3)(a) shall be treated as a reference to section 258 of the Companies Act 1985 (parent and subsidiary undertakings).

Shell banks, anonymous accounts etc.

16.—(1)   A credit institution must not enter into, or continue, a correspondent banking relationship with a shell bank.

---

[1] As substituted by the Treaty of Lisbon (Changes in Terminology) Order 2011 (SI 2011/1043) Pt 2 art.6(1)(c) (effective April 22, 2011).

(2)   A credit institution must take appropriate measures to ensure that it does not enter into, or continue, a corresponding banking relationship with a bank which is known to permit its accounts to be used by a shell bank.

(3)   A credit or financial institution carrying on business in the United Kingdom must not set up an anonymous account or an anonymous passbook for any new or existing customer.

(4)   As soon as reasonably practicable on or after 15th December 2007 all credit and financial institutions carrying on business in the United Kingdom must apply customer due diligence measures to, and conduct ongoing monitoring of, all anonymous accounts and passbooks in existence on that date and in any event before such accounts or passbooks are used.

(5)   A "shell bank" means a credit institution, or an institution engaged in equivalent activities, incorporated in a jurisdiction in which it has no physical presence involving meaningful decision-making and management, and which is not part of a financial conglomerate or third-country financial conglomerate.

(6)   In this regulation, "financial conglomerate" and "third-country financial conglomerate" have the meanings given by regulations 1(2) and 7(1) respectively of the Financial Conglomerates and Other Financial Groups Regulations 2004.

Reliance

17.—(1)   A relevant person may rely on a person who falls within paragraph (2) (or who the relevant person has reasonable grounds to believe falls within paragraph (2)) to apply any customer due diligence measures provided that—

(a)   the other person consents to being relied on; and

(b)   notwithstanding the relevant person's reliance on the other person, the relevant person remains liable for any failure to apply such measures.

(2)   The persons are—

(a)   a credit or financial institution which is an authorised person;

(aa)   *[As repealed by the Financial Services and Markets Act 2000 (Regulated Activities) (Amendment) (No.2) Order 2013 (SI 2013/1881) Sch.1(2) para.31 (effective July 26, 2013).]*

(b)   a relevant person who is—

(i)   an auditor, insolvency practitioner, external accountant, tax adviser or independent legal professional; and

(ii)[1]   supervised for the purposes of these Regulations by one of the bodies listed in Schedule 3;

(c)   a person who carries on business in another EEA state who is—

(i)   a credit or financial institution, auditor, insolvency practitioner, external accountant, tax adviser or independent legal professional;

(ii)   subject to mandatory professional registration recognised by law; and

(iii)   supervised for compliance with the requirements laid down in the money laundering directive in accordance with section 2 of Chapter V of that directive; or

(d)   a person who carries on business in a non-EEA state who is—

---

[1] As amended by the Money Laundering (Amendment) Regulations 2012 (SI 2012/2298) reg.5(b) (effective July 26, 2013).

      (i)   a credit or financial institution (or equivalent institution), auditor, insolvency practitioner, external accountant, tax adviser or independent legal professional;

      (ii)   subject to mandatory professional registration recognised by law;

      (iii) subject to requirements equivalent to those laid down in the money laundering directive; and

      (iv) supervised for compliance with those requirements in a manner equivalent to section 2 of Chapter V of the money laundering directive.

(3) In paragraph (2)(c)(i) and (d)(i), "auditor" and "insolvency practitioner" includes a person situated in another EEA state or a non-EEA state who provides services equivalent to the services provided by an auditor or insolvency practitioner.

(4) Nothing in this regulation prevents a relevant person applying customer due diligence measures by means of an outsourcing service provider or agent provided that the relevant person remains liable for any failure to apply such measures.

(5)[1] In this regulation, "financial institution" excludes—

    (a)   any money service business;

    (b)   any authorised payment institution, EEA authorised payment institution or small payment institution (within the meaning of the Payment Services Regulations 2009) which provides payment services mainly falling within paragraph 1(f) of Schedule 1 to those Regulations; and

    (c)[2] any electronic money institution or EEA authorised electronic money institution (within the meaning of the Electronic Money Regulations 2011) which provides payment services mainly falling within paragraph 1(f) of Schedule 1 to the Payment Services Regulations 2009.

Directions where Financial Action Task Force applies counter-measures

18. *[Repealed by the Money Laundering (Amendment) Regulations 2012 (SI 2012/2298) reg.6 (effective October 1, 2012).]*

PART 3

RECORD-KEEPING, PROCEDURES AND TRAINING

Record-keeping

19.—(1) Subject to paragraph (4), a relevant person must keep the records specified in paragraph (2) for at least the period specified in paragraph (3).

(2) The records are—

    (a)   a copy of, or the references to, the evidence of the customer's identity obtained pursuant to regulation 7, 8, 10, 14 or 16(4);

    (b)   the supporting records (consisting of the original documents or copies) in respect of a business relationship or occasional transaction which is the subject of customer due diligence measures or ongoing monitoring.

(3) The period is five years beginning on—

    (a)   in the case of the records specified in paragraph (2)(a), the date on which—

---

[1] As substituted by the Payment Services Regulations 2009 (SI 2009/209) Sch.6(2) para.6(b) (effective November 1, 2009).

[2] As inserted by the Electronic Money Regulations 2011 (SI 2011/99) Sch.4(2) para. 19(d) (effective April 30, 2011).

     (i)   the occasional transaction is completed; or

     (ii)   the business relationship ends; or

  (b)   in the case of the records specified in paragraph (2)(b)—

     (i)   where the records relate to a particular transaction, the date on which the transaction is completed;

    (ii)   for all other records, the date on which the business relationship ends.

(4)   A relevant person who is relied on by another person must keep the records specified in paragraph (2)(a) for five years beginning on the date on which he is relied on for the purposes of regulation 7, 10, 14 or 16(4) in relation to any business relationship or occasional transaction.

(5)   A person referred to in regulation 17(2)(a) or (b) who is relied on by a relevant person must, if requested by the person relying on him within the period referred to in paragraph (4)—

    (a)   as soon as reasonably practicable make available to the person who is relying on him any information about the customer (and any beneficial owner) which he obtained when applying customer due diligence measures; and

    (b)   as soon as reasonably practicable forward to the person who is relying on him copies of any identification and verification data and other relevant documents on the identity of the customer (and any beneficial owner) which he obtained when applying those measures.

(6)   A relevant person who relies on a person referred to in regulation 17(2)(c) or (d) (a "third party") to apply customer due diligence measures must take steps to ensure that the third party will, if requested by the relevant person within the period referred to in paragraph (4)—

    (a)   as soon as reasonably practicable make available to him any information about the customer (and any beneficial owner) which the third party obtained when applying customer due diligence measures; and

    (b)   as soon as reasonably practicable forward to him copies of any identification and verification data and other relevant documents on the identity of the customer (and any beneficial owner) which the third party obtained when applying those measures.

(7)   Paragraphs (5) and (6) do not apply where a relevant person applies customer due diligence measures by means of an outsourcing service provider or agent.

(8)   For the purposes of this regulation, a person relies on another person where he does so in accordance with regulation 17(1).

Policies and procedures

20.—(1)   A relevant person must establish and maintain appropriate and risk-sensitive policies and procedures relating to—

    (a)   customer due diligence measures and ongoing monitoring;

    (b)   reporting;

    (c)   record-keeping;

    (d)   internal control;

    (e)   risk assessment and management;

    (f)   the monitoring and management of compliance with, and the internal communication of, such policies and procedures,

in order to prevent activities related to money laundering and terrorist financing.

(2)   The policies and procedures referred to in paragraph (1) include policies and procedures—

    (a)   which provide for the identification and scrutiny of—

    (i)   complex or unusually large transactions;

    (ii) unusual patterns of transactions which have no apparent economic or visible lawful purpose; and

    (iii) any other activity which the relevant person regards as particularly likely by its nature to be related to money laundering or terrorist financing;

(b) which specify the taking of additional measures, where appropriate, to prevent the use for money laundering or terrorist financing of products and transactions which might favour anonymity;

(c) to determine whether a customer is a politically exposed person;

(d) under which—

    (i)   an individual in the relevant person's organisation is a nominated officer under Part 7 of the Proceeds of Crime Act 2002 and Part 3 of the Terrorism Act 2000;

    (ii) anyone in the organisation to whom information or other matter comes in the course of the business as a result of which he knows or suspects or has reasonable grounds for knowing or suspecting that a person is engaged in money laundering or terrorist financing is required to comply with Part 7 of the Proceeds of Crime Act 2002 or, as the case may be, Part 3 of the Terrorism Act 2000; and

    (iii) where a disclosure is made to the nominated officer, he must consider it in the light of any relevant information which is available to the relevant person and determine whether it gives rise to knowledge or suspicion or reasonable grounds for knowledge or suspicion that a person is engaged in money laundering or terrorist financing.

(3)   Paragraph (2)(d) does not apply where the relevant person is an individual who neither employs nor acts in association with any other person.

(4)   A credit or financial institution must establish and maintain systems which enable it to respond fully and rapidly to enquiries from financial investigators accredited under section 3 of the Proceeds of Crime Act 2002 (accreditation and training), persons acting on behalf of the Scottish Ministers in their capacity as an enforcement authority under that Act, officers of Revenue and Customs or constables as to—

(a) whether it maintains, or has maintained during the previous five years, a business relationship with any person; and

(b) the nature of that relationship.

(5)[1] A credit or financial institution must communicate where relevant the policies and procedures which it establishes and maintains in accordance with this regulation to its branches and subsidiary undertakings which are located outside the United Kingdom.

(5A)[2] A relevant person who is an issuer of electronic money must appoint an individual to monitor and manage compliance with, and the internal communication of, the policies and procedures relating to the matters referred to in paragraph (1)(a) to (e), and in particular to—

---

[1] As amended by the Recognised Auction Platforms Regulations 2011 (SI 2011/2699) Pt 4 reg.11(4) (effective December 12, 2011).

[2] As inserted by the Electronic Money Regulations 2011 (SI 2011/99) Sch.4(2) para.19(e) (effective April 30, 2011).

(a) identify any situations of higher risk of money laundering or terrorist financing;

(b) maintain a record of its policies and procedures, risk assessment and risk management including the application of such policies and procedures;

(c) apply measures to ensure that such policies and procedures are taken into account in all relevant functions including in the development of new products, dealing with new customers and in changes to business activities; and

(d) provide information to senior management about the operation and effectiveness of such policies and procedures at least annually.

(6) In this regulation—

"politically exposed person" has the same meaning as in regulation 14(4);
"subsidiary undertaking" has the same meaning as in regulation 15.

Training

21. A relevant person must take appropriate measures so that all relevant employees of his are—

(a) made aware of the law relating to money laundering and terrorist financing; and

(b) regularly given training in how to recognise and deal with transactions and other activities which may be related to money laundering or terrorist financing.

PART 4

SUPERVISION AND REGISTRATION

Interpretation

Interpretation

22.—(1) In this Part—

"Annex I financial institution" means any undertaking which falls within regulation 3(3)(a) other than—

(a) *[As repealed by the Financial Services and Markets Act 2000 (Regulated Activities) (Amendment) (No.2) Order 2013 (SI 2013/ 1881) Sch.1(2) para.31 (effective July 26, 2013).]*

(b) a money service business;

(c) an authorised person;

(d)[1] a bill payment service provider; or

(e)[2] a telecommunication, digital and IT payment service provider;

[As repealed by the Financial Services and Markets Act 2000 (Regulated Activities) (Amendment) (No.2) Order 2013 (SI 2013/1881) Sch.1(2) para.31 (effective July 26, 2013).]

---

[1] As inserted by the Payment Services Regulations 2009 (SI 2009/209) Sch.6(2) para.6(c) (effective November 1, 2009).

[2] As inserted by the Payment Services Regulations 2009 (SI 2009/209) Sch.6(2) para.6(c) (effective November 1, 2009).

[1]"recognised investment exchange" has the same meaning as in section 285 of the 2000 Act (exemption for recognised investment exchanges and clearing houses).

(2)   *[As repealed by the Financial Services and Markets Act 2000 (Regulated Activities) (Amendment) (No.2) Order 2013 (SI 2013/1881) Sch.1(2) para.31 (effective July 26, 2013).]*

Supervision

Supervisory authorities

23.—(1)   Subject to paragraph (2), the following bodies are supervisory authorities—

    (a)   the Authority is the supervisory authority for—

        [2](i)   credit and financial institutions which are authorised persons but not excluded money service businesses;

        (ii)   trust or company service providers which are authorised persons;

        (iii)   Annex I financial institutions;

        (iv)[3]   electronic money institutions;

        (v)[4]   auction platforms;

        (vi)[5]   credit unions in Northern Ireland;

        (vii)[6]   recognised investment exchanges.

    (b)   *[As repealed by the Financial Services and Markets Act 2000 (Regulated Activities) (Amendment) (No.2) Order 2013 (SI 2013/1881) Sch.1(2) para.31 (effective July 26, 2013).]*

    (c)   each of the professional bodies listed in Schedule 3 is the supervisory authority for relevant persons who are regulated by it;

    (d)   the Commissioners are the supervisory authority for—

        (i)   high value dealers;

        (ii)   money service businesses which are not supervised by the Authority;

        (iii)   trust or company service providers which are not supervised by the Authority or one of the bodies listed in Schedule 3;

        (iv)   auditors, external accountants and tax advisers who are not supervised by one of the bodies listed in Schedule 3;

        (v)[7]   bill payment service providers which are not supervised by the Authority;

---

[1] As inserted by the Money Laundering (Amendment) Regulations 2012 (SI 2012/2298) reg.7 (effective October 1, 2012).

[2] As amended by the Financial Services and Markets Act 2000 (Regulated Activities) (Amendment) (No.2) Order 2013 (SI 2013/1881) Sch.1(2) para.31 (effective July 26, 2013).

[3] As inserted by the Electronic Money Regulations 2011 (SI 2011/99) Sch.4(2) para.19(f) (effective April 30, 2011).

[4] As inserted by the Recognised Auction Platforms Regulations 2011 (SI 2011/2699) Pt 4 reg.11(5) (effective December 12, 2011).

[5] Possible drafting error—reg.23(1)(a)(v) purportedly inserted but that provision already exists so inserted after existing reg.23(1)(a)(v) by the Money Laundering (Amendment No.2) Regulations 2011 (SI 2011/2833) reg.2(a)(i) (effective March 31, 2012).

[6] As inserted by the Money Laundering (Amendment) Regulations 2012 (SI 2012/2298) reg.8 (effective October 1, 2012).

[7] As inserted by the Payment Services Regulations 2009 (SI 2009/209) Sch.6(2) para.6(d) (effective November 1, 2009).

    (vi)[1]   telecommunication, digital and IT payment service providers which are not supervised by the Authority.

    (vii)[2]   estate agents.

(e)   the Gambling Commission is the supervisory authority for casinos;

(f)   DETI is the supervisory authority for—

    (i)   *[As revoked by the Money Laundering (Amendment No.2) Regulations 2011 (SI 2011/2833) reg.2(a)(ii) (effective March 31, 2012).]*

    (ii)   insolvency practitioners authorised by it under article 351 of the Insolvency (Northern Ireland) Order 1989;

(g)   the Secretary of State is the supervisory authority for insolvency practitioners authorised by him under section 393 of the Insolvency Act 1986 (grant, refusal and withdrawal of authorisation).

(2)   Where under paragraph (1) there is more than one supervisory authority for a relevant person, the supervisory authorities may agree that one of them will act as the supervisory authority for that person.

(3)   Where an agreement has been made under paragraph (2), the authority which has agreed to act as the supervisory authority must notify the relevant person or publish the agreement in such manner as it considers appropriate.

(4)   Where no agreement has been made under paragraph (2), the supervisory authorities for a relevant person must cooperate in the performance of their functions under these Regulations.

[3](5)   For the purposes of this regulation, a money service business is an "excluded money service business" if it is an authorised person who has permission under the 2000 Act which relates to or is connected with a contract of the kind mentioned in paragraph 23 or paragraph 23B of Schedule 2 to that Act (credit agreements and contracts for hire of goods) but does not have permission to carry on any other kind of regulated activity.

[4](6)   Paragraph (5) must be read with—

(a)   section 22 of the 2000 Act,

(b)   any relevant order under that section, and

(c)   Schedule 2 to that Act.

Duties of supervisory authorities

24.—(1)   A supervisory authority must effectively monitor the relevant persons for whom it is the supervisory authority and take necessary measures for the purpose of securing compliance by such persons with the requirements of these Regulations.

(1A)[5]   The Authority, when carrying out its supervisory functions in relation to an auction platform—

(a)   must effectively monitor the auction platform's compliance with—

---

[1] As inserted by the Payment Services Regulations 2009 (SI 2009/209) Sch.6(2) para.6(d) (effective November 1, 2009).

[2] As inserted by the Public Bodies (Abolition of the National Consumer Council and Transfer of the Office of Fair Trading's Functions in relation to Estate Agents etc) Order 2014 (SI 2014/631) Sch.3 para.2 (effective March 31, 2014).

[3] As inserted by the Financial Services and Markets Act 2000 (Regulated Activities) (Amendment) (No.2) Order 2013 (SI 2013/1881) Sch.1(2) para.31 (effective July 26, 2013).

[4] As inserted by the Financial Services and Markets Act 2000 (Regulated Activities) (Amendment) (No.2) Order 2013 (SI 2013/1881) Sch.1(2) para.31 (effective July 26, 2013).

[5] As inserted by the Recognised Auction Platforms Regulations 2011 (SI 2011/2699) Pt 4 reg.11(6) (effective December 12, 2011).

      (i)   the customer due diligence requirements of Articles 19 and 20(6) of the emission allowance auctioning regulation;

     (ii)   the monitoring and record keeping requirements of Article 54 of the emission allowance auctioning regulation; and

   (iii)   the notification requirements of Article 55(2) and (3) of the emission allowance auctioning regulation; and

   (b)   may monitor the auction platform's compliance with regulations 20 and 21 of these Regulations.

(2)[1]   A supervisory authority which, in the course of carrying out any of its functions under these Regulations, knows or suspects that a person is or has engaged in money laundering or terrorist financing must promptly inform the National Crime Agency.

(3)   A disclosure made under paragraph (2) is not to be taken to breach any restriction, however imposed, on the disclosure of information.

(4)[2]   The functions of the Authority under these Regulations shall be treated for the purposes of Parts 1, 2 and 4 of Schedule 1ZA to the 2000 Act (the Financial Conduct Authority) as functions conferred on the Authority under that Act.

(5)[3]   The functions of the PRA under these Regulations shall be treated for the purposes of Parts 1, 2 and 4 of Schedule 1ZA to the 2000 Act (the Prudential Regulation Authority) as functions conferred on the PRA under that Act.

Disclosure by supervisory authorities

24A.—[4](1)   A supervisory authority may disclose to another supervisory authority information it holds relevant to its functions under these Regulations, provided the disclosure is made for purposes connected with the effective exercise of the functions of either supervisory authority under these Regulations.

(2)   Information disclosed to a supervisory authority under paragraph (1) may not be further disclosed by that authority, except—

   (a)   in accordance with paragraph (1);

 (aa)[5]   by the Authority to the PRA, where the information concerns a PRA-authorised person or a person who has a qualifying relationship with a PRA-authorised person;

   (b)   with a view to the institution of, or otherwise for the purposes of, any criminal or other enforcement proceedings; or

   (c)   as otherwise required by law.

Registration of high value dealers, money service businesses and trust or company service providers

Duty to maintain registers

25.—(1)   The Commissioners must maintain registers of—

---

[1] As amended by the Crime and Courts Act 2013 (c.22) Sch.8 para.190 (effective October 7, 2013).

[2] As amended by the Financial Services Act 2012 (Consequential Amendments and Transitional Provisions) Order 2013 (SI 2013/472) Sch.2 para.129 (effective April 1, 2013).

[3] As inserted by the Financial Services Act 2012 (Consequential Amendments and Transitional Provisions) Order 2013 (SI 2013/472) Sch.2 para.129 (effective April 1, 2013).

[4] As inserted by the Money Laundering (Amendment) Regulations 2012 (SI 2012/2298) reg.9 (effective October 1, 2012).

[5] As inserted by the Financial Services Act 2012 (Consequential Amendments and Transitional Provisions) Order 2013 (SI 2013/472) Sch.2 para.129 (effective April 1, 2013).

    (a)   high value dealers;

    (b)   money service businesses for which they are the supervisory authority;

    (c)   trust or company service providers for which they are the supervisory authority;

    (d)[1] bill payment service providers for which they are the supervisory authority; and

    (e)[2] telecommunication, digital and IT payment service providers for which they are the supervisory authority.

(2)   The Commissioners may keep the registers in any form they think fit.

(3)   The Commissioners may publish or make available for public inspection all or part of a register maintained under this regulation.

Requirement to be registered

26.—(1) A person in respect of whom the Commissioners are required to maintain a register under regulation 25 must not act as a—

    (a)   high value dealer;

    (b)   money service business;

    (c)   trust or company service provider,

    (d)[3] bill payment service provider; or

    (e)[4] telecommunication, digital and IT payment service provider,

unless he is included in the register.

(2)   Paragraph (1) and regulation 29 are subject to the transitional provisions set out in regulation 50.

Applications for registration in a register maintained under regulation 25

27.—(1) An applicant for registration in a register maintained under regulation 25 must make an application in such manner and provide such information as the Commissioners may specify.

(2)   The information which the Commissioners may specify includes—

    (a)   the applicant's name and (if different) the name of the business;

    (b)   the nature of the business;

    (c)   the name of the nominated officer (if any);

    (d)   in relation to a money service business or trust or company service provider—

        (i)   the name of any person who effectively directs or will direct the business and any beneficial owner of the business; and

        (ii) information needed by the Commissioners to decide whether they must refuse the application pursuant to regulation 28.

(3)   At any time after receiving an application and before determining it, the Commissioners may require the applicant to provide, within 21 days beginning with the date of being requested to do so, such further information as they reasonably consider necessary to enable them to determine the application.

---

[1] As inserted by the Payment Services Regulations 2009 (SI 2009/209) Sch.6(2) para.6(e) (effective November 1, 2009).

[2] As inserted by the Payment Services Regulations 2009 (SI 2009/209) Sch.6(2) para.6(e) (effective November 1, 2009).

[3] As inserted by the Payment Services Regulations 2009 (SI 2009/209) Sch.6(2) para.6(f) (effective November 1, 2009).

[4] As inserted by the Payment Services Regulations 2009 (SI 2009/209) Sch.6(2) para.6(f) (effective November 1, 2009).

(4)   If at any time after the applicant has provided the Commissioners with any information under paragraph (1) or (3)—

    (a)   there is a material change affecting any matter contained in that information; or

    (b)   it becomes apparent to that person that the information contains a significant inaccuracy,

he must provide the Commissioners with details of the change or, as the case may be, a correction of the inaccuracy within 30 days beginning with the date of the occurrence of the change (or the discovery of the inaccuracy) or within such later time as may be agreed with the Commissioners.

(5)   The obligation in paragraph (4) applies also to material changes or significant inaccuracies affecting any matter contained in any supplementary information provided pursuant to that paragraph.

(6)   Any information to be provided to the Commissioners under this regulation must be in such form or verified in such manner as they may specify.

Fit and proper test

28.—(1)   The Commissioners must refuse to register an applicant as a money service business or trust or company service provider if they are satisfied that—

    (a)   the applicant;

    (b)   a person who effectively directs, or will effectively direct, the business or service provider;

    (c)   a beneficial owner of the business or service provider; or

    (d)[1]   the nominated officer of the business or service provider,

is not a fit and proper person with regard to the risk of money laundering or terrorist financing.

(2)   *[Repealed by the Money Laundering (Amendment) Regulations 2012 (SI 2012/2298) reg.10 (effective October 1, 2012).]*

Determination of applications under regulation 27

29.—(1)   Subject to regulation 28, the Commissioners may refuse to register an applicant for registration in a register maintained under regulation 25 only if—

    (a)   any requirement of, or imposed under, regulation 27 has not been complied with;

    (b)   it appears to the Commissioners that any information provided pursuant to regulation 27 is false or misleading in a material particular; or

    (c)   the applicant has failed to pay a charge imposed by them under regulation 35(1).

(2)   The Commissioners must within 45 days beginning either with the date on which they receive the application or, where applicable, with the date on which they receive any further information required under regulation 27(3), give the applicant notice of—

    (a)   their decision to register the applicant; or

    (b)   the following matters—

        (i)   their decision not to register the applicant;

        (ii)   the reasons for their decision;

---

[1] As amended by the Money Laundering (Amendment) Regulations 2012 (SI 2012/2298) reg.10 (effective October 1, 2012).

(iii)[1] the right to a review under regulation 43A; and

(iv)[2] the right to appeal under regulation 43.

(3) The Commissioners must, as soon as practicable after deciding to register a person, include him in the relevant register.

Cancellation of registration in a register maintained under regulation 25

30.—(1)[3] The Commissioners must cancel the registration of a money service business or trust or company service provider in a register maintained under regulation 25(1) if, at any time after registration, they are satisfied that he or any person mentioned in regulation 28(1)(b), (c) or (d) is not a fit and proper person within the meaning of regulation 28.

(2)[3] The Commissioners may cancel a person's registration in a register maintained by them under regulation 25 if, at any time after registration—

(a) it appears to them that that any condition in regulation 29(1) is met; or

(b) the person has failed to comply with any requirement of a notice given under regulation 37.

(2A)[4] The Commissioners may cancel the registration of a money service business in a register maintained under regulation 25(1)(b) where the money service business—

(a) is providing a payment service in the United Kingdom, or is purporting to do so;

(b) is not included in the register of payment service providers maintained by the Authority under regulation 4(1) of the Payment Service Regulations 2009; and

(c) is not a person mentioned in paragraphs (c) to (h) of the definition of a payment service provider in regulation 2(1) of the Payment Services Regulations 2009, or a person to whom regulation 3 or 121 of those Regulations applies.

(3) Where the Commissioners decide to cancel a person's registration they must give him notice of—

(a) their decision and, subject to paragraph (4), the date from which the cancellation takes effect;

(b) the reasons for their decision;

(c)[5] the right to a review under regulation 43A; and

(d)[6] the right to appeal under regulation 43.

(4) If the Commissioners—

(a) consider that the interests of the public require the cancellation of a person's registration to have immediate effect; and

---

[1] As substituted by the Transfer of Tribunal Functions and Revenue and Customs Appeals Order 2009 (SI 2009/56) Sch.2 para.169 (effective April 1, 2009).

[2] As substituted by the Transfer of Tribunal Functions and Revenue and Customs Appeals Order 2009 (SI 2009/56) Sch.2 para.169 (effective April 1, 2009).

[3] As amended by the Money Laundering (Amendment) Regulations 2012 (SI 2012/2298) reg.11 (effective October 1, 2012).

[4] As inserted by the Payment Services Regulations 2012 (SI 2012/1791) reg.2 (effective October 1, 2012).

[5] As substituted by the Transfer of Tribunal Functions and Revenue and Customs Appeals Order 2009 (SI 2009/56) Sch.2 para.170 (effective April 1, 2009).

[6] As substituted by the Transfer of Tribunal Functions and Revenue and Customs Appeals Order 2009 (SI 2009/56) Sch.2 para.170 (effective April 1, 2009).

    (b)   include a statement to that effect and the reasons for it in the notice given under paragraph (3),

the cancellation takes effect when the notice is given to the person.

Requirement to inform the Authority

Requirement on authorised person to inform the Authority

    31.—(1)   An authorised person whose supervisory authority is the Authority must, before acting as a money service business or a trust or company service provider or within 28 days of so doing, inform the Authority that he intends, or has begun, to act as such.

    (1)   Paragraph (1) does not apply to an authorised person who—

        (a)   immediately before 15th December 2007 was acting as a money service business or a trust or company service provider and continues to act as such after that date; and

        (b)[1]   before 15th January 2008 informs the Financial Services Authority that he is or was acting as such.

    (3)   Where an authorised person whose supervisory authority is the Authority ceases to act as a money service business or a trust or company service provider, he must immediately inform the Authority.

    (4)   Any requirement imposed by this regulation is to be treated as if it were a requirement imposed by or under the 2000 Act.

    (5)   Any information to be provided to the Authority under this regulation must be in such form or verified in such manner as it may specify.

Registration of Annex I financial institutions, estate agents etc.

Power to maintain registers

    32.—(1)   The supervisory authorities mentioned in paragraph (2), (3) or (4) may, in order to fulfil their duties under regulation 24, maintain a register under this regulation.

    (2)   The Authority may maintain a register of Annex I financial institutions.

    (3)   *[As repealed by the Financial Services and Markets Act 2000 (Regulated Activities) (Amendment) (No.2) Order 2013 (SI 2013/1881) Sch.1(2) para.31 (effective July 26, 2013).]*

    (4)   The Commissioners may maintain registers of—

        (a)   auditors;

        (b)   external accountants; and

        (c)   tax advisers,

who are not supervised by the Secretary of State, DETI or any of the professional bodies listed in Schedule 3.

    (4A)[2]   The Commissioners may maintain a register of estate agents.

---

[1] As amended by the Financial Services Act 2012 (Consequential Amendments and Transitional Provisions) Order 2013 (SI 2013/472) Sch.2 para.129 (effective April 1, 2013).

[2] As amended by the Public Bodies (Abolition of the National Consumer Council and Transfer of the Office of Fair Trading's Functions in relation to Estate Agents etc) Order 2014 (SI 2014/631) Sch.3 para.2 (effective March 31, 2014).

(5)   Where a supervisory authority decides to maintain a register under this regulation, it must take reasonable steps to bring its decision to the attention of those relevant persons in respect of whom the register is to be established.

(6)   A supervisory authority may keep a register under this regulation in any form it thinks fit.

(7)   A supervisory authority may publish or make available to public inspection all or part of a register maintained by it under this regulation.

Requirement to be registered

33. Where a supervisory authority decides to maintain a register under regulation 32 in respect of any description of relevant persons and establishes a register for that purpose, a relevant person of that description may not carry on the business or profession in question for a period of more than six months beginning on the date on which the supervisory authority establishes the register unless he is included in the register.

Applications for and cancellation of registration in a register maintained under regulation 32

34.—[1](1) Regulations 27, 29 (with the omission of the words "Subject to regulation 28" in regulation 29(1)) and 30(2), (3) and (4) apply to registration in a register maintained by the Commissioners under regulation 32 as they apply to registration in a register maintained under regulation 25.

(2) Regulation 27 applies to registration in a register maintained by the Authority or under regulation 32 as it applies to registration in a register maintained under regulation 25 and, for this purpose, references to the Commissioners are to be treated as references to the Authority.

(3) The Authority may refuse to register an applicant for registration in a register maintained under regulation 32 only if—

(a) any requirement of, or imposed under, regulation 27 has not been complied with;

(b) it appears to the Authority that any information provided pursuant to regulation 27 is false or misleading in a material particular; or

(c) the applicant has failed to pay a charge imposed by the Authority under regulation 35(1).

(4) The Authority as the case may be, must, within 45 days beginning either with the date on which it receives an application or, where applicable, with the date on which it receives any further information required under regulation 27(3), give the applicant notice of—

(a) its decision to register the applicant; or

(b) the following matters—

(i) that it is minded not to register the applicant;

(ii) the reasons for being minded not to register him; and

(iii) the right to make representations to it within a specified period (which may not be less than 28 days).

(5) The Authority must then decide, within a reasonable period, whether to register the applicant and it must give the applicant notice of—

(a) its decision to register the applicant; or

(b) the following matters—

(i) its decision not to register the applicant;

(ii) the reasons for its decision; and

(iii) the right to appeal under regulation 44(1)(b).

(6) The Authority must, as soon as reasonably practicable after deciding to register a person, include him in the relevant register.

---

[1] As amended by the Financial Services and Markets Act 2000 (Regulated Activities) (Amendment) (No.2) Order 2013 (SI 2013/1881) Sch.1(2) para.31 (effective July 26, 2013).

(7)[1] The Authority may cancel a person's registration in a register maintained by them under regulation 32 if, at any time after registration—

    (a)   it appears to them that any condition in paragraph (3) is met; or

    (b)   the person has failed to comply with any requirement of a notice given under regulation 37.

(8) Where the Authority or proposes to cancel a person's registration, it must give him notice of—

    (a)   its proposal to cancel his registration;

    (b)   the reasons for the proposed cancellation; and

    (c)   the right to make representations to it within a specified period (which may not be less than 28 days).

(9) The Authority must then decide, within a reasonable period, whether to cancel the person's registration and it must give him notice of—

    (a)   its decision not to cancel his registration; or

    (b)   the following matters—

        (i)   its decision to cancel his registration and, subject to paragraph (10), the date from which cancellation takes effect;

        (ii)   the reasons for its decision; and

        (iii)   the right to appeal under regulation 44(1)(b).

(10) If the Authority—

    (a)   considers that the interests of the public require the cancellation of a person's registration to have immediate effect; and

    (b)   includes a statement to that effect and the reasons for it in the notice given under paragraph (9)(b),

the cancellation takes effect when the notice is given to the person.

(11) In paragraphs (3) and (4), references to regulation 27 are to be treated as references to that paragraph as applied by paragraph (2) of this regulation.

Financial provisions

Costs of supervision

35.—[2](1) The Authority and the Commissioners may impose charges—

    (a)   on applicants for registration;

    (b)   on relevant persons supervised by them.

(2) Charges levied under paragraph (1) must not exceed such amount as the Authority or the Commissioners (as the case may be) consider will enable them to meet any expenses reasonably incurred by them in carrying out their functions under these Regulations or for any incidental purpose.

(3) Without prejudice to the generality of paragraph (2), a charge may be levied in respect of each of the premises at which a person carries on (or proposes to carry on) business.

(4)[3] The Authority must pay to the Treasury any amounts received by the Financial Services Authority during the financial year beginning with 1st April 2012 year by way of penalties imposed under regulation 42 after deducting any

---

[1] As substituted by the Money Laundering (Amendment) Regulations 2012 (SI 2012/2298) reg.12 (effective October 1, 2012).

[2] As amended by the Financial Services and Markets Act 2000 (Regulated Activities) (Amendment) (No.2) Order 2013 (SI 2013/1881) Sch.1(2) para.31 (effective July 26, 2013).

[3] Reg.35(4)–(4D) substituted for reg.34(4) by the Payment to Treasury of Penalties Regulations 2013 (SI 2013/429) reg.2(1) (effective April 1, 2013).

amountsthe Financial Services Authority has, prior to 1st April 2013, applied towards expenses incurred by it in carrying out its functions under these Regulations or for any incidental purpose.

(4A)[1] The Authority must in respect of the financial year beginning with 1st April 2013 and each subsequent financial year pay to the Treasury any amounts received by it during the year by way of penalties imposed under regulation 42.

(4B)[2] The Treasury may give directions to the Authority as to how the Authority is to comply with its duties under paragraphs (4) and (4A).

4(C)[3] The directions may in particular—

(a) specify the time when any payment is required to be made to the Treasury, and

(b) require the Authority to provide the Treasury at specified times with information relating to penalties that the Authority has imposed under regulation 42.

(4D)[4] The Treasury must pay into the Consolidated Fund any sums received by them under this regulation.

(5) In paragraph (2), "expenses" in relation to the Authority includes expenses incurred by a local weights and measures authority or DETI pursuant to arrangements made for the purposes of these Regulations with the Authority—

(a) by or on behalf of the authority; or

(b) by DETI.

PART 5

ENFORCEMENT

Powers of designated authorities

Interpretation

[5]36. In this Part—

"designated authority" means—

(a) the Authority; and

(b) the Commissioners;

(c) *[As repealed by the Financial Services and Markets Act 2000 (Regulated Activities) (Amendment) (No.2) Order 2013 (SI 2013/ 1881) Sch.1(2) para.31 (effective July 26, 2013).]*

(d) *[Revoked by the Money Laundering (Amendment No.2) Regulations 2011 (SI 2011/2833) reg.2(b)(ii) (effective March 31, 2012).]*

"officer", except in regulations 40(3), 41 and 47 means—

(a) an officer of the Authority, including a member of the Authority's staff or an agent of the Authority;

---

[1] Reg.35(4)–(4D) substituted for reg.34(4) by the Payment to Treasury of Penalties Regulations 2013 (SI 2013/429) reg.2(1) (effective April 1, 2013).

[2] Reg.35(4)–(4D) substituted for reg.34(4) by the Payment to Treasury of Penalties Regulations 2013 (SI 2013/429) reg.2(1) (effective April 1, 2013).

[3] Reg.35(4)–(4D) substituted for reg.34(4) by the Payment to Treasury of Penalties Regulations 2013 (SI 2013/429) reg.2(1) (effective April 1, 2013).

[4] Reg.35(4)–(4D) substituted for reg.34(4) by the Payment to Treasury of Penalties Regulations 2013 (SI 2013/429) reg.2(1) (effective April 1, 2013).

[5] As amended by the Financial Services and Markets Act 2000 (Regulated Activities) (Amendment) (No.2) Order 2013 (SI 2013/1881) Sch.1(2) para.31 (effective July 26, 2013).

(b) an officer of Revenue and Customs;

(c) an officer of the Authority; or

(d) a relevant officer.

(e) *[Revoked by the Money Laundering (Amendment No.2) Regulations 2011 (SI 2011/2833) reg.2(c)(i) (effective March 31, 2012).]*

"recorded information" includes information recorded in any form and any document of any nature;

"relevant officer" means—

(a) in Great Britain, an officer of a local weights and measures authority;

(b) in Northern Ireland, an officer of DETI acting pursuant to arrangements made with the Authority for the purposes of these Regulations.

Power to require information from, and attendance of, relevant and connected persons

37.—(1) An officer may, by notice to a relevant person or to a person connected with a relevant person, require the relevant person or the connected person, as the case may be—

(a) to provide such information as may be specified in the notice;

(b) to produce such recorded information as may be so specified; or

(c) to attend before an officer at a time and place specified in the notice and answer questions.

(2)[1] For the purposes of paragraph (1)—

(a) "relevant person" includes a person whom a designated authority believes, or has reasonable grounds to suspect, is or has at any time been a relevant person; and

(b) a person is connected with a relevant person if the person is, or has at any time been, in relation to the relevant person, a person listed in Schedule 4 to these Regulations.

(3) An officer may exercise powers under this regulation only if the information sought to be obtained as a result is reasonably required in connection with the exercise by the designated authority for whom he acts of its functions under these Regulations.

(4) Where an officer requires information to be provided or produced pursuant to paragraph (1)(a) or (b)—

(a) the notice must set out the reasons why the officer requires the information to be provided or produced; and

(b) such information must be provided or produced—

(i) before the end of such reasonable period as may be specified in the notice; and

(ii) at such place as may be so specified.

(5) In relation to information recorded otherwise than in legible form, the power to require production of it includes a power to require the production of a copy of it in legible form or in a form from which it can readily be produced in visible and legible form.

---

[1] As substituted by the Money Laundering (Amendment) Regulations 2012 (SI 2012/2298) reg.13 (effective October 1, 2012).

(6) The production of a document does not affect any lien which a person has on the document.

(7) A person may not be required under this regulation to provide or produce information or to answer questions which he would be entitled to refuse to provide, produce or answer on grounds of legal professional privilege in proceedings in the High Court, except that a lawyer may be required to provide the name and address of his client.

(8) Subject to paragraphs (9) and (10), a statement made by a person in compliance with a requirement imposed on him under paragraph (1)(c) is admissible in evidence in any proceedings, so long as it also complies with any requirements governing the admissibility of evidence in the circumstances in question.

(9) In criminal proceedings in which a person is charged with an offence to which this paragraph applies—

(a) no evidence relating to the statement may be adduced; and

(b) no question relating to it may be asked,

by or on behalf of the prosecution unless evidence relating to it is adduced, or a question relating to it is asked, in the proceedings by or on behalf of that person.

(10) Paragraph (9) applies to any offence other than one under—

(a) section 5 of the Perjury Act 1911 (false statements without oath);

(b) section 44(2) of the Criminal Law (Consolidation)(Scotland) Act 1995 (false statements and declarations); or

(c) Article 10 of the Perjury (Northern Ireland) Order 1979 (false unsworn statements).

(11) In the application of this regulation to Scotland, the reference in paragraph (7) to—

(a) proceedings in the High Court is to be read as a reference to legal proceedings generally; and

(b)[1] an entitlement on grounds of legal professional privilege is to be read as a reference to an entitlement on the grounds of confidentiality of communications—

(i) between a professional legal adviser and his client; or

(ii) made in connection with or in contemplation of legal proceedings and for the purposes of those proceedings.

Entry, inspection without a warrant etc.

38.—(1) Where an officer has reasonable cause to believe that any premises are being used by a relevant person in connection with his business or professional activities, he may on producing evidence of his authority at any reasonable time—

(a) enter the premises;

(b) inspect the premises;

(c) observe the carrying on of business or professional activities by the relevant person;

(d) inspect any recorded information found on the premises;

(e) require any person on the premises to provide an explanation of any recorded information or to state where it may be found;

(f) in the case of a money service business or a high value dealer, inspect any cash found on the premises.

---

[1] As amended by the Money Laundering (Amendment) Regulations 2007 (SI 2007/3299) reg.2(b) (effective December 15, 2007).

(2) An officer may take copies of, or make extracts from, any recorded information found under paragraph (1).

(3) Paragraphs (1)(d) and (e) and (2) do not apply to recorded information which the relevant person would be entitled to refuse to disclose on grounds of legal professional privilege in proceedings in the High Court, except that a lawyer may be required to provide the name and address of his client and, for this purpose, regulation 37(11) applies to this paragraph as it applies to regulation 37(7).

(4) An officer may exercise powers under this regulation only if the information sought to be obtained as a result is reasonably required in connection with the exercise by the designated authority for whom he acts of its functions under these Regulations.

(5) In this regulation, "premises" means any premises other than premises used only as a dwelling.

Entry to premises under warrant

39.—(1) A justice may issue a warrant under this paragraph if satisfied on information on oath given by an officer that there are reasonable grounds for believing that the first, second or third set of conditions is satisfied.

(2) The first set of conditions is—

    (a) that there is on the premises specified in the warrant recorded information in relation to which a requirement could be imposed under regulation 37(1)(b); and

    (b) that if such a requirement were to be imposed—

        (i) it would not be complied with; or

        (ii) the recorded information to which it relates would be removed, tampered with or destroyed.

(3) The second set of conditions is—

    (a) that a person on whom a requirement has been imposed under regulation 37(1)(b) has failed (wholly or in part) to comply with it; and

    (b) that there is on the premises specified in the warrant recorded information which has been required to be produced.

(4) The third set of conditions is—

    (a) that an officer has been obstructed in the exercise of a power under regulation 38; and

    (b) that there is on the premises specified in the warrant recorded information or cash which could be inspected under regulation 38(1)(d) or (f).

(5) A justice may issue a warrant under this paragraph if satisfied on information on oath given by an officer that there are reasonable grounds for suspecting that—

    (a) an offence under these Regulations has been, is being or is about to be committed by a relevant person; and

    (b) there is on the premises specified in the warrant recorded information relevant to whether that offence has been, or is being or is about to be committed.

(6) A warrant issued under this regulation shall authorise an officer—

    (a) to enter the premises specified in the warrant;

    (b) to search the premises and take possession of any recorded information or anything appearing to be recorded information specified in the warrant or to take, in relation to any such recorded information, any other steps which may appear to be necessary for preserving it or preventing interference with it;

    (c)   to take copies of, or extracts from, any recorded information specified in the warrant;

    (d)   to require any person on the premises to provide an explanation of anyrecorded information appearing to be of the kind specified in the warrant or to state where it may be found;

    (e)   to use such force as may reasonably be necessary.

(7)[1]   Where a warrant is issued by a justice under paragraph (1) or (5) on the basis of information on oath given by an officer of the Authority, for "an officer" in paragraph (6) substitute "a constable".

  (8)   In paragraphs (1), (5) and (7), "justice" means—

    (a)   in relation to England and Wales, a justice of the peace;

    (b)   in relation to Scotland, a justice within the meaning of section 307 of the Criminal Procedure (Scotland) Act 1995 (interpretation);

    (c)   in relation to Northern Ireland, a lay magistrate.

(9)[2]   In the application of this regulation to Scotland, the references in paragraphs (1), (5) and (7) to information on oath are to be read as references to evidence on oath.

Failure to comply with information requirement

40.—(1)   If, on an application made by—

    (a)   a designated authority; or

  [3](b)   a local weights and measures authority or DETI pursuant to arrangements made with the Authority—

       (i)   by or on behalf of the authority; or

      (ii)   by DETI,

it appears to the court that a person (the "information defaulter") has failed to do something that he was required to do under regulation 37(1), the court may make an order under this regulation.

  (2)   An order under this regulation may require the information defaulter—

    (a)   to do the thing that he failed to do within such period as may be specified in the order;

    (b)   otherwise to take such steps to remedy the consequences of the failure as may be so specified.

  (3)   If the information defaulter is a body corporate, a partnership or an unincorporated body of persons which is not a partnership, the order may require any officer of the body corporate, partnership or body, who is (wholly or partly) responsible for the failure to meet such costs of the application as are specified in the order.

  (4)   In this regulation, "court" means—

    (a)   in England and Wales and Northern Ireland, the High Court or the county court;

---

[1] As amended by the Money Laundering (Amendment) Regulations 2007 (SI 2007/3299) reg.2(c) (effective December 15, 2007).

[2] As amended by the Money Laundering (Amendment) Regulations 2007 (SI 2007/3299) reg.2(b) (effective December 15, 2007).

[3] As amended by the Financial Services and Markets Act 2000 (Regulated Activities) (Amendment) (No.2) Order 2013 (SI 2013/1881) Sch.1(2) para.31 (effective July 26, 2013).

(b)[1] in Scotland, the Court of Session or the sheriff court.

Powers of relevant officers

41.—[2](1) A relevant officer may only exercise powers under regulations 37 to 39 pursuant to arrangements made with the Authority—

    (a) by or on behalf of the local weights and measures authority of which he is an officer ("his authority"); or

    (b) by DETI.

(2) Anything done or omitted to be done by, or in relation to, a relevant officer in the exercise or purported exercise of a power in this Part shall be treated for all purposes as having been done or omitted to be done by, or in relation to, an officer of the Authority.

(3) Paragraph (2) does not apply for the purposes of any criminal proceedings brought against the relevant officer, his authority, DETI or the Authority, in respect of anything done or omitted to be done by the officer.

(4) A relevant officer shall not disclose to any person other than the Authority and his authority or, as the case may be, DETI information obtained by him in the exercise of such powers unless—

    (a) he has the approval of the Authority to do so; or

    (b) he is under a duty to make the disclosure.

Civil penalties, review and appeals

Power to impose civil penalties

42.—(1)[3, 4] A designated authority may impose a penalty of such amount as it considers appropriate on a person (except an auction platform) who fails to comply with any requirement in regulation 7(1), (2) or (3), 8(1) or (3), 9(2), 10(1), 11(1), 14(1), 15(1) or (2), 16(1), (2), (3) or (4), 19(1), (4), (5) or (6), 20(1), (4) or (5), 21, 26, 27(4) or 33.

(1A)[5] A designated authority may impose a penalty of such amount as it considers appropriate on an auction platform which fails to comply with—

    (a) the customer due diligence requirements of Article 19 or 20(6) of the emission allowance auctioning regulation;

    (b) the monitoring and record keeping requirements of Article 54 of the emission allowance auctioning regulation; or

    (c) regulation 20(1), (4) or (5) or 21 of these Regulations.

(1B)[6] A designated authority may impose a penalty of such amount as it considers appropriate on a person who fails to comply with any requirement of a notice given under regulation 37(1).

---

[1] As amended by the Money Laundering (Amendment) Regulations 2007 (SI 2007/3299) reg.2(d) (effective December 15, 2007).

[2] As amended by the Financial Services and Markets Act 2000 (Regulated Activities) (Amendment) (No.2) Order 2013 (SI 2013/1881) Sch.1(2) para.31 (effective July 26, 2013).

[3] As amended by the Recognised Auction Platforms Regulations 2011 (SI 2011/2699) Pt 4 reg.11(7) (effective December 12, 2011).

[4] As amended by the Money Laundering (Amendment) Regulations 2012 (SI 2012/2298) reg.14 (effective October 1, 2012).

[5] As inserted by the Recognised Auction Platforms Regulations 2011 (SI 2011/2699) Pt 4 reg.11(7) (effective December 12, 2011).

[6] As inserted by the Money Laundering (Amendment) Regulations 2012 (SI 2012/2298) reg.14 (effective October 1, 2012).

(1C)[1]   In paragraphs (1), (1A) and (1B), "appropriate" means effective, proportionate and dissuasive.

(2)[2, 3]   The designated authority must not impose a penalty on a person under paragraph (1), (1A) or (1B) where there are reasonable grounds for it to be satisfied that the person took all reasonable steps and exercised all due diligence to ensure that the requirement would be complied with.

(3)   In deciding whether a person has failed to comply with a requirement of these Regulations, the designated authority must consider whether he followed any relevant guidance which was at the time—

  (a)   issued by a supervisory authority or any other appropriate body;
  (b)   approved by the Treasury; and
  (c)   published in a manner approved by the Treasury as suitable in their opinion to bring the guidance to the attention of persons likely to be affected by it.

(4)[4]   In paragraph (3), an "appropriate body" means any body which regulates or is representative of any trade, profession, business or employment carried on by the person.

(4A)[5]   Where the Authority proposes to impose a penalty under this regulation on a PRA authorised person or on a person who has a qualifying relationship with a PRA-authorised person, it must consult the PRA.

(5)   Where the Commissioners decide to impose a penalty under this regulation, they must give the person notice of—

  (a)   their decision to impose the penalty and its amount;
  (b)   the reasons for imposing the penalty;
  (c)[6]   the right to a review under regulation 43A; and
  (d)[7]   the right to appeal under regulation 43.

[8](6)   Where the Authority or DETI proposes to impose a penalty under this regulation, it must give the person notice of—

  (a)   its proposal to impose the penalty and the proposed amount;
  (b)   the reasons for imposing the penalty; and
  (c)   the right to make representations to it within a specified period (which may not be less than 28 days).

---

[1] As inserted by the Money Laundering (Amendment) Regulations 2012 (SI 2012/2298) reg.14 (effective October 1, 2012).
[2] As amended by the Recognised Auction Platforms Regulations 2011 (SI 2011/2699) Pt 4 reg.11(7) (effective December 12, 2011).
[3] As amended by the Money Laundering (Amendment) Regulations 2012 (SI 2012/2298) reg.14 (effective October 1, 2012).
[4] As substituted by the Money Laundering (Amendment) Regulations 2007 (SI 2007/3299) reg.2(e) (effective December 15, 2007).
[5] As inserted by the Financial Services Act 2012 (Consequential Amendments and Transitional Provisions) Order 2013 (SI 2013/472) Sch.2 para.129 (effective April 1, 2013).
[6] As substituted by the Transfer of Tribunal Functions and Revenue and Customs Appeals Order 2009 (SI 2009/56) Sch.2 para.171 (effective April 1, 2009).
[7] As substituted by the Transfer of Tribunal Functions and Revenue and Customs Appeals Order 2009 (SI 2009/56) Sch.2 para.171 (effective April 1, 2009).
[8] As amended by the Financial Services and Markets Act 2000 (Regulated Activities) (Amendment) (No.2) Order 2013 (SI 2013/1881) Sch.1(2) para.31 (effective July 26, 2013).

¹(7)   The Authority or DETI, as the case may be, must then decide, within a reasonable period, whether to impose a penalty under this regulation and it must give the person notice of—

    (a)   its decision not to impose a penalty; or

    (b)   the following matters—

        (i)   its decision to impose a penalty and the amount;

        (ii)   the reasons for its decision; and

        (iii)   the right to appeal under regulation 44(1)(b).

(8)   A penalty imposed under this regulation is payable to the designated authority which imposes it.

Appeals against decisions of the Commissioners

43.—²(1)   This regulation applies to decisions of the Commissioners made under—

    (za)³   regulation 28, to the effect that a person is not a fit and proper person;

    (a)   regulation 29, to refuse to register an applicant;

    (b)   regulation 30, to cancel the registration of a registered person; and

    (c)   regulation 42, to impose a penalty.

(2)   Any person who is the subject of a decision to which this regulation applies may appeal to the tribunal in accordance with regulation 43F.

(3)   The provisions of Part 5 of the Value Added Tax Act 1994 (appeals), subject to the modifications set out in paragraph 1 of Schedule 5 to these Regulations, apply in respect of appeals to a tribunal made under this regulation as they apply in respect of appeals made to the tribunal under section 83 (appeals) of that Act.

(4)   A tribunal hearing an appeal under paragraph (2) has the power to—

    (a)   quash or vary any decision of the supervisory authority, including the power to reduce any penalty to such amount (including nil) as it thinks proper, and

    (b)   substitute its own decision for any decision quashed on appeal.

(5)   The modifications in Schedule 5 have effect for the purposes of appeals made under this regulation.

(6)   For the purposes of appeals under this regulation, the meaning of "tribunal" is as defined in section 82 of the Value Added Tax Act 1994.

Offer of review

43A.—⁴(1)   The Commissioners must offer a person (P) a review of a decision that has been notified to P if an appeal lies under regulation 43 in respect of the decision.

(2)   The offer of the review must be made by notice given to P at the same time as the decision is notified to P.

(3)   This regulation does not apply to the notification of the conclusions of a review.

---

¹ As amended by the Financial Services and Markets Act 2000 (Regulated Activities) (Amendment) (No.2) Order 2013 (SI 2013/1881) Sch.1(2) para.31 (effective July 26, 2013).
² As substituted by the Transfer of Tribunal Functions and Revenue and Customs Appeals Order 2009 (SI 2009/56) Sch.2 para.172 (effective April 1, 2009).
³ As amended by the Money Laundering (Amendment) Regulations 2012 (SI 2012/2298) reg.15 (effective October 1, 2012).
⁴ As inserted by the Transfer of Tribunal Functions and Revenue and Customs Appeals Order 2009 (SI 2009/56) Sch.2 para.173 (effective April 1, 2009).

Review by the Commissioners

43B.—[1](1) The Commissioners must review a decision if—

(a) they have offered a review of the decision under regulation 43A, and

(b) P notifies the Commissioners accepting the offer within 30 days from the date of the document containing the notification of the offer.

(2) But P may not notify acceptance of the offer if P has already appealed to the tribunal under regulation 43F.

(3) The Commissioners shall not review a decision if P has appealed to the tribunal under regulation 43F in respect of the decision.

Extensions of time

43C.—[2](1) If under regulation 43A, the Commissioners have offered P a review of a decision, the Commissioners may within the relevant period notify P that the relevant period is extended.

(2) If notice is given the relevant period is extended to the end of 30 days from—

(a) the date of the notice, or

(b) any other date set out in the notice or a further notice.

(3) In this regulation "relevant period" means—

(a) the period of 30 days referred to in regulation 43B(1)(b), or

(b) if notice has been given under paragraph (1) that period as extended (or as most recently extended) in accordance with paragraph (2).

Review out of time

43D.—[3](1) This regulation applies if—

(a) the Commissioners have offered a review of a decision under regulation 43A, and

(b) P does not accept the offer within the time allowed under regulation 43B(1)(b) or 43C(2).

(2) The Commissioners must review the decision under regulation 43B if—

(a) after the time allowed, P notifies the Commissioners in writing requesting a review out of time,

(b) the Commissioners are satisfied that P had a reasonable excuse for not accepting the offer or requiring review within the time allowed, and

(c) the Commissioners are satisfied that P made the request without unreasonable delay after the excuse had ceased to apply.

(3) The Commissioners shall not review a decision if P has appealed to the tribunal under regulation 43F in respect of the decision.

Nature of review etc.

43E.—[4](1) This regulation applies if the Commissioners are required to undertake a review under regulation 43B or 43D.

---

[1] As inserted by the Transfer of Tribunal Functions and Revenue and Customs Appeals Order 2009 (SI 2009/56) Sch.2 para.173 (effective April 1, 2009).

[2] As inserted by the Transfer of Tribunal Functions and Revenue and Customs Appeals Order 2009 (SI 2009/56) Sch.2 para.173 (effective April 1, 2009).

[3] As inserted by the Transfer of Tribunal Functions and Revenue and Customs Appeals Order 2009 (SI 2009/56) Sch.2 para.173 (effective April 1, 2009).

[4] As inserted by the Transfer of Tribunal Functions and Revenue and Customs Appeals Order 2009 (SI 2009/56) Sch.2 para.173 (effective April 1, 2009).

(2)   The nature and extent of the review are to be such as appear appropriate to the Commissioners in the circumstances.

(3)   For the purpose of paragraph (2), the Commissioners must, in particular, have regard to steps taken before the beginning of the review—

    (a)   by the Commissioners in reaching the decision, and

    (b)   by any person in seeking to resolve disagreement about the decision.

(4)   The review must take account of any representations made by P at a stage which gives the Commissioners a reasonable opportunity to consider them.

(5)   The review may conclude that the decision is to be—

    (a)   upheld,

    (b)   varied, or

    (c)   cancelled.

(6)   The Commissioners must give P notice of the conclusions of the review and their reasoning within—

    (a)   a period of 45 days beginning with the relevant date, or

    (b)   such other period as the Commissioners and P may agree.

(7)   In paragraph (6) "relevant date" means—

    (a)   the date the Commissioners received P's notification accepting the offer of a review (in a case falling within regulation 43A), or

    (b)   the date on which the Commissioners decided to undertake the review (in a case falling within regulation 43D).

(8)   Where the Commissioners are required to undertake a review but do not give notice of the conclusions within the time period specified in paragraph (6), the review is to be treated as having concluded that the decision is upheld.

(9)   If paragraph (8) applies, the Commissioners must notify P of the conclusion which the review is treated as having reached.

Bringing of appeals against decisions of the Commissioners

43F.—[1](1)   An appeal under regulation 43 is to be made to the tribunal before—

    (a)   the end of the period of 30 days beginning with the date of the document notifying the decision to which the appeal relates, or

    (b)   if later, the end of the relevant period (within the meaning of regulation 43C).

(2)   But that is subject to paragraphs (3) to (5).

(3)   In a case where the Commissioners are required to undertake a review under regulation 43B—

    (a)   an appeal may not be made until the conclusion date, and

    (b)   any appeal is to be made within the period of 30 days beginning with the conclusion date.

(4)   In a case where the Commissioners are requested to undertake a review in accordance with regulation 43D—

    (a)   an appeal may not be made—

        (i)   unless the Commissioners have decided whether or not to undertake a review, and

        (ii)   if the Commissioners decide to undertake a review, until the conclusion date; and

---

[1] As inserted by the Transfer of Tribunal Functions and Revenue and Customs Appeals Order 2009 (SI 2009/56) Sch.2 para.173 (effective April 1, 2009).

(b) any appeal is to be made within the period of 30 days beginning with—
  (i) the conclusion date (if the Commissioners decide to undertake a review), or
  (ii) the date on which the Commissioners decide not to undertake a review.

(5) In a case where regulation 43E(8) applies, an appeal may be made at any time from the end of the period specified in regulation 43E(6) to the date 30 days after the conclusion date.

(6) An appeal may be made after the end of the period specified in paragraph (1), (3)(b), (4)(b) or (5) if the tribunal gives permission to do so.

(7) In this regulation conclusion date means the date of the document notifying the conclusions of the review.

Appeals

44.—(1) A person may appeal from a decision by—
  (a) *[Revoked by the Transfer of Tribunal Functions and Revenue and Customs Appeals Order 2009 (SI 2009/56) Sch.2 para.174 (effective April 1, 2009).]*
  [1](b) the Authority or DETI under regulation 34 or 42.

(2) An appeal from a decision by—
  (a) *[Revoked by the Transfer of Tribunal Functions and Revenue and Customs Appeals Order 2009 (SI 2009/56) Sch.2 para.174 (effective April 1, 2009).]*
  (b)[2] the Authority is to the Upper Tribunal;
  (c) *[As repealed by the Financial Services and Markets Act 2000 (Regulated Activities) (Amendment) (No.2) Order 2013 (SI 2013/1881) Sch.1(2) para.31 (effective April 1, 2009).]*
  (d) DETI is to the High Court.

(3) *[Revoked by the Transfer of Tribunal Functions and Revenue and Customs Appeals Order 2009 (SI 2009/56) Sch.2 para.174 (effective April 1, 2009).]*

(4) The provisions of Part 9 of the 2000 Act (hearings and appeals), subject to the modifications set out in paragraph 2 of Schedule 5, apply in respect of appeals to the Financial Services and Markets Tribunal made under this regulation as they apply in respect of references made to that Tribunal under that Act.

(5) *[Revoked by the Transfer of Functions of the Consumer Credit Appeals Tribunal Order 2009 (SI 2009/1835) Sch.2 para.1(b) (effective September 1, 2009: repeal has effect subject to transitional provisions and savings specified in SI 2009/1835 Sch.4).]*

(6) *[Revoked by the Transfer of Tribunal Functions and Revenue and Customs Appeals Order 2009 (SI 2009/56) Sch.2 para.174 (effective April 1, 2009).]*

(7) *[As repealed by the Financial Services and Markets Act 2000 (Regulated Activities) (Amendment) (No.2) Order 2013 (SI 2013/1881) Sch.1(2) para.31 (effective April 1, 2009).]*

(8) The modifications in Schedule 5 have effect for the purposes of appeals made under this regulation.

---

[1] As amended by the Financial Services and Markets Act 2000 (Regulated Activities) (Amendment) (No.2) Order 2013 (SI 2013/1881) Sch.1(2) para.31 (effective July 26, 2013).
[2] As substituted by the Transfer of Tribunal Functions Order 2010 (SI 2010/22) Sch.3 para.141 (effective April 6, 2010).

Criminal offences

Offences

45.—(1)[1, 2]   A person (except an auction platform) who fails to comply with any requirement in regulation 7(1), (2) or (3), 8(1) or (3), 9(2), 10(1), 11(1)(a),(b) or (c), 14(1), 15(1) or (2), 16(1), (2), (3) or (4), 19(1), (4), (5) or (6), 20(1), (4) or (5), 21, 26, 27(4) or 33 is guilty of an offence and liable—

    (a)   on summary conviction, to a fine not exceeding the statutory maximum;

    (b)   on conviction on indictment, to imprisonment for a term not exceeding two years, to a fine or to both.

(1A)[3]   An auction platform which fails to comply with the customer due diligence requirements of Article 19 or 20(6) of the emission allowance auctioning regulation, the monitoring and record keeping requirements of Article 54 of that regulation, or regulation 20(1), (4) or (5) or 21 of these Regulations, is guilty of an offence and liable—

    (a)   on summary conviction, to a fine not exceeding the statutory maximum;

    (b)   on conviction on indictment, to imprisonment for a term not exceeding two years, to a fine or to both.

(2)[4]   In deciding whether a person has committed an offence under paragraph (1) or (1A), the court must consider whether he followed any relevant guidance which was at the time—

    (a)   issued by a supervisory authority or any other appropriate body;

    (b   approved by the Treasury; and

    (c)   published in a manner approved by the Treasury as suitable in their opinion to bring the guidance to the attention of persons likely to be affected by it.

(3)   In paragraph (2), an appropriate body means any body which regulates or is representative of any trade, profession, business or employment carried on by the alleged offender.

(4)   A person is not guilty of an offence under this regulation if he took all reasonable steps and exercised all due diligence to avoid committing the offence.

(5)   Where a person is convicted of an offence under this regulation, he shall not also be liable to a penalty under regulation 42.

Prosecution of offences

46.—(1)   Proceedings for an offence under regulation 45 may be instituted by—

    (a)[5]   order of the Commissioners;

    (b)   *[As repealed by the Financial Services and Markets Act 2000 (Regulated Activities) (Amendment) (No.2) Order 2013 (SI 2013/1881) Sch.1(2) para.31 (effective July 26, 2013).]*

    (c)   a local weights and measures authority;

---

[1] As amended by the Recognised Auction Platforms Regulations 2011 (SI 2011/2699) Pt 4 reg.11(8) (effective December 12, 2011).

[2] As amended by the Money Laundering (Amendment) Regulations 2012 (SI 2012/2298) reg.16 (effective October 1, 2012).

[3] As inserted by the Recognised Auction Platforms Regulations 2011 (SI 2011/2699) Pt 4 reg.11(8) (effective December 12, 2011).

[4] As amended by the Recognised Auction Platforms Regulations 2011 (SI 2011/2699) Pt 4 reg.11(7) (effective December 12, 2011).

[5] As amended by the Public Bodies (Merger of the Director of Public Prosecutions and the Director of Revenue and Customs Prosecutions) Order 2014 (SI 2014/834) Sch.3 para.21 (effective March 27, 2014).

(d) DETI;

(e) the Director of Public Prosecutions; or

(f) the Director of Public Prosecutions for Northern Ireland.

(2) Proceedings for an offence under regulation 45 may be instituted only against a relevant person or, where such a person is a body corporate, a partnership or an unincorporated association, against any person who is liable to be proceeded against under regulation 47.

(3) Where proceedings under paragraph (1) are instituted by order of the Commissioners, the proceedings must be brought in the name of an officer of Revenue and Customs.

(4)–(5) *[As repealed by the Financial Services and Markets Act 2000 (Regulated Activities) (Amendment) (No.2) Order 2013 (SI 2013/1881) Sch.1(2) para.31 (effective July 26, 2013).]*

[1](6) A local weights and measures authority must, whenever the Authority requires, report in such form and with such particulars as the Authority requires on the exercise of its functions under these Regulations.

(7) Where the Commissioners investigate, or propose to investigate, any matter with a view to determining—

(a) whether there are grounds for believing that an offence under regulation 45 has been committed by any person; or

(b) whether such a person should be prosecuted for such an offence,

that matter is to be treated as an assigned matter within the meaning of section 1(1) of the Customs and Excise Management Act 1979.

(8) Paragraphs (1) and (3) to (6) do not extend to Scotland.

(9)[2] In its application to the Commissioners acting in Scotland, paragraph (7)(b) shall be read as referring to the Commissioners determining whether to refer the matter to the Crown Office and Procurator Fiscal Service with a view to the Procurator Fiscal determining whether a person should be prosecuted for such an offence.

Offences by bodies corporate etc.

47.—(1) If an offence under regulation 45 committed by a body corporate is shown—

(a) to have been committed with the consent or the connivance of an officer of the body corporate; or

(b) to be attributable to any neglect on his part,

the officer as well as the body corporate is guilty of an offence and liable to be proceeded against and punished accordingly.

(2) If an offence under regulation 45 committed by a partnership is shown—

(a) to have been committed with the consent or the connivance of a partner; or

(b) to be attributable to any neglect on his part,

the partner as well as the partnership is guilty of an offence and liable to be proceeded against and punished accordingly.

(3) If an offence under regulation 45 committed by an unincorporated association (other than a partnership) is shown—

---

[1] As amended by the Financial Services and Markets Act 2000 (Regulated Activities) (Amendment) (No.2) Order 2013 (SI 2013/1881) Sch.1(2) para.31 (effective July 26, 2013).
[2] As inserted by the Money Laundering (Amendment) Regulations 2007 (SI 2007/3299) reg.2(f) (effective December 15, 2007).

    (a)   to have been committed with the consent or the connivance of an officer of the association; or

    (b)   to be attributable to any neglect on his part,

that officer as well as the association is guilty of an offence and liable to be proceeded against and punished accordingly.

(4)   If the affairs of a body corporate are managed by its members, paragraph (1) applies in relation to the acts and defaults of a member in connection with his functions of management as if he were a director of the body.

(5)   Proceedings for an offence alleged to have been committed by a partnership or an unincorporated association must be brought in the name of the partnership or association (and not in that of its members).

(6)   A fine imposed on the partnership or association on its conviction of an offence is to be paid out of the funds of the partnership or association.

(7)   Rules of court relating to the service of documents are to have effect as if the partnership or association were a body corporate.

(8)   In proceedings for an offence brought against the partnership or association—

    (a)   section 33 of the Criminal Justice Act 1925 (procedure on charge of offence against corporation) and Schedule 3 to the Magistrates' Courts Act 1980 (corporations) apply as they do in relation to a body corporate;

    (b)   section 70 (proceedings against bodies corporate) of the Criminal Procedure (Scotland) Act 1995 applies as it does in relation to a body corporate;

    (c)   section 18 of the Criminal Justice (Northern Ireland) Act 1945 (procedure on charge) and Schedule 4 to the Magistrates' Courts (Northern Ireland) Order 1981 (corporations) apply as they do in relation to a body corporate.

(9)   In this regulation—

"officer"—

    (a)   in relation to a body corporate, means a director, manager, secretary, chief executive, member of the committee of management, or a person purporting to act in such a capacity; and

    (b)   in relation to an unincorporated association, means any officer of the association or any member of its governing body, or a person purporting to act in such capacity; and

"partner" includes a person purporting to act as a partner.

PART 6

MISCELLANEOUS

Recovery of charges and penalties through the court

48.   Any charge or penalty imposed on a person by a supervisory authority under regulation 35(1) or 42(1) is a debt due from that person to the authority, and is recoverable accordingly.

Obligations on public authorities

49.—(1)[1] The following bodies and persons must, if they know or suspect or have reasonable grounds for knowing or suspecting that a person is or has engaged in money laundering or terrorist financing, as soon as reasonably practicable inform the National Crime Agency—

(a) the Auditor General for Scotland;

(b) the Auditor General for Wales;

(c) the Authority;

(d) the Bank of England;

(e) the Comptroller and Auditor General;

(f) the Comptroller and Auditor General for Northern Ireland;

(g) the Gambling Commission;

(h) *[As repealed by the Financial Services and Markets Act 2000 (Regulated Activities) (Amendment) (No.2) Order 2013 (SI 2013/1881) Sch.1(2) para.31 (effective July 26, 2013).]*

(i) the Official Solicitor to the Supreme Court;

(j) the Pensions Regulator;

(ja)[2] the PRA;

(k) the Public Trustee;

(l) the Secretary of State, in the exercise of his functions under enactments relating to companies and insolvency;

(m) the Treasury, in the exercise of their functions under the 2000 Act;

(n) the Treasury Solicitor;

(o) a designated professional body for the purposes of Part 20 of the 2000 Act (provision of financial services by members of the professions);

(p) a person or inspector appointed under section 65 (investigations on behalf of Authority) or 66 (inspections and special meetings) of the Friendly Societies Act 1992;

(q) an inspector appointed under section 49 of the Industrial and Provident Societies Act 1965 (appointment of inspectors) or section 18 of the Credit Unions Act 1979 (power to appoint inspector);

(r)[3] an inspector appointed under section 431 (investigation of a company on its own application), 432 (other company investigations), 442 (power to investigate company ownership) or 446 (investigation of share dealing) of the Companies Act 1985 or under Article 424, 425, 435 or 439 of the Companies (Northern Ireland) Order 1986;

(s) a person or inspector appointed under section 55 (investigations on behalf of Authority) or 56 (inspections and special meetings) of the Building Societies Act 1986;

(t) a person appointed under section 167 (appointment of persons to carry out investigations), 168(3) or (5) (appointment of persons to carry out investigations in particular cases), 169(1)(b) (investigations to support overseas regulator) or 284 (power to investigate affairs of a scheme) of

---

[1] As amended by the Crime and Courts Act 2013 (c.22) Sch.8 para.190 (effective October 7, 2013).

[2] As amended by the Financial Services Act 2012 (Consequential Amendments and Transitional Provisions) Order 2013 (SI 2013/472) Sch.2 para.129 (effective April 1, 2013).

[3] As amended by the Companies Act 2006 (Consequential Amendments and Transitional Provisions) Order 2011 (SI 2011/1265) art.30 (effective May 12, 2011).

the 2000 Act, or under regulations made under section 262(2)(k) (open-ended investment companies) of that Act, to conduct an investigation; and

(u)   a person authorised to require the production of documents under section 447 of the Companies Act 1985 (Secretary of State's power to require production of documents), Article 440 of the Companies (Northern Ireland) Order 1986 or section 84 of the Companies Act 1989 (exercise of powers by officer).

(2)   A disclosure made under paragraph (1) is not to be taken to breach any restriction on the disclosure of information however imposed.

Disclosure by the Commissioners

49A.—[1](1)[2]   The Commissioners may disclose to the Authority information held in connection with their functions under these Regulations if the disclosure is made for the purpose of enabling or assisting the Authority to discharge any of its functions under the Payment Services Regulations 2009 or the Electronic Money Regulations 2011.

(2)   Information disclosed to the Authority under subsection (1) may not be disclosed by the Authority or any person who receives the information directly or indirectly from the Authority except—

(a)   to, or in accordance with authority given by, the Commissioners;

(b)   with a view to the institution of, or otherwise for the purposes of, any criminal proceedings;

(c)   with a view to the institution of any other proceedings by the Authority, for the purposes of any such proceedings instituted by the Authority, or for the purposes of any reference to the Tribunal under the Payment Services Regulations 2009; or

(d)   in the form of a summary or collection of information so framed as not to enable information relating to any particular person to be ascertained from it.

(3)   Any person who discloses information in contravention of subsection (2) is guilty of an offence and liable—

(a)   on summary conviction, to imprisonment for a term not exceeding three months, to a fine not exceeding the statutory maximum, or to both;

(b)   on conviction on indictment, to imprisonment for a term not exceeding two years to a fine, or to both.

(4)   It is a defence for a person charged with an offence under this regulation of disclosing information to prove that they reasonably believed

(a)   that the disclosure was lawful; or

(b)   that the information had already and lawfully been made available to the public.

---

[1] As inserted by the Payment Services Regulations 2009 (SI 2009/209) Sch.6(2) para.6(g) (effective March 2, 2009).

[2] As amended by the Electronic Money Regulations 2011 (SI 2011/99) Sch.4(2) para.19(g) (effective February 9, 2011).

Transitional provisions: requirement to be registered

50.—[1](1) Regulation 26 does not apply to an existing money service business, an existing trust or company service provider, an existing high value dealer, an existing bill payment service provider or an existing telecommunication, digital and IT payment service provider until—

    (a)   where it has applied in accordance with regulation 27 before the specified date for registration in a register maintained under regulation 25(1) (a "new register")—

        (i)   the date it is included in a new register following the determination of its application by the Commissioners; or

        (ii)   where the Commissioners give it notice under regulation 29(2)(b) of their decision not to register it, the date on which the Commissioners state that the decision takes effect or, where a statement is included in accordance with paragraph (3)(b), the time at which the Commissioners give it such notice;

    (b)   in any other case, the specified date.

  (2) The specified date is—

    (a)   in the case of an existing money service business, 1st February 2008;

    (b)   in the case of an existing trust or company service provider, 1st April 2008;

    (c)   in the case of an existing high value dealer, the first anniversary which falls on or after 1st January 2008 of the date of its registration in a register maintained under regulation 10 of the Money Laundering Regulations 2003;

    (d)   in the case of an existing bill payment service provider or an existing telecommunication, digital and IT payment service provider, 1st March 2010.

  (3) In the case of an application for registration in a new register made before the specified date by an existing money service business, an existing trust or company service provider, an existing high value dealer, an existing bill payment service provider or an existing telecommunication, digital and IT payment service provider, the Commissioners must include in a notice given to it under regulation 29(2)(b)—

    (a)   the date on which their decision is to take effect; or

    (b)   if the Commissioners consider that the interests of the public require their decision to have immediate effect, a statement to that effect and the reasons for it.

  (4) In the case of an application for registration in a new register made before the specified date by an existing money services business or an existing trust or company service provider, the Commissioners must give it a notice under regulation 29(2) by—

    (a)   in the case of an existing money service business, 1st June 2008;

    (b)   in the case of an existing trust or company service provider, 1st July 2008; or

    (c)   where applicable, 45 days beginning with the date on which they receive any further information required under regulation 27(3).

  (5) In this regulation—

---

[1] As amended by the Payment Services Regulations 2009 (SI 2009/209) Sch.6(2) para.6(h) (effective November 1, 2009).

"existing bill payment service provider" and "existing telecommunication, digital and IT payment service provider" mean a bill payment service provider or a telecommunication, digital and IT payment service provider carrying on business in the United Kingdom immediately before 1st November 2009;

"existing money service business" and an "existing high value dealer" mean a money service business or a high value dealer which, immediately before 15th December 2007, was included in a register maintained under regulation 10 of the Money Laundering Regulations 2003;

"existing trust or company service provider" means a trust or company service provider carrying on business in the United Kingdom immediately before 15th December 2007.

Minor and consequential amendments

51. Schedule 6, which contains minor and consequential amendments to primary and secondary legislation, has effect.

SCHEDULE 1

ACTIVITIES LISTED IN POINTS 2 TO 12 AND 14 OF ANNEX I TO THE CAPITAL
REQUIREMENTS DIRECTIVE

Regulation 3(3)(a)

2. Lending including, inter alia: consumer credit, mortgage credit, factoring, with or without recourse, financing of commercial transactions (including forfeiting).

3. Financial leasing.

4.[1] Payment services as defined in Article 4(3) of Directive 2007/64/EC of the European Parliament and of the Council of 13 November 2007 on payment services in the internal market.

5.[2] Issuing and administering other means of payment (including travellers' cheques and bankers' drafts) insofar as this activity is not covered by point 4.

6. Guarantees and commitments.

7. Trading for own account or for account of customers in:

(a) money market instruments (cheques, bills, certificates of deposit, etc.);

(b) foreign exchange;

(c) financial futures and options;

(d) exchange and interest-rate instruments; or

(e) transferable securities.

8. Participation in securities issues and the provision of services related to such issues.

9. Advice to undertakings on capital structure, industrial strategy and related questions and advice as well as services relating to mergers and the purchase of undertakings.

10. Money broking.

11. Portfolio management and advice.

12. Safekeeping and administration of securities.

---

[1] As substituted by the Payment Services Regulations 2009 (SI 2009/209) Sch.6(2) para.6(i) (effective November 1, 2009).

[2] As amended by the Payment Services Regulations 2009 (SI 2009/209) Sch.6(2) para.6(h) (effective November 1, 2009).

14. Safe custody services.

15.[1] Issuing electronic money.

SCHEDULE 2

FINANCIAL ACTIVITY, SIMPLIFIED DUE DILIGENCE AND POLITICALLY EXPOSED PERSONS

Regulations 4(1)(e) and (2), 13(6) and (8) and 14(5).

Financial activity on an occasional or very limited basis

1. For the purposes of regulation 4(1)(e) and (2), a person is to be considered as engaging in financial activity on an occasional or very limited basis if all the following conditions are fulfilled—

(a) the person's total annual turnover in respect of the financial activity does not exceed £64,000;

---

[1] As inserted by the Electronic Money Regulations 2011 (SI 2011/99) Sch.4(2) para.19(h) (effective April 30, 2011).

F 116/36/1
[NEXT TEXT PAGE IS F 116/37]

   (b)   the financial activity is limited in relation to any customer to no more than one transaction exceeding 1,000 euro, whether the transaction is carried out in a single operation, or a series of operations which appear to be linked;

   (c)   the financial activity does not exceed 5% of the person's total annual turnover;

   (d)   the financial activity is ancillary and directly related to the person's main activity;

   (e)   the financial activity is not the transmission or remittance of money (or any representation of monetary value) by any means;

   (f)   the person's main activity is not that of a person falling within regulation 3(1)(a) to (f) or (h);

   (g)   the financial activity is provided only to customers of the person's main activity and is not offered to the public.

Simplified due diligence

2. For the purposes of regulation 13(6), the conditions are—

   (a)[1]   the authority has been entrusted with public functions pursuant to the Treaty on European Union, the Treaty on the Functioning of the European Union or EU secondary legislation;

   (b)   the authority's identity is publicly available, transparent and certain;

   (c)   the activities of the authority and its accounting practices are transparent;

   (d)[2]   either the authority is accountable to an EU institution or to the authorities of an EEA state, or otherwise appropriate check and balance procedures exist ensuring control of the authority's activity.

3. For the purposes of regulation 13(8), the conditions are—

   (a)   the product has a written contractual base;

   (b)   any related transaction is carried out through an account of the customer with a credit institution which is subject to the money laundering directive or with a credit institution situated in a non-EEA state which imposes requirements equivalent to those laid down in that directive;

   (c)   the product or related transaction is not anonymous and its nature is such that it allows for the timely application of customer due diligence measures where there is a suspicion of money laundering or terrorist financing;

   (d)   the product is within the following maximum threshold—

      (i)   in the case of insurance policies or savings products of a similar nature, the annual premium is no more than 1,000 euro or there is a single premium of no more than 2,500 euro;

      (ii)   in the case of products which are related to the financing of physical assets where the legal and beneficial title of the assets is not transferred to the customer until the termination of the contractual relationship (whether the transaction is carried out in a single operation or in several operations which appear to be linked), the annual payments do not exceed 15,000 euro;

      (iii)   in all other cases, the maximum threshold is 15,000 euro;

   (e)   the benefits of the product or related transaction cannot be realised for the benefit of third parties, except in the case of death, disablement, survival to a predetermined advanced age, or similar events;

   (f)   in the case of products or related transactions allowing for the investment of funds in financial assets or claims, including insurance or other kinds of contingent claims—

      (i)   the benefits of the product or related transaction are only realisable in the long term;

      (ii)   the product or related transaction cannot be used as collateral; and

      (iii)   during the contractual relationship, no accelerated payments are made, surrender clauses used or early termination takes place.

Politically exposed persons

4.—(1) For the purposes of regulation 14(5)—

   (a)   individuals who are or have been entrusted with prominent public functions include the following—

---

[1] As substituted by the Treaty of Lisbon (Changes in Terminology or Numbering) Order 2012 (SI 2012/1809) Sch.1(2) para.1 (effective August 1, 2012: substitution has effect subject to savings specified in SI 2012/1809 art.2(2)).

[2] As substituted by Treaty of Lisbon (Changes in Terminology) Order 2011 (SI 2011/1043) Pt 2 art.6(1)(c) (effective April 22, 2011).

    (i)   heads of state, heads of government, ministers and deputy or assistant ministers;

    (ii)   members of parliaments;

    (iii) members of supreme courts, of constitutional courts or of other high-level judicial bodies whose decisions are not generally subject to further appeal, other than in exceptional circumstances;

    (iv) members of courts of auditors or of the boards of central banks;

    (v)   ambassadors, chargés d'affaires and high-ranking officers in the armed forces; and

    (vi) members of the administrative, management or supervisory bodies of state-owned enterprises;

(b)   the categories set out in paragraphs (i) to (vi) of sub-paragraph (a) do not include middle-ranking or more junior officials;

(c)   immediate family members include the following—

    (i)   a spouse;

    (ii)   a partner;

    (iii) children and their spouses or partners; and

    (iv) parents;

(d)   persons known to be close associates include the following—

    (i)   any individual who is known to have joint beneficial ownership of a legal entity or legal arrangement, or any other close business relations, with a person referred to in regulation 14(5)(a); and

    (ii)   any individual who has sole beneficial ownership of a legal entity or legal arrangement which is known to have been set up for the benefit of a person referred to in regulation 14(5)(a).

(2)   In paragraph (1)(c), "partner" means a person who is considered by his national law as equivalent to a spouse.

SCHEDULE 3[1]

PROFESSIONAL BODIES

Regulations 17(2)(b), 23(1)(c) and 32(4)

1.   Association of Accounting Technicians

2.   Association of Chartered Certified Accountants

3.   Association of International Accountants

4.   Association of Taxation Technicians

5.   Chartered Institute of Management Accountants

6.   Chartered Institute of Public Finance and Accountancy

7.   Chartered Institute of Taxation

8.   Council for Licensed Conveyancers

9.   Faculty of Advocates

10. Faculty Office of the Archbishop of Canterbury

11. General Council of the Bar

12. General Council of the Bar of Northern Ireland

13. Insolvency Practitioners Association

14. Institute of Certified Bookkeepers

15. Institute of Chartered Accountants in England and Wales

16. Institute of Chartered Accountants in Ireland

17. Institute of Chartered Accountants of Scotland

18. Institute of Financial Accountants

19. International Association of Book-keepers

---

[1] As substituted by the Money Laundering (Amendment) Regulations 2012 (SI 2012/2298) Sch.1 para.1 (effective October 1, 2012).

20. Law Society

21. Law Society of Northern Ireland

22. Law Society of Scotland

SCHEDULE 4

CONNECTED PERSONS

Regulation 37(2)

Corporate bodies

1. If the relevant person is a body corporate ("BC"), a person who is or has been—
    (a) an officer or manager of BC or of a parent undertaking of BC;
    (b) an employee of BC;
    (c) an agent of BC or of a parent undertaking of BC.

Partnerships

2. If the relevant person is a partnership, a person who is or has been a member, manager, employee or agent of the partnership.

Unincorporated associations

3. If the relevant person is an unincorporated association of persons which is not a partnership, a person who is or has been an officer, manager, employee or agent of the association.

Individuals

4. If the relevant person is an individual, a person who is or has been an employee or agent of that individual.

SCHEDULE 5

MODIFICATIONS IN RELATION TO APPEALS

Regulation 44(8)

[Not reproduced.]

SCHEDULE 6

MINOR AND CONSEQUENTIAL AMENDMENTS

Regulation 51

[Not reproduced.]

THE EUROPEAN COMMUNITIES (LAWYER'S PRACTICE) (SCOTLAND) REGULATIONS 2000

(SSI 2000/121)

F2.4

The Scottish Ministers, in exercise of the powers conferred upon them by section 2(2) of the European Communities Act 1972 and all other powers enabling them in that behalf, hereby make the following Regulations:

PART I

INTRODUCTORY

Citation, commencement, transitional and extent

1.—(1)   These Regulations may be cited as the European Communities (Lawyer's Practice) (Scotland) Regulations 2000 and shall come into force on 22nd May 2000, except for regulations 21 and 22, which shall come into force on 22nd November 2000.

(2)[1]   Where, on 22nd May 2000, a European lawyer is practising professional activities under his home professional title on a permanent basis in Scotland or commences such practice by 21st November 2000, he shall apply to be registered in accordance with regulation 16 by 21st November 2000 where he intends to practise those activities on a permanent basis after that date.

(3)[2]   On or after 22nd November 2000, a European lawyer shall not practise as referred to in paragraph (2) without being registered in accordance with regulation 16, unless he was already practising before that date and has made an application for registration which has not been determined.

(4)[3]   In paragraphs (3) and (5), an application for registration shall, as at a particular date, be taken not to have been determined if as at that date the applicant—

   (a)   has not received a rejection of his application and the period for such a rejection or a deemed rejection has not yet expired; or

   (b)   is appealing against a rejection of the application(including a deemed rejection) and the appeal has not been determined.

---

[1] With regard to "relevant lawyers" (SSI 2004/302, reg.2(2)) for "22nd May 2000", where it occurs substitute "16th September 2004"; for "21st November 2000", wherever it occurs, substitute "15th March 2005"; and for "22nd November 2000", wherever it occurs, substitute "16th March 2005" (The European Communities (Lawyer's Practice) (Scotland) Amendment Regulations 2004, SSI 2004/302, reg.2(4)).
[2] With regard to "relevant lawyers" (SSI 2004/302, reg.2(2)) for "22nd May 2000", where it occurs substitute "16th September 2004"; for "21st November 2000", wherever it occurs, substitute "15th March 2005"; and for "22nd November 2000", wherever it occurs, substitute "16th March 2005" (The European Communities (Lawyer's Practice) (Scotland) Amendment Regulations 2004, SSI 2004/302, reg.2(4)).
[3] With regard to "relevant lawyers" (SSI 2004/302, reg.2(2)) for "22nd May 2000", where it occurs substitute "16th September 2004"; for "21st November 2000", wherever it occurs, substitute "15th March 2005"; and for "22nd November 2000", wherever it occurs, substitute "16th March 2005" (The European Communities (Lawyer's Practice) (Scotland) Amendment Regulations 2004, SSI 2004/302, reg.2(4)).

(5)[1]   Regulations 21(1)(b) and 22 shall not apply to a European lawyer whilst that lawyer satisfies all the following conditions—

(a)   immediately before 22nd November 2000 he was practising on a permanent basis in any part of the United Kingdom;

(b)   before 22nd November 2000 he applied for registration to any of the barristers' professional bodies or England and Wales or Northern Ireland solicitors' professional bodies, or to the Faculty of Advocates or the Law Society of Scotland; and

(c)   his application for registration has not yet been determined.

(6)   These Regulations extend to Scotland and insofar as they extend beyond Scotland they do so only as a matter of Scots law.

Interpretation

2.—(1)   In these Regulations, unless the context otherwise requires—

"advocate" means a member of the Faculty of Advocates;

"barrister" means a person who is a barrister of England and Wales or, as the case may be, Northern Ireland, and practising as such;

"barristers' professional bodies" means the Inns of Court and the General Council of the Bar of England and Wales and the Executive Council of the Inn of Court of Northern Ireland;

"competent authority", in relation to Scotland, means either of the bodies designated as a competent authority by regulation 4 to undertake the activities required by the Directive set out in that regulation;

"the Directive" means of the European Communities Parliament and Council Directive No.98/5/EC to facilitate practice of the profession of lawyer on a permanent basis in certain states other than the State in which the professional qualification was obtained;

"England and Wales or Northern Ireland registered European lawyer" means a European lawyer who is registered with one of the barristers' professional bodies or England and Wales or Northern Ireland solicitors' professional bodies and whose registration has not been withdrawn or suspended;

"England and Wales or Northern Ireland solicitors' professional bodies" means the Law Society and the Law Society of Northern Ireland respectively;

"European lawyer" has the meaning given in paragraphs (2) and (3);

"home State" means the State in paragraph (4) in which a European lawyer acquired his authorisation to pursue professional activities and, if he is authorised in more than one of those States, it shall mean any of those States;

"home professional title" means, in relation to a European lawyer, the professional title or any of the professional titles specified in relation to his home State in paragraph (4) under which he is authorised in his home State to pursue professional activities;

"Irish barrister" means a European lawyer who is authorised in the Republic of Ireland to pursue professional activities under the professional title of barrister and whose home State is the Republic of Ireland;

---

[1] With regard to "relevant lawyers" (SSI 2004/302, reg.2(2)) for "22nd May 2000", where it occurs substitute "16th September 2004"; for "21st November 2000", wherever it occurs, substitute "15th March 2005"; and for "22nd November 2000", wherever it occurs, substitute "16th March 2005" (The European Communities (Lawyer's Practice) (Scotland) Amendment Regulations 2004, SSI 2004/302, reg.2(4)).

"Irish solicitor" means a European lawyer who is authorised in the Republic of Ireland to pursue professional activities under the professional title of solicitor and whose home State is the Republic of Ireland;

"member of the professional body" means a practising solicitor or advocate, as the case may be;

"professional body" means the Law Society of Scotland or the Faculty of Advocates;

"Qualification Regulations" means the European Communities (Recognition of Professional Qualifications) Regulations 1991;

"registered European lawyer" means a European lawyer who is registered with a professional body in accordance with regulation 17 and whose registration has not been withdrawn or suspended;

"solicitor" shall have the same meaning as in section 65(1) of the Solicitors (Scotland) Act 1980;

"supreme court" means the Court of Session, the High Court of Justiciary, the Lands Valuation Appeal Court, the House of Lords (hearing an appeal from the Court of Session) or the Judicial Committee of the Privy Council (hearing a reference or an appeal under the Scotland Act 1998).

(2)   In these Regulations, "European lawyer" means a person who is—

(a)   a national of the United Kingdom or of a State listed in paragraph (4);

(b)   authorised in any of the States listed in paragraph (4) to pursue professional activities under any of the professional titles appearing in that paragraph; and

(c)   subject to paragraph (3), not a solicitor or advocate, or under the law of England and Wales or Northern Ireland, a solicitor or barrister.

(3)   Where a person is a European lawyer registered with more than one of the following—

(a)   the Law Society of Scotland or the Faculty of Advocates; or

(b)   the England and Wales or Northern Ireland solicitors' professional bodies or the barristers' professional bodies, and subsequently acquires the title used by members of one of the bodies referred to in sub paragraph (b) then notwithstanding paragraph (2)(c), that person shall continue to fall within the definition of a European lawyer in relation to the relevant professional body referred to in sub paragraph (a) for the period that he remains registered with that other professional body.

(4)   The States and professional titles referred to in the definition of European lawyer in paragraph (1) are as follows—

State	Professional titles
Belgium	Avocat/Advocaat/Rechtsanwalt
Denmark	Advokat
Germany	Rechtsanwalt
Greece	Dikegoros
Spain	Abogado/Advocat/Avogado/Abokatu
France	Avocat
Republic of Ireland	Barrister/Solicitor
Italy	Avvocato
Luxembourg	Avocat
Netherlands	Advocaat
Austria	Rechtsanwalt

State	Professional titles
Portugal	Advogado
Finland	Asianajaja/Advokat
Sweden	Advokat
Switzerland[1]	Avocat/Advokat/Rechtsanwalt/Anwalt/ Fürsprecher/Fürsprech/Avvocato
Iceland[2]	Lögmaður
Liechtenstein[3]	Rechtsanwalt
Norway[4]	Advokat
Czech republic[5]	Advokát
Estonia[6]	Vandeadvokaat
Cyprus[7]	(Dikegoros)
Latvia[8]	Zvērināts advokāts
Lithuania[9]	Advokatas
Hungary[10]	Ügyvéd
Malta[11]	Avukat/Prokuratur legali
Poland[12]	Adwokat/Radca prawny
Slovenia[13]	Odvetnik/Odvetnica
Slovakia[14]	Advokát/Komerčný právnik"
Bulgaria[15]	

---

[1] As inserted by the European Communities (Lawyer's Practice) (Scotland) Amendment Regulations (SSI 2004/302) reg.3 (effective September 16, 2004).

[2] As inserted by the European Communities (Lawyer's Practice) (Scotland) Amendment Regulations (SSI 2004/302) reg.3 (effective September 16, 2004).

[3] As inserted by the European Communities (Lawyer's Practice) (Scotland) Amendment Regulations (SSI 2004/302) reg.3 (effective September 16, 2004).

[4] As inserted by the European Communities (Lawyer's Practice) (Scotland) Amendment Regulations (SSI 2004/302) reg.3 (effective September 16, 2004).

[5] As inserted by the European Communities (Lawyer's Practice) (Scotland) Amendment Regulations (SSI 2004/302) reg.3 (effective September 16, 2004).

[6] As inserted by the European Communities (Lawyer's Practice) (Scotland) Amendment Regulations (SSI 2004/302) reg.3 (effective September 16, 2004).

[7] As inserted by the European Communities (Lawyer's Practice) (Scotland) Amendment Regulations (SSI 2004/302) reg.3 (effective September 16, 2004).

[8] As inserted by the European Communities (Lawyer's Practice) (Scotland) Amendment Regulations (SSI 2004/302) reg.3 (effective September 16, 2004).

[9] As inserted by the European Communities (Lawyer's Practice) (Scotland) Amendment Regulations (SSI 2004/302) reg.3 (effective September 16, 2004).

[10] As inserted by the European Communities (Lawyer's Practice) (Scotland) Amendment Regulations (SSI 2004/302) reg.3 (effective September 16, 2004).

[11] As inserted by the European Communities (Lawyer's Practice) (Scotland) Amendment Regulations (SSI 2004/302) reg.3 (effective September 16, 2004).

[12] As inserted by the European Communities (Lawyer's Practice) (Scotland) Amendment Regulations (SSI 2004/302) reg.3 (effective September 16, 2004).

[13] As inserted by the European Communities (Lawyer's Practice) (Scotland) Amendment Regulations (SSI 2004/302) reg.3 (effective September 16, 2004).

[14] As inserted by the European Communities (Lawyer's Practice) (Scotland) Amendment Regulations (SSI 2004/302) reg.3 (effective September 16, 2004).

[15] As inserted subject to transitional provisions as specified in SSI 2007/358 reg.2(1) and (2) by the European Communities (Lawyer's Practice) (Scotland) Amendment Regulations (SI 2007/358) reg.3(2) (effective September 25, 2007).

State	Professional titles
Romania[1]	Avocat
Croatia[2]	Odvjetnik/Odvjetnica

---

[1] As inserted subject to transitional provisions as specified in SSI 2007/358 reg.2(1) and (2) by the European Communities (Lawyer's Practice) (Scotland) Amendment Regulations (SI 2007/358) reg.3(2) (effective September 25, 2007).
[2] As inserted by the European Union (Amendments in respect of the Accession of Croatia) (Scotland) Regulations 2013 (SSI 2013/177) reg.3 (effective July 1, 2013).

(5) For the purposes of regulations 4(2)(d), 5(3) and 24(1) registration with the Faculty of Advocates shall be construed as membership of it.

(6) Unless the context otherwise requires, any reference in these Regulations to a numbered regulation, Part or Schedule is a reference to a regulation or Part of, or a Schedule to, these Regulations and any reference in a regulation to a numbered paragraph is a reference to the paragraph bearing that number in that regulation.

NOTES
[1] As inserted by the European Communities (Lawyer's Practice) (Scotland) Amendment Regulations (SSI 2004/302) reg.3 (effective September 16, 2004).
[2] As inserted subject to transitional provisions as specified in SSI 2007/358 reg.2(1) and (2) by the European Communities (Lawyer's Practice) (Scotland) Amendment Regulations (SI 2007/358) reg.3(2) (effective September 25, 2007).

Purpose of Regulations
3.—(1) The purpose of these Regulations is to implement the Directive in or as regards Scotland.

(2) The provisions of these Regulations shall have effect for the purpose of facilitating the practice of the profession of lawyer on a permanent basis by a European lawyer registered or registering in Scotland.

(3) References in these regulations to practice or professional activities shall not include the provision of services by lawyers within the meaning of the European Communities (Services of Lawyers) Order 1978.

Competent authorities
4.—(1) The Law Society of Scotland is designated as the competent authority for the purposes of-
    (a) receiving applications for registration by European lawyers under Part III of these Regulations;
    (b) receiving applications from registered European lawyers for entry into the profession of solicitor;
    (c) the regulation of registered European lawyers registered with it; and
    (d) the provision of certificates attesting to registration of solicitors with it.

(2) The Faculty of Advocates is designated as the competent authority for the purposes of—
    (a) receiving applications for registration by European lawyers under Part III of these Regulations;
    (b) receiving applications from registered European lawyers for entry into the profession of advocate;
    (c) the regulation of registered European lawyers registered with it; and
    (d) the provision of certificates attesting to registration of advocates with it.

Exchange of information
5.—(1) In order to facilitate the application of the Directive and to prevent its provisions from being misapplied, a professional body may supply to or receive from-
    (a) another professional body;
    (b) the England and Wales or Northern Ireland solicitors' professional bodies or barristers' professional bodies; or
    (c) an authority in any of the States listed in regulation 2(4) which has been designated by that State under the Directive as a competent authority in that State,
any information relating to a European lawyer or to any person with whom he jointly practises.

(2) Subject to paragraph (1) or as otherwise required by law in the interests of justice, a professional body shall preserve the confidentiality of

any information received in accordance with paragraph (1) relating to a European lawyer or to any person with whom he jointly practises.

(3) A competent authority in Scotland shall provide a certificate attesting to the registration of a solicitor or advocate registered with it and his authorisation to practise when requested to do so by that solicitor or advocate or by a competent authority in a State listed in regulation 2(4).

PART II

PRACTICE OF PROFESSIONAL ACTIVITIES BY A REGISTERED EUROPEAN LAWYER

Practice of professional activities
   6.—(1) Subject to the provisions of these Regulations, a registered European lawyer shall be entitled to carry out under his home professional title any professional activities whether in Scotland or elsewhere that may lawfully be carried out by a member of the professional body with which he is registered and any enactment or rule of law or practice with regard to the carrying out of professional activities by members of that professional body shall be interpreted and applied accordingly.
   (2) A registered European lawyer who is in salaried employment may carry out professional activities whether in Scotland or elsewhere under his home professional title to the same extent that an employed member of the professional body with which he is registered may do so.

Title and description to be used by a registered European lawyer
   7.—(1) Where a registered European lawyer is engaged in any professional activities in pursuance of regulation 6(1) he shall comply with the requirements set out in paragraph (2).
   (2) The requirements referred to in paragraph (1) are that a registered European lawyer shall—
   (a) use his home professional title expressed in an officiallanguage of his home State in a manner which avoids confusion with the title of solicitor or advocate;
   (b) indicate the professional organisation by which he is authorised to practise or the court of law before which he is entitled to practise in that State;
   (c) indicate the professional body with which he is registered in Scotland and that he is a registered European lawyer with that body; and
   (d) if applicable indicate any England and Wales or Northern Ireland solicitors' professional bodies or barristers' professional bodies with which he may be registered and that he is an England and Wales or Northern Ireland registered European lawyer with that body or those bodies.

Joint practice
   8. Where a registered European lawyer carries out professional activities in pursuance of regulation 6(1) under his home professional title as part of a joint practice he shall do so to the same extent and in the same manner as a member of the professional body with which he is registered may do so, with—
   (a) a member of the professional body with which he is registered;
   (b) a registered European lawyer who is registered with the same professional body; or
   (c) any other person permitted by the professional body with which he is registered.

Name of joint practice
   9.—(1) Subject to paragraph (2), where a registered European lawyer is a member of a joint practice in his home State, he may use the name of that

practice with his home professional title when practising as a registered European lawyer.

(2) Rules of conduct of the professional body with which a registered European lawyer is registered may prohibit the use by him of the name of the joint practice of which he is a member in the home State to the extent that—

(a) that name is also used by persons who are not European lawyers or solicitors of any part of the United Kingdom; and

(b) those rules prohibit members of that professional body (whether or not practising as such) from using that name.

Notification of joint practice

10.—(1) Where a European lawyer is a member of a joint practice in his home State, he shall inform the professional body with which he intends to register and provide it with the following information:-

(a) the name of the joint practice;

(b) his place of business;

(c) the name and place of business of any member of his joint practice;

(d) any other relevant information about the joint practice requested by the professional body.

(2) A European lawyer shall notify that professional body of any changes in the information whether before or after registration.

Representation in legal proceedings

11.—(1) Subject to paragraphs (2) and (4), no enactment or rule of law or practice shall prevent a registered European lawyer from pursuing professional activities relating to the representation of a client in any proceedings before any court, tribunal or public authority (including addressing the court, tribunal or public authority) only because he is not a solicitor or advocate.

(2) In proceedings referred to in paragraph (1), where the professional activities in question may (but for these Regulations) be lawfully provided only by a solicitor or advocate, a registered European lawyer shall act in conjunction with a solicitor or advocate who is entitled to practise before the court, tribunal or public authority concerned and who could lawfully provide those professional activities.

(3) The solicitor or advocate referred to in paragraph (2) shall, where necessary, be answerable to the court, tribunal or public authority concerned in relation to the proceedings.

(4) A registered European lawyer shall not have a right of audience in a supreme court unless he has completed the course of training in evidence, pleading and practice in relation to that court which must be completed by any member of the professional body with which he is registered who seeks a right of audience in that court.

Property transactions

¹ **12.** A registered European lawyer is not entitled, by virtue of regulation 6(1), to prepare for remuneration any deed creating or transferring an interest in land unless he has a home professional title obtained in Denmark, the Republic of Ireland, Finland, Sweden, Cyprus, the Czech Republic, Hungary, Iceland, Liechtenstein, Norway or Slovakia.

NOTE
¹ As substituted by the European Communities (Lawyer's Practice) (Scotland) Amendment Regulations 2004 (SSI 2004/302) reg.4 (effective September 16, 2004).

Executries

¹ **13.** A registered European lawyer is not entitled, by virtue of regulation 6(1), to prepare for remuneration any deed for obtaining title to administer

the estate of a deceased person unless he has a home professional title obtained in Denmark, Germany, the Republic of Ireland, Austria, Finland, Sweden, Cyprus, the Czech Republic, Hungary, Iceland, Liechtenstein, Norway or Slovakia.

NOTE
[1] As substituted by the European Communities (Lawyer's Practice) (Scotland) Amendment Regulations 2004 (SSI 2004/302) reg.5 (effective September 16, 2004).

Legal aid
14. A registered European lawyer may provide professional activities by way of legal advice and assistance or legal aid under the Legal Aid (Scotland) Act 1986 and references to a solicitor, counsel or legal representative in that and any other enactment relating to legal advice and assistance or legal aid shall be interpreted accordingly.

PART III

REGISTRATION

Establishment and maintenance of registers of registered European lawyers
15. Each of the professional bodies shall establish and maintain a register of registered European lawyers.

Application to be entered on a register
16.—(1) Subject to paragraph (6) and regulation 18, a European lawyer who wishes to pursue professional activities under his home professional title on a permanent basis in Scotland or any other part of the United Kingdom shall apply to be entered on the register maintained by a professional body under regulation 15.

(2) A European lawyer who wishes to register with a professional body in accordance with paragraph (1) shall provide the professional body with certificates confirming his registration with the competent authority in each home State under whose home professional title he intends to practise.

(3) A professional body may require that the certificate referred to in paragraph (2) shall not have been issued more than three months before the date of the application under this regulation.

(4) An application for registration under this regulation shall comply with any applicable rules or regulations made by the relevant professional body and shall be accompanied by the appropriate fee.

(5) Subject to regulation 18, an application for registration under this regulation shall not be affected by any other application or registration with the barristers' professional bodies or the England and Wales or Northern Ireland solicitors' professional bodies.

(6) Paragraph (1) shall not apply to a European lawyer who wishes to pursue professional activities under his home professional title on a permanent basis in Scotland or any other part of the United Kingdom where that lawyer is an England and Wales or Northern Ireland registered European lawyer.

Registration by professional body
17.—(1) Subject to regulation 18, a professional body shall enter on its register the name of a European lawyer who applies to it in accordance with regulation 16.

(2) Where a professional body registers a European lawyer in accordance with paragraph (1), it shall inform the competent authority in the home state of the registration.

Restrictions on registration

18.—(1) A European lawyer shall not be registered at the same time both with the Law Society of Scotland and the Faculty of Advocates.

(2) An Irish solicitor shall not be entered on a register maintained under regulation 15 by the Faculty of Advocates.

(3) An Irish barrister shall not be entered on a register maintained under regulation 15 by the Law Society of Scotland.

(4) A European lawyer registered with any of the barristers' professional bodies shall not be entered on a register maintained under regulation 15 by the Law Society of Scotland.

(5) A European lawyer registered with any of the England and Wales and Northern Ireland solicitors' professional bodies shall not be entered on a register maintained under regulation 15 by the Faculty of Advocates.

Time limit for decision and notification by professional body

19.—(1) A professional body shall consider an application for registration under regulation 16 as soon as is reasonably practicable, and shall notify the

European lawyer of its decision, and if the application is rejected, or granted subject to conditions, the reasons upon which the rejection or the imposition of conditions is based, within four months of receipt of an application complying with regulation 16(2) and (4).

(2) Where the professional body fails to take a decision and notify the European lawyer within four months in accordance with paragraph (1), it shall be deemed to have taken a decision to reject his application and to have notified it to him on the last day of that period.

(3) Where the professional body withdraws or suspends a registration, it shall notify the European lawyer of its decision and the reasons upon which the withdrawal or suspension is based.

Appeal by European lawyer
   20.—(1) Within three months of the notification to him of the professional body's decision, or later with the permission of the Court of Session, the European lawyer may appeal against the decision by appeal in Form 41.19 to the Court of Session.

(2) The Court of Session may, for the purpose of determining any appeal under this Part—
   (a) order the professional body to register the European lawyer;
   (b) refuse the appeal; or
   (c) remit the matter to the professional body with such directions as it sees fit.

(3) The Court of Session shall give reasons for its decision.

Offence of pretending to be a registered European lawyer
   [1] **21.**—(1) A person who without being a registered European lawyer,
   (a) wilfully pretends to be a registered European lawyer or takes or uses any name, title, designation or description implying that he is a registered European lawyer whether in Scotland or elsewhere; or
   (b) subject to paragraph (2), carries on professional activities in Scotland under one of the professional titles listed in regulation 2(4) or under any name, designation or description implying that he is entitled to pursue those activities under one of those professional titles;
shall be guilty of an offence and liable on summary conviction to a fine not exceeding level 4 on the standard scale.

(2) Paragraph (1)(b) shall not apply to a person who satisfies any of the following conditions—
   (a) he is not a national of the United Kingdom or of any of the States listed in regulation 2(4);
   (b) he is a solicitor or advocate under the law of Scotland or a solicitor or barrister under the law of England and Wales or Northern Ireland;
   (c) he is an England and Wales or Northern Ireland registered European lawyer; or
   (d) he is providing services within the meaning of the European Communities (Services of Lawyers) Order 1978.

NOTE
   [1] Applies to "relevant lawyers" (SSI 2004/302, reg.2(2)) only as from March 16, 2005 (The European Communities (Lawyer's Practice) (Scotland) Amendment Regulations 2004, SSI 2004/302, reg.2(3)).

Fees, rewards, outlays and expenses of an unregistered European lawyer.
   [1] **22.** Where a European lawyer is carrying on professional activities under his home professionaltitle in Scotland any fees, rewards, outlays or expenses in respect of those activities shall not be recoverable by him or any other person unless that European lawyer is a registered European lawyer, or an England and Wales or Northern Ireland registered European lawyer.

NOTE
¹ Applies to "relevant lawyers" (SSI 2004/302, reg.2(2)) only as from March 16, 2005 (The European Communities (Lawyer's Practice) (Scotland) Amendment Regulations 2004, SSI 2004/302, reg.2(3)).

Evidence of registration
23. Any certificate purporting to be signed by an officer of a professional body and stating that a person—
 (a) is, or is not, registered as a European lawyer with that professional body; or
 (b) was, or was not, registered with that professional body during a period specified in the certificate,
shall, unless the contrary is proved, be evidence of that fact and be taken to have been so signed.

Publication of names of registered European lawyers
24.—(1) Where a professional body publishes the names of solicitors or advocates registered with it, it shall also publish the names of any European lawyers registered with it.
 (2) In this regulation, "publishes" or "publish" includes the provision of information to a legal publisher.

PART IV

REGULATION AND DISCIPLINE

Rules of professional conduct applicable
25. Where a registered European lawyer is practising under his home professional title whether in Scotland or elsewhere, he shall be subject to the same rules of professional conduct as a member of the professional body with which he is registered.

Disciplinary proceedings applicable
26.—(1) Where it is alleged that a registered European lawyer has failed to comply with the rules of professional conduct to which he is subject under regulation 25, he shall be subject to the same rules of procedure, penalties and remedies as a member of the professional body with which he is registered and shall, if appropriate, be subject to disciplinary proceedings brought by an appropriate authority.
 (2) Any sanction against a registered European lawyer in relation to disciplinary proceedings may include withdrawal or suspension of his registration.
 (3) The appropriate authority shall give reasons for its decision.
 (4) In this regulation, an appropriate authority means—
 (a) where the registered European lawyer is registered with the Law Society of Scotland, the Scottish Solicitors' Discipline Tribunal;
 (b) where the registered European lawyer is registered with the Faculty of Advocates, that body.

Disciplinary proceedings against a registered European lawyer
27.—(1) Where a professional body intends to begin disciplinary proceedings against a registered European lawyer, it shall–
 (a) inform the competent authority in his home State as soon as possible of the intention to begin those proceedings and furnish it with all the relevant details;
 (b) co-operate with that authority throughout those proceedings; and
 (c) inform that authority of the decision reached in those proceedings including the decision in any appeal, as soon as practicable after the decision is given.

(2) Subject to paragraph (3), where the competent authority in the registered European lawyer's home State withdraws his authorisation to practise under the home professional title either temporarily or permanently, his registration with the professional body shall be automatically withdrawn to the same extent.

(3) Where a registered European lawyer is authorised to practise under a home professional title in two or more home States, his registration shall be withdrawn in accordance with paragraph (2) if his authorisation to practise under a home professional title has been withdrawn in one or more of those home States.

(4) Where there is an appeal against a decision in disciplinary proceedings against a registered European lawyer, the body responsible for hearing the appeal shall afford the competent authority in the registered European lawyer's home State an opportunity to make representations in relation to that appeal.

Disciplinary proceedings against a solicitor or advocate
28. Where a professional body intends to begin disciplinary proceedings against a solicitor or advocate practising in a State listed in regulation 2(4), it shall inform the competent authority in that State of-
    (a) the intention to begin those proceedings and furnish it with all of the relevant details; and
    (b) the decision reached in those proceedings, including the decision in any appeal, as soon as practicable after the decision is given.

PART V

ENTRY INTO THE PROFESSION OF SOLICITOR OR ADVOCATE

Application by registered European lawyer
29.—(1) Where a registered European lawyer applies to the professional body with which he has been registered to become a solicitor or advocate, as the case may be, and that professional body requires him to pass an aptitude test under regulation 6(1)(b)(ii) of the Qualification Regulations, he may apply to the professional body for an exemption from that requirement on the grounds that he falls within paragraph (2) or (3) of this regulation.

(2) A person falls within this paragraph if—
    (a) he is a European lawyer and has been registered with that professional body for at least three years; and
[1] (b) he has for a period of at least three years effectively and regularly pursued in Scotland professional activities, in accordance with regulation 6, under his home professional title in the law of Scotland including EU law.

(3) A person falls within this paragraph if—
    (a) he is a European lawyer and has been registered with that professional body for at least three years;
    (b) he has for a period of at least three years effectively and regularly pursued in Scotland professional activities, in accordance with regulation 6, under his home professional title; and
    (c) he has for a period of less than three years effectively and regularly pursued in Scotland, professional activities, in accordance with regulation 6, under his home professional title in the law of Scotland.

NOTE
[1] As substituted by Treaty of Lisbon (Changes in Terminology) Order 2011 (SI 2011/1043) Pt 2 art.6(2)(a) (effective April 22, 2011).

Decision by professional body
30.—(1) Subject to paragraph (3), the professional body shall grant an

exemption applied for under regulation 29 if it considers that the requirements under paragraph (2) or (3) of regulation 29 have been met.

(2) The registration of a registered European lawyer shall cease from the date he is granted entry into the profession of solicitor or advocate.

(3) The professional body may refuse to grant an exemption if it considers that the registered European lawyer would be unfit to practise as a solicitor or advocate.

Evidence in support of application for exemption under regulation 29(2)
    31.—(1) Where a registered European lawyer makes an application under paragraph (2) of regulation 29, he shall provide the professional body with any relevant information and documentation which it may reasonably require.

(2) The professional body may verify the effective and regular nature of the professional activity pursued and may, if necessary, request the registered European lawyer to provide, orally or in writing, clarification of, or further details on, the information and documentation referred to in paragraph (1)

Evidence in support of application for exemption under regulation 29(3)
    32.—(1) Where a registered European lawyer makes an application under paragraph (3) of regulation 29, he shall provide the professional body with any relevant information and documentation it may reasonably require.

(2) In deciding whether to grant an application under paragraph (3) of regulation 29, the professional body shall take into account the professional activities the registered European lawyer has pursued during the period he has been registered and any knowledge and professional experience he has gained of, and any training he has received in, the law of Scotland, and the rules of professional conduct of the profession concerned.

(3) Subject to paragraph (4), in the case of an application under paragraph (3) of regulation 29, the professional body shall, by means of an interview, assess and verify the registered European lawyer's effective and regular professional activity and his capacity to continue that activity.

(4) Where a professional body believes that an interview is unnecessary and intends to grant an application under paragraph (3) of regulation 29, it may dispense with that requirement.

Meaning of "effectively and regularly pursued"
    33. For the purposes of regulations 29 to 32 activities shall be regarded as effectively and regularly pursued if they are actually exercised without any interruption other than that resulting from the events of everyday life.

Time limit for decision and notification by professional body
    34.—(1) A professional body shall consider an application under regulation 29 as soon as is reasonably practicable, and shall notify the applicant of its decision and, if the application is rejected, the reasons for the rejection, within four months of receipt of all the relevant information and documentation required under regulations 31 and 32.

(2) Where the professional body fails to take a decision and notify the registered European lawyer within four months in accordance with paragraph (1), it shall be deemed to have taken a decision to reject his application and to have notified it to him on the last day of that period.

Appeal by registered European lawyer
    35.—(1) Within three months of the notification to him of the professional body's decision, or later with the permission of the Court of Session, the registered European lawyer may appeal against the decision by appeal in Form 41.19 to the Court of Session.

(2) The Court of Session may, for the purpose of determining any appeal under this Part—
  (a) grant the exemption applied for;
  (b) refuse the appeal; or

(c) remit the matter to the professional body with such directions as the appeal body sees fit.

(3) The Court of Session shall give reasons for its decision.

Practice under the title of solicitor or advocate

36.—(1) This regulation applies where a registered European lawyer ("the lawyer") is granted entry into the profession of solicitor or advocate.

(2) Subject to paragraph (3), the lawyer shall be entitled to continue to practise in Scotland or elsewhere under his home professional title, and to use his home professional title, expressed in an official language of his home State, alongside the title of solicitor or advocate as the case may be, provided that he continues to be authorised in his home State to pursue professional activities under that title.

(3) For the purposes of rules of professional conduct, including those relating to disciplinary and complaints procedures, the lawyer's continuing practice in Scotland or elsewhere under his home professional title insofar as it relates to that lawyer's practice as a solicitor or advocate shall be deemed to form part of his practice as a solicitor or advocate, and those rules shall apply to his practice under his home professional title as they do to his practice as a solicitor or advocate.

(4) Where this regulation applies, a lawyer's registration in accordance with regulation 17 with the professional body whose title he has acquired shall cease from the date he is entitled to use that title.

PART VI

SUPPLEMENTARY PROVISIONS

Modification and extension of enactments

37.—(1) Schedule 1, which makes amendments to the Solicitors (Scotland) Act 1980, shall have effect.

(2) Schedule 2, which applies enactments, with modifications and extensions shall have effect in relation to registered European lawyers.

SCHEDULES

Regulation 37(1)   SCHEDULE 1

AMENDMENTS TO THE SOLICITORS (SCOTLAND) ACT 1980

[Not reproduced.]

Regulation 37(2)   SCHEDULE 2

APPLICATION, EXTENSION AND MODIFICATION OF ENACTMENTS TO REGISTERED EUROPEAN LAWYERS

PART I

SOLICITORS (SCOTLAND) ACT 1980

1.—(1) The provisions of the Solicitors (Scotland) Act 1980 shall have effect in relation to registered European lawyers as modified or extended by the provisions mentioned in these subparagraphs.

(2) Subsections (1) and (3) of section 2 shall apply to registered European lawyers as they apply to solicitors and any reference to a solicitor's practising certificate shall include reference to a registered European lawyer's registration certificate.

(3) The power to make regulations under section 5 shall also be exercisable in relation to registered European lawyers.

(4) The power to make rules under the following provisions:-

(a) section 34 (rules as to professional practice, conduct and discipline);
(b) section 35 (accounts rules);
(c) section 36 (interest on client's money);
(d) section 37 (accountant's certificates);
(e) section 44 (professional indemnity);
(f) section 52(2) (procedure on complaints to Tribunal);
(g) paragraph 4(1) and (4) of Part I of Schedule 3;

shall also be exercisable in relation to registered European lawyers and a reference in any of these provisions to a solicitor shall include a reference to a registered European lawyer and any references to a solicitor's practising certificate shall include references to a registered European lawyer's registration certificate.

(5) Any of the powers referred to in subparagraph (4) may be exercised so as to make different provision with respect to different categories of registered European lawyers and in different circumstances.

(6) Sections 20, 21, 30, 33A, 38 to 42, 42B, 42C, 51, 52(1), 53A to 54, 56, 56A, 60A to 64, Schedule 1 and paragraph 5 of Part II of Schedule 3 shall apply to registered European lawyers as they apply to solicitors and any references to a solicitor's practising certificate shall include references to a registered European lawyer's registration certificate.

(7) Sections 42A, 45, 46, 47 and 55 shall apply to registered European lawyers as they apply to solicitors and references in those sections to—

(a) the roll shall for this purpose include references to the register of European lawyers; and
(b) being struck off the roll shall for this purpose include references to being removed from the register of European lawyers.

(8) Section 43 shall apply to registered European lawyers as it applies to solicitors and references to a practising certificate shall include references to a registered European lawyer's registration certificate and references to the roll shall include references to the register of European lawyers and references to being struck off the roll shall include being removed from that register.

(9) Sections 53 and 55 and Schedule 4 shall apply to registered European lawyers as they apply to solicitors and any references in those sections and that Schedule to—

(a) solicitors shall include registered European lawyers;
(b) a solicitor's practising certificate shall include reference to a registered European lawyer's registration certificate;
(c) the roll shall include the register of European lawyers;
(d) enrolment shall include registration on the register of European lawyers; and
(e) being struck off the roll shall include being removed from that register.

PART II

OTHER ENACTMENTS AND PROVISIONS

1. In the Rehabilitation of Offenders Act 1974 (Exceptions Order) 1975 the reference to "solicitor" and "advocate" in Part 1 of Schedule 1 to the Order shall include reference to a registered European lawyer.

2. In the Estate Agents Act 1979[11] the reference to a practising solicitor in section 1(2)(a) (which exempts solicitors from that Act) shall include a reference to a registered European lawyer, and the partner of a registered European lawyer providing professional services in accordance with rules made under section 34 of the Solicitors (Scotland) Act 1980.

[1] 3. For the purposes of Part 20 of the Financial Services and Markets Act 2000 (provision of financial services by members of the professions), a registered European lawyer and any partner shall be treated as—

(a) a member of the profession in relation to which the Law Society of Scotland is established; and
(b) as subject to the rules of the Law Society of Scotland.

4. For the purposes of section 391 of the Insolvency Act 1986 (recognised professional bodies for insolvency practitioners) registered European lawyers and their partners shall be deemed to be—

(a) part of the solicitors' profession; and
(b) subject to the Law Society of Scotland's rules on the practice of their profession.
5. [*Repealed by the Financial Services and Markets Act 2000 (Consequential Amendments and Repeals) Order 2001 (SI 2001/3649) Pt 7(II) art.263(3) (effective December 1, 2001).*]
6.—(1) The Law Reform (Miscellaneous Provisions) (Scotland) Act 1990 shall be modified as follows.
(2) In section 33(5) in the definition of "practitioner" the references to "an advocate" and "a solicitor" shall be interpreted as including references to a registered European lawyer;
(3) In section 34(9) the references to "advocates" and "solicitors" shall be interpreted as including references to a registered European lawyer.

NOTE
[1] As substituted by the Financial Services and Markets Act 2000 (Consequential Amendments and Repeals) Order 2001 (SI 2001/3649) Pt 7(II) art.263(2) (effective December 1, 2001).

The European Communities (Lawyer's Practice) (Scotland) Amendment Regulations 2004

(SSI 2004/302)

[September 16, 2004]

The Scottish Ministers, in exercise of the powers conferred by section 2(2) of the European Communities Act 1972 and of all other powers enabling them in that behalf, hereby make the following Regulations:

Citation, commencement and interpretation
1.—(1) These Regulations may be cited as the European Communities (Lawyer's Practice) (Scotland) Amendment Regulations 2004 and shall come into force on 16th September 2004.
(2) In these Regulations, any reference to a regulation by number alone means the regulation so numbered in the European Communities (Lawyer's Practice) (Scotland) Regulations 2000.

Transitional provisions
2.—(1) In this regulation "relevant lawyer" means a European lawyer, as defined by the European Communities (Lawyer's Practice) (Scotland) Regulations 2000 as they are amended by these Regulations, who satisfies either or both of the conditions set out in paragraph (2) of this regulation.
(2) Those conditions are that—
(a) that person is a national of Switzerland, Iceland, Liechtenstein, Norway, the Czech Republic, Estonia, Cyprus, Latvia, Lithuania, Hungary, Malta, Poland, Slovenia or Slovakia; or
(b) that person is authorised in any of those States to pursue professional activities under any of the professional titles appearing in regulation 2(4) as it is amended by these Regulations, opposite the name of that State.
(3) Regulations 21 and 22 shall apply to a relevant lawyer only as from 16th March 2005.
(4) Regulation 1(2) to (5) shall apply to a relevant lawyer with the following modifications—
(a) for "22nd May 2000", where it occurs in paragraph (2), there shall be substituted "16th September 2004";
(b) for "21st November 2000", wherever it occurs, there shall be substituted "15th March 2005"; and
(c) for "22nd November 2000", wherever it occurs, there shall be substituted "16th March 2005".

Amendments to European Communities (Lawyer's Practice) (Scotland) Regulations 2000

3. In the table in regulation 2(4) (definition of European lawyer), after the entry relating to Sweden, there shall be inserted—

Switzerland	Avocat/Advokat/Rechtsanwalt/Anwalt/ Fürsprecher/Fürsprech/Avvocato
Iceland	Lögmaður
Liechtenstein	Rechtsanwalt
Norway	Advokat
Czech Republic	Advokát
Estonia	Vandeadvokaat
Cyprus	Δικηγόρος (Dikegoros)
Latvia	Zvērināts advokāts
Lithuania	Advokatas
Hungary	Ügyvéd
Malta	Avukat/Prokuratur legali
Poland	Adwokat/Radca prawny
Slovenia	Odvetnik/Odvetnica
Slovakia	Advokát/Komerčný právnik".

4. In regulation 12 (property transactions), for "or Sweden" there shall be substituted ", Sweden, Cyprus, the Czech Republic, Hungary, Iceland, Liechtenstein, Norway or Slovakia".

5. In regulation 13 (executries), for "or Sweden" there shall be substituted ", Sweden, Cyprus, Iceland, Liechtenstein, Norway or Slovakia".

The Solicitors (Scotland) Act 1980 (Foreign Lawyers and Multi-national Practices) Regulations 2004

(SSI 2004/383)

[October 1, 2004]

The Scottish Ministers, in exercise of the powers conferred by section 2(2) of the European Communities Act 1972 and all other powers enabling them in that behalf, hereby make the following Regulations:

Citation, commencement, extent and interpretation
1.—(1) These Regulations may be cited as the Solicitors (Scotland) Act 1980 (Foreign Lawyers and Multi national Practices) Regulations 2004 and shall come into force on 1st October 2004.

(2) These Regulations extend to Scotland and insofar as they extend beyond Scotland they do so only as a matter of Scots law.

(3) Expressions used in these Regulations have the same meanings as they have in the Solicitors (Scotland) Act 1980.

Amendment and modification of the 1980 Act
2. The Solicitors (Scotland) Act 1980 is amended and applied in accordance with these Regulations.

New section 23B
3. After section 23A insert—
"**23B.** Failure on the part of a registered foreign lawyer in practice to have in force a current registration certificate may be treated as professional misconduct for the purposes of Part IV.".

Amendment of section 26
4. In section 26 (offence for solicitors to act as agents for unqualified persons)—
  (a) in subsection (2), after "solicitor" in both places where it appears, insert ", registered foreign lawyer";
  (b) in subsection (3), after "incorporated practice" insert ", registered foreign lawyer, multi national practice".

Amendment of section 28
5. In section 28 (offence for solicitors who are disqualified to seek employment without informing employer)—
  (a) after paragraph (d) insert—
    " ; or
    (e) has had his registration as a registered foreign lawyer withdrawn; or
    (f) has been suspended from practice as a registered foreign lawyer,";
  (b) after "incorporated practice" insert "or multi-national practice".

Amendment of section 31
6. In section 31(1) (offence for unqualified persons to pretend to be solicitor or notary public)—
  (a) after paragraph (aa) insert—
    "(ab) pretends to be a registered foreign lawyer; or"; and
  (b) in paragraph (b), for "or registered European lawyer" substitute ", registered European lawyer or registered foreign lawyer".

Amendment of section 32
7. After section 32(3) (offence for unqualified person to prepare certain documents) insert—
    "(4) For the purposes of this section, "unqualified person" includes a registered foreign lawyer.".

New section 33B
8. After section 33A (privilege of incorporated practice from disclosure etc.) insert—
    "**33B.**—(1) Any communication made to or by a registered foreign lawyer in the course of his actings as such for a client shall in any legal proceedings be privileged from disclosure in like manner as if the registered foreign lawyer had at all material times been a solicitor acting for a client.
    (2) Any enactment or instrument making special provision in relation to a solicitor or other legal representative as to the disclosure of information, or as to the production, seizure or removal of documents, with respect to which a claim to professional privilege could be maintained, shall, with any necessary modifications, have effect in relation to a registered foreign lawyer as it has effect in relation to a solicitor.".

Amendment of section 34
9. After section 34(1A) (rules as to professional practice, conduct and discipline) insert—
    "(1B) Rules made under this section may—
    (a) prevent a solicitor from entering a multi-national practice without the approval of the Council; and
    (b) make different provision for the regulation of solicitors and registered foreign lawyers in a multi-national practice in the following different cases—
      (i)   where the principal place of business of the practice is

outside Scotland and it has a place of business in Scotland;
(ii)   where the principal place of business of the practice is in Scotland and it has a place of business outside Scotland;
(iii) where the principal place of business of the practice is in Scotland and it has no place of business outside Scotland.

(1C) For the purposes of subsection (1B)(b), the principal place of business of a multi-national practice shall be determined by the Council who shall take into account factors set out in rules which may be made under this section.".

Amendment of section 43

10. In section 43 (Guarantee Fund)—
(a) in subsection (2)(a), after "solicitor" in each place where it appears insert ", registered foreign lawyer"; and
(b) in subsection (3)—
   (i) at the end of paragraph (d) omit "or"; and
   (ii) after paragraph (e) insert—
      " ;
         (f) in respect of any act or default of a registered foreign lawyer, or any of his employees or partners, where such act or default takes place outside Scotland, unless the Council is satisfied that the act or default is closely connected with the registered foreign lawyer's practice, or any of his partners' practice, in Scotland; or
         (g) in respect of any act or default of any member, director, manager, secretary or other employee of an incorporated practice which is a multi-national practice, where such act or default takes place outside Scotland, unless the Council is satisfied that the act or default is closely connected with the incorporated practice's practice in Scotland.".

Amendment of section 60A

11. In section 60A (multi national practices)—
(a) in subsection (2), after paragraph (a) insert—
"(aa) the information which shall accompany such applications;";
(b) after subsection (4) insert—
"(4A) Any person may inspect the register of foreign lawyers during office hours without payment.

(4B) A registered foreign lawyer who wishes his name to be removed from the register of foreign lawyers may make an application to the Council in that behalf, and the Council shall, if the registered foreign lawyer satisfies the Council that he has made adequate arrangements with respect to the business that he has then in hand, remove the name of that foreign lawyer from the register of foreign lawyers.

(4C) On an application to the Council by a foreign lawyer whose name has been removed from the register of foreign lawyers under subsection (4B), the Council may, after such inquiry as they think proper, restore the name of the foreign lawyer to the register of foreign lawyers.

(4D) A foreign lawyer whose name has been removed (other than pursuant to an application made under subsection (4B)) from the register of foreign lawyers shall have his name restored to that register only if, on an application in that behalf made by him to the Tribunal and after such inquiry as the Tribunal thinks proper, the Tribunal so orders.

(4E) Rules made by the Tribunal under section 52 (procedure on complaints to the Tribunal) may—
(a) regulate the making, hearing and determining of applications under subsection (4D); and

(b) provide for payment by the applicant to the Council of such fee in respect of restoration to the register of foreign lawyers as the rules may specify.

(4F) Where, following an application under subsection (4), the Council decide not to enter the name of a foreign lawyer in the register of foreign lawyers the applicant may, within three months of the notification to him of the Council's decision (or later with the permission of the court), appeal to the court against the decision and, on such an appeal, the court may—

(a) order the Council to register the foreign lawyer;

(b) refuse the appeal; or

(c) remit the matter to the Council with such directions as it sees fit.

(4G) Sections 24A to 24G (registration certificates for registered European lawyers) shall apply to registered foreign lawyers as they apply to registered European lawyers and any reference in those sections (as so applied) to a registration certificate shall be construed as a reference to a registration certificate for a registered foreign lawyer."; and

(c) in subsection (5), omit paragraph (a).

Amendment of Schedule 3

12. After paragraph 1A of Schedule 3, insert—

"Contributions by registered foreign lawyers

1B.—(1) Subject to the provisions of this paragraph, paragraph 1 above shall apply to registered foreign lawyers as it applies to solicitors and in that paragraph as so applied references to a practising certificate shall be construed as references to a registered foreign lawyer's registration certificate.

(2) Where a registered foreign lawyer can prove that—

(a) he is covered by a guarantee provided in accordance with the rules of the legal profession of which he is a member; and

(b) the guarantee is equivalent in terms of the conditions and the extent of its cover to the Guarantee Fund,

then to the extent that there is such equivalence that lawyer shall be exempt from the requirements of paragraph 1.

(3) Where the equivalence referred to in sub paragraph (2) is only partial, the Society may specify the guarantee obligations a registered foreign lawyer is required to meet to comply with paragraph 1.

(4) The Council may, where it is satisfied that any acts or defaults on the part of a registered foreign lawyer would not result in a grant being made from the Guarantee Fund held under section 43, exempt that lawyer from the requirements of paragraph 1.

(5) Sub paragraphs (2), (6) and (8) of paragraph 1 shall not apply to registered foreign lawyers.".

Modification of provisions of the 1980 Act

13. Sections 30, 37, 38, 39, 39A, 40, 41, 42, 42A, 42B, 42C, 43, 45 (except subsection (4)), 47, 51 (except the references to a solicitor appointed under subsections (1) and (4)), 52(1), 53 (except subsections (2)(g), (6B) and (8)(b)), 53A, 53B, 53C, 54, 55 (except subsections (1)(ba) and (bb) and (3A)), 56, 56A, 61, 61A, 62A (except the references in that section to section 46), 63 and 64, paragraph 5 of Schedule 3 and Schedule 4 shall apply to registered foreign lawyers as they apply to solicitors and any reference in those sections as so applied—

(a) to a solicitor's practising certificate shall be construed as a reference to a registered foreign lawyer's registration certificate;

(b) to the roll shall be construed as a reference to the register of foreign lawyers;

(c) to enrolment shall be construed as a reference to registration on the register of foreign lawyers; and

(d) to being struck off the roll shall be construed as a reference to being removed from the register of foreign lawyers.

Rule-making powers

14.—(1) The power to make rules under—

(a) section 34 (rules as to professional practice, conduct and discipline);

(b) section 35 (accounts rules);

(c) section 36 (interest on client's money);

(d) section 37 (accountant's certificates);

(e) section 44 (professional indemnity);

(f) section 52(2) (procedure on complaints to the Tribunal) of; and

(g) paragraph 4(1) and (4) of Schedule 3 (Guarantee Fund—grants) to, the 1980 Act shall also be exercisable in relation to registered foreign lawyers and a reference in any of those provisions—

(i) to a solicitor shall include a reference to a registered foreign lawyer; and

(ii) to a solicitor's practising certificate shall include a reference to a registered foreign lawyer's registration certificate.

(2) Any of the powers referred to in paragraph (1) may be exercised so as to make different provision with respect to—

(a) different categories of registered foreign lawyer;

(b) different categories of incorporated practice; and

(c) different circumstances.

Modification of the Rehabilitation of Offenders Act 1974 (Exceptions) Order 1975

15. In the Rehabilitation of Offenders Act 1974 (Exceptions) Order 1975 the reference to "solicitor" in Part 1 of Schedule 1 shall include a reference to a registered foreign lawyer.

Modification of the Law Reform (Miscellaneous Provisions) (Scotland) Act 1990

16. Sections 33(5) and 34(9) of the Law Reform (Miscellaneous Provisions) (Scotland) Act 1990 shall apply to registered foreign lawyers as they apply to solicitors.

Proceeds of Crime Act 2002 (Money Laundering: Exceptions to Overseas Conduct Defence) Order 2006

(SI 2006/1070)

[May 15, 2006]

The Secretary of State, in exercise of the powers conferred upon him by sections 327(2A)(b)(ii), 328(3)(b)(ii) and 329(2A)(b)(ii) of the Proceeds of Crime Act 2002, makes the following Order:

1. This Order may be cited as the Proceeds of Crime Act 2002 (Money Laundering: Exceptions to Overseas Conduct Defence) Order 2006 and shall come into force on 15th May 2006.

2.—(1) Relevant criminal conduct of a description falling within paragraph (2) is prescribed for the purposes of sections 327(2A)(b)(ii), 328(3)(b)(ii) and 329(2A)(b)(ii) of the Proceeds of Crime Act 2002 (exceptions to defence where overseas conduct is legal under local law).

(2) Such relevant criminal conduct is conduct which would constitute an offence punishable by imprisonment for a maximum term in excess of 12 months in any part of the United Kingdom if it occurred there other than—

(a) an offence under the Gaming Act 1968;

(b) an offence under the Lotteries and Amusements Act 1976, or

(c) an offence under section 23 or 25 of the Financial Services and Markets Act 2000.

PRACTICE RULES, CODES AND REGULATIONS

EC QUALIFIED LAWYERS TRANSFER (SCOTLAND) REGULATIONS 1994

EC Qualified Lawyers Transfer (Scotland) Regulations 1994 made by the Council of the Law Society of Scotland in June 1994 with the concurrence of the Lord President of the Court of Session under section 5 of the Solicitors (Scotland) Act 1980.

F3.1

Title and commencement

1. These regulations may be cited as the EC Qualified Lawyers Transfer (Scotland) Regulations 1994 and shall come into operation on 1st July 1994.

Definitions and interpretation

2.—(1) In these Regulations, unless the context otherwise requires—

"the Act" means the Solicitors (Scotland) Act 1980;
"the Society" means The Law Society of Scotland;
"the Council" means the Council of the Society;
"the Directive" means the Directive of the Council of the European Communities for recognition of Higher Education Diplomas dated 21st December 1988 and numbered 89/48/EEC;
"applicant" means a person seeking admission as a solicitor in Scotland under these Regulations;
"the Test" means the qualified lawyers transfer test being the aptitude test defined in Article 1(g) of the Directive and being an assessment of competence in the subjects specified in these Regulations;
"the court" means the Court of Session.

(2) The provisions of the Interpretation Act 1978 shall apply to the interpretation of these Regulations as they apply to the interpretation of an Act of Parliament.

(3) The headings to these Regulations do not form part of these Regulations.

Scope of regulations

3. These Regulations shall apply to any lawyer making application for admission as a solicitor in Scotland pursuant to the Directive or legislation implementing the Directive in the United Kingdom.

Eligibility

4.—(1) An applicant shall submit his application in writing to the Society and shall—

    (i) make payment of such fee for assessment of his application by the Society as the Council shall from time to time prescribe; and

    (ii) provide such evidence as the Society may require that he

        (a) is a person to whom the Directive and in consequence these Regulations may apply; and

        (b) is a fit and proper person to be a solicitor.

(2) The Council shall within a period of four months after presentation by the applicant of all relevant documentation, issue a written statement giving its decision as to whether or not the applicant is eligible to seek admission as a solicitor in Scotland.

(3) Where it is established that an applicant is eligible to seek admission in terms of regulation 4(2), the Council shall specify those subjects (if any) in the Test which the applicant shall be required to pass and any other conditions which the applicant must satisfy, having regard to the nature and extent of the applicant's experience (if any) of legal practice in Scotland and any academic or other qualification in the law of Scotland.

The Test

5.—(1)   An applicant who has established his eligibility conform to regulation 4 shall be required to pass the Test in such subjects as are specified in the written statement referred to in regulation 4(2).

(2) The Test shall be an assessment by written and oral examination of an applicant's competence in the following subjects—

   (a) the Scottish law of Property including for this purpose the law of trusts and succession and family law;
   (b) the Scottish Legal System including for this purpose the law of evidence and civil and criminal procedure;
   (c) European Community Law and Institutions;
   (d) Professional Conduct including for this purpose a knowledge of the Solicitors' (Scotland) Accounts Rules in force from time to time; and
   (e) such other subjects as the Council may from time to time reasonably prescribe.

(3) The Council may delegate to appropriately qualified persons the examination of applicants taking the Test and the Test will be held at such times as the Council may determine.

(4) An applicant shall be required to give such notice of his intention to sit the Test and pay to the Society such fee for the Test as the Council shall from time to time prescribe.

(5) An applicant who has failed to pass the Test on four separate occasions shall not be again entitled to present himself for the Test.

(6) Unless the Council in exceptional circumstances otherwise determines, an applicant shall require to pass the Test at a single diet.

(7) The Council may at its sole discretion and subject to such reasonable conditions as it may impose, in what it deems to be appropriate circumstances, and taking into account the particular merits of an applicant, exempt him from all or any part of the Test or from the provisions of regulation 5(5).

Certificate of fitness
   6. Where an applicant has
   (a) passed or gained exemption from the Test or any part thereof; and
   (b) complied with any conditions imposed upon him by the Council in terms of these Regulations; and
   (c) satisfied the Council that he remains a fit and proper person to be a solicitor
he shall be entitled to obtain from the Council a certificate in terms of section 6(1)(b)(ii) of the Act and thereafter to call upon the Council to apply to the court on his behalf for admission as a solicitor in terms of section 6(3A) of the Act.

Application of these regulations
   7. These Regulations shall have effect in relation to applications for admission as a solicitor in Scotland received by the Society from applicants on or after 1st January 1994.

Revocation of 1990 regulations
   8. The EC Qualified Lawyers Transfer (Scotland) Regulations 1990 are hereby revoked.

Admission as Solicitor (Scotland) Regulations 2001

Rules dated 25th April 2001, made by the Council of The Law Society of Scotland with the concurrence of the Lord President of the Court of Session under section 5 of the Solicitors (Scotland) Act 1980.

PART I

INTRODUCTORY

Title and commencement
1. These Regulations may be cited as the Admission as Solicitor (Scotland) Regulations 2001 and shall come into operation on 1st May 2001.

Interpretation
2.—(1) In these Regulations, unless the context otherwise requires:—
    "Accreditation Procedure" means the procedure whereby the Council approves the courses offered by Universities in Scotland for the Degree of Bachelor of Laws and the courses offered by Universities, and other institutions, in Scotland for the Diploma;

"the Act" means the Solicitors (Scotland) Act 1980 (as amended);

"Certificate of Fitness" means a certificate issued by the Council under the hand of the Secretary that the person to whom the certificate applies has fulfilled the applicable conditions and requirements prescribed in these Regulations and in any enactment for admission as a solicitor in Scotland;

"the Council" means the Council of the Society or, where the Council has delegated powers for the consideration of applications under these Regulations, a Committee of the Council or such other body or individual to whom such powers have been delegated;

"degree" means a degree, other than an honorary degree, granted by a University;

"Degree in Law" means, until such date as the Accreditation Procedure first comes into effect, the degree of Bachelor of Laws (LL.B.) granted by one of the Universities of Aberdeen, Dundee, Edinburgh, Glasgow or Strathclyde and, after such date, the degree of Bachelor of Laws granted by any University in Scotland that is from time to time accredited by the Council in respect of the degree of Bachelor of Laws;

"Diploma" means, until such date as the Accreditation Procedure first comes into effect, the Diploma in Legal Practice granted by one of the Universities of Aberdeen, Dundee or Edinburgh or jointly by the Universities of Glasgow and Strathclyde and, after such date, the Diploma in Legal Practice granted by any University, or other institution, in Scotland that is from time to time accredited by the Council in respect of the Diploma in Legal Practice or granted jointly by any such University or other institution with any other such University or institution;

"the Directive" means Directive No. 98/5/EC of the European Parliament and Council and legislation and regulations (including regulations or rules of the Council) implementing that Directive in Scotland;

"employer" means a training solicitor who is a party to a training contract and references to "employ" and similar words include otherwise taking on a trainee under a training contract;

"Entrance Certificate" means a certificate issued by the Council under the hand of the Secretary to the effect that the person to whom the certificate applies has fulfilled the applicable conditions and requirements prescribed in these Regulations and in any enactment for admission as a solicitor in Scotland to entitle him to enter into a post-Diploma training contract or a non-Diploma training contract;

"Examiner" means an examiner appointed under regulation 19 of these Regulations;

"intrant" means a person seeking to become a solicitor in Scotland;

"non-Diploma training contract" means a training contract entered into between a training solicitor and an intrant who is exempt from holding a Diploma under these Regulations;

"post-Diploma training contract" means a training contract under regulation 7 of these Regulations which is entered into between a training solicitor and an intrant who holds an Entrance Certificate;

"practising certificate" has the meaning given by section 4 of the Act;

"pre-Diploma training contract" means a training contract which is entered into between a training solicitor and an intrant who is qualified under the provisions of regulation 11 of, and the Schedule to, these Regulations;

"Preliminary Entrance Certificate" means a certificate issued by the Council under the hand of the Secretary to the effect that the person to whom the certificate applies has fulfilled the applicable conditions and requirements prescribed in these Regulations and in any enactment for admission as a solicitor in Scotland to entitle him to enter into a pre-Diploma training contract;

"Professional Competence Course" means the professional competence course approved by the Council and offered by any University, or other institution, in Scotland that is from time to time approved by the Council in respect of that course or offered jointly by any such University or other institution with any other such University or institution;

"the 1986 Regulations" means the Admission as Solicitor (Scotland) Regulations 1986;

"the 1991 Regulations" means the Admission as Solicitor (Scotland) Regulations 1991;

"the 1994 Regulations" means the EC Qualified Lawyers Transfer (Scotland) Regulations 1994 and any other regulations from time to time applicable to an intrant making an application pursuant to the Directive referred to in regulation 3 of those regulations;

"the Secretary" means the Secretary of the Society and includes any person authorised by the Council to act on behalf of the Secretary for the purpose of these Regulations;

"the Society" means the Law Society of Scotland;

"the Society's examinations" means examinations set under regulation 21(1) of these Regulations;

"solicitor" means any person enrolled or deemed to have been enrolled as a solicitor in pursuance of the Act;

"Test of Professional Competence" means the test of professional competence set by, or on behalf of, the Society;

"trainee" means an intrant who is a party to a training contract;

"training contract" means a non-Diploma training contract, a post-Diploma training contract or a pre-Diploma training contract;

"training solicitor" means a solicitor who holds a practising certificate issued under section 14 of the Act and who:—

(a) is engaged as a principal in private practice; or

(b) is in employment as a solicitor,

and the expression "training solicitor" shall include a firm or an incorporated practice of solicitors as defined in the Act or a multi-national practice (as defined in the Act); and

"University" means:—

(a) any university in the United Kingdom; or

(b) the former Council for National Academic Awards; or

(c) any other University or institute recognised by the Council for the purposes of these Regulations.

(2) The provisions of the Interpretation Act 1978 shall apply for the interpretation of these Regulations as they apply to the interpretation of an Act of Parliament.

NOTE
[1] As amended by the Solicitors (Scotland) (Registered Foreign Lawyers) etc. Practice Rules 2005, Sch.5 (effective May 1, 2005).

Conditions precedent to admission
3. Subject to the provisions of section 6 of the Act and these Regulations, every intrant shall, as a condition precedent to his admission as a solicitor, comply with these Regulations so far as applicable to him and the Council may require any intrant to satisfy it by such means as it considers necessary as to such compliance.

Application of these Regulations
4.—(1) These Regulations shall apply to all intrants other than:—

(a) intrants (hereinafter referred to as "1986 intrants") who have presented themselves for any of the Society's examinations, obtained a Preliminary Entrance Certificate or obtained an Entrance Certificate under the 1986 Regulations;

(b) intrants (hereinafter referred to as "1991 intrants") who have presented themselves for any of the Society's examinations, obtained a Preliminary Entrance Certificate or obtained an Entrance Certificate under the 1991 Regulations;

(c) intrants eligible under the 1994 Regulations; and

(d) intrants eligible under the Directive.

(2) Any 1986 intrants or 1991 intrants who wish to do so may, by notice in writing to the Council, elect to proceed to admission under these Regulations but such election, once made, shall be irrevocable. In the absence of such an election, 1986 intrants shall proceed to admission under the 1986 Regulations and 1991 intrants shall proceed to admission under the 1991 Regulations.

(3) Notwithstanding regulation 4(1) of these Regulations, any person who is the subject of a decision by the Council made after the date these Regulations come into operation under the 1986 Regulations, the 1991 Regulations or the 1994 Regulations and who is aggrieved by that decision may, within 21 days of written intimation of the decision, appeal to the Court of Session.

PART II

ENTRANCE QUALIFICATIONS

(A) Entrance Certificate

Issue of Entrance Certificate

5.—(1) An intrant may not enter into either a post-Diploma training contract or a non-Diploma training contract unless he holds an Entrance Certificate.

(2) An intrant shall be entitled to an Entrance Certificate if he satisfies the Council that:—

(a) he is a fit and proper person to be a solicitor;

(b) (i) he holds a Degree in Law or a certificate that he is entitled to graduate in such a Degree notwithstanding that he has not so graduated; or (ii) he has served for a period of three years under a pre-Diploma training contract and has passed or obtained exemption from the Society's examinations; or (iii) he is an intrant to whom the provisions of any of regulations 29, 31, 32 or 33 of these Regulations apply; and

(c) unless exempt in terms of regulation 28(1) or Part V of these Regulations, he has obtained a Diploma.

Lapse of Entrance Certificate

6. An intrant's Entrance Certificate shall automatically lapse if he does not enter into either a post-Diploma training contract or a non-Diploma training contract within one year of the date of said Entrance Certificate or such extended period as may be permitted by the Council in any particular case.

(B) Post-Diploma training contract

Service under a post-Diploma training contract

7.—(1) Subject to regulation 28(1) and Part V of these Regulations, it shall be a requirement for admission as a solicitor in Scotland that an intrant shall serve under a post-Diploma training contract entered into with a training solicitor.

(2) The period of training under a post-Diploma training contract shall comprise two years of full-time training, provided always that any intrant may, with the written consent of the Council, undergo training on a part-time basis provided that the Council is satisfied that the total time spent working under such a post-Diploma training contract shall equate to two years of full-time training.

(3) Every post-Diploma training contract shall be in, or as nearly as may be in, such a form as the Council may from time to time prescribe.

Commencement of post-Diploma training contract
8.—(1) In the case of an intrant who is required to hold a Diploma, the commencement of his post-Diploma training contract shall be within a period of two years of the date of 1st January first occurring after the date when the intrant became entitled to the award of the Diploma provided that the Council may in its discretion extend such period but may, in granting such extension, impose such conditions as it thinks fit.

(2) In exercising its discretion under regulation 8(1) of these Regulations the Council shall have regard to the appropriateness of any work, paid or voluntary, and courses undertaken by the intrant since the intrant became entitled to the award of the Diploma and also the endeavours of the intrant to obtain a post-Diploma training contract.

Service elsewhere in Scotland and in other jurisdictions
9.—(1) Subject to the prior approval of the employer and the Council in each case, a trainee under a post-Diploma training contract may be permitted in order to extend the range of his training:—
  (a) to undertake legal work under appropriate supervision within Scotland on secondment; and/or
  (b) to undertake legal work under appropriate supervision for a period or periods not exceeding in the aggregate six months in any other part of the United Kingdom or any country which is a member of the European Union.
The period of any such secondment and such other period or periods of legal work shall be reckoned as part of the trainee's period of service under his post-Diploma training contract.

(2) A trainee may serve under a post-Diploma training contract at his employer's place of business outwith Scotland, but such a trainee shall not, without the prior approval of the Council, during the period of his post-Diploma training contract spend a period or periods exceeding in the aggregate six months at any such place of business outwith Scotland.

(C) Pre-Diploma training contract

Service under a pre-Diploma training contract
10.—(1) Any intrant who for the purpose of qualifying for an Entrance Certificate proposes to meet the requirements of regulation 5(2)(b)(ii) of these Regulations without obtaining a Degree in Law shall be required to enter into a pre-Diploma training contract with a training solicitor.

(2) The period of training under a pre-Diploma training contract shall comprise three years of full-time training, provided always that any intrant may, with the written consent of the Council, undergo training on a part-time basis provided that the Council is satisfied that the total time spent working under such a pre-Diploma training contract shall equate to three years of full-time training.

(3) Every pre-Diploma training contract shall be in, or as nearly as may be in, such form as the Council may from time to time prescribe and shall, subject to the provisions of regulation 17(1) of these Regulations, contain an obligation on the training solicitor to provide training for the intrant in:—
  (a) conveyancing;

(b) litigation; and
(c) either
    (i) trusts and executries; or
    (ii) where the training solicitor is not engaged in private practice, the
        legal work of the training solicitor.

(4) Subject to the consent of the employer, an intrant who is a party to a pre-Diploma training contract may be permitted to attend, during office hours, classes in law at a University or other institution.

(D) Preliminary Entrance Certificate

Issue of Preliminary Entrance Certificate
    11.—(1) An intrant may not enter into a pre-Diploma training contract unless he holds a Preliminary Entrance Certificate.

(2) An intrant shall be entitled to a Preliminary Entrance Certificate if he satisfies the Council that:—
    (a) he is a fit and proper person to be a solicitor; and
    (b) he is qualified under the provisions of the Schedule to these
        Regulations.

(3) The Council shall have power, in the case of an intrant who, being at least 21 years of age, satisfies the Council both that he is a fit and proper person to be a solicitor and, having regard to evidence of academic attainment and to any experience of legal work, as to his fitness to enter into a pre-Diploma training contract, to grant to such an intrant a Preliminary Entrance Certificate without requiring compliance with regulation (2)(b) of this regulation.

(4) In the event that any of the certificates referred to in paragraphs (a), (b) or (c) of the Schedule are no longer generally available, the Council may specify such alternative qualifications and/or levels of attainment for the purpose of those paragraphs as seem to it to be the nearest equivalent to those certificates and level of pass referred to in the Schedule.

(E) Non-Diploma training contract

Service under a non-Diploma training contract
    12.—(1) Subject to regulation 30 of these Regulations, an intrant who is exempt from holding a Diploma under regulation 28(1) or Part V of these Regulations shall serve under a non-Diploma training contract entered into with a training solicitor.

(2) The non-Diploma training contract shall be in similar terms to a post-Diploma training contract and shall be subject to the same conditions and requirements as are specified in these Regulations in relation to post-Diploma training contracts; provided that the minimum period of time which an intrant is required to serve under a non-Diploma training contract shall be either three years or, where applicable, the appropriate period specified in regulations 29, 31 or 32 of these Regulations.

(F) General provisions affecting training contract

Provisions as to training solicitors and intrants
    [1] **13.**—(1) A training solicitor shall not, without the consent in writing of the Council, employ any trainee, unless he is in practice as a solicitor at the time and has been in continuous practice for a period of at least three years immediately prior to his employing the trainee or, where the training solicitor is a firm or incorporated practice, at least one of the partners or directors (in the case of an incorporated practice which is a company) or members (in the case of an incorporated practice which is a limited liability partnership) thereof, as the case may be, has been in such continuous practice or, where the training solicitor is a multi-national practice, at least

one of the solicitors who is a member thereof has been in such continuous practice.

(2) The total number of intrants employed at any time under training contracts shall not, except with the consent of the Council, exceed:—

(a) in the case of a solicitor practising on his own under his own name or as a sole solicitor under a firm name, one;

(b) in the case of a firm or an incorporated practice of solicitors, twice the number of partners in the firm, or twice the number of directors (being individuals) of an incorporated practice which is a company, or twice the number of members (being individuals) of an incorporated practice which is a limited liability partnership, as the case may be;

² (ba) in the case of a multi-national practice, twice the number of solicitors who are members of the multi-national practice;

(c) in the case of a firm or an incorporated practice of solicitors having more than one office, within each such office, twice the number of solicitors having their principal place of business within that office but subject always, in respect of the firm or incorporated practice of solicitors as a whole, to the maximum specified by paragraph (b) above;

² (ca) in the case of a multi-national practice having more than one office, within each office, twice the number of solicitors having their principal place of business within that office, but subject always, in respect of the multi-national practice as a whole, to the maximum specified by paragraph (ba) above;

(d) in the case of a solicitor in employment, twice the number of solicitors employed by the solicitor's employer who are entitled, in terms of regulation 13(1) of these Regulations, to employ a trainee without the consent in writing of the Council but subject always, in respect of the solicitor's employer as a whole, (i) where the solicitor's employer falls within paragraph (a) or (b) above, to the maximum specified by, as the case may be, paragraph (a) or (b) above, and (ii) in any other case, to a maximum of twice the number of solicitors employed by the solicitor's employer who are so entitled;

(e) in the case of a solicitor in employment where the solicitor's employer has more than one office, within each such office, twice the number of solicitors having their principal place of business in that office but subject always, in respect of the solicitor's employer as a whole, to the maxima specified by paragraph (d) above; and

(f) in the case of any other solicitor, such number as the Council may in each case determine.

NOTES
¹ As amended by the Solicitors (Scotland) (Registered Foreign Lawyers) etc. Practice Rules 2005, Sch.5 (effective May 1, 2005).
² Inserted by the Solicitors (Scotland) (Registered Foreign Lawyers) etc. Practice Rules 2005, Sch.5 (effective May 1, 2005).

Registration of training contracts
14.—(1) For the purposes of these Regulations, the Council shall establish and maintain a register of pre-Diploma training contracts, a register of post-Diploma training contracts and a register of non-Diploma training contracts.

(2) Every training contract shall be produced by the intrant to the Council for registration within three months from its commencement and thereafter shall be presented for registration in the Books of Council and Session by the Society at the expense of the intrant.

(3) When an intrant produces his training contract to the Council, he shall pay such registration fee as the Council may from time to time prescribe.

(4) If an intrant's training contract and the prescribed registration fee are not presented to the Council within three months from the date of the commencement of the training contract, the period of service under the training contract shall for the purposes of these Regulations be reckoned, if the Council so directs, as commencing only from the date of presentation of the training contract to the Council or such earlier date as the Council may determine.

(5) Every assignation of a training contract shall, together with the relevant supporting documents, be produced by the trainee to the Council within six weeks from the date of assignation for registration in the relevant register of training contracts and, where the assignation has not been registered within said period, service after the assignation, but prior to its registration, shall be reckoned as part of the trainee's service under the training contract only to such extent as the Council may determine.

(6) Any person seeking registration of an assignation of a training contract shall pay to the Council such fee as it may from time to time determine.

Service under training contracts

15.—(1) The employer and the trainee shall each comply with their respective obligations under any training contract.

(2) For the purposes of these Regulations and subject to regulations 7, 9, 10 and 12 of these Regulations:—

    (a) a trainee during the term of his training contract shall not during office hours engage in any other gainful employment or otherwise absent himself from his employer's business without the prior consent of his employer and of the Council;

    (b) service by a trainee under a training contract shall be continuous, provided however that in exceptional circumstances, the Council may, in considering whether or not such service has been continuous and provided that the employer is prepared to certify the trainee's fitness to become a solicitor in due course or to continue as a solicitor, as the case may be, disregard short periods of absence by the trainee from employment, not exceeding an aggregate of six months; and

    (c) service by a trainee under a training contract shall be in Scotland.

Intervention in training contracts

16.—(1) The Council may make enquiries concerning any aspect of a training contract and the conduct of the parties to that contract and the Council shall be entitled to require the evidence of the employer, the trainee, any solicitor and any intrant and to call for and recover such evidence and documents from any such person as the Council thinks proper.

(2) If the Council, after enquiry and after affording the parties to the training contract the opportunity to make representations, is of the opinion that a party to a training contract is not, as a result of the acts or omissions of the other party to the training contract, receiving the benefits it should receive from that training contract, the Council may require that other party to take such steps as the Council may request to ensure that those benefits are so received.

(3) Without prejudice to the generality of regulation 16(2) of these Regulations, if:—

    (a) during the term of any training contract either the trainee or the employer has been continuously absent from the employer's place of business for an aggregate period of at least three months within any period of six months without reasonable cause; or

    (b) the Council, after enquiry and after affording the parties to the training contract the opportunity to make representations, is of the opinion that a training contract ought to be terminated, assigned or extended; or

(c) there is a dispute between the parties to a training contract

the Council may be notice in writing to the parties to the training contract require the termination of the training contract with effect from such date as may be specified in the notice or may require an assignation of the training contract or an extension to it, as the case may be, or may take such other action as it thinks fit. Where the Council has by notice required the termination of a training contract any service by the trainee under that training contract after the date specified in the notice shall not be reckoned as part of his period of service for the purpose of regulation 34 of these Regulations.

(4) Where, before the expiration of the period of service under a training contract, such training contract is terminated for any reason, an intrant shall be entitled and may be required, subject to such conditions as the Council may impose, to enter into a further training contract with another training solicitor.

(5) An employer shall be obliged to assign a post-Diploma training contract or non-Diploma training contract if called upon to do so by the Council.

(6) An intrant's Entrance Certificate may be withdrawn by the Council in such exceptional circumstances as the Council may in its sole discretion determine.

(7) If the Council after enquiry decides that a training solicitor would be unable to fulfil or is not fulfilling the proper obligations of an employer under a training contract either in relation to a particular application to employ a trainee or in relation to a particular training contract or generally, it shall intimate its decision to the solicitor and the solicitor, notwithstanding that he satisfies the provisions of regulation 13(1) of these Regulations, shall not thereafter engage or retain the services of any trainee without the consent in writing of the Council.

Consent to transfer of training contract

17.—(1) An employer under a pre-Diploma training contract shall, if requested by his trainee or if called upon to do so by the Council, assign such pre-Diploma training contract to another training solicitor, approved by the Council, to enable the trainee either to complete his training in the three areas of practice described in (a), (b) and (c)(i) of regulation 10(3) of these Regulations or to extend the range of his training generally, or for any other reason which the Council shall consider reasonable.

(2) A training contract shall not be assigned by the employer without the consent in writing of the Council.

(G) Professional Competence Course and Test of Professional Competence

Requirement

18. For an intrant to whom these Regulations apply it shall, subject to regulation 28(2) and (3) and Part V of these Regulations, be a requirement for admission as a solicitor in Scotland that he shall have:—
  (a) completed the Professional Competence Course or given the undertaking referred to in regulation 38(2)(b) of these Regulations; and
  (b) passed the Test of Professional Competence or given the undertaking referred to in regulation 38(2)(b) of these Regulations.

PART III

QUALIFICATIONS AND EXAMINATIONS

Appointment of Examiners

19.—(1) In order to test the suitability and qualifications of intrants, the Council shall from time to time nominate and appoint fit and proper persons to be Examiners and hold examinations in accordance with this part of these Regulations, which examinations shall be under the management and control of the Council.

(2) The Examiners shall comply with all directions that may be given by the Council with respect to the number of papers to be set on any subject, the number of questions to be set and to be answered and the percentage mark to be attained to qualify for a pass and any other matters in connection with the examinations.

(3) The Examiners shall be appointed for such period of time and be paid such remuneration as the Council may from time to time determine.

Eligibility of intrants
20. An intrant shall not be entitled to present himself for any of the Society's examinations unless he:—
  (a) holds a Preliminary Entrance Certificate and is serving under a pre-Diploma training contract or, that contract having terminated, had, prior to such termination, already presented himself for one or more of the Society's examinations; or
  (b) holds, or is entitled to graduate with, a Degree in Law which does not include passes in all the subjects in the syllabus prescribed by regulation 21(1) of these Regulations.

Examinations
21.—(1) The Society's examinations shall consist of examinations in the laws of Scotland in accordance with the syllabus prescribed by the Council from time to time.

(2) An intrant shall not be permitted to sit any one examination on more than four occasions or later than four years from the date of the first of the Society's examinations for which he presented himself except with the consent of the Council following on a recommendation by the Examiners, which consent may be given subject to such conditions as are deemed appropriate.

Award of distinction
22. A certificate of distinction in any subject may be awarded to an intrant at the discretion of the Examiners.

Conduct, dates and places of examinations
23.—(1) Diets for the Society's examinations shall be held in Edinburgh not less than twice each year and additional diets may be held in such circumstances as the Examiners, with the approval of the Council, may determine.

(2) Intrants intending to present themselves as candidates at any of the Society's examinations shall give three weeks' notice in writing of their intention to the Secretary, provided that the Examiners may at their discretion allow an intrant who has not given such notice to present himself for any examination.

(3) Every candidate shall be examined in writing and may be required by the Examiners to present himself for oral examination.

(4) Every candidate shall be required to advise the Society of any permanent change of address.

Fees
24. A candidate shall tender with his application to sit any examination such fee as may be prescribed by the Council from time to time.

PART IV

EXEMPTIONS

Faculty of Advocates' examinees
25. The Council may exempt from any of the Society's examinations an intrant who has obtained a pass in the corresponding examination in the examinations for admission to the Faculty of Advocates.

Corresponding passes
26. Where an intrant seeks exemption from any of the Society's examinations, provided the Council is satisfied that the intrant has passed a corresponding examination in the laws of Scotland to a standard approved by the Council, then the Council may grant such exemption.

Further exemptions for intrants from elsewhere in the UK
27. Where the terms of regulation 30 or 31 of these Regulations do not apply, the Council may, on application by an intrant who has passed the examinations required for admission as a solicitor or barrister in England and Wales or Northern Ireland within a reasonable time prior to such application, determine which of the Society's examinations, if any, such intrant shall be required to pass for the purposes of regulation 5(2)(b) of these Regulations and, notwithstanding regulation 20 of these Regulations, and subject always to such conditions as the Council may impose, including conditions as to the period of time during which the examinations must be passed, such an intrant shall be entitled to present himself for the Society's examinations.

Exemptions from Diploma, Professional Competence Course and Test of Professional Competence
28.—(1) An intrant who seeks to obtain a Certificate of Fitness under these Regulations and who satisfies the Council that there are exceptional circumstances which justify his being exempted from obtaining a Diploma may be granted a Certificate of Fitness on such conditions, including the passing of examinations, as the Council may in its discretion prescribe; provided that an intrant who receives such exemption shall be required to serve for a period of not less than three years under a non-Diploma training contract with a training solicitor, in terms similar to those of a post-Diploma training contract.

(2) An intrant who seeks to obtain a Certificate of Fitness under these Regulations and who satisfies the Council that there are exceptional circumstances which justify his being exempted from completing a Professional Competence Course may be granted a Certificate of Fitness on such conditions as the Council may in its discretion prescribe.

(3) An intrant who has become entitled to the award of the Diploma prior to 1st October 2000 shall be exempt from both passing the Test of Professional Competence and completing the Professional Competence Course.

PART V

REQUIREMENTS FOR SPECIAL INTRANTS

Scottish advocates
29. Notwithstanding any other provisions herein contained, but always without prejudice to regulation 41 of these Regulations, an intrant who is a member of the Faculty of Advocates, has had two years of recent active practice of Scots law since being called and who provides such evidence as the Council may require that he is a fit and proper to be admitted as a solicitor in Scotland shall be exempt from:—

(a) pre-Diploma training,
(b) the Society's examinations, and
(c) the Diploma

but he shall be required to complete the Professional Competence Course, pass the Test of Professional Competence and undergo six months of non-Diploma training prior to applying for admission in terms of regulation 34 of these Regulations.

English/Welsh and Northern Irish solicitors

30. Notwithstanding any other provisions herein contained, but always without prejudice to regulation 41 of these Regulations, an intrant who has been admitted as a solicitor in England and Wales or Northern Ireland and who provides such evidence as the Council may require that he is a fit and proper person to be admitted as a solicitor in Scotland shall be exempt from:—

(a) the Society's examinations,
(b) the Diploma,
(c) any period of training, and
(d) completing the Professional Competence Course and passing the Test of Professional Competence

but he shall be required to pass in such manner as the Council may require an intra-UK transfer test comprising examinations in conveyancing, trusts and succession, Scots criminal law, with civil and criminal evidence and procedure and (unless admitted as aforesaid prior to 1st January 1992) European Community law and institutions or such other examinations as may be prescribed by the Council from time to time prior to applying for admission in terms of regulation 34 of these Regulations.

English/Welsh and Northern Irish barristers

31. Notwithstanding any other provisions herein contained, but always without prejudice to regulation 41 of these Regulations, an intrant who is a member of the Bar in England and Wales or Northern Ireland, who provides such evidence as the Council may require that he is a fit and proper person to be admitted as a solicitor in Scotland and can demonstrate that he has had five years of recent active practice of law in the United Kingdom since his call to the Bar shall be exempt from:—

(a) pre-Diploma training,
(b) the Society's examinations, and
(c) the Diploma

but he shall be required to complete the Professional Competence Course, pass the Test of Professional Competence, pass in such manner as the Council may require an intra-UK transfer test comprising examinations in conveyancing, trusts and succession, Scots criminal law, with civil and criminal evidence and procedure and (unless called as aforesaid prior to 1st January 1992) European Community law and institutions or such other examinations as may be prescribed by the Council from time to time and undergo a period of six months of non-Diploma training, or such longer period as the Council may in its discretion determine, prior to applying for admission in terms of regulation 34 of these Regulations.

Colonial solicitors

32. Notwithstanding any other provisions herein contained, but always without prejudice to regulation 41 of these Regulations, an intrant to whom the Colonial Solicitors Act 1900, and any Order in Council made thereunder, apply and who provides such evidence as the Council may require that he is a fit and proper person to be admitted as a solicitor in Scotland shall be exempt from

(a) pre-Diploma training, and
(b) the Diploma

but he shall be required to complete the Professional Competence Course, pass the Test of Professional Competence, pass the Society's examinations and undergo one year of non-Diploma training prior to applying for admission in terms of regulation 34 of these Regulations.

Other overseas lawyers
33. Notwithstanding any other provisions herein contained, but always without prejudice to regulation 41 of these Regulations, a practising lawyer from outwith the United Kingdom to whom the Colonial Solicitors Act 1900, and any Order in Council made thereunder, the 1994 Regulations or the Directive do not apply shall be exempt from pre-Diploma training but he shall be required to satisfy the Council that he is qualified to undertake within the jurisdiction in which he qualified or practises professional work equivalent in its nature to that of a solicitor or advocate in Scotland, to provide such evidence as the Council may require that he is a fit and proper person to be admitted as a solicitor in Scotland and to pass the Society's examinations, gain the Diploma, complete the Professional Competence Course, pass the Test of Professional Competence and complete one year of post-Diploma training prior to applying for admission in terms of regulation 34 of these Regulations.

PART VI

PROCEDURE FOR ADMISSION AS SOLICITOR

Eligibility for Certificate of Fitness
34. Subject to the provisions of section 6 of the Act and these Regulations, an intrant shall be entitled to apply for a Certificate of Fitness for the purposes of section 6 of the Act if:—
(1)(a) he has passed or obtained exemption from all of the required Society's examinations; or
  (b) he has obtained or is entitled to obtain a Degree in Law which includes passes in subjects which the Council is satisfied correspond to all the subjects prescribed in the syllabus referred to in regulation 21(1) of these Regulations or, where such Degree does not include passes in subjects which correspond to all the subjects prescribed, he obtains passes in the remaining prescribed subjects in the Society's examinations, or otherwise passes corresponding subjects at the standard required for a Degree in Law; and
(2) he holds a Diploma, unless he is exempted from the requirement to hold a Diploma in terms of these Regulations; and
(3)(a) he has completed the Professional Competence Course, or is exempt therefrom, and has passed the Test of Professional Competence, or is exempt therefrom; or
  (b) he has complied with regulation 34(4)(a) or (c) of these Regulations; and
(4)(a) he has completed not less than one year of his two-year period of service under a post-Diploma training contract and has submitted to the Council:—
    (i) a declaration in conformity with regulation 36(1) of these Regulations;
    (ii) an undertaking in such form as the Council may prescribe that he will complete the remaining period of service under such training contract in fulfilment of his obligation under that training contract;
    (iii) an undertaking in conformity with regulation 38(1) of these Regulations; and
    (iv) undertakings in conformity with regulation 38(2) of these Regulations; or

(b) he has completed the full period of service under a post-Diploma training contract and has submitted to the Council a declaration in conformity with regulation 37 of these Regulations; or

(c) he has completed not less than two years of the full period of service under a non-Diploma training contract and he has submitted to the Council a declaration in conformity with regulation 36(2) of these Regulations and the undertakings referred to in regulation 34(4)(a) of these Regulations; or

(d) he has completed the full period of service under a non-Diploma training contract as is prescribed for him under these Regulations and has submitted to the Council a declaration in conformity with regulation 37 of these Regulations; or

(e) he is an intrant to whom regulation 33 of these Regulations applies and he has completed not less than one year of service under a post-Diploma training contract and has submitted to the Council a declaration in conformity with regulation 37 of these Regulations; and

(5) he has submitted to the Council such further evidence as it may require that he continues to be a fit and proper person to be admitted as a solicitor in Scotland.

Enquiries by Council

35. Without prejudice to any obligation in these Regulations on an intrant, including any intrant who is admitted as a solicitor by virtue of regulation 34(4)(a) or (c) of these Regulations while still a party to a post-Diploma training contract or a non-Diploma training contract, to satisfy the Council he is a fit and proper person to be admitted as, or be, a solicitor in Scotland, the Council may make enquiries concerning the intrant, both as regards those matters mentioned in regulation 36(3) of these Regulations and otherwise. For these purposes the Council shall be entitled to require the evidence of the intrant, his employer, any solicitor and any other intrant and to call for and recover such evidence and documents from any such person as the Council thinks proper.

Applicants admitted after one year of post-Diploma training or two years of non-Diploma training—employer's declaration

36.—(1) In the case of an intrant to whom regulation 34(4)(a) of these Regulations applies, the Council shall not grant a Certificate of Fitness to him unless he submits to the Council a declaration by his employer in such form as the Council may prescribe certifying that, during the first year of his post-Diploma training contract, he has fulfilled his obligations under such contract and is, in the opinion of his employer, a fit and proper person to be admitted as a solicitor in Scotland and, on completion of his full period of service under his post-Diploma training contract, such an intrant shall submit to the Council a declaration by his employer in such form as the Council may prescribe certifying that in his opinion the intrant continues to be a fit and proper person to be a solicitor in Scotland, provided always that, in any case where the employer of an intrant has declined to provide any such declaration, the Council may, after due enquiry and where it appears reasonable to do so, waive the requirement for such declaration from the employer, subject to such conditions as it may in its discretion determine.

(2) In the case of an intrant to whom regulation 34(4)(c) of these Regulations applies, the Council shall not grant a Certificate of Fitness to him unless he submits to the Council a declaration by his employer in such form as the Council may prescribe certifying that, during the first two years of his non-Diploma training contract, he has fulfilled his obligations under such contract and is, in the opinion of his employer, a fit and proper person to be admitted as a solicitor in Scotland and, on completion of his full period of service under his non-Diploma training contract, such an intrant

shall submit to the Council a declaration by his employer in such form as the Council may prescribe certifying that in his opinion the intrant continues to be a fit and proper person to be a solicitor in Scotland, provided always that, in any case where the employer of an intrant has declined to provide any such declaration, the Council may, after due enquiry and where it appears reasonable to do so, waive the requirement for such declaration from the employer, subject to such conditions as it may in its discretion determine.

(3) In forming an opinion whether the intrant is a fit and proper person to be admitted as a solicitor, the employer shall have regard not only to the moral character of the intrant but also to his aptitude for, and application to, his duties and his conduct generally.

Applicants admitted after two years of post-Diploma training or to whom regulation 33 applies—employer's declaration
37.—(1) In the case of an intrant to whom regulation 34(4)(b), (d) or (e) of these Regulations applies, the Council shall not grant a Certificate of Fitness to him unless he submits to the Council a declaration by his employer in such form as the Council may prescribe certifying that in his opinion the intrant has fulfilled his obligations under the training contract and is a fit and proper person to be admitted as a solicitor in Scotland, provided always that, in any case where the employer of an intrant has declined to provide any such declaration, the Council may, after due enquiry and where it appears reasonable to do so, waive the requirement for such declaration from the employer.

(2) In forming an opinion whether the intrant is a fit and proper person to be admitted as a solicitor, the employer shall have regard not only to the moral character of the intrant but also to his aptitude for and application to his duties and his conduct generally.

Undertaking by certain intrants
[1] **38.**—(1) In the case of an intrant to whom regulation 34(4)(a) or (c) of these Regulations applies, the intrant shall, before applying for a Certificate of Fitness, give an undertaking in such form as the Council may prescribe that he will not engage in professional practice on his own account and will only act as a professional assistant to a practising solicitor or a firm of practising solicitors or an incorporated practice (as defined in the Act) or a multi-national practice (as defined in the Act) in each case in Scotland. Such undertaking shall only bind the intrant until the date of grant of an employer's declaration that the intrant continues to be a fit and proper person to be a solicitor in Scotland pursuant to regulation 36(1) or (2) of these Regulations or the date the requirement for such a declaration is waived by the Council in terms of those regulations.

(2) Subject to regulation 38(4) of these Regulations, in the case of an intrant to whom regulation 34(4)(a) or (c) of these Regulations applies, the intrant shall, before applying for a Certificate of Fitness:—
  (a) give an undertaking in such form as the Council may prescribe that, if he has not on or before the last day of his service under his training contract completed the Professional Competence Course, he will not practise as a solicitor after that last day; and
  (b) give an undertaking in such form as the Council may prescribe that, if he has not on or before the last day of his service under his training contract passed the Test of Professional Competence, he will not practice as a solicitor after that last day.

(3) Undertakings given for the purpose of regulation 38(2) of these Regulations shall only bind the intrant until the later to occur of the date the intrant completes the Professional Competence Course and the date the intrant passes the Test of Professional Competence.

(4) An intrant who is exempt from completing the Professional Competence Course or who has, at the date he applies for a Certificate of

Fitness, completed the Professional Competence Course shall not be required to give the undertaking referred to in regulation 38(2)(a) of these Regulations and an intrant who is exempt from passing the Test of Professional Competence or who has, at the date he applies for a Certificate of Fitness, passed the Test of Professional Competence shall not be required to give the undertaking referred to in regulation 38(2)(b) of these Regulations.

NOTE
[1] As amended by the Solicitors (Scotland) (Registered Foreign Lawyers) etc. Practice Rules 2005, Sch.5 (effective May 1, 2005).

Applicants for admission after five years
39. Where an application for a Certificate of Fitness is made by an intrant under these Regulations more than five years after the date on which he became entitled to apply therefor, the Council may, after due enquiry and where it appears reasonable to do so, refuse the application or grant the application subject to such conditions as it may require.

PART VII

GENERAL

Right of appeal
40. Any person who is the subject of a decision by the Council under any of these Regulations and who is aggrieved by that decision may, within 21 days of written intimation of the decision, appeal to the Court of Session.

Council's discretion
41.—(1) The Council may in its discretion relieve any person from the consequences of any failure to comply with these Regulations where it is satisfied that such failure to comply is due to mistake, oversight or excusable cause, such not being wilful non-observance of these Regulations.

(2) The Council may, where the circumstances of a particular intrant are exceptional waive any provision of these Regulations applying to such intrant, provided that any such waiver may be subject to such conditions as the Council may in its discretion determine.

(3) The Council may, where the circumstances of a particular intrant are exceptional, determine that any of the exemptions provided by regulations 29, 30, 31, 32 and 33 of these Regulations shall not apply to such intrant.

(4) The Council may, where the circumstances of a particular intrant are exceptional, permit such intrant to depart from the terms of any undertaking given by him pursuant to regulation 38 of these Regulations.

Photograph
42. The Council may require any intrant to supply the Council with a recent photograph of the intrant for the purpose of verifying the identity of the intrant or otherwise and the Council may retain any photograph so supplied.

SCHEDULE

An intrant will be deemed to be duly qualified for the purposes of regulation 11(2)(b) of these Regulations if he complies with any of paragraphs (a) to (f) below:—

Scottish Certificate of Education

(a) (1) passes in at least five of the subjects in the Scottish Certificate of Education, as approved from time to time by the Universities Central Council on Admissions, at no more than two sittings, said passes to include:—

(i) a pass at Higher grade in English at not less than "B",
(ii) a pass at Higher grade in a subject chosen from one of the following groups:—
    (a) a group comprising mathematics or an approved science, or
    (b) a group comprising an approved language other than English, and
(iii) a pass at Higher, Ordinary or Standard grade in a subject chosen from the group not chosen under sub-paragraph (ii) above, provided that if at Ordinary or Standard grade, such pass is at not less than grade 3 and
  (2) a total of such points as the Council may from time to time determine in respect of the subjects passed, calculated as follows:—
    a pass at Higher grade at:—
      "A" being valued at three points,
      "B" being valued at two points, and
      "C" being valued at one point.
  Provided that if he has insufficient points or subject passes, he may add to these equivalent passes and points under (b)(1) and (2) below.

General Certificate of Education

(b) (1) passes in at least five of the subjects in the General Certificate of Education, as approved from time to time by the Universities Central Council on Admissions, at no more than two sittings, said passes to include:—
    (i) a pass at the Advanced level in English, at not less than "C" standard,
    (ii) a pass at the Advanced level in a subject chosen from one of the following groups:—
      (a) a group comprising mathematics or an approved science, or
      (b) a group comprising an approved language other than English, and
    (iii) a pass at the Advanced or Ordinary level or GCSE in a subject chosen from the group not chosen under subparagraph (ii) above; and
  (2) a total of such points as the Council may from time to time determine in respect of the subjects passed, calculated as follows:—
    a pass at the Advanced level at:—
      "A" being valued at four points,
      "B" being valued at three points,
      "C" being valued at two points, and
      "D" being valued at one point.
  Provided that if he has insufficient points or subject passes, he may add to these equivalent passes and points under (a)(1) and (2) above.

HND in Legal Studies

(c) a Scottish Higher National Diploma in Legal Studies from any College of Further Education approved by the Council offering such Diploma and also a pass in English at Higher grade in the Scottish Certificate of Education at not less than "B" or its equivalent.

University Degree

(d) a degree of any University, other than a Degree in Law, or an entitlement to graduate in such a degree notwithstanding that he has not so graduated.

Chartered Accountant

(e) membership of the Institute of Chartered Accountants of Scotland or of the Institute of Chartered Accountants in England and Wales or of the Association of Certified and Corporate Accountants.

Commissioned Officer

(f) a commission as a commissioned officer in one of the British armed services, where his commission has been obtained following study at a Royal Naval, Army or Royal Air Force college.

In this Schedule references to the Scottish Certificate of Education shall be construed as including the Scottish Qualifications Certificate.

Admission as Solicitor (Scotland) Regulations 2011

Regulations dated September 2011, made on behalf of the Council of the Law Society of Scotland by the Regulatory Committee formed in accordance with section 3B(1) of the Solicitors (Scotland) Act 1980 and with the concurrence of the Lord President of the Court of Session in terms of section 5 of the said Act.

PART 1

INTRODUCTORY

Title and commencement
1. These Regulations may be cited as the Admission as Solicitor (Scotland) Regulations 2011 and shall come into operation on 1 September 2011.

Interpretation
2.—(1) In these Regulations, unless the context otherwise requires—
"Accreditation Procedure" means the procedure whereby the Council approves (i) the courses offered by Universities for the Foundation Programme and (ii) the courses offered by Universities, and other institutions, for PEAT 1;
"Accredited" means approved in terms of the Accreditation Procedure;
"the Act" means the Solicitors (Scotland) Act 1980;
"Authorisation Procedure" means the procedure whereby the Council approves a provider of TCPD;
"Authorised" means approved in terms of the Authorisation Procedure;
"Certificate of Fitness" means a certificate issued by the Council that the person to whom the certificate applies has fulfilled the applicable conditions and requirements prescribed in these Regulations and in any enactment for admission as a solicitor in Scotland;
"the Council" means the Council of the Society;
"degree" means a degree, other than an honorary degree, awarded by a University;
"the Directive" means Directive No 98/5/EC of the European Parliament and Council and legislation and regulations (including regulations or rules of the Council) implementing that Directive in Scotland;
"employer" means a training solicitor who is party to a training contract and references to
"employ" and similar words include otherwise taking on a trainee under a training contract;
"Entrance Certificate" means a certificate issued by the Council to the effect that the person to whom the certificate applies has fulfilled the applicable conditions and requirements prescribed in these Regulations to entitle him to enter into a standard training contract or a non-PEAT 1 training contract;
"Examiner" means an examiner appointed under regulation 20;
"Foundation Programme" means the academic learning stage of professional legal education and training at degree or degree-equivalent level;
"Foundation Programme Qualification" means:
    (a) the degree of Bachelor of Laws or other Foundation Programme qualification awarded by a University, or jointly

by any University and any other University, that is from time to time Accredited in respect of such degree or other Foundation Programme qualification; or

(b) the Society's examinations;

"incorporated practice" has the meaning given in section 34(1A)(c) of the Act;

"intrant" means a person seeking to become a solicitor in Scotland;

"licensed provider" means licensed legal services provider construed in accordance with Part 2 of the Legal Services (Scotland) Act 2010;

"multi-national practice" has the meaning given in section 65(1) of the Act;

"non-PEAT 1 training contract" means a training contract entered into between a training solicitor and an intrant who is exempt from obtaining a PEAT 1 Qualification and who holds an Entrance Certificate;

"PEAT" means professional legal education and training comprising PEAT 1 and PEAT 2;

"PEAT 1" means the vocational learning stage of professional legal education and training;

"PEAT 1 Qualification" means the Diploma in Legal Practice or other PEAT 1 qualification awarded by a University or other institution, or jointly by any University or other institution and any other University or other institution, that is from time to time Accredited in respect of such Diploma or other PEAT 1 qualification;

"PEAT 2" means the work-based learning stage of professional legal education and training;

"PEAT 2 Outcomes" means such outcomes as shall be prescribed by the Council from time to time under the core headings of professionalism, professional communication, professional ethics and standards and business, commercial and practice awareness;

"practice unit" means (i) a sole practitioner, (ii) a firm of regulated persons, (iii) an incorporated practice, (iv) a multi-national practice, (v) a licensed provider, (vi) a solicitor in employment, otherwise than in private practice, being the sole solicitor within the employing organisation or (vii) two or more solicitors in employment, otherwise than in private practice, within the same employing organisation;

"practising certificate" means the certificate referred to in section 4 of the Act;

"pre-PEAT 1 training contract" means a training contract entered into between a training solicitor and an intrant who is qualified under the provisions of regulation 11 and who holds a Preliminary Entrance Certificate;

"Preliminary Entrance Certificate" means a certificate issued by the Council to the effect that the person to whom the certificate applies has fulfilled the applicable conditions and requirements prescribed in these Regulations to entitle him to enter into a pre-PEAT 1 training contract.

"principal" means a solicitor who is a sole practitioner or is a partner in a firm of regulated persons or a licensed provider or a multi-national practice or is a director of an incorporated practice or multi-national practice or licensed provider which is a company or is a member of an incorporated practice or multi-national practice or licensed provider which is a limited liability partnership;

"registered European lawyer" has the meaning given in section 65(1) of the Act;

"registered foreign lawyer" has the meaning given in section 65(1) of the Act;

"regulated person" means a solicitor, a registered European lawyer, a registered foreign lawyer and/or a practice unit;

"required TCPD" means, in relation to (i) a standard training contract, sixty hours over the term of that contract of which a minimum of forty hours shall be provided by an Authorised provider of TCPD, (ii) a standard training contract as specified in regulation 33, thirty hours over the term of that contract, of which a minimum of twenty hours shall be provided by an Authorised provider of TCPD, and (iii) a non-PEAT 1 training contract, such number of hours as shall be prescribed by the Council from time to time;

"the 2001 Regulations" means the Admission as Solicitor (Scotland) Regulations 2001;

"the 1994 Regulations" means the EC Qualified Lawyers Transfer (Scotland) Regulations 1994 and any other regulations from time to time applicable to an intrant making an application pursuant to Directive 2005/36/EC of the European Parliament and Council;

"the Secretary" means the Secretary of the Society or any person authorised by the Council to act on behalf of the Secretary for the purposes of any of these Regulations;

"the Society" means the Law Society of Scotland;

"the Society's examinations" means the examinations set under regulation 22(1);

"solicitor" means any person enrolled as a solicitor in terms of the Act;

"standard training contract" means a training contract entered into between a training solicitor and an intrant who has obtained a PEAT 1 Qualification and who holds an Entrance Certificate;

"trainee" means an intrant who is a party to a training contract;

"TCPD" means continuing professional development training for trainees;

"training contract" means a non-PEAT 1 training contract, a standard training contract or a pre-PEAT 1 training contract;

"training supervisor" means a natural person who is a training solicitor, who has been in continuous practice as a solicitor for a period of at least three years immediately prior to designation and who is designated by a practice unit in terms of regulation 14(2);

"training solicitor" means
    (a) a solicitor who holds a practising certificate and who—
        (i) is engaged as a principal in private practice; or
        (ii) is in employment as a solicitor, otherwise than in private practice, and
    (b) a practice unit; and

"University" means—
    (a) any university in the United Kingdom; or
    (b) any other university or institution of equivalent standing recognised by the Council for the purposes of these Regulations.

(2) The provisions of the Interpretation Act 1978 shall apply to the interpretation of these Regulations as they apply to the interpretation of an Act of Parliament.

(3) The headings to these Regulations do not form part of these Regulations.

(4) Reference to a Part is to a Part of these Regulations.

Conditions precedent to admission

3. Subject to the provisions of section 6 of the Act and these Regulations, every intrant shall, as a condition precedent to his admission as a solicitor, comply with these Regulations so far as applicable to him and the Council may require any intrant to satisfy it by such means as it considers necessary as to such compliance.

Application of these Regulations, Revocations and Savings
   4.—(1) These Regulations shall apply to all intrants other than—
   (a) intrants who have, prior to the date of commencement of these Regulations, commenced or completed service under a post-Diploma training contract or a non-Diploma training contract (as those terms are defined in the 2001 Regulations), who shall proceed to admission under the 2001 Regulations;
   (b) intrants eligible under the 1994 Regulations; and
   (c) intrants eligible under the Directive.
   (2) Where these Regulations apply to an intrant, and that intrant has obtained an Entrance Certificate or a Preliminary Entrance Certificate under the 2001 Regulations, that Certificate shall be treated in all respects as satisfying the requirements as to Entrance Certificates or Preliminary Entrance Certificates of these Regulations and shall have effect as if it had been granted under these Regulations.
   (3) Where these Regulations apply to an intrant, and that intrant has obtained or obtains a Degree in Law or a Diploma or has completed or completes his period of service under a pre-Diploma training contract (as those terms are defined in the 2001 Regulations), that Degree in Law, Diploma or pre-Diploma training contract (as the case may be) shall be treated in all respects as satisfying the requirements of these Regulations in respect of a Foundation Programme Qualification, a PEAT 1 Qualification or a pre-PEAT 1 training contract (as the case may be) and shall have effect as if it had been obtained or completed under these Regulations.
   (4) A registered foreign lawyer shall be responsible, as a member of a multi-national practice, for the compliance of that multi-national practice with any obligation placed upon it by these Regulations as a training solicitor, including without limitation, the obligations placed upon it by regulations 13(1), 13(2), 14(2), 14(5), 17(1), 17(3), 17(5), 17(7), 18, 35, 36(3) and 37(2).
   (5) The Admission as Solicitor (Scotland) Regulations 1986 and the Admission as Solicitor (Scotland) Regulations 1991 are hereby revoked: provided that such revocation shall not -
   (a) affect the validity of any application or determination made, certificate granted or other thing done under those Regulations and such application, determination, certificate or thing shall have effect as if it were made, granted or done under these Regulations;
   (b) cause the interruption of time periods nor affect any obligation to deliver any declaration, application or any other document, information or thing to the Council or the Society nor the rights of the Council or the Society against any person in respect of his failure to deliver such a declaration, application, document, information or thing; or
   (c) affect the taking or continuation of any proceedings by, or the exercise or continued exercise of any power available to, the Society, the Council or any other person in respect of any act or thing done or omitted to be done under, any breach of, or any matter arising from, those Regulations.

PART 2

ENTRANCE QUALIFICATIONS AND TRAINING CONTRACTS

(A) Entrance Certificate

Issue of Entrance Certificate
   5.—(1) An intrant may not enter into either a standard training contract or a non-PEAT 1 training contract unless he holds an Entrance Certificate. An intrant shall apply for an Entrance Certificate not less than four weeks

prior to the proposed date of commencement of service under a standard training contract or a non-PEAT 1 training contract.

(2) An intrant shall be entitled to an Entrance Certificate if he satisfies the Council that:

   (a) he is a fit and proper person to be a solicitor;

   (b) (i) he holds a Foundation Programme Qualification or a certificate that he is entitled to graduate with such a Qualification notwithstanding that he has not so graduated; (ii) he has served for a period of three years under a pre-PEAT 1 training contract and has passed or obtained exemption from the Society's examinations; (iii) he is an intrant to whom the provisions of regulation 28 apply and who has passed such of the Society's examinations as the Council shall have determined within such time period as it may have determined in terms of that regulation; or (iv) he is an intrant to whom the provisions of regulations 30, 32 or 33 apply; and

   (c) unless exempt in terms of regulations 29, 30 or 32, he has obtained a PEAT 1 Qualification.

Lapse of Entrance Certificate

6. An intrant's Entrance Certificate shall automatically lapse if he does not enter into either a standard training contract or a non-PEAT 1 training contract within one year of the date of said Entrance Certificate or such extended period as may be permitted by the Council in any particular case on cause shown.

(B) Standard training contract

Service under a standard training contract

7.—(1) Subject to regulations 29, 30, 31 and 32, it shall be a requirement for admission as a solicitor in Scotland that an intrant shall serve under a standard training contract entered into with a training solicitor.

(2) Subject to regulation 33, the period of training under a standard training contract shall comprise two years of full-time training, provided always that an intrant may, at any time, with the prior written consent of the Council, undergo training on a part-time basis provided that the Council is satisfied that the total time spent working under such a standard training contract shall equate to two years of full-time training.

(3) Every standard training contract shall be in, or as nearly as may be in, such form as the Council may from time to time prescribe.

Commencement of standard training contract

8.—(1) In the case of an intrant who is required to hold a PEAT 1 Qualification, the commencement of his standard training contract shall be within a period of two years of the date of 1 January first occurring after the date when the intrant became entitled to the award of the PEAT 1 Qualification provided that the Council may in its discretion extend such period but may, in granting such extension, impose such conditions as it thinks fit.

(2) In exercising its discretion under regulation 8(1) the Council shall have regard to the appropriateness of any work, paid or voluntary, and courses undertaken by the intrant since the intrant became entitled to the award of the PEAT 1 Qualification and also to the endeavours of the intrant to obtain a standard training contract.

Service elsewhere in Scotland and in other jurisdictions

9.—(1) Subject to the consent of the employer and the prior consent in writing of the Council in each case, a trainee under a standard training contract may be permitted, in order to extend the range of his training:

(a) to undertake legal work under appropriate supervision within Scotland on secondment; and/or

(b) to undertake legal work under appropriate supervision for a period or periods not exceeding in the aggregate six months in any other part of the United Kingdom or any other country which is a member of the European Union.

The period of any such secondment and such other period or periods of legal work shall be reckoned as part of the trainee's period of service under the standard training contract.

(2) A trainee may, subject to the consent of the employer, serve under a standard training contract at his employer's place of business outwith Scotland, but such a trainee shall not, during the period of his standard training contract and without the prior consent in writing of the Council, spend a period or periods exceeding in the aggregate six months at any such place of business outwith Scotland.

(C) Pre-PEAT 1 training contract

Service under a pre-PEAT 1 training contract
10.—(1) Any intrant who, for the purpose of qualifying for an Entrance Certificate, proposes to meet the requirements of regulation 5(2)(b)(ii) shall be required to enter into a pre-PEAT 1 training contract with a training solicitor.

(2) The period of training under a pre-PEAT 1 training contract shall comprise three years of full-time training, provided always that an intrant may, at any time, with the prior written consent of the Council, undergo training on a part-time basis provided that the Council is satisfied that the total time spent working under such a pre-PEAT 1 training contract shall equate to three years of full-time training.

(3) Every pre-PEAT 1 training contract shall be in, or as nearly as may be in, such form as the Council may from time to time prescribe and shall, subject to the provisions of regulation 18(1), contain an obligation on the training solicitor to provide training for the intrant in—

(a) conveyancing;

(b) litigation; and

(c) either
   (i) trusts and executries; or
   (ii) where the training solicitor is not engaged in private practice, the legal work of the training solicitor.

(4) Subject to the prior consent of the employer, an intrant who is a party to a pre-PEAT 1 training contract may be permitted to attend, during office hours, classes in law at a University or other institution.

(5) Subject to the consent of the employer and the prior consent in writing of the Council in each case, a trainee under a pre-PEAT 1 training contract may be permitted, in order to extend the range of his training—

(a) to undertake legal work under appropriate supervision within Scotland on secondment; and/or

(b) to undertake legal work under appropriate supervision for a period or periods not exceeding in the aggregate six months in any other part of the United Kingdom or any other country which is a member of the European Union.

The period of any such secondment and such other period or periods of legal work shall be reckoned as part of the trainee's period of service under the pre-PEAT 1 training contract.

(6) A trainee may, subject to the consent of the employer, serve under a pre-PEAT 1 training contract at his employer's place of business outwith Scotland, but such a trainee shall not, during the period of his pre-PEAT 1 training contract and without the prior consent in writing of the Council,

spend a period or periods exceeding in the aggregate six months at any such place of business outwith Scotland.

(D) Preliminary Entrance Certificate

Issue of Preliminary Entrance Certificate

11.—(1) An intrant may not enter into a pre-PEAT 1 training contract unless he holds a Preliminary Entrance Certificate. An intrant shall apply for a Preliminary Entrance Certificate not less than four weeks prior to the proposed date of commencement of service under a pre-PEAT 1 training contract.

(2) An intrant shall be entitled to a Preliminary Entrance Certificate if he satisfies the Council that he—

(a) is a fit and proper person to be a solicitor; and

(b) has attained such educational qualifications as shall be prescribed from time to time by the Council.

(3) The Council may, in the case of an intrant who satisfies the Council, having regard to evidence of academic attainment and to any experience of legal work, as to his fitness to enter into a pre-PEAT 1 training contract, grant to such an intrant a Preliminary Entrance Certificate without requiring compliance with regulation 11(2)(b).

(4) An intrant's Preliminary Entrance Certificate shall automatically lapse if he does not enter into a pre-PEAT 1 training contract within one year of the date of said Preliminary Entrance Certificate or such extended period as may be permitted by the Council in any particular case on cause shown.

(E) Non-PEAT 1 training contract

Service under a non-PEAT 1 training contract

12.—(1) An intrant who is exempt from obtaining a PEAT 1 Qualification under regulations 29, 30 or 32 shall serve under a non-PEAT 1 training contract entered into with a training solicitor.

(2) A non-PEAT 1 training contract shall be in similar terms to a standard training contract and shall be subject to the same conditions and requirements as are specified in these Regulations in relation to standard training contracts including, for the avoidance of doubt, regulation 9; provided that the period of time which an intrant is required to serve under a non-PEAT 1 training contract shall be as specified in regulations 29, 30 or 32, as the case may be.

(F) General provisions affecting training contracts

Provisions as to training solicitors and intrants

13.—(1) A training solicitor shall not, without the prior consent in writing of the Council, employ any trainee, unless he is in practice as a solicitor at the time and has been in continuous practice as a solicitor for a period of at least three years immediately prior to his employing the trainee or, where the training solicitor is a practice unit, at least one of the principals thereof has been in such continuous practice.

(2) The total number of intrants employed at any time under training contracts shall not, except with the prior consent in writing of the Council, exceed—

(a) in the case of a solicitor practising on his own under his own name or as a sole solicitor under a firm name, one;

(b) in the case of a practice unit (other than a sole practitioner, a sole solicitor in employment otherwise than in private practice, or two or more solicitors in employment otherwise than in private practice), twice the number of principals within the practice unit who are (a) natural persons and (b) solicitors;

(c) in the case of a practice unit (as specified in paragraph (b)) having more than one office, within each such office, twice the number of solicitors having their principal place of business within that office but subject always, in respect of the practice unit as a whole, to the maximum specified by paragraph (b);

(d) in the case of a solicitor in employment otherwise than in private practice, twice the number of solicitors employed by the solicitor's employer who are entitled, in terms of regulation 13(1), to employ a trainee without the prior consent in writing of the Council but subject always, in respect of the solicitor's employer as a whole, (i) where the solicitor's employer falls within paragraph (a) or (b), to the maximum specified by, as the case may be, paragraph (a) or (b), and (ii) in any other case, to a maximum of twice the number of solicitors employed by the solicitor's employer who are so entitled;

(e) in the case of a solicitor in employment otherwise than in private practice, where the solicitor's employer has more than one office, within each such office, twice the number of solicitors having their principal place of business within that office but subject always, in respect of the solicitor's employer as a whole, to the maxima specified by paragraph (d); and

(f) in the case of any other solicitor, such number as the Council may in each case determine.

Training supervisors

14.—(1) By each date set out in regulation 14(2) a practice unit which is a training solicitor and which employs or intends to employ trainees, or which has training solicitors who employ or intend to employ trainees within the practice, shall designate a training supervisor.

(2) A practice unit shall designate a training supervisor, and shall notify the Council of the identity of the person so designated—

(a) not later than 28 days after the date of commencement of these Regulations where, at such date, it employs trainees, or

(b) not later than 28 days after the commencement of service under a training contract by a trainee where, at the date of commencement of these Regulations, it does not employ trainees.

(3) A practice unit which, at any date referred to in regulation 14(2), is a solicitor who is a sole practitioner or a solicitor in employment, otherwise than in private practice, being the sole solicitor within the employing organisation shall be deemed, provided that solicitor has been in continuous practice as a solicitor for a period of at least three years immediately prior to designation, to have designated that solicitor as its training supervisor at that date.

(4) A training supervisor shall have the following responsibilities:-

(a) acting as a named point of contact for the Council with the practice unit in respect of trainees in that practice unit,

(b) the supervision of trainees in that practice unit, and

(c) overseeing (i) the completion by trainees in that practice unit of the required TCPD and (ii) the assessment of achievement of the PEAT 2 Outcomes by the trainees in that practice unit.

(5) A practice unit shall notify the Council of any change in the identity of a person designated as a training supervisor in terms of regulation 14(2) not later than 28 days after the date of such change.

(6) The Council may publish, and may from time to time amend, guidance in relation to the training of training supervisors. The Council may publish such guidance both in relation to training upon designation as training supervisor and training on an ongoing basis.

Registration of training contracts

15.—(1) For the purposes of these Regulations, the Council shall establish and maintain a register of pre-PEAT 1 training contracts, a register of standard training contracts and a register of non-PEAT 1 training contracts.

(2) Every training contract shall be produced by the trainee to the Council for registration within three months from its commencement and thereafter shall be presented for registration in the Books of Council and Session by the Society at the expense of the trainee.

(3) When a trainee produces his training contract to the Council, he shall pay such administration fee as the Council may from time to time prescribe.

(4) If a trainee's training contract and the prescribed administration fee in terms of regulation 15(3) are not produced to the Council within three months from the date of the commencement of the training contract, the period of service under the training contract shall for the purposes of these Regulations be reckoned, if the Council so directs, as commencing only from the date of production of the training contract together with the prescribed administration fee to the Council or such earlier date as the Council may determine.

(5) Subject to compliance with the requirements of regulation 18 as to the approval or consent of the Council, every assignation of a training contract shall, together with the relevant supporting documents and the prescribed administration fee in terms of regulation 15(6), be produced by the trainee to the Council for registration within six weeks from the date of assignation and where the assignation, together with the relevant supporting documents and the prescribed administration fee, has not been produced within the said period, service after the assignation, but prior to its registration, shall be reckoned as part of the trainee's service under the training contract only to such extent as the Council may determine.

(6) When a trainee produces an assignation of his training contract to the Council, he shall pay such fee as the Council may from time to time prescribe.

Service under training contracts

16.—(1) The employer and the trainee shall each comply with their respective obligations under any training contract.

(2) For the purposes of these Regulations but subject to regulations 7, 9, 10 and 12—

  (a) during the term of his training contract a trainee shall not, during office hours, engage in any other gainful employment or otherwise absent himself from his employer's business without the consent of his employer and the prior consent in writing of the Council;

  (b) service by a trainee under a training contract shall be continuous, provided that the Council may, in considering whether or not such service has been continuous and provided that the employer is prepared to certify the trainee's fitness to become a solicitor in due course or to continue as a solicitor, as the case may be, disregard short periods of absence by the trainee from employment, not exceeding six months in aggregate; and

  (c) service by a trainee under a training contract shall be in Scotland.

Intervention in training contracts

17.—(1) The Council may make enquiries concerning any aspect of a training contract and the conduct of the parties to that contract and the Council shall be entitled to require the evidence of the trainee, his employer, any solicitor, registered foreign lawyer, registered European lawyer and any other intrant and to call from and recover such evidence and documents from any such person as the Council thinks proper.

(2) If the Council, after due enquiry and after affording the parties to the training contract the opportunity to make representations, is of the opinion that a party to a training contract is not, as a result of the acts or omissions of the other party to the training contract, receiving the benefits it should

receive from that training contract, the Council may require that other party to take such steps as the Council may request to ensure that those benefits are so received.

(3) Without prejudice to the generality of regulation 17(2), if—

(a) during the term of any training contract either the trainee or the employer has been continuously absent from the employer's place of business for an aggregate period of at least three months within any period of six months without reasonable cause; or

(b) the Council, after enquiry and after affording the parties to the training contract the opportunity to make representations, is of the opinion that a training contract ought to be terminated, assigned, or extended; or

(c) there is a dispute between the parties to the training contract

the Council may by notice in writing to the parties to the training contract require the termination of the training contract with effect from such date as may be specified in the notice or may require an assignation of the training contract or an extension to it, as the case may be, or may take such other action as it thinks fit. Where the Council has by notice required the termination of a training contract any service by the trainee under that training contract after the date specified in the notice shall not be reckoned as part of his period of service for the purpose of regulation 34.

(4) Where, before the expiration of the period of service under a training contract, such training contract is terminated for any reason, an intrant shall be entitled and may be required, subject to such conditions as the Council may impose, to enter into a further training contract with another training solicitor.

(5) An employer shall be obliged to assign a standard training contract or non-PEAT 1 training contract if called upon to do so by the Council.

(6) An intrant's Entrance Certificate or Preliminary Entrance Certificate may be withdrawn by the Council in such exceptional circumstances as the Council may in its sole discretion determine.

(7) If the Council after enquiry decides that a training solicitor would be unable to fulfil or is not fulfilling the proper obligations of an employer under a training contract either in relation to a particular application to employ a trainee or in relation to a particular training contract or generally, it shall intimate its decision to the training solicitor and the training solicitor, notwithstanding that he satisfies the provisions of regulation 13(1), shall not thereafter engage or retain the services of any trainee without the consent in writing of the Council.

Consent to assignation of training contract

18.—(1) An employer under a pre-PEAT 1 training contract shall, if requested by his trainee or if called upon to do so by the Council, assign such pre-PEAT 1 training contract to another training solicitor, approved in writing by the Council, to enable the trainee either to complete his training in the three areas of practice described in (a), (b) or (c)(i) of regulation 10(3) or to extend the range of his training generally, or for any other reason which the Council shall consider reasonable.

(2) A training contract shall not be assigned by the employer without the prior consent in writing of the Council, and may not be assigned during the final three months of its term.

(3) If a standard training contract or non-PEAT 1 training contract is assigned in terms of regulation 18(2), the previous employer under that training contract shall submit to the Council such documentation and other evidence as is required to enable his former trainee under that training contract to apply for a Certificate of Fitness, including an employer's declaration in terms of regulation 36(1)(a), 36(2)(a) or 37(1)(a) (as the case may be), provided that the previous employer shall not require to submit such documentation and other evidence if the former trainee applies for a

Certificate of Fitness more than three months after the date of assignation of the training contract.

(G) PEAT 2 Outcomes/required TCPD

Requirement

19. For an intrant to whom these Regulations apply it shall, subject to regulation 31, be a requirement for admission as a solicitor in Scotland that he shall have achieved the PEAT 2 Outcomes and completed the required TCPD or given the undertaking referred to in regulation 38(2).

Part 3

Society's Examinations

Appointment of Examiners

20.—(1) The Council shall from time to time nominate and appoint suitably qualified persons to be Examiners and conduct examinations in accordance with this Part, which examinations shall be under the management and control of the Council.

(2) The Examiners shall comply with all directions that may be given by the Council with respect to the number of papers to be set on any subject, the number of questions to be set and to be answered and the percentage mark to be attained to qualify for a pass and any other matters in connection with the examinations.

(3) The Examiners shall be appointed for such period of time and be paid such remuneration as the Council may from time to time determine.

Eligibility of intrants

21. An intrant shall not be entitled to present himself for any of the Society's examinations unless—

    (a) he holds a Preliminary Entrance Certificate and is serving under a pre-PEAT 1 training contract or, that contract having terminated, has already presented himself for one or more of the Society's examinations;

    (b) he holds, or is entitled to graduate with, a Foundation Programme Qualification which does not include the achievement of outcomes equivalent to passes in all the subjects in the syllabus prescribed by regulation 22(1); or

    (c) the Council has determined that he may pursuant to regulation 28.

Examinations

22.—(1) The Society's examinations shall consist of examinations in the laws of Scotland in accordance with a syllabus prescribed by the Council from time to time.

(2) An intrant shall not be permitted to sit any one examination on more than four occasions or later than four years from the date of the first of the Society's examinations for which he presented himself except with the prior consent in writing of the Council following on a recommendation by the Examiners, which consent may be given subject to such conditions as the Council may determine.

Award of distinction

23. A certificate of distinction in any subject may be awarded to an intrant at the discretion of the Examiners.

Conduct, date and places of examination

24.—(1) Diets for the Society's examinations shall be held in Edinburgh not less than twice each year and additional diets may be held in such circumstances as the Examiners, with the approval of the Council, may determine.

(2) Intrants intending to present themselves as candidates at any of the Society's examinations shall give four weeks' notice in writing of their intention to the Secretary, provided that the Examiners may at their discretion allow an intrant who has not given such notice to present himself for any examination.

(3) Every candidate shall be examined in writing and may be required by the Examiners to present himself for oral examination.

(4) Every candidate shall be required to advise the Secretary of any permanent change of address.

Fees
25. A candidate shall tender with his notice of intention to sit any examination such fee as may be prescribed by the Council from time to time.

PART 4

EXEMPTIONS

Faculty of Advocates' examinees
26. The Council may exempt from any of the Society's examinations an intrant who has obtained a pass in the corresponding examination in the examinations for admission to the Faculty of Advocates.

Corresponding passes
27. Where an intrant seeks exemption from any of the Society's examinations, the Council may grant such exemption provided the Council is satisfied that the intrant has passed a corresponding examination in the laws of Scotland to a standard approved by the Council.

Further exemptions for intrants from elsewhere in UK
28. Where the terms of regulation 31 or 32 do not apply, the Council may, on application by an intrant who has passed the examinations required for admission as a solicitor or barrister in England and Wales or Northern Ireland within a reasonable time prior to such application, determine which of the Society's examinations, if any, such intrant shall be required to pass for the purposes of regulation 5(2)(b). Subject always to such conditions as the Council may determine, including conditions as to the period of time during which the examinations must be passed, such an intrant shall be entitled to present himself for the Society's examinations in accordance with regulation 24.

Exemptions from PEAT 1 Qualification
29. An intrant who seeks to obtain an Entrance Certificate and who satisfies the Council that there are exceptional circumstances which justify his being exempted from obtaining a PEAT 1 Qualification may be granted an Entrance Certificate on such conditions, including the passing of examinations, as the Council may in its discretion prescribe; provided that an intrant who receives such exemption shall be required to achieve the PEAT 2 Outcomes and complete the required TCPD and to serve for a period of not less than three years under a non-PEAT 1 training contract.

PART 5

REQUIREMENTS FOR SPECIAL INTRANTS

Scottish Advocates
30. Notwithstanding any other provision of these Regulations, but

without prejudice to regulation 41, an intrant who is a member of the Faculty of Advocates, has had two years of recent active practice of Scots law since being called and who provides such evidence as the Council may require that he is a fit and proper person to be admitted as a solicitor in Scotland shall be exempt from—

(a) pre-PEAT 1 training,
(b) obtaining a Foundation Programme Qualification, and
(c) obtaining a PEAT 1 Qualification,

but he shall be required to achieve the PEAT 2 Outcomes and complete the required TCPD and to serve for a period of six months under a non-PEAT 1 training contract prior to applying for admission in terms of regulation 34.

English/Welsh and Northern Irish solicitors
31. Notwithstanding any other provision of these Regulations, but without prejudice to regulation 41, an intrant who has been admitted as a solicitor in England and Wales or Northern Ireland and who provides such evidence as the Council may require that he is a fit and proper person to be admitted as a solicitor in Scotland shall be exempt from:-

(a) obtaining a Foundation Programme Qualification,
(b) obtaining a PEAT 1 Qualification,
(c) any period of training, and
(d) achieving the PEAT 2 Outcomes and completing the required TCPD,

but he shall be required to pass an intra-UK transfer test comprising examinations in conveyancing, trusts and succession, Scots criminal law, civil and criminal evidence and procedure and (unless admitted as such a solicitor prior to 1 January 1992) European Union law and institutions, or such other examinations as may be prescribed by the Council from time to time prior to applying for admission in terms of regulation 34.

English/Welsh and Northern Irish barristers
32. Notwithstanding any other provision of these Regulations, but without prejudice to regulation 41, an intrant who is a member of the Bar in England and Wales or Northern Ireland, has had five years of recent active practice of law in the United Kingdom since being called and who provides such evidence as the Council may require that he is a fit and proper person to be admitted as a solicitor in Scotland shall be exempt from—

(a) pre-PEAT 1 training,
(b) obtaining a Foundation Programme Qualification, and
(c) obtaining a PEAT 1 Qualification,

but he shall be required to pass an intra-UK transfer test comprising examinations in conveyancing, trusts and succession, Scots criminal law, civil and criminal evidence and procedure and (unless called to the Bar prior to 1 January 1992) European Union law and institutions or such other examinations as may be prescribed by the Council from time to time and to achieve the PEAT 2 Outcomes and complete the required TCPD and to serve for a period of six months under a non-PEAT 1 training contract, or such longer period as the Council may in its discretion determine, prior to applying for admission in terms of regulation 34.

Non UK/EU/EEA lawyers
33. Notwithstanding any other provision of these Regulations, but without prejudice to regulation 41, an intrant who has been admitted as a practising lawyer in a jurisdiction outwith the United Kingdom and to whom the 1994 Regulations or the Directive do not apply, shall be exempt from service under a pre-PEAT 1 training contract, but shall be required to satisfy the Council that he is qualified to undertake within the jurisdiction in which he qualified or practises professional work equivalent to that of a solicitor or advocate in Scotland, to provide such evidence as the Council may require that he is a fit and proper person to be admitted as a solicitor in

Scotland, to pass the Society's examinations, obtain a PEAT 1 Qualification and to achieve the PEAT 2 Outcomes and complete the required TCPD and to serve for a period of one year under a standard training contract prior to applying for admission in terms of regulation 34.

PART 6

PROCEDURE FOR ADMISSION AS SOLICITOR

Eligibility for Certificate of Fitness
34. Subject to the provisions of section 6 of the Act and these Regulations, an intrant shall be entitled to apply for a Certificate of Fitness for the purposes of section 6 of the Act if:
(1) (a) he has passed or obtained exemption from all of the required Society's examinations; or
    (b) he holds, or is entitled to graduate with, or is exempt under these Regulations from obtaining, a Foundation Programme Qualification; and
(2) he holds or is exempt under these Regulations from obtaining a PEAT 1 Qualification; and
(3) (a) he has completed the required TCPD or is exempt therefrom; or
    (b) he has complied with regulation 34(4)(a) or (c); and
(4) (a) he has completed not less than one year of the two-year period of service under a standard training contract and has submitted to the Council—
      (i) a declaration in terms of regulation 36(1)(a);
      (ii) an undertaking in such form as the Council may prescribe that he will complete the remaining period of service under such training contract in fulfilment of his obligations under that training contract;
      (iii) an undertaking in terms of regulation 38(1); and
      (iv) an undertaking in terms of regulation 38(2); or
    (b) he has completed the full period of service under a standard training contract and has submitted to the Council a declaration in terms of regulation 37; or
    (c) he has completed not less than two years of the full period of service under a non-PEAT 1 training contract pursuant to regulation 29 and he has submitted to the Council a declaration in terms of regulation 36(2)(a) and the undertakings referred to in regulation 34(4)(a)(ii) to (iv); or
    (d) he has completed the full period of service under a non-PEAT 1 training contract pursuant to regulations 29, 30 or 32 and has submitted to the Council a declaration in terms of regulation 37; or
    (e) he has completed the full period of service under a standard training contract pursuant to regulation 33 and has submitted to the Council a declaration in terms of regulation 37; and
(5) he has submitted to the Council such further evidence as it may require that he continues to be a fit and proper person to be admitted as a solicitor in Scotland.

Enquiries by Council
35. Without prejudice to any obligation in these Regulations on an intrant (including any intrant who is admitted as a solicitor by virtue of regulation 34(4)(a) or (c) while still a party to a standard training contract or a non-PEAT 1 training contract) to satisfy the Council he is a fit and proper person to be admitted as, or be, a solicitor in Scotland, the Council may make enquiries concerning the intrant, both as regards those matters mentioned in regulation 36(3) and otherwise. For these purposes the Council shall be

entitled to require the evidence of the intrant, his employer, any solicitor, registered foreign lawyer, registered European lawyer and any other intrant and to call for and recover such evidence and documents from any such person as the Council thinks proper.

Applicants admitted after one year of service under a standard training contract or two years of service under a non-PEAT 1 training contract— employer's declaration

36.—(1) In the case of an intrant to whom regulation 34(4)(a) applies:
(a) the Council shall not grant a Certificate of Fitness to him unless he submits to the Council a declaration by his employer in such form as the Council may prescribe certifying that, during the first year of his standard training contract, the intrant has fulfilled his obligations under that contract and has undertaken a minimum of twenty hours of TCPD and is, in the opinion of his employer, a fit and proper person to be admitted as a solicitor in Scotland; and
(b) on completion of his full period of service under his standard training contract, the intrant shall submit to the Council a declaration by his employer in such form as the Council may prescribe certifying that the intrant has fulfilled his obligations under that contract and has achieved the PEAT 2 Outcomes and that, in the employer's opinion, the intrant continues to be a fit and proper person to be a solicitor in Scotland, provided always that, in any case where the employer of an intrant has declined to provide any such declaration, the Council may, after due enquiry and where it appears reasonable to do so, waive the requirement for such declaration from the employer, subject to such conditions as it may in its discretion determine.
(2) In the case of an intrant to whom regulation 34(4)(c) applies—
(a) the Council shall not grant a Certificate of Fitness to him unless he submits to the Council a declaration by his employer in such form as the Council may prescribe certifying that, during the first two years of his non-PEAT 1 training contract, the intrant has fulfilled his obligations under that contract and has undertaken a minimum of thirty hours of TCPD and is, in the opinion of his employer, a fit and proper person to be admitted as a solicitor in Scotland; and
(b) on completion of his full period of service under his non-PEAT 1 training contract, the intrant shall submit to the Council a declaration by his employer in such form as the Council may prescribe certifying that the intrant has fulfilled his obligations under that contract and has achieved the PEAT 2 Outcomes and that, in the employer's opinion, the intrant continues to be a fit and proper person to be a solicitor in Scotland, provided always that, in any case where the employer of an intrant has declined to provide any such declaration, the Council may, after due enquiry and where it appears reasonable to do so, waive the requirement for such declaration from the employer, subject to such conditions as it may in its discretion determine.
(3) In forming an opinion whether the intrant is a fit and proper person to be admitted as a solicitor, the employer shall have regard not only to the moral character of the intrant but also to his aptitude for, and application to, his duties and his conduct generally.

Applicants admitted after the required period of service under a standard training contract or the required period of service under a non-PEAT 1 training contract—employer's declaration

37.—(1) In the case of an intrant to whom regulation 34(4)(b), (d) or (e) applies, the Council shall not grant a Certificate of Fitness to him unless—
(a) he submits to the Council a declaration by his employer in such form as the Council may prescribe certifying that the intrant has fulfilled

his obligations under the training contract and has achieved the PEAT 2 Outcomes and is, in the opinion of his employer, a fit and proper person to be admitted as a solicitor in Scotland; and
(b) he has completed the required TCPD,
provided always that, in any case where the employer of an intrant has declined to provide a declaration, the Council may, after due enquiry and where it appears reasonable to do so, waive the requirement for such declaration from the employer, subject to such conditions as it may in its discretion determine.

(2) In forming an opinion whether the intrant is a fit and proper person to be admitted as a solicitor, the employer shall have regard not only to the moral character of the intrant but also to his aptitude for, and application to, his duties and his conduct generally.

Undertakings by certain intrants
38.—(1) In the case of an intrant to whom regulation 34(4)(a) or (c) applies, the intrant shall, before applying for a Certificate of Fitness, give an undertaking in such form as the Council may prescribe that he will not engage in professional practice on his own account and will only act as a professional assistant to a practice unit in Scotland. Such undertaking shall only bind the intrant until the first to occur of—
(a) the date of grant of an employer's declaration pursuant to regulation 36(1)(b) or (2)(b);
(b) the date the requirement for such a declaration is waived by the Council pursuant to those regulations; and
(c) the date of lapse of the intrant's practising certificate current at the last day of his service under his training contract.

(2) In the case of an intrant to whom regulation 34(4)(a) or (c) applies, the intrant shall, before applying for a Certificate of Fitness, give an undertaking in such form as the Council may prescribe that, if he has not on or before the last day of his service under his training contract completed the required TCPD, he will not practise as a solicitor after that last day.

(3) An undertaking given in terms of regulation 38(2) shall only bind the intrant until the date the intrant has completed the required TCPD.

Application for admission after five years
39. Where an application for a Certificate of Fitness is made by an intrant under these Regulations more than five years after the date on which he became entitled to apply for such a Certificate, the Council may, after due enquiry and where it appears reasonable to do so, refuse the application or grant the application subject to such conditions as it may determine.

PART 7

GENERAL

Right of Appeal
40.—(1) Any person who is the subject of a decision by the Council under these Regulations and who is aggrieved by that decision may, within 21 days of written intimation of that decision, appeal to the Council.

(2) Any such appeal shall be in writing and shall set out, in sufficient detail, the grounds of appeal and the remedy sought.

(3) Any such appeal will be considered by the Council as soon as reasonably practicable and a written determination issued, within 21 days of consideration of the appeal by the Council, to the person who intimated the appeal.

(4) In considering any such appeal, the Council will ensure that no person who was party to the decision appealed against shall participate in the determination of the appeal. The Council may take evidence, written or

oral, from any person in its determination of the appeal.

(5) Any person who is the subject of a determination by the Council on an appeal and who is aggrieved by that determination may, within 21 days of written intimation of the determination, appeal to the Court of Session.

Council's discretion

41.—(1) The Council may in its discretion relieve any person from the consequences of any failure to comply with these Regulations where it is satisfied that such failure to comply is due to mistake, oversight or excusable cause.

(2) The Council may, where the circumstances of a particular intrant are exceptional, waive any provision of these Regulations applying to such intrant, provided that any such waiver may be subject to such conditions as the Council may in its discretion determine.

(3) The Council may, where the circumstances of a particular intrant are exceptional, determine that any of the exemptions provided by regulations 30, 31, 32 and 33 shall not apply to such intrant.

(4) The Council may, where the circumstances of a particular intrant are exceptional, permit such intrant to depart from the terms of any undertaking given by him pursuant to regulation 38.

Photograph

42. The Council may require any intrant to supply the Council with a recent photograph of the intrant for the purpose of verifying the identity of the intrant or otherwise and the Council may retain any photograph so supplied.

Solicitors (Scotland) (Continuing Professional Development) Regulations 1993

Regulations dated 29th July 1993 made by the Council of the Law Society of Scotland with the concurrence of the Lord President of the Court of Session under section 5 of the Solicitors (Scotland) Act 1980.

1.—(1) These Regulations may be cited as the Solicitors (Scotland) (Continuing Professional Development) Regulations 1993.

(2) These Regulations shall come into operation on 1st November 1993.

2.—(1) In these Regulations unless the context otherwise requires:—
"the Act" means the Solicitors (Scotland) Act 1980;
"the Council" means the Council of the Law Society of Scotland;
"solicitor" means a solicitor holding a practising certificate under the Act;
"continuing professional development" means relevant education and study by a solicitor to develop his or her professional knowledge, skills and abilities.

(2) The Interpretation Act 1978 applies to the interpretation of these Regulations as it applies to the interpretation of an Act of Parliament.

3. From 1st November 1993 every solicitor shall undertake continuing professional development the nature and timing of which shall be prescribed by the Council from time to time.

4. Every solicitor shall keep a record of continuing professional development undertaken to comply with these Regulations and produce that record to the Council on demand.

5. The Council shall have power to waive any of the provisions of these

Regulations in any particular circumstances or case and to revoke such a waiver.

6. Breach of any of these Regulations may be treated as professional misconduct for the purposes of Part IV of the Act (Complaints and Disciplinary Proceedings).

Law Society of Scotland Guidelines for Compliance with Continuing Professional Development Regulations

The regulations came into full effect on November 1, 1996. They apply to solicitors holding a Practising Certificate. The Guidelines will be reviewed periodically and may be amended in the light of experience.

Annual Requirements

Solicitors to whom the Regulations and Guidelines apply will require to undertake a minimum of 20 hours Continuing Professional Development (CPD) in each practice year. A minimum of 15 hours must be verifiable CPD and up to five hours can be by Private Study (except for authors of published books or articles – see below).

Definition

In the Regulations CPD is defined as *"relevant education and study by a solicitor to develop his or her professional knowledge, skills and abilities"*. This means education and training in:

(1) Specific updates on law, legal knowledge or legal procedure
(2) Management and organisation
(3) Professional skills
(4) Client care
(5) Ethics, attitudes and values
(6) Risk management
(7) Commercial awareness
(8) Development towards a particular milestone (e.g. Solicitor Advocate training)
(9) Any area designed to improve an individual's ability to operate properly and effectively as a solicitor.

Planning, Recording and Justifying

Solicitors are required to plan their annual CPD at the start of each practice year. Planning should take into account the learning needs of the individual solicitor and the sorts of activities that he or she intends to undertake (e.g. Risk Management Training, People Management Training; An update on a specific area of law) rather than focus unduly on exact activities on specific dates.

Solicitors are required to record the CPD they undertake in a practice year. Solicitors are encouraged to record any CPD hours they undertake over the minimum 20 hours.

Solicitors are required to justify—or reflect upon—the CPD activity that they undertake.

Method

The Society wishes solicitors to have as much control over their own development as possible. The parameters are therefore expressed in broad outline.

Verifiable CPD

A minimum of 15 hours of CPD per annum must meet the criteria of Verifiable CPD. By verifiable, the Society means that the CPD activity should meet the following criteria:
  (i) Have educational aims and objectives relevant to your development;
  (ii) Have clearly anticipated outcomes;
  (iii) Have quality controls;
  (iv) Be able to be evidenced.

Note: The Society has published a document called *CPD Requirements and Guidance for Scottish Solicitors* and a *Continuing Professional Development Handbook* both of which give further detail.

Private study

No more than five hours private study per annum will count towards fulfilling the CPD requirement. Private study includes:
  (i) The reading of relevant periodicals and books
  (ii) Writing relevant books or articles in periodicals or text books which are published (in which case the time occupied may be up to ten hours of the total CPD requirement for the particular practice year)

Note: This is not exhaustive but merely illustrative.

Double Training Relief

Solicitors who require to undertake compulsory training other than by reason of the Continuing Professional Development Regulations may count such training as part of the requirement for CPD in that particular practice year. The following are some examples. They are not an exhaustive list:

Practice Management Course: Solicitors who require to attend a Practice Management Course by virtue of Rule D2.2 of the Law Society of Scotland Practice Rules 2011.

Extended Rights of Audience: Solicitors who require to attend a Training Course in terms of either Rule C4.1 or Rule C4.2 of the Law Society of Scotland Practice Rules 2011.

Monitoring and Enforcement

Solicitors will be expected to complete their annual record honestly and truthfully, and will be required—upon request—to produce their record.

The Society will study in detail a sample of a minimum 5 per cent of solicitors on an annual basis to ensure compliance with the Regulations.

If a solicitor has not complied with the requirement and is not entitled to an exemption, further time will be given for compliance as a first sanction and independent evidence of verifiable CPD will require to be produced to show that compliance has been achieved. Continual failure may be referred to the Practising Certificate Committee of the Society for consideration as professional misconduct.

There are no formal exemptions in the Regulations from the CPD requirements although solicitors can apply to the Registrar for a waiver. Circumstances where a waiver may be considered include but are not limited to redundancy and retirement.

The following waivers do apply:
  1. Solicitors suffering long-term illness for ten weeks or more in respect of the same illness in any practice year may reduce their CPD requirement in proportion to the number of weeks worked during the practice year, rounded up to the nearest complete hour. To calculate

the required number of hours, divide the number of weeks worked by 2.6 and round up to the nearest whole number (e.g. solicitors who work between 37 and 39 weeks in a practice year will require to undertake 15 hours CPD that year).

2. Solicitors on maternity/paternity/adoption leave may reduce their CPD requirement in proportion to the number of weeks worked in the practice year rounded up to the nearest complete hour in accordance to the formula above.

3. Solicitors admitted during the practice year (November 1 to October 31) may reduce their requirement in proportion to the number of weeks working in the practice year rounded up to the nearest complete hour in accordance to the formula above.

4. Trainees admitted during the practice year are not required to undertake any CPD until the start of the practice year following the date on which their training contract ends assuming that the solicitor has been admitted and holds a Practising Certificate.

Note: In all of the above the proportions of Verifiable CPD and private study must be reduced pro-rata.

   [NEXT TEXT PAGE IS **F** 272/1]

The Scottish Solicitors' Discipline Tribunal Procedure Rules 2005

with the concurrence of the Lord President of the Court of Session under section 52 of the Solicitors (Scotland) Act 1980

PART I—INTRODUCTORY

1.—(1) These Rules may be cited as the Scottish Solicitors' Discipline Tribunal Procedure Rules 2005 and shall come into force on 1st April 2005.

(2)The Interpretation Act 1978, shall apply to the interpretation of these Rules as it applies to the interpretation of an Act of Parliament.

PART II—COMPLAINTS AGAINST SOLICITORS

2. Save as hereinafter provided, any complaint against a solicitor or a former solicitor for professional misconduct or in respect of inadequate professional services or any complaint against an incorporated practice or multi-national practice of failure to comply with any relevant statutory provisions or rules, shall be in writing under the hand of the complainer in the Form No I set out in the Schedule annexed to these Rules, and shall be sent to or lodged with the Clerk to the Tribunal. Along with the complaint the complainer shall also send to or lodge with the Clerk an affidavit by the complainer stating in concise numbered paragraphs the matters of fact on which he bases his complaint, and the specific charge(s) of professional misconduct and/or inadequate professional services and that the same to the best of his knowledge and belief are true, which affidavit shall be in the Form No II set out in the said Schedule to these Rules.

Where the complainer is the Council of the Law Society of Scotland (hereinafter referred to as "the Society") it shall not be necessary that the complaint be supported by an affidavit, but the complaint shall contain a statement setting forth in concise numbered paragraphs the matters of fact on which the Society bases its complaint and the specific charge(s) of professional misconduct and/or inadequate professional services.

Where a solicitor or former solicitor in respect of whom a complaint of inadequate professional services is made was, at the time when the services were provided, an employee of another solicitor or solicitors, the instance of the complaint shall contain the name of that other solicitor or those other solicitors.

Where a complaint may result in an order affecting the Investment Business Certificate of a firm, the instance of the complaint shall contain the names of all the solicitors who are partners in that firm.

Where the respondent is an incorporated practice or multi-national practice, the instance of the complaint shall contain the names of all the solicitors who are or at the time when the services were provided were members of that incorporated practice or multi-national practice and any associated incorporated practice or multi-national practice.

If a report is made to the Tribunal under section 51 of the Solicitors (Scotland) Act 1980 as amended ("the 1980 Act") by any of the parties referred to in that section, it shall not be necessary that such report be supported by an affidavit, and the report shall be dealt with as if it were a complaint and affidavit.

3. Where a complaint is made to the Tribunal by a person other than the Society or a person mentioned in section 51(3) of the 1980 Act, the Tribunal may remit the complaint to the Society whether or not the complaint is made in accordance with rule 2.

4. On receiving a complaint made, in the opinion of the Tribunal, in accordance with rule 2 the Tribunal shall consider the same, and it may from time to time and either before or after fixing a day for the hearing require the complainer to supply such further information and documents in support of the complaint as it thinks fit. In any case where, in the opinion of the Tribunal, no *prima facie* case against the solicitor, or former solicitor, or the incorporated practice or multi-national practice and all solicitors whose names appear in the instance of the complaint is disclosed the Tribunal shall give notice to the complainer and provide him with an opportunity to make representation in writing within seven days of such notice before making any order in writing dismissing the complaint.

5. If, in the opinion of the Tribunal, any complaint as originally lodged with the Clerk to the Tribunal or as supplemented in accordance with the procedure in rule 4 discloses a *prima facie* case the Tribunal shall serve a full copy of the complaint and affidavit as lodged or of the complaint as made by the Society and (in the appropriate case) as supplemented and shall allow answers to be lodged within such time as the Tribunal may appoint. If answers are lodged, a full copy thereof shall be sent by the party lodging said answers to the complainer, and a certificate that this has been done shall be sent to the Clerk of the Tribunal. On the expiry of the date appointed for lodging answers and whether answers have been lodged or not, the Tribunal, if on considering the documents lodged is of the opinion that no further action by it is called for, shall give notice to the complainer and provide him with an opportunity to make representation in writing within seven days of such notice before making any order dismissing the complaint; but otherwise the Tribunal shall fix a day for hearing the complaint and shall serve a notice thereof on the complainer and on the solicitor, or former solicitor, or the incorporated practice or multi-national practice and all solicitors whose names appear in the instance of the complaint. The day, time and place to be fixed for the hearing shall be in the discretion of the Tribunal, but parties concerned shall receive at least twenty-one days' notice thereof, unless all parties and the Tribunal agree to proceed on shorter notice.

6. The notice to be given to the parties under rule 5 may be in the Forms Nos III, IV, V set out in the Schedule to these Rules, and shall be sent by recorded delivery post or intimated by sheriff officer to the solicitor or former solicitor or the incorporated practice or multi-national practice and all solicitors whose names appear in the instance of the complaint and to the complainer at the respective addresses given in the complaint; said notice shall require the complainer and the respondents respectively to furnish to the Clerk to the Tribunal and also to each other a list of all documents on which they respectively propose to rely, and also a list of all witnesses whom they respectively propose to examine. Such lists shall, unless otherwise ordered by the Tribunal, be furnished by the complainer and by the respondents respectively in the case of lists of documents at least fourteen days, and in the case of lists of witnesses at least four days, before the day fixed for the hearing and so far as practicable each list of documents sent to the other party shall be accompanied by a copy of the documents referred to therein provided that if such lists are not furnished as aforesaid, the Tribunal at the hearing may have regard to any prejudice which may have been occasioned to the party not receiving the list or lists timeously.

7. Any party may inspect the documents contained in the list to be furnished by another party in terms of rule 6; the said documents shall be lodged with the Clerk to the Tribunal at least ten days before the date fixed for the hearing. If any party desires production of any documents, he may not later than seven days before the date fixed for the hearing send a list of such documents to the other party with a request that the same shall be lodged forthwith. In the event of the other party declining or failing to comply with the said request, the party requiring production shall be entitled to apply for and to obtain from the Tribunal an order on the other party to produce the said documents, if after considering the written submissions of the parties the Tribunal is of opinion that it is necessary for the proper consideration of the complaint that production should be made.

8. Each of the parties shall be in attendance and any incorporated practice or multi-national practice shall be represented on the day and at the time and place fixed for the hearing and shall then be prepared to lead all competent evidence. If any party fails to appear or any incorporated practice or multi-national practice fails to be represented at the hearing the Tribunal may, upon formal proof that the notice of the day fixed for the hearing has been duly posted or intimated to that party or incorporated practice or multi-national practice as the case may be in terms of rule 5, proceed to hear and determine the complaint in the absence of the party who failed to appear or incorporated practice or multi-national practice which has failed to be represented.

9. In any case in which the solicitor or former solicitor does not appear or any incorporated practice or multi-national practice is not represented and the Tribunal under rule 8 determines to proceed in the absence of such solicitor or former solicitor or representative of an incorporated practice or multi-national practice, as the case may be, the Tribunal may, either as to the whole case or as to any particular fact or facts, proceed and act upon evidence given by affidavit.

10. The Tribunal shall announce its decision as soon as reasonably practicable after the complaint has been considered by it. If the decision of the Tribunal is not pronounced on the day of the hearing it shall not be necessary to hold a hearing for the purpose of announcing the decision, but whether such a hearing be held or not, a copy of the decision certified by the Clerk to the Tribunal shall in accordance with the provisions of paragraph 15 of the Fourth Schedule to the 1980 Act be sent forthwith to each party with an intimation of the right of appeal competent under the provisions of section 54 of the 1980 Act. Where the decision of the Tribunal is pronounced outwith a hearing, the Tribunal shall arrange to hear parties on the matter of expenses.

11. Where any report is made to the Tribunal in pursuance of section 51 of the 1980 Act, the Tribunal, if it thinks fit, may appoint a solicitor to act as prosecutor in the complaint, and the expenses of such a solicitor, so far as not recoverable from the solicitor or former solicitor or any incorporated practice or complained against, shall be paid out of the funds of the Tribunal.

12. No complaint shall be withdrawn after it has been received by the Clerk to the Tribunal, except by the special leave of the Tribunal. Application for leave to withdraw shall be made not later than the day fixed for the hearing, unless the Tribunal otherwise directs. In granting leave to withdraw the Tribunal may attach such terms as to expenses or otherwise as it thinks fit.

13. The procedures in rules 2-12 shall apply equally to complaints in respect of conveyancing and executry practitioners in respect of the regulation, making, hearing and determining of inquiries under subsection (2A) of section 20 of the Law Reform (Miscellaneous Provisions) Scotland Act 1990 and to registered foreign lawyers, subject to the amendment of Forms Nos I, II, III, IV and V as appropriate.

PART III—CONVICTIONS

14. Where information is received by the Society from which it appears that a solicitor or former solicitor has, whether before or after enrolment, been convicted by any court of an act involving dishonesty, or sentenced to a term of imprisonment of not less than two years or an incorporated practice or multi-national practice has been convicted by any court of an offence which may render it unsuitable to continue to be recognised under section 34(1A) of the 1980 Act, the Society shall, as soon as may be, submit the information in the form of a complaint to the Tribunal so that the Tribunal may take such action, if any, as it thinks proper under section 53(1)(b) of the 1980 Act.

15. The Tribunal shall cause to be sent to the solicitor, former solicitor or incorporated practice or multi-national practice concerned particulars of the information submitted by the Society and shall invite the respondent to submit in writing to the Tribunal within such period as it may determine any explanations or observations which the respondent may wish to offer.

16. After the expiration of that period, whether such explanations or observations have been lodged or not, the Tribunal shall fix a date for the hearing of the case, and shall give not less than twenty-one days' notice thereof in writing to the respondent. The day, time and place of the hearing shall be in the discretion of the Tribunal.

17. The Tribunal shall announce its decision as soon as reasonably practicable after the hearing. It shall not be necessary to hold a hearing for the purpose of announcing the decision. A copy of the decision certified by the Clerk to the Tribunal shall in accordance with the provision of paragraph 15 of the Fourth Schedule to the 1980 Act be sent forthwith to the respondent with an intimation of the right to appeal competent under the provisions of section 54 of the 1980 Act. Where the decision of the Tribunal is pronounced outwith a hearing, the Tribunal shall arrange to hear parties on the matter of expenses.

18. The procedures in rules 14-17 shall apply equally in respect of convictions of conveyancing and executry practitioners in respect of regulating the making, hearing and determining of inquiries under subsection (2A) of section 20 of the Law Reform (Miscellaneous Provisions) Scotland Act 1990 and in relation to registered foreign lawyers.

PART IV—APPEALS BY SOLICITORS

19. Every appeal to the Tribunal shall be in writing in the Form No VI set out in the Schedule annexed to these Rules and shall be accompanied by a copy of the determination or direction appealed against, and any relative schedule or report and shall be sent to or lodged with the Clerk to the Tribunal within twenty-one days of the date on which the decision of the Society was sent to the appellant.

20. The respondents to an appeal shall be the Society and such other party, if any, who may have complained to the Society under section 42A(1)(a) of the 1980 Act.

21. On receiving a notice of appeal made, in the opinion of the Tribunal, in accordance with rule 19 the Tribunal shall consider the same, and it may from time to time and either before or after fixing a date for the hearing require the appellant to supply such further information and documents in support of the appeal as it thinks fit. In any case where in the opinion of the Tribunal the appeal is manifestly ill-founded or if the appellant fails to comply with any of these Rules, the Tribunal shall give notice to the appellant and provide him with the opportunity to make representation within seven days of such notice in writing before making any order in writing dismissing the appeal.

22. If in the opinion of the Tribunal, any appeal as originally lodged with the Clerk to the Tribunal or as supplemented does not fall to be dismissed under rule 21, the Tribunal shall serve upon each of the respondents a full copy of the statement of appeal and (in the appropriate case) as supplemented and shall allow answers to be lodged within such time as the Tribunal may appoint. If answers are lodged, a full copy shall be sent by each respondent lodging answers to the appellant, and a certificate that this has been done shall be sent by such respondents to the Clerk to the Tribunal. On the expiry of the date appointed for lodging answers and whether answers have been lodged or not, the Tribunal if on considering the documents lodged is of the opinion that no further action by it is called for, shall give notice to the appellant and provide him with the opportunity to make representation in writing within seven days of such notice before making any order dismissing the appeal; but otherwise the Tribunal shall fix a date for hearing the appeal and shall serve a notice thereof on the appellant and on each respondent. The day, time and place to be fixed for the hearing shall be in the discretion of the Tribunal, but the parties concerned shall receive at least twenty-one days' notice thereof, unless all parties and the Tribunal agree to proceed on shorter notice.

23. The notices to be given to parties under rule 22 may be in the Forms Nos VII, VIII and IX set out in the Schedule to these Rules and shall be sent by recorded delivery post to the appellant and to each of the respondents.

24. The Tribunal may on the application of a party *ex proprio motu* require any party to produce any document within such period as the Tribunal may determine.

25. Each of the parties shall be in attendance on the day and at the time and place fixed for the hearing. If any party fails to appear at the hearing the Tribunal may, upon formal proof that the notice of the day fixed for the hearing has been duly posted or intimated to that party in terms of rule 22, proceed to hear and determine the appeal in the absence of that party.

26. The Tribunal shall announce its decision as soon as reasonably practicable after the appeal has been considered by it. If the decision of the Tribunal is not pronounced on the day of the hearing it shall not be necessary to hold a hearing for the purpose of announcing the decision but whether such a hearing be held or not, a copy of the decision certified by the Clerk to the Tribunal shall, in accordance with the provisions of paragraph 15 of the Fourth Schedule to the 1980 Act be sent forthwith to the appellant and each respondent with an intimation of the right of appeal competent under the provisions of section 54 of the 1980 Act. Where the decision of the Tribunal is pronounced outwith a hearing, the Tribunal shall arrange to hear parties on the matter of expenses.

27. No appeal shall be withdrawn after it has been received by the Clerk to the Tribunal except by the special leave of the Tribunal. In granting leave to withdraw, the Tribunal may attach such terms as to expenses or otherwise as it shall think fit.

28. The procedures in rules 19-27 shall apply equally to appeals by conveyancing and executry practitioners in respect of regulating the making, hearing and determining of appeals under subsection (11)(b) of section 20 of the Law Reform (Miscellaneous Provisions) Scotland Act 1990 and in respect of registered foreign lawyers, subject to the amendment of Forms Nos VI, VII, VIII and IX as appropriate.

PART V—RESTORATION TO THE ROLL OF SOLICITORS

29. An application to the Tribunal for restoration to the Roll of Solicitors under section 10 of the 1980 Act by a person who has been struck off the Roll by order of the Tribunal shall be in writing in the Form No X set out in the Schedule to these Rules and shall be verified by affidavit in the Form No XI set out in the said Schedule. The application shall set forth the occupation or occupations of the applicant since his name was struck off the Roll. The application and affidavit shall be sent to or lodged with the Clerk to the Tribunal and shall be supported by letters from two solicitors who at the date of application are in practice and who declare that they know the applicant.

30. The Tribunal may if it thinks fit, require the applicant to give notice by advertisement or otherwise as it may direct that an application for restoration to the Roll has been made by the applicant and that the same will be disposed of by the Tribunal on a date appointed for the hearing. If any person desires to object to the application he shall give notice in writing to the solicitor and to the Clerk to the Tribunal at least ten days before the day fixed for the hearing, specifying the grounds of his objection. Styles of notice for such objection are in Form No XII Nos 1 and 2, set out in the Schedule to these Rules.

31. The Tribunal shall afford to the applicant an opportunity of being heard by the Tribunal and of adducing evidence. The Tribunal may require such evidence as it thinks necessary concerning the identity and character of the applicant, his conduct since his name was struck off the Roll and his suitability for restoration to the Roll and for this purpose may receive written or oral evidence.

32. If the objector appears on the day fixed for the hearing and if the Tribunal is of the opinion, after considering the notice of objection and after hearing the solicitor (if it thinks fit to do so) that the notice discloses a *prima facie* case for inquiry, the Tribunal shall afford to the objector an opportunity of being heard by the Tribunal and of adducing evidence.

33. Subject to the foregoing provisions, the procedure of the Tribunal in connection with applications for restoration to the Roll shall be such as the Tribunal may determine.

34. A copy of the decision of the Tribunal in the application, certified by the Clerk to the Tribunal shall, in accordance with the provision of paragraph 15 of the Fourth Schedule to the 1980 Act, be sent forthwith to the applicant with an intimation of the right of appeal competent under the provisions of section 54 of that Act.

35. In all cases in which the final decision whether by the Tribunal or by the court is to order restoration to the Roll, such decision shall be intimated to the Registrar of Solicitors who shall forthwith give effect thereto.

36. An applicant shall as a condition of having his name restored to the Roll of Solicitors pay to the Registrar of Solicitors, where the name of the applicant was struck off the Roll by order of the Discipline Tribunal, a fee of £500 or such other sum as may be fixed from time to time by the Tribunal.

37. The procedures in rules 29-36 shall apply equally to registered foreign lawyers seeking to make application for restoration to the Register of Foreign Lawyers.

PART VI—GENERAL

38. The Tribunal may appoint from its number a Chairman and Vice Chairmen, any one of whom may preside at hearings of the Tribunal. In the event of the Tribunal being unable to reach a majority decision the Chairman shall have a casting vote.

39. The Tribunal may hear all proceedings in public or in private as it thinks fit and may pronounce its decision in public or in private as it thinks fit. Where any party wishes any proceedings to be heard in private, a motion shall be submitted to the Tribunal in writing, not less than fourteen days prior to the date of the hearing.

40. The Tribunal may on its own motion, or on the application of the parties, or one of them, at any time and from time to time, postpone or adjourn a hearing upon such terms as to expenses or otherwise as, to the Tribunal, shall appear just. It shall not do so at the request of one party only unless, having regard to the grounds upon which, and the time at which, such request is made and to the convenience of the parties, it deems it reasonable to do so. The Chairman may, in regard to the foregoing, exercise the functions of the Tribunal who shall give to the parties such notice of any postponed or adjourned hearing as it deems to be reasonable in the circumstances.

41. If it shall appear to the Tribunal that the allegation contained in a complaint, affidavit, statement or report should be amended or added to, the Tribunal may permit such amendment or addition, and it may also require the same to be embodied in a further complaint, affidavit, statement or report, if in the judgment of the Tribunal such amendment or addition is not within the scope of the original complaint, affidavit, statement or report, provided always that if, in consequence of such amendment or addition, any party applies for an adjournment, the Tribunal may at its discretion grant an adjournment of the hearing, upon such terms as to the Tribunal shall appear just. Upon a hearing, the Tribunal may permit an appellant to amend his statement of appeal or a respondent to amend or withdraw his answers, provided always that if in consequence of such amendment or withdrawal any party applies for an adjournment the Tribunal may at its discretion grant an adjournment of the hearing, upon such terms as to the Tribunal shall appear just.

42. Shorthand notes of proceedings before the Tribunal may be taken by a shorthand writer appointed by the Tribunal or if no shorthand writer be available for any date appointed for a hearing the proceedings may be recorded electronically; the notes may be transcribed if the Tribunal thinks fit, and if transcribed any party to the proceedings shall be entitled to inspect the transcript thereof. The shorthand writer or transcriber of the recorded proceedings shall, if required, supply to the Tribunal and to any person entitled to be heard upon an appeal against a decision of the Tribunal, but to no other person, a copy of the transcript if made, on payment of his charges.

43. The Tribunal may from time to time dispense with any requirements of these Rules respecting notices, affidavits, documents, service or time, where it appears to the Tribunal to be just to do so.

44. The Tribunal may extend, and with consent of parties may at their discretion reduce, the time for doing anything under these Rules.

45. All complaints, reports, affidavits and statements of appeal shall be filed by the Clerk to the Tribunal. The Tribunal may order that any books, papers or other exhibits produced or used at a hearing before it shall be retained by the Clerk to the Tribunal until the time for appealing has expired, or if notice of appeal is given, until the appeal is heard or otherwise disposed of.

46. All orders, determinations, directions and decisions of the Tribunal shall be signed on behalf of the Tribunal by its Chairman or other member presiding or in the event of indisposition of such person by another member present and a copy of such orders or decisions purporting to be signed by the Chairman or other member shall be *prima facie* evidence of the due making thereof. Prior to any appeal being lodged or intimation being made to the Council of the Law Society in terms of paragraph 16 of the Fourth Schedule to the 1980 Act the Chairman or other member presiding may correct any clerical error contained in an order or decision and the order or decision so amended shall of new be intimated to the parties.

47. The Clerk to the Tribunal includes any depute clerk authorised by the Tribunal to act on its behalf.

48. The Tribunal may direct that any question of fact or law which appears to be in issue may be decided at a preliminary hearing. If in the opinion of the Tribunal, a decision on that question substantially disposes of the whole case, the Tribunal may treat the preliminary hearing as a hearing of the case and may give such direction as it thinks fit to dispose of the case. The decision of the Tribunal relating to any preliminary issue may be given orally at the end of the hearing or reserved and, in any event, whether there has been a hearing or not, must be recorded as soon as possible in a document which, save in the case of a decision by consent, must also contain a statement of reasons for the decision and must be signed by the Chairman or other member presiding.

49. If any direction given to a party under these Rules is not complied with by that party, the Tribunal may before or at the hearing dismiss the whole or part of the complaint/submission/appeal/application, strike out the whole or part of the written submission of the party who has not complied and, where appropriate, direct that such party shall be barred from contesting the complaint/submission/appeal/application altogether; but the Tribunal must not dismiss, strike out or give such a direction as aforesaid unless it has sent notice to the party who has not complied, giving that party an opportunity to comply within the period specified in the notice or to establish why the Tribunal should not dismiss, strike out or give such a direction as aforesaid.

50. Where two or more complaints have been lodged in respect of the same respondent the Tribunal may, on the application of a party to the proceedings or on its own initiative, direct that the complaints be conjoined and heard together.

51. If after commencement of any hearing, a member is absent, the proceedings may, with the consent of the parties be heard by the remaining members present, provided that the Tribunal is still properly constituted as provided in paragraph 5 of Schedule 4 to the 1980 Act and the Tribunal shall be deemed to be properly constituted.

52. Without prejudice to any other powers it may have, the Tribunal may exclude from any hearing, or part of it, any person (including a party to the proceedings or the party's representative) whose conduct has disrupted the hearing or whose conduct has otherwise interfered with the administration of justice. It the Tribunal decides to exclude a party it must allow the party's representative sufficient time to consult with the party.

53. If the Chairman is satisfied that any party is unable through physical or mental sickness or impairment to attend the Tribunal and that the party's inability is likely to continue for a long time, the Chairman may make such arrangements as may appear best suited, in all the circumstances of the case, for disposing fairly of the complaint/submission/appeal/application.

54. The Scottish Solicitors' Discipline Tribunal Rules 2002 are hereby revoked without prejudice to any order, reference or appointment made or instruction given or finding pronounced or other thing done thereunder and such order, reference, appointment, instruction, finding or other thing so far as the same could have been made, given, pronounced or done under these

Rules shall have effect as if made, given, pronounced or done under these Rules.

SCHEDULE

FORM I

FORM OF COMPLAINT

To the Scottish Solicitors' Discipline Tribunal, constituted under the Solicitors (Scotland) Act 1980.

COMPLAINT by A.B. against C.D.

I, the undersigned A.B. hereby request that C.D. of
            be required to answer the allegations contained in the affidavit which accompanies this application, and that the Tribunal issues such Order under section 53 of the Solicitors (Scotland) Act 1980, in the matter as it may think right.

Dated ....

....Signature

....Address

....Designation

FORM II

FORM OF AFFIDAVIT BY COMPLAINER

At   the   day of   in presence of   , one of Her Majesty's Justices of the Peace for   , compeared A.B. of   , who being solemnly sworn and interrogated, depones as follows, viz.:—

1. C.D.   has been employed by him in a professional capacity for the last ten years (or as the case may be).

2. (*Here state the facts concisely in numbered paragraphs, and show the deponent's means of knowledge.*)

All which is truth as the deponent shall answer to God.

FORM III

THE SCOTTISH SOLICITORS' DISCIPLINE TRIBUNAL

(Notice of Complaint)

Complaint by A.B.

against

C.D.

To: C.D. of

TAKE NOTICE that a complaint has been made by A.B. of   to the Scottish Solicitors' Discipline Tribunal, constituted under the Solicitors (Scotland) Act 1980, requesting that you be required to answer the allegations contained in the complaint whereof a copy accompanies this notice, and that the Tribunal may issue such Order under section 53 of the Solicitors (Scotland) Act 1980, in the matter as it thinks right.

The Tribunal has appointed that answers to the complaint shall be lodged with the Clerk at   within fourteen days from the date hereof, and that a copy of such answers shall, at the same time, be intimated to

Dated this   day of   20   .

....
Clerk to the Tribunal

(*N.B.*—A print of the Rules made under the said Act is sent herewith for your information and guidance.)

FORM IV

THE SCOTTISH SOLICITORS' DISCIPLINE TRIBUNAL

(Notice to respondent of date fixed for the hearing)

Complaint by A.B.

against

C.D.

To: C.D. of

TAKE NOTICE that the Scottish Solicitors' Discipline Tribunal has fixed the   day of   at   within   for the hearing of this complaint, and if you fail then to appear the Tribunal may in accordance with the Rules made under the Solicitors (Scotland) Act 1980, proceed in your absence.

You are required by the said Rules to furnish to the said A.B. and to the Clerk to the Tribunal at   at least fourteen days before the said   day of   , a list of all the documents on which you propose to rely. Under the said Rules the said A.B. is also required to furnish you with a list of documents on which he proposes to rely. The said documents must be lodged with the Clerk to the Tribunal at least ten days before the date fixed for the hearing.

Either party may inspect the documents included in the list furnished by the other. A copy of any document mentioned in the list of either party must, on application and at the expense of the party requiring it, be furnished to that party by the other within three days after receipt of the application.

If either party desires production of any documents not included in the other party's list he may, not later than seven days before the date fixed for the hearing, send a list of such documents to the other party with a request that the same shall be lodged forthwith, and not later than four days before the date fixed for the hearing. In the event of the other party declining or failing to comply with the said request, the party requiring production shall be entitled to apply for and to obtain from the Tribunal an order on the other party to produce the said documents, if after considering the written submissions of the parties the Tribunal is of the opinion that it is necessary for the proper consideration of the complaint that production should be made.

Dated this   day of   20   .

....
Clerk to the Tribunal

FORM V

THE SCOTTISH SOLICITORS' DISCIPLINE TRIBUNAL

(Notice to the complainer of the date fixed for the hearing)

To: A.B. of

TAKE NOTICE that answers to your complaint have/have not been lodged and that the   day of   20   has been fixed by the Scottish Solicitors' Discipline Tribunal for the hearing of your complaint against C.D., Solicitor of   .
The Tribunal will sit at   within   .
    You are required by the Rules made under the Solicitors (Scotland) Act 1980, to furnish to the said C.D. and to the Clerk to the Tribunal at   at least fourteen days before the   said day of   a list of all the documents on which you propose to rely, and at least fourteen days before the said date a list of the witnesses whom you propose to examine. So far as practicable said list of documents sent to C.D. shall be accompanied by a copy of the documents referred to therein. The said documents must be lodged with the Clerk to the Tribunal at least ten days before the date fixed for the hearing. Under the Rules of the Tribunal the said C.D. is also required to furnish, within the said respective periods, a list of the documents (if any) on which he proposes to rely, and a list of the witnesses (if any) whom he proposes to examine. The said documents must be lodged with the Clerk to the Tribunal at least ten days before the date fixed for the hearing. Under the Rules of the Tribunal the said C.D. is also required to furnish, within the said respective period, a list of documents (if any) on which he proposes to rely, and a list of witnesses (if any) whom he proposes to examine.
    Either party may inspect the documents included in the list furnished by the other. A copy of any document mentioned in the list of either party must, on the application and at the expense

of the party requiring it, be furnished to that party by the other within three days after receipt of a written request therefore. If either party desires production of any documents he may, not later than seven days before the date fixed for the hearing, send a list of such documents to the other party with a request that the same shall be lodged forthwith, and not later than four days before the date fixed for the hearing. In the event of the other party declining or failing to comply with the said request, the party requiring production shall be entitled to apply for and to obtain from the Tribunal an order on the other party to produce the said documents, if after considering the written submissions of the parties the Tribunal is of the opinion that it is necessary for the proper consideration of the complaint that production should be made.

In the event of a party complained of not appearing, and of the Tribunal being asked to proceed in his absence, you must be prepared to prove that any notice on which you rely was duly served on the solicitor in accordance with the Rules issued under the said Act.

Dated this   day of   20

....
Clerk to the Tribunal

FORM VI

THE SCOTTISH SOLICITORS' DISCIPLINE TRIBUNAL

FORM OF APPEAL TO THE TRIBUNAL

To the Scottish Solicitors' Discipline Tribunal constituted under the Solicitors (Scotland) Act 1980

APPEAL by A.B. against a determination/direction/order
of the Council of the Law Society of Scotland
dated

I, the undersigned A.B., hereby appeal against the determination/direction/order of the Council of the Law Society of Scotland dated   and intimated to me on   a copy of which is produced herewith.

The grounds of my appeal are as follows *(here state concisely in numbered paragraphs, the grounds of the appeal)*.

I hereby request the Tribunal *(here state the Order which you wish the Tribunal to pronounce in your favour)*.

In the consideration of the matter by the Council of the Law Society, the complainer was *(name and address of the party or parties whose complaint to the Law Society resulted in the decision appealed against)*.

Dated ....

.... Signature

[Address and

.... [place or places

[of business

FORM VII

FORM OF INTIMATION OF APPEAL

APPEAL by A.B. against a determination/direction/order
of the Council of the Law Society of Scotland dated

To: The Secretary
The Law Society of Scotland
or
C.D. *of*

TAKE NOTICE that an appeal has been lodged with the Scottish Solicitors' Discipline Tribunal by A.B. against a determination/direction/order of the Council of the Law Society of Scotland dated   . A copy of the statement of appeal accompanies this notice.

The Tribunal has appointed that answers to the statement of appeal shall be lodged with the Clerk at   within   days from the date hereof, and that a copy of such answers shall, at the same time, be intimated to   .

Dated this   day of   20

....
Clerk to the Tribunal

FORM VIII

FORM OF NOTICE TO AN APPELLANT OF DATE FIXED FOR THE HEARING OF AN APPEAL

To A.B. of

TAKE NOTICE that answers to your statement of appeal have been lodged by
and   and that the   day of has been fixed for the hearing of your appeal. The
Tribunal will sit at   at
and if you fail then to appear the Tribunal may in accordance with the Rules made under the
Solicitors (Scotland) Act 1980 proceed in your absence.

You are required by the said Rules to furnish to   and to   and to the Clerk to
the Tribunal at
at least fourteen days before the said day of a list of all the documents on which you propose to
rely. The said documents must be lodged with the Clerk to the Tribunal at least seven days
before the date fixed for the hearing.

Dated this   day of   20

....
Clerk to the Tribunal

FORM IX

FORM OF NOTICE TO THE RESPONDENT OF DATE FIXED FOR THE HEARING OF AN APPEAL

APPEAL by   against a determination/direction/orde
of the Council of the Law Society of Scotland dated

TAKE NOTICE that the Scottish Solicitors' Discipline Tribunal has fixed the day of
at   within   for the hearing of this appeal, and if you fail then to appear, the
Tribunal may in accordance with the Rules made under the Solicitors (Scotland) Act 1980
proceed in your absence.

You are required by the said Rules to furnish to   and to
and to the Clerk to the Tribunal at   at least fourteen days before the said
day of a list of all the documents on which you propose to rely. The said documents must be
lodged with the Clerk to the Tribunal at least seven days before the date fixed for the hearing.

Dated this   day of   20

....
Clerk to the Tribunal

FORM X

FORM OF APPLICATION BY A SOLICITOR FOR RESTORATION TO ROLL OF SOLICITORS

To the Scottish Solicitors' Discipline Tribunal constituted under the Solicitors (Scotland) Act 1980

1. I, the undersigned A.B. hereby apply to the Discipline Tribunal under section 10 of the Solicitors (Scotland) Act, 1980, for an order restoring my name to the Roll of Solicitors.

2. I was admitted a Solicitor on the   day of   in the year   .

3. On   in the year   , I was struck off the Roll of Solicitors by order of the Discipline Committee/Tribunal.

4. Since then my occupations have been as follows:—

(Here specify in the case of each employment the name and address of the employer, the nature of the work on which the applicant was employed and the period of employment.)

5. The following persons are prepared on request to testify to the Discipline Tribunal concerning my identity and character, my conduct since my name was struck off from the Roll and my suitability for restoration to the Roll.

(Here state the names and addresses of the persons prepared to testify.)

.... *Signature*

.... *Address*

FORM XI

**FORM OF AFFIDAVIT BY APPLICANT FOR RESTORATION
TO ROLL OF SOLICITORS**

At   on the   day of   in presence of   , one of Her Majesty's
Justices of the Peace for   compeared A.B. of   who being solemnly sworn
and interrogated, depones as follows, viz.:—

1. The deponent, was admitted as a Solicitor on the   day of   in the
year   , and on the   day of in the year   , was struck off the Roll of
Solicitors by order of the Solicitors' Discipline (Scotland) Committee/the Scottish Solicitors'
Discipline Tribunal.

2. The particulars of his occupations since then as set forth in the application for restoration to
the Roll now produced, and marked "A", are true.

3. The deponent is not aware and does not know of any cause of complaint or proceedings
which might have arisen out of his conduct since his name was struck off the Roll.

All which is truth as the deponent shall answer to God.

FORM XII

**FORMS OF NOTICE OF OBJECTION TO AN APPLICATION BY
A SOLICITOR FOR THE RESTORATION OF HIS NAME TO
THE ROLL OF SOLICITORS**

No. 1

FORM OF NOTICE TO BE GIVEN TO THE SOLICITOR

To C.D. of   , Solicitor.

TAKE NOTICE that I object to the application made by you to the Scottish Solicitors'
Discipline Tribunal for restoration of your name to the Roll of Solicitors, on the following
grounds, viz.:—

(The grounds of objection to be stated in articulate numbered paragraphs.)

Dated ....

....*Signature*

.... *Address*

.... *Designation*

No. 2

FORM OF NOTICE TO BE GIVEN TO THE TRIBUNAL

To the Scottish Solicitors' Discipline Tribunal.

TAKE NOTICE that I object to the application made by C.D. of
to the Scottish Solicitors' Discipline Tribunal for restoration of his name to the Roll of
Solicitors, on the following grounds, viz.:—

(The grounds of objection to be stated in articulate numbered paragraphs.)

Dated ....

.... *Signature*

.... *Address*

.... *Designation*

Scottish Solicitors' Discipline Tribunal Rules 2008

Table of Contents

Schedule

The Scottish Solicitors' Discipline Tribunal, in exercise of the powers conferred upon it by section 52(2) of the Solicitors (Scotland) Act 1980 and with the concurrence of the Lord President of the Court of Session, hereby makes the following rules.

Part 1: Introductory

Citation, commencement and application

1.—(1) These rules may be cited as the Scottish Solicitors' Discipline Tribunal Rules 2008.

(2) These rules shall come into force on 1st October 2008.

(3) These rules shall apply to any complaint, appeal or application to which Parts 2, 3 or 4 apply which is made to the Tribunal on or after 1st October 2008, except any such complaint or appeal to which the 2005 Rules continue to apply by virtue of rule 57(2).

Interpretation

2.—(1) In these rules—

"the 1980 Act" means the Solicitors (Scotland) Act 1980 (c.5) ;

"the 1990 Act" means the Law Reform (Miscellaneous Provisions) (Scotland) Act 1990 (c.40):

"the 2007 Act" means the Legal Profession and Legal Aid (Scotland) Act 2007 (asp 5);

"the 2005 Rules" means the Scottish Solicitors' Discipline Tribunal Rules 2005;

"the 2008 Order" means the Legal Profession and Legal Aid (Scotland) Act 2007 (Transitional, Savings and Consequential Provisions) Order 2008;

"appellant" means, in relation to any appeal to which Part 3 applies, the practitioner, complainer or legal practice making the appeal;

"applicant" means, in relation to any application to which Part 4 applies, the solicitor, registered European lawyer or registered foreign lawyer, who wishes to have his name restored to the roll or register, as the case may be;

"case" means a complaint, appeal or application under Part 2, 3, or 4, as the case may be, and "part of a case" includes, without prejudice to that generality, the holding of any procedural meeting or preliminary hearing or the determination of any procedural or substantive issue about the case;

"Chairman" includes any other person presiding at the proceedings of the Tribunal;

"Clerk" means the Clerk to the Tribunal and includes any depute clerk appointed by the Tribunal;

"the Commission" means the Scottish Legal Complaints Commission;

"complainer" means the person who makes the complaint and, where the complaint is made by the person on behalf of another person, includes that other person;

"complaint" includes any expression of dissatisfaction;

"conduct complaint" has the meaning given by section 2(1)(a) of the 2007 Act;

"convener", in relation to a particular tribunal, shall be construed in accordance with rule 55(1);

"conveyancing practitioner" means a person registered under section 17 of the 1990 Act in the register of conveyancing practitioners;

"the Council" means the Council of the Law Society of Scotland;

"the court" means the Court of Session;

"decision" includes any decision, order, determination or direction;

"executry practitioner" means a person registered under section 18 of the 1990 Act in the register of executry practitioners;

"functions" includes powers and duties;

"legal practice" means—

(a) a firm of solicitors, whether or not since the time when it is suggested the conduct complained of occurred there has been any change in the firm by the addition of a new partner or the death or resignation of an existing partner or the firm has ceased to practise;

(b) an incorporated practice, whether or not since that time there has been any change in the persons exercising the management and control of the practice or the practice has ceased to be recognised by virtue of section 34(1A) of the 1980 Act or has been wound up;

(c) a multi-national practice, whether or not since the time when the conduct complained of took place there has been any change in the members of the partnership or body corporate or the practice has been wound up or otherwise ceased to practise;

"particular tribunal" shall be construed in accordance with rule 54(1);

"parties to a case" means

(a) in the case of a complaint, the principal complainer and the respondent or respondents;

(b) in the case of an appeal, the appellant and the respondent or respondents; and

(c) in the case of an application, the applicant and any objector or objectors;

"practising certificate" has the meaning given by section 4 of the 1980 Act;

"practitioner" means—

(a) a conveyancing practitioner, whether or not registered at the time when it is suggested the conduct complained of occurred and notwithstanding that subsequent to that time the practitioner has ceased to be so registered;

(b) an executry practitioner, whether or not registered at that time and notwithstanding that subsequent to that time the practitioner has ceased to be so registered;

(c) a registered European lawyer whether or not the European lawyer was registered with the Law Society of Scotland at the time the conduct complained of took place and notwithstanding that subsequent to that time the registration has been withdrawn or suspended;

(d) a registered foreign lawyer, whether or not the foreign lawyer was registered under section 60A of the 1980 Act at the time the conduct complained of took place and notwithstanding that subsequent to that time the registration has been withdrawn or suspended; and

(e) a solicitor, whether or not the solicitor had a practising certificate in force at that time and notwithstanding that subsequent to that time the name of the solicitor has been removed from or struck off the roll or the solicitor has ceased to practise or has been suspended from practice;

"preliminary hearing" shall be construed in accordance with rule 42;

"principal complainer" means the person who made the complaint but does not include any person on whose behalf the complaint is made;

"procedural hearing" shall be construed in accordance with rule 41;

"respondent" means—

(a)   in relation to any complaint to which Part 2 applies, the practitioner who, or the legal practice which, is the subject of the complaint; and

(b)   in relation to any appeal to which Part 3 applies which is made by a practitioner or legal practice, the Council and any complainer and, in relation to any such appeal which is made by a complainer, the Council, practitioner or legal practice and any other complainer;

"the roll" means the roll of solicitors kept by the Council by virtue of section 7(1) of the 1980 Act;

"secondary complainer" means any person on whose behalf a complaint is made;

"Tribunal" means the Scottish Solicitors' Discipline Tribunal and includes, in relation to a particular case or part of a case, a particular tribunal; and

"unsatisfactory professional conduct" has the same meaning as it has in section 46(1) of the 2007 Act.

(2) Unless the context otherwise requires, any reference in these rules

(a) to a numbered rule or Part refers to the rule or Part bearing that number in these rules; or

(b) to the schedule refers to the schedule to these rules,

and any reference in a rule to a numbered paragraph refers to the paragraph bearing that number in that rule.

Part 2: Procedure regarding complaints made to the Tribunal

Complaints to which Part 2 applies

3.—(1) This Part applies to any complaint made to the Tribunal—

(a) under section 51(1) or (1A) of the 1980 Act by the Council (whether or not on behalf of any other person); and

(b) under section 51(2) of that Act by any person mentioned in subsection (3) of that section.

(2) Without prejudice to the generality of section 51(1) or (1A) of the 1980 Act, the complaints which may be made by the Council under that section (whether or not on behalf of any other person) include any complaint alleging—

(a) that a practitioner may have been guilty of professional misconduct; or

(b) that a practitioner may have been convicted by any court of an act involving dishonesty or may have been sentenced to a term of

imprisonment of not less than 2 years; or
  (c) that a legal practice may have failed to comply with any provision of the 1980 Act or of rules made under that Act applicable to it; or
  (d) that a legal practice, which is an incorporated practice, may have been convicted by any court of an offence which renders it unsuitable to continue to be recognised under section 34(1A) of the 1980 Act.

Notification of certain complaints made by the Council
  4.—(1) Paragraph (2) shall apply in any case where—
    (a) a complaint is about to be made to the Tribunal by the Council (whether or not on behalf of any secondary complainer) that a practitioner may have been guilty of professional misconduct; and
    (b) the Council considers that there may be any person, or, as the case may be, any other person, who may have been directly affected by that misconduct and who might be eligible to seek compensation for any loss, inconvenience or distress resulting from it.
  (2) The Council shall—
    (a) inform any person who it considers may be so affected that it is proposing to make such a complaint and give that person an opportunity of deciding whether to request the Council to make the complaint on behalf of that person; and
    (b) include a statement in its complaint that it has done so.

Complaint made by the Council on behalf of others
  5. Where a complaint is made by the Council on behalf of any secondary complainer,
    (a) the Tribunal shall deal only with the Council except where it is otherwise expressly provided in these rules; and
    (b) it shall be the duty of the Council—
      (i) in the case where the complaint is that a practitioner may have been guilty of professional misconduct, to ascertain from every secondary complainer whether that secondary complainer claims to have been directly affected by that misconduct and wishes to seek compensation for any loss, inconvenience or distress resulting from it;
      (ii) to keep the secondary complainer informed of any action taken by the Tribunal which may affect the interests of that complainer;
      (iii) to take account, where relevant, of any comments made by the secondary complainer in any comments or representations made by the Council to the Tribunal;
      (iv) where the Council receives notice of the hearing under rule 11, to send a copy of that notice, by first class recorded delivery post, to every secondary complainer;
      (v) in a case where paragraph (b)(i) applies and the secondary complainer is claiming compensation, to include, along with the copy of the notice of the hearing, a notice that the secondary complainer is entitled to appear at the hearing, and to lead evidence, on the date, time and place appointed in that notice, and
      (vi) to inform the Clerk in writing before the hearing that the duties mentioned in (i) to (v) have been carried out.

Manner in which complaints are to be made
  6.—(1) Any complaint by the Council shall—

(a) be in writing;
(b) be in Form No 1 set out in the schedule, or as near thereto as circumstances permit;
(c) contain the name and address of the Council;
(d) indicate whether or not the complaint is made on behalf of any other person and, if so, the name and address (or the address last known to the Council) of any such secondary complainer;
(e) contain the name and address (or the address last known to the Council) of the respondent and, where the respondent is a legal practice, the names of all the solicitors who are, or were at the time of the conduct complained of, members of that practice;
(f) contain, in concise numbered paragraphs, the statements mentioned in paragraph (2);
(g) be signed on behalf of the Council; and
(h) be lodged with the Clerk.

(2) The statements which a complaint under paragraph (1) shall contain are—
(a) a statement of the specific complaint which is being made;
(b) a statement of the facts upon which the complaint is based;
(c) a statement that the complaint is one to which these rules apply and is not one to which the 2005 Rules apply by virtue of rule 57(2);
(d) in the case where the complaint is that a practitioner may have been guilty of professional misconduct, a statement indicating whether or not the Council or any secondary complainer is claiming to have been directly affected by that misconduct and is seeking compensation for any loss, inconvenience or distress resulting from it and, if so, a statement of the facts which are relied upon in support of that claim; and
(e) a statement indicating that the Council has complied with rule 4.

(3) Any complaint by any of the persons mentioned in section 51(3) of the 1980 Act shall be—
(a) in writing;
(b) contain the name and address of the principal complainer;
(c) contain the name and address (or the last address known to the principal complainer) of the incorporated practice which is the respondent;
(d) give a brief statement of the facts upon which the complaint is based;
(e) be signed by the principal complainer; and
(f) be lodged with the Clerk.

Complaint not properly made
7.—(1) Where the Tribunal considers that a complaint is not a complaint to which these rules apply but is one to which the 2005 Rules apply by virtue of rule 57(2), the Tribunal shall make an order dismissing the complaint, inform the Council accordingly and request the Council to submit the complaint under the 2005 Rules.
(2) Where the Tribunal considers that a complaint is not otherwise a complaint made in accordance with rule 6, the Tribunal may make an order dismissing the complaint and, where it does so, it shall inform the principal complainer accordingly and request the principal complainer to submit a new complaint which complies with that rule.

Whether complaint discloses *prima facie* case
8.—(1) Where the Tribunal does not dismiss the complaint under rule 7, the Tribunal shall consider whether the complaint discloses a *prima facie* case against the respondent.
(2) For this purpose, the Tribunal may require the principal complainer to

supply such further information and documents in support of the complaint as it thinks fit.

(3) Paragraph (4) applies in any case where the Tribunal considers that the complaint, together with any further information and documents submitted in accordance with paragraph (2), does not disclose a *prima facie* case against the respondent.

(4) The Tribunal shall give notice to the principal complainer that the complaint does not disclose a *prima facie* case against the respondent and provide the principal complainer with an opportunity to make representations in writing within 21 days from the date of sending of such notice.

(5) If, after considering any representations submitted in accordance with paragraph (4), the Tribunal remains of the view that the complaint does not disclose a *prima facie* case against the respondent, the Tribunal shall make an order dismissing the complaint and inform the principal complainer accordingly.

Lodging of answers

9.—(1) Paragraph (2) applies in any case where the Tribunal considers that the complaint, together with any further information and documents submitted in accordance with rule 8(2) or any representations submitted in accordance with rule 8(3), discloses a *prima facie* case against the respondent.

(2) The Tribunal shall send a copy of the complaint and of any such further information, documents and representations to the respondent, together with a notice allowing answers to be lodged with the Clerk within 21 days from the date of sending of such notice.

(3) The notice shall be in Form No 2 set out in the schedule, or as near thereto as circumstances permit.

(4) Any documents and notice sent in accordance with paragraph (2) shall be sent by first class recorded delivery post or intimated by sheriff officer to the respondent at the address given in the complaint.

(5) If the respondent lodges answers with the Clerk in accordance with paragraph (2), the respondent may, at the same time, lodge with the Clerk any documents upon which the respondent proposes to rely.

(6) The respondent shall, at the same time as lodging any answers and any documents with the Clerk, send a copy of those answers and documents to the principal complainer and shall also inform the Clerk in writing that this has been done.

Dismissal without hearing

10.—(1) If answers are lodged in accordance with rule 9, the Tribunal shall consider the complaint and the answers and any other documents lodged with the Clerk.

(2) If the Tribunal is then of the opinion that no hearing into the complaint is necessary because the complaint is without merit, the Tribunal shall give notice to the principal complainer accordingly and provide the principal complainer with an opportunity to make representations in writing within 21 days from the date of sending of such notice.

(3) If, after considering any representations submitted in accordance with paragraph (2), the Tribunal remains of the view that no hearing into the complaint is necessary because the complaint is without merit, the Tribunal shall make an order dismissing the complaint and inform the principal complainer and respondent accordingly.

Notice of the hearing

11.—(1) After the expiry of the date for lodging answers and irrespective of whether or not answers have been lodged, the Tribunal shall, if it does not dismiss the complaint in accordance with rule 10, appoint a date, time and place for the hearing of the complaint.

(2) The Tribunal shall give the principal complainer and respondent notice of the date, time and place of the hearing which notice shall be—

    (a) in Form No 3 set out in the schedule, or as near thereto as circumstances permit;

    (b) given not less than 21 days before the date of the hearing, unless both the principal complainer and respondent agree to a shorter period of notice; and

    (c) sent by first class recorded delivery post or intimated by the sheriff officer to the respondent and the principal complainer at their respective addresses given in the complaint.

(3) This rule is without prejudice to the powers of the Tribunal to hold a procedural hearing or a preliminary hearing under rule 41 or 42.

Production of lists of documents and witnesses and production of documents

12.—(1) The notice of the hearing given under rule 11 shall also require the principal complainer and the respondent—

    (a) to lodge with the Clerk

        (i) a list of all the documents on which they propose to rely at the hearing, together with those documents (or copies of them), not less than 14 days before the date of the hearing, or such longer or shorter period as the Tribunal may specify in the notice; and

        (ii) a list of witnesses on which they propose to rely at the hearing, not less than 7 days before the date of the hearing, or such longer or shorter period as the Tribunal may specify in the notice; and

    (b) at the same time, to send to the other party a copy of the lists and a copy of the documents lodged with the Clerk and shall also inform the Clerk in writing that this has been done.

(2) In the case where—

    (a) the complaint is made by the Council on behalf of any secondary complainer that the practitioner may have been guilty of professional misconduct; and

    (b) that secondary complainer claims to have been directly affected by that misconduct and is seeking compensation for any loss, inconvenience or distress resulting from it,

the list of witnesses lodged by the Council shall include, in a separate part, the name of any such secondary complainer and any other witnesses on which the Council proposes to rely in support of such a claim.

Production of other documents

13.—(1) The Tribunal may, on the application of either the principal complainer or the respondent, or on its own initiative, make an order requiring—

    (a) the respondent, or, as the case may be,

    (b) the principal complainer, and

    (c) in the case mentioned in rule 12(2), any secondary complainer,

to produce any document in their custody or under their control within such period as the Tribunal may determine, if it is of the opinion that it is necessary for the proper consideration of the complaint that the document should be made available.

(2) The parties are not obliged by such an order to produce any document which they would be entitled to refuse to produce in proceedings in any court in Scotland.

Presence of parties at the hearing

14.—(1) The persons mentioned in paragraph (2) are entitled to be present, whether or not they may also be represented, and to lead their evidence, on the date, time and place appointed for the hearing under rule 11.

(2) The persons mentioned are—
  (a) the principal complainer;
  (b) the practitioner, in the case where the respondent is a practitioner; and
  (c) in the case mentioned in rule 12(2), any secondary complainer.

(3) Where the respondent is a legal practice, the legal practice is entitled to be represented and to lead its evidence, on the date, time and place appointed for the hearing under rule 11.

(4) If any person fails to appear or to be represented at the hearing, the Tribunal may, after being satisfied that notice of the hearing has been duly posted or intimated to that person in accordance with rule 11(2) or, as the case may be, rule 5(b)(v), proceed to hear and determine the complaint in the absence of that person.

(5) In any case where the respondent fails to appear or to be represented at the hearing and the Tribunal decides to proceed to hear and determine the complaint in the absence of that respondent under paragraph (4), the Tribunal—
  (a) shall take into account all the documents lodged with the Clerk, whether by the principal or secondary complainer or by the respondent; and
  (b) may, either as to the whole complaint or as to some or all of the facts alleged in the statements contained in the complaint, proceed and act upon evidence given by affidavit but this is without prejudice to its power to take evidence orally.

Decision of Tribunal

15.—(1) Every decision by the Tribunal shall—
  (a) set out the facts proved;
  (b) have appended to it a note of the reasons for its decision;
  (c) be signed by the Chairman; and
  (d) subject to paragraph 14A of Schedule 4 to the 1980 Act, be published in full.

(2) A copy of any such decision purporting to be signed by the Chairman shall be *prima facie* evidence of the due making thereof.

(3) The Tribunal shall announce its decision as soon as reasonably practicable after the hearing has finished.

(4) If the decision of the Tribunal is not announced on the day of the hearing or any adjourned hearing, it shall not be necessary to hold a hearing for the purpose of announcing its decision.

(5) Irrespective of whether or not the decision is announced at a hearing, the Clerk shall forthwith send a copy of the decision certified by the Clerk to the principal complainer, any secondary complainer and the respondent, together with a notice intimating the right of appeal available from that decision to the Court of Session under the 1980 Act or the 1990 Act.

(6) Where the decision of the Tribunal is announced outwith a hearing, the Tribunal shall arrange to hear parties on the matter of expenses.

(7) This rule is without prejudice to paragraphs 13 to 15 of Schedule 4 to the 1980 Act and to those provisions as applied by section 21B of the 1990 Act.

Appointment of solicitor in certain complaints

16.—(1) Where a report is made to the Tribunal under section 51(2) of the 1980 Act by any of the persons mentioned in section 51(3) of that Act, the Tribunal may, if it thinks fit, appoint a solicitor to act as prosecutor in the complaint.

(2) The expenses of such a solicitor, so far as not recoverable from the respondent, shall be paid out of the funds of the Tribunal.

Duplication of complaints

17. Where two or more complaints have been lodged in respect of the same respondent, the Tribunal may, on the application of a party to the proceedings or on its own initiative, direct that the complaints be conjoined and heard together.

Remission of certain complaints after inquiry

18.—(1) Where, after holding an inquiry under section 53(1) of the 1980 Act or, as the case may be, section 20(2A) of the 1990 Act into a complaint of professional misconduct against a practitioner, the Tribunal—

    (a) is not satisfied that the practitioner has been guilty of professional misconduct; but

    (b) considers that the practitioner may be guilty of unsatisfactory professional conduct,

the Tribunal must remit the complaint to the Council in accordance with section 53ZA of the 1980 Act or, as the case may be, section 20ZA of the 1990 Act.

(2) Where the Tribunal remits a complaint to the Council under paragraph (1), the Tribunal may make available to the Council any of its findings in fact in its inquiry into the complaint.

Withdrawal of complaint

19.—(1) No complaint shall be withdrawn by the complainer after it has been received by the Clerk, except with the leave of the Tribunal.

(2) In granting leave to withdraw, the Tribunal may attach such terms as to expenses or otherwise as it thinks fit.

Part 3: Procedure regarding appeals made to the Tribunal

Appeals to which Part 3 applies

20.– (1) This Part applies to any appeal made to the Tribunal against a decision of the Council under the 1980 Act or the 1990 Act.

(2) Without prejudice to that generality, this Part applies to any appeal made to the Tribunal by—

    (a) a practitioner under section 42ZA(9) of the 1980 Act against a determination of the Council upholding a conduct complaint under section 42ZA(1) or (2), or a direction under section 42ZA(4), of that Act;

    (b) a complainer under section 42ZA(10)–(12) of the 1980 Act against a determination of the Council not upholding a conduct complaint under section 42ZA(1) or (2) or not making a direction under section 42ZA(4)(c) of that Act to pay compensation or against the amount of the compensation directed to be paid;

    (c) a practitioner under section 42ZD(1) of the 1980 Act against a direction made by the Council under section 42ZC(1) of that Act (direction regarding education or training);

    (d) a practitioner or legal practice under section 53D of the 1980 Act against a decision of the Council to suspend or withdraw an investment business certificate or impose conditions or restrictions on it;

    (e) a practitioner under section 20ZB(9) of the 1990 Act against a determination of the Council upholding a conduct complaint under section 20ZB(1) or (2), or a direction under section 20ZB(4), of that Act;

    (f) a complainer under section 20ZB(10)–(12) of the 1990 Act against a determination of the Council not upholding a conduct complaint under section 20ZB(1) or (2) or   not making a direction under section 20ZB(4) of that Act to pay compensation or against the amount of the compensation directed to be paid;

(g) a practitioner under section 20ZE(1) of the 1990 Act against a direction made by the Council under section 20ZD(1) of that Act (direction regarding education or training);

Manner in which appeals are to be made

21. Any appeal shall—

(a) be in writing;

(b) be in Form No 4 set out in the schedule, or as near thereto as circumstances permit;

(c) contain the name and address of the appellant and of every respondent;

(d) be accompanied by a copy of the decision appealed against;

(e) contain, in concise numbered paragraphs, a statement of the grounds upon which the appeal is made;

(f) be signed by the appellant; and

(g) be lodged with the Clerk within the time limit allowed by the statutory provision under which the appeal is made.

Appeal not properly made

22.—(1) Where the Tribunal considers that an appeal is not made timeously, the Tribunal shall dismiss the appeal and inform the appellant accordingly.

(2) Where the Tribunal considers that an appeal is not one to which these Rules apply but is one to which the 2005 Rules apply by virtue of rule 57(2), the Tribunal shall dismiss the appeal, inform the appellant accordingly and request the appellant to submit an appeal under the 2005 Rules.

(3) Where the Tribunal considers that an appeal is not made in accordance with rule 21, the Tribunal may dismiss the appeal but, if it does so, it shall inform the appellant accordingly and request the appellant to submit a new appeal which complies with that rule.

Whether appeal is manifestly unfounded

23.—(1) Where the Tribunal does not dismiss the appeal under rule 22, the Tribunal shall consider whether the appeal is manifestly unfounded.

(2) The Tribunal may require the appellant to supply such further information and documents in support of the appeal as it thinks fit.

(3) If the Tribunal considers that the appeal, together with any further information and documents submitted in accordance with paragraph (2), is manifestly unfounded, the Tribunal shall give notice to the appellant accordingly and provide the appellant with an opportunity to make representations in writing within 21 days from the date of sending of such notice.

(4) If, after considering any representations submitted in accordance with paragraph (3), the Tribunal remains of the view that the appeal is manifestly unfounded, the Tribunal shall make an order dismissing the appeal and inform the appellant accordingly.

Lodging of answers

24.—(1) Paragraph (2) applies in any case where the Tribunal considers that the appeal, together with any further information and documents submitted in accordance with rule 23(2) or any representations submitted in accordance with rule 23(3), does not fall to be dismissed under rule 23.

(2) The Tribunal shall send, by first class recorded delivery post, a copy of the appeal and of any such further information, documents and representations to every respondent named in the appeal, together with a notice allowing answers to be lodged with the Clerk before such date, not being less than 21 days from the date of sending of such notice, as the

Tribunal shall specify in the notice.

(3) The notice shall be in Form No 5 set out in the schedule, or as near thereto as circumstances permit.

(4) If any respondent lodges answers with the Clerk in accordance with paragraph (2), the respondent may, at the same time, lodge with the Clerk any documents upon which the respondent proposes to rely.

(5) Any respondent shall, at the same time as lodging any answers and any documents with the Clerk, send a copy of those answers and documents to the appellant and to any other respondent and shall also inform the Clerk in writing that this has been done.

Dismissal without hearing

25.—(1) Paragraph (2) shall apply in any case after the expiry of the date appointed for lodging answers irrespective of whether or not answers have been lodged.

(2) The Tribunal shall consider the appeal and the other documents lodged and, if it is of the opinion that no hearing into the appeal is necessary because the appeal is without merit, the Tribunal shall give notice to the appellant accordingly and provide the appellant with an opportunity to make representations in writing within 21 days from the date of sending of such notice.

(3) If, after considering any representations submitted in accordance with paragraph (2), the Tribunal remains of the view that no hearing into the appeal is necessary because the appeal is without merit, the Tribunal shall make an order dismissing the appeal and inform the appellant and the respondents accordingly.

Notice of the hearing

26.—(1) After the expiry of the date for lodging answers and irrespective of whether or not answers have been lodged, the Tribunal shall, if it does not dismiss the appeal in accordance with rule 25, appoint a date, time and place for the hearing of the appeal.

(2) The Tribunal shall give the appellant and each respondent notice of the date, time and place of the hearing which notice shall be—

    (a) in Form No 6 set out in the schedule, or as near thereto as circumstances permit;

    (b) given not less than 21 days before the date of the hearing, unless the appellant and every respondent agree to a shorter period of notice; and

    (c) sent by first class recorded delivery post or intimated by sheriff officer to the appellant and every respondent at their respective addresses given in the appeal.

(3) This rule is without prejudice to the powers of the Tribunal to hold a procedural hearing or a preliminary hearing under rule 41 or 42.

Production of lists of documents and witnesses and production of documents

27. The notice of the hearing given under rule 26 shall also require the appellant and every respondent—

    (a) to lodge with the Clerk—

        (i) a list of all the documents on which they propose to rely at the hearing, together with those documents (or copies of them), not less than 14 days before the date of the hearing, or such longer or shorter period as the Tribunal may specify in the notice; and

        (ii) a list of witnesses on which they propose to rely at the hearing, not less than 7 days before the date of the hearing, or such longer or shorter period as the Tribunal may specify in the notice; and

    (b) at the same time, to send to the other parties a copy of the lists and a copy of the documents lodged with the Clerk and shall also inform the Clerk in writing that this has been done.

Production of other documents

28.—(1) The Tribunal may, on the application of either the appellant or any respondent or on its own initiative require any party to produce any document in their custody or under their control within such period as the Tribunal may determine if it is of the opinion that it is necessary for the proper consideration of the complaint that the document should be made available.

(2) Parties are not obliged by such an order to produce any document which they would be entitled to refuse to produce in proceedings in any court in Scotland.

Presence of parties at the hearing

29.—(1) Subject to paragraphs (2) and (3), the appellant and every respondent are entitled to be present, whether or not they may also be represented, and to lead evidence, on the date, time and place appointed for the hearing under rule 26.

(2) The Council and, in the case where the appellant or respondent is a legal practice, the legal practice, are entitled to be represented, and to lead evidence, on the date, time and place appointed for the hearing.

(3) If any of the respondents do not wish to appear or be represented at the hearing, they shall notify the Clerk accordingly before the date appointed for the hearing.

(4) If any party fails to appear or to be represented at the hearing, the Tribunal may, after being satisfied that notice of the hearing had been duly posted or intimated to that person in accordance with rule 26(2), proceed to hear and determine the appeal in the absence of that person.

Decision of Tribunal

30.—(1) Every decision by the Tribunal shall—
    (a) set out the facts proved;
    (b) have appended to it a note of the reasons for its decision;
    (c) be signed by the chairman; and
    (d) subject to paragraph 14A of Schedule 4 to the 1980 Act, be published in full.

(2) A copy of any such decision purporting to be signed by the Chairman shall be *prima facie* evidence of the due making thereof.

(3) The Tribunal shall announce its decision as soon as reasonably practicable after the hearing has finished.

(4) If the decision of the Tribunal is not announced on the day of the hearing or any adjourned hearing, it shall not be necessary to hold a hearing for the purpose of announcing its decision.

(5) Irrespective of whether or not the decision is announced at a hearing, the Clerk shall forthwith send a copy of the decision certified by the Clerk to the appellant and every respondent, together with a notice intimating the right of appeal available from that decision to the Court of Session under the 1980 Act or the 1990 Act.

(6) Where the decision of the Tribunal is announced outwith a hearing, the Tribunal shall arrange to hear parties on the matter of expenses.

(7) This rule is without prejudice to paragraphs 13 to 15 of Schedule 4 to the 1980 Act and to those provisions as applied by section 21B of the 1990 Act.

Withdrawal of appeal

31.—(1) No appeal shall be withdrawn by the appellant after it has been received by the clerk, except with the leave of the Tribunal.

(2) In granting leave to withdraw, the Tribunal may attach such terms as to expenses or otherwise as it thinks fit.

Part 4: Procedure relating to applications to the Tribunal

Applications to which Part 4 applies

32. This Part applies to any application made to the Tribunal

    (a) under section 10(1) of the 1980 Act by a solicitor, whose name has been struck off the roll (other than by order of the court), to have his or her name restored on the roll;

    (b) under section 12D(1) of the 1980 Act by a registered European lawyer, whose name has been removed from the register, to have his or her name restored to the register; and

    (c) under section 60A(4D) of the 1980 Act by a foreign lawyer, whose name has been removed (other than by the Council under section 60A(4B) of that Act) from the register of foreign lawyers, to have his or her name restored to the register.

Manner in which applications are to be made

33. Any application shall—

    (a) be in writing;

    (b) be in Form No 7 set out in the schedule, or as near thereto as circumstances permit;

    (c) contain the name and address of the applicant;

    (d) set out the occupation or occupations of the applicant since being struck off the roll or removed from the register;

    (e) be supported by letters from two solicitors who at the date of the application are in practice and who declare that they know the applicant;

    (f) be signed by the applicant;

    (g) be sworn before a notary public or justice of the peace; and

    (h) be lodged with the Clerk.

Notice of the hearing

34.—(1) The Tribunal shall appoint a date, time and place for the hearing of the application.

(2) The Tribunal shall give the applicant notice of the date, time and place of the hearing which notice shall be—

    (a) in Form No 8 set out in the schedule, or as near thereto as circumstances permit;

    (b) given not less than 21 days before the date of the hearing; and

    (c) sent by first class recorded delivery post or intimated by sheriff officer to the applicant at the address given in the application.

(3) This rule is without prejudice to the powers of the Tribunal to hold a procedural hearing or a preliminary hearing under rule 41 or 42.

Notice of the application

35. The Tribunal may, if it thinks fit, require the applicant to give notice to the Council and by advertisement or otherwise as it may direct informing them—

    (a) that the applicant has made such an application to the Tribunal;

    (b) of the date, time and place which the Tribunal has appointed for the hearing of the application under rule 34; and

    (c) that, if any person desires to object to the application, the objector shall give notice in writing to the applicant and to the Clerk in Form No 9 set out in the schedule, or as near thereto as circumstances permit at least 10 days before the date appointed for the hearing specifying the grounds of the objection.

Procedure at hearing

36.—(1) At the hearing, the Tribunal shall afford the applicant an opportunity of being heard by the Tribunal and adducing evidence.

(2) The Tribunal may require such evidence as it thinks necessary concerning the identity and character of the applicant, the applicant's conduct since his or her name was struck off the roll or the register as the case may be and the applicant's suitability for restoration to the roll or the register and, for this purpose, may receive written or oral evidence.

(3) If any objector appears on the day appointed for the hearing and if the Tribunal is of the opinion, after considering the notice of objection and after hearing the applicant (if it thinks fit to do so), that the notice discloses a *prima facie* case for inquiry, the Tribunal shall afford the objector an opportunity of being heard by the Tribunal and adducing evidence.

Decision of Tribunal

37.—(1) Every decision by the Tribunal shall—
    (a) set out the facts proved;
    (b) have appended to it a note of the reasons for its decision;
    (c) be signed by the Chairman or other person presiding; and
    (d) subject to paragraph 14A of Schedule 4 to the 1980 Act, be published in full.

(2) A copy of any such decision purporting to be signed by the Chairman or other person presiding shall be *prima facie* evidence of the due making thereof.

(3) The Tribunal shall announce its decision as soon as reasonably practicable after the hearing has finished.

(4) If the decision of the Tribunal is not announced on the day of the hearing or any adjourned hearing, it shall not be necessary to hold a hearing for the purpose of announcing its decision.

(5) Irrespective of whether or not the decision is announced at a hearing, the Clerk shall, in accordance with paragraph 15 of Schedule 4 to the 1980 Act, forthwith send a copy of the decision certified by the Clerk to the applicant and any objector, together with a notice intimating any right of appeal available from that decision to the Court of Session under the 1980 Act.

(6) Where the decision of the Tribunal is announced outwith a hearing, the Tribunal shall arrange to hear parties on the matter of expenses.

(7) Where the Tribunal orders that the name of the applicant should be restored to the roll or the register, as the case may be, the Clerk shall send a copy of the decision to the appropriate registrar who shall forthwith give effect thereto.

(8) This rule is without prejudice to paragraphs 13 to 15 of Schedule 4 to the 1980 Act.

Fee in respect of restoration

38. As a condition of having the name of the applicant restored to the roll or the register, as the case may be, the applicant shall pay to the registrar a fee of £750 in respect of that restoration.

Part 5: General

Appointment of Chairman and Vice Chairmen

39. Without prejudice to paragraph 4 of Schedule 4 to the 1980 Act, the Tribunal may appoint from among its members persons to be the Chairman and Vice Chairmen of the Tribunal.

General procedure

40.—(1) Subject to the provisions of the 1980 Act and the 1990 Act and of these rules, the procedure for dealing with a case, including the procedure at any hearing, shall be such as the Tribunal may determine.

(2) The Tribunal may issue directions to the parties or to any of them as to how the case is to be dealt with.

Procedural hearing
41.—(1) The Tribunal may hold a procedural hearing to decide what should be the timetable and procedure applicable to that case.

(2) The Tribunal shall give the parties to the case an opportunity to attend the procedural hearing by giving them notice of the date, time and place of the hearing.

(3) The notice under paragraph (2) shall be—
    (a) given not less than 21 days before the date of the meeting, unless all the parties agree to a shorter period of notice; and
    (b) sent by first class recorded delivery post or intimated by sheriff officer to the parties at their respective addresses given in the complaint, appeal or application, as the case may be.

(4) Subject to paragraph (5), the decision of the Tribunal relating to any procedural issue may be given orally at the end of the meeting but must be recorded by the Clerk as soon as possible.

(5) Any decision of the Tribunal at a procedural hearing which substantially disposes of the whole case must comply with rule 15, 30 or 37, as the case may be.

Preliminary hearing
42.—(1) The Tribunal may direct that any question of fact or law which appears to be in issue may be decided at a preliminary hearing.

(2) The Tribunal shall give the parties to the case an opportunity to attend the preliminary hearing by giving them notice of the date, time and place of the hearing.

(3) The notice under paragraph (2) shall be—
    (a) given not less than 21 days before the date of the hearing, unless all the parties agree to a shorter period of notice; and
    (b) sent by first class recorded delivery post or intimated by sheriff officer to the parties at their respective addresses given in the complaint, appeal or application, as the case may be.

(4) If, in the opinion of the Tribunal, a decision on the question mentioned in paragraph (1) substantially disposes of the whole case, the Tribunal may treat the preliminary hearing as a hearing of the case and may give such direction as it thinks fit to dispose of the case.

(5) Subject to paragraph (4), the decision of the Tribunal relating to any preliminary issue may be given orally at the end of the hearing or reserved and, in any event, must be recorded as soon as possible in a document which is signed by the Chairman and sent to the parties of the case.

(6) Any decision of the Tribunal relating to any preliminary issue which substantially disposes of the whole case must comply with rule 15, 30 or 37, as the case may be.

Proceedings in public and private
43.—(1) Subject to paragraphs (2) and (3), the Tribunal shall hold the hearing, or any part of it, and pronounce its decision, in public.

(2) Where any party wishes the hearing or part of it to be heard in private, that party shall
    (a) submit a motion to the Clerk in writing, not less than 21 days prior to the date of the hearing; and
    (b) send a copy of that motion to the other parties in the case and inform them that if they want to object to the motion they should inform the Clerk not less than 14 days prior to the hearing.

(3) If any party objects to that motion, the Tribunal may, if it thinks fit, invite the parties to a procedural hearing to determine whether or not to grant the motion but any such procedural hearing shall be held not less than 7 days prior to the date of the hearing.

Postponement or adjournment of hearing or sisting of a case

44. The Tribunal may, on its own initiative or on the application of any of the parties, at any time and from time to time, postpone or adjourn a hearing, or sist a case, upon such terms as to expenses or otherwise as, to the Tribunal, shall appear just.

Amendment of complaint or appeal

45.—(1) If it appears to the Tribunal that any allegation contained in a complaint to which Part 2 applies should be amended,

    (a) the Tribunal may make or permit such amendment or

    (b) if the Tribunal considers that any such amendment is not within the scope of the original complaint, it may require it to be embodied in a new complaint.

(2) In any appeal to which Part 3 applies, the Tribunal may permit an appellant to amend his statement of appeal or a respondent to amend or withdraw his answers.

(3) If, in consequence of such amendment or withdrawal mentioned in paragraph (1) or (2), any party applies for an adjournment of the hearing, the Tribunal may grant such an adjournment under rule 44.

Record of proceedings

46.—(1) Shorthand notes of proceedings before the Tribunal may be taken by a shorthand writer appointed by the Tribunal or, if no shorthand writer be available for any date appointed for a hearing, the proceedings may be recorded electronically.

(2) The shorthand notes or the electronic recording may be transcribed if the Tribunal thinks fit, and, if transcribed, any party to the proceedings shall be entitled to inspect the transcript thereof.

(3) The shorthand writer or transcriber of the recorded proceedings shall, if required, supply to the Tribunal and to any person entitled to be heard upon an appeal against a decision of the Tribunal, but to no other person, a copy of the transcript if made, on payment of the charges of the shorthand writer or transcriber.

Waiver or variation of certain rules

47.—(1) The Tribunal may from time to time dispense with any requirements of these rules respecting notices, documents, service or time, where it appears to the Tribunal to be just to do so.

(2) The Tribunal may extend, or, with consent of parties, may reduce, the time for doing anything under these rules.

Documents

48.—(1) Any complaint, appeal or application under Part 2, 3, or 4 lodged with the Clerk shall be kept by the Clerk.

(2) Unless the Tribunal otherwise determines, any documents or other exhibits produced or used at the hearing before it shall be retained by the Clerk until the time for appealing has expired, or, if notice of appeal is given, until the appeal is heard or otherwise disposed of.

Clerical errors in decisions

49.—(1) The Chairman may correct any clerical error contained in the decision ("the original decision") even though a copy of that decision has been sent to the parties, provided that this is done before the expiration of the days of appeal and before any appeal is lodged against that decision.

(2) Where any clerical error contained in the decision is corrected in accordance with paragraph (1), the Clerk shall send a copy of the amended decision to the parties together with a notice informing them that they may appeal against that amended decision to the Court of Session.

(3) The notice referred to in paragraph (2) shall be in similar terms to the

notice which was sent, or would have been sent, to the parties under rule 15(5), 30(5) or 37(5), as the case may be, except that the time limit for appealing shall run from the date on which the amended decision is intimated to that party.

(4) This rule is without prejudice to paragraphs 14 and 14A of Schedule 4 to the 1980 Act and those provisions as applied by section 21B of the 1990 Act.

Sanction for non-compliance with direction etc

50.—(1) If any direction, order or other requirement given by the Tribunal to a party under these rules is not complied with by that party, the Tribunal may before or at the hearing—

    (a) dismiss or strike out the whole or part of the complaint, appeal or application or other submission made by that party, and, where appropriate,

    (b) direct that such party shall be barred from proceeding with, or contesting, the complaint, appeal or application altogether.

(2) Before taking any action under paragraph (1)(b) or (c), the Tribunal shall send a notice to the party who has not complied with that direction, order or other requirement, giving that party an opportunity—

    (a) to comply within the period specified in the notice, which period shall not be less than 21 days from the date of sending of such notice; or

    (b) to send representations in writing to the Tribunal within that period as to why the Tribunal should not take any action under that paragraph.

(3) This rule is without prejudice to any other power which the Tribunal may have to deal with the fact that a party may not have complied with any direction, order or other requirement given by the Tribunal, including the power—

    (a) to proceed in the absence of a party under rule 14(4) or 29(4); or

    (b) to exclude a party from the hearing under rule 52; or

    (c) to take account of that fact when making any order as to expenses under paragraph 19 of Schedule 4 to the 1980 Act.

Absence of member of the Tribunal

51. Without prejudice to paragraph 1B of Schedule 4 to the 1980 Act, if a member of the Tribunal is, after the commencement of the hearing, absent, the proceedings may be heard by the remaining members of the Tribunal who are present, provided that the Tribunal is still properly constituted as provided in paragraph 5 of Schedule 4 to the 1980 Act.

Exclusion of persons from the hearing

52.—(1) Without prejudice to any other powers it may have, the Tribunal may exclude from the hearing, or part of it, any person (including a party to the proceedings or the party's representative) whose conduct has, in the opinion of the Tribunal, disrupted the hearing or whose conduct has otherwise interfered with the administration of justice.

(2) If the Tribunal decides to exclude a party from the hearing or part of it, it must
allow the party's representative sufficient time to consult with the party.

Absence of party

53. If the Chairman is satisfied—

    (a) that any party is unable, through physical or mental sickness or impairment, to attend a hearing of the Tribunal; and

    (b) that the party's inability is likely to continue for over a month, the Chairman may make such arrangements as may appear best suited, in all the circumstances of the case, for disposing fairly of the complaint, appeal or application under Part 2, 3 or 4, as the case may be.

Exercise of functions of the Tribunal by a particular tribunal

54.—(1) The functions conferred by these rules upon the Tribunal may be exercised on behalf of the Tribunal, in relation to a particular case or part of a case, by any particular tribunal constituted in accordance with paragraph 5 of Schedule 4 to the 1980 Act to deal with that case or part.

(2) Where paragraph (1) applies, any reference in these rules to the Tribunal or the Chairman shall be construed as a reference to the particular tribunal and the convener or other person presiding at the proceedings of that particular tribunal.

(3) Subject to paragraph (4), the particular tribunal constituted to deal with any part of a case is not required to deal with all the proceedings relating to that case and, accordingly, different particular tribunals may be constituted to deal with different parts of that case.

(4) The particular Tribunal constituted to deal with any part of a case must complete that part by coming to a decision upon it before another particular tribunal is constituted to deal with any subsequent part of the case.

Appointment of convener to a particular tribunal

55.—(1) The members of a particular tribunal shall appoint one of their own number to preside as the convener of that tribunal but—

(a) where the Chairman of the Tribunal is a member of a particular tribunal, he or she shall be appointed as the convener of that particular tribunal; and

(b) where (a) does not apply but any person appointed as a Vice Chairman of the Tribunal is a member of a particular tribunal, he or she shall be appointed as the convener of that particular tribunal.

(2) Where any person appointed to be the convener of a particular tribunal is unable, for any reason, to be present at any part of the proceedings of that tribunal, the members of that tribunal may appoint one of their own number to be the convener but only for the purpose of those proceedings.

(3) In the event of a particular tribunal being unable to reach a majority decision, the convener shall have a casting vote.

Exercise of functions of the Tribunal by the Chairman or Vice Chairmen

56.—(1) The functions conferred by these rules upon the Tribunal prior to any hearing of any case may be exercised, on behalf of the Tribunal, by the Chairman or any of the Vice Chairmen of the Tribunal.

(2) Paragraph (1) applies irrespective of whether or not—

(a) the Chairman or the Vice Chairman is the convener or member of the particular tribunal constituted to exercise those functions; or

(b) a particular tribunal has been constituted to exercise those functions.

(3) In this rule, any reference to the Chairman shall not include a reference to the convener of a particular tribunal.

Revocation of the 2005 Rules with savings

57.—(1) Subject to paragraph (2), the 2005 Rules are hereby revoked.

(2) The 2005 Rules shall continue to apply on and after 1st October 2008 as if they had not been revoked to—

(a) any complaint, appeal or application made to the Tribunal before that date;

(b) any complaint made on or after 1st October 2008 by the Council to the Tribunal under section 51(1) or (1A) of the 1980 Act as part of the complaint process when dealing with a relevant complaint;

(c) any complaint made on or after 1ˢᵗ October 2008 by the Council to the Tribunal under section 53C of the 1980 Act (complaint that a solicitor has failed to comply with a direction given by the Council under section 42A etc in the case of inadequate professional services) as part of the complaint process when dealing with a relevant complaint;

(d) any appeal made to the Tribunal on or after 1ˢᵗ October 2008 where—

   (i) the appeal is made under section 42A(7) of the 1980 Act or section 20(11) of the 1990 Act (against a determination or direction of the Council under that section where the Council upholds a complaint of inadequate professional services); or

   (ii) the appeal is made under section 53D of the 1980 Act (against a decision of the Council to suspend or withdraw an investment business certificate or impose conditions or restrictions on it); and, in either case,

   (iii) the appeal is part of the complaint process when dealing with a relevant complaint.

(3) In this rule, "a relevant complaint" means a complaint made to the Council (whether before, on or after 1ˢᵗ October 2008) by a person with an interest which is a complaint to which, despite its repeal, section 33 of the 1990 Act continues to apply by virtue of Article 2 of the 2008 Order and to which Article 4(1) or (2) or both Articles 4(1) and (2) of the 2008 Order applies.

[Signature]

Signed on behalf of the Tribunal by

Chairman of the Tribunal

Date:

I concur

[signature]

the Lord President of the Court of Session

Date

SCHEDULE

FORM 1

SCOTTISH SOLICITORS' DISCIPLINE TRIBUNAL PROCEDURE RULES 2008

FORM OF COMPLAINT

to the

SCOTTISH SOLICITORS' DISCIPLINE TRIBUNAL

by

THE COUNCIL of the LAW SOCIETY of SCOTLAND, 26 Drumsheugh Gardens, Edinburgh
("the Council")

[on behalf of

C.D. [name and address of any person on whose behalf the complaint is made]

Secondary Complainer(s)]
[*Delete if inapplicable*]

against

E.F. [name and address (or last known address) of the person against whom the complaint is
made]

Respondent

[*Under the 2008 Rules, the person against whom a complaint may be made may be a practitioner or
a legal practice. A practitioner is defined as a person who is or was a solicitor, a registered
European lawyer, a registered foreign lawyer, and a conveyancing or executry practitioner. A legal
practice is defined as a firm of solicitors, an incorporated practice or a multi-national practice. In
the case of a complaint against a legal practice, please give the names and addresses of all the
partners or members of the practice at the relevant time.*]

To the Clerk to the Tribunal

1.   The Council hereby submits a complaint to the Scottish Solicitors' Discipline Tribunal
      ("the Tribunal") that E.F. [specify complaint which is being made, such as]

      [is a practitioner who may have been guilty of professional misconduct.]
      [is a practitioner who may have been convicted by any court of [specify offence] being an
      act involving dishonesty or may have been sentenced to a term of imprisonment of not
      less than 2 years.]
      [is a legal practice which may have failed to comply with [specify provision] which is a
      provision of the 1980 Act or of rules made under that Act applicable to it .]
      [is a legal practice which may have been convicted by any court of [specify offence] being
      an offence which renders it unsuitable to continue to be recognised under section 34(1A)
      of the 1980 Act or otherwise unsuitable to continue to practise.]

      [*Delete whichever is inapplicable*]

2.   [*Please indicate whether or not the complaint is made on behalf of any other person (the
      secondary complainer) and, if so, give the name and address of any such secondary
      complainer.*]

3.   The statement of facts upon which this complaint is based is as follows:

[Please give in short numbered paragraphs the facts upon which the complaint is based and which the complainer is willing to prove.]

4. The complaint is not one to which the Scottish Solicitors' Discipline Tribunal Rules 2005 apply by virtue of rule 57(2) of the Scottish Solicitors' Discipline Tribunal Rules 2008.

5. If the complaint is against a practitioner who may have been guilty of professional misconduct,

   [Please indicate whether or not the Council or any secondary complainer claims to have been directly affected by that misconduct and is seeking compensation for any loss, inconvenience or distress resulting from it and, if so give a statement of facts in support of that claim.]

6. The following is a list of the documents which accompany this complaint:

   [Please list any documents which accompany the complaint and which support the facts mentioned in paragraph 2 and, if relevant, paragraph 3.]

   ....
   Signed on behalf of the Council

   Date

FORM 2

SCOTTISH SOLICITORS' DISCIPLINE TRIBUNAL PROCEDURE RULES 2008

FORM OF NOTICE OF COMPLAINT

to the

SCOTTISH SOLICITORS' DISCIPLINE TRIBUNAL

relating to the

COMPLAINT

by

A.B. [name and address of the person making the complaint]

Principal Complainer

[on behalf of

C.D. [name and address of any person on whose behalf the complaint is made]

Secondary Complainer(s)]
[Delete if inapplicable]

against

E.F. [name and address (or last known address) of the person against whom the complaint is made]

Respondent

To E.F.

I attach a copy of a complaint which has made to the Scottish Solicitors' Discipline Tribunal ("the Tribunal") against you by A.B.

I also attach a copy of any further information, documents and representations which have been submitted by A.B. in accordance with the Scottish Solicitors' Discipline Tribunal Rules 2008.

If you wish to answer the complaint, you are required to do so by lodging answers in writing with the Clerk to the Tribunal within 21 days of the date of this notice. You may also lodge at the same time any documents you wish the Tribunal to take into account.

You should also send at the same time a copy of your answers and any documents to A.B. and inform the Clerk in writing that you have done so.

....
Clerk to the Tribunal

Date

Note: Relevant statutory references relating to the Tribunal and its powers are contained in sections 50–54 of the Solicitors (Scotland) Act 1980, as amended, Part 11 of the Law Reform (Miscellaneous Provisions) (Scotland) Act 1990, as amended and the Scottish Solicitors' Discipline Tribunal Rules 2008. A copy of the 2008 Rules is enclosed for your information and guidance.

Rule 11

FORM 3

SCOTTISH SOLICITORS' DISCIPLINE TRIBUNAL PROCEDURE RULES 2008

FORM OF NOTICE OF HEARING

by the

SCOTTISH SOLICITORS' DISCIPLINE TRIBUNAL

of the

COMPLAINT

by

A.B. [name and address of the person making the complaint]

Principal Complainer

[on behalf of

CD. [name and address of any person on whose behalf the complaint is made]

Secondary Complainer(s)]

[Delete if inapplicable]

against

E.F. [name and address of the person against whom the complaint is made]

Respondent

[This notice should be given not less than 21 days before the date appointed for the hearing unless both A.B. and E.F. agree a shorter period]

To A.B. and E.F.

The Scottish Solicitors' Discipline Tribunal ("the Tribunal") has appointed the hearing of the above complaint to take place on *[specify date]* at *[specify time]* at *[specify place]*.

You are entitled to be present at the hearing, irrespective of whether or not you are also represented, and you should be prepared to lead your evidence then. If you fail to appear at the hearing, the Tribunal may proceed to hear and determine the complaint in your absence.

You are required to lodge with the Clerk to the Tribunal—

(a)   a list of all the documents on which you propose to rely at the hearing, together with those documents (or a copy of them), not less than 14 days before the date of the hearing; and

(b)   a list of witnesses on which you propose to rely at the hearing, not less than 7 days before   the date of the hearing.

Note: The Tribunal may specify a longer or shorter period. Where A.B. is the principal complainer and there are secondary eomplainers who are claiming compensation, the list of witnesses should include any such secondary complainer.

You are also required to send to the other party at the same time a copy of the lists and of the documents lodged with the Clerk and to inform the Clerk in writing that you have done so.

If you want the other party to produce any document which is in the possession of the other party but which is not included in that other party's list, you may apply to the Tribunal for an order requiring that other party to produce that document. The Tribunal may make such an order if it is of the opinion that it is necessary for the proper consideration of the complaint that the document should be made available.

....

Clerk to the Tribunal

Date

Rule 21

FORM 4

SCOTTISH SOLICITORS' DISCIPLINE TRIBUNAL PROCEDURE RULES 2008

FORM OF APPEAL

to the

SCOTTISH SOLICITORS' DISCIPLINE TRIBUNAL

by

A.B. [name and address of the person making the appeal]

Appellant

against

the decision of the Council of the Law Society of Scotland dated *[specify date]*

To the Clerk to the Tribunal

I, A.B., hereby appeal to the Scottish Solicitors' Discipline Tribunal ("the Tribunal") against the decision of the Council of the Law Society of Scotland ("the Council") dated *[specify date]* and intimated to me on *[specify date]*, a copy of which is attached.

The grounds upon which the appeal is made are as follows:

[*Please give in short numbered paragraphs the grounds upon which the appeal is made.*]

The respondents in this appeal are—

(a)   the Council;

(b)   where the appeal is being made by a practitioner or a legal practice, the name and address of the person who made the original complaint to the Council ("the principal complainer") and any person on whose behalf that complaint was made ("the secondary complainer");

(b)   where the appeal is being made by a complainer, the name and address of the practitioner or legal practice and of any other complainer.

[*Delete whichever is inapplicable*]

Rule 24

FORM 5

SCOTTISH SOLICITORS' DISCIPLINE TRIBUNAL PROCEDURE RULES 2008

FORM OF NOTICE OF APPEAL

to the

SCOTTISH SOLICITORS' DISCIPLINE TRIBUNAL

by

A.B. [name and address of the person making the appeal]

Appellant

against

the decision of the Council of the Law Society of Scotland dated [*specify date*]

To every respondent

I attach a copy of an appeal which was made by A.B. to the Scottish Solicitors' Discipline Tribunal ("the Tribunal") against the decision of the Council of the Law Society of Scotland ("the Council") dated [*specify date*].

I also attach a copy of any further information, documents and representations which have been submitted by A.B. in accordance with the Scottish Solicitors' Discipline Tribunal Rules 2008.

If you wish to lodge answers to the appeal, you are required to do so by lodging answers in writing with the Clerk to the Tribunal within 21 days of the date of this notice. You may also lodge at the same time any documents you wish the Tribunal to take into account.

You should also send at the same time a copy of your answers and any documents to A.B. and any other respondent and inform the Clerk in writing that you have done so.

....

Clerk to the Tribunal

Date

Rule 26

FORM 6

SCOTTISH SOLICITORS' DISCIPLINE TRIBUNAL PROCEDURE RULES 2008

FORM OF NOTICE OF HEARING

by the

SCOTTISH SOLICITORS' DISCIPLINE TRIBUNAL

of the

APPEAL

by

A.B. [name and address of the person making the appeal]

Appellant

against

the decision of the Council of the Law Society of Scotland dated [*specify date*]

To A.B. and every respondent

The Scottish Solicitors' Discipline Tribunal ("the Tribunal") has appointed the hearing of the above appeal to take place on [*specify date*] at [*specify time*] at [*specify place*].

You are entitled to be present at the hearing, irrespective of whether or not you are also represented, and to lead your evidence then. If you fail to appear at the hearing, the Tribunal may proceed to hear and determine the appeal in your absence.

You are required to lodge with the Clerk to the Tribunal—

(a)   a list of all the documents on which you propose to rely at the hearing, together with those documents, not less than 14 days before the date of the hearing; and

(b)   a list of witnesses on which you propose to rely at the hearing, not less than 7 days before the date of the hearing.

[*The Tribunal may specify a longer or shorter period.*]

You are also required to send to the other parties to the appeal at the same time a copy of the lists and of the documents lodged with the Clerk and to inform the Clerk in writing that you have done so.

If you want any other party to produce any document which is not included in that other party's list, you may apply to the Tribunal for an order requiring that other party to produce that document. The Tribunal may make such an order if it is of the opinion that it is necessary for the proper consideration of the appeal that the document should be made available.

....
Clerk to the Tribunal
Date
Rule 33

FORM 7

SCOTTISH SOLICITORS' DISCIPLINE TRIBUNAL PROCEDURE RULES 2008

FORM OF APPLICATION

to the

SCOTTISH SOLICITORS' DISCIPLINE TRIBUNAL

by

A.B. [name and address of the applicant]

To the Clerk to the Tribunal

1.   I hereby apply to the Scottish Solicitors' Discipline Tribunal ("the Tribunal")

[under section 10(1) of the Solicitors (Scotland) Act 1980 for an order of the Tribunal to have my name restored to the roll of solicitors.]

[under section 12D(1) of the Solicitors (Scotland) Act 1980 for an order of the Tribunal to have my name restored to the register of European lawyers.]

[under section 60A(4D) of the Solicitors (Scotland) Act 1980 for an order of the Tribunal to have my name restored to the register of foreign lawyers.]

[Delete whichever is inapplicable]

2.   I was [admitted as a solicitor] [registered as a European lawyer] [registered as a foreign lawyer] on *[specify date]*.

3.   My name was [struck off the roll] [removed from the register] by order of the Tribunal on *[specify date]*.

4.   Since then, my occupation (s) have been as follows:

[Here specify in the case of each employment the name and address of the employer, the nature of the work on which the applicant was employed and the period of employment.]

5.   I am not aware and do not know of any cause of complaint or proceedings which might have arisen out of my conduct since my name was [struck off the roll] [removed from the register].

6.   My application is supported by letters from the following two solicitors who are currently in practice and who declare that they know me:

[Here state the name and address of the two solicitors and attach a copy of their letters].

At the day of ....in presence of.................,[notary public] [one of Her Majesty's Justices of the Peace for............], compeared A.B. who being solemnly sworn and interrogated, depones that the statements made in the above application are true as the deponent shall answer to God.

....
Signature

Date

Rule 34

FORM 8

SCOTTISH SOLICITORS' DISCIPLINE TRIBUNAL PROCEDURE RULES 2008

FORM OF NOTICE OF HEARING

by the

SCOTTISH SOLICITORS' DISCIPLINE TRIBUNAL

of the

APPLICATION

by

A.B. [name and address of the applicant]

To A.B.

The Scottish Solicitors' Discipline Tribunal ("the Tribunal") has appointed the hearing of the above application to take place on [*specify date*] at [*specify time*] at [*specify place*].

You are required to give notice to the Council of the Law Society of Scotland and by advertisement in the Journal of the Law Society of Scotland and in [specify any other newspapers or journal] informing them—

(a) of the application which you have made to the Tribunal;

(b) of the date, time and place which the Tribunal has appointed for the hearing of the application; and

(c) that, if any person desires to object to the application, the objector is to give you and the Clerk to the Tribunal notice in writing in Form No. 9 set out in the Schedule to the Scottish Solicitors' Discipline Tribunal Rules 2008 (or as near thereto as circumstances permit) at least 10 days before the date appointed for the hearing specifying the grounds of the objection.

....
Clerk to the Tribunal

Date

Rule 35

FORM 9

SCOTTISH SOLICITORS' DISCIPLINE TRIBUNAL PROCEDURE RULES 2008

FORM OF OBJECTION

to the

APPLICATION

by

A.B. [name and address of the applicant]

To the Clerk to the Tribunal and A.B.

I, C.D. [*specify designation and address*] hereby give notice that I object to the application made by A.B. to the Scottish Solicitors' Discipline Tribunal ("the Tribunal") for an order to have his or her name restored to the [roll of solicitors] [register of European/foreign lawyers] on the following grounds, namely:

[*Specify the grounds of objection in articulate numbered paragraphs.*]

....
Signature

Date

[NEXT TEXT PAGE IS **F 275**]

Code of Conduct for European Lawyers

This Code of Conduct for European Lawyers was originally adopted at the CCBE Plenary Session held on 28 October 1988, and subsequently amended during the CCBE Plenary Sessions on 28 November 1998, 6 December 2002 and 19 May 2006. The Code includes an Explanatory Memorandum which was updated during the CCBE Plenary Session on 19 May 2006.

CONTENTS

1. Preamble

1.1. The Function of the Lawyer in Society

In a society founded on respect for the rule of law the lawyer fulfils a special role. The lawyer's duties do not begin and end with the faithful performance of what he or she is instructed to do so far as the law permits.

A lawyer must serve the interests of justice as well as those whose rights and liberties he or she is trusted to assert and defend and it is the lawyer's duty not only to plead the client's cause but to be the client's adviser. Respect for the lawyer's professional function is an essential condition for the rule of law and democracy in society.

A lawyer's function therefore lays on him or her a variety of legal and moral obligations (sometimes appearing to be in conflict with each other) towards:

— the client;
— the courts and other authorities before whom the lawyer pleads the client's cause or acts on the client's behalf;
— the legal profession in general and each fellow member of it in particular;
— the public for whom the existence of a free and independent profession, bound together by respect for rules made by the profession itself, is an essential means of safeguarding human rights in face of the power of the state and other interests in society.

1.2.   The Nature of Rules of Professional Conduct

1.2.1. Rules of professional conduct are designed through their willing acceptance by those to whom they apply to ensure the proper performance by the lawyer of a function which is recognised as essential in all civilised societies. The failure of the lawyer to observe these rules may result in disciplinary sanctions.

1.2.2. The particular rules of each Bar or Law Society arise from its own traditions. They are adapted to the organisation and sphere of activity of the profession in the Member State concerned and to its judicial and administrative procedures and to its national legislation. It is neither possible nor desirable that they should be taken out of their context nor that an attempt should be made to give general application to rules which are inherently incapable of such application.

The particular rules of each Bar and Law Society nevertheless are based on the same values and in most cases demonstrate a common foundation.

1.3.   The Purpose of the Code

1.3.1. The continued integration of the European Union and European Economic Area and the increasing frequency of the cross-border activities of lawyers within the European Economic Area have made necessary in the public interest the statement of common rules which apply to all lawyers from the European Economic Area whatever Bar or Law Society they belong to in relation to their cross-border practice. A particular purpose of the statement of those rules is to mitigate the difficulties which result from the application of "double deontology", notably as set out in Articles 4 and 7.2 of Directive 77/249/EEC and Articles 6 and 7 of Directive 98/5/EC.

1.3.2. The organisations representing the legal profession through the CCBE propose that the rules codified in the following articles:

— be recognised at the present time as the expression of a consensus of all the Bars and Law Societies of the European Union and European Economic Area;
— be adopted as enforceable rules as soon as possible in accordance with national or EEA procedures in relation to the cross-border activities of the lawyer in the European Union and European Economic Area;
— be taken into account in all revisions of national rules of deontology or professional practice with a view to their progressive harmonisation.

They further express the wish that the national rules of deontology or professional practice be interpreted and applied whenever possible in a way consistent with the rules in this Code.

After the rules in this Code have been adopted as enforceable rules in relation to a lawyer's cross-border activities the lawyer will remain bound to observe the rules of the Bar or Law Society to which he or she belongs to the extent that they are consistent with the rules in this Code.

1.4. Field of Application Ratione Personae

This Code shall apply to lawyers as they are defined by Directive 77/249/EEC and by Directive 98/5/EC and to lawyers of the Observer Members of the CCBE.

1.5 Field of Application Ratione Materiae

Without prejudice to the pursuit of a progressive harmonisation of rules of deontology or professional practice which apply only internally within a Member State, the following rules shall apply to the cross-border activities of the lawyer within the European Union and the European Economic Area. Cross-border activities shall mean:

- (a) all professional contacts with lawyers of Member States other than the lawyer's own;
- (b) the professional activities of the lawyer in a Member State other than his or her own, whether or not the lawyer is physically present in that Member State.

1.6 Definitions

In this Code:

"Member State" means a member state of the European Union or any other state whose legal profession is included in Article 1.4.

"Home Member State" means the Member State where the lawyer acquired the right to bear his or her professional title.

"Host Member State" means any other Member State where the lawyer carries on cross-border activities.

"Competent Authority" means the professional organisation(s) or authority(ies) of the Member State concerned responsible for the laying down of rules of professional conduct and the administration of discipline of lawyers.

"Directive 77/249/EEC" means Council Directive 77/249/EEC of 22 March 1977 to facilitate the effective exercise by lawyers of freedom to provide services.

"Directive 98/5/EC" means Directive 98/5/EC of the European Parliament and of the Council of 16 February 1998 to facilitate practice of the profession of lawyer on a permanent basis in a Member State other than that in which the qualification was obtained.

2. General Principles

2.1. Independence

2.1.1. The many duties to which a lawyer is subject require the lawyer's absolute independence, free from all other influence, especially such as may arise from his or her personal interests or external pressure. Such independence is as necessary to trust in the process of justice as the impartiality of the judge. A lawyer must therefore avoid any impairment of his or her independence and be careful not to compromise his or her professional standards in order to please the client, the court or third parties.

2.1.2. This independence is necessary in non-contentious matters as well as in litigation. Advice given by a lawyer to the client has no value if the lawyer gives it only to ingratiate him- or herself, to serve his or her personal interests or in response to outside pressure.

2.2. Trust and Personal Integrity

Relationships of trust can only exist if a lawyer's personal honour, honesty and integrity are beyond doubt. For the lawyer these traditional virtues are professional obligations.

2.3. Confidentiality

2.3.1. It is of the essence of a lawyer's function that the lawyer should be told by his or her client things which the client would not tell to others, and that the lawyer should be the recipient of other information on a basis of confidence. Without the certainty of confidentiality there cannot be trust. Confidentiality is therefore a primary and fundamental right and duty of the lawyer.

The lawyer's obligation of confidentiality serves the interest of the administration of justice as well as the interest of the client. It is therefore entitled to special protection by the State.

2.3.2. A lawyer shall respect the confidentiality of all information that becomes known to the lawyer in the course of his or her professional activity.

2.3.3. The obligation of confidentiality is not limited in time.

2.3.4. A lawyer shall require his or her associates and staff and anyone engaged by him or her in the course of providing professional services to observe the same obligation of confidentiality.

2.4. Respect for the Rules of Other Bars and Law Societies

When practising cross-border, a lawyer from another Member State may be bound to comply with the professional rules of the Host Member State. Lawyers have a duty to inform themselves as to the rules which will affect them in the performance of any particular activity.

Member organisations of the CCBE are obliged to deposit their codes of conduct at the Secretariat of the CCBE so that any lawyer can get hold of the copy of the current code from the Secretariat.

2.5. Incompatible Occupations

2.5.1. In order to perform his or her functions with due independence and in a manner which is consistent with his or her duty to participate in the administration of justice a lawyer may be prohibited from undertaking certain occupations.

2.5.2. A lawyer who acts in the representation or the defence of a client in legal proceedings or before any public authorities in a Host Member State shall there observe the rules regarding incompatible occupations as they are applied to lawyers of the Host Member State.

2.5.3. A lawyer established in a Host Member State in which he or she wishes to participate directly in commercial or other activities not connected with the practice of the law shall respect the rules regarding forbidden or incompatible occupations as they are applied to lawyers of that Member State.

2.6. Personal Publicity

2.6.1. A lawyer is entitled to inform the public about his or her services provided that the information is accurate and not misleading, and respectful of the obligation of confidentiality and other core values of the profession.

2.6.2. Personal publicity by a lawyer in any form of media such as by press, radio, television, by electronic commercial communications or otherwise is permitted to the extent it complies with the requirements of 2.6.1.

2.7. The Client's Interest

Subject to due observance of all rules of law and professional conduct, a lawyer must always act in the best interests of the client and must put those interests before the lawyer's own interests or those of fellow members of the legal profession.

2.8. Limitation of Lawyer's Liability towards the Client

To the extent permitted by the law of the Home Member State and the Host Member State, the lawyer may limit his or her liabilities towards the client in accordance with the professional rules to which the lawyer is subject.

3. Relations with Clients

3.1. Acceptance and Termination of Instructions

3.1.1. A lawyer shall not handle a case for a party except on that party's instructions. The lawyer may, however, act in a case in which he or she has been instructed by another lawyer acting for the party or where the case has been assigned to him or her by a competent body.

The lawyer should make reasonable efforts to ascertain the identity, competence and authority of the person or body who instructs him or her when the specific circumstances show that the identity, competence and authority are uncertain.

3.1.2. A lawyer shall advise and represent the client promptly, conscientiously and diligently. The lawyer shall undertake personal responsibility for the discharge of the client's instructions and shall keep the client informed as to the progress of the matter with which the lawyer has been entrusted.

3.1.3. A lawyer shall not handle a matter which the lawyer knows or ought to know he or she is not competent to handle, without co-operating with a lawyer who is competent to handle it.

A lawyer shall not accept instructions unless he or she can discharge those instructions promptly having regard to the pressure of other work.

3.1.4. A lawyer shall not be entitled to exercise his or her right to withdraw from a case in such a way or in such circumstances that the client may be unable to find other legal assistance in time to prevent prejudice being suffered by the client.

3.2. Conflict of Interest

3.2.1. A lawyer may not advise, represent or act on behalf of two or more clients in the same matter if there is a conflict, or a significant risk of a conflict, between the interests of those clients.

3.2.2. A lawyer must cease to act for both or all of the clients concerned when a conflict of interests arises between those clients and also whenever there is a risk of a breach of confidence or where the lawyer's independence may be impaired.

3.2.3. A lawyer must also refrain from acting for a new client if there is a risk of breach of a confidence entrusted to the lawyer by a former client or if the knowledge which the lawyer possesses of the affairs of the former client would give an undue advantage to the new client.

3.2.4. Where lawyers are practising in association, paragraphs 3.2.1 to 3.2.3 above shall apply to the association and all its members.

3.3. Pactum de Quota Litis

3.3.1. A lawyer shall not be entitled to make a *pactum de quota litis*.

3.3.2. By "*pactum de quota litis*" is meant an agreement between a lawyer and the client entered into prior to final conclusion of a matter to which the client is a party, by virtue of which the client undertakes to pay the lawyer a share of the result regardless of whether this is represented by a sum of money or by any other benefit achieved by the client upon the conclusion of the matter.

3.3.3. "*Pactum de quota litis*" does not include an agreement that fees be charged in proportion to the value of a matter handled by the lawyer if this is in accordance with an officially approved fee scale or under the control of the Competent Authority having jurisdiction over the lawyer.

3.4. Regulation of Fees

A fee charged by a lawyer shall be fully disclosed to the client, shall be fair and reasonable, and shall comply with the law and professional rules to which the lawyer is subject.

3.5. Payment on Account

If a lawyer requires a payment on account of his or her fees and/or disbursements such payment should not exceed a reasonable estimate of the fees and probable disbursements involved.

Failing such payment, a lawyer may withdraw from the case or refuse to handle it, but subject always to paragraph 3.1.4 above.

3.6. Fee Sharing with Non-Lawyers

3.6.1. A lawyer may not share his or her fees with a person who is not a lawyer except where an association between the lawyer and the other person is permitted by the laws and the professional rules to which the lawyer is subject.

3.6.2. The provisions of 3.6.1 above shall not preclude a lawyer from paying a fee, commission or other compensation to a deceased lawyer's heirs or to a retired lawyer in respect of taking over the deceased or retired lawyer's practice.

3.7. Cost of Litigation and Availability of Legal Aid

3.7.1. The lawyer should at all times strive to achieve the most cost effective resolution of the client's dispute and should advise the client at appropriate stages as to the desirability of attempting a settlement and/or a reference to alternative dispute resolution.

3.7.2. A lawyer shall inform the client of the availability of legal aid where applicable.

3.8. Client Funds

3.8.1. Lawyers who come into possession of funds on behalf of their clients or third parties (hereinafter called "client funds") have to deposit such money into an account of a bank or similar institution subject to supervision by a public authority (hereinafter called a "client account"). A client account shall be separate from any other account of the lawyer. All client funds received by a lawyer should be deposited into such an account unless the owner of such funds agrees that the funds should be dealt with otherwise.

3.8.2. The lawyer shall maintain full and accurate records showing all the lawyer's dealings with client funds and distinguishing client funds from other funds held by the lawyer. Records may have to be kept for a certain period of time according to national rules.

3.8.3. A client account cannot be in debit except in exceptional circumstances as expressly permitted in national rules or due to bank charges, which cannot be influenced by the lawyer. Such an account cannot be given as a guarantee or be used as a security for any reason. There shall not be any set-off or merger between a client account and any other bank account, nor shall the client funds in a client account be available to defray money owed by the lawyer to the bank.

3.8.4. Client funds shall be transferred to the owners of such funds in the shortest period of time or under such conditions as are authorised by them.

3.8.5. The lawyer cannot transfer funds from a client account into the lawyer's own account for payment of fees without informing the client in writing.

3.8.6. The Competent Authorities in Member States shall have the power to verify and examine any document regarding client funds, whilst respecting the confidentiality or legal professional privilege to which it may be subject.

3.9. Professional Indemnity Insurance

3.9.1. Lawyers shall be insured against civil legal liability arising out of their legal practice to an extent which is reasonable having regard to the nature and extent of the risks incurred by their professional activities.

3.9.2. Should this prove impossible, the lawyer must inform the client of this situation and its consequences.

4. Relations with the Courts

4.1. Rules of Conduct in Court

A lawyer who appears, or takes part in a case, before a court or tribunal must comply with the rules of conduct applied before that court or tribunal.

4.2. Fair Conduct of Proceedings

A lawyer must always have due regard for the fair conduct of proceedings.

4.3. Demeanour in Court

A lawyer shall while maintaining due respect and courtesy towards the court defend the interests of the client honourably and fearlessly without regard to the lawyer's own interests or to any consequences to him- or herself or to any other person.

4.4. False or Misleading Information

A lawyer shall never knowingly give false or misleading information to the court.

4.5. Extension to Arbitrators etc.

The rules governing a lawyer's relations with the courts apply also to the lawyer's relations with arbitrators and any other persons exercising judicial or quasi-judicial functions, even on an occasional basis.

5.   Relations between Lawyers

5.1. Corporate Spirit of the Profession

5.1.1.   The corporate spirit of the profession requires a relationship of trust and co-operation between lawyers for the benefit of their clients and in order to avoid unnecessary litigation and other behaviour harmful to the reputation of the profession. It can, however, never justify setting the interests of the profession against those of the client.

5.1.2.   A lawyer should recognise all other lawyers of Member States as professional colleagues and act fairly and courteously towards them.

5.2. Co-operation among Lawyers of Different Member States

5.2.1.   It is the duty of a lawyer who is approached by a colleague from another Member State not to accept instructions in a matter which the lawyer is not competent to undertake. The lawyer should in such case be prepared to help that colleague to obtain the information necessary to enable him or her to instruct a lawyer who is capable of providing the service asked for.

5.2.2.   Where a lawyer of a Member State co-operates with a lawyer from another Member State, both have a general duty to take into account the differences which may exist between their respective legal systems and the professional organisations, competences and obligations of lawyers in the Member States concerned.

5.3. Correspondence between Lawyers

5.3.1.   If a lawyer intends to send communications to a lawyer in another Member State, which the sender wishes to remain confidential or without prejudice he or she should clearly express this intention prior to communicating the documents.

5.3.2.   If the prospective recipient of the communications is unable to ensure their status as confidential or without prejudice he or she should inform the sender accordingly without delay.

5.4. Referral Fees

5.4.1.   A lawyer may not demand or accept from another lawyer or any other person a fee, commission or any other compensation for referring or recommending the lawyer to a client.

5.4.2.   A lawyer may not pay anyone a fee, commission or any other compensation as a consideration for referring a client to him- or herself.

5.5. *Communication with Opposing Parties*

A lawyer shall not communicate about a particular case or matter directly with any person whom he or she knows to be represented or advised in the case or matter by another lawyer, without the consent of that other lawyer (and shall keep the other lawyer informed of any such communications).

5.6. *(Deleted by decision of the Plenary Session in Dublin on 6 December 2002)*

5.7. *Responsibility for Fees*

In professional relations between members of Bars of different Member States, where a lawyer does not confine him- or herself to recommending another lawyer or introducing that other lawyer to the client but instead him- or herself entrusts a correspondent with a particular matter or seeks the correspondent's advice, the instructing lawyer is personally bound, even if the client is insolvent, to pay the fees, costs and outlays which are due to the foreign correspondent. The lawyers concerned may, however, at the outset of the relationship between them make special arrangements on this matter. Further, the instructing lawyer may at any time limit his or her personal responsibility to the amount of the fees, costs and outlays incurred before intimation to the foreign lawyer of the instructing lawyer's disclaimer of responsibility for the future.

5.8. *Continuing Professional Development*

Lawyers should maintain and develop their professional knowledge and skills taking proper account of the European dimension of their profession.

5.9. *Disputes amongst Lawyers in Different Member States*

5.9.1. If a lawyer considers that a colleague in another Member State has acted in breach of a rule of professional conduct the lawyer shall draw the matter to the attention of that colleague.

5.9.2. If any personal dispute of a professional nature arises amongst lawyers in different Member States they should if possible first try to settle it in a friendly way.

5.9.3. A lawyer shall not commence any form of proceedings against a colleague in another Member State on matters referred to in 5.9.1 or 5.9.2 above without first informing the Bars or Law Societies to which they both belong for the purpose of allowing both Bars or Law Societies concerned an opportunity to assist in reaching a settlement.

Explanatory Memorandum

This Explanatory Memorandum was prepared at the request of the CCBE Standing Committee by the CCBE's deontology working party, who were responsible for drafting the first version of the Code of Conduct itself. It seeks to explain the origin of the provisions of the Code, to illustrate the problems which they are designed to resolve, particularly in relation to cross-border activities, and to provide assistance to the Competent Authorities in the Member States in the application of the Code. It is not intended to have any binding force in the interpretation of the Code. The Explanatory Memorandum was updated on the occasion of the CCBE Plenary Session on 19 May 2006.

The original versions of the Code are in the French and English languages. Translations into other Community languages are prepared under the authority of the national delegations.

Commentary on Article 1.1—The Function of the Lawyer in Society

The Declaration of Perugia, adopted by the CCBE in 1977, laid down the fundamental principles of professional conduct applicable to lawyers throughout the EC. The provisions of Article 1.1 reaffirm the statement in the Declaration of Perugia of the function of the lawyer in society which forms the basis for the rules governing the performance of that function.

Commentary on Article 1.2—The Nature of Rules of Professional Conduct

These provisions substantially restate the explanation in the Declaration of Perugia of the nature of rules of professional conduct and how particular rules depend on particular local circumstances but are nevertheless based on common values.

Commentary on Article 1.3—The Purpose of the Code

These provisions introduce the development of the principles in the Declaration of Perugia into a specific Code of Conduct for lawyers throughout the EU and the EEA, and lawyers of the Observer Members of the CCBE, with particular reference to their cross-border activities (defined in Article 1.5). The provisions of Article 1.3.2 lay down the specific intentions of the CCBE with regard to the substantive provisions in the Code.

Commentary on Article 1.4—Field of Application Ratione Personae

The rules are stated to apply to all lawyers as defined in the Lawyers Services Directive of 1977 and the Lawyers Establishment Directive of 1998, and lawyers of the Observer Members of the CCBE. This includes lawyers of the states which subsequently acceded to the Directives, whose names have been added by amendment to the Directives. The Code accordingly applies to all the lawyers represented on the CCBE, whether as full Members or as Observer Members, namely:

Austria	Rechtsanwalt;
Belgium	avocat / advocaat / Rechtsanwalt;
Bulgaria	advokat;
Croatia	odvjetnik;
Cyprus	dikegóros;
Czech Republic	advokát;
Denmark	advokat;
Estonia	vandeadvokaat;
Finland	asianajaja / advokat;
FYROMacedonia	advokat;
France	avocat;
Germany	Rechtsanwalt;
Greece	dikegóros;
Hungary	ügyved;
Iceland	lögmaður;

Ireland	barrister, solicitor;
Italy	avvocato;
Latvia	zvērināts advokāts;
Liechtenstein	Rechtsanwalt;
Lithuania	advokatas;
Luxembourg	avocat / Rechtsanwalt;
Malta	avukat, prokuratur legali;
Netherlands	advocaat;
Norway	advokat;
Poland	adwokat, radca prawny;
Portugal	advogado;
Romania	avocat;
Slovakia	advokát / advokátka;
Slovenia	odvetnik / odvetnica;
Spain	abogado / advocat / abokatu / avogado;
Sweden	advokat;
Switzerland	Rechtsanwalt/Anwalt/Fürsprech/Fürsprecher avocat / avvocato /advokat;
Turkey	avukat;
Ukraine	advocate;
United Kingdom	advocate, barrister, solicitor.

It is also hoped that the Code will be acceptable to the legal professions of other non-member states in Europe and elsewhere so that it could also be applied by appropriate conventions between them and the Member States.

Commentary on Article 1.5—Field of Application Ratione Materiae

The rules are here given direct application only to "cross-border activities", as defined, of lawyers within the EU and the EEA and lawyers of the Observer Members of the CCBE - see above on Article 1.4, and the definition of "Member State" in Article 1.6. (See also above as to possible extensions in the future to lawyers of other states.) The definition of cross-border activities would, for example, include contacts in state A even on a matter of law internal to state A between a lawyer of state A and a lawyer of state B; it would exclude contacts between lawyers of state A in state A of a matter arising in state B, provided that none of their professional activities takes place in state B; it would include any activities of lawyers of state A in state B, even if only in the form of communications sent from state A to state B.

Commentary on Article 1.6—Definitions

This provision defines a number of terms used in the Code, "Member State", "Home Member State", "Host Member State", "Competent Authority", "Directive 77/249/EEC" and "Directive 98/5/EC".The reference to "where the lawyer carries on cross-border activities" should be interpreted in the light of the definition of "cross-border activities" in Article 1.5.

Commentary on Article 2.1—Independence

This provision substantially reaffirms the general statement of principle in the Declaration of Perugia.

Commentary on Article 2.2—Trust and Personal Integrity

This provision also restates a general principle contained in the Declaration of Perugia.

Commentary on Article 2.3—Confidentiality

This provision first restates, in Article 2.3.1, general principles laid down in the Declaration of Perugia and recognised by the ECJ in the *AM&S* case (157/79). It then, in Articles 2.3.2 to 4, develops them into a specific rule relating to the protection of confidentiality. Article 2.3.2 contains the basic rule requiring respect for confidentiality. Article 2.3.3 confirms that the obligation remains binding on the lawyer even if he or she ceases to act for the client in question. Article 2.3.4 confirms that the lawyer must not only respect the obligation of confidentiality him- or herself but must require all members and employees of his or her firm to do likewise.

Commentary on Article 2.4—Respect for the Rules of Other Bars and Law Societies

Article 4 of the Lawyers Services Directive contains the provisions with regard to the rules to be observed by a lawyer from one Member State providing services on an occasional or temporary basis in another Member State by virtue of Article 49 of the consolidated EC treaty, as follows:

(a) activities relating to the representation of a client in legal proceedings or before public authorities shall be pursued in each Host Member State under the conditions laid down for lawyers established in that state, with the exception of any conditions requiring residence, or registration with a professional organisation, in that state;

(b) a lawyer pursuing these activities shall observe the rules of professional conduct of the Host Member State, without prejudice to the lawyer's obligations in the Member State from which he or she comes;

(c) when these activities are pursued in the UK, "rules of professional conduct of the Host Member State" means the rules of professional conduct applicable to solicitors, where such activities are not reserved for barristers and advocates. Otherwise the rules of professional conduct applicable to the latter shall apply. However, barristers from Ireland shall always be subject to the rules of professional conduct applicable in the UK to barristers and advocates. When these activities are pursued in Ireland "rules of professional conduct of the Host Member State" means, in so far as they govern the oral presentation of a case in court, the rules of professional conduct applicable to barristers. In all other cases the rules of professional conduct applicable to solicitors shall apply. However, barristers and advocates from the UK shall always be subject to the rules of professional conduct applicable in Ireland to barristers; and

(d) a lawyer pursuing activities other than those referred to in (a) above shall remain subject to the conditions and rules of professional conduct of the Member State from which he or she comes without prejudice to respect for the rules, whatever their source, which govern the profession in the Host Member State, especially those concerning the incompatibility of the exercise of the activities of a lawyer with the exercise of other activities in that state, professional secrecy, relations with other lawyers, the prohibition on the same lawyer acting for parties with mutually conflicting interests, and publicity. The latter rules are applicable only if they are capable of being observed by a lawyer who is not established in the Host Member State and to the extent to which their observance is objectively justified to ensure, in that state, the proper exercise of a lawyer's activities, the standing of the profession and respect for the rules concerning incompatibility.

The Lawyers Establishment Directive contains the provisions with regard to the rules to be observed by a lawyer from one Member State practising on a permanent basis in another Member State by virtue of Article 43 of the consolidated EC treaty, as follows:

(a)   irrespective of the rules of professional conduct to which he or she is subject in his or her Home Member State, a lawyer practising under his home-country professional title shall be subject to the same rules of professional conduct as lawyers practising under the relevant professional title of the Host Member State in respect of all the activities the lawyer pursues in its territory (Article 6.1);

(b)   the Host Member State may require a lawyer practising under his or her home-country professional title either to take out professional indemnity insurance or to become a member of a professional guarantee fund in accordance with the rules which that state lays down for professional activities pursued in its territory. Nevertheless, a lawyer practising under his or her home-country professional title shall be exempted from that requirement if the lawyer can prove that he or she is covered by insurance taken out or a guarantee provided in accordance with the rules of the Home Member State, insofar as such insurance or guarantee is equivalent in terms of the conditions and extent of cover. Where the equivalence is only partial, the Competent Authority in the Host Member State may require that additional insurance or an additional guarantee be contracted to cover the elements which are not already covered by the insurance or guarantee contracted in accordance with the rules of the Home Member State (Article 6.3); and

(c)   a lawyer registered in a Host Member State under his or her home-country professional title may practise as a salaried lawyer in the employ of another lawyer, an association or firm of lawyers, or a public or private enterprise to the extent that the Host Member State so permits for lawyers registered under the professional title used in that state (Article 8).

In cases not covered by either of these Directives, or over and above the requirements of these Directives, the obligations of a lawyer under Community law to observe the rules of other Bars and Law Societies are a matter of interpretation of any relevant provision, such as the Directive on Electronic Commerce (2000/31/EC). A major purpose of the Code is to minimise, and if possible eliminate altogether, the problems which may arise from "double deontology", that is the application of more than one set of potentially conflicting national rules to a particular situation (see Article 1.3.1).

Commentary on Article 2.5—Incompatible Occupations

There are differences both between and within Member States on the extent to which lawyers are permitted to engage in other occupations, for example in commercial activities. The general purpose of rules excluding a lawyer from other occupations is to protect the lawyer from influences which might impair the lawyer's independence or his or her role in the administration of justice. The variations in these rules reflect different local conditions, different perceptions of the proper function of lawyers and different techniques of rule-making. For instance in some cases there is a complete prohibition of engagement in certain named occupations, whereas in other cases engagement in other occupations is generally permitted, subject to observance of specific safeguards for the lawyer's independence.

Articles 2.5.2 and 3 make provision for different circumstances in which a lawyer of one Member State is engaging in cross-border activities (as defined in Article 1.5) in a Host Member State when he or she is not a member of the Host State legal profession.Article 2.5.2 imposes full observation of Host State rules regarding incompatible occupations on the lawyer acting in national legal proceedings or before national public authorities in the Host State. This applies whether the lawyer is established in the Host State or not.

Article 2.5.3, on the other hand, imposes "respect" for the rules of the Host State regarding forbidden or incompatible occupations in other cases, but only where the lawyer who is established in the Host Member State wishes to participate directly in commercial or other activities not connected with the practice of the law.

Commentary on Article 2.6—Personal Publicity

The term "personal publicity" covers publicity by firms of lawyers, as well as individual lawyers, as opposed to corporate publicity organised by Bars and Law Societies for their members as a whole. The rules governing personal publicity by lawyers vary considerably in the Member States. Article 2.6 makes it clear that there is no overriding objection to personal publicity in cross-border practice. However, lawyers are nevertheless subject to prohibitions or restrictions laid down by their home professional rules, and a lawyer will still be subject to prohibitions or restrictions laid down by Host State rules when these are binding on the lawyer by virtue of the Lawyers Services Directive or the Lawyers Establishment Directive.

Commentary on Article 2.7—The Client's Interest

This provision emphasises the general principle that the lawyer must always place the client's interests before the lawyer's own interests or those of fellow members of the legal profession.

Commentary on Article 2.8—Limitation of Lawyer's Liability towards the Client

This provision makes clear that there is no overriding objection to limiting a lawyer's liability towards his or her client in cross-border practice, whether by contract or by use of a limited company, limited partnership or limited liability partnership. However it points out that this can only be contemplated where the relevant law and the relevant rules of conduct permit—and in a number of jurisdictions the law or the professional rules prohibit or restrict such limitation of liability.

Commentary on Article 3.1—Acceptance and Termination of Instructions

The provisions of Article 3.1.1 are designed to ensure that a relationship is maintained between lawyer and client and that the lawyer in fact receives instructions from the client, even though these may be transmitted through a duly authorised intermediary. It is the responsibility of the lawyer to satisfy him- or herself as to the authority of the intermediary and the wishes of the client.

Article 3.1.2 deals with the manner in which the lawyer should carry out his or her duties. The provision that the lawyer shall undertake personal responsibility for the discharge of the instructions given to him or her means that the lawyer cannot avoid responsibility by delegation to others. It does not prevent the lawyer from seeking to limit his or her legal liability to the extent that this is permitted by the relevant law or professional rules—see Article 2.8.

Article 3.1.3 states a principle which is of particular relevance in cross-border activities, for example when a lawyer is asked to handle a matter on behalf of a lawyer or client from another state who may be unfamiliar with the relevant law and practice, or when a lawyer is asked to handle a matter relating to the law of another state with which he or she is unfamiliar.

A lawyer generally has the right to refuse to accept instructions in the first place, but Article 3.1.4 states that, having once accepted them, the lawyer has an obligation not to withdraw without ensuring that the client's interests are safeguarded.

Commentary on Article 3.2—Conflict of Interest

The provisions of Article 3.2.1 do not prevent a lawyer acting for two or more clients in the same matter provided that their interests are not in fact in conflict and that there is no significant risk of such a conflict arising. Where a lawyer is already acting for two or more clients in this way and subsequently there arises a conflict of interests between those clients or a risk of a breach of confidence or other circumstances where the lawyer's independence may be impaired, then the lawyer must cease to act for both or all of them.

There may, however, be circumstances in which differences arise between two or more clients for whom the same lawyer is acting where it may be appropriate for the lawyer to attempt to act as a mediator. It is for the lawyer in such cases to use his or her own judgement on whether or not there is such a conflict of interest between them as to require the lawyer to cease to act. If not, the lawyer may consider whether it would be appropriate to explain the position to the clients, obtain their agreement and attempt to act as mediator to resolve the difference between them, and only if this attempt to mediate should fail, to cease to act for them.

Article 3.2.4 applies the foregoing provisions of Article 3 to lawyers practising in association. For example a firm of lawyers should cease to act when there is a conflict of interest between two clients of the firm, even if different lawyers in the firm are acting for each client. On the other hand, exceptionally, in the "chambers" form of association used by English barristers, where each lawyer acts for clients individually, it is possible for different lawyers in the association to act for clients with opposing interests.

Commentary on Article 3.3—Pactum de Quota Litis

These provisions reflect the common position in all Member States that an unregulated agreement for contingency fees (*pactum de quota litis*) is contrary to the proper administration of justice because it encourages speculative litigation and is liable to be abused. The provisions are not, however, intended to prevent the maintenance or introduction of arrangements under which lawyers are paid according to results or only if the action or matter is successful, provided that these arrangements are under sufficient regulation and control for the protection of the client and the proper administration of justice.

Commentary on Article 3.4—Regulation of Fees

Article 3.4 lays down three requirements: a general standard of disclosure of a lawyer's fees to the client, a requirement that they should be fair and reasonable in amount, and a requirement to comply with the applicable law and professional rules. In many Member States machinery exists for regulating lawyers' fees under national law or rules of conduct, whether by reference to a power of adjudication by the Bar authorities or otherwise. In situations governed by the Lawyers Establishment Directive, where the lawyer is subject to Host State rules as well as the rules of the Home State, the basis of charging may have to comply with both sets of rules.

Commentary on Article 3.5—Payment on Account

Article 3.5 assumes that a lawyer may require a payment on account of the lawyer's fees and/or disbursements, but sets a limit by reference to a reasonable estimate of them. See also on Article 3.1.4 regarding the right to withdraw.

Commentary on Article 3.6—Fee Sharing with Non-Lawyers

In some Member States lawyers are permitted to practise in association with members of certain other approved professions, whether legal professions or not. The provisions of Article 3.6.1 are not designed to prevent fee sharing within such an approved form of association. Nor are the provisions designed to prevent fee sharing by the lawyers to whom the Code applies (see on Article 1.4 above) with other "lawyers", for example lawyers from non-Member States or members of other legal professions in the Member States such as notaries.

Commentary on Article 3.7—Cost of Litigation and Availability of Legal Aid

Article 3.7.1 stresses the importance of attempting to resolve disputes in a way which is cost-effective for the client, including advising on whether to attempt to negotiate a settlement, and whether to propose referring the dispute to some form of alternative dispute resolution.

Article 3.7.2 requires a lawyer to inform the client of the availability of legal aid where applicable. There are widely differing provisions in the Member States on the availability of legal aid. In cross-border activities a lawyer should have in mind the possibility that the legal aid provisions of a national law with which the lawyer is unfamiliar may be applicable.

Commentary on Article 3.8—Client Funds

The provisions of Article 3.8 reflect the recommendation adopted by the CCBE in Brussels in November 1985 on the need for minimum regulations to be made and enforced governing the proper control and disposal of clients' funds held by lawyers within the Community. Article 3.8 lays down minimum standards to be observed, while not interfering with the details of national systems which provide fuller or more stringent protection for clients' funds.

The lawyer who holds clients' funds, even in the course of a cross-border activity, has to observe the rules of his or her home Bar. The lawyer needs to be aware of questions which arise where the rules of more than one Member State may be applicable, especially where the lawyer is established in a Host State under the Lawyers Establishment Directive.

Commentary on Article 3.9—Professional Indemnity Insurance

Article 3.9.1 reflects a recommendation, also adopted by the CCBE in Brussels in November 1985, on the need for all lawyers in the Community to be insured against the risks arising from professional negligence claims against them. Article 3.9.2 deals with the situation where insurance cannot be obtained on the basis set out in Article 3.9.1.

Commentary on Article 4.1—Rules of Conduct in Court

This provision applies the principle that a lawyer is bound to comply with the rules of the court or tribunal before which the lawyer practises or appears.

Commentary on Article 4.2—Fair Conduct of Proceedings

This provision applies the general principle that in adversarial proceedings a lawyer must not attempt to take unfair advantage of his or her opponent. The lawyer must not, for example, make contact with the judge without first informing the lawyer acting for the opposing party or submit exhibits, notes or documents to the judge without communicating them in good time to the lawyer on the other side unless such steps are permitted under the relevant rules of procedure. To the extent not prohibited by law a lawyer must not divulge or submit to the court any proposals for settlement of the case made by the other party or its lawyer without the express consent of the other party's lawyer. See also on Article 4.5 below.

Commentary on Article 4.3—Demeanour in Court

This provision reflects the necessary balance between respect for the court and for the law on the one hand and the pursuit of the client's best interest on the other.

Commentary on Article 4.4—False or Misleading Information

This provision applies the principle that the lawyer must never knowingly mislead the court. This is necessary if there is to be trust between the courts and the legal profession.

Commentary on Article 4.5—Extension to Arbitrators etc.

This provision extends the preceding provisions relating to courts and other bodies exercising judicial or quasi-judicial functions.

Commentary on Article 5.1—Corporate Spirit of the Profession

These provisions, which are based on statements in the Declaration of Perugia, emphasise that it is in the public interest for the legal profession to maintain a relationship of trust and cooperation between its members. However, this cannot be used to justify setting the interests of the profession against those of justice or of clients (see also on Article 2.7).

Commentary on Article 5.2—Co-operation among Lawyers of Different Member States

This provision also develops a principle stated in the Declaration of Perugia with a view to avoiding misunderstandings in dealings between lawyers of different Member States.

Commentary on Article 5.3—Correspondence between Lawyers

In certain Member States communications between lawyers (written or by word of mouth) are normally regarded as to be kept confidential as between the lawyers. This means that the content of these communications cannot be disclosed to others, cannot normally be passed to the lawyers' clients, and at any event cannot be produced in court. In other Member States, such consequences will not follow unless the correspondence is marked as "confidential".

In yet other Member States, the lawyer has to keep the client fully informed of all relevant communications from a professional colleague acting for another party, and marking a letter as "confidential" only means that it is a legal matter intended for the recipient lawyer and his or her client, and not to be misused by third parties.

In some states, if a lawyer wishes to indicate that a letter is sent in an attempt to settle a dispute, and is not to be produced in a court, the lawyer should mark the letter as "without prejudice".

These important national differences give rise to many misunderstandings. That is why lawyers must be very careful in conducting cross-border correspondence.

Whenever a lawyer wants to send a letter to a professional colleague in another Member State on the basis that it is to be kept confidential as between the lawyers, or that it is "without prejudice", the lawyer should ask in advance whether the letter can be accepted on that basis. A lawyer wishing that a communication should be accepted on such a basis must express that clearly at the head of the communication or in a covering letter.

A lawyer who is the intended recipient of such a communication, but who is not in a position to respect, or to ensure respect for, the basis on which it is to be sent, must inform the sender immediately so that the communication is not sent. If the communication has already been received, the recipient must return it to the sender without revealing its contents or referring to it in any way; if the recipient's national law or rules prevent the recipient from complying with this requirement, he or she must inform the sender immediately.

Commentary on Article 5.4—Referral Fees

This provision reflects the principle that a lawyer should not pay or receive payment purely for the reference of a client, which would risk impairing the client's free choice of lawyer or the client's interest in being referred to the best available service. It does not prevent fee-sharing arrangements between lawyers on a proper basis (see also on Article 3.6 above).

In some Member States lawyers are permitted to accept and retain commissions in certain cases provided the client's best interests are served, there is full disclosure to the client and the client has consented to the retention of the commission. In such cases the retention of the commission by the lawyer represents part of the lawyer's remuneration for the service provided to the client and is not within the scope of the prohibition on referral fees which is designed to prevent lawyers making a secret profit.

Commentary on Article 5.5—Communication with Opposing Parties

This provision reflects a generally accepted principle, and is designed both to promote the smooth conduct of business between lawyers and to prevent any attempt to take advantage of the client of another lawyer.

Commentary on Article 5.6—Change of Lawyer

Article 5.6 dealt with change of lawyer. It was deleted from the Code on 6 December 2002.

Commentary on Article 5.7—Responsibility for Fees

These provisions substantially reaffirm provisions contained in the Declaration of Perugia. Since misunderstandings about responsibility for unpaid fees are a common cause of difference between lawyers of different Member States, it is important that a lawyer who wishes to exclude or limit his or her personal obligation to be responsible for the fees of a foreign colleague should reach a clear agreement on this at the outset of the transaction.

Commentary on Article 5.8—Continuing Professional Development

Keeping abreast of developments in the law is a professional obligation. In particular it is essential that lawyers are aware of the growing impact of European law on their field of practice.

Commentary on Article 5.9—Disputes amongst Lawyers in Different Member States

A lawyer has the right to pursue any legal or other remedy to which he or she is entitled against a colleague in another Member State. Nevertheless it is desirable that, where a breach of a rule of professional conduct or a dispute of a professional nature is involved, the possibilities of friendly settlement should be exhausted, if necessary with the assistance of the Bars or Law Societies concerned, before such remedies are exercised.

Solicitors (Scotland) (Standards of Service) 2008

These Standards of Service were adopted at the Special General Meeting of the Society on September 26, 2008.

"Lawyers help people at times of crisis and bereavement, they protect the rights of the vulnerable, and they support business and economic growth" (Justice Secretary, Kenny MacAskill, November 26, 2007).

Lawyers interact with a wide cross section of our society and fulfil a critical role in meeting the interests of that society. Their clients are entitled to expect a good level of professional service from their solicitor. This means the solicitor must demonstrate the appropriate legal knowledge and skill to address the needs of the client, must communicate effectively in a clear and understandable way with their clients and others, must do what they say they are going to do, and must treat their clients and all others with respect and courtesy at all times.

At the same time, a solicitor is required to comply with rules of professional conduct and behaviour, recognising that their professional obligations are not only to their clients, but to the courts, the legal profession and the public. Amongst other things, these rules regulate:

- Confidentiality and legal professional privilege.
- Trust and personal integrity.
- The interest of the client.
- Independence of the solicitor.
- Disclosure of interest.
- Relations with the Courts.
- Conflict of Interest.

Standards of service are based on broad principles recognising the range and variety of work which can be undertaken by a solicitor. The standards have equal application to an individual solicitor, whether as a partner in a firm or an employee, and to firms. The application of these standards requires the use of effective systems, good training and appropriate supervision.

At the heart of providing a legal service are the interests and needs of the client. The importance of those interests and needs means that solicitors must adhere to the following overriding principles:

- **Competence**
- **Diligence**
- **Communication**
- **Respect**

Competence

- Know and apply the relevant law.
- Keep up-to-date.
- Ensure that those to whom work is delegated are properly trained and supervised.

In deciding whether or not to agree to work for a client and in carrying out the work, a solicitor must consider the nature and complexity of the matter and must have the appropriate level of professional skills to do that work. This means that a solicitor must consider if he or she has the knowledge and experience needed. Given the range of specialised areas of legal work it is essential that a solicitor recognises the need to keep his/her knowledge up to date and to make an ongoing commitment to continuing professional development.

Where a solicitor delegates work, whether to another solicitor or solicitors or to paralegals or other members of staff, it is essential that such staff are properly trained and that there are in place systems to ensure that the delegated work is adequately supervised.

Diligence

- Deliver on commitments.
- Act in the best interests of each client.
- Maintain and review systems of work.
- Prompt and transparent fee arrangements.

It is expected that a solicitor will fulfil commitments made to the client, other solicitors and the court. By way of example, this would include responding to letters, e-mails and telephone calls within an appropriate or agreed timescale.

A solicitor must only agree to work for a client where the work can be done within a reasonable timescale. Where a solicitor considers, for example, that the service to a client would be inadequate because they already have so much work to do that it would not be dealt with within a reasonable period of time, they should not agree to take on the work.

The solicitor will at all times seek to do his or her best for the client. This will include identifying the client's objectives in relation to the work to be done, giving the client a clear explanation of the issues involved and the options available to the client, and agreeing with the client the next steps to be taken. In keeping the client informed, the solicitor must provide updates on progress.

With the increasing advancement of technology, it is expected that the solicitor will regularly look at ways in which technology can support client service. By way of example, this may include client reporting systems, file and data management systems and use of knowledge management systems.

At the conclusion of the work, or earlier if agreed, the solicitor will ensure that the fees to be charged are promptly notified to the client and that a clear explanation and breakdown is provided. If there is any variation from the fees previously discussed, the solicitor must explain the reasons for the variation. The solicitor must respond promptly to any clarification sought from the client.

Communication

- Use of clear language and explanation from the perspective of the client.
- Agreement on the means and frequency of communication between client and solicitor.
- Letters of engagement or their equivalent clearly explaining and defining the service to be carried out, how that work will be carried out, who is responsible and the cost associated with the service.
- How complaints will be handled in the event of dissatisfaction.

Whatever the nature of the work carried out by a solicitor, communicating effectively with the client is very important. Solicitors must make sure that they communicate clearly, effectively and in plain understandable language with their clients and others. This includes keeping clients informed regularly about progress with the matter. The overriding aim is to ensure that the client can gain a proper understanding of what is being communicated. This necessarily requires the communication to be tailored to suit the audience, their needs and interests. Communication requires the solicitor to listen to the client and understand their objectives.

Solicitors must send a letter to their clients as soon as possible after the first instruction providing information about:

(a) the work to be carried out;
(b) what the fees and other costs will be, or the basis upon which such fees and costs will be charged including where appropriate the hourly

rate to be charged. Where the client is receiving legal advice and assistance or legal aid, they should be told about any contribution that might be payable, the consequences of preserving or recovering property, and where appropriate their possible liability for the expenses of the other party;

(c) the name of the person or persons who will do the work ; and

(d) the name of the person the client should speak to if they are unhappy about the work done.

Clients who use a solicitor or firm regularly to carry out the same type of work should be sent such a letter whenever there is any change in the terms previously agreed with them.

Solicitors should advise their clients of any significant development in relation to the matter they are working on for them and explain matters clearly in order to allow clients to make informed decisions. Information should be clear, easy to understand and comprehensive and where necessary or appropriate confirmed in writing. In particular solicitors should advise clients in writing as soon as it becomes known that the cost of work will exceed any estimate previously provided.

The duty to communicate effectively includes the duty of solicitors to report to their clients at the appropriate time about all money related to their matter which is handled by the solicitor.

Respect

- Treat each person as an individual.
- Recognise diversity, different cultures and values.

The relationship between solicitor and client is a mutual one built upon trust and respect.

Relationships based on openness, trust and good communication enable the solicitor to work in partnership with the client to address their needs. Implicit within a good level of professional service provided by a solicitor is that each and every client will be treated respectfully and with courtesy, in recognition of their dignity and rights as individuals. The solicitor also has a responsibility to treat colleagues, other members of the legal profession and the public with similar politeness and respect.

This will require of the solicitor to listen to and understand the interests and needs of the client and to bring his or her knowledge and experience to the work.

The solicitor must treat clients fairly and in line with the law. The solicitor must not discriminate against clients because of their age, sex, race, ethnic origin, nationality, special needs or disability, sexuality, health, lifestyle, beliefs or any other relevant consideration.

F 358/36

PRACTICE RULES, CODES AND REGULATIONS

CODE OF CONDUCT FOR CRIMINAL WORK[1]

F3.11

The following Code contains a statement of good practice for those solicitors conducting criminal work. It does not have the status of a Practice Rule but may be referred to for guidance in assessing whether a solicitor's conduct meets the standard required of a member of the profession.

Article 1—Seeking Business

(1) *A solicitor shall seek or accept only those instructions which emanate from the client properly given and should not accept instructions given as a result of an inducement or subject to any improper constraint or condition.*

Guidance Note

This statement of good practice is a reminder that a solicitor is an officer of the court and as such has obligations and duties to the Court. It is a reminder that a solicitor should always act properly when dealing with criminal law work.

It is essential that a solicitor should at all times remain independent of the client and that the solicitor should be free to give appropriate legal advice. Accordingly no instructions should be accepted in circumstances where it could be alleged that inducements have been offered in exchange for instructions. It will be considered an inducement for a solicitor or firm of solicitors to advertise and/or have a general policy of non-collection of properly asessed contributions. No instructions should be accepted in circumstances where those instructions are subject for whatever reason to restrictions or constraints which compromise the solicitors freedom to give appropriate independent legal advice. It follows that a client should not be considered as a "friend" and that the solicitor must always remain "at arms length" from the client. This will ensure that both the client and the court can be confident that the advice tendered by the solicitor is impartial and independent.

A solicitor should accept instructions only from the client directly and not from a third party on behalf of the client. There may be circumstances in which a solicitor is asked by the family or a friend of the accused person to visit the accused in custody. It is the duty of every solicitor to check with the police station to ascertain if the person in custody has requested another solicitor or the duty solicitor. If the person in custody has indeed requested the services of another solicitor or the duty solicitor, then the solicitor contacted by the family or friend may not visit the police station.

Moreover, instructions must come directly from the person detained and not by virtue of the police arranging for a specific solicitor to be contacted who is unknown to and has not been requested by the accused.

Any instructions given as a result of an inducement by a third party on the solicitor's behalf must not be accepted. A solicitor will be deemed to be strictly liable for the actions of third parties who contact potential clients and any third party who contacts potential clients shall be deemed to have acted on the instructions of the solicitor whether or not the solicitor is instructed as a result of the third party's approach. If the client's co-accused is instructing a solicitor contact must be made through that solicitor. All reasonable steps must be taken to ascertain the identity of the co-accused's solicitor.

---

[1] Reproduced with kind permission of the Law Society of Scotland.

Solicitors are reminded of the terms of Section 31 of The Legal Aid (Scotland) Act 1986. Any contract of agency between a solicitor and a client which is based upon any inducement may be illegal and may be subject to action in the criminal or civil courts. Such contracts may also form the basis of a complaint of professional misconduct and may lead to disqualification in terms of Section 31.

Article 2—Conflict of Interest

(2) *A solicitor should not accept instructions from more than one accused in the same matter.*

Guidance Note

This statement reflects the awareness which solicitors have always had of the obvious potential conflict of interest that will arise when instructions are accepted from more than one accused person in the same case, even though that conflict may not arise and the defence is common to all accused. Nevertheless, solicitors should not place themselves in the position whereby they may obtain information confidential to the defence of one accused which at the same time may be detrimental to the defence of another.

Accordingly when it becomes apparent to the solicitor that he has received instructions from two or more parties in the same case a solicitor may accept instructions from one of the accused and any others must be told immediately that separate representation must be sought.

Solicitors are also reminded that great care must be taken in situations where one of the solicitor's clients gives evidence against another client of that solicitor. The client, who is acting as a witness, is entitled to have his confidentiality respected as against the interests of the accused. In some situations, such as where the accused is incriminating or attacking the character of the client, who is a witness, there will be a conflict of interest and the solicitor should not act.

A solicitor should not apply for a Legal Aid Certificate for more than one accused person in any matter. However, a duty solicitor should responsibly carry out his duties under the Legal Aid scheme and be aware of the terms of this statement.

A solicitor may suggest that an accused seeks representation from a particular solicitor but that alternative solicitor must be based within the same jurisdiction as the accused. However the choice of a solicitor always lies with the accused person and a solicitor must always ask an accused if he wishes a particular solicitor to be instructed before a recommendation can be made.

Article 3—Preparation and Conduct of Criminal Cases

(3) *A solicitor is under a duty to prepare and conduct criminal cases by carrying out work which is actually and reasonably necessary and having due regard to economy.*

Guidance Note

It is essential at each stage of the conduct of a criminal case that the necessary preparation is undertaken timeously. It is essential that a solicitor should use his best endeavours to discover all relevant information and evidence relating both to the Crown case and any substantive case for the defence.

The solicitor must remember that his primary duties are to the client and the court and ensure that the case is properly prepared and there is no prejudice to the client.

Every solicitor should carry out these duties in a responsible and professional manner. With these duties uppermost in mind, the solicitor must not view criminal cases only as a means of financial enrichment.

For the purposes of cases which are legally aided, this statement is declaratory of Regulation 7(1) of the Criminal Legal Aid (Scotland) (Fees) Regulations 1989. Regulation 7(1) states that "subject to the provisions of Regulations 4, 5, 6 and 9 and paragraph (2) of this Regulation, a solicitor shall be allowed such amount of fees as shall be determined to be reasonable remuneration for work actually and reasonably done, and travel and waiting time actually and reasonably undertaken or incurred, due regard being had to economy".

When requested, files and information should be provided to the Scottish Legal Aid Board.

Abuse of the Legal Aid system may be fraudulent and may be considered as professional misconduct and may lead to disqualification under Section 31 of the Legal Aid (Scotland) Act 1986.

Any complaints can be dealt with in terms of Section 31 of the Legal Aid (Scotland) Act 1986.

Article 4—Identification of Solicitors

(4) *A solicitor who seeks access to any party who is in custody should have in his possession a form of identification provided by the Law Society of Scotland and should exhibit this upon request.*

Guidance Note

This statement is designed to prohibit unqualified employees or individuals from attending meetings with persons in custody. It will ensure not only that impersonation of solicitors or trainees is made more difficult but also that only those persons qualified to provide independent legal advice are granted access. Acceptable forms of confirmation of identity include the production of a valid identification card issued by the Law Society of Scotland; of a valid CCBE card provided by the Law Society of Scotland or of a valid and current practising certificate together with a form of visual identification.

Article 5—Custody Visits

(5) *Only a solicitor or trainee solicitor who has been instructed to do so may visit the client in custody.*

Guidance Note

This Statement restricts access to a person in custody in a police office, prison and cell area.

There are occasions when a solicitor has taken instructions from the family or friend of an accused and has then visited a person in custody. It is the duty of every solicitor to check with the police station to ascertain if the person in custody has requested another solicitor or duty solicitor. If the person in custody has indeed requested the services of another solicitor or the duty solicitor, then the solicitor contacted by the family or friend may not visit the police station.

Moreover, instructions must come directly from the person detained and not by virtue of the police arranging for a specific solicitor to be contacted who is unknown to and has not been requested by the accused.

Article 6—Property to Persons in Custody

(6) A business card and legal documents should be the only items given by a solicitor to a person in custody.

Guidance Note

It has become apparent that certain solicitors have attended to the so called "needs" of their clients in custody by providing them with cigarettes, newspapers, meals, access to the solicitor's mobile phone and money. Actings of this sort may be a contravention of Section 41(1) of the Prisons (Scotland) Act 1989 which forbids certain forms of donation. In addition, this statement shall include the giving to family or friends of the person in custody any items for onward transmission.

Article 7—Legal Aid Mandates

(7) *All legal aid mandates requesting the transfer of papers and legal aid relating to a criminal matter shall be completed and executed by the assisted person in the form agreed by the Scottish Legal Aid Board and the Law Society of Scotland.*

Guidance Note

The matter is governed by the Criminal Legal Aid (Scotland) Regulations 1996, paragraph 17(3), which states "where an assisted person desires that a solicitor, other than the solicitor presently nominated by him shall act for him, he shall apply to the Board for authority to nominate another specified solicitor to act for him and shall inform the Board of the reason for his application; and the Board, if it is satisfied that there is good reason for the application, may grant the application".

It seems clear from a plain construction of this Regulation that changes of agency where the client is legally aided in a criminal case can only take place if the Board gives the client authority to nominate another specified solicitor. Until the Board gives its authority the client cannot instruct another solicitor unless he wishes to do so without the benefit of legal aid, which fact should be notified to the Board.

Therefore the chronology of transfers of agency in criminal cases should be (1) the client approaches his proposed new solicitor to ascertain if he is willing to act; (2) client applies to Board for authority to transfer the agency; (3) Board grants authority; (4) client instructs new solicitor; (5) new solicitor serves mandate on previous solicitor.

The Board's authority to transfer must ante-date any mandate.

The Statement would solve many issues including inducements to transfer agency and "mandate wars". Adoption of this interpretation would of course mean that legally aided clients and fee paying clients will not be treated precisely equally. However, that objection has to be seen in the light of the need to comply with the Regulations which effectively impose a statutory suspensive condition on any mandate and the requirement that solicitors will require to inform a transferring client that instructions cannot be accepted until the Regulations are complied with.

Any complaints about conduct under this section can be dealt with in terms of section 31 of the Legal Aid (Scotland) Act 1986.

Article 8—Consultation with clients at liberty

(8) *A solicitor should not consult with a client, who is at liberty unless the consultation takes place in (1) the solicitor's office; (2) a court; (3) a hospital; or (4) the locus; a solicitor may exceptionally attend the house of a client who is unable to attend the solicitor's office due to illness.*

Guidance Note

The solicitor should not visit a client within his home unless it is impossible for the client to attend the offices of the solicitor through ill health.

A solicitor leaves himself open to various allegations and indeed risks if he should attend at the home of a client. All solicitors should be aware that there is a risk. For example a solicitor could be within a house which contains drugs or stolen goods.

It will not always be possible to consult with an accused within a solicitor's own office. However, such consultations should take place within a similar office environment, such as the interview rooms within a Court building. However, it is accepted that there will be occasions when it is not possible or appropriate to interview a client within an office environment, for example when the client is in hospital. The onus is on a solicitor to justify an interview at any other place if called upon to do so. The geography and rural nature of Scotland will be taken into account.

Article 9—Expenses

(9) *No payments in money or kind should be made to an accused person, a member of the accused person's family or potential witnesses.*

Guidance Note

The only payments which a solicitor is entitled to make to an accused person, to members of his family or to witnesses are the legitimate expenses paid to witnesses who were cited to appear at Court on behalf of the defence. It is appropriate for a solicitor to advance travel vouchers to a witness who shall be travelling a significant distance.

Any payment of expenses made by a solicitor should be properly recorded and vouched.

If a plea of not guilty is tendered and the solicitor has not been paid the contribution in full by the intermediate diet, he/she should withdraw from acting, or if a decision is taken to continue to represent the client, should do so on a pro bono basis and not access any publicly funded assistance.

Article 10—Defence Witnesses

(10) *Only those witnesses relevant to a case should be cited to attend court.*

Guidance Note

Ideally, a witness should be interviewed before citation. A solicitor must take all reasonable steps to obtain directly from a witness the potential evidence in a case. It is accepted that this is not always possible and indeed a solicitor could leave himself open to criticism and complaint if he should not cite a witness when he has been specifically instructed to do so by an accused person. Nevertheless, a solicitor must at all times be in a position to justify the citation of all witnesses in a case.

Defence witnesses should be cited sufficiently far in advance of the Trial Diet to give them adequate warning of the requirement to attend court. Where possible, witnesses should be cited prior to the Intermediate Diet in order to ascertain at that stage whether there is any difficulty about the defence witnesses attendance at court for the Trial Diet. Common courtesy demands that defence witnesses should be given adequate notice of their requirement to attend court as witnesses.

In providing a citation, a solicitor should advise the witness of their right to claim legitimate expenses. These include travelling to and from Court. Neither witnesses nor indeed an accused person should be transported to Court by a solicitor.

In recent times it has been suggested that some persons with no involvement in a case have been cited to attend court only to provide these persons with expenses. Additionally, it has been asserted that parties have been brought to Court from custody, who have no relevance whatsoever to the case but who are cited simply to allow them to meet other prisoners at Court. Such actions cannot be tolerated.

Solicitors should make a point of speaking to defence witnesses at court in order, as a matter of courtesy, to advise them of the court procedure and the likely timetabling for the case in respect of which they have been cited.

Solicitors should advise their clients that they as professional persons ultimately take the decision as to which defence witnesses require to be cited. Solicitors are the judges of whether or not a particular witness's evidence is relevant. In addition, solicitors should ensure that legitimate expenses claimed by defence witnesses are paid promptly. Witnesses of course require to be advised that any claim for expenses require to be properly vouched.

A solicitor should keep a contemporaneous record of his actings and financial dealings in terms of this Code and provide this if so requested by the Law Society of Scotland.

Article 11—Documents and materials

(11.1) *A solicitor will receive in the course of defence work the documents, materials or recordings related to the cases in which he is instructed. These documents, materials and recordings will include those disclosed to the solicitor by the Crown Office and Procurator Fiscal Service ("COPFS"). A solicitor should not give a client, or any other third party, even on a temporary basis, copies of any documents, materials or recordings. There may be exceptional circumstances justifying a departure from this rule in a particular case and if the solicitor believes that such exceptional circumstances exist, he must refer the matter to the Professional Practice Department of the Law Society of Scotland for guidance. If items are to be given to the client or third party, the solicitor must explain that the items must retained securely by them; must be kept confidential; must not be revealed to others, let alone released to others; must not be copied and must be returned to the solicitor by a fixed date which must be as soon as possible having regard to the circumstances justifying giving the items to the client in the first place.*

(11.2) *Some documents, materials or recordings may be of a sensitive nature and should never be given to the client. These documents should only be shown to the client in circumstances where the solicitor is present and it is possible to exercise adequate supervision to prevent the client retaining possession of the material or making a copy of it. Before showing the client the material, the solicitor should* *ensure that he has redacted the material to obscure any information tending to identify the home address or contact details of a witness. Some examples of sensitive material or documents are listed below:-*

(a) *A precognition or statement of a victim of a sexual offence;*

(b) *A photograph or pseudo photograph of any such victim or a deceased victim;*

(c) *A medical or other report or statement relating to the physical or mental condition of any such victim or a deceased victim;*

(d) *Any document, other than a document served on the client by the Crown or by a co-accused, containing the addresses or telephone numbers of witnesses or their relatives/friends or information from which there addresses and telephone numbers can be deduced;*

(e) *Any video or audio recording of a statement made by a vulnerable witness; and*

(f) *Any record in relation to previous convictions or outstanding charges of complainers or witnesses.*

(11.3) *In the event of a solicitor ceasing to act on behalf of a client, that client being unrepresented, any documents, materials or recordings which had been disclosed should be returned to the COPFS. If there is a transfer of agency, the documents, materials or recordings should be transferred on receipt of a mandate to the new solicitor. When a case has been concluded, a solicitor holding material disclosed by the COPFS should arrange for the material to be stored securely or to be disposed of as confidential waste.*

Guidance Note

From time to time the Society has been asked to give its views of the practice of giving to accused persons, or other third parties, copies of the precognitions or statements of witnesses and of other documents associated with the accused's case. This is particularly relevant in view of the solicitors obligations in relation to the material received from the COPFS under disclosure arrangements which have been put in place following the judgements of the Judicial Committee of the Privy Council in the cases of *Holland v HMA,* 2005 S.L.T. 563 and *Sinclair v HM Advocate,* 2005 S.L.T. 513.

In the vast majority of criminal cases, the accused is in receipt of legal aid and it has been judicially declared that the accused has no proprietorial claim on the case papers. These belong to the solicitor.

The view of the Society is that solicitors should not give copies of precognitions, statements, documents or recordings to the accused or third parties unless there are exceptional circumstances justifying a departure from this general practice. Exceptional circumstances might include a case of particular complexity, necessitating giving the accused copies of documents to allow proper preparation. A fraud case, for instance, where documents were originally in the possession of the accused, might be such an exception. Another example would be a request from an appropriate investigative or statutory body, such as the Law Society of Scotland, the Scottish Criminal Cases Review Commission or the Scottish Legal Aid Board. Where a solicitor believes that there are exceptional circumstances, he must refer the matter to the Society's Professional Practice Department for guidance. If the solicitor does give access to copies of documents, materials or recordings, he must ensure that a written record is kept of the reason for the documents, materials or recordings being given to the client or third party and of the fact that the recipient has been advised of the terms of the Code and the conditions of possession.

Information contained in the documents, materials or recordings which is sensitive, should only ever be used or disclosed to others for the limited purpose of the preparation and conduct of the proceedings. This is designed to ensure that a solicitor can disclose sufficient information to enable proper preparation to take place, for example, by disclosing to an expert witness but to reinforce the clear rule that such material should not be made available to persons unconnected with the case.

The Code makes it clear that sensitive material should never be disclosed. There are unfortunate worrying examples of problems which can arise if the guidelines are not observed, for example, copies of witness statements could be circulated in the public domain leading to witnesses being intimidated. Statements of victims of sexual crimes could be used as a form of pornography within prison. An extract from a firearms register, complete with addresses and type of weapons, has already been circulated in a prison.

Any sensitive material held by the solicitor should be retained securely and, if it has been given to the solicitor on condition that it is returned, the solicitor should return it to the issuing authority in accordance with that undertaking, as soon as it is no longer required by the solicitor.

Where a solicitor ceases to act and another solicitor takes over acting, the solicitor should ensure security and confidentiality of the material concerned and either return the documents and materials to the COPFS or transfer them to the incoming solicitor.

Solicitors are reminded that in receiving documentation, material or recordings from the COPFS, or other third parties, that they are accepting an implied undertaking to comply with the terms of this Article.

Article 12—Retention of Papers

(12.1) *In general terms, the solicitor should be aware of the general guidelines on retention and destruction of papers as issued from time to time by the Law Society of Scotland.*

(12.2) In murder cases and other cases involving life imprisonment, the papers should be retained indefinitely.

(12.3) In other Solemn and in any Summary case, the papers should be retained for 3 years.

As a general rule, a solicitor might regard it as good practice in every case to retain indefinitely a copy of the Complaint or Indictment and a copy of the Legal Aid Certificate.

GUIDANCE NOTE
  Another issue associated with case papers is the question of the length of time such papers should be retained once a case has been concluded and how such papers should ultimately be destroyed if at all.
  The options for retention are—
  (1) indefinitely;
  (2) destruction after a fixed period;
  (3) destruction at the discretion of the solicitor; or
  (4) a combination of the above, depending on the nature of the case and the likelihood or risk that reference to the original case papers will be necessary.
The Society is conscious of the consequences of recommending retention of too many papers for too long, having regard to the difficulties of office storage and the expense of "off-site" storage. On the other hand, certain types of cases involve offences of such gravity, complexity or high public profile, that the possibility of issues arising in future years is a real one. Solicitors should be aware of the existence of the Scottish Criminal Cases Review Commission and for the need to retain files where solicitors believe that there is a possibility that it will be of future importance to the client. Other offences may have sentence implications in the short to mid-term: e.g. petitions for restoration of a driving licence after disqualification; reimposing the unexpired portion of a sentence after re-offending. Solemn cases might be expected to throw up more difficulties than Summary. In legally aided cases, solicitors are reminded that in terms of the Code of Practice in relation to Criminal Legal Assistance, issued by the Scottish Legal Aid Board, records shall be maintained and accessible for a period 3 years from the date of payment of the relevant account by the Board.

Destruction of case papers
  Solicitors should note that when case papers are being destroyed, it is vital that this is done in a comprehensive, secure and confidential way. If the solicitor does not destroy the papers personally, then they should be destroyed by a suitably qualified commercial firm.

Article 13—Precognition of Witnesses
(13) When carrying out precognition of witnesses, whether personally, through directly employed staff, or through external precognition agents, the nominated solicitor or instructing solicitor has responsibility for the manner in which contact is made with the witnesses and the manner in which the witnesses are actually precognosced. In particular, it is the duty of the solicitor to ensure that any matters associated with the witness of which he is aware which would affect the taking of the precognition or the mode of contact, such as age, disability or other vulnerable status, are taken into account by him and communicated to any precognition agent.

GUIDANCE NOTE
  When precognoscing witnesses, a solicitor has responsibility to ensure that this is done in a way which is as sympathetic as possible to the needs of the witness. A solicitor does not discharge this responsibility simply by passing to a precognition agent a copy of the list of witnesses and asking the

precognition agent to commence precognoscing them. Where a solicitor is aware of information about witnesses which would affect the way in which they ought to be contacted or the way in which they should be precognosced, such as that they are children, that they are disabled in some way or anything else, the solicitor has a duty to ensure that the precognition agent is equipped with enough information about the case to carry out the precognition work properly. A solicitor who fails to ensure that the precognition agent is aware of such sensitive information which is known to the solicitor does not thereafter avoid responsibility for distress or inconvenience etc. which is caused to the witness by a failure to observe the particular characteristics of the witness.

Every witness should be contacted in writing by the solicitor in advance with effective information about the process of precognition. This should include information about to whom to complain, if things are perceived to go wrong. There should be no "cold calling".

Notice should be given as to who will take the precognition and due regard should be had to the venue and timing for the convenience of the witness.

It should be pointed out that the witness may have a friend or supporter present, provided that person is not also a witness in the case under investigation.

Care should be taken with vulnerable witnesses or witnesses who might be subjected to intimidation. The nature of the charge should be considered and it might be appropriate to precognosce the reporting officer with a view to obtaining information about witnesses prior to precognoscing them.

It may be that in certain cases the gender of the precognition taker should be considered. Crimes of indecency may, at least as far as victims are concerned, be better precognosced by precognoscers of the same sex.

Prior to the taking of the precognition, the witness should be able to satisfy himself that the precognition taker is who he says he is. Those instructed by solicitors to obtain precognitions should carry identification and a letter of authority from the instructing solicitor.

In cases involving more than one accused, there will obviously be separate and different interests but liaison between solicitors can very often result in a witness only having to undergo one session rather than a number of separate sessions. Where possible, multiple precognitions of civilian witnesses by each accused should be avoided unless this is absolutely essential in the interests of justice and of the accused.

The witness should be given a copy of these guidelines.

Other Rules of Professional Conduct

A solicitor should at all times comply with good professional practice and the ethics of the solicitors' profession as set out in practice rules, other codes of conduct and textbooks on professional ethics.

GUIDANCE NOTE

The essence of professional ethics is such that it cannot be codified. Many texts provide guidance on the professional behaviour expected of solicitors. Solicitors have a duty to inform themselves of these texts and to approach their work in a manner consistent with the principles of good ethical practice. A solicitor acting outwith the terms of this Code may be called upon to justify his conduct.

Code of Ethics for Insolvency Practitioners

Definitions

Authorising body	A body declared to be a recognised professional body or a competent authority under any legislation governing the administration of insolvency in the United Kingdom.
Close or immediate family	A spouse (or equivalent), dependant, parent, child or sibling.
Entity	Any natural or legal person or any group of such persons, including a partnership.
He/she	In this Code, he is to be read as including she.
Individual within the practice	The *Insolvency Practitioner*, any principals in the *practice* and any employees within the *practice*.
Insolvency appointment	A formal appointment: (a) which, under the terms of legislation must be undertaken by an *Insolvency Practitioner*; or (b) as a nominee or supervisor of a voluntary arrangement.
Insolvency Practitioner	An individual who is authorised or recognised to act as an *Insolvency Practitioner* in the United Kingdom by an *authorising body*. For the purpose of the application of this Code only, the term *Insolvency Practitioner* also includes an individual who acts as a nominee or supervisor of a voluntary arrangement.
Insolvency team	Any person under the control or direction of an *Insolvency Practitioner*.
Practice	The organisation in which the *Insolvency Practitioner* practices.
Principal	In respect of a *practice*: (a) which is a company: a director; (b) which is a partnership: a partner; (c) which is a limited liability partnership: a member; (d) which is comprised of a sole practitioner: that person; Alternatively any person within the *practice* who is held out as being a director, partner or member.

PART 1: GENERAL APPLICATION OF THE CODE

The Practice of Insolvency

Introduction

100.1 This Code is intended to assist *Insolvency Practitioners* meet the obligations expected of them by providing professional and ethical guidance.

100.2 This Code applies to all *Insolvency Practitioners. Insolvency Practitioners* should take steps to ensure that the Code is applied in all professional work relating to an *insolvency appointment*, and to any professional work that may lead to such an *insolvency appointment*. Although, an *insolvency appointment* will be of the *Insolvency Practitioner* personally rather than his *practice* he should ensure that the standards set out in this Code are applied to all members of the *insolvency team*.

100.3 It is this Code, and the spirit that underlies it, that governs the conduct of *Insolvency Practitioners*. Failure to observe this Code may not, of itself, constitute professional misconduct, but will be taken into account in assessing the conduct of an *Insolvency Practitioner*.

Fundamental Principles

100.4 An *Insolvency Practitioner* is required to comply with the following fundamental principles:

(a) Integrity
An *Insolvency Practitioner* should be straightforward and honest in all professional and business relationships.

(b) Objectivity
An *Insolvency Practitioner* should not allow bias, conflict of interest or undue influence of others to override professional or business judgements.

(c) Professional Competence and Due Care
An *Insolvency Practitioner* has a continuing duty to maintain professional knowledge and skill at the level required to ensure that a client or employer receives competent professional service based on current developments in practice, legislation and techniques. An *Insolvency Practitioner* should act diligently and in accordance with applicable technical and professional standards when providing professional services.

(d) Confidentiality
An *Insolvency Practitioner* should respect the confidentiality of information acquired as a result of professional and business relationships and should not disclose any such information to third parties without proper and specific authority unless there is a legal or professional right or duty to disclose. Confidential information acquired as a result of professional and business relationships should not be used for the personal advantage of the *Insolvency Practitioner* or third parties.

(e) Professional Behaviour
An *Insolvency Practitioner* should comply with relevant laws and regulations and should avoid any action that discredits the profession. *Insolvency Practitioners* should conduct themselves with courtesy and consideration towards all with whom they come into contact when performing their work.

Framework Approach

100.6 The framework approach is a method which *Insolvency Practitioners* can use to identify actual or potential threats to the fundamental principles and determine whether there are any safeguards that might be available to offset them. The framework approach requires an *Insolvency Practitioner* to:

(a) take reasonable steps to identify any threats to compliance with the fundamental principles;
(b) evaluate any such threats; and
(c) respond in an appropriate manner to those threats.

100.7 Throughout this Code there are examples of threats and possible safeguards. These examples are illustrative and should not be considered as exhaustive lists of all relevant threats or safeguards. It is impossible to define every situation that creates a threat to compliance with the fundamental principles or to specify the safeguards that may be available.

Identification of threats to the fundamental principles

100.8 An *Insolvency Practitioner* should take reasonable steps to identify the existence of any threats to compliance with the fundamental principles which arise during the course of his professional work.

100.9 An *Insolvency Practitioner* should take particular care to identify the existence of threats which exist prior to or at the time of taking an *insolvency appointment* or which, at that stage, it may reasonably be expected might arise during the course of such an *insolvency appointment*. Sections 200 and 210 below contain particular factors an *Insolvency Practitioner* should take into account when deciding whether to accept an *insolvency appointment*.

100.10 In identifying the existence of any threats, an *Insolvency Practitioner* should have regard to relationships whereby the *practice* is held out as being part of a national or an international association.

100.11 Many threats fall into one or more of five categories:

(a) **Self-interest threats**: which may occur as a result of the financial or other interests of a *practice* or an *Insolvency Practitioner* or of a *close or immediate family* member of an *individual within the practice*;

(b) **Self-review threats**: which may occur when a previous judgement made by an *individual within the practice* needs to be re-evaluated by the *Insolvency Practitioner*;

(c) **Advocacy threats**: which may occur when an *individual within the practice* promotes a position or opinion to the point that subsequent objectivity may be compromised;

(d) **Familiarity threats**: which may occur when, because of a close relationship, an *individual within the practice* becomes too sympathetic or antagonistic to the interests of others; and

(e) **Intimidation threats**: which may occur when an *Insolvency Practitioner* may be deterred from acting objectively by threats, actual or perceived.

100.12 The following paragraphs give examples of the possible threats that an *Insolvency Practitioner* may face.

100.13 Examples of circumstances that may create self-interest threats for an *Insolvency Practitioner* include:

(a) An *individual within the practice* having an interest in a creditor or potential creditor with a claim which requires subjective adjudication.

(b) Concern about the possibility of damaging a business relationship.

(c) Concerns about potential future employment.

100.14 Examples of circumstances that may create self-review threats include:

(a) The acceptance of an *insolvency appointment* in respect of an *entity* where an *individual within the practice* has recently been employed by or seconded to that *entity*.

(b) An *Insolvency Practitioner* or the *practice* has carried out professional work of any description, including sequential *insolvency appointments*, for that *entity*.

Such self-review threats may diminish over the passage of time.

100.15 Examples of circumstances that may create advocacy threats include:

(a) Acting in an advisory capacity for a creditor of an *entity*.

(b) Acting as an advocate for a client in litigation or dispute with an *entity*.

100.16 Examples of circumstances that may create familiarity threats include:

(a) An *individual within the practice* having a close relationship with any individual having a financial interest in the insolvent *entity*.

(b) An *individual within the practice* having a close relationship with a potential purchaser of an insolvent's assets and/or business.

In this regard a close relationship includes both a close professional relationship and a close personal relationship.

100.17 Examples of circumstances that may create intimidation threats include:

(a) The threat of dismissal or replacement being used to:

   (i) Apply pressure not to follow regulations, this Code, any other applicable code, technical or professional standards.

   (ii) Exert influence over an *insolvency appointment* where the *Insolvency Practitioner* is an employee rather than *a principal* of the *practice*.

(b) Being threatened with litigation.

(c) The threat of a complaint being made to the *Insolvency Practitioner's authorising body*.

Evaluation of threats

100.18 An *Insolvency Practitioner* should take reasonable steps to evaluate any threats to compliance with the fundamental principles that he has identified.

100.19 In particular, an *Insolvency Practitioner* should consider what a reasonable and informed third party, having knowledge of all relevant information, including the significance of the threat, would conclude to be acceptable.

Possible Safeguards

100.20 Having identified and evaluated a threat to the fundamental principles an *Insolvency Practitioner* should consider whether there any safeguards that may be available to reduce the threat to an acceptable level. The relevant safeguards will vary depending on the circumstances. Generally safeguards fall into two broad categories. Firstly, safeguards created by the profession, legislation or regulation. Secondly, safeguards in the work environment. In the insolvency context safeguards in the work environment can include safeguards specific to an *insolvency appointment*. These are considered in section 200 below. In addition, safeguards can be introduced across the *practice*. These safeguards seek to create a work environment in which threats are identified and the introduction of appropriate safeguards is encouraged. Some examples include:

(a) Leadership that stresses the importance of compliance with the fundamental principles.

(b) Policies and procedures to implement and monitor quality control of engagements.

(c) Documented policies regarding the identification of threats to compliance with the fundamental principles, the evaluation of the significance of these threats and the identification and the application of safeguards to eliminate or reduce the threats, other than those that are trivial, to an acceptable level.

(d) Documented internal policies and procedures requiring compliance with the fundamental principles.

(e) Policies and procedures to consider the fundamental principles of this Code before the acceptance of an *insolvency appointment*.

(f) Policies and procedures regarding the identification of interests or relationships between *individuals within the practice* and third parties.

(g) Policies and procedures to prohibit individuals who are not members of the *insolvency team* from inappropriately influencing the outcome of an *insolvency appointment*.

(h) Timely communication of a *practice's* policies and procedures, including any changes to them, to all *individuals within the practice*, and appropriate training and education on such policies and procedures.

(i) Designating a member of senior management to be responsible for overseeing the adequate functioning of the safeguarding system.

(j) A disciplinary mechanism to promote compliance with policies and procedures.

(k) Published policies and procedures to encourage and empower individuals within the *practice* to communicate to senior levels within the *practice* and/or the *Insolvency Practitioner* any issue relating to compliance with the fundamental principles that concerns them.

PART 2: SPECIFIC APPLICATION OF THE CODE

Insolvency Appointments

200.1 The practice of insolvency is principally governed by statute and secondary legislation and in many cases is subject ultimately to the control of the Court. Where circumstances are dealt with by statute or secondary legislation, an *Insolvency Practitioner* must comply with such provisions. An *Insolvency Practitioner* must also comply with any relevant judicial authority relating to his conduct and any directions given by the Court.

200.2 An *Insolvency Practitioner* should act in a manner appropriate to his position as an officer of the Court (where applicable) and in accordance with any quasi-judicial, fiduciary or other duties that he may be under.

200.3 Before agreeing to accept any *insolvency appointment* (including a joint appointment), an *Insolvency Practitioner* should consider whether acceptance would create any threats to compliance with the fundamental principles. Of particular importance will be any threats to the fundamental principle of objectivity created by conflicts of interest or by any significant professional or personal relationships. These are considered in more detail below.

200.4 In considering whether objectivity or integrity may be threatened, an *Insolvency Practitioner* should identify and evaluate any professional or personal relationship (see section 220 below) which may affect compliance with the fundamental principles. The appropriate response to the threats arising from any such relationships should then be considered, together with the introduction of any possible safeguards.

200.5 Generally, it will be inappropriate for an *Insolvency Practitioner* to accept an *insolvency appointment* where a threat to the fundamental principles exists or may reasonably be expected might arise during the course of the *insolvency appointment* unless:

(a) disclosure is made, prior to the *insolvency appointment*, of the existence of such a threat to the Court or to the creditors on whose behalf the *Insolvency Practitioner* would be appointed to act and no objection is made to the *Insolvency Practitioner* being appointed; and

(b) safeguards are or will be available to eliminate or reduce that threat to an acceptable level. If the threat is other than trivial, safeguards should be considered and applied as necessary to reduce them to an acceptable level, where possible.

200.6 The following safeguards may be considered:

(a) Involving and/or consulting another *Insolvency Practitioner* from within the *practice* to review the work done.

(b) Consulting an independent third party, such as a committee of creditors, an *authorising body* or another *Insolvency Practitioner*.

(c) Involving another *Insolvency Practitioner* to perform part of the work, which may include another *Insolvency Practitioner* taking a joint appointment where the conflict arises during the course of the *insolvency appointment*.

(d) Obtaining legal advice from a solicitor or barrister with appropriate experience and expertise.

(e) Changing the members of the *insolvency team*.

(f) The use of separate *Insolvency Practitioners* and/or staff.

(g) Procedures to prevent access to information by the use of information barriers (e.g. strict physical separation of such teams, confidential and secure data filing).

(h) Clear guidelines for *individuals within the practice* on issues of security and confidentiality.

(i) The use of confidentiality agreements signed by *individuals within the practice*.

(j) Regular review of the application of safeguards by a senior *individual within the practice* not involved with the *insolvency appointment*.

(k) Terminating the financial or business relationship that gives rise to the threat.

(l) Seeking directions from the court.

200.7 As regards joint appointments, where an *Insolvency Practitioner* is specifically precluded by this Code from accepting an *insolvency appointment* as an individual, a joint appointment will not be an appropriate safeguard and will not make accepting the *insolvency appointment* appropriate.

200.8 In deciding whether to take an *insolvency appointment* in circumstances where a threat to the fundamental principles has been identified, the *Insolvency Practitioner* should consider whether the interests of those on whose behalf he would be appointed to act would best be served by the appointment of another *Insolvency Practitioner* who did not face the same threat and, if so, whether any such appropriately qualified and experienced other *Insolvency Practitioner* is likely to be available to be appointed.

200.9 *An Insolvency Practitioner* will encounter situations where no safeguards can reduce a threat to an acceptable level. Where this is the case, an *Insolvency Practitioner* should conclude that it is not appropriate to accept an *insolvency appointment.*

200.10 Following acceptance, any threats should continue to be kept under appropriate review and an *Insolvency Practitioner* should be mindful that other threats may come to light or arise. There may be occasions when the *Insolvency Practitioner* is no longer in compliance with this Code because of changed circumstances or something which has been inadvertently overlooked. This would generally not be an issue provided the *Insolvency Practitioner* has appropriate quality control policies and procedures in place to deal with such matters and, once discovered, the matter is corrected promptly and any necessary safeguards are applied. In deciding whether to continue an *insolvency appointment* the *Insolvency Practitioner* may take into account the wishes of the creditors, who after full disclosure has been made have the right to retain or replace the *Insolvency Practitioner*.

200.11 In all cases an *Insolvency Practitioner* will need to exercise his judgment to determine how best to deal with an identified threat. In exercising his judgment, an *Insolvency Practitioner* should consider what a reasonable and informed third party, having knowledge of all relevant information, including the significance of the threat and the safeguards applied, would conclude to be acceptable. This consideration will be affected by matters such as the significance of the threat, the nature of the work and the structure of the *practice*.

Conflicts of interest

200.12 An *Insolvency Practitioner* should take reasonable steps to identify circumstances that could pose a conflict of interest. Such circumstances may give rise to threats to compliance with the fundamental principles. Examples of where a conflict of interest may arise are where:

(a) An *Insolvency Practitioner* has to deal with claims between the separate and conflicting interests of entities over whom he is appointed.

(b) There is a succession of or there are sequential *insolvency appointments* (see section 280).

(c) A significant relationship has existed with the *entity* or someone connected with the *entity* (see also section 210).

200.13 Some of the safeguards listed at 200.6 may be applied to reduce the threats created by a conflict of interest to an acceptable level. Where a conflict of interest arises, the preservation of confidentiality will be of paramount importance; therefore, the safeguards used should generally include the use of effective information barriers.

Practice mergers

200.14 Where *practices* merge, they should subsequently be treated as one for the purposes of assessing threats to the fundamental principles. At the time of the merger, existing *insolvency appointments* should be reviewed and any threats identified. *Principals* and employees of the merged *practice* become subject to common ethical constraints in relation to accepting new *insolvency appointments* to clients of either of the former *practices*. However existing *insolvency appointments* which are rendered in apparent breach of the Code by such a merger need not be determined automatically, provided that a considered review of the situation by the *practice* discloses no obvious and immediate ethical conflict.

200.15 Where an *individual within the practice* has, in any former *practice*, undertaken work upon the affairs of an *entity* in a capacity that is incompatible with an *insolvency appointment* of the new *practice*, the individual should not work or be employed on that assignment.

Transparency

200.16 Both before and during an *insolvency appointment* an *Insolvency Practitioner* may acquire personal information that is not directly relevant to the insolvency or confidential commercial information relating to the affairs of third parties. The information may be such that others might expect that confidentiality would be maintained.

200.17 Nevertheless an *Insolvency Practitioner* in the role as office holder has a professional duty to report openly to those with an interest in the outcome of the insolvency. An *Insolvency Practitioner* should always report on his acts and dealings as fully as possible given the circumstances of the case, in a way that is transparent and understandable. An *Insolvency Practitioner* should bear in mind the expectations of others and what a reasonable and informed third party would consider appropriate.

Professional Competence and due care

200.18 Prior to accepting an *insolvency appointment* the *Insolvency Practitioner* should ensure that he is satisfied that the following matters have been considered:

(a) Obtaining knowledge and understanding of the *entity*, its owners, managers and those responsible for its governance and business activities.
(b) Acquiring an appropriate understanding of the nature of the *entity*'s business, the complexity of its operations, the specific requirements of the engagement and the purpose, nature and scope of the work to be performed.
(c) Acquiring knowledge of relevant industries or subject matters.
(d) Possessing or obtaining experience with relevant regulatory or reporting requirements.
(e) Assigning sufficient staff with the necessary competencies.
(f) Using experts where necessary.

(g) Complying with quality control policies and procedures designed to provide reasonable assurance that specific engagements are accepted only when they can be performed competently.

200.19 The fundamental principle of professional competence and due care requires that an *Insolvency Practitioner* should only accept an *insolvency appointment* when the *Insolvency Practitioner* has sufficient expertise. For example, a self interest threat to the fundamental principle of professional competence and due care is created if the *Insolvency Practitioner* or the *insolvency team* does not possess or cannot acquire the competencies necessary to carry out the *insolvency appointment*. Expertise will include appropriate training, technical knowledge, knowledge of the *entity* and the business with which the *entity* is concerned.

200.20 Maintaining and acquiring professional competence requires a continuing awareness and understanding of relevant technical and professional developments, including:

(a) Developments in insolvency legislation.
(b) Statements of Insolvency Practice.
(c) The regulations of their *authorising body*, including any continuing professional development requirements.
(d) Guidance issued by their *authorising body* or the Insolvency Service.
(e) Technical issues being discussed within the profession.

Section 210

Professional and personal relationships

210.1 The environment in which *Insolvency Practitioners* work and the relationships formed in their professional and personal lives can lead to threats to the fundamental principle of objectivity.

Identifying relationships

210.2 In particular, the principle of objectivity may be threatened if any *individual within the practice*, the *close or immediate family* of an *individual within the practice* or the *practice* itself, has or has had a professional or personal relationship which relates to the *insolvency appointment* being considered

210.3 Professional or personal relationships may include (but are not restricted to) relationships with—

(a) the *entity*;
(b) any director or shadow director or former director or shadow director of the *entity*;
(c) shareholders of the *entity*;
(d) any *principal* or employee of the *entity*;
(e) business partners of the *entity*;
(f) companies or entities controlled by the *entity*;
(g) companies which are under common control;
(h) creditors (including debenture holders) of the *entity*;
(i) debtors of the *entity*;
(j) *close or immediate family* of the *entity*(if an individual) or its officers (if a corporate body);
(k) others with commercial relationships with the *practice*.

210.4 Safeguards within the *practice* should include policies and procedures to identify relationships between *individuals within the practice* and third parties in a way that is proportionate and reasonable in relation to the *insolvency appointment* being considered.

Is the relationship significant to the conduct of the *insolvency appointment*?

210.5 Where a professional or personal relationship of the type described in paragraph 210.2 has been identified the *Insolvency Practitioner* should evaluate the impact of the relationship in the context of the *insolvency appointment* being sought or considered. Issues to consider in evaluating whether a relationship creates a threat to the fundamental principles may include the following:

   (a) The nature of the previous duties undertaken by a *practice* during an earlier relationship with the *entity*.
   (b) The impact of the work conducted by the *practice* on the financial state and/or the financial stability of the *entity* in respect of which the *insolvency appointment* is being considered.
   (c) Whether the fee received for the work by the *practice* is or was significant to the *practice* itself or is or was substantial.
   (d) How recently any professional work was carried out. It is likely that greater threats will arise (or may be seen to arise) where work has been carried out within the previous three years. However, there may still be instances where, in respect of non-audit work, any threat is at an acceptable level. Conversely, there may be situations whereby the nature of the work carried out was such that a considerably longer period should elapse before any threat can be reduced to an acceptable level.
   (e) Whether the *insolvency appointment* being considered involves consideration of any work previously undertaken by the *practice* for that *entity*.
   (f) The nature of any personal relationship and the proximity of the *Insolvency Practitioner* to the individual with whom the relationship exists and, where appropriate, the proximity of that individual to the *entity* in relation to which the *insolvency appointment* relates.
   (g) Whether any reporting obligations will arise in respect of the relevant individual with whom the relationship exists (e.g. an obligation to report on the conduct of directors and shadow directors of a company to which the *insolvency appointment* relates).
   (h) The nature of any previous duties undertaken by an *individual within the practice* during any earlier relationship with the *entity*.
   (i) The extent of the *insolvency team's* familiarity with the individuals connected with the *entity*.

210.6 Having identified and evaluated a relationship that may create a threat to the fundamental principles, the *Insolvency Practitioner* should consider his response including the introduction of any possible safeguards to reduce the threat to an acceptable level.

210.7 Some of the safeguards which may be considered to reduce the threat created by a professional or personal relationship to an acceptable level are considered in paragraph 200.6. Other safeguards may include:

   (a) Withdrawing from the *insolvency team*.
   (b) Terminating (where possible) the financial or business relationship giving rise to the threat.
   (c) Disclosure of the relationship and any financial benefit received by the *practice* (whether directly or indirectly) to the *entity* or to those on whose behalf the *Insolvency Practitioner* would be appointed to act.

210.8   An Insolvency Practitioner may encounter situations in which no or no reasonable safeguards can be introduced to eliminate a threat arising from a professional or personal relationship, or to reduce it to an acceptable level. In such situations, the relationship in question will constitute a *significant* professional relationship ("Significant Professional Relationship") or a *significant* personal relationship ("Significant Personal Relationship"). Where this is case the Insolvency Practitioner should conclude that it is not appropriate to take the *insolvency appointment*.

210.9   Consideration should always be given to the perception of others when deciding whether to accept an *insolvency appointment*. Whilst an Insolvency Practitioner may regard a relationship as not being significant to the *insolvency appointment*, the perception of others may differ and this may in some circumstances be sufficient to make the relationship significant.

Section 220

Dealing with the assets of an entity

220.1   Actual or perceived threats (for example self interest threats) to the fundamental principles may arise when during an *insolvency appointment*, an Insolvency Practitioner realises assets.

220.2   Save in circumstances which clearly do not impair the Insolvency Practitioner's objectivity, Insolvency Practitioners appointed to any *insolvency appointment* in relation to an *entity*, should not themselves acquire, directly or indirectly, any of the assets of an *entity*, nor knowingly permit *any individual within the practice*, or any *close or immediate family member* of the Insolvency Practitioner or of an *individual within the practice*, directly or indirectly, to do so.

220.3   Where the assets and business of an insolvent company are sold by an Insolvency Practitioner shortly after appointment on pre-agreed terms, this could lead to an actual or perceived threat to objectivity. The sale may also be seen as a threat to objectivity by creditors or others not involved in the prior agreement. The threat to objectivity may be eliminated or reduced to an acceptable level by safeguards such as obtaining an independent valuation of the assets or business being sold, or the consideration of other potential purchasers.

220.4   It is also particularly important for an Insolvency Practitioner to take care to ensure (where to do so does not conflict with any legal or professional obligation) that his decision making processes are transparent, understandable and readily identifiable to all third parties who may be affected by the sale or proposed sale.

Section 230

Obtaining specialist advice and services

230.1   When an Insolvency Practitioner intends to rely on the advice or work of another, the Insolvency Practitioner should evaluate whether such reliance is warranted. The Insolvency Practitioner should consider factors such as reputation, expertise, resources available and applicable professional and ethical standards. Any payment to the third party should reflect the value of the work undertaken.

230.2   Threats to the fundamental principles (for example familiarity threats and self interest threats) can arise if services are provided by a regular source independent of the *practice*.

230.3   Safeguards should be introduced to reduce such threats to an acceptable level. These safeguards should ensure that a proper business relationship is maintained between the parties and that such relationships are reviewed periodically to ensure that best value and service is being obtained in relation to each *insolvency appointment*. Additional safeguards may include clear guidelines and policies within the *practice* on such relationships. An Insolvency Practitioner should also consider disclosure of the existence of such business relationships to the general body of creditors or the creditor's committee if one exists.

230.4   Threats to the fundamental principles can also arise where services are provided from within the *practice* or by a party with whom the *practice*, or an *individual within the practice*, has a business or personal relationship. An Insolvency Practitioner should take particular care in such circumstances to ensure that the best value and service is being provided.

Section 240

Fees and other types of remuneration

Prior to accepting an insolvency appointment

240.1   Where an engagement may lead to an *insolvency appointment*, an Insolvency Practitioner should make any party to the work aware of the terms of the work and, in particular, the basis on which any fees are charged and which services are covered by those fees.

240.2   Where an engagement may lead to an *insolvency appointment*, Insolvency Practitioners should not accept referral fees or commissions unless they have established safeguards to reduce the threats created by such fees or commissions to an acceptable level.

240.3   Safeguards may include disclosure in advance of any arrangements. If after receiving any such payments, an Insolvency Practitioner accepts an *insolvency appointment*, the amount and source of any fees or commissions received should be disclosed to creditors.

After accepting an insolvency appointment

240.4   During an *insolvency appointment*, accepting referral fees or commissions represents a significant threat to objectivity. Such fees or commissions should not therefore be accepted other than where to do so is for the benefit of the insolvent estate.

240.5   If such fees or commissions are accepted they should only be accepted or the benefit of the estate; not for the benefit of the Insolvency Practitioner or the *practice*.

240.6   Further, where such fees or commissions are accepted an Insolvency Practitioner should consider making disclosure to creditors.

Section 250

Obtaining insolvency appointments

250.1   The special nature of *insolvency appointments* makes the payment or offer of any commission for or the furnishing of any valuable consideration towards, the introduction of *insolvency appointments* inappropriate. This does not, however, preclude an arrangement between an Insolvency Practitioner and an employee whereby the employee's remuneration is based in whole or in part on introductions obtained for the Insolvency Practitioner through the efforts of the employee.

250.2 When an Insolvency Practitioner seeks an *insolvency appointment* or work that may lead to an *insolvency appointment* through advertising or other forms of marketing, there may be threats to compliance with the fundamental principles.

250.3 When considering whether to accept an *insolvency appointment* an Insolvency Practitioner should satisfy himself that any advertising or other form of marketing pursuant to which the *insolvency appointment* may have been obtained is or has been:

    (a)   Fair and not misleading.

    (b)   Avoids unsubstantiated or disparaging statements.

    (c)   Complies with relevant codes of practice and guidance in relation to advertising.

250.4 Advertisements and other forms of marketing should be clearly distinguishable as such and be legal, decent, honest and truthful.

250.5 If reference is made in advertisements or other forms of marketing to fees or to the cost of the services to be provided, the basis of calculation and the range of services that the reference is intended to cover should be provided. Care should be taken to ensure that such references do not mislead as to the precise range of services and the time commitment that the reference is intended to cover.

250.6 An Insolvency Practitioner should never promote or seek to promote his services, or the services of another Insolvency Practitioner, in such a way, or to such an extent as to amount to harassment.

250.7 Where an Insolvency Practitioner or the *practice* advertises for work via a third party, the Insolvency Practitioner is responsible for ensuring that the third party follows the above guidance.

Section 260

Gifts and hospitality

260.1 An Insolvency Practitioner, or *a close or immediate family* member, may be offered gifts and hospitality. In relation to an *insolvency appointment*, such an offer will give rise to threats to compliance with the fundamental principles. For example, self-interest threats may arise if a gift is accepted and intimidation threats may arise from the possibility of such offers being made public.

260.2 The significance of such threats will depend on the nature, value and intent behind the offer. In deciding whether to accept any offer of a gift or hospitality the Insolvency Practitioner should have regard to what a reasonable and informed third party having knowledge of all relevant information would consider to be appropriate. Where such a reasonable and informed third party would consider the gift to be made in the normal course of business without the specific intent to influence decision making or obtain information the Insolvency Practitioner may generally conclude that there is no significant threat to compliance with the fundamental principles.

260.3 Where appropriate, safeguards should be considered and applied as necessary to eliminate any threats to the fundamental principles or reduce them to an acceptable level. If an Insolvency Practitioner encounters a situation in which no or no reasonable safeguards can be introduced to reduce a threat arising from offers of gifts or hospitality to an acceptable level he should conclude that it is not appropriate to accept the offer.

260.4   An Insolvency Practitioner should also not offer or provide gifts or hospitality where this would give rise to an unacceptable threat to compliance with the fundamental principles.

Section 270

Record keeping

270.1   It will always be for the Insolvency Practitioner to justify his actions. An Insolvency Practitioner will be expected to be able to demonstrate the steps that he took and the conclusions that he reached in identifying, evaluating and responding to any threats, both leading up to and during an *insolvency appointment*, by reference to written contemporaneous records.

270.2   The records an Insolvency Practitioner maintains, in relation to the steps that he took and the conclusions that he reached, should be sufficient to enable a reasonable and informed third party to reach a view on the appropriateness of his actions.

THE APPLICATION OF THE FRAMEWORK TO SPECIFIC SITUATIONS

Section 280

Introduction to specific situations

280.1   The following examples describe specific circumstances and relationships that will create threats to compliance with the fundamental principles. The examples may assist an Insolvency Practitioner and the members of the *insolvency team* to assess the implications of similar, but different, circumstances and relationships.

280.2   The examples are divided into three parts. Part 1 contains examples which do not relate to a previous or existing *insolvency appointment*. Part 2 contains examples that do relate to a previous or existing *insolvency appointment*. Part 3 contains some examples under Scottish law. The examples are not intended to be exhaustive.

Part 1: Examples that do not Relate to a Previous or Existing Insolvency Appointment

280.3   The following situations involve a professional relationship which does *not* consist of a previous *insolvency appointment*:

Insolvency appointment following audit related work

Relationship: The *practice* or an *individual within the practice* has previously carried out audit related work within the previous 3 years.

Response: A Significant Professional Relationship will arise: an Insolvency Practitioner should conclude that it is not appropriate to take the *insolvency appointment*.

Where audit related work was carried out more than three years before the proposed date of the appointment of the Insolvency Practitioner a threat to compliance with the fundamental principles may still arise. The Insolvency Practitioner should evaluate any such threat and consider whether the threat can be eliminated or reduced to an acceptable level by the existence or introduction of safeguards.

This restriction does not apply where the *insolvency appointment* is in a members' voluntary liquidation; an Insolvency Practitioner may normally take an appointment as liquidator. However, the Insolvency Practitioner should consider whether there are any other circumstances that give rise to an unacceptable threat to compliance with the fundamental principles. Further, the Insolvency Practitioner should satisfy himself that the directors' declaration of solvency is likely to be substantiated by events.

Appointment as Investigating Accountant at the instigation of a creditor

Previous relationship: The *practice* or an *individual within the practice* was instructed by, or at the instigation of, a creditor or other party having a financial interest in an entity, to investigate, monitor or advise on its affairs.

Response: A Significant Professional Relationship would *not* normally arise in these circumstances provided that—

(a) there has not been a direct involvement by *an individual within the practice* in the management of the entity; and

(b) the *practice* had its principal client relationship with the creditor or other party, rather than with the company or proprietor of the business; and

(c) the entity was aware of this.

An Insolvency Practitioner should however consider all the circumstances before accepting an *insolvency appointment*, including the effect of any discussions or lack of discussions about the financial affairs of the company with its directors, and whether such circumstances give rise to an unacceptable threat to compliance with the fundamental principles.

Where such an investigation was conducted at the request of, or at the instigation of, a secured creditor who then requests an Insolvency Practitioner to accept an *insolvency appointment* as an administrator or administrative receiver, the Insolvency Practitioner should satisfy himself that the company, acting by its board of directors, does not object to him taking such an *insolvency appointment*. If the secured creditor does not give prior warning of the *insolvency appointment* to the company or if such warning is given and the company objects but the secured creditor still wishes to appoint the Insolvency Practitioner, he should consider whether the circumstances give rise to an unacceptable any threat to compliance with the fundamental principles.

Part 2: Examples Relating to Previous or Existing Insolvency Appointments

280.6 The following situations involve a prior professional relationship that involves a previous or existing *insolvency appointment*:-

Insolvency appointment following an appointment as Administrative or other Receiver

Previous appointment: An *individual within the practice* has been administrative or other receiver.

Proposed appointment: Any insolvency appointment.

Response: An Insolvency Practitioner should not accept any insolvency appointment.

This restriction does not, however, apply where the *individual within the practice* was appointed a receiver by the Court. In such circumstances, the Insolvency Practitioner should however consider whether any other circumstances which give rise to an unacceptable threat to compliance with the fundamental principles.

Administration or Liquidation following appointment as Supervisor of a Voluntary Arrangement

Previous appointment: An *individual within the practice* has been supervisor of a company voluntary arrangement.

Proposed appointment: Administrator or liquidator.

Response: An Insolvency Practitioner may normally accept an appointment as administrator or liquidator. However the Insolvency Practitioner should consider whether there are any circumstances that give rise to an unacceptable threat to compliance with the fundamental principles.

Liquidation following appointment as Administrator

Previous Appointment: An *individual within the practice* has been administrator.

Proposed Appointment: Liquidator.

Response: An Insolvency Practitioner may normally accept an appointment as liquidator provided he has complied with the relevant legislative requirements. However, the Insolvency Practitioner should also consider whether there are any circumstances that give rise to an unacceptable threat to compliance with the fundamental principles.

Conversion of Members' Voluntary Liquation into Creditors' Voluntary Liquidation

Previous appointment: An *individual within the practice* has been the liquidator of a company in a members' voluntary liquidation.

Proposed appointment: Liquidator in a creditors' voluntary liquidation, where it has been necessary to convene a creditors' meeting.

Response: Where there has been a Significant Professional Relationship, an Insolvency Practitioner may continue or accept an appointment (subject to creditors' approval) only if he concludes that the company will eventually be able to pay its debts in full, together with interest.

However, the Insolvency Practitioner should consider whether there are any other circumstances that give rise to an unacceptable threat to compliance with the fundamental principles.

Bankruptcy following appointment as Supervisor of an Individual Voluntary Arrangement

Previous appointment: An *individual within the practice* has been supervisor of an individual voluntary arrangement.

Proposed Appointment: Trustee in bankruptcy.

Response: An Insolvency Practitioner may normally accept an appointment as trustee in bankruptcy. However, the Insolvency Practitioner should consider whether there are any circumstances that give rise to an unacceptable threat to compliance with the fundamental principles.

Part 3: Examples in Respect of Cases Conducted Under Scottish Law

Sequestration following appointment as Trustee under a Trust Deed for creditors

Previous appointment: An *individual within the practice* has been trustee under a trust deed for creditors.

Proposed appointment: Interim trustee or trustee in sequestration.

Response An Insolvency Practitioner may normally accept an appointment as an interim trustee or trustee in sequestration. However, the Insolvency Practitioner should consider whether there are any circumstances that give rise to an unacceptable threat to compliance with the fundamental principles.

Sequestration where the Accountant in Bankruptcy is Trustee following appointment as Trustee under a Trust Deed for creditors

Previous appointment: An *individual within the practice* has been trustee under a trust deed for creditors.

Proposed appointment: Agent for the Accountant in Bankruptcy in sequestration.

Response: An Insolvency Practitioner may normally accept an appointment as agent for the Accountant in Bankruptcy. However, the Insolvency Practitioner should consider whether there are any circumstances that give rise to an unacceptable threat to compliance with the fundamental principles.

THE LAW SOCIETY OF SCOTLAND PRACTICE RULES 2011

Index

F3.13

Rules dated 27 May 2011, made by the Council of the Law Society of Scotland under:
  (a) in the case of all rules in Section A of these rules (save for rules 3.1.5, 3.1.6, 3.1.7 to 3.1.12 (inclusive), 3.1.14 and 3.3 in that Section), all rules in

Section B of these rules (save for rules 6 and 7 in that Section), all rules in Section C of these rules (save for rules 2 and 4 in that Section) and all rules in Section D of these rules (save for rules 6, 7 and 9 in that Section), section 34(1) of the Solicitors (Scotland) Act 1980 (in this preamble "the Act") and approved by the Lord President of the Court of Session ("the Lord President") in terms of section 34(3) of the Act;

(b)   in the case of rule 3.1.5 in Section A of these rules and rule 6 in Section D of these rules, regulation 16 of the European Communities (Lawyer's Practice) (Scotland) Regulations 2000 (SSI 2000 No.121) and section 24A of the Act;

(c)   in the case of rule 3.1.6 in Section A of these rules, sections 34(1), 35(1), 37(6) and 43 of, and Schedule 3 to, the Act and approved by the Lord President in terms of section 34(3) of the Act;

(d)   in the case of rules 3.1.7 in Section A of these rules and rule 7 in Section D of these rules, section 60A(2) of the Act and approved by the Lord President in terms of section 34(3) of the Act;

(e)   in the case of rules 3.1.8 to 3.1.12 (inclusive), 3.1.14 and 3.3 in Section A of these rules, sections 34, 35, 36 and 37 of, and paragraphs 4(1) and (4) of Schedule 3 to, the Act and approved by the Lord President in terms of section 34(3) of the Act; and also with the concurrence of the Lord President in terms of sections 5 and 44 of the Act;

(f)   in the case of rule 6 in Section B of these rules, sections 34(1), 35(1), 37(6) and 43 of, and paragraph 4(4) of Part 1 of Schedule 3 to, the Act and approved by the Lord President in terms of section 34(3) of the Act;

(g)   in the case of rule 7 in Section B of these rules, section 44 of the Act with the concurrence of the Lord President in terms of the section;

(h)   in the case of rule 2 in Section C of these rules, section 34(1) of the Act and approved by the Lord President in terms of section 34(3) of the Act and by the Financial Services Authority in terms of section 332(5) of the Financial Services and Markets Act 2000;

(i)   in the case of rules 4.1 and 4.2 in Section C of these rules, section 25A(4) of the Act and approved by the Lord President in terms of section 34(3) of the Act and by the Scottish Ministers (following consultation with the Office of Fair Trading) in terms of sections 25A(9) and 64B of the Act;

(j)   in the case of rule 4.3 in Section C of these rules, section 25A(6) of the Act and approved by the Lord President in terms of section 34(3) of the Act;

(k)   in the case of rule 4.4 in Section C of these rules, section 25A(5) of the Act and approved by the Lord President in terms of section 34(3) of the Act and by the Scottish Ministers (following any consultation with the Office of Fair Trading required in terms of section 25A(11) of the Act) in terms of section 64B of the Act; and

(l)   in the case of rule 9 in Section D of these rules, section 34 of the Act and approved by the Scottish Ministers (following consultation with the Office of Fair Trading) in terms of section 34(3A) of the Act.

Section A: General Provisions

Citation and Commencement

1.1   These rules may be cited as the Law Society of Scotland Practice Rules 2011.

1.2   These rules shall come into operation on 1 November 2011.

Definitions and Interpretation

2.1 In these rules, unless stated to the contrary or the context otherwise requires, terms listed in the first column of Schedule 1 to these rules shall have the meanings respectively ascribed to them in the second column of Schedule 1.

2.2 The provisions of the Interpretation Act 1978 shall apply to these rules as they apply to an Act of Parliament.

2.3 Neither the headings to these rules nor the headings to the Schedules to these rules nor the Index at the start of the document containing these rules shall form part of these rules.

2.4 Unless the context otherwise requires, any reference in these rules to a:
  (a) Section identified by a letter refers to the Section bearing that letter in these rules;
  (b) numbered rule within a Section of these rules refers to the rule bearing that number in the same Section; or
  (c) numbered Schedule refers to the Schedule bearing that number in the Schedules to these rules.

Application

3.1 Save where and to the extent stated to the contrary in any of these rules:
  3.1.1 if you are a solicitor the following rules apply to you:

  (a) all rules in Section A;
  (b) rules 1 and 8.3 in Section B;
  (c) rules 1, 3 and 9 in Section D;
  3.1.2 if you are a practising solicitor the following rules apply to you:

  (a) all rules in Section A;
  (b) all rules in Section B save for rules 5 and 7;
  (c) all rules in Section D save for rules 2.2, 2.3, 4, 5, 6 and 7;
  3.1.3 if you are a practising solicitor who is a manager the following rules apply to you:

  (a) all rules in Section A;
  (b) all rules in Section B;
  (c) all rules in Section D save for rules 6 and 7;
  3.1.4 if you are a practising solicitor (including, for the avoidance of any doubt, a manager):

  (a) conducting cross-border practice, then rule 1 in Section C shall also apply to you;
  (b) seeking to carry on or carrying on incidental financial business, then rule 2 in Section C shall also apply to you;
  (c) seeking to provide or providing legal aid, then rule 3 in Section C shall also apply to you;
  (d) seeking to exercise or exercising rights of audience, then rule 4 in Section C shall also apply to you;
  3.1.5 if you are a European lawyer seeking registration as a registered European lawyer then all rules in Section A and rule 6 in Section D apply to you;
  3.1.6 if you are a registered European lawyer then the same rules apply to you as would apply to a practising solicitor of equivalent status engaged in the same work save that:

(a) rule 7 in Section B, rules 4.1 and 4.2 in Section C and rule 1 in Section D shall not apply to you;

(b) rule 6 in Section D shall also apply to you;

(c) in their application to you these rules shall be construed subject to any contrary provision contained in the Directive, the European Lawyer Regulations or rule 6 in Section D;

3.1.7 if you are a foreign lawyer seeking registration as a registered foreign lawyer then all rules in Section A and rule 7 in Section D apply to you;

3.1.8 if you are a registered foreign lawyer the following rules apply to you:

(a) all rules in Section A;

(b) rules 1, 6 & 7 in Section B;

(c) rules 3, 4, 7, 8.2 and 9.1 in Section D;

3.1.9 if you are a registered foreign lawyer acting in pursuance of the Scottish practice of a multi-national practice the following rules apply to you, insofar as you are so acting:

(a) all rules in Section A;

(b) all rules in Section B save for rules 4, 5, 8.3 and 8.4;

(c) rules 3, 4, 7, 8.2 and 9 in Section D;

3.1.10 if you are a registered foreign lawyer who is a member of a Scottish multi-national practice the following rules apply to you:

(a) all rules in Section A;

(b) all rules in Section B save for rule 8.4.2;

(c) all rules in Section D save for rules 1, 2.1, 6 and 8.1;

3.1.11 if you are a registered foreign lawyer conducting cross-border practice, then rule 1 in Section C shall also apply to you;

3.1.12 if you are a registered foreign lawyer who is a member of a Scottish multi-national practice seeking to carry on or carrying on incidental financial business, then rule 2 in Section C shall also apply to you;

3.1.13 if you are a practice unit (excepting (i) a multi-national practice which is not a Scottish multi-national practice; and (ii) a licensed provider) the same rules apply to you as would apply to a practising solicitor who is also a manager engaged in the same work save that:

(a) rule 4 in Section C and rules 1, 2.1 and 2.2 in Section D shall not apply to you; and

(b) rule 5 in Section D shall only apply to you if you are, or seek to form, an incorporated practice;

3.1.14 if you are a multi-national practice which is not a Scottish multi-national practice but which is acting in pursuance of a Scottish practice the following rules apply to you insofar as you are so acting:

(a) all rules in Section A;

(b) all rules in Section B save for rules 4, 5, 8.3 and 8.4;

(c) rules 3, 4, 8, and 9 in Section D;

(d) when conducting cross-border practice, rule 1 in Section C;

(e) when seeking to provide or providing legal aid, rule 3 in Section C.

3.2 Subject to rule 3.3, where any of these rules apply (or are stated to apply) to a practice unit the managers of the practice unit shall ensure that the practice unit complies with same and the relevant rules shall also apply to the managers of the practice unit.

3.3   Reference in any of these rules to a multi-national practice shall not, of itself, apply that rule to any registered foreign lawyer who is a member of that multi-national practice where that rule would not otherwise apply to him. However, where any of these rules applies to a multi-national practice, no registered foreign lawyer or other regulated person who is a member of that multi-national practice (or of a member body of that multi-national practice) shall cause or knowingly permit that multi-national practice not to comply with that rule so far as it is applicable to that multi-national practice, even where that rule or regulation does not apply to him.

Failure to Comply

4.   Failure to comply with these rules may be treated as professional misconduct or unsatisfactory professional conduct.

Waiver

5.1   Subject to rule 5.2 the Council shall have the power to waive any of the provisions of these rules in any particular circumstances or case, provided that such waiver may be made subject to such conditions as the Council may in its discretion determine.

5.2   Rule 5.1 shall not apply to the rules listed in Schedule 2. The Council shall have no power to waive any of the rules so listed.

Revocation and Savings

6.1   The rules and regulations listed in Schedule 3 are hereby revoked and such revocation shall have the equivalent effect as would the repeal of an enactment by an Act of Parliament pursuant to section 16 of the Interpretation Act 1978.

6.2   Without prejudice to the generality of rule 6.1 but for the avoidance of any doubt, such revocation shall not:
  (a)   affect the validity of any application or determination made, certificate granted or other thing done under the rules and regulations listed in Schedule 3 and such application, determination, certificate or thing shall have effect as if it were made, granted or done under these rules;
  (b)   cause the interruption of time periods nor affect any obligation to deliver any certificate, application or any other document, information or thing to the Council or the Society nor the rights of the Council or the Society against any person in respect of his failure to deliver such a certificate, application, document, information or thing; or
  (c)   affect the taking or continuation of any proceedings by, or the exercise or continued exercise of any power available to the Society, the Council or any other person in respect of any act or thing done or omitted to be done under, any breach of, or any matter arising from, any of the rules and regulations listed in Schedule 3.

Communication and Notices

7.1   Subject to rule 7.2, where any of these rules permits or requires the Society or the Council to give or send a notice to, or serve a notice on, any person then such notice shall be:
  (a)   in writing;
  (b)   signed by the Secretary;

(c)   addressed to such person at the business address (or, in the case of such person not having intimated a current business address, the address for correspondence) most recently intimated, in writing, to the Society by such person;

(d)   sent by recorded delivery post or delivered by hand to the addressee at that address;

(e)   deemed to have been received by the addressee (i) in the case of a notice sent by recorded delivery post, on the expiry of the period of forty eight hours after the time of posting; or (ii) in the case of a notice delivered by hand, at the time of delivery as evidenced by a written acknowledgment of such delivery at a stated date and time, signed by the addressee or by a person holding himself out as authorised to accept such delivery on behalf of the addressee.

7.2   Where the person referred to in rule 7.1 is a practice unit then any such notice shall be addressed:

(a)   in the case of a notice permitted or required pursuant to rule 6 in Section B, to the practice unit care of the Cashroom Manager, as defined in that rule, at the business address most recently intimated, in writing, to the Society by such manager;

(b)   in the case of a notice permitted or required pursuant to rule 5 in Section B or related to any complaint received or referred to the Society in respect of a practice unit, to the practice unit care of the Client Relations Manager (or Lead Client Relations Manager, where the practice unit has one) at the business address most recently intimated, in writing, to the Society by such manager;

(c)   in the case of a notice permitted or required pursuant to rule 3 in Section C, to the practice unit care of the Compliance Manager at the relevant business address most recently intimated, in writing, to the Society by such manager;

(d)   in all other cases, to all of the managers of the practice unit as most recently intimated, in writing, to the Society at the appropriate business address most recently intimated, in writing, to the Society by such managers.

Provided that nothing in this rule 7 shall prevent the Council or the Society from addressing any notice in respect of a practice unit to all of the managers of that practice unit in accordance with paragraph (d) of this rule 7.2 should the Council or the Society, at their discretion, deem that appropriate.

7.3   Where any of these rules permits or requires a person to give or send a notice to, or serve a notice on, the Society or the Council then such notice shall be—

(a)   addressed to the Secretary at the principal business address of the Society most recently intimated generally by the Society;

(b)   sent by recorded delivery post or delivered by hand to the addressee at that address;

(c)   deemed to have been received by the addressee (i) in the case of a notice sent by recorded delivery post, on the expiry of the period of forty eight hours after the time of posting; or (ii) in the case of a notice delivered by hand, at the time of delivery as evidenced by a written acknowledgment of such delivery at a stated date and time, signed by the addressee or by a person holding himself out as authorised to accept such delivery on behalf of the addressee.

7.4   Where any of these rules permits or requires the Society or the Council to intimate any decision, matter or thing to any person then such intimation may be in whatever form the Society or the Council may deem appropriate, subject to the taking of reasonable precautions to protect the confidentiality of any material which the Society or Council knows to be confidential. Without prejudice to the foregoing generality, such intimations may be made by email to the email address most recently provided to the Society by the addressee and, in the case of intimations to practice units and those within them and to the public generally, may be deemed to have been made by the inclusion of the decision, matter or thing in the information available from time to time on any website of the Society.

Section B: Fundamental Principles And Client Care

Rule B1: Standards of Conduct

Application

1.1   Save when and to the extent engaged in cross-border practice you shall comply with the standards of conduct set out in this rule 1.

Trust and personal integrity

1.2   You must be trustworthy and act honestly at all times so that your personal integrity is beyond question. In particular, you must not behave, whether in a professional capacity or otherwise, in a way which is fraudulent or deceitful.

Independence

1.3   You must give independent advice free from external influences or personal interests which are inconsistent with these standards. It is your duty not to allow your independence to be impaired irrespective of the nature of the matter in which you are acting.

The interests of the client

1.4.1   You must act in the best interests of your clients subject to preserving your independence and complying with the law, these rules and the principles of good professional conduct.

1.4.2   You must not permit your own personal interests or those of the legal profession in general to influence your advice to or actings on behalf of clients.

1.4.3   You must at all times do, and be seen to do, your best for your client and must be fearless in defending your client's interests, regardless of the consequences to yourself (including, if necessary, incurring the displeasure of the bench). But you must also remember that your client's best interests require you to give honest advice however unwelcome that advice may be to the client and that your duty to your client is only one of several duties which you must strive to reconcile.

Proper instructions

1.5.1   You are the agent of your client and must have the authority of your client for your actings. You must not accept improper instructions, for example to assist a client in a matter which you know to be criminal or fraudulent, but you may properly advise on the legal consequences of a proposed course of action or on the scope or application of the law to particular circumstances.

1.5.2 You may decline to accept new instructions, whether from a new or established client, without giving a reason for doing so, provided the refusal to act is not motivated by discrimination in breach of rule 1.15.

Confidentiality

1.6 You must maintain client confidentiality. This duty is not terminated by the passage of time. You must also supervise your employees to ensure that they keep client matters confidential. Only the client, Acts of the legislature, subordinate legislation or the court can waive or override the duty of confidentiality. The duty does not apply to information about any crime a client indicates they will commit.

Conflict of Interest

1.7.1 You must not act for two or more clients in matters where there is a conflict of interest between the clients or for any client where there is a conflict between the interest of the client and your interest or that of your practice unit.

1.7.2 Even where there is only a potential conflict of interest you must exercise caution. Where the potential for conflict is significant, you must not act for both parties without the full knowledge and express consent of the clients.

Disclosure of Interest

1.8 Where you are consulted about a matter in which you have, or your practice unit has, a personal or a financial interest, the position must be made clear to the client as soon as possible. If the interest is such that you cannot reasonably give independent advice, you must decline to act and advise the client to seek appropriate advice elsewhere.

Effective communication

1.9.1 You must communicate effectively with your clients and others. This includes providing clients with any relevant information which you have and which is necessary to allow informed decisions to be made by clients. It also includes accounting to clients for funds passing through your hands. Information must be clear and comprehensive and, where necessary or appropriate, confirmed in writing.

1.9.2 You must advise your clients of any significant development in relation to their case or transaction and explain matters to the extent reasonably necessary to permit informed decisions by clients regarding the instructions which require to be given by them. In particular you must advise clients in writing when it becomes known that the cost of work will materially exceed any estimate that has been given and must also advise the client in writing when the limit of the original estimate is being approached.

Competence, diligence and appropriate skills

1.10 You must only act in those matters where you are competent to do so. You must only accept instructions where the matter can be carried out adequately and completely within a reasonable time. You must exercise the level of skill appropriate to the matter.

Professional fees

1.11.1 The fees you charge must be fair and reasonable in all the circumstances.

1.11.2   When the work is to be charged at an hourly rate, you must inform the client what that hourly rate will be and of any change to the hourly rate.

Withdrawing from acting if instructions are accepted

1.12   You must not cease to act for clients without just cause and without giving reasonable notice, or in a manner which would prejudice the course of justice. So far as possible, the client's interests should not be adversely affected, but you are entitled to exercise your rights in law to recover your justified fees and outlays.

Relations with the courts

1.13.1   You must never knowingly give false or misleading information to the court. You must maintain due respect and courtesy towards the court while honourably pursuing the interests of your clients.

1.13.2   You must not do or say anything which could affect evidence or induce a witness, a party to an action, or an accused person to do otherwise than give in evidence a truthful and honest account of that person's recollection.

1.13.3   As far as reasonably practical, you must give reasonable notice to witnesses of court hearings and when questioning witnesses, treat them with appropriate respect and courtesy.

1.13.4   Where you appear against a person who represents him or herself, you must avoid taking unfair advantage of that person and must, consistently with your duty to your client, co-operate with the court in enabling that person's case to be fairly stated and justice to be done. However you must not sacrifice the interests of your client to those of the person representing him or herself.

1.13.5   In rule 1.13 references to the "court" include tribunals and other bodies or persons exercising judicial or determinative functions.

Relations between regulated persons

1.14.1   You must act with other regulated persons in a manner consistent with persons having mutual trust and confidence in each other. You must not knowingly mislead other regulated persons or, where you have given your word, go back on it.

1.14.2   Other than as permitted by rule 3, you may only communicate with a person known or believed to be the client of another regulated person ("the other regulated person") if:
  (a)   the other regulated person has agreed to the communication;
  (b)   the other regulated person confirms that he or she is no longer acting;
  (c)   you are serving a court document or formal notice;
  (d)   you are sending a fee note (or a reminder letter with regard to a fee note which remains unpaid) to a former client;[1]
  (e)   you have (i) warned the other regulated person in writing that a reply to correspondence is needed within a specified and reasonable length of time and that if no reply is received within that time, you will write direct to the other regulated person's client; and (ii) no reply has been received within that time; or

---

[1] As amended by the Law Society of Scotland Practice (Amendment) Rules 2012 (effective November 1, 2012).

(f)   you are not already acting for another party in the matter and the person has sought advice from you.

1.14.3   In respect of rules 1.14.1 and 1.14.2 references to regulated persons shall be deemed to include advocates, English/Welsh solicitors, Northern Ireland solicitors, Isle of Man advocates, Jersey solicitors and Guernsey, Alderney and Sark advocates.

Diversity

1.15.1   You must not discriminate on the grounds of age, disability, gender reassignment, marriage and civil partnership, pregnancy and maternity, race, religion or belief, sex or sexual orientation in your professional dealings with other lawyers, clients, employees or others.

1.15.2   Where you act in a managerial capacity or supervise others you must ensure that:
(a)   there is no unlawful discrimination in employment including recruitment, training, employment terms, promotion, advancement and termination of employment;
(b)   those you manage or supervise do not discriminate unlawfully;
(c)   you and those you manage or supervise, have appropriate awareness and understanding of the issues surrounding equal opportunities, unlawful discrimination, equality and diversity; and
(d)   there is no unlawful discrimination in the provision of legal services, and that those to whom legal services are provided can access them in a manner most appropriate to their needs.

Rule B2: Conflict of Interest

2.1.1   In this rule 2.1, unless the context otherwise requires, terms listed in the first column of rule 2.1.1 shall have the meanings respectively ascribed to them in the second column of that rule:

Term	Definition
client	includes prospective client
connected	parties are connected if at least one of them is a body corporate and one is controlled by the other or both are controlled by the same third person;
established client	a person for whom you have or your practice unit has acted on at least one previous occasion
employed regulated person	a regulated person employed by his employer for the purpose, wholly or partly, of offering legal services to the public whether or not for a fee
practice unit	as defined in Schedule 1 but including, for the purposes of this rule 2, any office at which that practice unit carries on practice and any practice unit in which that practice unit has a direct interest through one or more of its managers
transaction	includes a contract and any negotiations leading thereto

2.1.2   You shall not act for two or more parties whose interests conflict.

2.1.3   Without prejudice to the generality of rule 2.1.2, where you are an employed regulated person and your only or principal employer is one of the parties to a transaction you shall not act for any other party to that transaction; provided always that you may, where no dispute arises or appears likely to arise between the parties to that transaction, act for more than one party thereto, if and only if:

    (a)   the parties are associated companies, public authorities, public bodies, or government departments or agencies; or

    (b)   the parties are connected.

2.1.4   Without prejudice to the generality of rule 2.1.2, a regulated person, or two or more regulated persons practising either as manager or employee in the same practice unit or in the employment of the same employer shall not, at any stage, act for both seller and purchaser in the sale or purchase or conveyance of heritable property, or for both landlord and tenant, or assignor and assignee in a lease of heritable property for value or for lender and borrower in a loan to be secured over heritable property; provided, however, that where no dispute arises or might reasonably be expected to arise between the parties and that, other than in the case of exception (a) hereto, the seller or landlord of residential property is not a builder or developer, this rule shall not apply if:

    (a)   the parties are associated companies, public authorities, public bodies, or government departments or agencies;

    (b)   the parties are connected;

    (c)   the parties are related by blood, adoption or marriage or civil partnership, one to the other, or the purchaser, tenant, assignee or borrower is so related to an established client; or

    (d)   both parties are established clients or the prospective purchaser, tenant, assignee or borrower is an established client; or

    (e)   there is no other regulated person in the vicinity whom the client could reasonably be expected to consult; or

    (f)   in the case of a loan to be secured over heritable property, the terms of the loan have been agreed between the parties before the regulated person has been instructed to act for the lender, and the granting of the security is only to give effect to such agreement.

2.1.5   In all cases falling within exceptions detailed at paragraphs (c), (d) and (e) of rule 2.1.4 both parties shall be advised by the regulated person at the earliest practicable opportunity that the regulated person, or his practice unit, has been requested to act for both parties, and that if a dispute arises, they or one of them will require to consult an independent regulated person, which advice shall be confirmed by the regulated person in writing as soon as may be practicable thereafter.

2.1.6   Unless the contrary be proved, for the purposes of rules 2.1.3 and 2.1.4, you shall be presumed to be acting for a party for whom you prepare an offer, whether complete or not, in connection with a transaction of any kind specified in this rule 2.1, for execution by that party.

2.1.7   [1]When you are acting on behalf of a party or prospective party to a transaction of any kind you shall not issue any deed, writ, missive or other document requiring the signature of an unrepresented party to that party without informing that party in writing that:

    (a)   such signature may have certain legal consequences, and

    (b)   he should seek independent legal advice before signature.

---

[1] As amended by the Law Society of Scotland Practice (Amendment) Rules 2013 r.2 (effective June 3, 2013).

2.1.8 Where a practice unit knowingly intends to act on behalf of two or more prospective purchasers or tenants (other than prospective joint purchasers or tenants) of heritable property (in this rule 2.1.8 referred to as "the clients"), the clients shall be informed of such intention, and a single natural person shall not, where he has given any advice to one of the clients with respect to the price or rent to be offered, or with respect to any other material condition of the prospective bargain, give advice to another of the clients in respect of such matters.

Drafting Wills

2.2.1 In this rule 2.2, unless the context otherwise requires, terms listed in the first column of rule 2.2.1 shall have the meanings respectively ascribed to them in the second column of that rule:

Term	Definition
business partner	a partner in any form of partnership or a co-director of any corporate body in either case providing legal services or associated with the provision of such services
connected person	your spouse, civil partner, cohabitant, ascendant, descendant or sibling; your business partner, employer, employee or fellow employee; or the spouse, civil partner, cohabitant, ascendant, descendant or sibling of your business partner, employer, employee or fellow employee

2.2.2 You shall not knowingly act on instructions in relation to the preparation of testamentary writings which could reasonably be perceived to give unfair benefits to you or those connected with you by family or professional relationships.

2.2.3 Without prejudice to the generality of rule 2.2.2, you shall not knowingly accept instructions from or give instructions to a business partner, employer, employee or fellow employee or act yourself to prepare a testamentary writing for a client ("the testator") if either of the following circumstances apply:
- (a) it contains a bequest in your favour or in favour of a connected person unless that bequest falls within one or more of the following exceptions:
  - (i) the bequest is of token sums or items not exceeding £250 in total value or such other sum as may be fixed by the Council from time to time; or
  - (ii) the bequest is to the spouse, civil partner or cohabitant of the testator provided that, if the testator has issue at the date of execution of the testamentary writing, either those issue are all apparently the issue of both the testator and the recipient of the bequest, or, if the testator has other issue, appropriate provision is also made for those other issue; or
  - (iii) the bequest is to a person related to the testator and is not to any significant degree disproportionately large as compared to that of (1) any other person in the same degree of relationship to the testator or (2) any person, who under the law relating to intestacy is, or could be, a representative of, or represented by, any other person in the same degree of relationship to the testator; or
- (b) it contains a direction that you or your practice unit or an entity in which your practice unit has a financial interest are to undertake the administration of the testator's estate.

Rule B3: Advertising and Promotion

3.1 Subject to rules 3.2 and 3.5, you shall be entitled to advertise and promote your services in any way you think fit.

3.2 You shall not make a direct or indirect approach whether verbal or written to any person whom you know or ought reasonably to know to be the client of another regulated person with the intention to solicit business from that person.

3.3 Rule 3.2 shall not preclude the general circulation (being circulation

to a group of persons, including bodies corporate, who can be categorised by a common description) of material promoting your services whether or not the persons to whom it is directed are established clients.

3.4 No-one shall be in breach of this rule 3 by reason only of his claim to be a specialist in any particular field of law or legal practice, provided that:

(a) the onus of proof that any such claim is justified shall be on the person making it; and

(b) any advertisement or promotional material issued by or on behalf of any person making any such claim shall otherwise conform to the requirements of rule 3.5.

3.5 Any advertisement or promotional material issued by you or on your behalf or any promotional activity by you or on your behalf shall be decent and shall not:

(a) contain any inaccuracy or misleading statement;

(b) be of such nature or character or be issued or done by such means as may reasonably be regarded as bringing the profession into disrepute;

(c) identify any client or item of his business without the prior written consent of the client; or

(d) be defamatory or illegal.

3.6 Any advertisement, promotional material or promotional activity of or by you (whether or not you are named or referred to therein) and any advertisement, promotional material or promotional activity of or by a third party which relates to your services shall be presumed to have been issued or promoted with your authority.

3.7.1 Where an advertisement or promotional material or activity of or by you, or by a third party which relates to your services, is deemed by the Council to contravene any of these rules, the Council may by way of notice duly given to you require you forthwith, or from such date as the notice may stipulate, to withdraw, terminate or cancel the advertisement or promotional material or activity as the case may require and not to repeat the same during the currency of the notice.

3.7.2 It shall be your duty to comply with any notice duly given to you under this rule 3.7. If you are aggrieved by the terms of any such notice you may, within 14 days of the date thereof, make written representations concerning that notice to the Council, which shall, within two months of the receipt of such representations, either confirm or withdraw such notice; provided that should the Council neither confirm nor withdraw such notice within the two month period, that notice shall be deemed to have been withdrawn at the expiry of that period.

Rule B4: Client Communication

4.1 In this rule 4, unless the context otherwise requires, terms listed in the first column of rule 4.1 shall have the meanings respectively ascribed to them in the second column of that rule:

Term	Definition
advice and assistance	advice and assistance as defined in section 6(1) of the 1986 Act to which Part II of the 1986 Act applies
client	a person who instructs a regulated person or to whom a regulated person tenders for business

F 514   *Solicitors: Practice Rules and Regulations*

| legal aid | the meaning given to it in section 41 of the 1986 Act |
| special urgency work | the meaning given to it in Regulation 18 of the Civil Legal Aid (Scotland) Regulations 2002 (SSI 2002 No.494) |

4.2 When tendering for business or at the earliest practical opportunity upon receiving instructions to undertake any work on behalf of a client, you shall provide the following information to the client in writing:

(a) an outline of the work to be carried out on behalf of the client;

(b) save where the client is being provided with legal aid or advice and assistance, details of either-

    (i) an estimate of the total fee to be charged for the work, including VAT and outlays which may be incurred in the course of the work; or

    (ii) the basis upon which a fee will be charged for the work, including VAT and outlays which may be incurred in the course of the work;

(c) if the client is being provided with advice and assistance or legal aid—

    (i) where advice and assistance is being provided, details of the level of contribution required from the client, and

    (ii) where civil legal aid, special urgency work or advice and assistance is being provided, an indication of the factors which may affect any contribution which may be required from the client or any payment which may be required from property recovered or preserved;

(d) the identity of the person or persons who will principally carry out the work on behalf of the client; and

(e) the identity of the person whom the client should contact if the client becomes concerned in any way with the manner in which the work is being carried out.

4.3 Where a client regularly instructs you in the same type of work, he need not be provided with the information set out in rule 4.2 in relation to a new instruction to do that type of work, provided that he has previously been supplied with that information in relation to a previous instruction to do that type of work and is informed of any differences between that information and the information which, if this rule 4.3 did not apply, would have been required to be provided to him in terms of rule 4.2.

4.4 Where there is no practical opportunity for you to provide the information set out in rule 4.2 to a client before the conclusion of the relevant work for that client then that information need not be provided to that client.

4.5 Where a client is a child under the age of 12 years then the information set out in rule 4.2 need not be provided to that client.

Rule B5: Client Relations Manager

5.1.1 In this rule 5, unless the context otherwise requires terms listed in the first column of rule 5.1.1 shall have the meanings respectively ascribed to them in the second column of that rule:

Term	Definition
practice unit	as defined in Schedule 1 but including, for the purposes of rules 5.2.4, 5.2.5, 5.2.6, 5.4.2 and 5.5, a practice unit which

Release 115: January 2012

	is dissolved or ceases to carry on business
manager	as defined in Schedule 1 but including, for the purposes of rules 5.2.4, 5.2.5, 5.2.6 and 5.4.2, a person who was such a manager in a practice unit which is dissolved or ceases to carry on business

5.2.1 By each date set out in rule 5.2.2 a practice unit shall designate one of its managers as its Client Relations Manager, who shall be responsible for dealing with complaints made to that practice unit.

5.2.2 A practice unit shall designate a person in terms of rule 5.2.1 within 28 days of—
(a) the date of its commencing practice on its own account; and
(b) every subsequent date when the office of Client Relations Manager in the practice unit becomes vacant.

5.2.3 A practice unit which is a regulated person who is a sole practitioner at any date referred to in 5.2.2 shall be deemed to have designated that regulated person as its Client Relations Manager at that date.

5.2.4 In the event of dissolution or cessation of the business of a practice unit, that practice unit shall, within 28 days after the date of dissolution or cessation (whichever is the earlier), designate one of its managers as its Client Relations Manager and notify the Council in writing of the information set out in rule 5.4.1 in, or substantially in, such form as may be prescribed from time to time by the Council.

5.2.5 Until a practice unit designates a Client Relations Manager and notifies the Council in accordance with rule 5.2.4, or if it does not so designate and notify, the Client Relations Manager designated by that practice unit in terms of rule 5.2.1 shall, notwithstanding the dissolution or cessation of business, continue to be responsible for dealing with complaints made against that practice unit, whether they have been made before or after the dissolution or cessation.

5.2.6 A Client Relations Manager responsible in terms of rule 5.2.4 or 5.2.5 for dealing with complaints made against a practice unit shall continue to be responsible for:
(a) complaints made in the period of two years after the date of dissolution or cessation of that practice unit; and
(b) complaints made before that date
until such date as those complaints are concluded.

5.3.1 Where a practice unit has more than one place of business, it may designate a Client Relations Manager in respect of each place of business. Each Client Relations Manager shall be responsible for dealing with complaints in relation to a specified place or places of business.

5.3.2 No practice unit may designate more than one Client Relations Manager in respect of any place of business.

5.3.3 Where a practice unit has two or more Client Relations Managers, it shall designate one Client Relations Manager as the lead Client Relations Manager. The lead Client Relations Manager shall be responsible for dealing with complaints in any case of doubt as to which Client Relations Manager is responsible.

5.4.1 A practice unit shall except as provided in rule 5.2.4, within 28 days of the designation of a Client Relations Manager, notify the Council in writing of the following information in, or substantially in, such form as may be prescribed from time to time by the Council:
(a) the name and address of the practice unit;
(b) the name, address, telephone number and email address of the person so designated;

    (c) the address of the place(s) of business for which the person so designated is responsible;

    (d) whether or not any other managers of the practice unit have been so designated;

    (e) whether or not the person in respect of which the notification is given has been designated as lead Client Relations Manager for the practice unit.

5.4.2 A practice unit shall, within 28 days of any change in any of the information provided to the Council in accordance with this rule 5.4 or rule 5.2.4, notify the Council in writing of such change in, or substantially in, such form as may be prescribed from time to time by the Council.

5.5.1 A practice unit shall ensure that its Client Relations Manager or Managers maintains a central record of each complaint and the way it is dealt with.

5.5.2 A practice unit shall ensure that the procedure to be followed by it when handling complaints is set out in writing.

5.5.3 Any client or former client of a practice unit who requests a copy of the procedure referred to in rule 5.5.2 from that practice unit shall be supplied with a copy of it within 28 days of such request.

Rule B6: Accounts, Accounts Certificates, Professional Practice and Guarantee Fund

Part I—General

Definitions and Interpretation

6.1.1 In this rule 6, unless the context otherwise requires, terms listed in the first column of rule 6.1.1 shall have the meanings respectively ascribed to them in the second column of that rule:

Term	Definition
2001 Rules	the Solicitors (Scotland) Accounts, Accounts Certificate, Professional Practice and Guarantee Fund Rules 2001;
accounting period	(a) a period not exceeding six months in duration, or a period not exceeding twelve months in duration in the case of a practice unit which has not at any time during that period held clients' money, the first such period commencing on the expiry of the immediately preceding accounting period (under the 2001 Rules) after the commencement of this rule 6 and each period thereafter commencing on the expiry of the immediately preceding period; or
	(b) where there is no such immediately preceding accounting period a period not exceeding six months in duration, or a period not exceeding twelve months in duration in the case of a practice unit which has not at any time during that period held clients' money, the first such period commencing on the date on which Part II of this rule 6 applies to the practice unit or, having ceased to

apply, applies again to that practice unit and each period thereafter commencing on the expiry of the immediately preceding period;

accounting records — all documents or permanent records held on a durable medium and commonly used for book-keeping systems (whether manual, mechanical or computerised), including, without limitation, client due diligence documents and client financial information obtained for the purposes of compliance with the Money Laundering Regulations, books and accounts, cash books, ledgers, loose-leaf books and cards, bank passbooks, loose leaf bank statements, deposit receipts, vouchers, documents of joint deposit, building society pass books, local authority deposits, statements of account and statements of bank overdrafts or loans whether in the name of a practice unit or in the name of or for a client or clients;

balance its books — to prepare and bring to a balance a trial balance being a schedule or list of balances both debit and credit extracted from the accounts in both practice unit and client ledgers and including the cash and bank balances from the cash book;

bank — the meaning given in sections 35(2) and (2A) of the 1980 Act;

building society — a building society within the meaning of the Building Societies Act 1986;

Certificate — a certificate in such form as the Council may from time to time prescribe and different forms may be prescribed for different circumstances;

client account — a current, deposit, or savings account or other form of account or a deposit receipt at a branch of a bank in the United Kingdom in the name of the practice unit in the title of which the word "client", "trustee", "trust", or other fiduciary term appears and includes an account or a deposit receipt with a bank, a deposit, share or other account with a building society, a current or general account with a building society operating such an account within the bankers automated clearing system or an account showing sums on loan to a local authority being in such cases in name of the practice unit for a client whose name is specified in the title of the account or receipt;

clients' money	money (not belonging to him) received by a regulated person whether as a regulated person or as a trustee in the course of his practice;
durable medium	any method by which information is stored in a way accessible for future reference for no less than the required retention period and which allows the unchanged reproduction of the information stored by visual record and by immediately available print-out;
holding ledger	a ledger, within the client ledgers, containing details of funds received which are to be held as undelivered, and specifying to whose order those funds are held and for what purpose;
independent legal professional	the meaning given in regulation 3(9) of the Money Laundering Regulations;
local authority	a council within the meaning of the Local Government etc. (Scotland) Act 1994;
Money Laundering Regulations	the Money Laundering Regulations 2007 (S.I. 2007 No. 2157);
other financial institution	a financial institution as defined in regulation 3(3) of the Money Laundering Regulations, but not including a bank or building society;
print-out	a printed or typewritten copy of any information stored in a durable medium;
required retention period	in relation to rules 6.7, 6.8 and 6.9, a period equal to the remainder of the financial year of the practice unit and a further six financial years of that practice unit;

Application of rules

6.2.1 Parts II and III of rule 6 shall not apply to a regulated person who is in any of the employments mentioned in sub-sections (4)(a), (b) and (c) of section 35 of the 1980 Act so far as regards monies received, held or paid by him in the course of that employment.

6.2.2 Parts IV, V and VI of rule 6 shall not apply to such a regulated person as is referred to in rule 6.2.1 so far as regards anything done or omitted to be done by him in the course of that employment.

6.2.3 Subject to rules 6.2.1 and 6.2.2, where any of the provisions of rule 6 are stated to apply to a practice unit:
(a) they shall also apply to the managers of the practice unit; and
(b) no regulated person within the practice unit shall cause or knowingly permit the practice unit not to comply with any such provision.

Part II—Accounts Rules

Clients' money to be paid into client account or holding ledger

6.3.1 Subject to the provisions of rule 6.6 every practice unit shall—
(a) ensure that at all times the sum at the credit of the client account,

or where there are more such accounts than one, the total of the sums at the credit of those accounts, shall not be less than the total of the clients' money held by the practice unit;

(b) pay into a client account without delay any sum of money exceeding £50 (or such other amount as the Council may from time to time prescribe) held for or received from or on behalf of a client; and

(c) pay into a client account, and make an entry in a holding ledger in respect of, any electronic transfer of funds received from or pursuant to instructions of a third party, that is required by that third party or pursuant to instructions received on behalf of that third party to be held as undelivered pending settlement of a transaction.

6.3.2 Where money is held by the practice unit in a client account in which the name of the client is specified and where no money is due to that client by the practice unit or the amount due is less than the amount in the specified client account, the sum in that account or, as the case may be, the excess, shall not be treated as clients' money for the purposes of rule 6.3.1(a).

6.3.3 Nothing contained in rule 6.3 shall:

(a) empower a practice unit, without the express written authority of the client, to deposit any money held by the practice unit for that client with a bank or on share, deposit or other account with a building society or on loan account with a local authority in the name of the practice unit for that client, except on such terms as will enable the amount of the share or deposit or loan or any part thereof to be uplifted or withdrawn on notice not exceeding one calendar month;

(b) relieve a practice unit of its responsibilities to the client to ensure that all sums belonging to that client and held in a client account in terms of rule 6 are available when required for that client or for that client's purpose; and

(c) preclude the overdrawing by a practice unit of a client account in which the name of the client for whom it is held is specified where that client has given written authority to overdraw, and an overdraft on such account shall not be taken into account to ensure compliance with rule 6.3.1(a).

Duty to rectify breaches

6.4.1 A practice unit shall remedy any breach of rule 6 promptly upon discovery and shall, without limitation, replace any money improperly withheld or withdrawn from a client account.

Drawings from client account

6.5.1 So long as money belonging to one client is not withdrawn without his written authority for the purpose of meeting a payment to or on behalf of another client, there may be drawn from a client account:

(a) money required for payment to or on behalf of a client;

(b) money required for or to account of payment of a debt due to the practice unit by a client or in or to account of repayment of money expended by the practice unit on behalf of a client;

(c) money drawn on a client's authority (including complying with lender instructions where the lender is a client);

(d) money properly required for or to account of payment of the practice unit's professional account against a client which has been debited to the ledger account of the client in the practice unit's books and where a copy of said account has been rendered;

(e) money for transfer to a separate client account kept or to be kept for the client only; and

(f) any fee taken as permitted by rule 6.11.

6.5.2 Where money drawn from a client account by cheque is payable to a person's account with any bank, building society or other financial institution, the cash book and ledger entries relating thereto and said cheque shall include the name of the person whose account is to be credited with the payment.

Exceptions from Rule 6.3

6.6.1 Notwithstanding any of the provisions of this Part of rule 6, a practice unit shall not be obliged to pay into a client account, but shall be required to record in its accounting records, clients' money:

(a) in the form of cash which is without delay paid in cash to the client or a third party on the client's behalf;

(b) in the form of a cheque or draft or other bill of exchange which is endorsed over to the client or to a third party on the client's behalf and which is not passed by the practice unit through a bank account;

(c) which it pays without delay into a separate bank, building society or local authority deposit account opened or to be opened in name of the client or of some person named by the client;

(d) which the client for his own convenience has requested the practice unit in writing to withhold from such account;

(e) for or to account of payment of a debt due to the practice unit from the client or in repayment in whole or in part of money expended by the practice unit on behalf of the client;

(f) expressly on account of a professional account incurred to the practice unit by the client, or as an agreed fee or to account of an agreed fee for business done by the practice unit for the client where a copy of said account has been rendered; or

(g) in the form of a third-party cheque to be passed on by the practice unit.

Accounts required to be kept in books of practice unit

6.7.1 A practice unit shall at all times keep properly written up such accounting records as are necessary:

(a) to show all its dealings with—

   (i)   clients' money;

   (ii) any other money dealt with by it through a client account;

  (iii) any bank overdrafts or loans procured by it in its own name for behoof of a client or clients; and

  (iv) any other money held by the practice unit in a separate account in the title of which the client's name is specified; and

(b) (i) to show separately in respect of each client all money of the categories specified in sub-paragraph (a) which is received, held or paid by it on account of that client; and

   (ii) to distinguish all money of the said categories received, held or paid by it from any other money received, held or paid by it; and

(c) to demonstrate compliance with the Money Laundering Regulations.

6.7.2 Without prejudice to rule 6.7.1, this rule 6.7 shall apply to money received or payments made by a practice unit or any of its managers or employees or any other person acting on its behalf by virtue of any power of attorney in favour of any of them.

6.7.3 All dealings referred to in rule 6.7.1 shall be recorded:

(a) in a clients' cash book, or a clients' column of a cash book, or

(b) in a record of sums transferred from the ledger account of one client to that of another, as may be appropriate, and in addition in a clients' ledger or a clients' column of a ledger.

6.7.4 Every practice unit shall:

(a) at all times keep properly written up such accounting records as are necessary to show the true financial position of the practice unit; and

(b) balance its books monthly and on the last day of each accounting period.

6.7.5 A practice unit shall retain, for at least the required retention period from the date of the last entry therein, all accounting records required to be kept by it under rule 6.7.

6.7.6 A practice unit shall:

(a) retain paid cheques;

(b) retain a digital image of the front and back of each cheque supplied by the relevant bank or building society; or

(c) have in place an arrangement with the relevant bank or building society for the production, promptly upon request, of a digital image of the front and back of each cheque so requested;

in each case for at least the required retention period from the date of the cheque.

Client bank statements to be regularly reconciled

6.8.1 Every practice unit shall within one month of the coming into force of rule 6 or of its commencing practice, and thereafter at intervals not exceeding one month, cause the balance between the client bank lodged and drawn columns of its cash book or the balance of its client bank ledger account as the case may be to be agreed with its client bank statements and shall retain such reconciliation statements showing this agreement for at least the required retention period from the dates they were respectively carried out.

6.8.2 On the same date or dates specified in rule 6.8.1 every practice unit shall extract from its clients' ledger a list of balances due by it to clients and prepare a statement comparing the total of the said balances with the reconciled balance in the client bank account and retain such lists of balances and statements for at least the required retention period from the dates they were respectively carried out.

Client funds invested in specified accounts

6.9.1 Every practice unit shall within three months of the coming into force of rule 6 or of its commencing practice, and thereafter at intervals not exceeding three months and coinciding with the date of a reconciliation in terms of rule 6.8, cause the balance between the client deposited and withdrawn columns of its cash book or the balance on its client invested funds ledger account as the case may be to be agreed with its client passbooks, building society printouts, special deposit accounts, local authority deposits, joint deposits or other statements or certificates and shall retain such reconciliation statements showing this agreement for at least the required retention period from the dates they were respectively carried out.

6.9.2 On the same date or dates specified in rule 6.9.1 every practice unit shall extract from its client ledger a list of funds invested by it in its name for specified clients and prepare a statement comparing the total of the said balances with the reconciled investment funds and retain such lists of balances and statements for at least the required retention period from the dates they were respectively carried out.

Interest to be earned for a client

6.10.1 Where a practice unit holds money for or on account of a client and, having regard to the amount of such money and the length of time for which it or any part of it is likely to be held, it is reasonable that interest should be earned for the client, the practice unit shall as soon as practicable place such money or, as the case may be, such part thereof, in a separate interest bearing client account in the title of which the client's name is specified and shall account to the client for any interest earned thereon, failing which the practice unit shall pay to the client out of its own money a sum equivalent to the interest which would have accrued for the benefit of the client if the sum it ought to have placed in such an interest bearing client account under rule 6.10 had been so placed.

6.10.2 Notwithstanding rule 6.10.1, interest shall not require to be earned for a client where the amount of interest which could be earned would be likely to be less than such amount as the Council may from time to time prescribe.

6.10.3 Nothing in rule 6.10 shall affect any arrangement in writing, whenever made, between a practice unit and its client as to the application of a client's money or interest thereon provided such arrangement was made prior to the said application.

6.10.4 For the purposes of rule 6.10 only, money held by a practice unit for or on account of a client:
 (a) for the purpose of paying stamp duty, recording dues or other outlays on behalf of the client; or
 (b) for or to account of the practice unit's professional account where said account has been rendered,
shall not be regarded as clients' money.

Client balances held after the conclusion of a matter

6.11.1 Subject to the provisions of rule 6.11, a practice unit shall:
 (a) return money held for or on account of a client promptly as soon as there is no longer any reason to retain that money; and
 (b) promptly pay to a client any money received for or on account of that client after a practice unit has already accounted to that client.

6.11.2 Rule 6.11.1 shall not apply to any matter in respect of which a practice unit acted for a client, which concluded or substantially concluded prior to the coming into operation of this rule 6, until 31 October 2013.

6.11.3 Notwithstanding rule 6.11.1, if a practice unit no longer has an up-to-date address or other contact details for a client and the balance held for or on account of that client is equal to or more than £10 (or such other amount as the Council may from time to time prescribe) ("the prescribed minimum") and less than £50 (or such other amount as the Council may from time to time prescribe) ("the prescribed maximum"), the practice unit may either remit the balance to the Office of the Queen's and Lord Treasurer's Remembrancer or to a registered charity of the practice unit's choice. A practice unit may not take any fee from the balance.

6.11.4 If the balance held for or on account of a client is equal to or more than the prescribed maximum, a practice unit shall use reasonable endeavours, having regard to the actual amount of money held, to trace the client. A practice unit may charge a reasonable fee for work undertaken to trace the client.

6.11.5 Notwithstanding rule 6.11.1, if, having used reasonable endeavours in terms of rule 6.11.4, a practice unit cannot trace the client, the practice unit shall remit the balance held for or on account of that client (after deducting any fee as permitted by paragraph (4)) to the Office of the Queen's and Lord Treasurer's Remembrancer.

6.11.6 A practice unit who remits a balance in terms of rule 6.11.5 shall maintain a record of the action taken by or on behalf of the practice unit to trace the client.

6.11.7 Notwithstanding rule 6.11.1, whether or not a practice unit has an up-to-date address or other contact details for a client, and where the balance held for or on account of that client is less than the prescribed minimum, the practice unit may take that balance to a fee and may aggregate that balance with other balances which are less than the prescribed minimum in a single fee, provided that such single fee includes a list of each of the balances and related clients which are included.

Duty not to act dishonestly

6.12.1 A regulated person shall not act, or omit to act, in a manner which is dishonest, reckless or intentionally misleading in respect of:
  (a) the writing up of accounting records in respect of clients' money or of his practice;
  (b) balancing his books; or
  (c) the financial affairs of his clients or of his practice.

Cashroom Manager

6.13.1 Within one month of the coming into force of rule 6 or of its commencing practice on its own account every practice unit shall designate one or more of its managers as Cashroom Manager. A Cashroom Manager will be responsible for the supervision of the staff and systems employed by the practice unit to implement the provisions of rule 6 and for securing compliance by the practice unit with the provisions of rule 6. In the case of a sole practitioner, the sole practitioner shall be the Cashroom Manager.

6.13.2 A Cashroom Manager shall use reasonable endeavours to acquire and maintain the skills necessary to discharge his responsibilities throughout the period during which he is so designated.

6.13.3 A Cashroom Manager shall:
  (a) use reasonable endeavours to advance and maintain the competence of all officers and employees of the practice unit;
  (b) adequately supervise or arrange for the adequate supervision of all such officers and employees; and
  (c) adequately train or arrange for the adequate training of all such officers and employees;
in each case so far as the duties of such officers and employees involve compliance with rule 6.

Savings of right of regulated person against client

6.14.1 Nothing in rule 6 shall deprive a regulated person of or prejudice him with reference to any recourse or right in law, whether by way of lien, set-off, counter-claim, charge or otherwise, against monies standing to the credit of a client account or against monies due to a client by a third party.

Part III—Accounts Certificate

Obligation to deliver a Certificate

6.15.1 A practice unit shall deliver to the Council within one calendar month (or within such other period as the Council may prescribe) of the completion of each accounting period a Certificate in respect of that accounting period.

6.15.2 The Council shall be entitled to use the information contained in the

Certificate to monitor compliance by the practice unit with rule 6, and to assess levels of risk in order to allow the Society effectively to target its regulatory activity. The Council may request a practice unit to provide a Certificate on a more frequent basis than provided for in terms of rule 6.15.1, and/or a Certificate containing more or less detailed information, according to its assessment of that practice unit's risk profile.

6.15.3 The Council may, in any case on cause satisfactory to it being shown, extend the period within which a Certificate is required to be delivered, but such extension shall in no case exceed three months from the date on which the Certificate should have been delivered.

6.15.4 If a practice unit fails to deliver a Certificate by the expiry of any extension period under rule 6.15.3 the Council will determine whether further action is to be taken against the practice unit or its managers in respect of such failure.

Who may sign a Certificate

6.16.1 Subject to rules 6.16.2 and 6.16.3, all sections of a Certificate required under rule 6 must be signed by two managers, one of whom must be a current Cashroom Manager.

6.16.2 Except where it is not required because the practice unit does not hold clients' money, the section of a Certificate relating to rule 6.23 must be signed by a current Cashroom Manager and the current Money Laundering Reporting Officer, provided that if the current Money Laundering Reporting Officer is also the only Cashroom Manager and is not a sole practitioner, it must also be signed by another manager.

6.16.3 A sole practitioner must sign all sections of the Certificate.

Where a practice unit practises in two or more places

6.17.1 In the case of a practice unit which has two or more places of business and where separate books and accounts are maintained for each such place of business a separate Certificate shall be submitted in respect of each such place of business. In any such case the client account balance shall be struck on the same date in respect of each place of business.

Part IV—Inspections and Investigations

Inspections and investigations on behalf of Council

6.18.1 In rule 6.18, unless the context otherwise requires, "practice information" means accounting records and any other documents, records, correspondence and information concerning the conduct of a regulated person's practice.

6.18.2 The Council may carry out two types of investigation in terms of rule 6.18, namely:
  (a) a routine investigation, referred to in rule 6.18.3 as an inspection; and
  (b) a non-routine investigation, referred to in rule 6.18.4 as an investigation.

6.18.3 For the purposes of enabling:
  (a) the Council to ascertain whether or not rule 6 is being complied with;
  (b) the Society to discharge its duties as supervisory authority under the Money Laundering Regulations;
  (c) the Council to protect the Guarantee Fund;
  (d) the Council to promote high standards of financial compliance by the profession; and
  (e) the Society to assist the profession,

the Council may, by giving notice, require any regulated person to produce practice information for the inspection of a person authorised by the Council and at a date, time and place to be fixed by the Council. If the place fixed by the Council for the inspection requires the transfer to that place of practice information in physical form, the Council shall, on such conditions as to the cost and distance of such transfer as it may from time to time prescribe, pay the reasonable expenses incurred by the regulated person in respect of such transfer.

6.18.4 If at any time there is a reasonable apprehension on the part of the Council:

(a) that a regulated person has not complied with, is not complying with or may not comply with rule 6, or

(b) that the practice of the regulated person has been, is being or may be being carried on in such a manner as may put at risk the interests of the public or the interests of the profession,

the Council may authorise a person to conduct such investigation of the regulated person and his practice as the Council may consider appropriate. The Council shall give notice of its authorisation of such a person to conduct such investigation and of the date, time and place of such investigation.

6.18.5 The Council may, in any case on cause satisfactory to it being shown, extend the period within which a regulated person may produce practice information as required by a person authorised by the Council under rule 6.18.3 or 6.18.4, but such extension shall in no case exceed three months from the date on which practice information should have been produced.

6.18.6 If a regulated person fails to produce practice information prior to the expiry of any extension period under rule 6.18.5, the Council will determine whether further action is to be taken against the regulated person in respect of such failure.

6.18.7 A regulated person shall provide a person authorised by the Council under rule 6.18.3 or 6.18.4 reasonable co-operation in the conduct of that person's inspection or investigation (as the case may be) including, without prejudice to the foregoing generality, the production of practice information as such person may reasonably require and, in the case of an investigation, the granting of authorisation (including by way of mandate) to contact clients or third parties for the production by such clients or third parties of documents, records and other information as such person may reasonably require.

6.18.8 Any person authorised by the Council under rule 6.18.3 shall report to the Council on the result of his inspection to the extent he considers it necessary to do so. Any person authorised by the Council under rule 6.18.4 shall report to the Council on the result of his investigation.

6.18.9 Where, following an inspection of practice information in terms of rule 6.18.3 or an investigation in terms of paragraph 6.18.4, or following any further inspection or investigation in terms of this paragraph, it appears to the Council that the regulated person has not complied with rule 6 or that the practice of the regulated person has been or is being carried on in such a manner as may put at risk the interests of the public or the interests of the profession, the Council may by giving notice instruct a further inspection of the practice information of the regulated person or a further investigation.

6.18.10 If the Council instructs a further inspection of the practice information of the regulated person or a further investigation under rule 6.18.9, the Council may by giving notice, require the regulated person to pay, or may agree with the regulated person that he will pay, the reasonable costs of any such further inspection or investigation, provided always that such notice is given to the regulated person, or such agreement is reached with the regulated person, not more than twelve months after the date of the immediately preceding inspection or investigation.

6.18.11 The costs referred to in rule 6.18.10 shall be determined by reference to a daily rate which shall be prescribed by the Council from time to time. The amount of any such costs shall be intimated by the Secretary to the regulated person following such further inspection or investigation.

6.18.12 It shall be the duty of a regulated person upon whom a notice in terms of rule 6.18.10 has been served, or with whom an agreement in terms of rule 6.18.10 has been reached, to make payment of the amount of costs intimated in terms of rule 6.18.11. The regulated person shall make such payment in accordance with the payment terms stated in the invoice issued by the Society in respect of such costs.

6.18.13 Any sum paid by a regulated person in terms of rule 6.18.12 shall accrue to the Society.

Part V—Professional Practice

Bridging Loans

6.19.1 A regulated person shall not enter into or maintain any contract or arrangement with a bank or other lender in terms of which the regulated person may draw down loan or overdraft facilities in his name on behalf of clients unless:

(a) the regulated person shall, in every case before drawing down any sums in terms of such contract or arrangement have intimated in writing to the bank or other lender:

    (i) the name and present address of the client for whom the loan or overdraft facilities are required; and

    (ii) the arrangements for repayment of the loan or overdraft facilities; and

(b) the contract or arrangement does not impose personal liability for repayment of any such loan or overdraft facilities on the regulated person.

6.19.2 A regulated person who has entered into a contract or arrangement with a bank or other lender under rule 6.19.1 shall obtain a closing statement from the bank or other lender upon termination of such contract or arrangement.

Borrowing from clients

6.20.1 A regulated person shall not borrow money from his client unless his client is in the business of lending money or his client has been independently advised in regard to the making of the loan. Such advice must be given in advance of the transaction, and must not be given by another regulated person in the same practice unit.

6.20.2 In rule 6.20, "client" shall mean a person for whom a regulated person or another regulated person in the same practice unit is currently acting or for whom either of such persons have acted on at least one previous occasion.

Prohibition on regulated person acting for lender to the regulated person or connected persons

6.21.1 No regulated person shall act for or pursuant to the written requirements of a lender in the constitution, variation, assignation or discharge of a standard security securing a loan which has been

advanced or is to be advanced to or has been guaranteed or is to be guaranteed by:
(a) the regulated person, where he is a manager,
(b) the regulated person's spouse or civil partner or cohabitee, where the regulated person is a manager,
(c) another manager in the practice unit of which the regulated person is a manager,
(d) the spouse or civil partner or cohabitee of any such other manager,
(e) any manager of the practice unit which employs the regulated person, or the spouse or civil partner or cohabitee of any such manager,
(f) any practice unit which employs the regulated person,
(g) any practice unit of which the regulated person or his spouse or civil partner or cohabitee is a manager,
(h) any practice unit of which any of the persons specified in sub-paragraphs (a) to (g) is a manager, or
(i) any company in which any person specified in sub-paragraphs (a) to (h) holds shares, whether directly or indirectly, other than a holding amounting to not more than 5% of the issued shares in a public company quoted on a recognised stock exchange.

6.21.2 For the avoidance of doubt, rule 2.1.4(f) in Section B shall not apply to any such loan as is referred to in rule 6.21.1.

6.21.3 For the purposes of rule 6.21 "loan" shall include an obligation ad factum praestandum or any obligation to pay money and "lender" shall include any person to whom said obligation is owed.

6.21.4 Rule 6.21 shall not apply if:
(a) the lender to any of the persons specified in rule 6.21.1 is the regulated person, or
(b) in relation to the discharge of a standard security, the borrower's obligations under that standard security have been fully implemented before the regulated person or his practice unit is in possession of the executed discharge.

Powers of Attorney

6.22.1 Rule 6.22 shall, subject to rule 6.22.2, apply to monies received or payments made by a regulated person by virtue of any power of attorney in his favour.

6.22.2 In the event of any power of attorney granted in favour of a regulated person continuing to have effect by virtue of sections 15 or 88 of the Adults with Incapacity (Scotland) Act 2000 any money of the granter held or received by the regulated person shall be clients' money.

[1] 6.22.3 Every regulated person (except any regulated person who is in any of the employments mentioned in sub-sections (4)(a), (b) and (c) of section 35 of the 1980 Act) shall deliver to the Council a list of any powers of attorney in the regulated person's favour held or granted during an accounting period, the list to be as set out in the Certificate.

6.22.4 In this rule 6.22 reference to a power of attorney "in favour of a regulated person" and cognate expressions shall:
(a) include reference to such a power in favour of a company, partnership, limited liability partnership, trust or other entity (whether or not having legal personality) in which the regulated person participates, whether as director, shareholder, member, partner, trustee or otherwise and which carries on activities in the course of the regulated person's practice; and
(b) not include reference to such a power the sole purpose of which is to authorise the submission of a stamp duty land tax return or the authentication or registration of a document created as an

electronic communication within the ARTL system (as defined in section 28(1) of the Land Registration (Scotland) Act 1979).

NOTE
[1] As amended by the Law Society of Scotland Practice (Amendment) Rules 2012 (effective November 1, 2012).

Money laundering
6.23.1 Every independent legal professional who is regulated by the Society shall comply with the provisions of the Money Laundering Regulations.
6.23.2 A regulated person shall demonstrate to the Society on request that the information held by him or by his practice unit is sufficient to evidence compliance with the provisions of Part 7 of the Proceeds of Crime Act 2002 and Part 3 of the Terrorism Act 2000.

Part VI—Guarantee Fund

Definitions and Interpretation for Part VI
6.24.1 In this Part of rule 6 unless the context otherwise requires, terms listed in the first column of rule 6.24.1 shall have the meanings respectively ascribed to them in the second column of that rule:

Term	Definition
authorised person	the solicitor to the Guarantee Fund or such other individual as may from time to time be specified by the Society;
loss	pecuniary loss by reason of dishonesty on the part of any regulated person in practice in the United Kingdom, or any employee of such regulated person in connection with the practice of the regulated person, and whether or not he had a practising certificate in force when the act of dishonesty was committed, and notwithstanding that subsequent to the commission of that act he may have died or had his name removed from or struck off the roll of solicitors (or register of registered European lawyers, register of registered foreign lawyers or register of incorporated practices, as appropriate) or may have otherwise ceased to practice or be entitled to practice.

Payments into and out of the Guarantee Fund
6.25.1 There shall be carried to the credit of the Guarantee Fund:
(a) all contributions paid by regulated persons under section 43 of, and Schedule 3 to, the 1980 Act;
(b) all interest, dividends and other income, and accretions of capital arising from investments of the Guarantee Fund;
(c) all moneys borrowed for the purposes of the Guarantee Fund;
(d) all sums received by the Society in respect of contracts of insurance entered into under paragraph 3 of Schedule 3 to the 1980 Act;
(e) all sums recovered by the Society in consequence of the provisions of sub-paragraph (2) of paragraph 4 of Schedule 3 to the 1980 Act; and
(f) any other moneys which may belong or accrue to the Guarantee Fund or be received by the Society in respect of the Guarantee Fund.

6.25.2 There shall from time to time be paid out of the Guarantee Fund:
  (a) the expenses of constituting and administering the Guarantee Fund, including the remuneration of officers and employees of, and other expenses incurred by, the Society in relation to the Guarantee Fund under or in the exercise of powers conferred by the 1980 Act;
  (b) all grants made by the Society under section 43 of the 1980 Act;
  (c) all premiums payable by the Society under contracts of insurance entered into under paragraph 3 of Schedule 3 to the 1980 Act;
  (d) all interest and other sums payable in respect of sums borrowed by the Society for the purposes of the Guarantee Fund; and
  (e) any other moneys payable out of the Guarantee Fund in accordance with the 1980 Act or any rules relating to the Guarantee Fund made thereunder.
6.25.3 Any person who wishes to apply to the Society for a grant from the Guarantee Fund in respect of a loss shall, as soon as is reasonably practicable after the date on which the loss first came to his or her knowledge and in any event within 12 months of that date, make an application in such form as may from time to time be prescribed by the Council and shall deliver the same to the authorised person.
6.25.4 The Council shall be entitled to treat an application as having been abandoned if such documents and other evidence as the Council may demand in terms of paragraph 4(1) of Schedule 3 to the 1980 Act are not produced to it within three months (or such longer period as the Council may have agreed with the applicant) provided that on the expiry of such period, the Council shall issue a reminder letter to the applicant allowing a further period of not less than 14 days for the production of such documents and other evidence.

Council may require institution of proceedings
6.26.1 The Council may, before deciding whether or not to make a grant out of the Guarantee Fund in respect of any application, require the applicant to institute civil proceedings (including, where appropriate, insolvency proceedings) in respect of the loss or to take steps with a view to the institution of criminal proceedings in respect of the dishonesty leading to the loss or with a view to the making by the Council of a complaint to the Scottish Solicitors' Discipline Tribunal.

Rule B7: Professional Indemnity Insurance

Master Policy
7.1.1 In this rule 7.1, unless the context otherwise requires, terms listed in the first column of rule 7.1.1 shall have the meanings respectively ascribed to them in the second column of that rule:

Term	Definition
acceptable alternative insurer	a person so designated by the Council in terms of this rule 7.1
authorised insurer	any person permitted under the Financial Services and Markets Act 2000 to carry on liability insurance business or pecuniary loss insurance business
brokers	the brokers from time to time appointed by the Council to act on behalf of the Society and its members in relation to any master policy entered into by the Society in terms of this rule 7.1

7.1.2 The Society shall take out and maintain with authorised insurers to be determined from time to time by the Council a master policy in terms to be approved by the Council to provide indemnity against such classes of professional liability as the Council may decide. The Council at its discretion may amend the terms of the master policy from time to time.

7.1.3 Subject to rule 7.1.6, the master policy shall provide indemnity for all regulated persons to whom this rule 7.1 applies and for such former regulated persons and other parties as may be mentioned in the master policy.

7.1.4 The limits of indemnity and the self-insured amounts under the master policy shall be as may be determined from time to time by the Council. Nothing in this rule 7.1 shall prohibit any regulated person from arranging with the insurers to extend the cover provided by the master policy if and on such terms as the insurers may agree.

7.1.5 Subject to rule 7.1.7, every regulated person to whom this rule 7.1 applies shall be obliged to be insured under the master policy and:

   (a) to comply with the terms of the master policy and of any certificate of insurance issued to him thereunder; and

   (b) to produce along with each application for a practising certificate a certificate from the brokers certifying that the regulated person in question is insured under the master policy for the practice year then commencing or the part thereof still to run as the case may be, or such other evidence of such insurance as may be acceptable to the Council.

7.1.6 The master policy need not provide indemnity for any regulated person to whom this rule 7.1 applies who is a member of a multi-national practice.

7.1.7 Where in terms of rule 7.1.6 no indemnity is provided by the master policy in respect of a regulated person to whom this rule 7.1 applies:

   (a) that regulated person shall not be obliged to comply with rule 7.1.5; and

   (b) that regulated person shall be obliged to be insured with an acceptable alternative insurer, in terms equivalent to the terms of the master policy or acceptable to the Council; and:

      (i) shall comply with the terms of that insurance policy and of any certificate of insurance issued to him thereunder; and

      (ii) shall produce along with each application for a practising certificate (or, if he is a registered foreign lawyer, registration certificate) a certificate certifying that he is insured for the practice year in question or the part thereof still to run as the case may be, or such other evidence of such insurance as may be acceptable to the Council.

7.1.8 The Council shall designate an authorised insurer or authorised insurers as an acceptable alternative insurer or as acceptable alternative insurers for the purposes of rule 7.1.7.

7.1.9 The Council is hereby empowered to take such steps as it may consider expedient in order to:

   (a) ascertain whether or not this rule 7.1 is being complied with; or

   (b) satisfy itself with regard to any matters arising out of the master policy or any insurance policy taken out in accordance with rule 7.1.7.

Contingency Fund

7.2.1 In this rule 7.2, unless the context otherwise requires terms listed in the first column of rule 7.2.1 shall have the meanings respectively ascribed to them in the second column of that rule:

Term	Definition
contingency fund	the fund which was established in terms of rule 6(2) of the Solicitors (Scotland) Professional Indemnity Insurance Rules 1995 for the purpose of refunding to practice units such portion of the premiums paid by them as was attributable to circumstances intimated in accordance with the master policy if and when the brokers were satisfied that no claim would result from such circumstances
contingency fund monies	the monies which remain in the contingency fund as at 1 September 2007
professional indemnity purpose	any purpose concerning indemnity for regulated persons and former regulated persons or the Society against any class of professional liability which is not otherwise funded: (a) in terms of rules made under section 44 of the 1980 Act; or (b) by the Society in terms of arrangements for such indemnity in respect of its activities.

7.2.2 The Society shall manage and administer the contingency fund monies.
7.2.3 The Society may use the contingency fund monies for any professional indemnity purpose.
7.2.4 The Society may use the contingency fund monies to pay costs and expenses reasonably incurred in connection with their management and administration of those monies or with their use for any professional indemnity purpose.

Rule B8: Miscellaneous Client Protection Requirements

Written Fee Agreements
8.1 No agreement in writing between you and your client as to your fees in respect of any work done or to be done by you for your client entered into in terms of section 61(A)(1) of the 1980 Act shall contain a consent to registration for preservation and execution.

ARTL Mandates
8.2.1 In this rule 8.2, unless the context otherwise requires terms listed in the first column of rule 8.2.1 shall have the meanings respectively ascribed to them in the second column of that rule:

Term	Definition
ARTL System	the same meaning as in section 28(1) of the Land Registration (Scotland) Act 1979
electronic communication	the same meaning as in s15(1) of the Electronic Communications Act 2000
the Keeper	the Keeper of the Registers of Scotland
the Land Register	the Land Register of Scotland

mandate	a mandate in the form prescribed from time to time by the Council

8.2.2 You shall neither authenticate, nor apply for registration in the Land Register of, a document created as an electronic communication within the ARTL System on behalf of any person unless you have obtained a mandate in your favour subscribed by that person authorising the authentication and registration of that document.

8.2.3 You shall, within 14 days of applying for registration in the Land Register within the ARTL System, send the principal of each mandate obtained in terms of rule 8.2.2 to the Keeper for archiving and return to you.

8.2.4 You shall retain the principal of each mandate obtained in your favour in terms of rule 8.2.2 in accordance with guidance issued from time to time by the Council.

Industrial Action

8.3.1 In this rule 8.3, unless the context otherwise requires, terms listed in the first column of rule 8.3.1 shall have the meanings respectively ascribed to them in the second column of that rule:

Term	Definition
courts	the civil and criminal courts in Scotland, the Supreme Court, the Judicial Committee of the Privy Council, the Court of Justice of the European Communities and the European Court of Human Rights
dispute	a "trade dispute" as defined in section 244 of the Trade Union and Labour Relations (Consolidation) Act 1992
industrial action	an act done or taken by a regulated person in contemplation or furtherance of a dispute

8.3.2 Subject to rules 8.3.3 and 8.3.4, you may take industrial action.

8.3.3 Notwithstanding that you are taking or have taken industrial action, you will (a) fulfil your professional duties to the courts or to the Scottish Parliament and to the Parliament of the United Kingdom of Great Britain and Northern Ireland, and (b) fulfil any personal obligation undertaken by you other than an obligation which is imposed upon you under the terms and conditions of your employment.

8.3.4 Notwithstanding that you are about to take, are taking or have taken industrial action, you will take all reasonable steps open to you to secure the consent of the appropriate body organising such industrial action to your acting as a regulated person (a) where a failure to do so could result in danger to any member or members of the public and (b) where a failure to do so would cause serious damage to a party other than your employer.

Appearance in a Superior Court

8.4.1 Where in the course of advising a client you identify a situation which may require appearance in a Superior Court in circumstances where such appearance is restricted to a solicitor advocate or an advocate, you shall advise your client:
(a) that appearance is so restricted;

(b)   that the decision whether a solicitor advocate or an advocate should be instructed is entirely that of the client.

8.4.2   Where you are unable, in a difficult or urgent situation, to secure representation for a person wishing to be represented by a solicitor advocate before any court you shall inform the Secretary of the situation.

Section C: Specialities

Rule C1: Cross-Border Practice

1.1   In this rule 1 unless the context otherwise requires, terms listed in the first column of rule 1.1 shall have the meanings respectively ascribed to them in the second column of that rule:

Term	Definition
the Code	the Code of Conduct for lawyers in the European Union adopted by the Council of the Bars and Law Societies of the European Union on 28 October 1988 as amended on 28 November 1998, 6 December 2002 and 19 May 2006, and as the same may be varied, supplemented, amended, consolidated or replaced from time to time

1.2   When conducting cross-border practice you shall observe and be bound by the terms of the Code at all times.

Rule C2: Incidental Financial Business

Part I—General

Definitions and interpretation[1, 2]

2.1.1   In this rule 2, unless the context otherwise requires, terms listed in the first column of rule 2.1.1 shall have the meanings respectively ascribed to them in the second column of that rule:

Term	Definition
accounting period	in respect of a licensed person, a period not exceeding six months immediately following the previous accounting period, the first such accounting period commencing on the date on which an incidental financial business licence has been granted to that licensed person or, having been withdrawn, suspended or not renewed, is granted again to that licensed person or is reinstated following suspension
the Act	the Financial Services and Markets Act 2000
the Amendment (No 1) Order	the Financial Services and Markets Act 2000 (Regulated Activities) (Amendment) (No 1) Order 2003

---

[1] As amended by the Law Society of Scotland Practice Rules (Amendment (No.1) Rules 2013 (effective April 1, 2014).
[2] As amended by the Law Society of Scotland Practice Rules (Amendment (No.1) Rules 2013 (effective April 1, 2014).

Term	Definition
the Amendment (No 2) Order	the Financial Services and Markets Act 2000 (Regulated Activities) (Amendment) (No 2) Order 2003
bankruptcy proceedings	an award of sequestration, bankruptcy order or equivalent in any other jurisdiction
consumer credit activity	any of the following regulated activities

i. credit broking (Chapter 6A of Part 2 of the Order)
ii. operating an electronic system in relation to lending (Chapter 6B of Part 2 of the Order)
iii. activities in relation to debt (Chapter 7B of Part 2 of the Order)
iv. regulated credit agreements (Chapter 14A of Part 2 of the Order)
v. regulated consumer hire agreements (Chapter 14B of Part 2 of the Order)
vi. specified activities in relation to information (Part 3A of the Order)

Term	Definition
contract of insurance	the meaning given by article 3(1) of the Order
contract of long-term care insurance	the meaning given by article 1(4) of the Amendment (No 2) Order
contract of long-term insurance	the meaning given by article 3(1) of the Order
Directive	Directive 2002/92/EC of the European Parliament and of the Council of the European Union on insurance mediation
exempt person	a person who is exempt from the general prohibition as a result of an exemption order made under section 38(1) of the Act or as a result of section 39(1) or 285(2) or (3) of the Act
the FCA	the Financial Conduct Authority
the general prohibition	the meaning given by section 19(2) of the Act
Incidental Financial Business Compliance Certificate	a certificate so designated by the Council in such form as the Council may from time to time prescribe
incidental financial business licence	a licence granted by the Council in terms of Part III of this rule 2
insurance intermediary	a person who carries on insurance mediation activity
insurance mediation activity	any of the following regulated activities carried on in relation to a contract of insurance or rights to or interests in a life policy:

i. dealing in investments as agent (Article 21 of the Order)
ii. arranging (bringing about) deals in investments (Article 25(1) of the Order)
iii. making arrangements with a view to transactions in investments (Article 25(2) of the Order)

Term	Definition
	iv. assisting in the administration and performance of a contract of insurance (Article 39A of the Order)
	v. advising on investments (Article 53 of the Order)
	vi. agreeing to carry on a regulated activity in (i) to (v) (Article 64 of the Order)
licensed person	a practice unit which is licensed by the Society to carry on incidental financial business in terms of this rule 2
long-term care insurance mediation activity	the meaning given by article 22 of the Amendment (No 2) Order
mortgage mediation activity	in relation to regulated mortgage contracts, has the meaning given by article 26 of the Amendment (No 1) Order
officer	a manager
the Order	the Financial Services and Markets Act 2000 (Regulated Activities) Order 2001
personal recommendation	a recommendation given to a specific person, and "personally recommending" shall be interpreted accordingly
regulated activity	the meaning given by section 22 of the Act
regulated mortgage contract	the meaning given by article 61(3) of the Order
retail client	a client who is a natural person who is acting for purposes which are outside his trade, business or profession

2.1.2 References in this rule 2 to incidental financial business or regulated activities carried on by a practice unit shall include such business or activities carried on by an individual as an officer or an employee of the practice unit and employees shall include solicitor and non-solicitor employees and consultants.

Purpose and scope of rule 2

2.2.1 This rule 2 makes provision for the carrying on by practice units of incidental financial business.

2.2.2 This rule 2 applies in respect of practice units where the activities constituting incidental financial business are the only regulated activities carried on by the practice unit (other than regulated activities in relation to which it is an exempt person).

2.2.3 This rule 2 applies in respect of incidental financial business carried on in, into or from the United Kingdom, and to practice units carrying on incidental financial business which is insurance mediation activity in or into another Member State.

Part II—Incidental Financial Business

Prohibition on carrying on incidental financial business

2.3 No practice unit shall carry on incidental financial business unless it has been licensed by the Society to do so in terms of this rule 2.

Criteria for carrying on incidental financial business

2.4 Subject to rules 2.2.2 and 2.3, a practice unit may carry on incidental financial business:

(a) to the extent that there is not in force a direction of the FCA under section 328(1) of the Act or an order of the FCA under section 329(1) of the Act preventing the practice unit from carrying on a regulated activity or regulated activities;

(b) to the extent that the regulated activities are not of a description, nor do they relate to an investment of a description, specified in any order made by the Treasury under section 327(6) of the Act;

(c) provided that the practice unit must not receive from a person other than its client any pecuniary reward or other advantage, for which it does not account to its client, arising out of its carrying on any regulated activity;

(d) provided that the manner of the provision by the practice unit of any service in the course of carrying on a regulated activity must be incidental to the provision by it of professional services;

(e) provided that the practice unit carries on only regulated activities which arise out of, or are complementary to, the provision by it of a particular professional service to a particular client; and

(f) provided that the practice unit is controlled or managed by officers who are regulated persons.

Part III—Licences

Application for licence

2.5.1 An application for an incidental financial business licence may be made by a practice unit by submitting to the Secretary at the same time:

(a) a completed form of application in such form as the Council may from time to time prescribe; and

(b) the fee to be prescribed from time to time by the Council in connection with such application.

2.5.2 At any time after receiving an application and before determining it, the Council may require the applicant to furnish additional information and such additional information shall be in such form or verified in such manner as the Council may specify.

Grant and refusal

2.6.1 Subject to rule 2.6.2, the Council may, on an application duly made in accordance with rule 2.5.1, grant or refuse to grant an incidental financial business licence or may grant such licence subject to such conditions or restrictions as it considers appropriate.

2.6.2 The Council shall refuse to grant an incidental financial business licence unless it is satisfied that:

(a) the applicant is a practice unit; and

(b) the main business of the applicant is the practice of professional services which are subject to supervision and regulation by the Society.

2.6.3 The Council shall advise an applicant for an incidental financial business licence, in writing, whether it has been granted an incidental financial business licence, in which case the date of grant shall be specified, as shall any conditions or restrictions which the Council considers appropriate in respect of that licence, or whether it has been refused an incidental financial business licence, in which case the reasons for refusal shall be given.

2.6.4 In the event that the Council shall have granted an incidental financial business licence to an applicant, it shall, at the same time as so advising the applicant in terms of rule 2.6.3, issue to the applicant a certificate confirming that the applicant is licensed to carry on incidental financial business.

2.6.5 The Council shall cause to be kept in respect of each practice year a register of applications for incidental financial business licences and of licences granted. The register shall be in such form as the Council may determine.

Duration, renewal and annual fee

2.7.1 An incidental financial business licence shall expire at the end of each practice year and shall require to be renewed annually. The fee for the renewal of an incidental financial business licence shall be payable annually on or before 1st November. For the avoidance of doubt, the certificate referred to in rule 2.6.4 shall not require to be reissued upon the renewal of an incidental financial business licence.

2.7.2 The amount of the fee referred to in rule 2.7.1 shall be such as the Council may from time to time prescribe.

Withdrawal, suspension and lapse[1]

2.8.1 An incidental financial business licence shall lapse automatically upon the licensed person ceasing to practise as a regulated person or ceasing to be a practice unit.

2.8.2 An incidental financial business licence shall lapse automatically upon the licensed person becoming authorised by the FCA to carry on regulated activities.

2.8.3 An incidental financial business licence shall lapse automatically upon a direction under section 328(1) or an order under section 329(1) of the Act being made in relation to the licensed person, such lapse to be to the extent necessary to secure compliance with the direction or order.

2.8.4 An incidental financial business licence granted to an incorporated practice shall lapse automatically on the revocation of the recognition of that incorporated practice.

2.8.5 An incidental financial business licence granted to a practice unit which is a sole practitioner shall be suspended automatically on the suspension of the practising certificate of that sole practitioner and an incidental financial business licence granted to a practice unit which has two or more managers (but is not an incorporated practice) shall be suspended automatically on the suspension of the practising certificates of the managers of that practice unit.

2.8.6 Any suspension of an incidental financial business licence pursuant to rule 2.8.5 shall continue to have effect only while the practising certificates of the relevant managers remain suspended.

2.8.7 An incidental financial business licence may be suspended by the Council if, within 30 days of the due date for payment of any fee required under rule 2.7.1, payment has not been made, provided that such suspension shall cease to have effect on payment being made.

2.8.8 An incidental financial business licence may be suspended by the Council if the licensed person has not, within one month (or within such extended period as the

---

[1] 2.8.1–2.8.12 as substituted by the Law Society of Scotland Practice (Amendment) Rules 2012 (effective November 1, 2012).

Council may have authorised in terms of rule 2.19) of the completion of its accounting period, delivered to the Council an Incidental Financial Business Compliance Certificate in accordance with Part V of this rule 2 , provided that such suspension shall cease to have effect on the date of the production to the Council of an Incidental Financial Business Compliance Certificate.

2.8.9 An incidental financial business licence may be suspended or withdrawn by the Council if the licensed person has failed to comply with any provision of this rule 2 other than those provisions failure to comply with which may result in suspension pursuant to rules 2.8.7 or 2.8.8, provided that an incidental financial business licence may be withdrawn by the Council if the licensed person has had its incidental financial business licence suspended pursuant to rule 2.8.7 or rule 2.8.8 on two or more occasions. In exercising its discretion to suspend or withdraw in such circumstances, the Council shall have regard to the materiality of any such failure to comply and to any previous failures to comply.

2.8.10 The Council shall advise the licensed person of any suspension or withdrawal pursuant to rules 2.8.7, 2.8.8 or 2.8.9 by notice, which notice shall specify the date upon which the suspension or withdrawal shall take effect. In the case of a suspension, the licensed person may represent either orally or in writing to the Council that such suspension should be terminated and, in considering any such representation, the Council shall have regard to the efforts made by the licensed person to remedy the failure to comply which gave rise to the suspension.

2.8.11 Where an incidental financial business licence has lapsed or has been or is to be withdrawn or suspended, whether automatically or otherwise, the Council may direct the licensed person whose incidental financial business licence has lapsed or has been or is to be withdrawn or suspended, to take such action and make such arrangements as are necessary, in the view of the Council, to ensure the speedy and satisfactory completion and/or transfer to another licensed person of clients' outstanding incidental financial business.

2.8.12 Any licensed person whose incidental financial business licence has lapsed or is withdrawn or suspended in terms of this rule 2.8 may, in a case of automatic lapse or suspension, within 21 days of the occurrence of the event which has given rise to such lapse or suspension and, in a case of withdrawal or suspension by the Council, within 21 days of being notified by the Council of such withdrawal or suspension, appeal to the Court of Session.

Notification of changes to information, section 328 directions and section 329 orders

2.9.1 A licensed person shall notify the Secretary in writing of any change to the information provided to the Society on the form of application submitted in terms of rule 2.5.1 or to the additional information (if any) provided in terms of rule 2.5.2.

2.9.2 The notification referred to in rule 2.9.1 shall be given by the licensed person within one month of any change referred to in rule 2.9.1.

2.9.3 A licensed person shall notify the Secretary in writing in the event that a direction of the FCA under section 328(1) or an order under section 329(1) of the Act is made in relation to the licensed person.

2.9.4 The notification referred to in rule 2.9.3 shall be given by the licensed person within one month of the direction or order referred to in rule 2.9.3 being made, and shall be accompanied by a copy of the direction or order.

2.9.5 A licensed person shall notify the Secretary in writing in the event that the licensed person becomes authorised by the FCA to carry on regulated activities.

2.9.6 The notification referred to in rule 2.9.5 shall be given by the licensed person within one month of the authorisation referred to in rule 2.9.5 coming into effect, and shall be accompanied by a copy of the certificate of authorisation.

Part IV—Insurance Mediation Activity

Registration for the purposes of insurance mediation activity

2.10.1 Every practice unit which carries on incidental financial business which is insurance mediation activity shall give the Council the details required by the Council of the officer responsible for the conduct of that business.

2.10.2 The Council shall notify the FCA of any details disclosed to it pursuant to paragraph 2.10.1.

2.10.3 Every practice unit which carries on any incidental financial business which is insurance mediation activity shall give the Council the details required by the Council of those persons involved in that business, which may include details of any criminal record and of any bankruptcy proceedings in relation to those persons.

2.10.4 The details required to be given to the Council in terms of this rule may form part of the information required by the form of application referred to in rule 2.5.1, and changes in those details shall be notified to the Council in terms of rule 2.9.1.

2.10.5 As required by the Directive, no practice unit may carry on insurance mediation activity until it appears on the FCA exempt professional firm (EPF) register.

Requirement of good repute

2.11.1 No person having a criminal record disclosing a serious criminal offence involving any crime against property or related to financial activities shall be involved in insurance mediation activity on behalf of any practice unit, whether as an officer, employee, consultant or otherwise.

2.11.2 No person who is subject to bankruptcy proceedings shall be involved in insurance mediation activity on behalf of any practice unit, whether as an officer, employee, consultant or otherwise.

Prohibition on carrying on business

2.12 No licensed person shall carry on incidental financial business which is insurance mediation activity if it is not registered with the FCA for that purpose.

Provision of information

2.13.1 Subject to rule 2.13.2, where a contract of insurance is to be concluded with a client in relation to which a licensed person has conducted insurance mediation activity, the information set out in Schedule A to this rule 2 must be provided to the client:

(a) on paper or other durable medium available and accessible to the client;

(b) in a clear and accurate manner, comprehensible to the client; and

(c) in an official language of the Member State of the Community or in any other language agreed by the licensed person and the client.

2.13.2 The information to be provided pursuant to rule 2.13.1:

(a) may be provided orally if:

    (i) the client requests this; or

    (ii) the client requires immediate cover; and

(b)   need not be provided before the conclusion of the contract if the contract is concluded by telephone at the client's request and the client gives his explicit consent to receiving limited information after the conclusion of the contract.

2.13.3   Where rule 2.13.2 applies, the client must be provided with the information set out in Schedule A to this rule 2, in a manner which complies with paragraphs (a) to (c) of rule 2.13.1, immediately after the conclusion of the contract.

2.13.4   If the contract is concluded by a licensed person acting as an insurance intermediary by telephone with a retail client, the retail client must be informed on initial contact of:

(a)   the name of the licensed person and, if the call is initiated by the insurance intermediary, the commercial purpose of the call; and

(b)   where relevant, the identity of the person in contact with the retail client and his link with the licensed person.

2.13.5   Where the contact of a licensed person with a client is limited to introducing that client to another insurance intermediary, the client must be given the information specified in paragraph 1 to 5, 8 and 9 of Schedule A to this rule 2 on initial contact. The information may be provided orally or in writing.

2.13.6   Where the information required to be supplied pursuant to rule 2.13.5 is given orally, the information must also be provided by the licensed person, in a manner which complies with sub-paragraphs (a) to (c) of rule 2.13.1 immediately after the initial contact with the client.

2.13.7   Where a licensed person acts as an insurance intermediary in relation to a contract of insurance, and selects contracts from a limited number of insurance undertakings or from a single insurance undertaking then it must maintain, and keep up to date, for each type of contract of insurance that it deals with, a list of insurance undertakings that it selects from or deals with and the relevant list must be made available to any client, in writing, on request.

Scope of services

2.14   Where a licensed person acts as an insurance intermediary and holds itself out as providing advice to clients on particular types of contracts of insurance on the basis of a fair analysis of the market, it must not provide such advice unless it has analysed a sufficiently large number of contracts available in the relevant sector or sectors of the market to be able to give advice on a contract of insurance which is adequate to meet the client's needs.

Statement of demands and needs

2.15.1   Where a licensed person makes a personal recommendation to a client of a specific contract of insurance, or arranges for a client to enter into a specific contract of insurance, it must, before the conclusion of that contract, provide the client with a statement of his demands and needs in respect of that insurance contract. In addition to stating the demands and needs of the client, the statement must:

(a)   confirm whether the licensed person has personally recommended that contract; and

(b)   explain the reasons for personally recommending that contract.

2.15.2   The statement referred to in rule 2.15.1 must reflect the complexity of the contract of insurance proposed.

2.15.3   Unless rule 2.15.4 applies, the statement referred to in rule 2.15.1 must be provided in writing.

2.15.4 A licensed person may provide the statement referred to in rule 2.15.1 orally if:

(a) the client requests it; or

(b) immediate cover is necessary;

but in both cases the licensed person must provide that statement in writing immediately after the conclusion of the contract.

Notification of establishment and services in other Member States

2.16.1 Any licensed person intending to exercise its right under article 6(1) of the Directive to carry on business for the first time in or into a Member State (other than the United Kingdom) shall notify the FCA of that intention and whether such business will be conducted through a branch or on a services basis.

2.16.2 A licensed person who has complied with rule 2.16.1 may commence business one month after the date on which it is notified by the FCA that the FCA has informed the competent authorities of the Member State in or into which that licensed person intends to carry on business of that licensed person's intention. If those competent authorities do not wish to be informed of that licensed person's intention, that licensed person may commence business immediately upon notification by the FCA of that fact to that licensed person.

Part V—Compliance and Monitoring

Obligation to deliver Incidental Financial Business Compliance Certificate

2.17.1 Every licensed person shall deliver to the Secretary, within one calendar month of the completion of each accounting period, an Incidental Financial Business Compliance Certificate in respect of that period.

2.17.2 An Incidental Financial Business Compliance Certificate shall be signed by an officer of the licensed person.

Where a licensed person practises in two or more places

2.18 In the case of a licensed person which has two or more places of business and where separate financial business records are maintained by the licensed person for each place of business, a separate Incidental Financial Business Compliance Certificate shall be delivered in respect of each place of business.

Power of Council to extend period of time referred to in rule 2.17.1

2.19 The Council may, in any case on satisfactory cause shown, extend the period of one calendar month within which an Incidental Financial Business Compliance Certificate requires to be delivered provided that such extension shall in no case exceed three months from the date of completion of the relevant accounting period.

Inspections by Council

2.20.1 To enable the Council to ascertain whether or not a licensed person is complying with this rule 2, the Council may, by notice, require that licensed person to produce at a time to be fixed by the Council and at a place to be fixed by the Council documents, records and other information concerning the conduct of its practice in relation to this rule 2 including, without prejudice to the foregoing generality, files and relative correspondence (in this rule 2 referred to as "documents, records and other information"), for inspection by a person or persons appointed by the Council. If the place fixed by the Council for the inspection requires the transfer to that place of documents, records and other information in physical form, the Council shall, on such conditions as to the cost and distance of such transfer as it may from time to time prescribe, pay the reasonable expenses incurred by the licensed person in respect of such transfer.

2.20.2 If at any time there is a reasonable apprehension on the part of the Council that a practice unit has not complied with, is not complying with or may not comply with this rule 2, including, but without prejudice to the foregoing generality, by carrying on incidental financial business in contravention of rule 2.3 or 2.12 the Council may, by notice, require that practice unit to produce at a time to be fixed by the Council and at a place to be fixed by the Council, documents, records and other information for inspection by a person or persons appointed by the Council.

2.20.3 It shall be the duty of a licensed person or a practice unit or solicitor to provide a person or persons appointed by the Council under rules 2.20.1 or 2.20.2 reasonable co-operation in the conduct of that person's or persons' inspection including, without prejudice to the foregoing generality, the production of documents, records and other information as such person or persons may reasonably require.

2.20.4 Any person or persons appointed by the Council under rules 2.20.1 or 2.20.2 shall report to the Council upon the result of his inspection.

2.20.5 Where, following an inspection of the documents, records and other information of a licensed person or practice unit in terms of rules 2.20.1 or 2.20.2, it appears to the Council that the licensed person or practice unit has not complied with this rule 2, the Council may instruct a further inspection of the documents, records and other information of the licensed person or practice unit and, if it so instructs, the Council may by notice require the licensed person or practice unit to pay to the Council the reasonable costs of such further inspection, provided always that such notice is given to the licensed person or practice unit not more than one year after the date of the inspection first referred to in this rule 2.20.5. The amount of such sum shall be fixed by the Council and intimated to the licensed person or practice unit following such further inspection.

2.20.6 It shall be the duty of a licensed person or practice unit upon whom a notice in terms of rule 2.20.5 has been served to make payment forthwith of the amount so intimated.

2.20.7 Where a licensed person carries out a consumer credit activity it must comply with any relevant FCA conduct of business rules relating to that activity as if it were authorised by the FCA.

Part VI—Misconduct, Disclosure, Training and Records

Terms of business

2.21 Whenever it intends or expects to carry out incidental financial business for a client, a licensed person shall so advise its client by sending to that client terms of business which contain, in a manner that is clear, fair and not misleading, the statements and the information specified in Schedule B to this rule 2 and/or such other statements or information as the Council may from time to time prescribe.

Disclosure

2.22.1 For the avoidance of doubt, but with the exception of the terms of business referred to in rule 2.21, a practice unit shall not be required to make any disclosure to the effect that it is a licensed person or otherwise on its stationery or any other material which it may publish.

2.22.2 A licensed person shall display at each of its places of business its certificate (or a copy thereof) issued pursuant to rule 2.6.4, confirming that the licensed person is licensed to carry on incidental financial business.

Training

2.23   In respect of the carrying on of incidental financial business by it, a licensed person shall:

(a)   advance and maintain the competence of all officers and employees carrying on incidental financial business;

(b)   ensure that all officers and employees carrying on incidental financial business remain competent for the functions they carry out;

(c)   ensure that all officers and employees carrying on incidental financial business are adequately supervised in relation to the attainment and maintenance of competence;

(d)   ensure that the training for and the competence of all officers and employees carrying on incidental financial business are regularly reviewed;

(e)   in dealing with the commitments set out in paragraphs (a) to (d), take account of the level of competence that is necessary having regard to the nature of its business and the role of all officers and employees carrying on incidental financial business; and

(f)   ensure that a reasonable proportion of the officers of the practice unit who are responsible for insurance mediation activity and all other persons directly involved in insurance mediation activity demonstrate the knowledge and ability necessary for the performance of their duties, having regard to the nature of the business and the roles of those persons.

Record keeping requirements

2.24   In respect of the carrying on of incidental financial business by it, a licensed person shall:

(a)   ensure that all instructions from clients to carry out specific incidental financial business are performed as soon as possible unless it would be contrary to the best interests of the client to do so;

(b)   retain records of all statements of demands and needs made in accordance with rule 2.15 in connection with personal recommendations made to clients in the course of insurance mediation activity for at least three years from the date on which the personal recommendation was made;

(c)   retain records of all instructions from clients to carry out specific incidental financial business on their behalf and all instructions from the licensed person to any third party to effect such incidental financial business for at least a period equal to the remainder of the financial year of the licensed person and a further six financial years of that person from the date of the instruction;

(d)   retain records of any pecuniary award or other advantage received by the licensed person as a result of carrying on incidental financial business on behalf of a client and records of the accounting by the licensed person to its client in respect of such pecuniary award or other advantage for at least a period equal to the remainder of the financial year of the licensed person and a further six financial years of that person from the date of the accounting;

(e)   take appropriate technical and organisational measures to ensure the safe keeping of assets held by the licensed person on behalf of its clients or third parties; and

(f)   ensure that, where the licensed person takes the advice of a third party authorised by the FCA to carry on regulated activities, that such third party provides independent advice.

Distance marketing of financial services

2.25 Licensed persons shall comply with the terms of the Financial Services (Distance Marketing) Regulations 2004 (SI 2004 No. 2095) so far as applicable to them.

F3.14

SCHEDULE A TO RULE 2[1]

Information to be Disclosed Before or Immediately after Conclusion of a Contract of Insurance

Rule 2.13.1

1. The name and address of the licensed person.

2. The licensed person's statutory status as a person licensed by the Society to conduct incidental financial business, including insurance mediation activity. This must be done by using the standard statement contained in PROF 4.1.3 R (2) of the FCA's Professional Firms Sourcebook relating to insurance mediation and mortgage activities.

3. The fact that items 1 and 2 may be checked on the FCA's register by visiting the FCA's website *http://www.fca.gov.uk* or by contacting the FCA on 0845 606 9966.

4. Whether the licensed person has any holding, direct or indirect, representing more than 10 per cent of the voting rights of or the capital in an insurance undertaking.

5. Whether an insurance undertaking or parent of an insurance undertaking has a holding, direct or indirect, representing more than 10 per cent of the voting rights of or capital in the licensed person.

6. In relation to the contract of insurance provided, whether the licensed person has selected or dealt with the contract;

    (a)   on the basis of a fair analysis of the market; or

    (b)   from a limited number of insurance undertakings; or

    (c)   from a single insurance undertaking.

If sub-paragraph (b) or (c) applies, the licensed person must also disclose whether it is contractually obliged to conduct insurance mediation activity in this way.

7. If the contract of insurance provided has not been selected on the basis of a fair analysis of the market, the client can request a copy of the list of the insurance undertakings the licensed person selects from or deals with in relation to that contract.

8. The details referred to in paragraph (d) of Schedule B.

9. The details referred to in paragraph (e) of Schedule B.

SCHEDULE B TO RULE 2[2]

Terms of Business

Rule 2.21

The terms of business referred to in rule 2.21 shall contain the following statements and disclosures:

---

[1] As amended by the Law Society of Scotland Practice Rules (Amendment (No.1) Rules 2013 (effective April 1, 2014).

[2] As amended by the Law Society of Scotland Practice Rules (Amendment (No.1) Rules 2013 (effective April 1, 2014).

(a) a statement as to the nature of the specific incidental financial business activities carried on by the licensed person for the client and the fact that these are limited in scope;

(b) a statement that the licensed person is licensed by the Law Society of Scotland to carry on incidental financial business;

(c) a statement that the licensed person is not authorised by the Financial Services Authority under the Financial Services and Markets Act 2000;

(d) disclosure of the compensation arrangements in respect of the carrying on of incidental financial business by that licensed person, making reference to the licensed person's professional indemnity insurance under the Law Society of Scotland's Master Policy (or the equivalent cover in respect of a registered European lawyer or registered foreign lawyer, as appropriate) and to the Scottish Solicitors Guarantee Fund (or the equivalent cover in respect of a registered European lawyer or registered foreign lawyer, as appropriate); and

(e) disclosure of the complaints procedure which is operated by the licensed person, which shall include details of the licensed person's internal complaints procedure and details of the right of a client to complain to Scottish Legal Complaints Commission, The Stamp Office, 10–14 Waterloo Place, Edinburgh. EH1 3EG. Tel: 0131 201 2130.

Rule C3: Civil Legal Aid[1]

Interpretation

3.1 In this rule 3, unless the context otherwise requires, terms listed in the first column of rule 3.1 shall have the meanings respectively ascribed to them in the second column of that rule:

Term	Definition
ABWOR	advice and assistance provided to a person by taking on his behalf any step in instituting, conducting or defending proceedings (a) before a court or tribunal; or (b) in connection with a statutory enquiry whether by representing him in those proceedings or by otherwise taking any steps on his behalf (as distinct from assisting him in taking such a step on his behalf)
advice and assistance	advice and assistance on a civil matter within the meaning of section 6 of the 1986 Act and to which Part II of the 1986 Act applies excepting any matter arising out of Chapters 2 and 3 of the Children (Scotland) Act 1995 and the Children's Hearings (Scotland) Act 2011
associated practising solicitor	in relation to a practice unit, a practising solicitor who: (a) is a manager of that practice unit, (b) is an employee of that practice unit, or (c) is a consultant to that practice unit

---

[1] As substituted by the Law Society of Scotland Practice (Amendment) Rules 2012 (effective November 1, 2012).

Term	Definition
the Board	the Scottish Legal Aid Board, established by the 1986 Act
civil legal aid	the meaning given to it in Part III of the 1986 Act
compliance	compliance in all material respects, and "comply" shall be construed accordingly
compliance certificate	a certificate awarded by the Council in terms of rule 3.5
employee	includes an associate
the Fund	the meaning given to it in section 4(1) of the 1986 Act
legal aid	(i) advice and assistance and (ii) civil legal aid
legal aid files	in relation to a practice unit:

(a) any files, papers or documents or copies thereof,

(b) copies in printed format of any data held in any way, and

(c) copies other than in printed format of any data held in any way

relating to the provision (whether current or past) of legal aid by that practice unit or the procedures followed, or to be followed, in doing so

practising solicitor	as defined in Schedule 1 but including a registered European lawyer providing or seeking to provide legal aid pursuant to regulation 14 of the European Lawyer Regulations provided that nothing in these rules shall confer on any registered European lawyer any entitlement to practice under the title of "solicitor"
registered practice unit	a practice unit that is registered
registration	registration with the Board as a practice unit for the purpose of providing legal aid, and "registered" shall be construed accordingly
relevant date	the relevant date as defined in rule 3.6
reviewer	a person appointed by the Council in terms of rule 3.14

Provision of legal aid

3.2.1 No practising solicitor shall:
(a) grant any application for advice and assistance;
(b) sign any application for civil legal aid as a practising solicitor nominated by the applicant; or
(c) sign any application for ABWOR as a practising solicitor nominated by the applicant

unless he satisfies a condition set out in rule 3.2.2, and provided that rule 3.8 does not apply to him.

3.2.2 A practising solicitor satisfies a condition set out in this rule 3.2.2 if he is acting:
(a) as a registered practice unit;
(b) as a manager of a registered practice unit; or
(c) as an employee of a registered practice unit; or
(d) as a consultant to a registered practice unit; or
(e) in the course of his employment by the Board; or

(f)   pursuant to the terms of an exemption granted to him by the Council in terms of rule 3.15.

3.2.3   No practising solicitor or practice unit shall apply to the Board for the registration of a practice unit which does not hold a compliance certificate.

Quality Assurance Scheme

3.3.1   The Council shall publish, and may from time to time amend, guidance in relation to the provision of legal aid which shall set out the standards expected of practising solicitors and practice units in relation to the carrying out of such work. The Council may publish separate guidance in relation to the provision of different types of legal aid. In providing legal aid, practising solicitors and practice units shall comply with that guidance.

3.3.2   Every practice unit applying for or holding a compliance certificate shall designate one of its managers as Compliance Manager, to whom notices and other communications to the practice unit from the Society, the Council or the Board which are related to (i) this rule 3; (ii) the practice unit's compliance certificate (or any application for same); or (iii) otherwise related to the practice unit's registration or its provision of legal aid, may be addressed

3.3.3   The designation required by rule 3.3.2 shall be made and intimated in writing to the Society (which intimation shall include full contact details for the manager so designated):

(a)   in the case of a practice unit which is applying for a compliance certificate, on submission of the application for same;

(b)   in every other case, within 28 days of these rules coming into operation.

3.3.4   Any change to the identity or contact details of a Compliance Manager shall be intimated to the Society, in writing, within 28 days of the effective date of the change.

Obligation on practice units to ensure compliance with guidance

3.4   A practice unit shall ensure compliance with the guidance published in terms of rule 3.3 by any person undertaking any activity pursuant to the provision of legal aid by that practice unit.

Applications

3.5.1   The Council shall, subject to rule 3.5.3, on application for a compliance certificate being made by or on behalf of a practice unit, make such enquiry as to the ability of that practice unit to comply with the guidance published in terms of rule 3.3 as the Council thinks fit, which may include interviewing any practising solicitor who is, or is to be, an associated practising solicitor of that practice unit, and a review of that practice unit pursuant to rules 3.13.1 and 3.13.2. That enquiry may be made on behalf of the Council by a reviewer. If that enquiry and review, if any, demonstrate that the practice unit complies, or will when it begins to provide legal aid comply, with the guidance published pursuant to rule 3.3, the Council shall award a certificate to that effect to that practice unit, starting on the date the practice unit was reviewed pursuant to rules 3.13.1 and 3.13.2, or, if it has not been so reviewed, stating that fact and starting on such date as the Council considers appropriate. If that enquiry and review, if any, do not demonstrate that the practice unit complies, or will when it begins to provide legal aid comply with the guidance published pursuant to rule 3.3, the Council shall, subject to rule 3.9, reject the application.

3.5.2   A practice unit may within six months of the relevant date apply for a review pursuant to rule 3.13.3, and provided that no previous review of that practice unit has been made pursuant to rule 3.13.3 since that date, the Council shall, subject to rule 3.13.4, instruct a review of that practice unit pursuant to rule 3.13.3 to be carried out not more than 12 months after the relevant date.

3.5.3   No application made pursuant to rule 3.5.2 shall be considered by the Council if it is made by a practice unit:

(a)   having a compliance certificate on which a note has been made pursuant to rule 3.6; or

(b)   within six months of

(i)   renunciation of the compliance certificate of that practice unit pursuant to rule 3.7.2; or

(ii)   rejection of any application by that practice unit in terms of rule 3.5.1; or

(c)   within 12 months of withdrawal of the compliance certificate of that practice unit pursuant to rule 3.6 or 3.7.1.

3.5.4   Applications made pursuant to rules 3.5.1 and 3.5.2 shall be in the form determined by the Council from time to time.

Requirement for further review and withdrawal of compliance certificate on failure to apply or pay for further review

3.6   If, having regard to the results of a review carried out pursuant to rule 3.13.2(a) (an extended review), or to rule 3.13.3(b) (a special review), together with other relevant information, the Council decides that a practice unit should be further reviewed pursuant to rule 3.13.3 (a final review), then it shall make a note to that effect on the compliance certificate of that practice unit. If that practice unit has not:

(a)   made any application in terms of rule 3.5.2 within six months of the date the decision is made to make such a note (the date of such decision being the "relevant date"), or

(b)   in a case where the instruction of a review pursuant to rule 3.13.3 is made conditional by the Council on payment of or agreement to pay the sum as provided for in rule 3.13.4, paid that sum to the Council by the date required by the Council,

the Council may withdraw the compliance certificate of that practice unit and if it does so, it shall notify the practice unit of the withdrawal of the compliance certificate and the compliance certificate shall cease to have effect three working days after receipt of that notice.

Withdrawal and renunciation of compliance certificate

3.7.1   If, having regard to the results of a review carried out pursuant to rule 3.13.3 (a final review), the Council decides that a practice unit does not comply with the guidance published pursuant to rule 3.3, then it shall withdraw the compliance certificate of that practice unit. The Council shall notify the practice unit of the withdrawal of the compliance certificate and the compliance certificate shall cease to have effect three working days after receipt of that notice, and the provisions of rule 3.8 shall apply.

3.7.2 A practice unit may renounce its compliance certificate at any time by giving notice to that effect to the Council. A notice of renunciation shall take effect from the date on which it is received by the Council, and the compliance certificate of that practice unit shall be withdrawn and cease to have effect from that date, and the provisions of rule 3.8 shall apply.

Effect of withdrawal or renunciation of compliance certificate

3.8.1 If the compliance certificate of a practice unit has been withdrawn pursuant to rule 3.6 or renounced pursuant to rule 3.7.2, then with effect from the date specified in rule 3.6, 3.7.1 or 3.7.2, as the case may be, on which that compliance certificate ceases to have effect, no associated practising solicitor shall
  (a) grant any application for advice and assistance,
  (b) sign any application for civil legal aid as a practising solicitor nominated by the applicant, or
  (c) sign any application for ABWOR as a practising solicitor nominated by the applicant .

3.8.2 No later than 28 days from the date in rule 3.8.1 each associated practising solicitor to a practice unit to which rule 3.8.1 applies who has granted any application for advice and assistance or has signed any application for ABWOR or civil legal aid as a practising solicitor nominated by the applicant or is otherwise providing legal aid shall:
  (a) cease the provision of legal aid,
  (b) in each case involving advice and assistance or ABWOR, notify the client in receipt of advice and assistance or ABWOR in writing that he and his practice unit must cease to act for that client, and
  (c) in each case involving civil legal aid, notify the applicant and (where the compliance certificate has been renounced) the Board in writing that he and his practice unit must cease to act for the applicant and supply to the Board a statement of his reasons for ceasing to act.

3.8.3 Each associated practising solicitor referred to in rule 3.8.2 shall, in each case involving civil legal aid, co-operate with the applicant and the Board in the transfer of civil legal aid files to another practising solicitor nominated by the applicant in terms of an application made by the applicant to the Board and granted by the Board.

3.8.4 No practice unit to which rule 3.8.1 applies and no associated practising solicitor shall apply to the Board for payment out of the Fund, from any contribution, expenses recovered or from any property recovered or preserved, of any fees or outlays incurred in respect of any legal aid which is provided by that associated practising solicitor after the expiry of the 28 day period referred to in rule 3.8.2.

Giving of Reasons

3.9 Where the Council is minded to:
  (a) reject an application in terms of rule 3.5.1, or
  (b) make a note on a compliance certificate pursuant to rule 3.6, or
  (c) withdraw a compliance certificate pursuant to rule 3.7.1

then it shall give notice of that fact to the relevant practice unit and supply that practice unit with copies of any information it proposes to rely on in coming to any such decision (with any deletions necessary to protect the identity of any person as appropriate), including, any report made in terms of rule 3.13.8, and shall have regard to written representations made to it by or on behalf of that practice unit, any associated practising solicitor and any other interested person.

Appeals

3.10.1   Where the Council has:
(a)   rejected an application in terms of rule 3.5.1,
(b)   withdrawn a compliance certificate pursuant to rule 3.6 or rule 3.7.1,

a practice unit which is the subject of any such decision and which is aggrieved by it may, within 21 days of written intimation of that decision, appeal to the Outer House of the Court of Session. The decision of the Outer House in relation to such an appeal shall be final.

3.10.2   For the avoidance of doubt, in circumstances where a compliance certificate has been withdrawn in terms of rule 3.7.1 and an appeal against that decision is made in terms of rule 3.10.1, the provisions of rule 3.8 shall continue to apply.

Updating of Certificate

3.11   Where, a review of a practice unit having a compliance certificate has been carried out pursuant to rule 3.13, and the Council is satisfied that such a practice unit complies with the guidance published pursuant to rule 3.3, the Council shall update the compliance certificate of that practice unit to show the date of that review.

Register of practice units holding compliance certificate, and of associated solicitors

3.12.1   The Council shall maintain a register of practice units in relation to which a compliance certificate is in effect.

3.12.2   The Council shall maintain a register of practising solicitors who carry out legal aid work and are associated with registered practice units.

3.12.3   All registered practice units will maintain a complete and accurate list of the name and contact details of all practising solicitors associated with the practice unit who carry out legal aid work. The Compliance Manager of each registered practice unit will supply a copy of the relevant list to the Society within 28 days of these rules coming into force. Any application for a compliance certificate must be accompanied by a list of the names and contact details of all practising solicitors associated with the applicant practice unit who it is intended will carry out legal aid work, if the application is granted. Any changes to any information contained in any list provided to the Society pursuant to this rule shall be intimated by the relevant Compliance Manager to the Society, in writing, within 28 days of the effective date of the change.

3.12.4   The Council may supply copies of entries in the register in rule 3.12.1 and 3.12.2 to such persons as it thinks fit.

Reviews

3.13.1   To enable it to ascertain whether a practice unit which holds, or has applied for, a compliance certificate complies, or will comply, with the guidance published pursuant to rule 3.3, the Council may instruct a review of that practice unit ("a routine review") by a reviewer specified by the Council. Where that practice unit has any legal aid files the Council may by notice to the practice unit require the practice unit and any associated practising solicitor to deliver to the reviewer, or so far as it or he is able, to procure that any other person so delivers, by a date and to an address to be specified by that reviewer, the legal aid files specified by him. The reviewer shall review any such legal aid files, and carry out such other enquiry as he sees fit, with the object of ascertaining whether that practice unit complies or will comply with the guidance published pursuant to rule 3.3. Where that practice unit does not have any legal aid files, the reviewer shall carry out such enquiry as he thinks fit with the object of ascertaining whether that practice unit complies or will comply with the guidance published pursuant to rule 3.3.

3.13.2   Where,

(a)   following a routine review in terms of rule 3.13.1, it appears to the Council that a review ("an extended review") at the premises of any practice unit is necessary or desirable to determine whether that practice unit complies or will comply with the guidance published pursuant to rule 3.3, or

(b)   on the basis of information received by it, it appears to the Council that a review ("a special review") at the premises of any practice unit is necessary or desirable to determine whether that practice unit complies or will comply with the guidance published pursuant to rule 3.3, or

(c)   the Council reaches agreement to do so with a practice unit that would otherwise be subject to a routine review, the Council may by notice to the practice unit require the practice unit or any associated practising solicitor to allow, or so far as it or he is able, to procure that any other person allows, access for that purpose by a reviewer on a date or dates to be specified by the Council to any premises, legal aid files or person. Where that practice unit has any legal aid files, the reviewer shall visit the premises, may review all or any such files and may carry out such other enquiry as he thinks fit with a view to ascertaining whether that practice unit complies or will comply with the guidance published pursuant to rule 3.3. Where that practice unit has no legal aid files, the reviewer shall visit the premises and carry out such enquiry as he thinks fit with a view to ascertaining whether that practice unit complies or will comply with the guidance published pursuant to rule 3.3.

3.13.3   A review in terms of this paragraph ("a final review"), which shall only be instructed pursuant to rule 3.5.2 subject to rule 3.13.4, is a review of a practice unit by a reviewer specified by the Council. The Council may by notice to the practice unit require it or any associated practising solicitor to allow, or so far as it or he is able, to procure that any other person allows, access by that reviewer to any premises, legal aid files or person. Where a practice unit has any legal aid files, the reviewer shall visit the premises, may review all or any such files and may carry out such other enquiry as he thinks fit with a view to ascertaining whether that practice unit complies or will comply with the guidance published pursuant to rule 3.3. Where that practice unit has no legal aid files, the reviewer shall visit the premises and carry out such enquiry as he thinks fit with a view to ascertaining whether that practice unit complies or will comply with the guidance published pursuant to rule 3.3

3.13.4   The Council may make the instruction pursuant to rule 3.5.2 of a review of a practice unit in terms of rule 3.13.3 conditional upon that practice unit paying or agreeing to pay to the Council such sum as may be required to meet the fees and costs incurred in connection with that review. The amount of such sum shall be fixed by the Council.

3.13.5   Where a practice unit that would otherwise be subject to a review in terms of rule 3.13.1 reaches agreement with the Council that it is instead reviewed in terms of rule 3.13.2 pursuant to a request by that practice unit, the agreement of the Council to do so may be made conditional upon that practice unit paying or agreeing to pay to the Council such sum as may be required to meet the fees and cost incurred in connection with that review. The amount of such sum shall be fixed by the Council.

3.13.6 A practising solicitor who is a manager shall ensure that the sum required to be paid by him or that practice unit in terms of rules 3.13.4 or 3.13.5 is paid.

3.13.7 A practising solicitor shall comply with all requirements made in terms of rules 3.13.1 to 3.13.3, and shall give reasonable co-operation to any reviewer acting in the course of any review or enquiry in terms of this rule 3.13.

3.13.8 Where:

(a) a reviewer has completed a routine, extended, special or final review of a practice unit, or

(b) any matter arises which in the opinion of a reviewer requires to be brought to the attention of the Council; or

(c) the Council requests it,

that reviewer shall make a written report to the Council on that review or matter or pursuant to that request.

Reviewers

3.14.1 In order to carry out reviews in terms of rule 3.13 and any other enquiry permitted or required in terms of these rules, the Council may appoint any person who consents to such appointment as a reviewer. Such a person shall be a practising solicitor.

3.14.2 A reviewer shall comply with any directions that may be given by the Council in respect of matters connected with reviews in terms of rule 3.13 or any other enquiry permitted or required in terms of this rule 3.

3.14.3 A reviewer shall be appointed for such term and be paid such remuneration as the Council may from time to time determine.

Exemption

3.15.1 The Council may exempt any practising solicitor from the requirement to satisfy the conditions contained in (a) to (e) of rule 3.2.2, subject to such conditions, if any, as it considers appropriate.

3.15.2 The Council may, where the circumstances of any practice unit are exceptional, consider any application made by such practice unit pursuant to rule 3.5.1 notwithstanding the provisions of rule 3.5.3, subject to such conditions, if any, as it considers appropriate.

Rule C4: Solicitor Advocates

Rights of Audience in the Civil Courts

Interpretation

4.1.1 In this rule 4.1, unless the context otherwise requires, terms listed in the first column of rule 4.1.1 shall have the meanings respectively ascribed to them in the second column of that rule:

Term	Definition
applicant	a solicitor who seeks a right of audience in the Court

Term	Definition
course of training	a course of training in evidence, procedure and pleadings in relation to proceedings in the Court
Court	the Court of Session, the Supreme Court and the Judicial Committee of the Privy Council
knowledge	knowledge of the practice, and procedures of and professional conduct in the Court
relevant date	the date on which the applicant informs the Council that he seeks a right of audience in the Court
right of audience	a right of audience in the Court

Course of Training in Evidence, Pleading and Procedure

4.1.2 The following matters are to be included in the course of training:
- (a) the preparation and submission to the persons conducting the course of examples of the forms and style of written pleadings used in the presentation of cases in the Court of Session;
- (b) the practical applications of the law of evidence in connection with the presentation of cases in the Court of Session;
- (c) the procedure employed in the Court;
- (d) the presentation by applicants to the persons conducting the course of examples of oral advocacy in the manner required in the Court.

4.1.3 The following methods of instruction are to be employed in the course of training:
- (a) lectures, the provision of written instructional material, and audio-visual or other practical demonstration by the persons conducting the course of training in relation to any of the matters specified in rule 4.1.2;
- (b) attendance for a period, to be specified by the course convener, of up to six days sitting in on proceedings in the Court of Session, not being proceedings involving the applicant or any member or employee of the applicant's practice unit unless the convener shall direct otherwise, in both or either of the Outer House (including the Commercial Court) and the Inner House, observing, with or without the supervision of the persons conducting the course of training, the manner in which cases are conducted in that court;
- (c) discussion of the applicant's performance by those conducting the course, and the provision of comment and criticism by them upon the applicant's presentation of oral advocacy;
- (d) consideration by those conducting the course of the applicant's written work and the provision of criticism and comment thereon.

4.1.4 The persons who conduct the course of training, including the course convener, shall be:
- (a) solicitors or advocates of at least 5 years standing; or
- (b) persons who have been employed at a university in Scotland for at least 5 years full-time during the last 10 years;

and who have experience in the matters specified in rule 4.1.2.

Demonstration of Knowledge

4.1.5 An applicant's knowledge shall be demonstrated by evidence that he has:

(a) passed in not more than two attempts a written examination on such matters set by examiners appointed by the Council within thirty months of the relevant date; or

(b) passed examinations for admission to the Faculty of Advocates which are considered by the Council to be equivalent to the written examination referred to above.

4.1.6 The examiners appointed by the Council for the purposes of rule 4.1.5 shall be solicitors with a right of audience in the Court, or advocates, or professors of law in a university in Scotland, in each case of at least 10 years standing.

Rights of Audience in the Criminal Courts

Interpretation

4.2.1 In this rule 4.2, unless the context otherwise requires, terms listed in the first column of rule 4.2.1 shall have the meanings respectively ascribed to them in the second column of that rule:

Term	Definition
applicant	a solicitor who seeks a right of audience in the Court
course of training	a course of training in evidence, procedure and pleadings in relation to proceedings in the Court
Court	the High Court of Justiciary and the Judicial Committee of the Privy Council
Knowledge	knowledge of the practice and procedures of and professional conduct in the Court
relevant date	the date on which the applicant informs the Council that he seeks a right of audience in the Court
right of audience	a right of audience in the Court

Course of Training in Evidence and Pleading

4.2.2 The following matters are to be included in the course of training:

(a) the practical applications of the law of evidence in connection with the presentation of cases in the Court;

(b) the procedure employed in the Court;

(c) the presentation by applicants to the persons conducting the course of examples of oral advocacy in the manner required by the Court.

4.2.3 The methods of instruction to be employed in the course of training are:—

(a) lectures, the provision of written instructional material and audio visual or other practical demonstration by the persons conducting the course upon the matters specified in rule 4.2.2;

(b) attendance for a period, to be specified by the course convener, of up to six days sitting in on proceedings in the High Court of Justiciary, not being proceedings involving the applicant or any member or employee of the applicant's practice unit unless the convener shall direct otherwise, observing, with or without the supervision of the persons conducting the course of training, the manner in which cases are conducted in that court;

(c)   discussion of the applicant's performance by the persons conducting the course based on observation and assessment of the applicant's presentation of oral advocacy.

4.2.4   The persons who conduct the course of training shall be:
(a)   solicitors or advocates of at least 5 years standing; or
(b)   persons who have been employed at a university in Scotland for at least 5 years full-time during the last 10 years;

and who have experience in the matters specified in rule 4.2.2.

Demonstration of Knowledge

4.2.5   An applicant's knowledge shall be demonstrated by evidence that he has:—
(a)   passed in not more than two attempts a written examination set by examiners appointed by the Council within 30 months of the relevant date; or
(b)   passed examinations for admission to the Faculty of Advocates which are considered by the Council to be equivalent to the written examination referred to above.

4.2.6   The examiners appointed by the Council for the purposes of rule 4.2.5 shall be solicitors with a right of audience in the Court or advocates or Professors of Law in a university in Scotland, in each case of at least 10 years standing.

Order of Precedence, Instructions and Representation

Interpretation

4.3.1   In this rule 4.3, unless the context otherwise requires, terms listed in the first column of rule 4.3.1 shall have the meanings respectively ascribed to them in the second column of that rule:

Term	Definition
instructions	(a) where a regulated person has on behalf of a practice unit arranged with another practice unit for the representation of his client before a Superior Court by a solicitor advocate;
	the agreement for representation between the two practice units; or
	(b) where a client has arranged on his own behalf with a practice unit his representation before a Superior Court by a solicitor advocate;
	the agreement for representation between him and the practice unit
solicitor advocate	as defined in Schedule 1 but including a registered European lawyer exercising rights of audience pursuant to regulation 6 or 11 of the European Lawyer Regulations provided that nothing in these rules shall confer on any registered European lawyer any entitlement to practise under the title of solicitor or advocate or any combination of same

4.3.2   In this rule 4.3 obligations and duties stated to be imposed on solicitor advocates shall not apply to an employed solicitor advocate whose contract of employment prevents him from acting for persons other than his employer.

Order of precedence of court

4.3.3 Where a solicitor advocate accepts instructions to appear in a Superior Court, those instructions shall:

(i)   take precedence over any other professional obligation;

(ii)   themselves be in the following order of precedence:

        (a)   where the solicitor advocate has rights of audience in the civil courts only:

              Court of Justice of European Communities
              European Court of Human Rights
              Supreme Court/Judicial Committee of the Privy Council
              Inner House of the Court of Session
              Outer House of the Court of Session;

        (b)   where the solicitor advocate has rights of audience in the High Court of Justiciary only:

              High Court of Justiciary exercising its appellate jurisdiction
              High Court of Justiciary;

        (c)   where the solicitor advocate has rights of audience in all courts:

              Court of Justice of European Communities
              European Court of Human Rights
              Supreme Court/Judicial Committee of the Privy Council
              High Court of Justiciary exercising its appellate jurisdiction
              High Court of Justiciary
              Inner House of the Court of Session
              Outer House of the Court of Session.

Subject to the above order of precedence instructions shall take priority according to the date, or, if on the same date, the time when they are delivered, or, if orally transmitted, when they have been accepted by the solicitor advocate.

Priority of instructions
4.3.4 Notwithstanding the general rule stated in rule 4.3.3 the solicitor advocate shall have regard to the following considerations in determining which instructions are to be accepted:
  (a) the seriousness, importance or value of the case;
  (b) in the case of an appeal, that the solicitor advocate has appeared for the client in the lower court;
  (c) in the case of an adjourned diet or continued hearing, that the solicitor advocate appeared at the previous diet or hearing;
  (d) in the case of a debate on the pleadings, that the solicitor advocate was responsible for drafting or revising the pleadings, particularly where a difficult or delicate point of law is involved to which the solicitor advocate has already devoted a substantial amount of time and research;
  (e) in the case of a proof or trial, that the solicitor advocate was involved to a substantial extent in drafting the pleadings, debating the pleadings, consulting with the client or advising on the pre-trial or pre-proof preparations;
  (f) that the client has, for the purposes of the case, come to rely on the advice and guidance of the solicitor advocate to an unusual extent;
  (g) that because of the nature or circumstances of the case, or because of the limited time available, it would be unusually difficult for either counsel or another solicitor advocate adequately to prepare for appearance;
  (h) that a suitable fee has been tendered with instructions or conversely that the instructions were given on the basis of an agreement with the client that no fee or only a modified fee will be paid.
If in doubt as to what his decision should be, the solicitor advocate should consult the Secretary.

Cancellation of instructions
4.3.5 Acceptance of instructions involves a professional commitment on which the client and the court are entitled to rely. A solicitor advocate is not entitled without good cause to cancel instructions once accepted so as to relieve himself of that professional commitment.
4.3.6 In considering whether, and if so when, to cancel instructions after having accepted them, a solicitor advocate should have in mind the following considerations:
  (a) so long as instructions to do so have been accepted and not cancelled a solicitor advocate owes a duty to the client and the court to attend in court when the case is called;
  (b) a solicitor advocate owes a duty to the client and the court to ensure, as far as he can, that the case is properly prepared and properly presented;
  (c) a solicitor advocate owes a duty to the client and the court to remain in attendance until the trial or hearing has been completed;
  (d) a solicitor advocate owes a duty to his fellow solicitor advocates to avoid placing them unnecessarily in a position where they have to take over his cases at short notice and face the client and the court without adequate time for preparation.

It may also be appropriate to take into account the considerations mentioned in rule 4.3.4.

4.3.7 Where a solicitor advocate has been instructed by a regulated person and has:
  (a) an actual clash of commitments he shall, subject to rule 4.3.10, without delay intimate the cancellation of the instructions with which he cannot comply and return the relevant papers; or
  (b) a foreseeable clash of commitments he shall, subject to rule 4.3.10, immediately inform the instructing regulated person of the situation and comply with any subsequent instructions as to alternative arrangements in the event of his being unable to appear.

4.3.8 Where a solicitor advocate has been instructed directly by a client and has:
  (a) an actual clash of commitments; or
  (b) a foreseeable clash of commitments;
  he shall, subject to rule 4.3.10, immediately inform the client of the situation, and comply with any subsequent instructions as to alternative arrangements in the event of his being unable to appear.

4.3.9 In the case of proceedings before the High Court of Justiciary on appeal, there is a particular obligation on the solicitor advocate who represented the appellant at the trial and has recommended an appeal to present that appeal.

Securing representation

4.3.10 Where a solicitor advocate is unable, in a difficult or urgent situation, to secure representation for a person wishing to be represented by a solicitor advocate before any court he shall inform the Secretary of the situation.

Conduct of Solicitor Advocates

Interpretation

4.4.1 In this rule 4.4, unless the context otherwise requires, terms listed in the first column of rule 4.4.1 shall have the meanings respectively ascribed to them in the second column of that rule:

solicitor advocate	as defined in Schedule 1 but including a registered European lawyer exercising rights of audience pursuant to regulation 6 or 11 of the European Lawyer Regulations provided that nothing in these rules shall confer on any registered European lawyer any entitlement to practice under the title of solicitor or advocate or any combination of same
counsel	a solicitor advocate or an advocate

Propriety of conduct

4.4.2 Where you are in any doubt as to the propriety of any course of conduct you should:
  (a) seek the advice of the Secretary;
  (b) explain the position to the Secretary including anything which may be relevant to the advice sought.

Acceptance of instructions

4.4.3 You accept that it is the responsibility of the Council to make rules to secure, through the Secretary whom failing such of its officers as it thinks appropriate, that, where reasonably practicable, any person wishing to be represented before a court by a solicitor advocate is so represented.

4.4.4 You shall not accept instructions as a solicitor advocate (as opposed to a solicitor or registered European lawyer) without satisfying yourself that it is proper for you to accept them. You shall be entitled at all stages of the case at your sole discretion to decide whether you require the assistance of a representative of your practice unit or of the instructing regulated person in connection with the preparation of the case and also at consultations with the client and at the presentation of the case in court.

4.4.5 There are circumstances in which you are entitled and indeed bound to refuse instructions.

4.4.6 You may not allow your personal interests to affect the performance of your professional duty. Accordingly, you should not accept instructions to act in your professional capacity in circumstances where you have a direct personal interest in the outcome. Where you have, or may have, an indirect personal interest in the outcome (e.g. where you are asked to act for a company in which you are a major shareholder or for an organisation in which you hold office although unremunerated), you should consult the Secretary before accepting instructions. Where a conflict of personal interest arises later, you should inform the instructing regulated person or client and cancel instructions.

4.4.7 You may not accept instructions on any basis which would deprive you of the responsibility for the conduct of the case or fetter your discretion to act in consultation with the client in accordance with your professional judgment and public duty.

4.4.8 You must not accept instructions to act in circumstances where, in your professional opinion, the case is unstatable in law or where the case is only statable if facts known to you are misrepresented to, or concealed from, the court. If such circumstances arise after you have accepted instructions, you should decline to act further. There may, however, be exceptional circumstances in which it is proper for you, in order to assist the court, to present a case which you believe to be unstatable in law. In such circumstances, you must explain to the client that you cannot do more than explain the client's position to the court, and that you will be bound to draw the court's attention to such statutory provisions or binding precedents as have led you to the conclusion that the case is unstatable.

Duty in relation to other members of the legal profession
4.4.9 You have a duty of loyalty to professional colleagues.

4.4.10 The efficient conduct of litigation under the adversarial system depends on mutual trust between those acting for different parties. Discussion and negotiation between professional colleagues may achieve settlement of a case or at least dispose of incidental points which would otherwise take up time and cause unnecessary expense. It is therefore essential that counsel should be able to discuss cases with each other on the basis that confidence will be respected and that agreements and undertakings will be honoured.

4.4.11 It must, however, also be remembered that all have a duty to act in the best interests of the respective clients. You cannot assume that everything said to opposing professional colleagues will be treated in confidence. It is therefore desirable, at the outset of such discussions that the basis of the discussion be clarified. If it is intended to disclose information on a basis of confidence, this should be stated. Correspondingly, if one party to the discussion is not prepared to treat information as confidential he should say so before the information is disclosed.

4.4.12 Where an agreement is reached following such discussions or an undertaking is given by one counsel to another it is binding in honour between them and should be reported as soon as possible so that it can, if necessary, be incorporated in a formal exchange of letters. Alternatively, a joint minute should be drafted and initialled by counsel who should also bear in mind that once recorded in writing the written agreement supersedes the verbal agreement.

Duties in relation to an instructing agent

4.4.13 When instructed by a regulated person you must respect the fact that the regulated person's relationship with the client is different from, and likely to be more continuing than, your own. You should do nothing, beyond what your professional duty requires, to upset the agent-client relationship or destroy the trust which the client has in the regulated person.

4.4.14 When you have reason to believe that a regulated person has been guilty of professional misconduct (as opposed to professional negligence) you have a duty to the client, the court and the profession to take appropriate action. If the matter comes to your knowledge in the course of proceedings in court, it may be necessary to take immediate action, and if an adjournment is necessary for this purpose, it should be asked for. If the matter does not call for immediate action, you should consult the Secretary before making any formal complaint or report.

4.4.15 If you feel compelled to criticise the conduct of a regulated person in respect of something falling short of professional misconduct, you should avoid doing so in the presence of the client and should in any event ask the regulated person to explain what he has done and why before criticising his conduct.

4.4.16 Where instructed by a regulated person or directly by a client you should consider carefully whether you should attend a consultation without your instructing regulated person or another representative of your practice unit or of the instructing practice unit being present. The presence of the regulated person or representative will protect both you and the regulated person should a dispute arise later as to what advice you gave or what instructions you were given by the client.

4.4.17 In exceptional circumstances, it may be unavoidable that a solicitor advocate instructed by a regulated person has to speak to the client without the regulated person being present. Such an occasion will however be rare, and when it arises the regulated person should be told as soon as possible what transpired.

Duties in relation to the client

4.4.18 *Confidentiality.* It is your fundamental duty not to disclose or use any information communicated to you in your professional capacity other than for the purpose for which it was communicated to you, so long as it remains in confidence and has not otherwise been made public. Any conversations relating to a case which take place between a solicitor advocate and those representing the other side, including Crown counsel, are confidential and should not be revealed to anyone other than the client or those who are professionally concerned with the case. If you wish to discuss a case with a colleague, for example, for the purpose of seeking his advice about law, you should do so only in terms which do not disclose, or risk disclosure of, the identity of the client or other parties involved. This applies equally where you are asked to give a written opinion or to advise in consultation. There may be good reasons, unknown to you, why the client or instructing regulated person would not even wish it to be known that your advice has been sought. Idle gossip about cases and clients, even if the facts are publicly known, is damaging to your reputation and that of the profession.

4.4.19 *Duty to uphold the interests of the client.* You should remember that the client relies on you to exercise your professional skill and judgment in the client's best interests. You must at all times do, and be seen to do, your best for the client and you must be fearless in defending your client's interests, regardless of the consequences to yourself (including, if necessary, incurring the displeasure of the bench). But you must also remember that your client's best interests require you to give honest advice however unwelcome that advice may be to the client and that your duty to the client is only one of several duties which you must strive to reconcile.

4.4.20 *Conflict between client and instructing regulated person (e.g. where the client may have a claim for professional negligence against his agent).* Where it appears to you that a conflict of interest has arisen or may arise between the client and the instructing regulated person, it is your duty to take steps to ensure that the client is so advised in order that he can get the advice of another regulated person. It will depend on the circumstances how this can be done. The great majority of instructing regulated persons can be relied upon, when the conflict has been pointed out, to take the necessary steps themselves. It will therefore normally be inappropriate to mention the matter in the presence of the client. But it may be necessary to record your advice as to the existence of a conflict in a formal note and to ask the instructing regulated person to send it to the client, or to deal with the matter at consultation with the client. In extreme cases, it may be your duty to refuse to act further on the instructions of the regulated person concerned, but before doing so you should where practicable intimate in writing to the instructing regulated person that it is your intention to refuse to act further.

4.4.21 *Cancellation of instructions.* In any case where you feel obliged to cancel instructions, you must do so without delay and take such steps as are necessary to ensure that the client, and where appropriate the instructing regulated person, knows why you have withdrawn. Where you feel obliged to cancel in the course of a trial or other hearing, you must formally intimate to the court that you have cancelled instructions and are withdrawing from acting and must protect the interests of the client by moving for an adjournment so that the client can get other advice. You are under no obligation to explain in detail to the court or tribunal your reasons for cancellation, since to do so may prejudice your client, and you should not yield to pressure to do so. If in doubt as to whether you are entitled or bound to cancel you should seek the advice of the Secretary, and if necessary obtain an adjournment to do so.

Special duties in criminal cases

4.4.22 *Pleas.* Where the Crown offers to accept a reduced or restricted plea, you have a duty to advise the accused of that offer and to obtain his instructions about it. Likewise, where any limited offer to plead is made by an accused, it should (if considered in law to be appropriate) be conveyed to the Crown for consideration, without delay. For avoidance of doubt, it is prudent to obtain written instructions from the accused, for the tendering of a plea. In no circumstances should you tender any plea on behalf of the accused unless instructions to do so have been obtained.

4.4.23 In advising as to the possible consequences of a plea of guilty, you should refrain from making any positive forecast of the possible sentence beyond drawing the attention of the accused to the normally anticipated range of sentences in the circumstances of that particular case. You may also discuss any current case law indicating that a discount sentence may be expected when a plea of guilty is tendered at an appropriate stage.

4.4.24 *Confessions.* Where an accused person makes a confession to you and you are satisfied in law that such confession amounts to guilt, you must explain to the accused (if he is not pleading guilty) that the conduct of his defence will be limited by that confession. It must be emphasised to the accused that no substantive defence involving an assertion or a suggestion of innocence will be put forward on his behalf and that, if he is not satisfied with this, he should seek other advice. You should consider whether it is advisable to obtain confirmation in writing from the accused that he has been so advised and that he accepts such an approach to the conduct of his defence.

4.4.25 So long as an accused maintains his innocence, your duty lies in advising him on the law appropriate to his case and the conduct thereof. You may not put pressure on him to tender a plea of guilty, whether to a restricted charge or not, so long as he maintains his innocence. Nor should you accept instructions to tender a plea in mitigation on a basis inconsistent with the plea of guilty. You should always consider very carefully whether it is proper, in the interests of justice, to accept instructions to tender a plea of guilty. You should ensure that the accused is fully aware of the consequences and should insist that the instructions to plead guilty are recorded in writing.

4.4.26 *Acting for co-accused.* Save in the most exceptional circumstances, you should not accept instructions to act for more than one accused or appellant.

The duty to the court

4.4.27 *Duties in relation to matters of law.* Where you are aware of a previous decision binding on the court, or of a statutory provision relevant to a point of law in issue, it is your duty to draw that decision or provision to the attention of the court whether or not it supports your argument and whether or not it has been referred to by your opponent.

4.4.28 Where there is no contradictor, you should inform the court of authorities relevant to that case, even when such authority may be against your interest.

Duties in relation to matters of fact

4.4.29 In relation to matters of fact, you should have two principles in mind:

(a) it is for the court, not for you, to assess the credibility and reliability of witnesses; and

(b) you must not, directly or indirectly, deceive or knowingly mislead the court.

4.4.30 *In court.* When conducting a case in court, you should base your questions upon your instructions, the precognitions and the productions supplemented by information obtained at consultation and, after evidence has been led, upon the evidence.

4.4.31 You should not state your personal opinion on matters of fact. It is particularly important to observe this rule when addressing a jury. You must not make observations on matters of fact which are not based on, or justified by, the evidence. In a criminal trial, you should not under any circumstances express either directly or indirectly a personal belief in the innocence of the accused.

4.4.32 You may not be a party to the giving of evidence which you know to be perjured evidence, or to any other course that would enable a case to be put forward on behalf of a client which the client has informed you is unfounded in fact.

4.4.33 You may not put to a witness any question suggesting that the witness has been guilty of a crime, fraud or other illegal or improper conduct unless you have personally satisfied yourself that there is evidence which could, if necessary, be led in support of the suggestion.

4.4.34 *Interviewing witnesses.* There is no general rule that you may not discuss the case with a potential witness, but when instructed by a regulated person, you are entitled to insist that you accept instructions on the basis that you will not do so.

4.4.35 In cases where you have not accepted instructions on such a basis you must avoid doing or saying anything which could have the effect of, or could be construed as, inducing the client or skilled witness to "tailor" his evidence to suit the case.

4.4.36 Once a proof or trial has begun, you must not interview any potential witness in relation to what has been said in court in the absence of that witness.

4.4.37 Some cases cannot be properly prepared or conducted if the foregoing rules against interviewing potential witnesses are followed strictly according to the letter. The client may be accompanied at consultation by a relative or friend who is also a potential witness. Where the client is a corporate persona, those who can speak for the corporation may also be potential witnesses, although in that case it is usually better to discuss the case with someone who is not personally involved and can take a more objective view of it. Some witnesses may be witnesses to fact as to part of their evidence and expert witnesses giving opinion evidence as to another part. It may be essential in a case raising technical issues to discuss points arising from the evidence with a skilled witness who has not yet given evidence. In such cases, you must use your discretion. But you should always act according to the spirit of the rule—namely, that you should not under any circumstances do or say anything which might suggest to the witness that he should give evidence otherwise than in accordance with his honest recollection or opinion.

4.4.38 You may not, except with the consent of your opponent and of the court, communicate with any witness, including your client, once that witness has begun to give evidence until that evidence is concluded.

4.4.39 As to interviewing the client or witnesses in the absence of an instructing agent, see rule 4.4.16 and 4.4.17.

4.4.40 *Confessions to a solicitor advocate by accused persons.* It follows from the provisions of rules 4.4.24 and 4.4.25 that, where an accused person has admitted that he committed the act with which he is charged (whether or not the admission is an explicit admission of guilt in law), you may not conduct the defence on a basis inconsistent with that admission. Thus, you may not put to a witness any question suggesting, or tending to suggest, that the accused did not commit the act. A fortiori, you may not seek to set up a special defence of alibi or incrimination.

4.4.41 Subject to the rule stated in rule 4.4.40, you may
    (a) take any proper objection to the jurisdiction of the court, to the competency or relevancy of the indictment, or to the admissibility of evidence;
    (b) test the evidence for the prosecution by cross-examination;
    (c) cross-examine or lead evidence in support of a special defence of insanity or (depending on the tenor of the accused's admission) self-defense;

    (d) cross-examine or lead evidence for the purpose of explaining the actings of the accused or supporting a plea in mitigation;

    (e) make submissions as to the sufficiency in law of the evidence to support a verdict of guilty.

4.4.42 *Ex parte statements of fact by a solicitor advocate at the bar.* The court frequently must rely on statements as to matters of fact made at the bar, for example, in the Motion Roll and certain types of Petition procedure. Such statements are made on the responsibility of the solicitor advocate as an officer of the court and you must therefore be scrupulously careful that anything stated as fact is justified by the information in your possession. If the court asks a question which you cannot answer on the information in your possession, you must say that you cannot answer it and, if necessary, ask leave to take instructions on the matter. This rule applies whether or not the opposing party is represented in court.

4.4.43 *Pleadings.* You must have a proper basis for stating a fact in any pleadings, such as on precognition or in the light of consultation with the client.

The duty of courtesy

4.4.44 Discourtesy is as offensive in court as it is outside, and is detrimental to your reputation and that of the bench, to the interests of the client and to public confidence in the administration of justice.

4.4.45 In the examination of witnesses, and particularly in the cross-examination of hostile witnesses, you must remember that the law places you in a privileged position which you should not abuse, for example, by bullying or insulting behaviour or by making offensive or personal remarks.

4.4.46 You should seek to uphold a relationship of mutual trust and courtesy with the bench.

4.4.47 A failure to appear in court on time should always, as a matter of courtesy, be the subject of an apology. If the court is still sitting, and has not yet passed on to other business, the proper time to make the apology is at once on arrival in court. The apology should always be in open court to the bench. It is not sufficient to offer an apology through the Macer or Clerk of Court.

The duty to attend court

4.4.48 It is your duty to arrange your affairs so as to avoid a reasonably foreseeable clash of commitments.

4.4.49 Having accepted instructions to appear, it is your responsibility to ensure, unless (in a civil case only) other arrangements have been made with an instructing regulated person, that you are present in court on the day and at the time appointed and thereafter until the trial or hearing is concluded. Where unforeseen circumstances make it impossible for you to be present you must ensure that someone else is present at or before the time appointed to explain your absence and, if necessary, to move for an adjournment. If you are unable to ensure that someone else is present you must contact the Secretary.

4.4.50 Since instructions to appear in the High Court of Justiciary and the Inner House take precedence over instructions to appear in the Outer House, it follows that if you have accepted instructions to appear in the High Court or the Inner House, including instructions for the Single Bills, it is your duty to ensure that you are present there at the appointed time, even though you also have instructions to appear in the Outer House. If a clash of commitments appears likely you should ensure that someone else is present to appear in the Outer House in your place and, if necessary, to move for an adjournment until you are free to appear there. If you are unable to ensure that someone else is present you must contact the Secretary. If a conflict arises due to unforeseen circumstances and you find yourself still detained in the Outer House when you must appear in the High Court or the Inner House, you should inform the Lord Ordinary that you require to go to the High Court or the Inner House as the case may be and ask for an adjournment so that you can do so.

4.4.51 If you are engaged in a proof or other hearing in the Outer House and expect to be in difficulty because you are required to attend elsewhere in the Outer House to deal with an important matter on the Motion Roll on the same day, you or a representative from your practice unit should inform the Clerk of Court as soon as possible so that the judge concerned may be alerted to the problem and take such action as is appropriate. It has been accepted that in such circumstances the start of the proof might reasonably be delayed until your business in the other court has been completed.

4.4.52 Where you are a senior solicitor advocate appearing with a junior solicitor advocate you should only be absent from court if you are satisfied that your junior will be present and will be able to deal properly with any matter which may arise.

Responsibility for pleadings and presentation in civil actions

4.4.53 If you draft any pleadings you accept personal responsibility to the court for their contents, except where your draft has been altered without your knowledge and consent. Where you find that pleadings drafted by you have been altered without your knowledge and consent, it is your professional duty to consider whether you can support the case on the basis of the pleadings so altered.

4.4.54 You should not sign in your own name pleadings drafted by someone else save in exceptional circumstances. Papers may be signed in that way provided you are satisfied that the solicitor advocate for whom you sign cannot reasonably be found and you are also satisfied that the paper is in proper form for submission to the court. In the case of pleadings drafted by others, before you sign same or otherwise agree to speak to same you have a professional duty to consider whether you can support the pleadings on the basis of the available information. If you cannot, you must insist that the pleadings are revised and, if not, refuse to act further.

Speculative actions

4.4.55 In speculative actions, you have a particular responsibility to the court both with regard to your own assessment of the merits of the case and with regard to the advice which you give. The nature of the responsibility undertaken by counsel and solicitor was stated thus by Lord President Normand (X Insurance Co v A & B 1936 SC 225, 239):

"It has long been recognised by the Courts that this is a perfectly legitimate basis on which to carry on litigation and a reasonable indulgence to people who while they are not qualified for admission to [Legal Aid] are nevertheless unable to finance a costly litigation.

But it is equally recognised that there is involved in such business a grave risk of abuse unless it is carried out with strict regard to honour by all who are professionally concerned in it. Before acting in business of this kind it is the imperative duty of the solicitor and of the counsel to consider whether the party for whom they are to act has a reasonable prospect of success.

The reasons for this are obvious, and need no discussion. If a solicitor, when asked to conduct the case on a speculative footing, is, after consideration, unable to advise that there is a reasonable prospect of success, he should refuse to conduct the case. But, if he has reasonable doubts about the prospects of success, he is justified in consulting counsel. If counsel advises that the action may properly be raised, the solicitor is entitled to follow his advice, and in the future conduct of the action he is bound to act in accordance with counsel's instructions. If he does this after having fairly disclosed to counsel all the information at his disposal, he will not be exposed to a charge of professional misconduct. In order that the prospects of success may be fairly estimated by the solicitor and by counsel in their turn, it is in most cases, where questions of fact are involved, a necessary precaution that fair and honest precognitions of the chief witnesses who will be relied on should be taken at the outset." (See also the opinion of Lord Fleming at 250–251.)

Criminal appeals
4.4.56 In advising on criminal appeals, you have a duty, first, to consider whether there are grounds for an appeal which you are prepared to state to the court and, second, if in your opinion there are none, to refuse to act further in the case: Scott v HM Advocate 1946 JC 68 per Lord President Normand at 69.
4.4.57 Having advised that an appeal is statable, you may later come to the view that it is not. If so, you must promptly inform your client that you can no longer act in the case.

Opposing a party litigant
4.4.58 Where you appear against a party litigant, you must avoid taking unfair advantage of the party litigant and must, consistently with your duty to the client, co-operate with the court in enabling the party litigant's case to be fairly stated and justice to be done. But you must not sacrifice the interests of the client to those of the party litigant.

SECTION D: REQUIREMENTS OF AND RESTRICTIONS ON PRACTICE

Rule D1: Practising Certificates

Application for practising certificate
1.1 A solicitor who wishes to obtain a practising certificate for a practice year shall complete and submit an application in, or substantially in, such form as may be prescribed from time to time by the Council.

Issue of practising certificate
1.2.1 Subject to sections 14(2) and 15 of the 1980 Act and to rule 1.3, on receipt of an application which has been duly completed, the Council shall issue a practising certificate to the applicant without delay.
1.2.2 A practising certificate shall be in, or substantially in, such form as may be prescribed from time to time by the Council.

Professional Indemnity Insurance
1.3 The Council shall not issue a practising certificate to any solicitor making an application unless he provides, with his application:
    (a) evidence that a certificate of insurance has been issued to the practice unit of which he is a manager for the practice year for which the application is made, in terms of the master policy taken out and maintained by the Society pursuant to rule 7.1.2 in Section B; or
    (b) where rule 7.1.6 in Section B applies, evidence that a certificate of

insurance satisfying the requirements of rule 7.1.7(b) in Section B has been issued to him or the multi-national practice of which he is a manager for the practice year for which the application is made; or
(c) a declaration that he is not a manager.

Register of applications and practising certificates issued
1.4.1 The Council shall keep, in respect of each practice year, a register of the applications and of practising certificates issued.
1.4.2 The register shall be in, or substantially in, such form as may be prescribed from time to time by the Council.
1.4.3 The register shall be open for inspection by any person within office hours without payment.

Rule D2: Practising as a Manager

Restriction on practice
2.1.1 In this rule 2, unless the context otherwise requires, terms listed in the first column of rule 2.1.1 shall have the meanings respectively ascribed to them in the second column of that rule:

Term	Definition
grouping	any entity, whether or not having legal personality, formed under the law of a Member State, within which lawyers pursue their professional activities jointly under a joint name

2.1.2 You shall not practise as a manager unless you hold an unrestricted practising certificate.
2.1.3 Subject as aftermentioned, you shall not practise as a manager unless you have been employed as a solicitor or European lawyer for a cumulative period of three years, one year of which shall immediately precede your commencing practice as a manager.
[1] 2.1.4 Rule 2.1.3 shall not apply if you become and remain a manager of a practice unit or a grouping which has as one of its managers at least one other solicitor or European lawyer who has practised as a manager (which term shall include, in the case of a European lawyer, being a partner, director or member of a grouping) for a period of not less than three years prior to your becoming such a manager.
2.1.5 Employment shall only be counted for the purpose of rule 2.1.3 if at the time:—
  (a) subject to rule 2.1.6, you (being a solicitor) held an unrestricted practising certificate; or
  (b) you (being a European lawyer) held an authority to practise free from conditions equivalent to those referred to in the definition of "unrestricted practising certificate" in Schedule 1.
2.1.6 Employment that would otherwise have counted for the purpose of rule 2.1.3 shall not be so counted if at the time you were bound by an undertaking given pursuant to the Admissions Regulations.
2.1.7 Notwithstanding any other provision in this rule 2.1, you shall not practise as a manager if you are prohibited from so doing in terms of the Admissions Regulations.
2.1.8 Rule 2.1.3 shall not apply to you if you commenced practice as a manager before 30 November 2001 provided that you have practised as a manager within the period of the last five years; provided also that, for the purposes of this rule 2.1.8, the practice as a "manager" of a European lawyer shall include being a partner, director or member of a grouping of lawyers.

NOTE
[1] As amended by the Law Society of Scotland Practice (Amendment) Rules 2012 (effective November 1, 2012).

Practice management course
2.2.1 In this rule 2.2, unless the context otherwise requires terms listed in the first column of rule 2.2.1 shall have the meanings respectively ascribed to them in the second column of that rule:

Term	Definition
practice management course	a course of practical training in the management of practice units, the duration, form and content of which shall be prescribed by the Council from time to time

2.2.2 Subject to rule 2.2.3, if you become a manager of a practice unit you shall be obliged to attend a practice management course within a period not exceeding twelve months after the date on which you became such a manager, or such other period as may be determined by the Council in any particular case.
2.2.3 Rule 2.2.2 shall not apply to you if you:
    (a) attended a practice management course within twelve months preceding the date on which you became a manager; or
    (b) had been a manager within the period of three years preceding that date.

Associates, Consultants and Employees
2.3.1 You shall not cause or permit the name of any person to appear on the nameplate or professional stationery of the practice unit of which you are a manager unless that person is:
    (a) a manager of that practice unit,
    (b) a consultant to that practice unit,
    (c) an associate of that practice unit, or
    (d) an employee of that practice unit.
2.3.2 Where you cause or permit the name of a consultant, associate or employee to appear on nameplate or professional stationery, the status and designation of such consultant, associate or employee shall be unambiguously stated in such a manner as to distinguish clearly such consultant, associate or employee from the managers of the practice unit.
2.3.3 In the event that the Council shall determine that you have contravened rules 2.3.1 or 2.3.2, the Council may, by notice duly given to you, require you, from such date as the notice may stipulate, to amend the relevant nameplate or professional stationery in such a manner as shall comply with rules 2.3.1 and 2.3.2.

Rule D3: Prohibition on Association with Disqualified Persons
3.1 In this rule 3, unless the context otherwise requires, terms listed in the first column of rule 3.1 shall have the meanings respectively ascribed to them in the second column of that rule:

Term	Definition
disqualified person	(a) in the case of a solicitor or former solicitor, a person who is disqualified from practising as a solicitor by reason of the fact that his name has been struck off the roll of solicitors or that he is sus-

pended from practising as a solicitor;

(b) in the case of a registered foreign lawyer or formerly registered foreign lawyer, a person whose name has been removed from the register of foreign lawyers by the Scottish Solicitors' Discipline Tribunal or whose certificate of registration as a registered foreign lawyer has been suspended in accordance with section 24F of the 1980 Act;

(c) in the case of a registered European lawyer or formerly registered European lawyer, a person whose name has been removed from the register of European lawyers by the Scottish Solicitors' Discipline Tribunal or whose certificate of registration as a registered European lawyer has been suspended in accordance with section 24F of the 1980 Act;

or

(d) in the case of any practice unit which requires, in order to be permitted to practise as such a practice unit, any form of recognition, registration or licence granted by the Council or the Society or any other regulatory body, any such practice unit in respect of which such recognition, registration or licence has been revoked, withdrawn or suspended.

3.2 Without prejudice to the restrictions contained in section 47 of the 1980 Act (restrictions on employing solicitor struck off or suspended), you shall not, in connection with your practice as a regulated person, without the prior written permission of the Council, which may be given for such period and subject to such conditions as the Council thinks fit, associate in business with or provide facilities for any person whom you know to be a disqualified person.

Rule D4: Practice Unit Information

Initial notification, annual confirmation and changes

New practice units
4.1.1 The managers of a practice unit which commences practice after the date these rules come into operation shall ensure that the Council is informed of such commencement of practice and certain information in relation to the practice unit and those within it within 7 days of the date of such commencement by the completion and submission (on behalf of the practice unit) of an initial notification form in such form as may be prescribed from time to time by the Council.

Existing practice units
4.1.2 The Council may issue forms seeking confirmation that the information similar in nature to that to be supplied in respect of new practice units pursuant to rule 4.1.1 held by the Council in respect of practice units which commenced practice prior to the coming into operation of these rules remains complete and correct. Such forms shall be as prescribed from time to time by the Council. The managers of each practice unit shall ensure that any form so issued to the practice unit is completed and submitted to the Council (on behalf of the practice unit) within 28 days of its receipt.

All practice units
4.1.3 No more than once in each practice year the Council may issue a confirmation form to each practice unit. Such form shall seek confirmation that the information held by the Council provided pursuant to rules 4.1.1 or 4.1.2 remains complete and correct and shall take such form as may be prescribed from time to time by the Council. The managers of each practice unit shall ensure that any confirmation form so issued to the practice unit is completed and submitted to the Council (on behalf of the practice unit) within 28 days of its receipt.
4.1.4 The managers of every practice unit shall ensure that the Council is advised of any change to any information submitted to the Council pursuant to any of rule 4.1 within 28 days of the effective date of such change by the completion and submission (on behalf of the practice unit) of the appropriate change notification form (which shall be in such form as may be prescribed from time to time by the Council).

Notification of cessation of trading
4.2.1 The managers of a practice unit which they intend to cease trading shall ensure that the Council is informed of that intention not less than 28 days prior to the planned date of cessation by the completion and submission (on behalf of the practice unit) of a cessation notification form in such form as may be prescribed from time to time by the Council.
4.2.2 Every manager of a practice unit to which rule 4.2.1 applies shall provide such further information to the Council as the Council may reasonably request within such periods as the Council may reasonably stipulate, all in order that the Council may ascertain that the managers and the practice unit are complying with these rules and have made appropriate arrangements to ensure compliance by the practice unit, former practice unit and any of its managers or former managers with such of these rules as will continue to apply to such parties following the cessation of trading intimated pursuant to rule 4.2.1.

Rule D5: Incorporated Practices

Interpretation
5.1 In this rule 5, unless the context otherwise requires, terms listed in the first column of rule 5.1 shall have the meanings respectively ascribed to them in the second column of that rule:

Term	Definition
1986 Act	the Company Directors Disqualification Act 1986 and shall include that Act as applied to limited liability partnerships and any legislation in any other jurisdiction having equivalent effect
registrar of companies	the registrar or other officer performing under the Companies Act 2006 the duty of registration of companies or of registration of limited liability partnerships, as the case may be

Permission
5.2 Subject to the provisions of rule 5, you may trade as a body corporate in terms of section 34(1A) of the 1980 Act provided:—
   (a) any such body corporate has been recognised by the Council as an incorporated practice;
   (b) the control of any such body corporate is exclusively by solicitors, firms of solicitors, registered European lawyers, registered foreign lawyers or other incorporated practices;
   (c) the membership of any such body corporate is restricted to solicitors, firms of solicitors, registered European lawyers, registered foreign lawyers or other incorporated practices;
   (d) no person shall control such body or be a member or director of such body if he is prohibited from practising as a manager in terms of rule 2.1; and
   (e) the registered office of any such body corporate is situated in Scotland.

Application
5.3 If you wish to form an incorporated practice you shall, at least one month prior to the anticipated date of commencement of business as such incorporated practice, submit to the Council:
   (a) in all cases—
      (i) the names, designations and business addresses (and, where appropriate, registered offices) of all persons who will be members of the incorporated practice;
      (ii) the proposed name, and address of the registered office, of the incorporated practice;
      (iii) a completed application for recognition as an incorporated practice in such form as may be prescribed from time to time by the Council; and
      (iv) the fee to be prescribed from time to time by the Council in connection with such application;
   (b) in the case of an incorporated practice which is to be a company—
      (i) the names, designations and business addresses (and, where appropriate, registered offices) of all persons who will be directors of the incorporated practice; and
      (ii) a draft of the memorandum and articles of association of the incorporated practice;
   (c) in the case of an incorporated practice which is to be a limited liability partnership, a draft of the incorporation document of the incorporated practice; and
   (d) in the case of an incorporated practice to be incorporated with limited liability, an irrevocable undertaking to the Council by each of the persons who will be members of the incorporated practice that he or it or they will jointly and severally along with

the other members of the incorporated practice reimburse to the Society grants paid out of the Guarantee Fund to a person who has suffered pecuniary loss by reason of dishonesty on the part of the incorporated practice or any member, director, manager, secretary or other employee thereof and that to any extent to which the Society shall have been unable to recover the amount of said grants from the incorporated practice or any liquidator or administrator thereof (which undertaking may provide that the granter shall have no liability in terms of the undertaking to reimburse the Society for grants paid out in respect of dishonesty that takes place subsequent to the granter ceasing to be a member of the relevant incorporated practice).

Memorandum and Articles of Association
5.4.1 The memorandum and articles of association of an incorporated practice which is a company shall contain provisions which show that it complies and will continue to comply with this rule 5 (as in force from time to time) including, without prejudice to the foregoing generality, provisions to the following effect:—
   (a) that no person shall be appointed or re-appointed or act as a director unless he is a member of the incorporated practice duly qualified to be a member within the meaning of sub-paragraph (d) of this rule 5.4.1;
   (b) that no person other than a person duly qualified to act as a director may be appointed as an alternate director;
   (c) that a director or alternate director shall vacate office if he ceases to be a member of the company or to be qualified to act as a director;
   (d) that no person shall be qualified to be a member of the incorporated practice or (subject to sub-paragraph (f) of this rule 5.4.1) enjoy any of the rights of members (i) if that person is prohibited from practising as a manager in terms of rule 2.1 and (ii) unless he or it is a solicitor, registered European lawyer or registered foreign lawyer or firm of solicitors or an incorporated practice;
   (e) that (subject to sub-paragraph (f) of this rule 5.4.1) any member who ceases to be duly qualified within the meaning of sub-paragraph (d) of this rule 5.4.1 shall forthwith transfer his or its shares or other interest in the incorporated practice to another person who is so qualified, or otherwise cease to be a member of the incorporated practice;
   (f) that, in the case of an incorporated practice which has a share capital, the executor of a deceased member of the incorporated practice shall have no voting rights in respect of his membership of the incorporated practice; and
   (g) that, in the case of an incorporated practice limited by guarantee, membership shall cease on death.
5.4.2 The memorandum and articles of association of an incorporated practice which is a company shall contain provisions to anticipate and to deal with the situation where for whatever reason there is no longer a person qualified to do so in terms of rule 5.2 exercising the day to day management and control of the incorporated practice. Without prejudice to the foregoing, the memorandum and articles shall contain specific provisions for:—
   (a) the operation in the situation aforesaid of all client accounts in the name of the incorporated practice; and
   (b) suitable arrangements in the situation aforesaid for making available to its clients or to some other regulated person instructed by its clients or itself:—

     (i) all deeds, wills, securities, papers, books of account, records, vouchers and other documents in its possession or control which are held on behalf of its clients or which relate to any trust of which it is sole trustee or co-trustee only with one or more of its employees; and

     (ii) all sums of money due from it or held by it on behalf of its clients or subject to any trust as aforesaid.

5.4.3 The memorandum and articles of association of an incorporated practice which is a company shall be only in terms previously approved by the Council, following submission of a draft thereof in terms of rule 5.3 (b)(ii), and thereafter no such incorporated practice shall alter its memorandum and articles without the prior consent of the Council.

5.4.4 The Council may charge a fee to be prescribed from time to time by the Council in respect of its examination and, if thought fit, its approval of the memorandum and articles of association of an incorporated practice which is a company or any alteration thereof and such fee shall be in addition to the fee referred to in rule 5.3 (a)(iv).

Undertaking to Council

5.5 Every person who becomes a member of an incorporated practice which is incorporated with limited liability shall grant an undertaking to the Council on the same terms as the undertaking described in rule 5.3(d).

Ongoing Provisions

5.6.1 The members and directors of an incorporated practice which is a company shall ensure that the conditions of its memorandum and articles of association are given effect to at all times and without delay.

5.6.2 The Council may at any time require an incorporated practice which is a company to demonstrate that the requirements of rule 5.4 are being complied with.

5.6.3 Incorporated practices shall notify the Council, within fourteen days of such change, of:—

(a) any change in the address of the registered office of the incorporated practice; and

(b) any change in the members or directors of an incorporated practice.

5.6.4 Incorporated practices shall send to the Secretary a copy of all documents which require to be filed with the registrar of companies or the Accountant in Bankruptcy contemporaneously with the despatch of such documents to the registrar of companies or the Accountant in Bankruptcy.

5.6.5 Incorporated practices shall send to the Secretary a copy of all certificates issued by the registrar of companies forthwith upon receipt thereof by the incorporated practice.

5.6.6 No person who is not a member of an incorporated practice (and duly qualified to be such a member in terms of rule 5.2) shall enjoy any of the rights of membership except (subject to rule 5.4.1(f)) an executor of a deceased member of the incorporated practice qua executor of that member.

5.6.7 Where a member of an incorporated practice dies or for any other reason ceases to hold a current practising certificate or, as the case may be, has its certificate of recognition revoked under rule 5.9 the incorporated practice shall immediately take the necessary steps, whether in terms of its memorandum or articles of association or otherwise, to ensure compliance with this rule 5.

5.6.8 No person shall be appointed or shall act as a director of an incorporated practice which is a company unless he is a member thereof.

5.6.9 Every incorporated practice to which these rules apply shall require to be insured against such classes of professional liability as are indemnified by the Master Policy (as referred to in rule 7 in Section B) and the Council shall prescribe from time to time the limits of indemnity and self-insured amounts applicable to incorporated practices and may prescribe different limits for different incorporated practices or classes of incorporated practices.

5.6.10 The Council shall maintain a list containing the names and places of business of all incorporated practices, which list shall be open for inspection at the office of the Society during the office hours by any person without payment of any fee.

Company Directors Disqualification Act 1986

5.7.1 In the event that a disqualification order under the 1986 Act is made against a person who is a member or a director of an incorporated practice, whether in respect of his conduct in relation to any incorporated practice of which he is a member or director, or otherwise, that person shall, forthwith upon such order being made, notify the Council and shall supply a copy of the order to the Council.

5.7.2 Subject to rule 5.7.3, the consent of the Council shall be required:
(a) for any such person as is referred to in rule 5.7.1 to become or remain a member or director of an incorporated practice; and
(b) for any other person against whom a disqualification order under the 1986 Act has been made to become a member or director of an incorporated practice.

5.7.3 The consent of the Council shall not be required pursuant to rule 5.7.2 if, and to the extent that, the court has given its consent to any such person as is specified in rule 5.7.2 becoming or remaining a director of an incorporated practice which is a company or a member of an incorporated practice which is a limited liability partnership.

5.7.4 Any person who requires the consent of the Council pursuant to rule 5.7.2 shall provide all reasonable co-operation with any request from the Council for information and documentation regarding the circumstances of the relevant disqualification order.

5.7.5 In giving or refusing its consent pursuant to rule 5.7.2, the Council shall have regard to the facts and circumstances surrounding the making of the relevant disqualification order and to the terms thereof, to the interests of the public in relation to the profession of the person concerned and to the effect of any refusal of consent on the person concerned and on any incorporated practice of which he may be a member or director. Any consent may be given subject to such conditions as the Council considers it appropriate to impose.

5.7.6 In the event, and to the extent, that the Council shall refuse a consent pursuant to rule 5.7.2(a) or shall give such a consent subject to conditions which require the person to whom it is given to cease to be a member and/or a director of an incorporated practice which is a company and/or a member of an incorporated practice which is a limited liability partnership, the person affected shall immediately cease to be such a member and/or director and/or member of such incorporated practice.

5.7.7 For the avoidance of doubt, any person against whom a disqualification order under the 1986 Act is made which prohibits that person from being a director of an incorporated practice which is a company or from being a member of an incorporated practice which is a limited liability partnership shall immediately cease to be such a director or member and shall not seek to apply for the consent of the Council in respect of that particular disqualification pursuant to rule 5.7.2.

5.7.8 In rules 5.7.1, 5.7.2 and 5.7.5, references to the term "member" in connection with an incorporated practice shall include reference both to membership of an incorporated practice which is a company and to membership of an incorporated practice which is a limited liability partnership.

Recognition

5.8.1 The Council shall consider every application made to it in terms of rule 5, and, if the Council is satisfied by the applicant(s) that a body corporate has complied in all respects with the requirements of rule 5, the Council shall issue to the applicant(s) a certificate recognising the proposed body corporate as an incorporated practice which certificate shall state:—

(a) the name and registered number of the incorporated practice;

(b) whether the incorporated practice will carry on business with liability which is unlimited or limited by guarantee or limited by share capital or as a limited liability partnership; and

(c) the date of the certificate of recognition.

5.8.2 The certificate of recognition or a true copy of it shall at all times be displayed at every place of business of the incorporated practice.

5.8.3 An incorporated practice which proposes to re-register as unlimited under section 102 or as limited under section 105 of the Companies Act 2006 shall, before applying for re-registration under section 103 or section 106 of that Act, as appropriate, submit to the Council an application to be allowed to re-register accordingly. Such application shall be in the form mutatis mutandis required by rule 5.3 for the recognition of an incorporated practice in the form proposed after re-registration. If the Council is satisfied by the applying incorporated practice that it has complied in all respects with the requirements of rule 5, the Council shall issue to the applying incorporated practice a certificate entitling it to apply for or to resolve to be re-registered as aforesaid and containing the information specified in rule 5.8.1. The incorporated practice shall not apply for or resolve to be re-registered as aforesaid until such certificate has been issued and shall so apply or resolve within one month of the date of such certificate. The certificate of authorisation for re-registration or a true copy of it shall at all times be displayed at every place of business of the incorporated practice along with the certificate of recognition.

Revocation of Certificate of Recognition

5.9 A certificate of recognition of an incorporated practice may be revoked by the Council if:

(a) recognition of the incorporated practice was granted by the Council by reason of error or fraud;

(b) an incorporated practice goes into liquidation (other than members' voluntary liquidation approved by the Council for the purpose of amalgamation or reconstruction) or if a provisional liquidator, receiver or judicial factor is appointed to such incorporated practice or if an administrator within the meaning of the Insolvency Act 1986 is appointed to such incorporated practice or if such incorporated practice enters into a voluntary arrangement under Part I of the Insolvency Act 1986, or if such incorporated practice is struck off the register of companies or the register of limited liability partnerships;

(c) control of an incorporated practice ceases for any reason, however temporarily, to be exclusively by persons duly qualified to exercise such control in terms of rule 5; or

(d) such incorporated practice has failed to comply with any of the provisions of rule 5.

Rule D6: Registration of European Lawyers

Definitions

6.1 In this rule 6, unless the context otherwise requires, terms listed in the first column of rule 6.1 shall have the meanings respectively ascribed to them in the second column of that rule:

Term	Definition
applicant	a European lawyer who wishes to pursue professional activities under his home professional title on a permanent basis in Scotland and who wishes to apply pursuant to regulation 16 of the European Lawyer Regulations to be entered on the register established and maintained by the Society pursuant to regulation 15 of the European Lawyer Regulations and section 12A of the 1980 Act
home State	the meaning given in paragraph (1) of regulation 2 of the European Lawyer Regulations
home professional title	the meaning given in paragraph (1) of regulation 2 of the European Lawyer Regulations

Purpose of regulations

6.2 The purpose of the European Lawyer Regulations is to implement the Directive in Scotland. This rule 6 makes provision in respect of applications for registration with the Society by European lawyers pursuant to regulation 16 of the European Lawyer Regulations and in respect of applications for, and the issue of, certificates of registration for registered European lawyers pursuant to section 24A of the 1980 Act.

Application for registration

6.3 An applicant shall apply in writing to the Society for registration by completing (so far as applicable to him) and submitting an application in such form as the Council shall from time to time prescribe, and by making payment of such fee(s) as the Council shall from time to time prescribe.

Determination of application

6.4 The Council shall determine an application pursuant to rule 6.3 in accordance with the European Lawyer Regulations.

Entry on register and issue of certificate of registration to applicant

6.5 If the Council grants an application pursuant to rule 6.3 it shall:

(a) cause the name of the applicant to be entered on the register of European lawyers established and maintained by the Society pursuant to regulation 15 of the European Lawyer Regulations and section 12A of the 1980 Act; and

(b) subject always to the provisions of rules 6.8 and 6.9, cause a certificate of registration to be issued to the applicant.

Application for Certificate of Registration by Registered European Lawyer
   6.6 A registered European lawyer who wishes to obtain a certificate of registration shall apply for the same by completing (so far as applicable to him) and submitting a form in such form as may be prescribed from time to time by the Council and by making payment of such fee(s) as the Council shall from time to time prescribe.

Issue of Certificate of Registration to Registered European Lawyer
   6.7 Subject always to the provisions of rules 6.8 and 6.9 and to the provisions of the 1980 Act and the European Lawyer Regulations in respect of withdrawal or suspension of registration the Council shall, on receipt of an application pursuant to rule 6.6 which has been duly completed and submitted, cause a certificate of registration to be issued to the registered European lawyer without delay. Any such certificate may, in accordance with the provisions of the 1980 Act, and in particular section 24C thereof, be issued subject to conditions.

Professional Indemnity Insurance
   6.8 The Council shall not issue a certificate of registration to any applicant making application pursuant to rule 6.3 or to any registered European lawyer making application pursuant to rule 6.6 unless he provides, along with his application:
   (a) evidence that a certificate of professional indemnity insurance has been issued to him or to the practice unit in or for which he practises being insurance which is equivalent in terms of the conditions and extent of its cover to the professional indemnity insurance which is required of solicitors in Scotland by the Council; or
   (b) evidence that he is covered by professional indemnity insurance taken out in accordance with the professional rules of his home State and that such insurance is equivalent in terms of the conditions and the extent of its cover to the insurance referred to in paragraph (a) of this rule 6.8; or
   (c) where the insurance referred to in paragraph (b) of this rule 6.8 is less than equivalent in terms of the conditions and the extent of its cover to the insurance referred to in paragraph (a) of this rule 6.8, evidence of the conditions and extent of cover of professional indemnity insurance taken out in accordance with the professional rules of his home State and, to the extent of the lack of equivalence, evidence that a certificate of insurance has been issued as specified in paragraph (a) of this rule 6.8.

Guarantee Fund
   6.9 The Council shall not issue a certificate of registration to any applicant making application pursuant to rule 6.3 or to any registered European lawyer making application pursuant to rule 6.6 unless he provides, along with his application:
   (a) a contribution by him or by the practice unit in or for which he practises to the Society on behalf of the Guarantee Fund in terms of section 43 of, and Schedule 3 to, the 1980 Act; or
   (b) evidence that he is covered by a guarantee taken out in accordance with the professional rules of his home State and that such guarantee is equivalent in terms of the conditions and the extent of its cover to the Guarantee Fund; or
   (c) where the guarantee referred to in paragraph (b) of this rule 6.9 is less than equivalent in terms of the conditions and the extent of

its cover to the Guarantee Fund, evidence of the conditions and extent of cover of the guarantee taken out in accordance with the professional rules of his home State and to the extent of the lack of equivalence:

    (i) a contribution as specified in paragraph (a) of this rule 6.9; or

    (ii) evidence that a guarantee (other than such as is specified in paragraph (a) of this rule 6.9) has been issued to him or the practice unit in or for which he practises.

Register of Applications and Certificates of Registration Issued

6.10 The Council shall cause to be kept in respect of each practice year a register of applications for certificates of registration and of certificates issued. The register shall be in such form as the Council may determine.

6.11 Subject to the provisions of the 1980 Act and the European Lawyer Regulations in respect of withdrawal or suspension of registration, the duration of registration shall be until the end of the practice year current when the relevant application is granted.

Rule D7: Registration of Foreign Lawyers

Definitions

7.1 In this rule 7, unless the context otherwise requires, terms listed in the first column of rule 7.1 shall have the meanings respectively ascribed to them in the second column of that rule:

Term	Definition
applicant	a person who wishes to become a registered foreign lawyer or a registered foreign lawyer who wishes to renew his registration
home jurisdiction	a jurisdiction in which a foreign lawyer is a member of a legal profession
home professional title	a professional title used by a foreign lawyer as a member of a legal profession in his home jurisdiction
register	the register of foreign lawyers established and maintained by the Council pursuant to section 60(A)(2) of the 1980 Act, and "registered" and "registration" shall be construed accordingly

Application for registration

7.2 An applicant shall apply in writing to the Society for registration by completing (so far as applicable to him) and submitting an application in such form as the Council shall from time to time prescribe, and by making payment of such application fee(s) as the Council shall from time to time prescribe.

Requirements for registration

[1] 7.3.1 No applicant shall be registered unless:

    (a) he has completed an application form in terms of rule 7.2;

    (b) he has paid such application fee(s) as the Council has prescribed in accordance with rule 7.2;

    (c) he is a foreign lawyer;

    (d) he has satisfied the Council:

(i)   that he is a fit and proper person to be a registered foreign lawyer;

(ii) that the legal profession of which he is a member is so regulated as to make it appropriate for the applicant to be registered for the relevant purpose; and

(iii) that he is, or will on registration become, a manager of a multi-national practice or have an interest in a licensed provider as a solicitor investor in terms of section 67(6) of the Legal Services (Scotland) Act 2010;

(e) he provides such evidence as may be required by the Council that he has satisfied its requirements as to the professional indemnity insurance cover required of registered foreign lawyers as they apply to him;

(f) he provides such evidence as may be required by the Council that he has satisfied its requirements as to the guarantee fund cover required of registered foreign lawyers as they apply to him;

(g) he is not an advocate and has made a declaration to that effect; and

(h) he is not a European Lawyer registered with the Society or the Faculty of Advocates, and has made a declaration to that effect.

NOTE
[1] As amended by the Law Society of Scotland Practice (Amendment) Rules 2012 (effective November 1, 2012).

7.3.2 The Council shall, where satisfied that an applicant complies with rule 7.3.1, register that applicant.

7.3.3 The Council shall consider an application pursuant to rule 7.3.1 as soon as is reasonably practicable, and shall notify the applicant of its decision within three months of receipt of that application.

7.3.4 If the Council does not notify the applicant of its decision within the period specified in rule 7.3.3, the applicant may, within three months of the end of that period, apply to the Court of Session which may, on such application, make such order as it sees fit.

Entry on register
7.4.1 If the Council grants an application pursuant to rule 7.3, it shall cause the name of the applicant to be entered on the register.

7.4.2 Subject to rule 7.5, the duration of registration shall be until the end of the practice year current when the relevant application is granted.

Removal from register
7.5 A person shall be removed from the register if he ceases to comply with any requirement set out in rule 7.3.1.

Rule D8: Multi-national Practices

Entering a Multi-national practice

Definitions
8.1.1 In this rule 8.1, unless the context otherwise requires, terms listed in the first column of rule 8.1.1 shall have the meanings respectively ascribed to them in the second column of that rule:

Term	Definition
enter a multi-national practice	to become a manager of a multi-national practice whether by joining a multi-national practice or by being a manager of a practice unit which becomes a multi-national practice

Restriction

8.1.2 You may not enter a multi-national practice having any place of business in Scotland unless you obtain the approval of the Council in terms of rule 8.1.3.

Application

8.1.3 If you wish to seek the approval of the Council in terms of rule 8.1.2 you shall, at least three months prior to the anticipated date of your entering the multi-national practice, submit to the Council an application in such form as may be prescribed from time to time by the Council. Where more than one person is seeking the approval of the Council in terms of this rule then those persons may jointly submit an application in terms of this rule.

Giving of approval

8.1.4 Where the Council is satisfied, on receiving your application in terms of rule 8.1.3:

(a) that you will on its approval being given be a manager of a multi-national practice, and

(b) that the multi-national practice of which you will be a manager is or will be so regulated as to make it appropriate for you to be allowed to enter it, the Council may approve your entering that practice.

8.1.5 Where you have been given approval to enter into a practice in terms of rule 8.1.4, the Council may withdraw that approval if at any time it ceases to be satisfied that either of the conditions set out in rule 8.1.4 remains true.

Charging of fees
8.1.6 The Council may charge a fee to be prescribed from time to time by the Council in respect of its examination of an application submitted in terms of rule 8.1.3.

Provision of information
8.1.7 While you remain a manager of a multi-national practice, you shall inform the Council of any changes to the information which was supplied by you in any application made to the Council to enter into that multi-national practice in terms of rule 8.1.3.
8.1.8 If you cease to be a manager of a multi-national practice you shall inform the Council of that fact.

Approved multi-national practices
8.1.9 The Council may maintain a list of multi-national practices which regulated persons may enter without seeking its approval in terms of rule 8.1.2, and may require the managers of any multi-national practice wishing to be added to or to remain on any such list to supply such information as it may require.

Multi-national practice—Principal Place of Business

Definitions and Interpretation
8.2.1 In this rule 8.2, unless the context otherwise requires, terms listed in the first column of rule 8.2.1 shall have the meanings respectively ascribed to them in the second column of that rule:

Term	Definition
location	in relation to a person, the place of business at which that person primarily practises or, if there is no such place of business, the place of business at which he is based or from which he is managed
new determination	a determination that the principal place of business of a multi-national practice is a place of business other than that provisionally determined in accordance with rule 8.2.6

8.2.2 A person is "associated with" a multi-national practice if:
(a) he is a manager of that multi-national practice;
(b) he is an employee of that multi-national practice; or
(c) he is a consultant to that multi-national practice.

Determinations
8.2.3 The Council may, on application made in terms of rule 8.2.13, determine the principal place of business of a multi-national practice.
8.2.4 The Council shall determine the principal place of business of a multi-national practice whose principal place of business has not been determined in accordance with an application made in terms of rule 8.2.13.

8.2.5   Subject to rule 8.2.18, the Council may change its determination of the principal place of business of a multi-national practice.

Provisional determinations

8.2.6   The Council may, on application made in terms of rule 8.2.14, provisionally determine the principal place of business of a proposed multi-national practice.

8.2.7   Where the principal place of business of a multi-national practice has been provisionally determined that place of business shall be treated as the principal place of business of that multi-national practice.

8.2.8   The Council may change or revoke any provisional determination made in accordance with rule 8.2.6.

8.2.9   Following the constitution of a multi-national practice whose principal place of business has been provisionally determined in accordance with rule 8.2.6:

(a)   the provisional determination may not be revoked; and

(b)   the Council shall confirm the provisional determination or make a new determination;

and such confirmation or new determination shall be treated as a determination made in accordance with rule 8.2.3.

Relevant factors

8.2.10   In determining the principal place of business of a multi-national practice in terms of rule 8.2.3 or 8.2.4 or in changing any such determination in terms of rule 8.2.5 or in confirming a provisional determination or making a new determination in terms of rule 8.2.9, the Council shall have regard to the following:

(a)   any election made by or behalf of the multi-national practice;

(b)   the locations of the place or places of business of the multi-national practice;

(c)   the number of solicitors holding a practising certificate who are associated with the multi-national practice both as an absolute number and as a proportion of the total number of solicitors and foreign lawyers associated with that multi-national practice;

(d)   the number of solicitors holding a practising certificate who are managers of the multi-national practice both as an absolute number and as a proportion of the total number of managers of that multi-national practice;

(e)   the locations of the solicitors and foreign lawyers associated with the multi-national practice and the identity of the legal professions of which those foreign lawyers are members;

(f)   the locations of the managers of the multi-national practice;

(g)   the identity of the persons exercising management control over the multi-national practice, the number of them who are practising solicitors and each of their locations;

(h)   the law applicable to the constitutive documents or arrangements of the multi-national practice; and

(i)   the law practised by the multi-national practice.

8.2.11   In determining the principal place of business of a multi-national practice, the Council may have regard to any other factor which it considers relevant.

8.2.12   In provisionally determining the principal place of business of a proposed multi-national practice in terms of rule 8.2.6 or in changing or revoking that provisional determination in terms of rule 8.2.8, the Council shall have regard to the factors set out at rules 8.2.10 and 8.2.11 as they may be ascertained in relation to the proposed multi-national practice from the information supplied to it in or in connection with an application in terms of rule 8.2.14 and other information available to it.

Application

8.2.13 If you are a manager of a multi-national practice you may seek a determination of the principal place of business of that multi-national practice by the Council in terms of rule 8.2.3.

8.2.14 If you propose to be a manager of a proposed multi-national practice you may seek a provisional determination of the principal place of business of that proposed multi-national practice by the Council in terms of rule 8.2.6.

8.2.15 If you seek a determination by the Council in terms of rule 8.2.3 or 8.2.6 you shall submit to the Council an application in such form as may be prescribed from time to time by the Council and shall, upon request by the Council, supply any other information required by the Council in connection with that application.

Charging of fees

8.2.16 The Council may charge a fee to be prescribed from time to time by the Council in respect of its examination of an application submitted in terms of this rule 8.2.

Provision of information

8.2.17 The Council may require any regulated person who is a manager of or associated with a multi-national practice or who proposes to be a manager of or associated with a proposed multi-national practice to supply it with any information it considers necessary in connection with:

(a) any determination in terms of rule 8.2.3 or 8.2.4; or

(b) any possible change in determination in terms of rule 8.2.5; or

(c) any provisional determination in terms of rule 8.2.6; or

(d) any possible change or revocation of a provisional determination in terms of rule 8.2.8; or

(e) the confirmation of a provisional determination or the making of a new determination in accordance with rule 8.2.9.

Notice

8.2.18 Where the Council is minded to change its determination of the principal place of business of a multi-national practice in terms of rule 8.2.5 it shall give notice of that fact to the relevant multi-national practice, together with copies of any information it proposes to rely on in making that change (with any deletions necessary to protect the identity of any person as appropriate). In making its decision as to whether to change its determination of the principal place of business of that multi-national practice, the Council shall have regard to any written representations made to it by or on behalf of that practice.

Rule D9: Multi-disciplinary Practices

Prohibition on multi-disciplinary practices

9.1.1 In this rule 9 unless the context otherwise requires, terms listed in the first column of rule 9.1.1 shall have the meanings respectively ascribed to them in the second column of that rule:

Term	**Definition**
legal relationship	membership of a partnership or a joint venture which is not a partnership, or membership or directorship of a body corporate

Term	Definition
multi-disciplinary practice	means a body corporate or partnership: (a) having as one of its managers a regulated person; and (b) which offers services, including professional services, such as are provided by individual solicitors, to the public; and (c) where a regulated person carries out, or supervises the carrying out, or makes provision of legal services.

9.1.2   Subject to rule 9.1.3, you shall not form a legal relationship with a person or body who is not a regulated person with a view to your jointly offering professional services as a multi-disciplinary practice to any person or body.

9.1.3   Nothing in this rule 9.1 shall prohibit you from being a member, director or employee of, or partner or investor in, a licensed provider.

Prohibition on the sharing of fees

9.2.1   In this rule 9.2, unless the context otherwise requires, terms listed in the first column of rule 9.2.1 shall have the meanings respectively ascribed to them in the second column of that rule:

Term	Definition
citizens advice body	as defined in s65(1) of the 1980 Act
law centre	as defined in s65(1) of the 1980 Act
lawyer	an advocate, a law centre, a citizens advice body, a licensed provider (or a member, director or employee of, or partner or investor in, a licensed provider) or a legal practitioner offering legal services to the public who is qualified and licensed to practise in accordance with the law of a legal jurisdiction other than that of Scotland, and includes a firm of lawyers, a European Economic Interest Group the membership of which is exclusively lawyers, an incorporated practice of lawyers and any association (whether corporate or unincorporate) consisting exclusively of lawyers or exclusively of lawyers and regulated persons
overheads	costs and expenses incurred by a practice unit in the running of its business which may include the costs of services provided to the practice unit (including services in relation to the advertisement and promotion of the practice unit) but shall exclude any payment purely for the introduction or referral of clients or business to the practice unit or any of its directors, members or employees save for any fee paid by the practice unit for its inclusion on a panel of legal advisers to whom referrals of business may be made provided that such fee is not expressed as a proportion of the fees generated from the business so referred
unqualified person	as defined in s65(1) of the 1980 Act

9.2.2 You shall not share with any unqualified person any profits or fees or fee derived from any business transacted by you of a kind which is commonly carried on by regulated persons in Scotland in the course of or in connection with their practice; provided always that:

(a) a practice unit may pay its overheads out of income from fees; and

(b) the provisions of this rule shall not apply to the sharing of profits or fees where:

    (i) a person who has ceased to practise as a regulated person shall receive from any regulated person a share of the profits or fees of the latter, as a price or value of the business which he has transferred to the latter or shall receive a share of such profits as a voluntary or other allowance out of the profits or fees of a business in which he had been a manager; or

    (ii) the widow, widower, civil partner, heirs, executors, representatives, next of kin or dependants of any deceased regulated person receive from any regulated person who has purchased or succeeded to the business of such deceased regulated person or from any practice unit of which such deceased regulated person was a manager at his death any share of the profits of such business; or

    (iii) the salary of any employee of a regulated person is partly or wholly paid in the form of a percentage on the profits of such regulated person's business or any part thereof; or

    (iv) such profits or fees are received by any public officer in respect of work done in the course of his duty; or

    (v) an agreement for sharing such profits or fees is made between a regulated person and a lawyer; or

    (vi) such profits or fees are received by an officer of a public body who is a regulated person or by the public body and are dealt with in accordance with statutory provisions.

Schedule 1: Defined Terms[1]

Term	Definition
1980 Act	the Solicitors (Scotland) Act 1980
1986 Act	the Legal Aid (Scotland) Act 1986
Admissions Regulations	Admission as Solicitor (Scotland) Regulations 2001 as the same may be varied, supplemented, amended, consolidated or replaced from time to time
advice and assistance	either or both of (i) advice and assistance on a civil matter or on a matter arising out of Part II of the Children (Scotland) Act 1995 and (ii) assistance by way of representation on a civil matter, within the meaning of section 6 of the 1986 Act, and to which Part II of the 1986 Act applies
advocate	a member of the Faculty of Advocates
associate	a regulated person, holding an unrestricted practicing certificate who is in the employment of a practice unit

---

[1] As amended by the Law Society of Scotland Practice Rules (Amendment (No.1) Rules 2013 (effective April 1, 2014).

Term	Definition
	whether full time or part-time and who has been afforded the status of "associate" of that practice unit;
certificate of registration	where the context relates to a European lawyer, a certificate of registration issued in accordance with the 1980 Act and rule 6 in Section D of the foregoing rules in, or substantially in, such form as may be prescribed from time to time by the Council; or, where the context relates to a foreign lawyer, a certificate of registration issued in accordance with the 1980 Act and rule 7 in Section D of the foregoing rules in, or substantially in, such form as may be prescribed from time to time by the Council
children's legal aid	legal aid to which section 29 of the 1986 Act applies
civil legal aid	the meaning given to it in Part III of the 1986 Act
Client Relations Manager	a manager of a practice unit so designated by that practice unit in terms of rule 5 in Section B
cohabitant	the same meaning as in the Family Law (Scotland) Act 2006
company	the meaning given in section 1 of the Companies Act 2006
Compliance Manager	a manager of a practice unit so designated by that practice unit in terms of rule 3 in Section C
consultant	a regulated person, holding an unrestricted practicing certificate who, not being a manager of a practice unit, makes his services and advice available to a practice unit or causes or permits his name to be associated with that practice unit
Council	the Council of the Society
cross-border practice	(a) all professional contacts with lawyers of Member States (which expression shall, for the purposes of this definition of "cross-border practice", include member states of the European Economic Area) other than the United Kingdom; and (b) the professional activities of a regulated person in a Member State other than the United Kingdom whether or not the regulated person is physically present in that Member State
Directive	Directive No. 98/5/EC of the European Parliament and Council to facilitate practice of the profession of lawyer on a permanent basis in certain states other than the state in which the professional qualification was obtained
European lawyer	the meaning given in paragraphs (2) and (3) of regulation 2 of the European Lawyer Regulations
European Lawyer Regulations	European Communities (Lawyer's Practice) (Scotland) Regulations 2000 (SSI 2000/121)
foreign lawyer	a person who is not a solicitor or an advocate but who is a member, and entitled to practise as such, of a legal profession regulated within a jurisdiction outwith Scotland

Term	Definition
Guarantee Fund	the Scottish Solicitors Guarantee Fund as referred to in section 43 of the 1980 Act
inadequate professional services	professional services which are in any respect not of the quality which could reasonably be expected of a competent regulated person and includes any element of negligence in respect of or in connection with the services; and cognate expressions are to be construed accordingly
incidental financial business	regulated activities which may, as a result of Part XX of the Financial Services and Markets Act 2000 and rule 2 in Section C of the foregoing rules, be carried on by a practice unit without breaching the general prohibition and includes, without limitation, consumer credit activity, insurance mediation activity, long-term care insurance mediation activity and mortgage mediation activity, all as defined in that rule 2
incorporated practice	a body corporate recognised by the Council in terms of section 34(1A) of the 1980 Act and rule 5 in Section D of the foregoing rules as being suitable to undertake the provision of professional services such as may be provided by solicitors
legal aid	(i) advice and assistance, (ii) civil legal aid and (iii) children's legal aid
licensed provider	licensed legal services provider construed in accordance with Part 2 of the Legal Services (Scotland) Act 2010
limited liability partnership	a body corporate incorporated under the Limited Liability Partnerships Act 2000
manager	a sole practitioner, a partner in a firm of solicitors, a member or director of an incorporated practice which is a company, a member of an incorporated practice which is a limited liability partnership; a member of a multi-national practice; or a solicitor, registered European lawyer or registered foreign lawyer who is either (a) a partner in a licensed provider which is a partnership; (b) a member or director of a licensed provider which is a company; or (c) a member of a licensed provider which is a limited liability partnership; provided that (i) for the purposes of rule 7.1 in Section B of the foregoing rules; and (ii) for the purposes of rule 3.1.3 in Section A of the foregoing rules but only in so far as same relates to the application of that rule 7.1, "manage" shall be construed so as to include persons held out to the public as a manager regardless of their actual status provided that a regulated person shall not be regarded as so held out by reason only (a) that he is a member of a multi-national practice which is not a Scottish multi-national practice; or (b) that he practises only as a consultant or associate to a practice unit or that he uses his own name when carrying out work for a practice unit of which he is an

Term	Definition
	employee (provided that, in all cases, if his name appears on the nameplate and professional stationery of a practice unit his status and designation are unambiguously stated thereon in compliance with rule 2.3 in Section D of the foregoing rules)
Member State	a member state of the European Union
multi-national practice	(a) a partnership whose members are regulated persons and include registered foreign lawyers; or (b) a body corporate whose members include registered foreign lawyers, and membership of which is restricted to regulated persons
practice unit	a sole practitioner, firm of regulated persons, incorporated practice, multi-national practice or licensed provider
practice year	the year commencing on 1st November and ending on the subsequent 31st October
practising certificate	(a) in relation to a solicitor, a certificate issued by the Council in accordance with the provisions of Part II of the 1980 Act authorising a person to practise as a solicitor; or (b) in relation to a registered European lawyer or a registered foreign lawyer, the relevant certificate of registration
practising solicitor	a solicitor who holds a practising certificate under the 1980 Act
principal place of business	the principal place of business of a multi-national practice as determined by the Council in terms of rule 8.2 in Section D of the foregoing rules
registered European lawyer	a person registered with the Society in accordance with regulation 17 of the European Lawyer Regulations
registered foreign lawyer	a foreign lawyer who is registered under section 60A of the 1980 Act
regulated person	a solicitor, a registered European lawyer, a registered foreign lawyer or a practice unit
rights of audience	a right of audience in the Court of Session, the Supreme Court and the Judicial Committee of the Privy Council or, as the case may be, the High Court of Justiciary and the Judicial Committee of the Privy Council
Scottish multi-national practice	a multi-national practice having its principal place of business in Scotland
Scottish practice	the practice of a multi-national practice which is not a Scottish multi-national practice in so far as that multi-national practice is acting in pursuance of the practice carried on in or from Scotland (or which is carried on outwith Scotland but which relates to a Scottish matter)

Term	Definition
	of any solicitor, registered European lawyer, member body or registered foreign lawyer who is a member of that multi-national practice
Secretary	the Secretary of the Society or any person authorised by the Council to act on behalf of the Secretary for the purposes of any of the foregoing rules
Society	the Law Society of Scotland
solicitor	any person enrolled as a solicitor in pursuance of the 1980 Act
solicitor advocate	a solicitor who has been granted rights of audience
Superior Court	the Court of Justice of European Communities, European Court of Human Rights, Court of Session, the Supreme Court, the Judicial Committee of the Privy Council and the High Court of Justiciary

unrestricted practising certificate

(i) where the context relates to the practising certificate of a solicitor, such a certificate free of conditions imposed in terms of section 15 or other relevant sections of the 1980 Act or any regulations made thereunder, or by the Scottish Solicitors' Discipline Tribunal or by the Court of Session; or

(ii) where the context relates to the practising certificate or certificate of registration of a registered European lawyer or of a registered foreign lawyer, such a certificate free of conditions imposed in terms of section 24C or other relevant sections of the 1980 Act or any regulations made thereunder, or by the Scottish Solicitors' Discipline Tribunal or by the Court of Session

unsatisfactory professional conduct

professional conduct which is not of the standard which could reasonably be expected of a competent and reputable regulated person but which does not amount to professional misconduct and which does not comprise merely inadequate professional services; and cognate expressions are to be construed accordingly

Parliament House Book R.126: May 2014

SCHEDULE 2

RULES IN RESPECT OF WHICH COMPLIANCE MAY NOT BE WAIVED

Section B Rule 1
Section B Rule 8.4.2
Section C Rule 2 to the extent that any waiver would be incompatible with the requirements of the Directive (as defined in that rule)
Section C Rule 4.1
Section C Rule 4.2

SCHEDULE 3

REVOCATIONS

Solicitors (Scotland) (Standards of Conduct) Practice Rules 2008
Solicitors (Scotland) Practice Rules 1986
Solicitors (Scotland) (Drafting Wills) Practice Rules 2010
Solicitors (Scotland) (Advertising and Promotion) Practice Rules 2006
Solicitors (Scotland) (Client Communication) Practice Rules 2005
Solicitors (Scotland) (Client Relations Partner) Practice Rules 2005
Solicitors (Scotland) (Client Relations Partner) Practice (Amendment) Rules 2007
Solicitors (Scotland) Accounts, Accounts Certificate, Professional Practice and Guarantee Fund Rules 2001
Solicitors (Scotland) Accounts, Accounts Certificate, Professional Practice and Guarantee Fund (Amendment) Rules 2004
Solicitors (Scotland) Accounts, etc (Amendment) Rules 2006
Solicitors (Scotland) Accounts, etc (Amendment) Rules 2007
Solicitors (Scotland) Accounts etc (Amendment No.2) Rules 2007
Solicitors (Scotland) Professional Indemnity Insurance Rules 2005
Solicitors (Scotland) Professional Indemnity Insurance Contingency Fund Rules 2007
Solicitors (Scotland) Professional Indemnity Insurance Contingency Fund (Amendment) Rules 2007
Solicitors (Scotland) (ARTL Mandates) Rules 2006
Solicitors (Scotland) (Industrial Action by Solicitors) Practice Rules 2003
Solicitors (Scotland) (Industrial Action by Solicitors) Practice (Amendment) Rules 2008
Solicitors (Scotland) (Written Fee Charging Agreements) Practice Rules 1993
Solicitors (Scotland) (Supreme Courts) Practice Rules 2003
Solicitors (Scotland) (Cross-Border Code of Conduct) Practice Rules 2003
Solicitors (Scotland) (Incidental Financial Business) Practice Rules 2004
Solicitors (Scotland) (Civil Legal Aid and Advice and Assistance) Practice Rules 2003
Solicitors (Scotland) (Civil Legal Aid and Advice and Assistance) (Amendment) Rules 2004
Solicitors (Scotland) (Rights of Audience in the Court of Session, the House of Lords and the Judicial Committee of the Privy Council) Rules 2002
Solicitors (Scotland) (Rights of Audience in the High Court of Justiciary and the Judicial Committee of the Privy Council) Rules 2002
Solicitors (Scotland) Order of Precedence, Instructions and Representation Rules 1992
Solicitors (Scotland) Rules of Conduct for Solicitor Advocates 2002
Solicitors (Scotland) Practising Certificate Rules 2007
Solicitors (Scotland) (Restriction on Practice) Practice Rules 2001
Solicitors (Scotland) (Practice Management Course) Practice Rules 2004
Solicitors (Scotland) (Associates, Consultants and Employees) Practice Rules 2001
Solicitors (Scotland) (Restriction on Association) Practice Rules 2004
Solicitors (Scotland) (Incorporated Practices) Practice Rules 2001
European Lawyers (Registration) (Scotland) Regulations 2001
Registered European Lawyers (Rules of Professional Conduct) (Scotland) Rules 2001
Solicitors (Scotland) (Foreign Lawyers) (Registration) Rules 2004
Solicitors (Scotland) (Registered Foreign Lawyers) etc Practice Rules 2005
Solicitors (Scotland) (Multi-National Practices) Practice Rules 2005
Solicitors (Scotland) (MNP Principal Place of Business) Practice Rules 2005
Solicitors (Scotland) Incorporated Practices, Foreign Lawyers Registration and Multi-National Practices (Amendment) Rules 2010
Solicitors (Scotland) (Multi-Disciplinary Practices) Practice Rules 1991
Solicitors (Scotland) Practice Rules 1991

Solicitors (Scotland) (EU Services Directive) Practice Rules 2009
Solicitors (Scotland) (Miscellaneous Amendments) Rules 2006

CONSTITUTION OF THE LAW SOCIETY OF SCOTLAND

Scheme under the Solicitors (Scotland) Act 1980, approved at a General Meeting of the Society held on 23rd September 1988 and having, by virtue of section 1 of, and Schedule 1 to, the said Act, effect as if enacted in that Act.

Title and Interpretation

Title

1.—(1)   This Scheme may be cited as the Constitution of the Law Society of Scotland.

(2)   This constitution shall come into operation on 1st November 1988.

Interpretation

2.—[1](1)   In this Constitution unless the context otherwise requires:—

"the 1990 Act" means the Law Reform (Miscellaneous Provisions) (Scotland) Act 1990;[2]
"the 2010 Act" means the Legal Services (Scotland) Act 2010; and[3]
"the Act" means the Solicitors (Scotland) Act 1980;
"the Council" means the Council of the Society;
"financial year" means the period of twelve months ending on 31st October.
"a lay member", means a member of Council who is a person who appears to the Council to be qualified to represent the interests of the public in relation to the provision of legal services in Scotland or, having regard to the Society's functions, appears to the Council to be suitable in other respects, but is not a:
  (a)   member of the Society,
  (b)   member of the Faculty of Advocates,
  (c)   conveyancing or executry practitioner as defined in section 23 of the 1990 Act,
  (d)   person having a right to conduct litigation or a right of audience by virtue of section 27 of the 1990 Act,
  (e)   confirmation agent as defined in section 90(4) of the 2010 Act, or will writer as defined in section 101(3) of the 2010 Act.
"a member of the Society" means a solicitor who in terms of Section 2(1) of the Act has in force a practising certificate, and any other solicitor who has paid the current annual membership subscription to the Society and whose name appears upon the Roll of Solicitors kept by the Council;
"place of business", in relation to a member of the Society means the member's place of business, or if the member has more than one place of business, the member's principal place of business, as specified in the member's practising certificate, if the member has one, or in a notice of change of place of business given by the member to the Society after the issue of the member's practising certificate, if the member has given such a notice, or if the member

---

[1] As amended by a Resolution of the members of the Law Society of Scotland to amend the Constitution of the Law Society of Scotland (effective May 2004).
[2] As inserted by a Resolution of the members of the Law Society of Scotland to amend the Constitution of the Law Society of Scotland (effective June 2011).
[3] As inserted by a Resolution of the members of the Law Society of Scotland to amend the Constitution of the Law Society of Scotland (effective June 2011).

does not have a place of business, his residence, and references to the constituency in which a member practises shall be construed as a reference to the constituency in which such member has his place of business;

"the President" means the chairman of the Society provided for in terms of paragraph 2(c) of Schedule 1 to the Act and includes, in the case of the absence of the President or his inability to act as President, the Vice-President;[1]

"the Secretary" means the Secretary of the Society and includes any person authorised by the President to act on behalf of the Secretary;

"the Society" means The Law Society of Scotland established by the Solicitors (Scotland) Act 1949;

"the Vice-President" means the vice-chairman of the Society provided for in terms of paragraph 2(c) of Schedule 1 to the Act;[2]

(2)   The Interpretation Act 1978 applies to the interpretation of this Constitution as it applies to the interpretation of an Act of Parliament.

Constitution and Election of Members of Council

Constitution of the Council

3.[3]   The Council shall consist of the following persons:

(1)   not more than 31 members of the Society elected in accordance with the provisions in this Constitution,

(2)   not more than 10 lay members appointed by the Council in accordance with the Act,

(3)   not more than 6 other members of the Society who may be co-opted by the Council, and

(4)   such *ex officiis* members as there may be from time to time in terms hereof.

(5)   The provisions of this Article are subject to the transitional and savings provisions as contained in Part III of the First Schedule to this Constitution.

Election of members of Council by constituencies

4.—(1)[4]   For the purpose of the election of members of Council, there shall be the several geographical constituencies listed in the first column of Part 1 of the First Schedule to this Constitution, and there shall be a separate election in each constituency. For the purposes of this Article and of the First and Second Schedules to this Constitution, a member of the Society having a place of business which is not in any such constituency shall be treated as having a place of business within such constituency as such member may select.

(2)   A member of the Society shall be entitled to vote in the constituency in which such member's place of business is situated and in that constituency only.

---

[1] Inserted by a Resolution of the members of the Law Society of Scotland to amend the Constitution of the Law Society of Scotland (effective May 2004).
[2] Inserted by a Resolution of the members of the Law Society of Scotland to amend the Constitution of the Law Society of Scotland (effective May 2004).
[3] As substituted by a Resolution of the members of the Law Society of Scotland to amend the Constitution of the Law Society of Scotland (effective June 2012).
[4] As substituted by a Resolution of the members of the Law Society of Scotland to amend the Constitution of the Law Society of Scotland (effective May 2004).

(3)   The members of the Society in each of the several constituencies shall elect the number of members of Council as set out in the second column of the said Part of the said Schedule opposite to the constituency.

(4)   Constituencies shall be arranged in three groups as set out in Part II of the said Schedule and the Council shall arrange that in each year there will be an annual election in one of such groups taken in rotation.

(5)–(6)   *[Revoked by the Law Society of Scotland (effective June 2011).]*

Term of office of members of Council

5.—[1](1)   An elected member of Council shall retire from office on the day immediately before the day fixed by the Council for the annual election of members of the Council in the third year after such member's election. A retiring member shall be eligible for re-election.

(2)   Members of the Society appointed by the Council in accordance with Article 3(2), or co-opted by the Council in accordance with Article 3(3), shall hold office for such term not exceeding three years as the Council may fix, and different terms may be fixed for different persons, but there shall be no limitation upon the number of terms for which such a person may be appointed or co-opted.

Date of election of members of Council

6.   The annual election of members of Council in terms of Article 4(4) hereof shall be held in the month of May in each year on a date to be fixed by the Council.

Returning officer

7.   The Secretary shall act as returning officer for the election in each constituency.

Conduct of election

8.—(1)   Subject to the provisions of this Constitution the election of members of Council for a constituency shall be conducted in accordance with the provisions of the Second Schedule hereto and of any regulations made thereunder.

(2)[2]   No election held under this Constitution shall be invalidated by reason of any misdescription or non-compliance with the provisions thereof or of any regulations thereunder or by reason of any miscount or of the nondelivery, loss or miscarriage of any document or information required to be sent under this Constitution or regulations thereunder, if it appears to the Returning Officer that the election was conducted substantially in accordance with this Constitution and the regulations and that the result of such misdescription, non-compliance, miscount, non-delivery, loss or miscarriage does not affect the return of any candidate at the election.

Expenses of election, co-option and appointment

9.   All expenses properly incurred by the returning officer or by the Society in relation to the election, co-option or appointment of members of Council shall be paid by the Society.

---

[1] As amended by a Resolution of the members of the Law Society of Scotland to amend the Constitution of the Law Society of Scotland (effective June 2011).

[2] As amended by a Resolution of the members of the Law Society of Scotland to amend the Constitution of the Law Society of Scotland (effective April 2014).

Failure of constituency to elect members of Council

10.[1]   If the members of the Society in a constituency fail to elect the number of members of Council for the constituency as herein prescribed, the Council may fill the vacancy by appointing a member of the Society to be a member of Council representing the constituency. Such member of the Society shall have his place of business within such constituency or as close thereto as may be reasonably practicable.

Casual vacancies in Council

11.—[2](1)   A member of Council may at any time resign from office by a notice in writing signed by such member and delivered to the Secretary. The resignation shall take effect upon the delivery of the notice or on a date not later than the end of that member's term of office in terms of Article 5 hereof specified by such member in such notice, whichever is the later.

(2)   The office of a member of Council shall be vacated if such member is absent, without leave of the President, from three consecutive meetings of the Council, with effect from the conclusion of that third meeting of Council. Such leave may be given retrospectively.

(3)   Council may by a majority of three-quarters of members present and voting, suspend a member of Council from attendance at meetings of Council and its committees.

(4)   If the office of a member of Council becomes vacant before the expiration of that member's term of office, whether by death, resignation or otherwise:

    (a)   in the case of a member elected from a constituency—

        (i)   where the vacancy arises at least three months before the date on which the vacating member would have reached the end of their term in the ordinary course, there shall be an election in that constituency as soon as practicable, on a date to be fixed by the Council and conducted in the same manner as an election in ordinary course,

       (ii)[3]   where the vacancy arises within three months of the date on which the vacating member would have reached the end of their term in the ordinary course, the vacancy shall be filled at the election to take place on the date to be fixed by the Council in terms of Article 6 of this Constitution,

    and the provisions of this Constitution, including the Second Schedule hereto relating to elections, shall apply, subject to any necessary modifications;

    (b)   in the case of a lay member appointed by Council, the Council shall appoint a new lay member as soon as practicable, on a date to be fixed by Council.

---

[1] As amended by a Resolution by the members of the Law Society of Scotland to amend the Constitution of the Law Society of Scotland (effective May 2004).

[2] As amended by a Resolution of the members of the Law Society of Scotland to amend the Constitution of the Law Society of Scotland (effective June 2011).

[3] As amended by a Resolution of the members of the Law Society of Scotland to amend the Constitution of the Law Society of Scotland (effective April 2014).

(5) A person elected or appointed to fill a casual vacancy under paragraph (4) shall hold office only for the unexpired period of office for the member in whose place such person is elected or appointed, as appropriate, and shall be eligible for re-election or re-appointment.

Meetings of Society

Meetings of Society

12.—(1) General Meetings of the Society shall comprise the Annual General Meeting and Special General Meetings.

(2) An Annual General Meeting shall be held each year at such time on such date and at such place as the Council may appoint but not more than 15 months after the last preceding Annual General Meeting.

(3) Special General Meetings of the Society shall be convened by the Secretary on the instructions of the President or of the Council or on a requisition signed by not less than 20 members of the Society. The requisition must state the objects of the meeting. It must be deposited with the Secretary and may consist of several documents in like form each signed by one or more requisitionists. A Special General Meeting required by requisition shall be held within 28 days of receipt of the requisition at such time on such date and at such place as the President, whom failing the Vice-President, may appoint.

(4)[1] Fourteen days' notice at least (exclusive of the day on which the notice is sent but inclusive of the day for which the notice is given), specifying the place, day, and hour of any General Meeting and the business to be considered shall be given to each member of the Society. A notice of a General Meeting shall be deemed to have been effected at the expiration of 24 hours after the notice is sent. The accidental omission to give notice of a meeting to, or the non-receipt of notice of a meeting by any member shall not invalidate the proceedings at the meeting.

(5)[2] A lay member of Council is entitled to attend a General Meeting of the Society.

Proceedings at General Meetings of the Society

13.—(1) The President, whom failing the Vice-President, shall preside at a General Meeting, and if at any meeting neither the President nor the Vice-President is present, the members present shall choose one of their number who is a member of Council to preside.

(2) The business of the Annual General Meeting shall be to consider the Report of the Council, the statement of accounts of the Society and the report of the auditors thereon, to elect auditors, and any other business specified in the notice of the meeting. A copy of the Report of the Council shall be made available to the members of the Society on the Society's website from the date the notice of the Annual General Meeting is sent to the members of the Society. If, after the notice of Annual General Meeting has been sent to the members of the Society, a member requests a copy of the Report, the Council shall promptly send a copy to the member. At the option of the member that copy shall be sent either in paper or electronic form to the member at his place of business.

---

[1] As amended by a Resolution of the members of the Law Society of Scotland to amend the Constitution of the Law Society of Scotland (effective April 2014).

[2] As amended by a Resolution of the members of the Law Society of Scotland to amend the Constitution of the Law Society of Scotland (effective June 2011).

(3)   The Council shall include in the notice of the Annual General Meeting any item relating to the business of the Society specified in a requisition made by not less than 10 members of the Society and received by the Secretary not less than 42 days before the meeting. The business of any Special General Meeting shall be to consider only the business specified in the notice of meeting.

(4)   No business shall be transacted at any General Meeting unless a quorum of members of the Society is present within half an hour after the time appointed for the meeting. Twenty members personally present shall be a quorum. A meeting at which a quorum is not present, if not convened on a requisition shall stand adjourned to a day and hour to be fixed by the majority of the members present, and if convened on a requisition shall fail and not be held.

(5)   Subject to the provisions of this Constitution and to any directions given by the Society in General Meeting, the Council may make standing orders with regard to the conduct of the business at meetings of the Society, including the adjournment of meetings.

(6)   Subject to the provisions of paragraph 5 of Schedule 1 to the Act, no resolution passed at a General Meeting shall be binding on the Society until it has been adopted by the Council or has been confirmed at the next General Meeting, and it shall be the duty of the Council, if it does not adopt the resolution, to bring the same before the next General Meeting accordingly, but this provision shall not apply to a resolution proposed by the Council and passed at the meeting at which it has been proposed.

Voting at General Meetings

14.—(1)   At any General Meeting a resolution put to the vote of the meeting shall be decided by a show of hands unless a poll is (before or on the declaration of the result of the show of hands) demanded by at least three members present in person and unless a poll is so demanded a declaration by the chairman of the meeting that a resolution has, on a show of hands, been carried or carried unanimously or by a particular majority or lost, and an entry to that effect in the minutes of the proceedings of the Society shall be conclusive evidence of the fact, without proof of the number or proportion of the votes recorded in favour of, or against, that resolution: always provided that a poll may not be demanded in the case of a resolution with regard to the appointment of a chairman of the meeting or the adjournment of the meeting or in the case of a motion that the question be now put or that the meeting move to the next business.

(2)   If a poll is demanded, it shall be taken at once in such manner as the chairman directs, and the result of the poll shall be deemed to be the resolution of the meeting at which the poll was demanded.

(3)   In the case of an equality of votes, whether on a show of hands or on a poll, the chairman of the meeting at which the show of hands takes place or at which the poll is taken shall be entitled to a second or casting vote.

(4)   On a show of hands every member present in person shall have one vote.

(5)   On a poll, votes may be given either personally or by proxy.

(6)   The instrument appointing a proxy shall be deposited with the Secretary at any time after the notice is sent calling the General Meeting and not less than 48 hours before the time for holding the meeting or adjourned meeting at which the person named in the instrument proposes to vote, and in default the instrument of proxy shall not be treated as valid. A proxy must be a member of the Society.

President, Vice-President, Past President and Honorary Vice-President of the Society

President, Vice-President, Past President and Honorary Vice-President

15.—[1](1)[2]   The Council shall at its first meeting after the 1st day of November in each year, receive nominations for the office of President and Vice-President and shall thereafter elect at its first meeting after the 1st day of December in each year one of its number who has been a member of Council for at least three years to be President of the Society, and another of its number who has also been a member of Council for at least three years to be Vice-President of the Society, to hold office as from the date of the first meeting of the Council held after the next annual election of members of the Council; provided always that if at or prior to the latter date the President, the President elect, the Vice President or the Vice President elect (which positions for the purposes of this provision are referred to as "the offices") ceases to be a member of Council as the result of his retiral in terms of article 5(1) he shall nevertheless be ex officio a member of Council whilst the holder of any one or more of the offices, or at or prior to the latter date the President elect or Vice-President elect ceases to be a member of Council, for any other cause, his election as the President or the Vice President shall be void as at the date of such cessation, and the Council shall at its first meeting held not less than four weeks after the date of such cessation, proceed to a new election of President or Vice-President as the case may be. Provided that if there are two or more nominations for either office the resulting competition shall be decided by ballot. If there are three or more nominations for either office the election shall be conducted by the single transferable vote method.

(1A)   Only solicitor members of Council are eligible for election as President or Vice-President.

(2)   Notwithstanding Article 5 hereof, the President and Vice-President shall hold office until the date from which their respective successors take office. A President or Vice-President shall cease to hold office if he ceases to be a member of the Society. The President shall be eligible for re-election to that office for each of the two succeeding years, but shall not again be eligible to be President until a period of at least two years has elapsed since he last held that office.

(3)   The Vice-President shall not again be eligible to be Vice-President until at least one year has elapsed since he last held that office.

(4)   The President or Vice-President may resign at any time from office as such by a signed notice in writing delivered to the Secretary, and the resignation shall take effect upon the delivery of the notice or on a date not later than the date on which he would otherwise have demitted office specified in the said notice, whichever is the later.

(5)

    (a)   On a casual vacancy occurring in the office of President or Vice-President at a time when there is a President elect or Vice-President elect as the case may be appointed to take up office in the ensuing month of May, the President elect or Vice-President elect shall immediately assume office as President or Vice-President as the case may be; and the resulting additional period of office, which will terminate at the first

---

[1] As amended by a Resolution of the members of the Law Society of Scotland to amend the Constitution of the Law Society of Scotland (effective September 2012).

[2] As amended by a Resolution of the members of the Law Society of Scotland to amend the Constitution of the Law Society of Scotland (effective May 2013).

meeting of the Council held after the next annual election of members of the Council, shall be disregarded in applying the provisions of Articles 15(2) and 15(3) hereof.

(b) On a casual vacancy occurring in the office of President at a time when there is no President elect, the Vice-President shall assume the additional office of Interim President until the next meeting of the Council held less than four weeks after the date of the occurrence of the said vacancy, when the Council shall elect a new President.

(c) On a casual vacancy occurring in the office of Vice-President at a time when there is no Vice-President elect, the Council shall as soon as practicable appoint one of its solicitor members to fill the vacancy until the date of the first meeting of the Council held after the next annual election of members of the Council.

(6) From the date upon which the President ceases to hold office as such except when he has resigned in terms of Article 15(4) hereof he shall serve as Past President of the Society for a period of one year. If the Past President is not or if during his period of office he should cease to be a member of Council, he shall ex officio be a member of Council until the expiry of his period of office. The Past President may resign as provided in Article 15(4) hereof and shall cease to hold office if he ceases to be a member of the Society.

(7) The Council may at any meeting elect one of its solicitor members or a former one of its solicitor members to be Honorary Vice-President of the Society to hold office until the next annual election of members of Council and to carry out such duties as may from time to time be prescribed by the Council. If the Honorary Vice-President is not a member of Council or if during his period of office he should cease to be a member of Council, he shall ex officio be a member of Council until the expiry of his period of office. An Honorary Vice-President shall not be eligible for re-election as such. An Honorary Vice-President may resign as provided in Article 15(4) hereof and shall cease to hold office if he ceases to be a member of the Society.

Admission of Honorary and Other Members of Society

Honorary members of Society

16.—(1) The Council may admit as an honorary member of the Society any person of distinction in the legal profession whether or not such person is or has been a member of the Society.

(2) Unless he is a member of the Society an honorary member shall have no right to vote at meetings of the Society or in elections of members of Council and shall not be liable in payment of any annual subscription to the Society.

Admission as members of solicitors exempt from holding practising certificates

17. The Council shall, on application and on payment of the annual subscription, admit as a member of the Society any solicitor who is exempt from taking out a practising certificate.

Honorary Presidents of Society

Honorary Presidents

18. *[Deleted by a Resolution of the members of the Law Society of Scotland to amend the Constitution of the Law Society of Scotland (effective May 2004).]*

Secretary and Staff

Secretary and staff

19.—(1)   The Council shall appoint a Secretary of the Society who shall be chief executive officer of the Council and it shall pay a suitable remuneration for his services and may make such provision for pension or other rights for his benefit as it thinks proper. The Secretary shall perform such duties as the Council may from time to time determine.

(2)   The Council shall appoint such other staff as it thinks necessary for the efficient discharge of the functions of the Society and of the Council, and shall pay to every member of staff appointed under this Article suitable remuneration and may make such provision for pension or other rights for his benefit as it thinks proper.

Accounts

Accounts

20.—(1)   The Council shall keep proper books of accounts with regard to all sums of money received and expended by the Society, the Council and staff of the Society, and the matters in respect of which the receipt and expenditure take place.

(2)   The Council shall keep such bank accounts in name of the Society as the Council may determine, and, save as otherwise directed by the Council, there shall be paid into the said bank accounts all sums received by the Society or the Council or staff of the Society or otherwise all payments due to be met by the Society or the Council or otherwise payable out of the funds of the Society. The Council may give directions with respect to keeping, paying money into, and operating on the several bank accounts.

Accounts to be made up yearly and submitted for audit

21.—(1)   Immediately after the end of each financial year the Council shall cause the accounts of the Society for that year to be brought to a balance and a balance sheet prepared.

(2)   The Council shall cause the accounts for the financial year to be audited as soon as practicable after the end of the year by the auditors appointed by the Society at the Annual General Meeting. A copy of the accounts, or an abstract thereof, and of the auditors' certificate thereon shall be made available to the members of the Society on the Society's website from the date the notice of the Annual General Meeting at which the statement of accounts of the Society and the report of the auditors thereon are to be considered is sent to the members of the Society. If, after the notice of the Annual General Meeting has been sent to the members of the Society, a member requests a copy of the accounts, or an abstract thereof, and of the auditor's certificate thereon to the member. At the option of the member that copy shall be sent either in paper or electronic form to the member at his place of business.

(3)   If a vacancy arises in the office of auditor of the accounts of the Society between Annual General Meetings, the Council may appoint an auditor to fill the vacancy until the next Annual General Meeting and fix the remuneration.

Miscellaneous

Committees and Sub-Committees of the Council

22.[1]   Any notice or other document or information required by or under this Constitution to be given to a member of the Society may, without prejudice to any other competent method of communication, be given to such member by email to an email address of such member provided by such member to, or lawfully known to, the Society.

The Regulatory Committee

23.—[2](1)   The regulatory committee is to have the responsibility to exercise the Council's regulatory functions (as defined in section 3F of the Act) independently and on behalf of Council, and:
(a)   to determine the Society's strategy in regulatory matters,
(b)   to set performance targets for the regulatory system, and
(c)   to make regular reports to Council on regulatory matters.

(2)   The regulatory committee is to have 10 members appointed by the Council. Five members are to be members of the Society. Five members are to be lay members, as defined in Article 2. The members of the regulatory committee may, but need not, be members of the Council.

(3)   The committee's Convener shall be a lay member chosen by the committee members.

(4)   Any sub-committee of the regulatory committee (a) need not be chaired by a lay member of that committee and (b) may co-opt members from outside the membership of that committee.

Notice to members of Society

24.   Any notice or other document required by or under this Constitution to be sent to a member of the Society shall be sent to such member at his place of business.

Council may hold referendum of members of the Society

25.   The Council may if it thinks fit and shall on a requisition signed by not fewer than 50 members of the Society and deposited with the Secretary ascertain the views of the members of the Society at any time on any question affecting the Society or the members thereof by holding a referendum of its members and the Council shall make such arrangements as it considers proper for that purpose, including issuing to every member of the Society a voting paper and arranging for the scrutiny of voting papers. The Council shall include in its annual report a report of any referendum taken during the year.

---

[1] As amended by a Resolution of the members of the Law Society of Scotland to amend the Constitution of the Law Society of Scotland (effective April 2014).
[2] As inserted by a Resolution of the members of the Law Society of Scotland to amend the Constitution of the Law Society of Scotland (effective June 2011). The following articles are renumbered accordingly.

Standing orders

26.—[1](1)   Subject to the provisions of this Constitution, the Council may by standing orders make provision with respect to—

    (a)   keeping minutes of General Meetings of the Society; and

    (b)   any other matters which the Council considers would facilitate the conduct of business of meetings of the Society, or of the Council, or of any committee or sub-committee of the Council.

(2)   Standing orders made under this Article or under any other provision of this Constitution may be varied or revoked at any time by the Council.

Validity of acts of Council

27.[2]   The acts and proceedings of the Council shall not be invalidated by any vacancy among its members or by any defect in the election, appointment, co-option or qualification of any member.

Expenses of members of Council and committees

28.   There shall be paid to the members of the Council and of committees thereof such travelling and other expenses in respect of attendance at meetings as may be approved by the Council.

Common Seal of Society

Common seal of Society

29.   The Secretary shall be responsible for the custody of the common seal of the Society. The seal shall not be affixed to any instrument except by order of the Council or of a committee of the Council specifically authorised for the purpose.

FIRST SCHEDULE[3]

PART I

The Council Constituencies

1.   Subject to Part III of this Schedule, the geographical constituencies referred to in article 4.1 are set out in column (i) below and the maximum number of members of the Council to be elected for each of them is set out opposite in column (ii) below.

(i) (Geographical constituencies)	(ii) (Maximum number of members)
The Sheriff Court Districts of:	
Glasgow and Strathkelvin	5
Perth	1
Greenock, Kilmarnock & Paisley	2
Cupar, Dunfermline & Kirkcaldy	2

---

[1] As substituted, September 1, 2003.
[2] As amended by a Resolution of the members of the Law Society of Scotland to amend the Constitution of the Law Society of Scotland (effective June 2011).
[3] As amended by a Resolution of the members of the Law Society of Scotland to amend the Constitution of the Law Society of Scotland (effective June 2012).

(i)	(ii)
(Geographical constituencies)	(Maximum number of members)
Edinburgh	5
Aberdeen, Banff, Peterhead, Stonehaven	2
Ayr, Dumfries, Kirkcudbright & Stranraer	2
Airdrie, Hamilton and Lanark	2
Dingwall, Dornoch, Elgin, Inverness Kirkwall, Lerwick, Lochmaddy, Portree, Stornoway, Tain & Wick	2
Duns, Haddington, Jedburgh, Peebles & Selkirk	2
Campbeltown, Dumbarton, Dunoon, Fort William, Oban & Rothesay	2
Arbroath, Dundee & Forfar	1
Alloa, Falkirk, Linlithgow and Stirling	2
England & Wales	1

PART II

GROUPING OF CONSTITUENCIES FOR PURPOSES OF ARTICLE 4 SO AS TO DETERMINE THE ROTATION OF THE ELECTIONS OF MEMBERS OF THE COUNCIL

Group 1
Glasgow & Strathkelvin
Perth
Greenock, Kilmarnock & Paisley
Cupar, Dunfermline & Kirkcaldy

Group 2
Edinburgh
Aberdeen, Banff, Peterhead, Stonehaven
Ayr, Dumfries, Kirkcudbright & Stranraer
Airdrie, Hamilton & Lanark

Group 3
Dingwall, Dornoch, Elgin, Inverness, Kirkwall, Lerwick, Lochmaddy, Portree, Stornoway, Tain & Wick
Duns, Haddington, Jedburgh, Peebles & Selkirk
Campbeltown, Dumbarton, Dunoon, Fort William, Oban & Rothesay
Arbroath, Dundee & Forfar
Alloa, Falkirk, Linlithgow & Stirling
England & Wales

PART III
1. Notwithstanding the provisions of Part II of this Schedule:
    (a) Each of the constituencies described in Part I of this Schedule shall come into effect as follows:

    (i)   Those constituencies included in Group 1 in terms of Part II of this Schedule shall come into effect no later than 31 May 2013;

    (ii)   Those constituencies included in Group 2 in terms of Part II of this Schedule shall come into effect no later than 31 May 2014;

    (iii)   Those constituencies included in Group 3 in terms of Part II of this Schedule shall come into effect no later than 31 May 2015.

  (b) The provisions of the Constitution in force as at 31 May 2012 shall continue to have effect until the dates specified in the foregoing sub paragraph.

2. Where a vacancy arises in any constituency constituted prior to 31 May 2012, within the six months immediately prior to the scheduled date of effect of the reformed constituency, the arrangements for election shall be in respect of the reformed constituency.

SECOND SCHEDULE[1]

PART I

RULES WITH REGARD TO THE ELECTION OF MEMBERS OF COUNCIL

Roll of electors and returning officer

1. The Secretary shall prepare, for each election, a roll of electors identifying every member of the Society who, on the date six weeks before the date of the election, had his place of business in the constituency for which the election is to be held. The Secretary shall appoint, for each election, a returning officer and a deputy returning officer who shall exercise the functions conferred by this Schedule. References in this Schedule to the returning officer shall include the deputy returning officer.

Notice of election

2. The returning officer shall on or before a date not later than five weeks before the day of the elections in the various constituencies concerned give notice, in such manner as the Council may determine, of election of the members of Council for those constituencies, including the date by which nominations must be received by the returning officer (being not less than three weeks before the day of election) and instructions on the nomination and voting process in such form as the Council may determine.

Nominations

3. No person may be elected a member of Council unless a nomination in respect of such person is received by the returning officer on or before the date specified in the notice of election. No person may be nominated as a candidate for election by a constituency unless he is a member of the Society having a place of business in the constituency for which the election is to be held. A nomination in respect of a candidate must have two proposers being electors within the constituency and must contain a statement by the candidate that he consents to be nominated and that, if elected, he will act as a member of Council. No proposer may propose more candidates than there are members of Council to be elected by a constituency, and if he does, his proposal shall be inoperative in all but those nominations up to the

---

[1] As amended by a Resolution by the members of the Law Society of Scotland to amend the Constitution of the Law Society of Scotland (effective April 2014).

permitted number which are first received. A nomination may be withdrawn at any time before the latest date for receipt of nominations.

Uncontested elections

4. If on the last date for receipt of nominations the number of persons validly nominated for a constituency does not exceed the number of persons to be elected by the constituency, the returning officer shall give notice in such manner as the Council may determine declaring the return of the persons nominated as members of Council and that no voting will take place in the constituency.

Voting in contested elections

5.—(1) If on the last date for receipt of nominations the number of persons validly nominated for a constituency exceeds the number of members to be elected by the constituency, the members of Council shall be elected by the first past the post method in accordance with the following provisions of this Schedule and with the provisions of any regulations made under paragraph 8.

(2) The returning officer shall, on or before a date to be determined by the Council (being not less than 10 days before the day of election), notify each elector on the roll of electors in the various constituencies concerned that voting in the relevant election is open. Such notification shall also contain the name, place of business and date of admission of each candidate and such other information relating to the candidates as the Council may determine, the date and time that voting closes and instructions on how to vote in such form as the Council may determine. The voting process shall, so far as reasonably practicable, ensure anonymity of voting.

(3) The returning officer shall, in the case of each constituency, immediately after the date and time that voting closes, arrange for the votes (providing the same are valid) to be counted and shall then declare the result of the election in such manner as the Council may determine.

Power to returning officer to cancel election

6. Notwithstanding anything in this Schedule, if after the last date for receipt of nominations a candidate withdraws with the result that the number of the remaining candidates does not exceed the number of persons to be elected by the constituency, the returning officer may cancel the election and give notice in such manner as the Council may determine declaring the return of the remaining candidates as members of Council.

Provisions in case of death of candidate

7. If a candidate validly nominated dies on or before the last date for receipt of nominations his nomination shall be treated as having been withdrawn, but if such a candidate dies after that date, but before the declaration of the result of the election under paragraph 5(3), the returning officer shall order a fresh election to be held.

Power to make regulations varying for certain purposes provisions of schedule

8. Notwithstanding anything in this Schedule, the Council may make regulations containing consequential amendments to the provisions of this Schedule as appear to the Council to be necessary to give full effect to those provisions.

Decision of returning officer final

9. Any question arising with regard to the validity of a nomination, a vote, or otherwise in connection with an election under this Constitution shall be determined by the returning officer, whose decision shall be final.

Standing Orders of the Law Society of Scotland

Standing Orders made by the Council of the Law Society of Scotland in terms of Article 25 of the Constitution of the Society.

Interpretation

1.—(1) "the Act" means the Solicitors (Scotland) Act 1980; and other expressions used in these Orders shall have the same respective meanings as in the Constitution of the Society.

(2) The Interpretation Act 1978 applies to the interpretation of these Standing Orders as it applied to the interpretation of an Act of Parliament.

(3) In these Orders, references to "the Secretary" include, in the event of the Secretary's absence or incapacity, the Registrar or any other person authorised by the President to act on behalf of the Secretary.

(4) These Orders may be cited as the Law Society of Scotland Standing Orders, 2004, and have effect to regulate all proceedings of the Society on and after 1 April 2004.

CONDUCT OF BUSINESS AT GENERAL MEETINGS OF SOCIETY

Authority of the Chair

2. The decision of the Chairman of a General Meeting of the Society on any question relating to procedure or order at the meeting shall be final and conclusive.

Motions and Amendments at Meetings of Society

3.(a) Every motion submitted to a General Meeting, except those relating to routine matters or the conduct or procedure of the meeting, shall be in writing and signed by the mover, who shall be a member, and shall relate to business specified in the notice calling the meeting.

  (b) In the case of any motion, any member may propose—
    (i) an amendment of the motion by substitution, deletion and/or addition,
    (ii) the direct negative,
    (iii) that the debate be adjourned, or
    (iv) that the question be now put or that the meeting move to the next business.

  (c) All proposals under 3(b)(i), (iii) and (iv) but not (ii) shall require a seconder.

  (d) Movers of motions and of proposals under 3(b)(i), (ii) or (iii) shall be allowed five minutes to speak and other speakers shall be allowed three minutes. The Chairman may, at his discretion, allow a specific extension of time to any speaker.

  (e) Without the permission of the Chairman, no member shall be entitled to speak more than once on any motion or on any proposal under 3(b)(i), (ii) or (iii) (unless on a point of order or information) except that movers of motions and of proposals under 3(b)(i), (ii) or (iii) may reply, and shall be allowed three minutes therefor. In replying, members shall confine themselves to answering previous speakers and shall not introduce new matter. Movers of motions shall have the opportunity of closing the debate.

  (f) Proposers and seconders of a proposal under 3(b)(iv) shall not be permitted initially to speak in support of the proposal. When the proposal has been proposed and seconded, the Chairman will ask the meeting whether any member wishes to move the direct negative and, if he does, whether he has the support of one other member. If no member and supporting member wishes so to do, the proposal will be stated by the Chairman to have been carried unanimously. If the direct negative is moved and supported as aforesaid the proposer of the proposal will be allowed three minutes to speak to the proposal and the seconder two minutes to speak to it. The mover of the direct negative will be allowed three minutes to speak in support of the negative and the said supporting member two minutes to speak to it. No other member will be allowed to speak and, at the conclusion of the four speeches herein referred to, the proposal will forthwith be put to the meeting.

(g) Points of order shall be confined strictly to the conduct or procedure of the meeting.

(h) No motion or proposal may be withdrawn except with the concurrence of its seconder and, in the case of a motion, by permission of the meeting.

(i) No member shall unless with the permission of the Chairman move more than once that any one motion be amended.

Adjournment of General Meetings of the Society and suspension of Standing Orders

4. (a) The Chairman may with the consent of any General Meeting of the Society at which a quorum is present, and shall, if so instructed by the meeting, adjourn the meeting from time to time and from place to place, but no business shall be transacted at any adjourned meeting other than the business left unfinished at the meeting at which the adjournment took place. When a meeting is adjourned for more than 14 days, seven days' notice of the adjourned meeting shall be given to each member but, save as aforesaid, it shall not be necessary to give any notice of an adjournment. It shall not be necessary in any case to give notice of the business to be transacted at an adjourned meeting.

(b) At any General Meeting of the Society a motion to suspend Standing Orders may be made and may be spoken to only by the mover who shall be allowed five minutes for that purpose. Such a motion if seconded shall be put forthwith to the meeting and shall not be passed unless it be supported by two-thirds of the members voting thereon. Any such suspension shall relate to one item of business only, or shall be for a fixed period of time not extending beyond the conclusion of that General Meeting.

Minutes of General Meeting of the Society

5.—(1) Minutes shall be kept by or on behalf of the Secretary recording—

(a) the names and places of business of the members present at each meeting; and

(b) all resolutions and proceedings at such meetings of the Society.

(2) The minutes of each General Meeting of the Society shall be submitted to the following Annual General Meeting of the Society and if approved as a true record shall be signed by the Chairman of the meeting to which it relates or the Chairman of the meeting at which the minute is approved.

MEETINGS OF THE COUNCIL

Ordinary Meetings of the Council

6.—(1) Subject to the other provisions of these Orders, ordinary meetings of the Council shall be held at the office of the Society, or at such other place as the Council may from time to time determine, and the Council shall hold not less than seven meetings in each year for the transaction of Council business.

(2) The Secretary shall call a meeting of the Council—

(a) on being required so to do by the President (or, in the event of the absence or incapacity of the President, the Vice-President), such meeting to be held at a date and time directed by the President or Vice-President or

(b) on receiving a requisition in writing for that purpose, specifying the business proposed or to be transacted at the meeting, signed by not less than nine members of the Council, which meeting shall be held within 14 days of receipt of the requisition at a date and time directed by the President or (in the event of absence or incapacity of the President) the Vice-President.

(3) A member of Council who wishes an item of business to be considered at an ordinary meeting of the Council shall give notice thereof in writing to the Secretary and such item shall (if the notice is received at least two days before the date when, in the ordinary course of events, notice of the meeting would be issued) be included in the agenda in the next notice issued under paragraph (4) of this Order.

(4) The Secretary shall give to every member of the Council written notice of the time and place of every ordinary meeting of Council, and—

(a) such notice shall be deemed to have been duly given if it is sent by ordinary mail (or a document exchange in which the addressee has provided an address to be used for the purpose) to the place of business of the member so that it would arrive, in the ordinary course of events, at least seven days before the date of the meeting,

(b) the notice shall specify the business proposed to be transacted at the meeting, but the President (or person actually presiding at the meeting of the Council) may, if it appears to him that any additional item of business should receive consideration, allow that matter to be dealt with although not mentioned in the notice.

Special Meetings of the Council

7.—(1) Notwithstanding anything in Order 6—

(a) if the President (or, in the event of the absence or incapacity of the President, the Vice-President) considers that any item of business is of such urgency that the giving of notice in accordance with paragraph 6(4) would be prejudicial to the interests of the public or of the solicitors' profession, he may require the Secretary to call a meeting of the Council to be held on giving not less than three days' notice;

(b) a meeting called under this paragraph shall conduct only the item of business for which it was called.

(2) Notwithstanding any of the other provisions of these Orders

(a) in the event that a matter arises which, in the opinion of the President or the Vice-President or the immediate Past President, or in their absence the Secretary, requires powers of discretion to be exercised by the Council in terms of section 38, 39A, 40, 41, 45 or 46 of the Solicitors (Scotland) Act 1980 more urgently than is allowed for by the foregoing provisions of this Order, the Secretary shall call a meeting of the Council for the purpose of dealing with such matter and the following provisions of this paragraph shall apply to that meeting;

(b) such a meeting may be held on giving not less than 24 hours notice, and shall conduct only the item of business for which it was called.

Notice may be given by facsimile or email

8.—(1) This Order applies to all meetings of the Council.

(2) Notwithstanding any other provision of these Orders as to the form of a notice of a meeting or as to the manner and time of its delivery

(a) any notice calling a meeting [to which this Order applies] [of the Council] shall be in writing but may be given by facsimile transmission or by email to the facsimile number or email address given to the Society by a member of Council for this purpose;

(b) any notice sent by facsimile or by email shall be deemed to have been received by the addressee immediately on sending whether or not it is actually received;

Attendance by Audio Conference

9.—(1) This Order applies to all meetings of the Council.

(2) A meeting to which this Order applies may consist of a conference between members of Council who are not all in one place, but each of whom is able to speak to each of the others and to be heard by all of the others simultaneously and a member of Council taking part in such a meeting shall be deemed to be present in person at the meeting and accordingly shall be entitled to vote and to be counted in the quorum.

Proceedings at meetings of the Council

10.—(1) The President (or, in the event of the absence or incapacity of the President, the Vice-President) shall preside at each meeting of the Council, but if both be not present the members present shall choose one of their number to preside; in the following provisions of the Order, "the Chairman" means the person in fact presiding over a meeting in accordance with this paragraph.

(2) No business shall be transacted at a meeting of the Council unless at least nine members are present.

(3) The decision of the Chairman on any question relating to procedure or order at the meeting shall be final.

(4) Except where different provision is expressly made, or the context otherwise requires, the procedures for the conduct of business of the Council shall be those applicable to the conduct of business at General Meetings of the Society.

(5) Questions coming and arising before the Council shall, except in so far as may be otherwise expressly provided, be decided by a majority of the members voting on the question. In the event of an equality of votes, the Chairman shall be entitled to a second or casting vote.

(6) The Council may adjourn a meeting of the Council to any other day, hour and place.

(7) A motion the purport of which, in the opinion of the Chairman, is to alter or rescind a decision of the Council, shall not be competent within three months from the date of the passing of that decision.

(8) The Secretary shall keep (or cause to be kept) Minutes of all meetings of the Council, and—

    (a) the Minutes of each meeting shall record the names of members attending, and all resolutions and proceedings at, that meeting,

    (b) subject to sub-paragraph (c) below, the Minutes of each meeting shall be submitted to the following meeting for confirmation (either as written or with such amendments as the Council shall direct) of their factual accuracy, but draft minutes approved by the Chairman shall be sufficient evidence of the proceedings pending such confirmation,

    (c) a meeting called in terms of Order 7(1) or 7(2) shall not consider the Minutes of any earlier meeting; any Minutes which, apart from this sub-paragraph, would be submitted to such a meeting shall be submitted to the next meeting called in terms of Order 6(4).

Elections of President and Vice-President

[1] **11.** The principles which must be followed in the election of the President and Vice-President under Article 15(1) of the Constitution are—

    (a) All members of the Council, including lay members, have one vote, and

    (b) Voting is a by a ballot system to be agreed by the Council at its first meeting after the first day in October each year.

NOTE

[1] As amended by a Resolution of the Law Society of Scotland (effective October 2012).

APPOINTMENT OF COUNCIL COMMITTEES

Constitution of Committees and Sub-Committees

12.—(1) The Council may, in terms of Article 22(1) of the Society's Constitution, constitute such committees and sub-committees as are necessary or convenient to carry out the work of the Council, and shall specify (and may from time to time amend) the remit of each committee and sub-committee that it constitutes.

(2) A committee may, unless its remit provides otherwise, constitute such sub-committees as are necessary or convenient to carry out the work of the committee, and shall specify (and may from time to time amend) the remit of each sub-committee that it constitutes.

(3) A sub-committee constituted by a committee shall not have any remit beyond that of the committee which constituted it.

(4) In this Order, "remit" means a written statement setting out the functions, powers, duties and responsibilities of a committee or sub-committee and regulating its membership and procedures.

Membership of Committees and Sub-Committees

13.—(1) Each committee and sub-committee constituted by the Council shall have such members as the Council, on the nomination of the Nominations Committee, shall from time to time appoint; the Council shall appoint one of the members to be Convener of the committee except for the Regulatory Committee which shall appoint one of its lay members as its Convener.

(2) Each sub-committee constituted by a committee shall have a Convener appointed by the Council, on the nomination of the Nominations Committee and such other members (subject to the terms of its remit) as may from time to time be appointed by the Council.

(3) The Regulatory Committee and the sub-committees of the Regulatory Committee shall have at least 50% of their membership as lay members.

(4) A committee or sub-committee (or the Convener thereof) shall, of its remit so provides, have the power to co-opt any person as a member for a specified purpose or for a specified period of time not exceeding one year.

(5) A member of a committee or sub-committee need not be a member of the Council or of the Society, and a committee or sub-committee may have a majority of members who are not members of the Council or the Society.

(6) The President and Vice-President shall, by virtue of their respective offices, be members of all committees and sub-committees, except for the Regulatory Committees and the sub-committees of the Regulatory Committee.

(7) Conveners and Vice-Conveners shall hold office from the dates specified in their respective appointments until (unless a different date is specified is the appointment) 31 May next following their appointment, or (in either case) until the earlier occurrence of one of the following events—

(a) resignation;

(b) death or mental incapacity;

(c) removal by a resolution of the Council supported by two-thirds of the Council members voting thereon;

(d) in the case of a member who is a solicitor, striking off or suspension from practice

but a Convener or Vice-Convener retiring by reason of the expiry of his period of appointment shall be eligible to be re-appointed.

(8) Subject to paragraph (6) above, members of committees shall hold office for three years (or such shorter period, if any, as is specified in their appointments) or until the earlier occurrence of one of the following events—

(a) resignation;

(b) death or mental incapacity;

(c) removal by a resolution of the Council supported by two-thirds of the Council members voting thereon;

(d) in the case of a member who is a solicitor, striking off or suspension from practice;

but a member retiring by reason of the expiry of his period of appointment shall be eligible to be re-appointed.

(9) Notwithstanding any other provision of this Order, a member of a committee shall be deemed to have resigned if he is absent from three successive meetings of the Committee; but this paragraph shall not apply if such absence was with the approval (which may be given retrospectively)

(a) in the case of a Convener, of the President;

(b) in any other case, of the Convener of the committee or sub-committee.

Committee Secretaries

14. Each committee and sub-committee shall have a committee secretary, being a member of the Society staff assigned for that purpose by or on behalf of the Secretary of the Society.

Savings for Existing Committees

15. Nothing in Orders 12 and 13 affects the constitution or membership of committees and sub-committees which were in existence on 31 March 2004, save that the members of such committees and sub-committees shall remain in office until 31 May 2004 or until the earlier occurrence of one of the following events

(a) resignation;

(b) death or mental incapacity;

(c) removal by a resolution by the Council supported by two-thirds of the Council members voting thereon;

(d) in the case of a member who is a solicitor, striking off or suspension from practice;

but a member retiring by reason of the passage of time shall be eligible to be re-appointed.

CONDUCT OF COMMITTEE BUSINESS

Meetings of Committees

16.—(1) In this Order, and in Order 17, unless the context requires otherwise—

(a) references to the Convener include (if the Convener is absent or unable to act) the Vice-Convener or, if the relevant committee has no Vice-Convener, the Committee Secretary;

(b) references to a committee include (unless the context requires otherwise) a sub-committee.

(2) Subject to the following provisions of this Order, each committee shall meet as often as is necessary for the effective performance of its remit.

(3) The dates, times and places of meetings shall be such as the committee may determine or otherwise as directed by the Convener.

(4) The Committee Secretary shall call a meeting of a committee

(a) upon being required to do so by the President or by the Convener of that committee, such meeting to be held at a date, time and place specified by the President or the Convener or

(b) on receiving a request in writing for that purpose, specifying the business proposed to be transacted at the meeting, signed by not less than one quarter of the members of the committee, such meeting to be held within ten days of the receipt of the request, at a date, time and place specified by the Convener.

(5) The Committee Secretary shall give to every member of the committee

written notice of the time and place of every meeting of the committee, and—

    (a)   such notice shall be deemed to have been duly given if it is sent by ordinary mail (or a document exchange in which the addressee has provided an address to be used for the purpose) to the address provided by the member for that purpose so that it would arrive, in the ordinary course of events, at least seven days before the date of the meeting.

    (b)   the business proposed to be transacted at the meeting shall be specified in the notice or in a separate notice sent (in similar manner) so as to arrive, in the ordinary course of events, at least three days before the meeting; but the Convener (or person actually presiding at the meeting) may, if it appears to him that any additional item of business should receive consideration, allow that matter to be dealt with although not mentioned in the notice.

  (6)   Notwithstanding anything in paragraph (4) of this Order—

    (a)   if the Convener considers that any item of business is of such urgency that the giving of notice in accordance with paragraph (5) would be prejudicial to the interests of the public or of the solicitors' profession, he may require the Committee Secretary to call a meeting of the committee to be held on giving not less than three days' notice;

    (b)   a meeting called under this paragraph shall conduct only the item of business for which it was called.

  (7)   Order 8, paragraph 2 applies to all committee meetings.

  (8)   Order 9, paragraph 2 applies to all committee meetings.

Procedure at Meetings

17.—(1)   The Convener (or, in the event of the absence or incapacity of the Convener, the Vice-Convener, if there is one) shall preside at each meeting of the committee, but if both be not present the members present shall choose one of their number to preside (in which event, references in this Order to "the Convener" include the person so chosen).

  (2)   Except where different provision is expressly made, or the context otherwise requires, the procedures for the conduct of the business of a committee shall be those applicable to the conduct of the business of the Council.

  (3)   No business shall be transacted at a meeting of a committee unless at least three members are present except for a meeting of the Regulatory Committee or a sub-committee of the Regulatory Committee for which the quorum will be four members of whom two are lay members.

  (4)   The Committee Secretary shall keep, or cause to be kept, Minutes of all meetings of the committees, and

    (a)   the Minutes of each meeting shall record the names of members attending, and all resolutions and proceedings at, that meeting;

    (b)   the Minutes of each meeting shall be submitted to the following meeting for confirmation (either as written or with such amendments as the Committee shall direct) of their factual accuracy, but draft minutes approved by the Convener shall be sufficient evidence of the proceedings pending such confirmation.

  (5)   Subject to paragraph (3) of this Order, a committee may meet and conduct business notwithstanding any vacancy in its membership.

  (6)   The provisions of this Order have effect subject to any contrary or inconsistent provisions made by the Council in the remit of any committee.

PRACTICE GUIDELINES

LAW SOCIETY GUIDANCE

LAW SOCIETY GUIDANCE

LAW SOCIETY GUIDANCE

LAW SOCIETY GUIDANCE

LAW SOCIETY GUIDANCE

LAW SOCIETY GUIDANCE

LAW SOCIETY GUIDANCE

LAW SOCIETY GUIDANCE

LAW SOCIETY GUIDANCE

LAW SOCIETY GUIDANCE

LAW SOCIETY GUIDANCE

LAW SOCIETY GUIDANCE

LAW SOCIETY GUIDANCE

LAW SOCIETY GUIDANCE

LAW SOCIETY GUIDANCE

LAW SOCIETY GUIDANCE

LAW SOCIETY GUIDANCE

LAW SOCIETY GUIDANCE

LAW SOCIETY GUIDANCE

LAW SOCIETY GUIDANCE

LAW SOCIETY GUIDANCE

LAW SOCIETY GUIDANCE

LAW SOCIETY GUIDANCE

LAW SOCIETY GUIDANCE

LAW SOCIETY GUIDANCE

LAW SOCIETY GUIDANCE

LAW SOCIETY GUIDANCE

LAW SOCIETY GUIDANCE

LAW SOCIETY GUIDANCE

LAW SOCIETY GUIDANCE

LAW SOCIETY GUIDANCE

LAW SOCIETY GUIDANCE

LAW SOCIETY GUIDANCE

LAW SOCIETY GUIDANCE

LAW SOCIETY GUIDANCE

LAW SOCIETY GUIDANCE

LAW SOCIETY GUIDANCE

LAW SOCIETY GUIDANCE

LAW SOCIETY GUIDANCE

LAW SOCIETY GUIDANCE

LAW SOCIETY GUIDANCE

LAW SOCIETY GUIDANCE

LAW SOCIETY GUIDANCE

LAW SOCIETY GUIDANCE

LAW SOCIETY GUIDANCE

LAW SOCIETY GUIDANCE

LAW SOCIETY GUIDANCE

LAW SOCIETY GUIDANCE

LAW SOCIETY GUIDANCE

LAW SOCIETY GUIDANCE

Contents

Purpose and Status of Guidance

The purpose of Guidance is to assist solicitors and others providing legal services to meet the standards of good professional and ethical practice. Some of the Guidance explains or illustrates the ways in which the Practice Rules are applied or interpreted. Some of the Guidance is not specific to a particular Rule or Rules but relates to the carrying out of a particular type of service or applies to particular circumstances only. Therefore it may be necessary to consider different parts of the Guidance depending on the matter in hand. Although much of it contains suggestions as to other areas which may be of relevance it is obviously not possible to predict every circumstance in which guidance may be required and use of the A-Z index by subject matter is therefore recommended.

Whilst the Guidance does not have a status equivalent to the Rules, it is principally intended to assist you with the interpretation of the Rules and the identification of good practice. You must exercise your professional judgement in considering what parts of the Guidance may be relevant in all the circumstances of any particular case so you ensure compliance with the Rules.

Guidance related to Rule A5: Waiver

Guidance on the circumstances in which a waiver request may be granted may be found in the guidance related to the specific rule in respect of which a waiver is sought.

Section B: Fundamental Principles and Client Care

Guidance related to Rule B1.1: Application

The standards of conduct contained in rule B1 do not apply when you are engaged in cross-border practice. Note that this term does not encompass transactions or activity between the constituent parts of the United Kingdom. When engaged in cross-border practice you must comply with rule C1 instead.

The principles which apply are broadly similar, however, the Code of Conduct which applies to cross-border practice is that adopted by the Council of the Bars and Law Societies of the European Union and is therefore not wholly within the control of the Society. Minor discrepancies are, therefore, inevitable and you should consider the appropriate rule and Code in detail.

Guidance related to Rule B1.3: Independence—outsourcing

It is important to remember that you must maintain your ability to give independent advice free from external influences where you are providing outsourced services to other legal service providers.

Guidance related to Rule B1.4: The Interests of the Client

Supervision of non-solicitor employees

It is emphasised that the obligation in rule B1.4.1 (to "act in the best interests of your clients subject to preserving your independence and complying with the law, these rules and the principles of good professional conduct") extends to practice units as well as individual solicitors. The managers of a practice unit are responsible for matters done in the name of the practice unit, whoever actually carries them out.

In particular, the manager responsible for a specific department should ensure that all staff in that department have adequate training in any relevant professional practice rules and practice guidance, and that there is adequate supervision of staff in carrying out work. If there is no manager directly responsible, the duty of supervision will rest with all the managers of the practice unit.

This Rule applies equally to staff whether directly employed or sub-contracted.

Guidance related to Rule B1.5: Vulnerable Clients Guidance

1. Introduction

1.   You are reminded that a solicitor must (a) have instructions from his or her client and (b) be satisfied when taking instructions, that his or her client has the capacity to give instructions to relation to that matter. If there is any doubt as to a client's capacity to instruct in a particular case, advice should be sought from the medical profession.

2.   "Rule" and "Rules" refer to the Law Society of Scotland Practice Rules 2011. "Must" refers to a binding obligation under statute, regulations, Rules or the like. "Should" refers to good practice: failure to comply may be taken into account in disciplinary or other proceedings. Where a solicitor considers that particular circumstances justify departure from this guidance, a written record of those circumstances and the reasons for the departure should be kept.

3.   This guidance has been issued following publication of a report by the Mental Welfare Commission for Scotland ("MWC") on "An investigation into the response by statutory services and professionals to concerns raised in respect of Mr and Mrs D" (published 13th February 2012) ("the D Report"), as has the related "Guidance on Continuing and Welfare Powers of Attorney ("the POA guidance"). While vulnerability is a particular potential concern in relation to such Powers of Attorney, it can be equally important in relation to Wills, gifts, guarantees, and the like. Vulnerability may be relevant to any contemplated act or transaction about which a solicitor may be consulted or instructed. This guidance accordingly addresses vulnerability generally.

4.   This guidance should be read subject to the terms of relevant Rules and guidance published by the Society thereon. It is not the purpose of guidance to state or interpret the law, and it should not be read as seeking to do so: this guidance assumes compliance with Rule B 1.10—see paragraph 11 below.

Capacity and incapacity

5.   Solicitors should balance the positive obligation to facilitate valid and competent acts and transactions against the negative obligation to avoid purported acts or transactions which are incompetent, void or voidable.

6.   Solicitors should as far as reasonably practicable assist vulnerable clients to express their wishes, understand relevant advice, give valid instructions, and carry through valid acts and transactions. Where appropriate, solicitors should take advice as to optimum place, time and other arrangements for advising and taking instructions. A person confused by a lengthy or complex document, or unable to sustain the concentration necessary to understand it, may nevertheless be able to understand (and if so desired, validly execute) a simple and straightforward document which is nevertheless adequate for its intended purpose. Under Rule B 1.9.1 solicitors must communicate effectively with their clients; therefore if a client is capable of understanding, a solicitor must communicate by whatever means is necessary to enable the client to understand. Assistance with communication is addressed in paragraph 15 below.

7.   The definition of incapacity in the Adults with Incapacity (Scotland) Act 2000 ("2000 Act") applies for the purposes of that Act, but it may reasonably be referred to for guidance in determining capacity for other purposes. Note that the definition includes "incapable of acting", which may include acting to resist undue influence or other vitiating factors, or acting so as to adhere to and implement otherwise valid decisions, or to maintain consistency.

8.   A solicitor may, and in some circumstances should, seek and carefully consider expert guidance. However the solicitor retains responsibility for compliance with all relevant Rules and should not abdicate responsibility to the expert. Solicitors should not simply rely upon the legal presumption of capacity. On the contrary, they "must …. be satisfied when taking instructions, that his or her client has the capacity to give instructions in relation to that matter" (guidance related to Rule B 1.5).

9.   In cases of doubt as to the extent to which, and circumstances in which, capacity can be exercised, or conversely as to the extent to which incapacity prevents a contemplated act or transaction, the advice of a medical practitioner or clinical psychologist should be sought. It may be necessary to approach someone with particular specialist expertise. The solicitor should not seek a generalised and simplistic verdict of "capable" or "incapable". The solicitor should explain the act or transaction contemplated and the legal requirements for it to be valid. The solicitor should explain any indications of relevant capacity or incapacity of which the solicitor is aware, and any steps which the solicitor proposes in order to facilitate exercise of capacity.

Vulnerability generally

10. The possibility of vulnerability should be considered whenever a solicitor is consulted or instructed in any matter. Often the solicitor will be able to decide quickly and confidently that there is no question of vulnerability; but solicitors should always be alert to any indications of possible vulnerability.

11. A solicitor "must only act in those matters where you are competent to do so" (Rule B 1.10). However solicitors must not discriminate contrary to Rule B 1.15.1. They may accordingly require to refer to another solicitor whose particular skills are required in determining capacity, identifying vulnerability, or in advising and acting for a particular client (including the requirement to communicate effectively – see paragraph 6 above).

12. Indications of possible vulnerability may arise from the normal process of ascertaining a client's wishes and intentions, exploring circumstances, and advising as to merits, risks, advantages and disadvantages of a proposed act or transaction, or of alternatives. However, on the one hand an apparently unwise act or transaction may represent a client's valid and competent choice; while conversely an apparently wise act or transaction could be invalid through lack of relevant capacity, or undue influence, or other vitiating factors

Influence and undue influence

13. Influence, even powerful influence, is not necessarily undue influence. A client may attend to make a Will or grant a Power of Attorney only because someone has strongly influenced them that they ought to do so. Influence may be powerful but benign. Or it may be subtle, but undue. Influence to make a Will, but not as to who should benefit or who should be appointed executor, or to grant a Power of Attorney, but not as to whom to appoint, is unlikely to be undue. If however (in those examples) influence seeks to affect choice of beneficiaries, executor(s) or attorney(s), it is likely to be undue, particularly where the influencer or someone connected to the influencer so benefits, though the extent of realistic (or sensible) choice in the matter may also be relevant. The solicitor should use reasonable endeavours to ascertain such matters from the client.

14. While a solicitor must not act in accordance with purported instructions which the client does not have capacity to give validly, there is no equivalent direct prohibition where the solicitor detects undue influence or other vitiating factors. Where a solicitor believes that a purported act or transaction will be voidable on grounds of undue influence or other vitiating factors, the solicitor may decline to act in accordance with such instructions, but is not bound to do so unless the solicitor reasonably considers that to facilitate the act or transaction would put the solicitor in breach of the requirement of Rule B 1.4.1 to act in the best interests of the client. If the solicitor declines, the solicitor should explain the reasons. If the solicitor acts, the solicitor should warn the client that the purported act or transaction may be voidable and (if such be the case) may prove to be contrary to the client's interests. The solicitor should also obtain the client's authorisation to disclose such advice and the reasons for it, should the validity of the act or transaction be put in issue following impairment of capacity or death of the client.

15. A dominated client may deny or conceal undue influence. Where there is a possibility of vulnerability, the client should be seen alone except where the client reasonably prefers someone to give support, or to assist communication, in which case such third party should if at all possible be neutral in relation to the matter in hand. Undue influence can be exercised regardless of presence, though the effect may be greater if the influencer is present, or present elsewhere in the building, or is the initiator, or brings the client and then leaves.

16. A client who is subject to two different spheres of influence may express different, or even contradictory, wishes or make contradictory purported decisions when the client perceives himself (or herself) to be within each of those spheres of influence. This is a clear indication of incapacity to resist influence. However, while inability to resist influence may indicate incapacity, the concepts of undue influence and other vitiating factors are of course not dependent upon incapacity and may apply in cases where capacity is not impaired.

Who is my client?

17. The granter of a Power of Attorney, Will, guarantee, a document (including a Deed of Trust) incorporating a gift, or other document is the solicitor's client. All relevant Rules should be complied with in relation to that client – including Rule B 4.2 (providing written intimation in accordance with that Rule "when tendering for business or at the earliest practicable opportunity upon receiving instructions"); Rule B 6.23.1 (compliance with Money Laundering Regulations); and Rules B 1.4.1, 1.9.1, 1.10 and 1.15.1 (all referred to above). Of particular importance in the context of vulnerable clients are Rule B 1.5.1: "You are the agent of your client and must have the authority of your client for your actings … "; Rule B 1.7.1, under which solicitors must not act where there is a conflict of interest; and Rule B 1.7.2, under which solicitors must exercise caution where there is a potential conflict of interest and, if the potential for conflict is significant, not act for both parties without the full knowledge and express consent of the clients. If there is doubt as to capacity to instruct, that should be resolved before accepting engagement if a new client, or before accepting instructions from an existing client.

18. Where a solicitor issues any document for signature to a party or prospective party "to a transaction of any kind" the solicitor should consider Rule B 2.1.7. "Issue" means issuing in any way, including giving the document to the client or other third party to take to the proposed signatory. In the case of continuing and/or welfare Powers of Attorney, Wills and gratuitous documents, these should only be prepared by a solicitor acting for the granter or donor. A solicitor may occasionally prepare a Power of Attorney for commercial purposes, which is not a continuing or welfare Power of Attorney, or include such power in a longer document, when not acting for the proposed granter. Even in that situation, the solicitor should carefully consider whether he or she can properly proceed if the proposed granter is not separately represented. In any event, the solicitor should consider Rule B 2.1.7. Similar considerations may apply in relation to other documents, such as guarantees.

19. Proposed appointees under the Adults with Incapacity (Scotland) Act 2000 should be referred to relevant Codes of Practice and other material available on the Public Guardian's website, as may be appropriate.

Indicators

20. The following possible situations and indicators are offered as examples, not as a comprehensive list.

Some categories of situations

The situations are described simplistically in that they are stated as applying with certainty, whereas in practice they will present with varying degrees of probability.

Type A: Capable client making own independent decisions, has justified faith in competence and trustworthiness of proposed appointee. (Capacity and no undue influence)

Type B: Client dominated by proposed appointee, nevertheless capable and proposed appointee competent and motivated to act properly. (Capacity and influence, influence not undue or malign)

Type C: Client capable and not subject to undue influence, but instructions seem unwise. (The solicitor's role is to advise, perhaps in strong terms, but in this situation there are no grounds for refusing to act. It is wise to record concerns, advice given, and reasons for acting. See also paragraph 12 above)

Type D: Client of limited but sufficient capacity, vulnerable to undue influence but not in fact unduly influenced. (The solicitor must respect and if necessary support the client's capacity, without discrimination on grounds of the client's disability)

Type E: Client subject to influence which is undue and malign, not benign, and unable to resist it through incapacity or facility or the dominance of the influencer(s). (Regardless of level of capacity to consult and instruct, the solicitor will not be able to implement instructions)

Type F: Presents as any of types A – D, but there is in fact undue and malign influence which may be covert or deliberately concealed (including by the person influenced)

Difficulty: Strong influence is not necessarily undue influence (see paragraph 13 above). It may be necessary to try to assess the motives and intentions of an influencer (or influencers) whom the solicitor may not even have met.

Who has approached the solicitor ("initiator")?
1. Client who is well known? Be alert to possible changes in capacity, vulnerability.
2. A new client? Be alert to possible incapacity or vulnerability.
3. Neutral person on behalf of the client? Be careful—see below if there is possible significant influence.
4. Proposed appointee or donee on behalf of the client? Be very careful—(but this could still be a type A or B, or even D, situation).
5. Initiator reluctant to "stay completely out of the way" when instructions are taken? Be very careful.
4. Initiator resistant to possibility of joint appointment or additional donees? Be very careful.

Other possible indicators
1. Any references to family disunity? Be very careful.
2. Initiator a dominant personality? Be very careful.

3. Client appears to be very influenced by initiator? Be very careful, and if initiator is proposed appointee or donee—danger sign!
4. Client "doesn't want to upset" proposed appointee or donee? Danger sign!
5. Client "doesn't want to upset" family or others? Be very careful.
4. Proposed appointee or donee seems largely motivated by need to mitigate tax, avoid means-testing? Danger sign!

Possibility of some form of "mental disorder" (broadly defined)? Investigate.

Diagnosis or information that there is some degree of "mental disorder"? Enquire, take great care, but the solicitor has a duty to help clients exercise such capacity and autonomy as they can. Consider simple form of document.

Illiteracy, communication difficulties, sensory impairments, other physical issues, frailty? The solicitor's approach needs to be supportive, facilitative, well-informed and careful.

Guidance related to Rule B1.6: Confidentiality Generally

Confidentiality is related to conflict of interest but is also a separate and distinct question. The position is set out in rule B1.6 which states "You must maintain client confidentiality. This duty is not terminated by the passage of time. You must also supervise your employees to ensure that they keep client matters confidential. Only the client, Acts of the legislature, subordinate legislation or the court can waive or override the duty of confidentiality. The duty does not apply to information about any crime a client indicates they will commit."

This obligation to supervise extends to all outsourced providers of your business operations and services.

Confidentiality is a privilege which is exercisable by the client and which can therefore be waived by the client. It covers matters which are actually confidential and not in the public domain. For example, the contents of a document which has been registered in a public register can never be confidential, although the circumstances in which it was entered into, the advice given to the client and the instructions which were received from the client will be confidential so far as not set out in the document.

Specific situations

1. Party in dispute with former client

Where a practice unit used to act for one party and is now instructed by another party with whom the original client is in dispute, if the original client has instructed a new solicitor there will be no breach of rule B2.1 (Conflict of Interest) but you may not be able to act for the new client. If you are in possession of confidential information about your original client which would be of benefit to the new one, you must make certain that this is not disclosed and not made use of or used. The best way to achieve this is to decline to act for the new client.

You should always remember the client's perception of the matter which will be different from your own. He may make a complaint which will now go to the Scottish Legal Complaints Commission. While it will be a matter for your own judgment, you would not be criticised for declining to act. If the former client has not yet instructed a new solicitor, you should exercise even more caution before accepting new instructions as the original client may wish to instruct you in the matter anyway.

2. Solicitor moving practice unit

A solicitor who had moved from one firm to another was the subject of a case in England in 1995. He had had been a partner in one of the foremost firms specialising in the field of intellectual property and a firm which at all times had acted for the plaintiff in a patent case. The solicitor was not in any way involved in those proceedings and was engaged on work for different clients. He left the firm to join a different firm who were acting for the defendant in the patent case.

The plaintiff sought an injunction to prevent the individual solicitor—but not his new firm—being involved in any part of the patent case on the grounds that he might be in possession of confidential information. The High Court in London did not grant the injunction and set out the test relating to solicitors who move firms. A solicitor will only be disqualified from acting in a contentious matter against his previous firm's clients if he or she has (or there is a real risk that he or she has) relevant confidential information; that is, information which was confidential at the time of communication and which remains both confidential and relevant. The onus of proof is on the solicitor. While the matter has not been tested in the courts in Scotland the test set down in England is a valid one.

Information barriers and informed consent

The question of information barriers (or Chinese Walls as they were called in the speeches) was considered at length by the House of Lords in the case of *Bolkiah (Prince Jefri) v KPMG* [1999] 2W.L.R. 215—also [1999] 1 ALL E.R. 517. Lord Hope of Craighead (at page 217) stated that the solicitor's duty to preserve confidentiality "extends well beyond that of refraining from deliberate disclosure" and encompasses a duty to ensure "that the former client is not put at risk that confidential information which the solicitor has obtained from that relationship may be used against him in any circumstances". If the Court is satisfied that there is no risk of disclosure, it will not intervene.

Lord Millett stated (at pages 226–227): "It is in any case difficult to discern any justification in principle for a rule which exposes a former client without his consent to any avoidable risk, however slight, that information which he has imparted in confidence in the course of a fiduciary relationship may come into the possession of a third party and be used to his disadvantage. Where in addition the information in question is not only confidential but also privileged, the case for the strict approach is unanswerable. Anything less fails to give effect to the policy on which legal professional privilege is based. It is of over-riding importance for the proper administration of justice that a client should be able to have complete confidence that what he tells his lawyer will remain secret. This is a matter of perception as well as substance. It is of the highest importance to the administration of justice that a solicitor or other person in possession of confidential and privileged information should not act in any way that might appear to put that information at risk of coming into the hands of someone with an adverse interest.... The Court should intervene unless it is satisfied that there is no risk of disclosure. It goes without saying that the risk must be a real one and not merely fanciful or theoretical, but it need not be substantial."

He also said that the Court should restrain the firm from acting for the second client unless satisfied on the basis of clear and convincing evidence that effective measures have been taken to ensure that no disclosure would occur. Although there is no rule of law that Chinese Walls or other arrangements of a similar kind are insufficient to eliminate the risk, the starting point must be that unless special measures are taken information moves within a firm. He approved of the terms of a consultation paper prepared by the Law Commission in England in 1992 which described Chinese Walls as normally involving some combination of the following:

1. The physical separation of the various departments in order to insulate them from each other—this often extends to such matters of detail as dining arrangements;

2. An education programme, normally recurring, to emphasise the importance of not improperly or inadvertently divulging confidential information;

3. Strict and carefully defined procedures for dealing with a situation where it is felt that the Walls should be crossed and the maintaining of proper records where this occurs;

4. Monitoring by compliance officers of the effectiveness of the Walls;

5. Disciplinary sanctions where there has been a breach of "the Wall".

In a subsequent case, also in England, the High Court held that where cases were being handled by two separate departments and all documentation was in hard copy only there was clear departmental and physical separation of the matters and that the information barrier was entrenched within the firm's organisation structure (*Current Law* March 2000 page 147 item 460). In another case the Court of Appeal held that where a solicitor had no recollection of ever representing a party and checks on records held at her firm revealed no potential conflict of interest or risk of injustice, the solicitor should not be prevented from acting for the other party (*Current Law* February 2000 page 73 item 226). In both these cases, *Prince Jefri* was followed.

Although *Prince Jefri* was an English case dealing with a firm of Chartered Accountants, there can be no doubt that the same approach would be taken to a firm of solicitors in Scotland. It follows therefore that if there is a risk of inadvertent disclosure of confidential information then that is an unacceptable risk. The only way in which it could be avoided with certainty is for the firm declining to act for clients in circumstances where the clients themselves may perceive there to be a risk of a breach of confidentiality.

3. Police enquiries and/or Production Orders/Search Warrants

The Professional Practice Department regularly receives calls from solicitors who have been asked to give a statement either to the police or the Procurator Fiscal. The authorities on confidentiality were reviewed in the reported case of *Micosta v Shetland Islands Council*, 1983 S.L.T. 483 where Lord President Emslie giving the opinion of the court, stated the general rule that communications passing between a party and his law agent are confidential. He then went on to say: "So far as we can discover from the authorities the only circumstances in which the general rule will be superseded are where fraud or some other illegal act is alleged against a party and where his law agent has been directly concerned in the carrying out of the very transaction which is the subject matter of enquiry". In the particular case the court refused a motion to open up a confidential envelope which had been recovered by specification in a civil action.

The principle was taken slightly further by Lord Macfadyen in the case of *Conoco v The Commercial Law Practice* in 1996. In that case the Commercial Law Practice had been consulted by a client who had asked them to write to Conoco without mentioning his name but advising them that he was aware of circumstances in which they had made substantial overpayments on a contract which he would be willing to provide further information about in return for a proportion of what was recovered.

Instead of responding positively to this invitation, Conoco brought a petition under the Administration of Justice Act to require the solicitors to disclose their client's name and address, which was granted. Lord Macfadyen stated: "The public policy consideration which underlies the fraud exception may be capable of extension to a situation in which a party and his solicitor, not themselves either guilty of fraud or involved in carrying out a fraudulent transaction, are involved in a transaction the purpose of which is to derive for the client benefit from his knowledge of a fraud committed by another party."

If you are presented with a Production Order by the police you should pay close attention to what is called for in such an order and only deliver that. If asked to give a statement simply confirming that this is the file/these are the papers called for in the Order you should do so.

If you are asked to give a statement to the Police or the Procurator Fiscal in relation to a matter where the information sought is not already in the public domain (for instance having been disclosed in open court, or published in a public register) but is actually confidential, the Professional Practice Committee's view is that you should offer to be precognosced on oath before the sheriff. If you answer a question on the direction of the court you would not be subject to a complaint of breach of confidentiality, as thematter is fundamentally one of law not of practice. In 1999 The High Court of Justiciary refused a Bill of Suspension in the case of *Kelly* and Sarwar where the solicitor appealed against a citation to give a precognition on oath.

You should not hand over your file or papers to the Police or the Fiscal unless they have obtained a warrant or a Production Order. If the authorities complain about the difficulty in obtaining an order, then a fortiori you should not hand over your papers voluntarily.

If you are cited to give evidence at a trial you must appear but again should follow the judge's directions. If you are required to answer a question you should do so. Whether the evidence is admissible is a matter for the court to determine and might form grounds of appeal.

4. Statement to other solicitors

You may be asked to give a statement to other solicitors. If they are now instructed by your former client you can treat the request as a waiver of confidentiality by the client and give a statement. You can also hand over copies of documents, but should seek a written mandate from the former client before handing over original documents.

If the request comes from a solicitor acting for your former client's opponent in a civil matter you should decline the request—even if the allegation is that you did not give proper advice to your former client—unless and until you either have the former client's authority to do so, preferably in writing, or have been ordered by the court to do so, e.g. having been cited to give evidence and required by the judge to answer the question. If you are a Crown witness in a criminal case and are asked to give a statement to the solicitor acting for a party other than your former client you can confirm what you have told the police or the Procurator Fiscal but cannot do more than that without your client's authority.

5. Crime about to be committed

You may receive information from your client about a crime which he is threatening to commit. In those circumstances the client is not entitled to the privilege of confidentiality and as stated in the rule you would be quite entitled, and some would say obliged, to draw the circumstances to the attention of the authorities. For example, if Thomas Hamilton—who had consulted a number of different solicitors about different matters—had advised any of them of his intentions at Dunblane primary school, those solicitors would have been duty bound to alert the authorities so as to prevent the tragic events from happening.

6. Insolvent client

You may find yourself asked to produce information to a trustee in sequestration, receiver, administrator or a liquidator. If you acted for the bankrupt or the company which has gone into administration or liquidation, the trustee, administrator or liquidator steps into the client's shoes and is entitled to all the papers which you hold for the client— although in a sequestration only so far as relating to the bankrupt's financial affairs. You do not need to take your client's instructions on whether such information should be given.

You should however be careful to separate out papers in relation to individual directors or shareholders where you were acting for a company and only deliver those papers in relation to your acting for the company— unless of course the same person has been appointed trustee to the individual directors or shareholders.

7. Statutory requirements

Some statutes, most notably the Proceeds of Crime Act 2002, require solicitors and others to breach confidentiality. If such a statutory obligation exists or the person seeking the information has statutory authority for the request, you should comply with it.

8. Civil court matters

Finally, if you are cited as a witness in a civil case you must attend court and can answer questions posed by the agent or advocate acting for your client or former client. However, if you feel that the answer to a question from the person acting for any other party would breach client confidentiality you should seek directions from the judge and follow those. If you are served with a Specification of Documents or similar order you should comply with it but should put the documents in a "confidential" envelope if the court order was not granted on your own client's motion. You should be given an opportunity to be heard on whether the confidential envelope should be opened up, in which case you can refer the court to the *Micosta* case (see para.3 above).

Guidance related to Rule B1.6: Confidentiality: Notifications to ICO

The Society continues to receive enquiries, especially from criminal practitioners, about whether they should have notified the Information Commissioner's Office ("ICO") under the Data Protection Act.

All solicitors should notify the ICO and risk a substantial fine if they do not. In particular, taking up the new Crown Office disclosure procedures— by electronic means called Pendrive—means it is essential for a solicitor's practice to notify.

The ICO is targeting unregistered solicitors' and accountants' firms on a regional basis and has contacted legal firms across Scotland. The ICO has previously stated that as many as one third of solicitors' firms may still be unregistered. Letters have been sent to advise firms that they are not registered. If there is no response within three weeks, a second letter warns that failure to reply within a further 14 days will result in details being passed on to the investigations team.

This obligation extends to any outsourced providers of your services.

Guidance related to Rule B1.6: Comments to the Media by Solicitors

The law and the legal profession are of significant interest to the media and their readers, listeners and viewers. Solicitors can work effectively with journalists in responding to their inquiries, as well as act as legal commentators and assist in conveying accurate information to the public.

When presenting information to the media in relation to your clients' affairs you are acting in a professional capacity. You should conduct yourself in your public appearances and public statements in the same manner as you would with your fellow practitioners and with the courts.

In making a public statement concerning a client's affairs, you must (1) have your client's authority to do so; (2) be satisfied that any communication is in the client's best interests; (3) ensure it is based upon an accurate appreciation of the facts and is not misleading; and (4) in relation to a case which has been decided in court, make clear that the views expressed are those of the client and not your views. You should not permit your personal interests or those of other causes to conflict with the client's interests.

Guidance related to Rule B1.6: Company Audit Enquiries

Solicitors acting for companies should maintain records of incidents of non-compliance by the company of laws and regulations which have been reported to them or discovered by then in the course of acting for the company.

If in the course of conducting an audit, the auditors request details of any actual or potential non-compliance with the laws and regulations which are central to the conduct of the company's business of which the practice unit is aware, care should be taken in responding. First, solicitors should not respond to such enquiries without the client company's express agreement. Secondly, some requests for information may go beyond those to which it is appropriate for the company's legal adviser to reply. Information which has traditionally been requested of solicitors as legal advisers to companies has included information as to titles, outstanding fees and any consultation with the solicitor with regard to litigation involving the company. It is appropriate to respond to these types of question. It must be stressed, however, that requests for information falling outwith these areas such as whether the solicitor is aware of any matter where the company may have failed to comply with the law or regulatory standards, or whether the solicitor is aware of any contingent liability other than litigation matters which he or she has been consulted on, should always be referred to the company's directors and no response should be made other than on the specific instructions of directors. Failure to do so could potentially open a company's legal adviser to risk.

Provision of an auditor's letter or certificate is an important step in the audit process which has to be handled with care, takes time and carries significant risk for the solicitor giving it. For all these reasons, he or she is entitled to make an appropriate charge.

Guidance related to Rule B1.8: Disclosure of interest—outsourcing

This obligation extends to any outsourced providers of your business operations and services and as a result, you should ensure that systems are in place to identify and respond to any so identified!

Guidance related to Rule B1.9: Dispute Resolution

Solicitors should have a sufficient understanding of commonly available alternative dispute resolution options to allow proper consideration and communication of options to a client in considering the client's interests and objectives.

A solicitor providing advice on dispute resolution procedures should be able to discuss and explain available options, including the advantages and disadvantages of each, to a client in such a way as to enable the client to make an informed decision as to the course of action and procedure he or she should pursue to best meet their needs and objectives, and to instruct the solicitor accordingly.

A solicitor providing advice on dispute resolution procedures is also expected to be able to identify where alternative methods of dispute resolution may not be in the best interests of the client. For example, this may be a particular consideration for mediation or arbitration in the context of family disputes or other situations where one party may be at risk of violence or intimidation by the other.

Guidance related to Rule B1.10: Competence, Diligence and Appropriate Skills

Change in specialism by means of a conversion course

The Society is keen to make the professional support it offers to members, through the challenges of the recession, as relevant as possible.

For those seeking re-employment or making career choices, encouragement has been given to consider continuing with a current specialism or changing focus to another area of the law.

The Professional Practice Committee has noted that various training providers, in responding to the current practice and employment market, are advertising courses to appeal to those wishing to change specialism. The Committee has concerns about the promotion of a change in specialism by means of a short conversion course, particularly in the context of issues arising out of diversification that are beginning to filter through to the Complaints and Guarantee Fund Committees.

Whilst the Professional Practice Committee wants to encourage members, who are considering how best they can diversify, it wishes to remind all solicitors that you must only act in those matters where they are competent to do so and must exercise the level of skill appropriate to the matter; all as provided in rule B1.10.

Guidance related to Rule B1.14: Defenders Contacting Pursuers' Agents Direct

It has come to the attention of the Professional Practice Committee that there is an increasing tendency for defenders to telephone pursuers' agents direct to discuss active cases.

To date the problem has arisen mainly in relation to repossession litigation situations, but also where defenders' telephone firms which are either acting for inhibiting creditors or in relation to mortgage to rent cases.

The essential problem in many of the cases is that the defenders are already represented by solicitors and this is known to the pursuers' agents. Indeed in some of the cases the defenders' solicitors have actually (according to the defenders) encouraged the defender clients to telephone the pursuers' solicitors.

It is clearly unprofessional for a defender's solicitor to encourage his client to telephone the solicitor on the other side, as this puts undue pressure on the pursuer's solicitor to act in a manner contrary to his duty under rule B1.14 which sets out the very limited circumstances where a solicitor may communicate with a person known or believed to be the client of another solicitor.

Guidance related to Rule B1.14: Settlements—Holding Items as Undelivered

The Professional Practice Committee and the Council confirm that where money or deeds are sent to be held as undelivered pending purification of a condition, they should be so held if the condition is not purified. Settlement will not take place until they can be treated as delivered.

For more guidance on this matter in a conveyancing context, refer to Cheques to be Held as Undelivered but note that the core principle, as set out above, is of general application and is not restricted to conveyancing transactions.

Guidance related to B1.15: Diversity—outsourcing

This obligation extends to any outsourced providers of your business operations and services and as a result, you should ensure that systems are in place to ensure that such providers comply with all requirements in relation to this Rule.

Guidance Related to Rule B2.1: Conflict of Interest Generally

Conflict of interest generally

It is a well established principle that solicitors should not act for clients where there is a conflict of interest between them. This is codified in rule B2.1.2 which states that: "You shall not act for two or more parties whose interests conflict." That statement is entirely unqualified and is the guiding principle which governs the rest of rule B2.1. Conflict of interest is amplified in rule B1.7 which states that:

> "1.7.1   You must not act for two or more clients in matters where there is a conflict of interest between the clients or for any client where there is a conflict between the interest of the client and your interest or that of your practice unit.
>
> 1.7.2   Even where there is only a potential conflict of interest you must exercise caution. Where the potential for conflict is significant, you must not act for both parties without the full knowledge and express consent of the clients."

The rules do not contain a definition of conflict of interest. It has been said that it is hard to define but you know it when you see it. Unfortunately some only seem to see it long after it has appeared and when it is too late. There are three elements that need to be considered. First, if you would give different advice to different clients about the same matter there is a conflict of interest between them. It does not matter that the clients may be agreed about what they wish to do. Second, if your actings on behalf of one client would have an adverse impact on a matter you are dealing with for another client, there is a conflict, even if on the face of it the matters are unrelated. Third, if you are unable to disclose relevant information to one client because of a duty of confidentiality to another client there is a conflict of interest. This also means that if you cannot act for one of them you cannot breach confidentiality in telling them about that.

Conflict of interest is not a matter for the judgment of the client—it is a matter for your judgment. Only you have the breadth of experience, training and knowledge to fully advise a client where his interest lies. Jane Ryder in her book *Professional Conduct for Scottish Solicitors* states: "Where facts are disclosed to a solicitor on behalf of one client which may be prejudicial if disclosed to another client without the authority of the first, there is almost certainly a conflict of interest…the critical test is whether the solicitor can adequately discharge all duties to his or her respective clients equally?" (pages 61 and 62).

The Discipline Tribunal have expressed concern in their Annual Reports about continuing failure to recognise a conflict of interest and follow the appropriate rules.

This obligation extends to all outsourced providers of your services. Specifically they should be required to have systems in place to ensure that they comply with Rule 1.7.1 and 1.7.2.

Rule B1.7 is based on the CCBE Code of Conduct for European Lawyers. The latter states (at 3.2) that: "A lawyer may not advise, represent or act on behalf of two or more clients in the same matter if there is a conflict, or a significant risk of a conflict, between the interests of those clients. A lawyer must cease to act for both or all of the clients concerned when a conflict of interest arises between those clients and also whenever there is a risk of a breach of confidence or where the lawyer's independence may be impaired. A lawyer must also refrain from acting for a new client if there is a risk of breach of a confidence entrusted to the lawyer by a former client or if the knowledge which the lawyer possesses of the affairs of the former client would give an undue advantage to the new client".

Many foreign jurisdictions prohibit lawyers acting for two parties to a matter even where there is only a potential conflict of interest, unless the clients consent to it. Such consent has to be informed consent which means explaining to the clients the implications of the common representation and the advantages and risks involved. Rule B1.7 deals with this in Scotland. Caution must be exercised and where the potential conflict is significant, informed consent of all clients affected must be obtained. The question of informed consent is considered in some detail in some American states. For example, in Massachusetts they take the view that, "when a disinterested lawyer would conclude that the client should not agree to the representation under the circumstances, the lawyer involved cannot properly ask for such agreement or provide representation on the basis of the client's consent. When more than one client is involved, the question of conflict must be resolved as to each client. Moreover there may be circumstances where it is impossible to make the disclosure necessary to obtain consent". These considerations are equally relevant to Scotland.

This brings us to the conflict between confidentiality and disclosure.

These two fundamental principles underpin the practice of a solicitor. The privilege of confidentiality is recognised by the courts as being essential to provide a basis of trust between solicitor and client to ensure that the advice given by a solicitor to a client is based on a full disclosure of the facts. Apart from exceptional circumstances clients can expect that what they disclose to their solicitor will not be passed on to anyone without their knowledge and consent. At the same time solicitors are charged with the equally important duty to clients to act in their best interest, which requires solicitors to disclose to their client all and any relevant information within the solicitor's knowledge to enable the client to make an informed decision on the matter in hand.

The nature of these two duties is such that, apart from exceptional circumstances such as the future commission of a crime, neither can take precedence over the other. It follows therefore that if a solicitor has information which would be relevant to a client but which he requires to keep confidential in the interests of another client, there is a conflict of interest between those clients. That applies to all solicitors within the practice unit unless there are formal Chinese Walls as described in the reported case *Bolkiah v KPMG* [1999] 2 W.L.R. 215—see also Guidance on Confidentiality.

Turning now to some specific situations in which actual or potential conflict of interest arises:

Conflict of interest in civil court matters

1. Matrimonial

It is trite to say that you should not sue your own client, but the question of conflict in court matters goes further than that. In matrimonial cases (including civil partnership and co-habiting couples) the same firm of solicitors should not act for both parties in negotiating a separation agreement—or even in preparing a document that reflects the parties' own agreement. The parties have separate interests and the same practice unit should not act for both of them. If one of them refuses to get separate independent advice, they cannot be forced to do so but you should ensure that you only act for one.

You would be entitled to deal with the other as an unrepresented party—in which case you must (in terms of rule B2.1.7), advise the unrepresented party in writing when sending a document for signature that such signature would have legal consequences and they should seek independent legal advice before signing. It is also prudent to say in terms that you are not acting for or advising that party on the matter. You should not spell out what the consequences might be as that would be giving advice. If the unrepresented party does not obtain separate advice and signs and returns the document to you, you would be entitled to treat it as delivered on behalf of your client and to deal with it accordingly (*Inglis v Inglis* 1999 S.L.T. 59).

In 1998 the Discipline Tribunal found a solicitor guilty of professional misconduct for failing to comply with the then equivalent of rule B2.1.7 and said that whatever pressures might be put upon the solicitor "where professional obligations arise it is not sufficient for a solicitor merely to follow the instructions of his client".

In many separations the jointly owned home will require to be sold. The Professional Practice Committee first issued a Guideline about this in 1994. The current version states that unless the parties have agreed in writing how the sale proceeds will be distributed (either as part of a wider agreement or as a separate standalone agreement) neither of the solicitors firms acting for the individuals should act in the sale. A separate firm should be instructed. In a reported case (*Dawson v. R. Gordon Marshall & Co.* , 1996 G.W.D. 1243) Lord Osborne held that by not accounting to the husband for his share of the proceeds in accordance with the title, the solicitors had acted improperly. In that case the solicitors in fact had retained the balance of the proceeds and were in a position to implement the court's decree but they also required to meet the expenses of a defended proof in the Court of Session.

If the parties have reached written agreement dealing with the free proceeds, and that means an agreement signed by the parties themselves, the solicitor acting for one of the parties in the matrimonial affairs may act in the sale but must account to both parties in accordance with the signed agreement. He cannot accept unilateral instructions from one of them to alter that. That would be a conflict situation requiring him to immediately withdraw from acting. The mirror image is that if you are consulted by a couple in connection with the sale of their jointly owned property and at that time or subsequently you discover that they are either separated or in the process of splitting up you would be entitled to accept the instructions to act in the sale, but you would require to advise each of them to seek separate independent advice in relation to their personal position. Unless and until a written agreement dealing with the free proceeds is intimated to you at the time or before the sale settles you require to account to the parties in accordance with the title. You cannot under any circumstances accept unilateral instructions to do otherwise. If both parties wish some other division, that needs to be confirmed by both in writing. It is not something which the practice unit acting in the sale can give any advice about.

If the property is not in joint names there is a clear conflict of interest between each of the couple and you could not act for both of them at any stage.

2. Other civil court cases

The real questions are whether there is an actual conflict of interest—or a significant potential conflict—and whether you have confidential information which would be of benefit to the other party. You also need to have regard to other people in the practice unit who may be dealing with a different matter. As an example, a question arose some years ago in a large city firm where the Court department acting in an action for payment lodged an inhibition against the defender company, but the Conveyancing department were acting for that company in a totally unrelated transaction. It is important to have a system which will disclose any matter in which the firm are acting—or have acted—for the party with whom your client is in dispute.

3. Criminal matters—Acting for co-accused

The Code of Conduct for Criminal Work (which continues to be unaffected by rule B1) states in art.2: "A solicitor should not accept instructions from more than one accused in the same matter." There is always a potential for conflict between co-accused. For example, if one pleads guilty he becomes a compellable witness against the other. Witnesses do not always come up to precognition. A solicitor who accepts instructions and subsequently has to abandon one of the clients is placed in a compromised position not only by virtue of having potentially breached the practice rules but also by virtue of being likely to possess confidential information relating to the client for whom he has had to cease acting. Unlike the rules the Code is a statement of best practice and there may be particular circumstances where you can act for co-accused but you need to consider the specific facts and exercise your professional judgment and also obtain the clients' informed consent. Rule C4.4 prohibits solicitor advocates from acting for more than one accused person "save in the most exceptional circumstances".

Conflict of interest in conveyancing

Conflict in conveyancing transactions is dealt with in rules B2.1.4 to 2.1.6. Rule B2.1.4 is without prejudice to the generality of rule B2.1.2 (see above) and has the effect—reading short—that the same individual solicitor or practice unit shall not at any stage (see below) act for both seller and purchaser, landlord and tenant, or assignor and assignee in a lease of heritable property for value, provided that where no dispute arises or might reasonably be expected to arise, and the seller of residential property is not a builder or developer, the rule shall not apply in certain particular situations. It is worth bearing in mind that when something goes wrong and a complaint is made to the Society or a claim is made under the Master Policy, the circumstances will be looked at with the benefit of hindsight. With hindsight it is clear that the disputes that regularly arise in conveyancing transactions are all disputes which could reasonably have been foreseen, such as difficulties with the title; unauthorised alterations; or problems with the purchaser's funding. If a dispute does arise in the middle of a transaction where the same individual or practice unit is acting for both sides, the party acting must take immediate steps to cease acting for at least one of the parties and advise them that they should consult an independent solicitor. It is almost always a mistake to attempt to resolve matters and you are generally digging a deeper hole for yourself if you try to do so. It must always be remembered that the rules are there not only for the protection of clients but also for your protection.

The exceptions to the general prohibition in rule B2.1.4 are—again reading short—(a) associated companies or public bodies; (b) connected parties; (c) parties related by blood, adoption marriage or civil partnership; (d) established clients; and (e) where there is no other solicitor in the vicinity whom the client could reasonably be expected to consult.

Categories (a) and (b) of the exemptions do not cause any difficulties but "associated companies" means companies in the same group structure, not merely ones which have some or all of the directors and/or shareholders in common. Category (c), parties related by blood etc., is not restricted to any particular degree of relationship but it is unwise to stray beyond the forbidden degrees of marriage/civil partnership.

The most commonly used exemption is the established client—category (d). An established client is defined as "a person for whom you have or your practice unit has acted on at least one previous occasion". The Professional Practice Committee is of the view that this does not mean that you require to have ceased acting in the previous matter—it can be a continuing matter. It must however be a matter in respect of which you have opened a file with something that the client could be charged for even if he has not in fact been charged for it or may never be charged for it.

Category (e)—no other solicitor in the vicinity—has been interpreted by the Committee as restricted to isolated rural and island communities. It is not applicable anywhere in central Scotland. The matter was raised in connection with a small Highland town which had one full-time and one part-time solicitors' practice. The Committee decided that this exemption was not available even in that situation, where the nearest other town with a firm of solicitors was nine miles away.

In every case where you are acting for both parties by virtue of categories (c), (d) or (e) of rule B2.1.4, rule B2.1.4 requires that both parties be advised by you at the earliest practicable opportunity that you have been requested to act for them and that if a dispute arises they or one of them will require to consult an independent solicitor. You must confirm this advice in writing "as soon as may be practicable thereafter". This does not mean when the offer has been submitted or is about to be submitted. It means when you are first instructed by the purchaser in respect of a property you are selling or in which you know you are to be instructed by the seller if the sale is being dealt with by an external estate agent. Advising both clients that you are acting for both is clearly necessary to obtain informed consent.

These letters, formerly known as Rule 5(2) letters, are mandatory and even if you are entitled to act and there is no conflict of interest, failure to send out such a letter is a breach of the rule. Although you may think that that will not matter if there is no actual difficulty, when the Society's Financial Compliance Inspectors carry out a routine inspection of your practice unit they will ask for files where the firm has acted for both buyer and seller and report back to the Society where no such letters appear in the file. That may lead by itself to a complaint of professional misconduct. Indeed in its Annual Report for 1998 the Discipline Tribunal highlighted a case where they found a solicitor guilty of misconduct for not complying with this rule. The Tribunal said: "It does not mitigate the gravity of any breach that none of the clients involved had been prejudiced or were dissatisfied with the solicitor's conduct of the transaction".

"At any stage"

As mentioned above, rule B2.1.4 prohibits you from acting "at any stage". This is interpreted strictly. For example:

(1)   Acting as an estate agent only is acting at a stage for the seller even if all offers are to be submitted to a different firm of solicitors. You would not be entitled to act or give any advice to a prospective purchaser who does not fall within one of the exemptions, but note later comments on the potential availability of waivers in certain circumstances.

(2)   Giving advice about a mortgage or finance for a property is acting at a stage. Again you would only be able to give such advice to a prospective purchaser who is an established client or in respect of whom one of the other exemptions is available. This means you have to be careful about what you say in your property particulars if you are selling the property. If you market your mortgage advice service in your property particulars you must include a notice that you may not be able to act for the recipient.

Builders and developers

Of course you cannot give any advice to a purchaser at all if you are acting for a seller of residential property who is a builder or developer. Firstly, a Housing Association is a developer. Secondly, a person who is by trade a builder or developer selling in the course of his business houses or plots which are part of a larger development is clearly a developer, but such a person selling a site or house as a single unit and not part of a larger development has also been treated by the Discipline Tribunal as a developer. For example a builder selling a house which has been bought as a trade-in would still be a builder for the purposes of rule B2.1.4.

Thirdly, a person who is not by trade a builder or developer but is selling individual plots or houses which are part of a larger development has the temporary status of a developer (e.g. a farmer selling residential plots in a field).

However a person who is not by trade a builder or developer but is selling a single plot or site is not regarded as a developer. A solicitor acting for such a seller who is consulted by the purchaser would be entitled to act for the purchaser if he falls within one of the exemptions to the rule. That is again always provided there is no actual conflict of interest between the parties and no dispute is reasonably likely to arise—which will remain a matter for the judgment of the solicitor—and provided informed consent is obtained. In such transactions there could well be conflicting interests e.g. rights of access; other servitudes; maintenance of private roadway; etc. The safest way to avoid such difficulties is to decline to accept instructions in the first place.

Conflict of interest in relation to loans

1.   General

Rule B2.1.4 also deals with acting for lender and borrower. In terms of rule B2.1.4 (f) the terms of the loan must have been agreed between the parties before you are instructed by the lender and the granting of the security must only be to give effect to such agreement. You must always remember that the lender is also a client. The lender/borrower rule is still subject to the question of an actual conflict of interest or a dispute which may reasonably be likely to arise. Difficulties have arisen in a number of cases which have been reported—mainly in relation to commercial securities, but the lessons are also relevant to domestic security transactions. There are some extremely valuable articles by Professor Robert Rennie in the Journal of

April 1994 (the lenders need to know); February 1995 (the expanding duty of care) and October 1995 (certificates of title). There was also a useful item in the *Caveat* column in the Journal of February 1995 at page 71.

2. Commercial securities

In relation to commercial securities there is a specific Practice Guideline advising that banks would normally instruct their own solicitors except in what they regarded as de minimis cases (now below £250,000). The Guideline gives a number of examples where there is a greater scope for conflict of interest in commercial transactions.

3. Home secured for business loan

Another area of difficulty in relation to loans is where the jointly owned home is to be put up as security for a business loan to only one of the owners. There is a clear conflict of interest between the owners and you should not act for both of them. Not only must you make it clear that you are not acting for the owner who is not getting the benefit of the loan, when sending the standard security for signature by that person you must accompany it with a letter in terms of rule B2.1.7 as stated earlier (see Matrimonial). In the case of *Smith v the Bank of Scotland* (1997 S.L.T. 1061) the House of Lords decided that the lender has a duty to advise such a joint owner to seek independent advice. This will only focus attention back on the solicitor acting for the lender. In *Forsyth v Royal Bank of Scotland* (2000 S.L.T. 1295) Lord Macfadyen decided that the lenders had a valid security where the same solicitors acted for lender, borrower and guarantor. While this is all very well for the lender, it leaves the solicitor open to a claim and/ or complaint from the guarantor.

The matter was further considered by the English Courts in *Royal Bank of Scotland v Etridge* [2001] UKHL 44 and *Zwebner v Mortgage Corporation Ltd* [1998] P.N.L.R. 769 in relation to the duties owed to a spouse who is asked to put up her share of the matrimonial home as security. (See Article by Alistair Sim in Journal of March 1999 at page 40, also on *www.lawscot.org.uk*).

4. House purchase funded by relative

A further specific area in relation to loans to be wary of is the house purchase (e.g. by an entitled tenant) which is being funded by other members of the family. There are clearly different interests to be protected in these situations. The entitled tenant is entitled to the discount as a statutory right. He or she may also be entitled to security of tenure. The person putting up the money is entitled to have that investment protected or at least to get advice about that. Should this be by Standard Security? What about interest and terms of repayment? It is essential to recognise that these interests may not have been addressed by the parties themselves, and you need to make sure that these matters are fully understood by the parties and that there is no dispute between them about what is to happen before you can act.

5. Ranking Agreements

There is a conflict of interest between lenders in relation to a Ranking Agreement and you should not act for more than one lender even in de minimis cases.

Consideration should also be given to whether there is a conflict of interest between lender and borrower in relation to a Ranking Agreement. Whether there is will depend on the particular circumstances of each case, and if you are instructed to act for both the borrower and one of the lenders you should exercise your own professional judgment about that. As stated in rule B1.7.2, informed consent of the clients must be obtained if there is a significant potential for conflict of interest.

6. Your own security

Finally, in relation to loans—and not strictly speaking conflict of interest—the Society gets a considerable number of enquiries from solicitors about their own purchase and sale. The matter is governed by rule B6.21 (Accounts etc rules). That rule means that the practice unit cannot act for the lender in the creation, variation or discharge of a Standard Security where the borrower is a manager, the spouse of a manager, or a company or a partnership in which either of them have an interest. The definition of loan is wide enough to include a guarantee or a loan to children, parents or others. In relation to discharges there is an exception where the borrower's obligations under the Standard Security have been fully implemented before a discharge is obtained from the lender. That means where the loan has been repaid in the natural course or out of funds not deriving from the sale of the property. For further guidance see Guidance related to Rule B6 (the Accounts Rules).

Conflict of interest in relation to commercial matters

In a small jurisdiction like Scotland where there is a relatively small number of firms dealing with major commercial clients it is not uncommon for a practice unit to be instructed by two or more different clients seeking to bid for the same project. There is clearly a significant potential conflict of interest between such clients and an obligation to keep matters confidential which may give rise to tension with the duty of disclosure. This has not been the subject of previous specific guidance from the Society but now comes within rule B1.7.2. If clients give informed consent to information barriers—or Chinese Walls as they were described in the *Bolkiah* case—and those barriers are properly put in place, the firm may act for different clients competing with each other for the same project if bids are to be submitted at a closing date. However, if one client wishes to make a pre-emptive bid that would be an actual conflict of interest. The Society accept that clients in business, particularly substantial clients, are better able to give informed consent in such circumstances than ordinary members of the public. (See also separate Guidance on Confidentiality where the *Bolkiah* case is considered in more detail).

Waivers

The Council have the power to grant a waiver and the Society's Professional Practice department receives several waiver requests every week. Waivers are quite regularly granted in respect of rule B2.1.4 but not for rules B2.1.2, B2.1.5, or B2.1.7. For more information on the circumstances where waivers are granted see Journal of September 2002 Pg 47. It should be noted that rule B1 may not be waived and that rule must be complied with at all times.

As detailed above the Professional Practice Committee has always been of the view that acting for the seller as an estate agent only is acting "at any stage", even if all offers are to be submitted to a different firm of solicitors. However, where solicitors are only providing estate agency services to a builder/developer in respect of properties being sold at a fixed price with a standard missive which will be submitted to and negotiated with a different firm of solicitors, it may be appropriate for a waiver to be granted to allow the firm which supplied those estate agency services to act for an established client who wishes to purchase one of the properties, provided that the solicitors seeking the waiver have satisfied themselves that there is no actual conflict of interest between the parties and no advice on the value or price will be sought by the developer from the solicitor acting as estate agent. Requests for such waivers should be submitted to the Society's Professional Practice department. It is stressed that this does not constitute any change to Rule B2.1.

Getting it wrong

As stated above, if it goes wrong it will all be looked at with the benefit of hindsight. A breach of the conflict of interest rules will lead to a double deductible (double excess) as well as a potential finding of professional misconduct.

Although in many situations the clients will want it all done as cheaply as possible, that is their problem.

The golden rule in this, as in all other professional practice matters, is never to convert your client's problem into your own professional problem. If you are faced with a finding of professional misconduct and/or an expensive insurance claim, it could be the most costly fee you have ever earned.

Guidance related to Rule B2.1: Conflict of Interest in Commercial Securities

The Society believes that a definition of a commercial security transaction is helpful:

> "A commercial security transaction relates to the secured lending to a customer of a bank or other lending institution where the purpose of the loan is clearly for the customer's business purposes."

Scottish banks have policies whereby in commercial security transactions the banks instruct separate practice units to represent them. Borrowers instruct their own solicitors. The banks' solicitors will usually recover their fees and outlays from the borrowers. Other banks operating in Scotland and members of the British Bankers Association adopt similar policies.

Notwithstanding this general policy, Scottish banks wish to reserve the right to instruct the borrowers' solicitors to act for them, in what the banks describe as de minimis cases. Each bank may adopt a different policy on what constitutes a de minimis case. De minimis cases are currently commonly understood (from the lenders' viewpoint) to include loans not exceeding £250,000.

Regardless of the banks' views or internal policies regarding what is or is not "de minimis", solicitors must consider each case on its own merits having regard to the particular facts and circumstances.

We remind you that, should you receive instructions to act for a lender and a borrower in any transaction, including a commercial security transaction, you must exercise your judgment having regard to the provisions of rule B2.1 as to whether you can act properly for both parties. In exercising that judgment you should take account of the whole facts and circumstances. There follow a number of examples of conflicts of interest which can arise. The list is not exhaustive but may assist you in exercising your professional judgment.

Remember that, should you decide to act for both lender and borrower (even in what purports to be a de minimis case) and a claim arises, you may have exposed yourself and your firm to the risk of bearing a double excess/deductible and the possibility of a loading on your firm's Master Policy premium.

Please do not hesitate to contact the Professional Practice Team if you require further advice or guidance.

Examples of conflicts of interest in commercial security transactions

The following illustrate some of the instances where lenders and borrowers have separate interests in commercial security transactions:

1. **Disclosure of all relevant circumstances** Either:

      (i)   the solicitor may know more of the borrower's position than has been communicated to the lender or vice versa; or (ii) there may have been a reluctance by the borrower or lender fully to disclose their respective positions because of dual representation.

          These circumstances may affect the extent to which impartial "best advice" can be given.

2.   **Ongoing negotiations** Negotiations between the borrower and lender may have only reached the "Outline Terms" stage. Further detailed consideration or negotiation of covenants, undertakings or events of default may be required. In such negotiations the borrower and lender may have different negotiating strengths and so there may be competing pressures on the solicitor as to whose interests are to be promoted.

3.   **Defects in title/due diligence package** A borrower may be prepared to "live with" a minor defect in title or some lack of planning or building consent whereas a lender may take an entirely different stance.

4.   **Security by companies** Apart from the complexities and time restraints affecting registration of security granted by companies, companies may well be subject to negative or restrictive covenants or powers affecting the security on which the borrower, but not necessarily the lender, may be prepared to take a commercial view. In these circumstances separate advice may be required.

5.   **Competing creditors' ranking agreements** The circumstances as to the inter-relationship/enforcement of security between lenders may merit separate advice. A solicitor may be involved in preparing a ranking agreement and negotiating its terms on points which have a bearing on the borrower's position.

6.   **Security over commercial property** The permitted use, associated licences/quotas and specific standard conditions may merit separate advice. Particular risks arise on the transfer of a licence where the lender's interests may conflict with the borrower's commercial ambitions.

7.   **Leased property as security** The circumstances in which a lender requires protection in the event of irritancy may merit separate advice. Invariably the borrower is trying to strike the best deal while for his occupancy while the lender needs protection in the event of the borrower's failure through insolvency or otherwise.

8.   **Enforcement of security** The solicitor acting for both borrower and lender may be placed in difficulty in the event of subsequent enforcement of a security. For whom does the solicitor act in such circumstances? Do both clients know and understand their respective positions?

9.   **Powerful clients** A major business client may bring subtle or even open pressures to bear on a solicitor to follow a particular course or to turn a blind eye to a matter which could prejudice a lender's position, for example, discrepancies between a valuation and the purchase price.

10.   **"All sums due" securities** Solicitors should advise fully joint obligants (for example, husbands and wives) of the nature of an "all sums due" security. In particular it should be drawn to their attention that additional loans, for example in respect of one obligant's business, may give rise to further secured borrowings without the other obligant requiring to sign the documentation. In such circumstances there is also a conflict of interest between the joint obligants.

Guidance related to Rule B2.1: Mandates in Executries

Where there is a combination of solicitor and non-solicitor executors, a solicitor executor should not use his power as executor to secure the continuity of his acting as solicitor in the winding up of the estate. In such circumstances the solicitor may either cease acting or resign as executor.

If the solicitor ceases to act but remains as executor, he should bow to the wishes of the other executors on which practice unit should take over the administration of the estate. Failure to do so gives rise to a conflict between the interests of the executors and the interests of the practice unit.

If the solicitor decides to resign, he should obtain a receipt and comply with any mandate if the remaining executors resolve that another practice unit should act.

Guidance related to Rule B2.1: Acting as Director of Client Company

From time to time the Society is asked to provide guidance to solicitors who have been asked to act as a director of a company which is also a client of the practice unit (and also where a company of which the solicitor is a director becomes a client of the practice unit). This is a complex subject and it is impossible to provide more than an indication of the main points which a solicitor in this position should bear in mind. Many practice units have their own policies on this, and this guidance is not intended to displace them in any respect. The Society would appreciate any comments with a view to improving this guidance.

There is no prohibition on a solicitor acting as a director of a client company, but there are a number of issues of which a solicitor should be aware if asked to act in this capacity. A directorship should not be accepted or retained if any of these give rise to difficulty.

Know the law

The law relating to the duties and responsibilities of a company director, and the inherent risks of that office, is complex. A solicitor asked to act as a director of any company (not just a client) should only accept office if he or she is fully aware of the relevant law. A director also has to keep abreast of changes in company law which occur very frequently.

Conflict of interest

A director is obliged by statute to disclose to the directors of the company any arrangement or transaction between the company and the director or any firm of which he is a member (Sections 182 to 187 of the Companies Act 2006). This applies, in particular, to the provision of legal services to the company.

The Articles of the company may impose additional conditions beyond those required by statute.

A solicitor acting as a director of a client company must be aware that there is an inherent conflict of interest between the solicitor and his or her practice unit with respect to fees for legal services and related matters. The solicitor should ensure that any decision on these matters is taken by the directors other than himself or herself.

As a director, a solicitor's primary duty is to the company in which he holds that office. This may give rise to particular difficulties (1) if the company is a wholly owned subsidiary and there is conflict between the interests of the subsidiary and the parent company and (2) where a solicitor director has confidential information about another client which is relevant to the interests of the company.

Point (2) is a particular instance of the circumstances considered by the House of Lords in *Hilton v. Barker Booth* [2005] 1 All ER 657 in which a solicitor was found liable in damages to a client from whom information was withheld on the grounds of a duty of confidentiality to another client.

Privileged communications

Another issue which needs careful thought is the matter of legal professional privilege, particularly in relation to EU competition issues. The European Court of Justice has recently reaffirmed (in *Akzo Nobel Chemicals Ltd v The Commission*) that in an EU context legal privilege only applies to the extent that the lawyer is independent—i.e. not bound to his client by a relationship of employment. The Commission accepted in its submission that it is possible for documents written by in-house lawyers in preparation for legal proceedings to be subject to privilege but not other documents, and the court appears to have accepted that argument. While this decision obviously applies to executive directors, it is possible that the court could extend it to non-executive directors, particularly if there is an issue of breach of competition law before the court.

Risk areas

As noted above, it is impossible in guidance such as this to give a full account of the risks and responsibilities borne by a company director. The following may be taken as indications of the main areas—

1. Legislation contains numerous criminal offences which arise if a director is responsible for the company's failure to observe the provisions of the legislation, as well as his or her own failure to do so.

2. A director may be subject to a claim by a member (or a liquidator etc) that an act or omission in which he or she participated amounts to a breach of duty and this may expose the director to liability to compensate the company.

3. It is important for a director, whatever the terms of his or her appointment, to participate fully in the management of the company and, in particular, to ensure that he or she receives and understands regular management accounts where the company is actively trading.

4. If the company goes into insolvent liquidation the liquidator may consider imposing personal liability on a director in respect of his or her failure to take adequate steps to protect the interests of creditors.

5. If the company goes into insolvent liquidation, administration or receivership all current directors and those who held office in the recent past will automatically be the subject of a report to the Secretary of State on whether proceedings to disqualify them from holding the office of director (and certain other offices) should be taken, on the grounds that the conduct of the director makes him or her unfit to hold that position. This constitutes a particular risk for those solicitors whose practice units have become limited liability partnerships. Disqualification as a company director also disqualifies the individual from being a member of an LLP (and vice versa).

6. The duties, responsibilities and risks of a company director also extend to "shadow directors" i.e. persons on whose instructions the board of a company is accustomed to act. The definition contains an exception, however, for professional advice. This exception may be lost if the person in question is actually a director, and in those circumstances, his or her

practice unit may be deemed to be a "shadow director" of the company and exposed to the same risks as outlined above.

7.   It would be imprudent for a solicitor to act as a nominee director for another person.

Guidance related to Rule B2.1: Pre-nuptial, Cohabitation and Separation Agreements

After extensive discussion and consideration the view of the Society is that in general there is a clear conflict and the same solicitor should not advise both parties in relation to preparation of a cohabitation agreement. The Society acknowledge that the consequences of this view may be some added expense for cohabiting couples but the priority has to be the independent protection of their interests. However there will be many situations where a couple may be buying property with little or no deposit in which case need for a formal written co-habitation agreement is considerably reduced.

Separated Spouses/Civil Partners (for the avoidance of doubt reference to "Spouses" includes "Civil Partners")

1.   Acting in preparation of Separation Agreement

There is a clear conflict of interest and the same practice unit should not act for both spouses in relation to a separation agreement. Even if the spouses have agreed on matters, a practice unit should act for only one of them in preparing an actual agreement. If the other refuses to seek separate advice, the practice unit can deal with that spouse as an unrepresented party and follow the appropriate guidance.

2.   Sale of jointly owned property

Unless the parties have agreed in writing (i.e. an agreement signed by the parties themselves) how the sale proceeds will be distributed, neither of the practice units acting for the individual spouses in their matrimonial affairs should act in the sale. A separate practice unit should be instructed. The agreement to be signed does not have to be a full separation agreement. It may be an agreement about the free proceeds alone. It would not be improper for the practice unit acting for one of the spouses to accept instructions from both parties to market the property, but unless there is a signed agreement by the time an offer is received, they should not act in the conveyancing.

Where a practice unit is acting in the sale of jointly owned property and in the course of the transaction it transpires that the spouses have separated or are about to separate, the practice unit can continue to act in the sale, but cannot act for either of them in relation to their matrimonial affairs. The clients must be referred to other agents for such advice. The practice unit acting in the sale should distribute the free proceeds in accordance with the title, or in accordance with the spouses' subsequent written agreement. The practice unit cannot advise either of the spouses on such an agreement as there is a clear conflict of interest between them in relation to that.

If the agreement between the parties is that the free proceeds of sale should be held on deposit in the joint names of the parties, the consequences should be fully explained to each of the parties and their informed consent obtained to such an agreement.

3. Sale of property in name of one spouse.

There is a clear conflict of interest between the spouses and the same practice unit should not act for both of them. The practice unit acting for the entitled spouse may accept instructions in the sale of the property, but must not act for the non-entitled spouse.

4. Where there is a signed Agreement

If the parties have signed an agreement dealing with the free proceeds, the solicitors or legal advisers acting for one of the spouses may act in the sale but must account to the parties in accordance with the signed agreement. They cannot accept unilateral instructions from one of the parties to alter that. There is a clear conflict of interest between the parties in that event. Where solicitors or legal advisers are not acting in the sale, they are able to accept instructions from their own client to do diligence on the dependence of an action or in execution of an agreement.

5. Cohabitation Agreements

There is an obvious concern that there is a conflict in situations between two parties who are not married and who are cohabiting or about to cohabit. The Family Law (Scotland) Act 2006 provides for cohabitation agreements to be prepared, effectively dealing with issues arising relating to property on separation. These are a statutory creation.

There is a clear conflict of interest in representing the parties in a cohabitation agreement or prenuptial agreement and they should be treated precisely the same as separation agreements under this guidance.

Where parties are subject to a cohabitation agreement which deals with the disposal of the property and the appropriate trigger event has occurred in regard to disposal of the property then this should be treated as a separation agreement for the purposes of this guidance.

Given that a cohabitation agreement may be given effect to possibly years after it is drawn it is inappropriate to provide in such an agreement for a particular agent to carry out work in the future.

Guidance related to Rule B2.1: Conflict of Interest Guidance on Corporate Guarantees Sought by Banks

The Professional Practice Committee have considered issues arising out of instructions by banks to solicitors in relation to loans or overdraft facilities being provided to Directors of Companies where the bank are seeking a Guarantee from the Company itself. Such instructions contain requests for the solicitors' view on whether an opinion expressed in a resolution of the Company under Section 172(1) of the Companies Act 2006 "is justifiable in the circumstances"; and/or state that the bank are "entirely" relying on the solicitors to obtain all necessary documents to ensure that there is no risk of the bank lending being set aside and/or the transaction being deemed voidable or the banks security position generally being in anyway prejudiced if the transaction has been entered into in contravention of the 2006 Act "or any associated reason". The instructions went on to say that the bank would not be under any obligation or expectation to make any additional enquiries or scrutinise the documentation themselves.

The Committee agreed that imposing such terms and requirements on solicitors creates a conflict of interest between the solicitors and their clients, the bank or its customers. As the clear intention of the bank is to claim against the solicitor if the bank cannot recover from the company under the Guarantee, solicitors will be concerned about their own exposure in the event of the company's default.

The Society's Practice Rules on Standards of Conduct prohibit solicitors from acting for any client where there is a conflict between the interests of the client and the interests of the solicitor or their practice unit (Rule B1.7).

The Committee's guidance is therefore that solicitors should not accept instructions containing such onerous requirements.

If a solicitor is asked to confirm that a Resolution under the Companies Act has been passed in particular terms, the solicitor should insist on sight of either the signed written Resolution or Notices and Minutes of the General Meeting at which such a resolution was passed, and should not rely only on confirmation from the Directors or Secretary that such a Resolution has been passed.

Guidance related to Rule B2.2: Drafting Wills

Drafting wills

Rule B2.2 is a restatement of The Solicitors (Scotland) (Drafting Wills) Practice Rules 2010 ("the 2010 Rules") with one amendment (the addition of the word "knowingly" before the word "act" in rule B2.2.2, added for clarity and consistency with B2.2.3). The purpose of the rule is substantially the same as para.8 of the Schedule to the Standards of Conduct Practice Rules 2008 (that dealt with the drafting of a will containing a legacy in favour of a solicitor or a closely connected person) but avoiding the unnecessarily restrictive and inflexible effects of para.8.

Rule B2.2.3 is the substantive rule. That rule specifically prohibits solicitors from preparing testamentary writings that contain—

(a) a bequest in favour of themselves or a connected person, subject to only certain exceptions (see below); or

(b) a direction to the executor that the solicitor's practice unit, or an entity, such as a Trustee company in which the practice unit has a financial interest, is to administer the testator's estate.

The aims in drafting rule B2.2 were to replace para.8 with provisions that are more appropriate and specific; to avoid concerns that arise out of the testamentary writing rather than who benefits by it, and to avoid inoffensive situations being debarred with testators being sent away unnecessarily to another practice unit.

Interpretation

"Business partner" does of course include members of an LLP.

"Connected person": includes "employee or fellow employee". The consultation process highlighted concerns in the profession about inappropriate pressures being applied to more junior solicitors by fellow employees to prepare testamentary writings in which the fellow employees are disproportionately benefitted. Additionally an employer solicitor should not accept instructions in relation to a testamentary bequest in favour of an employee who is to be disproportionately benefitted.

That said, a solicitor's employees and their relatives are a potential client base and the purpose of the rule is not to prohibit a solicitor from acting for such clients, rather the prohibition will only operate in very particular circumstances. Further it is always open to the solicitor to seek a waiver.

Rule B2.2 applies to ALL solicitors in their own right, so whilst locums are included in the category of employees, agency solicitors, as self-employed sub-contractors, are still subject to the rule.

General prohibition

Rule B2.2.2 is general in its terms and precludes anything reasonably perceived as allowing solicitors or those connected with them by family or professional relationship to exercise undue influence and obtain an unfair advantage. This covers situations not otherwise specifically prescribed in terms of the rule. The family and professional relationship defines the connection, and it is deliberately a wide term.

Exceptions to the Prohibition

There are three exceptions to the specific prohibition in rule B2.2.3(a). Whilst what is prohibited is quite wide, the exceptions are also very wide; the intention being that rule B2.2 will permit everything that is reasonable and fair.

Exception (i)

The bequest is of token sums or items not exceeding £250 in total value.

A token legacy (not a share of the residue) has long been recognised as reasonable. The average cost of instructing another solicitor to prepare a codicil (for such a bequest) is the benchmark for the upper limit for a token legacy.

The figure of £250 is the total value at the time the testamentary writing is executed.

Exception (ii)

The bequest is to the spouse, civil partner or cohabitant of the testator, subject to provisos.

"Cohabitant" (as defined in the Family Law (Scotland) Act 2006) is included as an exception.

The two provisos are essentially exceptions to the exception.

The first is "if the testator has issue at the date of execution of the testamentary writing, these issue are all apparently the issue of both the testator and the recipient of the bequest".

It should be entirely open to a testator to leave everything to their partner, if that partner is also the parent of all the testator's children. It is presumed that it is solely up to parents to make their own choices as to provision for their own children, whose rights are in any event protected to an extent by their entitlement to claim legal rights on both parents' estates.

An example of what would be a breach of the rule is a solicitor whose spouse has a child by a previous relationship preparing a testamentary writing for their partner in which the solicitor benefits to the exclusion of that child.

If the solicitor were to survive their spouse, then under the will the solicitor would inherit. It would then be open to them to cut out the deceased spouse's child. It is not appropriate that the solicitor prepares that testamentary writing. The spouse should receive independent advice as to that possible consequence.

The second proviso is an alternative namely "or if the testator has other issue, appropriate provision is also made for those other issue."

On "appropriate provision" it is impossible to be exhaustively prescriptive. However a simple and important example would be to leave the residue in liferent to the solicitor partner and in fee to the children including children of the testator's previous relationship (with no power to the liferenter to get a full advance of capital). Appropriate provision could also be a lump sum to the new partner and the residue to the children or vice versa, or some other kind of proportionate division between the new partner and the children. Much would depend on the size of the estate and the age of the children, which is why it is not appropriate to try to be exhaustive. Initially it must be for the solicitor to decide what is appropriate, but it should be borne in mind that in the event of a complaint this would be examined objectively and it may thus be preferable to send the testator elsewhere or seek a waiver from the Society.

The purpose of rule B2.2 is not to prevent testamentary writings being made; it is simply to prevent solicitors putting themselves in an invidious position.

While appropriate provision could rarely mean "nil" a testator may explain that she has already by lifetime gift made very large provision for her children and thus wishes to leave what is left to her new partner, who may be within the definition of "connected person" to the solicitor preparing the testamentary writing. That might well be appropriate but is exactly the type of case where the solicitor should either send the testator elsewhere or seek a waiver or at least guidance from the Society.

Exception (iii)

The bequest is to a person related to the testator and is not to any significant degree disproportionately large as compared to that of (1) any other person in the same degree of relationship to the testator or (2) any person, who under the law relating to intestacy is, or could be, a representative of, or represented by, any other person in the same degree of relationship to the testator.

The representation point, which has been carefully thought through, is actually quite permissive. Once the exception was drafted a classic family tree was constructed and the provision thoroughly tested out with the solicitor in all the various permutations. To achieve the principle of complete flexibility regarding bequests to a family that includes a solicitor it was found necessary to include a provision for representation.

As an example there would be no difficulty in a solicitor making a testamentary writing for a parent leaving everything to the other parent whom failing all their children. However, if for what might be a very good reason, the parent wishes to benefit the solicitor son or daughter at the expense of one or more of their other children, the parent should be sent to a different practice unit to prepare the testamentary writing. Another example would be a solicitor's parent leaving a pecuniary legacy of a specific sum to each of their grandchildren. The solicitor may have more children than his/ her siblings, but if the legacy is the same to each grandchild that would not breach the rule.

The aim in relation to this exception is to leave it quite widely permissive as long as the bequest is not disproportionately large in favour of the solicitor (or connected person). In relation to the wording 'significant degree' the intention is to allow a modest difference in value between or amongst specific items taken by different beneficiaries. For example if a mother has a number of items of jewellery and leaves some specific items to each of her two daughters, one of whom is married to a solicitor, that solicitor could prepare the testamentary writing even if the jewellery to be left to his wife is worth slightly more than the jewellery left to the other daughter, but not if it is worth twice as much. It is a means of allowing solicitors to exercise professional judgment and avoid unnecessary applications for waiver.

Prohibition of a Direction

Rule B2.2.3 (b) prohibits a solicitor from preparing a testamentary writing that contains a direction to the executors to instruct that solicitor's practice unit or Trustee company, and no other practice unit, in the administration of the estate. Such clauses are a clear example of a solicitor benefitting from the testamentary writing and have been criticised by the courts in recent years, notably by Sheriff John Baird in the JG Application (AW1259/09) "reported" by Sheriff Baird himself in March 2009. It is only a Direction that is struck at. This rule does not prevent a testator from nominating the solicitor or their Trustee company as one of the executors, or even as the sole executor, with the usual professional remuneration. Nor would it be a breach of the rule if the solicitor executor in exercise of that power decides to act as solicitor in the administration of the testator's estate. What is prohibited is a direction to any other executors that they must instruct the solicitor who prepared the testamentary writing.

An in-house solicitor who is employed by a bank is not precluded from drafting a testamentary writing in terms of which it is provided that the bank will administer the Estate, so long as the solicitor is not appointed as an executor.

Waivers

The Council has power to grant a waiver which may be subject to conditions. In practice this power is delegated to the Professional Practice (Rules and Waivers) Sub-Committee of the Regulatory Committee, which meets monthly except in August. A specific reason should be given for seeking the waiver, and the request is likely to be continued for such information if it is not provided initially. There is no power to grant a general waiver. Each specific case would require a particular waiver.

It is appreciated that a testamentary writing may require to be completed within a timescale that does not allow for the grant of a waiver in which case the safest and recommended course is for the testator to be referred elsewhere.

Rule B2.2 is not retrospective nor does it mean that a solicitor cannot prepare his own testamentary writing whatever the circumstances.

Guidance related to Rule B3: Advertising Fees

Where your fees for your services are advertised either by you or by a third party and whether or not you are named in such an advertisement the advertisement must include mention of outlays and VAT with no less prominence than the fees. Where "legal fees" or similar expressions are used, the fees quoted should be the fees to be charged by you and the figure quoted should not conceal a commission or referral fee to be paid to a third party. Any such commission or referral fee should be shown separately.

Failure to mention outlays and VAT with no less prominence than the fees may be regarded as misleading and inaccurate and therefore in breach of rule B3.5. In terms of rule A4, such a breach may be treated as professional misconduct.

Systems should be put in place to ensure that any outsourced provider of your services complies with this Rule.

Guidance related to Rule B3: Mandates

It is difficult to draw lines between a response to advertising, competitive quoting and touting. It remains the case, however that you should not directly approach someone else's client. We therefore have to look at both sides of the Mandate situation, the obtaining of a Mandate and the response to a Mandate.

Obtaining mandates

Since you cannot approach another solicitor's client other than as part of a general circulation, mailshot or advert, the initial approach must come from the client. The exception to this, the situation of practice units breaking up, is considered below. There may be a variety of reasons why a client may wish to change solicitors.

(a) Client moving

The simplest situation which will seldom cause any difficulties is the obvious one of the client moving from one part of the country to another and wanting to instruct a local solicitor, e.g. in an ongoing matrimonial case.

(b) Client dissatisfied

The client may or may not be moving but wants a new solicitor. This should be straightforward enough but points to note include:

Ensuring that the instruction to the new solicitor is from the client as opposed to a relative or friend who has suggested the change of solicitor; and the client should be asked if the dissatisfaction should be communicated to the previous solicitor and, if so, whether in general or detailed terms.

(c) New cases

For a variety of reasons, (moving, dissatisfaction, lower quote, personal connection or recommendation) a client may give instructions to a new solicitor at the beginning of a new piece of business although that client was represented by a different solicitor in previous matters. Most commonly this would be the situation where a property has been bought using one solicitor and a few years later is to be sold through another who then has to obtain the titles. Obviously if the titles are with a Bank or Building Society the new solicitor just requests them and gets on with it and no Mandate is needed. If the titles are with the previous solicitor a Mandate will be required.

The situations outlined at (a), (b) and (c) above are relatively straightforward. For whatever reason the client has instructed a new solicitor. Things are much less straightforward, however, in the situation where the solicitor's practice unit is breaking up. There are two slightly different situations here. One is a partner (referred to in the rules as a manager) leaving the continuing practice unit and the other is the practice unit itself dissolving.

Partner moving to another practice unit

The partners of the practice unit involved should attempt to agree on the procedure to be adopted in advising clients of the change in the practice unit. In some cases it may be agreed amongst the partners that the departing partner should carry on with certain cases. In others it may be desired to leave it to their clients to decide whether to stay or go with the departing partner. It makes sense to agree the approach in advance. An unseemly squabble may well alienate the client from all of the partners. The terms of a joint communication should be agreed and sent to the client who should be invited to indicate a preference to stay with the established practice unit or go with the departing partner. In an age of ever increasing competitiveness, however, it may be that the established practice unit and the departing partner wish to set out their respective stalls in their own distinct ways. It is to be hoped that they can at least agree to send their letters in the same envelope.

Particular difficulties arise where there is no co-operation between the departing and remaining partners. Some take the view that all clients are clients of the firm rather than individual partners and maintain that a departing partner has no right to try to take clients away from the continuing practice unit. If that were the case then the departing partner would not be allowed to seek Mandates from the clients. The Professional Practice Committee has reaffirmed its view however that subject to what the partners may themselves have agreed a departing partner is entitled to contact clients for whom he or she has acted personally as the responsible partner and invite them to continue to be clients at the new practice unit.

The right to contact clients applies both while the departing partner is still a partner of the practice unit whose clients are being contacted; and also for a reasonable time after the partner has left. What is a reasonable time will depend on the circumstances but in a case in the early 1990's the Committee decided that 3 months was still within a reasonable time.

Associates and assistants moving to another practice unit

All of the above applies only to partners, (i.e. partners in the previous practice unit). Unless there is a specific agreement which allows it, a departing Assistant/ Associate is not entitled to contact clients of his or her employers to seek Mandates with the sole exception of those who are Nominated Solicitors on a Legal Aid Certificate. The Professional Practice Committee accepts that an Assistant may very well attract business to a practice unit. However it is the practice unit, and the partners thereof, who have the authority to deal with the clients. An Associate/ Assistant does not act for the client. It is anticipated, however, that where there is a significant element of delectus personae the clients may wish to follow the Assistant elsewhere. The approach has to be from the client however.

Nominated solicitors

In terms of the Legal Aid Act, legal aid is available through individual solicitors not practice units. The Court of Session has held that so long as a nominated solicitor remains in that position he is under a clear professional duty to render all normal services provided by a solicitor. It follows that an employed solicitor who is a nominated solicitor is obliged to advise the client of a move and if the client wishes, is entitled to continue as nominated solicitor.

Dissolution of Practice Units

Occasionally a practice unit may be dissolved completely with various partners going in various directions. If the practice unit ceases to exist then it can only be the personal relationship between an individual partner and the client which is important. In most cases arrangements would be made for each partner to take certain files etc. and the client would be advised of this and given an opportunity to instruct otherwise.

In the odd situation where there is no agreement between the partners the proper course is for the client to be advised of the position, told the new business addresses of all the relevant partners and asked to choose which, if any, to instruct to hold files etc. All of the partners of the dissolving practice unit have a duty to ensure proper arrangements are made for the retention of all necessary files and documents.

Receiving Mandates

The simple rule (except that there is no specific practice rule on the matter) is, and always has been, that when you receive a Mandate you must respond to it timeously either by sending the items requested to the new solicitor or stating that you are exercising a lien pending settlement of fees and outlays. A delay in doing so will normally be misconduct. You cannot retain papers, even if you have a right of lien, if to do so would prejudice the client (e.g. in a continuing Court case or transaction) but you can offer to deliver the papers reserving your right of lien and requesting the papers to be returned when the case is concluded. If that is accepted by the new solicitor he/she will be bound by it. It must be stressed that prejudice is more than inconvenience and will depend on the particular circumstances of the matter, but would involve the loss of a right; decree passing against the client; or the like. It would not cover having to incur extra costs.

Any solicitor receiving a Mandate will usually want to know why. Sometimes the reason is obvious but various questions and problems can arise.

Did the new solicitor tout for the business?

It is not for the established solicitor to judge. You may suspect and if you have evidence you may report but you must, in any event, take the Mandate at face value and hand over the papers.

There is an outstanding fee note. (See also Guidance on charging for delivery/lending files/deeds)

You can exercise your lien but you must still respond to the Mandate by writing to the new solicitor immediately to say you are doing so.

Work has been done for which a fee will be payable but no fee note has been sent out

One sometimes gets the response when sending a Mandate that the file has been sent to the Law Accountants and will be forwarded in due course once the fee has been advised and paid. Whether this is acceptable depends on the case in question. If a few weeks without the file will make no great difference then it may be acceptable for the established solicitor to do this but if the new solicitor needs the file quickly it is not. The file etc. can be delivered reserving the right of lien. A reasonable time to render an account is in order but it should not exceed four weeks unless the circumstances are truly exceptional. It may be that having extracted such information as required the new solicitor does not need the actual file in which case it should be returned. This imposes a duty on the new solicitor to say whether the file is needed urgently and to return the file for feeing as soon as reasonably practicable. If the new solicitor gives an undertaking (not the client's undertaking) that the account will be paid out of the proceeds of the matter in hand, that should normally be accepted by the original solicitor and the file and papers delivered.

It is improper to exercise a lien over the file or papers if you already have sufficient funds in hand to meet your fees and outlays (e.g. in an executry).

Mandate dated before the original solicitor's last meeting with or last instructions from the client

In these circumstances it is quite proper (although not obligatory) to seek confirmation from the client as to which solicitor he wishes to act. That may be done in writing, by telephone or in person. If the client confirms the mandate in favour of the new solicitor, that is the end of the matter and the original solicitor cannot pursue it further.

Confidential social work reports or court documents

If the papers contain a confidential social work report or court document which the original solicitor has seen as an officer of the court, but which the client now wishes to see as a party litigant, the solicitor should not pass it to the former client.

Lack of capacity

Where a mandate is received in respect of a client who has been medically certified as incapax the solicitor is entitled to regard the mandate as void until satisfied that the client has regained capacity.

To whom should a fee note be sent when a Mandate is received?

Views differ but the Professional Practice Committee decided in March 1997 that it is not a breach of what was then Article 9 of the Code of Conduct (now rule B1.14) for a solicitor to send a fee note direct to the former client. This followed the view that the debt was due by and would require to be enforced directly against the client. If a lien is being exercised the new solicitor should be informed anyway. If a lien is not being exercised it might be wondered whether there is a duty on the established solicitor to tell the new solicitor that a fee note has been/is being sent. One doubts if it could be categorised as misconduct not to tell the new solicitor this was being done but it might be seen as a matter of professional courtesy. It should be emphasised, however, that if anything at all is to be sent directly to a client who has instructed a new solicitor then there should be nothing in that communication which invites the former client to resume the original connection. If fee notes can be sent direct to the client after a Mandate it seems to follow that reminders can also be sent direct but these should be just that, reminders and nothing more. Any invitation to discuss or the like would be a breach of rule B1.14 and any such matters should be raised through the new solicitor.

Can the established solicitor ask why the Mandate has been sent?

Yes, but only after the mandate has been implemented. Implementation means delivery of the papers and not simply telling the new solicitor that a lien is being exercised. The idea behind this is that no undue pressure should be brought to bear on the client and the danger of that happening clearly still exists while the established solicitor still holds the papers.

To whom should the request for reasons be made?

Having implemented a Mandate the original solicitor may write to the former client making a reasonable enquiry as to why the client has instructed a new solicitor. The solicitor can ask for information but must not in any way invite the former client to resume the original connection. Many solicitors may disagree with the view that the solicitor can write directly to the former client at all. On the other hand it may be one of the few ways in which touting might come to light. The current position is, therefore, that the established solicitor can write directly to the client once the Mandate has been implemented but must be extremely careful in the wording of any such communication. It would, for example, be in order to ask if the client was unhappy with some aspect of the service he had received.

Criminal legal aid cases

Specific rules apply and are set out at Article 7 of the Code of Conduct for Criminal Work.

Civil legal aid cases

Again specific rules apply relating to SLAB's approval of the transfer of Legal Aid Certificates.

In both criminal and civil cases the guidance on request for reasons would apply. With regard to the payment of fees, it can be a source of great frustration in Advice and Assistance cases that SLAB will not consider an account until the whole matter is completed. The original solicitor may have no way of knowing the matter has been completed unless this information is received from the new solicitor and is therefore entitled to exercise a lien until a satisfactory undertaking from the original solicitor is received. There is a clear duty on the new solicitor to tell the original solicitor when the account can be submitted or to pay the account out of the proceeds recovered or preserved.

Assistants moving to another practice unit

As noted above, the general rule here is that the client is a client of the firm practice unit and not the individual and so the Assistant should not approach the client. A Mandate received in these circumstances however still has to be treated at face value and still has to be implemented, although the former Assistant's conduct could be brought to the attention of the Scottish Legal Complaints Commission.

Partial Mandates and General Mandates

A difficulty which may occasionally arise is the situation where the client wants a particular practice unit to do a particular transaction without in any way intending to shift allegiance in general. Sometimes this has not been reflected in the Mandate which followed which might request all title deeds and documents leading to misunderstandings and quite possibly a falling out between solicitors, none of which tends to impress the client very greatly. It is not uncommon these days for clients to use different solicitors for different types of business or even for the same type and a new solicitor should not simply assume that he or she is going to be acting for a new client in all matters. This difficulty could be addressed by producing a pro forma Mandate along the following lines:

I hereby authorise and instruct you to send:
* All title deeds and documents and files
* The title deeds of (specify property)
* The documents and papers relating to (specify matter concerned) held by you to (new solicitors)
* Delete where applicable.

Separate record of the date on which a Mandate is implemented

Following the delivery of a file and any other documents in implement of a Mandate the original solicitor should retain the Mandate and a separate record of the date on which the Mandate was implemented to include a general description of what was delivered in implement of the Mandate.

Guidance related to Rule B3: Mandates in Criminal Work

Mandates in criminal work (article 7 of the Code of Conduct for Criminal Work)

All Mandates requesting the transfer of papers and legal aid relating to a criminal matter shall be completed and executed by the assisted person in the form agreed by the Scottish Legal Aid Board and the Law Society of Scotland. The Mandate should include the place and date of signing and a full explanation as to why the Mandate has been issued.

The matter is governed by the Criminal Legal Aid (Scotland) Regulations 1987, paragraph 17(3), which states where an assisted person desires that a solicitor, other than the solicitor presently nominated by him shall act for him, he shall apply to the Board for authority to nominate another specified solicitor to act for him and shall inform the Board of the reason for his application; and the Board, if it is satisfied that there is good reason for the application and, in the case of Legal Aid made available under Sections 24 or 25 of the Act that it is in the interests of justice or, as the case may be, is reasonable, for him to receive or continue to receive Criminal Legal Aid, may grant the application.

It seems clear from a plain construction of this Regulation that changes of agency where the client is legally aided in a criminal case can only take place if the Board gives the client authority to nominate another specified solicitor. Until the Board gives its authority the client cannot instruct another solicitor unless he wishes to do so without the benefit of Legal Aid, which fact should be notified to the Board.

Therefore the chronology of transfers of agency in criminal cases should be (1) the client approaches his proposed new solicitor to ascertain if he is willing to act; (2) client applies to Board for authority to transfer the agency; (3) Board grants authority; (4) client instructs new solicitor; (5) new solicitor serves Mandate on previous solicitor.

The Board's authority to transfer must antedate any Mandate.

This Statement would solve many issues including inducements to transfer agency and Mandate wars. Adoption of this interpretation would of course mean that legally aided clients and fee paying clients will not be treated precisely equally. However, that objection has to be seen in the light of the need to comply with the Regulations which effectively impose a statutory suspensive condition on any Mandate and the requirement that solicitors will require to inform a transferring client that instructions cannot be accepted until the Regulations are complied with.

Form of Mandate approved by the Council

Dear Sir,

I write to inform you that the Scottish Legal Aid Board has transferred Legal Aid Certificate No. from you to my new nominated solicitor who is. I authorise and instruct you to transfer to all papers, documents and files which you hold on my behalf in relation to this matter.

Yours faithfully

Guidance related to Rule B4: Client Communication Generally

This rule requires solicitors to provide information in writing to clients about certain specific matters namely:

1. An outline of the work to be done;
2. An estimate of the total fee including VAT and outlays or the basis upon which the fee will be charged, including VAT and outlays;
3. Details of any contribution towards Legal Advice & Assistance or Legal Aid and details of the effect of preservation or recovery of any property if relevant;
4. Who will do the work;
5. Who the client(s) should contact if they wish to express concern about the manner in which the work is being carried out.

With certain exceptions (see below) this information must be provided at the earliest practicable opportunity upon receiving instructions. It does not have to be contained in a single letter to comply with the rule, but unless there is a particular reason why it cannot be done in a single letter, there is a risk of omitting certain of the information if it is done in different stages.

If a practice unit is tendering for new business, either from an established client or a new client, the information can be given when tendering. If it is, and the tender is accepted, there is no need to repeat the information subsequently.

It is quite in order to give the client more information than is necessary to comply with the rule, but the rule sets out the minimum requirement.

To avoid any risk of misunderstanding or confusion, the outline of the work to be done must provide sufficient information so the scope of the work and the significant elements covered can be clearly identified. However it need not rehearse in detail every step to be taken in progressing and completing the work where that information is not required to enable the client to check that your description of work to be done meets with his intentions. You should always bear in mind your obligation to communicate effectively with your client and others in terms of Rule B 1.9.

Care should be taken in relation to providing information on "who will do the work" when this involves an outsourced provider. This matter should also be considered in relation to the provision of this type of information in Letters of Engagement and formal commissioning documentation and tenders.

Exceptions

There are only three automatic exceptions to the rule:
1. First where a client regularly instructs you in the same type of work, the information does not have to be provided repeatedly but it will have to be provided on at least the first occasion, and it will have to be updated if there is a change in the information previously provided.
2. The second exception is where there is no practical opportunity for the information to be provided before the conclusion of the work. That means where the work is completed at a single meeting. For example a client who may be about to go on holiday and wishes to make a will may have instructions implemented immediately and sign the will at the first meeting. Where you are receiving instructions on an agency basis it is not necessary to provide information to the principal solicitor acting, although it is prudent to have an agreed basis of charging for agency work.
3. The third exception is children under the age of 12. If the client is the child's parent or guardian (for example in a personal injury case) the information will still need to be provided. This exception does not, however, in any way depart from or dilute your obligation to communicate effectively with your

client in terms of Rule B 1.9. Where your client is under the age of 12 special considerations may apply which may suggest that a method of communication other than correspondence is likely to be more effective or more appropriate. That is a matter on which you should exercise your professional judgement in all the circumstances of the particular case.

Fees

As there is no Law Society Table of Fees, it is not appropriate to refer to fees recommended by the Society. If, for example in executries, the file is to be feed by an external fee charger such as an Auditor or Law Accountant, the basis on which the external fee charger will be asked to fee up the file needs to be stated to the client.

As well as the hourly rate any commission which will be charged on capital transactions or on the sale of a house would need to be included. In any matter where the account is being rendered on a detailed basis, the charges for letters, drafting papers, etc will need to be expressed as well as the hourly rate. They can be in a separate schedule referred to in the basic letter. If hourly rates are reviewed during the course of the work, the clients will need to be told about any increase or there is a risk that practice units will be unable to charge the higher rate.

In terms of Section 61A of the Solicitors (Scotland) Act 1980, where a solicitor and client enter into a written fee charging agreement it is not competent for the Court to refer any dispute in the matter to the Auditor for taxation. Where an hourly rate is specified, and that is accepted in writing, the client would still be entitled to seek a taxation, but would not be able to challenge the agreed hourly rate at such a taxation.

It should be made clear at the outset whether the fee quoted is the fee to be charged or only an estimate. If it is not stated as an estimate and the client accepts it in writing, that could be regarded as a written fee charging agreement under Section 61A of the 1980 Act. If a client has been given an estimate, they must be advised in writing when it becomes known that the cost of work will materially exceed such an estimate and when the limit of the original estimate is being approached.

Information should be clear, and terms with which the client may not be familiar such as "outlays" may need to be briefly explained. If a payment to account is required, that should be clearly stated, as well as the consequences of failing to pay it on time. For example in a Court matter if the client is advised that failure to make a payment to account will lead to you withdrawing from acting, there is unlikely to be a professional difficulty about withdrawing from acting in compliance with that. However if the consequence is not stated, and the proof is approaching, you could be vulnerable to a complaint if you withdraw at a late stage to the potential prejudice of the client.

If the clients costs are to be paid by a third party such as a Trade Union or Legal Expenses Insurer, specific details of the basis of charging do not need to be set out when writing to the individual client but any part of the fee which that client may be asked to pay should be included—such as a success fee in a speculative action.

While it is not strictly necessary under the rule, it is also strongly recommended that any potential liability for other people's costs should be explained. This would include a tenant's liability to meet a landlord's fees as well as the potential liability for expenses in a Court action.

Executries and Trusts

In executries where the only executors are solicitors in the practice unit, the information should be provided to the residuary beneficiaries, as they will be meeting the fees out of their shares of the residue. In other executries the information should be provided to the non solicitor executors.

Legal Aid

It is not necessary to comply with the rule for you to explain the statutory payment scheme to Legal Aid clients in relation to Legal Advice & Assistance or Legal Aid. You may wish to forward copies of leaflets provided by SLAB to clients in receipt of Advice & Assistance or Legal Aid. If you do wish to communicate detailed advice to clients about Advice & Assistance or Legal Aid, including for example the client's requirement to report changes in circumstances, that is optional and may be done in a separate letter.

Waivers

The Council have power to grant a waiver which may be subject to conditions. In practice this power is delegated to the Professional Practice (Rules and Waivers) Sub-Committee of the Regulatory Committee, which meets monthly except in August. A specific reason should be given for seeking the waiver, and the request is likely to be continued for such information if it is not provided initially.

Failing to Comply with the Rules

Breach may be treated as professional misconduct. For the avoidance of doubt, an occasional failure to send the information required, or sending information which does not fully comply with the rule, is likely to be dealt with in the first instance as a matter for professional practice guidance. However regular failure to provide the information required may lead to a formal complaint about your conduct, which may be categorised as professional misconduct.

Guidance related to Rule B4: Engagement Waiver for Mortgage Lenders

The Professional Practice Committee considers that it is unnecessary to provide written information as required by rule B4 at least in domestic security transactions, as lenders are setting out the terms of the relationship in their instructions to solicitors and fees will require to be paid by the borrower.

In these circumstances the Committee has granted a general waiver where practice units are acting for both the lender and borrower in domestic conveyancing transactions. Where the practice unit is only acting for the lender, or is acting in a commercial security, the rule still applies.

Guidance related to Rule B4: Terms of Business—Client Funds

During October 2008 there was uncertainty about the stability of banks and the Society sought the opinion of the Dean of Faculty. That opinion can be summarised as follows:

Common law duties of accounting for client funds

In the Dean's view the basic duty is that of the solicitor of ordinary skill acting with ordinary care as set out in *Hunter v Hanley* , 1955 S.C. 200. The contract of agency between solicitor and client is fiduciary but in the Dean's view that does not equate to an absolute duty to account to clients for client funds which have been deposited in accordance with the Society's Accounts Rules. If the solicitor has actual or constructive knowledge of a material risk of failure of a particular bank, a question of negligence might arise.

In the Society's view, actual or constructive knowledge of a material risk of failure means such knowledge of a specific and material risk for a bank. Mere knowledge of speculation in the media or on the internet would be unlikely to amount to actual or constructive knowledge.

The Accounts Rules

In response to the suggestion that the Society's Accounts Rules, and in particular Rule 4(3)(b) (in the 2001 Rules, now Rule B6.3.3(b)), create an obligation to guarantee clients' funds the Dean confirmed that such an obligation is not created by the Accounts Rules. The wording in the relevant rule that nothing contained in the rule shall relieve a solicitor or practice unit of responsibilities must refer to responsibilities to be found elsewhere and not within the Accounts Rules.

Terms of business

In the light of the Dean's opinion and having regard to his advice the Professional Practice Committee agreed that further guidance on terms of business is appropriate. You should advise clients in your standard terms of business of the identity of the bank or banks in which any funds held for the client will be deposited. The terms of business should further say that if clients wish their funds to be deposited in a different bank or banks they will need to give you specific instructions to that effect.

Guidance related to Rule B4: Closing of Files

There is a professional duty upon a solicitor to advise a client in writing that the file will be closed in the absence of his instructions within a specific period of time.

This is clearly sound common sense in the situation where the solicitor is sitting waiting for further instructions. There must be some way of bringing the matter to a close so that the filing cabinet can be cleared of dormant files, accounts can be rendered either to the client or SLAB and both solicitor and client know the matter has come to an end. However there are cases such as old conveyancing transactions after the delivery of the Search and other cases where the matter is obviously concluded where the duty is not the same.

In cases where the matter in which the solicitor was instructed has not come to an obvious and natural conclusion there is a duty upon a solicitor to advise the client in writing that the file will be closed in the absence of his instructions within a specific period of time.

Guidance related to Rule B4: Interest on Invested Funds

Interest on invested funds and commission arrangements on designated client accounts "Global Investments Schemes"

Unless agreed otherwise and set out in Terms of Business or a separate letter which provides either that no interest will be earned because of current bank interest rates, or that some of the interest will be retained by the practice unit, then the matter is covered by Rule B6.10 (the Accounts etc rules). This requires interest to be earned but includes a provision that practice units and clients can agree in writing what interest will be earned on clients' invested funds, provided that agreement is made in writing in advance of the funds being deposited.

Rule B1 (the Standards of Conduct rules) are also relevant. Solicitors are the agents of their clients and must put the clients' interest ahead of their own; must avoid a conflict between their practice unit's interest and that of the client; must disclose a financial interest; and must charge fees which are fair and reasonable in all the circumstances.

An arrangement whereby the practice unit receives all or even half of the interest earned on invested funds, no matter how little that is, could leave the practice unit open to a complaint.

The Society is often asked for advice in relation to solicitors setting up and operating "global" investment schemes, where the practice unit has an option of how much interest is payable to the client and how much to the practice unit.

The Society does not approve or disapprove of any individual scheme offered by specific providers. The following guidance relates to "global investment schemes" generally.

Separate accounting

While the funds invested for clients earn interest based on the total sum invested for all clients, it is essential that individual accounts are maintained for each client.

The statements produced must specify the name of the client in the title and the interest applied to that client must be directly applied to that account. This is no different from any other invested funds account or statement.

Interests of the clients

The interests of the client must come first. If there is an element of discretion in how much interest is paid to the client and therefore how much commission is paid to the practice unit, you must ensure that the client gets at least as good a rate as they would if you did not have that discretion.

In general terms, they should earn at least an equivalent to the current available "high street" rate of interest.

Disclosure

There is a requirement to disclose to the client that your practice unit will benefit from a share of the interest payable on their invested funds.

It would normally be sufficient to include a section within your terms of business explaining when funds held for a client would require to be invested to earn interest for that client and outlining the way the scheme operates.

The fact that the total interest earned is shared between your practice unit and the client should be specifically disclosed.

The practice unit may refer to the rate paid to the practice unit as a percentage of the rate paid to the client in relation to the base rate, which would avoid the need for constant amendments with each rate change.

If clients request more specific information you should provide it.

Including the information in terms of business will only work if all clients are issued with terms of business, at commencement of a transaction and regardless of the nature of the business undertaken. In terms of rule B4 there is already a requirement to provide written information to clients in all cases, with very limited exceptions.

Written approval

Duplicate copies of the disclosure, however it is made, should be issued for signature and return to be held on file. This is to satisfy the requirement of Rule B6.10.3 in relation to an arrangement in writing with your client.

Clients for whom funds are already held invested or where funds may be invested during the course of a transaction that has already commenced will need to be informed of the nature of the scheme. In such cases the terms of business letter will have been issued prior to implementation of the scheme and an alternative disclosure is required.

It may be practical to retain any sums currently invested, but which will be uplifted in the short term, outwith the scheme to avoid having to contact the client and provide information regarding this scheme.

Further questions

Any further questions should be directed to the Financial Compliance Department of the Society.

Interest rate change

Due to the recent interest rate decline, confirmation from the bank is required to ensure that the practice unit is not receiving more interest than the client under such global schemes. It may be necessary, in the event that no interest is payable, to shop around or persuade the practice unit's existing bank to pay some interest to avoid having to move the accounts elsewhere. Any further questions regarding interest should be directed to the Professional Practice Department of the Society.

Guidance related to Rule B5:Client Relations Manager

1. Records to be kept (Rule B5.5.1)

It is not intended that the record keeping exercise should simply be an administrative one. Experience shows that keeping records of complaints received can assist a practice unit in identifying areas which need to be improved in the service to clients and often point up either problems with systems or the way in which a member of staff may be dealing with matters. It is considered that the Client Relations Manager of a practice unit should hold a record of all complaints received even if the practice unit itself splits into various different departments for business. That way the Client Relations Manager can get an overview of the work being carried out and where difficulties may be arising.

The central record itself could take various forms. It is accepted that the central record might simply be a file retained by the Client Relations Manager with the correspondence received in connection with complaints showing what has happened and how they have been dealt with. However, either instead of or in addition to that, a number of practice units keep a central summary record of complaints which they have received.

That record could show the following information:
1. The name of the client.
2. The type of business giving rise to the concern.
3. The name of the individual involved.
4. The concerns expressed by the client.
5. The action taken to deal with the complaint.
6. Any other issues arising.

This type of record does help a Client Relations Manager see at a glance if there is a common theme to complaints being made, or common issues that might need to be tackled. It is recommended that records of individual complaints should be retained for five years from the date the matter is resolved or closed.

2. Written procedure (Rule B5.5.2)

In September 2001 a protocol was published in the Journal (page 8) for handling complaints within firms. The principles set out in that protocol have not altered in the intervening years. It is believed that where a client wants to make a complaint they should be given clear written information about what to do, who to contact, and how to set out the complaint. It is suggested that the written procedure should be kept as simple as possible and can be contained either in a leaflet or on a single A4 sheet of paper which can be handed to a client who indicates they wish to make a complaint.

The essentials of the procedure are considered to be as follows:
1. Who should the client contact in the first instance if they have a concern?
    It could be the solicitor they are instructing, the departmental head or the Client Relations Manager.
2. What should they do if they are dissatisfied with the answer they receive?
    At that stage should they contact the Client Relations Manager or if they have been to the Client Relations Manager they can be advised to contact the Scottish Legal Complaints Commission.
3. What information does the practice unit need from them to enable them to investigate the complaint?
4. What timescales will be involved in dealing with the complaint?
5. Will the matter be dealt with in writing or will the complainer be offered a meeting to discuss matters?
6. How will the matter be finalised?
7. Will a letter or other form of communication be sent confirming the outcome of any attempt to resolve matters or set out, if matters are not resolved, why they have not been resolved?

There is a need to be aware of the Equality Act 2010 and to vary the procedure if the client seeking to express concern either has difficulty in reading or writing, or has language or other difficulties which would make communications in writing a barrier to them.

Guidance related to Rule B6: Accounts, Accounts Certificates, Professional Practice & Guarantee Fund

Part I—General

Cashroom Managers remain responsible for Account Rules compliance whatever method they use to achieve that compliance. In particular, they need to ensure compliance with Rule 6.13.1 the supervision of staff and systems, Rule 6.13.2 to acquire and maintain skills necessary to discharge their responsibilities, and Rule 6.13.3 the need to advance and maintain the competence of others and supervision and adequately train.

In addition, the selection of the outsourced provider should include consideration of insurance cover provided. It is also important to consider the impact on clients that there could be third party fraud by outsourced staff not covered by the Guarantee Fund.

Part II—Accounts Rules

Client's money to be paid into client account or holding ledger

Rule 6.3.1(a)

Do I have to keep all my client funds in the client bank account?

Yes. You must always have sufficient funds in the client bank account to cover all of the client credit balances.

Can I offset sums due by clients to me?

Offsetting sums due to you can only be done where you have the legal right to offset for sums due to/by the same client.

What do I do if I know the practice unit is in deficit?

If there is not sufficient funds in the bank account to cover all the correct credit balances, the position must be rectified without delay. All rule breaches are to be disclosed on the next Accounts certificate to be submitted. If the deficit is ongoing, you are advised to inform Financial Compliance department for advice.

Rule 6.3.1(b)

When do the accounts rules require me to pay money into a client account?

When the solicitor receives more than £50 from a client and the money does not belong to the solicitor, it must be lodged in a client bank account without delay. This normally means on the same day.

Will the minimum sum always be £50?

The rule gives the Council the authority to change this amount from time to time.

Rule 6.3.1(c)

When do I use the holding ledger?

When electronic transfers are to be held as undelivered pending settlement of a sale transaction. When settlement has been agreed, the funds can then be credited to the ledger of the seller.

Can this account be used for other purposes?

No

Why are electronic transfers to be held as undelivered pending settlement of the transaction?

The solicitor cannot credit the client ledger of the seller until settlement has been agreed.

Rule 6.3.3(c), 6.7.1 & 6.19.1 & 2

Can I arrange bridging or other loan accounts on behalf of clients?

Yes—provided you have written authority from the client and made disclosure of the client details to the lender. You must record the outstanding balance and reconcile it on a monthly basis with a bank statement to the same date. Closing statements must be obtained following repayment of the outstanding sum.

Rule 6.3 and 6.23.1 & 2—Acceptance of funds unrelated to a legal transaction

Can I accept funds into my client account which are not related to any legal transaction or service involving my practice unit?

Yes.

However solicitors are encouraged not to act as a bank for their clients due to the potential Money Laundering Regulations 2007 and Proceeds of Crime Act 2002 implications. Should solicitors choose to accept funds from a client which are not related to any legal transaction or service involving the practice unit they should ensure that they have fully complied with the Money Laundering Regulations and the Proceeds of Crime Act.

These would still be "client funds", therefore you have the same obligations as for all funds held on behalf of client.

Terms of Business are necessary for each financial transaction.

Duty to rectify breaches

Rule 6.4.1

Prompt action is required under this rule to rectify any accounts rules breaches which are discovered. This applies to breaches identified in any way including the practice unit's own review work, disclosures on Accounts Certificates, and Law Society of Scotland inspections.

Can I arrange to pay my own money into the client bank account?

Rectifying a breach can include introducing your own money to the client account to cover any deficit identified. Many solicitors also hold a float or surplus money in the client bank account. These funds are usually held to take care of minor mistakes on the solicitor's part i.e. paying outlays for clients who have not yet put them in funds. Using such a surplus as a routine source of funding for clients' outlays has sometimes led to unintended shortages therefore continued vigilance is necessary.

Drawings from client account

Rule 6.5.1

If I am carrying out an inter-client transfer, what do I have to do?

Always remember the prohibition on using one client's money for the benefit of another client. This is only allowed if it is authorised in writing. The fact that the accounts rules allow such payments if authorised in writing should not result in the practice unit overlooking the potential conflict of interest in such a transaction.

Remember that all inter-client transfers must be separately recorded under the terms of Rule 6.7.3(b).

Rule 6.5.1

What monies can be paid from the client bank account without the client's specific written authority?

Any sums due to be paid on behalf of the client where an account has been submitted to the solicitor for work instructed on behalf of a client or for a debt due to the solicitor where the client has received an accounting or to transfer money into the named client bank account to be held for the client or money paid in by the solicitor including sums paid into the account in error.

Rule 6.5.1(c)

I see the rule refers to money drawn on a client's authority. Does this have to be in writing?

Although the authority can be oral, confirmation should be obtained to vouch that authority has been obtained. If questions are raised by the client at a later date, you will need this written authority to rely on.

If I have a client's written authority can I make payments from the client account to third parties?

The rule does not specifically prevent this. However the Society's guidance is generally that a practice unit should not act as a bank for clients. Our recommendation is that practice units should return funds to their clients in such situations and the clients can then make payments to any third parties.

Where a practice unit does agree to make such payments, the practice unit should take steps to ensure that it has taken the Money Laundering Regulations and Proceeds of Crime legislation into consideration in order to protect the practice unit.

You may wish to state in your Terms of Business that your practice unit will not make payments from the client account to third parties. This would reduce the practice unit's exposure to money laundering or Proceeds of Crime risks.

How do I ensure that I am complying with lender instructions when the lender is a client?

All instruction of lenders must be followed. These may be stated within the offer of loan, by letter, within the Council of Mortgage Lenders' Handbook (both parts where applicable), Building Society Association handbook, or in any other form.

Financial Compliance inspections and the Guarantee Fund Sub Committee will pay particular attention to compliance with lender handbook sections which are focused on reducing the risk of fraud. This includes provisions which require solicitors to disclose key facts which lenders should be aware of when making their lending decisions. Solicitors must ensure that they maintain their knowledge of the relevant lender handbooks when they are updated.

Rule 6.5.1(d)

Does this rule mean that I can take fees from a client account?

Yes—provided the solicitor has carried out the work and raised a note of fees due and sent it to the client. The amount of the fee should be charged to the client ledger and then an equivalent sum of money can be transferred to the practice unit's account.

Fees cannot be taken from loan funds held for settlement as this money is only to be used in payment towards the price of property.

How is a fee justified?

Any solicitor seeking to take a fee from a client balance must be able to justify the work carried out and demonstrate the nature and extent of that work. The solicitor must be able to show when the work was carried out and that it was carried out with the authority of, and on the instruction of, the client. It must be possible to identify the fee earners who carried out the work and a record of this should be maintained on the file. The fee note itself should identify the work done, the matter to which it relates, and the fee being charged. It is also expected that a solicitor will be able to produce some form of documentary evidence (for example a paper file or electronic database) to demonstrate the work carried out and which supports the taking of a fee from a client balance.

What happens if a client's address is unknown, after the work is completed, but before the fee note is rendered?

An investigation must be carried out to trace the client and reasonable endeavours must be used to trace the client, details of which should be retained on file. If the client's new address can be ascertained, then the fee note (in relation to a fee that can be justified) can be rendered to the new address and the fee can be taken from the client balance. If the client cannot be traced, despite reasonable endeavours being made, then it may be possible to send out the fee note to the client's last known address, and fees taken where the fee can be justified. In that connection, however, the solicitor sending out the fee note must be acting with the utmost good faith, and the fee note itself could still be challenged by the client if the client subsequently becomes aware of it and disagrees with it. Furthermore, it is good professional practice to render a fee note as soon as possible after the work is completed, to minimise the risk of this situation occurring.

Can a fee be taken more than 5 years after the work that it relates to has been completed?

Solicitors are directed to the terms of the Prescription and Limitation (Scotland) Act 1973, Section 6 and Schedules 1 and 2, which determines the conditions where the 5 year prescriptive period in respect of an obligation arising from a contract (i.e. for legal services) applies.

Rule 6.5.1 (f)

When is it acceptable to take a fee in terms of Rule 6.5.1(f) from client balances held after the conclusion of a matter?

This is explained in Rule 6.11.

Rule 6.5.2

How should a cheque to a bank or building society be designated?

You should ensure that the name of the person whose account is being credited is shown as part of the payee information on the payee line of the cheque. The account number may also be shown, however this is not a requirement of the rule.

Exceptions from Rule 6.3

What should I do if I find that I have received funds which are not to be lodged in the general client account but are to be paid onwards to the client or a third party on the same day?

It is necessary to record the receipt and payment of the funds as a cross entry on the client's ledger account. This discloses the whole sequence of financial dealings on behalf of a client on the ledger card.

Accounts to be kept in books of a solicitor

Rule 6.7.1—6.7.4

The rule requires solicitors to keep "properly written accounting records as are necessary" at all times. What does this mean in practice?

All transactions carried out by the practice unit must be recorded correctly in the books of the practice unit, and the books must be kept up to date. This generally means on a daily basis. The practice unit should ensure that it is able to comply with this rule during periods of staff holidays or illness.

How do I get professional help in setting up and maintaining my accounting records?

You need to determine what level of assistance you need to comply with the rule.

Solicitors considering carrying out their own accounting work should consider whether it is realistic to expect that they will have the time (and skills) to carry out this work adequately.

You should consider the adequacy of the qualifications and experience of any person you are planning to engage to provide you with accounting support. You can also seek information from accountancy bodies such as ICAS and SOLAS.

How quickly would I be expected to make available my accounting records?

This rule requires accounting records to be "properly written up" at all times, the accounting records should therefore be available immediately. Rule 6.1.1 defines the "durable medium" on which accounting records may be stored and notes that printouts from such a medium must be immediately available.

It is therefore vital that the books of the practice unit are held by the practice unit. If the cashroom function of the practice unit is outsourced, the organisation providing the service must also provide the books to the practice unit.

How can I ensure that my accounting records will be immediately available?

You must ensure that whatever approach is taken to the storage of accounting records that these records are immediately available. If you retain accounting records internally this means that you must establish systems to ensure that you can retrieve records whenever required. If you choose to use an external physical storage option you need to ensure that your terms of business with that provider are sufficient to achieve the immediate availability of the accounting records.

Rule 6.7.1(c)

How do accounting records demonstrate compliance with the Money Laundering Regulations?

Accounting records as defined in Rule 6.1.1 include "client due diligence documents and client financial information obtained for the purposes of compliance with the Money Laundering Regulations". The rationale for this definition is that such due diligence work and information gathering needs to be carried out before the commencement of a business relationship and as required throughout that relationship. No accounting entries should take place before this work is completed. This requires no additional work for a solicitor beyond what is already required to comply with the Money Laundering Regulations.

Rule 6.7.4(a)

What is meant by the "true financial position"?

All income, expenditure, assets and liabilities of the practice unit must be shown correctly on the records together with details of every transaction which takes place so that the true financial position of the practice unit can be established using this information.

Rule 6.7.5

How long must I keep the accounting records?

Accounting records must be retained for at least the required retention period from the date of the last entry. The required retention period is defined in Rule 6.1.1 as being a period equal to the remainder of the financial year of the practice unit and a further six financial years of the practice unit.

Rule 6.7.6

What evidence of paid cheques does this rule require me to keep?

Either the actual paid cheques or digital copies of both sides of all cheques, supplied by your bank, or an arrangement as set out in the rule.

Why does the digital image need to show the front and back of a cheque?

The back of a paid cheque will often show details of the account which has been credited with the funds. This is an important element of the audit trail.

How long do I need to ensure that images of cheques (whether in the form of physical copies or digital images) are kept?

The required retention period set out in Rule 6.1.1 applies to cheques and therefore the response given above for Rule 6.7.5 is also relevant here.

Client bank statements to be regularly reconciled

Rule 6.8.1

How often should I carry out these reconciliations?
You must reconcile your general client bank ledgers with the bank statements every month at the same date as the other monthly procedures.

Is there any merit in doing a more frequent reconciliation?
If the practice is very busy, carrying out this reconciliation on a daily or weekly basis may be beneficial in reducing the month end work to more manageable levels. However, there must always be reconciliations to the monthly procedures date.

How long should I retain the documented reconciliation and supporting papers?
Six full years plus the current ongoing year.

Is it useful to have an independent review of completed reconciliations?
An independent review of reconciliations can be useful but individual practice units will need to decide if this is necessary or beneficial for them. In a larger practice unit it is likely that it will be possible to have reconciliations reviewed by a member of staff who was not involved in its preparation. If this is possible within the practice unit, it is recommended that this takes place. A smaller practice unit would benefit if an independent review could be achieved by having a DCP review reconciliations completed by a cashier.

Should completed reconciliations be signed off by the preparer and reviewer?
It is good practice to have completed reconciliations signed off by the preparer and reviewer as an audit trail of their work

Rule 6.8.2

All points noted for Rule 6.8.1 also apply to Rule 6.8.2

If the comparison of the client credit balances with the reconciled client bank balance identifies a client account deficit what action is required?
You must immediately rectify the deficit. This may have to be done by introducing your own funds.

Any deficit should also be disclosed on your practice unit's next Accounts Certificate.

Client funds invested in specified accounts

Rule 6.9.1

How often do I need to carry out the reconciliation of ledger balances for monies held in specific accounts for named clients to bank statements/ passbooks etc
You must carry out this reconciliation on a quarterly basis.
All guidance applicable to Rule 6.8.1 also applies to this rule.

Interest to be earned for a client

Rule 6.10.1

How does this rule work?
The Society has opted to avoid stating fixed periods and levels of client balances regarding the earning of interest. Instead, sums must now be

invested when the amount of interest which could be earned exceeds the level prescribed by Council which is currently £100. The prescribed level is stated on the Society's Financial Compliance webpage and should be checked regularly. Your practice unit needs to estimate the likely level of interest which would be earned given the amount held, the expected time period that the amount is to be held and the prevailing interest rate at the time. Regular review should take place to ensure that decisions remain valid, taking into account factors such as changes in interest rates or changed expectations regarding how long funds are to be held.

Rule 6.10.2

Does the rule require interest to be earned on trivial client balances?
No. The prescribed level of interest likely to be earned (above which investment is expected) is set by Council at what is regarded as a practical and reasonable level.

If a solicitor feels that the prescribed minimum is set at too low a level, the Solicitor should contact the Society's Director of Financial Compliance who will consult with the Guarantee Fund Sub Committee on the issue.

Rule 6.10.3

Is there flexibility regarding earning interest for a client?
Yes. Rule 6.10.1 sets a standard approach which should be adhered to in the absence of any other approach being agreed with the client. Rule 6.10.3 allows a solicitor to agree other approaches in writing with a client. For instance if a solicitor and a client are happy with the arrangements for earning interest under the previous Rule 11 then this provides the flexibility to allow that arrangement to continue.

If the arrangement is set out in the Terms of Business issued to clients, a signed copy must be held so that this evidences a written arrangement agreed between the practice unit and the clients.

The client's written agreement to any arrangement must be held.

This would apply to interest arrangements for any "Global Investment Schemes" where it would be necessary to disclose to your clients that your practice unit will benefit from a share of interest payable on their invested funds. In such schemes the interest of the client must come first and you should ensure that the client gets as least as good a rate as they would have if the funds were not invested in the proposed scheme.

Client balances held after the conclusion of a matter

Rules 6.11.1 to 6.11.7

The requirements of the rule and guidance apply to balances held in general accounts or in invested accounts.

Rule 6.11.1

Why do I need to manage client balances which are retained by my practice unit after the conclusion of matters?
These balances remain the property of your clients and must be returned to them promptly as soon as there is no longer any reason to retain the money. It is expected that in most cases where a matter has concluded, balances should not be required after two months.

Practice units should carry out a monthly review of balances held by them so that balances which are no longer required can be identified and then returned promptly. Such a review will also identify balances where the practice unit decides that there is a continuing good reason to hold the balance within the practice unit. In such cases, the practice unit should document the review they have undertaken to record the reason why it is not appropriate to return the balance to the client.

By carrying out a monthly review as noted above and then acting on the results of the review to dispose of old and small balances promptly and in accordance with the rule, practice units will no longer build up old balances which are no longer required for a transaction. After 1 November 2013, when all such balances existing at 31 October 2011 should have been dealt with (see the next paragraph), all balances older than two months should be known to be required for a transaction.

Rule 6.11.2

Why is there a 2013 date for the application of this rule for matters concluded prior to the implementation date of these rules?
It has been recognised that for some practice units making this rule immediately applicable to all matters, whether concluded before or after the implementation date, would present a challenge as they may have significant numbers of relevant balances to clear. Such practice units should use this period to proactively deal with the balances they hold for matters concluding before the implementation date for these rules and that these will be cleared in accordance with the rule by or in advance of the 2013 date noted.

Rules 6.11.3 to 6.11.7

Detailed Guidance on the Operation of Rules 6.11.3 to 6.11.7

Rule 6.11.3

Rule 6.11.3 refers to small balances within the stated limits whether in general client accounts or whether invested. (The stated limits can be varied by Council. The Society will consult with the QLTR before Council is asked to approve changes to these limits.) Guidance will be updated to reflect any changes in the stated limits, but solicitors should take steps to ensure that they are referring to the up to date limits when dealing with balances.

Sums between £10 and less than £50

What does the Rule allow?
Where the practice unit does not hold up-to-date address or other contact details for the client, the rule allows these sums to be paid either to the QLTR or a registered charity of the solicitor's choice (but subject to the requirement to comply with the law regarding Crown property—see below).

What should be included in Terms of Business?
A practice unit should include in its Terms of Business that where the address or contact details provided by a client are found not to be current then no further efforts need be made to find new contact details for the client before the practice unit can dispose of the balances in accordance with the rule. (Again this is subject to the requirement to comply with the law regarding Crown property.)

Accountability
Solicitors should be aware that they are accountable for their decisions to submit funds within this range to registered charities or the QLTR. Solicitors may need to reimburse their clients at a later date, for example if it turns out that they did have current contact details or did not address the treatment of funds in their Terms of Business.

Funds within this range will not be returned by the QLTR at a later date as the QLTR's administration fee is £50 and it is unlikely that a registered charity will be willing or able to return funds at a later date.

QLTR and Crown Property
The rule allows solicitors to dispose of such balances by submitting them to registered charities or the QLTR.

In most cases solicitors will not have the information available to be sure that the funds represent Crown property. This is because for funds between these values, the rule accepts that it is not economically practicable to carry out further investigations to find an up to date client address or other contact details. Therefore the solicitor in most cases will simply be disposing of funds where the address on file is no longer up to date and no further work can be justified to find a new address.

However in some cases, it will be clear that the balances represent Crown property. It is also possible to clarify if certain balances represent Crown property by carrying out some straightforward steps.

If it is clear that a balance represents Crown Property then this supersedes the ability under this rule to send funds to a registered charity. In these cases it will only be appropriate to send funds to the QLTR. This would apply where a company or limited liability partnership was known to be dissolved.

For corporate clients generally, a solicitor should, in any case of uncertainty, ascertain the status of the company (or LLP) through a Companies House Direct search (which can be done online at no cost) as part of the process of deciding how to dispose of the balances covered by this part of the rule. Where the search discloses that the company (or LLP) is dissolved then the balance represents Crown property and can only be submitted to the QLTR. Such balances cannot be submitted to a registered charity. Similarly, where the search discloses that the company is in administration, receivership, liquidation or other insolvency process, balances should be submitted to the company, followed by the words "(In Receivership)" or as appropriate.

Steps to be followed to successfully submit funds to the QLTR are included in this guidance at "**What process should be followed to submit funds to the QLTR?**" below.

Why can I not take a fee for the work outlined in sending balances to QLTR or a registered charity?
All that is required under Rule 6.11.3 is the identification of balances within certain parameters and the despatch of these balances to the chosen destination. No additional work is required to trace the client (other than that associated with dissolved companies or companies the subject of an insolvency process) and no further value can be added by the solicitor. In these circumstances it would not be appropriate to take a fee.

What do I do if a client comes to me after I have sent their balance to a registered charity?
You should explain the process you undertook to contact them (although the rules do not require this for balances of between £10 and less than £50, you may wish to keep a record of that process) and the Terms of Business agreed with the client. The decision to send funds to a charity is your decision and at your risk. You are unlikely to be able to recover these funds from a charity and may have to repay the funds to your former client.

Sums of £50 and more

Rule 6.11.4

How much work do I need to do to attempt to trace a client for a balance above the prescribed maximum?

The rule requires you to use reasonable endeavours to trace the client. What is reasonable will vary depending on the level of the balance with more work being reasonable as the value of the balances increases. Solicitors should document the work they have done to trace clients and to justify any fee taken.

What process should be followed to submit funds to the QLTR?

Rules 6.11.3 and 6.11.5 and balances for untraced beneficiaries

The following process should be followed when submitting funds to the QLTR pursuant to rule 6.11.3 or 6.11.5. Credit balances which are held in respect of untraced beneficiaries, or in other circumstances, and which may be substantial sums, may also be remitted to the QLTR. In the event that the client or beneficiary is found or appears at a later date then the funds may be recovered from the QLTR (but note that the QLTR will not normally repay funds more than 10 years after the date they were received by her). An administration fee will be deducted by the QLTR.

Where funds were held for a *client or an untraced beneficiary*, the following information requires to be provided to the QLTR when submitting the funds to the QLTR:

- name of client/beneficiary, and any information as to what the funds related to
- last known address of client/beneficiary
- details of the efforts made to trace the client/beneficiary (where the amount is less than £50 this will comprise an explanation as to why the last contact details for the client/beneficiary are no longer considered to be up to date).

Where such funds are remitted to the QLTR, if a refund is subsequently sought it is the QLTR's practice to refund the money to the practice unit which submitted the payment rather than direct to the client/beneficiary who may have reappeared.

Where funds were held for a *dissolved company (or LLP)*, evidence of dissolution (which can be obtained from the Companies House Website as indicated above) requires to be provided to the QLTR when submitting the funds to the QLTR.

There are forms which may be used when submitting funds to QLTR For individual's balances QLTR 1 and for Dissolved Scottish Company balances QLTR 2.

The QLTR address is:

> Queen's and Lord Treasurer's Remembrancer Office,
> Unit 5, 14a South St Andrew Street,
> Edinburgh
> EH2 2AZ.

NOTE: the QLTR will accept a composite cheque for various balances held so long as any permitted fee deductions are taken from each balance and a breakdown, to include the appropriate information required above, is provided with the cheque.

Rule 6.11.6

Why do I need to keep a record of my efforts to trace a client?

You are taking a decision about the disposal of money which does not belong to you. Despite your efforts the client may come forward in the future seeking recovery of their funds. It is therefore in your interests to retain a documented audit trail of what you did to trace the client.

Duty not to act dishonestly

Rule 6.12.1

What sort of behaviour is covered by this rule?

The rule is self-explanatory regarding dishonesty. However as noted, the rule also covers behaviour which is intentionally misleading. An example of the type of behaviour which would be likely to be considered as a breach of this rule would be the deliberate falsification of records and the presentation of these to another person or organisation (such as the Society's inspectors) as being accurate documents.

Cashroom Manager

Rule 6.13.1

I'm not Cashroom Manager, so why do I need to worry about compliance?

All partners/directors ("managers" using the terminology of the rules) are responsible for ensuring compliance with the Accounts Rules.

Rule 6.13.1

Can you explain the role of the Cashroom Manager and how it interacts with the other partners and their responsibilities?

The Cashroom Manager is a signatory to all sections of the Accounts Certificate and has accepted supervisory responsibilities on behalf of the partnership or incorporated practice. More than one Cashroom Manager can be appointed at any one time but there should be clear definition of their individual roles. Sharing or rotating of tasks can be arranged if suitable to the practice unit and the managers.

Rule 6.13.2

What skills will a Cashroom Manager need to have?

The rule requires a Cashroom Manager to use reasonable endeavours to acquire and maintain the skills necessary to discharge the responsibilities of the role. A Cashroom Manager would be expected to have an understanding of the Accounts Rules and how they are applied in the practice unit. The depth of the understanding which is necessary will vary with the support which is available from other staff or advisors who have relevant skills such as cashroom staff and the degree to which the Cashroom Manager has to personally carry out cashroom tasks in the practice unit. The Cashroom Manager should have sufficient supervisory skills to ensure that he can be satisfied with the operations of the cashroom whether through direct supervision or through assurance received from other staff or systems in the practice unit.

One way in which a Cashroom Manager can demonstrate reasonable endeavours is by attending relevant training events.

Rule 6.13.3(a) & (c)

What is the role of the Cashroom Manager in training of staff?

Rule 6.13 places a responsibility on a Cashroom Manager to use reasonable endeavours to ensure that officers and employees have an adequate understanding of the application of the accounts rules in so far as their duties involve compliance with the rules. The Cashroom Manager will clearly want to be satisfied that officers and employees with cashroom roles have detailed knowledge of the rules and how they are applied in the practice unit. The Cashroom Manager will wish to ensure that adequate accounts rules induction training for new cashroom staff/staff changing roles and ongoing update training is in place for all cashroom staff.

For other officers and employees outwith the cashroom, varied levels of accounts rules knowledge will be needed and the Cashroom Manager should be satisfied that a training structure is in place to deliver this training on an initial and ongoing basis.

Does the Cashroom Manager need to deliver accounts rules training personally?

No. A Cashroom Manager can do this if they have the time and skills to do so. However the rule acknowledges that in many cases this will not be practical or necessary and that the Cashroom Manager will instead arrange for the training to be provided.

In some specialist areas such as the Money Laundering Regulations, it would be reasonable for training to be the responsibility of the Money Laundering Reporting Officer. However it would be good practice for the Cashroom Manager to liaise with the officer responsible for such specialist areas to assure himself that adequate training arrangements were in place.

Rule 6.13.3(a) & (b)

What is the role of the Cashroom Manager in the supervision of officers and employees?

The Rule places a supervisory responsibility on the Cashroom Manager "in each case so far as the duties of such officers and employees involve compliance with the rules". The Cashroom Manager will clearly need to implement a robust and evidenced supervisory process for the cashroom. However the cashroom is not the only part of the practice unit which ensures adherence to the accounts rules and it cannot operate in isolation from the rest of the practice unit. The Cashroom Manager should take steps to become aware of and ascertain the adequacy of supervisory arrangements in place to ensure accounts rules compliance amongst staff outwith the cashroom including those in specialist areas such as conveyancing or those required to apply the Money Laundering Regulations.

Does the Cashroom Manager need to deliver all supervision personally?

No. A Cashroom Manager can put in place a supervisory structure to ensure that such tasks are undertaken by suitably skilled staff at various levels. The Cashroom Manager should ensure that such a structure delivers regular and reliable assurance to him that supervisory work is being carried out. This could take various forms (eg: submission of completed control checklists, review of key documents for evidence of supervisory checks, occasional review of reconciliations). Whatever approach is taken it would be prudent for the Cashroom Manager to evidence whatever supervisory work he carries out as part of the practice unit's overall control audit trail.

In some specialist areas such as a conveyancing department the Cashroom Manager would not have the primary supervisory responsibility. However as the work of such a department involves complying with certain accounts rules and impacts on the operation of the cashroom it would be good practice for the Cashroom Manager to liaise with the officer responsible for the area to assure himself that suitable supervisory arrangements are in place. This would also be an opportunity to raise any issues regarding the linkages between the two departments.

Part II—Accounts Rules

Obligation to deliver a certificate

Rule 6.15.1

Why do I need to deliver certificates?

Certificates are the method by which solicitors provide certain assurances to the Society regarding client monies and various related processes. The Society uses this information to monitor practice units' compliance with rules, assess risk and to help it make decisions regarding regulatory matters such as inspection scheduling.

What happens if I have breached the Accounts Rules?

You should take steps to correct the breach or breaches and write to the Financial Compliance Department explaining the position. You should explain the nature of the breach, what steps you have taken to resolve it and provide a timescale within which the resolution will be in place. You should also disclose the breach or breaches in the Accounts Certificate, where there is a section to record the issues. If you are unsure how to resolve the breach(s) you should liaise with your cashroom staff or accountant initially. However you may also contact the Financial Compliance Department for assistance.

I hold no client funds—do I need to deliver a certificate?

Yes—but not as frequently as a practice unit which does hold client funds. Within Rule 6.1.1, the accounting period referred to in this rule is defined. For practice units holding no client funds an accounting period as defined as "a period not exceeding 12 months in duration". Reducing the certificate frequency for practice units which hold no client funds is a proportionate reflection of the risks faced by such practice units. However the Society still wishes to receive certificates on a 12 monthly basis to confirm that client funds are not held. The certificates to be delivered by practice units which hold no client funds are much shorter and simpler than the certificates required from other practice units.

If during the accounting period a practice unit begins to hold client money (having previously reported on a certificate that it does not hold client money), then the Society should be informed of this as soon as possible and the position reported on the next certificate due.

What is the accounting period referred to in the rule?

This is defined in Rule 6.1.1 as being a period not exceeding six months in duration for practice units holding client money. You should set up an accounting period of no more than six months from the start of a new practice and report in the approved style within one month of the accounting period end. Certificates should be for consecutive periods of time, without gaps or overlaps, and should not cover more than six months.

Rule 6.15.2

In what circumstances would the Society require a certificate on a more frequent basis than is normally required?

This might be required where significant rule breaches had been identified in an inspection and it was felt necessary to closely monitor progress in rectifying the rule breaches through the submission of very regular Accounts Certificates.

In what circumstances would the Society require a certificate containing more detailed information than is normally required?

The situation noted above might also lead to a more detailed certificate being required. In both of these situations it is envisaged that this will be applied in exceptional cases in response to risks identified.

Rule 6.15.3

If I am aware that I will not be able to deliver a certificate within the required time period—what should I do?

You should communicate with the Financial Compliance Department in advance to explain the difficulty you are having and to seek an extension to the period. You will be required to provide a satisfactory reason as to why an extension should be granted. No extension can be granted beyond three months after the date on which the certificate would have initially been due.

Rule 6.15.4

What happens if I do not submit a certificate within the required time period?

Reminders will be issued following any missed deadlines including cases when extensions have been granted. If reminders do not result in the certificate being submitted then the case will be brought to the attention of the Guarantee Fund Sub Committee to decide on the appropriate action. This can include inviting solicitors to a Guarantee Fund Interview prior to potentially deciding on any required disciplinary action.

Who may sign a Certificate

Rule 6.16.1 to 3

This rule is self-explanatory. Sign off as outlined in the rule by the Cashroom Manager and Money Laundering Reporting Officer is required to ensure that the certificate has been reviewed and endorsed by those officers with these regulatory responsibilities.

Where solicitor practices in two or more places

Rule 6.17.1

What happens when the practice unit operates separate accounting systems at any branch or has more than one set of accounting records?

You must provide an Accounts Certificate for each set of accounting records. All Accounts Certificates for the same business must be submitted with information to the same date.

Part III—Inspections and Investigations

Inspections and investigations on behalf of the Council

Why are inspections necessary?

The purposes of inspections are listed at Rule 6.18.3. Inspections are the method by which the Society has chosen to fulfil the requirements listed. Inspections are scheduled according to various factors including the time since a previous inspection of the practice unit, whether the practice unit is a new one and various other factors including for instance, findings from an early inspection or intelligence received.

Who will receive notices related to accounts rules issues, inspections etc?

Notices will be sent to the Cashroom Manager as the nominated person responsible for securing compliance with the provisions of these rules. The Cashroom Manager is expected to make other managers, officers and employees aware of the contents of the notice as appropriate. For instance it would be appropriate to tell other managers, the Money Laundering Reporting Officer and cashroom staff that the Society had notified that an inspection was to take place on a specific date.

The Society may send notices to all managers (partners/directors) when this is felt to be necessary.

Rule 6.18.1

Why is "practice information" required for an inspection/investigation not simply limited to the accounting records?

Completion of an inspection/investigation will frequently require information to be provided which is not accounting information.

Rule 6.18.3

How will I be informed that my practice unit will be inspected and what notice will I be given?

A Cashroom Manager will receive a formal notice of an inspection. Usually this will be two to three weeks in advance of the inspection date. A Cashroom Manager is expected to tell other managers (partners/director/ members) and relevant staff about a planned inspection.

Where considered necessary, the Society may notify all managers that an inspection has been scheduled.

Rule 6.18.3

Can an inspection take place without notice?

Yes, the Society can fix the time and place of the inspection.

Rule 6.18.3

What will I be expected to do in advance of an inspection?

The letter intimating the inspection will include information as to the books and records which are required. You are expected to have these available at the commencement of the inspection.

A pre-visit questionnaire will also be enclosed for completion prior to commencement of the inspection.

Rule 6.18.3

Who will decide where and when an inspection will take place?

The notice received from the Society will specify the time and a place for the inspection. In nearly all cases inspection will take place at the practice unit's place of business. However the rule allows the Council to fix a time and place for the inspection and from time to time it may not be appropriate to offer any flexibility regarding the timing or to progress the inspection at the practice unit's normal place of business. This may arise for various reasons including that it is economically not viable for the inspectors to travel to some locations to carry out inspections of very small scale practice units or where the Society has identified health and safety concerns regarding a practice unit's place of business. In these cases the Society will nominate the alternative location for the inspection. Where this requires files, accounting information etc to be transported to/from the alternative location, the Society will reimburse the reasonable costs of the transportation.

Rule 6.18.4 & 6.18.7

What does the Society mean when it notifies that an Investigation is to take place?

This means that the Council has concerns regarding rule non-compliance or the wider manner in which a practice unit is being operated. In these cases a routine inspection is unlikely to be sufficient to address the concerns of Council. It is likely that information will be sought which is not normally required for an inspection. This may include information which can only be provided by third parties such as clients, lenders, and banks. Therefore the Society may require the practice unit to grant authorisation for such third parties to be contacted by the person conducting the investigation. Rule 6.18.7 outlines that reasonable co-operation is required from solicitors regarding the completion of the investigation and this includes the granting of this authorisation.

Rule 6.18.5 & 6.18.6

Can an inspection/investigation be postponed at the solicitor's request?

The Society will generally want to carry out an inspection at the time selected. However if you feel that there is a good reason why a postponement should take place you should contact the Financial Compliance Department to explain this and to discuss the possibility of a postponement. If a postponement is granted this cannot be for more than three months from the original date selected.

It is unlikely to be possible to postpone an investigation as concerns will already have been identified as set out above. Similarly some inspections may be scheduled as a result of risk factors identified which would mean that postponement would be difficult to grant.

If a three-month postponement is granted and the solicitor is unwilling or unable to supply practice information allowing an inspection to proceed, the case will be brought to the attention of the Guarantee Fund Sub Committee.

Rule 6.18.7

What is meant by reasonable co-operation with an inspection or investigation?

The following would be expected if reasonable co-operation was being provided;
- timely and accurate responses to reasonable requests for information within reasonable timescales. What is considered to be reasonable will vary depending on the urgency of the situation. For instance it would be reasonable for the Society to require a very prompt response as part of an urgent investigation or where significant issues such as deficits have been identified
- solicitors and staff making themselves available to discuss inspection or investigation matters
- assistance in overcoming problems encountered during an inspection/ investigation
- timely, complete and accurate responses to post inspection or investigation correspondence
- very prompt responses to information requests and correspondence where it is made clear that the matter is urgent/concerns a significant issue This would be applicable in many parts of an Investigation where the risk level is clearly high.
- timely granting authorisation to contact third parties such as clients and lenders as part of an approved Investigation

Rule 6.18.10

Why do reinspections/further investigations result in charges to the solicitor?

When a reinspection or a further investigation is approved by the Council it is not appropriate for the costs incurred in carrying out this work to be met by the profession as a whole. The reinspection or further investigation costs are being incurred because there is evidence of rule breaches within a practice unit and it is therefore appropriate that the practice unit meets the costs associated with this. The costs are therefore invoiced to the relevant practice unit based on a daily charge out rate agreed by Council from time to time.

Rule 6.18.12

How quickly do I need to pay such a charge?

You should pay the charge in accordance with the stated invoice terms. If you are experiencing difficulty in paying the charge you should contact the Society to explain the position and the Society will consider options such as accepting payment by instalments. The Society will issue reminders regarding overdue invoices and will then consider the use of the debt collector or any other appropriate means to achieve recovery.

Part IV—Professional Practice

Bridging loans

Rule 6.19.1

How do I deal with bridging loans?

You must not enter into a bridging loan agreement on behalf of a client in circumstances which may impose on you a personal liability for repayment in the event of default by the client. Bridging loans must always be in writing and you must give the lender full details of the client and what the arrangements are for repayment.

Can I lend money to a client?

Yes—but you should consider whether a conflict of interest might arise.

Rule 6.19.2

What do I need to do following redemption of a bridging loan arranged on behalf of a client?

You must ensure that you hold a receipt/closing statement showing that redemption of the bridging loan has been paid in full.

Borrowing from clients

Rule 6.20.1

Can I borrow money from a client?

No—unless the client has been independently advised about the loan or is in the business of lending money. (NB Personal and business loans are not covered by the Guarantee Fund.)

(NB the client must have been independently advised before the loan proceeds. Offering the client the opportunity to take independent advice which they acknowledge but decline to take is insufficient to comply with this Rule).

Prohibition on regulated person acting for lender to the regulated person or connected persons

These notes have been prepared with the help of the director of professional practice. If you are unsure how your specific case is affected by the rule, enquiries are welcomed before you begin to act.

Rule 6.21.

(a) Creation, variation and assignation of securities

What loans are affected?

Secured loans to any of the managers (principals) in the practice or their spouse or civil partner, or any partnership of which they or their spouse or civil partner are a partner or any company in which they or their spouse or civil partner are shareholders (except holdings of less than 5% of quoted companies).

Can we act for the managers (principals) or their spouse or civil partner?

Yes—the rule only prohibits acting for the lender.

Can we act for the lender if the borrower is a consultant, associate or employee of the practice unit?

Yes—provided the consultant, associate or employee is not married to, or a civil partner of, a manager in the practice and provided no manager, or spouse or civil partner of a manager, is guaranteeing the loan.

Can we act for the lender where the borrower is the parent, brother, sister, son or daughter of a manager?

Yes—provided that no manager, or spouse or civil partner of a manager, will be guaranteeing the loan.

Why are guarantors included?

Rule 22 (3) defines "loan" as including any obligation to pay money. That includes a guarantee of a loan to somebody else, even though it is only a contingent obligation.

Can we act in a variation or assignation of an existing standard security?

Again, the practice unit can act for the borrower, but not for the lender as the rule applies equally to variations and assignations as it does to the constitution of a standard security.

(NB—Reference is made to the instructions in the CML Lenders' Handbook concerning when a practice unit is entitled to act for both the lender and employees of the practice unit and care should be taken to ensure these instructions are fully adhered to).

(b)   Discharging secured loans

What about discharges?

The practice unit may not act for the lender until the borrower's obligations have been fully implemented.

At what stage in relation to a discharge does a solicitor act for a lender?

Only at the stage where the discharge has been executed and is held by the solicitor on behalf of the lender before the loan has been repaid in full. Drafting the discharge is done on behalf of the borrower, not the lender.

Can I send the discharge direct to the lender for execution?

Yes—but you must advise them not to return it to you but to either retain it until the loan has been redeemed or to send it to their own agents for onward delivery to you only after the loan has been redeemed.

(c)   Other queries

If I am buying a property with the aid of a secured loan, can the seller's solicitors act for the lender?

No—the Society's Professional Practice Committee takes the view that there is a conflict of interest between the seller and the lender to a purchaser.

If I am buying property and another practice unit is acting for the lender, can the lenders forward the loan funds direct to my practice unit or do they have to go through their own solicitors first?

The loan funds can be remitted direct to your practice unit if another practice unit is acting for the lender. Receipt of the loan funds does not of itself constitute acting for the lender.

Who should I contact at the Law Society if I am still in doubt about rule 6.21?

You should contact the Professional Practice Department.

Powers of attorney

Rule 6.22

Do I need to keep a list of powers of attorney?

Yes—the Cashroom Manager must keep an up-to-date list of active and dormant powers of attorney in the name of any solicitor for submission with the accounts certificate.

Do I need to include powers of attorney held for clients specifically for the purposes of submitting the SDLT 1 on behalf of clients or relative to ARTL?

No—powers of attorneys for these two areas are excluded under rule 6.22.4(b).

Rules 8(2) and 23

What records do I have to keep to operate a power of attorney?

A clear record of money paid in or out of the client's own bank account should be kept in a client ledger and cash book. Where you have exclusive control of the client's bank account then that bank balance should be treated as client funds which should be included in invested funds held for named clients.

What effect does the Adults with Incapacity (Scotland) Act 2000 have?

If you are dealing with a continuing power of attorney, you must ensure that client funds are treated as client monies and are recorded in the invested funds records and reconciled.

Money Laundering

6.23.1

Which regulated persons are affected by rule 6.23.1?

Regulation 3(9) of the Money Laundering Regulations 2007 defines "independent legal professional" and identifies which regulated persons and practice units are therefore affected by this rule.

If I do not come under the definition of "independent legal professional" am I still required to carry out customer due diligence measures for clients?

No—while a regulated person who is not an independent legal professional under the Regulations is not required to carry out customer due diligence measures under this rule, it is still advisable for all regulated persons to ensure that they know their clients.

(NB—Regulated persons should be mindful of acting for non-existent principals)

Does the Society offer guidance for compliance with the Money Laundering Regulations 2007?

Yes—both the Professional Practice Department and the Financial Compliance Department offer general and specific guidance for compliance with the Money Laundering Regulations. Furthermore the Society adopted the guidance issued by the Joint Money Laundering Steering Group.

6.23.2

Which regulated persons are affected by rule 6.23.2?

All—Part 7 of the Proceeds of Crime Act 2002 and Part 3 of the Terrorism Act 2000 affect everybody (even non-solicitors).

How do I ensure compliance with rule 6.23.2?

A regulated person must be able to demonstrate appropriate action following the discovery of suspicious activity during a transaction.

The regulated person should take steps to alleviate the suspicions associated with the transaction by questioning their client about the transactions. Where the response received from the client is reasonable and alleviates all suspicions the regulated person should make appropriate file notes and hold any documentation to verify the explanation of client on the file.

Where the response from the client intensifies the suspicions already held the regulated person should be able to evidence that a SAR has been submitted to SOCA.

(NB Regulated persons should be mindful of tipping off under S.333 of the Proceeds of Crime Act 2002 if they choose to question the client rather than submit a SAR to SOCA)

If I have complied with Part 7 of the Proceeds of Crime Act 2002 will I have complied with rule 6.32.2?

Not necessarily—this rule is primarily about record keeping and what information the regulated person holds in regard to a suspicious transaction.

A prosecution for a breach of Part 7 of the Proceeds of Crime Act 2002 is not necessary for the solicitor to have failed to hold sufficient evidence to demonstrate compliance with this rule.

Part V—Guarantee Fund

Guarantee Fund

Rule 6.24.1—6.26.1

The Society's policies regarding the application of the Guarantee Fund rules are contained within the Guarantee Fund Guidelines which can be obtained from the Solicitor to the Guarantee Fund within the Financial Compliance Department and are available on the Society's website.

Guidance related to Rule B7.1: Criminal Court Undertaking

Under the Society's arrangements for the Master Policy for Professional Indemnity Insurance firms whose activities are restricted to criminal court work only throughout the practice year are entitled to a discount on their Master Policy premium.

This restriction is very narrowly defined and those who engage in any legal activity outwith what might be truly described as "criminal court work" are not eligible for the discount. Extradition cases are covered by the criminal court discount under the Master Policy. This discount will also apply to the situation where at a sentencing diet in a criminal case the Crown serves a Prosecutor's Statement for proceeds of crime.

For the avoidance of doubt the Society consider that the following matters are NOT within the acceptable definition of criminal court work for the purposes of the discount. Accordingly those claiming the discount should not act in such matters:

- Appearances before a Sheriff at a hearing to establish the facts following a reference from a children's panel—See *S v Miller No.2* , 2001 S.L.T. 1304.
- Representing police officers at a disciplinary hearing.
- Representing members of the Armed Forces at Courts Martial.
- Appearances at a Fatal Accident Inquiry.
- Confiscation Orders in relation to the assets of convicted criminals.
- Appearances before a Sheriff in relation to an application for the grant of an Antisocial Behaviour Order (ASBOs) are civil matters. For the avoidance of doubt representing an offender who has been charged with a criminal offence following the breach of an Antisocial Behaviour Order is within the definition of "Criminal Court work".

Guidance related to Rule B7.1: Outsourcing

All outsourced providers must be made aware of the terms of the master policy and current certificate of insurance.

Guidance related to Rule B8.2: ARTL Mandates

Please refer to the Guidance on Registration of Deeds: ARTL

Note that in terms of Rule B8.2.4 you are required to retain the principal of each mandate obtained in your favour in terms of rule B8.2.2 in accordance with guidance issued from time to time by the Council.

Section C: Specialities

Guidance related to Rule C1: Cross-Border Practice

The standards of conduct contained in rule B1 do not apply when you are engaged in cross-border practice. Note that this term does not encompass transactions or activity between the constituent parts of the United Kingdom. When engaged in cross-border practice you must comply with rule C1 instead. The principles which apply are broadly similar; however, the Code of Conduct which applies to cross-border practice is that adopted by the Council of the Bars and Law Societies of the European Union and is therefore not wholly within the control of the Society. Minor discrepancies are, therefore, inevitable and you should consider the appropriate rule and Code in detail.

Visit the CCBE website to learn more.

Guidance related to Rule C2: Incidental Financial Business Generally

1. Regulatory framework

1. The Financial Services Authority (FSA) is the principal regulator for investment business in the United Kingdom. Its powers are set out in the Financial Services and Markets Act 2000 ("the Act").

The Act provides that no individual or firm may carry on a regulated activity unless that individual/firm is authorised by the FSA.

Regulated activities are defined in the Financial Services and Markets Act 2000 (Regulated Activities) Order 2001 which has been amended by various Orders including the Financial Services and Markets Act 2000 (Regulated Activities) (Amendment No.1) Order 2003 to include mortgage business and by the Financial Services & Markets Act 2000 (Regulated Activities) (Amendment No.2) Order 2003 to include insurance business.

An individual solicitor or firm of solicitors can undertake certain regulated activities and thereby be exempt from the requirement to be authorised by the FSA if that solicitor/firm is licensed by the Society under Part XX of the Financial Services and Markets Act 2000. The Part XX regime allows the establishment of exempt professional firms (exempt from the FSA's regime) to undertake exempt regulated activities provided such activities are an integral part of a solicitor's professional services. For the purposes of the Part XX regime, the Society is a Designated Professional Body and licenses firms to conduct exempt regulated activities.

The Society's regime is known as the "Incidental Financial Business (IFB) Regime" effective from 31st October 2004 and this regime replaces the Incidental Investment Business Regime which has been in operation since 1st December 2001. The IFB regime allows firms to conduct certain activities which would otherwise require FSA authorisation. The essence of these incidental financial business activities is that they are integral to the professional services provided to clients and are not conducted on a standalone basis. Furthermore, such activities must not be marketed on a standalone basis.

As the FSA's regime has been expanded to include mortgage and insurance business, there has been a similar expansion to the Society's IFB regime so that it incorporates investment, mortgage and general insurance business.

There are four options open to firms of Scottish solicitors under the UK's investment business regulatory regime and these are—
- FSA authorisation.
- An IFB Licence from the Society.
- Acting as an introducer to an independent financial adviser—this option can be undertaken in connection with either of the first two options.
- None of the above.

It is important to recognise the wide definition of a regulated activity which includes—
- advising on investments, mortgages and general insurance.
- making arrangements in investment, mortgages and general insurance.
- selling investments, mortgages and general insurance.

The definition of regulated activities is therefore very wide and is not confined only to the giving of advice but includes making arrangements in the following product areas—

Insurance products

Includes after the event legal expenses insurance, Bonds of Caution, building insurance, defective title indemnity insurance, household contents insurance, missing beneficiary indemnity insurance, term assurance, unoccupied property insurance and warranty insurance.

Investment products

Includes shares, fixed interest stock, individual savings accounts, pension and collective investment schemes, unit trusts and open-ended investment companies.

Regulated mortgage contract is one which is secured by a first legal mortgage on land which is in the United Kingdom and where at least 40% of the land is, or is to be used, as a dwelling by the borrower.

2. Direct authorisation by the FSA

There are currently just around 80 firms of Scottish solicitors authorised for investment business by the FSA. The FSA has its own rules and procedures for those firms which it authorises.

An application for authorisation should be made direct to the FSA whose contact details are:

> The Financial Services Authority,
> 25 The North Colonnade,
> Canary Wharf,
> London.
> E14 5HS

FSA switchboard number—020.7066.1000

Website address—*www.fsa.gov.uk*

A firm which is authorised by the FSA will be able to give its own specific advice on individual investment products and investment companies. Furthermore an FSA authorised firm will also be able to give specific advice on mortgage lenders and mortgage products.

A firm which is authorised by the FSA for investment business cannot also be authorised for incidental financial business by the Society. A firm's FSA authorisation also covers such a firm for incidental financial business as the Society's "incidental regime" does not cover any incidental financial business conducted by FSA authorised firms. The relevant FSA rules cover the incidental financial business of FSA authorised firms.

3. Incidental Financial Business ("IFB") Regime

The IFB regime incorporates four types of incidental business as follows—
* Incidental insurance business
* Incidental investment business
* Incidental long-term care insurance business
* Incidental mortgage business

The Scottish Legal Complaints Commission will have responsibility for handling any complaints arising from any of the above four types of incidental financial business, at least initially.

Before looking at the specific types of business which may be conducted under this regime it is necessary to highlight the conditions which must be followed if a practice unit is to be licensed for IFB.

Conditions for conducting Incidental Financial Business

A practice unit's incidental financial business services must be an integral part of its professional services. A practice unit cannot have stand-alone incidental financial business.

1. The incidental financial business conducted must be linked to the provision of a particular professional service to a particular client.

2. A practice unit licensed for incidental financial business cannot also be authorised by the FSA and must not hold itself out as being so authorised.

3. Any commission, financial or other pecuniary benefit received from third parties due to the conduct of incidental financial business belongs to the client. This means that any commission arising from the incidental financial business must either be given to the client or the client can agree to the commission being offset against his/her fees. However, the client must agree to this offsetting in writing in advance. Typically, this can be arranged by a pro forma letter signed by the client agreeing to this offsetting. Such a letter can be sent to the client for signing along with the terms of business letter.

4. The practice unit's income from incidental financial business cannot account for more than 50% of the practice unit's total income.

The above conditions must be met in relation to the four types of incidental financial business which may be conducted. Each of these four categories of incidental financial business are explained below—

Incidental Insurance Business

The regulation of insurance business as a category of incidental financial business has brought more practice units into this regulatory regime than under the previous regime. This is because of the wide definition of insurance business within the legislation.

The legislation refers to insurance business as "insurance mediation". The insurance business which falls into the incidental financial business regime consists of the following activities—

*   introducing, proposing or carrying out other work preparatory to the conclusion of contracts of insurance.
*   concluding contracts of insurance.
*   assisting in the administration and performance of contracts of insurance, in particular in the event of a claim.

A practice unit will be conducting insurance business under the IFB Licence when, in connection with its professional services it introduces, sells, arranges and advises on general insurance, such as after the event legal expenses insurance, buildings insurance, contaminated land insurance, defective title indemnity insurance, household contents insurance, missing beneficiary indemnity insurance, trustees indemnity insurance and unoccupied property insurance. Significantly, as the definition of insurance mediation includes "assisting in the administration and performance of contracts of insurance, in particular in the event of a claim" where a practice unit acts for an insured in bringing a claim against his/her own insurer, this activity when undertaken in conjunction with professional services will fall into the new regime. Where a practice unit acts for an insurance company in the defence of a claim, this activity will not fall under the new regime if the activity is covered by the exemption in Article 39B of the Regulated Activities Order 2001. This Article provides an exemption where a practice unit "manages claims on behalf of an insurer" as part of the practice unit's professional services. It should be noted that where a practice unit acts for a third party in an insurance claim such an activity will not fall under the definition of insurance mediation as the third party is not making a claim under his/her own insurance policy. An example of such a third party claim is where a pedestrian is injured in a road traffic accident and then he/she wishes to bring a personal injury claim against the car driver who caused the accident.

The insurance element of the incidental financial business regime does allow a practice unit to give its own advice and recommendations to a client on a specific contract of insurance. A practice unit therefore can give its own advice on insurance contracts or insurance companies under the IFB regime.

Incidental Investment Business

The following activities are examples of what may constitute investment incidental financial business—

1. arranging for the purchase or sale of shares on the instructions of clients without providing advice on those shares. Such arrangements may arise within an executry or trust work.
2. discussing with a client investment advice which has been provided by an independent financial adviser. The practice unit may comment upon such advice and, acting on the client's instructions, carry out investment arrangements based on the advice.
3. a practice unit undertaking matrimonial work can obtain the advice of an independent financial adviser regarding the matrimonial investment assets. The practice unit can comment upon the advice in negotiating a financial settlement in the matrimonial work on the client's instruction.
4. a practice unit at its own initiative can advise a client that the investment advice or investment arrangements provided by another person do not appear to be in the client's best interest and that the client should seek further independent financial advice.

A practice unit under this section of the IFB regime may not give its own specific advice on investment products or investment companies. A practice unit may, however, give generic advice on the range of investment products and investment companies.

Incidental Long-Term Care Insurance Financial Business

This section of the IFB regime allows a practice unit to introduce, arrange or advise on long-term care insurance policies, products and providers.

Incidental Mortgage Financial Business

The IFB regime for incidental mortgage financial business came into force on 31st October 2004.

A practice unit which wishes to arrange a mortgage on the instructions of a client will be able to undertake such arrangements through this element of the IFB regime. However, a practice unit will not be able to give its own advice on a specific mortgage product, or mortgage lenders to a client and such specific advice will have to come from an independent mortgage adviser. On receipt of such third-party advice a practice unit will be able to discuss the advice with a client and acting on the client's instructions arrange a mortgage.

4. Introductions

A practice unit either with or without an IFB Licence may undertake introductory business where a client is referred to an independent financial adviser. There are different rules depending on the type of financial business which is introduced. The types of financial business which may be introduced can be categorised as follows—

Introductory Insurance Business—either general insurance or long-term care insurance

If a practice unit wishes to introduce clients to an independent insurance broker for any contract of insurance a practice unit will require an IFB Licence. This is because the general statutory provisions on introductions under Article 33 of the Regulated Activities Order are disapplied for insurance mediation.

Introductory Investment Business

A practice unit may introduce a client to an independent financial adviser. The practice unit making the introduction must do no more than bring together the client and the independent financial adviser to whom the introduction is made. Any commission arising from the introduction can be retained by the practice unit.

Introductory Mortgage Business

A practice unit may introduce a client to an independent mortgage broker. There are two principal conditions which apply to such introductions which are—

- a practice unit must not receive any money paid by the borrower in connection with the introduction; and
- before making the introduction the practice unit must disclose to the borrower details of any payment or any other reward which may arise out of the introduction.

5. Incidental Financial Business Practice Rules

(a) **Application for an Incidental Financial Business Licence** An application for an IFB Licence must be made by a practice unit to the Society by submitting an application form in a form specified by the Council.

  The application form requires details of the manager within the practice unit who will have overall responsibility for the conduct of insurance mediation where a practice unit wishes to undertake incidental insurance or incidental long-term care insurance. No person having a criminal record disclosing a serious criminal conviction, involving any crime against property or related to financial services can fulfil this role. No person who is subject to bankruptcy proceedings can fulfil this role. These prohibitions are requirements of the Insurance Mediation Directive from which the Society's IFB Rules are derived.

  The application form also seeks notification to the Society of those persons within the practice unit (solicitors and non-solicitors) who are to be individually licensed for each incidental financial business activity. Each person identified must indicate which incidental financial business activities will be undertaken by ticking one or more of the appropriate boxes. The options are— incidental investment business (IB); incidental insurance business (IM); incidental long-term care insurance (LTC) and incidental mortgage business (MMA).

No person who wishes to conduct incidental insurance or long-term care insurance work can undertake such work where they have a criminal record (as defined above) or where they have been subject to bankruptcy proceedings.

The application form asks the practice unit to provide the date from which the new Incidental Financial Business Licence is required.

(b) **Duration of an Incidental Financial Business Licence** The Licence runs for the normal twelve month term of the Society's practice year, from 1st November to 31st October.

(c) **Renewal of an Incidental Financial Business Licence** A practice unit's IFB Licence will be renewed annually. If a practice unit does not wish to renew its IFB Licence, notice of this intention and the date from when the Licence is to be revoked must be sent to the Society.

(d) **Annual fee for an Incidental Financial Business Licence** The annual fee for an IFB Licence will be set at the Society's Special General Meeting in September each year.

(e) **Display of the Incidental Financial Business Certificate** A practice unit must display at its place of business its Incidental Financial Business Certificate (or a copy). A practice unit will be issued with an Incidental Financial Business Certificate after it first applies to be licensed for such work from the Society.

(f) **Notification to the Society in changes of personnel who undertake Incidental Financial Business** A practice unit must notify the Society in writing of any changes to the list of personnel originally provided to the Society of those who conduct incidental financial business within a practice unit. This notification must be made to the Society within one month of any change to the original list of licensed individuals.

(g) **Specific Rule requirements for insurance mediation activity (general insurance and long-term care insurance)**

- every practice unit which undertakes incidental general insurance or incidental long-term care insurance must appoint a manager who has overall responsibility for the conduct of such work within the practice unit. This person will be referred to as the Insurance Mediation Officer. It is this person who will be identified on the FSA's website as being responsible for insurance mediation within a practice unit.
- A practice unit will not be able to undertake any form of insurance mediation work (general insurance or long-term care insurance) until that practice unit is registered on the FSA's Register for this work. It is the Society which has responsibility for transmitting this information on practice units and their insurance mediation officer to the FSA. The Society will update the information on the FSA's Register on a weekly basis.
- Provision of information—certain information requires to be provided to a client where a practice unit concludes a contract of insurance for a client. The information which requires to be provided is set out in pro forma style in Schedule 1 to this guidance to Rule C2. The information can be provided orally if the client requests this or if the client requires immediate cover. Furthermore, where the contract is concluded by telephone and the client agrees to receiving limited information after the conclusion of the contract, the general information to be provided in writing need not be given.

- Scope of services—where a practice unit acts as an insurance intermediary providing advice on particular types of insurance a practice unit must have undertaken an appropriate analysis of the insurance market to show that the advice given on a particular contact of insurance is adequate to meet a client's needs. A record should be made of how a practice unit has undertaken an appropriate analysis of the insurance market.
- Statement of demands and needs—where a practice unit makes a personal recommendation to a client of a specific contract of insurance or arranges for a client to enter into a specific contract of insurance, before the conclusion of that contract the client must be provided with a statement of his demands and needs in respect of that insurance contract. This statement is in essence a "reason why letter" explaining to the client why a particular contract of insurance has been recommended by the practice unit. The letter should also clearly state the demands and needs of the client. A pro forma style of this statement is provided in Schedule 2 to this guidance on rule C2.

(h) **Incidental Financial Business Compliance Certificate** A practice unit is required to submit an Incidental Financial Business Compliance Certificate for each six-month period within a practice unit's financial year. The form of Compliance Certificate which must be submitted to the Society is specified by the Council. The Compliance Certificate requires the following information—

- The accounting period to which the Certificate relates.
- Confirmation that the practice unit fulfils the criteria for carrying out IFB in terms of the rules and has complied with the rules.
- Date and signing of the Certificate by a manager.

The Society's team of inspecting accountants will monitor a practice unit's compliance with the rules as part of the Society's [two-yearly] cycle of Accounts Rules inspection.

(i) **Terms of business** Whenever a practice unit undertakes incidental financial business a terms of business letter must be issued to a client. A pro forma style of terms of business letter for incidental financial business is provided in Schedule 3 to this guidance.

(j) **Disclosure on a practice unit's notepaper** A practice unit is not required to state on its notepaper that it is licensed by the Society for incidental financial business. No such disclosure on a practice unit's notepaper is required due to the requirement to issue terms of business letters.

(k) **Training** There is no requirement to undertake an investment business exam or any specified level of investment business CPD for those individuals who are licensed to conduct incidental financial business. The training obligations for individuals who undertake incidental financial business are set out in general terms in rule C2.23. The responsibility is on practice units and those licensed individuals to ensure that they keep themselves up to date on incidental financial business matters.

(l) **Record keeping requirements** The record keeping requirements are set out in rule C2.24. The general obligations are as follows—

- Best execution—instructions from clients to carry out specific incidental financial business should be arranged with due timeliness.
- Records of statements of demands and needs—these must be kept for a minimum of three years from the date on which a practice unit's

personal recommendation on a specific contract of insurance or the arrangements to enter into a specific contract of insurance have been made.

- Records of a client's instructions—a practice unit must retain records of instructions from clients to carry out specific incidental financial business and instructions from the practice unit to any third party to effect or arrange such incidental financial business. These records must be retained for at least six years from the date of the instruction.
- Records of accounting to clients for commission etc—a practice unit must retain records of how it has accounted to its clients for any IFB commission or other pecuniary reward from third parties. Such records must be kept for at least six years from the date of accounting. This record keeping can be achieved by retaining copies of the letter and payment details where commission is paid direct to the client. Alternatively, where the commission is deducted from a practice unit's fee note, a copy of the fee note detailing this deduction is sufficient.
- Safe-keeping of assets—where a practice unit holds for safe-keeping purposes documents of title i.e. share certificates, a practice unit should ensure that at all times such documents are readily accessible and are separately identifiable from any of the practice unit's own investments. A practice unit should also ensure that storage facilities are appropriate to the value and risk of loss of the investments to be safe-guarded and provide protection from damage, misappropriation or other losses. Where a practice unit uses a third party custodian to safe-keep such documents a practice unit must be satisfied that such a third party is suitable to act as a custodian.

Schedule 1

Style of information letter to be used before or immediately after the conclusion of a contract of insurance with a client.

1. The practice unit of AB has its principal place of business at..........
2. The practice unit of AB is not authorised by the Financial Services Authority. However, the practice unit is included on the Register maintained by the Financial Services Authority so that this practice unit can carry on insurance mediation activities, which is broadly the advising on, selling and administration of insurance contracts. This part of our business, including arrangements for complaints or redress if something goes wrong, is regulated by the Law Society of Scotland. The Register can be accessed via the Financial Services Authority website.
3. The information provided in parts 1 and 2 above may be checked on the FSA's Register by visiting the FSA's website or by contacting the FSA on 0845 606 1234.
4. The practice unit of AB does not have any holding, direct or indirect, representing more than 10% of the voting rights of, or the capital in, an insurance undertaking.
5. No insurance undertaking or parent of an insurance undertaking has a holding, direct or indirect, representing more than 10% of the voting rights of or capital in this practice unit.
6. The contract of insurance on which this practice unit has provided advice or arranged has been selected [on the basis of a fair analysis of the insurance market. This analysis was undertaken by reviewing the range of insurance

products on the market] or [from a limited number of insurance undertakings] or [from a single insurance undertaking] *[Note, if the practice unit adopts either of these last two approaches then it must also disclose whether it is contractually obliged to conduct insurance mediation in this way].*

7. The practice unit of AB has Professional Indemnity Insurance under the Law Society of Scotland of Scotland's Master Policy. The current level of indemnity on the Master Policy is £2m per claim. The practice unit of AB is also covered by the Scottish Solicitors Guarantee Fund which is a fund established by Section 43 of the Solicitors (Scotland) Act 1980 for the purpose of making grants in order to compensate persons who, in the opinion of the Council of the Law Society of Scotland suffer pecuniary loss by reason of dishonesty on the part of a Scottish solicitor in connection with the practice of the solicitor.

8. Any complaint which you may have about any service provided by the practice unit should be directed to the manager within AB. Furthermore, you have a right to complain to the Scottish Legal Complaints Commission, The Stamp Office, 10-14 Waterloo Place, Edinburgh. EH1 3EG. Tel: 0131 528 5111

Schedule 2

Style of Statement of Demands & Needs when advising on or arranging a specific contract of insurance.

1. The practice unit of AB has recommended that you (name of client) take out a contract of insurance for household contents with CD insurance company of (insert address of insurance company).

2. The demands and needs of (client's name) in respect of this insurance contract are that insurance cover is required for your household contents for your newly purchased property.

3. The practice unit has recommended the household insurance contract of CD insurance company because *[insert reasons for recommendation which should relate to the insurance contract meeting the client's insurance needs].*

Schedule 3

Style of Terms of Business letter for incidental financial business.

1. The specific incidental financial business undertaken by this practice unit will be the sale of a ABC shares in DE through stockbrokers FG on your instructions. The practice unit has limited its incidental financial business activities to arranging the sale of these shares given the limited scope of activities allowed under the incidental financial business regime.

2. The practice unit of AB is licensed by the Law Society of Scotland to carry on incidental financial business under the Solicitors (Scotland) (Incidental Financial Business) Practice Rules 2004.

3. The practice unit of AB is not authorised by the Financial Services Authority under the Financial Services and Markets Act 2000.

4. The practice unit of AB has Professional Indemnity Insurance under the Law Society of Scotland of Scotland's Master Policy. The current level of indemnity on the Master Policy is £2m per claim. The practice unit of AB is also covered by the Scottish Solicitors' Guarantee Fund which is a fund

established by Section 43 of the Solicitors (Scotland) Act 1980 for the purpose of making grants in order to compensate persons who, in the opinion of the Council of the Law Society of Scotland suffer pecuniary loss by reason of dishonesty on the part of a Scottish solicitor in connection with the practice of the solicitor.

Any complaint which you may have about any service provided by the practice unit should be directed to the manager within AB. Furthermore, you have a right to complain to the Scottish Legal Complaints Commission, The Stamp Office, 10-14 Waterloo Place, Edinburgh, EH1 3EG. Tel: 0131 528 5111

Guidance related to Rule C2: Pension Sharing on Divorce

Under the Welfare Reform and Pensions Act 1999 the following guidance in relation to the requirements of the financial services legislation has been given to the Society. There are three stages to be considered separately in this area.

The first stage is the gathering of information about the value of the assets including the pension. This stage is not of itself Investment Business and can be done by a solicitor. Valuation methods used should be in accordance with the pension regulations, such as the cash equivalent method.

The second stage is the important decision whether to opt for earmarking, sharing or offsetting, pension entitlement. A practice unit may give generic advice on the general nature of these options provided a practice unit holds an Incidental Financial Business Licence from the Society.

Only those practice units which are licensed by the Financial Services Authority are permitted to give specific investment advice on each of these options a client should pursue with regard to Pension Sharing on Divorce.

It should be borne in mind in all cases that, even where pension sharing is not used, clients may require pensions and other investment advice in their changed marital and financial status.

Guidance related to Rule C3: Peer Review Criteria Guidance

This guidance is issued by the Council of the Law Society of Scotland in terms of Rule C3 of the Law Society of Scotland Practice Rules 2011, in order to set out the standards expected of solicitors and practice units in relation to the carrying out of civil legal assistance work. In providing civil legal assistance, solicitors are required to comply with these guidelines.

The purpose of peer review of selected files is to review the quality of the work carried out on behalf of the client and the Scottish Legal Aid Board, based on the evidence contained within the file. It is therefore necessary for solicitors to manage their files so that they are sufficiently well organised for the peer reviewer to be able to read them, and so that there is sufficient evidence on each file to enable the peer reviewer to satisfy him/herself that the criteria have been met. Where files have been held electronically, it is necessary for them to be printed for submission for peer review.

The Society has published a detailed Peer Review Manual to assist solicitors in fulfilling the requirements of civil quality assurance. It is a comprehensive guide to the civil quality assurance scheme, covering the process of peer review, the requirements of the scheme and themes arising from previous cycles of reviews.

What follows is an outline of the criteria to be applied by the peer reviewer in civil and in children's legal assistance cases, with additional explanation where relevant, and an indication of the scoring system to be applied.

All criteria will be applied by the peer reviewer where relevant to the file being reviewed; not all criteria will apply to every file. The file will be scored against each of the criteria below according to the following marking scale.

1. *Below requirements*
2. *Meets requirements*
3. *Exceeds requirements*

The standard to be applied is that of the reasonable competence to be expected of a solicitor of ordinary skills.

When considering the advice given or actions taken in the course of a case, there will be circumstances in which differing interpretations might legitimately be taken by solicitors applying their professional judgement: the reviewer should not attempt to second-guess the acting solicitor. Professional judgement should only be called into question where, in the reviewer's opinion, no reasonable solicitor would have conducted the case in the way demonstrated by the contents of the file.

In addition to the three point scale, two other marks are available for particular criteria:

C Cannot Assess / Not Enough Information

N/A Not Applicable

An additional score should also be given for the file as a whole, based on a five-point scale (with 1 indicating very poor performance and 5 excellent performance).

The criteria follow a broad chronology to ensure proper consideration is given to key aspects of the case. In addition, criteria 9 to 13 should be applied to the case as a whole.

Guidance on the application of individual criteria is provided as required below each criterion.

Several criteria use the terms accurate and/or appropriate:

- in determining whether advice is accurate, the reviewer should consider whether it is *factually* and *legally* acceptable, bearing in mind the test in Hunter v Hanley;
- in considering whether it is appropriate, the reviewer should have regard to the circumstances of the case and the level of information available to the solicitor and take into account ethical, practical, tactical and legal considerations.

Criteria for Civil Legal Assistance Cases

Initial meeting(s)

1. How effective were the solicitor's initial fact and information gathering skills, including the identification of any additional information required and the taking of steps necessary to obtain it?

1 2 3 C N/A

2. Was the client given accurate and appropriate advice regarding

    a) the potential case, including whether it is stateable

        1 2 3 C N/A

    b) the client's eligibility for advice and assistance, especially if the client is not admitted

        1 2 3 C N/A

    c) legal aid more generally, including the application of regulation 18 and advice and assistance, including possible clawback and the impact of legal aid on expenses

1 2 3 C N/A

For the avoidance of doubt, where relevant to the case in question, general guidance should be given on the question of clawback.

3. Is there evidence on file or in a letter to the client of:—
    a)   a terms of engagement letter, where applicable

    1 2 3 C N/A

    There are some situations where letters of engagement are not required e.g. if the case began before 1st August 2005, if the client regularly instructs the solicitor in the same type of business, if there is no practical opportunity for the solicitor to send one—as will usually be the case in minimum fee cases and where the client is a child under 12.

    b)   a note of agreed actions?

    1 2 3 C N/A

    c)   a request to the client for further information to be obtained from the client, where required

    1 2 3 C N/A

    d)   an assessment as to whether any urgent steps were required/appropriate

    1 2 3 C N/A

Continuing Work

4. Did the solicitor take appropriate steps to carry out further investigation to progress matters for the client within a reasonable timescale?

1 2 3 C N/A

5. Did the solicitor communicate appropriately with others, and where appropriate, pursue settlement or agreement on relevant issues?

1 2 3 C N/A

6. Did the solicitor give appropriate advice to the client, where relevant, on alternative options, such as litigation and mediation?

1 2 3 C N/A

7. Has the solicitor
    a)   identified the need for appropriate experts, other reports or counsel

    1 2 3 C N/A

    b)   applied for sanction / increase(s) in authorised expenditure in accordance with the guidelines, and if granted, instructed / obtained the appropriate experts / Counsel / reports?

    1 2 3 C N/A

8. Is there evidence of adequate preparation for each diet, debate or proof, to include (as appropriate) the list of witnesses, productions and list of authorities as appropriate to the facts of the case?

1 2 3 C N/A

Throughout the case

Having considered the specific aspects of the case set out in the preceding criteria, the reviewer should apply criteria 9 to 13 to the case as a whole, covering activity carried out under both advice and assistance and civil legal aid where relevant.

9.
a)   After the initial meeting(s), did the solicitor make use of, and provide accurate and appropriate advice to the client on, legal aid and advice and assistance, in accordance with the relevant guidelines?

    1 2 3 C N/A

This assessment should include: consideration of relevant changes in circumstances that may impact on eligibility for legal aid (merits and means); timeous application for increases in authorised expenditure or for sanction for experts/counsel/ unusual work; preparation and submission of application for civil legal aid (including the initial application, provision of any additional information required and review of refusal/reassessment of means if appropriate); submission of accurate and appropriate staged reports to SLAB.

b)   After the initial meeting(s), did the solicitor give accurate and appropriate legal advice to the client?

1 2 3 C N/A

Matters not relating to legal aid, to prevent duplicate marking with criteria 2.

10.   Did the solicitor take steps identified/agreed with the client, within a reasonable timescale given the circumstances of the case?

1 2 3 C N/A

The timescale within which the solicitor would be expected to act will vary with the circumstances of the case. However, in assessing criterion 10, the reviewer should also have regard to issues such as the need for work to be carried out under special urgency, for example, where there is a danger that the action will become time-barred.

11.   Did the solicitor keep the client informed of progress / advised as to next steps / further procedure and provide accurate and appropriate advice, including following the receipt of substantive correspondence (including offers / proposals from the opponent?

1 2 3 C N/A

Substantive should be interpreted to include any significant correspondence that might have a bearing on the solicitor's advice to the client or the progress of the case. For the avoidance of doubt, this would include copy pleadings, any offers/ proposals received from the opponent, or responses to any offers/ proposals made by the acting solicitor.

12.   Where an offer/proposal is made, is there evidence of accurate and appropriate advice having been given to the client on the terms of the offer/ proposal, its reasonableness and the consequences for the client of acceptance/rejection, including the potential impact of expenses/clawback?

1 2 3 C N/A

Conclusion of the case

13.

a)   Has the solicitor taken appropriate steps to close the file and communicate that to the client?

1 2 3 C N/A

b)   Where judgement is issued, has the solicitor advised the client as to the judgement, including advice on expenses, property recovered and preserved, diligence on decree, prospects of appeal?

1 2 3 C N/A

For the avoidance of doubt, it would not be considered adequate in explaining expenses / property recovered and preserved for the solicitor to provide the client with a copy of the relevant Scottish Legal Aid Board leaflet.

14.   Has the account been submitted to SLAB in accordance with guidelines and necessary and appropriate steps been taken in relation to recovery of expenses / handling of property recovered and preserved?

1 2 3 C N/A

In assessing this criteria reviewers should check that any accounting to the client and any fee charged to the client has been dealt with appropriately.

Overall mark for file

1 2 3 4 5

Having considered each of the individual criteria, including those applicable to throughout the case, the reviewer should allocate an additional mark for the file as a whole.

Comments on file/case overall

The reviewer should provide brief comments on the case. These should focus on any criteria on which a score of 1 is provided. If applicable, the reviewer should explain why a "fail" score has been given and suggest areas for improvement and ways in which these might be achieved. These comments will provide an initial indication to the firm/solicitor involved as to any particular issues that require to be addressed. Where any high scores are given, these should also be drawn to the solicitor's/firm's attention.

Criteria for Children's Legal Assistance Cases

Initial meeting(s)

Considering the time, place and circumstances of instruction, and the age and maturity of the client:

1. How effective were the solicitor's initial fact and information gathering skills, including the identification of any additional information required and the taking of steps necessary to obtain it?

    1 2 3 C N/A

2. Did the solicitor give accurate and appropriate advice to the client regarding

(a)   The relevant section(s) of Part II of the Children's (Scotland) Act 1995

    1 2 3 C N/A

(b)   the client's eligibility for advice and assistance

    1 2 3 C N/A

(c)   the legal aid application, including the use of Regulation 8

    1 2 3 C N/A

3. Is there evidence of a note of agreed actions with the client, where appropriate?

    1 2 3 C N/A

Continuing Work

4. Did the solicitor take appropriate steps to carry out further investigation and communicate appropriately with others in order to progress matters for the client within a reasonable timescale?

    1 2 3 C N/A

5. Did the solicitor take appropriate steps to advise the client and, where appropriate, inform the client as to the date, time and place of hearings?

    1 2 3 C N/A

6.

a)   Has the solicitor identified the need for appropriate experts, other reports or Counsel?

    1 2 3 C N/A

b)   Has the solicitor applied for sanction / increase(s) in authorised expenditure in accordance with the guidelines, and, if granted, instructed / obtained the appropriate experts / counsel / reports?

1 2 3 C N/A

7. Is there evidence of adequate preparation for each court appearance, to include (as appropriate) the list of witnesses, productions and list of authorities as appropriate to the facts of the case?
1 2 3 C N/A

Throughout the case

8.

a) After the initial meeting(s), did the solicitor make use of, and provide accurate and appropriate advice to the client on, legal aid and advice and assistance, in accordance with the relevant guidelines?
1 2 3 C N/A

b) After the initial meeting(s), did the solicitor give accurate and appropriate legal advice to the client?
1 2 3 C N/A

9. Did the solicitor take steps identified/agreed with the client, within a statutory or reasonable timescale given the circumstances of the case?
1 2 3 C N/A

10. Did the solicitor keep the client informed of progress / advised as to next steps / further procedure and provide accurate and appropriate advice throughout the case, including the final outcome?
1 2 3 C N/A

Conclusion of the case

11. Has the solicitor advised the client as to the judgement or decision, and any further procedure to follow, e.g. on the prospects for appeal?
1 2 3 C N/A

12. Has the account been submitted to the Scottish Legal Aid Board in accordance with guidelines?
1 2 3 C N/A

Overall mark for file

1 2 3 4 5

Comments on file/case overall

The reviewer should provide brief comments on the case. These should focus on any criteria on which a score of 1 is provided. If applicable, the reviewer should explain why a "fail" score has been given and suggest areas for improvement and ways in which these might be achieved. These comments will provide an initial indication to the firm/solicitor involved as to any particular issues that require to be addressed. Where any high scores are given, these should also be drawn to the solicitor's/firm's attention.

Section D: Requirements of and Restrictions on Practice

Guidance related to Rule: D1: PC Renewal

Practising certificate renewal or PC renewal is required on expiry of existing certificates on 31 October in each year. See the Society's website for a variety of links dealing with PC renewal.

Paper renewal

Application forms are distributed to the profession during the first week of October. If you have not received your application form by mid-October, you should contact the records section of the Registrar's Department on 0131 226 7411 or send an email.

For information on practising certificate renewals, you can download our guidance material from the website and visit our FAQs page.

Online renewal

Members can opt in to online Practising Certificate renewal. Online renewal is only available to members renewing Practising Certificates expiring October 31. For members whose employer pays their fees the employer requires to opt in to online renewal for all staff. Other members who are not associated with any employer in our records can opt in to online renewal as individuals. You must login on our website to opt in between 5 and 16 September.

See the Online Renewal "How to" Guide and the Online Renewal Troubleshooting Guide on the Society's website.

Renewal fees

The fees agreed at the 23 September 2011 SGM remain unchanged from the previous year.

Guarantee Fund contribution 2011/12

The Guarantee Fund contribution for 2011/12 is £50 lower than the 2010/11 contribution. However the current charge has been separated between a contribution to the Guarantee Fund and an Accounts Fee. The Accounts Fee reflects cost of the inspection regime—it is not an additional charge.

We made making this change because the Scottish Government expressed the view that only costs and income which can be directly attributed to the Guarantee Fund claims process should be allocated to the accounts of the Guarantee Fund. This view was accepted by the Society for future years.

The details
- The costs of the inspection regime will no longer be charged to the Guarantee Fund. They will instead be charged to the Society budget from 2011/12 and approved through the Society's budgeting process. The inspection regime costs include the costs of the financial compliance and interventions teams.
- The income to cover these costs will be covered by a new charge called the Accounts Fee (which is reflected in the Legal Services Act) which is charged to the same population as the Guarantee Fund contribution and represents income to the Society and not the Guarantee Fund.
- The Guarantee Fund contribution for 2011/12 is lower than in the previous year as fewer costs are to be funded from this subscription.
- The main cost now met by the Guarantee Fund is therefore grant expenditure. The grants forecast for 2011/12 is shown on the attached schedule. Representatives of Chubb (the providers of the fund's Stop Loss insurance) have recently reviewed the approach to budgeting for grant expenditure and did not raise any suggested improvements to the process.
- The breakdown of the 2011/12 proposal

Income Type	2010/11	2011/12
GF Subscription	630	239
Accounts Fee—approved through LSS budgeting process	—	341
Total	630	580

If you have any queries about the new arrangements, please email us at fincomp@lawscot.org.uk.

Guidance related to Rule D5: Trust and Company Service Providers

The Money Laundering Regulations 2007 require trust and company service providers to be registered with HMRC or a professional regulatory body. The purpose of registration, which is set out in Regulation 24 of the 2007 Regulations, is monitoring by the supervisory authority, and the only power to monitor which the Society has under the Solicitors (Scotland) Act 1980 is in respect of sole practitioners, firms of solicitors, and incorporated practices.

It remains the Society's position that if a practice unit has one or more of these ancillary companies, the company's activities are not "monitored" by the Society unless it is recognised in its own right as an incorporated practice under rule D5. If practice units wish the Society to be the supervisory authority for such a company under Part 4 of the 2007 Regulations they should apply for recognition as an incorporated practice.

Guidance related to Rule D7 / D8: Registration of Foreign Lawyers and Multi-national Practices

Registration of foreign lawyers and multi-national practices

There is no bar to lawyers qualified in another jurisdiction working in Scotland, provided they do not describe themselves as "solicitors" and do not do certain types of work reserved by statute for Scottish qualified solicitors (S32 of the Solicitors (Scotland) Act 1980). Those are broadly conveyancing of land and/or buildings; litigation (civil or criminal); and obtaining confirmation in favour of executors (the Scottish equivalent of probate). They can enter into partnerships with Scottish qualified solicitors in an MNP by becoming registered foreign lawyers.

Rule D7: Registration of foreign lawyers

This provides for the registration of foreign lawyers, ie lawyers from jurisdictions outwith Scotland (including England and Wales). It is a requirement of the 1980 Act that foreign lawyers must be registered with the Society before they can enter into MNPs with Scottish solicitors or incorporated practices.

Rule D8.1: Entering a multi-national practice

In summary, this rule governs the entering into of MNPs by solicitors, firms of solicitors and incorporated practices. The rule requires solicitors, firms of solicitors and incorporated practices to seek the approval of the Council prior to entering into an MNP. In order to be able to give that approval, the Council requires to be satisfied that the applicant solicitor (or firm or incorporated practice) will become a member of an MNP as that term is defined in section 65 of the 1980 Act. The Council also has to be satisfied that the MNP of which that solicitor (or firm or incorporated practice) will be a member is or will be so regulated as to make it appropriate for solicitors to be allowed to enter it.

In order to qualify as an MNP in terms of section 65 of the 1980 Act, all of the foreign lawyers within the practice must be registered by the Society, and hence this rule should be read along with rule D7. As mentioned, this provides for the registration of foreign lawyers and contains two important safeguards for the profession. The first is that anyone who wishes to become a registered foreign lawyer must satisfy the Council that he is a fit and proper person. Secondly, he must also satisfy the Council that the legal profession of which he is a member is so regulated as to make it appropriate for him to be allowed to enter into MNPs with Scottish solicitors. The registration rules also contain provisions in respect of professional indemnity insurance and guarantee fund matters.

Rule D8.2: Multi-national practice—Principal place of business

This rule is the primary means of determining how many of the Society's rules are applied to registered foreign lawyers. Generally, a higher degree of regulation is imposed on registered foreign lawyers in an MNP whose principal place of business is located in Scotland.

Guidance related to Rule D9.2: Prohibition on the Sharing of Fees

Rule D9.2 prohibits solicitors and others from sharing "with any unqualified person any profits or fees or fee derived from any business transacted by you of a kind which is commonly carried on by regulated persons in Scotland in the course of or in connection with their practice"; with certain limited exceptions. Those exceptions are, broadly, (a) payment of overheads (as defined in the rule) and (b) retired partners ("managers" in the rule) and their executors, heirs or representatives; employees who are wholly employed in the practice unit; public officers in respect of work done in the course of their duty; and other lawyers—including lawyers in other jurisdictions—and law centres, citizens advice bodies and licensed legal services providers and those within them.

The Professional Practice Committee take the view that the principal type of arrangement which the rule prohibits is an arrangement to pay commission for the introduction of business on a case by case basis. Solicitors are entitled to pay for the cost of marketing or promoting the practice unit as part of their overheads. They are entitled to pay a fee to be included on a panel to whom referrals will be made provided that that fee is not expressed as a specific sum per referral or as a percentage of the fees chargeable for referred business. A flat fee is not in breach of the rules and that may be a fee which is reviewed periodically.

You are entitled to pay for the provision of services to the practice unit as part of overheads. Even if the service is provided by the person who introduces the client, you are entitled to pay for the service. However the service must be a real service and not merely the introduction of the client. The Committee has also decided that the carrying out of a money laundering check by the introducer would not, however, be a service for which payment could be made as that is an obligation on solicitors themselves in terms of the Accounts Rules (Rule B6). Services which have been accepted as not breaching the rules have included carrying out hearing tests; taking statements of witnesses; obtaining photographs of a locus; and completing a detailed client questionnaire relating to the particular matter in which the solicitor is instructed. The introduction of capital in return for a percentage of fees would be regarded as breaching the practice rules, but the provision of loan funds with a variable rate of interest expressed as a percentage of the funds advanced would not.

The inclusion of a commission paid to an introducer as an outlay in a solicitor's fee note—and not a hidden part of the fee—would not be in breach of the rules however the position would have to be made clear to the client at the outset in the terms of business.

Finally solicitors and others are of course entitled to receive commission from third parties for the introduction of business, but the existence of such arrangements should be disclosed to the client although the actual amount of commission does not need to be disclosed unless the client specifically seeks that information. Such commission received must relate to any work undertaken by the solicitors in connection with the business referred. If no work has been undertaken, unless the commission is of a nominal amount it should be accounted for to the client.

Section E: General Guidance on Client Care and Practice Management

Division A: Standards of Service

"Lawyers help people at times of crisis and bereavement, they protect the rights of the vulnerable, and they support business and economic growth." (Justice Secretary, Kenny MacAskill, 26 November 2007)

Lawyers interact with a wide cross section of our society and fulfil a critical role in meeting the interests of that society. Their clients are entitled to expect a good level of professional service from their solicitor. This means the solicitor must demonstrate the appropriate legal knowledge and skill to address the needs of the client, must communicate effectively in a clear and understandable way with their clients and others, must do what they say they are going to do, and must treat their clients and all others with respect and courtesy at all times.

At the same time, a solicitor is required to comply with rules of professional conduct and behaviour, recognising that their professional obligations are not only to their clients, but to the courts, the legal profession and the public. Amongst other things, these rules regulate:

- Confidentiality and legal professional privilege
- Trust and personal integrity
- The interest of the client
- Independence of the solicitor
- Disclosure of interest
- Relations with the Courts
- Conflict of Interest

Standards of service are based on broad principles recognising the range and variety of work which can be undertaken by a solicitor. The standards have equal application to an individual solicitor, whether as a partner in a firm or an employee, and to firms. The application of these standards requires the use of effective systems, good training and appropriate supervision.

All outsourcing providers should be made aware of the Standards of Service and required to comply with them.

At the heart of providing a legal service are the interests and needs of the client. The importance of those interests and needs means that solicitors must adhere to the following overriding principles:

- Competence.
- Diligence.

- Communication.
- Respect.

Competence
- Know and apply the relevant law
- Keep up-to-date
- Ensure that those to whom work is delegated are properly trained and supervised

In deciding whether or not to agree to work for a client and in carrying out the work, a solicitor must consider the nature and complexity of the matter and must have the appropriate level of professional skills to do that work. This means that a solicitor must consider if he or she has the knowledge and experience needed. Given the range of specialised areas of legal work it is essential that a solicitor recognises the need to keep his/her knowledge up to date and to make an ongoing commitment to continuing professional development.

Where a solicitor delegates work, whether to another solicitor or solicitors or to paralegals or other members of staff, it is essential that such staff are properly trained and that there are in place systems to ensure that the delegated work is adequately supervised.

Diligence
- Deliver on commitments
- Act in the best interests of each client
- Maintain and review systems of work
- Prompt and transparent fee arrangements

It is expected that a solicitor will fulfil commitments made to the client, other solicitors and the court. By way of example, this would include responding to letters, e-mails and telephone calls within an appropriate or agreed timescale.

A solicitor must only agree to work for a client where the work can be done within a reasonable timescale. Where a solicitor considers, for example, that the service to a client would be inadequate because they already have so much work to do that it would not be dealt with within a reasonable period of time, they should not agree to take on the work.

The solicitor will at all times seek to do his or her best for the client. This will include identifying the client's objectives in relation to the work to be done, giving the client a clear explanation of the issues involved and the options available to the client, and agreeing with the client the next steps to be taken.

In keeping the client informed, the solicitor must provide updates on progress.

With the increasing advancement of technology, it is expected that the solicitor will regularly look at ways in which technology can support client service. By way of example, this may include client reporting systems, file and data management systems and use of knowledge management systems.

At the conclusion of the work, or earlier if agreed, the solicitor will ensure that the fees to be charged are promptly notified to the client and that a clear explanation and breakdown is provided. If there is any variation from the fees previously discussed, the solicitor must explain the reasons for the variation. The solicitor must respond promptly to any clarification sought from the client.

Communication

- Use of clear language and explanation from the perspective of the client
- Agreement on the means and frequency of communication between client and solicitor
- Letters of engagement or their equivalent clearly explaining and defining the service to be carried out, how that work will be carried out, who is responsible and the cost associated with the service
- How complaints will be handled in the event of dissatisfaction

Whatever the nature of the work carried out by a solicitor, communicating effectively with the client is very important. Solicitors must make sure that they communicate clearly, effectively and in plain understandable language with their clients and others. This includes keeping clients informed regularly about progress with the matter. The overriding aim is to ensure that the client can gain a proper understanding of what is being communicated. This necessarily requires the communication to be tailored to suit the audience, their needs and interests. Communication requires the solicitor to listen to the client and understand their objectives.

Solicitors must send a letter to their clients as soon as possible after the first instruction providing information about:

(a) the work to be carried out;

(b) what the fees and other costs will be, or the basis upon which such fees and costs will be charged including where appropriate the hourly rate to be charged. Where the client is receiving legal advice and assistance or legal aid, they should be told about any contribution that might be payable, the consequences of preserving or recovering property, and where appropriate their possible liability for the expenses of the other party;

(c) the name of the person or persons who will do the work; and

(d) the name of the person the client should speak to if they are unhappy about the work done.

Clients who use a solicitor or firm regularly to carry out the same type of work should be sent such a letter whenever there is any change in the terms previously agreed with them.

Solicitors should advise their clients of any significant development in relation to the matter they are working on for them and explain matters clearly in order to allow clients to make informed decisions.

Information should be clear, easy to understand and comprehensive and where necessary or appropriate confirmed in writing. In particular solicitors should advise clients in writing as soon as it becomes known that the cost of work will exceed any estimate previously provided.

The duty to communicate effectively includes the duty of solicitors to report to their clients at the appropriate time about all money related to their matter which is handled by the solicitor.

Respect

- Treat each person as an individual
- Recognise diversity, different cultures and values

The relationship between solicitor and client is a mutual one built upon trust and respect.

Relationships based on openness, trust and good communication enable the solicitor to work in partnership with the client to address their needs. Implicit within a good level of professional service provided by a solicitor is that each and every client will be treated respectfully and with courtesy, in recognition of their dignity and rights as individuals. The solicitor also has a responsibility to treat colleagues, other members of the legal profession and the public with similar politeness and respect.

This will require of the solicitor to listen to and understand the interests and needs of the client and to bring his or her knowledge and experience to the work.

The solicitor must treat clients fairly and in line with the law. The solicitor must not discriminate against clients because of their age, sex, race, ethnic origin, nationality, special needs or disability, sexuality, health, lifestyle, beliefs or any other relevant consideration.

Division B: The Management of Files, Papers and Information

The ownership and destruction of files

All outsourcing providers should be made aware of these provisions and required to comply with them.

The following information is based on an Opinion from the Dean of Faculty provided to the Society in June 2000.

Who owns what in files?

The answer is not entirely straightforward and drawing on the opinion of Counsel the Society has produced this guidance which we hope will deal with the main queries which arise:

Finished documents or drafts/notes

Material Ordinarily Owned by Client
- Documents produced by the client or produced by the solicitor for the client.
- Written Opinions (whether principals or copies) but not preparatory personal notes prepared for the solicitor's benefit.
- Draft formal documents and deeds. (These may be of evidential importance to the client in the event of the loss or destruction of the principals.)
- Written submissions tendered in Court, but not detailed research notes and other documents generated for the solicitor's own personal use. Precognitions taken by the solicitor or obtained from other parties but see Article 11 of the Code of Conduct for Criminal Work where they may contain sensitive material and where it might be inappropriate to pass this information to clients. See *Swift v. Bannigan* 1991 S.C.L.R. 604, although the Dean had reservations about this case.
- Original letters received from and copy letters to third parties.
- Copies of letters written to the client, although if these have been retained by the solicitor as part of a private record or if the contents relate exclusively to the contractual relationship between the solicitor and the client, the solicitor may own them.
- Notes of meetings and telephone calls, which constitute the solicitor's work on behalf of the client.
- Files and documents received under a mandate.

Material Ordinarily Owned by Solicitor
- Original letters received by the solicitor from the client.
- Notes of meetings and telephone calls, which form part of the solicitor's preparatory work.
- Inter-office memoranda.

Sensitive material and precognitions in criminal cases should be dealt with in accordance with Article 11 of the Code of Conduct for Criminal Work.

Mandates

It is matter of judgment whether a file should be copied, but copying is prudent. The costs should be borne by the solicitor.

If a mandate is received from one of two or more clients and the consent of the other cannot be obtained the file can be exhibited or copies offered at the client's expense, provided that nothing is disclosed or copied which is confidential to the other party. See also the next paragraph "Multiple Clients" and Guidance on Charging for Lending or Delivery of Files.

Multiple clients

Issues of confidentiality, duties of disclosure and informed consent of multiple clients must be borne in mind.

Where a matter develops to the extent that a solicitor cannot continue acting for multiple clients due to a conflict of interest arising or developing, care must be taken with the nature of the material copied or delivered.

Any release of correspondence or documents must either be with the consent of all or the file should be divided into parts relevant to each client, e.g. in the lender/ borrower situation the file should be divided into those parts belonging to the lender and borrower respectively.

Where there are common documents they can be copied to all clients.

If a lien is to be exercised, the solicitor cannot prejudice one client, e.g. a lender if that client has no liability for fees. If one client requests a file where fees are due by the other, the file should be forwarded under reservation of the lien so that it cannot be passed on to new agents.

A file can be delivered subject to an undertaking to produce it to "the other side" if called upon.

Each client has the right to inspect documents in which he or she has a proprietary interest and also to receive copies at his or her own expense.

Destruction of files

The Terms of Business letter should include information about the intention to destroy files and/or papers after conclusion of a transaction after a certain period to provide evidence of consent to destruction.

The following points should be noted:
(1) The client's informed consent should be obtained before the files and papers may be safely destroyed. The client's documents may be returned, by agreement. However, it may be prudent to retain copies.
(2) Documents that may be relevant to a claim should prima facie be kept for at least the period of long negative prescription if the claim has not previously been disposed of.
(3) Documents containing client's tax or VAT affairs must be retained for at least the relevant statutory subscribed period.
(4) There is no specific date beyond which the obligation to hold a client's own

documents can be said to expire. Deeds or other documents constituting or evidencing rights should be preserved indefinitely but it is virtually impossible to predict when they might turn out to be of value. There is therefore a risk attached to destroying them.

(5)   In storing and insuring files and papers, solicitors are providing clients with a continuing service for which they can properly charge.

(6)   The client might be advised in writing again prior to the file being destroyed, that this is about to happen in accordance with the agreed Terms of Business letter. This is a matter of judgment.

(7)   At the end of each transaction a letter might be sent to the client to advise as to the location of title deeds and/or other important documents or confirmation of what is to happen to these.

(8)   The Master Policy Insurers have clarified that destruction of the file will not affect the insurance position but clients could take issue with the fact that the file had been destroyed if their position was prejudiced.

(9)   Destruction of the client's property without consent could expose the solicitor to liability and damages.

(10)   Solicitors must ensure that sensitive or privileged documents and files are not disposed of in any way which might compromise them.

(11)   Document shredding within the office or by a reliable specialist contractor would appear to be the safest option.

Fire, flood etc

If clients' files and/or documents are destroyed by fire, flood or other disaster, you should inform the Society's Registrar Department of such an incident within a reasonable length of time. You will not be required to list the destroyed files and/or documents, but of course may do so if you wish.

Electronic storage of files

Electronic storage of files on CD or on a server may be a practical way of dealing with storage. Commercial firms provide these services and give the option of destroying paper files after calculating and assessing the risk.

Alistair Sim from Marsh has written an article about the scanning of files and the paperless office, see Journal March 2001, p.42.

Where it is not possible to store files electronically without time limit the Society has issued the following guidance for solicitors:

This is guidance only. The onus rests with the solicitor as to whether or not it is safe to dispose of a file in any particular case and, in considering that, the solicitor should always have regard to the nature of the transaction and the circumstances.

•   Files should only be destroyed under the direct instructions of the manager of the practice unit.

•   Consent of the clients should be obtained before files are destroyed.

•   Information on this should be contained in a Terms of Business letter.

•   Care must be taken to ensure that no important papers such as confirmations, decrees, etc., which should normally be kept separate from other correspondence are in any file being destroyed.

•   So far as financial records are concerned regard should be had to the terms of rule B6 and the relative Guidance.

Suggested timing in different categories

Simple debt collection

On completion, i.e. after the time for appeal has elapsed.

Divorce and consistorial matters

Five years after final completion, e.g. after maintenance, residence and contact orders, etc., have ceased to have effect, or children have reached majority.

Civil court cases

Ten years after completion.

Criminal cases

Murder and other cases involving life imprisonment—the papers should be retained indefinitely.

Solemn cases

Files should be kept for the duration of the sentence if more than three years.

Summary cases

The papers should be retained for three years. A copy of the complaint or indictment and a copy of the legal aid certificate should be kept indefinitely.

Executries

Ten years after completion although an executry may never be complete. Relevant documents and papers might be sent to the Executor for safekeeping since unclaimed legal rights never prescribe.

Continuing trusts

Ten years after the termination of the Trust.

Conveyancing transactions

Purchase

Ten years after completion—although the file may be of use until the property is subsequently disposed of.

Sale

One year later after completion (i.e. after implementing Letter of Obligation; dealing with any funds retained; and after Missives have ceased to have effect).

Company work

Ten years after completion.

Endowment and investment business

Practice units should retain all files in relation to endowment and investment business until such time as the policy in question has matured.

Other correspondence files

Five years after completion of the business.

Financial records

In terms of rule B6 bank reconciliations and vouchers (cheques and invoices) should be retained for 3 years and ledgers/accounts for the balance of the practice year and a further 6 years.

Money laundering—Customer due diligence records

In terms of Regulation 19 of The Money Laundering Regulations 2007 records relating to customer due diligence should be retained for five years. This continues the requirement under the previous Regulations to retain such records for five years.

Note: Certain records need to be kept for different periods to comply with HMRC / Statutory requirements.

IMPORTANT NOTES
- When files, papers and/or documents are destroyed a separate record should be retained of the date of destruction to include a general description of what was destroyed.
- In all cases, important papers such as confirmations, decrees, etc., should be retained indefinitely and should be kept separately from the correspondence. The whereabouts of these documents should be set out in a closing letter once the transaction has been completed so that there is no dubiety about who holds them. Documents containing client's tax and VAT affairs must be retained for at least the relevant statutory periods.

Division B: Lenders' Requests for Solicitor Files

Requests by Lenders for Files where a Solicitor has acted for borrower and lender—March 2012

Background

The issue of requests by lenders or their solicitors for copies of files where the same solicitor had acted for lender and borrower in a purchase was discussed recently at the Professional Practice Committee.

When a borrower defaults on a secured loan, the lender repossesses the property with a view to selling it. If the lender sustains a loss on the sale it may, and often does, look to see whether it has a remedy against the solicitor who acted on its behalf in putting the security in place. Lenders know that solicitors carry Professional Indemnity Insurance against which the lender will hope a sustainable claim can be made. In the majority of cases the lenders are looking to see whether the solicitor has complied with the lenders' contractual instructions, in particular the CML Handbook.

The first step lenders take in looking at a possible claim is to ask for a copy of the solicitor's file. In the context of such a request the crucial question is to establish what the lender is entitled to demand to see, and whether solicitors are contractually obliged to send a copy of their file to a lender in such a situation.

Counsel's opinion

The Committee agreed that Senior Counsel's Opinion should be obtained on this important matter, and that is now available.

In summary, counsel was asked to advise on three separate situations—

a)   Where the terms of neither the CML Handbook nor the BSA Mortgage Instructions apply (the basic case);
b)   Where the CML Handbook (or the BSA Mortgage Instructions) does apply; and
c)   Where the purchaser/borrower client has given consent to disclosure of the whole file to the lender.

Counsel's preliminary comment is that such a request from a lender is undoubtedly a "fishing expedition" which would not be permitted by the Court in a petition brought under section 1 of the Administration of Justice (Scotland) Act,1972.

He then confirmed the Society's position published in the Guideline on Ownership and Destruction of Files that in considering a request from a lender for the contents of the file, the solicitor has to divide up the documents into three categories: documents that are the property of the borrower client, documents that are the property of the lender client and documents which belong to the solicitor himself. The timing of instructions from the lender is relevant, as no documents in the file can belong to the lender until the lender instructs the solicitor, although the lender may have a valid right to sight of some of them.

The initial instructions from the borrower will belong to the solicitor himself as the addressee of the letter or email. So also do private notes and memoranda written for the solicitor's own benefit; not by way of a record of material events, but as preparatory work designed to put the solicitor in a position to provide advice or draft the necessary documents.

In Counsel's view, much of the conveyancing work in the file will be work in which both the lender and the borrower will have a legitimate interest.

The basic case

The lender will own only the correspondence (including e-mail) into which it entered with the solicitor, any documents it sent the solicitor with its instructions, correspondence between third parties and the solicitor directed to the constitution of the standard security, any notes of meetings or telephone conversations on that subject, the drafts of the standard security (as also the drafts and engrossments of any other securities it was to receive to secure its lending) and a copy of the appropriate Land Certificate to show the requisite entry in the Charges Section of that Certificate.

The documents concerned with the conclusion of the contract of sale of the heritage and the transfer of that heritage (in the condition, and with the validity of title thereto, for which the borrower had contracted) are in counsel's view documents owned by the borrower client who has the primary, and greater, interest in them. The lender has a legitimate interest in matters relating to the purchase which may affect its position and about which the lender needs to know for the purpose of protecting its security. It should be informed about such matters by its solicitor, but that that does not entitle the lender to sight of the underlying documentation, which belongs to the borrower.

In counsel's opinion, no implied authority is deemed by the law to exist by which the borrower is held to grant the lender permission to receive, or even to see, all the underlying legal material which belongs to the borrower and the contents of which are confidential to him.

Where the CML Handbook/BSA Mortgage instructions apply

The material provisions are clause 14.3.2 of the C.M.L. Handbook and clause E28 in the B.S.A. Mortgage Instructions, which are in the same terms.

Counsel states that these clauses do not amount to a contractual permission to the solicitor (still less a contractual obligation on him) to disclose the whole file to the lender on the footing that all the documents comprised therein are as much the lender's property as they are the borrower's. In counsel's words "It is critical to the construction of the common clause to bear in mind that it forms part of the contract between the solicitor and the bank, and that the borrower is not party thereto. It cannot, therefore, detract from the property rights of the borrower."

He adds "In short, I do not think that these two provisions widen the rights of the bank to see contents of the solicitor's file which the bank does not already have the right to inspect as their owner. They make no material difference to the position outlined in the basic case."

Where the borrower client has consented to release of the file, or a copy of it

Counsel saw this in a different light. With the exception of those documents in the file which belong to the solicitor, (to which the consent of the borrower client to release does not apply), the solicitor is obliged to allow the bank to see the whole contents of the file. It is a client's prerogative to waive his rights to confidentiality. As such a waiver must be "voluntary, informed and unequivocal" [*Millar v Dickson* 2002 SC(PC) 30], the solicitor has a duty to both clients to advise the borrower about the meaning and possible consequences of the waiver.

Counsel added however "Aside from material in which the lender has a proprietary interest, it can be entitled to see material belonging to another person only with the consent of him to whom the material belongs. Since actual (as opposed to deemed) contractual arrangements are very variable in their terms, on a basis which would be of general application, I can only advise that the solicitor consider carefully the correct construction of any arrangement said to embody or imply such consent in order to judge whether it does in fact convey such a consent, and, if it does, to determine its scope."

Finally on this aspect, the solicitor must check through the whole file to satisfy himself that in exhibiting the contents to the lender he will not disclose material which does not fall within the ambit of that consent.

Document control and file tracking

When a solicitor takes control of files from another solicitor for any reason and in any situation (including but not limited to receipt of files either in implement of a Mandate or where files are taken over from a ceased practice) the solicitor receiving the files should keep a record of all the files received. This should include where the files are stored; such as within the office; electronically; off-site or with a named storage provider. The solicitor who receives a Mandate should comply with the last paragraph under the heading "Receiving Mandates" of the Society's Guidance on Mandates.

Scanning and archiving documents

All outsourcing providers should be made aware of these provisions and required to comply with them.

Electronic storage of files may be a practical way of dealing with storage.

(1)   Scanned documents should preferably be scanned into a native PDF format (100% compatible with the Acrobat standard). Failing that they should certainly be in a format that allows output in PDF. This reflects the Court Technology Forum view that Adobe Acrobat PDF is the de facto cross platform standard.

(2) Subject to compliance with this guidance, retaining a scanned copy having destroyed the original will be deemed compliant with the guidance on the Ownership and Destruction of Documents. It is prudent to keep original documents in a "buffer" following scanning for a period of 28 days prior to destruction so that they might be retrieved within that timescale if there is a problem, error, or client query in the interests of risk management. If an original document has not been scanned it should be retained in paper form in terms of that guidance.

(3) In the event that original documents are to be destroyed (either at point of receipt or at a later date) the intent to do so should be intimated in writing to the client. Tacit consent such as by accepting terms of engagement is acceptable.

(4) The normal duties of care and confidentiality in the storage of clients papers in terms of the rules would, for the avoidance of doubt, apply to scanned archive material. Offsite electronic copies of the scanned archive should form part of the practice unit's contingency planning strategy.

(5) Documents should be scanned before at least one witness and where technology permits would benefit from a digital encrypted signature certifying them a true copy (Adobe Acrobat Professional 8 or later permits this on a batch basis) or alternatively supported by a signed daily logbook certifying authenticity.

(6) Although documents which have only ever existed electronically may be printed and scanned, they should be retained in original format where possible or converted into PDF electronically thus retaining their "Metadata" with its forensic benefits.

(7) Where a mandate is received or clients request a copy of the file the practice unit's obligations in that regard should be covered in terms of engagement. The Society would expect files to be made available within the Society's recommended retention periods. If the terms of engagement are silent on the point, a client is entitled to request the file in either paper or electronic form and any cost of printing from electronic to paper should be borne by the practice unit.

(8) If the practice unit merges with or is taken over by another practice unit care should be taken to ensure systems used to hold scanned documents are compatible and that a paper copy can be printed if required. If new technology supersedes an existing system, scanned material should be transferred to it or a means of reading and printing the material retained.

Terms of Engagement should include clarification on:
(1) Whether the practice unit intends to scan and destroy original documents in accordance with the Society's guidance
(2) The practice unit's policy in relation to when original documents are destroyed; for example, immediately upon receipt, or on closure of the file, or on the expiry of the Society's recommended retention periods.
(3) Advice that there is a risk that in any subsequent dispute or court case electronic copies may not have the same status as original documents potentially reducing their evidential value.
(4) The practice unit's policy in relation to documents submitted by clients which are not to be destroyed.
(5) Whether or not the practice unit keep original documents in a "buffer" for a period prior to destruction.
(6) The practice unit's policy in relation to mandate requests and if necessary costs associated with paper copies being produced.

(7) The practice unit's policy in relation to retention of electronic documentation. For example whether the electronic copies will be retained beyond the Society's recommended retention periods or not.

Electronic communications

1.1 Rule B1.9.1 provides that "You must communicate effectively with your clients and others."

1.2 Rule B1.14.1 provides "You must not knowingly mislead other regulated persons or where you have given your word go back on it".

Practice management

2.1 A written e-mail policy intimated in writing to everyone in the practice unit is good risk management. It should be reviewed regularly and it should link to other relevant policies (for example, equal opportunities, copyright infringement or IT security policies).

2.2 A properly intimated and enforced policy is of particular importance if practice units intend to monitor employee communications.

2.3 E-mails should include the same information as provided on letterhead. For incorporated practice units, the requirements of the Companies Act 2006 and Limited Liability Partnerships (Application of Companies Act 2006) Regulations 2009 should be considered.

2.4 Professional solicitor correspondence is generally confidential and may attract legal professional privilege. Although there is some doubt as to the legal effect of such clauses it is good risk management to include a warning to this effect in e-mails. Automatic inclusion of a warning is recommended.

2.5 Routine monitoring of e-mail to ensure professional standards are being maintained and the advice given is appropriate and adequate is good practice but must be carried out only in accordance with relevant legislation: there is no blanket right for practice units to monitor and intercept emails. The principles of any monitoring should be outlined in the practice unit's email policy. The relevant legislation to consider includes:

- Regulation of Investigatory Powers Act 2000 (RIPA)
- Data Protection Act 1998 (DPA)
- the Telecommunications (Lawful Business Practice) (Interception of Communications) Regulations 2000 (LBP Regulations)

2.6 If private e-mails may be intercepted and read, the practice unit's email policy should ensure the freely given consent of staff. Practice units should consider the implications of consent being withdrawn. It is possible to monitor emails without consent but only provided the requirements of the LBP Regulations (and, in particular, Reg. 3(2)) are met. The Information Commissioner also publishes useful guidance on DPA aspects of workplace monitoring, including email monitoring, within the Employment Practices Code available for download on the ICO's website *www.ico.gov.uk*.

Professional undertakings and contracts

3.0 Professional undertakings may be given by unsecured e-mail but practice units should be cautious when accepting them: it is not difficult to fake both content and sender. The act of typing a name into an electronic document, including an e-mail, may of itself be a form of electronic signature, depending on the particular circumstances. The use of digital signatures may also provide assurance for the recipient of the authenticity of e-mail. If encryption is widely adopted it might bring with it the additional benefit of improved confidentiality.

3.1 Practice units receiving a professional undertaking by e-mail should check that the context provides reasonable assurance of its authenticity and should consider the need for a check by telephone or fax that it came from its purported sender.

3.2 Although some special rules apply to those contracts which require to be in writing, in general a contract may be formed by email or other electronic means. The same risks and considerations of intention, clarity and authority (actual or ostensible) therefore apply to email as to any other form of communication and firms should seek wherever possible to mitigate these risks. Accordingly care should be taken, possibly by the inclusion of a standard disclaimer to the effect that e-mails are not contractual except perhaps where accompanied by a digitally encrypted signature. The law in this area is not mature and the best advice would appear to be to minimise any risk of misunderstanding.

3.3 There is a duty on a solicitor to follow up a fax or email (unless the email contains a digital signature creating a binding contract) of a contractual document with the original as soon as possible. If the solicitor is instructed by the client not to send the hard copy that fact must be communicated to the other solicitor immediately and the first solicitor must withdraw from acting if the client cannot be persuaded to withdraw such instructions. Furthermore, if a solicitor is not sure if a contractual document can be sent, a fax or email should not be sent of it. It has been held in the Sheriff Court that a bargain was concluded where the final Missive was communicated by fax.

Statutory Obligations

4.0 Solicitors will generally be required to notify as data controllers under the DPA and comply with the relevant regulation. It is prudent to appoint a specific person within the practice unit to manage this.

4.1 Practice units should also note that the DPA requires data controllers to take appropriate steps to secure personal data. Most unencrypted e-mail is vulnerable to unauthorised access and alteration as it passes over the Internet.

4.2 The Regulation of Investigatory Powers Act 2000 which applies to the whole of the UK creates several offences including interception of a communication in the course of its transmission without lawful authority. The Regulation of Investigatory Powers (Scotland) Act 2000 should also be considered. The offences potentially apply to a practice unit's monitoring and recording of e-mail communications sent and received by staff. The LBP Regulations set out various circumstances in which monitoring and recording of e-mail for business related purposes is deemed to have lawful authority. Monitoring and recording e-mail will also generally involve the processing of personal data under the DPA.

4.3 Article 8 of the European Convention on Human Rights (ECHR) provides that "everyone has the right to respect for his private and family life, his home and his correspondence". The right to privacy extends to the workplace. Whilst practice units are not public authorities and therefore the Human Rights Act 1998 does not apply to them directly, the Courts are increasingly taking human rights cases into account in their decisions. Employment tribunals considering any claim made by a disgruntled employee are required to have regard to the Articles of the ECHR in the course of their decision making.

4.4 Directive 2000/31/EC (the E-Commerce Directive) applies to solicitors' services provided electronically from or within the EU, except for litigation and notarial work. It also applies to electronic advertising, including websites.

Broadly:

(a) The Society's rules will apply to the exclusion of other professional rules if a practice unit in the UK provides electronic services (even an e-mail sent from a lap-top while a solicitor is on a visit to France).

(b) If a solicitor based at an office in an EU state other than the UK provides electronic services (even an e-mail sent from a lap-top while a solicitor is on a visit to London) the professional rules of that EU state will apply, to the exclusion of the other professional rules.

(c) solicitors providing services electronically or advertising electronically must provide customers with certain information:

　　(i) name, address, e-mail address and VAT number;
　　(ii) where price is referred to, clear indications of price;
　　(iii) professional details, as follows:
　　　　• If the office is in the UK, the client must be told that the service is provided by Scottish solicitors, regulated by the Society, and how to access the Society's rules. This can be done by providing a link to *www.lawscot.org.uk*.
　　　　• If the solicitor is based at an office in another EU state, the client must be told that the service is provided by a Scottish

solicitor, registered with (for example) the Athens Bar, and how to access the rules of that Bar. It is recommended that all e-mails providing electronic services (as opposed to merely communicating by email) include this information or a link to it.

4.5 If electronic trading is carried out, (very unlikely in the present context) suppliers must provide a description of:

(i)   the technical steps required to enter into the contract;

(ii)   how end users may correct any inputting errors; and

(iii) how end users can access and store the terms of the contract made.

Good practice

5.0 E-mail presents new problems because it can arrive unseen by other members of staff. Arrangements should be made to check incoming e-mails where the recipient may be absent. Automated "out of office" responses should be used where appropriate.

5.1 Most practice units print e-mails and file a copy in their paper records, although by doing so, evidence contained in the email header is lost. The header includes a trail of the computers from which the email was sent, through which it has been routed, times and other information. This information would be useful evidence in the event of a dispute. Usually a paper print contains none of these details. Consideration should be given to electronic archiving and storage of significant and substantive e-mails (including e-mails that are subject to statutory retention periods) to retain this forensic evidence.

5.2 Where some correspondence about a matter is stored electronically and the rest is on paper, practice units should ensure that none of the material will be overlooked if responsibility for a matter is transferred (perhaps temporarily). Practice units should also be confident that they know what information their systems record. If not, an audit may be appropriate.

5.3 Practice units should note the risk of filtering out legitimate client correspondence using spam filters. If practice units use spam filters they should warn clients not to assume that every e-mail will be received. They should explain that important communications should always be followed up with a phone call, fax or printed copy by post.

5.4 Practice units who are themselves considering e-mail marketing campaigns should familiarise themselves with the requirements of the law on the matter and also consider relevant professional rules of conduct. Electronic marketing includes not only email but also text messages, faxes and other electronic means of communication. Usually express consent must be obtained from the recipient, although there can be limited exemptions for existing clients. The relevant legislation includes the Privacy and Electronic Communications (EC Directive) Regulations 2003 (as amended) and useful guidance on the practical implications of these Regulations and the DPA on electronic marketing may be found on the Information Commissioner's website *www.ico.gov.uk.*

5.5 Care should be taken using "Reply to All" given that this will generally include Bcc (Blind Courtesy Copy) parties who you cannot identify and who you or your client may not wish to see your response.

Charging for lending or delivering files, titles and other papers

Where a solicitor is asked to lend titles or other documents to another solicitor a fee may properly be charged for such lending to cover both the delivery and return of the documents. If more than three documents are lent, a fee for an inventory may properly be charged.

Delivering documents in response to client's mandate

Where files or documents are delivered by one solicitor to another in accordance with the client's written instructions or mandate, a fee may properly be charged including a fee for an inventory if more than three documents are delivered. No charge should be made for delivering such papers direct to the client or former client, but any outlay incurred in posting or delivering by courier may properly be recovered from the client or former client. As the fee is payable for delivering material, it is not chargeable before the material is delivered and therefore any attempt to exercise a lien over the material before it is delivered in respect of this fee would be improper. The fee is chargeable to the client, not to the new practice unit.

Amount of fee which may be charged

The Society is not in a position to give guidance on the amount of fee which may be charged in either of the above situations, but in terms of rule B1.11, the fees charged shall be fair and reasonable.

It should be noted that where the Council are satisfied that a solicitor has issued an account for fees and outlays of an amount which is grossly excessive, whether or not the account has been paid, the Council may, in terms of Section 39A of the Solicitors (Scotland) 1980, withdraw the solicitor's practising certificate but only after enquiry and after giving the solicitor an opportunity of being heard. What is grossly excessive is a matter to be determined by the Auditor of the Court of Session at taxation.

Division C: Fees

Form of Business Accounts and Taxation

Notes:
1. This guidance does *not* apply to the taxation of solicitors' accounts remitted to the Auditor of the Court of Session in terms of Rule 42.7 of the Rules of the Court of Session or to a Sheriff Court Auditor in terms of the Act of Sederunt (Solicitor and Client Accounts in the Sheriff Court) 1992 (SI 1992 No 1434);
2. This guidance is shortly to be amended—see the related Alert.

1. Business accounts—preparation and presentation

(a) The form in which a solicitor presents a business account is a matter for the solicitor's personal preference but if the person liable to pay requires details, the solicitor must give a narrative or summary sufficient to indicate the nature and the extent of the work done. If a breakdown is requested the solicitor should give such information as can readily be derived from the records, such as the total recorded time spent, the number and length of meetings, the number of letters and of telephone calls. No charge may be made for preparing the note of fee or for the provision of such information. However if having been given such information the party paying insists on a fully itemised account, the cost of preparing that may be charged to them.

(b)   A solicitor may submit his file to a Sheriff Court Auditor or a law accountant for assessment of the fee either before or after the note of fee is issued, but it is stressed that a unilateral reference of this kind does not constitute a taxation. Such an assessment of a fee must never be represented as a taxation; as having any official status; or as being final and binding. The fee for such a reference is not chargeable to the party paying unless that has been included in the terms of business intimated to the client at the outset. If a note of fee which has been assessed requires to be taxed (see 2 below), it should be taxed by a different Auditor from the one who originally assessed it.

Where a solicitor acts:
- as an administrator of a client's funds under a power of attorney where the granter is incapable; or
- in a representative capacity, e.g. a sole executor

he may consider having a fee note prepared or the file assessed by an Auditor of Court or independently assessed.

2.   Joint remit for taxation

A solicitor and client may agree that the solicitor's fee should be taxed by an Auditor of Court in advance of a note of fee being issued. They should sign a joint remit to the Auditor in the following form:

(place) (date). I, AB (client) and we, Messrs E & F, Solicitors, hereby request the Auditor of the (Sheriff Court of .... /Court of Session) to tax the remuneration due and payable to the Solicitors for their whole work and responsibility in connection with (matter) and agree that the Auditor's decision on matters of taxation will be final and binding. [In executry add—The Auditor's fee for carrying out the taxation will be payable out of the estate before distribution to residuary beneficiaries]

Signed: AB, E & F

(This precise wording however is not essential. All the Auditor requires is to be satisfied that both parties accept that the taxation will be binding. Any reasonable written record of such an agreement will be sufficient for the Auditor.)

A formal diet of taxation will not usually be required in these cases. Note that the client is entitled to refer a complaint of inadequate service to the Scottish Legal Complaints Commission irrespective of the outcome of the taxation.

3.   Taxation of disputed business accounts

(a)   If an account continues to be disputed, the solicitor must inform the paying party of the availability of taxation by the Auditor of the Court of Session or by a Sheriff Court Auditor and of the procedure involved. If the payer requests a taxation without a fully itemised account, the solicitor may have such an account prepared at his own expense. That full account may be submitted for taxation even if it is for a greater amount than the original note of fee.

(b)   A solicitor who is a co-executor with an unqualified person must not make a unilateral reference to an Auditor for taxation. Such a reference needs the concurrence of the other executor.

(c)   When the party paying, whether client or third party, requires that the solicitor's account be taxed, the solicitor cannot refuse to agree to taxation unless the solicitor and client have entered into a written fee charging agreement in which the actual fee has been agreed, as opposed to the basis on which the fee is to be charged. Failure to agree to taxation may be treated as unsatisfactory conduct.

(d) The solicitor and client should agree which Auditor will tax the account, failing which the account should be taxed by the Auditor of the Court of Session.

(e) The solicitor must then forthwith submit the file and all relevant information including the note of fee or detailed account to the Auditor. The Auditor will establish whether the client wishes to proceed by way of oral or written representations. In most cases there will be a diet of taxation which, in a taxation by a Sheriff Court Auditor, must be intimated to the client by the solicitor.

Evidence of such intimation, which may be by ordinary first class post, may be required if the client does not appear at the diet. In a taxation before the Auditor of the Court of Session the diet will be intimated to parties by the Auditor. In either case both parties will be entitled to present oral submissions at the diet, but if either of the parties wishes to make written submissions, the auditor will ensure that each party is fully aware of the other's representations.

(f) The Auditor's decision on matters of taxation will be final and binding. However the client is entitled to refer a complaint of inadequate service to the Scottish Legal Complaints Commission irrespective of the outcome of the taxation.

4. Taxation of other business accounts

Taxation is necessary by law and in practice in certain circumstances. The accounts of a solicitor acting for:

- an administrator of a company under the Insolvency Acts;
- a liquidator appointed by the court;
- a creditors' voluntary liquidator;
- a trustee in bankruptcy;
- a judicial factor, guardian or curator

must be taxed by an Auditor of Court.

5. Expenses of taxation

The Auditor will charge a fee for the taxation. It will usually be 4 per cent of the amount of the account as presented for taxation and may attract VAT.

In the case of disputed business accounts, any award of expenses of the taxation—not only the Auditor's fee (which may be apportioned between the solicitor and the client) but also the time and expenses of parties attending—is wholly within the discretion of the Auditor. If the matter is settled within the seven days preceding the diet of taxation the Auditor may still charge a proportion of his fee, not exceeding 50%, at his discretion.

[1]Division D: Executry and Trust Accounting

Following consideration of the propriety of a solicitor seeking discharges from beneficiaries in relation to their administration of an Executry or a Trust the Professional Practice (Rules and Waivers) sub-committee has approved the following Guidance.

---

[1] In view of correspondence received following publication of this Guidance, the whole matter will be reviewed again by the Professional Practice (Rules & Waivers) sub-committee. In the meantime this Guidance is suspended and there is no requirement to follow it from the date of its issue until further notice.

It is entirely appropriate and prudent for an Executor or Trustee and their solicitor to send a final accounting to beneficiaries setting out the extent of the beneficiaries' interest and to seek approval of such accounting by the beneficiaries before embarking on a final distribution and settlement.

It is inappropriate however to go beyond an approval of the accounting and require such beneficiaries to (1) approve the whole actings of the Executor/Trustee and their solicitor; (2) discharge the Executor/Trustee and their solicitor from all claims competent to the beneficiaries against the Executor/Trustee and their solicitor; and (3) require that the beneficiaries free and relieve the Executor/Trustee and their solicitor from and against all claims and demands which could be made against them in connection with their intromissions with the Estate/Trust.

Once an Executor/Trustee completes the administration of an Executry/ Trust their powers and duties automatically terminate. If however there remains Estate to be administered or Trust purposes to be fulfilled their powers and duties continue and it is not appropriate that these are prematurely discharged. Nor is it appropriate that the beneficiaries indemnify the Executor/Trustee or their solicitor against any negligent administration.

Such approvals, discharges and indemnifications will relate to duties and functions about which the beneficiaries are unlikely to have any detailed knowledge or understanding.

If the solicitors have not acted for the beneficiaries, applications for such approvals, discharges and indemnifications would require a written warning under Rule B2.1.7. Even if it is recommended to such beneficiaries that they obtain independent legal advice regarding the request for such approvals, discharges and indemnifications it is inappropriate to expect beneficiaries to incur the additional expense of obtaining such independent legal advice to ensure that they are properly informed before signing.

To delay making settlement to a beneficiary pending receipt of such an approval, discharge or indemnification may well render the solicitor vulnerable to a complaint of inadequate professional service.

Division E: Guidance on Referral of Clients for Financial Advice

The Retail Distribution Review ("RDR") of the Financial Conduct Authority ("FCA") has new definitions for financial advisers. Advisers will broadly either be "independent" or "restricted". To come within the former category such an adviser will have to provide advice on the whole of the financial services market. Other advisers will be "restricted" advisers.

The FCA definition of "independent" is different from the definition used in the Society's Standard of Conduct which provides:

"You must give independent advice free from external influences or personal interests which are inconsistent with these standards. It is your duty not to allow your independence to be impaired irrespective of the nature of the matter in which you are acting."

The Society envisages two common circumstances which may apply to a practice which refers clients for financial advice to existing advisers under the RDR and these are—

1.   A practice continues to refer clients to an adviser which meets the new FCA definition of "independent". No changes in client arrangements are needed

2.   A practice refers clients to an existing adviser which was "independent" (under the pre-RDR regime) but the adviser is "restricted" under the RDR regime. In such circumstances a practice need take no further action provided the adviser continues to be FCA authorised and there is no change to the services provided by the adviser. It would only be where such a practice has concerns about the adviser following its re-classification post RDR that further examination of the adviser's suitability for the client should be considered.

Division F: Outsourcing

General statement on "outsourcing"

The Society has seen an increase in the use of outsourcing by the profession and as a result has decided to generate this General Statement and additional Advice and Assistance.

Members are reminded of the need to comply with all relevant legislation, including Data Protection legislation and EU Anti-Competition legislation.

Outsourcing can also be referred to as sub-contracting and falls into two categories or types: outsourcing of

(a)   business operational functions such as HR, payroll and Cashroom and

(b)   aspects of legal service provision such as legal research and document production.

It is essential for members to remember that, whoever undertakes these functions, the obligation to meet regulatory requirements and professional rules continues to rest with them as members of the Society. In addition, it is not permissible to outsource reserved matters unless to another entity regulated by the Society.

As a result, contractual arrangements with outsourced providers should ensure that they are required to comply with the Practice Rules.

In addition, it is essential to ensure that the Society continues to have access to all data, information and documents required for all regulatory inspection and compliance. This includes access to confidential passwords and user names.

Section F: Guidance Relating to Particular Types of Work

Division A: Criminal Work

The Code of Conduct for Criminal Work

The following Code contains a statement of good practice for those solicitors conducting criminal work. It does not have the status of a Practice Rule but may be referred to for guidance in assessing whether a solicitor's conduct meets the standard required of a member of the profession.

Article 1—Seeking business

A solicitor shall seek or accept only those instructions which emanate from the client properly given and should not accept instructions given as a result of an inducement or subject to any improper constraint or condition.

Guidance re Article 1

This statement of good practice is a reminder that a solicitor is an officer of the court and as such has obligations and duties to the Court. It is a reminder that a solicitor should always act properly when dealing with criminal law work.

It is essential that a solicitor should at all times remain independent of the client and that the solicitor should be free to give appropriate legal advice. Accordingly no instructions should be accepted in circumstances where it could be alleged that inducements have been offered in exchange for instructions. No instructions should be accepted in circumstances where those instructions are subject for whatever reason to restrictions or constraints which compromise the solicitor's freedom to give appropriate independent legal advice. It follows that a client should not be considered as a "friend" and that the solicitor must always remain "at arm's length"' from the client. This will ensure that both the client and the court can be confident that the advice tendered by the solicitor is impartial and independent.

A solicitor should accept instructions only from the client directly and not from a third party on behalf of the client. There may be circumstances in which a solicitor is asked by the family or a friend of the accused person to visit the accused in custody. It is the duty of every solicitor to check with the police station to ascertain if the person in custody has requested another solicitor or the duty solicitor. If the person in custody has indeed requested the services of another solicitor or the duty solicitor, then the solicitor contacted by the family or friend may not visit the police station. Moreover, instructions must come directly from the person detained and not by virtue of the police arranging for a specific solicitor to be contacted who is unknown to and has not been requested by the accused. Any instructions given as a result of an inducement by a third party on the solicitor's behalf must not be accepted. A solicitor will be deemed to be strictly liable for the actions of third parties who contact potential clients and any third party who contacts potential clients shall be deemed to have acted on the instructions of the solicitor whether or not the solicitor is instructed as a result of the third party's approach. If the client's co-accused is instructing a solicitor contact must be made through that solicitor. All reasonable steps must be taken to ascertain the identity of the co-accused's solicitor.

Solicitors are reminded of the terms of Section 31 of The Legal Aid (Scotland) Act 1986. Any contract of agency between a solicitor and a client which is based upon any inducement may be illegal and may be subject to action in the criminal or civil courts. Such contracts may also form the basis of a complaint of professional misconduct and may lead to disqualification in terms of Section 31.

Article 2—Conflict of interest
A solicitor should not accept instructions from more than one accused in the same matter.

Guidance re Article 2
This statement reflects the awareness which solicitors have always had of the obvious potential conflict of interest that will arise when instructions are accepted from more than one accused person in the same case, even though that conflict may not arise and the defence is common to all accused. Nevertheless, solicitors should not place themselves in the position whereby they may obtain information confidential to the defence of one accused which at the same time may be detrimental to the defence of another. Accordingly when it becomes apparent to the solicitor that he has received instructions from two or more parties in the same case a solicitor may accept instructions from one of the accused and any others must be told immediately that separate representation must be sought.

Solicitors are also reminded that great care must be taken in situations where one of the solicitor's clients gives evidence against another client of that solicitor. The client, who is acting as a witness, is entitled to have his confidentiality respected as against the interests of the accused. In some situations, such as where the accused is incriminating or attacking the character of the client, who is a witness, there will be a conflict of interest and the solicitor should not act.

A solicitor should not apply for a Legal Aid Certificate for more than one accused person in any matter. However, a duty solicitor should responsibly carry out his duties under the Legal Aid scheme and be aware of the terms of this statement.

A solicitor may suggest that an accused seeks representation from a particular solicitor but that alternative solicitor must be based within the same jurisdiction as the accused. However the choice of a solicitor always lies with the accused person and a solicitor must always ask an accused if he wishes a particular solicitor to be instructed before a recommendation can be made.

Article 3—Preparation and conduct of criminal cases
A solicitor is under a duty to prepare and conduct criminal cases by carrying out work which is actually and reasonably necessary and having due regard to economy.

Guidance re Article 3
It is essential at each stage of the conduct of a criminal case that the necessary preparation is undertaken timeously. It is essential that a solicitor should use his best endeavours to discover all relevant information and evidence relating both to the Crown case and any substantive case for the defence. The solicitor must remember that his primary duties are to the client and the court and ensure that the case is properly prepared and there is no prejudice to the client.

Every solicitor should carry out these duties in a responsible and professional manner. With these duties uppermost in mind, the solicitor must not view criminal cases only as a means of financial enrichment. For the purposes of cases which are legally aided, this statement is declaratory of Regulation 7(1) of the Criminal Legal Aid (Scotland) (Fees) Regulations 1989. Regulation 7(1) states that "subject to the provisions of Regulations 4, 5, 6 and 9 and paragraph (2) of this Regulation, a solicitor shall be allowed such amount of fees as shall be determined to be reasonable remuneration for work actually and reasonably done, and travel and waiting time actually and reasonably undertaken or incurred, due regard being had to economy".

When requested, files and information should be provided to the Scottish Legal Aid Board.

Abuse of the Legal Aid system may be fraudulent and may be considered as professional misconduct and may lead to disqualification under Section 31 of the Legal Aid (Scotland) Act 1986.

Any complaints can be dealt with in terms of Section 31 of the Legal Aid (Scotland) Act 1986.

Article 4—Identification of solicitors
A solicitor who seeks access to any party who is in custody should have in his possession a form of identification provided by the Law Society of Scotland and should exhibit this upon request.

Guidance re Article 4
This statement is designed to prohibit unqualified employees or individuals from attending meetings with persons in custody. It will ensure not only that impersonation of solicitors or trainees is made more difficult but also that only those persons qualified to provide independent legal advice are granted access. Acceptable forms of confirmation of identity include the production of a valid identification card issued by the Law Society of Scotland; of a valid CCBE card provided by the Law Society of Scotland or of a valid and current practising certificate together with a form of visual identification.

Article 5—Custody visits
Only a solicitor or trainee solicitor who has been instructed to do so may visit the client in custody.

Guidance re Article 5
This Statement restricts access to a person in custody in a police office, prison and cell area.

There are occasions when a solicitor has taken instructions from the family or friend of an accused and has then visited a person in custody. It is the duty of every solicitor to check with the police station to ascertain if the person in custody has requested another solicitor or duty solicitor. If the person in custody has indeed requested the services of another solicitor or the duty solicitor, then the solicitor contacted by the family or friend may not visit the police station.

Moreover, instructions must come directly from the person detained and not by virtue of the police arranging for a specific solicitor to be contacted who is unknown to and has not been requested by the accused.

Article 6—Property to persons in custody

A business card and legal documents should be the only items given by a solicitor to a person in custody.

Guidance re Article 6

It has become apparent that certain solicitors have attended to the so called "needs" of their clients in custody by providing them with cigarettes, newspapers, meals, access to the solicitor's mobile phone and money. Actings of this sort may be a contravention of Section 41(1) of the Prisons (Scotland) Act 1989 which forbids certain forms of donation. In addition, this statement shall include the giving to family or friends of the person in custody any items for onward transmission.

Article 7—Legal aid mandates

All legal aid mandates requesting the transfer of papers and legal aid relating to a criminal matter shall be completed and executed by the assisted person in the form agreed by the Scottish Legal Aid Board and the Law Society of Scotland.

Guidance re Article 7

The matter is governed by the Criminal Legal Aid (Scotland) Regulations 1996, paragraph 17(3), which states "where an assisted person desires that a solicitor, other than the solicitor presently nominated by him shall act for him, he shall apply to the Board for authority to nominate another specified solicitor to act for him and shall inform the Board of the reason for his application; and the Board, if it is satisfied that there is good reason for the application, may grant the application".

It seems clear from a plain construction of this Regulation that changes of agency where the client is legally aided in a criminal case can only take place if the Board gives the client authority to nominate another specified solicitor. Until the Board gives its authority the client cannot instruct another solicitor unless he wishes to do so without the benefit of legal aid, which fact should be notified to the Board.

Therefore the chronology of transfers of agency in criminal cases should be (1) the client approaches his proposed new solicitor to ascertain if he is willing to act; (2) client applies to Board for authority to transfer the agency; (3) Board grants authority; (4) client instructs new solicitor; (5) new solicitor serves mandate on previous solicitor.

The Board's authority to transfer must ante-date any mandate.

The Statement would solve many issues including inducements to transfer agency and "mandate wars". Adoption of this interpretation would of course mean that legally aided clients and fee paying clients will not be treated precisely equally. However, that objection has to be seen in the light of the need to comply with the Regulations which effectively impose a statutory suspensive condition on any mandate and the requirement that solicitors will require to inform a transferring client that instructions cannot be accepted until the Regulations are complied with. Any complaints about conduct under this section can be dealt with in terms of section 31 of the Legal Aid (Scotland) Act 1986.

Article 8—Consultation with clients at liberty

A solicitor should not consult with a client, who is at liberty unless the consultation takes place in (1) the solicitor's office; (2) a court; (3) a hospital;

or (4) the locus; a solicitor may exceptionally attend the house of a client who is unable to attend the solicitor's office due to illness.

Guidance re Article 8

The solicitor should not visit a client within his home unless it is impossible for the client to attend the offices of the solicitor through ill health.

A solicitor leaves himself open to various allegations and indeed risks if he should attend at the home of a client. All solicitors should be aware that there is a risk. For example a solicitor could be within a house which contains drugs or stolen goods.

It will not always be possible to consult with an accused within a solicitor's own office. However, such consultations should take place within a similar office environment, such as the interview rooms within a Court building. However, it is accepted that there will be occasions when it is not possible or appropriate to interview a client within an office environment, for example when the client is in hospital. The onus is on a solicitor to justify an interview at any other place if called upon to do so. The geography and rural nature of Scotland will be taken into account.

Article 9—Expenses

No payments in money or kind should be made to an accused person, a member of the accused person's family or potential witnesses.

Guidance re Article 9

The only payments which a solicitor is entitled to make to an accused person, to members of his family or to witnesses are the legitimate expenses paid to witnesses who were cited to appear at Court on behalf of the defence. It is appropriate for a solicitor to advance travel vouchers to a witness who shall be travelling a significant distance. Any payment of expenses made by a solicitor should be properly recorded and vouched.

Article 10—Defence witnesses

Only those witnesses relevant to a case should be cited to attend court.

Guidance re Article 10

Ideally, a witness should be interviewed before citation. A solicitor must take all reasonable steps to obtain directly from a witness the potential evidence in a case. It is accepted that this is not always possible and indeed a solicitor could leave himself open to criticism and complaint if he should not cite a witness when he has been specifically instructed to do so by an accused person. Nevertheless, a solicitor must at all times be in a position to justify the citation of all witnesses in a case.

Defence witnesses should be cited sufficiently far in advance of the Trial Diet to give them adequate warning of the requirement to attend court. Where possible, witnesses should be cited prior to the Intermediate Diet in order to ascertain at that stage whether there is any difficulty about the defence witnesses' attendance at court for the Trial Diet. Common courtesy demands that defence witnesses should be given adequate notice of their requirement to attend court as witnesses.

In providing a citation, a solicitor should advise the witness of their right to claim legitimate expenses. These include travelling to and from Court. Neither witnesses nor indeed an accused person should be transported to Court by a solicitor.

In recent times it has been suggested that some persons with no involvement in a case have been cited to attend court only to provide these persons with expenses. Additionally, it has been asserted that parties have been brought to Court from custody, who have no relevance whatsoever to the case but who are cited simply to allow them to meet other prisoners at Court. Such actions cannot be tolerated.

Solicitors should make a point of speaking to defence witnesses at court in order, as a matter of courtesy, to advise them of the court procedure and the likely timetabling for the case in respect of which they have been cited. Solicitors should advise their clients that they as professional persons ultimately take the decision as to which defence witnesses require to be cited. Solicitors are the judges of whether or not a particular witness's evidence is relevant. In addition, solicitors should ensure that legitimate expenses claimed by defence witnesses are paid promptly. Witnesses of course require to be advised that any claim for expenses require to be properly vouched. A solicitor should keep a contemporaneous record of his actings and financial dealings in terms of this Code and provide this if so requested by the Law Society of Scotland.

Article 11—Documents and materials

11.1 A solicitor will receive in the course of defence work the documents, materials or recordings related to the cases in which he is instructed. These documents, materials and recordings will include those disclosed to the solicitor by the Crown Office and Procurator Fiscal Service ("COPFS"). A solicitor should not give a client, or any other third party, even on a temporary basis, copies of any documents, materials or recordings. There may be exceptional circumstances justifying a departure from this rule in a particular case and if the solicitor believes that such exceptional circumstances exist, he must refer the matter to the Professional Practice Department of the Law Society of Scotland for guidance. If items are to be given to the client or third party, the solicitor must explain that the items must be retained securely by them; must be kept confidential; must not be revealed to others, let alone released to others; must not be copied and must be returned to the solicitor by a fixed date which must be as soon as possible having regard to the circumstances justifying giving the items to the client in the first place.

11.2 Some documents, materials or recordings may be of a sensitive nature and should never be given to the client. These documents should only be shown to the client in circumstances where the solicitor is present and it is possible to exercise adequate supervision to prevent the client retaining possession of the material or making a copy of it. Before showing the client the material, the solicitor should ensure that he has redacted the material to obscure any information tending to identify the home address or contact details of a witness. Some examples of sensitive material or documents are listed below—

    (a) A precognition or statement of a victim of a sexual offence;

    (b) A photograph or pseudo photograph of any such victim or a deceased victim;

    (c) A medical or other report or statement relating to the physical or mental condition of any such victim or a deceased victim;

    (d) Any document, other than a document served on the client by the Crown or by a co-accused, containing the addresses or telephone numbers of witnesses or their relatives/friends or information from which their addresses and telephone numbers can be deduced;

    (e) Any video or audio recording of a statement made by a vulnerable witness; and

    (f) Any record in relation to previous convictions or outstanding charges of complainers or witnesses.

11.3 In the event of a solicitor ceasing to act on behalf of a client, that client being unrepresented, any documents, materials or recordings which had been disclosed should be returned to the COPFS. If there is a transfer of agency, the documents, materials or recordings should be transferred on receipt of a mandate to the new solicitor. When a case has been concluded, a solicitor holding material disclosed by the COPFS should arrange for the material to be stored securely or to be disposed of as confidential waste.

Guidance re Article 11

From time to time the Society has been asked to give its views of the practice of giving to accused persons, or other third parties, copies of the precognitions or statements of witnesses and of other documents associated with the accused's case. This is particularly relevant in view of the solicitor's obligations in relation to the material received from the COPFS under disclosure arrangements which have been put in place following the judgements of the Judicial Committee of the Privy Council in the cases of *Holland v HM Advocate*, 2005 S.L.T. 563 and *Sinclair v HM Advocate*, 2005 S.L.T. 513.

In the vast majority of criminal cases, the accused is in receipt of legal aid and it has been judicially declared that the accused has no proprietorial claim on the case papers. These belong to the solicitor.

The view of the Society is that solicitors should not give copies of precognitions, statements, documents or recordings to the accused or third parties unless there are exceptional circumstances justifying a departure from this general practice. Exceptional circumstances might include a case of particular complexity, necessitating giving the accused copies of documents to allow proper preparation. A fraud case, for instance, where documents were originally in the possession of the accused, might be such an exception. Another example would be a request from an appropriate investigative or statutory body, such as the Law Society of Scotland, the Scottish Criminal Cases Review Commission or the Scottish Legal Aid Board. Where a solicitor believes that there are exceptional circumstances, he must refer the matter to the Society's Professional Practice Department for guidance. If the solicitor does give access to copies of documents, materials or recordings, he must ensure that a written record is kept of the reason for the documents, materials or recordings being given to the client or third party and of the fact that the recipient has been advised of the terms of the Code and the conditions of possession.

Information contained in the documents, materials or recordings which is sensitive, should only ever be used or disclosed to others for the limited purpose of the preparation and conduct of the proceedings. This is designed to ensure that a solicitor can disclose sufficient information to enable proper preparation to take place, for example, by disclosing to an expert witness but to reinforce the clear rule that such material should not be made available to persons unconnected with the case.

The Code makes it clear that sensitive material should never be disclosed. There are unfortunate worrying examples of problems which can arise if the guidance is not observed, for example, copies of witness statements could be circulated in the public domain leading to witnesses being intimidated. Statements of victims of sexual crimes could be used as a form of pornography within prison. An extract from a firearms register, complete with addresses and type of weapons, has already been circulated in a prison.

Any sensitive material held by the solicitor should be retained securely and, if it has been given to the solicitor on condition that it is returned, the solicitor should return it to the issuing authority in accordance with that undertaking, as soon as it is no longer required by the solicitor.

Where a solicitor ceases to act and another solicitor takes over acting, the solicitor should ensure security and confidentiality of the material concerned and either return the documents and materials to the COPFS or transfer them to the incoming solicitor.

Solicitors are reminded that in receiving documentation, material or recordings from the COPFS, or other third parties, that they are accepting an implied undertaking to comply with the terms of this Article.

Article 12—Retention of papers

12.1   In general terms, the solicitor should be aware of the general guidance on retention and destruction of papers as issued from time to time by the Law Society of Scotland.

12.2   In murder cases and other cases involving life imprisonment, the papers should be retained indefinitely.

12.3   In other Solemn and in any Summary case, the papers should be retained for 3 years. As a general rule, a solicitor might regard it as good practice in every case to retain indefinitely a copy of the Complaint or Indictment and a copy of the Legal Aid Certificate.

Guidance re Article 12

Another issue associated with case papers is the question of the length of time such papers should be retained once a case has been concluded and how such papers should ultimately be destroyed if at all.

The options for retention are—
(1)   indefinitely;
(2)   destruction after a fixed period;
(3)   destruction at the discretion of the solicitor; or
(4)   a combination of the above, depending on the nature of the case and the likelihood or risk that reference to the original case papers will be necessary.

The Society is conscious of the consequences of recommending retention of too many papers for too long, having regard to the difficulties of office storage and the expense of "off-site" storage. On the other hand, certain types of cases involve offences of such gravity, complexity or high public profile, that the possibility of issues arising in future years is a real one. Solicitors should be aware of the existence of the Scottish Criminal Cases Review Commission and for the need to retain files where solicitors believe that there is a possibility that it will be of future importance to the client. Other offences may have sentence implications in the short to mid-term: e.g. petitions for restoration of a driving licence after disqualification; reimposing the unexpired portion of a sentence after re-offending. Solemn cases might be expected to throw up more difficulties than Summary. In legally aided cases, solicitors are reminded that in terms of the Code of Practice in relation to Criminal Legal Assistance, issued by the Scottish Legal Aid Board, records shall be maintained and accessible for a period of 3 years from the date of payment of the relevant account by the Board.

Destruction of case papers

Solicitors should note that when case papers are being destroyed, it is vital that this is done in a comprehensive, secure and confidential way. If the solicitor does not destroy the papers personally, then they should be destroyed by a suitably qualified commercial firm.

Article 13—Precognition of Witnesses

When carrying out precognition of witnesses, whether personally, through directly employed staff, or through external precognition agents, the nominated solicitor or instructing solicitor has responsibility for the manner in which contact is made with the witnesses and the manner in which the witnesses are actually precognosced. In particular, it is the duty of the solicitor to ensure that any matters associated with the witness of which he is aware which would affect the taking of the precognition or the mode of contact, such as age, disability or other vulnerable status, are taken into account by him and communicated to any precognition agent.

Guidance re Article 13

All outsourcing providers (including external precognition agents) should be made aware of the provisions of Article 13 and required to comply with them.

When precognoscing witnesses, a solicitor has responsibility to ensure that this is done in a way which is as sympathetic as possible to the needs of the witness. A solicitor does not discharge this responsibility simply by passing to a precognition agent a copy of the list of witnesses and asking the precognition agent to commence precognoscing them. Where a solicitor is aware of information about witnesses which would affect the way in which they ought to be contacted or the way in which they should be precognosced, such as that they are children, that they are disabled in some way or anything else, the solicitor has a duty to ensure that the precognition agent is equipped with enough information about the case to carry out the precognition work properly. A solicitor who fails to ensure that the precognition agent is aware of such sensitive information which is known to the solicitor does not thereafter avoid responsibility for distress or inconvenience etc. which is caused to the witness by a failure to observe the particular characteristics of the witness.

Every witness should be contacted in writing by the solicitor in advance with effective information about the process of precognition. This should include information about to whom to complain, if things are perceived to go wrong. There should be no "cold calling".

Notice should be given as to who will take the precognition and due regard should be had to the venue and timing for the convenience of the witness.

It should be pointed out that the witness may have a friend or supporter present, provided that person is not also a witness in the case under investigation.

Care should be taken with vulnerable witnesses or witnesses who might be subjected to intimidation. The nature of the charge should be considered and it might be appropriate to precognosce the reporting officer with a view to obtaining information about witnesses prior to precognoscing them. It may be that in certain cases the gender of the precognition taker should be considered. Crimes of indecency may, at least as far as victims are concerned, be better precognosced by precognoscers of the same sex. Prior to the taking of the precognition, the witness should be able to satisfy himself that the precognition taker is who he says he is. Those instructed by solicitors to obtain precognitions should carry identification and a letter of authority from the instructing solicitor. In cases involving more than one accused, there will obviously be separate and different interests but liaison between solicitors can very often result in a witness only having to undergo one session rather than a number of separate sessions. Where possible, multiple precognitions of civilian witnesses by each accused should be avoided unless this is absolutely essential in the interests of justice and of the accused.

The witness should be given a copy of Article 13 and this guidance.

Other Rules of Professional Conduct

A solicitor should at all times comply with good professional practice and the ethics of the solicitors' profession as set out in practice rules, other codes of conduct and textbooks on professional ethics.

The essence of professional ethics is such that it cannot be codified. Many texts provide guidance on the professional behaviour expected of solicitors. Solicitors have a duty to inform themselves of these texts and to approach their work in a manner consistent with the principles of good ethical practice. A solicitor acting outwith the terms of this Code may be called upon to justify his conduct.

Correspondence between Prisoners and Legal Advisers

When writing to a prisoner client the letter should be sealed in a plain envelope addressed to the prisoner. That envelope should also bear the name, address and telephone number of the firm and a reference number, the words "legal correspondence" and the signature of the legal adviser or his/her assistant. Alternatively, this information could be contained in a

covering letter to the prison authorities. In either case, the correspondence should be addressed to the Governor of the establishment concerned and on receipt at the prison the outer envelope would be opened and the inner envelope passed unopened to the prisoner.

This will ensure that legal correspondence between solicitors and their clients remain confidential.

Precognosing Untried Prisoners

It is frequently the case that in preparing defence precognitions a statement will have to be taken from a witness who is an untried prisoner. Almost without exception an untried prisoner will have a solicitor representing him.

An untried prisoner on remand must be known to be represented by a solicitor and that another solicitor seeking to take a statement from such a person in connection with another case should not communicate directly with the untried prisoner but should request permission to precognosce him through his own solicitor. The precognoscing solicitor should only discuss the case in which he is involved and should not attempt to discuss the case in which the witness is himself or herself awaiting trial. (See rules B1.14 and B3.2).

Division B: Immigration

Immigration practitioners

The following guidance constitutes an amplification of the standard of practice that the Society considers essential for the compliance with the rules of professional conduct when undertaking immigration, nationality and asylum work and contains best practice advice. The guidance may be taken into account by the Society or by others in connection with the investigation and determination of complaints (including those made by third parties) alleging inadequate professional service and/or unsatisfactory professional conduct or professional misconduct arising from immigration, nationality and asylum work.

The following guidance applies to solicitors and registered European lawyers (RELs) and to registered foreign lawyers (RFLs) when in practice with solicitors/RELs, and to anyone, including non-solicitors, supervised by solicitors or RELs.

General duties

1. When engaged in the conduct of activities as advisers and representatives in the field of immigration, nationality and asylum and practice related matters you are expected to maintain the standards of the profession.

In particular:

- (a) You should give sound advice having familiarised yourself with the relevant law, the immigration rules, and details of any published concessions outside the rules.
- (b) You should at all times show sensitivity to the particularly vulnerable position of those seeking immigration advice. You should pay due regard to the related difficulties faced by such a client, and should ensure that the client fully understands the implications of any decision or proposed course of action, making full use of an interpreter for translation purposes only as necessary.
- (c) You must not deceive or deliberately mislead the immigration authorities or the courts or knowingly allow yourself to be used in any such way.
- (d) You should consider whether, by virtue of your knowledge, skills and experience, you are competent to act in the particular case, and must

not take on cases outside your area of competence or beyond your caseload capacity.

(e) You must maintain proper records of your professional dealings, including records of the matters set out below.

Fees

2. You must give advance information about fees and outlays.

3. The question of whether the client is eligible for advice and assistance under the "pink form scheme" should be explored and discussed with the client at the outset. If eligible for advice and assistance the client should be advised accordingly. If eligible for advice and assistance but the client does not wish to obtain advice and assistance, you should ensure that the client signs a written statement to the effect that the client understands the client's entitlement to legal advice and assistance but does not wish to apply for it. In that event or where the client is ineligible for legal advice and assistance and a fee is due to be charged, the best information possible about the likely overall costs should be supplied to the client, in writing, with a description of the work to be carried out to be specified and the method of calculation of such fee. Where the fee is likely to exceed the estimate a written revision of the estimate should be given.

4. Where a charge is to be made to a client for the provision of legal services, a written estimate of the costs should be supplied to the client at the outset of the matter to which the charge relates, with a description of the work to be done to a specified stage and the method of calculation of such fee (unless the fee is fixed) and the likely overall cost including outlays and VAT. Where the fee is likely to exceed the estimate given or requires variation, a written revision of the estimate and mode of calculation should be given as soon as it becomes apparent that the original estimate is likely to be exceeded or requires revision, and in any event before it is in fact exceeded.

Appeals

5. In the conduct of appeals you must take all reasonable steps to comply with the rules of procedure and with practice notes both to protect the interest of the client and to meet obligations to the court. "Court" includes tribunal.

6. You must not withdraw from acting except for good reason and upon reasonable notice, recording the reasons for withdrawing from acting in the file. Where, for good reason, whether the client has been granted advice and assistance by the Scottish Legal Aid Board or otherwise, you decide to withdraw from acting for the client, it must be with as much notice to the client as possible in all the circumstances. Issues of merits, funding and arrangements to provide advocacy must be addressed as soon as reasonably practicable so as to avoid damage either to the client's interests or to the effective operation of the court. Such advice as may be appropriate should be given to the client for alternative representation. Notice of withdrawal from representation must be promptly given to the court in such manner as to minimise prejudice to the client.

7. If you are without funds to cover a hearing it is unacceptable for you to withdraw from acting so close to the date of the hearing as to prevent the client having any opportunity of seeking to find alternative representation, or to hinder the court in adequately disposing of matters pending.

Lien (privately funded)

8. If the client withdraws instructions just before a hearing date and a successor solicitor is appointed, the Society recommends the papers be released to the successor solicitor, subject to a satisfactory undertaking as to costs being given in lieu of the exercise of a lien.

Standard of work

9. You should not normally agree to represent a client where adequate preparation of a case is not possible, but in cases of urgency you may agree to act or continue to act for the purpose of applying for an adjournment. Where an adjournment is refused, you must consider whether continuing to act compromises effective standards of representation. If so, you should then not participate further in the hearing.

Supervision

10. You must ensure that all staff are properly supervised. There is a general duty to ensure that a practice is properly supervised, managed, and compliant with any quality assurance criteria in force. Every office must have at least one solicitor or REL qualified to supervise with that office being that solicitor's or REL's usual place of work. When the solicitor or REL qualified to supervise at an office is away for any reason, suitable arrangements must be in place to ensure that duties to clients and others are met.

11. Solicitors and RELs must be confident that non-solicitor staff providing immigration, nationality or asylum advice to clients are of good standing and repute and have proper knowledge and experience of the work for which they are being recruited. Non-solicitor staff must also be properly supervised under a supervising solicitor's or REL's direction.

12. Solicitors and RELs must exercise great care in the recruitment of non-solicitor staff whom it is intended will undertake immigration work, so as to avoid employing unsuitable staff. Before employing non-solicitor staff thorough enquiries should be made as a matter of course about the prospective employee's background, including whether the prospective employee has been the subject of any disciplinary charge upheld by the First-Tier Tribunal (Immigration Services); and references should be sought.

13. Non-solicitor staff include paralegals; legal executives; clerks from time to time working away from the office, for example attending with clients at Home Office interviews, attending clients at detention centres or at court; persons working out of solicitors' offices (even if only in the office for a few hours each week); and any person paid by a solicitor or REL to undertake immigration work or where there is any arrangement, however vague, between a practice unit and a non-solicitor, for the purposes of gain. Even if it could be argued that there is not strictly an employer/employee relationship, for example if a person is an independent self-employed contractor working in the name of the practice unit, that person is the responsibility of the manager(s) of the practice unit when engaged to carry out work on behalf of the practice unit and proper supervision must be exercised. The term "non-solicitor staff" should not be taken to include RELs, RFLs, members of the Faculty of Advocates or trainee solicitors under a training contract registered with the Law Society of Scotland.

14. When you are instructing firms of solicitors in another part of the United Kingdom you are not responsible for supervision of the staff of such other firm or any person instructed by such other firm to carry out any part of such instructions. Paragraphs 10-13 of this guidance do not apply when a solicitor in another part of the United Kingdom is instructed.

15. Persons qualified to provide immigration advice or immigration services under Part V of the Immigration and Asylum Act 1999 include those authorised to practise as solicitors in Scotland by the Law Society of Scotland or those working under the supervision of such persons. The Society may treat failure to supervise properly as unsatisfactory professional conduct or professional misconduct. In considering any complaint received by the Office of the Immigration Services Commissioner in connection with an alleged failure of a solicitor or REL to supervise properly, the Commissioner may also apply this guidance.

Interrelation between Guidance and other Practice Rules etc

16. Solicitors and others engaged in immigration, nationality and asylum work remain subject to all practice rules, codes of conduct and any other professional or regulatory rules which may apply to them in any capacity and to any contractual terms. In particular, solicitors and others should have regard to their obligation to communicate effectively with their client in terms of Rule B1.9 (Standards of Conduct—Effective Communication). In the context of the provision of immigration advice or immigration services this may well include an obligation to advise the client periodically that information is still awaited from the relevant authorities. They should also note the terms of Rule B1.14.2 (Standards of Conduct—Relations between regulated persons) which prohibits communication with a person known or believed to be the client of another regulated person save in certain limited circumstances. They should take reasonable steps to satisfy themselves that any person approaching them for immigration, nationality or asylum advice or services is not already represented by another solicitor, REL or RFL before accepting instructions from such person.

Division C: Conveyancing

Fixed price offers

The use of fixed price offers should be considered carefully. Problems can arise when two or three prospective purchasers attempt to express interest simultaneously or when offers are submitted subject to conditions.

A sale advertised at a fixed price is an invitation to prospective purchasers to submit offers at that price. In the view of the Conveyancing Committee that does not imply an undertaking on the part of the solicitor that the first such offer will be accepted.

If a solicitor is instructed to advertise a property at a fixed price, the Property Particulars should state if the date of entry is material and whether offers subject to survey, subject to finance being obtained, subject to the purchaser's own house being sold or subject to some other suspensive condition will be considered. Other matters material to the seller should also be clearly stated.

Gazumping, gazundering and closing dates

Where a solicitor for a seller has intimated verbally or in writing to the solicitors or a prospective purchaser that their client's offer is acceptable— whether after a closing date or otherwise—the seller's solicitor should not accept subsequent instructions from the seller to accept an offer from another party unless and until negotiations with the original offeror have fallen through for bona fide reasons unconnected with the possible offer from another party. The solicitor should advise the seller to instruct another solicitor if he wishes to accept the later offer.

Solicitors acting for prospective purchasers of residential property whose offer is accepted—either verbally or in writing—should withdraw from acting if the client subsequently wishes to re-negotiate the price downwards without having made the offer subject to a satisfactory valuation or obtaining satisfactory finance. If there is a valid issue arising out of an unforeseen problem with the title that would not require the agents to withdraw.

Where an offer has been submitted subject to survey, and the survey discloses a problem, e.g. unauthorised alterations; new windows; damp or rot requiring specialist treatment—the solicitors would be entitled to accept instructions to seek to adjust the price in the light of that problem. However if the offer is only subject to survey and the survey discloses no such problem but the valuation is regarded as too low by the offeror, solicitors should not accept instructions to withdraw the original offer and re-submit a lower offer (unless the original offer was clearly subject to satisfactory valuation) but should refer the client to other solicitors if the client insists on doing so.

Purchasers' solicitors should advise the clients in advance of submitting an offer that if the client subsequently wishes to re-negotiate the price downwards without good reason, the solicitor will require to withdraw from acting.

There is no difficulty where a seller initiates renegotiation at a lower price if the prospective purchaser has withdrawn an offer due to an unsatisfactory survey, whether or not valuation was the sole issue.

There is no legal requirement on a selling solicitor to fix a Closing Date when more than one interest is noted.

Selling solicitors are entitled to accept their client's instructions to accept an incoming offer without having a Closing Date and without giving other parties who may have noted an interest an opportunity to offer although every effort should be made to give them such an opportunity if at all possible.

Where a client has instructed a solicitor to intimate a closing date to other solicitors who have noted interest, that solicitor should withdraw from acting if the selling client wishes to cancel the closing date and accept an offer submitted in advance of it unless the Closing Date is brought forward giving those who have noted an interest a reasonable opportunity to offer. Sellers' solicitors should therefore advise their clients of this in advance of fixing a closing date.

Where possible when fixing a Closing Date, the client should be advised to make him/herself available to consider the offers received. If this is not possible (e.g. Executries, Trusts, Companies etc.) prospective offerers should be told this when being advised of the Closing Date.

In taking instructions from the selling client to fix a Closing Date, solicitors should advise the client that, although not bound to accept the highest—or indeed any—offer, if the client instructs the solicitor to enter negotiations with a view to concluding a bargain with a party who has submitted an offer at the Closing Date, the solicitor will not be able to accept any subsequent instructions to enter negotiations with or accept an offer from another party unless and until negotiations with the original offerer have fallen through for bona fide reasons unconnected with the possible offer from another party. Unsuccessful offerers should, of course be advised as soon as possible after the Closing Date of the situation.

In the event of the selling client subsequently attempting to instruct the solicitor to discontinue such negotiations in order solely to enter into negotiations with or accept an offer from another party the solicitor should decline to act further in the sale unless the client reconsiders and adheres to the original instructions.

Where, at a Closing Date, two or more offers are received in terms that are such that they cannot be distinguished by the selling client, the solicitor may revert to those offerers and give them equal opportunity to revise their offer.

This guidance applies equally to solicitors acting as estate agents as well as solicitors acting in the conveyancing. Different considerations may apply however to sales of commercial property and to sellers owing statutory or fiduciary duties to others.

In the event of an unsuccessful prospective purchaser subsequently attempting to instruct the solicitor to submit a revised offer or formal amendment after a Closing Date has passed and without an express invitation by the seller's agent, the solicitor should decline to implement those instructions. The solicitor may accept instructions to intimate to the seller's agent that in the event of negotiations with the successful party falling through, the prospective purchaser would be willing to enter negotiations, but no indication of any increased bid should be given.

Solicitors acting for purchasers who have received a verbal or qualified acceptance—whether following a Closing Date or not—should advise clients that although an initial acceptance may have been given by the seller, the contract will not be binding until Missives are concluded. Solicitors acting for prospective purchasers should advise their clients that noting an interest may not guarantee the clients an opportunity to offer, and if the clients are not in a position to put in an early offer they may not be allowed an opportunity to submit an offer at all.

Avoidance of delay in concluding missives

It is common for Missives to be in an unconcluded state until shortly before or even at the date of entry. While solicitors require to have regard to the interests of their clients and to take their clients' instructions, they must have regard to the principles of good professional conduct and may not accept an improper instruction. They should not knowingly mislead professional colleagues and must act with fellow solicitors in a spirit of trust and co-operation (rule B1.14 (Standards of Conduct)).

In residential property transactions solicitors acting on behalf of both purchasers and sellers have a professional duty to conclude Missives without undue delay. Clients should be advised at the outset of this duty and of the consequences.

Where a solicitor for a purchaser is instructed to submit an offer but to delay concluding a bargain until some matter outwith the selling agent's control has been resolved e.g. the purchaser's own house has not been sold; a survey or specialist's report is required; or funding arrangements are to be confirmed these circumstances should be disclosed to the selling solicitor. If the purchaser instructs the solicitor not to disclose such matters to the selling solicitor, the purchaser's solicitor should withdraw from acting. To continue acting could amount to a breach of rule B1.14 by knowingly misleading a fellow solicitor. Where a purchaser instructs his solicitor to delay concluding a bargain without giving any reason the solicitor should similarly withdraw from acting.

Where a selling client instructs a solicitor to delay concluding a bargain having given an indication that an offer is to be accepted, the reason for that delay should be disclosed to the purchaser's solicitor. If the seller instructs the solicitor not to disclose the reason, or does not give a reason for such an instruction, the solicitor should also withdraw from acting.

If a solicitor whether for seller or purchaser withdraws from acting in terms of this guidance, the confidentiality of the client should not be breached without the client's authority but when intimating withdrawal that should be done by stating that it is in terms of this guidance.

Note: The Conveyancing Committee is of the view that this guidance does not require a solicitor or legal adviser to coerce a client into concluding an early bargain, but rather requires that if there is a delay, the reason for that delay should be disclosed at an early stage.

Delivery of missives—Thomas Park, Petitioner

The Conveyancing Committee has come to the view that this recent decision reinforces the legal position that delivery is required before a missive is binding. The Committee has also confirmed the Society's existing guidance on electronic communications. This guidance provides that there is a duty on a solicitor to follow up a fax or e-mail of a contractual document with the original as soon as possible. Furthermore if the solicitor is instructed by the client not to send the hard copy that fact must be communicated to the other solicitor immediately and the solicitor must withdraw from acting if the client cannot be persuaded to withdraw such instructions.

Standard missives

The Society fully supports the standard missive initiatives of faculties throughout the country. There are real and obvious benefits to the public and the profession in the standardisation of missives. Relevant documents can be found in Advice & Information and accessed via the links on the right hand side of the page on the Society's website. Note, however that the Society does not endorse or approve any particular standard missive or other document and the provision of such links should not be interpreted as implying any such approval or endorsement. You must exercise your own professional judgment in relation to assessing the appropriateness of any such standard missive or other document in the particular circumstances of each transaction.

A large part of Scotland is now covered by standard missives which reflect geographical and other localised differences and take account of different practices in different parts of the country.

Should any faculty wish to seek advice and guidance from the Society we are very willing to assist in facilitating the creation of additional and new standard missives in any way that we can.

Exhibition of title deeds

In a conveyancing transaction, the seller/landlord's solicitor should, other than in exceptional circumstances, forward the title deeds for examination by the purchaser/tenant's solicitor at the latter's office. If a title is likely to be in heavy demand, the seller/landlord's solicitor should make up sufficient sets of extracts and/or copies to ensure that the progress of transactions is not impeded by the unavailability of deeds. In such a case, it is acceptable to send copies of deeds, provided the originals or extracts are available for examination at the offices of the seller/landlord's solicitor if so desired. Exceptional circumstances would include, for example, the situation where an extract did not contain the plan annexed to the original deed, which was in particularly heavy demand, or in fragile condition; or where the number of relevant deeds involved would render compliance with this guidance impracticable.

Home Reports

Lifespan of reports

(1) Members should intimate to purchasing clients in writing that they should not rely upon reports more than 12 weeks old.

(2) Members should intimate to selling clients the Society's guidance in relation to purchasing clients so that they might consider the appropriateness of updating reports from time to time.

Making reports available to "interested parties"

(3) Parties who have formally "noted an interest" through solicitors or licensed conveyancers should be deemed to "have sufficient means to buy the house" and/or be "genuinely interested".

(4) Members should ensure that they ask sellers if there are any persons to whom the seller would not be prepared to sell the house prior to marketing property to avoid any difficulties.

Liability for information contained in Property Questionnaire

(5) Members should ensure that they have advised sellers in writing of their obligations in regard to the preparation of the property questionnaire and the importance of accurately and truthfully answering those questions, including clarifying for the client possible liability both in terms of the Property Misdescriptions Act 1991,The Housing (Scotland) Act 2006 and The Housing (Scotland) Act 2006 (Prescribed Documents) Regulations 2008.

(6) Members should make clear to selling clients completing such questionnaires that primary responsibility for the accuracy and truthfulness of those questionnaires rests with the client and that the member's only obligation in terms of compliance is to ensure that the copy which they offer members of the public who are purchasers is effectively a true copy of that form and therefore "authentic" in terms of the legislation and regulation.

(7) The Society take the view that members do not have an obligation to check the information contained in the property questionnaire and may accept the statements therein at face value except in circumstances where they are personally aware that the statement is untrue. (For example in a situation where the member or their firm carried out the remortgage in respect of a substantial extension to the property and the questionnaire states that there are no alterations.)

Who can complete the Property Questionnaire?

(8) Ideally the questionnaire should be signed by at least one principal owner acting under authority from any co-proprietors.

(9) In the view of the Society "Authorised persons" (for the purposes of the Regulation 5(2)) definitely includes those acting under a Power of Attorney, Deed of Trust, Court Order, Solicitors and Duly Authorised Officers of a Company, but may include others with a similar level of formal authority. Care should be taken in cases where only informal authority is available. In the interests of risk management the Society do not recommend that solicitors sign questionnaires on behalf of clients.

Deferred Payment Arrangements

(10) Terms of business should state or should include a separate covering document in relation to:
- **(a)** The price to be paid for the Home Report;
- **(b)** A clear statement of any financial interest the selling agent has in the Home Report provider;
- **(c)** Details of any deferred payment option including any discount for early payment and charges in relation to property where the sale does not proceed or the property is withdrawn;
- **(d)** Where a mandate is to be signed for payment a clear statement of the meaning and effect of such a mandate.

Withdrawn from the market

(11) In the view of the Society a property is not "sold" until a bargain is concluded. Property marked "under offer" is still technically available for sale (admittedly subject to a change of agent in terms of the Society's Closing Date Gazumping and Gazundering Guidelines). Accordingly for the purposes of Regulation 6(2)(b) property marked "under offer" should not be deemed "sold" and it should not be deemed "withdrawn from the market" until there is a concluded bargain. On this basis it is the view of the Society that where a property is marked "under offer" and negotiations fall through the existing Home Report could still be used in terms of Regulation 6(2)(b).

Annexation of the Home Report to offers

(12) While the Society accepts that it is a matter for individual members and their clients the Society does not recommend annexation of the Home Report to offers.

Conflict of interest

(13) In the interests of transparency where firms act for both buyer and seller in terms of the existing conflict rules they should clarify the source of the Home Report and any connection which their firm has with the supplier of the report.

(14) Where the selling solicitor is aware that multiple reports have been purchased by, or on behalf of the seller in an effort to obtain a report that portrays the property in the best light, the firm should not also represent a purchaser (notwithstanding the fact that an exemption under rule B2.1.4 of the Conflict of Interest Rules applies) without disclosing the full circumstances due to the clear conflict of interest between the parties.

(15) Where a purchaser is to be advised to seek an additional independent report in cases where the firm already acts for the seller the firm should not represent the purchaser due to the clear conflict of interest between the parties. Exemptions rely on the fact that the agent will not advise either party in relation to price. It is difficult to see how an additional independent report could be instructed without a discussion in relation to price.

Common repairs

The Scottish Consumer Council has recently published a report on the views and experiences of owner occupiers in Scotland who share common property with their council. Its recommendations include the following: "Solicitors should always make sure prospective purchasers are aware of the conditions contained in their title deeds about the management of repairs".

"The Law Society of Scotland should take steps to improve pre-purchase information given by solicitors about common repair responsibilities".

The Society's Conveyancing Committee is of the view that current best practice already covers this but feels it appropriate to bring practitioners' notice to the recommendations.

The report makes further recommendations to the Scottish Parliament, national bodies and local authorities.

Deeds of conditions for housing estates

Solicitors are reminded that they should draw to the attention of prospective purchasers the existence of a Deed of Conditions and to highlight any difficulties which may arise in such Deed and to comply with the conditions therein, including notification to the secretary of the Proprietors' Association of change of ownership.

Coal mining searches

Coal mining searches are considered by property professionals to be vital for anyone buying property in any coal mining area in Britain. The Coal Authority holds and maintains the national coal mining database and its Mining Reports Service provides a fast, accurate, property-specific and cost-effective coal mining search service for any individual property or site in Scotland, England or Wales.

The mining search includes information about any past, current or proposed surface and underground coal mining activity to affect a particular property or site. It also includes further property specific information about the existence of old shallow coal workings, old shafts and other entrances to mines, coal mining related ground fractures, subsidence damage claims, mine gas emissions and emergency call-out surface hazard incidents.

Practitioners can quickly establish whether a coal mining search is required by either:

- Referring to the Gazetteer of Scotland, which gives an indication of places that may, or may not, require a coal mining search to be carried out, or alternatively
- Using the Coal Authority's On-Line Post-Code Referral Service at *www.groundstability.com* which provides immediate on-line confirmation on entering a property post-code as to whether a search is necessary or not. By its nature, this electronic referral system is more precise than using the Directory listing of place names.

The Coal Authority's Scale of Charges lists current charges incurred when ordering coal mining reports and related services.

PART 1

Law Society of Scotland's Guidance Notes 2006

1. Introduction
   1.1 Solicitors should consider whether a coal mining search should be made in any particular transaction dealing with land in coal mining areas ("affected areas"), including purchase, mortgage, further advance or before any development takes place. If deemed necessary, it is recommended that the search be made before the conclusion of Missives or in appropriate cases that the Missives be made conditional on the report being satisfactory.
   1.2 For those solicitors not using electronic means, the enquiry should be in the form approved by the Society (ScotForm 2006) and the Coal Authority. The search should be made before the exchange of contracts or any binding obligation is entered into.
   1.3 Solicitors are recommended to submit a plan of the property with every postal search enquiry. Plans should be marked with the full boundary of the property and not just the property building footprint or other lesser area. Solicitors should retain a copy of the search form and plan.
   1.4 These Guidance Notes should be read in conjunction with the Coal Authority's Terms and Conditions 2006 and User Guide 2006 (refer to their website for details).

2. Preliminary enquiries
   2.1 If the property is in an affected area (see User Guide 2006, paragraph 2), it is suggested that a solicitor should, in addition to requesting a search from the Coal Authority, ask, as a preliminary enquiry of the seller, whether during the ownership of the seller or, to the seller's knowledge, his predecessors in title, the property has sustained coal mining subsidence damage and if so how any claim was resolved (by repair or payment in respect of the cost of remedial or redevelopment works or otherwise).
   2.2 If the report discloses a current "stop notice" concerning the deferment of remedial works or repairs affecting the property, or the withholding of consent to a request for preventive works affecting the property, it is recommended that the solicitor should ask preliminary enquiries of the seller as to the present position.

3. Reproduction of forms
   3.1 It is important that both sides of the ScotForm 2006 enquiry form are reproduced for retention and annexing to the reply when received. Solicitors are granted a non-exclusive licence to reproduce them. Any such form must follow precisely and in all respects the printed version (see the example in Part 5).
   3.2 The Coal Authority will reject any reproduction of the ScotForm 2006 enquiry form which does not comply with these requirements.

4. Mining surveys and site investigation
   4.1 Disclosure of a disused mine shaft or mine adit in a report, the existence of recorded shallow workings or possible unrecorded coal workings reported as believed to be at or close to the surface (such that future ground movement may still subsequently occur) and/or any other coal mining related hazard identified within the report, should be brought to the attention of the client. If further information or advice is required in addition to that available from the Coal Authority (e.g. further to that contained within a Coal Authority Interpretive Report, see paragraph 17 of the User Guide 2006), then solicitors should in these circumstances explain to clients that there are experienced mining surveyors and structural engineers able to advise as to what further enquiries, surveys or investigation should be made.

4.2 If a lender is involved in the transaction, solicitors should establish that the surveyor or engineer selected is acceptable to the lender and make arrangements to provide a copy of the search to them.

4.3 In most cases, but not all, the Coal Authority and not the adjacent surface landowner will own any shaft or adit. Clients should be advised accordingly and reminded that in these cases the permission of the Coal Authority must be sought before carrying out any works to locate, treat or in any other way interfere with former coal workings including disused coal mine shafts or adits.

5. Dealing with lenders

5.1 If domestic property which is the subject of a mining search is to be charged as security for a loan, it is suggested that a copy of the report should be sent to the lender as soon as received. Whether or not this is appropriate depends on the result of the search and the lenders' instructions. It is recommended that the solicitor should not comment substantively on the replies within the mining report but should recommend that they be referred to the lender's valuer for review and information.

5.2 Provided that a copy of the mining report has been so provided solicitors are not obliged to make any other reference to the replies in any mining report in a report on title to a lender except to refer to the existence of the search and the mining report.

5.3 The Royal Institution of Chartered Surveyors, the Council of Mortgage Lenders and the Association of British Insurers have been consulted with regard to these Guidance Notes in respect of, surveys of, loans granted on security of and insurance of, domestic properties in areas affected by coal mining and each such organisation has prepared separate guidance to its own members.

5.4 With regard to non-domestic property a similar procedure should be adopted. It is suggested that solicitors should, however, refer to the replies to the additional enquiries included in the mining reports for non-residential, commercial or development sites as these deal with legal matters (namely the withdrawal of support and the existence of working facilities orders).

5.5 When also acting for the lender it is suggested that solicitors should, in all cases, check whether the instructions from that lender require the solicitor to deal with the mining report in any other manner. If so, it is suggested that the solicitor should explain to the lender the basis upon which the solicitor is recommended by these paragraphs to proceed. It is important that solicitors should not attempt to perform the function of the client's valuer or surveyor with regard to the mining report.

6. Implementation of ScotForm (2006) enquiry form

6.1 ScotForm can also be used by Scottish solicitors in the event of them acting for clients purchasing property in England or Wales.

6.2 From 23rd October 2006, all ScotForm (2006) reports requested from the Coal Authority will be prepared in accordance with the Law Society's Guidance Notes 2006, the User Guide 2006 and the Coal Authority's Terms and Conditions 2006.

PART 2

User Guide 2006

1. Introduction

1.1 The past legacy and ongoing impact of coal mining can affect surface property. Consequently, property professionals agree that considering whether a coal mining search is necessary is an essential step for anyone buying or developing property in any coal mining area in Scotland.

1.2 The Coal Authority ("the Authority") holds and maintains the national coal mining database and their Mining Reports Service provides a fast, accurate and cost-effective coal mining search service. Mining reports provide property-specific information about past, current and future underground and surface coal mining activities affecting any individual property or site in Scotland.

1.3 Before making a search, it is suggested that users should familiarise themselves with this User Guide. For the purpose of this Guide, users should be taken to include solicitors, licensed conveyancers, surveyors, valuers, estate agents, lending organisations, insurers, surface developers and any other individual or organisation making a search with the Authority for their own or their clients use.

1.4 Solicitors should consider whether a coal mining search should be made in any particular transaction dealing with land in coal mining areas ("affected areas"), including purchase, mortgage, further advance or before any development takes place. If deemed necessary, it is recommended that the search be made before the conclusion of Missives or in appropriate cases that the Missives be made conditional on the report being satisfactory. It is also recommended that the search be made early enough to enable the results to be available to the client's valuer or surveyor so that s/he has the benefit of the search information to hand when carrying out any valuation for sale, purchase, mortgage or other valuation purpose.

1.5 This User Guide should be read in conjunction with the Law Society's Guidance Notes 2006 and the Authority's Terms and Conditions 2006.

2. Affected Areas

2.1 Whilst past and current coal mining activities are widespread, most of Scotland is not an affected area. It is suggested that a coal mining search may be required if the property is within an area which may be affected by previous, current or proposed working of coal. It is recommended that the user should not rely upon his/her own "local knowledge" in determining whether or not a search should be made.

2.2 Subject to paragraph 2.7 below, no coal mining search is required to be made in respect of property in any of the following Unitary Districts of Scotland:

- Aberdeenshire
- Angus
- City of Aberdeen
- City of Dundee
- Inverclyde

Moray
Orkney Islands
Shetland Islands
Western Isles

2.3 A coal mining search may be necessary in respect of properties in certain specified places in the following Unitary Districts, namely:

- Argyll & Bute
- Borders
- City of Edinburgh
- City of Glasgow
- Clackmannanshire
- Dumfries & Galloway
- East Ayrshire
- East Dunbartonshire
- East Lothian
- East Renfrewshire
- Falkirk
- Fife

Highland
Midlothian
North Ayrshire
North Lanarkshire
Perth and Kinross
Renfrewshire
South Ayrshire
South Lanarkshire
Stirling
West Dunbartonshire
West Lothian

2.4 The procedures for finding out which places within these Unitary Districts are deemed to be affected by coal mining are outlined at paragraph 3.1 of this User Guide.

2.5 Not all property located within an affected area is within the zone of likely physical influence on the surface of underground coal working.

Property which is within such a zone will not necessarily sustain subsidence damage but some support from the surface where the property is situated may have been or may be withdrawn in the future. Calculations relating to the likely zone of influence on the surface from mining activities will be based on the principle of 0.7 times the depth of the working allowing for seam inclination.

2.6 Licensed mine operators are required to give property owners advance notice of any proposals for underground coal mining operations which might result in subsidence affecting the property and of any decision not to proceed with the operations or anything which gives them reason to believe there is no longer any risk of the property being affected by subsidence and of the discontinuance of any operations which have been carried on.

2.7 When the Authority states, by whatever means, that the possibility of future coal working is unlikely, this does not and should not be deemed to affirm that no coal mining strata is present, nor that some part of any coal resources present will (subject to obtaining planning permission and a licence from the Authority) not be worked at some future date.

2.8 Responses to searches made for land and property lying outside of the Authority's defined coal mining areas will state that the property lies outside any defined coalfield area, and will not answer each individual question on Scot Form 2006.

3. Procedures for finding out whether a coal mining search may be necessary
    3.1 Users can establish whether a coal mining search is required by:—
- Using the Directory of Places in Part 4—an updated version of which is maintained by the Authority at *www.groundstability.com.*
- Using the Authority's Online Address Screening Service at *www.groundstability.com* which provides immediate online confirmation on entering a property address as to whether a coal mining search is recommended or not. By its nature, this electronic screening system is more precise than using a printed listing of place names.

4. How to use the published Directory listings
    4.1 The user should inspect the Directory of Places to ascertain whether the name of the place in which the property is situated is listed as either a place where a coal mining search may be required or whether it is listed as a place where a coal mining search is not required. If the place is listed as a place where a coal mining search may be required then it is suggested that a coal mining search should be made. Where a place is not listed, users should contact the Authority on 0845 762 6848 or by e-mail at groundstability@coal.gov.uk.

5. How to use the Authority's online address screening service
    5.1 To use the Authority's online address screening service:
1. Log onto the Authority's web-site at *www.groundstability.com* (a link is also available from the corporate web-site at *www.coal.decc*.
2. Enter the site as either a regular user (see paragraph 8 of this User Guide) or to simply use the service.
3. Select the premise type (e.g. residential or non-residential or site search)
4. Enter the house number or name and post-code in the boxes provided. If a post-code is not available then select "full address entry".
5. Where possible, confirm the corrected Royal Mail Postcode Address File (PAF) search address when prompted.
6. You will be immediately advised that, from the information available to the Authority, either:—
    (a) a search is not required for the property (with the option to

purchase a No Search Required Certificate to confirm this information, if required); or

(b) that a search is recommended (and given the option of report types and services available for purchase) and the facility to order reports online.

7. If users do not wish to make a search online they can exit the service at this stage, or search against other property addresses.

6. Search enquiries and types of report

6.1 Two types of search can be made (see paragraph 12 of the User Guide for fees):

1. **Residential Property Search**. This is available for single unit residential property, either existing or currently being built, i.e. having already been the subject in full or part of a previous development site search. By way of illustration, this includes any single unit domestic property (e.g. a house, flat or bungalow including any associated garage or car-parking space), a single plot on a multi-plot development site, a farmhouse or similar converted property up to a maximum of 25 hectares in extent.The mining report answers enquiries 1 to 11 of the ScotForm (2006) Enquiry Form, relating to:

- past, present and future underground coal mining;
- mine shafts and adits;
- coal mining geology;
- past, present and future opencast coal mining;
- coal mining subsidence (damage notice / claim / method of discharge of remedial obligations or claim / stop notice / request for preventive works);
- mine gas emissions, and
- incidents dealt with under the Authority's emergency surface hazard call out procedure.

Additional advice will be included, where appropriate, depending on the mining circumstances. All residential property searches will include insurance cover (see paragraph 20 of this User Guide).

If the search is for an existing single unit residential property and the homeowner intends having a conservatory or an extension built, then the residential search should still be appropriate. If major development works are intended then a non-residential search should be made.

2. **Non-Residential Property or Development Site Search**. This is available for non-domestic properties, i.e. non-residential, commercial or development and other sites. By way of illustration, this includes multiple residential property requests (e.g. a pair of semi-detached houses, a row of terraced houses or a block of flats), vacant land, public houses, shops, businesses, commercial property, industrial estates, rural estates, working farms and their associated outbuildings and land, pipelines, roads and similar linear structures up to 500 metres in extent, **any** sized development site from a single plot up to a maximum of 25 hectares in extent (see also paragraph 12.2 of the User Guide). The mining report answers enquiries 1 to 13 of the ScotForm (2006) Enquiry Form, including the Residential Property Search enquiries 1 to 11 and the additional enquiries relating to:

- withdrawal of support
- working facilities orders

Additional advice will be included from the Coal Authority, where appropriate, depending on the reported circumstances. The residential property search insurance **does not** cover non-residential or commercial land or property, or development sites.

6.2 With regard to withdrawal of support, users should be aware that statutory provisions may override the common law principles giving surface landowners a prima facie right of support. Such statutory provisions are contained in coal mining legislation such as:-

- Coal Industry Act 1994, section 38;

- Coal Industry Act 1975, section 2; and
- Coal Act 1938, Schedule 2, paragraphs 5 & 6.

The report will give details of any notice(s) given under the relevant legislation. The report will not give details of any rights contained in Title or Severance Deeds. Whether any support has or may be withdrawn can be answered only by reference to the records presently available to the Authority and, where appropriate, will be effectively answered under the past, present and future headings of the Scot Form 2006 report reply.

7 Overview of search methods

7.1 Searches can be made electronically using the Authority's online service or through a private sector search company. They can also be ordered by telephone and ordered and returned by email, post or fax. Details of each method are outlined below.

7.2 The vast majority of Coal Authority online, telephone and fax enquiries are returned within 24 to 48 hours. Most postal enquiries are dealt with within five working days of receipt. Whilst these turnaround times are typical, they cannot be guaranteed. It is therefore suggested that searches should be made as early as possible in the conveyancing process to avoid the consequence of any delay. This will ensure timely return of reports and avoid potential difficulties in meeting the user's own time schedules.

8. Ordering electronically (Coal Authority's Online Service)

8.1 The Coal Authority's Online Service is a quick, easy and convenient way for users to make searches and receive reports, either directly or through a private sector search company registered to use it.

8.2 To use the online service directly users will require the following:
- the postcode and house number or name of the property (or full postal address or description for any non-postcode property);
- an email address;
- contact details including name, address and telephone number;
- a credit or debit card (unless a monthly invoiced account is used);
- Netscape Browser version 4.0 or above/Microsoft Internet Explorer Browser version 5.0 or above.

8.3 Regular users can register online at www.groundstability.com and create their own unique user ID and password for unlimited subsequent access to the system and for reports to be dispatched using either their pre-recorded address details or be available to download.

8.4 Reports will be dispatched to users via email as a PDF or ZIPPED attachment (WinZip can be obtained from www.winzip.com). Users will need to have the Adobe Acrobat Reader to view these attachments (if you do not have this it can be downloaded from www.adobe.co.uk for free). Registered users are also able to download reports.

8.5 The majority of reports are returned within 24 to 48 hours, the remainder within 72 hours.

8.6 Payment for the reports is made via the WorldPay secure payment system or by monthly invoice. A monthly invoiced account arrangement is available but its use is subject to application, acceptance and a formal credit agreement with the Authority. The Authority reserves the right to carry out credit checks on account holders and applicants.

8.7 Where the WorldPay secure payment system is used, the Authority's Online Service will automatically link users to the WorldPay system when payment is required. For security reasons, no credit or debit card details are seen or stored by the Authority, and all payment transactions take place directly within the WorldPay system. For more information on the WorldPay system users can visit the Authority's or WorldPay website (www.worldpay.com).

8.8 The Authority's Online Service is based on postal address searching and is particularly suited for making searches on existing residential property. Searches can also be ordered for non-residential property, vacant land and development sites. However, when ordering non-residential property searches online, users should also send a location plan quoting the order confirmation number provided once the order is completed. This is necessary to enable the Authority to accurately define the property or site boundary. Location plans can be provided by email, fax or post at the preference of the user.

8.9 Once WorldPay confirms payment, or account holders receive confirmation that reports have been added to monthly invoices, reports will be automatically produced by the Authority. Users will therefore not be able to cancel orders after receiving confirmation that reports have been ordered.

8.10 Whilst it is not necessary to use the ScotForm (2006) search form when carrying out searches online, replies will be prepared in answer to the questions asked on this form and in accordance with the Law Society's Guidance Notes 2006, the User Guide 2006 and the Authority's Terms and Conditions 2006.

8.11 Registered users are also able to track the progress of searches made online with an option to request further copies of the search report, if required, by email or to be downloaded.

9. Ordering by telephone

9.1 Account and credit/debit card users can also order reports by telephone on 0845 762 6848. Users then have the option of having the reports returned by email, fax or post. The procedure is as follows:

9.2 Before calling, users need to have the following information to hand:

Account holders will need:
- customer account number; and
- the house number and postcode of the subject property (or full site description for non-addressable property).

Non-account holders will need:
- credit/debit card details;
- contact telephone number;
- the house number and postcode of the subject property (or full site description for non-addressable property);
- contact details of the preferred method of receiving the report(s), i.e. email, postal address or fax number.

9.3 Users should call the Authority on 0845 762 6848 and inform the customer service search assistant that they wish to order a ScotForm coal mining report(s) over the phone.

9.4 Callers should advise whether they are an account holder or not and, if so, provide their customer account number.

9.5 The search assistant will ask for the house number and postcode of each subject property and confirm the Royal Mail's Postcode Address File (PAF) corrected address. The facility is also available to order a non-PAF address, e.g. for a development plot or site, with users then forwarding a plan separately by e mail, fax or post (at the user's preference) delineating the boundaries of the site (see paragraph 9.8 below).

9.6 The search assistant will confirm the account holders' preferred method of receiving the report(s). Non-account holders will be asked for their preferred return route and asked for details, i.e. email, postal address or fax number.

9.7 The search assistant will digitise the property boundary, seeking any clarification as necessary.

9.8 Where the extent of the property boundary needs further clarification, users will be asked to provide a location plan by email, fax or post (at the user's preference) and given a reference number to quote.

9.9 Multiple requests can be accommodated.

9.10 For non-account holders, the search assistant will advise of the total fee for the report(s) ordered and request and input the user's credit or debit card details.

9.11 On successful credit/debit card authorisation, boundary digitisation will be confirmed and the coal mining report(s) will be passed for processing.

9.12 If the credit/debit card authorisation is unsuccessful, the process cannot proceed and the user will be asked to request the report(s) by another method, e.g. by post (see paragraph 10 of this User Guide).

9.13 Whilst it is not necessary to use the ScotForm (2006) form when carrying out searches by telephone, replies will be prepared in answer to the questions asked on the form and in accordance with the Law Society's Guidance Notes 2006, the User Guide 2006 and the Authority's Terms and Conditions 2006.

10. Searches by post

10.1 Searches can be made by completing the ScotForm (2006) search form. Copies of the form are available from the Law Society of Scotland, telephone 0131 226 7411. These can also be accessed and downloaded from the Authority's web-site at *www.groundstability.com*.

10.2 The search form must be completed (preferably in type or block capitals) by insertion of the full postal address including the postcode of the property. As full a description as possible should be given where the property address is not of the standard single number and postcode type. The search form should include the name and either the document exchange (DX) number of the user, or postal address. An email address is required if electronic return of the mining report is preferred, or a fax number. The request should also include the user's file reference and telephone number. Replies by email will be sent as a secure PDF file. *Please note that Legal Post do not currently provide any service for the return of mail from England & Wales. It is important therefore that Users provide either a Royal Mail, DX or email address.*

10.3 Users should indicate the mining report type required, i.e. whether it is for residential or for a non-residential site. The non-residential site searches attract a higher fee and will include replies to the Additional Enquiries 12 and 13 outlined in paragraph 6.1 above. It is inappropriate to request a residential property search for non-residential property sites and any such requests will be returned for resubmission and the correct fee. The search form also contains provision for the search to be expedited by fax on payment of an additional fee (see paragraph 11 below).

10.4 The search request should be sent with a plan of the property (see paragraph 10.5 below) and the appropriate fee to: *The Coal Authority, Mining Reports, DX 716176, Mansfield 5* or by post to *The Coal Authority, Mining Reports, 200 Lichfield Lane, Mansfield, Nottinghamshire, NG18 4RG*.

10.5 When searches are requested by post, users are recommended to submit a plan with every search application as it is likely to be replied to sooner than a search application without a plan. If a plan is not submitted there may be difficulties and delays in identifying the property or its extent, in which circumstances, the Authority may request that a plan be supplied with consequent delay in replying to the search application. When submitting requests for development site plots, the accompanying plan should show the plot boundary in relation to established surface features. The Authority will retain plans supplied.

10.6 No covering letter is required to be sent nor is it necessary to sign the search form. A copy of the search and plan should be retained and affixed to the replies when received. If photocopies of the form are used it is important that these are of good quality and both sides of the search form should be reproduced for retention and annexing to the reply when received.

10.7 A separate search is required to be made in respect of each individual property.

10.8 Poor quality photocopies of the search form may not be accepted and will be returned.

10.9 Users are asked:—

- not to staple anything to the form—cheques should be attached with a paper-clip or similar;
- not to send a covering letter;
- to write clearly—the form should be typed or written in block letters;
- to include a post-code where available;
- to complete all the entries on the form; and
- to enclose and sign an accompanying cheque and ensure it is for the correct fee.

11. Expedited search service

11.1 Notwithstanding the introduction of online services (which return the majority of reports within 24 to 48 hours), the Authority's Expedited Search service is still available, on payment of an additional fee.

11.2 In using this service a user may make a search by telephone, fax or by post and receive a mining report by fax within 48 hours. An additional fee is payable for expedition and this can be established by contacting the Authority's customer service team on 0845 762 6848 or visiting *www.groundstability.com*.

11.3 The Expedited search service is only available to credit account customers or where the full fee, including the expedite element, is paid in advance, i.e. either by credit or debit card (over the telephone) or by cheque (postal enquiries).

11.4 In order to make an **Expedited** Search by post, the form should be completed as normal with "Yes" selected against the "Expedited Search" field. Users should also add their fax number in full. In normal circumstances the replies will be returned by fax the same day or the next working day.

12. Fees

12.1 The current scale of charges for mining searches and other services is available on the Authority's website at *www.groundstability.com*. Advice is also available on contacting the Authority's customer service team on 0845 762 6848.

12.2 The actual fee payable for a report will depend on the method of ordering and whether it is for a residential property or for a non-residential, commercial or other site. Additional fees are payable for sites in excess of 25 hectares in extent and for linear property, like pipelines and roads etc, that exceed 500 metres in length. The fee in these circumstances will be the current Non- Residential Search fee for each 25 hectares or 500 metre length. No Search Required certificates (see paragraph 5.1 above) attract a lesser fee.

12.3 The fees charged in respect of searches and related services are reviewed from time to time. The Law Society will be consulted before any change is proposed. Notification by email, post or the publication on the Authority's website of a revised scale of charges constitutes notice of any fee change. Changed fees become payable from the date advised on any notification email, letter or website scale of charges.

12.4 For postal enquiries, the fee is payable when the search is made and should accompany the form. The reply will contain a VAT receipt for the fee. The VAT element of the fee should be treated by the user as an input for VAT purposes and VAT must be charged to the client. It should not be necessary to retain the receipted reply (nor a copy) for VAT purposes.

12.5 If, by mistake, a user makes a coal mining search in respect of property outside the affected areas, the Authority will reply but the fee will not be refunded.

12.6 The Authority will return any request received that encloses an incorrect fee, with a request for the correct fee.

12.7 The Authority cannot guarantee to cancel a search once a request has been made. No refund or transfer of any fee (or part thereof) will be made once a search has been logged onto the Authority's MRSDS computer systems for report production.

13. Paying for reports

13.1 Depending on the method used to search and to receive reports, various methods of payment are available. Payment can be made by:

- cheque in advance (for all postal enquiries) made payable to The Coal Authority;
- postal order;
- BACS or CHAPS transfer;
- credit or debit card; and
- customer credit account (telephone and on-line customers only).

14. Customer account facilities

14.1 Customer account facilities are available (subject to conditions) for users of the Authority's online and telephone services. To apply for a monthly invoiced account, telephone users will need to complete an application form which is available from the Authority on 0845 762 6848 or by email at groundstability@coal.gov.uk. Online users need to register at www.groundstability.com. Accounts will only be offered to those customers who satisfy the selection criteria and are subject to a formal credit agreement with the Authority. No account facility will be provided to users who are currently on the stop list of either the Authority's MRSDS system or the expedited service. Account facilities will only be provided to those users who request, on average, five or more reports each month.

14.2 The account facility terms and conditions are:

1. For each calendar month (or similar period) the Authority will issue to the account holder a statement with details of all reports dispatched to the account holder in the relevant month (or similar period) and an invoice showing the amount payable by the account holder.
2. The account holder shall pay to the Authority within 30 days of the date of each statement and invoice the total amount properly due and owing shown in each such statement and invoice without deduction or set off.

14.3 Payment can be made by credit or debit card, BACS transfer or by cheque payable to "The Coal Authority" sent to The Coal Authority, Finance Department, 200 Lichfield Lane, Mansfield, Nottinghamshire, NG18 4RG (or DX 716176 Mansfield 5).

14.4 In the event that the account holder does not pay the amount shown in any statement and invoice within the time specified in paragraph 14.2.2 above the Authority shall be entitled to:

- charge interest on the amount outstanding at the rate of five per cent per annum above the base rate announced from time to time by the Monetary Policy Committee of the Bank of England (or any replacement committee), from the date that it became due to the date of receipt;
- withdraw the account facility;
- withdraw any volume related discount entitlement.

14.5 As and when it deems it necessary to do so, the Authority reserves the right to make searches with credit reference agencies, who may keep a record of those searches and may share that information with other businesses. The Authority also reserves the right to make enquiries about your directors with credit reference agencies.

14.6 The Authority reserves the right to withdraw or suspend customer account facilities where the volumes of reports requested falls below, on average, five per month or for persistent late payment of invoices.

14.7 The decision of the Authority as to the amount, if any, of volume related discount available to high volume users of the Authority's electronic services, is final and not subject to negotiation. Late payment of invoices disqualifies the account holder to any volume related discount entitlement.

15. Plans

15.1 Users should ensure that the full boundary of the property is provided to the Authority and not just the property building footprint or other lesser area. When submitting requests for development site plots, the accompanying plan should show the plot boundary in relation to established surface features.

15.2 The Authority provides with each report a plan of the boundaries of the property in respect of which the report has been prepared. It is necessary for users to ensure that such boundaries correspond with those of the property. If the boundary of the property shown on the Authority plan does not so correspond, any discrepancy should be resolved by the user with the Authority. If users do not refer the discrepancy to the Authority within 28 days of the date of the report in question, users will have to make a fresh search with payment of the appropriate fee. The property will be located with reference to Ordnance Survey (OS) digital publications. The Authority cannot and does not warrant that the OS information is up-to-date, complete or accurate and accepts no liability for the plotted position of property as shown on published OS maps.

15.3 Ordnance Survey has undertaken a positional accuracy improvement programme of its mapping data. The Authority had no control over the timing of issue of positionally improved mapping data by OS or other users of that data. In some instances the relative position between surface features and coal mining and other features has altered as a consequence of this programme. The Authority has ensured that the integrity of its database has been maintained by replotting certain coal mining information to ensure that the relationship between that mining information and the improved OS surface positions is accurate. However, mining reports may still be produced against pre-improved OS mapping whilst the Authority updates its database in line with the OS changes.

16. Shafts and Adits

16.1 Shafts are vertical or near vertical entrances sunk from the surface to access underground mine workings. Adits are walkable entrances driven from the surface to access underground mine workings. Adits may be horizontal, or slope upwards or downwards. Shafts and adits may be collectively referred to as "mine entries".

16.2 The reply as to shafts and adits (within 20m of the boundary of the property) will be prepared only from the records in the possession of the Authority. These records may not be complete. The reporting distance of 20 metres is recommended and agreed with the Law Society, Royal Institution of Chartered Surveyors, Council of Mortgage Lenders and the Association of British Insurers. Given the indeterminate accuracy of many of the source records, the Authority is unable to take account of and reflect in reports any possible difference between the actual and plotted position of the mine entry or its likely size or depth. The approximate location of any such shaft or adit will be identified on a plan with the report at no extra cost. To aid clarity the mine entry symbols are not necessarily shown to the same scale as the plan. Distances are measured from the estimated centre of the shaft or centre point of an adit entrance.

16.3 References to a coal mine shaft within 20 metres of a property or its boundary does not necessarily mean that the property has or will have any instability problems. The number of cases where shafts affect the structure of a property are very low. The Authority provides an optional follow-up supplementary Interpretive Report Service for any user receiving a residential mining report which discloses a mine entry (shaft or adit)—see paragraph 17 of this User Guide.

16.4 Users are reminded that with effect from 31 October 1994 British Coal's interests in unworked coal and coal mines became vested in the Authority. In most cases, but not all, any shaft or adit will be owned by the Authority and not the adjacent surface landowner. In these cases the permission of the Authority must be sought before carrying out any works to locate, treat or in any other way interfere with disused coal mine shafts or adits.

17. Interpretive Reports
17.1 The Authority offers an Interpretive Report Service as a value-added optional extra for any user receiving a residential mining report which discloses a mine entry (shaft or adit). These interpretive reports provide more detailed analysis and advice about mine entries. This will include a risk assessment as to whether, in the expert opinion of the Coal Authority, the main building of the property is inside or outside the possible zone of ground movement from any reported mine entry. In carrying out this risk assessment, the Authority will take account of the geology beneath the property (based on additional data provided by the British Geological Survey where the Authority's data is incomplete), the possible difference between the actual and plotted position of the mine entry, its source and its likely size. Opinion will also be given where the main building is considered clear of the zone of ground movement but the possibility of coal mining subsidence damage to the garden areas or other buildings cannot be discounted. Where property lies inside the zone of influence of a mine entry, the Authority will provide comprehensive advice as to the rights of property owners and the remedial obligations of the Authority or licensed operators.

17.2 The Interpretive Report Service was created to resolve the difficulties being experienced in some parts of the country where properties lost value as a consequence of a mining report disclosing the presence of disused mine entries. Emphasis has been given to customer needs in the design, content and format of the report following extensive customer liaison, as well as with the Law Society, Council of Mortgage Lenders, Association of British Insurers and the Royal Institution of Chartered Surveyors, to ensure its introduction was beneficial to property professionals and the property buying public alike.

17.3 The initial residential report advises of the availability and cost of the Interpretive Report and the procedure for ordering one. The Authority aim to return the majority of Interpretive Reports within 48 hours.

17.4 Payment can be made by credit or debit card, by cheque or on account.

17.5 This service is not available for pre-build property or for non-residential property or sites.

18. Coal mining subsidence damage claims
18.1 In answer to enquiry 9 of the ScotForm (2006) enquiry form, the report will provide information about any claim for coal mining subsidence damage made or pursued since 1 January 1984. Where the Authority confirm that they have not received a damage notice or claim for a property since 1 January 1984 this should not be taken as necessarily inferring that a claim either has or hasn't been made prior to this date. When the first standard mining report enquiry form was introduced in 1989 it asked whether any claims had been made or pursued "in the last five years", i.e.

since 1984. All subsequent editions of the standard enquiry form have retained this 1984 start date.

18.2 If further subsidence damage claims information is required in addition to that provided in a report, the Authority need to manually search their records. Such further enquiries should be made under separate cover to The Coal Authority, Claims History Service, DX 716176 Mansfield 5 or by post to The Coal Authority, Claims History Service, 200 Lichfield Lane, Berry Hill, Mansfield, Nottinghamshire, NG18 4RG, enclosing the relevant fee or by telephone for payment by credit or debit card or for account customers. For advice on the current fee for this service contact the Authority's customer service team on 0845 762 6848 or check the Authority's website at *www.groundstability.com*.

Alternatively, it may be that such information can be obtained by other means such as preliminary enquiries of the present owner.

19. Time Validity

19.1 There is no time protection afforded by replies to ScotForm and other mining and reports. Whether a user can rely on a past report (of his/her own or another) depends upon all the circumstances of the case including how recently it was made, the content of the report, the nature of the property and the user's intentions in relation to it. Licensed operators plans for mining may change as may the other relevant information available to the Authority. If there is any doubt as to whether the previous replies remain valid, it is suggested that a new search should be made. Without prejudice to the generality of the foregoing, any report must not be relied upon in any event in excess of 90 days from its date of issue and must thereafter be verified as still being up-to-date, either by making a fresh search or by using any available update service provided by the Authority.

20. Scot Form (2006) reports insurance

20.1 Insurance cover will be provided to owners of property to mitigate against any loss of value, up to a maximum of £20,000, attributable to any material change of any of the information in a subsequent residential ScotForm (2006) report from that contained in the ScotForm (2006) report to which the insurance attaches. The period of insurance cover is the full term of ownership.

20.2 It is suggested that the report and insurance certificate should be kept with the title deeds. The insurance cover takes account of circumstances where a report was obtained by the seller of the property as part of a Purchaser's Information Pack or where the property is being sold by way of auction. Cover is also provided where a report is obtained in the event of a remortgage of the property or where the owner simply elects to obtain a fresh report.

20.3 The insurance does not cover non-residential property; neither does it cover physical damage to property caused by coal mining subsidence for which other more powerful remedies already exist, in particular, but not limited to, the Coal Mining Subsidence Act 1991.

The insurance is not a substitute for any normal homeowner building and contents insurance cover.

20.4 The insurance has been designed and arranged by Tyser (UK) Ltd, part of Tyser Group (Lloyd's insurance brokers, established 1820) and is underwritten by Groupama Insurance Company via Legal & Contingency Ltd. The insurance certificate provided with the residential report outlines the terms and conditions of this insurance.

Contaminated land

1. The contaminated land regime was brought into effect in Scotland on 14 July 2000. It applies to all land, whether residential, commercial, industrial or agricultural. It can affect owners, occupiers, developers and lenders. The legislation, which is contained in Part IIA, Environmental Protection Act 1990 and regulations and statutory guidance issued under it (see the Contaminated Land (Scotland) Regulations 2000 SI 2000/178 and the Scottish Executive Circular 1/2000, July 2000) is retrospective. It covers existing and future contamination.

2. Local authorities must inspect and identify seriously contaminated sites. They can issue remediation notices requiring action to remediate contamination, in the absence of a voluntary agreement to do so. In certain cases ("Special Sites") responsibility for enforcement lies with the Scottish Environment Protection Agency ("SEPA").

A negative reply to the standard local authority enquiries from the local authority may merely mean the site has not been inspected. It does not preclude a future inspection. It does not necessarily mean there is no problem.

Compliance can be costly, and may result in expenditure, which could exceed the value of the property.

Liability falls primarily on those who "cause or knowingly permit" contamination (a Class A person). If the authority cannot identify a Class A person, liability falls on a Class B person, the current owner, or occupier of the land. Class B persons include lenders in possession. There are complex exclusion provisions for transferring liability from one party to another. Some exclusions apply only on the transfer of land, or the grant of a lease. The applicability of any relevant exclusion needs to be considered before entering such transactions.

In every transaction you should consider whether contamination is an issue.

Conveyancing transactions

In purchases, heritable securities and leases, solicitors should address the issue of advising the client in relation to:
1. Potential liabilities associated with contaminated land, taking into account the client's own knowledge and expertise;
2. Raising specific observations with the seller at least if a substantive response is likely.

In all commercial cases, and if contamination is considered likely to be a risk in residential cases, (e.g. redevelopment of brown field land) solicitors should consider:—
3. Advising the client to consider making enquiries of statutory and regulatory bodies (under the changes to the Council of Mortgage Lenders Handbook, in all residential transactions the solicitor will need to ensure that the contaminated land questions for local authorities are on the property enquiry certificate and to consider undertaking an independent site history investigation, e.g. obtaining a site report from a commercial company).

In commercial cases, if there is a likelihood that the site is contaminated solicitors should consider:—
4. Advising the client to consider instructing an independent full site investigation;
5. Advising the client to use contractual protections.

For unresolved problems, solicitors should consider:—
6. Advising the client to withdraw;
7. Advising the client to consider obtaining insurance (increasingly obtainable for costs of remediation of undetected contamination and any shortfall in value because of undisclosed problems).

Specific Transactions
1. Leases
Consider the effect of the terms of the lease and advise.
2. Heritable Securities

Comply with the standing instructions of the heritable creditor.

In enforcement cases consider and advise client on the risk of the client becoming liable whether as a Class A or a Class B person.

3. Share Sales and Asset Purchases

Consider recommending the obtaining of specialist technical advice on potential liabilities, use of detailed enquiries, warranties and indemnities.

Other Relevant Legislation

Other legislation and common law liabilities (e.g. nuisance) may also be relevant when advising on environmental matters including:

- The Control of Pollution Act 1974
- The Health and Safety at Work etc Act 1974
- The Environmental Protection Act 1990
- The Radioactive Substances Act 1993
- The Environment Act 1995
- The Town and Country Planning (Scotland) Act 1997
- The Groundwater Regulations 1998
- The Pollution Prevention and Control Act 1999 and the Pollution Prevention and Control (Scotland) Regulations 2000, SI 2000/323

Letters of Obligation

View of Conveyancing Committee

The Conveyancing Committee is of the view that conveyancing transactions should be settled with a letter of obligation being granted by the solicitor personally. The practice is to grant the obligation on behalf of the client in relation to the charges register and company file. The view was expressed that selling solicitors should take care when granting letters of obligation that they only deal with matters over which they have control.

What is a classic letter of obligation?

The classic letter of obligation does not need to have any specific words, although it does need to fall within certain parameters. There are various styles, including those produced by the Property Standardisation Group. The letter contains an obligation on a solicitor to clear the record in the period from the date of a search to a date 14 days after settlement and also, if appropriate, to deliver a discharge of one or more security.

Is there anything needed to make the obligation classic apart from the actual obligation itself?

There are four conditions which must be complied with, where applicable. These are:—

- a search must have been carried out immediately prior to the date of entry including, in Sasine cases a search in the computerised presentment book. The CML Handbook provides that the search in the Personal Registers be no more than three working days' old but in all other cases the Conveyancing Committee accepts that both Property and Personal Register searches can be up to seven days' old (five working days' old); In calculating the number of days, the Committee considers that you should count from the settlement date back to the date to which the Search is certified as being correct (as opposed to the date on which it was issued).
- proper enquiry must be made of the client as to whether or not there are any outstanding securities. Even where the client is a receiver or liquidator or other insolvency practitioner the enquiry must be made of both the insolvency practitioner and of the original owner even although no response is received;
- the solicitor granting the obligation must be unaware of any other security; and

- the solicitor granting the obligation must in the case of an undertaking to deliver a discharge, have sufficient funds to pay off the loan(s).

If these conditions have been satisfied then the letter of obligation is a classic one.

What is the effect of a claim on a classic letter of obligation?

A claim can be made in the normal way but there is no penalty excess and no loading under the master policy for a claim under a classic letter of obligation.

What if these conditions are not complied with?

If the conditions are not complied with then the letter of obligation is called a "failed classic" and the normal excess and loading applies. It is "classic" because it contains the classic items but it is "failed" because the conditions (set out above) have not been satisfied.

What about where the letter of obligation contains other obligations, particularly where a solicitor has no control over the situation?

In this case the letter (or more accurately the relevant obligation in the letter) is called a "non-classic". Where a claim is made against such an obligation there will be a "double deductible". That means that double the normal excess will be applied to it. The grant of such non-classic obligations should, needless to say, never be given.

What about a letter of obligation which contains both classic and non-classic items? Does the whole thing become failed or non-classic?

A classic letter of obligation is always classic and has the same protections. If the letter contains other non-classic obligations then the classic elements of the letter remain protected and the non-classic elements will suffer the double deductible.

Is there an implied obligation on a solicitor to give a letter of obligation?

While there is no legal obligation to give a letter of obligation where missives are silent, there is a professional duty on a solicitor to grant a letter of obligation unless the solicitor advises to the contrary at the earliest possible opportunity. This expression "at the earliest possible opportunity" does not have a particular meaning but it is interpreted as being before conclusion of missives. This is because if a solicitor finds out before conclusion of missives that no letter of obligation will be given he or she can advise the client who can make an informed decision of whether or not to enter into the missives or to contract for a Register House settlement.

In some cases however, there are exceptions. Where someone conveys property as a gift the grantee takes it "warts and all" and is simply obtaining what is within the ownership of the granter of the gift and to the extent that the granter had power to grant it. There is therefore no obligation on the solicitor to give a letter of obligation in such a case.

Is it possible to contract out of giving a letter of obligation?

It is indeed possible to contract out of giving the obligation and this is most commonly found in articles of roup where one takes the title as it stands. It might seem rather odd not to give a classic obligation in such circumstances since a classic obligation attracts no excess or loading but for a classic letter to be given there needs to be a search and in a roup situation it may be contracted that no search is given. Where that is agreed in advance and where there is no search it is not appropriate to give a letter of obligation and there is clear notice in advance.

Do letters of obligation apply to the Charges Register?

The letter of obligation may contain a provision to show a clear search in the Charges Register and company file but there is no obligation on the solicitor to give a personal obligation to that effect and it should only be given on behalf of the client.

Whether the company is a UK company or a foreign company or an LLP or another corporate body one should never give a personal obligation for any company search.

However in missives, solicitors frame the clause obliging the client to supply company searches. It is reasonable to say that these searches should be brought down to the nearest reasonable point and in the Committee's view it is reasonable to order a charges search no more than three working days before settlement brought down to the date to which the registers have been brought down at the time of such order. (There is no objection to the parties contracting for a search more recent than that if circumstances require). If there were a breach of this then the clients' claim would be a normal claim in negligence for the search having been brought down too early. Liability for the "gap" period (between the date of the search and settlement and indeed until 14 days after settlement) is, however, a clients' risk.

What happens when the letter of obligation is breached?

A letter of obligation is a contract between the seller's solicitor and the purchaser, not the purchasers' solicitor. The remedy for the breach therefore is for the purchaser to sue the selling solicitor. If however, the obligation given by the solicitor mirrors an obligation in the missives then the seller and the seller's solicitor are jointly and severally liable.

When does the letter of obligation prescribe?

The prescriptive period of five years does not begin to run until the breach but that is likely to be soon after settlement since it covers only the "gap" period.

How long should the period be within the letter of obligation?

The Law Society and the insurers have agreed that the obligation may be given for a period of up to 14 days after settlement. However, practitioners must take all steps to stamp and register at the earliest possible opportunity. With SDLT online, this is much easier these days.

Should letters of obligation be given where there is no monetary consideration?

If there is a consideration for the property then a letter of obligation should be granted (subject to the issues above). If the grant of the disposition or lease or other document disposing of the property is in the nature of a gift then there should be no letter of obligation. However, where there is a consideration which is not conventional (such as a transfer of matrimonial property where one party is giving up rights or buying the other out or in the case of a disposal of land where one party is taking on onerous obligations (for example "cleaning up" contaminated land) then that would be treated as an onerous transaction and a letter of obligation should be given.

Is the grant of a letter of obligation where my client grants a Section 75 Agreement to a Local Authority in the same category?

The answer to this is "no". The master policy insurers only regard such letters as classic where they relate to disposals such as a lease, disposition or security. A section 75 agreement is in the nature of a deed of real burdens or servitude. While there is insurance for a letter of obligation in such circumstances a "double deductible" will be made, as the letter is not classic and outwith our control. The Property Law Committee therefore recommends that a letter of obligation should not be given in such circumstances.

What does one do when one is conveying a property under the Adults with Incapacity Legislation?

In such a case the letter of obligation should state at the heading the name of both the adult and the guardian. They should jointly be referred to as the client.

Are there any further checks one should make?

If there is a high value transaction then one should consider whether the

PI cover of the firm granting the letter of obligation is adequate. Although the letter may be classic and the insurers may be expected to pay out on it, they would only pay out to the extent of the cover.

Should there be an obligation to deliver a land certificate within a specific period?

If one gives an obligation to deliver a land certificate within a specific period then that is outwith one's control as only the Keeper has control of when the land certificate will be delivered. It is therefore perfectly reasonable to undertake to deliver the land certificate to the lender "as soon as received". Although slightly contradictory to the style of letter of obligation in the practice book issued by the Registers of Scotland the Committee is happy with this aspect.

Should an in-house lawyer give a letter of obligation?

An in-house lawyer is not covered by the master policy and therefore should not give a letter of obligation. However, it is only reasonable that the in-house solicitor must contract out in this situation and advise prior to missives being concluded that no solicitor's personal obligation will be given.

What are the pitfalls when acting for an insolvency practitioner?

There is really no harm in the solicitor of the insolvency practitioner giving the classic letter of obligation as long as they comply with the conditions which would include an attempt to contact the previous owner. Some receivers' solicitors are concerned that there might be a "Sharp v Thomson" type disposition in a drawer delivered but unrecorded. The Keeper however has confirmed that he will not exclude indemnity on that ground. The insurers do not add any further loading or penalty in those circumstances although they do expect the lawyer acting for the insolvency practitioner at least to make enquiries of the former directors or owner even although there may be no response.

If I am acting for a borrower, can I give a letter of obligation to the lender if I am not receiving a letter of obligation from the Seller's solicitor?

Just because there is no "back to back" obligation from the other side, so long as the purchaser to lender obligation complies with the "classic rules" then any claim will be honoured as a classic obligation.

What do I tell the client if no letter of obligation is to be given?

Often house builders' missives provide for letters of obligation not to be given or for these to be granted on behalf of the builder. This is unsatisfactory and has been raised with Homes for Scotland. There appears to be no immediate prospect of the situation changing. If a letter of obligation is not to be given then the client must be advised of the risks.

When do I get the letter of obligation when entering into a lease?

Very often a tenant takes entry on missives but the lease is not signed up until later. A letter of obligation can be granted at entry. If there is any doubt arrangements should be made to have the lease signed by all the parties in time for entry. If that is not possible then the Keeper will accept the missives (provided they comply with the self proving rules) for registration in the Land Register.

If the lease is for less than 20 years then the letter of obligation should just be given at entry, as a real right is obtained at that point.

Can I grant a letter of obligation on a second registration where the land certificate has not been issued?

The obligation to deliver a land certificate with no exclusion of indemnity is a clients' obligation. The solicitors' letter of obligation simply covers the "gap" period and therefore this situation is no different from any other.

Can I give an obligation to deliver a discharge of a notice of potential liability for costs, even although I withhold funds?

A letter of obligation should not be granted unless one is in control of the situation, so only where you are sure you can implement it should an obligation be given in such circumstances. In this case it would be appropriate where the factor has given confirmation that he will grant a discharge in exchange for a fixed sum and that sum has been retained at settlement.

Does ARTL make any difference to letters of obligation?

There is no change in relation to the classic letter of obligation except that with a paperless transaction or an electronic Land Certificate, it is acceptable to change the terminology so that after the words "Land Certificate to be issued" you may add the words "in either paper or electronic format".

What happens when the format of the forms change?

If the format of the form changed, as they have done recently, then it is perfectly acceptable to substitute the numbering. So, for example, in relation to a registered interest, references to questions "1 to 8" can now be "1 to 10".

What is the Letter of Obligation position when selling a company?

If property is acquired on the sale of a company then there is no conveyance of the property and no letter of obligation need be given. However, sometimes the purchaser's solicitor has to give a letter of obligation to its clients' funder. That is treated no differently from any other so long as it is in classic format and the checks have been carried out. The purchaser of the company may be able to obtain the appropriate property warranties from the seller of the shares. This will be the case very often but, even if it is not, it does not affect the position with the letter of obligation.

Postal Settlement

The Conveyancing Committee has considered the practice of some selling agents to insist on receipt of the settlement cheque before they forward the Disposition and other settlement items to the purchaser's solicitor. The result of this practice is that the purchaser's solicitor is unable to check these items until after the settlement cheque has been encashed.

The mechanics of settlement are a matter for agreement between the solicitors. However the Committee is of the view that, where postal settlement is envisaged, the preferable course of action is that the seller's Solicitor sends the executed deed and deliverable title deeds contemporaneously with the purchaser's solicitor sending the settlement cheque, each to be held by the receiving party as undelivered pending performance by the other side, such performance to be confirmed by an exchange of communications (telephone, fax or e-mail) on the settlement date itself. Such an arrangement requires to be agreed in the missives or between the parties and their agents in advance of settlement (see the guidance entitled "Cheques to be Held as Undelivered"). The Committee would encourage all practitioners to adopt this practice on the basis that exchanging a cheque for a disposition and titles on the day of settlement is good risk management.

Cheques to be Held as Undelivered

Where postal settlement of a transaction is envisaged arrangements for the sending of and intromission with funds and other settlement items require to be agreed in advance. It is not appropriate unilaterally to impose a condition, whether made verbally or in writing, after a contract such as for the sale of heritable property has become binding. In the absence of subsequent agreement, the missives prevail. It is professionally improper for an agent to impose a unilateral condition, the first intimation of which to the other side is in a letter or an email on the morning of settlement. Prior discussion and agreement is necessary if any such condition is to be effective.

It is recognised that in a postal settlement it is appropriate for the buyer's solicitor to send a cheque to be held as undelivered either pending fulfilment of conditions in the missives or pending confirmation that the solicitor is in funds and the cheque can be encashed. Both sides need to agree to this latter condition. This practice avoids alternative courses of action such as bridging or effecting settlement in person, all of which can be viewed as adding expense, though agents should consider the alternative of electronic transfer of funds (which may have certain advantages and disadvantages on which see the guidance entitled "Settlement, Loan Redemption and Remit of the Free Proceeds of Sale"). Assuming trust between practitioners, arrangements which rely on mutual acceptance of an undertaking not to cash the cheque or intromit with funds sent electronically can be made. This is analogous to the customary sending of the settlement cheque to be held as undelivered pending dispatch of a duly executed disposition, etc.

It is also important to bear in mind that the question of conditional delivery of a cheque is dealt with in s.21 of the Bills of Exchange Act 1882.

The Society's view is that it is improper professional practice for a purchasing agent to seek to impose unilaterally a condition making delivery and encashment of a settlement cheque conditional upon the purchasing agent authorising that. However, even though it is improper, that does not entitle the selling agent to cash the cheque in breach of such condition provided that it was sent subject to the words "to be held as undelivered". **The Professional Practice Committee and the Council confirm that where money or deeds are sent to be held as undelivered pending purification of a condition, they should be so held if the condition is not purified. Settlement will not take place until they can be treated as delivered,** with consequent penalty interest if provided for in the missives. The matter is one of practice between agents rather than of law.

Settlement, Loan Redemption and Remit of Free Proceeds of Sale

The Professional Practice Committee has seen an increasing number of requests for information or guidance on the question of whether settlement of house purchase and sale transactions should take place by cheque or electronic transfer. This is also getting to be a frequently asked question by clients, and the issues are not well understood.

Almost all transactions now settle by post. A solicitor can send a cheque subject to conditions but it is not practical to attach conditions at the time of sending an electronic transfer. It is perfectly proper to reach agreement with the other solicitor in advance of sending funds by electronic transfer that those funds will be held as undelivered pending fulfilment of certain conditions, but if that is not agreed in advance, it is too late to impose the condition at the time the funds are sent by electronic transfer.

If such pre-arranged conditions are not fulfilled, the solicitor receiving the funds would risk a finding of professional misconduct or unsatisfactory professional conduct if the funds are treated as delivered and paid out to clients or third parties.

An electronic transfer cannot be stopped, but if the buyer's solicitor does not receive the titles, Letter of Obligation, keys etc in return for a client's account cheque which has been sent to be held as undelivered he can either demand the return of a cheque or stop the cheque (in extreme circumstances). Settlement by cheque therefore protects the buyer by giving the buyer's solicitor control over the money even after the cheque has been sent. A seller's solicitor can also protect the seller by attaching conditions to deeds etc sent by post, including a condition about interest on the price if settlement has been delayed.

Traditionally, when a selling solicitor received and banked another solicitor's client account cheque, he could write his own client account cheques to redeem his client's loan or settle his client's purchase on the same day. Problems are encountered very occasionally if the solicitor receiving the cheque banks at the same branch of the same bank as the solicitor sending the cheque although that is rare.

Since the introduction of the cheque clearing process known as 2-4-6 there is a risk that the cheque sent out will be presented for payment at the sender's bank before the cheque paid in has cleared. The Professional Practice department at the Society has received a number of telephone calls from solicitors affected in this way.

These problems may be surmounted by either:

(1) clients arranging short term bridging loans or

(2) solicitors arranging a temporary facility with their own bank that would allow the bank to transfer sufficient funds into the client bank account to meet the presentation of an outgoing cheque where the incoming cheque has still to clear. Any interest payable could be charged to the client although that would have to be specified in the relevant Terms of Business.

If neither of these options is adopted, a third option namely:

(3) settlement by electronic transfer is suggested to avoid the possibility of a shortfall in the client account that may in turn lead to a failure to comply with Rule B6 (the Accounts etc rules).

If a selling solicitor is also purchasing for his client on the same day and wishes the sale to be settled by electronic transfer the selling solicitor should put a clause in the missives requiring the sale to be settled electronically. That will be subject to agreement by the buyer, but it must be in the missives or it cannot be insisted upon.

Subject to these considerations the Professional Practice Committee remains of the view that settlement by cheque between solicitors is in both clients' interests as the cheque can be sent in advance to be held as undelivered pending delivery of relevant items and/or confirmation that the sender is in funds, and the disposition can be sent in advance subject to the seller's conditions.

LENDERS and CLIENTS

The Committee agreed however that so far as settlement with the client and the lender are concerned the seller's agent should ascertain in advance whether the seller would prefer to meet the cost of an electronic transfer of funds or opt for the issue of a cheque in relation to (a) redemption of the loan (if the method is not prescribed by the lender) and (b) remit of the free proceeds of sale to the seller. Such instructions will of course be subject to the solicitor ensuring that there are sufficient cleared funds to meet whatever method of payment is adopted.

ENGLAND and WALES

If a client is purchasing a property in England or Wales out of the proceeds of sale of a property in Scotland, it is important to ascertain the requirements for settling the purchase at the earliest possible stage. Purchase and sale transactions routinely settle by electronic transfer in England and Wales and the client's English or Welsh Solicitor will assume that he will receive funds by electronic transfer. If there will not be sufficient time for a cheque to clear before funds are required in England or Wales, the selling solicitor should explain that to the client and conclude the bargain for the sale on the basis that settlement will be by electronic transfer or advise the client that he will need to arrange temporary bridging facilities to await cleared funds. Failure to address these issues at an early stage is likely to lead to a dissatisfied client and a possible complaint to the Scottish Legal Complaints Commission.

Registration of Deeds—Payment of Registration Dues by Direct Debit

Variable direct debit is a robust and secure means of payment, but the Society has issued guidance that the principal client bank account should never be subject to variable direct debit. A separate account should be opened from which to operate such payments. This will reduce the risk of an error causing a shortage on the client bank account and assist in the ease of reconciling the account.

Registration of Deeds—ARTL

Guidance

1. The Local Registration Authority (LRA—the person(s) responsible for Administering ARTL in the practice unit) should be solicitors.

2. Principal responsibility for compliance with the Keeper's Terms and Conditions shall rest on the Practice Administrator (PA). All managers in the practice unit or solicitors in the organisation registered to use ARTL should understand their joint general responsibility. In smaller practice units it is anticipated that the Local Registration Authority and Practice Administrator may be one and the same person.

3. The PA should understand his/her responsibility for the actions of parties who are given access to the system.

4. The PA and LRA should jointly (where these are separate persons) ensure compliance with procedures and that the integrity of the system and in particular usernames, passwords, smartcards and pin numbers in connection with the digital execution of documents are preserved.

5. Practice units should have contingency plans in place. They should incorporate specific provisions in connection with:
   — Sickness or absence of the PA or LRA.
   — Loss of access to the system.
   — General contingency planning issues.

6. All staff with access to the system should be made aware of the Keeper's Terms and Conditions, the Society's Guidance and Practice Notes and their obligations in respect of security of the ARTL system.

7. A policy should be adopted in regard to possession of mandates to execute documents electronically.

8. Direct debit payments should not be made on the principal client bank account. A separate subsidiary Client bank account holding only sums required to meet direct debit payments (and perhaps a small surplus where appropriate) should be operated for such purposes.

9. For the avoidance of doubt it should be noted that the following may give rise to conduct as well as service complaint issues:
   — Deliberately giving any other party access to your username, password, smartcard and/or pin number.
   — Execution of any document electronically without the appropriate authority.
   — Use of any other person's username, password, smartcard and/or pin number.
   — False declarations in the ARTL process.

ARTL PRACTICE NOTES

Introduction

Although ARTL represents a fundamental change in the process of Land Registration, the Law Society of Scotland has managed to introduce only one single Rule as a consequence. There are some issues that require Guidance and at a more basic level Practice Notes.

Terms Of Business

Whenever possible Terms of Business should specify whether ARTL is to be used or not. In the event that it is not possible to confirm the position when the Terms of Business are first issued, that fact should be made clear and the position clarified in an amendment to the Terms of Business as soon as possible. The ARTL process should be explained to the client with particular reference to the Mandate position and the different registration dues, but with the proviso that for reasons outwith the solicitor's control, the system may not be available in certain circumstances. It should be remembered that use of ARTL is dependent on the client being willing to sign the appropriate ARTL mandate.

Missives

Offers should state whether it is intended that ARTL is to be used in the transaction if it is available. Selling agents should at the earliest opportunity make clear whether or not it is intended to use the system. In the absence of a provision in the missives there will be no obligation on either party to use ARTL and the transaction may proceed under ARTL, or not, as may be agreed.

The standard missives contain examples of clauses which may be of assistance.

Conveyancing

Tell Me Don't Show Me

Underlying the ARTL application is the principle of "Tell Me Don't Show Me". This is already in use to a limited extent in several questions in the existing Land Register Forms 1 & 2 where the applicant's agent effectively certifies certain statements to be true without providing vouching to that effect. ARTL extends this principle and care should be taken when completing the application online that such statements can be properly certified. The application should be reviewed immediately prior to completion/submission to ensure such statements are still true at that time. Paragraphs 3 and 4 should be noted in terms of responsibility for this certification.

The buyer's agent may require sight of a copy of an ARTL Mandate obtained by the seller's agent in order to ensure that statements on the online application can properly be certified as true. The agents should ensure that there are adequate obligations in this regard.

Discharges

Where a practice unit has authority from a lender to execute discharges on their behalf, whether under ARTL or not, individual Mandates may not be required if the Council of the Law Society have granted a waiver in terms of the rules and the general mandate may be registered provided each execution of a discharge is vouched by an appropriate authority from a lender. To protect the integrity of the Register, it is imperative that discharges are promptly registered in such cases. Wherever possible discharges should be lodged electronically.

Delayed Discharges

ARTL envisages that discharges will be electronically executed and released for registration at settlement. Where this does not happen, discharges will have to be submitted by the seller's solicitor either under ARTL or on paper. It would be expected that Discharges would be registered within 14 days of settlement. Parties should ensure that there are adequate obligations in this regard. On submission by the seller's agent of the Discharge for registration, ARTL will acknowledge that to the seller's agent and intimate the fact to the purchaser's agent.

Letters of Obligation

Although registration in ARTL cases will be completed in most cases within 24 hours following submission of the application to the Keeper, a standard 14 day letter of obligation should be issued in normal form. This is likely to be reviewed once ARTL has been in operation for some time. To ensure that the letter of obligation is classic the usual checks should be made.

Mandates

Where Mandates are sent to clients for execution, a covering letter clearly explaining the meaning and import of the mandate and its effect should be sent. Where appropriate any other caveats relating to the execution of the document or its effect should be incorporated in that covering letter or intimated separately to the client prior to execution of the mandate. It is improper for an electronic signature to be applied without the appropriate authority. It may also be an offence. Care should be taken to ensure that:

— Mandates are in place
— They correctly identify the parties
— The parties have the capacity to grant such Mandates
— They have not been withdrawn
— They are sent to be archived by the Keeper within the 14 day time limit following registration

Unrepresented Borrowers

In addition to other guidance and practice notes, additional care should be taken to ensure that unrepresented borrowers are made aware that they are unrepresented and understand the meaning import and effect of that. The appropriate special mandate should be obtained for execution of documents in such cases.

Operational Issues

ARTL and PKI Administration

The Terms and Conditions of Use of ARTL and the PKI Policy Statement set out the responsibilities and obligations of practice units in relation to the use of ARTL, but the following is a list of issues which should be particularly considered. It is illustrative only and is not definitive:

Practice units should:
— Monitor the use of ARTL access by authorised users.
— Promptly remove access rights when users leave the firm.
— Ensure that the level of authority given to staff is commensurate with their knowledge and ability.
— Regularly review Risk Management issues.
— Where smartcards are lost or where the pin number or username and password may be compromised, withdraw access rights and replace them without delay.

ARTL Terms and Conditions

All staff with access to the system should be familiar with the Keeper's Terms and Conditions, rule B8.2, the Guidance and Practice Notes and the conditions of use of the PKI.

SDLT and Registration Dues

For the avoidance of doubt, the obligation in respect of all payments of registration dues and SDLT rests with the practice unit. In completing an ARTL application the practice unit accepts this responsibility and failure to meet this responsibility may have significant consequences including conduct issues.

Practice units should ensure before completing registration that they are in funds to meet these obligations.

Care should be taken in relation to the provision of cleared funds when settling a sale and purchase simultaneously and settlement is effected by means of cheque as SDLT and Registration Dues relating to the purchase will be deducted from the practice unit account by direct debit within three days following submission of the application.

Compliance Issues

Practice units should cooperate with the Keeper in any auditing or compliance procedures.

Practice units should comply with the Keeper's Terms and Conditions at all times.

Practice units should be aware of money laundering and other issues.

Managers, Senior staff, Organisations and practice units have a responsibility to preserve the integrity of the PKI signature and should make all users aware of their obligations to keep this secure. In particular they should remind staff of the duty to keep PIN numbers secret and prevent others having access to their Smartcards. If other users need access to the system they should be granted their own Smartcards and PINs.

Practice units should be aware of the data protection issues arising from the use of the ARTL system and in particular the addition of ARTL to their declaration of data use at next renewal should they hold Data Protection Act Registration.

Definitions

"ARTL" means the computer system provided by the Keeper of the Registers of Scotland ("the Keeper") to enable creation of electronic documents and the electronic generation and communication of an application for registration of an interest in land in the Land Register of Scotland and the automated registration of that interest.

"ARTL compatible" means, in respect of a transaction, one which is capable of being processed under ARTL as being of a kind, and falling within a geographical area, approved by the Keeper for such processing.

"practice units" shall include Organisations and in that context references to Managers shall include senior line management working in-house in Organisations who are themselves solicitors.

Retention of Funds

The Professional Practice Department at the Society receives a substantial number of inquiries about solicitors' obligations in relation to funds retained at settlement of conveyancing transactions (retentions). Solicitors frequently find that they are unable to get instructions from clients who either decline to reply to letters or who have disappeared. Some general guidance may be of assistance in these situations.

Where a sum of money is to be retained at settlement of a conveyancing transaction, the conditions upon which it is retained should be set out in writing at settlement. The agreement should specify the time limit for implementation. Matters should not be left to recollection of telephone conversations which may become vague with the passage of time.

If funds were retained pending fulfillment of certain conditions by the seller, they should be released when those conditions have been fulfilled in terms of the written agreement. The purchaser's solicitor does not need to seek instructions from his or her client at that stage.

Solicitors are entitled to rely upon agreements reached with other solicitors at settlement which set out conditions on which funds will be released. If the client instructs the solicitor not to release funds there could be a conflict of interest between solicitor and client requiring the solicitor to withdraw from acting.

It may be that the conditions for release of the funds have not been fulfilled by the seller. In these circumstances if the purchaser's solicitor produces vouching for the actual or estimated expenditure required to fulfil the conditions, the seller's agent does not require the seller's instructions to agree to the release of the funds as so vouched. Again solicitors are entitled to rely on the reciprocity of such agreements.

Implementation of Letters of Obligation in Land Registration Cases

An Edinburgh firm asked whether, in a land registration case, it was appropriate on delivery of the land certificate to return the letter of obligation marked as fully implemented. The firm on the other side of a particular transaction had declined to do so, on the basis that the Keeper might require to rectify the land certificate at a later stage. The Committee agreed that, where a land certificate had been issued without exclusion of indemnity, the proper practice was for the purchaser's solicitor to return the letter of obligation marked as implemented.

Identifying Mortgage Fraud

The recent slow down in the UK property market has exposed a rise in mortgage fraud by organised criminals and the potential vulnerability of professionals to be exploited by organised crime syndicates.

How is the fraud perpetrated?

- A criminal syndicate will usually organise finance on a number of properties. The buy-to-let market is particularly vulnerable to mortgage fraud, whether through new build apartment complexes or large scale renovation projects.
- The nominated purchasers, who are taking out the mortgage, are likely to have no beneficial interest in the property and may even be fictitious. This creates a real risk that a solicitor may enter into a contract on behalf of a non-existent principal and thus raises the possibility that the solicitor may be personally liable to implement the contract.
- The value of the property is inflated and a maximum loan-to-value will be taken out for the full inflated valuation.
- Often, mortgage payments are not met and the properties are allowed to deteriorate. The properties can also be used for other criminal or fraudulent activities such as drug production, unlicensed gambling and prostitution.
- When the lender seeks payment of the mortgage, the crime syndicate raises mortgages with another lender through further fictitious purchasers and effectively sells the property back to themselves, but at an even greater leveraged valuation.
- Because the second mortgage is inflated, the first mortgage is repaid together with the arrears, leaving a substantial profit. This may be repeated many times, until a lender finally calls up the security, only to find the property in disrepair and worth significantly less than the current mortgage and its arrears.

Using the services of professionals

Organised criminals will generally involve at least one professional at the centre of the fraud, to provide reassurance and direction to the other professionals instructed to act around the periphery. There is evidence that mortgage brokers and introducers have been used in this role in the past.

Mortgage lenders often rely on professionals to verify the legitimacy of a transaction and safeguard their interests. Lenders may not extensively verify the information they receive, especially in a rising market. They will subscribe to the CML Handbook and expect their solicitors to comply with their guidelines as a means of protecting their lending.

Solicitors are likely to be approached with packaged transactions and completed paper work. The lender will often have already received the loan applications, and granted the loan before the solicitor is instructed. The solicitor will simply be required to carry out the necessary conveyancing work to transfer title and complete the transaction.

The solicitor will be encouraged to complete the Certificate of Title at the gross price and not the actual price paid for the property after allowances and discounts, while being discouraged from complying with specific obligations in the CML Handbook (e.g. Para. 4 which requires solicitors to have had sight of the valuation report in every case; Para. 5.9 which requires solicitors to report in every case where the balance of the purchase price is not being provided by the borrower from his own funds; and Para.6.4 which requires disclosure of all incentives).

How are you affected?

If a mortgage has been obtained by fraud, it is then the proceeds of crime. If solicitors complete a property transaction where the mortgage has been obtained by fraud, you risk committing a principal money laundering offence. Courts will assume a high level of legal knowledge and education, and be less willing to accept claims that a solicitor was unwittingly involved in a fraud if they have not applied appropriate due diligence to a transaction.

How can you protect yourself?

Know the warning signs for fraudulent mortgage transactions. Ask yourself the following questions:

- Has the property been owned by the current owner for less than six months?
- Has the value of the property significantly increased in a short period of time?
- Does the client usually engage in property investment of this scale?
- Does the client seem unusually disinterested in their purchase?
- Does the client seem unusually disinterested in the amount of the fee?
- Is the mortgage for the full value of the property?
- Is the deposit being paid by someone other than the purchaser?
- If there is money left over from the mortgage after the purchase price has been paid, are you being asked to pay this money to the account of someone you don't know, or to the introducer, or to someone else on the client's instructions?
- Have you been asked to enter a price on the title that is greater than you know was paid for the property?

Where any of these warning signs exist, applying anti-money laundering checks and applying the requirements set out in the CML handbook will help you to understand whether you are involved in a legitimate transaction or if you are being used to facilitate mortgage fraud.

Relevant checks and procedures include:

Know your client and any beneficial owners—ascertain and verify the identity of the purchaser. Ensure the identities you have been given correspond with the information on the mortgage documents and any bank accounts relating to the transaction.

Undertake enhanced due diligence—many organised crime syndicates conducting mortgage fraud provide only paperwork, and avoid a meeting. If you do not meet your client, you are required under the Money Laundering Regulations 2007 to undertake Enhanced Due Diligence, and enhanced monitoring of the transaction.

Relying on other professionals—if you asked to use the reliance provisions in the Money Laundering Regulations 2007 to minimise client due diligence activities, consider who you are relying upon.
- Are they regulated for anti-money laundering purposes?
- Do you know them personally?
- Are they from an established firm?
- What is their reputation?
- Are they able to provide you with the client due diligence material they have?

Even if you rely on someone else, you are still responsible for ensuring due diligence has been appropriately conducted.

Reporting—if you suspect you are being asked to facilitate money laundering, you should consider making a disclosure to the Serious Organised Crime Agency.

Disclose material facts—inform your lender client providing the mortgage of all material facts as required under the CML Handbook.

Discount Standard Securities—Discharges
The Conveyancing Committee has agreed that a discount standard security in which the debtor's obligation was stated to subsist for a defined period of years would not require the registration of a discharge after the expiry of that defined time. The security would expire automatically after the period stated in the security had elapsed. However, in dealing with sales of properties where such securities had existed and had not been formerly discharged but had expire, the profession would require to ensure in missives that the obligation to provide a clear search was removed or qualified with regard to the standard security and that it was made clear to the purchaser and his agents *at that stage* that no discharge would be delivered.

Discharge of Standard Securities
1. Please refer to draft CML Guidance on Mortgage Redemption statements.

2. Solicitors should be aware that, since 1 September 2010, it has been the policy of Registers of Scotland that they will no longer delay the registration of any application pending receipt of a Discharge that has been marked "to follow". This may result in a Land Certificate being issued showing an outstanding standard security by the previous owner. However, it is possible to demonstrate that the prior standard security has been removed from the title sheet by obtaining a Form 12 report or a copy of the title sheet from Registers Direct (for which an additional fee is payable). If an application to register the discharge is submitted before the related application is completed the Registers will process them together.

3. Solicitors should also be aware that many lenders will refuse to release executed Discharges until they have received cleared funds to redeem the outstanding indebtedness. The Society is unable to insist or require lenders to exercise any expedition in the release of Discharges. (In cases of extreme delay, see Paragraph 4 below).

4. Solicitors frequently experience difficulty in obtaining Discharges from lenders, particularly those based in England, where Discharges are not required in the same format and the registers can be cleared more easily.

Section 18 of the Conveyancing and Feudal Reform (Scotland) Act 1970 effectively permits a debtor to apply to the local Sheriff Court and, on satisfying the Court that the debt has been redeemed, the Court will issue an order equivalent to a Discharge. Intimating in writing to the lender that you intend raising proceedings under section 18 and seeking expenses is often effective.

The 1970 Act outlines the procedure and you should also see Act of Sederunt (Sheriff Court Ordinary Cause Rules) 1993 No.1956 (S.223).

5. Many of the difficulties caused by the delay in the release of executed Discharges could be eradicated by the use of ARTL—see Guidance on ARTL.

Division D: Court Work

Duty to Lodge a Joint Minute and Move for Decree

The Professional Practice Committee has reaffirmed a Guideline originally published in December 1996. The Committee was asked for guidance about a divorce action where the wife defender had agreed terms with her husband in a Joint Minute which was signed by her solicitors. The action was allowed to proceed as undefended, but when the affidavits and Minute for Decree were lodged by the husband's solicitors, decree was not sought in terms of the Joint Minute, which had included a payment of periodical allowance.

The Committee agreed that a solicitor acting for a pursuer has a duty not only to lodge the Joint Minute, but also to seek decree in the terms of the Joint Minute. The solicitor for the defender is entitled to rely on that being done without requiring to check the Court Process.

Division E: Acting as Notary Public

1. General information

Responsibility for admission and registration of notaries lies with the Council of The Law Society of Scotland under the Law Reform (Miscellaneous Provisions) (Scotland) Act 1990. Petitions to the Court of Session for admission as a solicitor normally include an application for admission as a notary public. Prior to 1 November 2007 any solicitor on the roll of solicitors had the right to act as a notary. With effect from 1 November 2007 only solicitors holding a current practising certificate issued by The Law Society of Scotland have the right to act as a notary. See Legal Profession and Legal Aid (Scotland) Act 2007 (asp 5) Section 62. Accordingly most but not all solicitors are notaries public.

The Law Society of Scotland is a member of the United Kingdom Notarial Forum.

Current Notarial Functions

Oaths, affidavits and affirmations.

The Solicitors (Scotland) Act 1980 provides that these may be signed before a notary public. Such deeds should not relate to any matter in respect of the preservation of the peace, prosecutions, trial or punishment of an offence, or any proceedings before either house of Parliament or any committee thereof.

Affidavits under the Matrimonial Homes (Family Protection) (Scotland) Act 1981.

This role is changed by the Civil Partnerships Act 2004 and the Family Law (Scotland) Act 2006.

Foreign documents.
Documents for use in foreign jurisdictions often require execution before a notary. Care should be taken to ensure that you have your authority registered with the Foreign and Commonwealth Office before executing such documents.

Protests in maritime matters.
Protests for example against poor wind and weather conditions by a sea captain on arrival in port are signed before a notary public.

Notarial execution.
Signature on behalf of persons who are blind or unable to write. See the Requirements of Writing (Scotland) Act 1995.

Miscellaneous
Other functions include notarising entry of a person to overseas territories, notarising documents in connection with formation of overseas companies and drawing for repayment of bonds of debenture.

2. Guidance
When acting as a notary the following points should be addressed:
Is a notary required?
If so in what capacity?
Do you clearly understand the procedures in this particular case?
Are you disqualified in any way?

Jurisdiction
Is the matter governed by the jurisdiction where the document originated?
Is the matter governed by the jurisdiction where the notarial act is to take place?
A notary acting in Scotland on a Scottish matter presents no problem.
A notary acting in Scotland in a non Scottish matter requires care to ensure that there is no prohibition in the foreign jurisdiction on the Scottish notary acting.
A notary acting outwith Scotland in a Scottish matter. Generally notaries should defer to local notaries. See the Public Notaries Act 1801.
A notary acting outwith Scotland in a non Scottish matter. Generally a notary should not act.

Identity of the deponent
Proof of identity consistent with money-laundering standards should be seen and recorded. Often documents require the incorporation of a declaration by the notary that he/she is satisfied as to identity.

The deponent understands the document
It is essential the notary is satisfied on this point. Short documents should be read over and the deponent should be invited to formally acknowledge that they have read and understand the document. Unless the notary is fluent documents in foreign languages must be accompanied by a certified translation.
Some documents do not require administration of an oath. Where documents do require administration of an oath the deponent must be sworn. Although not strictly necessary it is good practice to have the deponent raise their right hand and repeat some form of words along the lines "I swear by Almighty God that the contents of this document are true." The phraseology should be varied to take account of persons of other religions. For those who do not wish to take a religious oath the words "solemnly and sincerely affirm" may be substituted for "swear by Almighty God". There is authority for the proposition that where this oath is not

actually formally sworn the document is void (*Blair v North British Mercantile Insurance Company*, 1889 16 R 325).

Execution

This depends on the jurisdiction and the type of deed. In some jurisdictions the notary and deponent require to sign on every page including schedules and annexations. If in doubt this is safe practice. It is essential that the document is executed in the presence of the notary and both signatures are applied contemporaneously. It has been held to be professional misconduct for a notary to send a document for signature by a client and subsequently apply the notarial signature.

Alterations should be initialled by both parties. Notaries should add the words "notary public" after their signature. If they are not fully designed in the body of the document a full designation is good practice. The application of the notarial seal is not necessary for Scottish purposes but may be necessary in other jurisdictions.

Apostilles

Certain documents for use abroad require a signature and notarial seal and to be "legalised" (authenticated) by the Foreign and Commonwealth office in London. See the Hague Convention on legalisation of foreign documents. Notaries should register their signature and seal with the Foreign and Commonwealth Office for this purpose. Thereafter notarised documents can be sent to the Foreign and Commonwealth Office Legalisation Office for the application of the Apostille together with payment of the relevant fee.

Subscription on behalf of grantors who are blind or unable to write

See the Requirements of Writing (Scotland) Act 1995 Ss 9(3) 9(4) 9(7) and Schedule 3.

Cases where a notary cannot act—normal conflict rules and guidance apply.

See *Gorries Trustees v Stivens Executrices*, 1952 S.L.T. 54 where a notarially executed will was void because the notary's partner was appointed trustee with power to charge fees.

See the Requirements of Writing (Scotland) Act 1995 s9(4) which provides that where a document confers on the relevant person or his or her spouse son or daughter a benefit in money or money's worth whether directly or indirectly it is invalid only to the extent that it confers such benefit.

Division F: Acting as Insolvency Practitioner

1. Licensing of Insolvency Practitioners

The Law Society of Scotland is a Recognised Professional Body under the Insolvency Act 1986.

The Society's status as an Insolvency Recognised Professional Body permits it to issue licences to those solicitors who wish to become insolvency practitioners in terms of the Insolvency Act 1986.

Information in relation to insolvency practitioners and how to obtain an insolvency licence is available from the Registrar.

2. Insolvency Code of Ethics

An Insolvency Code of Ethics has been agreed by all the Recognised Professional Bodies under the Insolvency Act 1986 and applies to all insolvency practitioners licensed by the Society. To view the Code of Ethics please go to the website of The Insolvency Service.

Professional Practice—Where Can I Find It?

Index to journal articles etc. on aspects of professional practice which are not available on the Law Society of Scotland website (see Note below). The index has been compiled by Bruce A. Ritchie, Director (Professional Practice), The Law Society of Scotland, who will be pleased to receive users' suggestions for further items for inclusion.

Note—Includes items not printed in the Parliament House Book or the Solicitors Professional Handbook.

OFFICE: 26 Drumsheugh Gardens, Edinburgh EH3 7YR. Tel. 0131 226 7411; fax. 0131 225 2934; LPI Edinburgh-1; email: lawscot@lawscot.org.uk

Website: *www.lawscot.org.uk*

Brussels Office Address—The Law Society of Scotland, 141/142 Avenue de Tervuren, 1150 Brussels Tel. 00 322 743 8585; fax 00 322 743 8586; email: brussels@lawsociety.org.uk

Note—the Practice Rules and Guidelines can be found on the Society's website at *www.lawscot.org.uk/rules_and_guidance/*

ADVERTISING
Consumer Credit (Advertisements) Regulations 1989 (SI 1989/1125).

A NON DOMINO
Law Society Journal, February 1997, p.72 (also on website).
Also *Aberdeen College v Stewart Watt Youngson* [2005] CSOH 31 and *Law Society Journal* July 2008 p.67.

BANKRUPTCY
Register of Undischarged Bankrupts, *Law Society Journal*, October 1990.

BUILDER/DEVELOPER
Law Society Journal, November 1994, p.423; March 2003 p.9; and *Journal Online News*, October 2007.

BUILDING SOCIETY FLOTATIONS/MERGERS
Law Society Journal, May 1997, p.206 (also an website).

BOOKS
Alan Paterson and Bruce Ritchie, *Law, Practice and Conduct for Solicitors* (Edinburgh: W. Green, 2006).

CERTIFICATE OF TITLE
See Commercial Securities.

CLIENT CARE
See Terms of Business.

CLOSING A FILE
Law Society Journal, April 1998, p.44.

CLOSING DATE GUIDELINES
Law Society Journal, February 1999, p.42.

CODE OF CONDUCT FOR CRIMINAL WORK
PH Book, Vol.1, F 2090. Also on *www.lawscot.org.uk* (Public Information | Using a Solicitor | Codes of Conduct).

COMMENTS TO THE MEDIA
Law Society Journal, June 2009, p.37.

COMMERCIAL SECURITY TRANSACTIONS
Articles—*Law Society Journal*, April 1994 ("Lenders' Need to Know"); February 1995 ("Expanding Duty of Care") and October 1995 ("Certificate of Title").

COMMON REPAIRS
Law Society Journal, October 1999, p.10.

COMPANY AUDIT ENQUIRIES
Law Society Journal, July 2000, p.41 and November 2001, p.9.

CONFIDENTIALITY
Micosta v Shetland Islands Council, 1983 S.L.T. 483.
Conoco v Commercial Law Practice—Journal, April 1996, p.132 also 1996 G.W.D. 12–731.
Bolkiah (The Prince Jefri Case) v KPMG [1999] 1 ALL E.R. 517.

CONFLICT OF INTEREST
Greens Property Law Bulletin, December 1994, p.7.
Law Society Journal, March 1999, p.40.
Marks & Spencer v Freshfields [2004] EWCA Civ. 741.

CONSUMER CREDIT LICENCE COVER
Law Society Journal, February 2009, p.28.

COURT WORK—DUTY TO LODGE JOINT MINUTE
Law Society Journal, June 1998, p.43.

CRIMINAL WORK
See Code of Conduct for Criminal Work.

DEED OF CONDITIONS FOR HOUSING ESTATES
Law Society Journal, October 1999, p.8.

DESTRUCTION OF FILES
Law Society Journal, November 2001, p.46.

DEVELOPERS
See Builder/Developer.

DISCOUNT STANDARD SECURITIES—DISCHARGES
Law Society Journal, January 1987, p.4 and July 1998, p.8.

DIVORCE—PENSION SHARING
Law Society Journal, June 2001, p.9 (also on website).

ELECTRONIC STORAGE OF FILES
See Storage of Files—Electronic.

ELECTRONIC TRANSFER OF FUNDS
Law Society Journal, July 2008, p.41.

EUROPEAN LAW—WHERE TO FIND IT
Law Society Journal, April 1994, p.127.

EXECUTRIES
"Solicitor required to implement Mandate from co-executor" *Law Society Journal*, July 1998, p.42.
Solicitor's duty to account to executors—not beneficiaries—*Loretto School v McAndrew & Jenkins*, 1992 S.L.T. 615.

FEES—LIABILITY FOR OTHER SOLICITORS' FEES
Solicitors (Scotland) Act 1980, s.30 (PH Book, Vol.1, Div.F).

FEES—DUTY TO AGREE TO TAXATION
Practice Guideline—Form of Accounts & Taxation (PH Book, Vol.1, Div.F).
See also Written Fee Charging Agreements.

FEES—SCHEME FOR ACCOUNTING FOR COUNSELS FEES
Scottish Law Directory Fees Supplement 2009, p.70.

FEU DUTY FACTORS
Law Society Journal, May 2000, p.6.

FIXED PRICE OFFERS
Law Society Journal, June 1998, p.42.

FOREIGN LAWYERS
See Multi National practices and also European Lawyers.

GUARANTORS
Borrower and Spouse—*Law Society Journal*, March 1999, p.40 and October 2003, p.34.

HELD AS UNDELIVERED
See settlement cheques.

INSOLVENCY
Ethics—PH Book, Vol. 1.
Searches—*Law Society Journal*, October 1999, p.14—Letter by The Accountant in Bankruptcy.

INVESTMENT BUSINESS
Law Society Journal, April 2004, p.44.

JOINT MINUTE
See Court Work.

LETTERS OF ENGAGEMENT
See Terms of Business.

LETTERS OF OBLIGATION
Law Society Journal, article of April 2003, p.26. See also: April 1973, p.121 (Professor Henry); May 1991, p.171; November 1993, p.431 (Professor Rennie).

MANDATES
From client—*Law Society Journal*, May 1998, p.46. (Also PH Book, Vol.1, F 1293).
In executries—*see* Executries.
From banks, creditors etc.—*Law Society Journal*, May 1993, p.185.

MEDIA
See Comments to the Media.

MISSIVES—AVOIDANCE OF DELAY
Law Society Journal, June 1998, p.42. (Also PH Book, Vol.1) (also on website).

NOTARY PUBLIC
Article—*Law Society Journal*, February 1997, p.50.

NOTES OF INTEREST
See Closing Dates.

NURSING HOME COMMISSION
Law Society Journal, October 1999, p.10.

OWNERSHIP OF FILES
Article—Law Society Journal, November 2001, p.46.

PERSONAL INJURY CASES
Pre Action Protocol—Law Society Journal, December 2005.
Protocol Fees—see www.lawscot.org.uk

PRECOGNITIONS IN CRIMINAL CASES NOT DELIVERABLE TO CLIENT
Swift v Bannigan, 1991 S.C.L.R. 604.

REDEMPTION STATEMENTS
Guidelines issued by Council of Mortgage Lenders (copies available from Professional
Practice Department).
Law Society Journal, July 2008, p.52 (in article on lender claims).

SEPARATED SPOUSES—SALE OF MARIMONIAL HOME
Dawson v R. Gordon Marshall & Co., 1996 G.W.D. 21–1243.

SETTLEMENT CHEQUES SENT TO BE HELD AS UNDELIVERED
Article—Law Society Journal, November 2008, p.31.
Greens Property Law Bulletin, August 1994, p.6.

SIGNATURE OF MISSIVES ETC.
Article—Law Society Journal, February 1991, p.73, "Who signs for the firm?" (signature
by assistant).
Article—Law Society Journal, April 1996, p.158, "Requirements of Writing (Scotland)
Act 1995".

SPECULATIVE ACTIONS
Solicitors (Scotland) Act 1980, s.61A (PH Book, Vol.1).
Court of Session, Rule 42.17 and the Scottish Law Directory Fees Supplement, p.44.
Sheriff Court—Act of Sederunt (Fees of Solicitors in Speculative Actions) 1992. (Scottish
Law Directory Fees Supplement, p.63).

STORAGE OF FILES—ELECTRONIC
Law Society Journal, December 2008, p.35.

WRITING DIRECT TO ANOTHER SOLICITOR'S CLIENT IMPROPER
Practice Rules, B1.14.2.

WRITTEN FEE CHARGING AGREEMENTS
Solicitors (Scotland) Act 1980, s.61A (PH Book, Vol.1).